1966	1968	1969	1970	1971	1972	1973	1974	1975	1976	1977	1978	1979
128.1	132.0	134.3	137.1	140.2	144.1	147.1	150.1	153.2	156.2	159.0	161.9	164.9
75.8	78.7	80.7	82.8	84.4	87.0	89.4	91.9	93.8	96.2	99.0	102.3	105.0
59.2	59.6	60.1	60.4	60.2	60.4	60.8	61.3	61.2	61.6	62.3	63.2	63.7
80.4	80.1	79.8	79.7	79.1	78.9	78.8	78.7	77.9	77.5	77.7	77.9	77.8
40.3	41.6	42.7	43.3	43.4	43.9	44.7	45.7	46.3	47.3	48.4	50.0	50.9
58.7	59.3	59.9	60.2	60.1	60.4	60.8	61.4	61.5	61.8	62.5	63.3	63.9
63.0	62.2	62.1	61.8	60.9	60.2	60.5	60.3	59.6	59.8	60.4	62.2	62.2
72.9	75.9	77.9	78.7	79.4	82.2	85.1	86.8	85.8	88.8	92.0	96.0	98.8
2.9	2.8	2.8	4.1	5.0	4.9	4.4	5.2	7.9	7.4	7.0	6.2	6.1
3.8	3.6	3.5	4.9	5.9	5.6	4.9	5.6	8.5	7.7	7.1	6.1	5.8
3.2	2.9	2.8	4.4	5.3	5.0	4.2	4.9	7.9	7.1	6.3	5.3	5.1
4.8	4.8	4.7	5.9	6.9	6.6	6.0	6.7	9.3	8.6	8.2	7.2	6.8
3.4	3.2	3.1	4.5	5.4	5.1	4.3	5.0	7.8	7.0	6.2	5.2	5.1
7.3	6.7	6.4	8.2	9.9	10.0	9.0	9.9	13.8	13.1	13.1	11.9	11.3
12.8	12.7	12.2	15.3	16.9	16.2	14.5	16.0	19.9	19.0	17.8	16.4	16.1
2.56	2.85	3.04	3.23	3.45	3.70	3.94	4.24	4.53	4.86	5.25	5.69	6.16
38.6	37.8	37.7	37.1	36.9	37.0	36.9	36.5	36.1	36.1	36.0	35.8	35.7
294	298	301	298	303	315	315	302	293	297	301	301	292
.8	1.7	.8	−.9	1.7	4.1	.0	−4.2	−3.0	1.5	1.2	.0	−3.1
1.25	1.60	1.60	1.60	1.60	1.60	1.60	2.00	2.10	2.30	2.30	2.65	2.90
4.0	3.4	.4	2.0	4.3	3.3	3.2	−1.7	3.5	3.4	1.7	1.1	−0.4
6.7	8.1	7.0	7.8	6.4	6.3	8.6	9.7	10.3	8.8	7.9	8.9	9.7
2.6	4.6	6.6	5.7	2.0	2.9	5.2	11.6	6.6	5.2	6.0	7.7	10.1
17.9	18.9	19.0	21.2	21.3	21.7	22.3	22.8	22.4	22.7	22.5	22.8	22.6
22.7	23.0	22.6	25.7	25.3	24.9	24.9	24.8	23.8	23.6	22.7	22.3	21.5
321	392	412	381	298	250	317	424	235	231	298	219	235
.10	.20	.16	.29	.19	.09	.08	.16	.09	.12	.10	.11	.09
68.3	70.2	71.8	73.5	72.7	72.3	71.8	73.5	72.8	72.7	72.2	71.9	72.3

[e]days idle in strikes involving 1,000 or more workers divided by total estimated working time   na data unavailable

CONTEMPORARY LABOR ECONOMICS

CONTEMPORARY LABOR ECONOMICS

Campbell R. McConnell
University of Nebraska

Stanley L. Brue
Pacific Lutheran University

David A. Macpherson
Florida State University

Irwin
McGraw-Hill

Boston Burr Ridge, IL Dubuque, IA Madison, WI New York San Francisco St. Louis
Bangkok Bogotá Caracas Lisbon London Madrid
Mexico City Milan New Delhi Seoul Singapore Sydney Taipei Toronto

Irwin/McGraw-Hill

A Division of The ***McGraw-Hill*** *Companies*

CONTEMPORARY LABOR ECONOMICS, FIFTH EDITION

This book is printed on acid-free paper.

1 2 3 4 5 6 7 8 9 0 QPF/QPF 9 3 2 1 0 9 8

ISBN 0–07–046040–X

Vice president and editorial director: *Michael W. Junior*
Publisher: *Gary Burke*
Senior sponsoring editor: *Lucille Sutton*
Marketing manager: *Nelson Black*
Project manager: *Sheila M. Frank*
Senior production supervisior: *Mary E. Haas*
Designer: *Francis Owens*
Supplement coordinator: *David A. Welsh*
Compositor: *York Graphic Services, Inc.*
Typeface: *10/12 Times Roman*
Printer: *Quebecor Printing Book Group/Fairfield, PA*

Cover image: *Ed Moses, Primal Strategies #4, 1997, acrylic and oil on canvas, 66 × 54 inches. Courtesy Brian Gross Fine Art, San Francisco*
Photograph: *Brian Forrest*

Library of Congress Cataloging-in-Publication Data

McConnell, Campbell R.
Contemporary labor economics / Campbell R. McConnell, Stanley L. Brue, David A. Macpherson. — 5th ed.
p. cm.
Includes index.
ISBN 0–07–046040–X
1. Labor economics. I. Brue, Stanley L., 1945– . II. Title.
HD4901.M15 1999
331—dc21 98-29110
CIP

www.mhhe.com

ABOUT THE AUTHORS

CAMPBELL R. McCONNELL earned his Ph.D. from the University of Iowa after receiving degrees from Cornell College and the University of Illinois. He taught at the University of Nebraska–Lincoln from 1953 until his retirement in 1990. He is also the coauthor of *Economics,* currently in its fourteenth edition and the leading introductory economics textbook. He has also edited readers for the principles and labor economics courses. He is a recipient of both the University of Nebraska Distinguished Teaching Award and the James A. Lake Academic Freedom Award and is past-president of the Midwest Economics Association. His primary areas of interest are labor economics and economic education. He has an impressive collection of jazz recordings and enjoys reading jazz history.

STANLEY L. BRUE did his undergraduate work at Augustana College (S.D.) and received his Ph.D. from the University of Nebraska–Lincoln, where he was a student of Professor McConnell. He teaches at Pacific Lutheran University, where he has received the Burlington Northern Faculty Achievement Award for classroom excellence and professional accomplishment. Professor Brue is a current national president and past member of the International Executive Board of Omicron Delta Epsilon International Honor Society in Economics. He is coauthor of the fourteenth edition of *Economics* (with Campbell R. McConnell) and *Economic Scenes: Theory in Today's World,* 5th ed. (with D. R. Wentworth), and author of *The Evolution of Economic Thought,* 5th ed. He has a special interest in the labor market aspects of public policies. For relaxation he enjoys travel, fishing and skiing with his family and friends.

DAVID A. MACPHERSON received his undergraduate degree and Ph.D. from The Pennsylvania State University. He teaches at Florida State University, where he received a Teaching Incentive Program award for teaching excellence. Professor Macpherson is the author of many articles in leading labor economics and industrial relations journals, including the *Journal of Labor Economics, Industrial and Labor Relations Review,* and the *Journal of Human Resources.* He is co-author (with Barry Hirsch) of the annual *Union Membership and Earnings Data Book: Compilations from the Current Population Survey,* published by the Bureau of National Affairs. He is also co-author of *Pensions and Productivity* (with Stuart Dorsey and Christopher Cornwell). His specialty is applied labor economics. His current research interests include pensions, discrimination, industry deregulation, labor unions, and the minimum wage. He enjoys listening to classic rock, seeing movies and plays, playing sports with his sons, and going to the seashore with his family.

CONTENTS

PREFACE

BACKGROUND AND PURPOSE

One of the benefits of authoring a text that has met the test of the market is the opportunity to revise. Revision provides for improvement—to delete the archaic and install the novel, to rectify errors of omission or commission, to rewrite misleading or obscure statements, to introduce more relevant illustrations, to bring more recent data to bear, to upgrade organizational structure, and to enhance pedagogical aids—in short, to build on an accepted framework of ideas. We feel that those who examine this new fifth edition of *Contemporary Labor Economics* will agree that we have fully exploited the opportunity afforded us.

Our basic purpose remains that of presenting the content of the "new" labor economics in a logical and readable fashion. While such traditional topics as labor law, the structure of unions, and collective bargaining have not been entirely crowded out, our focus is clearly on labor economics as an applied field of micro and macro theory. This volume is based on the assumption that labor economics has become less and less an area tangential to the core of analytical economics and increasingly a critical component of that core.

The level of analysis is tailored for the undergraduate student who has completed a standard sequence on macro and micro principles. The book is designed for a one-semester or one-quarter course, although appropriate supplementation can make it usable as the focal point of a two-semester course.

THE FIFTH EDITION

This new edition incorporates many significant changes, several of which were instigated by the comments of colleagues and students. We are especially grateful to the scholars acknowledged at the end of the preface who provided reviews of the fourth edition and commented on drafts of this edition.

The most visible and significant modifications and additions to *Contemporary Labor Economics* are as follows:

New Chapter

This edition introduces a new chapter (16) that focuses on job search within as well as outside the firm. The core of this new material was previously found in the discussions of internal labor markets (Chapter 16) and job search among the unemployed (Chapter 19). The fourth edition's material on dual labor markets and institutional economics has been deleted, as well as Chapter 20 which discussed wages and inflation.

New Topics and Expanded Discussions

New, revised, and expanded discussions permeate the fifth edition. Some of the more important changes are:

Public Policy Issues This edition includes a number of new discussions of public policy issues including welfare reform, the decline in pension coverage, the productivity of public capital, the minimum wage, the causes of growing wage inequality, and wage discrimination.

Applications We have increased the total number of "World of Work" applications from 62 to 70.

New World of Work Sections

Fourteen of the "World of Work" boxes are new to this edition. The new titles include: "The End of Welfare as an Entitlement"; "Working for Free"; "Smoking Is Bad for Your Financial Health"; "Are Fears of Downsizing Overblown?"; "Is the Decline of Unionization Increasing Inequality?"; "Does Health Insurance Cause 'Job Lock'?"; "Revitalization of Unions?"; "A Strike's Impact on Other Workers"; "What Do Government Workers Do?"; "Do Computers Expand Job Opportunities for Those with Spinal Cord Injuries?"; "It Pays to Be Good-Looking"; "How Do the Unemployed Search for Work?"; "Are Earnings Becoming Less Stable?"; and "Is Public Capital Productive?"

Global Perspectives

We included many global elements of labor markets when preparing the previous edition and have again done so by adding "Global Perspective" boxes to nearly every chapter. These boxes provide comparisons of labor market conditions in the United States with those in other countries. Examples: "Global Perspective" 3-2 examines differences in the labor force participation rate of prime-aged women. An international comparison of union membership rates is provided in "Global Perspective" 10-1. International productivity and unemployment rates are the subjects of "Global Perspectives" 18-1 and 19-1.

Web Emphasis

The text has a corresponding web site (http://garnet.acns.fsu.edu/~dmacpher/cle.htm), which provides supplementary material. This site includes updated data, interactive quizzes, instructor's manual content, a student discussion board, and links to relevant web sites to enhance the textbook. The data appendix now includes a list of web sites with labor economics related information.

ORGANIZATION AND CONTENT

The subject matter in this book generally proceeds from micro to macro topics. Figure 1-1 and the "Overview" section of Chapter 1 outline the organizational framework in some detail. Thus, we will simply call your attention to the figure here. We trust that Figure 1-1 and its accompanying discussion will provide a clear expression of our organizational approach. We fully recognize that other chapter orderings are possible and in fact may be optimal for many professors. Also, our bias has been to be inclusive in our presentation of topics. Professors can easily overcome this bias by selecting chapters for their own particular classes.

DISTINGUISHING FEATURES

At the hazard of immodesty, we feel that this volume embodies a number of features that distinguish it from other books in the field.

Content

In the area of subject matter, the emphasis in Chapter 6 and elsewhere on allocative efficiency is both unique and desirable. The efficiency emphasis makes students realize that *society* has an interest in how labor markets function. Chapter 7 brings together the literature on the principal-agent problem and the "new economics of personnel" in a single, focused chapter. Chapter 8 on the wage structure has been consistently praised by instructors for providing a thorough, systematic treatment of wage differentials and a simplified presentation of the hedonic wage theory. The comprehensive analysis of government's impact on labor markets found in Chapters 12 and 13 also sets this book apart.

The additional chapter on discrimination focuses direct attention on women and blacks in the labor market and the two discrimination chapters together provide extensive analysis of discrimination and antidiscrimination policies. Chapter 18 discusses job search within and outside the firm. Chapter 17 confines its focus almost entirely to the personal distribution of *earnings,* compared to the usual discussion of the distribution of *income* and the poverty problem. We believe this approach to be more relevant for a textbook on *labor* economics. The critical topic of labor productivity has been largely ignored or treated in a piecemeal fashion in other books. We have upgraded this topic by according it extensive treatment in Chapter 18. Chapter 19 on unemployment embodies the modern aggregate supply and demand model now common in principles texts to discuss the contending views of economists concerning natural versus cyclical unemployment. Finally, the appendix provides a comprehensive discussion of information sources that can be used to widen and deepen the reader's understanding of the field.

Organization and Presentation

We have put great stress on the logical organization of subject matter, not only chapter by chapter but within each chapter. We have sought to develop the subject matter logically from micro to macro, from simple theory to real-world complications, and from analysis to policy. Similarly, considerable time has been spent in seeking the optimal arrangement of topics within each chapter. Chapter subheadings have been used liberally; our feeling is that the student should always be aware of the organizational structure and directional flow of the subject matter.

Many of the key topics of labor economics will be intellectually challenging for most students. We have tried not to impair student understanding with clumsy or oblique exposition. Our purpose is to communicate effectively with students. To this end we have taken great care that our writing be clear, direct, and uncluttered. It is our goal that the material contained herein be highly accessible to the typical college undergraduate who has limited training in economics.

Pedagogical Features

We have included a variety of pedagogical devices that we feel will make significant contributions to student understanding. First, the introduction of each chapter contains a paragraph or so stating the goals of the chapter and, in many cases, relating it to prior or future chapters. Second, end-of-chapter summaries provide a concise, point by point recapitulation of each chapter. Third, key terms and concepts are highlighted at the end of each chapter, and a comprehensive glossary of these and other terms is located at the end of the book. Fourth, ample lists of questions are provided at the end of each chapter. These range from open-ended discussion questions to numerical problems that permit students to test their understanding of basic analytical concepts. Fifth, a list of basic references is provided at the end of each chapter for those ambitious students who seek greater breadth and depth of understanding. Sixth, we have used the inside covers of the book to present relevant historical statistics that we think will be valuable to both students and instructors. Seventh, the new within-chapter "Quick Review" summaries and "Your Turn" questions should help students identify key points and study for exams. Furthermore, as indicated previously, the appendix of the book lists and discusses various avenues by which the interested reader can update statistical materials found in the book and continue the learning process beyond the course. Finally, as also noted earlier, we have included 70 short "World of Work" minireadings in this edition.

Instructor's Manual

Contemporary Labor Economics is accompanied by a comprehensive Instructor's Manual by Norris Peterson of Pacific Lutheran University. Among other features, it contains chapter outlines and learning objectives, answers to end-of-chapter text questions, and chapter-by-chapter multiple choice questions.

ACKNOWLEDGMENTS

We would like to express our thanks for the many useful comments and suggestions provided by colleagues who reviewed previous editions of this text during the development stage, especially to Neil Alper, Northeastern University; John Antel, University of Houston; Martin Asher, Villanova University; Peter S. Barth, University of Connecticut-Storrs; Clive Bull, New York University; Vito Colapietro, William Jewell College; Robert Catlett, Emporia State University; David H. Ciscel, Memphis State University; Michael J. Dinoto, University of Idaho; Arthur Dobbelaere, Loyola University; Roger Frantz, San Diego State University; Scott Fuess, Jr., University of Nebraska; Robert Gitter, Ohio Wesleyan University; Lonnie M. Golden, University of Wisconsin; Richard Hansen, Southeast Missouri State University; Michael D. Harsh, Randolph–Macon College; Julia Heath, Memphis State University; Carl P. Kaiser, Washington and Lee University; Douglas Kruse, Rutgers University; Julia Lane, University of Louisville; Kevin Lang, Boston University; Eng Seng Loh, Kent State University; John Marcis, Virginia Commonwealth University; J. Peter Mattila, Iowa State University; Eric Nilsson, California State University–San Bernardino; Norris Peterson, Pacific Lutheran University; Jerry Petr, University of Nebraska–Lincoln; Blair Ruble, Social Sciences Research Council; Robert Simonson, Mankato State University; Timothy Schibik, University of Southern Indiana; Larry Singell, University of Oregon; Russell Snyder, Eastern Washington University; Steven Stern, University of Virginia; Wade Thomas, Ithaca College; William Torrence, University of Nebraska–Lincoln; and Ronald S. Warren, Jr., University of Georgia.

The fifth edition has benefited from the critiques and suggestions of Jack Hou, California State University–Long Beach; Laura Leete, Case Western Reserve University; Robert I. Lerman, The Urban Institute; Douglas Romrell, Utah State University; and Larry Singell, University of Oregon.

We are also greatly indebted to the many professionals at Irwin/McGraw-Hill—in particular, Lucille Sutton, Terry Routley, Mary Haas, Pat Anglin, Francis Owens, Lee Hertel, and Nelson Black—for their expertise in the production and marketing of this book.

Campbell R. McConnell
Stanley L. Brue
David A. Macpherson

CHAPTER 1

LABOR ECONOMICS: INTRODUCTION AND OVERVIEW

The core problem of economics permeates all of its specialized branches or subdivisions. This problem is that productive resources are relatively scarce or limited. Society's material wants—the desire of consumers, businesses, and governmental units for goods and services—exceed our productive capacity. That is, our economic system is incapable of providing all the products and services that individuals and institutions would like to have. Because absolute material abundance is impossible, society must make choices as to what goods and services should be produced, how they should be produced, and who should receive them. *Economics* is concerned with the discovery of rules or principles that indicate how such choices can be rationally and efficiently rendered. Since resources are scarce and wants are virtually unlimited, society needs to manage its resources as efficiently as possible to achieve the maximum fulfillment of its wants. Labor, of course, is one of society's scarce productive resources, and this book centers on the problem of its efficient use. ***Labor economics*** *examines the organization, functioning, and outcomes of labor markets; the decisions of prospective and present labor market participants; and the public policies relating to the employment and payment of labor resources.*

LABOR ECONOMICS AS A DISCIPLINE

How can a special field of economics concerned solely with labor be justified? What makes labor economics important as an area of inquiry? There are several answers to these questions.

Socioeconomic Issues

First, evidence of the importance of labor economics is all around us. We need simply glance at the newspaper headlines: "Senator calls for increase in minimum wage"; "General Motors cuts work force"; "Labor productivity slows"; "Teamsters gain wage hike"; "Growing wage inequality"; "President calls for more job training"; "Free-trade agreement: Boon or bane for employment?"; "Workplace safety improves"; "Gender discrimination charged"; "More single parents in labor force"; "Illegal immigration continues"; "High executive salaries questioned"; "Jobs shipped out to foreigners."

Moreover, labor economics helps us understand causes and outcomes of major socioeconomic "megatrends" occurring over the past several decades: the rapid rise in employment in the service industries; the surge in the number of female workers; the precipitous drop in union membership as a percentage of the workforce; the slowing of the rise in the average American worker's standard of living; the recent increase in immigration to the United States; and the expanding globalization of labor markets.

Quantitative Importance

A second justification for labor economics is quantitative. About three-quarters of the national income flows to workers as wages and salaries. Ironically, in the capitalistic economies of the world, the bulk of national income is received not as capitalist income (profit, rent, interest) but as wages! The primary source of income for the vast majority of households in the United States is from providing labor services. Quantitatively, labor is our most important economic resource.

Unique Characteristics

Finally, the markets in which labor services are "bought" and "sold" embody special characteristics and peculiarities calling for separate study. Labor market transactions are a far cry from product market transactions. As succinctly stated by the famous British economist Alfred Marshall:

> It matters nothing to the seller of bricks whether they are to be used in building a palace or a sewer: but it matters a greal deal to the seller of labor, who undertakes to perform a task of given difficulty, whether or not the place in which it is to be done is a wholesome and pleasant one, and whether or not his associates will be such as he cares to have.[1]

Or, as explained by a more recent observer:

> The labor market is a rich and complicated place. When a worker takes a job he expects to earn a wage, but will also care about rates of wage growth, fringe benefits, levels of risk, retirement practices, pensions, promotion and layoff rules, seniority rights, and

[1]Alfred Marshall, *Principles of Economics,* 8th ed. (London: Macmillan and Co., Limited, 1938), p. 566.

grievance procedures. In return the worker must give up some time, but he is also asked to upgrade his skills, train other workers, provide effort and ideas, and defer to authority in questions of how his time is spent.[2]

The complexity of labor markets means that the concepts of supply and demand must be substantially revised and reoriented when applied to labor markets. On the supply side, the labor services a worker "rents" to an employer are inseparable from the worker. Because a worker must spend 40 or so hours per week on the job delivering labor services, the nonmonetary facets of a job become extremely significant. Aside from remuneration, the worker is interested in a job's health and safety features, the arduousness of the work, stability of employment, and opportunities for training and advancement. These nonmonetary characteristics may well be as important as the direct pay. Indeed, a worker's social status, self-esteem, and independence may all depend on the availability of labor market work. Thus, the supply decisions of workers are more complex than the supply concept that applies to product markets.

Similarly, while the demand for a product is based on the satisfaction or utility it yields, labor is demanded because of its contribution—its productivity—in creating goods and services. Indeed, the demands for particular kinds of labor are derived from the demands for the products they produce. Society has a demand for automobile workers because there is a demand for automobiles. We have a demand for accountants because we value accounting services. The demand for labor is therefore an indirect or "derived" demand.

The point to be underscored is that an understanding of labor markets presumes an appreciation of the special attributes of labor supply and demand. Unique institutional considerations—such as labor unions and collective bargaining, the minimum wage, occupational licensing, and discrimination—all affect the functioning of labor markets and require special attention.

THE "OLD" AND THE "NEW"

The field of labor economics has long been recognized as a legitimate area of study. But the content or subject matter of the field has changed rather dramatically in the past two decades or so. If you were to go to the library and examine a labor text published 20 or 25 years ago, you would find its orientation to be highly descriptive and historical. Its emphasis would be on the history of the labor movement, a recitation of labor law and salient court cases, the institutional structure of labor unions, and the scope and composition of collective bargaining agreements. In short, the "old" study of labor was highly descriptive, emphasizing historical developments, facts, institutions, and legal considerations. A primary reason for this approach was that the complexities of labor markets seemed to make them more or less immune to economic analysis. To be sure, labor markets and unemployment were accorded some attention, but the analysis was typically minimal and superficial.

[2]H. Lorne Carmichael, "Self-Enforcing Contracts, Shirking, and Life Cycle Incentives," *Journal of Economic Perspectives.* Fall 1989, p. 65.

This state of affairs has changed significantly in recent decades. Economists have achieved important analytical breakthroughs in studying labor markets and labor problems. As a result, economic analysis has crowded out historical, institutional, legal, and anecdotal material. Labor economics increasingly has become applied micro and macro theory. The present volume focuses on the techniques and understandings associated with the "new" labor economics. This is not to say, however, that all descriptive aspects of the field have been discarded. As noted earlier, the unique institutional features of labor markets are a part of the justification for a special field of economics devoted to labor. Yet the focal point of our approach is the application of economic reasoning to labor markets and labor issues.

ECONOMIC PERSPECTIVE

Contemporary labor economics employs theories of *choice* to analyze and predict the behavior of labor market participants and the economic consequences of labor market activity. It attempts to answer such questions as: Why do some people decide to work while others do not? Why do some prospective labor market participants choose to delay their labor force entry to attend college? Why do some employers employ few workers and much capital while others use many workers and little capital? Why do firms lay off some workers during recessions but retain others? Labor economists also examine the *outcomes* of the choices made in the labor market. Why do some workers earn $5.15 an hour while others are paid $20 or $50 per hour? Why have women entered the labor force in record numbers during the past few decades? What impact, if any, does immigration have on the wages of native workers?

In short, contemporary labor economics focuses on choices—why they are made and how they generate particular outcomes. It therefore is important to be aware of three implicit assumptions underlying this ***economic perspective.***

Relative Scarcity

We know that land, labor, capital, and entrepreneurial resources are scarce, or limited, relative to the many individual and collective wants of society. This relative scarcity dictates that society must choose how and for what purpose labor and other resources should be allocated. Similarly, individuals face a relative scarcity of time and spendable income. They must choose, for example, how much time to devote to jobs, to work in the home, and to leisure. They must choose how much present income (goods and services) to forgo for the prospect of obtaining higher future earnings. They must decide which goods and services to buy and, consequently, which to forgo. Relative scarcity—of time, personal income, and societal resources—then, is a basic element of the economic perspective.

Purposeful Behavior

Because relative scarcity keeps us from having everything we want, we are forced to choose among alternatives. For every choice, say to work longer hours or to institute a national service program, something is gained and something else is sacrificed. This sacrifice—forgone leisure, forgone private-sector output—is an *opportunity cost.*

The economic perspective assumes that people compare costs with expected benefits. A worker will compare the extra utility (income) gained from an added hour of work with the value of the lost leisure. A firm will compare the added revenue from hiring a worker with the extra wage cost, and so forth. Thus, contemporary labor economics looks for purpose, or rationality, in labor market behavior and, for that matter, in many labor market institutions. Relative scarcity necessitates that choices be made; the economic perspective assumes that these choices will be made purposefully, rather than randomly or in a chaotic way.

To say that labor market participants behave rationally, however, is not to say that they always achieve their intended goals. Information is imperfect or imperfectly processed, unforeseen events occur, choices made by others positively or adversely affect the outcomes of our own choices. But even those choices that in retrospect were "poor" choices are assumed to have been made on the *expectation* of net gain.

Adaptability

Because relative scarcity forces people to make choices, and because choices are made purposefully, labor market participants respond to changes in perceived costs and benefits. Some workers will adjust the number of hours they desire to work when the wage rate they receive changes. Fewer people will decide to obtain a specific skill when the training cost rises or when the wage paid to those already possessing the skill falls. Firms will adjust their hiring when the demand for their product changes. Some workers will migrate from lower-paid regions to areas experiencing a significant rise in labor demand and therefore in wage rates. Union officials will lower their wage demands when the economy encounters recession and unemployment among union workers is high. Restated, the economic perspective assumes that workers, employers, and other labor market participants *adapt, adjust,* or *alter* their behaviors in response to changes in expected costs and expected gains. Contemporary labor economics sorts out these responses, finds predictable patterns, and, by so doing, adds to our understanding of the economy.

These three assumptions of the economic perspective—the scarcity of resources relative to wants, purposeful behavior based on comparisons of benefits and costs, and the adaptability of behavior to changing circumstances—underlie all that follows in this text.

QUICK REVIEW 1-1

- Labor economics examines the organization, functioning, and outcomes of labor markets; the decisions of prospective and present labor market participants; and the public policies relating to the employment and payment of labor resources.
- The new labor economics employs the economic perspective, which assumes that resources are scarce relative to wants, individuals make choices by comparing costs and benefits, and people respond to incentives and disincentives.

Your Turn: Which of these two statements best reflects the economic perspective? "Most workers in America would retire at age 65 even without pensions because this

1-1 age has long been the customary retirement age." "Most workers in America retire at age 65 because at this age they become eligible for private pensions and full social security benefits." (Answer: See page 625.)

OVERVIEW

Before plunging into the details of specific topics, let's pause for a brief overview of our field of study. This overview is useful for two closely related reasons. First, it provides a sense of direction. More specifically, it reveals the logic underlying the sequence of topics constituting each chapter. Second, the overview yields insights as to how the subject matter of any particular chapter relates to other chapters.[3]

[3]This text covers more topics in economics than most instructors will choose to cover in a single course. Also note that chapters and topics can be logically sequenced in numerous ways.

1-1 World of Work

GARY BECKER: NOBEL LAUREATE

Few economists were surprised when the University of Chicago's Gary Becker was named the winner of the 1992 Nobel Prize in economics. More than any other recent economist, Becker has extended the boundaries of economic analysis.

Becker's theories presume that individuals or households make purposeful choices in attempting to maximize their utility and that these choices depend heavily on incentives. His basic contribution has been to apply this perspective to aspects of human behavior that traditionally were believed to be noneconomic.

Becker's theory of marriage is illustrative. People allegedly seek marriage partners much like they search for jobs or decide which products to buy. Couples stop far short of obtaining complete information about each other before marriage. At some point the costs of obtaining additional information—the main cost being the benefits of marriage forgone—exceed the extra benefits of more information. After being married for months or years, however, a person learns additional information about his or her spouse's personality and attributes. This new information in some cases places the spouse in a less favorable light, ending the optimality of the original match and causing divorce.

Becker views the household as a little factory, allocating its time between labor market work, household production, and household consumption in producing utility-providing "commodities" (Chapter 3). Household's have fewer children—time-intensive "durable goods"—as the "price" of children rises. A major component of this "price" is the forgone earnings associated with having and caring for children (World of Work 3-4).

Becker's theory of human capital (Chapter 4) holds that decisions to invest in education and training are analogous to decisions by firms to purchase physical capital. Applying his approach to crime, Becker concludes that criminals rationally choose between crime and normal labor market work. Also, they respond to changes in costs and benefits, just as do noncriminals. Becker analyzes labor market discrimination (Chapter 14) as a preference or "taste" for which the discriminator is willing to pay.

Because Becker has invaded the traditional territories of sociology, anthropology, demography, and law, he has been called an "intellectual imperialist" (by both supporters and detractors!). But, as stated by Summers, there can be no doubt that Becker "has profoundly influenced the future of economics by demonstrating the breadth, range, and power of economic reasoning in a context that seemed unimagined a generation ago."*

*Lawrence Summers, as quoted in "An Economist for the Common Man," *Business Week,* October 26, 1992. For a more thorough review of Becker's contributions, see Stanley L. Brue, *The Evolution of Economic Thought,* 5th ed. (Fort Worth: Dryden Press, 1994), pp. 527–533.

Figure 1-1 is helpful in presenting the overview. Reading from left to right, we note that most aspects of labor economics can be fitted without too much arbitrariness under the headings of "microeconomics" or "macroeconomics." ***Microeconomics*** is concerned with the decisions of individual economic units and the functioning of specific markets. On the other hand, ***macroeconomics*** is concerned with the economy as a whole or with basic aggregates that constitute the economy. The determination of the wage rate and the level of employment in a particular market—carpenters in Oshkosh or retail clerks in Okoboji—are clearly microeconomic matters. In contrast, the consideration of the average level of real wages, the aggregate levels of employment and unemployment, and the overall price level are issues in macroeconomics. Because some topics straddle micro- and macroeconomics, the subject matter of individual chapters will sometimes pertain to both aspects of economics. However, it is fair to say that Chapters 2 to 16 address topics that are "mainly micro." Similarly, Chapters 17 to 19 are "mainly macro."

Figure 1-1 reemphasizes that microeconomics stresses the working of individual markets. The goal of Chapters 2 to 6 is to develop and bring together the concepts that underlie labor supply and demand. Specifically, in Chapter 2 we examine the simple theory of labor supply. Here we analyze the basic factors that determine whether or not a person will participate in the labor force and, if so, the number of hours that the individual would prefer to work. We also consider how various pay schemes and income maintenance programs might affect the person's decision to supply labor services.

In Chapter 3 we consider the major determinants of the aggregate amount of labor supplied: population; the labor force participation rates of various demographic groups; and hours of work. In particular, we examine labor supply from a household perspective and explore reasons for the rapid increase in the labor force participation of married women.

Chapter 4 introduces a qualitative dimension to labor supply. Workers can provide more productive effort if they have training. Thus, in Chapter 4 we examine the decision to invest in human capital—that is, in education and training—and explain why it is rational for different individuals to invest in different quantities of human capital.

We turn to the demand side of the labor market in Chapter 5. Here we systematically derive the short-run labor demand curve, explaining how the curve varies between a firm that is selling its product competitively and one that is not. The notion of a long-run demand curve is also explored, as is the concept of wage elasticity of demand. Several short applications of demand and elasticity then follow.

Chapter 6 combines labor supply and labor demand to explain how the equilibrium wage rate and level of employment are determined. An array of market models is presented, ranging from a basic perfectly competitive model to relatively complex bilateral monopoly and "cobweb" models. Because of the importance of using scarce resources prudently, the emphasis in Chapter 6 is on the efficiency with which labor is allocated. Is the "socially desirable" or "right" amount of labor employed in a particular labor market? If not, what is the efficiency loss to society?

Chapters 7 to 9 are important elaborations and modifications of Chapter 6's discussion of the working and outcomes of labor markets. In Chapter 6 worker compensation is treated as a standard hourly wage rate, for example, $10 per hour. In Chapter 7 we recognize that worker compensation also involves a whole range of fringe

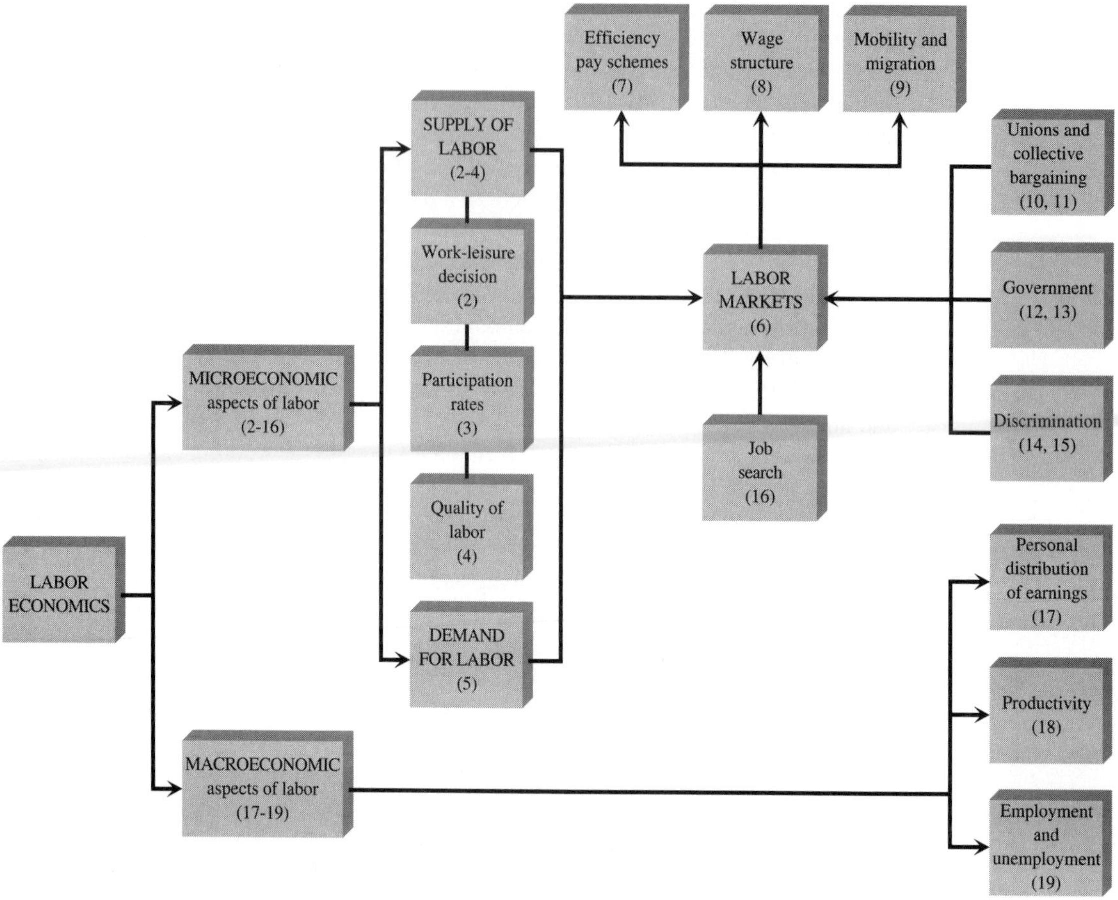

FIGURE 1-1 AN OVERVIEW OF LABOR ECONOMICS
This diagram shows how the chapters of this volume are divided between microeconomic and macroeconomic topics. Microeconomics focuses on the determinants of labor supply and demand and the ways supply and demand interact to determine wages rates and employment in various labor markets. In these labor markets, the types and composition of pay are determined, as is the wage structure. Some wage differences persist; others are eroded by mobility and migration. Labor unions, government, and discrimination all affect labor markets through either supply or demand. Macroeconomics stresses the aggregative aspects of labor markets and, in particular, the distribution of earnings, labor productivity, and the overall level of employment.

benefits, including health insurance, paid vacations, sick leave, contributions to pensions, and so forth. We will attempt to explain why different "compensation packages" might appeal to different workers. More important, Chapter 7 explains how pay schemes might be designed to promote worker efficiency and productivity.

In Chapter 8 we confront the complex topic of the wage structure. Why do different workers receive different wages? We find that wage differences are traceable to such factors as the varying working conditions and skill requirements of jobs, differences in the human capital and job preferences of workers, and imperfections in labor mobility and the flow of job information.

Chapter 9 continues our elaboration of the labor market, explaining how the movement of labor—from employer to employer, occupation to occupation, and place to place—can contribute to economic efficiency. This mobility is analyzed as an investment in human capital and has a variety of economic ramifications.

As Figure 1-1 suggests, Chapters 10 to 15 focus on a variety of real-world considerations that have a pervasive and profound impact on how wages are determined and the way labor markets operate. Specifically, in these chapters we examine in some depth how labor unions, government, and discrimination affect labor markets. Using the unionized models of labor markets in Chapter 6 as a springboard, Chapters 10 and 11 are concerned with unions and collective bargaining. In Chapter 10 we explore the demographics of trade union membership, discuss the size and institutional structure of the labor movement, note the unique characteristics of the collective bargaining transaction, and present a model of the bargaining process. Chapter 11 is devoted to the effects of unions and collective bargaining on the operation of labor markets. The discussion focuses on the impact of unions on wage rates, efficiency and productivity, firm profitability, and the distribution of earnings.

The direct and subtle ways government influences labor markets are the subject matter of Chapters 12 and 13. Chapter 12 considers government as a direct employer of labor and explores how government's fiscal functions affect labor markets. More specifically, we seek to determine how government expenditures and taxes alter wages and employment. In Chapter 13 our attention shifts to the impact of the legislative and regulatory functions of government on labor markets. What are the implications, for example, of minimum-wage legislation and regulations concerning worker health and safety?

In addition to labor unions and government, the "institution" of discrimination greatly affects labor markets. Thus, Chapter 14 introduces several models of race and gender discrimination that enable us to see how discrimination might alter labor market results. Chapter 15 presents facts and figures about differences in pay by race and gender and asks what part of these differences results from discrimination. This chapter also examines antidiscrimination policies and issues in some detail.

Job search behavior has important implications for issues such as unemployment and economic efficiency. Thus, Chapter 16 is devoted to job search within as well as outside a firm.

The next three chapters deal primarily with macroeconomic aspects and outcomes of labor markets. The personal distribution of earnings is the subject of Chapter 17. Here we discuss alternative ways of portraying the overall earnings distribution and measuring the degree of observed inequality. We then offer explanations for the pattern of earnings and discuss related topics such as the degree of mobility within the earnings distribution and the recent trend toward greater earnings inequality.

In Chapter 18 we consider productivity for the important reason that the average level of real wages and, thus, living levels are intimately related to it. The factors that contribute to the growth of productivity are examined, as are the systematic changes in productivity that occur over the course of the business cycle. The relationship of changes in productivity to the price level and the level of employment is also explained.

Chapter 19 is devoted to the problem of unemployment. Among other things, distinctions are made between frictional, structural, and cyclical unemployment. The distribution of unemployment by occupations and by demographic groups is considered, as are a variety of public policies designed to alleviate unemployment.

The Appendix falls outside of Figure 1-1's overview, but it is important for staying apprised of future developments in labor economics and continuing the study of the field. It lists and discusses sources of labor-related statistics; discusses bibliographic, technical, and nontechnical journals in the field; and cites advanced textbooks in labor economics along with books in the closely related fields of labor relations, collective bargaining, and labor law. Students doing term papers or other written assignments in labor economics will want to read this chapter at the outset. Appendix Table 1 lists numerous potential term paper topics that may be of interest.

1-2

PAYOFFS

What benefits might you derive from studying labor economics? The payoffs from a basic understanding of the field may be both personal and social. Labor economics yields information and develops analytical tools that may be useful in making personal and managerial decisions relevant to labor markets. Also, a grasp of the field puts one in a better position as a citizen and voter to develop informed positions on labor market issues and policies.

Personal Perspective

At the personal level, the vast majority of readers have already been labor market participants. You have worked summers, on part-time jobs, on your family farm, or perhaps in a school-related internship. Most of you will receive the bulk of your future incomes from the labor market. Thus, many of the topics addressed in this book will have immediate relevance to you. Such topics as job search, unemployment, migration, discrimination, unionism, and labor productivity, to enumerate only a few, will take on new meaning and relevance. For example, if you become a public schoolteacher or a state employee, what might you personally expect to gain in terms of salary and fringe benefits by unionization? To what extent does a college education contribute to higher earnings? That is, what rate of return can one expect from investing in higher education? What are the peculiarities of labor markets for college-trained workers? If you are a woman or member of a minority group, how might discrimination affect your access to specific occupations and your earnings? Similarly, some of you will find yourselves in managerial positions with responsibilities for personnel and labor relations. The background and analytical perspective provided by an understanding of labor economics should be useful in making rational managerial decisions concerning the hiring, firing, promotion, training, and remuneration of workers.

1-2 World of Work

LOTTO WINNERS: WHO QUIT?

Of the many reasons people work, monetary compensation usually is the leading incentive. Indeed, the word *compensation* implies that workers require reimbursement or indemnification—in this case, for the loss of utility associated with forgone leisure.

Although most of us profess to like our work, the economic perspective suggests that many of us would quit our jobs if we were assured of a substantial amount of nonlabor income each year. Quite simply, nonlabor income reduces our incentive to work. The greater the amount of nonlabor income, the greater the likelihood of our quitting our jobs.

A *Seattle Times* survey of lottery winners in the state of Washington supports this perspective. Three-quarters of the Lotto winners surveyed were employed when they won.

Observe in the accompanying figure that winners of "small" jackpots tended to continue to work. Only 7 percent of those winning jackpots of $1 million or less quit. Bear in mind that a $1 million jackpot, for instance, is paid as twenty annual payments of $40,000, with $10,000 more a year being withheld for taxes. Conversely, those who won large jackpots were much more likely to quit. Seventy-seven percent of the winners of jackpots of $4 million or more chose to quit. Note from the charts that the larger the jackpot winnings, the greater was the percentage of workers who opted out of the workforce.*

Source: Seattle Times survey. Reprinted with permission.

*A more extensive survey of lottery winners also supports this generalization. See Roy H. Kaplan, "Lottery Winners and Their Work Commitment," *Journal of the Institute for Socioeconomic Research,* Summer 1985, pp. 82–94.

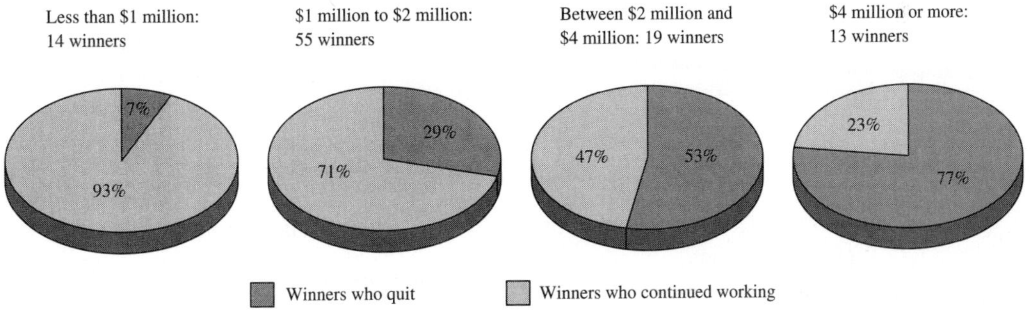

Social Perspective

From a societal viewpoint, a knowledge of labor economics should help make you a more informed citizen and more intelligent voter. The issues here are broad in scope and impact. Should unionization be encouraged or discouraged? Are unions on balance positive or negative forces in our society? Should government place limits on the salaries of executives, athletes, and entertainers? How might a given change in the tax structure—for example, to a more progressive federal income tax—affect incentives to work? Should government subsidize worker mobility? Should U.S. immigration policies be liberalized or made more restrictive? Should "comparable worth" legislation be passed to guarantee that women and minorities are paid the same wages as white males on "comparable" jobs? Should formal education and vocational training be given more or less public support? Is it desirable for employers to pay teenagers wage rates that are lower than the legislated minimum wage? While detailed and definitive answers to such questions cannot be guaranteed, an understanding of labor economics should provide valuable insights that should be helpful in formulating your opinions on these and similar issues.

CHAPTER SUMMARY

1 The relative scarcity of labor and other productive resources provides an incentive for society to use such resources efficiently.
2 The importance of labor economics is reflected in *(a)* current socioeconomic issues and problems, *(b)* the quantitative dominance of labor as a resource, and *(c)* the unique characteristics of labor supply and demand.
3 In the past two decades the field of labor economics has put greater emphasis on economic analysis and has deemphasized historical, institutional, and legal aspects.
4 The economic perspective assumes that *(a)* labor and other resources are relatively scarce, *(b)* individuals and institutions make rational or purposeful decisions, and *(c)* decisions are altered or adapted in the light of changing economic circumstances.
5 This volume examines a series of pertinent microeconomic and macroeconomic topics, as outlined in Figure 1-1.
6 An understanding of the content and analytical tools of labor economics contributes to more intelligent personal and social decisions.

TERMS AND CONCEPTS

labor economics	microeconomics
economic perspective	macroeconomics

Note: To aid you with terminology, we have included an extensive glossary at the end of this book.

QUESTIONS AND STUDY SUGGESTIONS

1 Why is economics a science of choices? Explain the kinds of choices confronting workers and employers in labor markets. Distinguish between microeconomics and macroeconomics.
2 In 1997 136 million workers were in the U.S. labor force, of which 6.7 million were unemployed. In view of these facts, how can economists say that labor is a scarce resource?
3 Indicate whether each of the following statements pertains to microeconomics or macroeconomics:
   a The unemployment rate in the United States was 4.9 percent in 1997.
   b Workers at the Sleepy Eye grain elevator are paid $8 per hour.
   c The productivity of American workers as a whole increased by less than 2 percent per year in the last decade.
   d The money or nominal wages of hospital orderlies increased by 3 percent in 1997.
   e The Alpo dog food plant in Bowser, Indiana, laid off fifteen workers last month.
4 Why must the concepts of supply and demand as they pertain to product markets be modified when applied to labor markets?

5 What is the relative importance of labor as an economic resource?
6 Briefly compare the "old" and the "new" labor economics.
7 What are the major features or assumptions of the economic perspective?
8 Briefly state and justify your position on each of the following proposals:
  a Women and minorities should be paid the same wage as white males, provided the work is comparable.
  b The United States should close its boundaries to all immigration.
  c The federal government should take measures to achieve the 4 percent unemployment rate specified by the Humphrey–Hawkins Act of 1978.
  d So-called "right-to-work laws," which specify that workers who refuse to join unions cannot thereby be deprived of their jobs, should be repealed.
  e Conditions of worker health and safety should be determined by the labor market, not by governmental regulation.
9 What benefits might accrue to you from studying labor economics?

SELECTED REFERENCES

Addison, John T., and W. Stanley Seibert: *The Market for Labor: An Analytical Treatment* (Santa Monica, Calif.: Goodyear Publishing Company, Inc., 1979), chap 1.

Fearn, Robert M.: *Labor Economics: The Emerging Synthesis* (Cambridge, Mass.: Winthrop Publishers, Inc., 1981), intro.

Fleisher, Belton M., and Thomas J. Kniesner: *Labor Economics: Theory, Evidence, and Policy,* 3d ed. (Englewood Cliffs, N.J.: Prentice-Hall, Inc., 1984), chaps. 1–2.

CHAPTER 2

THE THEORY OF INDIVIDUAL LABOR SUPPLY

In supplying labor, human beings are a curious and diverse lot. Adams moonlights at a second job, while Anderson takes numerous unpaid absences from his only job. College student Brown works full-time while attending school; roommate Bailey works part-time; and classmate Brinkman doesn't work at all. Conway quit her job to raise her young children; Cohen, also with young children, continues to work full-time in the workplace. Downy quickly grabs an opportunity for early retirement; Wong plans to work until she can no longer do so because of old age. Evans welcomes overtime work; Ebert, given an option, routinely rejects it. Fleming supplies more hours of labor when her wage rate rises; Hernandez cuts back on his work hours.

How are these diverse labor supply decisions made? How do individuals decide on the number of hours of labor, if any, to supply in the labor market? Our main goal in this chapter is to develop and apply a basic theory of individual labor supply that will help answer these questions.

Our discussion is organized as follows. First, we introduce a basic model of work–leisure choice so we can understand the critical variables determining an individual's optimal combination of work and leisure. Second, by changing the wage rate confronting the worker, we use the basic model to derive a short-run labor supply curve for the individual. Third, we extend our basic model by discussing a number of applications. In particular, we explain the case of labor force nonparticipation, that is, the circumstances that might cause a person to choose zero hours of labor market work. Next, the implications of the situation where the individual worker is confronted with a standard workday are discussed. Then we inquire whether different pay schemes affect the number of hours an individual might choose to work. And, finally, the basic model is modified to analyze the impact of an income maintenance program on work incentives.

THE WORK–LEISURE DECISION: BASIC MODEL

Imagine an individual with a certain amount of education and labor force experience and, therefore, a given level of skills. That individual, having a fixed amount of time available, must decide how that time should be allocated among *work* ("labor market activity") and *leisure* ("non-labor market activity"). In the present context, *work* is time devoted to a paying job. The term *leisure* is used here in a broad sense to include all kinds of activities for which the person does not get paid: for example, work within the household and time spent on consumption, education, commuting, rest, relaxation, and so forth.

2-1

Two sets of information are necessary to determine the optimal distribution of an individual's time between work and leisure. First, we require *subjective,* psychological information concerning the individual's work–leisure preferences. This information is embodied in *indifference curves.* Second, we need the *objective,* market information that is reflected in a *budget constraint.*

2-1 Global Perspective

ANNUAL HOURS OF WORK PER EMPLOYEE, 1995

Average hours worked per year differ substantially across countries. For example, the average U.S. employee works 408 more hours per year than the average Swedish worker.

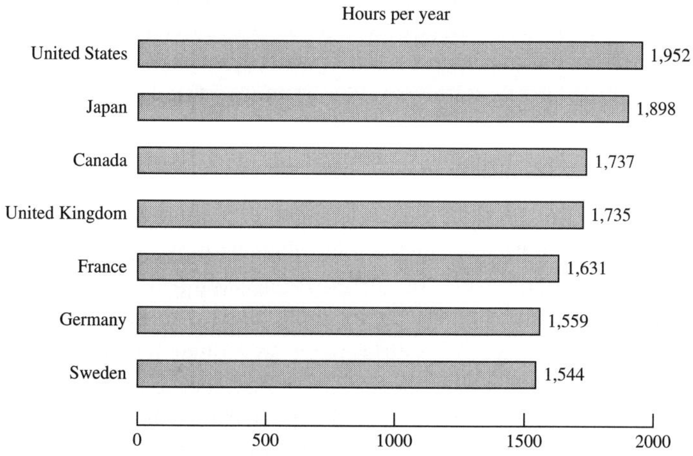

Source: Organization for Economic Cooperation and Development, *Employment Outlook,* July 1996, Table C. All data are for 1995, except Japanese data, which is for 1994.

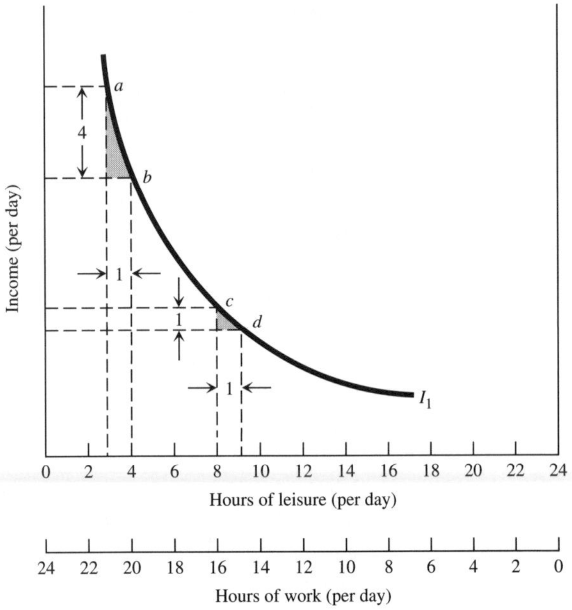

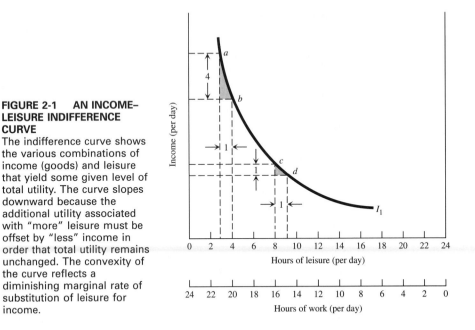

FIGURE 2-1 AN INCOME–LEISURE INDIFFERENCE CURVE
The indifference curve shows the various combinations of income (goods) and leisure that yield some given level of total utility. The curve slopes downward because the additional utility associated with "more" leisure must be offset by "less" income in order that total utility remains unchanged. The convexity of the curve reflects a diminishing marginal rate of substitution of leisure for income.

Indifference Curves

As applied to the work–leisure decision, an ***indifference curve*** *shows the various combinations of real income and leisure time that will yield some specific level of utility or satisfaction to the individual.* Curve I_1 in Figure 2-1 is illustrative. Note that we measure daily income on the vertical axis and hours of leisure, or non-labor market activities, from left to right on the horizontal axis. The second horizontal axis reminds us that, given the fixed 24 hours available each day, we may measure the number of hours of work from right to left. According to the definition of indifference curves, each combination of income and leisure designated by any point on I_1 is equally satisfactory; each point on the curve yields the same level of utility to the individual.

Indifference curves embody several salient properties.

1 Negative Slope The indifference curve slopes downward because real income from work, on the one hand, and leisure, on the other, are both sources of utility or satisfaction. In moving southeast down the curve, some amount of real income—of goods and services—must be given up to compensate for the acquisition of more leisure if total utility is to remain constant. Stated differently, the indifference curve is downward-sloping because, as an individual gets more of one "good" (leisure), some of the other "good" (real income) must be surrendered to maintain the same level of utility.

2 Convex to Origin A downward-sloping curve can be concave, convex, or linear. We note in Figure 2-1 that our indifference curve is *convex* (bowed inward) to the origin, or—alternatively stated—the absolute value of the curve's slope *diminishes* as we move down the curve to the southeast.

Why are indifference curves convex as viewed from the origin? We shall explain this characteristic in intuitive terms and then more technically. Both explanations are rooted in two considerations. First, the slope of the curve reflects an individual's subjective willingness to substitute between leisure and income. And, second, the individual's willingness to substitute leisure for income, or vice versa, varies with the amounts of leisure and income initially possessed.

The convexity of an indifference curve reflects the notion that an individual becomes increasingly reluctant to give up any good (in this case, income) as it becomes increasingly scarce. Consider the *ab* range of our indifference curve, where the individual has a relatively large amount of income and very little leisure. Here the individual would be willing to give up a relatively large amount of abundant income (4 units) in exchange for an additional unit, say an hour, of scarce leisure. The extra utility from the added hour of leisure will perfectly offset the loss of utility from having 4 fewer units of income. But now as we move down the curve to the *cd* range, we find that the individual's circumstances are different in that income is now relatively scarcer and leisure is more abundant. The individual is now willing to trade only a small amount of scarce income (1 unit) for an extra hour of leisure. As the individual obtains more leisure, the amount of income the person is willing to give up to gain still more units of leisure becomes smaller and smaller. Thus the indifference curve becomes flatter and flatter. By definition, a curve that flattens out as we move to the southeast is convex to the origin.

In more technical terms, the slope of the indifference curve is measured by the ***marginal rate of substitution of leisure for income*** (MRS *L,Y*). *The MRS L,Y is the amount of income one must give up to compensate for the gain of 1 more unit (hour) of leisure.* Although the slope of the indifference curve shown in Figure 2-1 is negative, it is convenient to think of the MRS *L,Y* as an absolute value. In these terms, MRS *L,Y* is large—that is, the slope of the indifference curve is steep—in the northwest or upper range of the curve. For example, we observe that MRS *L,Y* is 4/1, or 4 over the *ab* range of the curve. This high MRS *L,Y* occurs because the person has much income and very little leisure over this range of the curve. The subjective relative valuation of income is low at the margin and the subjective relative valuation of leisure is high at the margin. The individual therefore is willing to forgo a large number of units of income (4) for 1 additional unit of leisure.

In moving down the indifference curve to the southeast, the quantities of income and leisure change at each point so that the individual now has less income and more leisure. This fact means that relatively more abundant leisure now has less value at the margin and increasingly scarce income has more value at the margin. Over the *cd* range of the indifference curve, the individual is willing to forgo only a small amount of income (1 unit) for an additional hour of leisure. The slope of the curve or the MRS *L,Y* over this range is only 1/1, or 1. This slope (1) is smaller than the slope of the curve (4) in the *ab* range. This basic point is that MRS *L,Y*—the slope of the indifference curve—declines as one moves down the curve. Any curve whose slope or MRS *L,Y* declines as one moves southeast along it is, by definition, convex to the origin.

3 Indifference Map It is both possible and useful to consider an indifference map, which is a whole family or field of indifference curves, as shown in Figure 2-2. Each

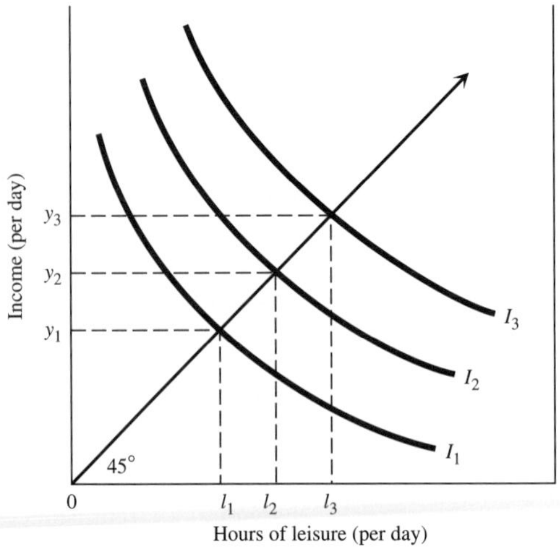

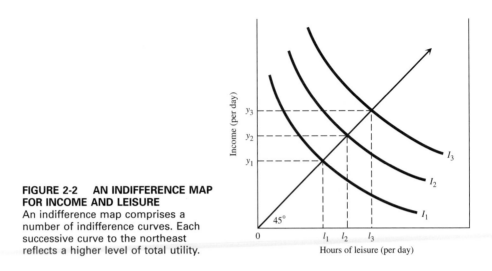

FIGURE 2-2 AN INDIFFERENCE MAP FOR INCOME AND LEISURE
An indifference map comprises a number of indifference curves. Each successive curve to the northeast reflects a higher level of total utility.

curve reflects some different level of total utility much like each contour line on a topographical map reflects a different elevation. Figure 2-2 illustrates only three of a potentially unlimited number of indifference curves. Every possible combination of income and leisure will lie on some indifference curve. Curves farther from the origin indicate higher levels of utility. This can be demonstrated by drawing a 45° diagonal from the origin and noting that its intersection with each successive curve denotes larger amounts of *both* income and leisure. The y_2l_2 combination of income and leisure is preferred to the y_1l_1 combination because the former indicates larger amounts of *both* income and leisure. Similarly, the y_3l_3 combination entails greater total utility than y_2l_2, and so on.[1] It is evident that an individual will maximize total utility by achieving a position on the highest *attainable* indifference curve.

4 Different Work–Leisure Preferences Just as the tastes of various consumers for specific goods and services vary greatly, so do individual preferences for work and leisure. Different preferences as to the relative desirability of work and leisure are reflected in the shape of one's indifference curves. In Figure 2-3(a) we present the indifference curves of a "workaholic" who places a low value on leisure and a high value on work (income). Note that the workaholic's curves are relatively flat, indicating that this individual would give up an hour of leisure for a relatively small increase in income. Figure 2-3(b) shows the indifference curves of a "leisure lover" who puts a high value on leisure and a low value on work (income). Observe that this individual's indifference curves are steep, which means that a relatively large increase in income must

[1]Indifference curves cannot intersect. We know that all points on any one curve reflect the same amount of utility, while any point above (below) that curve represents a larger (smaller) level of utility. If two indifference curves intersected, the level of utility would be the same at the point of intersection. However, at all other points the levels of utility would differ. Given the definition of an indifference curve, this is logically impossible.

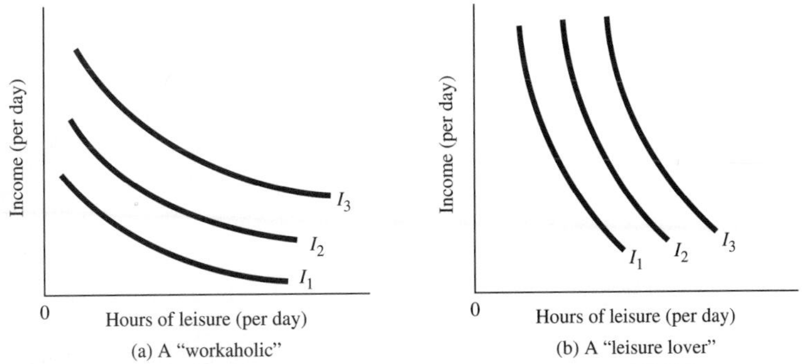

FIGURE 2-3 DIFFERENT PREFERENCES FOR WORK (INCOME) AND LEISURE
The shape of one's indifference curves depends on one's relative preferences for work (income) and leisure. In (a) we portray a "workaholic" who is willing to give up an hour of leisure for only a small increase in income. In comparison the "leisure lover" shown in (b) requires a large increase in income to sacrifice an hour of leisure or nonmarket time.

be realized to sacrifice an hour of leisure. In each case the indifference curves are convex to the origin, but the rate of decline of MRS L,Y is far greater for the leisure lover than for the workaholic.

Why the differences? In the first place, it may be purely a matter of tastes or preferences as rooted in one's personality. A second and related point is that the occupations of individuals differ. The flat curves of Figure 2-3(a) may pertain to a person who has a creative and challenging occupation: for example, a painter, ceramist, or musician. Work entails very little disutility, and hence it takes only a small increase in income to induce the artist to sacrifice an hour of leisure. Conversely, an unpleasant job in a coal mine or on an assembly line may elicit steep indifference curves. Such work involves substantial disutility, and a large increase in income is required to induce one to give up an hour of leisure. Finally, an individual's personal circumstances may affect his or her relative evaluations of labor market work and leisure. For example, a young mother with two or three preschool children or a college student may have relatively steep indifference curves because "leisure" (non-labor market time) is very valuable for child care and studying. Similarly, José may be married and therefore may have substantial financial obligations. Consequently, his indifference curves are relatively flat; he is quite willing to give up leisure for income. On the other hand, John is single and his financial responsibilities are less compelling. He is less willing to give up leisure for income, and his indifference curves are therefore relatively steep. In short, personality, the type of work under consideration, and personal circumstances may influence the shape of a person's indifference curves.

Budget Constraint

Our assertion that the individual maximizes utility by achieving a position on the highest *attainable* indifference curve implies that the choice of curves is constrained. Specifically, the individual is constrained by the amount of money income that is available. Let's assume for the moment that an individual's only source of money income is from work. In other words, we are assuming that the individual has no nonlabor income, no accumulated savings to draw on, and no possibility of borrowing funds. Let's also suppose that the wage rate confronting this person in the labor market is "given" in that the individual cannot alter the hourly wage paid for his or her services by varying the number of hours worked.[2] Thus we can draw a ***budget (wage) constraint*** *line, which shows all the various combinations of income (goods) and leisure that a worker might realize or obtain, given the wage rate.* If the going wage rate is \$1, we can draw a budget line from 24 hours on the horizontal leisure axis to \$24 on the vertical income axis in Figure 2-4. Given the \$1 wage rate, at the extremes an individual could obtain (1) 24 hours of leisure and no real income or (2) \$24 worth of real income and no leisure. The line connecting these two points reveals all other attainable options; for example, \$8 of real income and 16 hours of leisure, \$12 of income and 12 hours of leisure, and so forth. Observe that the absolute value of the slope of this budget line is 1, reflecting the \$1 wage rate. In moving northwest along the line, 1 hour of leisure must be sacrificed to obtain each \$1 of real income. This is true because the wage rate is \$1.

Similarly, we note that if the wage rate is \$2, the appropriate budget line would be anchored at 24 hours of leisure and \$48 of real income. The slope of this line is 2, again reflecting the wage rate. The budget constraints for wage rates of \$3 and \$4 are also shown in Figure 2-4. We observe that the budget lines fan out clockwise from the

[2]This assumption permits us to use a linear budget constraint.

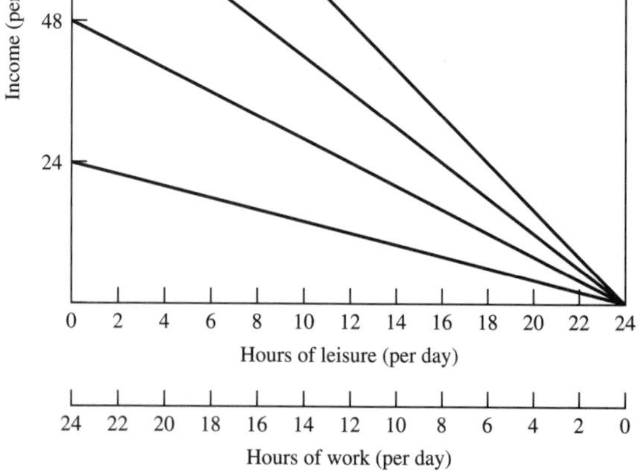

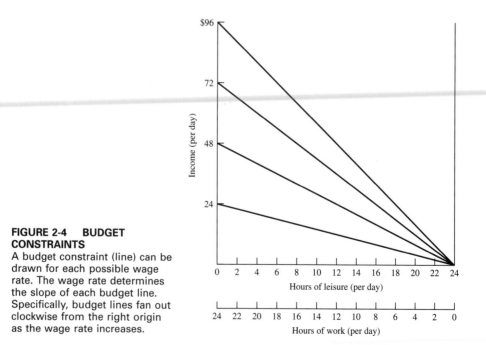

FIGURE 2-4 BUDGET CONSTRAINTS
A budget constraint (line) can be drawn for each possible wage rate. The wage rate determines the slope of each budget line. Specifically, budget lines fan out clockwise from the right origin as the wage rate increases.

right origin as the wage rate goes up. In each case the wage rate—the slope of the budget line—reflects the "objective" or market rate of exchange between income and leisure. If the wage rate is \$1, an individual can exchange 1 hour of leisure (by working) and obtain \$1 worth of real income. If the wage rate is \$2, 1 hour of leisure can be exchanged in the labor market for \$2 worth of real income, and so forth.[3]

Utility Maximization

The individual's optimal or utility-maximizing position can be determined by bringing together the subjective preferences embodied in the indifference curves and the objective market information contained in each budget line. This is in Figure 2-5, where we assume that the wage rate is \$2.

Recall that the farther the indifference curve is from the origin, the greater the person's total utility. Therefore, an individual will maximize total utility by attaining the highest possible indifference curve. Given the \$2 wage rate, no leisure–real income combination is attainable outside—to the northeast—of the resulting *HW* budget constraint. This particular budget constraint allows one to realize the highest attainable

[3]In equation form, the budget constraint is $Y = WH$, where Y = income, W = wage rate, and H = number of hours of work. Hence $Y = W(24 - L) = 24W - WL$, where L = number of hours of leisure and the slope of the budget line is $-W$.

FIGURE 2-5 UTILITY MAXIMIZATION: THE OPTIMAL CHOICE BETWEEN LEISURE AND INCOME
The optimal or utility-maximizing combination of leisure and income for the worker is at point u_1, where the budget constraint is tangent to the highest attainable indifference curve I_2.

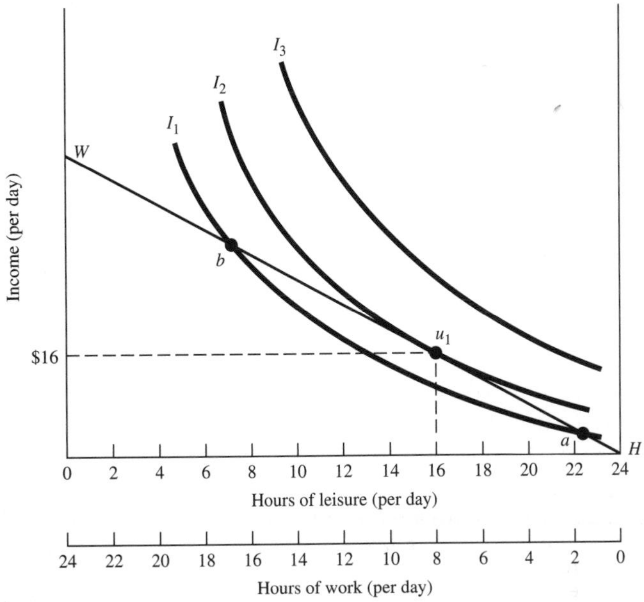

level of utility at point u_1, where the budget line just touches (is tangent to) indifference curve I_2. Of all the attainable positions on the various indifference curves, point u_1 is clearly on that curve that is farthest from the origin and therefore yields the highest achievable level of total utility. We observe that the individual will choose to work 8 hours, earning a daily income of \$16 and enjoying 16 hours of leisure.

It is important to recognize that at this optimal position, the individual and the market are in agreement as to the relative worth of leisure and real income at the margin. At u_1 the slope of indifference curve I_2 and the slope of the budget line are equal. The individual's preferences are such that he or she is subjectively willing to substitute leisure for income at precisely the same exchange rate as the objective information of the labor market requires. The ***optimal work–leisure position*** *it achieved where MRS L,Y (slope of the indifference curve) is equal to the wage rate (the slope of the budget line).* By definition, these slopes are only equal at the point of tangency.

We can reinforce our understanding of the optimal work–leisure position by considering briefly why points *a* and *b* are *not* optimal. Let's start with point *b,* where we note that indifference curve I_1 is steeper than the budget line or, more technically, MRS *L,Y* is greater than the wage rate. For example, the MRS *L,Y* might be 4 while the wage rate is \$2. What does this mean? It indicates that an additional hour of leisure is worth \$4 to this individual but that she will have to sacrifice only \$2 of income to obtain that extra hour of leisure. Acquiring something worth \$4 at the cost of something worth only \$2 is clearly a beneficial exchange. Thus, "trading" income (by working fewer hours) for leisure will be beneficial for her. These trades in effect move her down budget line *HW* and on to successively higher indifference curves. At point u_1 all such trades are exhausted, and this individual and the market are in agreement as to the value of work (income) and leisure at the margin. As noted earlier, at u_1 the MRS *L,Y* equals the wage rate. At this point the individual and the market agree that the marginal hour of leisure is worth \$2. Later we will note that at point *b* the individual will feel "overemployed" in that she can increase her total utility by working fewer hours, that is, by moving to a point such as u_1 where she has more leisure and less income.

The situation is just the opposite at point *a*. Here the slope of indifference curve I_1 is less than the budget line or, in other words, MRS *L,Y* is less than the wage rate. To illustrate, the wage rate is \$2 and the MRS *L,Y* might be only \$1. This indicates that an hour of leisure is worth only \$1 at the margin but that the individual can actually get \$2 worth of income by sacrificing an hour of leisure. Getting something worth \$2 by giving up something worth only \$1 is obviously a beneficial trade. In trading leisure for income (by working more hours) the individual moves up the *HW* budget line to preferred positions on higher indifference curves. Again, all such beneficial exchanges of leisure for income will be completed when point u_1 is achieved because here the MRS *L,Y* and the wage rate are equal. At u_1 leisure and income are of equal value at the margin. At point *a* the individual would feel "underemployed." She could increase her total utility by working more hours, that is, by moving to a point such as u_1 where she has less leisure and more income.

QUICK REVIEW 2-1

- An income–leisure indifference curve represents all combinations of income and leisure that provide equal total utility; its slope is called the marginal rate of substitution (MRS).
- Each successive curve to the northeast in an indifference map indicates a greater level of total utility.
- An income–leisure budget line reveals all combinations of income and leisure that a worker can achieve at a specific hourly wage rate.
- The utility-maximizing combination of income and leisure occurs at the point of tangency between the budget line and the highest attainable indifference curve; there, MRS L,Y (the slope of the indifference curve) equals the wage rate (the slope of the budget line).

Your Turn: Suppose that at a particular combination of income and leisure, the slope of the budget line is steeper than the slope of the indifference curve it intersects. How should the worker adjust work hours? (Answer: See page 625.)

Wage Rate Changes: Income and Substitution Effects

Will an individual choose to work more or fewer hours as the wage rate changes? It depends. Figure 2-6(a) repeats the u_1 utility-maximizing position of Figure 2-5, but adds four more budget lines and indicates the relevant optimal positions associated with each. We observe that for the wage rate increase that moves the budget line from W_1 to W_2, the optimal position moves from u_1 to u_2. On the horizontal axis we find that the individual chooses fewer hours of leisure and more hours of work. Similarly, the wage rate increase that shifts the budget constraint from W_2 to W_3 also entails more hours of work and fewer of leisure at u_3 than is the case at u_2. But the further wage rate boost reflected by the shift of the budget line from W_3 to W_4 produces an optimum at u_4 that involves less work and more leisure than the prior optimum u_3. Similarly, the wage increase depicted by the increase in the budget line from W_4 to W_5 causes a further reduction in hours of work at u_5.

This analysis suggests that *for a specific person, hours of work may for a time increase as wage rates rise, but beyond some point, further wage increases may lead to fewer hours of labor being supplied.* Indeed, we can translate the hours of work–wage rate combinations associated with the five optimal positions of Figure 2-6(a) into a diagram such as shown in Figure 2-6(b), which has traditional axes—measuring wage rates on the vertical axis and hours of labor supplied left to right on the horizontal axis. In so doing we find that this individual's labor supply curve is forward-rising for a time and then backward-bending. This curve is known as a ***backward-bending labor supply curve,*** the forward-rising portion being expected or taken for granted. We can envision an individual labor supply curve for each person in the economy. But keep in mind that each individual's preferences for work versus leisure are unique, and hence

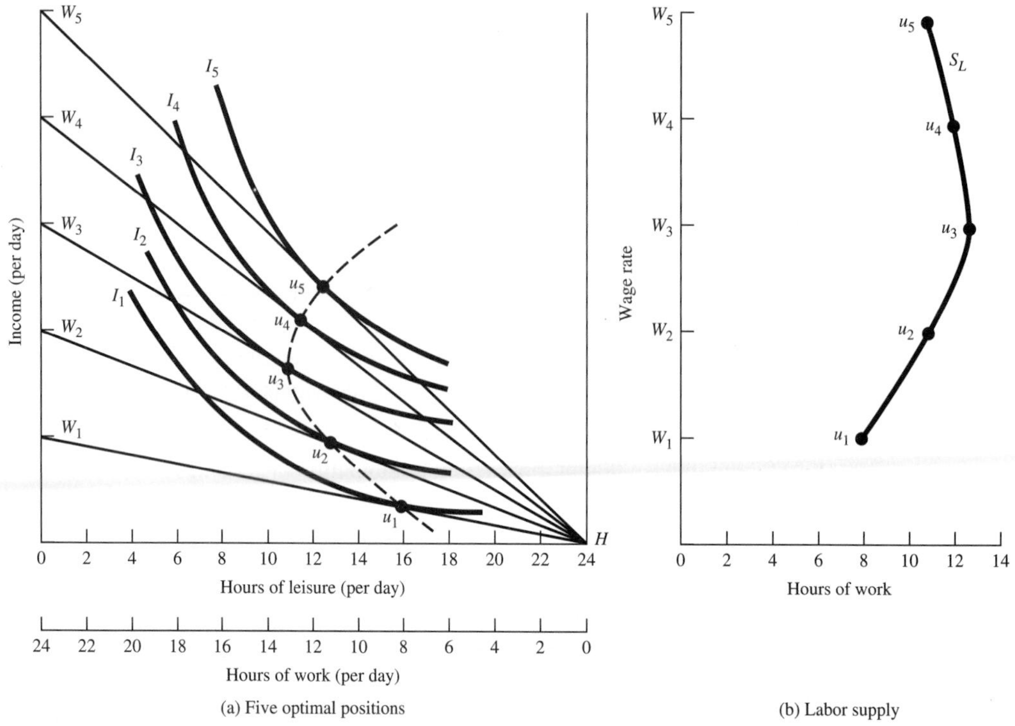

FIGURE 2-6 DERIVATION OF THE BACKWARD-BENDING LABOR SUPPLY CURVE
In (a) higher wage rates result in a series of increasingly steep budget lines whose tangencies with indifference curves locate a series of utility-maximizing positions. The movement from u_1 to u_2 and u_3 reveals that for a time higher wage rates are associated with longer hours of work, while the shifts from u_3 to u_4 and u_5 indicate that still higher wage rates entail fewer hours of work. The overall result is a backward-bending labor supply curve as shown in (b).

the exact location, shape, and point of the backward bend of the curve vary from person to person.

Why is a backward-bending labor supply curve a realistic possibility? The possibility can be explained in terms of the income and substitution effects. When the wage rate changes, these two effects tend to alter one's utility-maximizing position.

Income Effect *The **income effect** refers to the change in the desired hours of work resulting from a change in income, holding the wage rate constant.*[4] We shall discover that the income effect of a wage *increase* is found by isolating the increase in work hours resulting solely from the increase in potential income per hour of work, *as if the price of leisure (the wage rate) did not change.* A wage rate increase means that a larger

[4]In mathematical terms, income effect $= \left.\frac{\Delta H}{\Delta Y}\right| \overline{W} < 0$

where: H = hours of work, Y = income, $\overline{W}$ = constant wage.

money income is obtainable from a given number of hours of work. We would expect an individual to use a part of this enhanced income to buy goods and services: for example, a new stereo, movie tickets, and so on. But if we make the reasonable assumption that leisure is a *normal good*—a "good" of which more is consumed as income rises—then we can expect that a part of one's expanded income might be used to "purchase" leisure. Consumers do not derive utility from goods alone, but from combinations of goods and nonmarket time (leisure). A stereo or movie tickets yield satisfaction only if one has the time to enjoy them. How does one purchase leisure or nonmarket time? In a unique way: by working fewer hours. This means that when wage rates *rise,* and leisure is a normal good, the income effect results in a reduction in the desired number of hours of work.

Substitution Effect *The* ***substitution effect*** *indicates the change in the desired hours of work resulting from a change in the wage rate, keeping income constant.*[5] In the context of a wage rate increase, it evidences itself in an increase in the desired number of hours of work. When the wage rate increases, the relative price of leisure is altered. Specifically, an increase in the wage rate raises the "price" or opportunity cost of leisure. Because of the higher wage rate, one must now forgo more income (goods) for each hour of leisure consumed (not worked). The basic theory of economic choice implies that an individual will purchase less of any normal good when it becomes relatively more expensive. In brief, the higher price of leisure prompts one to consume less leisure or, in other words, to work more. The substitution effect merely tells us that when wage rates rise and leisure becomes more expensive, it is sensible to substitute work for leisure. For a wage *increase,* the substitution effect results in the person desiring to work more hours.[6]

Net Effect The overall effect of an increase in the wage rate on the number of hours an individual wants to work depends on the relative magnitudes of these two effects. Economic theory does not predict the outcome. *If the substitution effect dominates the income effect, the individual will choose to work more hours when the wage rate rises.* Dominance of the substitution effect is reflected in shifts from u_1 to u_2 to u_3 in Figure 2-6(a) and the upward-sloping portion of the labor supply curve in Figure 2-6(b). *But if the income effect is larger than the substitution effect, a wage increase will prompt the individual to work fewer hours.* The movements from u_3 to u_4 and u_5 in Figure 2-6(a) and the backward-bending portion of the labor supply curve in Figure 2-6(b) are relevant in this case.

[5]In mathematical terms, substitution effect = $\left.\frac{\Delta H}{\Delta W}\right|_{\bar{Y}} > 0$

where: H = hours of work, W = wage, $\bar{Y}$ = constant income.

[6]An alternative way to express the substitution effect is to say that a higher wage rate reduces the "price of income" since it now takes a smaller amount of work time to obtain $1 worth of goods. When the wage rate is $2 per hour, the "price" of $1 worth of income is one-half an hour of work time. But if the wage rate increases to $4 per hour, the "price" of $1 worth of income falls to one-quarter of an hour. Now that income is cheaper, it makes sense to purchase more of it. This purchase is made by working more hours and taking less leisure. The classic article is Lionel Robbins, "On the Elasticity of Demand for Income in Terms of Effort," *Economica,* June 1930, pp. 123–129.

TABLE 2-1 WAGE CHANGES AND HOURS OF WORK: SUBSTITUTION AND INCOME EFFECTS

(1) Size of effects	(2) Impact on hours of work (a) Wage rate increase	(b) Wage rate decrease	(3) Slope of labor supply curve
Substitution effect exceeds income effect	Increase	Decrease	Positive
Income effect equals substitution effect	No change	No change	Vertical
Income effect exceeds substitution effect	Decrease	Increase	Negative

Table 2-1 provides a useful summary and extension of our discussion of the implications of the relative sizes of the substitution and income effects for the desired hours of work. Columns 1, 2a, and 3 summarize the discussion we have just completed. Note from column 2a that this discussion was couched in terms of a wage rate *increase*. Columns 1, 2b, and 3 are important because they reveal that the impact of the substitution and income effects on hours of work is reversed if we assume a wage *decrease*. The income effect associated with a wage decline is such that the desired hours of work increase. That is, a decline in the wage rate will reduce an individual's income from a given number of hours of work, and we can expect the individual to purchase less leisure and therefore choose to work more hours. Similarly, in terms of a wage decline, the substitution effect evidences itself as a decline in work hours. A reduction in the wage rate makes leisure cheaper, prompting one to consume more of it. Once again, the final outcome depends on the relative strength of the two effects. You should study Table 2-1 carefully to be certain that you fully understand it.

Graphic Portrayal of Income and Substitution Effects

Figure 2-7 permits us to isolate graphically the income and substitution effects associated with a wage rate increase for a specific person. Remember that the substitution effect reflects the change in desired hours of work arising solely because an increase in the wage rate alters the relative prices of income and leisure. Therefore, to isolate the substitution effect, we must control for the increase in income created by the increase in the wage rate. Recall, too, that the income effect indicates the change in the hours of work occurring solely because the higher wage rate means a larger total income from any number of hours of work. In portraying the income effect, we must hold constant the relative prices of income and leisure or, in other words, the wage rate.

Consider Figure 2-7. As the wage rate increases and shifts the budget line from HW_1 to HW_2, the resulting movement of the utility-maximizing position from u_1 on I_1 to u_2 on I_2 is the consequence of the combined income and substitution effects. The *income effect* is isolated by drawing the budget line nW', which is parallel to HW_1 and tangent

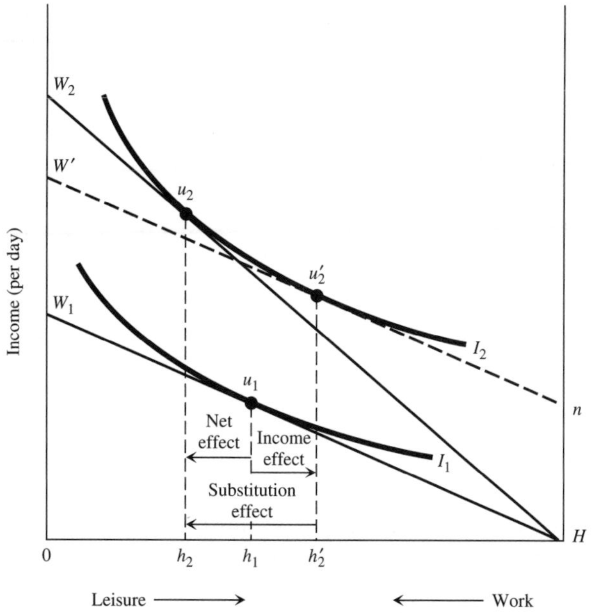

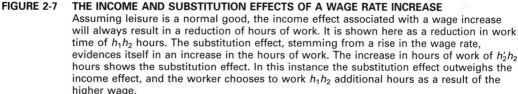

FIGURE 2-7 THE INCOME AND SUBSTITUTION EFFECTS OF A WAGE RATE INCREASE
Assuming leisure is a normal good, the income effect associated with a wage increase will always result in a reduction of hours of work. It is shown here as a reduction in work time of h_1h_2 hours. The substitution effect, stemming from a rise in the wage rate, evidences itself in an increase in the hours of work. The increase in hours of work of $h_2'h_2$ hours shows the substitution effect. In this instance the substitution effect outweighs the income effect, and the worker chooses to work h_1h_2 additional hours as a result of the higher wage.

to I_2 at point u_2'.The vertical distance Hn measures the amount of *nonlabor* income that would be required to make the individual just as well off (that is, attain the same total utility) at u_2' as at u_2. But by moving the individual from curve I_1 to curve I_2 with *nonlabor* income, we have left the wage rate, that is, the relative prices of leisure and goods, unchanged.[7] No substitution effect is involved here. The movement from u_1 to u_2' therefore measures or isolates the income effect. As noted earlier, this effect results in fewer work hours when analyzed from the vantage point of an increase in wage rates and hence an increase in income. Specifically, the income effect would result in the individual wanting to work h_1h_2' fewer hours.

The *substitution effect* is isolated as follows. The substitution effect occurs solely because the slope of the budget line—the relative prices of income and leisure—has been altered by the assumed increase in the wage rate. We are concerned with budget lines nW' and HW_2 because their comparison involves no change in the individual's well-being; they pertain to the same indifference curve I_2. Line nW', however, reflects

[7]Note that the slopes of HW_1 and nW' are the same; the lines are parallel, meaning the wage rate embodied in both budget lines is the same.

the original wage rate (also embodied in HW_1), while HW_2 mirrors the new higher wage rate. The movement from u_2' to u_2 on curve I_2 is the substitution effect. It is solely the result of a change in the relative prices of leisure and goods or, specifically, the fact that goods have become cheaper and leisure more expensive. It is no surprise that this prompts a substitution of work (goods) for leisure. For a wage rate increase, the hours of work rise (the substitution effect). In this case, the individual wishes to work $h_2'h_2$ more hours.

Keep in mind that the individual does not actually "move" to a new optimal position in two distinct steps, but rather goes directly from u_1 to u_2. We have conceptually isolated the income and substitution effects to stress that there are two opposing ways in which a wage increase affects the worker: by increasing money income *and* by increasing the relative price of leisure. Both effects are at work, but one effect may dominate the other.

In Figure 2-7, the income and substitution effects can be thought of in terms of a boating analogy. Assume that a boat is drifting on the ocean. Suppose that the tide moves the boat eastward while the surface wind blows it westward. Both forces are present, but whether the boat actually moves east or west depends on which of these forces are strongest. So it is also with the income and substitution effects of a wage change.

To summarize: In this instance the income effect is represented by the rightward horizontal movement from u_1 to u_2', that is, from Hh_1 to Hh_2' hours of work. The substitution effect is shown by the leftward horizontal movement from u_2' to u_2, that is, from Hh_2' to Hh_2 hours of work. In this case, the substitution effect (increased work hours) is larger than the income effect (reduced work hours). The net effect is an increase in hours of work from Hh_1 to Hh_2; at the higher wage rate, the individual wants to work h_1h_2 additional hours. This individual is clearly on the upward-sloping segment of his or her labor supply curve; the wage rate and the desired hours of work are directly related.

It is a worthwhile exercise for you to diagram and explain the case in which the income effect is larger than the substitution effect, causing the labor supply curve to be backward-bending. Questions 2 and 3 at the end of this chapter also are relevant.

Rationale for Backward-Bending Supply Curve

From Figure 2-6 we remember that for a time wage rate increases are initially associated with the desire to work more hours. Specifically, for the wage increases that shift the budget line from W_1 through W_3, the absolute value of the substitution effects must be greater than that of the income effects, yielding the forward-rising segment of the labor supply curve. But further increases in the wage rate that shift the budget line from W_3 through W_5 are associated with the choice to work fewer hours. The income effects associated with these wage rate increases are greater than the substitution effects, yielding the backward-bending segment of the labor supply curve.

What is the rationale for this reversal? The answer is that points u_1 and u_2 are at positions on indifference curves where the amount of leisure is large relative to the amount of income (goods). That is, u_1 and u_2 are located on relatively flat portions of indifference curves, where MRS *L,Y* is small because the individual is willing to give up substantial amounts of leisure for an additional unit of income or goods. This means that the substitution effect is large—so large that it dominates the income effect. The individual's labor supply curve is forward-rising; higher wage rates induce more hours of work. But points u_3, u_4, and u_5 are reached only after much leisure has been exchanged in the labor market for income. At these points, the individual has a relatively large amount of income and relatively little leisure. This is reflected in the relative steepness of the indifference curves. In other words, MRS *L,Y* is large, indicating that the individual is willing to give up only a small amount of leisure for an additional unit of income. This means that the substitution effect is small and in this case is dominated by the income effect. Consequently, the labor supply curve of the individual becomes backward-bending; rising wage rates are associated with fewer hours of work.

Empirical Evidence

What do empirical studies reveal about labor supply curves? The evidence differs rather sharply between males and females. Specifically, Killingsworth made an exhaustive survey of empirical work that led him to the conclusion that "male labor supply is much less sensitive to wage changes than is female labor supply. Indeed, the male labor supply curve appears to be gently backward-bending with respect to the wage, whereas the female schedule . . . is strongly positive sloped."[8] Apparently for men the income effect slightly dominates the substitution effect when wage rates rise. For women the substitution effect seems to dominate substantially the income effect.

Individual studies report various magnitudes of the labor supply responses of males and females. However, a careful review of nine empirical studies has led Borjas and Heckman to estimate that a 10 percent *increase* in male wage rates would *decrease* the amount of labor supplied by approximately 1 to 2 percent. Keeley[9] has offered the same general estimate for males as Borjas and Heckman, but also suggests that a 10 percent increase in wages would increase the hours of work of married women by about 10 percent.[10]

How might one explain the apparent differences in the labor supply responses of males and females to a wage change? The answer hinges on existing differences in the allocation of time. A very high percentage of adult males—over 90 percent—work full-time. Furthermore, men on the average do relatively little housework. Thus, increased hours of work in response to a wage rate increase would have to come at the expense of pure leisure, that is, nonproductive activities or rest and relaxation. Apparently, pure leisure and labor market work are not highly substitutable. The result is a small sub-

[8]Mark R. Killingsworth, *Labor Supply* (Cambridge: Cambridge University Press, 1983), p. 102. Also see Michael C. Keeley, *Labor Supply and Public Policy* (New York: Academic Press, 1981), chap. 4.

[9]George J. Borjas and James J. Heckman, "Labor Supply Estimates for Public Policy Evaluation," *Proceedings of the Industrial Relations Research Association* (Madison, Wis.: Industrial Relations Research Association, 1978), p. 331.

[10]Keeley, op. cit., p. 104. The ambitious, mathematically sophisticated reader should consult John Pencavel, "Labor Supply of Men: A Survey," pp. 3–102; and Mark R. Killingsworth and James J. Heckman, "Female Labor Supply: A Survey," pp. 103–204, in Orley Ashenfelter and Richard Layard (eds.), *Handbook of Labor Economics, Volume 1* (Amsterdam: North-Holland, 1986).

stitution effect for men and a nearly vertical or perhaps slightly backward-bending labor supply curve. In comparison, the labor market participation rate for women is significantly less than that for men; many women work part-time, and women assume major responsibility for work within the home. At the risk of oversimplification, this means that while men use their time in basically two ways (market work and pure leisure), women use their time in three (market work, work in the home, and pure leisure). For many married women, work in the home and work in the labor market are highly substitutable. That is, household work may be accomplished by doing it oneself *or* by working in the labor market and using a portion of one's earnings for hiring housecleaning and child care help and purchasing prepared meals. Thus when wage rates increase, many women substitute labor market work for work in the home. They enter the labor force, switch from part-time to full-time jobs, or increase their hours on full-time jobs.[11] In other words, a strong substitution effect occurs, which implies an upward-sloping labor supply curve for married women.

2-1

Elasticity versus Changes in Labor Supply

To this point, we have been discussing the direction in which wage changes cause an individual to alter the hours of work supplied. Implicitly, our discussion has focused

[11]Most of the gender differences in the labor supply result from differences in labor force participation between men and women, not from differences in the hours of work supplied by those working. See James J. Heckman, "What Has Been Learned about Labor Supply in the Past Twenty Years?" *American Economic Review,* May 1993, pp. 116–121.

2-1 World of Work

SLEEP TIME LINKED TO EARNINGS*

The horizontal axis in our graphs in this chapter measure leisure, which includes hours spent sleeping. If sleep time is biologically determined, then a worker has a fixed amount of nonsleep time to allocate between work and "waking leisure." But a novel study by Jeff Biddle and Daniel Hamermesh suggests that sleep time itself may be a matter of economic discretion.

Biddle and Hamermesh analyzed minute-to-minute diaries kept by 706 people between the ages of 23 and 65. They found that a 25 percent increase in wages reduced sleep time for the average worker by about 1 percent. A doubling of wages resulted, on average, in 20 fewer minutes of sleep time each night.

The researchers observed interesting differences in work–sleep choices between men and women. Higher wages reduced sleep time among men but did not increase hours worked. Instead, men substituted "waking leisure" for sleep time. Men apparently responded to the income effect of the wage increase by sleeping less as a way of freeing more time to enjoy the products made available by their increased income. Alternatively, women responded to wage increases by working more hours but not reducing their sleep time. Working women took their added work time from hours of "waking leisure." Why didn't women reduce their sleep time? The answer may lie in the fact that women, on average, slept 5 percent fewer hours than working men. Women may simply have been operating too close to their biological limits to reduce their sleep time further.

*Based on Jeff Biddle and Daniel Hamermesh, "Sleep and the Allocation of Time," *Journal of Political Economy,* October 1990, pp. 922–943.

on the wage elasticity of individual labor supply. More precisely, ***wage elasticity of labor supply*** is defined as follows:

$$E_S = \frac{\text{percentage change in quantity of labor supplied}}{\text{percentage change in the wage rate}} \tag{2-1}$$

Over specific ranges of an individual's labor supply curve, the elasticity coefficient given in equation (2-1) may be zero (perfectly inelastic), infinite (perfectly elastic), less than one (relatively inelastic), greater than one (relatively elastic), or negative (backward-bending). The elasticity will depend on the relative strengths of the income and substitution effects generated by a wage rate change. But these movements *along* an existing individual labor supply curve [as in Figure 2-6(b)] should not be confused with *shifts* in the entire supply curve. These shifts—increases or decreases in labor supply—occur in response to changes in either of two factors that we have heretofore held constant. First, changes in *nonlabor income* may shift an individual's labor supply curve. Receiving a large inheritance, winning a lottery, qualifying for a pension, or becoming eligible for welfare benefits may shift one's labor supply curve leftward, that is, cause a decrease in labor supply. Or conversely, the layoff of one's spouse or a significant decline in dividend income may produce an increase (rightward shift) in labor supply.

Second, a change in a person's indifference map—that is, in work–leisure preferences—may cause a shift in the labor supply curve. An improvement in working conditions, availability of child care, or large medical bills may change a person's indifference map in ways that increase his or her labor supply. Working in the opposite direction, the purchase of a product requiring leisure to enjoy or the attainment of a culturally acceptable retirement age may alter one's indifference map such that labor supply declines. A more detailed treatment of factors that shift the labor supply curve is found in Chapter 6.

To summarize: As Figure 2-6 suggests, given work–leisure preferences and nonlabor income, a change in wage rates traces out or locates the individual's labor supply curve. The elasticity of this curve for any particular wage change—that is, the sensitivity of hours one wants to work to a change in wages—depends on the relative sizes of the income and substitution effects. In contrast, changes in work–leisure preferences or in nonlabor income shift the location of one's labor supply curve.

QUICK REVIEW 2-2

- A change in the wage rate produces two simultaneous effects: *(a)* an income effect that, taken alone, changes a worker's desired hours of work in the opposite direction as the wage rate change, and *(b)* a substitution effect that, taken alone, changes a worker's desired hours of work in the same direction as the wage rate change.
- As the wage rate rises, the labor supply curve for a typical person first is positively sloped as the substitution effect swamps the income effect; eventually the curve becomes negatively sloped (turns backward) as the income effect of further wage rate hikes exceeds the substitution effect.

• The wage elasticity of supply is the percentage change in the quantity of labor supplied divided by the percentage change in the wage rate.

Your Turn: Suppose that an individual's wage rate decreases and the income effect dominates the substitution effect. What will be the impact on the desired hours of work? What is the relevant segment of the person's labor supply curve? (Answers: See page 625.)

APPLYING AND EXTENDING THE MODEL

The basic model just developed outlines the logic of the work–leisure decision, provides a rationale for an individual's backward-bending labor supply curve, and helps us understand changes in individual labor supply. Our goal now is to extend, embellish, and apply the basic work–leisure model. Specifically, we want to show that the work–leisure model is useful in delineating reasons for nonparticipation in the labor force, in explaining how a standard workweek might cause certain workers to feel overemployed or underemployed, and in comparing the impact that various pay schemes and income maintenance programs might have on work incentives.

Nonparticipants and the Reservation Wage

Figure 2-8 portrays the case of a nonparticipant, that is, an individual who decides *not* to be in the labor force. Note the following characteristics in Figure 2-8. First, the person's indifference curves are very steep, indicating that leisure (nonmarket time) is valued very highly relative to income. The marginal rates of substitution of leisure for income are high, meaning that the individual is very willing to forgo real income for leisure or nonmarket time. This might reflect the preferences of, say, a 20-year-old who deems it important to devote time and effort to attending college. Second, we note the availability of nonlabor income *HN*. (Ignore all other budget lines but *HNW* for the moment.) Perhaps this nonlabor income takes the form of an "intrahousehold transfer" to the young student from the earned income of parents. Finally, the relative flatness of the *NW* budget line indicates that the wage rate that this individual can earn in the labor market is relatively low. For example, the student may have modest skills and little or no labor market experience and therefore is not yet able to command a high wage rate by working.

The optimal position in Figure 2-8 is based on the same principle employed in Figure 2-5. Given budget line *HNW,* choose that position that puts one on the highest attainable indifference curve. In this case, the highest level of utility is achieved at point *N*. Here the budget constraint *HNW* touches I_3. At this point the individual is *not* participating in the labor market; all of this person's time is devoted to nonmarket activities. The technical reason is that at all points within the axes of the diagram, the person's indifference curves are more steeply sloped than the budget constraint. In other words, at all points within the diagram, the individual values leisure (nonmarket time) more highly at the margin than does the market. Note that in contrast to Figure 2-5, the op-

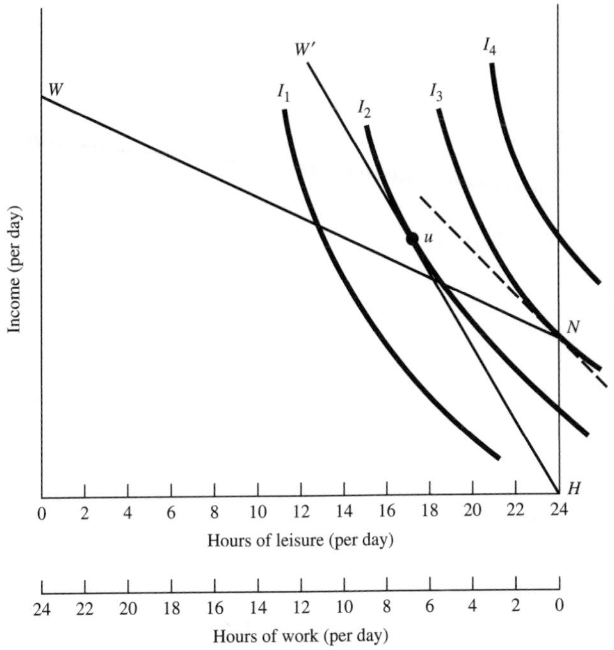

FIGURE 2-8 NONPARTICIPATION: THE COLLEGE STUDENT
A very high subjective evaluation of nonwork time (reflected in steep indifference curves), the availability of nonlabor income *(HN),* and low earning ability (*NW* is relatively flat) are all factors which are conducive to not participating in the labor force.

timal outcome at *N* is *not* a tangency position but rather a "corner" solution. At *N* the wage rate is less than MRS *L,Y*, which means that the individual values nonmarket time more highly than does the market. But given the fact that the individual is a nonparticipant, there is no further possible substitution of leisure for work to be made.

The importance of low earning capacity in the labor market and the availability of nonlabor income can be understood if we replace the original budget line *HNW* in Figure 2-8 with *HuW'*. This new budget line reduces nonlabor income to zero *and* assumes that a much higher wage rate can be garnered in the labor market. Suppose, for example, that our student is a highly skilled computer programmer who has immediate employment opportunities at a high wage. Or to make the point even more graphic, suppose that the student is a premier college basketball player who is sought by the National Basketball Association. We find that under these new conditions the individual would prefer to participate in the labor force. The optimal position will now be at *u,* where the person will want to work 6 or 7 hours per day.

Figure 2-8 also allows us to introduce the concept of the reservation wage, which is useful in understanding why some individuals participate in the labor force and others do not. In simple terms, the ***reservation wage*** *is the highest wage rate at which an individual chooses* not *to work or, if you prefer, the lowest wage rate at which one would decide to work.* When nonlabor income is *HN,* as in Figure 2-8, the reservation wage is that market wage rate implicit in the broken budget line that is equal to the slope of indifference curve I_3 at zero hours of work. At this particular wage rate, the value of work and the value of nonmarket time (leisure) are equal. If the market wage is below the reservation wage, the individual will clearly choose to be a nonparticipant. The relatively low market wage rate embodied in the *NW* segment of the *HNW* budget line demonstrates this decision *not* to be in the labor force. In nontechnical terms, at point *N* the value of nonmarket time to this individual exceeds the value of work, and therefore this person's well-being would be reduced by working. Conversely, if the market wage rate were above the reservation wage, the individual would be induced to become a labor market participant. You can demonstrate this by drawing a steeper budget line from point *N* that is tangent to I_4 at some point. With this steeper (higher market wage) budget line, we would find at point *N* that the value of work would be greater than the value of nonmarket time and that the individual's economic welfare would be enhanced by working.

Figure 2-9 illustrates another common instance of nonparticipation in the labor force. Here we assume that a rather elderly worker is initially participating in the labor force, working about 9 hours per day at optimal position *u* on indifference curve I_1. Suppose now that when the worker reaches age 65 a private or public pension of *HN* becomes available, *provided* the individual retires fully from work. In other words, the choice is between budget line *HW* and the associated optimal position at *u* or budget line *NN′* and the corner solution at point *N*. We find that *N* is preferable to *u* because it is associated with the higher indifference curve I_2. In this case, the availability of a pen-

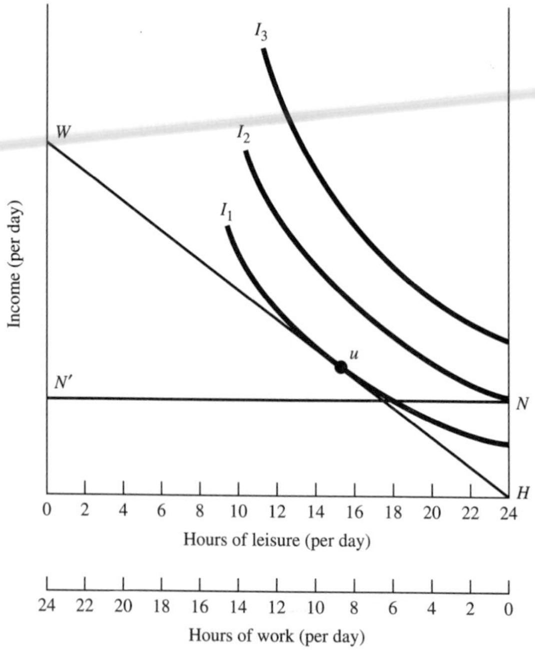

FIGURE 2-9
NONPARTICIPATION: PENSIONS AND THE ELDERLY
An elderly worker whose wage rate yields the budget line *HW* will be a labor force participant at *u*. However, when a pension of *HN* becomes available at, say, age 65, the individual will prefer to become a nonparticipant at point *N*.

sion—for example, Social Security benefits—induces the individual to become a nonparticipant. Stated differently, it shifts the person's labor supply curve [Figure 2-6(b)] leftward such that no labor is supplied at the market wage. Note that the decision to be a nonparticipant entails a *reduction* in money income but a more than compensating *increase* in leisure. The individual is better off at N than at u, even though income is reduced.

Empirical research confirms several generalizations arising from our discussion of Figures 2-8 and 2-9. First, other things being equal, full-time college attendance *is* a deterrent to labor force participation. This is also true of such things as the desire to care for one's preschool children. Stated alternatively, those who attach great marginal utility to nonmarket time (college attendance, child care) are more likely to be nonparticipants in the labor force. Second, other things being the same, the higher the nonlabor income available to a person from parents, spouses, Social Security benefits, private pensions, welfare, and other sources, the less likely it is that the person will be a labor force participant. Finally, all else being equal, the greater the opportunity cost of not working—that is, the higher the wage obtainable in the labor market—the more
2-2 likely it is that a person will be a labor force participant.[12]

Standard Workday

Our discussion thus far has implicitly assumed that workers can individually determine the number of hours they work. This is typically not the case. In the United States a "standard" workday of 8 hours (40 hours per week) has evolved. This is partly due to federal legislation that obligates employers to pay time and a half for hours worked in excess of 40 per week. Furthermore, industries whose technologies involve the continuous processing of goods or components are able to divide the workday into three 8-hour shifts.

Overemployment What may happen when a worker confronts a standard workday of HD hours, as illustrated in Figure 2-10? Consider first the solid indifference curves for Smith shown in the lower right-hand portion of the diagram. Smith's optimal position is at u_s, where he prefers to work only Hh_s hours per day. But this is not

[12]Numerous studies confirm these conclusions. For example, for a listing and review of the studies that examine the impact of social security (nonlabor income) on the participation decision, see Sheldon Danziger, Robert Haveman, and Robert Plotnick, "How Income Transfers Affect Work, Savings, and the Income Distribution," *Journal of Economic Literature,* September 1981, pp. 975–1028. This source also surveys studies on the labor supply impact of other sources of nonlabor income such as disability payments, unemployment compensation, and Aid to Families with Dependent Children benefits. This study and survey is updated and extended by Robert Moffitt, "Incentive Effects of the U.S. Welfare System: A Review," *Journal of Economic Literature,* March 1992, pp. 1–61. For an analysis of the impact of preschool children, education (market wage), and husband's income on the labor force participation of married females, see T. Aldrich Finegan, "Participation of Married Women in the Labor Force," in Cynthia B. Lloyd (ed.), *Sex, Discrimination, and the Division of Labor* (New York: Columbia University Press, 1975), pp. 30–31. Also relevant is Evelyn L. Lehrer, "The Impact of Children on Married Women's Labor Supply," *Journal of Human Resources,* Summer 1992, pp. 422–440. For an investigation of the impact of changes in marginal tax rates, see Nada Eissa, "Taxation and Labor Supply of Married Women: The Tax Reform Act of 1986 as a Natural Experiment," National Bureau of Economic Research Working Paper No. 5023, February 1995.

2-2 World of Work

THE CARNEGIE CONJECTURE*

In 1891 Andrew Carnegie, the well-known philanthropist and baron of U.S. Steel, asserted that "parents who leave their children enormous wealth generally deaden their children's talents and energies and tempt them to lead less productive lives." In the language of the work–leisure model, Carnegie was suggesting that large inheritances have a significant pure income effect. We know that, if leisure is a normal good, this effect may cause some workers to reduce their work hours or possibly withdraw from the labor force. Graphically, inheritances will produce an upward parallel shift in the wage rate line facing an individual. The result will be a decline in the optimal number of work hours.

In 1992 Holtz-Eakin, Joulfaian, and Rosen examined three years of data from tax returns for 4300 people receiving inheritances. Their findings lend general support to Carnegie's conjecture. For example, a single person receiving an inheritance of more than \$150,000 was about four times more likely to leave the labor force than a single person inheriting \$25,000. Specifically, 4.6 percent of people receiving inheritances of less than \$25,000 exited the labor force; 10 percent of the people getting inheritances between \$25,000 and \$150,000 left; and 18.2 percent of those inheriting \$150,000 or more quit their jobs.

Also, for families receiving large inheritances whose members continued to work, the growth of labor earnings slowed compared to families receiving lesser inheritances. This suggests that large inheritances may reduce work hours or the supply of effort, even when people receiving inheritances continue to work.

Two other findings of this study are of interest. First, people not working when they received large inheritances were less likely than those receiving smaller inheritances to enter the labor force in subsequent years. Second, people receiving larger inheritances were less likely to be working during the years immediately preceding the inheritance. Perhaps people *anticipating* large inheritances have lower incentives to work. An alternative explanation is that those expecting large inheritances can better afford to quit their jobs to attend to the needs of their dying parents.

Although inheritances reduce labor force participation, they do permit the children to attain higher indifference curves—to achieve greater total utility. Moreover, those taking extra "leisure" may use it for socially beneficial activities such as volunteer work and educational pursuits. The point is simply that nonlabor income—be it from lottery winnings, pensions, intrahousehold transfers, or inheritance—is an important factor in understanding labor supply behavior.

*Based on Douglas Holtz-Eakin, David Joulfaian, and Harvey S. Rosen, "The Carnegie Conjecture: Some Empirical Evidence," *Quarterly Journal of Economics,* May 1993, pp. 413–436.

a relevant choice; Smith can either work *HD* hours or not at all. That is, the relevant choice is between working the standard workday at *P* or being a nonparticipant at *N*. What to do? In this instance, it is preferable to work the standard workday because it entails a higher indifference curve I_{s2} as opposed to I_{s1}. Note once again that this is not a tangency position. At *P* the slope of I_{s2} is greater than the slope of the budget line *NW*. The marginal rate of substitution of leisure for income exceeds the wage rate, which means that the worker values leisure more highly at the margin than does the market. Clearly Smith would be better off at u_s with more leisure and less work per day.

Simply put, at point *P* in Figure 2-10 Smith will feel ***overemployed.*** Faced with a standard workday denying him added leisure, Smith may compensate by engaging in absenteeism; he may more or less habitually miss a day of work every week or so. In fact, the absence rate—the ratio of full-time workers with absences in a typical week to total full-time employment—was 3.9 percent in 1997. In that year lost work time

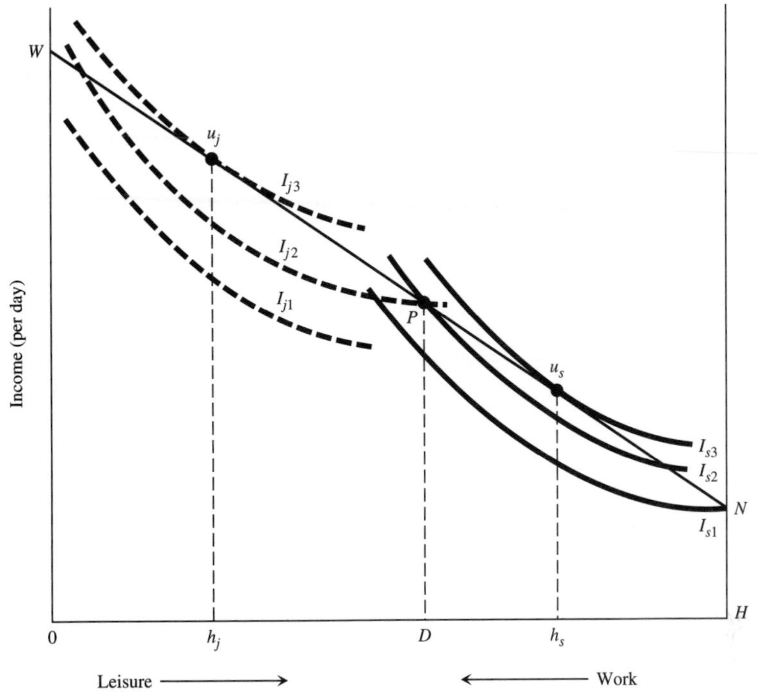

FIGURE 2-10 **OVEREMPLOYMENT AND UNDEREMPLOYMENT**
When confronted with a standard workday of *HD,* Smith (solid indifference curves) will feel overemployed while Jones (broken indifference curves) will feel underemployed.

from absences was 2.0 percent of total hours usually worked. Many of the absent workers are absent without pay. Also, the overemployed worker described in Figure 2-10 may have a relatively high rate of job turnover. The worker obtains more leisure by frequently being "between jobs." Of course, we have purposely ruled out the possibility of part-time employment, which would appeal to this overemployed worker.

Underemployment The broken indifference curves in the upper left-hand portion of Figure 2-10 portray the position of Jones, an ***underemployed*** worker. Jones would prefer to be at u_j, where she would work the long workday of Hh_j hours as opposed to the shorter standard workday of *HD* hours. Note again that *P* is not a tangency position. At *P* the slope of Jones' indifference curve I_{j2} is less than the budget line. Jones' marginal rate of substitution of leisure for income is less than the wage rate. Simply stated, at the margin Jones values leisure less highly than does the market. This means that Jones will feel *underemployed* at *P*. Jones may realize her desire for more work and less leisure by moonlighting, or taking a second job. You should use Figure 2-10 to demonstrate that Jones might be willing to take a second job even if the wage rate were less than that paid on the primary job. In fact, in 1997 some 8.0 million workers—approximately 6.1 percent of all employees—held multiple jobs.

Survey data suggest that the majority of workers are satisfied with the number of hours they work. In 1985 the Bureau of Labor Statistics surveyed some 84,000 workers, and almost two-thirds indicated that they would prefer to work their current number of hours at their present rate of pay, rather than work more or fewer hours at proportionately higher or lower earnings. Only 8 percent expressed a preference for shorter hours, with a proportionate decline in earnings. Approximately one-fourth of all surveyed workers wanted to work more hours, with a proportionate increase in earnings. Not surprisingly, this latter group was dominated by young workers and low-wage earners.[13]

2-3

Premium Pay versus Straight Time

While we ordinarily think of a worker receiving the same wage rate regardless of the number of hours worked, this is not always the case. Indeed, the Fair Labor Standards Act of 1938 specifies that those workers covered by the legislation must be paid a pre-

[13]Susan E. Shank, "Preferred Hours of Work and Corresponding Earnings," *Monthly Labor Review*, November 1986, pp. 40–44.

2-3 World of Work

MOONLIGHTING IS ON THE RISE*

The percentage of the employed labor force holding two or more jobs has increased steadily since 1975. In 1997, 6.1 percent of all employed people held multiple jobs, up from 5.4 percent in 1985 and 4.7 percent in 1975.

There are many motivations for moonlighting. Most fundamental, the limits on the available number of hours on the primary job may lead some workers to take second jobs (see Figure 2-10). Workers wanting to work more than 40 hours per week may be constrained by standard workweeks in their primary jobs. Also, workers who are unable to secure full-time employment may decide to take two or more part-time jobs. Another motivation for moonlighting may be that some second jobs enable workers to engage in activities of special interest. For example, a musician holding a full-time office job during the day may perform his music at night or a college professor desiring to apply her special expertise may serve as a consultant.†

The increase in moonlighting over the past two decades partly reflects the substantial growth of jobs during this period. In particular, more than 18 million new jobs were created in the 1980s, meaning that finding a second job became easier than before. Also, part-time jobs, temporary jobs, self-employment, and home-based work have increased faster than 9-to-5 jobs. These jobs are highly conducive to moonlighting.

Still another reason for the rise in moonlighting is that many peoples' wages on their primary jobs have not increased as rapidly as routine living expenses. For others, wages simply have not risen as fast as their aspirations for consumer goods. Of the moonlighters surveyed in 1979, 37 percent said they took a second job to meet routine living expenses or pay off debt; 40 percent of the moonlighters cited this reason in 1991. The increased frequency of this response may in part be explained by a surge in the number of households headed by women. Widowed, divorced, or separated women had a rate of multiple job holding of 7.4 percent in 1991, more than a full percentage point above the overall 6.2 percent rate. Almost two-thirds of these women said they were moonlighting to meet expenses or pay off debt.

*Data from John F. Stinson, "Multiple Jobholding Up Sharply in the Eighties," *Monthly Labor Review,* July 1990, pp. 3–10; and Bureau of Labor Statistics, *Employment and Earnings,* January 1998.

†Karen Smith Conway and Jean Kimmel, "Moonlighting Behavior: Theory and Evidence," W. E. Upjohn Institute Working Paper 92-09, June 1992.

mium wage—specifically, time and a half—for hours worked in excess of 40 per week. What impact does this premium pay provision have on the work–leisure decision? And how does it compare with a straight-time equivalent wage rate that provides an identical daily or weekly income from the same number of hours of work? Suppose, for example, that in a given industry a 10-hour workday (50-hour workweek) becomes commonplace. Does it make any difference with respect to work incentives to pay \$6 per hour for the first 8 hours of work and \$9 per hour for an additional 2 hours of overtime *or* to pay \$6.60 per hour for each 10 hours of work? Since both payment plans yield the same daily income of \$66, one is inclined to conclude that it makes no difference. But with the aid of Figure 2-11, we find that it *does* make a difference.

We assume in Figure 2-11 that a worker is initially at the optimal point u_1, where HW is tangent to indifference curve I_1. At u_1 the individual chooses to work Hh_1 hours, which we will presume to be the standard workday. Let us now suppose that the employer offers additional hours of overtime work at premium pay. This renders the u_1W segment of HW irrelevant, and the budget constraint now becomes Hu_1P. We observe that the optimal position will move to u_2 on the higher indifference curve I_2 and that the worker will choose to work h_1h_2 additional hours. Daily earnings will be u_2h_2.

Consider now the alternative of a straight-line equivalent wage, that is, a standard hourly wage rate that will yield the same daily income of u_2h_2 for the Hh_2 hours of work. The straight-time equivalent wage can be shown by drawing a new budget line HW' through u_2. The budget lines Hu_1P and HW' will both yield the same money income of u_2h_2 for Hh_2 hours of work. The important point is that if confronted with HW', the worker will want to move from u_2 to a new optimal position at u_3, where fewer hours than Hh_2 are worked. Stated differently, at u_2 indifference curve I_2 cuts

FIGURE 2-11 PREMIUM WAGES AND STRAIGHT-TIME EQUIVALENT
Premium wage rates for overtime work will be more conducive to more hours of work (Hh_2) than a straight-time wage rate that would yield an equivalent daily income (Hh_3).

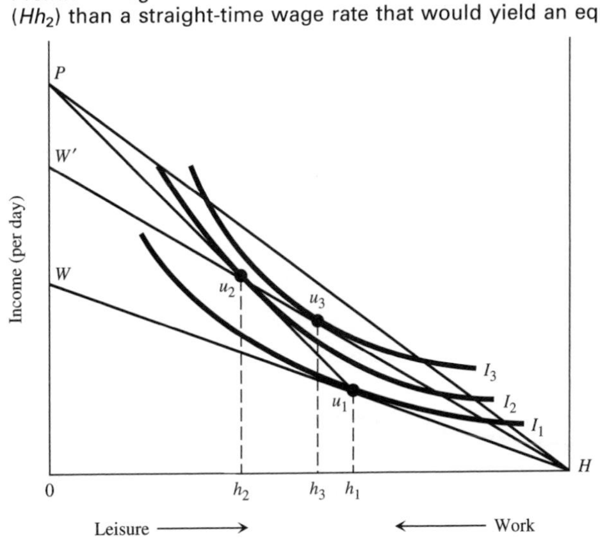

HW' from above; that is, MRS *L,Y* is greater than the wage rate. This means that the worker subjectively values leisure more highly at the margin than does the market, and, thus, u_2 is no longer the optimal position under a straight-time pay arrangement. Our worker will feel overemployed when working Hh_2 hours on a straight-time pay plan (recall Figure 2-10).

Conclusion: Premium wage rates for overtime work will call forth more hours of work than a straight-time wage rate that yields the same income at the same number of hours as that actually chosen by an individual paid the overtime premium. Why the difference? The use of premium pay will have a relatively small income effect because it applies only to hours worked in excess of Hh_1. In comparison, the straight-time equivalent wage will have a much larger income effect because it applies to *all* hours of work.[14] Figure 2-11 is essentially the labor market analog of price discrimination in the product market. Sellers of some products can obtain more revenue by charging different prices for different quantities of output. In the present analysis, we are observing that an employer can obtain a greater amount of labor for a given outlay by paying different wage rates for different hours of work.[15]

QUICK REVIEW 2-3

- Steep indifference curves, the availability of nonlabor income, and low earnings ability all contribute to nonparticipation in the labor force.
- The reservation wage is the lowest acceptable wage rate; below this wage a person would decide not to participate in the labor force.
- The standard 8-hour workday may leave some workers wanting additional hours of work (underemployed) and others wishing to work fewer hours (overemployed), depending on their indifference maps and earnings abilities.
- Premium wage rates for overtime work provide a greater incentive for additional hours of work than a straight-time wage rate yielding an equivalent daily income.

Your Turn: Suppose that you have a choice between two otherwise identical jobs, including hourly pay. In one job the employer sets the hours of work each week and in the other you select the number of hours. Which job would you prefer? Why? (Answer: See page 625.)

Income Maintenance Programs

There exist in the United States a variety of ***income maintenance programs***—also dubbed "welfare" or "public assistance" programs—whose purpose is to provide some

[14] Figure 2-11 is drawn so that for the straight-time equivalent wage the substitution effect dominates the income effect, and therefore the individual is on the forward-rising portion of her or his labor supply curve. This is the reason u_3 entails more hours of work than u_1. Such an outcome is not necessary. The diagram could have been drawn so that u_3 was to the right of u_1, in which case our basic conclusion would be even more evident.

[15] Kenneth E. Boulding, *Economic Analysis,* vol. 1, 4th ed. (New York: Harper and Row, 1966), p. 616. Our conclusion holds only if we restrict the employer from hiring additional workers.

minimum level of income to all families and individuals.[16] These programs include Supplementary Security Income, food stamps, and Medicaid. Our objective is to examine the possible effects of such programs on work incentives.

Three Basic Features Although details vary greatly, income maintenance programs have three basic features.

1 The Income Guarantee or Basic Benefit, B This is the amount of public subsidy an individual or family would be paid if no earned income were received.[17]

2 The Benefit-Reduction Rate, t This refers to the rate at which a family's basic benefit is reduced as earned income increases. For example, if t is .50, then a family's basic benefit will be reduced by \$.50 for every \$1.00 of wage income earned. This means that if the market wage rate is \$5.00, the family's *net* wage rate will be just \$2.50 when the benefit-reduction provision is taken into account. The critical point is that the benefit-reduction rate reduces one's net gain from work. Economists often refer to the benefit-reduction rate as an "implicit tax rate" because t has the same impact on the net income of a person participating in an income maintenance program as income tax rates have on the earnings of individuals not in the program.

3 The Break-Even Level of Income, Y_b The basic benefit and the benefit-reduction rate permit the calculation of the *break-even income.* This is the level of earned income at which the actual subsidy payment received by an individual or family becomes zero. It is that level of earned income at which an individual is dropped from an income maintenance program. As we shall see in a moment, the break-even income depends on the sizes of the basic benefit and the benefit-reduction rate.

Illustration A simple numerical illustration might be helpful in relating these concepts to one another. The ***actual subsidy payment*** S received by an individual can be determined by the following formula:

$$S = B - tY \tag{2-2}$$

where: B = basic benefit
t = benefit-reduction rate
Y = level of earned income

[16]Income maintenance programs are not to be confused with various "social insurance programs." Income maintenance programs are designed to assist families and individuals who have more or less permanent handicaps or dependent children. These programs are financed out of general tax revenues and are regarded as public charity. To qualify for aid, one must demonstrate economic "need." In contrast, social insurance programs (such as Old Age and Survivors Insurance and unemployment compensation) are tailored to replace a portion of the earnings lost due to retirement or temporary unemployment. They are financed by earmarked payroll taxes, and benefits are viewed as earned rights as a consequence of prior financial contributions. For thoughtful critiques of our public assistance programs, see Gary Burtless, "The Economist's Lament: Public Assistance in America," *Journal of Economic Perspectives,* Winter 1990, pp. 57–78; and Judith M. Gueron, "Work and Welfare: Lessons on Employment Programs," *Journal of Economic Perspectives,* Winter 1990, pp. 79–98.

[17]We simplify by assuming that no nonwage income in the form of, say, interest or dividends is received.

Thus, for example, if B is \$2,000, t is .50, and Y is \$2,000, then the actual subsidy payment received will be \$1,000. That is:

$$\$1{,}000 = \$2{,}000 - .50(\$2{,}000)$$

Furthermore, the break-even level of income can be calculated quite readily. A glance back at equation (2-2) suggests that S will become zero—that is, the break-even income will be reached—when earned income Y is equal to B/t.[18] For our illustrative numbers, B is \$2,000 and t is .50, so B/t—the break-even level of income—is therefore \$2,000/.50, or \$4,000. We verify this by substituting the relevant numbers into equation (2-2):

$$\$0 = \$2{,}000 - .50(\$4{,}000)$$

Let's now incorporate these concepts into Figure 2-12 to examine the impact of an income maintenance program on work incentives. The HW line shows us the budget constraint confronting the individual in the absence of an income maintenance program. The resulting optimal position is a u_1. For simplicity's sake, let's assume that the wage rate is \$1.00 per hour and that the individual chooses to work 40 hours per week. Over the 50-week workyear earned income would be \$2,000, as shown on the left vertical axis. Now suppose that an income maintenance program with the characteristics just described is enacted. The impact of this program is to change the budget constraint from HW to HBY_bW. Note that HB on the right vertical axis is the basic benefit; it is the amount of income subsidy the individual would receive if he or she had no earned income. The BY_b segment of the new budget constraint reflects the influence of the benefit-reduction rate. Specifically, the slope of the BY_b segment is measured by the *net* wage rate, that is, the market wage rate as it is reduced by the benefit-reduction rate. Thus, while the absolute value of the slope of HW is 1.00 (reflecting the \$1.00 wage rate), the slope of BY_b is only .50 (reflecting the \$.50 *net* wage rate).[19] The vertical distance between HW and BY_b is equal to S, the actual subsidy received. Point Y_b indicates the break-even level of income because at this point the individual's earned income is sufficiently large (\$4,000 in this case) so that the application of the .50 benefit-reduction rate causes the actual subsidy payment S to become zero [see equation (2-2)].

We observe in Figure 2-12 that the new optimal position is at u_2, where HBY_bW is tangent to indifference curve I_2. While the individual's total money income has increased (from h_1u_1 to h_2u_2), *earned* income and the number of hours worked have both declined (from h_1u_1 to h_2a and from Hh_1 to Hh_2, respectively). In our earlier analysis of a wage *increase* (Figure 2-7), we found that the net effect on hours of work (work

[18]The algebra is simple. By setting $S = 0$ in equation (2-2) we get $0 = B - tY$. Therefore, $tY = B$ and $Y = B/t$.

[19]As noted, the slope of BY_b reflects the *net* wage rate w_n, which is the wage rate w multiplied by $(1 - t)$; that is, $w_n = (1 - t)w$. In our example the slope of BY_b is $.50 = (1 - .5)1$. If the benefit-reduction rate were .25, the net wage rate and slope of BY_b would be $.75 = (1 - .25)1$. If the benefit-reduction rate were 1.00, BY_b would be horizontal.

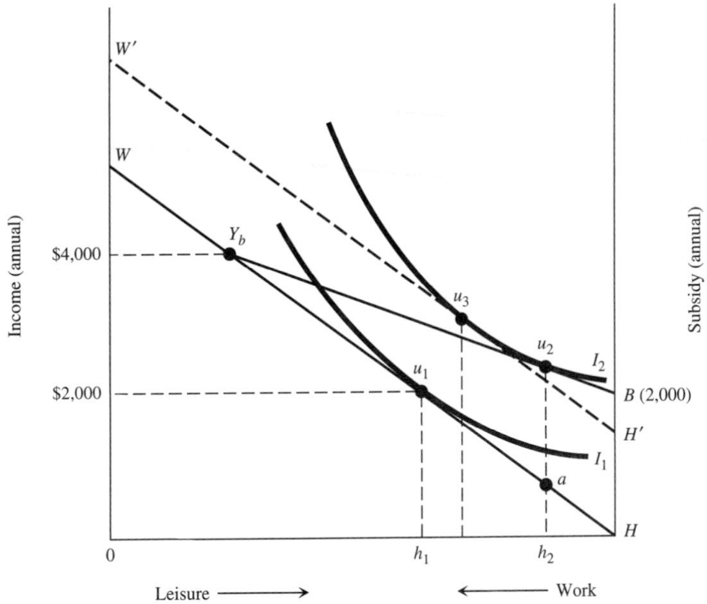

FIGURE 2-12 INCOME MAINTENANCE AND INCENTIVES TO WORK
An income maintenance program that incorporates both a basic benefit and a benefit-reduction rate will change the budget constraint from *HW* to HBY_bW. This alteration moves the utility-maximizing position from u_1 to u_2 and reduces hours of work.

incentives) depended on the relative sizes of the income effect (reduction in hours of work) and the substitution effect (increase in hours of work). *In the present case, the income and substitution effects both reduce hours of work.* The tendency for the income effect to reduce hours of work is no surprise. The income maintenance program increases money income, and assuming leisure is a normal good, some of that income is "spent" on leisure and therefore fewer hours are worked. But, curiously, the substitution effect also reduces hours of work. The presence of the benefit-reduction rate *reduces* the *net* wage rate; it makes BY_b flatter than *HW*. Even though the basic benefit raises total money income, the benefit-reduction feature means there has been an effective decrease in wage rates. Leisure is now cheaper—one sacrifices only $.50 by not working an hour rather than $1.00—and therefore leisure is substituted for work.

Recalling our earlier diagrammatic separation of the income and substitution effects (Figure 2-7), we can draw the broken line $H'W'$ parallel to *HW* and tangent to I_2 at u_3. The horizontal distance between u_1 and u_3 is the income effect, and the horizontal distance between u_3 and u_2 is the substitution effect. We observe that both reduce the amount of work supplied.[20]

[20]In contrast to other income maintenance programs, the Earned Income Tax Credit program, on net, increases the labor force participation of single women with children. See Nada Eissa, "Labor Supply Response to the Earned Income Tax Credit," *Quarterly Journal of Economics,* May 1996, pp. 605–637.

2-4

Controversy The various income maintenance programs have long been surrounded by controversy. This stems in part from fundamental ideological differences among policy makers. But it also reflects the fact that the accepted goals of income maintenance programs are in conflict with one another and that it is easy to disagree as to the proper or "optimal" trade-offs. In particular, it is generally agreed that income maintenance programs should (1) effectively get poor people out of poverty, (2) maintain incentives to work, and (3) achieve goals 1 and 2 at a "reasonable" cost. Figure 2-12 is a useful point of reference in explaining these goal conflicts.

Our analysis of Figure 2-12 has just made it clear that goals 1 and 2 are in conflict. The imposition of an income maintenance program triggers income and substitution effects, both of which are negative with respect to work. Furthermore, we might improve

2-4 World of Work

THE END OF WELFARE AS AN ENTITLEMENT

In August 1996, President Bill Clinton signed the Personal Responsibility and Work Opportunity Act, which fundamentally changed the welfare system in the United States. In recent years, the welfare system has been criticized for its inherent work disincentives and accused of encouraging dependency among benefit recipients. The welfare reform act attempts to correct these perceived deficiencies in several ways as well as shift more control over welfare to state governments.

A major goal of the legislation is to make receiving welfare a transition period before returning to work. The act requires welfare recipients, with few exceptions, to work after two years of receiving assistance. This provision is phased in so that by the year 2002, one-half of families must be working or have left the welfare rolls. Welfare recipients may meet the work provision by being employed, attending vocational training, or performing community service. By the year 2000, single parents must be working at least 30 hours per week and two-parent families at least 35 hours per week. The act also mandates a 5-year lifetime limit on the receipt of cash welfare payments (though states may exempt up to 20 percent of their recipients). It also provides child care and health insurance for families entering the job market. Finally, most forms of public assistance are denied to legal immigrants for five years, or until they become citizens.

The act also tries to encourage responsibility regarding parenthood. It includes provisions to help enforce the collection of child support payments. Teen pregnancy is discouraged with such measures as requiring that unmarried minor parents live with an adult and stay in school to receive assistance.

Much debate has occurred over the effects of the law. Supporters claim that the work requirements and incentives to reduce out-of-wedlock births will decrease welfare dependency and thus crime and other social problems. They also favor the act's provision of a fixed federal payment for welfare to states instead of the previous approach that tied payments to the amount spent on welfare. They claim this will provide incentives for states to reduce spending on welfare.[1]

Critics argue that the decrease in welfare spending will cause severe hardship for many families and poverty will increase, even if the changes cause some welfare recipients to leave the welfare rolls for work. One study forecasts that annual welfare spending will decrease by $16 billion when the legislation is fully implemented. As a result, an estimated 2.6 million more people will enter poverty, including 1.1 million children. More than one-fifth of all families with children will see their incomes fall by about $1,300 per year, on average, according to the study.[2]

[1]Robert Rector, "How Congress Reformed the Welfare System," in *Reviewing the Revolution: Conservative Successes in the 104th Congress.* Washington, D.C.: Heritage Foundation, 1996.

[2]Sheila Zedlewski, Sandra Clark, Eric Meier, and Keith Watson, "Potential Effects of Welfare Reform Legislation on Family Incomes," Urban Institute Working Paper, July 1996.

the effectiveness of the program in eliminating poverty by increasing the basic benefit, that is, by shifting the BY_b line upward in Figure 2-12. But this will clearly make the program more costly. On the one hand, a larger basic benefit would relocate point Y_b to the northwest on line *HW* and cause additional families to be eligible for subsidies. On the other hand, with a higher basic benefit, people already in the income maintenance program will each receive larger subsidy payments. Goal 1 conflicts with goal 3.

Finally, given the basic benefit, one might want to reduce the benefit-reduction rate (increase the slope of the BY_b line) to preserve incentives to work. A reduction in the benefit-reduction rate increases the net wage rate, boosting the "price" of leisure and inducing the substitution of work for leisure. The higher net wage rate may also prompt individuals who are currently not in the labor force to become participants (see Figure 2-8). However, the resulting increase in the slope of the BY_b line will extend point Y_b to the northwest along *HW,* making more families eligible for subsidies and therefore increasing program costs. An increase in the slope of the BY_b line will also boost costs by increasing the actual subsidy received for any given number of hours worked. Goal 2 conflicts with goal 3.[21]

Experimental Evidence Between 1968 and 1982 the federal government sponsored four income maintenance experiments. These were conducted in (1) New Jersey, (2) rural Iowa and North Carolina, (3) Gary, Indiana, and (4) Seattle and Denver. The main objective was to determine how families would adjust their labor supply in response to income subsidies. In each experiment a sample of households was selected and a fraction of the sample was provided with income maintenance involving a variety of basic benefits and benefit-reduction rates. The labor supply behavior of this "experimental" group was compared with that of the remaining families, which constituted a comparison or "control" group. The results of these experiments were consistent in confirming the negative effects on labor supply that the work–leisure theory (Figure 2-12) predicts. For the four programs as a whole:

> Husbands reduced labor supply by about the equivalent of two weeks [per year] of full-time employment. Wives and single female heads [of households] reduced labor supply by about the equivalent of three weeks of full-time employment. Youth reduced labor supply by about the equivalent of four weeks of full-time employment.[22]

The Seattle and Denver Income Maintenance Experiment (popularly known as SIME/DIME) was the largest of the four experiments. Carried out over the 1971–1982

[21]In fact, the effect of a reduction in the benefit-reduction rate on work incentives is more complex than our discussion suggests. On the one hand, a decline in the benefit-reduction rate will reduce the size of the negative income and substitution effects for those currently receiving benefits. Therefore, the hours of work for this group will increase. On the other hand, the lower benefit-reduction rate will extend program benefits to additional families that originally had not received benefits. The resultant income and substitution effects will both be negative for this group, causing them to work fewer hours. The overall impact on work incentives will depend on the average response of each group and their relative sizes. See Burtless, op. cit., pp. 68–70.

[22]Philip K. Robins, "A Comparison of the Labor Supply Findings from the Four Negative Income Tax Experiments," *Journal of Human Resources,* Fall 1985, p. 580.

period, SIME/DIME involved 4,800 families and a number of combinations of income guarantees (basic benefits) and benefit-reduction rates. The program lasted 3 years for some families, while other families were in a 5-year program. The basic benefits were relatively generous, providing families with incomes that were on average 115 percent of the poverty level.

Table 2-2 presents the percentage difference in hours worked by husbands in the experimental group. For those families in the 3-year program, the maximum decline in annual hours worked by experimental group husbands was 7.3 percent and occurred in both the second and third years. For those in the 5-year program, the maximum decline in the number of hours worked by husbands was 13.6 percent and happened in the fourth year. In absolute terms, these declines represent reductions in the number of hours worked of approximately 133 and 234 hours per year, respectively. The third row combines the 3- and 5-year groups and indicates that the work disincentive effect for husbands was about 9 percent of total hours in both the second and third years. Note, too, that for husbands in the 3-year program, the hours of work returned essentially to the same level as those in the control group in years 4 and 5. This strongly suggests that the reduction in hours that occurred during the experiment was attributable to the program and that once the program ended husbands fairly quickly adjusted their labor supply to altered economic incentives. Furthermore, a disaggregation of the data (not shown) indicates no statistically significant differences between white, black, and Hispanic husbands in their average work reductions.

What was the form of the reduction in hours? Did husbands in the experimental group work fewer hours per week? Or did they spend more time unemployed? The answer is the latter. That is, the availability of the income guarantee caused male workers who were out of work to spend more time between jobs than men in the control group.

Wives also responded to SIME/DIME by reducing hours of work outside the home. In fact, the relative decline for them was larger than that for husbands. For example, the decline for wives in the second year of the combined programs was 20.1 percent as compared to 9.0 percent for husbands. However, this translated into a smaller absolute decline in hours because on the average, women work outside the home fewer

TABLE 2-2 LABOR SUPPLY RESPONSE OF HUSBANDS (PERCENTAGE DIFFERENCE IN ANNUAL HOURS WORKED)

	Year				
	1	2	3	4	5
Three-year program	−1.6	−7.3	−7.3	−0.5	−0.2
Five-year program	−5.9	−12.2	−13.2	−13.6	−12.3
Combined programs	−3.1	−9.0	−9.3		

Source: Office of Income Security Policy of the U.S. Department of Health and Human Services, *Overview of the Seattle-Denver Income Maintenance Experiment Final Report,* May 1983, p. 13.

hours per year than men. Finally, the relative decline in hours for females who were family heads also exceeded that of married men. The second-year decline for the combined group of female family heads was 14.3 percent.[23]

CHAPTER SUMMARY

1 In the work–leisure choice model, an indifference curve shows the various combinations of real income and leisure that will yield a given level of utility to an individual. Indifference curves are convex to the origin, reflecting a diminishing marginal rate of substitution of leisure for income. Curves farther from the origin indicate higher levels of utility.

2 The budget (wage) constraint line shows the various combinations of real income and leisure that are obtainable at a given wage rate. The absolute value of the slope of the budget line reflects the wage rate.

3 The individual achieves an optimal or utility-maximizing position by selecting that point that puts him or her on the highest attainable indifference curve.

4 Changing the wage rate and observing predicted changes in one's optimal position suggest the possibility of a backward-bending individual labor supply curve.

5 The impact of a wage change on hours of work depends on the sizes of the income and substitution effects. The income effect measures that portion of a total change in desired hours of work that is due solely to the change in real income caused by the wage change. The substitution effect is the portion of a total change in desired hours of work that is due solely to the wage rate change, the level of real income or utility being held constant. For a wage increase (decrease), the income effect decreases (increases) while the substitution effect increases (decreases) desired hours of work.

6 Empirical evidence suggests that women are significantly more responsive to a wage change in their labor supply decisions than are men.

7 The responsiveness of the quantity of labor supplied to a given change in wage rates is measured by the elasticity of labor supply. It is calculated as the percentage change in quantity of labor supplied divided by the percentage change in the wage rate. In contrast, changes in nonlabor income or work–leisure preferences alter the location of an individual's labor supply curve.

8 The case of nonparticipants—individuals who choose not to do labor market work—is portrayed by a corner solution on the right vertical axis of the work–leisure model.

9 The reservation wage is the lowest wage rate at which a person would decide to work.

10 A worker may be overemployed or underemployed when forced to conform to a standard workday. A worker is overemployed (underemployed) when for the standard workday his or her marginal rate of substitution of leisure for income is greater (less) than the wage rate.

11 A system of premium pay—for example, time and a half for overtime work—has a more positive effect on work incentives than the straight-time wage rate, which would yield an equivalent income for the same hours of work.

12 Most income maintenance programs entail a basic benefit and a benefit-reduction rate from which the break-even level of income can be calculated. Because *(a)* the basic

[23]For a detailed evaluation of the income maintenance experiments, see Federal Reserve Bank of Boston, *Lessons from the Income Maintenance Experiments* (Boston: Federal Reserve Bank of Boston, 1986).

benefit causes only an income effect and *(b)* the benefit-reduction rate *reduces* the net wage rate, the income and substitution effects both contribute to a decline in desired hours of work.

13 Experimental studies confirm the major predictions of the work–leisure model concerning the effects of income maintenance programs on labor supply.

TERMS AND CONCEPTS

indifference curve
marginal rate of substitution of leisure for income
budget (wage) constraint
optimal work–leisure position
backward-bending labor supply curve
income effect
substitution effect
wage elasticity of labor
reservation wage
overemployment
underemployment
income maintenance program
income guarantee or basic benefit
benefit-reduction rate
break-even level of income
actual subsidy payment

QUESTIONS AND STUDY SUGGESTIONS

1 What information is embodied in *(a)* an indifference curve and *(b)* the budget line in the work–leisure model? Why are indifference curves *(a)* downward-sloping and *(b)* convex to the origin? Draw an indifference map and budget line and locate a worker's optimal position.

2 Indicate in each of the following instances whether the specified circumstances will cause a worker to want to work more or fewer hours.

a The wage rate increases and the substitution effect is greater than the income effect.
b The wage rate decreases and the income effect is greater than the substitution effect.
c The wage rate decreases and the substitution effect is greater than the income effect.
d The wage rate increases and the income effect is greater than the substitution effect.

3 Employ a diagram similar to Figure 2-5 to show an individual's leisure–income choices before and after a wage rate *decrease*. Isolate the income and substitution effects, indicate whether each increases or decreases hours of work, and use the two effects to explain the overall impact of the wage decline on hours of work. Is your worker on the forward-rising or backward-bending portion of the labor supply curve?

4 The "supply-side" economics of the Reagan administration (1981–1988) presumed that income tax cuts would stimulate incentives to work and thereby increase economic growth. Demonstrate this outcome with a work–leisure diagram. What does this outcome assume about the relative sizes of the income and substitution effects? Explain: "The predicted increase in work incentives associated with supply-side tax cuts might in fact be more relevant for women than for men."

5 Suppose Lauren is confronted with two options by her employer. First option: She may choose her own hours of work and will be paid the relatively low wage rate implied by budget line HW_1 shown in the accompanying diagram. Second option: She can work exactly *HR* hours and will be paid the relatively high wage rate implied by budget line HW_2. Which option will she choose? Justify your answer.

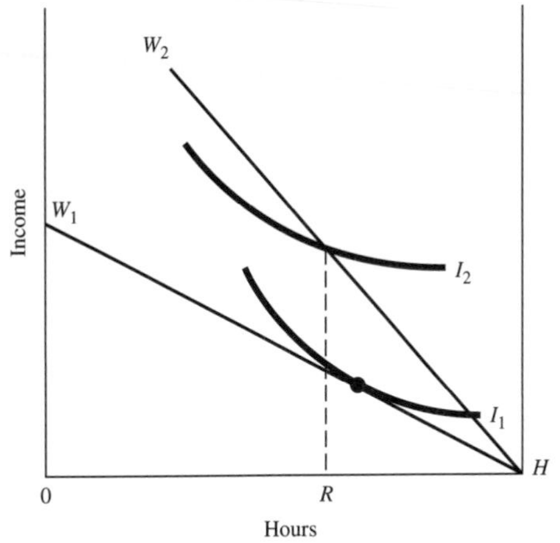

6 Use a work–leisure diagram that includes nonlabor income to portray an individual who is maximizing utility by working, say, 8 hours per day. Now compare the labor supply effects of imposing *(a)* a lump-sum tax, that is, a tax that is the same absolute amount at all levels of earned income; and *(b)* a proportional tax of, say, 30 percent on earned income. Do hours of work rise or fall in each case? Can you generalize these outcomes of *all* individuals in the economy? Explain.

7 What set of circumstances will tend to cause an individual to choose not to participate in the labor force? What generalizations can you formulate on the basis of *(a)* education, *(b)* the presence of preschool children, *(c)* level of spouse's income, *(d)* race, *(e)* location of a household (urban or rural) on the one hand and the probability that a married woman will be a labor force participant on the other?

8 What is the reservation wage? "Other things being equal, one's reservation wage increases as larger amounts of nonlabor income are realized." Do you agree? Explain. Redraw the indifference curves of Figure 2-8 to demonstrate that anything that lowers (raises) the value of nonmarket time will increase (reduce) the probability of labor force participation.

9 Using Figure 2-10, demonstrate that Smith has a stronger "taste" for leisure and a weaker "taste" for work than Jones. What factor(s) might underlie this difference in tastes? Redraw Smith's indifference curves to show the case where she would rather be a nonparticipant than work the standard *HD* workweek.

10 Use Figure 2-11 to explain the following statement: "Although premium wage rates for overtime work will induce workers to work more hours than would a straight-time equivalent wage rate, the latter will entail a higher level of well-being."

11 If an income maintenance program entails a \$3,000 basic benefit and a benefit-reduction rate of .30, what will be the size of the subsidy received by a family that earns

$2,000 per year? What will be the family's total income? What break-even level of income does this program imply?

12 In the accompanying diagram *WH* is the budget line resulting from labor market work. Describe the characteristics of the income maintenance programs implicit in budget lines *HBW′*, *HBYW*, and *HBW*. Given an individual's work–leisure preferences, which program will entail the strongest disincentives to work? Why? Which entails the weakest disincentives to work? Why? "The higher the basic benefit and the higher the benefit-reduction rate, the weaker the work incentive." Do you agree?

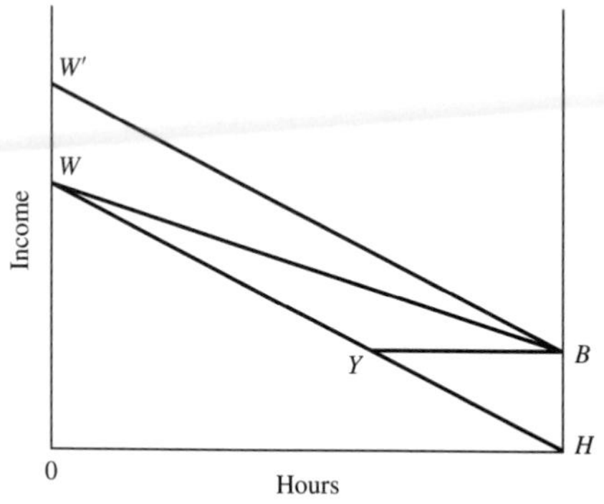

13 In the United States payments to disabled workers on the average replace about one-half of their former earnings. In some other countries such as Sweden and the Netherlands disabled workers receive as much as 70 to 90 percent of the average earnings. We also observe that the proportion of workers receiving disability benefits is much lower in the United States than in the latter two nations. Are these findings consistent with the work–leisure model? Explain.

14 Suppose Congress changed our social security law to allow recipients to earn as much as they wanted with no reduction in benefits. Use a work–leisure diagram to show the predicted effects on labor supply.

15 One way of aiding low-income families is to increase the minimum wage. An alternative is to provide a direct grant of nonlabor income. Compare the impact of these two options on work incentives.

16 Evaluate the following statements:

a "An employer might reduce worker absenteeism by changing from a standard wage rate to premium pay for hours that exceed a fixed minimum."

b "A worker who feels underemployed may moonlight even though the wage rate is somewhat lower than the one paid on the worker's first job."

c "Given the wage rate, an individual will always prefer a job on which the worker, as opposed to the employer, selects the number of hours worked."

d "If at all points within the work–leisure diagram a person's indifference curves are flatter than the budget constraint, then that individual will choose to be a nonparticipant."

e "The income effect of any given wage increase is larger for individuals who are currently working many hours than it is for those who are currently working few or no hours."

SELECTED REFERENCES

Final Report of the Seattle-Denver Income Maintenance Experiment, vol. 1 (Menlo Park, Calif.: SRI International, 1983).

Fleisher, Belton M., and Thomas J. Kniesner: *Labor Economics: Theory, Evidence, and Policy,* 3d ed. (Englewood Cliffs, N.J.: Prentice-Hall, Inc., 1984), chap. 4.

Heckman, James J.: "What Has Been Learned about Labor Supply in the Past Twenty Years?" *American Economic Review,* May 1993, pp. 116–121.

Keeley, Michael C.: *Labor Supply and Public Policy* (New York: Academic Press, 1981).

Killingsworth, Mark R.: *Labor Supply* (Cambridge: Cambridge University Park, 1983).

Moffitt, Robert: "Incentive Effects of the U.S. Welfare System: A Review," *Journal of Economic Literature,* March 1992, pp. 1–61.

CHAPTER 3

POPULATION, PARTICIPATION RATES, AND HOURS OF WORK

"The times they are a changin'."[1] The 1946–1964 baby boom that added about 76 million people to the labor force gave way to a "baby bust" that will mean much smaller increases in the labor force in the immediate future. During the past decade immigration added over 6 million people to the U.S. population. Disadvantaged groups such as blacks and Hispanics constitute a growing percentage of our labor force. Dual-worker families were 9 percent of all families in 1940; today they are over 42 percent.

The hustle-bustle of our lives has greatly increased as we juggle education, market work, household activities, and leisure. Divorces are much more common than in earlier periods. The percentage of families maintained by single mothers has doubled from 12 percent in 1970 to 26 percent today. Since 1950 women have increasingly participated in the labor force; meanwhile, the participation rates of older working-age men have declined. The workweek decreased by 20 percent during the first half of this century, but since then it has remained relatively constant.

These facts all relate to the supply of labor, examined more broadly here than in the previous chapter. For the economy as a whole, the concept of labor supply has many dimensions. As Figure 3-1 indicates, the aggregate of labor services available to a society depends on (1) the size and demographic composition of the population, which in turn depend on births, deaths, and net immigration; (2) the labor force participation rate, that is, the percentage of the working-age population that is actually working or seeking work; (3) the number of hours worked per week or year; and (4) the quality of the labor force. In this chapter we will consider the first three of these aspects of labor supply—population, participation rates, and hours of work. Labor quality will be analyzed in Chapter 4.

[1]Bob Dylan lyrics.

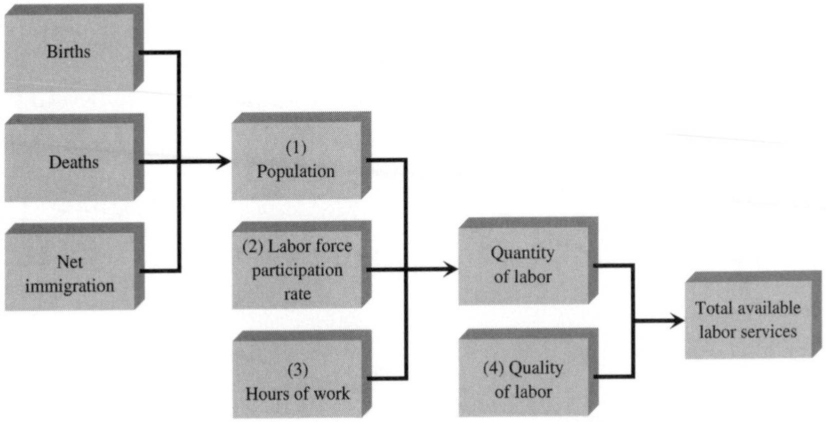

FIGURE 3-1 **DETERMINANTS OF THE TOTAL LABOR SERVICES AVAILABLE**
The total amount of labor services available in an economy depends on population size, the labor force participation rate, the length of the workweek and workyear, and the quality of the labor force.

Our discussion in this chapter is organized as follows. First, we will briefly examine the population base of the labor force. Second, as a prelude to examining participation rates, we will reorient our perspective from that of the individual to that of the household or family. The third and major segment of the chapter is concerned with labor force participation rates. How are participation rates measured? How has the aggregate participation rate changed secularly? What about the participation rates of major demographic groups? What short-run or cyclical changes occur in participation rates? Our fourth objective is to present and explain long-run trends in hours of work. Finally, we will examine the slowdown in population and labor force growth predicted for the near future and ponder its potential economic implications.

THE POPULATION BASE

As a broad generalization, the size of a nation's labor force depends on the size of its population and the fraction of its population participating in the labor market. Figure 3-2 portrays the growth of our population and labor force over the 1950–1997 period. Recalling Figure 3-1, we know that population grows partly as a result of natural increases—that is, the excess of births over deaths—and net immigration. Because death rates are less variable (declining slowly over time), most of the variations in our population growth have resulted from changes in birthrates and net immigration. For example, the 1946–1964 baby boom added almost 76 million people to our population who, some 20 years later, entered the labor force in extraordinarily large numbers. What caused the average workweek to decline from 50 hours to 40 hours early in this century? Why hasn't the workweek declined any further since then? Immigration—considered in detail in Chapter 9—has also fluctuated over time, largely as a consequence of changes in U.S. immigration policies. In some recent

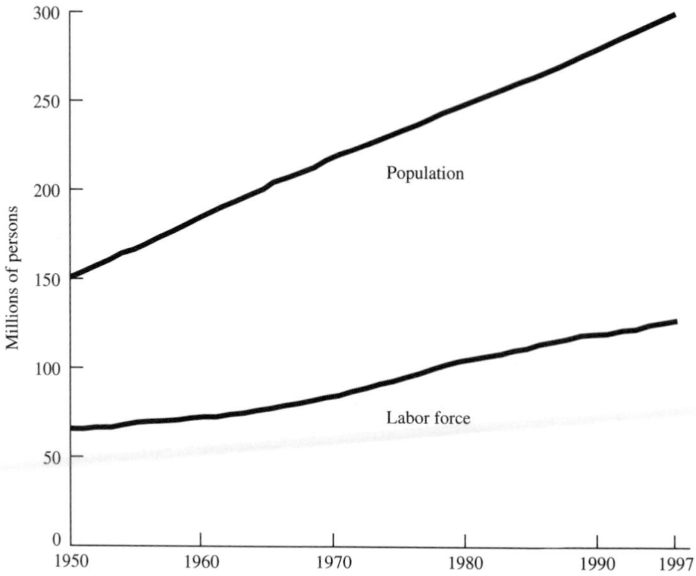

FIGURE 3-2 **POPULATION AND LABOR FORCE GROWTH, 1950–1997**
Population and labor force have both grown significantly in the United States, but rates of growth have varied from one period to another.

years immigration has accounted for as much as 20 to 25 percent of population growth.

3-1 Let's now consider a bit of economic theory that will be helpful in understanding participation rates.

BECKER'S MODEL: THE ALLOCATION OF TIME

In Chapter 2 we introduced a model in which an *individual* was making a choice between labor market work and leisure. While this model proved useful in generating an understanding of the work–leisure decision and a number of its implications, the model has been generalized and expanded by Becker (World of Work 1-1) and others.[2] This generalized ***model of the allocation of time*** is particularly useful in understanding the main topic at hand, labor force participation.

Two Fundamental Changes

The basic work–leisure choice model can be extended in two fundamental ways.

1 Household Perspective The first change is that it is frequently more informative to think of the household as the basic decision-making unit rather than the

[2]The landmark article is Gary Becker, "A Theory of the Allocation of Time," *Economic Journal*, September 1965, pp. 493–517. See also Staffan B. Linder, *The Harried Leisure Class* (New York: Columbia University Press, 1970).

3-1 World of Work

THE CHANGING FACE OF AMERICA*

In 1996 the Census Bureau issued a revised population forecast that suggests greater long-term growth of the U.S. population than did earlier estimates. The report also predicts even more diversity in the population than was projected earlier. By 2050 the U.S. population is expected to rise to 394 million from 263 million in 1995. This new projection for 2050 is up 56 million from earlier projections.

How will the composition of the population be different in 2050 compared to 1995? As shown in the accompanying pie charts, the population in 2050 is expected to be much more diverse. Asians, Hispanics, blacks, and other nonwhite groups will comprise nearly one-half of the population in 2050.

Although population growth will slow in the next decade or so, several factors will drive rapid increases in population in subsequent decades. Legislation in 1990 increased the number of legal immigrants to the United States. The Census Bureau now estimates that 820,000 immigrants will arrive each year, up from earlier estimates of 500,000. The number of Asians and Pacific Islanders will increase by 270 percent, to about 8 percent of the total population. Hispanics will overtake blacks as the nation's largest minority group, comprising an expected 24.5 percent of the population in 2050. The increase in Hispanics and Asians will also boost the nation's fertility rate—from 2.06 children per average woman today to 2.25 children.

If the Census Bureau's predictions are accurate, they have several important implications for the labor force. First, the projected slowdown in labor force growth through 2005—and the potential for labor shortages—should only be a short-term problem. Second, the higher immigration and greater fertility rates will slow and eventually reverse the present aging of the American population. This means, for example, that the ratio of receivers of Social Security benefits to the number of people paying into the system will not rise as fast as once expected. Third, a renewed emphasis on education and training will be necessary to prepare the growing number of racially diverse youth for high-quality jobs. Finally, workplaces will be transformed, with owners, managers, and workers increasingly being nonwhite. Greater tolerance for racial and ethnic differences will be an absolute necessity if the United States is to retain its high labor productivity and standard of living.

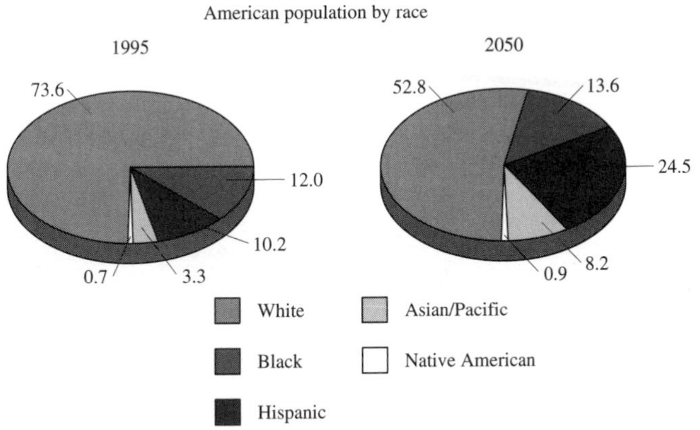

Source: U.S. Census Bureau.

*Based partly on U.S. Census Bureau, *Population Projections of the United States by Age, Sex, Race, and Hispanic Origin: 1995 to 2050; Current Population Reports,* ser. P-25, no. 1130, and "A Spicier Stew in the Melting Pot," *Business Week,* December 1992, pp. 29–30. Updated.

individual. Most people are members of households, and decisions as to how they spend their time are strongly influenced by the decisions of other household members. Decision making is interrelated; for example, a wife's decision as to whether she should seek labor market work may depend on whether her husband is currently employed, and vice versa.

2 Multiple Uses of Time In Becker's model of household allocation of time, the traditional work–leisure dichotomy is replaced by a more complex categorization of the uses of time. As Becker sees it, a household should be regarded as an economic unit that is *producing* utility-yielding "commodities." These utility-yielding *commodities* are produced by the household by combining *goods* (goods and services) with *time.* More generally, a household can use the time available to it in at least three basic ways. Time can be (1) sold in the labor market to obtain the money income required to purchase goods and services (labor market time), (2) used in household production (household production time), and (3) used in the actual consumption of goods and services (consumption time).

Thus, for the typical household, the commodity we call a meal is produced by combining certain goods acquired through the provision of labor market time (food bought at the supermarket) with household production time (the time it takes to prepare these goods as a meal) and consumption time (the time it takes to eat the meal). Because the total amount of time available to the household is limited, the alternative uses of time are competitive with one another. For example, other things being equal, the family in which both spouses engage in labor market work will have less time available for household production and consumption than the family with one nonworking spouse.

Commodity Characteristics

Commodities have two characteristics of considerable significance for any discussion of how a household might allocate its time in general and how it might make labor market participation decisions in particular. First, some commodities are relatively time-intensive, while others are relatively goods-intensive. ***Time-intensive commodities*** are composed of a large amount of time and a small amount of goods. Examples include such "pure" leisure activities as watching the sunset at the beach or dozing in a hammock.[3] ***Goods-intensive commodities*** require quite large amounts of goods and little time, for example, a meal at a fast food restaurant. One implication of this distinction is that as time becomes more valuable in the labor market (if wage rates increase), a household may sacrifice time-intensive commodities in favor of goods-intensive commodities in order to devote more time to labor market work.

The second characteristic of commodities is that, within limits, time and goods are usually substitutable in producing them. Thus, a specific commodity can be produced by the household with much time and a small amount of goods or vice versa. At one extreme a household can produce a meal with home-grown, home-prepared food. At

[3]In the Becker model we can think of leisure as the pleasurable consumption of time per se wherein the amount of goods required is nil.

the other extreme it can purchase a meal at a restaurant. The former is a highly time-intensive commodity, while the latter is a goods-intensive commodity.

Household Choices

In the Becker model, the household has a number of questions to answer as it seeks to maximize its utility. First, what commodities does it want to consume? Second, how does it want to produce these commodities? That is, to what extent should commodities be provided through labor market work as opposed to production in the home? Third, how should individual family members allocate their time among labor market work, home production, consumption, and other possible uses?

The third question is most relevant for the topic at hand.[4] The general principle employed in deciding how each household member should allocate his or her time is that of comparative advantage. The principle of comparative advantage says that an individual should specialize in that productive endeavor that can be performed with the greatest relative efficiency, or in other words, with the least opportunity cost. In apportioning its available time, a household should compare the productivity for each family member in all of the various market and nonmarket activities needing to be performed in producing commodities. The basic rule is that the more productive or proficient one is in a certain activity as compared to other family members, the greater the amount of one's time that should be devoted to that activity. Because each family member normally has different characteristics with respect to age, sex, educational attainment, and previous labor market and nonlabor market experience, at any point in time they will differ substantially in the relative efficiency of "producing" commodities (utility) from market and nonmarket activities. Obviously, the wife has a biologically determined comparative advantage in childbearing. Also, through socialization (role definition by society) or because of preferences, or both, many females develop a comparative advantage in other aspects of household production, for example, in homemaking activities such as cleaning, food preparation, and caring for children. Furthermore, we will find evidence in Chapter 15 suggesting that women are often discriminated against in the labor market. Because of such discrimination and assuming

[4]The second question will be treated in the ensuing discussion of the participation rates of the various subaggregates of the population. With regard to the first question, we will assume that the household's preferences for commodities are given, noting that in Becker's model the theory of consumer behavior must be modified to account for the economic value of time. More precisely, a household will be purchasing the utility-maximizing combination of goods $(a, b, \ldots, n)$ when the marginal utility of the last dollar spent on each is the same. Algebraically stated, utility is maximized when

$$\mathrm{MU}a/Pa = \mathrm{MU}b/Pb = \cdots = \mathrm{MU}n/Pn$$

where MU is marginal utility and P is product price. Becker contends that the appropriate prices to be used are *not* simply the market prices of each good but rather the "full price," that is, the market price of a good *plus* the market value of the time used in its consumption. Thus, if good a is a 2-hour concert whose price is \$8 and your time is worth \$10 per hour in the labor market, then the full price of the concert is \$28 = \$8 + (2 × \$10). Taking the value of time into account, the full prices of highly time-intensive goods will rise relatively and those of less time-intensive goods will fall relatively, generating a different utility-maximizing combination of goods than if only market prices were used.

that other things (such as education, job training, and labor market experience) are equal, many husbands can obtain more income and therefore more goods for the household from a given amount of labor market work than the wife. Historically, for many households the principle of comparative advantage led husbands to devote much of their time to labor market work, while their wives engaged in nonmarket work within the home. Similarly, we will find in Chapter 4 that children have a comparative advantage in acquiring education. Education is an investment in human capital, and other things being equal, the rate of return on that investment varies directly with the length of time a person will be in the labor market after his or her education is completed.[5]

3-1

Income and Substitution Effects Revisited

It is helpful in understanding Becker's model to reexamine the income and substitution effects within its more general framework.

Becker Income Effect Assume there is an increase in wage rates. The *income effect* indicates that the household now realizes a larger income for any number of hours of labor market work, and therefore the consumption of most goods will increase.[6] But the consumption of additional goods requires more time. Remember that goods must be combined with time to produce utility-yielding commodities. Therefore, with consumption time increasing, hours of work will tend to fall. Although the rationale is different, the income effect reduces hours of work as it did in the simpler model of Chapter 2.

Becker Substitution Effect There is also a more complex *substitution effect*. A higher market wage rate means that time is more valuable not only in the labor market but also in both the production and consumption activities occurring within the household. On the one hand, the household will substitute goods for time in the *production* of commodities as the wage rate rises. This implies that the household will produce commodities in less time-intensive ways. For example, the family may patronize fast-food restaurants with greater frequency and therefore spend less time in meal preparation within the home. On the other hand, with respect to *consumption,* the household will alter the mix of commodities it consumes, shifting from time-intensive to goods-intensive commodities as wage rates increase. Such time-intensive activities as vacations and playing golf may give way to the purchase of a work of art or racquetball. Or alternatively, a week's skiing in Colorado can be made less time-intensive for a Chicagoan by flying to the resort rather than driving. These adjustments in both the production and consumption of commodities release time for paid work in the labor market. Therefore, as in our simpler model, this more complex substitution effect increases hours of work when wage rates rise.

[5]For an interesting discussion of the *dis*advantages of intrahousehold specialization, see Francine D. Blau, Marianne A. Ferber, and Anne E. Winkler, *The Economics of Women, Men, and Work,* 3rd ed. (Englewood Cliffs, N.J.: Prentice-Hall, 1998), pp. 40–45.

[6]The exception, of course, is *inferior goods,* that is, goods the purchases of which decline as incomes increase.

3-1 **Global Perspective**

MEN AND WOMEN'S HOURS OF HOME WORK, 1995

Cross-country differences in the gender gap in home work time is largely due to variations in hours worked by men.

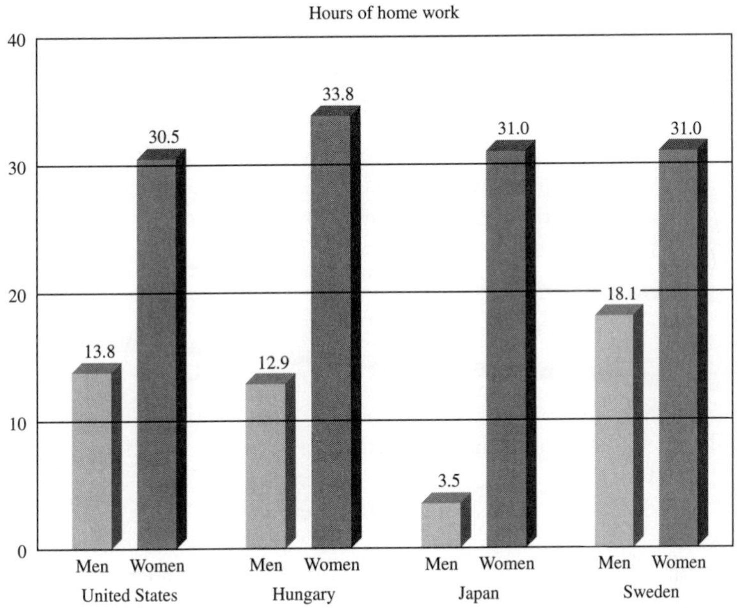

Source: F. Thomas Juster and Frank Stafford, "The Allocation of Time: Empirical Findings, Behavioral Models, and Problems of Measurement," *Journal of Economic Literature*, June 1991, pp. 471–522.

As in our simpler model, the net impact of the income and substitution effects on the hours of labor market work could be either positive or negative, depending on their relative magnitudes. But the alleged superiority of Becker's model is that it embodies a more comprehensive and more realistic portrayal of the uses of time. People do not merely divide their time between the assembly line and the hammock, as a narrow interpretation of Chapter 2's simpler model might imply. As noted earlier, the Becker model is a useful tool for understanding labor force participation rates, the topic to which we now turn.

QUICK REVIEW 3-1

- The population base underlying the total supply of labor depends on the birthrate, the death rate, and the rate of net immigration.
- The Becker model of the allocation of time regards households as economic units deciding how best to allocate their time among work, household production, and household consumption to obtain utility-yielding commodities.
- In the Becker income effect, a rise in the wage rate raises income, allowing the household to buy more goods; hours of work fall because these goods require more time to consume.
- In the Becker substitution effect, a rise in the wage rate increases hours of work because households substitute *(a)* goods for time in the production of commodities and *(b)* goods-intensive commodities for time-intensive commodities in consumption.

Your Turn: In general, women's educational levels and real wage rates have increased greatly over the past several decades. Also, women are increasingly participating in the workplace. What do these facts imply about the relative strengths of the Becker income and substitution effects? (Answer: See page 625.)

PARTICIPATION RATES: DEFINED AND MEASURED

The labor force participation rate is determined by comparing the actual labor force with the potential labor force or what is sometimes called the "age-eligible population."

In the United States we consider the ***potential labor force*** or age-eligible population to be the entire population *less* (1) young people under 16 years of age and (2) people who are institutionalized. Children—those under 16—are excluded on the assumption that schooling and child labor laws keep most of them out of the labor force.[7] Furthermore, that segment of the population that is institutionalized—in penal or mental institutions, nursing homes, and so on—is also not available for labor market activities.[8] The ***actual labor force*** consists of those people who are either (1) employed or (2) unemployed but actively seeking a job.[9] Thus in percentage form we can say that the ***labor force participation rate*** (LFPR) is:

$$\text{LFPR} = \frac{\text{actual labor force}}{\text{potential labor force}} \times 100 \tag{3-1}$$

[7]Although excluded from the official definition of the labor force, many persons under 16 years of age do engage in labor market activities.

[8]Since 1983 all armed forces personnel stationed in the United States have been considered to be members of the labor force, the rationale being that joining the military is a voluntary decision and therefore represents a viable labor market alternative. Prior to 1983 members of the military were not counted as part of the labor force. The Bureau of Labor Statistics now reports data for both the total labor force and the civilian labor force.

[9]More precise definitions will be introduced in Chapter 19. It should be noted that all part-time workers are included in the labor force.

or

$$\text{LFPR} = \frac{\text{noninstitutional population 16 years or over in the labor force}}{\text{noninstitutional population}} \times 100 \qquad (3\text{-}2)$$

In April 1998, for example:

$$\frac{136,379,000}{204,731,000} \times 100 = 66.6\%$$

Participation rates can be similarly determined for various subaggregates of the population, for example, married women, black teenage females, and so forth.

SECULAR TREND OF PARTICIPATION RATES

3-2

Let's now turn to the long-run or secular trend of participation rates in the United States as portrayed in Figure 3-3. You should be forewarned that the factors affecting participation rates are varied and complex; some are economic variables, while others are of an institutional, legal, or attitudinal nature. Thus, while the Becker model is useful in

3-2 World of Work

WORKING FOR FREE*

Millions of Americans work for free. They volunteer their time to a variety of organizations such as churches, charities, hospitals, and schools. Volunteer activity represents an important part of the U.S. economy. A study by Richard Freeman estimates that volunteers contributed $116 billion worth of their time in 1991, or 3.5 percent of total work time.

Standard neoclassical theory would predict that volunteers would tend to be those with a low opportunity cost of time such as low-wage workers or unemployed persons. However, few of the demographic characteristics of volunteers tend to be consistent with this hypothesis. They are employed with high wages, married, in high-income and larger families, aged 35 to 54, more educated, and professionals and managers.

What, then, explains why people volunteer their time? Freeman argues that people volunteer because they are asked to do so. He finds that people who were asked to volunteer in the past year were at least three times more likely to volunteer than those who were not asked to do so. Freeman argues this relationship exists because volunteering is a "conscience good." That is, people accede to such requests because they feel morally obligated to do so. In addition, the request carries some "social pressure" to accept if it comes from an employer, friend, co-worker, or family member. Does this mean this activity would increase dramatically if everyone were asked to volunteer? No, because those more likely to accept such a request are probably more likely to be asked.

Traditional economics is supported in one dimension. One may suspect that high-income individuals, due to their high opportunity costs of time, would tend to substitute monetary gifts for donations of time. Freeman does find some support for this conjecture.

*Richard B. Freeman, "Working for Nothing: The Supply of Volunteer Labor," *Journal of Labor Economics*, January 1997, pp. S140–S166.

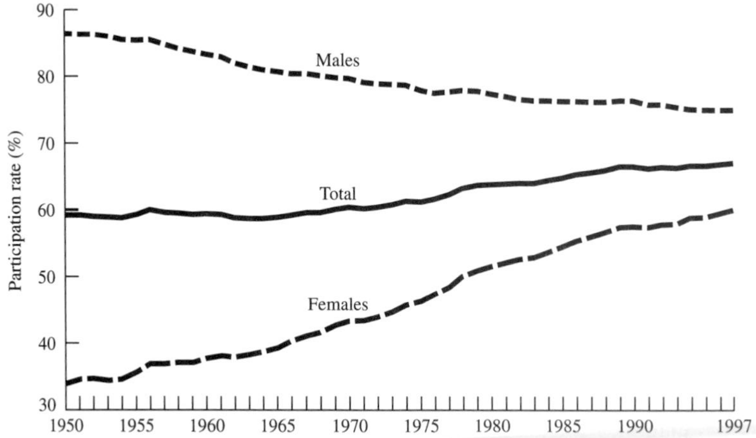

FIGURE 3-3 TOTAL, MALE AND FEMALE PARTICIPATION RATES, 1950–1997
The total or aggregate participation rate has slowly drifted upward over time. This is the net consequence of the rapidly rising female participation rate more than compensating for a declining male rate.

explaining many of the important changes in participation rates, it cannot be realistically expected to provide a complete understanding of all the forces at work.

Figure 3-3 reveals that the aggregate participation rate has gradually drifted upward since World War II. In 1950 about 60 percent of the age-eligible population were labor force participants. By 1997 that figure had increased to about 67 percent, with most of the rise occurring in the 1970s and 1980s. In Figure 3-3 we also observe that the participation rate of males has declined steadily. Specifically, male participation rates declined from about 86 percent in 1950 to approximately 75 percent in 1997. But concomitant increases in female participation rates have more than offset this decline. Female participation rates rose from about 34 percent in 1950 to about 59 percent in 1997. In short, male and female participation rates are tending to converge. It is important that we understand the major causal factors underlying these trends.

Declining Participation Rates of Older Males

Figure 3-4 shows male participation rates by age groups. The message here is that the participation rates of older males have declined markedly. We find a virtually uninterrupted reduction in the participation rates for males 65 and older over the entire 1950–1997 period.[10] We also observe a sharp 18 percentage point decline for males aged 55 to 64 over the past three decades.

A variety of factors have been cited to explain these declines. These include (1) rising real wages and earning, (2) the increasing availability of public and private pen-

[10]Economic incentives don't fully explain the spike in retirement at age 65. See Robin L. Lumsdaine, James H. Stock, and David A. Wise, "Why Are Retirement Rates So High at Age 65?" National Bureau of Economic Research Working Paper No. 5190, July 1995.

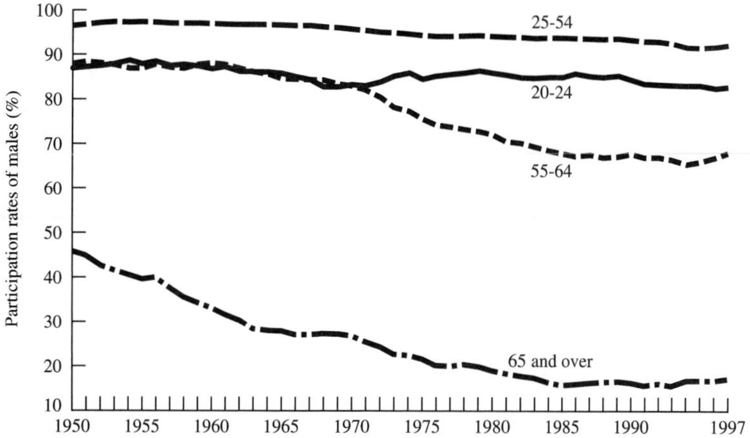

FIGURE 3-4 MALE PARTICIPATION RATES BY AGE GROUP, 1950–1997
While the participation rates of males in the 20-to-24 and 25-to-54 age groups have remained quite constant, the rates for older males have fallen significantly over the past 47 years.

sions, (3) an increasing access to disability benefits, and (4) the allocation of time over one's life cycle.

1 Rising Real Wages and Earnings Economic growth has been accompanied by rising real wages and earnings. For example, real gross domestic product per capita has increased about threefold since 1940. We know that rising real wages entail both income and substitution effects. In the case of older men, the income effect has dominated the substitution effect, and consequently, many have chosen more leisure in the form of retirement. In many instances, the deteriorating health of older males may also have induced retirement by increasing their preferences for leisure or, in terms of Chapter 2, by making their indifference curves steeper.[11] Put in simpler language, as our society has become more affluent over time, the secular increase in real wages and earnings has allowed more and more workers to accumulate sufficient wealth to retire at an earlier age. The average age of final retirement has fallen by between 4 and 5 years for both men and women since 1950.[12]

2 Social Security and Private Pensions An additional factor in explaining the declining participation rates of older males is the availability of Social Security and private pensions. Established in 1935, the social security program now provides

[11]Health status played a more important role in the labor force participation decisions of older men earlier in the century than now. See Dora L. Costa, "Health and Labor Force Participation of Older Men, 1900–1991," *Journal of Economic History,* March 1996, pp. 62–89.

[12]Murray Gendell and Jacob S. Siegel, "Trends in Retirement Age by Sex, 1950–2005," *Monthly Labor Review,* July 1992, pp. 22–29.

retirement benefits for older workers and their survivors in addition to income support in the case of disability or illness. Social Security retirement benefits have been characterized by both expanding coverage and increasingly generous levels, thereby providing an important source of nonlabor income that has induced large numbers of elderly male workers to withdraw from the labor force (see Figure 2-9). In recent years Social Security benefits have been rising faster than wages in real terms, which enhances the relative attractiveness of retirement. Furthermore, retirement benefits are subject to a substantial benefit-reduction rate—that is, an implicit tax on earned income—which further enhances the incentive for older workers to withdraw from the labor force. Thus, both the income *and* substitution effects associated with social security generate disincentives to work.

While federal legislation prohibits mandatory retirement, the availability of private pensions has been an inducement to early retirement. In 1950 only 16 percent of the labor force was covered by private pension plans; by 1994 41 percent of all workers were covered. Declining participation rates for the 55-to-64 age group undoubtedly reflect that many pension plans allow retirement with full or partial benefits on completion of a specified number of years—say, 20 or 30—of employment.

Research by Ippolito[13] suggests that approximately one-half of the decline in the participation rates of men aged 55 to 64 in the 1970–1986 period is attributable to two factors: (1) changes in the Social Security system that increased retirement benefits by about 50 percent, and (2) the alteration of private pension rules that encouraged early retirement.

Ruhm, however, finds that pensions have offsetting effects on the labor supply of older men.[14] He reports that pensions increase the participation of men in their late fifties and early sixties, but decrease the participation of men aged 65 to 69. He argues that this finding is the result of incentives included in pensions to retire in certain age ranges.

3 Disability Benefits Evidence also exists to suggest that the disability component of the Social Security program has become increasingly generous and is progressive in the sense that low-wage workers receive relatively larger benefits than high-wage workers. As a result, low-wage workers are more inclined to seek disability benefits as an alternative to labor market participation.[15] Because black workers are generally lower-income workers, this consideration may explain the larger decline in the participation rates of older black workers compared to older white workers.[16]

[13]Richard A. Ippolito, "Toward Explaining Earlier Retirement after 1970," *Industrial and Labor Relations Review,* July 1990, pp. 556–569. From a public policy perspective, however, it may be difficult to reverse the increase in early retirement by reducing Social Security benefits. See Alan B. Krueger and Jorn-Steffen Pischke, "The Effect of Social Security on Labor Supply: A Cohort Analysis of the Notch Generation," *Journal of Labor Economics,* October 1992, pp. 412–437.

[14]Christopher J. Ruhm, "Do Pensions Increase the Labor Supply of Older Men?" *Journal of Public Economics,* February 1996, pp. 157–175.

[15]One obvious solution to the problem of able individuals receiving disability benefits is to deny the benefit applications from such persons. Some evidence exists that program officials can fairly effectively screen out claims from able individuals. See Jonathan Gruber and Jeffrey D. Kubik, "Disability Insurance Rejection Rates and the Labor Supply of Older Workers," *Journal of Public Economics,* April 1997, pp. 1–23.

[16]See Donald O. Parsons, "Racial Trends in Male Labor Force Participation," *American Economic Review,* December 1980, pp. 911–920.

4 Life Cycle Considerations Let's consider a fourth and final factor that may account for the declining participation rates of older males. You may have recognized that the factors discussed thus far have centered on the income effect. The availability of nonlabor income in the form of public or private pensions, disability payments, or income from accumulated wealth generates a pure income effect that is sufficient to induce many older males to become nonparticipants. Some economists feel that a kind of substitution effect is also at work over time in encouraging older workers to withdraw from the labor force. In particular, they observe that the real earnings of many workers rise quite significantly until they reach, say, their mid-fifties, and then earnings grow slowly or gradually decline. A glance ahead at Figure 4-1 seems to confirm this trend of earnings. The alleged reason for the decline in the earnings of older workers is that, on average, their formal education and on-the-job training become obsolete and their mental and physical capabilities diminish. This means that in allocating time over one's lifetime, it is rational to work continuously and for long hours during one's younger years because one's earnings potential is high and therefore leisure is expensive. Conversely, as a person grows older, the earnings potential becomes smaller and leisure becomes relatively cheaper, meaning that one is inclined to substitute leisure for work. In the extreme, this substitution is complete and retirement is chosen.

3-3

3-3 World of Work

DOES TECHNOLOGICAL CHANGE INDUCE EARLY RETIREMENT?

It is conceivable that technological change might lead older workers to retire sooner than they otherwise might. Psychologists note that for many people, adapting to change becomes more difficult as they age. Thus, learning new techniques and adapting to new production methods may be more difficult for older workers than for younger ones. Also, older workers have less incentive to adapt to new technology; they have few years of work ahead of them in which to reap the benefits of new training. Workers nearing retirement thus may decide to retire early, concluding it is not worth the time and effort to learn the new technology.

Bartel and Sicherman* recently examined the relationship between rates of technological change in industries and the timing of retirement. They measured technological change as an industry's rate of productivity growth—its increases in output per worker hour—not explained by changes in the quantity and quality of capital and labor. According to this measure, the communications and machinery industries are examples of industries with high technological change.

Somewhat surprisingly, these researchers found that workers retired *later* in industries with high continuing rates of technological change. These industries require longer training periods and provide workers with more on-the-job training than other industries. Workers in these industries experience rising wages and apparently stay on their jobs longer to gain the returns on their training investments.

The authors discovered, however, that technological shocks—rapid, unexpected changes in an industry's rate of technological change—*do* induce older workers to retire early. These changes may require substantial new training and use of new equipment and techniques. Many older workers simply may conclude that "it isn't worth it" to undergo major retraining this late in their careers.

In brief, in industries characterized by expected, continuous technological change, workers adjust to new technology and have longer careers than workers in industries with lower rates of technological change. However, when confronted with technological shocks, older workers in all industries are more likely to retire earlier.

*Ann P. Bartel and Nachum Sicherman, "Technological Change and the Retirement Decisions of Older Workers," *Journal of Labor Economics,* January 1993, part 1, pp. 162–183.

Rising Female Participation Rates

Figure 3-5 portrays the participation rates of females by age groups. Excepting women aged 65 and over, the participation rates of all female age groups have increased over the 47 years shown. We observe particularly pronounced increases for the two younger age groups.

Most of the increase in female participation rates shown in Figure 3-5 has been accounted for by married women. For example, the total number of females in the labor force increased by approximately 45 million over the 1950–1997 period. Of this total increase about two-thirds were married women. In one sense, this is a surprising phenomenon. From the perspective of a household, one might have expected that the participation rate of married women would have declined since World War II as a consequence of the generally rising real wage rates and incomes of married males. And, indeed, cross-sectional (point-in-time) studies reveal that the participation rates of married women do in fact vary inversely with the husband's income. Our analysis in Chapter 2 suggests the reason: If leisure is a normal good, then a household will "purchase" more leisure as its income rises. Historically, this purchase of leisure was likely to be in the form of the wife's nonparticipation in the labor market. In terms of Figure 2-8, as the husband's income rises, an expanding intrahousehold transfer of income is available to the wife and the consequent income effect induces her to be a nonparticipant. This line of reasoning suggests that wives in lower-income families are likely to work in the labor market because of economic necessity, but as the husband's income increases, more families will enjoy the luxury of having the wife produce "commodities" at home.

How can this reasoning be reconciled with the evidence that the participation rates of married women have actually increased over time? The answer lies partly

FIGURE 3-5 FEMALE PARTICIPATION RATES BY AGE GROUP, 1950–1997
Aside from the 65 and older group, the participation rates of all women have risen over the past 46 years. The sharpest increases have been for younger women in the 20-to-24 and 25-to-54 age groups.

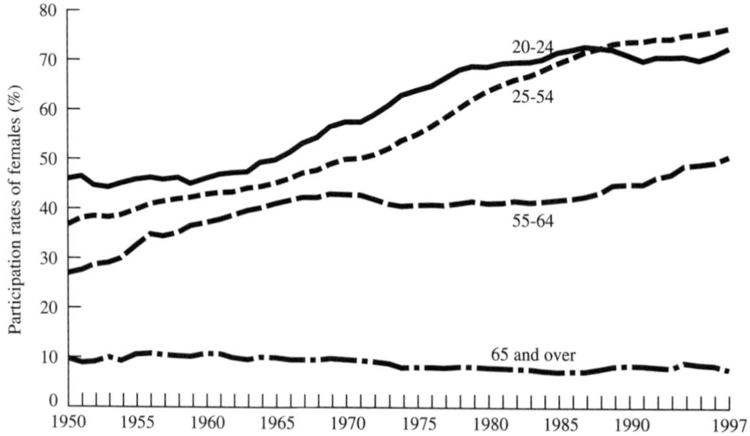

in the fact that cross-sectional studies do not have a time dimension and therefore ignore or hold constant certain variables other than the husband's income that might have an impact on a wife's decision to participate in the labor force. That is, a number of factors besides the husband's rising income have been influencing the participation rates of married women over time. These other factors have so strongly influenced women to enter the labor market that they have overwhelmed the negative effect on labor market work of the generally rising incomes of husbands. Also, during the past two decades, the real income growth of many husbands has slowed or even ceased.

3-2

Economists have cited several possible reasons for the rapid rise in women's labor force participation.[17]

[17]See T. Aldrich Finegan, "Participation of Married Women in the Labor Force," in Cynthia B. Lloyd (ed.), *Sex, Discrimination, and the Division of Labor* (New York: Columbia University Press, 1975), pp. 28–29; *Economic Report of the President, 1987* (Washington: U.S. Government Printing Office, 1987), chap. 7; and Barbara R. Bergmann, *The Economic Emergence of Women* (New York: Basic Books, 1986), chaps. 2–3. For a more detailed analysis, see James P. Smith and Michael P. Ward, "Time-Series Growth in the Female Labor Force," *Journal of Labor Economics*, Suppl. January 1985, pp. S59–S90.

3-2 Global Perspective

LABOR FORCE PARTICIPATION FOR WOMEN AGED 25 TO 54, 1995

Large variations exist in women's labor force participation rates across industrialized countries.

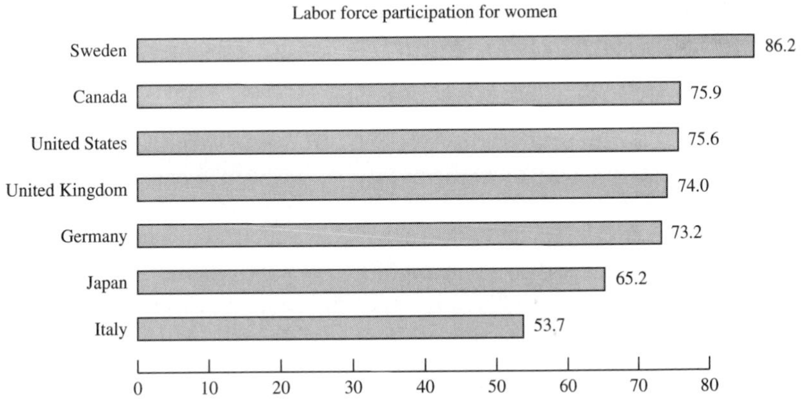

Source: Organization for Economic Cooperation and Development, *Employment Outlook,* July 1996, Table B.

1 Rising Real Wage Rates for Women There has been a long-run increase in the real wage rates that women can earn in the labor market. This is primarily a consequence of women having acquired more skills through education. As already noted, higher wage rates will generate both income and substitution effects within the framework of Becker's model. While the income effect will act to reduce hours of work, the substitution effects related to both production- and consumption-related activities within the home will tend to increase them. Goods will be substituted for time in the production of commodities *and* goods-intensive commodities will be substituted for time-intensive goods in the household's mix of consumer commodities. Both adjustments will free the wife's time from household activities so that she may spend more time in the labor market. Presumably the substitution effect has dominated the income effect for many women, causing their participation rates to rise. The income effect for married women may be small because its size will vary directly with the amount of time they are already devoting to labor market work. In the extreme, the income effect of a rise in wage rates will be nil for a married woman who is not currently participating in labor market work. A wage rate increase will increase a person's income only if the individual is currently providing hours of labor market work.

2 Changing Preferences and Attitudes Rising female participation rates may also be the result of a fundamental change in female preferences in favor of labor market work. First, the feminist movement of the 1960s may well have had the effect of altering the career objectives of women toward labor market participation. Similarly, antidiscrimination legislation of the 1960s—which specifies "equal pay for equal work" and presumably has made "men's jobs" more accessible—also *may* have made labor market work more attractive compared to work in the home.[18] Furthermore, aside from its positive impact on wage rates, greater education for women may have enhanced their "tastes" or preferences for labor market careers. More generally, society's attitudes about work have changed greatly. In the 1920s and 1930s there was general disapproval of married women working outside the home. A man would lose status and be regarded as a "poor provider" if his wife was "forced" to take a job. But in the post–World War II period an attitudinal turnabout has emerged such that labor force participation by married women is widely condoned and encouraged.

Reference to Figure 2-8 is helpful in distinguishing between how higher wage rates on the one hand and changing preferences on the other affect female participation rates. The availability of higher wage rates increases the slope of the budget line, which—given preferences—encourages labor market participation. Similarly, given the wage rates, a change in preferences favorable to market work makes the indifference curves flatter, which is also conducive to participation.

[18]Considerable disagreement exists as to whether gender discrimination has diminished significantly. For example, a glance ahead at Table 15-1 indicates that the female-male earnings gap persists.

3 Rising Productivity in the Household The use of more and technologically superior capital goods by businesses over time has been an important factor in increasing the productivity of work time and therefore in raising real wage rates. Larger amounts of improved machinery and equipment permit workers to produce a unit of output with less time. Similarly, the availability of more and better capital goods for household use has permitted households to reduce the amount of time needed to accomplish both production and consumption within the home. For example, supermarkets and the availability of home refrigerators and freezers greatly reduce the amount of time devoted to grocery shopping. The supermarket permits one-stop shopping, and refrigerators and freezers further reduce the number of shopping trips needed per week. Similarly, microwave ovens, vacuum cleaners, automatic clothes washers and dryers, and dishwashers have greatly reduced the amount of time involved in food preparation and housework. Fast-food restaurants circumvent the time-intensive activity of food preparation in the home. By providing direct and convenient transportation, the automobile has reduced the time required to attend a concert, movie, or football game. In terms of Becker's model, the increased availability of such household capital goods has increased productivity in the home, thereby freeing time from household production and consumption and allowing many women to engage in part- and full-time employment in the labor market.[19] Also, the increasing availability of child care centers has facilitated the transition of married women from work in the home to labor market work.

4 Declining Birthrates The presence of children—and particularly preschool children—is associated with low participation rates for wives. Child care is a highly time-intensive household productive activity that keeps many wives out of the labor force. While baby-sitters, nurseries, husbands, and child care centers can substitute for wives in caring for children, the expense and opportunity cost involved often discourage such substitutions. Over time, the widespread availability and use of birth control techniques, coupled with changing lifestyles, has reduced birthrates *and* compacted the span of time over which a family's children are born. While there were about 3.8 lifetime births per women in 1957 at the peak of the baby boom, that figure has declined to only 1.8 over the past decade. Fewer children reduce associated homemaking responsibilities and free married women for labor market work. Moreover, the compression of the time span over which children are born reduces the amount of time during which many women are absent from the labor force for child-raising responsibilities and is therefore more conducive to their pursuit of a labor market career.

Two points must be added. First, higher wage rates are associated with lower fertility rates. More-educated women who can command relatively high wage rates in the labor market tend to have fewer children than less-educated women for whom wages are low. Becker's model provides one explanation for this relationship. Child rearing is a highly time-intensive activity, and thus the opportunity cost of children—the

[19]For a detailed discussion of rising productivity in the home, see Bergmann, op. cit., chap. 12.

income sacrificed by not being in the labor market—is higher for more-educated women than for those who are less-educated.

The second point is that the presence of young children is currently less of an inhibitor to labor market participation than it has been in the recent past. In fact, the largest increases in labor force participation have been for wives with very young children. In 1996 61 percent of wives with preschool children participated in the labor force as compared to only 30 percent in 1970. Currently, more than one-half of all mothers return to work before their youngest child is 2 years old.

3-4

5 Rising Divorce Rates Marital instability as evidenced in rising divorce rates has undoubtedly motivated many women to establish and maintain labor market ties.

3-4 World of Work

ECONOMICS AND FERTILITY

In the past two decades some economists have attempted to explain birthrates in terms of the benefit-cost calculations of microeconomics. In particular, Gary Becker's economic view of the family has been extended to fertility and childbearing. Becker* and others contend that the decision to have children is analogous to a market transaction in which one purchases a capital good or a consumer durable good. Considered as a "capital good," a child may yield *benefits* in the form of future income flows for the parents. That is, the child may provide labor and thus income for a family farm or business. Or the child may provide transfer income when the parents are elderly and retired. As "consumer goods," children presumably yield a future stream of satisfactions or benefits in the same sense as an automobile or video recorder.

On the other hand, the decision to have a child implies both *direct* and *indirect* (opportunity) *costs.* The former involve expenditures for food, shelter, health care, day care, education, and so forth. The latter entail the cost or value of the time that parents devote to a child's care. One of the primary costs often is the forgone labor market income of the mother who remains out of the labor market to care for the child. Children are very time-intensive "commodities." Presumably, if the future stream of benefits is estimated to exceed the stream of costs, a couple will decide in favor of having a child. But if the costs exceed benefits, the couple will choose to forgo having the child.

Proponents of this microeconomic explanation of fertility argue that it explains why birthrates decline with economic growth. That is, high-income families (nations) tend to have fewer children (lower rates of population growth) than poor families (nations). Income and substitution effects are again relevant. Children are considered to be normal "goods," so that rising real incomes per se can be expected to *increase* birthrates. Wealthier families can afford to "purchase" more children. But this tendency is more than offset by the substitution effect. Specifically, the "price" of children has increased significantly, reflecting not merely higher direct costs but also higher opportunity costs due to the rising labor market wages available to wives.

Furthermore, Becker contends there is a quality–quantity trade-off for children just as there is for other goods. As incomes have risen, couples have opted for higher-quality (healthier, better-educated) children in the same way they have purchased higher-quality automobiles and housing. This choice has entailed the expenditure of more money and more time per child. For all of these reasons, the cost or price of children has increased substantially with a consequent large substitution effect. Put bluntly, the higher price of children allegedly has induced higher-income couples to substitute other goods and to therefore "buy" fewer children.

*See in particular Gary S. Becker, *The Economic Approach to Human Behavior* (Chicago: University of Chicago Press, 1976), part 6; and idem, *A Treatise on the Family* (Cambridge: Harvard University Press, 1981), chap. 5. Victor F. Fuchs, *How We Live* (Cambridge: Harvard University Press, 1983), chap. 2, is also relevant.

Divorce rates have grown rapidly in recent decades. Currently, statisticians estimate that almost one-half of all new marriages will end in divorce. The economic impact of divorce on women is often disastrous because relatively few women receive substantial alimony or child-support payments from their former husbands. All too often the options are poverty, welfare support, or labor market work. In short, more and more married women, not to mention women contemplating marriage, may participate in the labor force as a means of protecting themselves against the financial exigencies of potential divorce. In terms of Figure 2-8, divorced women find themselves with substantially less nonlabor income, and this reduction is an inducement to labor market work.

A word of caution: The cause-and-effect relationship between fertility, divorce rates, and labor force participation is complex and unclear. For example, declines in fertility resulting from more efficient and less costly birth control techniques undoubtedly encourage labor force participation. On the other hand, the initial choice of a woman to pursue a labor market career may precipitate the decision to have fewer children. Similarly, the increased likelihood of divorce will tend to reduce fertility because child care is more difficult after a marriage dissolves. Conversely, the presence of few or no children makes divorce less painful and less costly.[20]

6 Expanding Job Accessibility In addition to a decline in gender discrimination, a variety of other factors have made jobs more accessible to women. First, since World War II there has been a great expansion both absolutely and relatively in the kinds of employment that have traditionally been "women's jobs"; for example, clerical and secretarial work, retail sales, teaching, and nursing. Second, there has been a long-run shift of the population from farms and rural regions to urban areas, where jobs for women are more abundant and more geographically accessible. Third, the average length of the workweek has declined in full-time jobs *and* the availability of part-time jobs has increased. These latter two developments have made it easier for women to reconcile labor market employment with housekeeping tasks.

7 Attempts to Maintain Living Standards The growth of male earnings during the past two decades has been quite stagnant compared to earlier decades. In fact, for some men—particularly low-wage workers and those in industries hurt by imports—*real* weekly earnings are lower today than a decade, or even two decades, ago. Many households have adjusted to these realities by having both spouses work. That is, they have substituted labor market time for household production time to preserve the family's standard of living, that standard defined either absolutely or relative to other households.[21]

In this view, part of the more recent rise in the female labor force participation rate has been necessitated by the family's desire to "make ends meet." In some cases,

[20]For a further discussion, you might consult Blau and Ferber, op. cit., pp. 104, 264–267; and William R. Johnson and Jonathan Skinner, "Labor Supply and Marital Separation," *American Economic Review,* June 1986, pp. 455–469.

[21]Some doubt has been cast on the hypothesis that married women are increasing work effort in response to declining wages of husbands. See Chinhui Juhn and Kevin M. Murphy, "Wage Inequality and Family Labor Supply," *Journal of Labor Economics,* January 1997, pp. 72–97.

"making ends meet" implies paying for basic food, clothing, and shelter. In other instances, it means preserving middle- or upper-class lifestyles, including living in comfortable homes, driving nice cars, enjoying household electronic equipment, and taking family trips. Quite understandably, families look for ways to maintain their standards of living, whatever those levels might be. If spouses had not entered the labor force in record numbers during the past two decades, many households would have suffered absolute or relative declines in real income. Undoubtedly, many wives entered the labor force to prevent this from happening. Relatedly, couples may be concerned about their family income compared to other families. As a result, the entry of some women into the labor market may encourage other women to enter in order to maintain their families' relative income level.[22]

Relative Importance

Fuchs has analyzed the various factors that may have contributed to rising female participation rates, with a view to discerning their comparative significance.[23] He discounts the importance of such considerations as antidiscrimination legislation and the feminist movement, largely on the basis that their timing is bad. That is, the growth of female participation rates predates both the feminist movement and the passage of antidiscrimination laws (Chapter 15). It also predates the stagnant growth of real earnings experienced by many husbands during the past two decades. The problem with attributing rising participation rates for women to the availability of time-saving household goods and related innovations is that cause and effect are unclear. Did innovations such as clothes washers, freezers, fast-food restaurants, and supermarkets simply appear and thereby free up time that married women could devote to labor market work? Or were these innovations made largely in response to needs that arose when women decided for other reasons to enter the labor force? Fuchs believes that their growth in the United States is the *result* of the rising value of time and the rising female participation rates, rather than a causal factor.

More positively, Fuchs feels that rising real wage rates and the expansion of "women's jobs" in the service industries are the most important reasons for rising female participation rates. Better control of fertility is also deemed significant, but once again cause and effect are difficult to unravel. Do women first decide on labor force participation and, as a consequence of this decision, determine to have fewer children? Or does the decision to have smaller families precede the decision to enter the labor
3-3 force? Fuchs also contends that the growing probability of divorce compels women to achieve and maintain their ties to the labor market. Smith and Ward are in substantial agreement with Fuchs. Their research leads them to conclude that rising real wage rates directly (by creating incentives to work) and indirectly (by inducing lower birthrates)

[22]For some evidence consistent with this hypothesis, see David Neumark and Andrew Postlewaite, "Relative Income Concerns and the Rise in Married Women's Employment," National Bureau of Economic Research Working Paper No. 5044, February 1995.

[23]Victor R. Fuchs, *How We Live* (Cambridge: Harvard University Press, 1983), pp. 127–133.

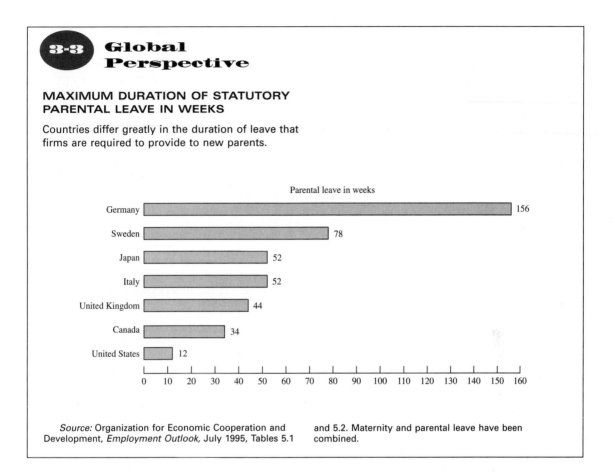

3-3 **Global Perspective**

MAXIMUM DURATION OF STATUTORY PARENTAL LEAVE IN WEEKS

Countries differ greatly in the duration of leave that firms are required to provide to new parents.

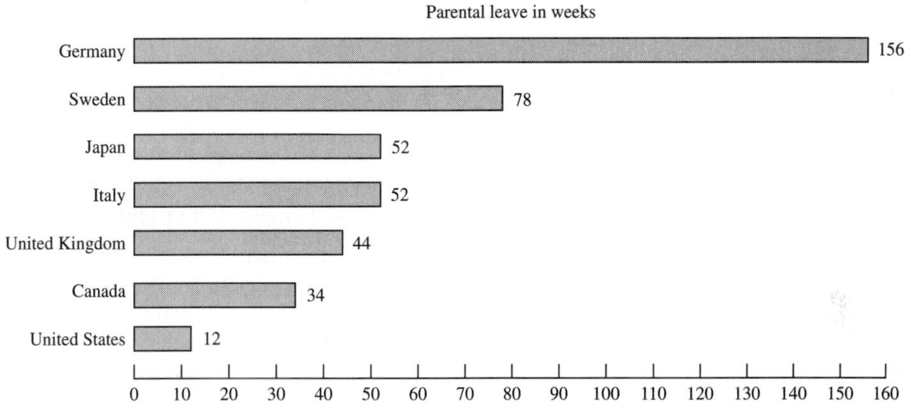

Source: Organization for Economic Cooperation and Development, *Employment Outlook,* July 1995, Tables 5.1 and 5.2. Maternity and parental leave have been combined.

3-5

have accounted for almost 60 percent of the increase in the female labor force that has occurred since World War II.[24]

Racial Differences

Important gender differences mark the effect of race on labor force participation rates.

Females The participation rates of black and white women are nearly identical. This situation was not always the case. In the past, the participation rate of black women exceeded that of white women. For example, in the mid-1950s, the difference between the participation rates of black and white women was 12 to 15 percentage points. The gap has been closed because the rise in the participation rate of women (discussed in

[24]Smith and Ward, op. cit., pp. S59–S90.

3-5 World of Work

FAMILY AND MEDICAL LEAVE ACT OF 1993

After eight years of debate, in 1993 Congress passed the Family and Medical Leave Act (FMLA). Passage of this act relates directly to the growing labor force participation of women. Increased participation in labor market work has left women with less time to care for newborn children, temporarily disabled spouses, and aging parents. Before passage of this law, many workers—both female and male—faced the prospect of permanent loss of their jobs if they had to leave work temporarily to care for loved ones.

FMLA permits workers to take up to 12 weeks a year of unpaid leave to care for (1) a spouse, a parent, or a child with a serious medical condition; (2) a newborn or newly adopted child; or (3) the worker's own serious health problem. Employees must provide 30 days' advance notice for foreseeable leaves. They retain their health insurance during their leaves and are guaranteed their original jobs or equivalent positions when they return to work.

FMLA covers employers with 50 or more workers within a 75-mile radius of the firm. Part-time employees and those who have been on the job for less than one year are excluded from eligibility. Also, firms can deny leaves to the highest-paid 10 percent of their salaried workers if allowing the leaves would create "substantial and grievous" injury to the business operation. The idea here is to exclude key management from the provisions of the act.

Debate has been considerable on the merits and impacts of FMLA. Critics claim that it raises costs to firms and discourages the hiring of women (the group predicted to make the heaviest use of the leave provisions). Proponents argue that the law is a way for employees to mesh work and nonwork responsibilities and decrease career interruptions for women. The result, they say, will be increased worker and family well-being.

The evidence so far indicates that the FMLA has had little impact. A 1995 study by the government's independent General Accounting Office reports that only 2 percent of the eligible workers have taken advantage of the act's provision for leave. Consistent with expectations, women were more likely to take a leave than men. Surprisingly, 59 percent took leave to tend their own health, not to care for others. Finally, the median leave was only 10 days, though the mean leave was 37 days. Relatedly, research by Ruhm and Teague (1997), using cross-country data on mandated family leaves, indicates such leaves have little impact on productivity.*

*Christopher J. Ruhm and Jacqueline L. Teague, "Parental Leave Policies in Europe and North America," in Francine Blau and Ronald Ehrenberg, eds., *Gender and Family Issues in the Workplace* (New York, NY: Russell Sage Foundation Press, 1997).

the previous section) has been concentrated among white women. Relatively little change has occurred in the participation of black women because their participation traditionally has been high.[25]

The decline in the racial gap in participation may be a critical factor in explaining why the ratio of black incomes to white incomes has increased only modestly in the past two decades or so. The income gains for black families, which may have resulted from antidiscrimination legislation and more enlightened attitudes toward minorities, may have been largely offset by the relatively larger numbers of white married women entering the labor force.[26]

[25]For a discussion of the reasons for the historical racial gap in participation, see Glen Cain, *Married Women in the Labor Force* (Chicago: University of Chicago Press, 1966), pp. 77–83.

[26]In this section we have focused on the factors that explain the rise in female labor market employment. For an interesting discussion of the effects of women's labor force participation on marriage, fertility, divorce, and the general well-being of family members, see Blau and Ferber, op. cit., chap. 9.

Males Since the 1950s a gap has evolved between the participation rates of black and white males. Thus, for example, in 1955 the participation rates of both groups were approximately 85 percent. But by 1997 the participation rate of white males was 76 percent compared to only 68 percent for black males.

Why the significantly lower participation rates for black men? There is no consensus on this question, but several hypotheses have been offered. First, a "demand-side" hypothesis suggests that the difference may be largely attributable to inferior labor market opportunities as reflected in relatively lower wage rates and poorer prospects for finding employment. On the average, blacks have less education and education that is allegedly of inferior quality compared to whites. Discrimination as embodied in lower wages, less desirable dead-end jobs, and the tendency for blacks to be the "last hired and first fired" are all inducements for blacks to remain outside of the labor force.[27] A "spatial mismatch" also may exist between black workers and employment opportunities in that jobs have been moved out of the central cities, where black populations are concentrated.

A second view explains the high labor market inactivity of blacks as residing primarily on the supply side of the market. Welch[28] has argued that nonlabor market opportunities may have improved for blacks, affording them more attractive alternatives to labor market work. What are those nonlabor market opportunities? One is the receipt of Social Security or public assistance. Indeed, we found in Chapter 2 that the increased availability and enhanced generosity of public income maintenance programs encourage income receivers of all races to withdraw from the labor force (see Figure 2-9 in particular). Because blacks are disproportionately represented among the lowest-income groups in our society, we would expect the participation rates of blacks to be less than those of whites.[29] Welch notes that in 1980 over 30 percent of black men aged 20 to 24 and almost 22 percent of black men aged 35 to 44 either received social security or public assistance or lived with someone who did. Comparable figures for white males were only 13 and 10 percent, respectively. Welch also ponders whether illegal activities are more attractive than labor market work for many black men. He points out that young black males are six to seven times as likely to be in jail as are whites. Thus, in 1980 some 4.6 percent of blacks aged 20 to 24 were incarcerated as compared to only 0.7 for whites. Since 1980, the incarceration rate has risen particularly for black males. By 1993, 7 percent of all black males over 18 were in jail.

[27]For more on this, see the discussion of secondary labor markets in Chapter 16 and Katharine L. Bradbury and Lynn E. Browne, "Black Men in the Labor Market," *New England Economic Review* (Federal Reserve Bank of Boston), March–April 1986, pp. 32–42.

[28]Finis Welch, "The Employment of Black Men," *Journal of Labor Economics,* January 1990, pp. S26–S74.

[29]This point is stressed by Richard Butler and James J. Heckman, "The Government's Impact on the Labor Market Status of Black Americans: A Critical Review," in Leonard J. Hausman (ed.), *Equal Rights and Industrial Relations* (Madison, Wis.: Industrial Relations Research Association, 1977), pp. 235–281. It is interesting to note that Butler and Heckman argue that the increase in the ratio of black to white average earnings that has occurred in recent years (Chapter 15) is *not* attributable to government antidiscrimination policies, but rather to income maintenance programs that reduce the supply of black labor market participants to the extent that their average wage rates have increased in comparison to those of whites.

Third, the differences in health status may play a role in the differences in the participation rates of older black and white males. Bound, Schoenbaum, and Waidmann conclude that racial differences in age, education, and health status can account for 44 percent of the black-white difference in participation of males aged 51 to 61.[30] Evidence exists that some of these health differences may partly be the result of black males holding more physically demanding and stressful jobs.

Finally, the relatively lower participation rate for black married males may also be a reflection of the relatively high participation rate of black wives noted earlier. In terms of Becker's model, black women may incur less discrimination in the labor market than black men, making it rational for relatively more black women and relatively fewer black men to participate in labor market work.

CYCLICAL CHANGES IN PARTICIPATION RATES

Our discussion has concentrated on long-term or secular changes in participation rates. We must now recognize that cyclical changes also occur. Let's consider how cyclical fluctuations might affect a family in which one spouse engages in labor market work while the other performs productive activities within the home. Assume that a recession occurs, causing the employed spouse to lose her or his job. The net effect on overall participation rates depends on the size of the added-worker effect and the discouraged-worker effect.

Added-Worker Effect

The ***added-worker effect*** is the idea that when the primary breadwinner in a family loses his or her job, other family members will temporarily enter the labor force in the hope of finding employment to offset the decline in the family's income. The rationale involved is reminiscent of Chapter 2's income effect. Specifically, one spouse's earned income may be treated as *nonlabor* income from the standpoint of the other spouse. In our illustration the nonemployed family member receives an intrahousehold transfer of some portion of the employed spouse's earnings. From the perspective of the person working in the home, this transfer is *nonlabor* income. In terms of Figure 2-8, the spouse's job loss will reduce nonlabor income as measured on the right vertical axis. Other things being equal, a decrease in nonlabor (transfer) income tends to cause one to become a labor force participant. This is the underlying rationale of the added-worker effect.[31]

Discouraged-Worker Effect

The ***discouraged-worker effect*** works in the opposite direction. The discouraged-worker effect suggests that during a recession some unemployed workers (for exam-

[30] John Bound, Michael Schoenbaum, and Timothy Waidmann, "Race and Education Differences in Disability Status and Labor Force Attachment in the Health and Retirement Survey," *Journal of Human Resources*, Suppl. 1995, pp. S227–S267.

[31] For an examination of the added worker effect, see Shelly Lundberg, "The Added Worker Effect," *Journal of Labor Economics*, January 1985, pp. 11–37.

ple, the unemployed spouse in our illustration) become so pessimistic about finding a job with an acceptable wage rate that they cease to actively seek employment and thereby temporarily become nonparticipants. This phenomenon can be explained in terms of Chapter 2's substitution effect. Recessions generally entail declines in the real wages available to unemployed workers and new job seekers, increasing the "price" of income (that is, increasing the amount of work time that must be expended to earn $1 of goods) and decreasing the price of leisure. This causes some workers to substitute leisure (nonparticipation) for job search. Other things being equal, a decrease in the wage rate will cause some individuals to withdraw from the labor force now that the wage rate available to them is lower. Remember that the substitution effect suggests that a *decline* in the wage rate available to a worker will lead to a *decrease* in the incentive to engage in labor market work.

Procyclical Labor Force Changes

These two effects influence participation rates and labor force size in opposite ways. The added-worker effect increases and the discouraged-worker effect decreases participation rates and labor force size during an economic downturn. Which effect is dominant? What actually happens to participation rates over the business cycle? Empirical research generally indicates that the discouraged-worker effect is dominant, as is evidenced by the fact that the aggregate labor force participation rate varies inversely with the unemployment rate. When the unemployment rate increases, the participation rate falls and vice versa.

Why does the discouraged-worker effect apparently outweigh the added-worker effect? Why does the size of the labor force vary in a procyclical fashion? The conventional wisdom is that the discouraged-worker effect applies to many more households than the added-worker effect. For example, if the nation's unemployment rate rises from, say, 6 to 9 percent, only those 3 percent or so of all families that now contain an additional unemployed member will be subject to the added-worker effect. On the other hand, worsening labor market conditions evidenced by the increase in the unemployment rate and decline in real wages may have a discouraging effect on actual and potential labor force participants in *all* households. Thus, as the economy moves into a recession, young people who are deciding whether to continue school or to drop out to seek employment will take note that wage rates are less attractive and jobs more difficult to find. Many of them will decide to stay in school rather than participate in the labor force.

Procyclical changes in the labor force size also have been explained in terms of the *timing* of labor force participation by some individuals. For example, many married women are marginally attached to the labor force in that they plan to engage in labor market work for, say, only one-half of their adult years. The other half of their time will be spent in household production. Given this planned overall division of time, it is only rational for such women to participate in the labor force in prosperous times when jobs are readily available and real wages are relatively high and, conversely, to be nonparticipants when unemployment is high and available wage rates are low.[32]

The procyclical changes in labor force size are of more than idle academic interest. Such changes have a significant bearing on the magnitude of the official unemployment rate and, hence, an indirect bearing on macroeconomic policy (Chapter 19). The apparent dominance of the discouraged-worker effect over the added-worker effect means that the labor force shrinks (or at least grows at a below-normal rate) during recession, and the official unemployment rate understates unemployment. During economic expansions, the discouraged-worker effect becomes an "encouraged-worker" effect and the added-worker effect becomes a "subtracted-worker" effect. The former dominates the latter, and the labor force expands as a result. This means there is a larger-than-normal increase in the labor force during an economic expansion that keeps the official unemployment rate higher than would otherwise be the case. In short, cyclical changes in participation rates cause the official unemployment rate to understate unemployment during a cyclical downswing and to overstate it during an upswing.

Postscript: Even though cyclical changes in the labor force have been studied by economists for over four decades, considerable disagreement remains as to the magnitude of such changes.[33] You should also be aware that unanimity does not exist that the discouraged-worker effect is dominant.[34]

QUICK REVIEW 3-2

- The labor force participation rate (LFPR) measures the percentage of the potential labor force that is either employed or officially unemployed.
- Two pronounced secular trends in LFPRs are the declining rates of older men and the rising rates of working-age women.
- The LFPRs for black women have consistently exceeded the rates for white women; the rates for black males have dropped far below those of white males.
- The overall LFPR falls as the economy recedes and rises as the economy expands, implying that the discouraged-worker effect (encouraged-worker effect) exceeds the added-worker effect (subtracted-worker effect).

Your Turn: Suppose that a hypothetical country has a total population of 100 million, of which 7 million are unemployed (but actively seeking work), 15 million are under

[32]See Jacob Mincer, "Labor-Force Participation and Unemployment: A Review of Recent Evidence," in R. A. Gordon and M. S. Gordon (eds.), *Prosperity and Unemployment* (New York: John Wiley & Sons, Inc., 1966), pp. 73–112.

[33]For one such estimate, see T. Aldrich Finegan, "Discouraged Workers and Economic Fluctuations," *Industrial and Labor Relations Review,* October 1981, pp. 88–102.

[34]See, for example, Michael C. Keeley, "Cyclical Unemployment and Employment: Effects of Labor Force Entry and Exit," *Economic Review* (Federal Reserve Bank of San Francisco), Summer 1984, pp. 5–25. This article contains a useful review of theory and evidence and an extensive bibliography. Also see William E. Cullison, "The Changing Labor Force: Some Provocative Findings," *Economic Review* (Federal Reserve Bank of Richmond), September–October 1989, pp. 30–36.

16 or institutionalized, 25 million are eligible to work but not in the labor force, and 53 million are employed. What is the LFPR? (Answer: See page 625.)

HOURS OF WORK: TWO TRENDS

Observe in Figure 3-1 that the total amount of labor supplied in the economy depends not only on the number of labor force participants but also on the average number of hours worked per week and per year by those participants. Therefore, let's now consider what has happened to hours of work over time.

Table 3-1 provides an overview of secular changes in the average workweek. The data show decade averages of the workweek and the workyear for production workers in U.S. manufacturing industries. Two important observations are apparent. First, hours of work declined steadily from 1900 to World War II. Note that the average workweek fell by almost 16 percent [(49.4 − 41.5)/49.4] over the 1910–1919 to 1940–1949 period.[35] Second, the average workweek and workyear changed very little after the 1940s. While there is no universally accepted explanation of these trends, interesting and plausible theories have been put forth.

[35]The shorter hours of the 1930s are largely explainable in terms of the Great Depression; the shorter workweek was widely instituted to spread the smaller demand for labor among more workers.

TABLE 3-1 DECADE AVERAGES OF WEEKLY AND YEARLY HOURS OF WORK FOR PRODUCTION WORKERS IN MANUFACTURING

Period	Workweek (hours)	Workyear (hours)
1910–1919	49.4	2630
1920–1929	44.7	2473
1930–1939	38.1	1971
1940–1949	41.5	2111
1950–1959	40.2	1991
1960–1969	40.6	2007
1970–1976	40.1	1955
1977–1997	40.7	—

Source: John Brack and Keith Cowling, "Advertising and Labour Supply: Workweek and Workyear in U.S. Manufacturing Industries, 1919–1976," *Kyklos,* no. 2, 1983, pp. 285–303. Workweek data for 1977–1997 are from *Employment and Earnings.*

Workweek Decline, 1900–1940

The pre–World War II decline in the workweek is explainable in terms of the basic work–leisure model described in Chapter 2. The essential contention is that the declining workweek is simply a supply response to historically rising real wages and earnings. More precisely, given (1) worker income–leisure preferences, (2) nonwage incomes, and (3) the assumption that leisure is a normal good, rising wage rates over time will reduce the number of hours individuals will want to work, provided the income effect exceeds the substitution effect. And, in fact, a substantial amount of empirical evidence indicates that the net effect of wage increases on hours of work has been negative.[36]

Post–World War II: Workweek Stability

But how does one explain the relative constancy of the workweek in the postwar era? Real wages have continued to rise, but either the substitution effect has somehow acted to offset the income effect, or perhaps some additional factors have been at work in recent decades to offset the tendency of higher wage rates to reduce the workweek. Let's survey a number of possible explanations.

1 FLSA Recall from Chapter 2 that the ***Fair Labor Standards Act of 1938*** (FLSA) required employees to pay a wage premium—specifically, one and one-half times a worker's base pay—for all hours worked in excess of 40 per week. This legislation tended not only to reduce the length of the workweek but also to standardize it at 40 hours.

2 Higher Tax Rates Another possible explanation is that marginal tax rates on income rose rapidly during and after World War II, with the result that given increases in gross (before-tax) wage rates have translated into smaller increases in net (after-tax) wage rates. Thus, the negative supply, or hours of work, response has been much smaller in the postwar era than in earlier decades.

3 Education Kniesner[37] has hypothesized that the supply of labor over time is positively related to education. Furthermore, he notes that increases in educational attainment have been much greater in the postwar period than in the prewar period; in the 1910–1940 period the increase in median years of schooling completed was only about 6 percent as compared to a 34 percent increase in the 1940–1970 period. Kniesner argues that these differences in educational attainment account for the two trends evidenced in Table 3-1.

[36]For a good discussion of these studies, see John T. Addison and W. Stanley Siebert, *The Market for Labor: An Analytical Treatment* (Santa Monica, Calif.: Goodyear Publishing Company, Inc., 1979), pp. 85–90.

[37]Thomas J. Kniesner, "The Full-Time Workweek in the United States, 1900–1970," *Industrial and Labor Relations Review,* October 1976, pp. 3–5. See also Ethel B. Jones, "Comment," and Kniesner, "Reply," *Industrial and Labor Relations Review,* April 1980, pp. 379–389.

Why might more education increase or sustain hours of work? First, a change in preferences may be involved. Education is a means of enhancing one's earning power in the labor market. Decisions to acquire more education may therefore reflect a change in tastes favoring a stronger commitment to labor market work. Second, more-educated workers generally acquire more-pleasant jobs, that is, jobs that are less physically demanding, less structured, more challenging, and so forth. Other things being equal, such job characteristics would make workers less willing to reduce the workweek. Finally, a more-educated work force may increase employer resistance to a declining workweek. The reason for this is that employers incur more fixed-cost expenditures in recruiting more-educated workers and in training them over their job tenures as compared to less-educated workers. A shorter workweek will increase these fixed costs per worker hour and thus will increase the overall hourly cost of any given quantity of labor. As their labor forces have become more educated, employers have stiffened their resistance to a shorter workweek.[38]

4 Advertising More recently Brack and Cowling[39] have tested the idea that advertising has induced the labor force to work longer hours than it otherwise would. Their argument is that advertising has both grown quantitatively and increased in effectiveness (largely because of television) in the post–World War II period. This has increased the desires of workers for more goods and services and therefore induced them to work more hours than would otherwise be the case.

The cumulative impact of advertising allegedly has been to generate a reemergence of a substitution effect powerful enough to prevent the continued fall in the workweek in the postwar period. This strengthening of the substitution effect has occurred because advertising has increased the marginal valuation of goods relative to leisure. In terms of the analysis in Chapter 2 (see Figure 2-5, for example), advertising has made worker indifference curves flatter, with the consequence that a given increase in wage rates may now leave desired hours of work unchanged, rather than reduced. Brack and Cowling conclude that "the growth in advertising . . . has exercised a cumulative impact on the desire to acquire goods and in consequence has created a reluctance to substitute leisure for income as the real wage rises."[40] They suggest that advertising has caused the workweek to be approximately 27 percent longer than it otherwise would have been.

5 "Catching Up" Still another explanation of the postwar stability of the workweek has been offered by Owen.[41] He reminds us that the postwar period followed a

[38]Employer resistance to a shrinking workweek may be reinforced by the greater growth of fringe benefits that has occurred in the postwar period (Chapter 7). Employer expenditures for such fringes as worker life and health insurance are also fixed costs on a per worker basis, and as with recruitment and training costs, a shortened workweek would entail higher hourly labor costs.

[39]John Brack and Keith Cowling, "Advertising and Labour Supply: Workweek and Workyear in U.S. Manufacturing Industries, 1919–1976," *Kyklos,* no. 2, 1983, pp. 285–303.

[40]Ibid., p. 300.

[41]John D. Owen, "Workweeks and Leisure: An Analysis of Trends, 1948–1975," *Monthly Labor Review,* August 1976, pp. 3–8.

decade and a half of depression and war. During the depression era of the 1930s most families were forced to curtail greatly their expenditures for consumer goods. And during the war years of the early 1940s many consumer durables were simply not available. Furthermore, birthrates declined in the 1930s because many couples found they simply could not afford children. Owen contends that in the immediate postwar period American households attempted to "catch up" on both consumption and childbearing and that, as a result, there was little demand for further reductions in the workweek. In other words, the immediate postwar period was characterized by both a consumer buying binge and a baby boom. The latter was particularly significant because unlike the purchase of a car or a television, the decision to have more children imposes higher household costs that extend over some two decades. Furthermore, the extension of the years of schooling during the postwar period added substantially to the cost of rearing each child. In short, Owen contends that catching up in terms of consumer goods and family size, coupled with more schooling, has made a declining workweek—and the attendant loss of earnings—less attractive.

CHAPTER SUMMARY

1 The aggregate quantity of labor supplied depends on population size, the labor force participation rate, and the number of hours worked weekly and annually.

2 It is fruitful to examine and explain participation rates in terms of Becker's time allocation model. This model views households as "producing" utility-yielding commodities by combining goods and time. In this context, household members allocate their time to labor market work, household production, and consumption on the basis of comparative advantage.

3 The labor force participation rate is the actual labor force as a percentage of the potential or age-eligible population.

4 In the post–World War II period the aggregate participation rate has drifted upward from about 59 percent in 1950 to about 67 percent in 1997. This is basically the result of an increase in the participation rates of women (particularly married women), which have more than offset the declining participation rates of males.

5 Older males account for most of the decline in male participation rates. The declining participation rates of older men are attributed to *(a)* rising real wages and earnings, *(b)* the availability of public and private pensions, *(c)* greater access to disability benefits, and *(d)* age-earnings profiles that suggest that the cost of leisure may decline for older workers.

6 Rising participation rates for women have been caused by *(a)* rising relative wage rates for women, *(b)* stronger female preferences for labor market work, *(c)* rising productivity within the household, *(d)* declining birthrates, *(e)* greater marital instability, *(f)* the greater accessibility of jobs, and *(g)* attempts to maintain family standards of living.

7 The participation rates of black women have been greater than those of white women, but the rates have tended to converge over time.

8 The participation rates of black males are significantly less than those of white males and the rates are diverging over time. Some analysts stress such demand-side factors as labor market discrimination, inferior educational opportunities, and the geographic inaccessibility of jobs in explaining lower black rates. Others focus on such supply-side factors as the availability of public assistance and illegal activities.

9 Cyclical changes in participation rates reflect the net impact of the added-worker and discouraged-worker effects. The added-worker effect suggests that when a family's primary breadwinner loses his or her job, other family members will become labor market participants in order to sustain the family's income. The discouraged-worker effect indicates that during recession, some unemployed workers will become pessimistic as to their prospects for reemployment and will therefore withdraw from the labor force. Most empirical studies suggest that the discouraged-worker effect is dominant, with the result that the aggregate labor force participation rate varies inversely with the unemployment rate.

10 The average workweek and workyear declined during the 1910–1940 period, but since World War II both have been quite stable. The earlier workweek and workyear declines have been explained in terms of the income effect's domination of the substitution effect as real wage rates have risen historically. The post–World War II stability of the workweek and workyear has been variously attributed to *(a)* enactment of the Fair Labor Standards Act, *(b)* higher income taxes, *(c)* increases in education, *(d)* the effect of advertising, and *(e)* the desire of households to catch up with respect to the low levels of consumption and the low birthrates of the pre–World War II era.

TERMS AND CONCEPTS

Becker's model of the allocation of time
time-intensive and goods-intensive commodities
potential and actual labor force
labor force participation rate
added-worker and discouraged-worker effects
Fair Labor Standards Act of 1938

QUESTIONS AND STUDY SUGGESTIONS

1 Briefly discuss the major components of aggregate labor supply. In terms of the projected labor shortage of the last half of the 1990s, explain how these components might interact with one another.

2 In what specific ways does Becker's model of the allocation of time differ from the simple work–leisure choice model? Compare the functioning of the income and substitution effects in each of the two models. Do the two effects have the same impact upon labor market work in both models?

3 In 1997, the United States had a population of 267 million, of which 64 million were either under 16 years of age or institutionalized. Approximately 137 million people were either employed or unemployed but actively seeking work. What was the participation rate in 1997?

4 What has happened to the aggregate labor force participation rate in the post–World War II period? To the participation rates of males and females?

5 What factors account for the declining participation rates of older males?

6 What factors account for the increase in the participation rates of married women? Use a work–leisure diagram (similar, for example, to Figure 2-8) to explain how *each* of these factors individually might alter either the indifference curves or the budget line of women and make labor force participation more likely.

7 Compare the participation rates of *(a)* white and black women and *(b)* white and black men. In each case explain any differences.

8 "The ratio of the incomes of black families to the incomes of white families has increased quite slowly in the past two or three decades, despite legislation and a variety of public policies to ameliorate discrimination. One may therefore conclude that government programs have failed to lessen racial discrimination." Discuss critically.

9 Use a work–leisure diagram to demonstrate that *(a)* if blacks have labor market opportunities that are inferior to those of whites and *(b)* nonlabor income is available in the form of, say, disability benefits, blacks will have lower participation rates even though the work–leisure preferences (indifference curves) of blacks and whites are identical.

10 "Empirical evidence for the United States suggests that labor force participation varies directly with unemployment." Do you agree? Explain in terms of the discouraged-worker and added-worker effects.

11 "The added-worker effect can be explained in terms of the income effect, while the discouraged-worker effect is based on the substitution effect." Do you agree?

12 What has happened to the length of the workweek and workyear during this century? Explain any significant trends.

13 The accompanying diagram restates the basic work–leisure choice model as presented in Chapter 2. Use this diagram to explain the declining workweek occurring in the pre–World War II period, making explicit the assumptions underlying your analysis. We noted in the present chapter that the stability of the workweek in the post–World War II era has been attributed by various scholars to such considerations as *(a)* higher taxes on earnings, *(b)* acquisition of more education, *(c)* advertising, and *(d)* compensation by households for low levels of consumption and low birthrates experienced in the pre–World War II period. Make alterations in the indifference curves or budget line of the diagram to indicate how *each* of these four factors might contribute to a relatively stable workweek despite rising before-tax real wages.

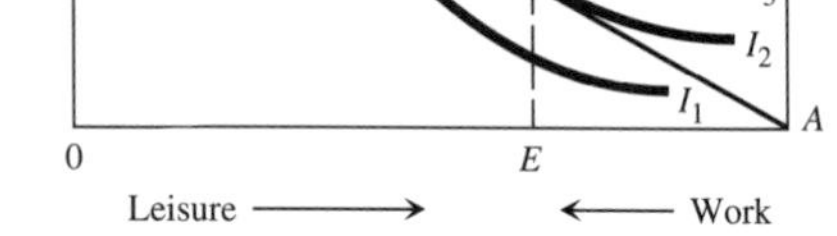

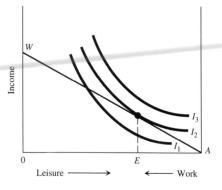

SELECTED REFERENCES

Bergmann, Barbara R.: *The Economic Emergence of Women* (New York: Basic Books, 1986), particularly chaps. 1–3.

Blau, Francine D., Marianne A. Ferber, and Anne E. Winkler: *The Economics of Women, Men, and Work,* 3rd ed. (Englewood Cliffs, N.J.: Prentice-Hall, 1998), chaps. 1–4.

Bowen, William G., and T. Aldrich Finegan: *The Economics of Labor Force Participation* (Princeton, N.J.: Princeton University Press, 1969).

Cain, Glen G.: *Married Women in the Labor Force* (Chicago: University of Chicago Press, 1966).

Economic Report of the President, 1987 (Washington, D.C., 1987), chap. 7.

Goldin, Claudia: *Understanding the Gender Gap: An Economic History of American Women* (Oxford: Oxford University Press, 1990).

Killingsworth, Mark: *Labor Supply* (Cambridge: Cambridge University Press, 1983), chaps. 2–3.

Layard, Richard, and Jacob Mincer (eds.): "Trends in Women's Work, Education, and Family Building," *Journal of Labor Economics, Supplement,* January 1985.

CHAPTER 4

LABOR QUALITY: INVESTING IN HUMAN CAPITAL

Education and training are much in the news. Not since the days of *Sputnik,* when the Soviet Union orbited the world's first satellite, has as much attention been given to improving our educational and training system. Today's threat is not space technology; rather it is the fear of being unable to compete effectively in the emerging global marketplace. Experts agree that to maintain our relative standard of living, we must upgrade the education and skill levels of our work force. They also agree that the dynamic aspects of global technological innovation and product competition have rendered many of our jobs less secure. Continuous education, training, and retraining will be crucial to keeping our work force fully employed.

In Chapters 2 and 3 we looked primarily at the decisions of whether and to what degree to participate in the labor market. Our emphasis there was on the work–leisure decision and the various participation rates. In this chapter we turn from the quantitative to the qualitative aspects of labor supply. Workers bring differing levels of formal educational attainment and skills to the labor market. They also acquire substantially different amounts of on-the-job training. A more-educated, better-trained person is capable of supplying a larger amount of useful productive effort than one with less education and training.

Any activity that increases the quality (productivity) of labor may be considered an investment in human capital. Human capital investments include expenditures not only on formal education and on-the-job training but also on health, migration, job search, and the preschool nurturing of children. Workers can become more productive by improving their physical or mental health and also by moving from locations and jobs where their productivity is relatively low to other locations and jobs where their productivity is relatively high. In fact, in Chapter 9 human capital theory will be the core concept used to analyze labor migration.

In the present chapter our focus is on investment in education and on-the-job training. First, we want to justify the notion that expenditures on education and training merit consideration as investment and to present some simple data showing the statistical relation between education and worker earnings. Second, we will present a basic model that will demonstrate how the rate of return on a human capital investment can be estimated. Next, we will examine and illustrate several important generalizations or predictions implicit in the human capital model. Fourth, the concept of the investment demand for human capital will be derived from the human capital model and combined with the supply of investment funds to explain why different individuals invest in substantially different amounts of education. Fifth, we will consider on-the-job training as a human capital investment. Finally, some of the criticisms and alleged shortcomings of human capital theory will be discussed.

INVESTMENT IN HUMAN CAPITAL: CONCEPT AND DATA

When a firm invests in physical capital, it is acquiring some asset that is expected to enhance the firm's flow of net profits over a period of time. For example, a company might purchase new machinery designed to increase output and therefore sales revenues over, say, the 10-year projected useful life of the machinery. The unique characteristic of investment is that *current* expenditures or costs are incurred with the intent that these costs will be more than compensated for by enhanced *future* revenues or returns. Analogously, investments are made in human capital. When a person (or a person's parents or society at large) makes a current expenditure on education or training, it is anticipated that the individual's knowledge and skills and therefore future earnings will be enhanced.[1] The important point is that expenditures on education and training can be fruitfully treated as ***investment in human capital*** just as expenditures on capital equipment can be understood as investment in physical capital.

Relevant data reveal three things. First, expenditures on education and training are substantial. In 1995 Americans spent some $514 billion on elementary, secondary, and higher education. In addition, an estimated $35 billion of direct costs are incurred each year by employers for on-the-job training.

Second, the educational attainment of the labor force has increased dramatically over time. For example, in 1970 over 36 percent of the civilian labor force had achieved less than a high school education, while a mere 14 percent had completed 4 or more years of college. Similar figures for 1995 were 11 and 28 percent, respectively.

Third, investments in education result in an enlarged flow of earnings. This tendency is reflected in the ***age-earning profiles*** of Figure 4-1, which show the lifetime earnings patterns of male workers who have attained various educational levels. Observe that the average earnings of more-educated workers exceed those of less-educated workers. Also, the earnings profiles of more-educated workers rise more rapidly than those

[1]As will be noted later, the payoff from an investment in education may also take nonmonetary forms, for example, obtaining a more pleasant job or a greater appreciation of literature and art.

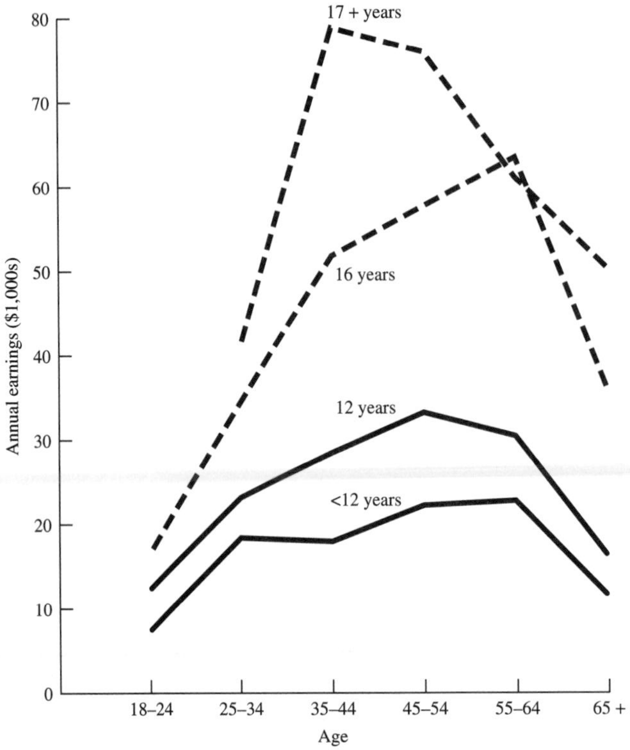

FIGURE 4-1 AGE-EARNINGS PROFILES BY YEARS OF EDUCATION
Age-earnings profiles (in this case for males in 1995) indicate that education "pays" in that more-educated workers obtain higher average annual earnings than less-educated workers of the same age group. (*Derived from U.S. Bureau of the Census, Educational Attainment in the United States: March 1995; Current Population Reports,* ser. P-20, no. 489, p. 52.)

of less-educated workers. Differences in the earnings of more- and less-educated workers tend to widen during workers' prime earning years.

Not shown, the age-earnings profiles of females display similar overall characteristics as those in Figure 4-1, but lie significantly below those of men. Also, the profiles for women are much flatter than those for men. We discuss these gender differences in earnings in detail in Chapter 15.[2]

[2]The fact that the age-earnings profiles ultimately decline must be interpreted with some care. While it is tempting to attribute the declining incomes of older workers to diminished physical vigor and mental alertness, the obsolescence of education and skills, or the decision to work shorter hours, the decline may be largely due to the character of the data. In particular, these data do *not* track the earnings of specific individuals through their lifetimes. Rather, these cross-sectional data show the earnings of different individuals of different ages in some particular year. Longitudinal data that do trace the earnings of specific persons over time indicate that earnings continue to increase until retirement. The declining segments of the age-earnings profiles in Figure 4-1 may occur because the U.S. economy has been growing and therefore each succeeding generation has earned more than the preceding one. Thus, the average 45-year-old college-educated worker has higher earnings as shown in the age-earnings profiles simply because he or she is a member of a more recent "generation" than a 65-year-old college-educated worker.

THE HUMAN CAPITAL MODEL

Let's now introduce a simple model to analyze the decision to invest in, say, a college education. Assume you have just graduated from high school and are deciding whether to go to college. From a purely economic standpoint, a rational decision will involve a comparison of the associated costs and benefits. The monetary costs incurred in the purchase of a college education are of two general types. On the one hand, there are *direct* or *out-of-pocket costs* in the form of expenditures for tuition, special fees, and books and supplies. Expenditures for room and board are *not* included as a part of direct costs because you would need food and shelter regardless of whether you attended college or entered the labor market. On the other hand, the *indirect* or *opportunity cost* of going to college is the earnings you give up by not entering the labor market after completing high school. For example, estimates suggest that indirect costs may account for as much as 60 to 70 percent of the total cost of a college education, at least at public universities. The economic *benefit* of investing in a college education, as we know from Figure 4-1, is an enlarged future flow of earnings.

This conception of a human capital investment decision is portrayed graphically in Figure 4-2. Curve *HH* represents your earnings profile if you decide not to attend college, but rather enter the labor market immediately on the completion of high school

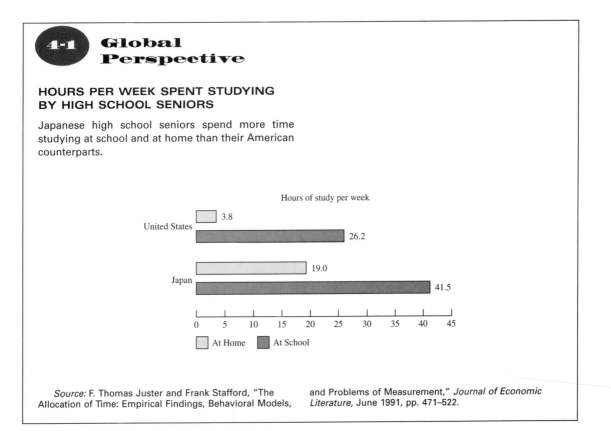

4-1 Global Perspective

HOURS PER WEEK SPENT STUDYING BY HIGH SCHOOL SENIORS

Japanese high school seniors spend more time studying at school and at home than their American counterparts.

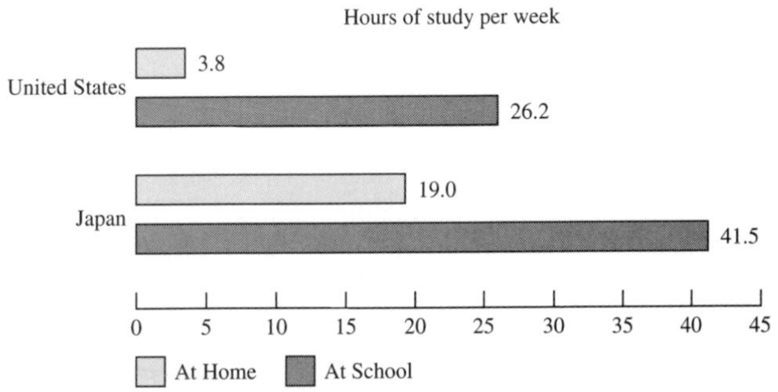

Source: F. Thomas Juster and Frank Stafford, "The Allocation of Time: Empirical Findings, Behavioral Models, and Problems of Measurement," *Journal of Economic Literature,* June 1991, pp. 471–522.

FIGURE 4-2 AGE-EARNINGS PROFILES WITH AND WITHOUT A COLLEGE EDUCATION
If an individual decides to enter the labor market after graduation from high school at age 18, the age-earnings profile will be *HH* in comparison with the *CC* profile if she or he had gone to college. Attending college entails both direct costs (tuition, fees, books) and indirect costs (forgone earnings). But on entering the labor market at age 22, the college graduate will enjoy a high level of annual earnings over her or his working life. To determine whether it is economically rational to invest in a college education, its net present value must be found by discounting costs and benefits back to the present (age 18).

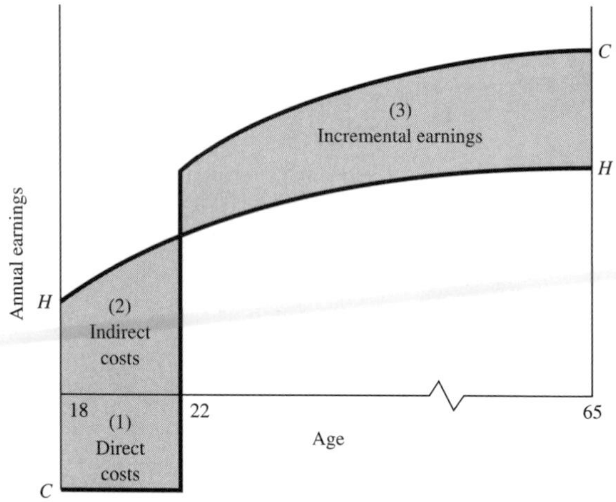

at age 18. The *CC* "curve" is your cost-earnings profile if you decide to undertake a 4-year college degree before entering the labor market. We note that area 1 below the horizontal axis represents the direct or out-of-pocket costs (the "negative income") incurred in attending college. Area 2 reflects the indirect or opportunity costs, that is, the earnings you forgo while attending college. The sum of areas 1 and 2 shows the total cost—your total investment—in a college education. Area 3—the difference between the *CC* and *HH* curves over ages 22 to 65—shows the gross *incremental* earnings which you will realize by obtaining a college degree; it shows how much *additional* income you will obtain as a college graduate over your work life as compared to what you would have earned with just a high school diploma. Your work life in this case is presumed to extend over the 43-year period from age 22 to age 65.

Discounting and Net Present Value

We know that to make a rational decision you will want to compare costs (areas 1 and 2) with benefits (area 3). But a complication arises at this point. The costs and benefits associated with investing in a college education accrue at different points in time. This is important because dollars expended and received at different points in time are of different value. A meaningful comparison of the costs and benefits associated with a college education requires that these costs and benefits be compared in terms of a common point in time, for example, the present. What we seek to determine from the vantage point of an 18-year-old youth is the net present discounted value, or simply the ***net present value,*** of the present and future costs *and* present and future benefits of a college education.

Time Preference Why do dollars earned (or expended) have a different value a year, or 2 or 3 years, from now than they have today? The immediate answer is that a positive interest rate is paid for borrowing or "renting" money. But this raises an additional question: *Why* is interest paid for the use or "rent" of money? The answer lies in the notion of ***time preference,*** that is, the idea that, given the choice, most people prefer the pleasure of indulgence today to the promise of indulgence tomorrow. Most individuals prefer present consumption to future consumption because, given the uncertainties and vagaries of life, the former seems more tangible and therefore more valuable. Time preference, in short, is the idea that people are impatient and subjectively prefer goods in the present over the same goods in the future. It follows that an individual must be "bribed" or compensated by an interest payment to defer present consumption or, alternatively stated, to save a portion of her or his income. If an individual equates $100 worth of goods today with $110 worth of goods a year from now, we can say that his or her time preference rate is 10 percent. The individual must be paid $10 or 10 percent as an inducement to forgo $100 worth of present consumption.

Present Value Formula Because the preference for present consumption necessitates payment of a positive interest rate, a dollar received a year from now is worth less than a dollar obtained today because a dollar received today can be loaned or invested at some positive interest rate and thereby can be worth more than a dollar a year from now. If the interest rate is 10 percent, one can lend $1 today and receive $1.10 at the end of the year; the $1.10 is comprised of the original $1 plus $.10 of interest. This can be shown algebraically as follows:

$$V_p(1 + i) = V_1 \qquad (4\text{-}1)$$

where V_p = present or current value, for example, $1.00 today
V_1 = value (of the $1.00) 1 year from now
i = interest rate

The $(1 + i)$ term indicates that one receives back the original or present value ($1.00) *plus* the interest. Substituting our illustrative numbers, we have

$$\$1.00\ (1.10) = \$1.10$$

This formulation tells us that, given a 10 percent interest rate, $1.10 received next year is the equivalent of $1.00 in hand today.

Equation (4-1) focuses on determining the *future* value of the $1.00 one has today. As indicated earlier, our goal is to determine the *present* (today's) value of expenditures and revenues incurred and received in the future. We can get at this by restating our original question. Instead of asking how much $1.00 obtained today will be worth a year from now, let's inquire how much $1.10 received a year from now would be worth today. In general terms, the answer is found by solving equation (4-1) for V_p. Thus

$$V_p = \frac{V_1}{(1 + i)} \tag{4-2}$$

Equation (4-2) is a ***discount formula*** for a 1-year period. Inserting our illustrative numbers:

$$\$1.00 = \frac{\$1.10}{1.10}$$

That is, \$1.10 received a year from now is worth only \$1.00 today if the interest rate is 10 percent.

Observing in Figure 4-2 that both costs and benefits are incurred over a number of years, we can extend the discounting formula of equation (4-2) as follows:

$$V_p = E_0 + \frac{E_1}{(1 + i)} + \frac{E_2}{(1 + i)^2} + \frac{E_3}{(1 + i)^3} + \cdots + \frac{E_n}{(1 + i)^n} \tag{4-3}$$

where the E's represent a stream of incremental earnings (E_0 being any additional income received immediately, E_1 the additional income received next year, E_2 the incremental earnings received two years from now, and so forth); n is the duration of the earnings stream or, in other words, the individual's expected working life, and i is the interest rate.[3] Observe that incremental earnings (or costs), E_0, incurred immediately need not be discounted. But the incremental earnings received next year, or 1 year hence, E_1, must be discounted 1 year. Note further that the denominator of the third term is squared, the fourth is cubed, and so forth. This is so because the values of E_2 and E_3 must be discounted 2 and 3 years, respectively, to determine their present value. Dividing E_2—the incremental earnings to be received 2 years hence—by $(1 + i)$ discounts the value of those earnings for the time elapsed in the first year, but *that* value must be again divided by $(1 + i)$ to find its present value because the time between the first and second year further diminishes the value.

Restating the formula for our high school graduate who enters the labor force at age 18, we have

$$V_p = E_{18} + \frac{E_{19}}{(1 + i)} + \frac{E_{20}}{(1 + i)^2} + \frac{E_{21}}{(1 + i)^3} + \cdots + \frac{E_{64}}{(1 + i)^{46}} \tag{4-4}$$

which can be more compactly stated as:

$$V_p = \sum_{n=18}^{64} \frac{E_n}{(1 + i)^{n-18}} \tag{4-5}$$

[3]We are sidestepping the troublesome problem of deciding which interest rate is appropriate. A small difference in the rate actually used can have a very substantial impact on the calculation of present value.

This formulation tells us that we are calculating the present value (V_p) of the sum ($\sum$) of the discounted incremental earnings (E_n) over the individual's working life, which runs from age 18 through age 64, after which time he or she retires when attaining age 65. Since n is 64 years of age, the $n = 18$ notation indicates that we are discounting future earnings over 46 (= 64 − 18) years of working life.

Figure 4-2 reminds us that the decision to invest in a college education entails both costs and benefits (enhanced earnings). How can both be accounted for in equation (4-3) or (4-4)? The answer is to treat costs as negative earnings. Thus, the "earnings" for the 4 years the individual is in college (E_0, E_1, E_2, and E_3) will be the negative sum of the direct and indirect costs incurred in each of those years. For each succeeding year until retirement, incremental earnings will be positive. We therefore are actually calculating the *net* present value of a college education in these two equations.

Decision Rule: $V_p > 0$ The relevant investment criterion or decision rule based on this calculation is that *the individual should make the investment if its net present value is greater than zero.* A positive value tells us that the present discounted value of the benefits exceeds the present discounted value of the costs, and when this is so—when benefits exceed costs—the decision to invest is economically rational. If the net present value is negative, then costs exceed benefits and the investment is not economically justifiable.

Illustration A truncated example may be helpful at this point. Assume that after graduating from high school Carl Carlson contemplates enrolling in a 1-year intensive course in data processing. The direct costs of the course are $1,000, and the opportunity cost is $5,000. Upon completion of the course, he has been promised employment with the Computex Corporation. Expecting to receive a large inheritance, he plans to work only 3 years and then retire permanently from the labor force. The incremental income he anticipates earning because of his data processing training is $2,500, $3,000, and $3,500 for the 3 years he intends to work. The relevant interest rate at this time is 10 percent. Is the decision to enroll in the data processing course rational? By substituting these figures in equation (4-3), we have

$$V_p = E_0 + \frac{E_1}{(1+i)} + \frac{E_2}{(1+i)^2} + \frac{E_3}{(1+i)^3}$$

$$V_p = -\$6{,}000 + \frac{\$2{,}500}{(1.10)} + \frac{\$3{,}000}{(1.10)^2} + \frac{\$3{,}500}{(1.10)^3}$$

$$V_p = -\$6{,}000 + \$2{,}273 + \$2{,}479 + \$2{,}630$$

$$V_p = \$1{,}382$$

Our formula shows that the present value of the benefits (the incremental earnings) totals $7,382 (= $2,273 + $2,479 + $2,630) and exceeds the present value of the costs of $6,000 by $1,382. This positive net present value indicates that it *is* economically rational for Carlson to make this investment in human capital.

Internal Rate of Return

An alternative means of making an investment decision involves calculating the ***internal rate of return,*** r, on a prospective investment and comparing it with the interest rate i. *By definition, the internal rate of return is that rate of discount at which the net present value of a human capital investment will be zero.*

Formula Instead of using the interest rate i in equation (4-3) to calculate whether the net present value is positive or negative, one determines what particular rate of discount r will equate the present values of future costs and benefits so that the net present value is zero. We must modify equation (4-3) as follows:

$$V_p = E_0 + \frac{E_1}{(1+r)} + \frac{E_2}{(1+r)^2} + \cdots + \frac{E_n}{(1+r)^n} = 0 \qquad (4\text{-}6)$$

Instead of solving for V_p as in equation (4-3), we solve for r, given the values of the E's and assuming V_p is zero. A moment's reflection makes clear that r indicates the maximum rate of interest that one could pay on borrowed funds to finance a human capital investment and still break even.

Decision Rule: $r = i$ The investment criterion or decision rule appropriate to this approach involves a comparison of the internal rate of return r with the interest rate i. *If* r *exceeds the market* i, *the investment is profitable and should be undertaken.* For example, if one can borrow funds at a 10 percent interest rate and make an investment that yields 15 percent, it is profitable to do so. But *if* r *is less than* i, *the investment is unprofitable and should not be undertaken.* If one can borrow money at a 10 percent rate and the prospective investment yields only 5 percent, it is not profitable to invest. As we will discover momentarily, investing in human capital is subject to diminishing returns and therefore r generally declines as the number of years of schooling increases (look ahead to Figure 4-4). In this case, given i, *it will be profitable to invest in all human capital investment opportunities up to the point where* r = i.

Generalizations and Implications

The explanatory power of the human capital model is considerable. Let's pause at this point to consider several generalizations that stem from the basic model as presented in Figure 4-2 and equations (4-3) and (4-6).

1 Length of Income Stream *Other things being equal, the longer the stream of postinvestment incremental earnings, the more likely the net present value of an investment in human capital will be positive.* Or, alternatively, the longer the earnings stream, the higher the internal rate of return. A human capital investment made later in life will have a lower net present value (and a lower *r*) simply because fewer years of work life and, hence, of positive incremental earnings will remain after completion of the investment. This generalization helps explain why it is primarily young people who go to college[4] and why younger people are more likely to migrate—to invest in geographic mobility—than older people. It also explains a portion of the earnings differential that has traditionally existed between women and men. In many cases, the participation of women in the labor force has been discontinuous. That is, many women work for a few years after the completion of formal schooling, then marry and stay out of the labor force for a time to bear and raise children. They then reenter the labor force sometime after the last child begins school. In equations (4-3) and (4-6), this means an abbreviated stream of earnings. This dampens the economic incentive of these particular women to invest in their own human capital by lowering the net present value or the rate of return. Furthermore, their discontinuous labor force participation inhibits employers from investing in their on-the-job training.

2 Costs *Other things being equal, the lower the cost of a human capital investment, the larger the number of people who will find that investment to be profitable.* If the direct or indirect costs of attending college were to fall, we would expect enrollment to rise. Illustration: The guaranteeing of student loans by the government eliminates the risk to the lender and lowers the interest rate charged for borrowing funds to attend college. By reducing the private direct cost[5] of a college education, such loan guarantees increase college enrollments.[6] Similarly, the state of the economy may influence college enrollments through its effects on the indirect or opportunity costs of attending college. For example, if recession reduces the earnings that high school graduates can achieve or, alternatively, reduces the probability of obtaining a job, the opportunity costs of attending college will fall and enrollments will rise. Lower costs increase the net present value of a college education, making the investment in education "profitable" for some who previously found it to be unprofitable. In fact, recession does have a positive effect on college enrollments.[7]

[4] While perhaps not rational in investment grounds, the decision of older people to return to college may be justified in terms of consumption (utility) criteria.

[5] Of course, there is no free lunch. Taxpayers (society as a whole) pay the costs associated with loan guarantees. But in calculating the cost of a college education from a *private* (as opposed to *social*) perspective, loan guarantees reduce the costs to the individual enrollee and increase the private net present value associated with a college education.

[6] Public subsidies appear to have large enrollment effects, particularly for low-income students and those attending community colleges. See Thomas J. Kane, "Rising Public College Tuition and College Entry: How Well Do Public Subsidies Promote Access to College?" National Bureau of Economic Research Working Paper No. 5164, July 1995.

[7] J. Peter Mattila, "Determinants of Male School Enrollments: A Time-Series Analysis," *Review of Economics and Statistics,* May 1982, pp. 242–251. In examining cyclical changes in male school enrollment, Mattila notes that a recession imposes both a discouraged-worker effect and an added-worker effect (Chapter 3) on young people. The former indicates that when jobs are unavailable, a youth may decide to attend school. The latter effect suggests that when a parent becomes unemployed, a youth may be unable to afford staying in school. Mattila finds that the discouraged-worker effect exceeds the added-worker effect for males ages 16 to 19, but there is no clear impact on males 20 to 21 years old.

A more subtle point ties in with our previous generalization that older individuals are less likely to invest in human capital. Our age-earnings profiles (Figure 4-1) reveal that earnings rise with age. Thus, the opportunity cost of attending college will be greater for older workers and, other things being equal, the net present value and the internal rate of return associated with human capital investments will be lower. In other words, there are two reasons older people are less likely to invest in a college education: (1) The length of their future earnings stream will be relatively short, and (2) their opportunity costs of attending college will be high.

3 Earnings Differentials Not only is the *length* of the incremental earnings stream critical in making a human capital investment decision, but so is the *size* of that differential. The generalization is that *other things being equal, the larger the college–high school earnings differential, the larger the number of people who will invest in a college education.* Empirical evidence confirms this generalization. Freeman has argued that in about 1970 the labor market for college graduates changed from one characterized by shortages to one of surpluses. One of the manifestations of this change was that the incremental earnings associated with a college education declined sharply. "Among all men in 1969, college graduates earned 53% more than high school graduates and 99% more than grade school graduates; in 1974 the premiums stood at 35% and 74% respectively."[8] One of the responses to this decline in earnings differentials was that in the early 1970s the proportion of young persons enrolling in college declined significantly. In 1969 some 60 percent of male high school graduates decided to go to college; by 1974 only 49 percent were enrolling in college. "Despite a 20% increase in the number of persons of college age, enrollment of 18- to 19-year-old men fell from 1,397,000 in 1969 to 1,262,000 in 1974.[9]

Empirical Data

Numerous empirical studies have estimated the returns of human capital investments at all educational levels. Here we concentrate on those showing private rates of return on investments in a college education.

Rate-of-Return Studies Speaking very generally, most rate-of-return studies have estimated such rates to be on the order of 10 to 15 percent. For example in his classic work Becker estimated the internal rate of return to be 14.5, 13.0, and 14.8 in 1939, 1949, and 1958, respectively.[10] Estimates by Freeman indicate the private rate of return ranged from 8.5 to 11 percent over the 1959–1974 period.[11] The social rate of return for the corresponding period was estimated to range from 7.5 to 11.1 percent. Card

[8]Richard B. Freeman, *The Overeducated American* (New York: Academic Press, 1976), p. 13.

[9]Ibid., p. 34. The indicated declines were undoubtedly influenced by changes in military conscription laws. A young man could obtain a draft deferment by attending college in 1969, but by 1974 the draft was inconsequential as a determinant of college attendance.

[10]Gary Becker, *Human Capital,* 2d ed. (New York: National Bureau of Economic Research, 1975).

[11]Richard B. Freeman, "Overinvestment in College Training?" *Journal of Human Resources,* Summer 1975, p. 296.

4-1

finds a return of 10 percent in 1976.[12] In a more recent study Angrist and Krueger find a private rate of return of 8 percent for 1980.[13] Kane and Rouse report a rate of return of 9 percent to higher education for 1986.[14]

The College Wage Premium Readers might have a special interest in the trend of the college wage premium in recent decades. We define the ***college wage premium*** *as the ratio of the earnings of college graduates to the earnings of high school graduates.* Figure 4-3 presents this wage premium over the 1967–1995 period for women and men. Data are for year-round, full-time workers age 25 or older. We observe that in 1967 the ratios for women and men were about 1.50, meaning that each group earned some 50 percent more than high school graduates of the same gender. The premium for women expanded to roughly 58 percent in 1970, although the premium for men fell to 45 percent. Then, during the 1970s the college wage premium for both groups declined noticeably. But since the late 1970s the wage premiums for women and men have increased sharply, rising from 37 percent to 84 percent for

[12]David Card, "Using Geographic Variation in College Proximity to Estimate the Return to Schooling," National Bureau of Economic Research Working Paper No. 4483, October 1993.

[13]Joshua D. Angrist and Alan B. Krueger, "Does Compulsory School Attendance Affect Schooling and Earnings?" *Quarterly Journal of Economics,* November 1991, pp. 979–1014.

[14]Thomas J. Kane and Cecilia Rouse, "Labor Market Returns to Two- and Four-Year Colleges," *American Economic Review,* June 1995, pp. 600–613.

4-1 **World of Work**

TWINS, EDUCATION, AND EARNINGS*

In August 1991 the sixteenth annual Twins Day Festival was held in Twinsburg, Ohio. The festival, the largest gathering of twins in the world, attracted more than 3,000 sets of twins, triplets, and quadruplets. It also attracted two labor economists, Ashenfelter and Krueger, who wanted to study the relationship between educational attainment and earnings.

Monozygotic (identical) twins result from the division of a single fertilized egg and are considered genetically identical. Studying identical twins who grow up together thus allows researchers to control for genetic endowments and family background. Such differences, of course, complicate comparisons of unrelated individuals.

Ashenfelter and Krueger interviewed about 500 twins over the age of 18, looking especially for identical twins with different levels of education. During the interviews the twins were separated and, as a cross-check, the questioners asked each twin to report on his or her own schooling level and that of the twin. About half the pairs of identical twins had the same schooling levels.

The authors discovered a relatively high variability of earnings among identical twins with the same education levels. Despite this fact, better-educated pairs of twins tended to have higher earnings levels than less-educated pairs. Also, individual twins having more education tended to have higher earnings than their twin brothers or sisters. On average, an additional year of schooling increased wages by 16 percent. This is a considerably higher estimate of the economic returns to education than found in previous studies, including those involving twins. Thus, this study lends support to the basic investment in human capital model.

*Based on Orley C. Ashenfelter and Alan B. Krueger, "Estimates of the Return to Schooling from a New Sample of Twins," *American Economic Review,* December 1994, pp. 1157–1173.

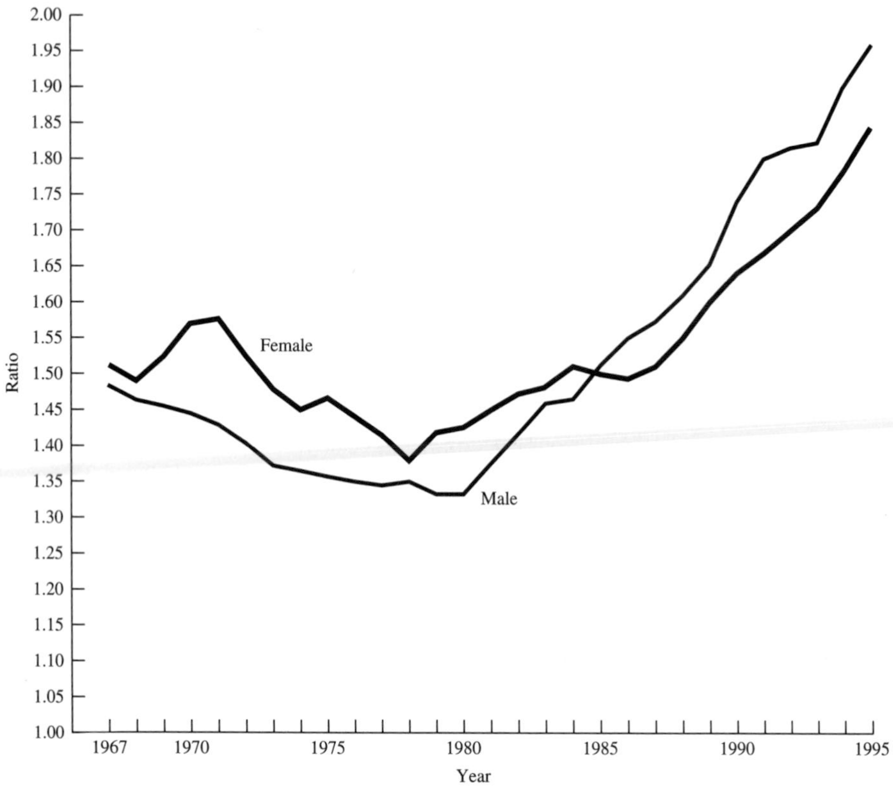

FIGURE 4-3 RECENT TRENDS IN COLLEGE WAGE PREMIUMS
The college wage premium—measured here as the ratio of earnings of college graduates to the earnings of high school graduates—has varied substantially over time. The premium for women rose in the late 1960s but then fell quite sharply in the 1970s. The premium for men drifted downward from 1967 to 1979. Since 1979 the wage premiums for both groups have increased dramatically. Changes in the college premium are generally explained by changes in the supply of and the demand for college- and high school-educated workers.

women and from 34 percent to 96 for men.[15] Studies have found that the most rapid rise in the wage premium has been for young college graduates with 1 to 5 years of experience.[16]

Explanations of changes in the college wage premium center on labor supply and demand. It is generally agreed that the declining premium in the 1970s resulted from the large influx of baby boomers completing college, coupled with a relatively stagnant demand for college graduates. There is less consensus as to why the college pre-

[15]Daniel E. Hecker, "Reconciling Conflicting Data on Jobs for College Graduates," *Monthly Labor Review,* July 1992, p. 5; and U.S. Bureau of the Census, *Educational Attainment in the United States,* various issues.

[16]Kevin Murphy and Finis Welch, "Wage Premiums for College Graduates: Recent Growth and Possible Explanations," *Educational Researcher,* May 1989, pp. 17–26.

mium soared in the 1980s. Murphy and Welch[17] explain the rapid increase in the wage premium in terms of huge increases in the demand for college-trained workers. In particular, changes in the structure of domestic industry (for example, the shift of employment to high technology industries) and changes in production techniques (for example, the greater use of computer-aided technologies) may have greatly increased the demand for college-trained workers.[18] Coupled with a slowdown in the growth of the college-educated workforce, the college premium has risen sharply.

Although the Murphy–Welch interpretation is generally accepted, some economists have pointed out that a growing number of college graduates are working in occupations where college degrees have not traditionally been required. This fact seems to contradict the idea of a growing demand for college graduates relative to their supply. Hecker[19] contends that the increasing college wage premium has resulted not from an increased demand for college-educated workers but from a declining demand for high school graduates, particularly males. In this view, a decline in the wages of high school graduates has pushed up the college wage premium.

Tyler, Murnane, and Levy argue that Hecker overstates the degree to which college graduates are taking jobs requiring only high school degrees.[20] They report that Hecker's assertion does not hold for young college graduates or for older female college graduates. For these workers, real earnings increased and the percent in high school-degree jobs declined during the 1980s. On the other hand, older male college graduates (45–54) are now more likely to be in high school-degree jobs than in the past.[21]

Caveats But all such empirical data must be interpreted with some care. First, we have no way of accurately predicting the future. Economists cannot accurately estimate what the future earnings of a new college graduate will be. Data used in research studies to calculate rates of return on human capital investments or the college wage premium are *historical* data. They represent the age-earnings profiles of *past* college graduates who obtained their education as far back as, say, 1950 or even earlier. The observation that college graduates in the labor market in 1995 received on average $14,000 more per year than the typical high school graduate is no guarantee that this difference will persist into the future. By 2000 or 2005 the amount of incremental income might have widened or diminished.

In fact, the rosy situation for college graduates will likely deteriorate somewhat in the near future. The proportion of 25-to-29 year olds with at least a college degree is projected to rise from 23 to 31 percent by the year 2000.[22] Mincer forecasts that if the

[17]Ibid., pp. 13–26.

[18]See Steven G. Allen, "Technology and the Wage Structure," National Bureau of Economic Research Working Paper No. 5534, April 1996.

[19]Hecker, op. cit., pp. 3–21.

[20]John Tyler, Richard J. Murnane, and Frank Levy, "Are More College Graduates Really Taking 'High School' Jobs?" *Monthly Labor Review,* December 1995, pp. 18–27.

[21]Erica L. Groshen and Colin Drozdowski provide a good summary of the various views on this topic in "The Recent Rise in the Value of Education: Market Forces at Work," *Economic Commentary,* Federal Reserve Bank of Cleveland, August 15, 1992. Of related interest is Nachum Sicherman, "'Overeducation' in the Labor Market," *Journal of Labor Economics,* April 1991, pp. 101–122.

[22]Jacob Mincer, "Investment in U.S. Education and Training," National Bureau of Economic Research Working Paper No. 4844, August 1994.

demand for college graduates remains steady during the 1990s, then the increased supply of such workers will decrease the college wage premium by 25 percent by the year 2002.

Also, while incremental earnings affect the decision to invest in a college education, the decision to invest in a college education affects incremental earnings. If college graduates have enjoyed a high earnings differential compared with high school graduates in the recent *past,* an increasing proportion of new high school graduates will invest in a college education. But this investment will increase the supply of college as opposed to high school graduates and will reduce the *future* earnings differential or college premium. A high rate of return in the recent past could contribute to a decreasing rate of return in the future.

Second, the historical data used in human capital studies are in the form of *average* (median) earnings, and the distribution of earnings by educational level around the average is wide. Although a given study may calculate that the average rate of return on a college education is 10 percent, some individuals may earn 30 or 50 percent, while the return may be negative for others. A significant percentage of those with only high school educations earn more than the median income of college graduates. And some college graduates earn less than the median income of high school graduates.

4-2

4-2

Third, the discussion so far has focused on the amount of schooling rather than the quality of schooling. We have implicitly assumed that the only relevant factor was the number of years students spend in school. However, the quality of the schooling will likely affect the rate of return to schooling. For example, higher quality teachers, better classroom resources, and greater studying by students should increase the rate of return to schooling.

Some recent evidence exists on how schooling inputs affect the rate of return.[23] A study by Card and Krueger indicates that higher teacher salaries and lower student-teacher ratios raise the return to schooling.[24] They also find that relative improvements in schooling quality among blacks account for 20 percent of the decline in the male black-white wage gap between 1960 and 1980.[25] However, Heckman, Layne-Farrar, and Todd conclude that schooling inputs have a more modest impact on the return to schooling than estimated by Card and Krueger.[26]

Private versus Social Perspective To this point we have viewed the human capital investment decision from a *personal* or ***private perspective.*** That is, we have viewed benefits and costs strictly from the standpoint of an individual who is contemplating a

[23]For a survey, see David Card and Alan B. Krueger, "School Resources and Student Outcomes: An Overview of the Literature and New Evidence from North and South Carolina," *Journal of Economic Perspectives,* Fall 1996, pp. 31–50.

[24]David Card and Alan B. Krueger, "Does School Quality Matter? Returns to Education and the Characteristics of Public Schools in the United States," *Journal of Political Economy,* February 1992, pp. 1–40.

[25]See David Card and Alan B. Krueger, "School Quality and Black/White Relative Earnings: A Direct Assessment," *Quarterly Journal of Economics,* February 1992, pp. 151–200.

[26]James J. Heckman, Anne Layne-Farrar, and Petra Todd, "Does Measured School Quality Really Matter? An Examination of the Earnings-Quality Relationship," in Gary Burtless (ed.), *Does Money Matter? The Effect of School Resources on Student Achievement and Adult Success,* (Washington, D.C.: Brookings Institution, 1996). For a similar conclusion, see Julian Betts, "Does School Quality Matter? Evidence from the National Longitudinal Survey of Youth," *Review of Economics and Statistics,* May 1995, pp. 231–250.

4-2 World of Work

HIGHER EDUCATION: MAKING THE RIGHT CHOICES

The accompanying table shows the annual salaries of 1996–97 college graduates by major. These data imply a number of questions. Does it matter which college or university one attends? Is choice of major as important as the table suggests? To what extent, if at all, does grade-point average affect earnings?

James and colleagues* have shed light on these and related questions by examining earnings data for 1,241 male college graduates who attended some 519 different colleges and universities and who have been out of college 7 to 9 years. They found that the choice of school had only a modest impact on future earnings. Attending a private eastern school (such as Harvard, Princeton, or Amherst) raises earnings by about 5 percent. In fact, attending any school that is highly selective of its student body tends to raise future earnings. Specifically, a 100-point increase in the average SAT score of the freshman class raises earnings by about 3 percent. Aside from the prestigious private eastern schools, the choice of a public or private institution has no statistically significant impact on future earnings. Further, it makes no difference whether one attends a small college or a large university. Nor does the presence of a graduate program or a strong research orientation affect the earnings of undergraduates when they complete their studies. Interestingly, a college or university's expenditures per pupil do not significantly affect future earnings of students.

Most of the variance in the earnings of college graduates is explained by such factors as choice of major (see table), the amount of mathematics taken, achieved grade-point average, and the acquisition of a postgraduate degree. For example, an increase in GPA by one letter grade increases earnings by about 9 percent. James and colleagues observe that a high GPA reflects not only the acquisition of specific knowledge, but that students possess innate ability and habits of discipline and perseverance that are valued in the labor market.

James and colleagues conclude that, while attending Harvard "appears to be a good investment, [attending] your local state university to major in engineering, to take lots of math, and preferably to attain a high GPA, is an even better private investment. Apparently, what matters most is not which college you attend, but what you do while you are there. . . ."†

*Estelle James, Nabeel Alsalam, Joseph Conaty, and DucLe To, "College Quality and Future Earnings: Where Should You Send Your Child to College?" *American Economic Review,* May 1989, pp. 247–252.

†Ibid., pp. 251–252.

ESTIMATED STARTING SALARIES FOR NEW COLLEGE GRADUATES, 1996–97

Academic major	Estimated starting salary	Academic major	Estimated starting salary
Chemical engineering	$42,758	Marketing/Sales	$28,658
Mechanical engineering	39,852	General business administration	28,506
Electrical engineering	39,811	Agriculture	26,415
Industrial engineering	37,732	Human resources management	26,024
Computer science	36,964	Retailing	25,856
Packaging engineering	35,353	Education	25,742
Materials and logistics management	34,520	Communications	25,224
Nursing	32,927	Hotel, restaurant, and institutional management	25,176
Civil engineering	32,170	Advertising	24,757
Mathematics	32,055	Social science	24,232
Physics	31,972	Liberal arts/Arts and letters	24,081
Geology	31,606	Natural resources	22,950
Chemistry	31,261	Human ecology/Home economics	22,916
Accounting	30,393	Telecommunications	22,447
Financial administration	30,054	Journalism	22,102

Source: L. Patrick Scheetz, *Recruiting Trends 1996–97* (East Lansing: Collegiate Employment Research Institute, Michigan State University, 1996).

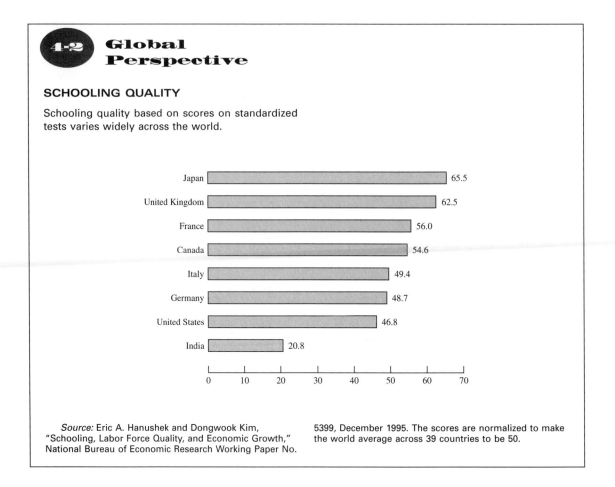

4-2 Global Perspective

SCHOOLING QUALITY

Schooling quality based on scores on standardized tests varies widely across the world.

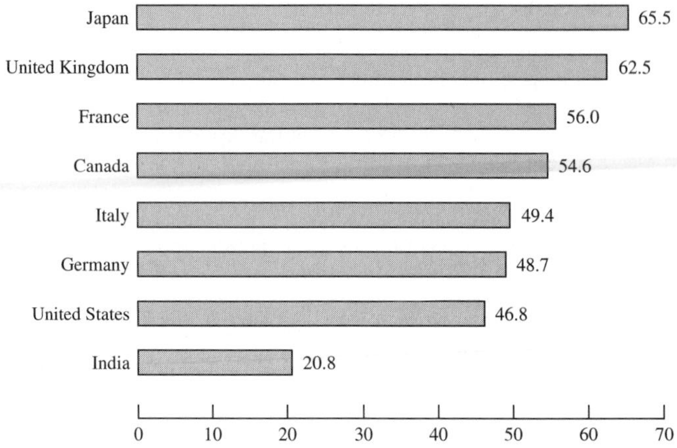

Source: Eric A. Hanushek and Dongwook Kim, "Schooling, Labor Force Quality, and Economic Growth," National Bureau of Economic Research Working Paper No. 5399, December 1995. The scores are normalized to make the world average across 39 countries to be 50.

human capital investment. The investment decision also can be viewed from a *public* or ***social perspective.*** In changing perspectives we can retain equations (4-3) and (4-6); however, we must alter our conceptions of costs and benefits. The private approach includes only those costs and benefits accruing to the individual. But from the social perspective the scope of relevant costs and benefits must be broadened. In particular, the private perspective excludes any public subsidies to education in calculating costs simply because such subsidies are *not* paid by the individual. Similarly, benefits (incremental earnings) should be calculated on an *after-tax* basis from the personal point of view. From the standpoint of society, costs should include any public subsidies to education, and benefits should be in terms of *before-tax* incremental earnings. Presumably the part of incremental earnings taxed away by government will be used to finance public goods and services beneficial to society as a whole.

Furthermore, most economists believe that education entails substantial *external* or *social benefits,* that is, benefits accruing to parties other than the individual acquiring the education. From a social perspective, these benefits should clearly be included in estimating the rate of return on human capital investments. What are these social benefits? First, it is well known that more-educated workers have lower unemployment rates than less-educated workers. Having high unemployment rates, poorly educated workers receive unemployment compensation and welfare benefits with greater frequency and may also find crime a relatively attractive alternative source of income. This means that society might benefit from investing in education by having to pay less taxes for social welfare programs, crime prevention, and law enforcement. Second, political participation and, presumably, the quality of political decisions might improve with increased literacy and education. More education might mean that society's political processes would function more effectively to the benefit of society at large. Third, there are intergenerational benefits; the children of better-educated parents grow up in a more desirable home environment and receive better care, guidance, and informal preschool education. Fourth, the research discoveries of highly educated people might yield large and widely disbursed benefits to society. Jonas Salk's discovery of an effective and economic polio vaccine is illustrative.[27]

Why is our distinction between private and social rates of return on human capital investments significant? First, the difference between the private and the social perspective is of potential importance because efficiency demands that the economy's total investment outlay be allocated so that rates of return on human and physical capital should be equal at the margin. If a given amount of investment spending is currently being allocated so that the rate of return on human capital investment is, say, 12 percent, while that on physical capital is only 8 percent, the society would benefit by relocating investment from physical to human capital. In making this comparison it is correct to use the social, rather than the private, rate of return. Thus, if we were to find that the *private* rate of return on human capital was in fact equal to the rate of return on physical capital, it would not necessarily be correct to conclude that investment resources were being efficiently divided between human and real capital. If the *social* rate of return was higher (lower) than the private rate, resources would have been underallocated (overallocated) to human capital investments. Incidentally, most studies of social rates of return yield rates that are quite comparable to those found in studies estimating private rates of return.

A second reason that the distinction between the private and social perspectives is important has to do with policy. The social or external benefits associated with education provide the rationale for the subsidization of education with public funds. In the interest of allocative efficiency, the size of these public subsidies to education should be determined on the basis of the magnitude of the associated social benefits.

QUICK REVIEW 4-1

- Human capital consists of the accumulation of prior investments in education, on-the-job training, health, and other factors that increase productivity.

[27]For more detailed discussions of the social and nonmarket benefits from education, see Burton A. Weisbrod, "Investing in Human Capital," *Journal of Human Resources,* Summer 1966, pp. 1–21; and Robert H. Haveman and Barbara W. Wolfe, "Schooling and Economic Well-Being: The Role of Nonmarket Effects," *Journal of Human Resources,* Summer 1984, pp. 377–406.

• The net present value method of computing the return on a human capital investment uses a market interest rate to discount the net earnings of the investment to its present value. If the net present value is positive, the investment should be undertaken.

• The internal rate of return method discovers the unique rate of discount that equates the present value of future earnings and the investment costs. If this internal rate of return exceeds the interest cost of borrowing, the investment should be undertaken.

• Private rates of return on investments in education are on the order of 10 to 15 percent and seem to be rising; social rates of return are thought to be similar.

Your Turn: Suppose the net present value of an educational investment is highly positive. What can you infer about the investment's internal rate of return relative to the interest cost of borrowing? (Answer: See page 625.)

HUMAN CAPITAL INVESTMENT AND THE DISTRIBUTION OF EARNINGS

Why do people vary significantly in the amounts of human capital that they acquire? Why is Nguyen a high school dropout, Brooks a high school graduate, and Hassan a Ph.D.? The reasons are many and complex, but by presenting a simple model of the demand for and the supply of human capital, we can gain valuable insights pertinent to this question. In so doing we shall also achieve some understanding as to why earnings are quite unequally distributed.

Diminishing Rates of Return

In Figure 4-4 we plot the marginal internal rate of return—the extra return from additional education—for a specific individual for successive years of education. For simplicity we have assumed that the rate of return falls continuously. In reality, the rate of return on the fourth year of, say, college—the year a student graduates—may yield a higher marginal return than the third year. But, in general, it is reasonable to assume that rates of return fall as more investment takes place. Why do these rates of return diminish? The answer is essentially twofold. On the one hand, investment in human capital (education) is subject to the law of diminishing returns. On the other hand, as additional education is undertaken, the attendant benefits fall and the associated costs rise so as to reduce the internal rate of return.

1 Diminishing Returns Investment in education is subject to the law of diminishing returns. The extra knowledge and skills "produced" by education or schooling become smaller and smaller as the amount of schooling is increased. This means that the incremental earnings from each additional year of schooling will diminish and therefore so will the rate of return. Explanation: Think of the individual as analogous to a firm that combines fixed resources with variable inputs to generate a certain output. An individual combines certain physical and mental characteristics with inputs of education or schooling to generate outputs of labor market skills. The individual's phys-

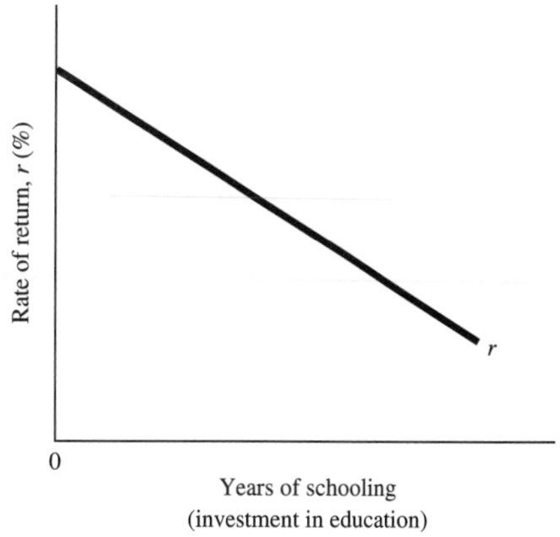

FIGURE 4-4 RATES OF RETURN FROM SUCCESSIVE YEARS OF SCHOOLING
The rate of return from investing in successive years of schooling diminishes because (1) such investment is subject to the law of diminishing returns and (2) costs rise and benefits fall as more education is obtained.

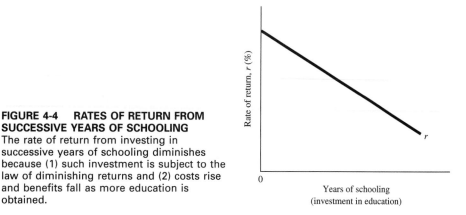

ical and mental characteristics—IQ, motor coordination, and so forth—are essentially fixed resources; these characteristics are determined by genes and the home environment. To these fixed resources we add variable inputs in the form of years of schooling. As with any other situation where a variable input is added to some fixed input, the resulting increases in the amount of human capital produced—the new knowledge and skills acquired by the individual—will ultimately decline. And diminishing returns will mean that the rate of return on successive human capital investments will also diminish.

2 Falling Benefits, Rising Costs We have already touched on the second reason the internal rate of return will decline as additional education is acquired. Costs tend to rise and benefits tend to fall for successive years of schooling. In addition to having essentially fixed mental and physical characteristics, the individual also possesses a fixed amount of time, that is, a finite work life. It follows that the more years one invests in education, the fewer one has during which one can realize the benefits of incremental income from that investment and, hence, the lower rate of return. The rate of return also declines because the costs of successive years of schooling tend to rise. On the one hand, the opportunity cost of one's time increases as more education is acquired. That is, an additional year of school has a greater opportunity cost for the holder of a bachelor's degree than for someone who has only a high school diploma. Similarly, the private direct costs of schooling increase. Public subsidies make elementary and high school education essentially free, but a substantial portion of the cost of college and graduate school is borne by the individual student. Studies confirm that the rate of return on schooling diminishes as the amount of schooling increases.

Demand, Supply, and Equilibrium

Next question: Why have we identified the curve labeled r in Figure 4-5 as a ***demand for human capital curve*** (D_{hc})? This identification is the result of applying the previously discussed decision rule, which says that investment is profitable if $r > i$ and unprofitable if $r < i$. Or, in the context of Figure 4-5, it is profitable to invest in human

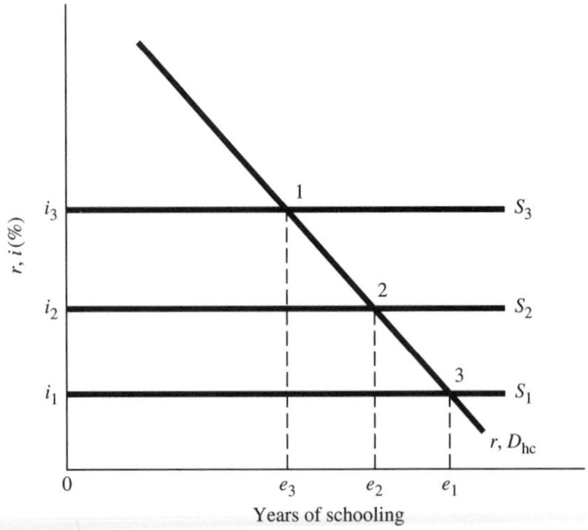

FIGURE 4-5 DERIVING THE DEMAND FOR HUMAN CAPITAL CURVE
Application of the $r = i$ rule reveals that the marginal internal rate of return curve is also the demand for human capital curve. Each of the equilibrium points (1, 2, 3) indicates the financial "price" of investing (i) on the vertical axis and the quantity of human capital demanded on the horizontal axis. This information on price and quantity demanded constitutes the demand curve for human capital.

capital or schooling up to the point where the marginal rate of return equals the interest rate or, in short, where $r = i$. Thus, in Figure 4-5 we assume that the individual is a "price taker" in borrowing funds for educational purposes and that needed amounts of money capital can be borrowed at a given interest rate. The horizontal line drawn at, say, i_2 indicates that the individual faces a perfectly elastic ***supply of investment funds*** S_2 at this interest rate. Our $r = i$ rule indicates that e_2 is the most profitable number of years of schooling in which to invest. Similarly, *if* the market rate of interest were higher at i_3, the application of the $r = i$ rule would make only e_3 years of schooling profitable. *If* the interest rate were lower at i_1, then it would be profitable to invest in e_1 years of schooling. By applying a selection of possible interest rates or money capital prices to the marginal rate of return curve, we locate a number of equilibrium points (1, 2, 3) that indicate the financial "price" of investing (various possible interest rates) on the vertical axis *and* the corresponding quantities of human capital demanded on the horizontal axis. Any curve containing such information on price and quantity demanded is, by definition, a demand curve—in this case the demand curve for human capital or schooling.

Differences in Human Capital Investment

The demand and supply curves of Figure 4-5 can be used to explain why different people invest in different amounts of human capital *and,* therefore, realize substantially different earnings. Our emphasis is on three considerations: (1) differences in ability, (2) differing degrees of uncertainty concerning the capacity to transform skills and knowledge into enhanced earnings due to discrimination, and (3) differing access to borrowed funds for human capital investment. The first two factors work through the demand side of the human capital market; the third works through the supply side.

1 Ability Differences Figure 4-6 embodies two different demand curves for human capital—D_A and D_B for Adams and Bowen, respectively—and a common supply

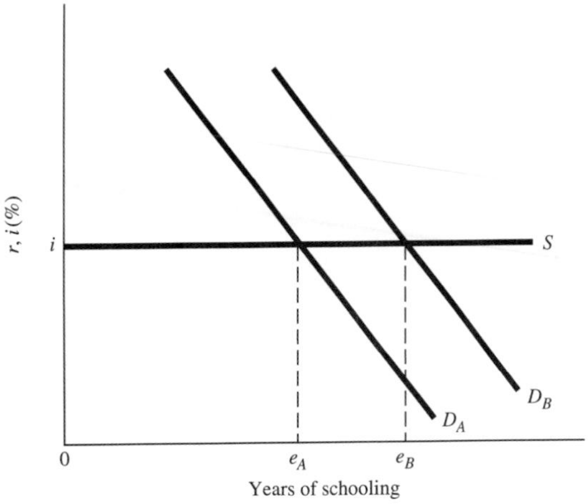

FIGURE 4-6 ABILITY, DISCRIMINATION, AND INVESTMENT IN HUMAN CAPITAL If Bowen has greater ability to translate schooling into increased labor market productivity and higher earnings than Adams, then Bowen's demand curve for human capital *(D_B)* will lie farther to the right than Adams' *(D_A)*. Given the interest rate, it will be rational for Bowen to invest in more education than Adams. Similarly, if Adams and Bowen are of equal ability but discrimination reduces the amount of incremental income Adams can obtain from additional education, it will be rational for Adams to invest in less education than Bowen.

curve. The common supply curve shows that money capital for investment in schooling is available to Adams and Bowen on identical terms. The key question is why Bowen's demand curve for human capital *(D_B)* is to the right of Adams' *(D_A)*. The answer may be that Bowen has greater abilities—better mental and physical talents and perhaps greater motivation and self-discipline—which cause any given input of schooling to be translated into a larger increase in labor market productivity and earning ability. That is, Bowen is more able than Adams to obtain enhanced earnings for each year of schooling; Bowen is capable of "getting more out of education" that is useful in the labor market than Adams. Thus, the rate of return on each year of schooling is higher, and Bowen's demand curve for human capital is therefore farther to the right. Given the interest rate and the perfectly elastic supply of financial capital, this means that Bowen will invest in e_B years of schooling, while Adams will choose to invest in only e_A years.[28]

Note that because it is rational for more-able people to obtain more education than less-able people, earnings differentials are compounded. Given the same amount of schooling, we would expect Bowen to earn more than Adams because of the former's greater innate ability. Because it is rational for Bowen to obtain more education than Adams, we would anticipate a further widening of the earnings differential.

2 Discrimination: Uncertainty of Earnings Let's now assume that Adams and Bowen are identical in terms of ability. But let's suppose that Adams is black or female and therefore is more likely to encounter discriminatory barriers to selling in the labor market the higher productivity acquired through education. In other words, Adams may encounter various forms of discrimination that reduce the likelihood of

[28]Some evidence indicates that less-educated persons obtain less education mainly because they have a higher discount rate (i.e., come from a poorer family or have a distaste for education), rather than because they lack ability. See David Card, "Earnings, Schooling, and Ability Revisited," *Research in Labor Economics,* Volume 16, 1995, pp. 23–48.

transforming the labor market skills acquired through education into incremental earnings. In equations (4-3) and (4-6), discrimination creates the probability that the flow of *E*'s to black (female) Adams will be smaller than those accruing to white (male) Bowen from the same amount of education. This means rates of return on each level of education are lower to Adams than to Bowen. In Figure 4-6, Adams' demand for human capital is less than Bowen's. Given equal access to funds for the financing of education, (the *iS* curve in Figure 4-6), Bowen will again find it rational to invest in more human capital than Adams. Discrimination, which reduces wages and earnings, also has the perverse impact of reducing the incentive for those discriminated against to invest in human capital.

3 Access to Funds This brings us to a final consideration. Figure 4-7 portrays the situation where the demand for human capital curves for Adams and Bowen are identical, but Bowen can acquire money capital on more favorable terms than Adams. Why the difference? Bowen may be from a wealthier family that is in a position to pledge certain financial or real assets as collateral and therefore obtain a lower interest rate. Under these conditions it is rational for Bowen to invest in more years of schooling than Adams.[29]

[29] A more elusive factor, one's *time preference,* also affects human capital investment. For example, Curt may be highly present-oriented in that he is relatively reluctant to sacrifice current consumption for future benefits. In terms of equation (4-3), Curt would in effect use a high interest rate in discounting the future flow of earnings. Other things being equal, this would reduce the present value of a human capital investment and decrease the likelihood that it would be undertaken. Conversely, Beth may be highly future-oriented in that she is quite willing to forgo current consumption for future benefits. She would use a low interest rate in discounting equation (4-3)'s future flow of earnings, tending to increase the present value of a human capital investment and enhancing the likelihood that it will be undertaken. The notion of time preference is helpful in explaining why individuals who are quite homogeneous with respect to ability and access to funds acquire much different amounts of human capital. This matter will be considered further in Chapter 8. For an examination of the effect of time preference, see William N. Evans and Edward Montgomery, "Education and Health: Where There's Smoke, There's an Instrument," National Bureau of Economic Research Working Paper No. 4949, December 1994.

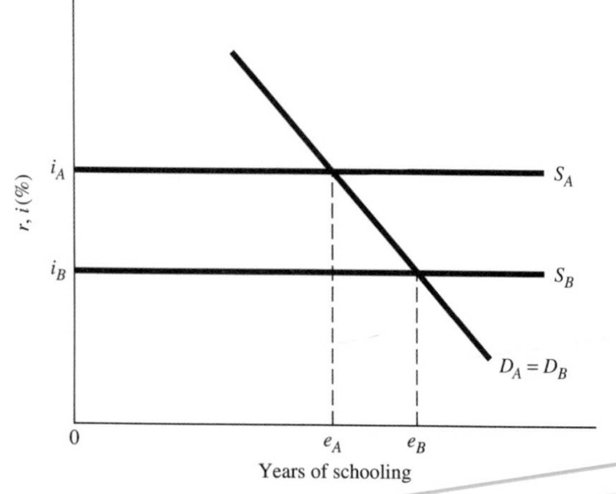

FIGURE 4-7 ACCESS TO FUNDS AND HUMAN CAPITAL INVESTMENT
If Bowen has access to financial resources on more favorable terms than Adams, it will be rational for Bowen to invest in a larger amount of education.

Interactions The basic point is that differences in ability, the impact of discrimination, and varying access to financial resources are all reasons various individuals find it rational to obtain different amounts of education. As shown in the age-earnings profiles in Figure 4-1, we note that these differences in educational attainment are important in generating inequality in the distribution of earnings. In fact, the factors that explain educational inequality may interact to generate greater earnings inequality than our discussion would suggest. For example, discrimination may not only influence the demand side of the human capital market to reduce the demands of blacks and females for education but may also appear on the supply side. If a lender reasons that discrimination makes it less likely that a black or a female will be able to achieve employment in the occupation for which he or she is training, the lender will compensate for this greater risk by charging a higher rate of interest. This causes the supply of investment funds curve for blacks and women to shift upward as in Figure 4-7, and the amount of education acquired will be further diminished. Similarly, individuals with greater ability may also enjoy lower financial costs. Greater ability may stem not simply from one's genetic inheritance but also from the quality of one's home environment. The child fortunate to be born into a high-income family may enjoy more and better preschool education, have greater motivation and self-discipline, and place a higher value on education in general. These considerations mean that the child may have greater ability to absorb education and to increase his or her labor market productivity and earnings. Being born into a high-income family also means a greater ability to finance education on favorable terms.[30]

The above comments correctly imply that public policy may also play a significant role in determining the amounts of human capital various individuals acquire and the consequent distribution of earnings. For example, to the extent that antidiscrimination policies have been effective, variations in individual demand curves for education have been reduced and so has earnings inequality. Scholarships based on student ability mean that those students with the strongest demand curves for human capital would also have the greatest access to funds, a combination that would increase inequality in the distribution of human capital and earnings. Conversely, scholarships on the basis of need or special education programs for youth from disadvantaged or minority families would reduce inequality in the dispersion of human capital and earnings.

Capital Market Imperfections

The capital market may include certain biases or imperfections causing it to favor investment in physical, rather than human, capital. Specifically, funds may be less readily available, or accessible only on less favorable terms, for investment in human capital as compared to real capital or the purchase of consumer durables. Perhaps the primary reason for this is that human capital is embodied in the borrower and therefore is not available as collateral on a loan. If one defaults on a house mortgage or an automobile loan, there is a tangible asset that the lender can repossess and sell to recover losses. But in a nation that rejects slavery and indentured servitude, there is no

[30]For an interesting discussion of how parents affect the earnings of their children, see Paul Taubman, *Income Distribution and Redistribution* (Reading, Mass.: Addison-Wesley Publishing Company, 1978), chap. 5.

designated asset for the lender to seize if the borrower fails to repay an educational loan. This increases risk to the lender and prompts the inclusion of a risk premium in the interest rate charged. Furthermore, we have noted that other things being equal, it is more rational for young people to make human capital investments than for old people. But young people are less likely to have established credit ratings or collateral assets to allow them to borrow on reasonable terms. Finally, the variation in returns on human capital investments is very large. Recall that although college graduates *on the average* earn substantially more than high school graduates, many college graduates earn less than the average high school graduate. This uncertainty of return may inflate the risk premium charged for human capital loans.[31]

The relative unsuitability of the capital market for educational loans has one or two important consequences. First, because of the problems and uncertainties just noted, financial institutions may choose *not* to make human capital loans. This means that the amount of human capital investment that individuals can undertake will depend on their, or their families', income and wealth. Thus, well-to-do families can finance the college educations of their children by the relatively painless process of reducing their volume of saving. But poor families cannot save and, therefore, the financing of a college education implies a possibly severe cut in living standards.[32] These circumstances may perpetuate a vicious circle. Individuals and families with little human capital (education) may be poor; being poor, it is extremely difficult for them to finance the acquisition of additional human capital.

Capital market imperfections have a second important implication. If it is in the social interest to achieve a balance or equilibrium between investment in real capital and human capital, then government may have to offset the imperfections by subsidizing or providing human capital loans. Ideally, an equilibrium between investment in real and human capital would occur when the last dollar spent on human capital contributes the same amount to the domestic output as the last dollar expended on real capital. But the higher interest rates charged for educational loans will restrict expenditures on human capital so that the relative contribution of the last unit to the national output will exceed that of the last unit of real capital. This indicates that investment resources are being underallocated to human capital. This rationale in part lies behind the loan guarantees and financial resources that government has provided to stimulate educational loans.

QUICK REVIEW 4-2

- The rate of return from investing in successive units of human capital declines—that is, the investment demand curve is downsloping—because opportunity costs rise and marginal benefits fall as more investment occurs.

[31]For a further discussion of capital market imperfections, see Lester Thurow, *Investment in Human Capital* (Belmont, Calif.: Wadsworth Publishing Company, Inc., 1970), pp. 77–83.

[32]Even publicly supported colleges and universities that feature relatively low tuition and fees may attract few students from low-income families simply because their families may not be able to afford the opportunity costs (see Figure 4-2). A very poor family may not be able to forgo the income that a son or daughter can earn by entering the labor market immediately upon graduating from high school. Federal education loan programs have mitigated this problem in recent years.

- The optimal level of investment in human capital occurs where the marginal rate of return, r, equals the interest rate, i (price of investing).
- It is rational for people having greater ability to obtain more education than others; conversely, those who are discriminated against in the labor market have less incentive to invest in human capital.
- People who have greater access to financial funding for investment on more favorable interest terms will rationally invest more in education than others.
- Imperfections in the capital market may bias investment toward physical capital rather than human capital.

Your Turn: In equilibrium, the marginal rates of return, r, for those with more ability to extract earnings from formal education and those with less ability are equal (see Figure 4-6). So why do people with greater ability get more formal education? (Answer: See page 625.)

ON-THE-JOB TRAINING

Much of the usable labor market skills that workers possess are acquired not through formal schooling but rather through ***on-the-job training.*** Such training may be somewhat formal; that is, workers may undertake a structured trainee program or an apprenticeship program. On the other hand, on-the-job training is often highly informal and therefore difficult to measure or even detect. Less-experienced workers often engage in "learning by doing"; they acquire new skills by simply observing more-skilled workers, filling in for them when they are ill or on vacation, or engaging in informal conversation during coffee breaks.

Costs and Benefits

Like formal education, on-the-job training entails present sacrifices and future benefits. It thus is an investment in human capital and can be analyzed through the net present value and internal rate of return frameworks (equations 4-3 and 4-6). In deciding whether or not to provide on-the-job training, a firm will weigh the expected added revenues generated by the training against the costs of providing it. If the net present value of the training investment is positive, the firm will invest; if it is negative, it won't. Alternatively, the firm will invest if the internal rate of return of the investment exceeds the interest cost of borrowing.

For employers, providing training may involve such direct costs as classroom instruction or increased worker supervision, along with such indirect costs as reduced worker output during the training period. Workers may have to accept the cost of lower wages during the training period. The potential benefit to firms is that a trained workforce will be more productive and will therefore make greater contributions to the firm's total revenue. Similarly, trained workers can expect higher wages because of their enhanced productivity.

General and Specific Training

To understand how the associated costs and benefits are distributed among workers and employers we must distinguish between two polar types of on-the-job training. At one extreme, ***general training*** *refers to the creation of skills or characteristics that are equally usable in* all *firms and industries.* Stated differently, general training enhances the productivity of workers to all firms. At the other end of the continuum, ***specific training*** *is training that can be used* only *in the particular firm that provides that training.* Specific training increases the worker's productivity only in the firm providing that training. In practice, most on-the-job training contains elements of both general and specific training, and it is therefore difficult to offer unequivocal examples. Nevertheless, we might venture that the capacity to concentrate on a task for a reasonable period of time, to show up for work regularly and be punctual, to read, to perform simple mathematical manipulations, and to follow instructions all constitute general training. Similarly, gaining word processing, carpentry, or accounting skills would be considered general training. Alternatively, the ability to perform an assembly procedure unique to a firm's product exemplifies specific training. The training of personnel to answer toll-free telephone questions about a firm's products is another example of specific training.

The distinction between general and specific training is important for at least two reasons. First, it is helpful in explaining whether the worker or the employer is more likely to pay for on-the-job training. Second, it is useful in understanding why employers might be particularly anxious to retain certain of their trained workers.

Distributing Training Costs

Analyzing whether workers or firms pay the costs of on-the-job training gets a bit complex. Let's start by looking at pure cases and then modify our analysis to account for real-world observations. We begin with two broad generalizations, each based on the assumptions that markets are competitive and that workers are perfectly mobile. First, *the worker will pay for general training through lower wages during the training period.* Second, *the firm must bear the cost of specific training.*

General training gives a worker skills and understanding that are transferable; they can be sold to other firms at a higher wage rate. If the employer were to bear the cost, the worker might leave the firm's employment after completion of the training and thus deprive the employer of any return (benefit) on the training investment. Or, alternatively, in the posttraining period the employer would have to pay a wage rate commensurate with the worker's higher productivity, eliminating any possible return on the training investment to the employer. Therefore, if general on-the-job training is undertaken, it is paid for by the worker in the form of a reduced wage rate during the training period.

On the other hand, a specific skill is not transferable or salable by a worker. Thus, the worker will not pay for such training. If a worker is fired or laid off at the end of a period of specific training, the worker has gained nothing of value to sell in the labor market. The cost is borne by the employer. This typically means that the employer will pay a wage rate in excess of the worker's contribution to the firm's revenue during the training period. Figure 4-8 is useful in elaborating these generalizations.

General Training Figure 4-8(a) shows the case of general training. Here W_u and MRP_u indicate what wage rate and marginal revenue product would be for an untrained worker. ***Marginal revenue product*** *is the increase in a firm's total revenue associated with the employment of a given worker.*[33] The employment of an additional worker will add to a firm's total output and therefore to its revenue. This addition to its revenue is the MRP.

In Figure 4-8(a) the wage rate and marginal revenue product *during* training are represented by W_t and MRP_t, while W_p and MRP_p are the posttraining wage rate and marginal revenue product. MRP_t is below that for an untrained worker because during the training period the worker is diverting time from production to learning. It is important to stress that the higher posttraining marginal revenue product (MRP_p) is relevant

[33]This concept will be explored in more detail in Chapter 5.

FIGURE 4-8 WAGE RATES AND MARGINAL REVENUE PRODUCTS FOR GENERAL AND SPECIFIC TRAINING

(a) *General training.* Because general training is salable to other firms and industries *(W_p = MRP_p)*, workers normally must pay for such training that a firm provides. This payment is in the form of a reduced wage *($W_t < W_u$)* during the training period. A possible exception is where the firm faces a legal minimum wage and needs to provide remedial basic education to have a qualified work force. The firm may conclude that it can pay a wage rate above W_t in the training period and recoup its investment by paying a wage rate slightly below W_p in the posttraining period. Workers facing high costs of job search and relocation may not leave for jobs paying W_t. (b) *Specific training.* Specific training is not transferable to other firms; therefore, the employer must pay for such training. During the training period the employer pays a wage rate in excess of the worker's marginal revenue product *($W_u > MRP_t$)*. In the posttraining period the employer receives a return on specific training because the worker's marginal revenue product will exceed his or her wage rate *($MRP_p > W_u$)*. Because the employer's return on specific training varies directly with the length of the posttraining period, the employer might voluntarily pay an above-competitive wage *(W'_p as compared to W_u)* in order to reduce worker turnover. [Adapted from John T. Addison and W. Stanley Siebert, *The Market for Labor: An Analytical Treatment* (Santa Monica, Calif.: Goodyear Publishing Company, 1979), p. 114.]

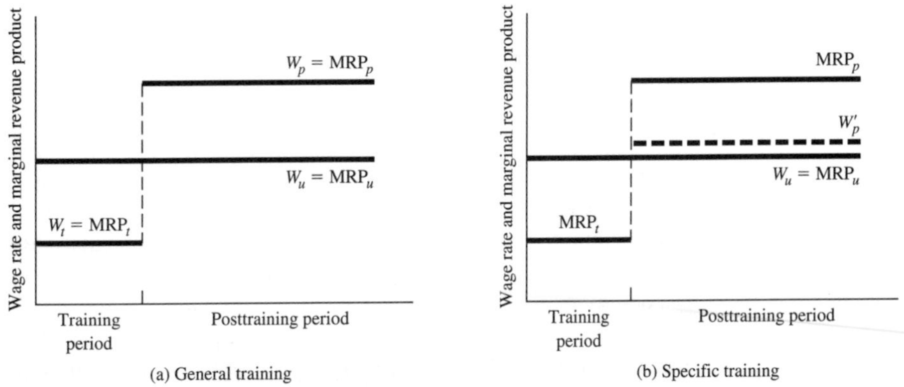

to all firms because the training is general. Competing firms will therefore bid up the wage rate of this trained worker until it is equal to MRP_p. It is precisely for this reason—that competition will force the posttraining wage rate upward into equality with the posttraining marginal revenue product—that the employer will normally *not* be willing to pay for general training. The employer has no opportunity to obtain a return on its training investment by paying a wage rate less than the worker's marginal revenue product. Why should the employer bear general training costs when the benefits accrue solely to the trained employee in the form of higher wages? To repeat: The worker pays for general training costs by accepting a wage below that of the untrained worker (W_t as compared to W_u) during the training period. Incidentally, the fact that competition will bid a worker's wage rate up into equality with his or her higher posttraining marginal revenue product (MRP_p), and thereby preclude a return to the employer, explains why general education typically occurs in schools and not on the job.

Specific Training Figure 4-8(b) pertains to specific training. Again, W_u and MRP_u are the wage rate and marginal revenue product of an untrained worker, and MRP_t and MRP_p, respectively, show marginal revenue productivity during and after specific training. In contrast to Figure 4-8(a), the posttraining marginal revenue product applies *only to this firm.* The worker has acquired specific training that will increase productivity in *this* firm; but by definition, specific training is *not* transferable or useful to other firms. Because specific training is not transferable—that is, it will not allow the worker to obtain a higher wage rate as the consequence of labor market competition for his or her services—the worker will refuse to pay for such training and will not accept a lower wage during the training period. Note that during the training period the wage rate will remain at W_u, which means that the employer must bear the cost of the training by paying a wage rate that is in excess of the worker's marginal revenue product (MRP_t). However, because specific training is not transferable—that is, it does not increase the worker's marginal revenue product to other firms—the employer need not increase the wage rate above W_u in the posttraining period. Thus, from the employer's standpoint, training imposes a flow of costs (W_u exceeds MRP_t) in the training period that is followed by a flow of benefits or incremental revenues (MRP_p exceeds W_u) in the posttraining period. As shown in equation (4-3), if the net present value of these flows is positive, the firm will find it profitable to undertake a given program of specific training for its workers. Indeed, you have undoubtedly noticed that Figure 4-8(b) resembles Figure 4-2.

Modifications

Our discussion of general and specific training merits modifications in some important ways. First, let's again look at general training [Figure 4-8(a)]. Recently, some firms have begun providing new employees with general training—remedial reading, writing, and mathematics—to compensate for a decline in the quality of primary and secondary education. These firms have been forced to provide this general training to ensure themselves a sufficient number of qualified workers. Usually, these firms reduce the wage during the training period, as suggested in Figure 4-8. But, in other instances, the legal minimum wage (Chapter 13) precludes this strategy. Thus, some firms may have to pay part of the training costs themselves.

In Figure 4-8(a), we are suggesting that the minimum wage may force some firms offering general training to pay more than W_t during the training period. How is it possible for these firms to recoup these general training expenses? Won't employees take their services elsewhere if they are paid less than W_p after completion of the training? The answer is that, in the real world, workers are not perfectly mobile; it is costly to change jobs and to relocate geographically. Thus, these firms may be able to recoup their investments in general training through paying less than the workers' marginal productivity during part or all of the posttraining period. The extra pay the worker could get by changing jobs may not be sufficient to cover the worker's job search and relocation costs.

We also need to modify our discussion of Figure 4-8(b). We have observed that in the posttraining period the employer realizes a return from specific training by paying a wage (W_u) that is less than each worker's contribution to the firm's total revenue (MRP_p). The total amount of revenue or profit derived from this discrepancy will vary directly with the length of time the worker remains employed by the firm. In short, the employer has a financial interest in lowering the turnover or quit rates of workers with specific training. The employer might accomplish this by voluntarily paying a wage rate somewhat higher than the worker could obtain elsewhere, for example, W_p' rather than W_u. Stated differently, the wage in the posttraining period is likely to be set so as to divide the gains from specific training between employer and employee. Specific training is one of a number of considerations that changes labor from a variable input to a *quasi-fixed* factor of production.[34]

A final comment: On the average, those individuals who receive the largest amount of formal education also receive more on-the-job specific training. This is not surprising. A person who has demonstrated his or her trainability by completing, say, a college degree is more likely to be selected by an employer for specific on-the-job training than someone with only a high school diploma. Why? Because that individual will be trainable at a lower cost. Indeed, Figure 4-8(b) implies that on-the-job training will have a higher rate of return to employers when workers can absorb training in a short period of time. A college degree is evidence of the capacity to absorb training quickly. The fact that persons with more formal education on the average receive more on-the-job training helps explain why age-earnings profiles of more highly educated workers rise faster than those of less-educated workers (See Figure 4-1).

QUICK REVIEW 4-3

- Because general training is salable to other firms, workers must normally pay for it indirectly through reduced pay during the training period.

[34]The classic study is Walter Oi, "Labor as a Quasi-Fixed Factor," *Journal of Political Economy,* December 1962, pp. 538–555.

• Specific training is not transferable to other firms; therefore, the employer normally must pay for it, recouping the investment cost in later periods by paying these workers less than their MRPs.

• Faced with a legal minimum wage, some firms needing qualified workers may pay for general training, recouping their expenses by paying workers less than their MRPs during the posttraining period. Because of high job search and relocation costs, many workers will stay at their jobs, even though they might be able to earn more elsewhere.

• The employer's return on specific training varies directly with the length of the posttraining period; thus, the employer may pay a higher-than-competitive wage to reduce worker turnover and increase its return on its investment.

Your Turn: Suppose that after graduation you take a job with an employer that offers to pay full tuition for employees wishing to return to school to get an MBA degree during nonwork hours. You are *not* required to continue working for the firm after getting your MBA. What type of training is this, and who do you think actually pays for it? (Answers: See page 625.)

Increasing Importance and Empirical Evidence

In 1991, nearly 50 million American workers reported participating in training to improve their job skills. This represented 41 percent of the labor force, up from 35 percent in 1983. College-educated workers, who comprise only 25 percent of total employment, accounted for 37 percent of the on-the-job training. An equal percentage of men and women received training while at work. In 1991, 40 percent of white workers, 34 percent of black workers, and 28 percent of Hispanic workers reported engaging in training while working.[35]

Concomitant to the increases in training has been a kaleidoscope of new research on this topic. A few of the recent findings are as follows. Workers with postsecondary education receive more training than those with less education.[36] Training leads to improvements in job performance as measured by performance rating scores and positively effects wage growth.[37] The likelihood of participating in employer-provided training program is greater in larger firms than in smaller ones.[38]

The accumulation of on-the-job training raises a worker's real wages. Specifically, 10 years of job seniority increases the real wage for the typical male worker by more than 25 percent.[39]

[35]Thomas Amirault, "Training to Qualify for Jobs and Improve Skills," *Monthly Labor Review,* September 1992, pp. 31–36.

[36]Joseph G. Altonji and James R. Spletzer, "Worker Characteristics, and the Receipt of On-the-Job Training," *Industrial and Labor Relations Review,* October 1991, pp. 58–79. Also, see Lisa M. Lynch and Sandra E. Black, "Beyond the Incidence of Training: Evidence from a National Employer's Survey," National Bureau of Economic Research Working Paper No. 5231, August 1995.

[37]Ann Bartel, "Training, Wage Growth and Job Performance: Evidence from a Company Database," *Journal of Labor Economics,* July 1995, pp. 401–425.

[38]Alphonse G. Holtmann and Todd L. Idson, "Employer Size and On-the-Job Training Decisions," *Southern Economic Journal,* October 1991, pp. 339–355.

[39]Robert H. Topel, "Specific Capital, Mobility, and Wages: Wages Rise with Job Seniority," *Journal of Political Economy,* February 1991, pp. 145–176.

Wages rise particularly rapidly in the first few years on the job, which is the period when training is likely to take place.[40] Youths without college degrees in Britain receive much more postschool training than similar youths in the United States.[41] Firms with below-average productivity growth are more likely to institute new training programs for their employees than other firms. These training programs pay off—they 4-3 bring productivity growth up to the level of comparable businesses.[42] Gender and racial differences in the amounts of, and returns to, on-the-job training account for part of the gender and racial wage gaps.[43]

CRITICISMS OF HUMAN CAPITAL THEORY

A number of criticisms have been made of the human capital model and its applications. The first two criticisms discussed here are concerned with measurement problems and suggest that estimates of the rates of return on investments in education are likely to be biased. Two other criticisms also have implications for measuring the rate of return on human capital investments, but are more profound in that they challenge the very concept or theory of investing in human capital.

Investment or Consumption?

One criticism of measuring the rate of return on human capital investment is that it is *not* correct to treat all expenditures for education as investment because, in fact, a portion of such outlays are consumption expenditures. The decision to attend college, for example, is based on broader and more complex considerations than expected increases in labor productivity and enhanced earnings. Some substantial portion of one's expenditures on a college education yields consumption benefits either immediately or in the long run.[44] Expenditures for courses on Shakespeare, ceramics, music appreciation, and so forth, yield both immediate and long-run consumption benefits by enlarging an individual's range of interests, tastes, and activities. It is true, of course, that a course in nineteenth-century English literature not only yields consumption benefits but also enhances the capacity of oral and written expression. And this ability has value in the labor market; it increases productivity and earnings. The problem, however, is that there

[40]James N. Brown, "Why Do Wages Rise with Tenure? On-the-Job Training and the Life Cycle Wage Growth Observed within Firms," *American Economic Review,* December 1989, pp. 971–991.

[41]David G. Blanchflower and Lisa M. Lynch, "Training at Work: A Comparison of U.S. and British Youth," in Lisa M. Lynch (ed.), *Training and the Private Sector* (Chicago: University of Chicago Press, 1994), pp. 233–260.

[42]Ann Bartel, "Productivity Gains from the Implementation of Employee Training Programs," *Industrial Relations,* October 1994, pp. 411–425. For a survey of earlier research on training, see Charles Brown, "Empirical Evidence on Private Training," in *Investing in People,* Background Papers vol. 1, Commission on Workforce Quality and Labor Market Efficiency, U.S. Department of Labor, 1989, pp. 301–330.

[43]Reed Neil Olsen and Edwin A. Sexton, "The Returns to On-the-Job Training: Are They the Same for Blacks and Whites?" *Southern Economic Journal,* October 1994, pp. 328–42; and Reed Neil Olsen and Edwin A. Sexton, "Gender Differences in the Returns to and Acquisition of On-the-Job Training," *Industrial Relations,* January 1996, pp. 59–77.

[44]Interestingly, a recent study indicates that light to moderate high school employment has positive effects on later economic outcomes and does not just provide resources for current consumption. See Christopher J. Ruhm, "Is High School Employment Consumption or Investment?" *Journal of Labor Economics,* October 1997, pp. 735–776.

4-3 World of Work

JOB TRAINING: LESSONS FROM GERMANY?*

Germany has an elaborate youth apprenticeship program that may provide important lessons for the United States. The German program encourages non-college-bound students ages 15 to 19 to undertake on-the-job training. Participants usually sign individual contracts with participating employers who agree to train them for 2 to 3 years in a particular occupation. Typically, apprentices spend 1 day a week in a public vocational school and the other 4 work days in apprenticeship training. About 66 percent of German workers are graduates of these programs.

Apprentices choose 1 of 380 occupations for training and are paid 20 to 25 percent of the salaries of the certified graduates. Participants virtually are guaranteed full-time jobs at full pay if they perform their work satisfactorily and pass the apprenticeship tests. Therefore, this German program provides smooth transitions from formal education to job training and from job training to full-time employment. In contrast, many American high school dropouts and high school graduates experience long periods of unemployment or aimless wandering from job to job.

City and regional chambers of industry and commerce organize the apprenticeship system. These coalitions of governmental, business, and union representatives "register the apprenticeship contracts, certify training companies, regulate and supervise the program, settle disputes, establish examination boards staffed by volunteers, organize midterm and final examinations (88% pass), and issue certificates recognized all over Germany and, increasingly, across Europe."†

The annual cost of training the 1.5 million German apprentices is about $28 billion. These trainees in turn produce about $10 billion of output each year. The net annual cost of the program therefore is $18 billion, or about $11,000 per trainee per year. Most of these costs are borne by the participating companies, which treat the net training expense as an investment in human capital. While trainees are not obligated to stay with the firms that trained them, most workers do. Thus, firms recoup their investments through higher productivity over the workers' careers.

Could the German apprenticeship model be implemented in the United States? Most observers strongly doubt it. The German model tracks children at age 10 into three levels of later education and training: college, skilled trades, and lower-skilled office jobs. This early tracking runs counter to the American view of education, which emphasizes the liberal arts. Also, the German apprenticeship program relies heavily on widespread union involvement. But only 14 percent of the American labor force is unionized, far less than the 40 percent in Germany. Another difference is that German children are required by law to attend school or training programs until they are 18 years old. Finally, American antitrust laws restrict the type of industry associations that allow German firms to pool the costs and benefits of worker training.

Despite these differences, a consensus is emerging that more apprenticeship options such as those in Germany should be made available for American students who do not plan to attend college. In 1993 the Clinton administration proposed the creation of a modest, first-step apprenticeship plan. The resulting legislation, the School to Work Opportunities Act of 1994, attempts to ease the transition to the work force for youth through a variety of methods including apprenticeships.

*Based on Wilfried Prewo, "The Sorcery of Apprenticeship," *Wall Street Journal,* February 12, 1993, p. A10. Also relevant is Margaret Hilton, "Shared Training: Learning from Germany," *Monthly Labor Review,* March 1991, pp. 33–37.

†Ibid., p. A10.

is no reasonable way of determining what portion of the expense on a literature course is investment and what part is consumption. The main point is that by ignoring the consumption component of educational expenditures and considering *all* such outlays as investment, empirical researchers *understate* the rate of return on educational investments. In other words, by overstating the investment costs we understate the return on that investment.

Nonwage Benefits

In calculating the internal rate of return, most researchers simply compare the differences in the earnings of high school and college graduates. But the jobs of high school and college graduates differ in other respects. First, the fringe benefits associated with the jobs obtained by college graduates are more generous—both absolutely and as a percentage of earnings—than those received by high school graduates. By ignoring fringe benefits, empirical studies *understate* the rate of return on a college education. Second, the jobs acquired by college graduates are generally more pleasant and interesting than those of high school graduates. This means that a calculated rate of return based on incremental earnings *understates* the total benefits accruing from a college education.

The Ability Problem

Two other related criticisms, labeled the *ability problem* and the *screening hypothesis,* question the very concept of human capital investment. We first consider the ***ability problem.***

It is widely recognized that average incomes vary directly with the level of education. But it is less well accepted that a strong, clear-cut cause-effect relationship exists between the two. Critics of human capital theory doubt that the observed income differential is solely—or even primarily—the result of the additional education. To state the problem somewhat differently, the "other things being equal" assumption underlies the simple model of Figure 4-2 and the conclusions derived from it. Critics of human capital theory contend that "other things" in fact are not likely to be equal. It is widely acknowledged that those who have more intelligence, more self-discipline, and greater motivation—not to mention more family wealth and better job market "connections"—are more likely to go to college. If we could somehow blot out all of the knowledge and understanding that college graduates acquired in college, we would still expect this group to earn larger incomes than those who decided *not* to attend college. Thus, one can argue that although college graduates earn higher incomes than high school graduates, a substantial portion of that incremental income is *not* traceable to the investment in a college education. In other words, people with high abilities tend to do well in the labor market; the fact that they also attend college may be somewhat incidental to this success. "The only reason that education is correlated with income is that the combination of ability, motivation, and personal habits that it takes to succeed in education happens to be the same combination that it takes to be a productive worker.[45] This criticism implies that if a substantial portion of the incremental earnings enjoyed by college graduates is attributable to their *ability* and not to their *schooling,* then estimated rates of return on investing in a college education will be *overstated.*

Accepting the validity of the criticism, a number of researchers have tried to determine what portion of incremental earnings derives from human capital investment as

[45]Alice M. Rivlin, "Income Distribution—Can Economics Help?" *American Economic Review,* May 1975, p. 10.

opposed to differences in ability and other personal characteristics. For example, a study of identical twins concludes that ability bias plays a small role in the measurement of the rate of return to schooling.[46] Other studies using other approaches reach a similar conclusion.[47]

It is also worth observing that the causal relationship between education and earnings has important implications for public policy. *If* human capital theorists are correct in arguing that education is the sole or primary cause of higher earnings, then it makes sense to provide more education and training to low-income workers if society chooses to reduce poverty and the degree of income inequality. On the other hand, *if* high incomes are caused primarily by ability, independent of education and training, then a policy of increased spending on the education and training of low-income groups may be of limited success in increasing their incomes and alleviating income inequality.

The Screening Hypothesis

The ***screening hypothesis*** is closely related to the ability problem. This hypothesis suggests that education affects earnings, not primarily by altering the labor market productivity of students but by grading and labeling students in such a way as to determine their job placement and thereby their earnings.[48] It is argued that employers use educational attainment—for example, the possession of a college degree—as an inexpensive means of identifying workers who are likely to be of high quality. A college degree or other credential thus becomes a ticket of admission to higher-level, higher-paying jobs where opportunities for further training and promotion are good. Less-educated workers are screened from these positions, not necessarily because of their inability to perform the job but simply because they do not have the college degree to give them access in the position. The incremental income enjoyed by college graduates might be a payment for being credentialed rather than a reward for being more productive.

Viewed from a private perspective, screening should have no effect on the internal rate of return. Whether one is admitted to a higher-paying position because of the knowledge and skills acquired in college or because one possesses the necessary credential (a college degree), the fact remains that having attended college typically results in higher earnings. But from a social perspective, the screening hypothesis, if valid, is very important. One might well question the expenditure of $514 (in 1995) on elementary, secondary, and higher education if the payoff is merely to signal employ-

[46]Orley Ashenfelter and Alan Krueger, "Estimates of the Economic Returns to Schooling from a New Sample of Twins," *American Economic Review,* December 1994, pp. 1157–1173.

[47]For example, see McKinley Blackburn and David Neumark, "Omitted-Ability Bias and the Increase in the Return to Schooling," *Journal of Labor Economics,* July 1993, pp. 521–544; and Joshua D. Angrist and Alan B. Krueger, "Estimating the Payoff to Schooling Using the Vietnam-Era Draft Lottery," National Bureau of Economic Research Working Paper No. 4067, May 1992.

[48]Michael Spence, "Job Market Signaling," *Quarterly Journal of Economics,* August 1973, pp. 355–374. For a survey of the screening literature, see Andrew Weiss, "Human Capital vs. Signalling Explanations of Wages," *Journal of Economic Perspectives,* Fall 1996, pp. 133–154.

ers that certain workers are above-average in terms of intelligence, motivation, and self-discipline. To the extent that a college graduate's incremental earnings stem from screening, the social rate of return of investing in a college education will be *overstated.*

To what extent are the higher earnings of more-educated workers due to education augmenting the productivity of workers, as the human capital view suggests? Similarly, to what degree are the higher earnings of such individuals attributable to the screening hypothesis, which indicates that schooling serves the function of merely identifying more productive workers? Does schooling produce skills or merely serve to identify preexistent skills? Empirical evidence is mixed. For example, research by Taubman and Wales suggests that as much as 50 percent of the effect of education on earnings might result from screening.[49]

On the other hand, studies by Altonji and Pierret, Wolpin, and Wise question the importance of screening. Altonji and Pierret argue that signaling is likely to be an important part of the return to schooling only to the extent that firms lack good information about the productivity of new workers and that they learn slowly over time.[50] They find evidence that firms do screen young workers on the basis of education, but that employers learn quickly about worker productivity. Altonji and Pierret's calculations suggest that the screening component of the return to schooling is probably only a small part of the difference in wages associated with education. Wolpin has reasoned that if education is a screening device, workers who are to be screened in the process of job acquisition will be prone to purchase more schooling than those workers who are not screened. He notes that while salaried workers are screened, self-employed workers are not. Therefore, if schooling is a screening device, salaried workers will tend to purchase more schooling than the self-employed. But he finds that in fact the two groups of workers acquire about the same amount of education, which Wolpin regards as "evidence against a predominate screening interpretation" of the positive association between schooling and earnings.[51] Similarly, Wise has argued that if education does affect worker productivity as the human capital theory suggests, then college degrees of differing quality *and* student performance while attending college should be reflected in salary differentials. That is, if human capital theory is correct, workers with bachelor degrees from high-quality institutions *and* workers who achieved higher grade-point averages should be more productive and therefore earn higher salaries. Examining data for some 1,300 college graduates employed by Ford Motor Company, Wise found a "consistent positive relationship between commonly used measures of academic achievement [institutional quality and grade-point average] and rates of salary increase."

[49]Paul Taubman and Terence Wales, "Higher Education, Mental Ability and Screening," *Journal of Political Economy,* January–February 1973, pp. 28–55. Also see Paul W. Miller and Paul A. Volker, "The Screening Hypothesis: An Application of the Wiles Test," *Economic Inquiry,* January 1984, pp. 121–127.

[50]Joseph G. Altonji and Charles R. Pierret, "Employer Learning and the Signaling Value of Education," in I. Ohashi and T. Tachibonoki (eds.), *Employment Adjustment, Incentives, and Internal Labor Markets,* New York, McMillan Publishing, forthcoming.

[51]Kenneth Wolpin, "Education and Screening," *American Economic Review,* December 1977, pp. 949–958.

4-4

Wise concludes that a "college education is not only a signal of productive ability, but in fact enhances this ability."[52]

Recapitulation

There is no question that human capital theory has been the basis for important insights and the cornerstone for a myriad of revealing empirical studies. But as the ability problem and the screening hypothesis suggest, human capital theory is not univer-

[52]David A. Wise, "Academic Achievement and Job Performance," *American Economic Review,* June 1975, pp. 350–366. For evidence that education per se, as opposed to ability to screening, enhances earnings in two less-developed nations (Kenya and Tanzania), see M. Boissiere, J. B. Knight, and R. H. Sabot, "Earnings, Schooling, and Cognitive Skills," *American Economic Review,* December 1985, pp. 1016–1030.

4-4 World of Work

THE RADICAL CRITIQUE OF HUMAN CAPITAL THEORY*

The radical critique of human capital theory is largely a philosophical attack that, while not rejecting the notion that schooling affects worker productivity, contends that schooling influences productivity much differently than hypothesized by human capital theory. Radical economists insist that a highly educated, highly skilled workforce is *not* necessarily a profitable workforce. Profitable production in a capitalist system requires that, in addition to technical skills, workers have "appropriate" attitudes and personality traits. More specifically, the capitalist system needs workers who will submit to hierarchical systems of authority and control, accept a structure of unequal economic rewards, and respond positively to the incentive mechanisms through which enterprises extract useful labor from them. To radical economists, the function of schooling—of human capital investment—is to inculcate these kinds of attitudes and values that are consistent with and therefore sustain and perpetuate the capitalist system. Put bluntly, the function of schooling in the United States is to generate a disciplined, obedient, and well-motivated workforce that accepts the capitalist ideology and fits the needs of capitalist enterprises. Human capital theorists fail to recognize that a basic function of education is "social reproduction," that is, the preservation of the capitalist system and the class distinctions peculiar to it. Human capital theory is therefore held to be incomplete, superficial, and quite irrelevant in explaining the amounts and kinds of education that we have in the United States.

How do schools develop those attitudes and personality traits that capitalist employers desire? First, radicals point out that American schools embody systems of authority, control, and motivation paralleling those in the job structures of business enterprises. "Good" students are those who, instead of thinking for themselves, accept the authoritarian hierarchy of teachers and administrators found in schools. Discipline, punctuality, responsibility, and dependability are earmarks of superior students and later of superior workers. Similarly, the system of grading that rewards certain classroom behaviors and penalizes others, ostensibly on the basis of merit, conditions students to acquiesce in the unequal structure of economics rewards that they will later encounter in the labor market. Thus, the education system functions so that individuals with lower grades, lower test scores, and smaller amounts of education come to believe that their subsequent lower earnings are fair.

*This synopsis is based on Samuel Bowles and Herbert Gintis, "The Problem with Human Capital Theory: A Marxian Critique," *American Economic Review,* May 1975, pp. 74–82; Samuel Bowles and Herbert Gintis, *Schooling in Capitalist America* (New York: Basic Books, 1976); and Herbert Gintis, "Education, Technology, and the Characteristics of Worker Productivity," *American Economic Review,* May 1971, pp. 266–279.

sally accepted, and some who accept it do so only with reservations. While there is almost universal agreement as to the positive association between education and earnings, there is disagreement as to the *reasons* for this association. Empirical testing is usually indirect in that it is first determined that those with more education and training have higher earnings, and then it is *inferred* that the additional education and training increase worker productivity and thereby cause the enhanced earnings. But the issue remains: Does education increase one's productivity? Or do those who acquire more education earn more simply because they are more able and more motivated? Do educational degrees simply identify productive workers?[53]

Most economists reject the various criticisms of human capital theory, believing that education and training directly increase productivity and earnings. But they also recognize that not all investments in education and training have a positive net present value; some investments are poor ones, and others have sharply diminishing returns. Thus, human capital theory cannot be used uncritically as a basis for public policy. For example, taken alone, massive government investments in human capital to increase economic growth may yield disappointing results. Such policies need to be balanced against alternative policies promoting new technology and greater investment in physical capital.

CHAPTER SUMMARY

1. Expenditures on education and training that increase one's productivity and future earnings in the labor market can be treated as a human capital investment decision.
2. The decision to invest in a college education entails both direct (out-of-pocket) and indirect (forgone earnings) costs. Benefits take the form of future incremental earnings.
3. There are two basic methods of comparing the benefits and costs associated with a human capital investment. The net present value approach uses a discounting formula to compare the present value of costs and benefits. If net present value is positive, it is rational to invest. The internal rate of return is the rate of discount at which the net present value of the investment is zero. If the internal rate of return exceeds the interest rate, it is rational to invest.
4. Most empirical studies suggest that the rate of return on investing in a college education has ranged from 10 to 15 percent.
5. The college wage premium—the percentage differential in the earnings of college and high school graduates—has varied significantly over time, rising rapidly since 1979. Changes in the supply of and the demand for college and high school graduates can be used to explain changes in the college wage premium.
6. From a private perspective, the human capital decision excludes public subsidies to education, considers after-tax earnings, and ignores any social or external benefits associated with education. The social perspective includes public subsidies and external benefits and considers before-tax earnings.

[53]For excellent elaborations of the criticisms of human capital theory, see Bobbie McCrackin, "Education's Contribution to Productivity and Economic Growth," *Economic Review* (Federal Reserve Bank of Atlanta), November 1984, pp. 8–23; and Gian Singh Sahota, "Theories of Personal Income Distribution: A Survey," *Journal of Economic Literature*, March 1978, pp. 11–19.

7 The demand for human capital curve and the supply of investment funds curve can be combined to explain why various people invest in different amounts of human capital. Ability differences, discrimination, and varying access to financial resources all help explain differences in education and earnings among individuals.

8 The money market may provide funds for human capital investment on less favorable terms than for investment in physical capital, providing some justification for public subsidization of human capital investments.

9 It is useful to distinguish between general and specific on-the-job training. General training generates workers skills that are useful in all firms and industries. Specific training is useful only in the specific firm providing that training. Given competitive markets, workers will normally pay for general training provided by a firm by accepting lower wages during the training period. An exception may occur where firms must pay a legal minimum wage. Employers pay for specific training. Seeking to retain trained workers, employers may share with workers the increases in total revenue resulting from specific training.

10 Criticisms of human capital theory include the following: *(a)* By failing to recognize that a part of the expenditures on education are consumption rather than investment, empirical studies understate the rate of return on education; *(b)* empirical studies understate the rate of return on a college education by not taking into account that the jobs of college graduates are more pleasant and entail superior fringe benefits than the jobs of high school graduates; *(c)* to the extent that the incremental earnings of college graduates are due to their greater ability and not to schooling per se, the rate of return on a college education will be overstated; *(d)* if a portion of the incremental earnings of college graduates is attributable to screening, the social rate of return on a college education will be overstated.

TERMS AND CONCEPTS

investment in human capital
age-earnings profiles
net present value
time preference
discount formula
internal rate of return
college wage premium
private and social perspectives
demand for human capital curve
supply of investment funds
capital market imperfections
on-the-job training
general versus specific training
marginal revenue product
ability problem
screening hypothesis

QUESTIONS AND STUDY SUGGESTIONS

1 Why might the decision to undertake an educational program be treated as an investment? From a private perspective, what are the costs and benefits associated with obtaining a college education? What are the costs and benefits from a social perspective? Explain why it is necessary to determine the present value of costs and benefits in making a rational human capital investment decision.

2 What is the internal rate of return on a human capital investment? Given the internal rate of return, what is the appropriate investment criterion? Compare this to the criterion relevant to the present value approach.

3 Floyd is now working on a job that pays $8,000 per year. He is contemplating a 1-year automobile mechanics course that entails costs of $1,000 for books and tuition. Floyd estimates that the course will increase his income to $13,000 in each of the 3 years following completion of the course. At the end of those 3 years, Floyd plans to retire to a commune in Boulder, Colorado. The current interest rate is 10 percent. Is it economically rational for Floyd to enroll in the course?

4 Comment on each of the following statements:

a Given the work-life cycle of the "traditional" woman, it may be rational for women to invest in less human capital than men.

b Older workers are less mobile geographically than younger workers.

c An economic recession tends to stimulate college enrollments.

d One of the disadvantages of social security's benefit-reduction rate (reducing benefits when earnings exceed a certain level during retirement years) is that it biases investment away from human capital and toward bonds and stocks.

e The age-earnings profiles of Figure 4-1 clearly indicate that people with more education earn more than people with less education; therefore, personal spending on education is always a good investment.

5 What is the college wage premium? Can you explain why the premium *(a)* declined in the 1970s and *(b)* increased in the 1980s and 1990s?

6 Assume that a recent high school graduate reads in a magazine that the rate of return on a college education has been estimated to be 15 percent. What advice would you give the graduate in using this information as he or she decides whether or not to attend college?

7 Why is the internal rate of return from human capital investment subject to diminishing returns? Explain the rationale for identifying the "diminishing rate of returns to education curve" as the "demand for human capital curve." Combine the demand for human capital curve with a "supply of investment funds curve" to explain why various individuals find it rational to invest in different amounts of human capital. What are the implications of your answer for the personal distribution of income? Do you think that the educational system in the United States contributes to more or less equality in the distribution of earnings? Explain. If you wanted to reduce the degree of inequality in the distribution of earnings, what policy recommendations would you make?

8 Why might funds be available on less favorable terms for human capital investments than for physical capital investments? In your judgment, does this difference justify public subsidy in the form, say, of federal guarantees of loans to college students? What are some of the external benefits associated with education? Do you feel that these benefits justify public subsidies to education? Can you provide a rationale for the argument that public subsidies should diminish as students advance to higher and higher educational levels?

9 Describe the expected effects that college scholarships based on *(a)* student ability and *(b)* student need are likely to have on the distribution of earnings.

10 Distinguish between general and specific on-the-job training. Who normally pays for general training? Specific training? Why the difference? Are there any exceptions to these generalizations? Explain.

11 As the diagram indicates, the distribution of "ability" (here measured by IQ scores) is normal or bell-shaped, but the distribution of earnings is skewed to the right. Can you use human capital theory to reconcile these two distributions?

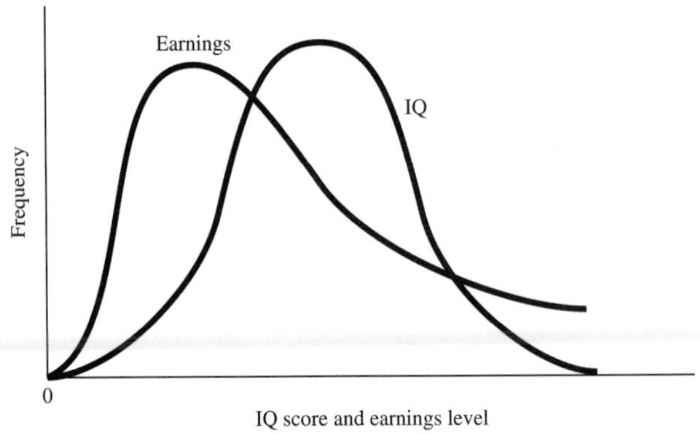

12 Data show that the age-earnings profiles of women are considerably lower and flatter than those for men. Can you explain these differences?

13 Indicate the implications of each of the following for estimates of the rate of return on a college education: *(a)* the screening hypothesis, *(b)* the possibility that a portion of one's expenditures on college should be considered as consumption rather than investment, *(c)* the fact that people who go to college are generally more able than those who do not and *(d)* the fact that jobs acquired by college graduates generally entail larger fringe benefits than the jobs of high school graduates. What implications do the ability problem and the screening hypothesis have for public policy toward education?

SELECTED REFERENCES

Becker, Gary, S.: *Human Capital,* 2d ed. (New York: National Bureau of Economic Research, 1975).

Bowen, Howard R.: *Investment in Learning* (San Francisco: Jossey-Bass Publishers, 1977).

Freeman, Richard B.: *The Overeducated American* (New York: Academic Press, 1976).

Levin, Henry M., et al.: "Symposium on the Economics of Education," *Educational Researcher,* May 1989, pp. 13–62.

Marshall, Ray, and Marc Tucker: *Thinking for a Living: Education and the Wealth of Nations* (New York: Basic Books, 1992).

Schultz, T. W.: "Investment in Human Capital," *American Economic Review,* March 1961, pp. 1–17.

Taubman, Paul: *Income Distribution and Redistribution* (Reading, Mass.: Addison-Wesley Publishing Company, 1978), chaps. 3 and 4.

Thurow, Lester: *Investment in Human Capital* (Belmont, Calif.: Wadsworth Publishing Company, Inc., 1970).

CHAPTER 5

THE DEMAND FOR LABOR

The previous three chapters have examined the supply of labor. In the present chapter our attention shifts to the demand side of the labor market. Why do Microsoft, Mobil, and Motorola wish to employ those willing to supply their particular labor services? How is Mattel's demand for labor affected by increases in the demand for the toys that it produces? What factors alter Maytag's and McDonald's demand for labor? Why might Monsanto adjust its level of employment more than Merck when wage rates change for a particular type of labor?

Answers to these and related questions motivate our discussion of labor demand. Then, in Chapter 6, we will combine our understanding of labor demand and labor supply to explain how wage rates are determined.

The specific goals of the present chapter are as follows. Our first objective is to explain how the short-run demand curve for labor is derived. In this discussion we note how a firm's short-run demand curve relates to the marginal productivity of labor and the way in which it varies according to whether a firm is selling its output in a competitive or noncompetitive product market. Next, the long-run demand for labor is presented and compared with the short-run demand curve. Third, we examine the process by which the labor demand curves of individual firms are summed to obtain the market demand curve for a particular type of labor. Fourth, the principal factors influencing the elasticity of demand for labor are enumerated and explained. Next, we discuss the factors that cause the market demand for labor curve to shift leftward or rightward.
5-1 Finally, we provide several real-world examples to help illustrate and reinforce the central ideas discussed in this chapter.

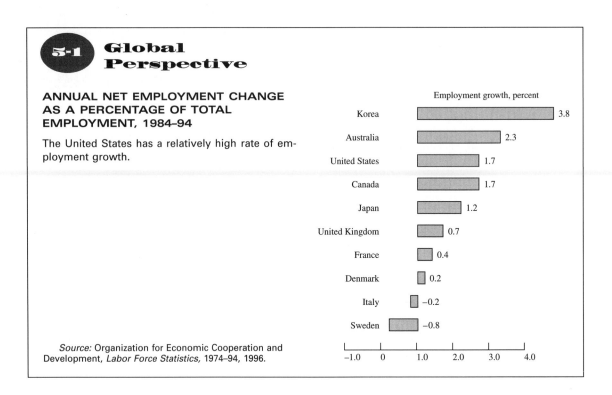

5-1 Global Perspective

ANNUAL NET EMPLOYMENT CHANGE AS A PERCENTAGE OF TOTAL EMPLOYMENT, 1984–94

The United States has a relatively high rate of employment growth.

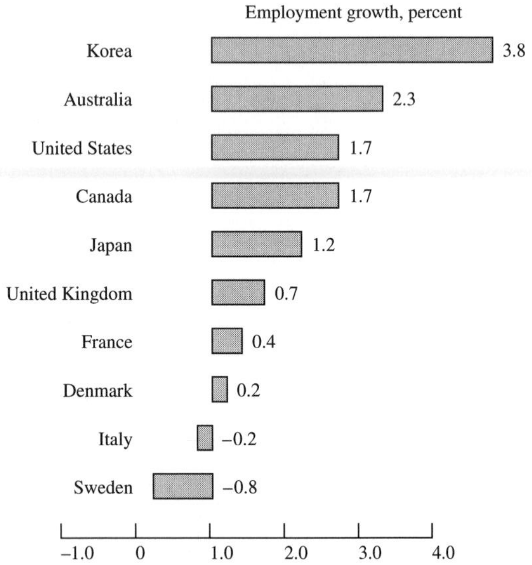

Source: Organization for Economic Cooperation and Development, *Labor Force Statistics,* 1974–94, 1996.

DERIVED DEMAND FOR LABOR

It should be noted at the outset that the demand for labor, or for any other productive resource, is a ***derived demand.*** This means that the demand for labor depends on, or is derived from, the demand for the product or service it is helping to produce or provide. In manufacturing labor is demanded for the contribution it makes to the production of such products as automobiles, television sets, or loaves of bread. Thus, a decrease in the demand for, say, automobiles will reduce the demand for automobile workers. In the service sector labor is demanded by firms because it directly provides benefits to consumers. An increase in the demand for child care services, for example, will increase the derived demand for child care workers.

The fact that the demand for labor is a derived demand means that the strength of the demand for any particular type of labor will depend on (1) how productive that labor is in helping to create some product or service and (2) the market value of that item. If type A labor is highly productive in turning out product X, and if product X is highly valued by society, then a strong demand for type A labor will exist. Conversely, the demand will be weak for some kind of labor that is relatively unproductive in producing a good or service that is not of great value to society.

These observations point the way for our discussion. We will find that the immediate determinants of the demand for labor are labor's marginal productivity and the value (price) of its output. Let's begin by examining the short-run production function for a typical firm and then introduce the role of product price. Although our discussion will be cast in terms of a firm producing a particular good, bear in mind that the concepts developed apply equally to firms hiring workers to "produce" services.

A FIRM'S SHORT-RUN PRODUCTION FUNCTION

A ***production function*** is a relationship between quantities of resources (inputs) and the corresponding production outcomes (output). We will assume that the production process entails just two inputs—labor L and capital K. To simplify further, let's suppose that a single type of labor is being employed or, in other words, that the firm is hiring homogeneous inputs of labor. Furthermore, initially we examine the firm as it operates in the short run, *a period in which at least one resource is fixed.* In this case the fixed resource is the firm's stock of capital—its plant, machinery, and other equipment. As shown in equation (5-1)

$$TP_{SR} = f(L, \overline{K}) \tag{5-1}$$

the firm's total product in the short run (TP_{SR}) is a function of a variable input L (labor) and a fixed input K (capital).

Total, Marginal, and Average Product

What happens to the total product (output) as successive inputs of labor are added to a fixed plant? The answer is provided in Figure 5-1, where the upper graph (a) shows a short-run production function or total product (TP) curve and the lower graph (b) displays the corresponding curves for the marginal product of labor (MP) and the average product of labor (AP).

In the short run, ***total product*** (TP) shown in (a) is *the total output produced by each combination of the variable resource (labor) and the fixed amount of capital.* The ***marginal product*** (MP) of labor is *the change in total product associated with the addition of one more unit of labor.* It is the absolute change in TP and can be found by drawing a line tangent to the TP curve at any point and then determining the slope of that line. For example, notice line mm', which is drawn tangent to point Z on the TP curve. The slope of mm' is zero, and this is the marginal product MP as shown at point z on the MP curve in the lower graph. The ***average product*** (AP) of labor is *the total product divided by the number of labor units.* Geometrically, it is measured as the slope of any straight line drawn from the origin to or through any particular point on the TP curve. For example, observe line $0a$, which radiates from the origin through point Y on TP. The slope ($\Delta TP/\Delta L$) of $0a$ tells us the AP associated with this particular combination of TP and labor input L. For example, if TP were 20 at point Y, and L were 4, then AP would be 5 (= 20/4). This is the value of the slope of line $0a$, which as measured from the origin is the *vertical* "rise" (= 20) divided by the *horizontal* "run" (= 4). If we assume that labor units are labor hours, rather than workers, then this slope measures output per worker hour.

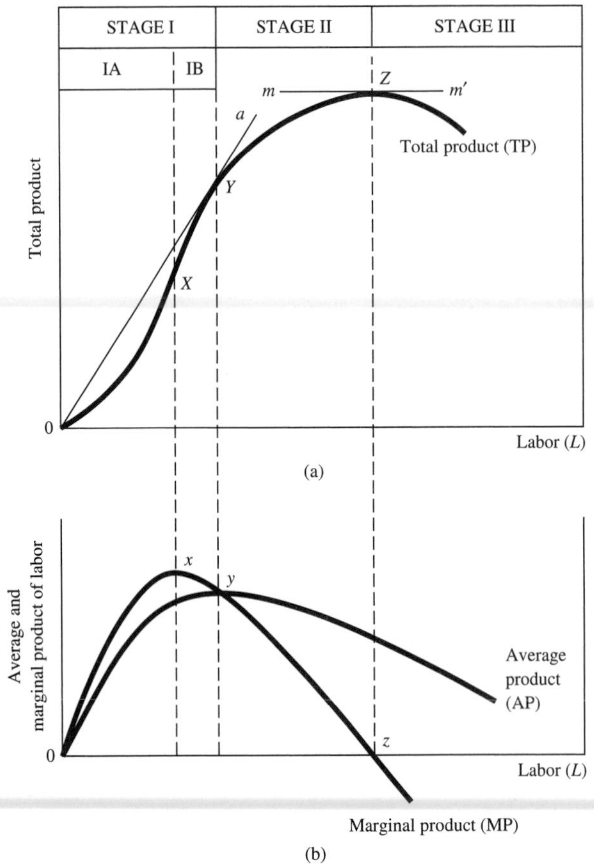

FIGURE 5-1 **A FIRM'S SHORT-RUN PRODUCTION FUNCTION**
As labor is added to a fixed amount of capital, total product will eventually increase by diminishing amounts, reach a maximum, and then decline as shown in (a). Marginal products in (b) reflect the changes in total product associated with each additional input of labor. The relationship between marginal product and average product is such that MP intersects AP where AP is at its maximum. The *yz* segment of the MP curve in stage II is the basis for the short-run labor demand curve.

Stages of Production

The relationships between total, marginal, and average products are important. To show these relationships *and* to permit us later to isolate the region in which the firm will operate if it decides to do so, we have divided the total product curve (TP) into three stages, but we have also subdivided stage I into two parts. Over segment $0X$ of the TP curve—or stated alternatively, within part IA of stage I—the total product curve is increasing at an *increasing* rate. As observed in the lower graph, this implies that MP ($= \Delta TP/\Delta L$) necessarily is rising. For example, suppose that the TPs associated with the first three workers were 3, 8, and 15, respectively. The corresponding MPs would be 3 (= 3 − 0), 5 (= 8 − 3), and 7 (= 15 − 8). Note, too, from the lower graph that because MP exceeds average product (AP), the latter also is rising. This is a matter of arithmetic necessity: Whenever a number that is greater than the average of some total is added to that total, the average must rise. In the present context, marginal product is the addition to total product while average product is the average of total product. Hence, when MP exceeds AP, then AP must rise.[1]

Next, observe segment *XY*—or stage IB—of the production function in Figure 5-1(a). The total product curve is now such that TP is still increasing as more workers are hired, but at a *decreasing* rate, and therefore MP (graph b) is declining. Notice that MP reached its maximum at point *x* in the lower graph and that this point corresponds to point *X* on the production function. But beyond points *X* and *x*, MP falls. We see, however, that even though MP is now falling, it still is above AP, and hence AP continues to rise. Finally, observe that the end of range IB of stage I is marked by the point at which AP is at its maximum and just equals MP (point *y*). The fact that AP is at a maximum at point *Y* on the TP curve is confirmed by ray 0*a*. The slope of 0*a*—which, remember, measures AP—is greater than would be the slope of any other straight line drawn between the origin and a specific point on the TP curve.

In stage II, later referred to as the zone of production, total product continues to rise at a diminishing rate. Consequently, MP continues to decline. But now AP also falls because MP finally is less than AP. Again, simple arithmetic tells us that when a number (MP) that is less than the current average of a total is added to that total (TP), then the average (AP) must fall.

At the dividing line between stages II and III, TP reaches its maximum point *Z* and MP becomes zero (point *z*), indicating that beyond this point additional workers detract from total product. In stage III, TP falls and MP is therefore negative, the latter causing AP to continue to decline.

Law of Diminishing Marginal Returns

Why do TP, MP, and AP behave in the manner shown in Figure 5-1? Let's focus on marginal product, keeping in mind that changes in MP are related to changes in TP and AP. Why does MP rise, then fall, and eventually become negative? It is *not* because the quality of labor declines as more of it is hired; remember that all workers are assumed to be identical. Rather, the reason is that the fixed capital at first gets used increasingly productively as more workers are employed but eventually becomes more and more burdened. Imagine a firm that possesses a fixed amount of machinery and equipment. As this firm hires its initial workers, each worker will contribute more to output than the previous worker because the firm will be better able to use its machinery and equipment. Time will be saved because each worker can specialize in a task and will no longer have to scramble from one job operation to another. Successively greater increases in output will occur because the new works will permit

[1]You raise your cumulative grade-point average by earning grades in the most recent (marginal) semester that are higher than your current average.

capital equipment to be used more intensively during the day. Thus, for a time the added, or marginal, product of extra workers will rise.

These increases in marginal product cannot be realized indefinitely. As still more labor is added to the fixed machinery and equipment, the ***law of diminishing marginal returns*** will take hold. This law states that *as successive units of a variable resource (labor) are added to a fixed resource (capital), beyond some point the marginal product attributable to each additional unit of the variable resource will decline.* At some point labor will become so abundant relative to the fixed capital that additional workers cannot add as much to output as did previous workers. For example, an added worker may have to wait in line to use the machines. At the extreme, the continuous addition of labor will so overcrowd the plant that the marginal product of still more labor will become negative, reducing total product (stage III).

Zone of Production

The characteristics of TP, MP, and AP discussed in Figure 5-1 are summarized in Table 5-1. In reviewing this table, notice that stage II of the production function is designated as the ***zone of production.*** To see why, let's establish that the left-hand boundary of stage II in Figure 5-1 is where the efficiency of labor—as measured by its average product—is at a maximum. Similarly, the right-hand boundary is where the efficiency of the fixed resource capital is maximized. Notice first that at point *Y* on TP and *y* on AP and MP, total product *per unit of labor* is at its maximum. This is shown both by ray 0*a*, which is the steepest line that can be drawn from the origin to any point on TP, and by the AP curve, since AP *is* TP/*L*. Next, note that at point *Z* on TP and *z* on MP, total product is at a maximum. Because capital (*K*) is fixed, this implies that the average product of *K* is also at a maximum. That is, total product *per unit of capital* is greater at the right-hand boundary of stage II than at any other point. The generalization here is that if a firm chooses to operate, *it will want to produce at a level of*

TABLE 5-1 PRODUCTION FUNCTION VARIABLES: A SUMMARY

			Total product, TP_L	Marginal product, MP_L	Average product, AP_L
	STAGE I	**IA**	Increasing at an increasing rate	Increasing and greater than AP	Increasing
		IB	Increasing at a decreasing rate	Declining but greater than AP	Increasing
Zone of Production	**STAGE II**		Increasing at a decreasing rate	Declining and less than AP	Declining
	STAGE III		Declining	Negative and less than AP	Declining

output where changes in labor contribute to increasing efficiency of either labor or capital.[2]

This is *not* the case in either stage I or III. In stage I, additions to labor *increase* both the efficiency of labor *and* the efficiency of capital. The former can easily be seen by the rising AP curve; the latter is true since capital is constant and TP is rising, thereby increasing the average product of capital (= TP/*K*). The firm therefore will desire to move at least to the left-hand boundary of stage II.

What about stage III? Inspection of Figure 5-1(a) and (b) shows that the addition of labor *reduces* the efficiency of *both* labor and capital. Notice that the average product of labor is falling. Also, because there is less total product than before, the TP/*K* ratio is declining. Stated differently, the firm will not operate in stage III because it can *add* to the efficiency of labor and capital and to its total product by *reducing* employment.

Conclusion? The profit-maximizing or loss-minimizing firm that chooses to operate will face a marginal product curve indicated by line segment *yz* in Figure 5-1(b). *This MP curve is the underlying basis for the firm's short-run demand for labor curve.*

SHORT-RUN DEMAND FOR LABOR: THE PERFECTLY COMPETITIVE SELLER

To see how segment *yz* in Figure 5-1(b) relates to labor demand, let's next (1) transform the TP and MP information in that figure to hypothetical numbers via a table and (2) convert our analysis from output to monetary terms. Employers, after all, make their decisions on how many workers to hire in terms of *revenues* and *costs,* rather than in output terms.

Consider Table 5-2. Columns 1 to 3 are merely numerical illustrations of the relationships within the zone of production, showing total and marginal product but omitting average product. To simplify, we have identified only the range of labor inputs over which diminishing marginal productivity sets in. Recalling our earlier discussion of the demand for labor as a derived demand, note that column 4 shows the price of the product that is being produced. The fact that this $2 price does not decline as more output is produced and sold indicates that the firm is selling its output in a perfectly competitive market. In technical terms, the firm's *product* demand curve is perfectly elastic; the firm is a "price taker." For example, this firm may be one that is selling standardized products such as grain or fresh fish.

Multiplying column 2 by column 4, we obtain total revenue (sometimes called "total revenue product") in column 5. From these total revenue data we can easily compute ***marginal revenue product*** (MRP), which is *the increase (change) in total revenue resulting from the employment of each additional labor unit.* These figures are shown in column 6. The MRP schedule shown by columns 1 and 6 is strictly

[2]This generalization applies only to a competitive firm. For an imperfectly competitive firm such as a monopoly, *only* stage III is necessarily a nonprofit maximizing area. In maximizing profits, a monopolist may restrict output and therefore employment to some point in stage I.

TABLE 5-2 DEMAND FOR LABOR: FIRM SELLING IN A PERFECTLY COMPETITIVE PRODUCT MARKET (HYPOTHETICAL DATA)

(1) Units of labor, L	(2) TP	(3) MP	(4) Product price, P	(5) Total revenue, TR	(6) MRP ($\Delta TR/\Delta L$)	(7) VMP ($MP \times P$)
4	15		$2	$30		
5	27	12	2	54	$24	$24
6	36	9	2	72	18	18
7	42	6	2	84	12	12
8	45	3	2	90	6	6
9	46	1	2	92	2	2

proportionate to the MP schedule, shown by columns 1 and 3. In this case, MRP is *twice* as large as MP because price is $2.

Columns 1 and 6—the MRP schedule—constitute the firm's ***short-run labor demand curve.*** To justify and explain this assertion we must first understand the rule that a profit-maximizing firm will apply in determining the number of workers to employ. *A profit-maximizing employer should hire workers so long as each successive worker adds more to the firm's total revenue than to its total cost.* We have just noted that the amount that each successive unit of labor adds to total revenue is measured by MRP. The amount that a worker adds to total costs is measured by ***marginal wage cost*** (MWC), defined as *the change in total wage cost resulting from the employment of one more labor unit.* Thus, we can abbreviate our rule by saying that the profit-maximizing firm should hire units of labor up to the point at which MRP = MWC.[3] If at some level of employment MRP exceeds MWC, it will be profitable to employ more labor. If for some level of employment MWC exceeds MRP, the firm will increase its profits by hiring less labor.

Let's now assume that the employer for whom Table 5-2 is relevant is hiring labor under purely competitive conditions. This means the firm is a "wage-taker" in that it employs a negligible portion of the total labor supply and therefore exerts no perceptible influence upon the wage rate. Perhaps this firm is, say, a fish-processing firm that is hiring people to clean fish. The market wage rate is "given" to the employer, and it follows that total wage cost (the wage bill) increases by the amount of the wage rate W for each additional unit of labor hired. In other words, the wage rate and marginal wage cost are equal. We can thus modify our MRP = MWC rule for the firm hiring competitively and restate it as the MRP = W rule. The profit-maximizing firm that is a perfectly competitive employer of labor should employ units of labor up to the point at which marginal revenue product MRP equals the wage rate W.

We now can apply the MRP = W rule to demonstrate our earlier assertion: The MRP schedule shown in columns 1 and 6, derived directly from the MRP data from the zone

[3]The rationale for this rule is the same as that for the marginal revenue equals marginal cost (MR = MC) rule, which identifies the profit-maximizing output in the product market. The difference is that the MRP = MWC rule is in terms of *inputs* of labor, while the MR = MC rule is in terms of *outputs* of product.

of production, *is* the firm's short-run labor demand curve. The MRP data from columns 1 and 6 are graphed in Figure 5-2 to demonstrate this point. This schedule and curve indicate the amount of labor this firm would demand at several separate competitively determined wage rates. First, let's suppose that the wage rate is $23.9\bar{9}, an amount infinitesimally less than $24. This firm will decide to employ 5 units of labor because it either adds to profits or subtracts from losses by hiring these units of labor. But the firm will not employ the sixth, seventh, and further units because MRP < *W* for each of them.

Next, suppose that the wage rate falls to $11.99. The MRP = *W* rule indicates that the firm will now also hire the sixth and seventh units of labor. If the wage rate falls further to, say, $1.99, it will employ 9 units of labor. We conclude then that *the MRP curve in Figure 5-2 is the firm's short-run labor demand curve* because each point on it indicates the quantity of labor that a firm will demand at each possible wage rate that might exist. Any curve which embodies this information on wage rate and quantity of labor demanded is, by definition, the firm's labor demand curve.

One further point needs to be made: Where there is perfect competition in the product market, a firm's marginal revenue product or labor demand curve is also the ***value of marginal product*** (VMP) curve. *The value of marginal product is the extra output in dollar terms that accrues to society when an extra unit of labor is employed.* Columns 1 and 7 in Table 5-2 show the VMP schedule in our example. Notice that VMP is determined by multiplying marginal product MP (column 3) by the product price (column 4). We observe in this case that VMP, the value of the marginal product, is identical to MRP, the extra revenue accruing to the firm when it adds a unit of labor

FIGURE 5-2 THE LABOR DEMAND CURVE OF A PERFECTLY COMPETITIVE SELLER
Application of the MRP = *W* rule reveals that the MRP curve is the firm's short-run labor demand curve. Under perfect competition in the product market, MRP = VMP and the labor demand curve slopes downward solely because of diminishing marginal productivity.

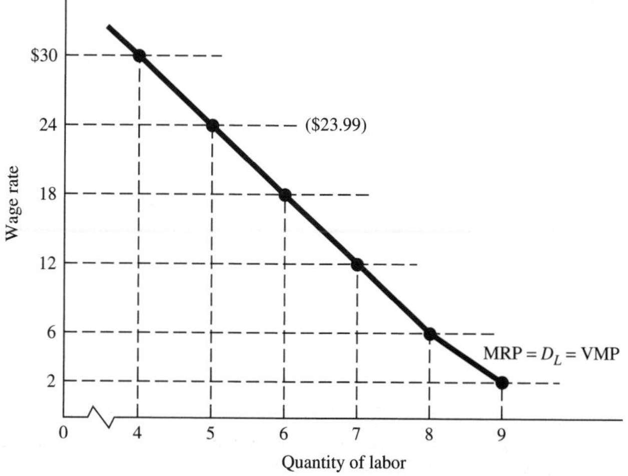

(column 6). For this reason we label the demand for labor curve in Figure 5-2 as VMP, as well as MRP.

What is the logic underlying the equality of VMP and MRP where perfect competition prevails in the product market? Because the competitive firm is a price-taker, it can sell as many units of output as it desires at the market price (= \$2). The sale of *each* additional unit of the product adds the product price (= \$2) to the firm's total revenue; therefore, the seller's *marginal revenue* (MR) is constant and is equal to the product price. In this situation, the extra *revenue* to the firm from employing an additional labor unit (= MR × MP) equals the social *value* of the extra output (= P × MP) contributed by that unit of labor.

SHORT-RUN DEMAND FOR LABOR: THE IMPERFECTLY COMPETITIVE SELLER

Most firms in our economy do *not* sell their products in purely competitive markets; rather, they sell under imperfectly competitive conditions. That is, the firms are monopolies, oligopolies, or monopolistically competitive sellers. When a firm can set its price—rather than being forced to accept a market-determined price—it has some monopoly power.

The change in assumptions about product market conditions from pure competition to imperfect competition alters our analysis in an important way. Because of product uniqueness or differentiation, the imperfectly competitive seller's product demand curve is downward-sloping rather than perfectly elastic. This means that the firm must lower its price to sell the output contributed by each successive worker. Furthermore, because we assume that the firm cannot engage in price discrimination, it must lower the price not only on the last unit produced but also on all other units, which otherwise would have commanded a higher price. The sale of an extra unit of output therefore does *not* add its full price to the firm's marginal revenue, as it does in perfect competition. To obtain the marginal revenue for the imperfectly competitive seller, one must subtract the potential revenue lost on the other units from the new revenue gained from the last unit. Because marginal revenue is less than the product price, the imperfectly competitive seller's marginal revenue product (= MR × MP) is less than that of the perfectly competitive seller (= P × MP). Recall that the perfectly competitive firm suffers no decline in marginal revenue as it sells the extra output of added workers.

Conclusion: The MRP or labor demand curve of the purely competitive seller falls for a *single* reason—marginal product diminishes as more units of labor are employed. But the MRP or labor demand curve of the imperfectly competitive seller declines for *two* reasons—marginal product falls as more units of labor are employed *and* product price declines as output increases. Table 5-3 takes this second consideration into account. The production data of columns 1 to 3 are precisely the same as in Table 5-2, but in column 4 we recognize that product price must be lowered to sell the marginal product of each successive worker.

It is worth reemphasizing that the lower price accompanying each increase in output applies not only to the output produced by each additional worker but also to all prior units that otherwise could have been sold at a higher price. For example, the fifth

TABLE 5-3 DEMAND FOR LABOR: FIRM SELLING IN AN IMPERFECTLY COMPETITIVE PRODUCT MARKET (HYPOTHETICAL DATA)

(1) Units of labor, L	(2) TP	(3) MP	(4) Product price, P	(5) Total revenue, TR	(6) MRP ($\Delta TR/\Delta L$)	(7) VMP ($MP \times P$)
4	15		$2.60	$39.00		
5	27	12	2.40	64.80	$25.80	$28.80
6	36	9	2.20	79.20	14.40	19.80
7	42	6	2.10	88.20	9.00	12.60
8	45	3	2.00	90.00	1.80	6.00
9	46	1	1.90	87.40	−2.60	1.80

worker's marginal product is 12 units, and these 12 units can be sold for $2.40 each or, as a group, for $28.80. This is the value of the marginal product (VMP) of labor, that is, the value of the added output from society's perspective (column 7). But the MRP of the fifth worker is only $25.80. Why the $3.00 difference? The answer is that in order to sell the 12 units associated with the fifth worker, the firm must accept a $.20 price cut on *each* of the 15 units produced by the previous workers—units that could have been sold for $2.60 each. Thus, the MRP of the fifth worker is only $25.80 [= $28.80 − (15 × $.20)]. Similarly, the sixth worker's MRP is only $14.40. Although the 9 units produced are worth $2.20 each in the market and therefore their VMP is $19.80, the worker does *not* add $19.80 to the firm's total revenue when account is taken of the $.20 price cut that must be taken on the 27 units produced by the previous workers. Specifically, the sixth worker's MRP is $14.40 [= $19.80 − (27 × $.20)]. The other MRP figures in column 6 of Table 5-3 are similarly explained. Comparison of columns 6 and 7 reveals that at each level of employment, VMP—the value of the extra product to buyers—exceeds MRP—the extra revenue to the firm. The efficiency implications of this difference will be examined in Chapter 6.

As in the case of the purely competitive seller, application of the MRP = W rule to the MRP curve will yield the conclusion that the MRP curve *is* the firm's labor demand curve. However, by plotting the imperfectly competitive seller's MRP or labor demand curve D_L in Figure 5-3 and comparing it with the demand curve in Figure 5-2, we find visual support for an important generalization: *All else being equal, the imperfectly competitive seller's labor demand curve is less elastic than that of the purely competitive seller.* It is not surprising that the firm that possesses monopoly power is less responsive to wage rate changes than the purely competitive seller. The tendency for the imperfectly competitive seller to add fewer workers as the wage rate declines is merely the labor market reflection of the firm's restriction of output in the product market. Other things being equal, the seller possessing monopoly power will find it profitable to produce less output than a purely competitive industry. In producing this smaller output, the seller with monopoly power will employ fewer workers.

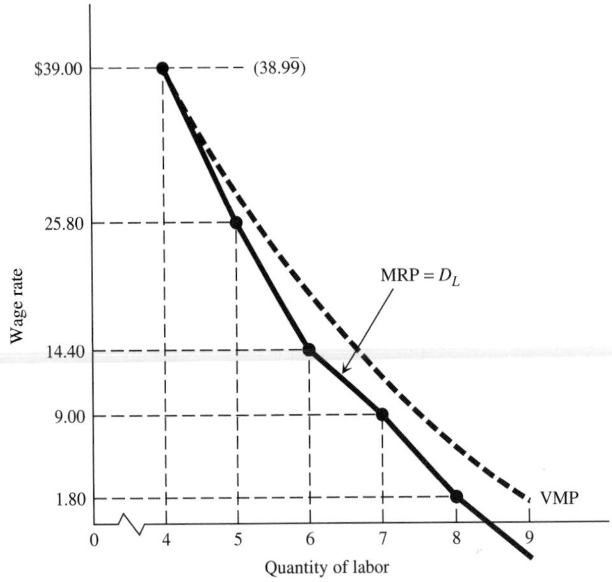

FIGURE 5-3 THE LABOR DEMAND FOR AN IMPERFECTLY COMPETITIVE SELLER
Under imperfect competition in the product market, the firm's demand curve will slope downward because marginal product diminishes as more units of labor are employed *and* because the firm must reduce the product price on all units of output as more output is produced. Also, the MRP (= MR × MP) for the imperfect competitor is less than the VMP (= P × MP) at all levels of employment beyond the first unit.

Finally, notice that the VMP schedule that is also plotted in Figure 5-3 lies to the right of the firm's D_L = MRP curve. This visually depicts our previous conclusion: The marginal revenue accruing to an imperfectly competitive seller from hiring an additional unit of labor is less than the market value of the extra output the unit of labor helps produce [(MRP = MR × MP) < (VMP = P × MP)].

QUICK REVIEW 5-1

- The demand for labor is derived from the demand for the product or service which it helps produce.
- As labor is added to a fixed amount of capital, the total product of labor first increases at an increasing rate, then increases at a diminishing rate, and then declines; this implies that the marginal product of labor first rises, then falls, and finally becomes negative.
- Because a perfectly competitive firm will hire employees up to where WR = MRP, the MRP curve is the firm's labor demand curve.
- The labor demand curve for an imperfectly competitive seller will not be as strong as for a perfectly competitive seller because the former must lower its product price on all units of output as more output is produced (MR < P).

Your Turn: Assume labor is the only variable input and that an additional unit of labor increases total output from 65 to 73 units. If the product sells for $4 per unit in a perfectly competitive market, what is the MRP of this additional worker? Would MRP be higher or lower than this amount if the firm were a monopolist and had to lower its price to sell all 73 units? (Answers: See page 625.)

THE LONG-RUN DEMAND FOR LABOR[4]

Thus far, we have derived and discussed the firm's short-run production function [equation (5-1)] and demand for labor, which presuppose that labor is a variable input and that the amount of capital is fixed. We now turn to the long-run production relationship shown in equation (5-2), where we find that *both* labor and capital are variable. Once again we assume that L and K are the only two inputs and that labor is homogeneous.

$$\mathrm{TP}_{\mathrm{LR}} = f(L, K) \tag{5-2}$$

The ***long-run demand for labor*** *is a schedule or curve indicating the amount of labor that firms will employ at each possible wage rate when both labor and capital are variable.* The long-run labor demand curve declines because a wage change produces a short-run output effect and a long-run substitution effect, which together alter the firm's optimal level of employment.

Output Effect

As it relates to labor demand, the ***output effect*** (also called the scale effect) is *the change in employment resulting solely from the effect of the wage change on the employer's costs of production.* This effect is present in the short-run period and is demonstrated in Figure 5-4. Under normal circumstances, a decline in the wage rate shifts a firm's marginal cost curve downward, as from MC_1 to MC_2. That is, the firm can produce any additional unit of output at less cost than before. The reduced marginal cost (MC_2) relative to the firm's marginal revenue (MR) means that marginal revenue now exceeds marginal costs for each of the Q_1 to Q_2 units. Adhering to the MR = MC profit-maximizing rule, the firm will now find it profitable to increase its output from Q_1 to Q_2. To accomplish this it will wish to expand its employment of labor.

Substitution Effect

As it relates to long-run labor demand, the ***substitution effect*** is *the change in employment resulting solely from a change in the relative price of labor, output being held*

[4]We provide a more advanced derivation of the long-run demand for labor curve in the Appendix of this chapter. There, and in the discussion that follows, we ignore the long-run "profit-maximizing effect" of a wage rate change. For simplicity, we focus on the short-run output effect and the long-run substitution effect.

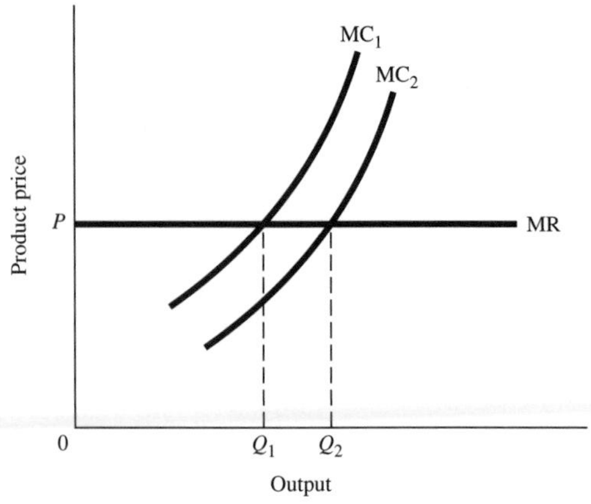

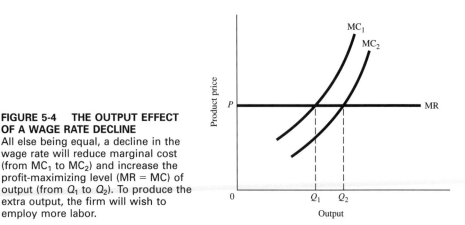

FIGURE 5-4 THE OUTPUT EFFECT OF A WAGE RATE DECLINE
All else being equal, a decline in the wage rate will reduce marginal cost (from MC_1 to MC_2) and increase the profit-maximizing level (MR = MC) of output (from Q_1 to Q_2). To produce the extra output, the firm will wish to employ more labor.

constant. In the short run, capital is fixed, and therefore, substitution in production between labor and capital *cannot* occur. In the long run, however, the firm can respond to a wage reduction by substituting the relatively less-expensive labor in the production process for some types of capital. This fact means that the long-run response to a wage change will be greater than the short-run response. In other words, the long-run demand for labor will be more elastic than the short-run demand curve.

The Combined Effects

In Figure 5-5 the substitution and output effects are summarized. In Figure 5-6 we use these ideas to depict a long-run labor demand curve D_{LR}. Initially, suppose that the firm faces the short-run labor demand curve D_{SR} and also that the initial equilibrium wage rate and equilibrium quantity of labor are W_1 and Q as shown by point *a*. Now suppose that the wage rate declines from W_1 to W_2, resulting in an *output effect* that increases employment to Q_1 at *b*. In the long run, however, capital is variable, and therefore, a *substitution effect* also occurs that further increases the quantity of labor employed to Q_2 at point *c*. While the short-run adjustment is from *a* to *b,* the additional long-run adjustment is from *b* to *c*. The locus of the long-run adjustment points *a* and *c* determines the location of the *long-run* demand for labor curve. As observed in Figure 5-6, the long-run curve D_{LR} is more elastic than the short-run labor demand curve.

Other Factors

Several other factors tend to make a firm's long-run labor demand curve more elastic than its short-run curve. Three such factors in particular deserve mention.

1 Product Demand As we will explain shortly in our discussion of the determinants of the elasticity of labor demand, *product demand* is more elastic in the long run than in the short run, making the demand for labor more elastic the longer the period

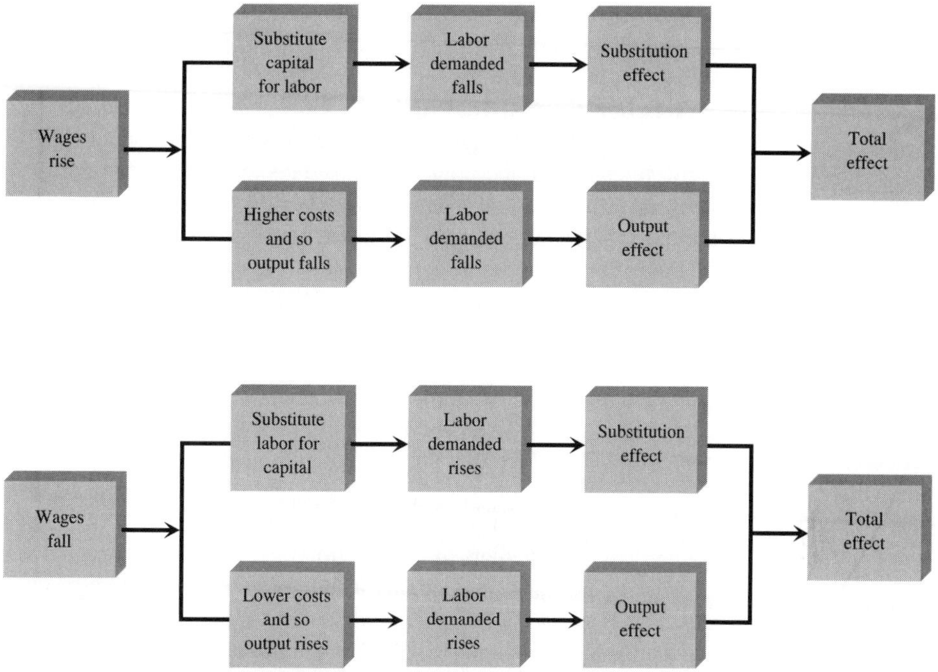

FIGURE 5-5 SUMMARY OF SUBSTITUTION AND OUTPUT EFFECTS
Labor demand curves slope downward because of the substitution effect and the output effect. For a wage increase, firms tend to (1) substitute away from labor toward capital, and (2) output falls because of higher production costs. The combined effect is less labor demanded.

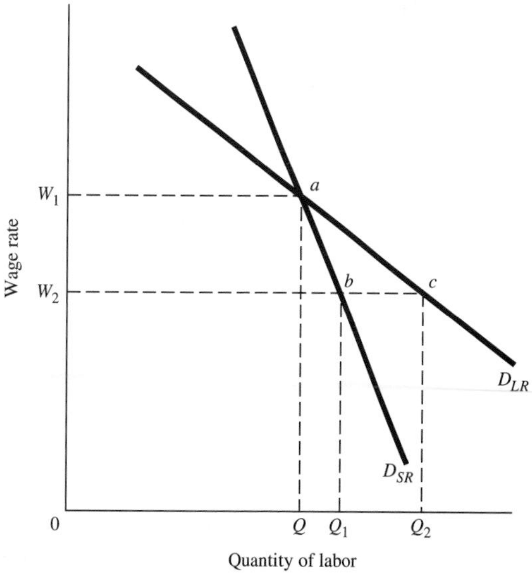

FIGURE 5-6 THE LONG-RUN LABOR DEMAND CURVE
A wage reduction from W_1 to W_2 increases the equilibrium short-run quantity of labor from Q to Q_1 *(output effect)*. In the long run, however, the firm also substitutes labor for capital, resulting in a *substitution effect* of Q_1Q_2. The long-run labor demand curve therefore results from both effects and is found by connecting points such as *a* and *c*.

of time. Other things being equal, the greater the consumer response to a product price change, the greater the firm's employment response to a wage rate change.

2 Labor–Capital Interactions Under production conditions described as "normal," a change in the quantity of one factor causes the marginal product of another factor to change in the same direction. This idea relates to the demand for labor as follows. Let's again assume that the wage rate for a particular type of labor falls, causing the quantity of labor demanded in the short run to rise. This increase in the quantity of labor itself becomes important to the long-run adjustment process, since it increases the marginal product and, hence, the MRP of capital. Just as the MRP of labor *is* the firm's short-run demand for labor, the MRP of capital *is* the firm's short-run demand for capital (labor being constant). Given the price of capital, we would therefore expect more capital to be employed, which in turn will increase the marginal product and demand for labor. Thus, the long-run employment response resulting from the wage decrease will be greater than the short-run response.

3 Technology In the long run, the technology implicitly assumed constant when we constructed our short-run production function can be expected to change in response to major, permanent movements in relative factor prices. Investors and entrepreneurs direct their greatest effort toward discovering and implementing new technologies that reduce the need for relatively higher-priced inputs. When the price of labor falls relative to the price of capital, these efforts get channeled toward technologies that economize on the use of capital and that increase the use of labor. The long-run response to the wage rate decline therefore exceeds the short-run response.

Important point: We have cast our entire discussion of the downward-sloping long-run labor demand curve in terms of a wage *decline*. You are urged to reinforce the conclusion that labor demand is more elastic in the long run than in the short run by analyzing the short- versus long-run effects of an *increase* in the wage rate.

THE MARKET DEMAND FOR LABOR

We have now demonstrated that the MRP curve derives from the MP curve in the firm's zone of production and *is* the firm's short-run demand curve for labor. We also have established that a firm's long-run demand for labor is more elastic than the short-run demand. Let's next turn our attention to the market demand for labor. At first thought, we might reason that the total or ***market demand for labor*** of a particular type can be determined by simply summing (horizontally on a graph) the labor demand curves of all firms which employ this kind of labor. Thus, if there were, say, 200 firms with labor demand curves identical to the firm portrayed in Table 5-2, we would simply multiply the amounts of labor demanded at the various wage rates by 200 and thereby determine the market demand curve. However, this simple process ignores an important aggregation problem. The problem arises because certain magnitudes (such as product price), which are correctly viewed as constant from the vantage point of the *individual firm,* must be treated as variable from the standpoint of the *entire market.*

To illustrate, let's suppose there are, say, 200 competitive firms, each with a labor demand curve identical to that shown earlier in Figure 5-2. Assume also that these firms are all producing a given product that they are selling in competition with one another. From the perspective of the *individual firm,* when the wage rate declines, the use of more labor will result in a *negligible* increase in the market supply of the product and, therefore, no change in product price. But because *all firms* experience the lower wage rate and respond by hiring more workers and increasing their outputs, there will be a *substantial* increase in the supply of the product. This change in supply will reduce the product price. This point is critical because, as we showed earlier in Table 5-2, product price is a determinant of each firm's labor demand curve. Specifically, a lower product price will reduce MRP and shift the labor demand curve of each firm to the left. This implies that the market demand for labor is in fact *less elastic* than that yielded by a simple summation of each firm's labor demand curve.[5]

Consider Figure 5-7 in which the diagram on the left (a) shows labor demand for one of the 200 firms and the diagram on the right (b) shows the market demand for labor. The individual firm is initially in equilibrium at point *c,* where the wage rate is W_1 and employment is Q_1. The labor demand curve D_{L1} is based on a product price of \$2.00, as shown in column 4 of Table 5-2. If the wage rate falls to W_2, ceteris paribus

[5]If *all* employers are monopolists in their distinct product markets, our conclusion does not hold. As pointed out in the discussion of Figure 5-3, the monopolist's labor demand curve already incorporates the declines in product price that accompany output increases. Thus, to get the market labor demand curve, one can sum the labor demand curves of the monopolists.

FIGURE 5-7 THE MARKET DEMAND CURVE FOR LABOR

The market demand curve for labor is less elastic than the simple horizontal summation of the labor demand curves of the individual employers. A lower wage includes all firms to hire more labor and produce more output, causing the supply of the product to increase. The resulting decline in product price shifts the firms' labor demand curves to the left. Consequently, total employment rises from *C* to *E* in graph (b), rather than from *C* to *E*′.

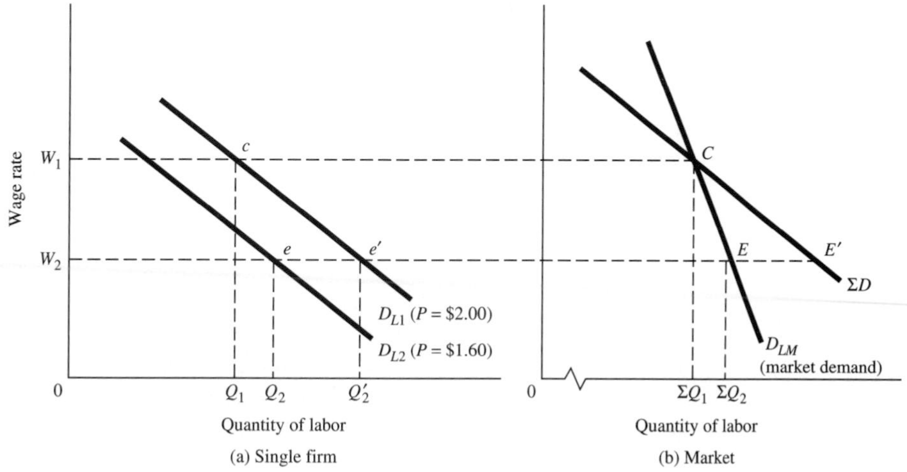

(other things being equal), the firm would now find it profitable to move to a new equilibrium at e', where it would hire Q_2' workers. But our ceteris paribus assumption does *not* hold in the context of a number of firms that are hiring this kind of labor to produce some particular product. The lower wage induces *all* of the firms to hire more labor. This increases output or product supply, which then reduces product price. This lower price—say $1.60 as compared to the original $2.00—feeds back to the labor demand curve for each firm, shifting those curves leftward as indicated by the move from D_{L1} to D_{L2} in Figure 5-7(a). In effect, each firm then recalculates its MRP or labor demand using the new lower price. Thus, each firm achieves equilibrium at point e by hiring only Q_2, as opposed to Q_2', workers at the wage rate W_2. The market labor demand curve in Figure 5-7(b) is therefore *not* curve CE', the simple horizontal summation of the demand for labor curves for all the 200 firms. Rather, it is the horizontal summation of all quantities, such as Q_1 at wage rate W_1 on D_{L1}, *and* the summation of all quantities, such as Q_2 at wage rate W_2, that fall on the "price-adjusted" market demand curve that cuts through points CE in Figure 5-7(b). As shown there, the correct price-adjusted market demand curve CE is less elastic than the incorrect "simple summation" CE' curve.

QUICK REVIEW 5-2

- The long-run demand curve for labor is more elastic than the short-run curve because in the long run there are both output and substitution effects; only an output effect occurs in the short run.
- The output effect of a wage rate change is the change in employment resulting from a change in the employer's costs of production; the substitution effect is the employment change caused by the altered price of labor relative to the price of capital.
- The market demand curve for labor is less elastic than the simple summation of the labor demand curves of individual employers; by inducing all firms to hire more labor and produce more output, the lower wage increases product supply, reduces product price, and lowers each firm's MRP.

Your Turn: In the 1970s, the United Automobile Workers greatly increased wage rates in the American auto industry. Referring to the output and substitution effects, explain how these high wages might have contributed to the decline in auto employment experienced by General Motors, Ford, and Chrysler in the 1980s. (Answer: See page 625.)

5-1

ELASTICITY OF LABOR DEMAND

We have concluded that the long-run demand curve is more elastic than the short-run curve and that the market demand for labor is less elastic than a curve derived by a simple summation of labor demand curves of individual firms. These references to elasticity raise an important unanswered question: What determines the *sensitivity* of em-

5-1 World of Work

COMPARATIVE ADVANTAGE AND THE DEMAND FOR LABOR

As it applies to international trade, the principle of comparative advantage states that total output will be greatest when each good is produced by that nation with the lower opportunity cost. For example, suppose that in the United States 15 units of chemicals must be sacrificed to produce 1 unit of raincoats, whereas in South Korea 10 units of chemicals must be sacrificed for each unit of raincoats. The opportunity cost of a unit of raincoats in South Korea thus is lower (= 10 units of chemicals) than it is in the United States (= 15 units of chemicals). South Korea, therefore, should specialize in raincoats. Similarly, the United States should specialize in producing chemicals since it has lower opportunity costs (= 1/15 raincoats) than South Korea (= 1/10 raincoats). South Korea will specialize in raincoats and trade them for chemicals; the United States will specialize in chemicals and trade them for raincoats.

How will this specialization and trade affect labor demand in the United States and South Korea? Most obviously, the demand for workers employed in the production of chemicals will rise in the United States and the demand for workers who produce raincoats will fall. The opposite outcomes will occur in South Korea. Because international trade causes both positive and negative shifts in the demand for labor, the impact on the total demand for labor in each country is uncertain. It is clear, however, that specialization will increase the total output available in the two nations. Specialization promotes the expansion of relatively efficient industries that have a comparative advantage and indirectly causes the contraction of relatively inefficient industries. This means that specialization shifts resources—including labor—toward more productive uses. If the total number of workers remains constant in each nation, each worker on average will be able to buy more output. That is, either wages will rise or the prices of goods will fall such that real earnings (= nominal earnings/price level) will increase.

It is important to note that comparative advantage, not differences in wage rates between two nations, drives international trade. Low wage rates in South Korea do *not* give it a special international advantage. High American wage rates do *not* condemn the United States to be a net importer of goods. Even if low wages in South Korea would have permitted it to produce chemicals more cheaply in dollar terms than the United States, South Korea would still benefit by specializing in raincoats and buying chemicals from the United States. By so doing, South Korea could reduce its true costs of obtaining chemicals (raincoats forgone), just as trade permits the United States to get raincoats at a lower true cost (chemicals forgone) than if it had to use domestic resources for this purpose.

ployment to a change in the wage rate; that is, what determines the ***elasticity of labor demand?*** Let's examine this topic in more detail.

The Elasticity Coefficient

The sensitivity of the quantity of labor demanded to wage rate changes is measured by the ***wage elasticity coefficient*** E_d, as shown in equation (5-3).

$$E_d = \frac{\text{percentage change in quantity of labor demanded}}{\text{percentage change in the wage rate}} \tag{5-3}$$

Since the wage rate and the quantity of labor demanded are inversely related, the elasticity coefficient will always be negative. By convention, the minus sign is taken as understood and therefore is ignored. Also, you should be aware that percentage calculations present a "reversibility" problem. For example, a wage rate increase from \$5 to

\$10 is a *100 percent* increase, while a wage decrease from \$10 to \$5 is only a *50 percent* decline. Economists therefore use the *averages* of the two wages and the *averages* of the two quantities as the bases when computing wage elasticity coefficients. In terms of our previous example, a wage change from \$10 to \$5 and one from \$5 to \$10 are each considered to be 67 percent changes {= \$5/[(\$10 + \$5)/2]}.

The equation that incorporates the averaging technique when computing wage elasticity is known as a *midpoints formula* and is shown as equation (5-4).

$$E_d = \frac{\text{change in quantity}}{\text{sum of quantities/2}} \div \frac{\text{change in wage}}{\text{sum of wages/2}} \qquad (5\text{-}4)$$

Demand is *elastic*—meaning that employers are quite responsive to a change in wage rates—if a given percentage change in the wage rate results in a larger percentage change in the quantity of labor demanded. In this case the absolute value of the elasticity coefficient will be greater than 1. Conversely, demand is *inelastic* when a given percentage change in the wage rate causes a smaller percentage change in the amount of labor demanded. In this instance E_d will be less than 1, indicating that employers are relatively insensitive to changes in wage rates. Finally, demand is *unit elastic*—meaning that the coefficient is 1—when a given percentage in the wage rate causes an equal percentage change in the amount of labor demanded.

The Total Wage Bill Rules

You may recall from basic economics that the price elasticity of demand for a product can be determined by observing what happens to total revenue when product price changes. Similar rules, called the ***total wage bill rules,*** are used to assess the wage elasticity of demand.

Consider Figure 5-8, which displays two separate labor demand curves D_{L1} and D_{L2}. Suppose initially that the wage rate is \$8, at which the firm hires 5 units of labor. The *total wage bill,* defined as $W \times Q$, in this case is \$40 (= \$8 × 5). This amount also happens to be the *total wage income,* as viewed by the five workers. Now let's suppose the wage rate rises to \$12. This increase produces two opposing effects on the wage bill. The higher wage rate tends to increase the wage bill, but the decrease in employment tends to reduce it. With D_{L1}, the firm responds to the \$4 higher wage rate by reducing the amount of labor employed from 5 to 2 units. The wage increase boosts the wage bill by \$8 (= \$4 × 2), while the decline in employment lowers it by \$24 (= \$8 × 3). The net effect is that the wage bill falls by \$16 from \$40 (= \$8 × 5) to \$24 (= \$12 × 2). *When labor demand is elastic, a change in the wage rate causes the total wage bill to move in the opposite direction.*

On the other hand, notice that for labor demand, D_{L2}, the \$4 higher wage adds more to the wage bill (\$4 × 4 = \$16) than the 1-unit decline in employment subtracts (\$8 × 1 = \$8), causing the total wage bill to rise from \$40 (= \$8 × 5) to \$48 (= \$12 × 4). *When labor demand is inelastic, a change in the wage rate causes the total wage bill to move in the same direction.* Finally, *where labor demand is unit elastic (= 1), a change in the wage rate leaves the total wage bill unchanged.*

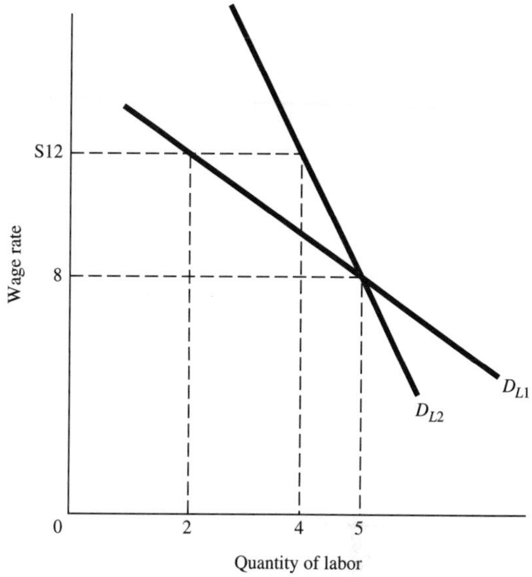

FIGURE 5-8 THE TOTAL WAGE BILL RULES
If a change in the wage rate causes the total wage bill ($W \times Q$) to change in the opposite direction, then labor demand is elastic. This is the case along the \$8 to \$12 segment of D_{L1}, where the total wage bill falls from \$40 (= \$8 × 5) to \$24 (= \$12 × 2) when the wage rate rises from \$8 to \$12. In the case of labor demand D_{L2}, however, this same wage increase causes the total wage bill to rise from \$40 to \$48 (= \$12 × 4). This second situation supports the generalization that when demand is inelastic, the wage rate and the total wage bill change in the same direction.

We can confirm the results of the total wage bill tests by using the midpoints formula [equation (5-4)] to compute elasticity coefficients for the appropriate segments of D_{L1} and D_{L2} in Figure 5-8. The \$8 to \$12 wage change is a 40 percent increase {= \$4/[(\$8 + \$12)/2]}, while we see from D_{L1} that the 3-unit change in quantity is an 86 percent decline {= 3/[(5 + 2)/2]}. Because the percentage decrease in quantity exceeds the percentage increase in the wage, labor demand is elastic (the wage bill falls as the wage increases). In the case of D_{L2}, the same 40 percent rise in the wage produces only a 22 percent employment decline {= 1/[(5 + 4)/2]}; hence, demand is inelastic (the wage bill increases as the wage rises).

Determinants of Elasticity

What determines the elasticity of the market demand for labor? The theoretical generalizations are as follows.[6]

1 Elasticity of Product Demand Because the demand for labor is a derived demand, the elasticity of demand for labor's output will influence the elasticity of demand for labor. Other things being equal, *the greater the price elasticity of product demand, the greater the elasticity of labor demand.* It is quite simple to see why this is so. If the wage rate falls, the cost of producing the product will decline. This means a decline in the price of the product and an increase in the quantity demanded. If the

[6]These generalizations were developed in 1890 by Alfred Marshall in his *Principles of Economics* (London: Macmillan Publishing Company, 1890) and refined by John R. Hicks, *The Theory of Wages,* 2d ed. (New York: St. Martin's Press, 1966), pp. 241–247. For this reason they are often referred to as the "Hicks-Marshall rules of derived demand."

elasticity of product demand is great, that increase in the quantity of the product demanded will be large and thus necessitate a large increase in the quantity of labor to produce that additional output. This implies an elastic demand for labor. But if the demand for the product is inelastic, the increase in the amount of the product demanded will be small, as will be the increase in the quantity of labor demanded. This suggests that the demand for labor would be inelastic.

This generalization has two noteworthy implications. First, other things being equal, the greater the monopoly power an individual firm possesses in the product market, the less elastic is its demand for labor. This is confirmed by Figures 5-2 and 5-3, discussed previously. Recall that in Figure 5-2 the firm is selling its product in a perfectly competitive market, implying that it is a price-taker facing a perfectly elastic product demand curve. The resulting demand for labor curve slopes downward solely because of diminishing returns. Contrast that curve to the one for the imperfectly competitive seller shown in Figure 5-3. This firm's product demand curve is less elastic, as evidenced by marginal revenue being less than price (Table 5-3). Thus, the labor demand curve in Figure 5-3 also is less elastic; it slopes downward not only because of diminishing marginal productivity but also because of the less than perfectly elastic product demand, meaning that product price falls with increased output.

A second implication is that labor demand will be more elastic in the long run than in the short run. One reason that wage elasticity tends to be greater in the long run is because price elasticity of product demand is greater in the long run. Consumers are often creatures of habit and only slowly change their buying behavior in response to a price change. Coffee drinkers may not immediately reduce their consumption when the price of coffee rises; but given sufficient time, some may acquire a taste for, say, tea. Another factor at work here is that some products are mainly used in conjunction with costly durable goods. For example, when the price of electricity rises, people who have electric furnaces and other appliances do not respond by greatly reducing their consumption of electricity. But as time transpires, the elasticity of the demand for electricity—*and the elasticity of the derived demand for workers in that industry*—becomes greater. People eventually replace their electric furnaces and water heaters with devices that use natural gas, solar energy, wood, or even coal.

2 Ratio of Labor Costs to Total Costs In general, all other things being the same, *the larger the proportion of total production costs accounted for by labor, the greater will be the elasticity of demand for labor.*[7] The rationale here is straightforward. Compare these two cases. Case one: If labor costs were the only production cost—that is, if the ratio of labor to total costs were 100 percent—then a 20 percent increase in the wage rate would increase unit costs by 20 percent. Given product demand, this large cost increase eventually would cause a considerable increase in product price, a sizable reduction in sales of output, and, therefore, a large decline in the employment of labor. Case two: If labor costs were only 10 percent of total cost, then the same 20

[7]Technical note: This proposition assumes that the product demand elasticity is greater than the elasticity of substitution between capital and labor. See Hicks, op. cit., pp. 241–247.

percent increase in the wage rate would increase total unit costs by only 2 percent. Assuming the same product demand as in case one, this relatively small cost increase will generate a relatively modest decline in employment. Case one implies a more elastic demand for labor than case two. The same 20 percent wage increase caused a larger percentage decline in employment in case one than in case two.

Many service industries such as education, temporary workers, and building maintenance exemplify situations in which firms' labor costs are a large percentage of total costs. In these industries wage increases translate into large cost increases, resulting in relatively elastic labor demand curves. Conversely, highly capital-intensive industries such as electricity generation and brewing are examples of markets in which labor costs are small relative to total costs. Labor demand curves in these industries are relatively inelastic.

3 Substitutability of Other Inputs Other things being equal, *the greater the substitutability of other inputs for labor, the greater will be the elasticity of demand for labor.* If technology is such that capital is readily substitutable for labor, then a small increase in the wage rate will elicit a substantial increase in the amount of machinery used and a large decline in the amount of labor employed. Conversely, a small drop in the wage rate will induce a large substitution of labor for capital. The demand for labor will tend to be elastic in this case. In other instances, technology may dictate that a certain amount of labor is more or less indispensable to the production process; that is, the substitution of capital for labor is highly constrained. In the extreme, the production process may involve fixed proportions; for example, three airline pilots—no more and no less—may be required to fly a commercial airliner. In this case, a change in the wage rate will have little short-run effect on the number of pilots employed, and this implies an inelastic demand for labor.

It is worth noting that *time* plays an important role in the input substitution process, just as it does in the previously discussed process through which consumer goods are substituted for one another. The longer the period of elapsed time since a wage rate was changed, the more elastic are labor demand curves. For example, a firm's truck drivers may obtain a substantial wage increase with little or no immediate decline in employment. But over time, as the firm's trucks wear out and are replaced, the company may purchase larger trucks and thereby be able to deliver the same total output with significantly fewer drivers. Alternatively, as the firm's trucks depreciate, it might turn to entirely different means of transportation for delivery. Or, in the case of airline pilots, new aircraft may be developed that require only two pilots, rather than three. Recent versions of Boeing aircraft are good examples.

4 Supply Elasticity of Other Inputs The fourth determinant of the elasticity of demand for labor is simply an extension of the third determinant. The generalization is that other things being equal, *the greater the elasticity of the supply of other inputs, the greater the elasticity of demand for labor.* In discussing our third generalization, we implicitly assumed that the prices of nonlabor inputs—say, capital—are unaffected by a change in the demand for them. But this may not be realistic.

To illustrate, assume once again that an increase in the wage rate prompts the firm to substitute capital for labor. This increase in the demand for capital will leave the price of capital unchanged only in the special case where the supply of capital is perfectly elastic. But let's suppose the supply of capital curve slopes upward, so that an increase in demand would increase its price. Furthermore, the less elastic the supply of capital, the greater the increase in the price of capital in response to any given increase in demand. Any resulting change in the price of capital is important because it will retard or dampen the substitution of capital for labor and reduce the elasticity of demand for labor. More specifically, if the supply of capital is inelastic, a given increase in the demand for capital will cause a large increase in the price of capital, greatly retarding the substitution process. This implies that the demand for labor will be inelastic. Conversely, if the supply of capital is highly elastic, the same increase in demand will cause only a small increase in the price of capital, only dampening the substitution process slightly. This suggests that the demand for labor will be elastic.

Estimates of Wage Elasticity

Hamermesh has summarized and compared more than 100 studies of labor demand and has concluded that the overall long-run labor demand elasticity in the United States is 1.0.[8] This coefficient implies a unitary elastic labor demand curve, which means that for every 10 percent change in the wage rate, employment changes in the opposite direction by 10 percent. Hamermesh concludes that about two-thirds of the long-run elasticity response takes the form of the output effect, with the other third consisting of the substitution effect. Other studies generally support Hamermesh's estimates, although problems of statistical design and incomplete data make research in this area difficult.

Studies also reveal that labor demand elasticities vary greatly by industry, type of labor, and occupational group. For example, Clark and Freeman estimate that the wage elasticity for all U.S. manufacturing is about 1.[9] Ashenfelter and Ehrenberg find that the wage elasticity in public education is 1.06.[10] Other studies show that the elasticity of labor demand is higher for teenagers than for adults, is greater for production workers than for nonproduction workers, is higher for low-skilled workers than for high-skilled workers, and is larger in nondurable goods industries than in durable goods industries.

Significance of Wage Elasticity

Of what practical significance are such estimates of labor demand elasticity? The answer is that private and public policies might be greatly affected by the size of the wage rate–employment trade-off suggested by the elasticity estimates.

[8] Daniel S. Hamermesh, *Labor Demand,* (Princeton, N.J.: Princeton University Press, 1993), chap. 3.

[9] Kim B. Clark and Richard B. Freeman, "How Elastic Is the Demand for Labor?" *Review of Economics and Statistics,* November 1980, pp. 509–520.

[10] Orley Ashenfelter and Ronald G. Ehrenberg, "The Demand for Labor in the Public Sector," in Daniel Hamermesh (ed.), *Labor in the Public and Nonprofit Sectors* (Princeton, N.J.: Princeton University Press, 1975), p. 71.

In the private sphere, a union's bargaining strategy might be influenced by the elasticity of labor demand for its workers. We might expect a union of higher-skilled engineers in the aerospace industry (where the demand for labor is inelastic) to bargain more aggressively for higher wages than a union of restaurant workers (where the demand for labor is elastic). The reason? A given percentage increase in wage rates will give rise to a smaller decline in employment for the higher-skilled engineers than for the lower-skilled restaurant workers.

Similarly, a union will wish to know something about its employer's wage elasticity before agreeing to a wage reduction purportedly necessary to save jobs threatened by intense import competition. The more elastic the employer's demand for labor, the greater the likelihood that the union will agree to a wage concession. Under conditions of elastic labor demand, the wage cut will be more effective in preserving jobs than when demand is inelastic.

The effectiveness and impact of government policies often depend on the elasticity of labor demand. The employment consequences of a rise in the minimum wage rate, for example, will depend on the elasticity of demand for workers affected by the change. Similarly, the effectiveness of a program providing wage subsidies to employers who hire disadvantaged workers will depend on the elasticity of labor demand in the industries employing low-skilled labor. The more elastic the labor demand, the greater will be the increase in employment resulting from the wage subsidies.

DETERMINANTS OF DEMAND FOR LABOR

The movement along a labor demand curve implied by the concept of elasticity is quite distinct from an increase or decrease in labor demand. The latter imply shifts of the demand for labor curve either rightward or leftward. What factors will cause such shifts? The major ***determinants of labor demand*** are product demand, productivity, the number of employers, and the prices of other resources.

Product Demand

A change in the demand for the product that a particular type of labor is producing, all else being equal, will shift the labor demand curve in the same direction. For example, suppose that in Table 5-2 and Figure 5-2 an increase in product demand occurs, causing the product price to rise from \$2 to \$3. If we plotted the *new* MRP data onto Figure 5-2, we would observe that the demand for labor curve shifted rightward. A decline in the demand for the product would likewise shift the labor demand curve leftward.

Productivity

Assuming that it does not cause a fully offsetting change in product price, a change in the marginal product of labor (MP) will shift the labor demand curve in the same direction. Again return to Table 5-2 and Figure 5-2. Suppose that technology improves, shifting the entire production function (column 2 in relationship to column 1 in

Table 5-2) upward. More concretely, let's assume a doubling of the total product produced by each worker in combination with the fixed capital. Clearly, MP in column 3 and consequently MRP in column 6 would increase. If the new MRP data were plotted in Figure 5-2, we would observe that labor demand had shifted rightward. Conversely, a decline in productivity would shift the labor demand curve leftward.

Number of Employers

Recall that we found the market demand for labor in Figure 5-7 by summing horizontally the "price-adjusted" labor demand curves possessed by individual employers. *Assuming no change in employment by other firms, a change in the number of firms employing a particular type of labor will change the demand for labor in the same direction.* In terms of Figure 5-7, D_{LM} will shift rightward if additional firms enter this labor market to hire workers, and shift leftward if firms leave, all else being equal.

Prices of Other Resources

Changes in the prices of other inputs such as capital, land, and raw materials can shift the demand curve for labor. To illustrate this idea, we focus solely on changes in the price of capital. Normally, labor and capital are *substitutes in production,* meaning that a given quantity of output can be produced with much capital and little labor *or* much labor and little capital. Now suppose that the price of capital falls. Our task is to determine the impact of this price decline on the demand for labor.

Gross Substitutes[11] If labor and capital are ***gross substitutes,*** the decline in the price of capital will result in a *decrease* in the demand for labor. *Gross substitutes are inputs such that when the price of one changes, the demand for the other changes in the same direction.* This correctly implies that here the substitution effect outweighs the output effect. The decline in the price of capital lowers the marginal cost of producing the output, which taken alone would result in an expansion of output and an *increase* in the demand for labor (the output effect). But the lower-priced capital is substituted for labor, which taken alone would *reduce* the demand for labor (the substitution effect). Where labor and capital are gross substitutes, this latter substitution effect swamps the output effect and labor demand falls. Example: The decline in the price of security equipment used by businesses to protect against illegal entries has reduced the demand for night guards.

Gross Complements If, on the other hand, labor and capital are ***gross complements,*** a decline in the price of capital will *increase* the demand for labor. *Gross complements are inputs such that when the price of one changes, the demand for the other*

[11]The term *gross* as a modifier of *substitutes* and *complements* in this discussion is in keeping with terminology used in advanced economics. As used here, the concepts are *gross* because they encompass both substitution and output effects. So-called *net* substitutes and complements, on the other hand, focus only on substitution effects, holding output constant.

changes in the opposite direction. In this case of a decline in the price of capital, the output effect outweighs the substitution effect and the demand for labor increases. Restated, the fall in the price of capital reduces production costs and increases sales so much that the increased demand for labor that results overwhelms the substitution of capital for labor occurring in the production process. When labor and capital are gross complements, a decrease (increase) in the price of capital increases (decreases) the demand for labor. Example: The decline in the price of telephone switching equipment over the decades increased the demand for communications workers.

Thus far we have assumed that labor and capital are substitutes in production. What can we conclude about the impact of a change in the price of capital on the demand for labor in the extreme case in which labor and capital are *not* substitutable in the production process? Suppose instead that labor and capital are *pure complements in production,* meaning they are used in direct proportion to one another in producing the output. An example would be crane operators and cranes; more cranes mean more operators on a one-for-one basis. The decline in the price of capital in this instance will unambiguously increase the demand for labor. Pure complements in production are always gross complements because there is no substitution effect. The lower price of capital will reduce the firm's marginal cost and cause it to increase its output, bolstering its demand for labor.

Generalizations: *(1) A change in the price of a resource that is a substitute in production for labor may change the demand for labor either in the same or in the opposite direction, depending on whether the resources are gross substitutes or gross complements, respectively; (2) a change in the price of a resource that is a pure complement in production (used in a fixed proportion with labor) will change the demand for labor in the opposite direction—it will always be a gross complement.*

QUICK REVIEW 5-3

- Wage elasticity measures the sensitivity of the amount of labor demanded to wage rate changes; it is the percentage change in quantity of labor demanded divided by the percentage change in price.
- When changes in the wage rate cause the wage bill $(W \times Q)$ to move in the opposite direction, labor demand is elastic; when the wage bill remains constant, labor demand is unit elastic; and when the wage bill moves in the same direction, labor de-
5-2 mand is inelastic.
- The major determinants of wage elasticity are the *(a)* elasticity of product demand, *(b)* ratio of labor costs to total costs, *(c)* substitutability of other inputs, and
5-3 *(d)* the supply elasticity of other inputs.
- The factors that shift the labor demand curve include *(a)* changes in product demand, *(b)* changes in labor productivity, *(c)* changes in the number of employers, and *(d)* the changes in the prices of other inputs.

Your Turn: Suppose that the price of capital falls relative to the wage rate and, as a result, the demand for labor increases. Are these inputs gross substitutes, or are they gross

5-2 Global Perspective

PART-TIME EMPLOYMENT AS A PERCENTAGE OF TOTAL EMPLOYMENT, 1995

The use of part-time workers varies substantially across countries.

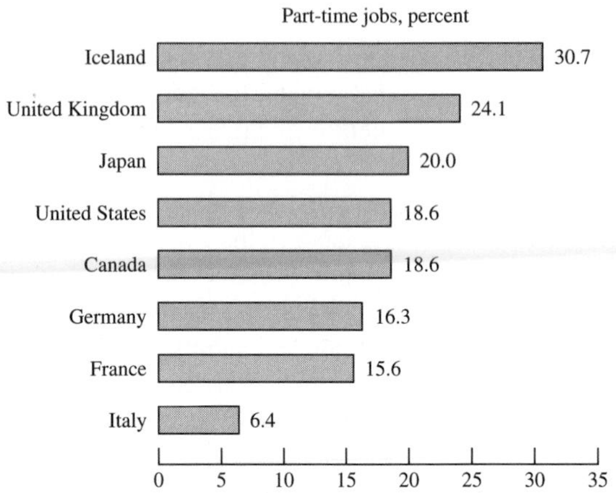

Source: Organization for Economic Cooperation and Development, *Employment Outlook,* July 1996, Table E.

5-3 Global Perspective

TEMPORARY EMPLOYMENT AS A PERCENTAGE OF TOTAL EMPLOYMENT

The United States has low rate of employment in jobs with time-limited contracts relative to other countries.

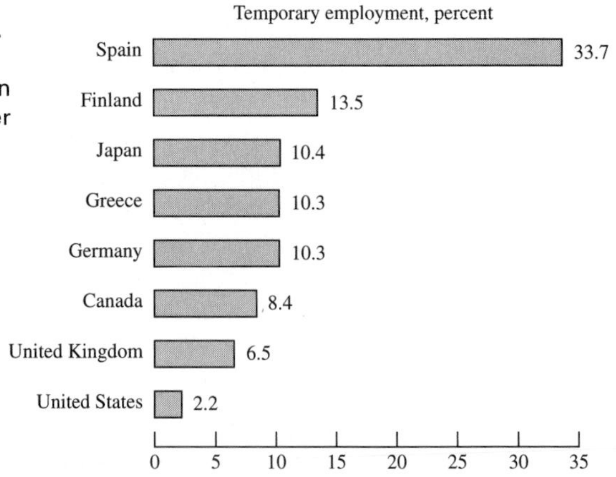

Source: Organization for Economic Cooperation and Development, *Employment Outlook,* July 1996, Table 5.1.

complements? What can you infer about the relative strengths of the output and sub-
5-2 stitution effects? (Answers: See page 625.)

REAL-WORLD APPLICATIONS

The concepts of labor demand and the elasticity of labor demand have great practical significance, as seen in the following examples.

American Automobile Industry

In 2005 there are expected to be 225,000 fewer workers in the American automobile industry than in 1979. Several factors help explain this dramatic decline in jobs. First, foreign competition, particularly from Japanese producers, has reduced the demand for American cars. The share of total American automobile sales accounted for by General Motors, Ford, and Chrysler has fallen from about 80 percent in 1979 to less than 65 percent today. This decline in demand for American autos has sharply reduced the derived demand for American autoworkers.

Another factor at work has been the spread of robotic technology in auto manufacturing. Industrial robots and assembly-line labor are gross substitutes, meaning that lower prices of robots have produced substitution effects exceeding output effects. The net effect has been a decline in the demand for autoworkers. Coupled with the reduced demand for the product, the substitution of robots for workers has sharply reduced em-
5-3 ployment in the industry.

Fast-Food Workers

In the past several years, McDonald's and other fast-food establishments have undertaken advertising campaigns to attract homemakers and older people to work in their restaurants. One important reason for these efforts has been the rapid increase in the demand for fast-food workers. The labor force participation rate of women and the number of two-worker families has increased, raising the opportunity cost of time (recall the Becker model in Chapter 3). In Becker's terms, people have substituted goods (restaurant meals) for time (home-prepared meals) in producing "commodities." The increase in the demand for restaurant meals has increased the demand for fast-food workers. Because the labor supply of traditional fast-food workers—teenagers—has not kept pace, many restaurants are now recruiting homemakers and semiretired workers.

Personal Computers

The last decade has seen a remarkable drop in the average price of personal computers and an equally amazing rise in the computing power of the typical machine. The effects of these developments on labor demand have been pervasive. For example, the demand for workers in some segments of the computer industry has significantly increased. Between 1983 and 1994, employment in the computer services industry

5-2 World of Work

THE RISING DEMAND FOR CONTINGENT WORKERS

One of the rather dramatic labor market changes of recent years has been that many employers have reduced the size of their full-time "core" workforces. Simultaneously, they have increased the use of contingent workers (part-time, temporary, and subcontracted workers). A February 1995 government survey indicated 4.9 percent of the workforce is employed in jobs that they expect to last less than 1 year. Currently, part-time workers comprise 18.6 percent of the American labor force, up from 15.6 percent in 1973. A 1995 Conference Board study of 93 major multinational companies revealed that use of contingent workers is rising quickly in such companies. By the year 2000 more than one-third of these multinationals expect contingent workers to comprise at least one-tenth of their workforce. The corresponding figure for 1995 was one-fifth.

The ranks of involuntary part-time workers jumped by more than 120 percent from 1970 to 1990. The number of voluntary part-timers grew by about 70 percent. These percentages compare to the 54 percent growth of employment in general over this period. Today, part-time workers comprise almost one-fifth of the American labor force.

Why has the demand for contingent workers increased so rapidly? Several factors have been at work. These workers are usually paid less than full-time workers, and this pay gap has been expanding. Also, increasingly expensive fringe benefits such as health insurance are minimal or nonexistent for many contingent workers. For example, retail stores provide health insurance for only 10 percent of their part-time workers, compared to nearly 50 percent of their full-time workers.

A second and closely related reason for the growing demand for contingent workers in that these workers give firms more flexibility in responding to changing economic conditions. As product demand shifts, firms can readily increase or decrease the sizes of their workforces through altering their part-time, temporary, and subcontracted employment. This flexibility enhances the competitive positions of the firms and improves their ability to succeed in international markets.

Many contingent workers, of course, voluntarily choose their labor force status. Part-time jobs provide greater opportunities for workers to be employees in an environment compatible with other goals. Students can combine work with education; workers with children can balance labor market work and work in the home.

But the contingency workforce also entails problems and costs. While lower costs and greater flexibility may benefit employers, this obviously means lower earnings and greater employment insecurity to workers. Often these workers get permanently stuck in low-paid temporary jobs. The possible effect of part-time work on productivity is also worrisome. Are contingency workers motivated to do quality work? Can they be trusted with proprietary secrets? Are firms willing to train and develop part-timers? There is also the social issue of how to provide increasingly expensive health care and adequate retirement income for contingency workers who lack these benefits.

The contingent workforce, for employers as well as workers, may be a mixed blessing.*

*The pros and cons of the growing contingent labor force are discussed in more detail in Richard S. Belous, *The Contingent Economy: The Growth of the Temporary, Part-Time and Subcontracted Workforce* (Washington, D.C.: National Planning Association, 1989). Also of interest is Chris Tilly, "Continuing Growth of Part-Time Employment," *Monthly Labor Review,* March 1991, pp. 10–18. For a series of articles covering contingent workers, see *Monthly Labor Review,* October 1996.

(programming and software) expanded at an annual 8 percent growth rate. Apple Corporation, which was founded in 1976, boasted 15,500 workers in 1996. Microsoft, a major producer of software, employed 19,600 people in 1996, up from 476 workers in 1983.

In some offices, personal computers have been gross substitutes for labor, thus reducing the demand for labor and allowing these firms to use fewer workers to produce

5-3 World of Work

ARE FEARS OF DOWNSIZING OVERBLOWN?*

In recent years many well-publicized, massive layoffs have occurred at large American companies. These layoffs have built up a public perception that firms have been restructuring and reducing their workforces in reaction to increased competition much more now than ever before. It is also typically believed that the laid-off workers are now likely to be white-collar workers and that they suffer severe economic hardship.

Henry Farber has attempted to assess the accuracy of these beliefs using data covering the period of 1981–95. He concludes that the layoff rate in the 1990s is up somewhat but not dramatically from the 1980s. Between 1991 and 1995 15.8 percent of men and 14.3 percent of women suffered a job loss. Contrary to perceptions, he reports, younger and less-educated workers continue to suffer the highest rate of job loss. The rate of job loss has increased the most, however, for older and more-educated workers.

Farber finds the economic consequences of job loss, such as continued unemployment and earning losses, are substantial but have not risen across time. For example, 26 percent of workers who were laid off between 1993 and 1995 were not reemployed when they were interviewed in February 1996. Among full-time workers who were reemployed in a full-time job, 28 percent suffered an earnings decrease of at least 20 percent on their new job compared to their old job. More-educated workers, however, are more likely to obtain reemployment and suffer a smaller proportional earnings loss than their less-educated counterparts.

A surprisingly common response to layoffs appears to be self-employment, as 7.3 percent of laid-off workers become self-employed within 2 years of being laid off. For example, laid-off workers can become consultants, sometimes for the firm that fired them. More-educated and older workers are the most likely to turn to self-employment.

*Based on Henry S. Farber, "The Changing Face of Job Loss in the United States, 1981–1995," *Brookings Papers on Economic Activity, Microeconomics,* 1997, pp. 55–142 and U.S. Department of Labor, "Worker Displacement during the Mid-1990s (Based on Revised Estimates)," News Release 96-446, October 25, 1996.

their outputs. But in other instances, computers and labor have proven to be gross complements. The decline in computer prices has reduced production costs to the extent that product prices have dropped, product sales have increased, and the derived demand for workers has risen. Also, keyboard personnel and computers are pure complements. Thus, there is no substitution effect; a keyboard worker is needed for each computer.

Today 51 million people work with personal computers at least sometime during the day. Krueger has estimated that workers who use computers earn 10 to 15 percent more than otherwise similar workers who do not use this technology.[12]

Minimum Wage

As we detail in Chapter 12, federal law prohibits employers from paying covered workers less than $5.15 per hour. Critics contend that an above-equilibrium minimum wage moves employers upward along their downsloping labor demand curves and causes unemployment, particularly among teenage workers. Workers who remain employed at

[12] Alan B. Krueger, "How Computers Have Changed the Wage Structure: Evidence from Microdata, 1984–1989," *Quarterly Journal of Economics,* February 1993, pp. 33–60.

the minimum wage will receive higher incomes than otherwise. The amount of income lost by job losers and the income gained by those who keep their jobs will depend on the elasticity of demand for minimum-wage labor. Studies have generally found that a 10 percent increase in the minimum wage reduces employment from 1 to 3 percent, meaning that demand is inelastic. Thus, the minimum wage increases the wage income to minimum-wage workers as a group (increases the wage bill). The case made by critics of the minimum wage would be stronger if the demand for low-wage labor were elastic.

Bank Tellers

Between 1990 and 1995, 40,000 bank tellers lost their jobs, and half of the remaining bank tellers could lose their jobs by the year 2005. Three factors have been causing this employment decline. First, banks have been replacing branch offices with automated teller machines (ATMs) since ATMs serve customers more cheaply than tellers. The number of bank branches is forecasted to fall in half by 2005 from the current level of 52,000 branches. On the other hand, the number of ATMs is predicted to rise by 50 percent to 103,000 by the year 2000. As a consequence, fewer bank tellers are needed to staff bank branches. Second, new technology lets customers bank by telephones and personal computers. Thus, banks are able to further substitute electronic machinery for bank tellers. Third, the direct deposit of paychecks and benefit checks is increasing. This reduction in the number of check cashers will further reduce the demand for bank tellers.

Defense Cutbacks

The end of the Cold War and the resulting reductions in American defense spending have substantially reduced labor demand by the military. An estimated 800,000 to 1 million *military* jobs were lost between 1993 and 1998. Also, the federal spending cuts on defense will significantly reduce the demand for labor in industries producing aircraft, missiles, tanks, and related military hardware. Recent estimates are that 1 million defense-related *civilian* jobs were lost between 1993 and 1998. Hooker and Knetter report that this decline in defense spending has increased the national unemployment rate by 0.2 to 0.4 percentage points.[13] The downsizing of the military amounts to a 3-percentage point decline in defense spending's share of the gross domestic product over a 10-year period. Other parts of the federal budget, however, have increased to help offset the declines in defense spending. For example, spending on infrastructure (such as roads, bridges, and ports) and health care has greatly increased. This increased spending has raised the demand for construction and health care workers.

[13]Mark Hooker and Michael Knetter, "Unemployment Effects of Military Spending: Evidence from a Panel of States," National Bureau of Economic Research Working Paper No. 4889, October 1994.

CHAPTER SUMMARY

1 The demand for labor is a derived demand and therefore depends on the marginal productivity of labor and the price or market value of the product.

2 The segment of the marginal product curve that is positive and lies below the average product curve is the basis for the short-run labor demand curve. More specifically, the short-run demand curve for labor is determined by applying the MRP = W rule to the firm's marginal revenue product data.

3 Other things being equal, the demand for labor curve of a perfectly competitive seller is more elastic than that of an imperfectly competitive seller. This difference occurs because the imperfectly competitive seller must reduce product price to sell additional units of output, while the purely competitive seller does not. This also means that the imperfectly competitive seller's marginal revenue product curve lies to the left of the corresponding value of marginal product curve, while marginal revenue product and the value of the marginal product are identical for the perfectly competitive seller.

4 A firm's long-run labor demand curve is more elastic than its short-run curve because in the long run the firm has sufficient time to adjust nonlabor inputs such as capital. In the short run a wage change produces only an output effect; in the long run it also creates a substitution effect. Additionally, such factors as product demand elasticity, labor–capital interactions, and technology contribute to the greater long-run wage elasticity.

5 The market demand for a given type of labor is less elastic than a simple horizontal summation of the short- or long-run demand curves of individual employers. The reason for this is that as employers as a group hire more workers and produce more output, product supply will increase significantly and product price will therefore decline.

6 The elasticity of labor demand is measured by comparing the percentage change in the quantity of labor demanded with a given percentage change in the wage rate. If the elasticity coefficient is greater than 1, demand is relatively elastic. If it is less than 1, demand is relatively inelastic. When demand is elastic, changes in the wage rate cause the total wage bill to change in the *opposite* direction. When demand is inelastic, changes in the wage rate cause the total wage bill to move in the *same* direction.

7 The demand for labor generally is more elastic *(a)* the greater the elasticity of product demand, *(b)* the larger the ratio of labor cost to total cost, *(c)* the greater the substitutability of other inputs for labor, and *(d)* the greater the elasticity of supply of other inputs.

8 The location of the labor demand curve depends on *(a)* product demand, *(b)* the marginal productivity of labor, *(c)* the number of employers, and *(d)* the prices of other inputs. When any of these determinants of demand change, the labor demand curve shifts to a new location.

9 Labor and capital can either by substitutes or pure complements in production. If they are substitutes in production, they can be either gross substitutes or gross complements. When the price of a gross substitute changes, the demand for the other resource changes in the same direction. When the price of gross complement changes, the demand for the other resource changes in the opposite direction.

10 The concepts of labor demand, changes in labor demand, and the elasticity of labor demand have great applicability to real-world situations.

TERMS AND CONCEPTS

derived demand
production function
total product
marginal product
average product
law of diminishing marginal returns
zone of production
marginal revenue product
short-run labor demand curve
marginal wage cost
value of marginal product
long-run demand for labor
output effect
substitution effect
market demand for labor
elasticity of labor demand
wage elasticity coefficient
total wage bill rules
determinants of labor demand
gross substitutes
gross complements

QUESTIONS AND STUDY SUGGESTIONS

1 Graph a short-run production function (one variable resource) showing the correct relationships between total product, average product, and marginal product.

2 "Only that portion of the MP curve that lies below AP constitutes the basis for the firm's short-run demand curve for labor." Explain.

3 Explain how marginal revenue product is derived. Why is the MRP curve the firm's short-run labor demand curve? Explain how and why the labor demand curves of a perfectly competitive seller and an imperfectly competitive seller differ.

4 Given the data in Table A, complete the labor demand schedule shown in Table B. Contrast this schedule to the value of marginal product schedule that would exist given these data. Explain why the labor demand and VMP schedules differ.

TABLE A

Inputs of labor	Total product	Product price
0	0	$1.10
1	17	1.00
2	32	.90
3	45	.80
4	55	.70
5	62	.65
6	68	.60

TABLE B

Labor demand schedule	
Wage rate	Quantity demanded
$18	
14	
11	
6	
2	
1	

5 Explain how each of the following would affect the demand schedule that you derived in question 4: *(a)* an increase in the price of a gross substitute for labor, *(b)* a decrease in the price of a pure complement in production with labor, *(c)* a decrease in the demand for the product which the labor helps to produce.

6 Referring to the output and substitution effects, explain why an increase in the wage rate for autoworkers will generate more of a negative employment response in the long run than in the short run. Assume there is no productivity increase and no change in the price of nonlabor resources.

7 "It would be incorrect to say that an industry's labor demand curve is simply the horizontal sum of the demand curves of the individual firms." Do you agree? Explain.

8 Suppose that marginal productivity tripled while product price fell by one-half in Table 5-2. What would be the net impact on the location of the short-run labor demand curve in Figure 5-2?

9 Use the concepts of *(a)* substitutes in production versus pure complements in production and *(b)* gross substitutes versus gross complements to assess the likely impact of the rapid decline in the price of computers, word processors, and related office equipment on the labor demand for secretaries.

10 Use the total wage bill rules and the labor demand schedule in question 4 to determine whether demand is elastic or inelastic over the \$6 to \$11 wage-rate range. Compute the elasticity coefficient using equation (5-4).

11 The productivity of farm labor has increased substantially since World War II. How can this be reconciled with the fact that labor has moved from agricultural to nonagricultural occupations over this period?

12 Contrast and explain changes in the demand for automobile workers and fast-food workers from 1979 to the present. Explain: "Workers, not consumers, bore the major burden of the federal luxury tax on expensive pleasure boats." Why is the elasticity of labor demand crucial to the debate on the effects of increasing the minimum wage?

SELECTED REFERENCES

Ehrenberg, Ronald G., and Robert S. Smith: *Modern Labor Economics,* 6th ed. (New York: HarperCollins, 1997), chap. 4.

Fleisher, Belton M., and Thomas J. Kniesner: *Labor Economics: Theory, Evidence, and Policy,* 3d ed. (Englewood Cliffs, N.J.: Prentice-Hall, 1984), chap. 3.

Hamermesh, Daniel S.: "The Demand for Labor in the Long Run," in Orley Ashenfelter and Richard Layard (eds.), *Handbook of Labor Economics* (Amsterdam: North-Holland, 1986).

Hamermesh, Daniel S.: "Econometric Studies of Labor Demand and Their Application to Policy Analysis," *Journal of Human Resources,* Fall 1976, pp. 507–525.

Hamermesh, Daniel S.: *Labor Demand* (Princeton, N.J.: Princeton University Press, 1993).

Hicks, John R.: *The Theory of Wages,* 2d ed. (London: Macmillan Publishing Company, 1964), chap. 1.

Rothschild, K. W.: *The Theory of Wages* (New York: Augustus M. Kelly, 1967), chap. 2.

APPENDIX: Isoquant–Isocost Analysis of the Long-Run Demand for Labor

A more advanced derivation of the firm's long-run downward-sloping labor demand curve is based on (1) isoquant and (2) isocost curves.

ISOQUANT CURVES

An ***isoquant curve*** *shows the various possible combinations of two inputs that are capable of producing a specific quantity of physical output.* By definition, then, output is the same at all points on a *single* isoquant. For example, total output is 100 units of some product or service on curve Q_{100} in Figure 5-9 when 20 units of capital are combined with 7 units of labor *or* when 10 units of capital and 15 units of labor are employed.* Isoquants—or equal output curves—possess several other characteristics.

1 Downward Slope Assuming that capital and labor are substitutes in production, if a firm employs less capital *(K),* then, to maintain a specific level of output, it must employ more labor *(L).* Conversely, to hold total output constant, using less of *L* will require it to employ more of *K*. There is thus an *inverse* relationship between *K* and *L* at each output level, implying a downward-sloping isoquant curve.

2 Convexity to the Origin Isoquants are convex to the origin because capital and labor are not perfect substitutes for one another. For example, an excavating company can substitute labor and capital to produce a specific level of "output," say, clearing 1,000 acres of wooded land in a fixed amount of time. But labor and capital are not perfectly substitutable for this purpose. To understand this and see why the firm's isoquant curve is convex to the origin, compare the following circumstances. First, suppose that the firm is using a single bulldozer and hundreds of workers. Clearly, an extra bulldozer would compensate, or substitute, for many workers in producing this output. Contrast that to a second situation in which the firm has, say, 100 bulldozers but only relatively few workers. The addition of still another machine would have a

*For simplicity we will assume that the only two resources are capital and labor, and disregard all combinations of capital and labor that are not within a firm's zone of production.

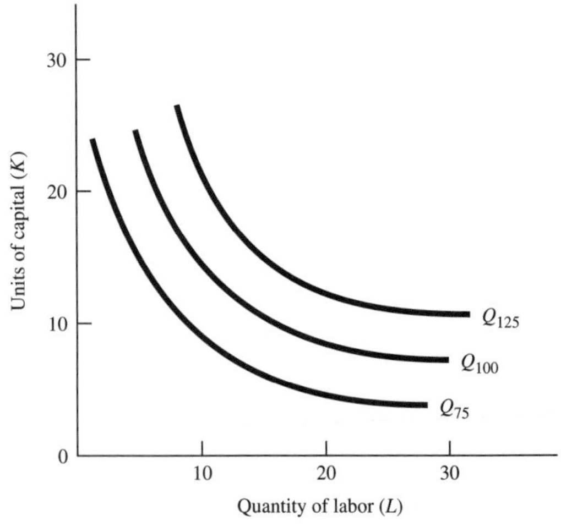

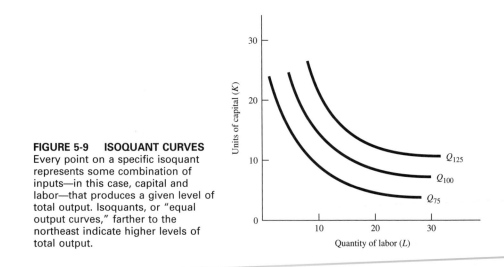

FIGURE 5-9 ISOQUANT CURVES
Every point on a specific isoquant represents some combination of inputs—in this case, capital and labor—that produces a given level of total output. Isoquants, or "equal output curves," farther to the northeast indicate higher levels of total output.

relatively low substitution value; for example, it might compensate for only one or two workers. Why? The firm already has numerous bulldozers; it needs people to operate them, supervise the operation, and cut down the trees that cannot be bulldozed.

This same concept can be viewed in the opposite way. When the firm is employing only a small amount of labor and a large amount of equipment, an extra worker will possess a relatively high substitution value, that is, compensate for the reduction of a large amount of capital. As more labor is added, however, the decrease in capital permitted by an added unit of labor will decline. Stated in technical terms, the absolute value of the ***marginal rate of technical substitution*** of labor for capital will fall as more labor is added. This MRTS L, K, shown symbolically in equation (5-5), is the absolute value of the slope of the isoquant at a given point.

$$\text{MRTS } L, K = \frac{\Delta K}{\Delta L} \tag{5-5}$$

Returning to Figure 5-9, we see that each isoquant is convex to the origin. As one moves along, say, Q_{75}, from left to right, the absolute value of the slope of the curve which declines; in other words, the curve gets flatter. A curve that gets flatter (whose absolute slope declines) as one moves southeast is convex to the origin.

3 Higher Output to the Northeast Each isoquant further to the northeast reflects combinations of K and L that produce a greater level of total output than the previous curve. Isoquant Q_{125} represents greater output than Q_{100}, which in turn reflects more output than Q_{75}, and so forth. Two other points are relevant here. First, we have drawn only three of the many possible isoquant curves. Second, just as "equal elevation" lines on a contour map never intersect, neither do these "equal output" lines.

ISOCOST CURVES

A profit-maximizing firm will seek to minimize the costs of producing a given output. To accomplish this task, it will need to know the prices of K and L. These prices will enable the firm to determine the various combinations of K and L that are available to it for a specific expenditure. For example, if the prices of K and L and \$6 and \$4 per unit, respectively, then the input combinations that can be obtained from a given outlay, say, \$120, would be \$6 times the quantity of K plus \$4 times the quantity of L. Then one possibility would be to use 20 units of K (= \$120 = \$6 × 20) and no labor. At the other extreme, this firm could use zero units of capital and 30 units of labor (= \$120 = 30 × \$4). Another such combination would be 10K and 15L. In Figure 5-10 we plot these three points and connect them with a straight line. This line is an ***isocost curve;*** *it shows all the various combinations of capital and labor that can be purchased by a particular outlay, given the prices of K and L.* Note that the absolute value of the slope of this "equal expenditure" line is the ratio of the price of labor to the price of capital; that is, the slope is $^2/_3$ (= \$4/\$6).

The location of a particular isocost curve depends on (1) the total expenditure and (2) the relative prices of L and K. Given the prices of K and L, the greater the total

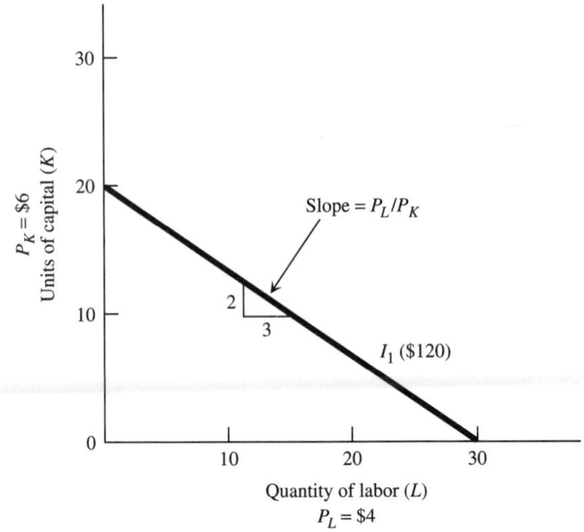

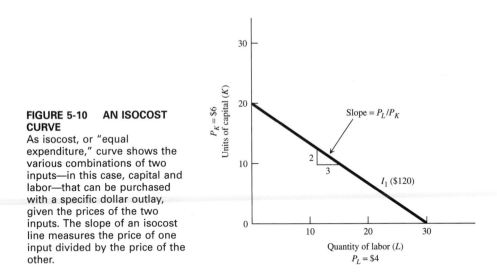

FIGURE 5-10 AN ISOCOST CURVE
As isocost, or "equal expenditure," curve shows the various combinations of two inputs—in this case, capital and labor—that can be purchased with a specific dollar outlay, given the prices of the two inputs. The slope of an isocost line measures the price of one input divided by the price of the other.

expenditure, the farther the isocost curve will lie outward from the origin. If the total outlay were enlarged from \$120 to \$150, and the prices of K and L remained unchanged, then the isocost curve shown in Figure 5-10 would shift outward in a parallel fashion. Similarly, a smaller outlay would shift it inward. Second, the location of an isocost curve depends on the relative prices of L and K. Given the total expenditure, the higher the price of L relative to the price of K, the *steeper* the isocost curve; the lower the price of L relative to the price of K, the *flatter* the curve.

LEAST-COST COMBINATION OF CAPITAL AND LABOR

By overlaying the isocost curve in Figure 5-10 onto Figure 5-9's isoquant "map," we can determine the firm's cost-minimizing combination of K and L for a given quantity of total output. Stated somewhat differently, this allows us to determine the lowest cost *per unit of output*. This ***least-cost combination of resources*** occurs at the *tangency point* of the isoquant curve Q_{100} and the isocost curve I_1 (point a) in Figure 5-11. At point a the slope of the isoquant, the MRTS, L, K, just equals the ratio of the prices of labor and capital—the slope of the isocost curve. The firm will use 10 units of capital and employ 15 units of labor. This expenditure of \$120 is the minimum outlay possible in achieving this level of output. To reinforce this proposition, you should determine why combinations of K and L represented by other points on Q_{100} are *not* optimal.

DERIVING THE LONG-RUN LABOR DEMAND CURVE

Earlier in this chapter we derived a *short-run* labor demand curve by holding capital constant, adding units of labor to generate a marginal product schedule, multiplying MP times the extra revenue gained from the sale of additional product, and graphing the resulting marginal revenue product schedule. By applying the W = MRP rule, we

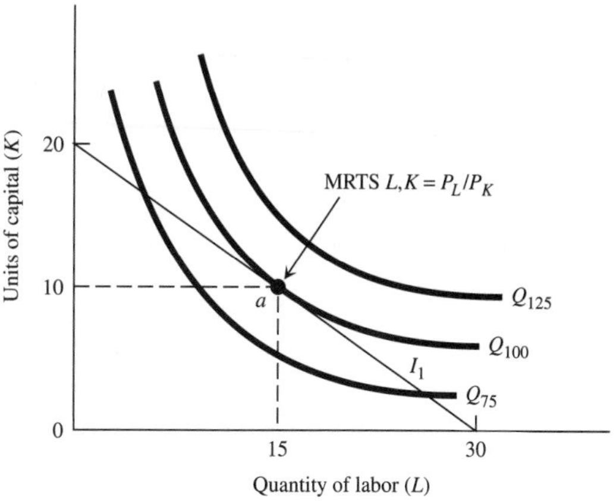

FIGURE 5-11 THE LEAST-COST COMBINATION OF CAPITAL AND LABOR
The least-cost combination of capital and labor used to produce 100 units of output is at point *a*, where the isocost line is tangent to isoquant Q_{100}. At *a*, the marginal rate of technical substitution of labor for capital (MRTS *L*, *K*) equals the ratio of the price of labor to the price of capital. In this case, the firm will use 10 units of capital, employ 15 units of labor, and in the process expend $120.

demonstrated that the MRP curve *is* the short-run labor demand curve. Now we derive a *long-run* labor demand curve directly from our isoquant–isocost analysis. In Figure 5-12(a) we reproduce our $120 isocost line I_1 and the isoquant Q_{100}, which is tangent to it at point *a.* We then drop a perpendicular dashed line down to the horizontal axis of graph (b), which also measures units of labor, but measures the price of labor, or wage rate, vertically. Recall that the price of *L* is assumed to be $4, at which the optimal level of employment is 15 units of labor. This gives us point *A* in the lower graph.

Now suppose that some factor, say out-migration, reduces labor supply and increases the price of labor from $4 to $12. We need to ascertain graphically the effect of this increase of the wage rate on the quantity of labor demanded. To accomplish this, let's proceed in several steps. First, we must draw a new isocost curve, reflecting the new ratio of the price of *L* to *K*. Inasmuch as the price of labor is now $12 while the price of *K* is assumed to remain constant at $6, the new isocost curve will have a slope of 2 (= $12/$6). Because we wish initially to hold the level of output constant at Q_{100}, we construct isocost curve I_2 that has a slope of 2 and is tangent to Q_{100} at point *b* in Figure 5-12(a).

Our next step is to determine the new combination of *K* and *L* that would be used *if* output were to be held constant. This is shown at point *b,* where the marginal rate of technical substitution on isoquant curve Q_{100} equals the slope of isocost curve I_2 (20*K* and 7*L*). Notice what has happened thus far: In response to the higher wage rate, the firm has substituted more capital (+ 10) for less labor (− 8). This is the ***substitution effect*** of the wage increase. It is defined as *the change in the quantity of an input demanded resulting from a change in the price of the input, with the output remaining constant.*

The final step is to acknowledge that the increase of the price of labor from $4 to $12 will cause the firm to reassess its profit-maximizing level of output. In particular, production costs are now higher and, given product demand, the firm will find it profitable to produce less output. Let's assume that this reevaluation results in the firm's decision to reduce its output from Q_{100} to Q_{75}. Given the new $12 to $6 price ratio of *L* and *K,* we simply push the I_2 line inward in a parallel fashion until it is tangent with

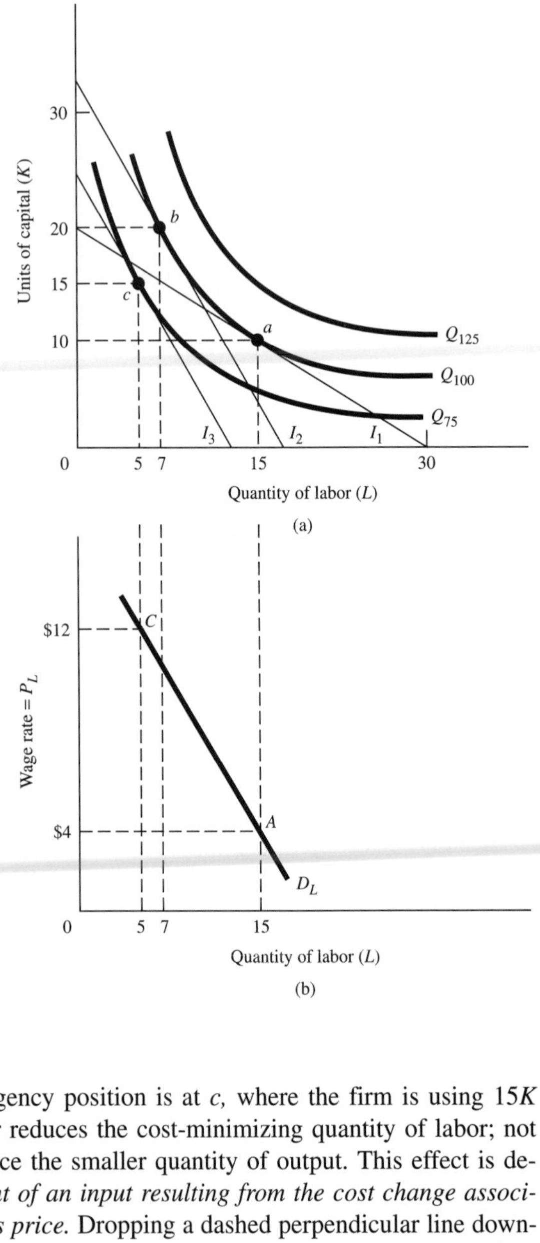

FIGURE 5-12 DERIVING THE LONG-RUN LABOR DEMAND CURVE
When the price of labor rises from \$4 to \$12, the substitution effect causes the firm to use more capital and less labor, while the output effect reduces the use of both. The labor demand curve is determined in (b) by plotting the quantity of labor demanded before and after the increase in the wage rate from \$4 to \$12.

this lower isoquant. The new tangency position is at *c*, where the firm is using 15*K* and 5*L*. This ***output effect*** further reduces the cost-minimizing quantity of labor; not as much labor is needed to produce the smaller quantity of output. This effect is defined as *the change in employment of an input resulting from the cost change associated with the change in the input's price.* Dropping a dashed perpendicular line downward from point *c*, we derive point *C* in the lower graph. At the new wage rate of \$12, the firm desires to hire only 5 units of labor. By finding a series of points such as *a* and *c* in the upper graph and *A* and *C* in the lower one, and then by determining the locus of these latter points, we derive a long-run labor demand curve such as D_L in graph (b). This curve slopes downward because of both a *substitution effect* (− 8 labor units) and an *output effect* (− 2 units).

APPENDIX SUMMARY

1 An isoquant curve shows the various possible combinations of two inputs that are capable of producing a specific quantity of physical output.
2 An isocost curve shows the various combinations of two inputs that a firm can purchase with a given outlay or expenditure.
3 The firm's cost-minimizing combination of inputs in achieving a given output is found at the tangency point between the isocost and isoquant curve, that is, where the marginal rate of technical substitution of labor for capital (slope of the isoquant curve) equals the ratio of the input prices (slope of the isocost curve).
4 Changing the price of either input while holding the price of the other resource and the level of output constant produces a new isocost curve that has a new tangency position on the given isoquant curve. This generates a *substitution effect* that results in the use of less of the resource that rose in price and more of the resource that did not experience a price change.
5 An increase in the price of a resource also increases the cost per unit of the product. This creates an *output effect* tending to reduce the employment of both labor and capital.
6 A downward-sloping long-run labor demand curve can be derived by plotting the wage rate–quantity combinations associated with changing the price of labor (wage rate).

APPENDIX TERMS AND CONCEPTS

isoquant curve
marginal rate of technical substitution
isocost curve
least-cost combination of resources
substitution effect
output effect

APPENDIX QUESTIONS AND STUDY SUGGESTIONS

1 Explain why isoquant curves for inputs that are substitutes in production *(a)* are negatively sloped, *(b)* are convex to the origin, and *(c)* never intersect.
2 Suppose that the quantity of capital is fixed at 10 units in Figure 5-9. Explain, by drawing a horizontal line rightward from 10*K*, the short-run law of diminishing marginal returns discussed in the body of this chapter. Hint: Observe the distance between the isoquants along your horizontal line.
3 Explain how each of the following, other things being equal, would shift the isocost curve shown in Figure 5-10: *(a)* a decrease in the price of *L*, *(b)* a simultaneous and proportionate increase in the prices of both *K* and *L*, and *(c)* an increase in the total outlay, or expenditure, from \$120 to \$150.
4 Explain graphically how isoquant–isocost analysis can be used to derive a long-run labor demand curve. Distinguish between the *substitution* and *output* effects.
5 By referring to Figure 5-12(a), explain the impact of the increase of the price of labor on the cost-minimizing quantity of capital. What can you conclude about the relative strengths of the substitution and output effects as they relate to the demand for capital in this specific situation?
6 Is labor demand *(a)* elastic, *(b)* unit elastic, or *(c)* inelastic over the \$4 to \$12 wage-rate range of D_L in Figure 5-12(b)? Explain by referring to the total wage bill rules (Figure 5-8) and the midpoint formula for elasticity [equation (5-4)].

CHAPTER 6

WAGE DETERMINATION AND THE ALLOCATION OF LABOR

Something quite remarkable happens in the United States every workday. Nearly 135 million of us go to work sometime, somewhere, during the day. We work at an amazing array of jobs; we are carpenters, secretaries, executives, professional athletes, lawyers, dock workers, farm hands, geologists, hair stylists, nurses, managers, truck drivers, and professors. And the list goes on and on. Equally remarkable are the pay differences among us. Professional baseball players make, on average, \$350 an hour; fast-food employees, \$6 per hour.

Who or what determines the occupational composition of the total jobs in the economy? What mechanisms allocate us to our various occupations and specific workplaces? How are occupational and individual wage rates determined? In this chapter we combine labor supply (Chapters 2–4) and labor demand (Chapter 5) into basic models that help us answer these important questions.

First, we examine the elements of a perfectly competitive labor market, focusing on wage and employment determination, the hiring decision by the individual firm, and allocative efficiency. Second, we assess the impact of product market monopoly on a firm's hiring conduct and on allocative efficiency. The third section of the chapter explores a labor market in which a monopsonist—a single buyer—is the sole employer of a particular type of labor. Next, we consider the ways unions might increase wage rates by altering labor supply or demand. Fifth, we develop a bilateral monopoly model where power exists on both the buyer and seller sides of the labor market. Finally, we present a model in which labor supply adjustments are sluggish and delayed in response to a change in labor demand, resulting in alternating periods of labor shortages and surpluses.

A caution: In reading this chapter be aware that we are assuming for simplicity that all compensation is paid in the form of the wage rate. In Chapter 7 we will relax this assumption, specifically looking at the composition of pay and the economics of fringe benefits.

THEORY OF A PERFECTLY COMPETITIVE LABOR MARKET

A ***perfectly competitive labor market*** has the following characteristics that contrast it with other labor markets: (1) a large number of firms competing with one another to hire a specific type of labor to fill identical jobs; (2) numerous qualified people who have identical skills and independently supply their labor services; (3) "wage-taking" behavior—that is, neither workers nor firms exert control over the market wage; and (4) perfect, costless information and labor mobility.

Let's examine the components, operation, and outcomes of this stylized labor market in some detail. Specifically, we will divide our discussion into three subsections: the labor market, the hiring decision by an individual firm, and allocative efficiency.

The Labor Market

The competitive market for a specific type of labor can best be analyzed by separating it into two parts: labor demand, which reflects the behavior of employers; and labor supply, deriving from the decisions of workers.

Labor Demand and Supply Recall from the previous chapter (Figure 5-7) that the market demand for a particular type of labor is found by summing over a range of wage rates the "price-adjusted" amounts of labor that employers desire to hire at each of the various wage rates. Also remember, specifically from Chapter 2, that *individual* labor supply curves are normally backward-bending. Can we then conclude that the *market* supply of a particular grade of labor is also backward-bending? In most labor markets this is not the case; market supply curves generally slope upward and to the right, indicating that collectively workers will offer more labor hours at higher relative wage rates. Why is this so?

Figure 6-1 helps explain the positive relationship between the wage rate and the quantity of labor hours supplied in most labor markets. Graph (a) displays five separate backward-bending *individual* labor supply curves in a specific labor market, while graph (b) sums the curves horizontally to produce a *market* labor supply curve.[1] Notice from their respective labor supply curves, S_A and S_B that at wage W_1, Adams will offer 4 hours of labor and Bates 6 hours. We simply sum these outcomes (4 + 6) to get point x at wage W_1 on the market labor supply curve shown in graph (b). Now let's suppose that the wage rate rises from W_1 to W_2 in this labor market while all other

[1]We are assuming that while all these workers have identical skills, they have differing preferences for leisure, differing levels of nonwage income, and so forth. Thus, their reservation wages and individual labor supply curves differ.

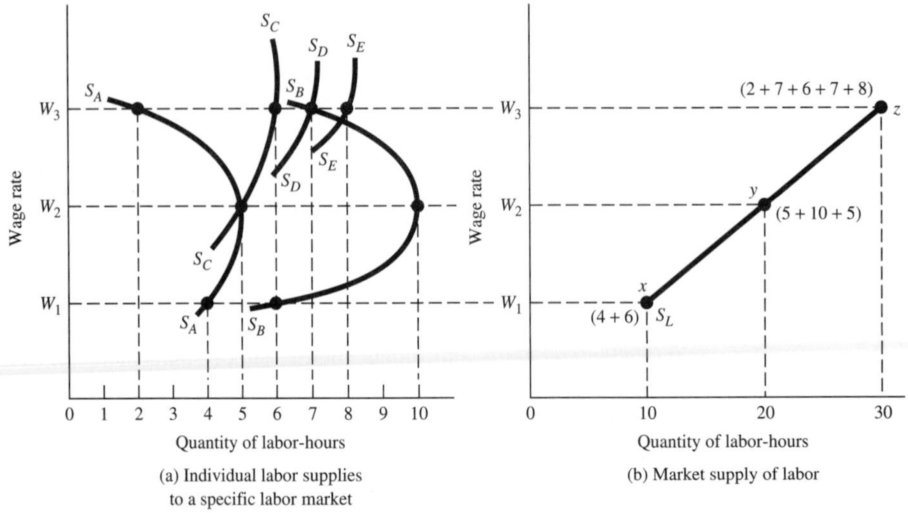

FIGURE 6-1 THE MARKET SUPPLY OF LABOR
Even though specific individuals normally have backward-bending labor supply curves, market labor supply curves generally are positively sloped over realistic wage ranges. Higher relative wages attract workers away from household production, leisure, or their previous jobs. The height of the market labor supply measures the opportunity cost of using the marginal labor hour in this employment. The shorter the time period, the less elastic this curve.

wage rates remain constant. Adams will increase her hours from 4 to 5 and Bates will work 10 hours rather than 6. We know from previous analysis that this implies that for these two workers, substitution effects exceed income effects over the W_1 to W_2 wage range. But also notice that at W_2, a third worker—Choy (S_C)—chooses to participate in this labor market, deciding to offer 5 hours of labor. Presumably, he is attracted away from either another labor market, household production, or leisure by the W_2 wage rate. Thus, the total quantity of hours supplied is 20 (= 5 + 10 + 5), as shown by point *y* in the right-hand graph. Finally, observe wage rate W_3, at which Adams and Bates choose to work fewer hours than previously, but Choy decides to offer 6 hours, and two new workers—Davis (S_D) and Egan (S_E)—now enter this labor market. The total number of hours, as observed at point *z* on the market labor supply curve, is now 30 (= 2 + 7 + 6 + 7 + 8).

Conclusion? Even though specific people may reduce their hours of work as the market wage rises, labor supply curves of specific labor markets generally are positively sloped over realistic wage ranges. *Higher relative wages attract workers away from either household production, leisure, or other labor markets and toward the labor market in which the wage increased.*

The vertical height of the market labor supply curve *xyz* measures the opportunity cost of employing the last labor hour in this occupation. For example, point *y* on S_L in Figure 6-1(b) indicates that wage rate W_2 is necessary to entice the twentieth hour of labor. Where there is competition in product and labor markets, perfect information, and costless migration, the value of the alternative activity that that hour previously produced—either as utility from leisure or output from work in a different occupation—is equivalent to W_2. To attract 30 hours of labor compared to 20, the wage must rise to W_3 (point z) because the twenty-first through thirtieth hours generate more than W_2 worth of value to workers and society in their alternative uses. To attract these hours to this labor market, these opportunity costs must be compensated for via a higher wage rate. *In perfectly competitive product and labor markets, labor supply curves measure marginal opportunity costs.*

One final point needs to be emphasized concerning market labor supply. The shorter the time period and the more specialized the variety of labor, the less elastic the labor supply curve. In the short run increases in the wage may not result in significant increases in the number of workers in a market, but in the long run human capital investments can be undertaken that will allow greater responsiveness to the higher relative wage (Chapter 4).

Equilibrium Figure 6-2 combines the market labor demand and supply curves for a specific type of labor and shows the equilibrium wage W_0 and the equilibrium quantity of labor Q_0. If the wage were W_{es}, an *excess supply*, or surplus, of labor $(b - a)$ would occur, driving the wage down to W_0. If instead the wage rate were W_{ed}, an *excess demand,* or shortage $(e - c)$, of workers would develop, and the wage would increase to W_0. Wage W_0 and employment level Q_0 is the only wage–employment combination at which the market clears. At W_0 the number of hours offered by labor suppliers just matches the number of hours that firms desire to employ.

Determinants The supply and demand curves in Figure 6-2 are drawn holding all factors other than the wage rate for this variety of labor constant. But a number of other factors—or ***determinants of labor supply and demand***—can change and cause either rightward or leftward shifts in the curves. We discussed many of these factors in

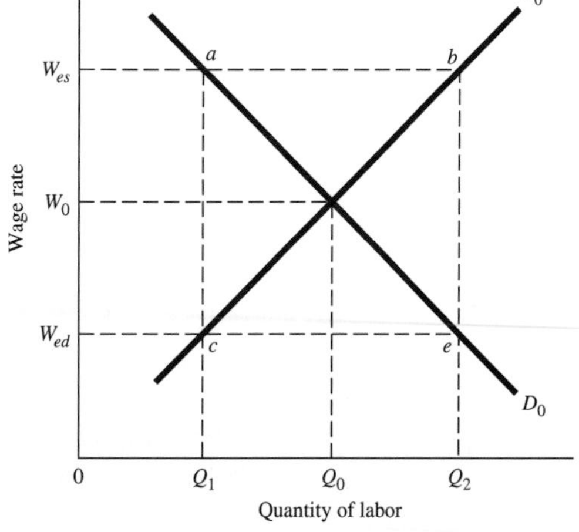

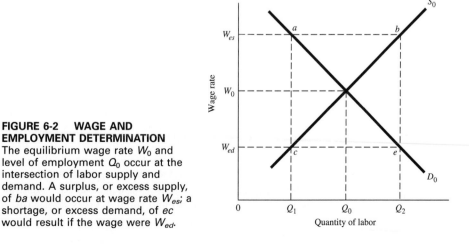

FIGURE 6-2 WAGE AND EMPLOYMENT DETERMINATION
The equilibrium wage rate W_0 and level of employment Q_0 occur at the intersection of labor supply and demand. A surplus, or excess supply, of *ba* would occur at wage rate W_{es}; a shortage, or excess demand, of *ec* would result if the wage were W_{ed}.

TABLE 6-1 THE DETERMINANTS OF LABOR SUPPLY AND DEMAND

Determinants of labor supply

1. **Other wage rates**
   An increase (decrease) in the wages paid in other occupations for which workers in a particular labor market are qualified will decrease (increase) labor supply.
2. **Nonwage income**
   An increase (decrease) in income other than from employment will decrease (increase) labor supply.
3. **Preferences for work versus leisure**
   A net increase (decrease) in people's preferences for work relative to leisure will increase (decrease) labor supply.
4. **Nonwage aspects of the job**
   An improvement (worsening) of the nonwage aspects of the job will increase (reduce) labor supply.
5. **Number of qualified suppliers**
   An increase (decrease) in the number of qualified suppliers of a specific grade of labor will increase (decrease) labor supply.

Determinants of labor demand

1. **Product demand**
   Changes in product demand that increase (decrease) the product price will raise (lower) the marginal revenue product (MRP) of labor and therefore increase (decrease) the demand for labor.
2. **Productivity**
   Assuming that it does not cause an offsetting decline in product price, an increase (decrease) in productivity will increase (decrease) the demand for labor.
3. **Prices of other resources**
   Where resources are *gross complements* (output effect > substitution effect), an increase (decrease) in the price of a substitute in production will decrease (increase) the demand for labor; where resources are *gross substitutes* (substitution effect > output effect), an increase (decrease) in the price of a substitute in production will increase (decrease) the demand for labor. An increase (decrease) in the price of a pure complement in production will decrease (increase) labor demand (no substitution effect; therefore a gross complement).
4. **Number of employers**
   Assuming no change in employment by other firms hiring a specific grade of labor, an increase (decrease) in the number of employers will increase (decrease) the demand for labor.

Chapters 2 and 5; they are simply formalized in Table 6-1 here. The distinction between "changes in demand" versus "changes in quantity demanded" *and* "changes in supply" versus "changes in quantity supplied" apply to the labor market as well as the product market. Changes in the determinants of labor demand and supply shown in the table shift the entire curves; these curve shifts are designated as "changes in labor demand" and "changes in labor supply." Changes in the wage rate, on the other hand, cause movements *along* demand and supply curves; that is, the quantity of labor demanded or supplied changes. But in the short run changes in the wage rate normally do not cause shifts of the curves themselves.

To demonstrate how a competitive market for a particular type of labor operates and to emphasize the role of the determinants of supply and demand, let's suppose that the labor market in Figure 6-3 is characterized by labor demand D_0 and labor supply S_0, which together produce equilibrium wage and employment levels W_0 and Q_0 (point *c*). Next, assume that demand declines for the product produced by firms hiring this labor, reducing the price of the product and thus the ***marginal revenue product*** (MRP) of labor (demand determinant 1, Table 6-1). Also, let's suppose that simultaneously the federal government releases findings of a definitive research study that concludes that the considerable health and safety risks that were heretofore associated with this occupation are in fact minimal. Taken alone, this information will increase the relative nonwage attractiveness of this labor and shift the labor supply curve rightward—say, from S_0 to S_1 (supply determinant 4, Table 6-1).

Now observe that at the initial wage rate W_0 the number of workers seeking jobs in this occupation (point *b*) exceeds the number of workers that firms wish to hire (point *a*). How will the market adjust to this surplus? Because wages are assumed to be perfectly flexible, the wage rate will drop to W_1, where the labor market will once again clear (point *e*). Figure 6-3 illustrates two generalizations. First, taken alone, a decline in labor demand reduces *both* the wage rate and quantity of labor employed. Second, an increase in labor supply—also viewed separately—reduces the wage rate and increases equilibrium quantity. In this case the net outcome of the simultaneous changes in supply and demand is a decline in the wage rate from W_0 to W_1 and a fall in the quantity of labor offered and employed from Q_0 to Q_1. The latter occurred because the decrease in demand was greater than the increase in labor supply. At W_1 the Q_1Q_0

FIGURE 6-3 CHANGES IN DEMAND, SUPPLY, AND MARKET EQUILIBRIUM
Changes in labor supply and demand create initial shortages or surpluses in labor markets, followed by adjustments to new equilibrium wage rates and employment. Here, the decline in demand from D_0 to D_1 and increase in supply from S_0 to S_1 produce an initial excess supply of *ab* at wage W_0. Consequently, the wage rate falls to W_1, and because the decline in demand is large relative to the increase in supply, the equilibrium quantity falls from Q_0 to Q_1.

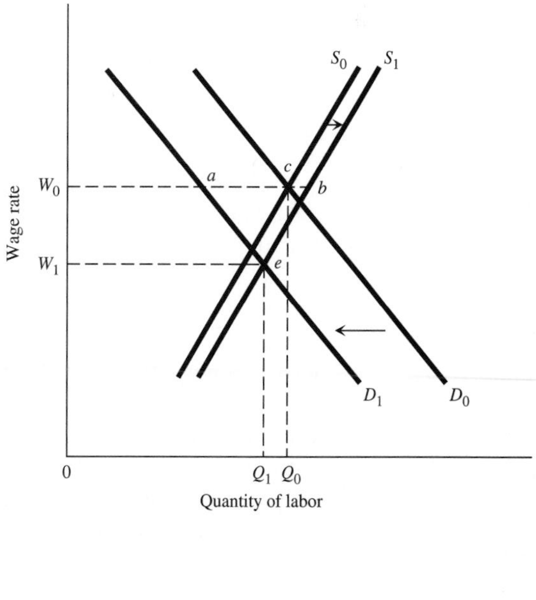

6-1 **World of Work**

THE STAGNATION OF REAL EARNINGS, 1979–1997

In the past century, the secular trend of real hourly wages and real weekly earnings for Americans has been upward. Increases in labor demand have outpaced increases in labor supply, advancing nominal wages faster than the price level.

But this positive trend in real wages has not been steady or uninterrupted. A troublesome fact is that inflation-adjusted hourly wages and weekly earnings have been stagnant since 1979. Specifically, in 1997 the average real hourly wage (1982 dollars) in all private nonagricultural industries was $7.50, down from $8.17 in 1979. In 1997 average weekly real earnings were $261, compared with $292 in 1979.

This stagnation of real earnings implies that, in the aggregate, increases in the demand for U.S. labor did not keep pace with increases in labor supply. Although the labor demand and supply curves clearly shifted rightward—total employment rose by about 33 million workers—the average real wage fell.

Several factors help explain the 1979–97 real wage decline. Perhaps of most significance were two supply-side factors: the rapid increase in the labor force associated with the baby boom and the surge in the labor force participation of females, particularly married women. To a lesser extent, rapid immigration during this period also expanded labor supply.

On the demand side, foreign competition placed great downward pressure on U.S. wages. The related sharp decline in unionism may have contributed to the slide in real wages. With weakened or nonexistent unions, gains in labor productivity are less likely to be translated into gains in real wages. Similarly, deregulation of the airline, trucking, and banking industries fostered greater product market competition, which in turn reduced real wages in these industries.

Other factors are involved. The rapid increase in low-paid part-time employment ("World of Work" 5-2) undoubtedly contributed to the decline in the *average* hourly wage. The rise in the part-time work force also helps explain why average weekly hours fell from 35.7 in 1979 to 34.6 in 1997. This increase accounts for part of the decline in average weekly real earnings. Finally, the rising expense of employer-paid health insurance benefits severely limited the ability of firms to increase real wages.

workers formerly employed in this market were not sufficiently compensated for their opportunity costs, and they left this occupation for either leisure, household production, or other jobs.

6-1

The Hiring Decision by an Individual Firm

Given the presence of, say, market wage W_0 or W_1 in Figure 6-3, how will a firm operating in a perfectly competitive labor and product market decide on the quantity of labor to employ? The answer can be found in Figure 6-4. Graph (a) portrays the labor market for a specific occupational group, and graph (b) shows the labor supply and demand curves for an individual firm hiring this labor. Because this particular employer is just one of many firms in this labor market, its decision on how many workers to employ will not affect the market wage. Instead, this firm is a "wage-taker" in the same sense that a perfectly competitive seller is a "price-taker" in the product market. The single employer in (b) has no incentive to pay more than the equilibrium wage W_0 because at the W_0 wage, it can attract as many labor units as it wants. On the other hand, if it offers a wage below W_0, it will attract *no* units of labor. All workers who possess this skill have marginal opportunity costs of at least W_0; they can get a minimum of W_0 in

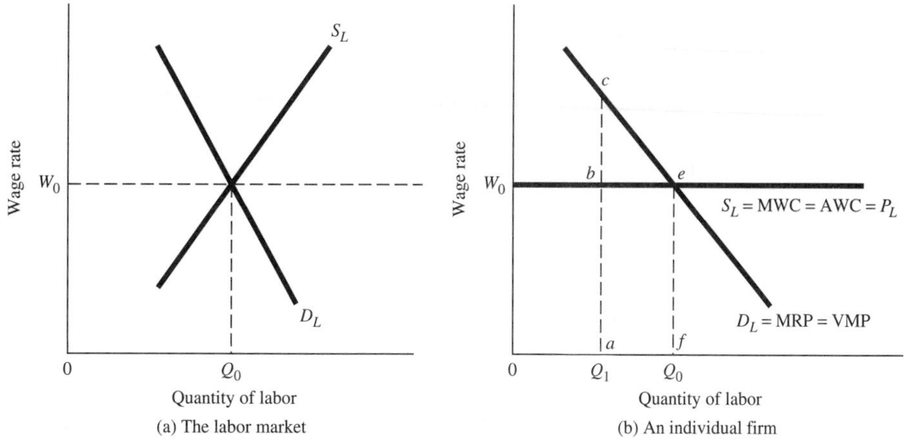

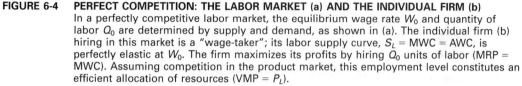

FIGURE 6-4 PERFECT COMPETITION: THE LABOR MARKET (a) AND THE INDIVIDUAL FIRM (b)
In a perfectly competitive labor market, the equilibrium wage rate W_0 and quantity of labor Q_0 are determined by supply and demand, as shown in (a). The individual firm (b) hiring in this market is a "wage-taker"; its labor supply curve, S_L = MWC = AWC, is perfectly elastic at W_0. The firm maximizes its profits by hiring Q_0 units of labor (MRP = MWC). Assuming competition in the product market, this employment level constitutes an efficient allocation of resources (VMP = P_L).

alternative employment. Consequently, the horizontal wage line W_0 in Figure 6-4(b) *is* this firm's labor supply curve *(S_L)*. You will observe that it is perfectly elastic.

Curve S_L in graph (b) also indicates this firm's average wage cost and marginal wage cost. ***Average wage cost*** (AWC) is *the total wage cost divided by the number of units of labor employed.* ***Marginal wage cost*** (MWC), on the other hand, is *the absolute change in total wage cost resulting from the employment of an additional unit of labor.* To see why average and marginal wage costs are equal in this case, suppose that the firm hires 100 labor hours at $8 per hour. The total hourly wage bill will be $800 (= $8 × 100). What will be the average wage cost and marginal wage cost? Answer: AWC = $8 (= $800/100); MWC (extra cost of the last worker hour) = $8 (= $800 − $792). And if the firm hires 200 labor hours? Answer: total wage cost = $1,600; AWC = $8 (= $1,600/200); MWC = $8 (= $1,600 − $1,592). For all levels of employment, W = $8 = MWC = AWC = S_L in this labor market.

Recall from Chapter 5 that in the short run a firm's demand for labor curve *is* its marginal revenue product curve. Thus, this firm can compare the additional revenue (MRP) obtained by hiring 1 more unit of labor with the added cost (MWC) or, in this case, the wage rate (W = MWC). If MRP > W, it will employ the particular hour of labor; on the other hand, if MRP < W, it will not. To generalize: *The profit-maximizing employer will obtain its optimal level of employment where MRP = MWC.* We label this equality the ***MRP = MWC rule.***

The profit-maximizing quantity is Q_0 in Figure 6-4(b). To confirm this, observe level Q_1 where MRP, as shown by the vertical distance *ac,* exceeds MWC (distance *ab*). Clearly this firm will gain profits if it hires this unit of labor because it can sell the added product produced by this worker for more than the wage W_0 (= MWC). This is true for all units of labor up to Q_0, where MRP and MWC are equal (distance *fe*). Beyond Q_0, diminishing returns finally reduce marginal product (MP) to the extent that MRP (= MP × *P*) lies below the market wage W_0 (= MWC). Thus, this firm's total profit will fall if it hires more than Q_0 worker hours.

Allocative Efficiency

We stressed at the outset of Chapter 1 that labor is a scarce resource and it therefore behooves society to use it efficiently. How do we define an efficient allocation of labor? Is labor efficiently allocated in the perfect competition labor market just discussed? And what about the noncompetitive labor market models to follow?

Labor Market Efficiency Let's first bring the notion of allocative efficiency into focus. An ***efficient allocation of labor*** is realized when workers are being directed to their highest valued uses. Labor is being allocated efficiently when society obtains the largest amount of domestic output from the given amount of labor available. Stated technically, available labor is efficiently allocated when its value of marginal product or VMP—the dollar value to society of its marginal product—is the same in all alternative employments.

This assertion can be demonstrated through a simple example. Suppose that type *A* labor (for example, assembly line labor) is capable of producing both product *x* (say, autos) and product *y* (say, refrigerators). Suppose the available amount of type *A* labor is currently allocated so that the value of marginal product of labor in producing autos is \$12 and its value of marginal product in producing refrigerators is \$8. In short, VMP_{Ax} (= \$12) > VMP_{Ay} (= \$8). This is *not* an efficient allocation of type *A* labor because it is not making the maximum contribution to domestic output. It is clear that by shifting a worker from producing *y* (refrigerators) to making *x* (autos), the domestic output can be increased by \$4 (= \$12 − \$8). This reallocation will cause a movement down the VMP curve for *x* and up the VMP curve for *y*. That is, VMP_{Ax} will fall and VMP_{Ay} will rise. The indicated reallocation from *y* to *x* should continue until the VMP of type *A* labor is the same for both products, or, $VMP_{Ax} = VMP_{Ay}$. In our example, this might occur where, say, $VMP_{Ax} = VMP_{Ay} = \$10$. When this equality is achieved, there is no further reallocation of labor that will cause a net increase in the domestic output.

If we expand our example from just two products to any number of products, that is, *n* products, we can state the condition for allocative efficiency for any given type of labor by the following equation:

$$VMP_{Ax} = VMP_{Ay} = \ldots = VMP_{An} = P_{LA} \qquad (6\text{-}1)$$

where *A* is the given type of labor; *x, y, . . . n* represent all possible products that labor might produce; and VMP is the value of labor's marginal product in producing the various products.

Observe that in equation (6-1) we have made the VMPs of labor equal not only to one another, but also to the ***price of labor*** P_L. Why so? The reason is that we take into consideration that type *A* labor will be made available in this labor market only if the price of labor is sufficiently high to cover the opportunity costs of those supplying their labor services. Type *A* labor may be used in non-type *A* work, household production (child care, meal preparation, etc.), or pure leisure. Indeed, the optimal position in Chapter 2's work–leisure model (specifically, point u_1 in Figure 2-5) defines an efficient allocation of labor (time) between labor market and nonlabor market activities. In Figure 6-1 we found that such individual work–leisure allocations—along with wage opportunities in other labor markets—are reflected in the labor supply curve within a competitive labor market. Thus, equation (6-1) tells us that human resources are efficiently allocated when the value of the last units of labor in various labor market uses (producing goods *x, y, . . . n*) are all equal and these values in turn are equal to the opportunity cost of labor P_L (the marginal value of alternative work, non-labor market production, and leisure). Alternatively, an *underallocation* of a particular type of labor to labor market production occurs when its VMP in any employment exceeds P_L; an *overallocation* occurs when its VMP in any labor market employment is less than P_L.

Perfect Competition and Allocative Efficiency Having defined allocative efficiency, let's consider our second question: Do perfect competitive labor markets result in an efficient allocation of labor? Figure 6-5 is simply an expansion of Figure 6-4 to show the equilibrium positions of representative firms from several competitive industries; that is, industries producing *x, y,* and *n* with type *A* labor. Note that equilibrium for the three representative firms occurs at employment levels Q_{Ax}, Q_{Ay}, and Q_{An}, respectively. The equilibrium positions are the result of each firm's desire to maximize profits by equating the MRPs of *A* with the MWC of *A*. But perfect competition in the hiring of labor means that P_{LA} equals the MWC of *A*. Similarly, perfect competition

FIGURE 6-5 **PERFECT COMPETITION AND AN EFFICIENT ALLOCATION OF LABOR**
Representative firms producing goods such as *x, y,* and *n* maximize profits by employing type *A* labor where the marginal revenue product of labor (MRP) equals the marginal wage cost (MWC). Perfect competition in the product market ensures that MRP equals the value of marginal product (VMP), and perfect competition in the labor market means that MWC equals the price of labor *(P_L)*. Thus, VMP matches P_L in each use, satisfying the condition for efficiency in the allocation of type *A* labor: $VMP_{Ax} = VMP_{Ay} = \ldots = VMP_{An} = P_L$.

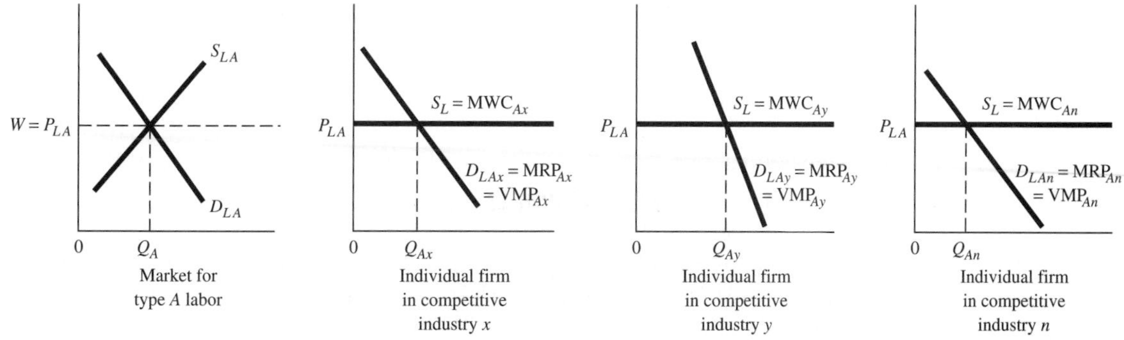

in the sale of the three products means that the MRP of *A* equals its VMP for all three products. Thus, each firm maximizes profits where MWC = MRP. But because P_{LA} = MWC *and* MRP = VMP for all competitive firms using type *A* labor, we find that equation (6-1) is fulfilled. In short, competitive labor markets *do* result in an efficient allocation of labor. This is an example of Adam Smith's famous concept of the "invisible hand." In competitive labor and product markets, pursuit of private self-interest (profit maximization) furthers society's interest (an efficient allocation of scarce resources). It is as if there is an unseen coordinator moving resources to where they are most beneficial to society.

With this understanding of allocative efficiency and its realization when perfect competition prevails, let's now seek to determine whether noncompetitive labor markets are consistent with an efficient allocation of labor.

WAGE AND EMPLOYMENT DETERMINATION: MONOPOLY IN THE PRODUCT MARKET

To this point we have assumed that the employers hiring labor in a perfectly competitive labor market are "price-takers" in the product market; that is, they do not possess monopoly power. But recall from Chapter 5, specifically Table 5-3 and Figure 5-3, that if a firm is a monopolist in the sale of its product, it will face a downward-sloping product demand curve. This means that increases in its output will require price reductions, and because the lower prices will apply to all the firm's output, its marginal revenue (MR) will be less than its price. Consequently, MRP_L (= MP × MR) will fall for two reasons: (1) MP will decline because of diminishing returns (also true for perfect product market competition), *and* (2) MR will decline more rapidly than price as more workers are hired (in perfect competition, MR is constant and equals product price *P*).

The labor market consequences of product market monopoly are shown in Figure 6-6. Here we assume that the labor market is perfectly competitive but that one particular firm hiring this type of labor is a monopolist in the sale of its product. Restated, this type of labor is used by thousands of firms, not just this monopolist, and thus there is competition in the labor market.

Figure 6-6 indicates that this monopolist is a "wage-taker" and therefore faces the perfectly elastic labor supply curve shown as S_L. This supply curve coincides with the firm's marginal wage cost (MWC) and its average wage cost (AWC), just as it did in our previous model.

Labor demand curve D_c is the MRP curve that would have existed had there been competition rather than monopoly and therefore no decline in marginal revenue as the firm increased its employment and output. This MRP curve would be equal to VMP; the firm's revenue gain from hiring one more worker would equal society's gain in output. On the other hand, demand curve D_m is the *monopolist's* MRP curve. In this case, MRP *does not equal* VMP. The value of the extra output of each worker to the monopolist is less than the value to society. The reason again: The monopolist's sale of an additional unit of output does not add the full amount of the product's price to

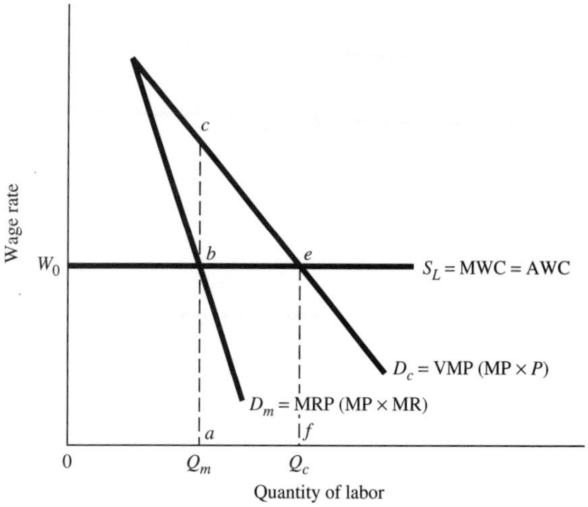

FIGURE 6-6 WAGE RATE AND EMPLOYMENT DETERMINATION: MONOPOLY IN THE PRODUCT MARKET Because a product market monopolist faces a downward-sloping demand curve, increased hiring of labor and the resulting larger output force the firm to lower its price. And because it must lower its price on all units, its marginal revenue (MR) is less than the price. Thus, the firm's MRP curve (MP × MR) lies below the VMP curve (MP × *P*), and this employer hires Q_m rather than Q_c units of labor. An efficiency loss to society of *bce* results.

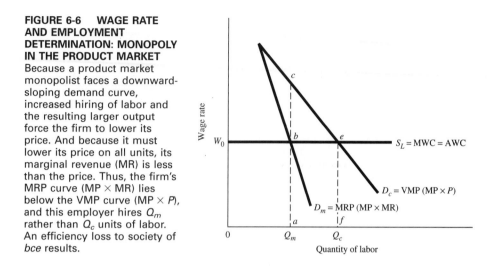

its marginal revenue. Thus, MRP (= MR × MP)—the value to the firm—is less than VMP (= *P* × MP)—the value to society.[2]

Several noteworthy outcomes of monopoly in the product market are evident in Figure 6-6. First, the monopolist's labor demand curve D_m is *less elastic* than the competitive curve D_c. Second, the monopolist behaves in the same way as the competitor by determining its profit-maximizing level of employment where MRP = MWC. Nevertheless, this equality produces a lower level of employment—Q_m in this case—than would occur under competitive product market conditions *(*Q_c*)*. Third, the wage paid by the monopolist is the same as that paid by competitive firms. Without unions, both are wage-takers.[3] Fourth, labor resources are misallocated. To understand why, recall that in a perfectly competitive labor market the price of labor *(*$P_L = W$*)* reflects the marginal opportunity cost to society of using a resource in a particular employment. Also remember that the VMP of labor is a measure of the added contribution to output of a worker in a specific employment. Notice in the figure VMP > P_L (W_0) for the Q_m through Q_c workers. This implies that too few labor resources are being

[2]If you are not clear on this point, review Table 5-3 and Figure 5-3.

[3]For evidence supporting this theoretical prediction, see Leonard W. Weiss, "Concentration and Labor Earnings," *American Economic Reviews,* March 1966, pp. 96–117.

The less elastic labor demand curve possessed by the monopolist, however, may increase the collective bargaining power of unions and result in a higher wage for workers in monopolized product markets. For evidence of a positive impact of monopoly power on wages, see James A. Dalton and Edward J. Ford, "Concentration and Labor Earnings in Manufacturing and Utilities," *Industrial and Labor Relations Review,* October 1977, pp. 45–60; John E. Kwoka, "Monopoly, Plant and Union Effects on Worker Wages," *Industrial and Labor Relations Review,* January 1983, pp. 251–257; James E. Long and Albert N. Link, "The Impact of Market Structure on Wages, Fringe Benefits, and Turnover," *Industrial and Labor Relations Review,* January 1983, pp. 239–250; John S. Heywood, "Labor Quality and the Concentration-Earnings Hypothesis," *Review of Economics and Statistics,* May 1986, pp. 342–346; Dale L. Belman, "Concentration, Unionism, and Labor Earnings: A Sample Selection Approach," *Review of Economic Statistics,* August 1988, pp. 391–397; and S. Nickell, J. Vainiomaki, and S. Wadwani, "Wages and Product Market Power," *Economica,* November 1994, pp. 457–473.

allocated to this employment and therefore too many are allocated somewhere else. Assuming costless labor mobility, if Q_mQ_c (or *be*) workers were reallocated from alternative activities to work in this industry, the *net* value of society's output would rise by area *bce*. These workers would contribute output valued at *acef* in this employment—the value of the total product added—while they previously contributed output valued at area *abef*—the opportunity cost to society of using them here.[4]

QUICK REVIEW 6-1

- Changes in the determinants of labor supply and demand (Table 6-1) shift the labor supply and demand curves and produce new equilibrium wage-employment levels.
- The perfectly competitive firm is a "wage-taker" whose labor supply curve is perfectly elastic (WR = MWC = AWC); it maximizes profit at the level of employment where marginal wage cost equals marginal revenue product (MWC = MRP).
- By equating the value of the marginal product of labor (= VMP_L) and the opportunity cost of labor (= P_L), perfect competition in product and labor markets creates allocative efficiency.
- Because a product market monopolist's MRP (= MP × MR) curve lies below the VMP (= MP × *P*) curve, employment is less in the monopolized industry than it would be if the industry were competitive.

Your Turn: Assume that perfectly competitive firms are employing labor in profit-maximizing amounts. Now suppose that, all else being equal, the market supply of this labor increases. How will the firms respond? How will they know when to stop responding? Explain, referring to MRP and MWC. (Answers: See page 626.)

6-2

MONOPSONY

Thus far, we have assumed that the labor market is perfectly competitive. Now we wish to analyze a labor market where either a single firm is the sole hirer of a particular type of labor or two or more employers collude to fix a below-competitive wage. These market circumstances are called ***pure monopsony*** and ***joint monopsony,*** respectively. For purposes of simplicity, our discussion will be confined to pure forms of monopsony, but keep in mind that monopsony power, much the same as monopoly power, extend beyond the *pure* model to include weaker forms of market power.

We will again assume that (1) there are numerous qualified, homogeneous workers who act independently to secure employment in the monopsonized labor market, and (2) information is perfect and mobility is costless. But unlike the perfect competitor, the monopsonist is a "wage-setter"; it can control the wage rate it pays by adjusting

[4]We are assuming that the monopoly firm cannot "price discriminate." If it could charge purchasers the exact price they would be willing to pay rather than do without the product, MRP would coincide with VMP in Figure 6-6. The firm would now find it profitable to hire Q_c (rather than Q_m) workers and labor resources would be allocated efficiently (Q_c).

6-2 World of Work

ARE CHIEF EXECUTIVES OVERPAID?

Chief executive officers (CEOs) of many large U.S. corporations earn multimillion-dollar annual salaries. For example, in 1996 the 30 highest-paid U.S. executives received more than $30 million each of annual compensation (salary, bonuses, and stock options). Are these sky-high salaries based on marginal revenue product, as in Figure 6-4's competitive market? That is, does such a salary reflect the CEO's contribution to the firm's output and thus to its revenues?

Those who answer affirmatively point out that decisions made by the CEOs of large corporations affect the productivity of every employee in the organization. Good decisions enhance productivity throughout the organization; bad decisions reduce productivity. Only executives who have consistently made good business decisions attain the top positions in large corporations. Because the supply of these people is highly limited and their marginal productivity is great, top CEOs earn enormous salaries.

Also, some economists note that CEO pay may be like the prizes professional golfers and tennis players receive for winning tournaments. These high prizes are designed to promote the productivity of all those who aspire to achieve them (Chapter 7). In corporations the top prizes go to the winners of the "contests" among managers to attain, at least eventually, the CEO positions. Thus, high CEO pay may not derive solely from the CEO's *direct* productivity. Instead, it may exist because the high pay creates incentives that raise the productivity of scores of other corporate employees who seek to achieve the top position. Thus, in this view, the high CEO pay remains grounded on high productivity.

Critics of existing CEO pay acknowledge that CEOs deserve higher salaries than ordinary workers or typical managers, but they note that CEO pay in other industrial nations, including Japan and Germany, is far lower than in the United States. Also, in these countries the ratios of CEO salaries to average salaries are far less than in the United States.

So why have multimillion-dollar salaries emerged here? The answer, say critics, is that corporations, although owned by their stockholders, are controlled by corporate boards and professional executives. Because many board members are present or past CEOs of other corporations, they often exaggerate CEO importance and, consequently, overpay their own CEOs. These overpayments are at the expense of the stockholders.

In brief, critics believe that multimillion-dollar CEO pay bears little relationship to wages determined in competitive markets (Figure 6-4). It is clear from our discussion that this issue remains unsettled.

the amount of labor it hires, much as a product market monopolist can control its price by adjusting its output.

Table 6-2 contains the elements needed to examine labor supply and demand, wage and employment determination, and allocative outcomes in the monopsony model. Comprehension of the table will greatly clarify the graphic analysis that follows.

Notice in Table 6-2 that columns 1 and 2 indicate that the firm must increase the wage rate it pays in order to attract more units of labor toward this market and away from alternative employment opportunities. We assume that this firm cannot "wage discriminate" when hiring additional workers; it must pay the higher wage *to all workers,* including those who could have been attracted at a lower wage. This fact is reflected in column 3, where total wage cost (TWC) is shown. The values for TWC are found by *multiplying* the units of labor times the wage rate, rather than by summing the wage column. For example, if the monopsonist hires 5 units of labor, it will have to pay $5 for each, for a total of $25. Next, notice the marginal wage cost (MWC) shown in column 4. The extra cost of hiring, say, the fifth unit of labor ($9) is more

TABLE 6-2 WAGE AND EMPLOYMENT DETERMINATION: MONOPSONY (HYPOTHETICAL DATA)

(1) Units of labor	(2) (AWC) Wage	(3) TWC	(4) MWC	(5) (VMP) MRP
1	$1	$1	$1	$7
2	2	4	3	6
3	3	9	5	5
4	4	16	7	4
5	5	25	9	3
6	6	36	11	2

than the wage paid for that unit ($5). Each of the 4 labor units that could have been attracted at $4 must now also be paid $5. The $1 extra wage paid for each of these workers (= $4 total) plus the $5 paid for the fifth worker yields the $9 MWC in column 4. To generalize: *The monopsonist's marginal wage cost exceeds the wage rate because it must pay a higher wage to attract more workers, and it must pay this higher wage to all workers.*

Finally, note column 5 in Table 6-2, which shows the marginal revenue product (MRP) of labor. We know that the MRP schedule is the firm's short-run demand for labor curve. In this case we can avoid unnecessary complexity by assuming that the monopsonist is selling its product in a perfectly competitive market, and therefore MRP = VMP. We will soon discover, however, that the monopsonist will disregard this MRP schedule once it selects its profit-maximizing level of employment.

Figure 6-7 shows the monopsony model graphically. The labor supply curve slopes upward because the monopsonist is the only firm hiring this labor and hence faces the market labor supply curve. Notice that S_L is also the firm's average wage cost (AWC) curve (total wage cost/quantity of labor). Marginal wage cost (MWC) lies above and rises more rapidly than S_L because the higher wage rate paid to attract an additional worker must also be paid to all workers already employed. As we previously indicated, the marginal revenue curve MRP is the competitive labor demand curve and also measures the value of the marginal product of labor, VMP.

What quantity of labor will this monopsonistic firm hire, and what wage will it pay? To maximize profits, the firm will equate MWC with MRP, as shown at point *a,* and employ Q_1 units of labor. To understand this, suppose that the firm employed Q_c units of labor rather than Q_1. The MWC of the Q_c unit is shown by point *b* on the MWC curve, but the MRP of the extra labor is only *c*. Thus, the firm would lose profits equal to area *abc* by its action. To repeat: *The monopsonist, like the perfect competitor, finds its profit-maximizing employment level where MRP equals MWC.*

Having decided to hire Q_1 units of labor, the monopsonist's effective labor demand becomes a single point *e* rather than the entire curve D_L. This point lies along the market labor supply curve S_L, allowing the firm to set the wage at W_1. The market clears at this wage; the quantity of labor demanded by the firm, Q_1, equals the amount of la-

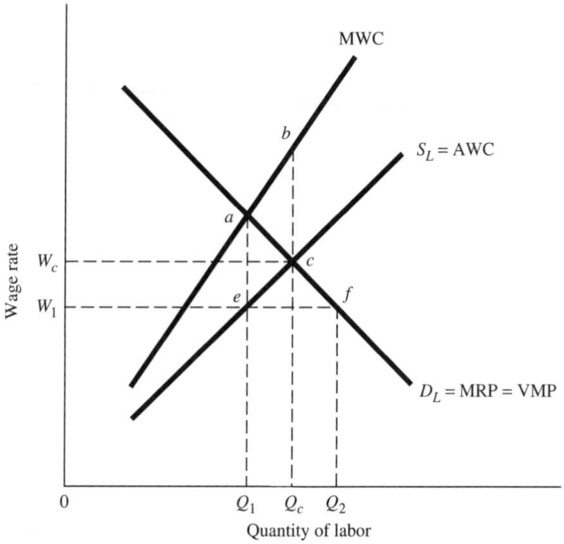

FIGURE 6-7 WAGE RATE AND EMPLOYMENT DETERMINATION: MONOPSONY
The firm's MWC lies above the S_L = AWC curve in a monopsonistic labor market. The monopsonist equates MRP with its MWC at point *a* and chooses to hire Q_1 units of labor. To attract these workers it need only pay W_1 an hour, as shown by point *e*. The firm thus pays a lower wage rate (W_1 rather than W_c) and hires fewer units of labor (Q_1 as compared to Q_c) than firms in a competitive labor market. Society loses area *eac* because of allocative inefficiency.

bor that suppliers are willing to offer. This equilibrium wage corresponds to that in Table 6-2 (circled row of data). Notice from point *f* on the MRP = VMP curve in Figure 6-7, however, that this monopsonist would prefer to hire Q_2 units of labor *if* it could hire each unit at a W_1 wage. Thus, the monopsonist may perceive a shortage of this type of labor. It would like more units of labor at the W_1 wage than it can get, but its self-interest keeps it from raising the wage above W_1. This may explain why monopsony markets, such as the one for nurses, are characterized by chronically unfilled job vacancies.[5] If we transformed this labor market into a perfectly competitive one, the equilibrium wage and quantity of labor would be W_c and Q_c units, respectively (point *c*). But as previously indicated, it simply is not profitable for this monopsonist to hire the Q_c units of labor and pay W_c to all Q_c workers. Instead, it restricts the quantity of labor hired and pays (1) a lower-than-competitive wage (W_1 compared to W_c) and (2) a wage below the MRP of the last unit of labor employed (*e* as opposed to *a*).

It is easy to see the basic divergence between the monopsonist's profit-maximizing goal and society's desire to maximize the total value of its output. Indeed, MRP equals

[5]The traditional view is that the labor market for nurses is monopsonistic. Hospitals are relatively few, particularly in small and medium size cities. See Richard Hurd, "Equilibrium Vacancies in a Labor Market Dominated by Non-Profit Firms: The 'Shortage' of Nurses," *Review of Economics and Statistics,* May 1973, pp. 234–240. More recent research, however, questions whether monopsony exists in the market for nurses. See Barry T. Hirsch and Edward J. Schumacher, "Monopsony Power and Relative Wages in the Labor Market for Nurses," *Journal of Health Economics,* October 1995, pp. 443–476.

MWC at Q_1 units of labor, but VMP is greater than the supply price of labor, W_1 ($= Q_1e$). Remember that the market labor supply curve reflects the price of labor in terms of the value of the output which the labor can produce in the next best employment opportunity. We observe that along segment *ac* of the VMP curve, the value of the marginal product of the Q_1Q_c labor units exceeds the opportunity cost to society of using that labor in this specific employment (shown by *ec* on the supply of labor curve). Therefore, if society reallocated this labor from the alternative employments and to this market, it would gain output of more value than it would forgo. The labor would contribute total output shown by area Q_1acQ_c in Figure 6-7. Society would forgo area Q_1ecQ_c of domestic product elsewhere, and thus, the net gain would be area *eac*. This latter triangle then identifies the allocative cost to society of the monopsonized labor market. Labor is underallocated to the goods and services produced in monopsonized industries.

Several attempts have been made to identify and measure monopsony power in real-world labor markets. Monopsony outcomes are not widespread in the U.S. economy.[6] A large number of potential employers exists for most workers, particularly when these workers are occupationally and geographically mobile (Chapter 9). Also, strong labor unions counteract monopsony power in many labor markets (Chapters 10 and 11).

Table 6-3 provides a matrix showing the wage outcomes of the three labor market models discussed thus far. The outcome in the bottom right corner of the matrix sim-

[6]For a sampling of studies on monopsony, see G. W. Scully, "Pay and Performance in Major League Baseball," *American Economic Review,* December 1974, pp. 915–930; R. L. Bunting, *Employer Concentration in Local Labor Markets* (Chapel Hill: University of North Carolina Press, 1962); J. H. Landon and R. N. Baird, "Monopsony in the Market for Public School Teachers," *American Economic Review,* December 1971, pp. 966–971; James Luizer and Robert Thornton, "Concentration in the Labor Market for Public School Teachers," *Industrial and Labor Relations Review,* July 1986, pp. 573–584; and William N. Boal, "Testing for Employer Monopsony in Turn-of-the-Century Coal Mining," *Rand Journal of Economics,* Autumn 1995, pp. 519–536.

TABLE 6-3 WAGE OUTCOMES OF LABOR MARKETS WITHOUT UNIONS

		Product market structure (firm)	
		Perfect competitor in sale of product (MR = P)	Monopolist in sale of product (MR < P)
Labor market structure (firm)	Perfect competitor in hire of labor (MWC = *W*)	*W* = MRP = VMP (Figure 6-4)	*W* = MRP *W* < VMP (Figure 6-6)
	Monopsonist in hire of labor (MWC > *W*)	*W* < MRP (= VMP) (Figure 6-7)	*W* < MRP (< VMP)

6-3

ply extends the monopsony outcome to a market where the monopsonist is an imperfect competitor in the sale of the product. You are urged to study each part of this table carefully.

UNIONS AND WAGE DETERMINATION

We assumed throughout the previous discussion that workers *independently* supplied their labor services and therefore competed for available jobs. But in some labor markets workers have organized into unions to "sell" their labor services *collectively.* These unions can increase the wage rate paid to those members who have jobs by (1)

6-3 World of Work

PAY AND PERFORMANCE IN PROFESSIONAL BASEBALL

Professional baseball has provided an interesting "laboratory" in which the predictions of orthodox wage theory have been empirically tested. Until 1976 professional baseball players were bound to a single team through the so-called "reserve clause" that prevented players from selling their talents on the open (competitive) market. Stated differently, the reserve clause conferred monopsony power on the team that originally drafted the player. Labor market theory (Figure 6-7) would lead us to predict that this monopsony power would permit teams to pay wages less than a player's marginal revenue product (MRP). However, since 1976 major league players have been able to become "free agents" at the end of their sixth season of play and at that time can sell their services to any team. Theory suggests that free agents should be able to increase their salaries and bring them more closely into accord with their MRPs. Research tends to confirm both of the indicated predictions.

Scully[*] found that before baseball players could become free agents their salaries were substantially below their MRPs. He estimated a player's MRP as follows. First, he determined the relationship between a team's winning percentage and its revenue. Then he estimated the relationship between various possible measures of player productivity and a team's winning percentage. He found the ratio of strikeouts to walks for pitchers and the slugging averages for hitters (all nonpitchers) to be the best indicators of a player's contribution to the winning percentage. These two estimates were combined to calculate the contribution of a player to a team's total revenue.

Scully discovered that prior to free agency the estimated MRPs of both pitchers and hitters were substantially greater than player salaries. Even the lowest-quality pitchers received on the average salaries amounting to only about 54 percent of their MRPs. "Star" players were exploited more than other players. The best pitchers received salaries that were only about 21 percent of their MRPs, according to Scully. The same general results applied to hitters. For example, the least productive hitters on the average received a salary equal to about 37 percent of their MRPs.

Sommers and Quinton[†] assessed the economic fortunes of 14 players who constituted the "first family" of free agents. In accordance with the predictions of labor market theory, their research indicated that the competitive bidding of free agency brought the salaries of free agents more closely into accord with their estimated MRPs. Although MRP and salary differences were found to be larger for hitters, Sommers and Quinton concluded that the overturn of the monopsonistic reserve clause forced owners to pay players more closely in relation to their contribution to team revenues.

Thanks largely to free agency, the average salary in major league baseball had soared to $1,383,578 for the 1997 season.

[*]Gerald W. Scully, "Pay and Performance in Major League Baseball," *American Economic Review,* December 1974, pp. 915–930.

[†]Paul M. Sommers and Noel Quinton, "Pay and Performance in Major League Baseball: The Case of the First Family of Free Agents," *Journal of Human Resources,* Summer 1982, pp. 426–435.

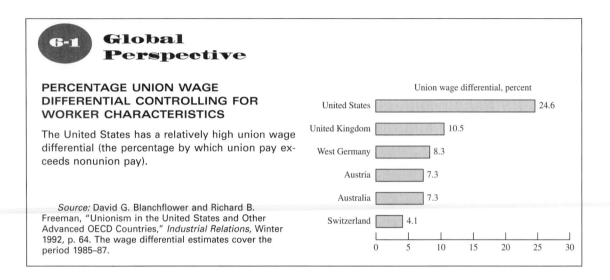

6-1 Global Perspective

PERCENTAGE UNION WAGE DIFFERENTIAL CONTROLLING FOR WORKER CHARACTERISTICS

The United States has a relatively high union wage differential (the percentage by which union pay exceeds nonunion pay).

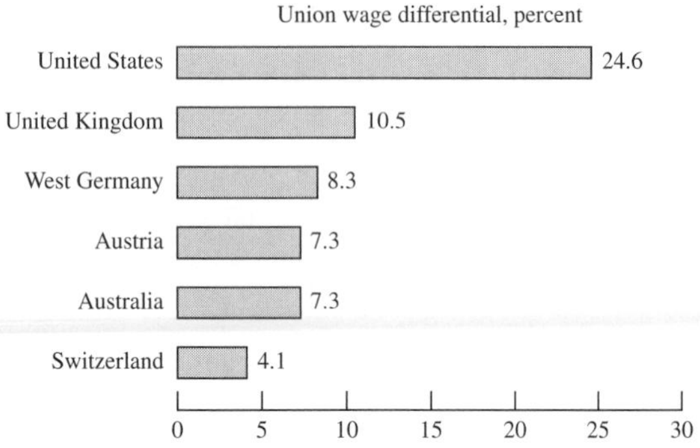

Source: David G. Blanchflower and Richard B. Freeman, "Unionism in the United States and Other Advanced OECD Countries," *Industrial Relations,* Winter 1992, p. 64. The wage differential estimates cover the period 1985–87.

6-1

increasing the demand for labor, (2) restricting the supply of labor, and (3) bargaining for an above-equilibrium wage.

Increasing the Demand for Labor

To the limited extent that a union is able to increase the demand for labor, it can raise *both* the market wage rate and the quantity of labor hired. This is shown in Figure 6-8, where an increase in labor demand from D_0 to D_1 results in a rise in the wage rate from W_0 to W_1 and an increase in employment from Q_0 to Q_1. The more elastic the supply of labor, the less the increase in the wage rate relative to the rise in employment.

Is the Q_1 level of employment an overallocation of labor to this use? It depends. If Q_0 is indeed the efficient level of employment, then triangle *abc* represents an efficiency loss resulting from the union's actions. The opportunity cost of the Q_0Q_1 units of labor—shown by segment *ab* of *S*—exceeds the VMP of labor—shown by segment *ac* of D_0. But Q_0 need not be the efficient allocation of labor in all instances to which this model applies. We will highlight one such circumstance in the following discussion.

A union can increase labor demand through actions that alter one or more of the determinants of labor demand (Table 6-1). Specifically, it can try to (1) increase product demand, (2) enhance labor productivity, (3) influence the price of related resources, and (4) increase the number of "buyers" of its specific labor services. Let's analyze these actions and cite examples of each.

1 Increasing Product Demand Unions do not have direct control over the demand for the product they help produce, but they can influence it through (a) product advertising and (b) political lobbying.

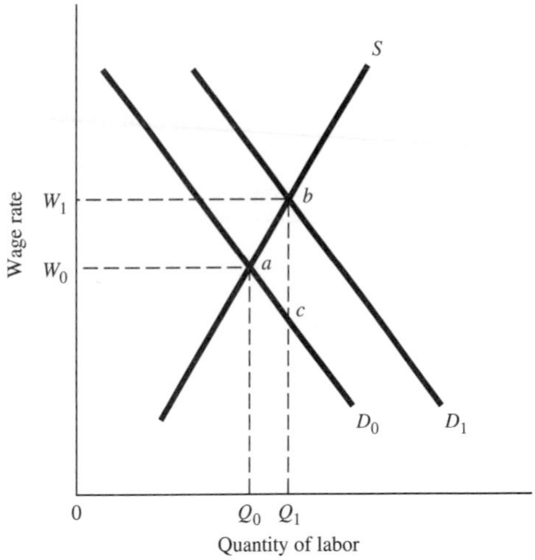

FIGURE 6-8 UNION TECHNIQUES: INCREASING THE DEMAND FOR LABOR
To the extent that unions can increase the demand for union labor (D_0 to D_1), they can realize higher wage rates (W_0 to W_1) and increased employment (Q_0 to Q_1).

First, unions can advertise the product. One example is the activity of the locals of the International Ladies Garment Workers Union (ILGWU) that have joined their employers in financing advertising campaigns to bolster the demand for their products. The ILGWU also participated in a multimedia campaign to persuade consumers to "look for the union label." A second example is the $2 million "Call or Buy Union" campaign begun by the Communications Workers Union (CWA) in 1984. The purpose was to convince telephone users to choose the long-distance services provided by AT&T Communications and Western Union Corporation, which together provided nearly 100,000 CWA jobs. That advertising was designed to increase the demand for union-produced goods and services and boost the demand for union workers.

Of considerably more significance is political lobbying by unions to increase the demand for union-made goods and services. For example, unions often actively support proposed legislation that would increase government purchases of the products they make. It is not surprising to see construction union lobbying for new highway projects, urban mass-transit proposals, plans to revitalize urban areas, or flood control and related water projects. Nor is it unusual to discover teachers' organizations pushing for legislation to increase government spending on education.

For similar reasons, unions also lobby for legislation that bolsters private-sector demand for union-made products. For example, unions in the aerospace industry strongly supported legislation granting interest rate subsidies to foreign purchasers of commercial airplanes produced in the United States.

Still another way unions may increase product demand is through their political support for laws that increase the price of goods that are close substitutes for those made by union members. For instance, the United Auto Workers (UAW) joined the major U.S. auto companies in proposing tariffs and import quotas on imported motor vehicles. These trade barriers increase the price of a substitute good, adding to the demand for (and price of) domestically produced autos. This then raises the demand for UAW members.

Finally, some unions recognize that they can enhance the demand for their own labor by lobbying successfully for legislation that *reduces* the price of goods or services that are *complements* to the services they render. For example, unions representing restaurant employees often resist attempts to increase city excise taxes levied on hotels and motels. The lower lodging prices help attract convention business, which increases the demand for restaurant meals and the derived demand for restaurant workers.

6-4

2 Enhancing Productivity We know that the strength of labor demand in a specific occupation depends partly on productivity (MP). Firms control most of the factors that determine worker productivity. But two possible ways unions might be able to influence output per worker hour are participation in joint labor–management committees on productivity—sometimes called "quality circles"—and "codetermination," which consists of direct worker participation in the decision processes of the firms. The latter also is sometimes called "worker democracy." The purpose of both approaches is to improve internal communication within the firm and increase productivity through more emphasis on teamwork and profit incentives.

In many cases, unions have resisted participation in quality circles and codetermination, contending that these programs circumvent the collective bargaining process

6-4 World of Work

INFLUENCING THE DEMAND FOR LABOR: UNIONS AND MUNICIPAL EXPENDITURES*

Downward-sloping labor demand curves mean that reductions in employment are likely to accompany union-negotiated wage rate increases. This problem can be particularly acute for unions in city government, where budgets are based on available tax revenues. Therefore, it is in the interest of municipal unions to try to find ways to shift the demand curve rightward for the services of their members (Figure 6-8).

How might municipal unions increase labor demand in their departments and thereby improve wage and employment combinations? First, municipal unions can act as a voting bloc or pressure group in support of candidates for mayor, city council, or department head who favor expanding those city services provided by union members. Second, municipal unions may mount publicity campaigns to gain public support for expenditure bills favorable to their departments. Finally, the political atmosphere within government may permit union leaders to engage in so-called "end-run bargaining." This type of bargaining involves appealing to legislators or superiors as a way to maneuver around administrative personnel who stand in the way of union goals. Hence, unions may be able to gain larger expenditures for their own departments.

Valletta used data for about 700 cities to test the hypothesis that municipal unions increase the demand for municipal services. He found that, other things being equal, municipal unionism increased expenditures by about 10 to 15 percent, on average, as compared to nonunionized departments. Because these higher expenditures in large part took the form of increased employment, Valletta was able to conclude that municipal unions shifted the labor demand curve to the right.

Did unions increase the overall expenditures by government in the cities studied? Valletta discovered that they did not; collective bargaining contracts were *not* associated with greater total city expenditures. Rather, the larger expenditures in the unionized departments apparently reduced either wages or employment in nonunionized departments within the same cities.

*Based on Robert G. Valletta, "The Impact of Unionism on Municipal Expenditures and Revenues," *Industrial and Labor Relations Review,* April 1989, pp. 430–442.

and undermine union authority. In other instances, unions have agreed to participate on an experimental basis. To the extent that either approach raises the marginal product of labor, the demand for labor will increase, improving the union's prospect for negotiating a wage increase.[7] This rightward shift in the labor demand curve does not produce the efficiency loss *abc* in Figure 6-8. The higher level of employment results from the increased productivity of labor, not from an artificial distortion of the allocation of society's resources.

3 Influencing the Prices of Related Inputs Where labor and some other resource are gross substitutes (substitution effect > output effect), unions can bolster the demand for their own labor by raising the relative price of the other resource. Unions do not have direct control over prices of alternative resources, but there are examples of political actions by unions that might influence such prices. First, unions—generally being populated by higher-paid, skilled workers—may support increases in the minimum wage as a way to raise the relative price of substitutable less-skilled, nonunionized labor. As a simple example, suppose that two less-skilled workers can produce the same amount of output in an hour—say, 1 unit—as one skilled union laborer, but that the hourly pay for the unskilled workers is \$2 while the union scale is \$5. Obviously, firms would hire unskilled workers (per unit wage cost of output = \$4). Now assume that unions successfully lobby for a \$3 per hour minimum wage for all workers. Assuming that skilled and unskilled workers are substitutes in production and also gross substitutes, this increase in the price of unskilled workers will increase the demand for skilled, union workers. The reason is that now each unit of the product can be produced at less cost by hiring one union worker at \$5 an hour rather than employing two unskilled workers at \$6 (= 2 × \$3).

The ***Davis–Bacon Act*** (1931) and its amendments provide another example of how unions might be able to increase the price of a resource that is a substitute in production with labor, in this case the price of *skilled nonunion* labor. The act, which has strong union support, requires contractors engaged in federally financed projects to pay "prevailing wages." The latter, in effect, are union wages since the formula for determining prevailing wages mandates that the wage rate that occurs with the greatest frequency be observed. Because nonunion firms normally pay their workers less than the union scale, the act has the effect of raising the price of nonunion labor. Where union and nonunion labor are gross substitutes, the demand for union labor rises, enabling unions to bargain for higher wages without fear of losing federal work to nonunion firms.[8]

Unions also can increase the demand for their labor through support of government actions that *reduce* the price of resources that are complements in production with labor. As one example, affected unions occasionally argue against rate increases proposed by electric or natural gas utilities, particularly when the industries where they work use

[7]For one study that finds a positive impact on productivity from cooperative union-management programs, see Michael Schuster, "The Impact of Union-Management Cooperation on Productivity and Employment," *Industrial and Labor Relations Review,* April 1983, pp. 415–430.

[8]For empirical evidence in support of the hypothesis that the Davis–Bacon Act increases union wages by increasing union bargaining power, the reader should consult John F. O'Connell, "The Effect of Davis–Bacon on Labor Cost and Union Wages," *Journal of Labor Research,* Summer 1986, pp. 239–253.

substantial amounts of these energy sources. Where labor and energy inputs are pure complements in production and thus gross complements, these price increases will reduce the demand for labor through a significant output effect (higher production costs).

4 Increasing the Number of Employers Unions can increase the demand for their labor by lobbying for government programs that encourage new employers to establish operations in a local area. For example, unions might favor the issuing of industrial revenue bonds to build industrial parks and property tax breaks to attract domestic or foreign manufacturers.

As a more specific example, the United Auto Workers unsuccessfully lobbied Congress to pass "domestic content" legislation that would have required that substantial portions of automobiles sold in the United States be produced here. This restricted U.S. auto firms from moving the manufacture of major auto components abroad and encouraged foreign firms to locate operations in the United States. In both cases, the domestic demand for U.S. unionized autoworkers would be strengthened.

Restricting the Supply of Labor

Unions also can boost wages by reducing the *supply* of labor. By referring back to Figure 6-2, you will observe that a union can obtain a higher wage rate if it can shift the labor supply curve leftward. However, the union must accept a decrease in employment in achieving this wage hike. Fortunately for the union, the restriction of labor supply is more likely to occur in a dynamic context wherein the effect is merely to restrict the growth of job opportunities.

In Figure 6-9 we depict a dynamic labor market in which both labor demand and supply are increasing. Let's suppose that demand is rising because of increases in product demand and productivity, while supply is increasing because of population growth, which is expanding the number of persons qualified to supply this labor. In the absence of the union, the increases in demand (D_0 to D_1) and supply (S_0 to the broken line S_1) would raise the wage rate and level of employment from W_0 to W_1 and Q_0 to Q_1, respectively (point *a* to *c*).

Now let's introduce the union and suppose that it takes actions that keep labor supply from expanding to S_1. The result? The market wage will rise to W_u, not W_1, and the quantity of labor hired will be Q_u, as opposed to Q_1. This union has increased the wage rate by restricting the growth of labor supply. In this case, the action also slows the growth rate of employment—$(Q_u - Q_0)/Q_0$ compared to $(Q_1 - Q_0)/Q_0$. The greater the elasticity of labor demand, of course, the greater the negative employment impact of a given supply restriction. Finally, the union action causes an efficiency loss of triangle *ebc*. If the Q_uQ_1 workers had been employed here, they would have contributed more to the value of society's output (segment *bc* of D_1) than they would have added in their best alternative employment (segment *ec* of S_1).

Unions can restrict labor supply by taking actions or supporting government policies that alter one or more of the determinants of labor supply (Table 6-1). One of these factors in particular—reducing the number of qualified suppliers—is most easily influenced by unions. One other—influencing nonwage income—is also of some significance.

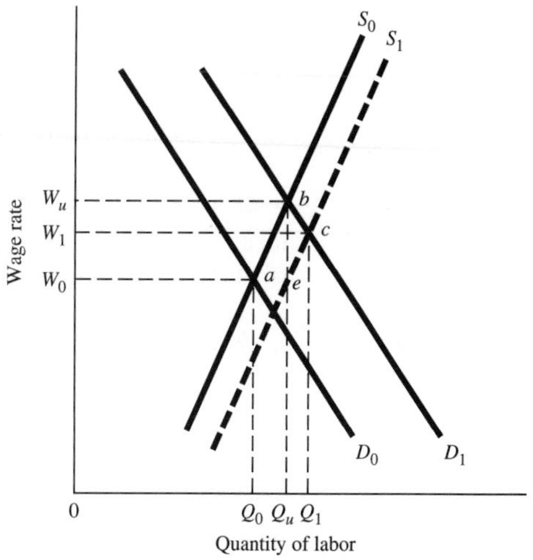

FIGURE 6-9 UNION TECHNIQUES: RESTRICTING THE SUPPLY OF LABOR
In a dynamic labor market characterized by normal expansions of labor demand and supply, such as D_0 to D_1 and S_0 to S_1, a union or professional organization may be able to increase wage rates (W_1 to W_u) through action that restrict normal increases in labor supply. (S_0 rather than S_1). However, these actions also slow the rate of growth of union employment $[(Q_u - Q_0)/Q_0$ compared to $(Q_1 - Q_0)/Q_0]$.

1 Reducing the Number of Qualified Suppliers of Labor One way that unions in general can limit the supply of qualified workers in a specific labor market is to restrict the overall "stock" of qualified workers in the nation. This partially explains why organized labor has strongly supported (a) limited immigration, (b) child labor laws, (c) compulsory retirement, and (d) shorter workweeks.

Unions also can restrict labor supply for particular labor by limiting entry into the occupation itself. For example, craft unions composed of workers of a specific skill—such as plumbers, carpenters, or bricklayers—and some professional groups such as the American Medical Association allegedly have controlled access to training and established extraordinarily long apprenticeship programs to limit labor supply. Thus, this type of unionism is sometimes referred to as ***exclusive unionism;*** the supply restriction derives from actions that "exclude" potential workers from participating in the trade or profession.

Of perhaps greater importance, unions and professional groups have been able to limit entry to certain jobs through ***occupational licensure,*** *which is the enactment of laws by government to force practitioners of a trade to meet certain requirements.* These requirements may specify the level of educational attainment or amount of work experience needed and may also include the passing of an examination to obtain a license. State licensing boards have wide discretion in establishing the tests and standards needed to qualify for a license. In fact, there is evidence suggesting that some boards adjust the "pass rate" as a way to control the rate of entry into the licensed occupation.[9] Furthermore, the licensing requirements may include a minimum residency stipulation that inhibits the flow of qualified workers between states. Hence,

[9]Alex Maurizi, "Occupational Licensing and the Public-Interest," *Journal of Political Economy,* March/April 1974, pp. 399–413.

occupational licensure restricts labor supply and increases the wage rate as shown in Figure 6-9.

A final means by which unions may limit labor supply to an occupation is through discrimination by race or gender. Some predominantly male craft unions and professional organizations have explicitly or implicitly argued that their particular type of work is "too physical" or "too stressful" to be performed by females and then have taken such actions as instituting overly rigorous physical requirements to make it difficult for women to enter the trade or occupation. Some craft unions also have engaged in racial segregation, perhaps resulting from the direct economic self-interest evident in Figure 6-9.[10]

2 Influencing Nonwage Income Unions and professional organizations may also improve their wages by affecting the nonwage income determinant of labor supply. They may be able to accomplish this through legislation that provides income to unemployed workers, partially disabled workers, and older citizens. Stated differently, among the several reasons that labor unions generally support increased unemployment compensation, workers' compensation, and Social Security retirement benefits is the fact that these sources of nonwage income reduce labor force participation (Chapter 2) and therefore raise the before-tax wages to those employed. This is *not* to suggest that this is a primary reason for such support; after all, union members must join others in paying for government transfers through higher taxes (lower after-tax wages). Rather, it *is* to imply that such support is consistent with Figure 6-9.

Bargaining for an Above-Equilibrium Wage

In addition to restricting the supply of labor to an occupation (shifting the labor supply curve leftward), some unions are successful at enlisting as union members a large percentage of the available workers in an industry or occupation. Through recruitment of union members, an *industrial union* can gain control over a firm's labor supply. During negotiations the union therefore can credibly threaten to withhold labor—to strike—unless the employer increases its wage offer. Because these unions attempt to attract or "include" all potential industry workers into the union, this form of unionism is called ***inclusive unionism.*** Examples of industrial unions that control high percentages of industry labor supply within the domestic economy include the United Auto Workers and the United Steelworkers of America (USA).

The impact of control over labor supply by a union is shown graphically in Figure 6-10. Suppose that employers in this labor market act independently and that in the absence of the union the competitive equilibrium wage rate and level of employment are W_c and Q_c. Now suppose that a union forms and successfully bargains for the higher, above-equilibrium wage rate W_u. This in effect makes the labor supply curve perfectly

[10]For evidence of discrimination by unions, see Orley Ashenfelter, "Discrimination and Trade Unions," in Orley Ashenfelter and Albert Rees (eds.), *Discrimination in Labor Markets* (Princeton, NJ: Princeton University Press, 1973). The economic aspects of labor market discrimination will be examined in detail in Chapters 14 and 15.

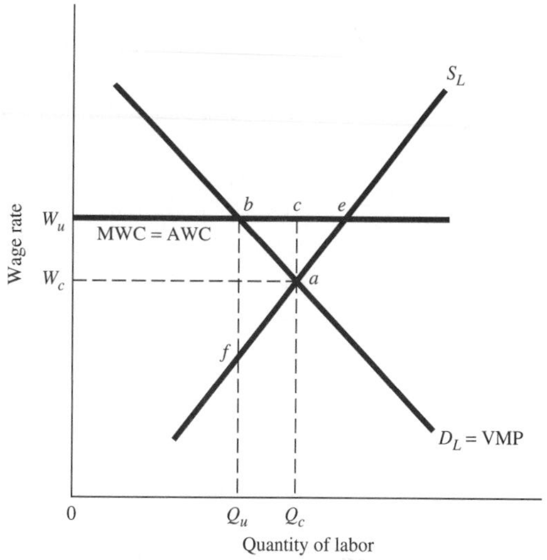

FIGURE 6-10 UNION TECHNIQUES: BARGAINING FOR A HIGHER WAGE
By organizing all available workers and securing union shops, inclusive unions may successfully bargain for a wage rate, such as W_u, that is above the competitive wage rate W_c. The effects are to make the labor supply curve perfectly elastic between W_u and point *e* (MWC = AWC = S_L), to reduce employment from Q_c to Q_u, and to create an efficiency loss of area *fba*. The more elastic the labor demand, the greater the employment and allocative impacts.

elastic over the W_ue range. If employers hire any number of workers within this range, they must pay the union scale W_u or the union will withdraw *all* labor via a strike. If the employers desire more than *e* workers, however, say because of a major expansion of labor demand during the life of the union contract, they will need to pay wages above the union's scale to attract workers away from alternative jobs paying more than W_u.

Notice the *postunion* employment outcome in Figure 6-10. Employers respond to the union-imposed wage rate W_u by discharging *cb* workers (Q_cQ_u). Furthermore, the higher wage attracts *ce* additional job seekers to the occupation. Thus, excess labor supply *be* exists at the union-imposed wage. The greater the elasticity of demand, the wider the range *cb.* The more elastic the preunion supply of labor, the greater the gap *ce.*

This model enables us to understand several observed labor market phenomena and union actions. First, it explains why some unionized labor markets are characterized by chronic "waiting lists" for jobs. Second, and closely related, it clarifies why labor organizations place great emphasis on gaining *union security* provisions in labor contracts. The union's bargaining power relies to a greater extent on the credibility of its threat to call for a strike and on its ability to withhold the firm's entire labor supply once a work stoppage occurs. A ***union shop clause*** permits the firm to hire nonunion workers, but requires that workers join the union following a probationary period. These clauses typically increase the percentage of workers who are union members. Thus, a strike occurring when the existing contract expires is likely to deprive the firm of such a substantial portion of its labor supply that the firm will be forced to curtail or cease production. The potential or actual loss of profit from a threatened or actual strike increases the union's bargaining power and improves the union's chances of getting an above-equilibrium wage, such as W_u in Figure 6-10.

Third, the distance *bc* in Figure 6-10 sheds light on why unions are interested in securing contract provisions that reduce the elasticity of labor demand. The lower this elasticity, the smaller the number of displaced workers from any given wage increase. Recall that one major determinant of the elasticity of labor demand is the substitutability of other inputs. What contract provisions might reduce the substitution of capital for union labor? What provisions might limit the substitution of nonunion labor for union workers? Examples of the first include provisions limiting new technology, requiring redundant labor ("featherbedding"), and providing for supplementary unemployment benefits (SUBs). By dictating the pace of the introduction of new technology and engaging in featherbedding, the union can temporarily reduce the elasticity of labor demand—that is, slow the substitution of capital for labor in response to wage increases. SUBs and severance pay provisions perform a similar function; if high enough, they raise the "effective price" of any capital used to replace union labor. Examples of contract provisions that reduce the substitutability of nonunion and union labor include clauses preventing subcontracting and plant relocation. Both are sometimes used to "economize" on the use of union labor following union-imposed wage increases. But by preventing such actions, the union at least temporarily reduces the elasticity of labor demand.

The employment impact of the union-imposed above-equilibrium wage in Figure 6-10 will be greater as time transpires. For example, the firm may resist continuing the contract provisions that keep the short-run demand curve inelastic. Alternatively, foreign or nonunion competition may arise in response to the high product prices in unionized industries. On the other hand, in a growing economy the demand curves for most types of labor gradually shift rightward over time. Instead of an absolute decline in the number of jobs in the unionized labor market, the outcome may simply be a slower rate of growth of job opportunities. In this respect, no specific layoff of existing union workers is observed. This may explain why some union leaders have in the past erroneously concluded that demand for labor curves are highly inelastic.

A final observation from Figure 6-10 is that given homogeneous workers, a union-imposed above-equilibrium wage creates a misallocation of labor resources. Notice that the value of the marginal product *b* exceeds the marginal opportunity cost of labor *f* at wage W_u and quantity Q_u. If Q_uQ_c workers were transferred from competitive labor
6-5 markets to this one, society would experience a net gain in the value of its output equal to area *fba*.[11]

BILATERAL MONOPOLY

In the previous section we assumed that a union had gained control over the supply of labor in an otherwise competitive labor market. But what if a monopsonist and a strong industrial union coexist in a labor market? This situation is characteristic of some U.S. labor markets. For example, in the eastern coal industry the United Mine Workers (UMW) union confronts a "multiemployer" bargaining unit in negotiating a standard labor contract. In the labor market for automobile workers, the UAW bargains indi-

[11]A more complete analysis of the efficiency losses created by unions is provided in Chapter 11.

6-5 World of Work

HAS DEUNIONIZATION INCREASED EARNINGS INEQUALITY?*

One of the major economic trends of the past two decades has been the sharp rise in earnings inequality. One measure of inequality is the income quintile ratio, which is the average income of the families in the top 20 percent of all families divided by the average income of families in the bottom 20 percent. This ratio rose from 5.92 in 1974 to 10.02 in 1994. Over the same period unionization declined rapidly. In 1974 23.6 percent of wage and salary workers were union members; by 1994 union membership had dropped to 15.5 percent.

In theory, unionism has ambiguous effects on income inequality. On one hand, unions increase income inequality because they raise the wages of union workers relative to their nonunion counterparts and because they are made up largely of higher-paid blue-collar workers. On the other hand, unions lower income inequality since they equalize wages within and across firms with unionized workers. In addition, unions tend to lower the wage gap between white-collar and blue-collar workers because they raise the relative wages of their mainly blue-collar members. Though unions have uncertain effects in theory on income inequality, the evidence generally indicates they tend to reduce income inequality.

How much has the decline in unionization contributed to the increased income inequality? Asher and Defina conclude that about 10 percent of the rise in earnings inequality among all workers and about 20 percent of the rise in inequality among mature male workers are the results of declining unionism. Other factors, such as greater demand for skilled workers due to improvements in technology as well as an increased supply of low-skilled workers because of growth in immigration, also contributed to the rise in inequality.

*Based on Martin A. Asher and Robert H. Defina, "Has Deunionization Led to Higher Earnings Inequality?" *Business Review,* November/December 1995, pp. 3–12; and Barry T. Hirsch and David A. Macpherson, *Union Membership and Earnings Data Book: Compilations from the Current Population Survey (1998 edition),* (Washington, DC: Bureau of National Affairs, 1998).

vidually with the "Big Three" U.S. auto manufacturers. Similarly, the Communication Workers union negotiates with regional telephone service monopsonists, and the players' associations of various professional sports bargain against unified team owners. Will the wage be below or above the competitive equilibrium wage in these ***bilateral monopoly*** situations?[12] The answer is that the wage outcome is *indeterminate;* the negotiated wage rate may be either above, below, or equal to the competitive wage rate. Let's explore why.

In Figure 6-11 we combine the monopsony model (Figure 6-7) and the union model (Figure 6-10) to illustrate bilateral monopoly. For simplicity, we once again assume that the product is sold in a perfectly competitive market (MRP = VMP). If monopsony alone existed in this market, the wage rate would be W_m and the level of employment would be Q_1. On the other hand, if the union could set any wage rate it desired, it might select W_u.[13] Neither the employer nor the union, however, can impose its desired wage on the other in this situation. If the monopsonist offers W_m, the union may threaten to withhold the supply of labor via a strike. If the union demands W_u, the monopsonist may resist, believing that it is too costly to pay the wage rate relative to

[12]It is important to note that we are using the term *monopoly* conceptually here. Legally, labor unions are not monopolies and are not subject to the antitrust laws when engaged in their normal activities. Congress and the courts have declared that "labor is not an article of commerce."

[13]In Chapter 10 we will analyze the criteria that a union might use to determine this wage rate.

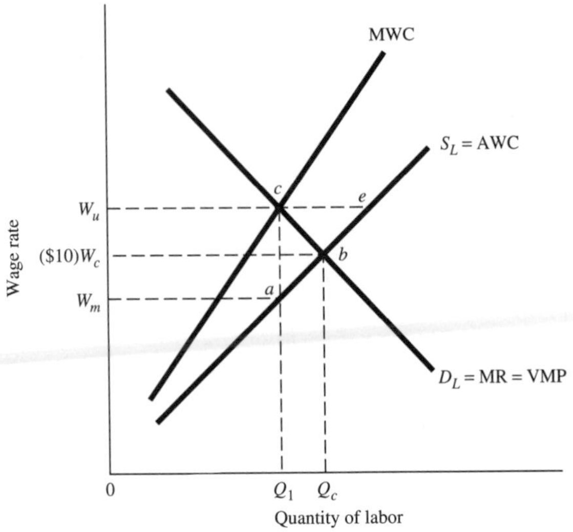

FIGURE 6-11 BILATERAL MONOPOLY IN THE LABOR MARKET
When a monopsonistic employer must "buy" labor services from a "monopolistic" union, the wage rate and employment outcomes are indeterminate. However, if the union negotiates a wage above W_m but below W_u, employment will increase and allocative efficiency will improve relative to the situation under monopsony alone (W_m, Q_1).

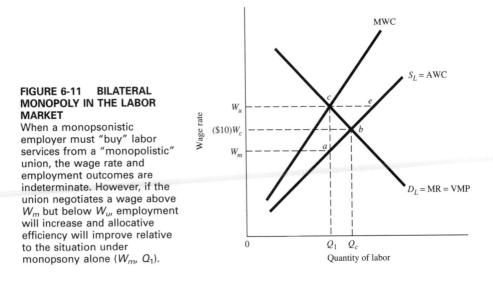

the expected costs associated with either allowing the strike or locking out workers. Thus, we are left with a *range* of possible wage outcomes—W_m to W_u—and the mutual interest of the two parties will normally result in a negotiated wage rate acceptable to each. The final wage will depend on the relative bargaining strength and prowess of each party (Chapter 10).

Careful scrutiny of the bilateral monopoly situation shown in Figure 6-11 reveals several interesting points. First, it is entirely possible that the negotiated wage will be at or near the wage rate W_c, which would have occurred if *neither* monopsony nor union power existed in the market. In that case the quantity of labor hired would be Q_c (point *b*). The perfectly elastic segment of S_L would now be W_cb, which means that the coincident MWC intersects MRP at the Q_c level of employment. And because perfect competition is assumed to exist in the product market, labor resources would be efficiently allocated.

Second, the union may be able simultaneously to increase (1) the wage rate, (2) the level of employment, and (3) allocative efficiency. Notice that any increase in the wage above W_m but below W_u causes the firm to increase its employment beyond Q_1. Why? Once the firm agrees to one of these wage rates, its incentive to restrict employment disappears; at the negotiated wage, its marginal wage cost (MWC) and average wage cost (AWC) become perfectly horizontal overlaying lines. Therefore, the firm equates the negotiated wage (MWC) with the marginal revenue product (MRP) and hires more workers than it would if its MWC exceeded its AWC. For example, if the negotiated wage is W_c, and this happens to be $10 an hour, then from the firm's perspective, the MWC and AWC are also $10 per hour. The firm will operate where MRP and this wage rate are equal and hire *b* rather than *a* units of labor. Notice also that area *abc* portrays the efficiency loss associated with either wage rate W_m or W_u. If the union negotiates a wage above W_m but below W_u, this area will diminish. In the case of W_c, it disappears! Hence, the presence of unions in monopsonized labor markets may enhance allocative efficiency. Galbraith has called this tendency ***countervailing power,*** or offsetting power.

A caution: Some economists reject the proposition that countervailing power is the actual outcome in circumstances of bilateral monopoly. Adams and Brock, for example, argue that where firms possessing monopsony power also dominate their product markets, countervailing power gives way to ***coalescing power.*** This coalescing power results from tacit vertical collusion between the union and the firm to suppress competition in the firm's product market. More concretely, the union and firm may jointly use their political power to secure government regulation of entry into the industry, tariff protection, domestic content legislation, and so on, which increase both product prices *and* wages.[14]

A final observation from Figure 6-11 is that even though the low monopsony wage W_m and the high union wage W_u result in the same employment level (Q_1), at wages W_m through W_c the labor market clears (although there may be a "perceived" shortage). But for wages above W_c unemployment occurs. For example, at wage W_u the firm hires only *c* units of labor, but *e* units are supplied. Some of the *ce* suppliers may be willing to wait for job turnover to enable them to gain employment in this market. Since they are in the labor force and seeking work, they are officially unemployed.

Table 6-4 summarizes the wage and employment outcomes under unionism both where competitive hiring and monopsony exist. This table merits careful review.

[14]Walter Adams and James W. Brock, "Tacit Collusion and the Labor-Industrial Complex," *Nebraska Law Review,* 1983, pp. 623–707.

TABLE 6-4 WAGE (*W*) AND EMPLOYMENT (*Q*) OUTCOMES OF LABOR MARKETS WITH UNIONS

		Labor market structure (firms): Perfect competition in hire of labor	Labor market structure (firms): Monopsonist
Labor market structure (workers)	No union	Competitive *W* and *Q* (Figure 6-4)	Less than competitive *W*; reduced *Q* (Figure 6-7)
Labor market structure (workers)	Union	Higher than competitive *W*; reduced *Q* (Figures 6-9 and 6-10); increased *Q* (Figure 6-8)	Indeterminate *W* and *Q* (Figure 6-11)

QUICK REVIEW 6-2

- A monopsonist pays a lower wage rate and employs fewer workers than firms hiring in a competitive labor market; this outcome is allocatively inefficient.
- Unions can raise the wage rate by increasing labor demand through actions that *(a)* increase product demand, *(b)* enhance productivity, *(c)* alter the prices of related inputs, and *(d)* increase the number of employees.
- Unions can increase the wage rate by restricting labor supply; actions include *(a)* reducing the number of qualified labor suppliers, and *(b)* influencing nonwage income.
- Unions can raise the wage rate by gaining control over a firm's potential labor supply and threatening to withhold labor unless an acceptable negotiated wage rate is obtained.
- When a monopsonistic employer faces a "monopolistic" union, the wage rate and employment outcomes are indeterminate; they are set through collective bargaining.

6-6 **Your Turn:** Why does the monopsonist's MWC curve lie above the market labor supply curve? Isn't this a disadvantage to the monopsonist? (Answers: See page 626.)

WAGE DETERMINATION: DELAYED SUPPLY RESPONSES

The standard supply and demand model of the labor market (Figures 6-2 and 6-3) assumes that suppliers of labor respond quickly to changes in the market wage rate brought about by changes in labor demand. When the market wage rate rises in relative terms, more workers offer their labor services in that market. When the market wage falls, fewer workers supply their labor services there. Movements of this sort along a market supply of labor curve bring the quantity of labor supplied into equality with the quantity of labor demanded at the equilibrium wage rate. In brief, the labor market immediately clears.

Although rapid supply responses are indeed characteristic of some labor markets, in other situations labor supply adjustments are less rapid than the standard model suggests. In fact, in some cases supply adjustments may take several years. Our attention now turns to a model of one of these slowly adjusting labor markets.

Cobweb Model

Consider Figure 6-12, where we depict the market for new engineers who are recent college graduates. Suppose that labor demand and supply initially are D and S, respectively. Also assume that the market is presently in equilibrium at a, where the wage rate is W_0 and the level of employment is Q_0.

Now suppose that an unexpected increase in the demand for engineers occurs, perhaps because of the emergence of new technologies. In the standard labor market model the market would quickly clear at the intersection of supply S and demand D_1. But the

6-6 World of Work

NAFTA AND AMERICAN LABOR*

After much national and congressional debate, in late 1993 Congress passed the North American Free Trade Agreement (NAFTA). This agreement will eliminate tariffs and other trade barriers among the United States, Canada, and Mexico over a 15-year period. NAFTA will constitute the world's largest free-trade zone, covering 360 million people. Economists generally agree that this trade pact will raise the standard of living of U.S. citizens and Mexicans, mainly through increased output and lower product prices. But how will NAFTA affect employment and wages, the subjects of this chapter?

Employment effects. The congressional Joint Economic Committee surveyed 16 studies of NAFTA and concluded that, during its first five years, NAFTA would produce anywhere from a net gain or a net loss of 200,000 U.S. jobs. The Congressional Budget Office, evaluating 32 studies of NAFTA, reached a similar conclusion. Since the U.S. economy typically creates about 2 million net new jobs annually, NAFTA's impact on employment is relatively slight.

Nevertheless, NAFTA is expected to produce differential impacts on various U.S. labor markets. Employment will likely increase in industries that export to Mexico, where tariffs historically have been high. For example, U.S. employment in industries such as computers, telecommunications, and financial services will rise. This will happen because Mexican imports will rise along with its national income. Conversely, the demand for U.S. labor and hence U.S. employment may decrease in industries such as apparel and food processing. These low-wage industries have long enjoyed protection from U.S. trade barriers, including those against imports from Mexico.

Wage effects. Foreign investment from the United States and other advanced economies should bolster the demand for Mexican labor and eventually boost Mexican wages significantly. On the other hand, NAFTA will only slightly raise the average wage in the United States—perhaps as little as 0.5 percent during the first five years. Also, lower product prices will benefit U.S. and Mexican workers in their capacity as consumers.

Some specific U.S. workers may experience wage gains from NAFTA; others may suffer wage declines. The "winners" will be workers in industries where U.S. exports rise. The "losers" may be less-skilled U.S. workers who are in direct competition with Mexican workers. Some employers of these workers may well seek wage cuts, perhaps threatening to move their operations to Mexico. It must be emphasized, however, that the low wages in Mexico have largely resulted from very low Mexican productivity (output per worker). The Mexican wage advantage, like that in other developing nations, is thus partly illusory. Labor cost per unit of output—the critical determinant of competitiveness—depends not only on wages but also on productivity (Chapter 18). Thus, the number of U.S. firms relocating to Mexico is not expected to be substantial.

*For a series of studies examining the effects of NAFTA, see Nora Lustig, Barry P. Bosworth, and Robert Z. Lawrence (eds.), *North American Free Trade: Assessing the Impact* (Washington, DC: Brookings Institution, 1992).

market for new engineers and other highly trained professionals is atypical. It is not unusual in these markets to observe 4- or 5-year delays in the supply response to the new labor market conditions. Students currently enrolling in engineering schools will not graduate and enter the labor force for several years.

In the immediate market period the number of new engineers available remains temporarily fixed at Q_0. The immediate market period is a time period so short that there is no quantity-supplied response to a change in the wage rate. We might therefore envision a vertical *immediate-market-period labor supply curve* emanating upward from Q_0 through *a* and *b*. Supply curve *S*, on the other hand, may be thought of as the *long-run supply curve;* it indicates the *eventual* response of labor suppliers to changes in wage rates. Here, the long run entails a 4- to 5-year period.

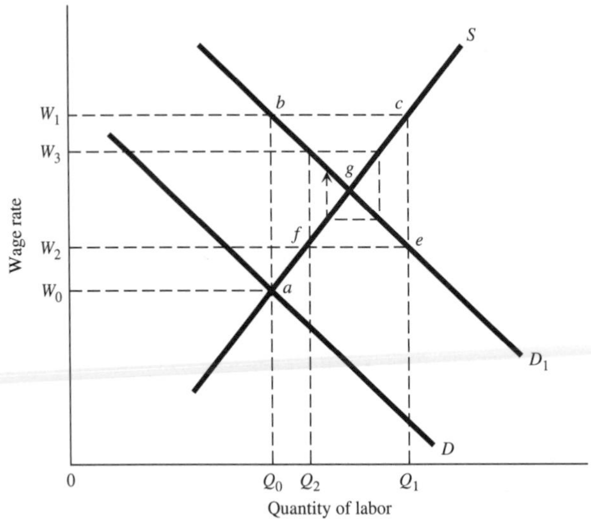

FIGURE 6-12 COBWEB MODEL
The market for highly trained professionals such as engineers is characterized by delayed supply responses to changes in demand and wage rates. Because the quantity of labor supplied temporarily is fixed at Q_0, the wage rate rises to W_1 when demand changes from D to D_1. At wage rate W_1, Q_1 engineers eventually are attracted to this profession. With supply fixed at Q_1, however, the wage rate falls to W_2. Given this wage rate, the quantity of engineers available eventually falls to Q_2. This cycle repeats until equilibrium is achieved in this case at the intersection of S and D_1.

Given that Q_0 engineers are now in the labor force and that demand now is D_1, a *shortage* of workers will occur at W_0 and the market wage rate will shoot upward to W_1. This wage rate will eliminate the shortage, since at point *b*, demand curve D_1 intersects the vertical immediate-market-period labor supply curve comprised of Q_0ab.

This is only the beginning of the story. Because of the high wage rate W_1, numerous new students will flock to the field of engineering. When they graduate some 5 years hence, Q_1 engineers will be available in the labor market. This supply response is determined at *c* on the long-run supply curve *S* and results from the previous wage rate W_1. In effect, the vertical immediate-market-period labor supply curve shifts rightward in a parallel fashion from Q_0 to Q_1.

Now that the quantity of labor supplied is again temporarily fixed—this time at Q_1—a *surplus* of *bc* engineers occurs at W_1. The wage rate consequently drops to W_2 (point *e* on D_1). Here, the new immediate-market-period supply curve going upward from Q_1 through *e* and *c* cuts the demand curve D_1 at *e,* and the surplus is eliminated.

This scenario continues. Although the new starting wage rate W_2 is considerably lower than W_1, it will not immediately elicit a decline in the number of new engineers offering their labor services. Recent graduates holding engineering degrees are not likely to abandon their careers in response to lower relative salaries. Moreover, wage rate W_2 in all likelihood is higher than wage rates available to engineers in nonengineering jobs. The relatively low wage rate W_2, however, *does* affect the decisions of beginning college students who are planning their academic programs. The poor starting pay will discourage these students from opting to become engineers. In 4 or 5 years colleges will confer fewer engineering diplomas during their graduation ceremonies. We see that the number of new engineers in this labor market falls from Q_1 to Q_2, the latter being determined at f on long-run supply curve S. Given demand D_1, a shortage of fe engineers occurs and the wage rate responds by rising from W_2 to W_3.

The cycle just described repeats itself. The quantity of labor *demanded* in each period depends on the wage rate at that time; the quantity of labor *supplied* in each period results from the wage rate during the previous period when education and career decisions were originally made. In this instance, equilibrium eventually is achieved at the intersection of the long-run labor supply curve S and demand curve D_1. You are urged to carry the analysis forward through another cycle to test your understanding of this unusual model. The adjustment path toward equilibrium at g results in a cobweb pattern and for that reason this model is called a ***cobweb model.***

Two further observations merit comment. It is entirely possible for still another shift in labor demand to occur before the cobweb path is completed to g. Thus, a new set of cobweb adjustments may be necessitated. Also, the elasticities of the demand and supply curves might be such that the market does not move to the ultimate equilibrium at g, but rather continues to oscillate between periodic shortages and surpluses.

Evidence and Controversy

Cobweb models help explain adjustments in several labor markets having long training periods and highly specialized labor. For example, historical cobweb adjustments have been found in the markets for new engineers, lawyers, and physicists.[15]

But not all economists find the cobweb model to be persuasive. Some critics question the relevancy of the model to the majority of today's labor markets for the college-trained workforce. You will note that in the model labor market participants are assumed to adjust their career decisions to changes in *starting salaries.* Some economists suggest that the more likely scenario is that college students look to the present value of *lifetime earnings streams* (Chapter 4) in making education and career decisions.[16] Other critics assert that today's students are highly attuned to the possible boom–bust potential in some labor markets. Therefore, they form *rational expectations* about the end result of any sudden change in the demand for labor and adjust their supply responses accordingly. If either of these two related criticisms are correct, the abrupt changes in immediate-market-period supply in the cobweb model and the resulting

[15]Richard B. Freeman, "A Cobweb Model of the Starting Salary of New Engineers," *Industrial and Labor Relations Review,* January 1976, pp. 236–248; Freeman, "Legal Cobwebs: A Recursive Model of the Market for New Lawyers," *Review of Economics and Statistics,* May 1975, pp. 171–180; Freeman, "Supply and Salary Adjustments to the Changing Science Manpower Markets: Physics, 1948–1973," *American Economic Review,* March 1975, pp. 27–39.

[16]Mark Berger has presented evidence supporting this view. See his "Predicted Future Earnings and Choice of College Major," *Industrial and Labor Relations Review,* April 1988, pp. 418–429. Also see Dennis Hoffman and Stuart Low, "Rationality and the Decision to Invest in Economics," *Journal of Human Resources,* Fall 1983, pp. 480–496; and Gary Zarkin, "Occupational Choice: An Application to the Market for Public School Teachers," *Quarterly Journal of Economics,* May 1985, pp. 409–446.

oscillating path to equilibrium are less likely to occur. That is, equilibrium is more likely to be achieved without the cobweb effects.

In any event, the cobweb model is important because it reminds us that labor supply adjustments are not always as immediate or as certain as our basic labor market model predicts. The upshot is that many labor markets may better be characterized as moving toward allocative efficiency (VMP = P_L) than as having actually achieved it.

CHAPTER SUMMARY

1 In a competitive labor market, the demand for labor is a "price-adjusted" summation of labor demand by independently acting individual employers, and the supply of labor is a summation of the responses of individual workers to various wage rates. Market supply and demand determine an equilibrium wage rate and level of employment.

2 The vertical height of the market labor supply curve measures the opportunity cost to society to employing the last worker in some specific use (P_L). The vertical height of the labor demand curve indicates the extra revenue the employer gains by hiring that unit of labor (MRP) and, given perfectly competitive markets, the value of that output to society (VMP).

3 The locations of the supply and demand curves in the labor market depend on the determinants of each (Table 6-1). When one of these determinants changes, the affected curve shifts either rightward or leftward, altering the equilibrium wage and employment levels.

4 The individual firm operating in a perfectly competitive labor market is a "wage-taker." This implies that its MWC equals the wage rate W; that is, the supply of labor is perfectly elastic. This firm maximizes its profits by hiring the quantity of labor at which MRP = MWC, or MRP = W.

5 An efficient allocation of labor occurs when the VMPs of a particular type of labor are equal in various uses and these VMPs also equal the opportunity cost P_L of that labor. Perfectly competitive product and resource markets result in allocative efficiency. By maximizing profits where MRP = MWC, firms also equate VMP and P_L, because MRP = VMP and MWC = P_L.

6 Monopoly in the product market causes marginal revenue to fall faster than product price as more workers are hired and output is expanded. Because product price P exceeds marginal revenue MR, it follows that MRP (= MP × MR) is less than VMP (= MP × P). The result is less employment and an underallocation of labor resources relative to the case of perfect competition in the product market.

7 Under monopsony MWC > S_L (or P_L) because the employer must bid up wages to attract a greater quantity of labor and pay the higher wage to *all* workers. Consequently, it will employ fewer workers than under competitive conditions and pay a wage rate below the MRP of labor. This underallocation of labor resources (VMP > P_L) reduces the total value of output in the economy.

8 Unions can increase the wage rate paid to those members who are employed by *(a)* increasing the demand for labor, *(b)* restricting the supply of labor, and *(c)* bargaining for an above-equilibrium wage. To increase the demand for labor, unions try to increase product demand, enhance productivity, influence the price of related inputs, and increase the number of employers. To restrict labor supply, unions attempt to affect the number of qualified suppliers, nonwage income, and alternative wages. To control labor supply, unions organize "inclusively" and bargain for union shops.

9 Bilateral monopoly is a labor market situation in which a union that controls labor supply faces a monopsonistic employer or coalition of employers. Although the wage rate and employment outcomes are indeterminate, the possibility arises that through collective bargaining a union may be able to enhance simultaneously *(a)* its wage rate, *(b)* the level of employment, and *(c)* allocative efficiency.

10 The cobweb model traces out labor supply adjustments to changes in labor demand and wage rates in markets characterized by long training periods. The equilibrium wage rate is achieved only after a period of oscillating wage rate changes caused by recurring labor shortages and surpluses.

TERMS AND CONCEPTS

perfectly competitive labor market
determinants of labor supply and demand
marginal revenue product
average wage cost
marginal wage cost
MRP = MWC rule
efficient allocation of labor
price of labor
pure monopsony
joint monopsony
Davis–Bacon Act
exclusive unionism
occupational licensure
inclusive unionism
union shop clause
bilateral monopoly
countervailing power
coalescing power
cobweb model

QUESTIONS AND STUDY SUGGESTIONS

1 List the distinct characteristics of a perfectly competitive labor market and compare them to the characteristics of monopsony.

2 Explain why most market labor supply curves slope upward and to the right, even though individual labor supply curves are presumed to be backward-bending. How does the height of a market labor supply curve relate to the concept of opportunity costs?

3 What effect will each of the following have on the market labor demand for a specific type of labor?

a An increase in product demand that increases product price
b A decline in the productivity of this type of labor
c An increase in the price of a gross substitute for labor
d A decline in the price of a gross complement for labor
e The demise of several firms that hire this labor
f A decline in the market wage rate for this labor
g A series of mergers that transforms the product market into a monopoly

4 Predict the impact of each of the following on the equilibrium wage rate and level of employment in labor market A:

a An increase in labor demand and supply in labor market A
b The transformation of labor market A from a competitive to a monopsonistic market

5 Assume a "surplus" of doctors exists. Use labor market supply and demand graphics to depict this outcome. How would the market remedy this situation in the short run and the long run?

6 Answer the following questions on the basis of the table shown below. Q_B is type *B* labor, and VMP_{Bx} *and* VMP_{By} are the industry values of the marginal products of this labor in producing *x* and *y*, the only two goods in the economy.

Q_B	VMP_{Bx}	VMP_{By}
1	$18	$23
2	15	19
3	12	15
4	9	11
5	6	9
6	3	5

a Explain why the VMPs in the table decline as more units of labor are employed.
b If the supply price or opportunity cost of labor P_L is $9, how many units of type *B* labor need to be used in producing *x* and *y* to achieve an efficient allocation of labor? What will be the combined total value of the two outputs?
c Suppose that P_L is $15 and that presently 5 units of labor are being allocated to producing *x*, while 2 units are being allocated to *y*. Is this an efficient allocation of labor? Why or why not? If not, what is the efficient allocation of type *B* labor?
d Suppose that P_L is $25 and that 3 units of labor are being allocated to producing *x*, while 6 units are being allocated to producing *y*. Explain why this is not an efficient allocation of labor. What *is* the efficient allocation of this type labor? What gain in the total value of leisure, alternative outputs, or home production results from this reallocation of labor?
e Suppose that product *x* is sold in a perfectly competitive product market. Also ignore the VMP_{By} column and assume that the VMP_{Bx} schedule is representative of each firm hiring workers in a perfectly competitive labor market. If the market wage rate is $12, what will be each firm's MWC? What will be their MRPs at their profit-maximizing level of employment? Explain why an efficient allocation of labor will occur in this industry.

7 Complete the following table for a single firm operating in labor market A and product market AA.

Units of labor	Wage rate (*W*)	Total wage cost	MWC	MRP	VMP
1	$10			$16	$16
2	10			14	15
3	10			12	14
4	10			10	12
5	10			8	10
6	10			6	8

a What, if anything, can one conclude about the degree of competition in labor market A and product market AA?
b What is the profit-maximizing level of employment? Explain.
c Does this profit-maximizing level of employment yield allocative efficiency? Explain.

8 Use the production data shown on the left and the labor supply data on the right for a single firm to answer the following questions. Assume that this firm is selling its product for $1 per unit in a perfectly competitive product market.

Units of labor	Total product
0	0
1	13
2	25
3	34
4	42
5	46
6	48

Units of labor	Total product
0	—
1	$1
2	2
3	3
4	4
5	5
6	6

a How many workers will this firm choose to employ?
b What will be its profit-maximizing wage rate?
c What labor market model do these data best describe?

9 Assume a firm *(a)* is a monopsonist in hiring labor, *(b)* is selling its product as a monopolist, and *(c)* faces no union. Portray this market graphically. Correctly label *all* relevant curves, show the equilibrium wage rate and level of employment, and indicate the efficiency loss (if any).

10 Under what elasticity of labor demand conditions could a union restrict the supply of labor—that is, shift the supply curve leftward—and thereby increase the collective wage income (wage bill) of those workers still employed?

11 Use graphic analysis to explain how a union in a monopsonized labor market might simultaneously enhance *(a)* its wage rate, *(b)* employment, and *(c)* allocative efficiency.

12 Explain why there may be an "appearance" of chronic shortages in some monopsonized labor markets, while in some bilateral monopoly markets chronic surpluses often exist.

13 Explain how each one of the following contract provisions might affect the *elasticity* of labor demand during the period of the labor contract:
a Layoff and severance pay
b Prevention of subcontracting
c The limiting of plant shutdown or relocation

14 Use graphical analysis to show how an unexpected *decline* in labor demand may set off a cobweb adjustment cycle in a labor market for highly trained professionals. In explaining your graph, distinguish between the immediate-period supply curve and the long-run supply curve.

SELECTED REFERENCES

Boal, William M., and Michael R. Ransom: "Monopsony in the Labor Market," *Journal of Economic Literature,* March 1997, pp. 86–112.

Bunting, Robert L.: *Employer Concentration in Local Labor Markets* (Chapel Hill: University of North Carolina Press, 1962).

Fleisher, Belton M., and Thomas J. Kneisner: *Labor Economics: Theory, Evidence, and Policy,* 3d ed. (Englewood Cliffs, NJ: Prentice-Hall, Inc., 1984), chaps. 5 and 6.

Freeman, Richard B.: *The Overeducated American* (New York: Academic Press, 1976).

Rottenberg, Simon (ed.): *Occupational Licensure and Regulation* (Washington, DC: American Enterprise Institute for Public Policy Research, 1980).

CHAPTER 7

ALTERNATIVE PAY SCHEMES AND LABOR EFFICIENCY

Most of you will be seeking full-time employment when you graduate from college. Let's suppose that you are offered a job relating to your college major. Before accepting this particular job offer, what information about the compensation package would you want to know? Our surmise is that, first, you would want to know about the annual salary or the hourly wage. What else? No doubt, you would seek information about the fringe benefit package. How good are the medical benefits? Is there disability insurance? Are there paid vacations? Does the firm contribute to a pension plan?

In Chapter 6 we identified and explained several basic models of wage determination. Our assumption in those models was that all compensation was in the form of an hourly wage rate, say, \$10 per hour. But, as the previous paragraph suggests, in reality fringe benefits constitute an important element of our compensation. Additionally, firms are not indifferent as to the composition of the total compensation they pay; for example, they may wish to structure their pay package in special ways to enhance work effort and reduce turnover.

The goal of this chapter is to examine pay packages that are more complex in composition and purpose than the standard hourly wage rate. We begin by developing a model of the optimal level of fringe benefits and then use it to explain the historical growth of such benefits. Next, we introduce the notions of "principals" and "agents" and note the so-called "principal–agent problem" relating to divergent interests of the firm and the worker. After defining these new terms, we examine several pay-for-performance plans. These include piece rates, commissions, royalties, raises and promotions, personal and team bonuses, profit sharing, and tournament pay. Then we look at efficiency wage theories in which the productivity of labor depends on the wage rate itself. This discussion is followed by a section of life-cycle pay schemes where portions of wage payments are deferred to later years.

Throughout the discussion our focus will be on how the structure and timing of pay can promote worker well-being and labor efficiency. In short, this chapter treats topics related to the "new economics of personnel" and extends our understanding of labor market efficiency.

ECONOMICS OF FRINGE BENEFITS

We begin by analyzing the economics of the fringe benefit portion of total compensation. *Total compensation* comprises wage earnings and the costs of fringe benefits. ***Fringe benefits*** include public (legally mandated) programs such as Social Security, unemployment compensation, and workers' compensation. They also include many private nonmandatory programs such as private pensions, medical and dental insurance, paid vacations, and sick leave. We will find that fringe benefits can increase the utility that workers receive from a given amount of total compensation. Fringe benefits also can benefit the firm by permitting it to retain and attract high-quality workers.

Fringe Benefits: Facts

Fringe benefits constitute a significant portion of total compensation, and they have grown rapidly as a percentage of total compensation during the past several decades.

1 Fringe Benefits as a Proportion of Total Compensation The Bureau of Labor Statistics (BLS) has broken down employee compensation within private industry.[1] Although confined to the private sector, this breakdown provides a rough sketch of the relative size of fringe benefits in pay packages for the total economy. As revealed in Figure 7-1, *wages and salaries* constitute about 72 percent of total compensation in private industry, while *employee fringe benefits* account for about 28 percent.

It is instructive to examine the various fringe benefit components of the compensation pie. Observe from Figure 7-1 that *legally required benefits* comprise over 9 percent of total compensation. These benefits include Social Security, railroad retirement and supplemental retirement, federal and state unemployment insurance, workers' compensation, and state temporary disability insurance benefits. *Paid leaves,* which include paid vacations, paid holidays, paid sick leave, and the like, account for 6.4 percent of total employee compensation. Note that *insurance benefits*—for life, health, and sickness and accident insurance—comprise a 6.5 percent share.

The remaining three slices of the employee compensation pie are *retirement and savings benefits* (3.1 percent), which include retirement plans and saving thrift plans; *supplemental pay* (2.8 percent), comprised of premium pay for overtime and work on holidays, shift differentials, nonproduction bonuses, and lump-sum payments; and *other*

[1]U.S. Bureau of Labor Statistics, *New Employer Costs for Employee Compensation,* U.S. Department of Labor, 96-424.

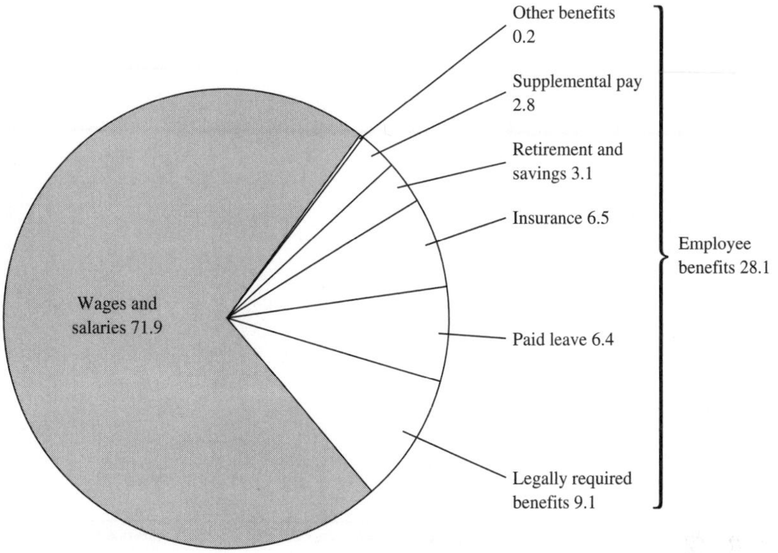

FIGURE 7-1 **COMPONENTS OF TOTAL COMPENSATION (PRIVATE INDUSTRY, IN PERCENT)**
Fringe benefits account for more than one-fourth of the total compensation in private industry. (*Source:* Bureau of Labor Statistics. Data are for March 1996.)

benefits (0.2 percent), which include severance pay, supplemental unemployment benefits, and merchandise discounts in department stores.

The composition of total compensation varies greatly by industry. For example, the fringe benefits proportion of employee compensation is larger (1) in high-paid industries than in low-paid ones; (2) in goods-producing industries compared to service industries; and (3) in transportation and public utilities compared to retail trade. The proportion and specific types of benefits also vary by industry. For example, paid leaves comprise about 8 percent of total compensation in transportation and public utilities, while they are only about 4 percent in retail trade.

Finally, the BLS data reveal that the composition of total compensation also differs by occupational group. For example, because of legally mandated fringe benefits, the fringe benefit share of total compensation is greater for blue-collar workers than for white-collar workers. As another example, legally required benefits are a significantly higher percentage of total pay for transportation workers than for executives.

2 Fringe Benefit Growth Fringe benefits have grown significantly as a component of total employee compensation during the past several decades. This growth is shown in Figure 7-2, where we see that fringe benefits for all workers have expanded from less than 3 percent of total compensation in 1929 to more than one-quarter of total pay in 1996.

Why are fringe benefits a significant component of total compensation? What explains their rapid growth? A model of optimal fringe benefits will help us answer these questions.

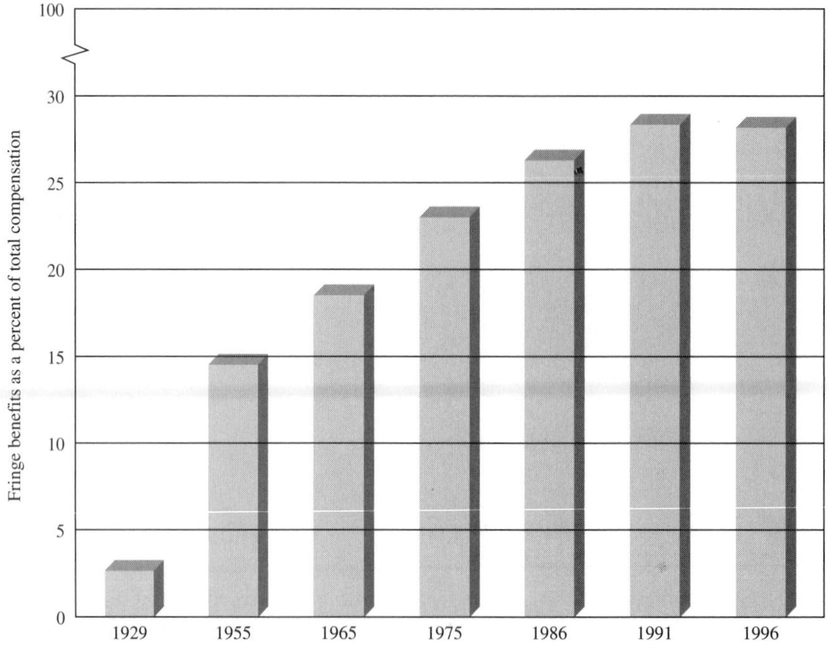

FIGURE 7-2 RELATIVE GROWTH OF FRINGE BENEFITS
Fringe benefits have increased dramatically as a percent of total compensation since 1929. (*Source:* Bureau of Labor Statistics, *Employee Benefits in a Changing Economy: A BLS Chartbook,* September 1992, p. 3.), updated.

THEORY OF OPTIMAL FRINGE BENEFITS

The theory of optimal fringe benefits is a variation of the income–leisure choice problem encountered in Chapter 2. There, we saw that a budget constraint (wage rate line) limited the worker to specific combinations of earnings and leisure (Figure 2-5). The worker chose the single combination of these two "goods" that provided the highest utility. This choice was made on the basis of the worker's subjective evaluation of the trade-off between earnings and leisure in relationship to the objectively determined budget constraint.

In a similar way we might think of a worker facing a choice between wages and fringe benefits. The worker's preferences for these two "goods" are reflected in an *indifference map.* The budget constraint takes the form of the employer's total compensation line, or an *isoprofit curve.*[2]

[2]The analysis that follows was developed by Ronald G. Ehrenberg and Robert S. Smith. See Smith and Ehrenberg, "Estimating Wage-Fringe Trade-Offs: Some Data Problems," in Jack E. Triplett (ed.), *The Measurement of Labor Cost* (Chicago: University of Chicago Press, 1983), pp. 347–367; and Ehrenberg and Smith, *Modern Labor Economics,* 6th ed. (Reading, MA: Addison-Wesley, 1997), pp. 271–278.

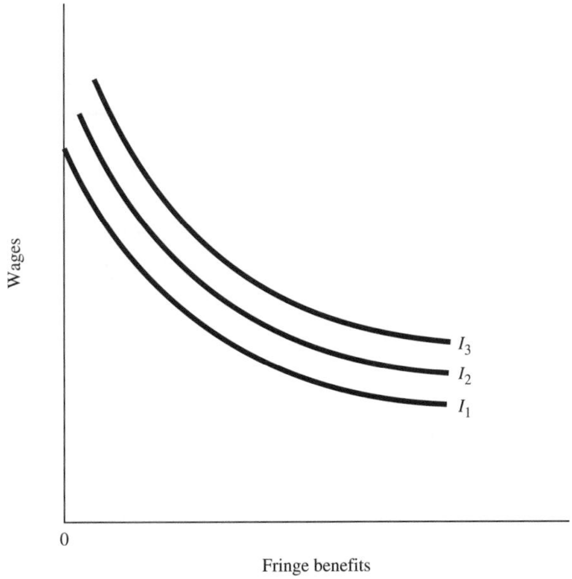

FIGURE 7-3 A WORKER'S INDIFFERENCE MAP FOR WAGES AND FRINGE BENEFITS
Each indifference curve shows the combinations of wages and fringe benefits that yield a specific level of total utility. Indifference curves farther to the northeast in the indifference map represent higher levels of total utility; therefore, they are preferred by the worker.

Worker's Indifference Map

Each indifference curve shown in Figure 7-3 displays combinations of wages and fringe benefits yielding the same level of satisfaction or utility to the worker. Thus, a single indifference curve such as I_1 reflects a constant level of total utility. As we move northeast from the origin, each successive indifference curve entails a higher level of total utility.

The downward slope of each indifference curve indicates that workers view wages and fringes as each yielding utility and therefore being somewhat substitutable. At first thought this may seem surprising because most fringes are ***in-kind benefits****—benefits in the form of a specific kind of good or service.* Would not a worker (consumer) always be better off with—and therefore prefer—an additional dollar's worth of (cash) wages rather than an additional dollar's worth of some specific fringe benefit? One dollar in cash wages represents generalized purchasing power that can be spent on $1 worth of whatever good or service is most preferred by (yields the most marginal utility to) the consumer. An in-kind fringe benefit, on the other hand, ties the individual to the particular good or service. In fact, that good or service may provide little or no marginal utility, or satisfaction, to a particular worker. An on-the-job day care center yields little satisfaction to a worker who does not have children or to an older worker whose children are grown. An older worker with false teeth may derive little or no utility from a program of dental insurance. Nevertheless, there are two major reasons that workers are in fact willing to sacrifice some of their wages to obtain a package of fringe benefits.

First, and undoubtedly of greatest consequence, certain fringe benefits entail a large tax advantage to workers. For example, workers do not pay taxes on the deferred income benefits embodied in private pension plans until those benefits are actually received. Pensions allow principal, interest, and dividends to accumulate at a pretax growth rate rather than a posttax pace. Also, since the worker's earned income will likely fall to zero at retirement, the income provided by the pension plan might be taxed at a lower marginal tax rate (say, 15 percent) than the same amount paid as wages during the worker's active work life (for example, 28 or 36 percent). In short, pensions are a means of deferring income to achieve lower tax rates. The after-tax value of $1 of pension contribution is perceived to be greater than the after-tax value of $1 of current wage income. Similarly, premiums paid by employers for health and life insurance are subject neither to the Social Security tax nor the personal income tax.[3]

Second, workers may be willing to substitute fringe benefits for a part of their wages as a way to guard against their own tendency to purchase goods that provide more immediate gratification than, say, health insurance or pension annuities. People may realize that their cash earnings have a way of getting spent on other items such as cars, boats, clothing, and vacations. Thus, they are willing to sacrifice some of their earnings to get health and pension benefits that they know are important for their futures. By accepting pay packages that contain fringe benefits, workers ensure that insurance, pension, and other benefits are available when they are needed.

Observe that the indifference curves not only slope downward but are convex as viewed from the origin (as was the case in our income–leisure diagrams in Chapter 2). Stated technically, the marginal rate of substitution of fringe benefits for wages falls as more benefits are added. When a person has few fringe benefits, the worker is willing to trade off a large amount of wages for an additional unit of fringe benefits. But as the amount of fringe benefits rises, the marginal utility of still more fringe benefits falls, and the person is less willing to sacrifice wage payments to attain still more units of them.

Employer's Isoprofit Curve

For a given level of output, a firm will wish to minimize its total compensation per hour of work to help maximize its profits. In Figure 7-4 we show a firm's ***isoprofit curve,*** *WF,* which *indicates the various combinations of wages and fringe benefits providing a given profit.* We assume for simplicity that competition in the product market has resulted in a *normal profit.* We also suppose that competition in the labor market has forced this firm to pay the total compensation indicated by the combinations of wages and fringes demonstrated by curve *WF.* That is, *WF* shows the combinations of wages and fringe benefits that allow the firm to maintain a normal profit, given the "prices" of wages and fringe benefits.

[3]For studies examining the role of taxes in employee demand for fringe benefits, see Stephen A. Woodbury and Daniel S. Hamermesh, "Taxes, Fringe Benefits, and Faculty," *Review of Economics and Statistics,* May 1992, pp. 287–296; and Stephen A. Woodbury and Wei-Jang Huang, *The Tax Treatment of Fringe Benefits* (Kalamazoo, MI: W. E. Upjohn Institute, 1991).

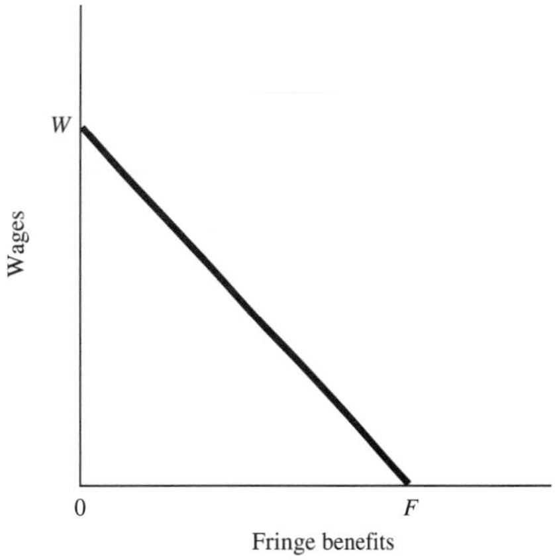

FIGURE 7-4 AN EMPLOYER'S ISOPROFIT CURVE (NORMAL PROFIT)
An isoprofit curve portrays the various combinations of wages and fringe benefits that yield a specific level of profits. We assume that competition will result in a normal profit. Thus, *WF* shows the various combinations of wages and fringes the firm can afford to provide, given the "prices" of the alternative forms of compensation.

Close inspection of this isoprofit line in Figure 7-4 reveals that its slope is -1. In this example, a \$1 reduction in wages accompanied by a \$1 increase in fringe benefits leaves the total compensation to the worker—and thus the total profits to the firm—unchanged. The firm's total compensation and profits are the same if it pays $0W$ wages and 0 fringe benefits or 0 wages and $0F$ fringe benefits. Similarly, total compensation is the same for all other combinations of wages and fringe benefits indicated by line *WF*.

Wage–Fringe Optimum

Noting that the axes of Figure 7-3 and 7-4 are the same, we can now determine the worker's utility-maximizing combination of wages and fringe benefits. Of all the attainable combinations of wages and fringe benefits along line *WF* in Figure 7-5, combination W_0 and F_0 yields the worker the greatest satisfaction, or utility. Specifically, the utility-maximizing combination is the one tangent to the highest attainable indifference curve (I_2 at *b*). To test this proposition, note that points *a* (all wage payments and no fringes) and *c* (relatively low wage payments and high fringes) are inferior to point *b*. That is, at these points the worker is on lower-than-attainable indifference curve I_1. This person can attain the higher indifference curve I_2 if the wages–fringes combination is appropriately adjusted from point *a* or *c* toward *b*.

Although indifference maps vary among individual workers, we will suppose for simplicity that this worker's preferences for wage payments and fringe benefits are representative of the average worker. Differing indifference maps among workers—and therefore differing wage–fringe optimums—are discussed in Chapter 8.

Causes of Fringe Benefit Growth

Let's next consider the implications of a lower "price" for fringe benefits. In Figure 7-6 we have drawn a new normal-profit isoprofit line *WF′* that has a flatter slope than

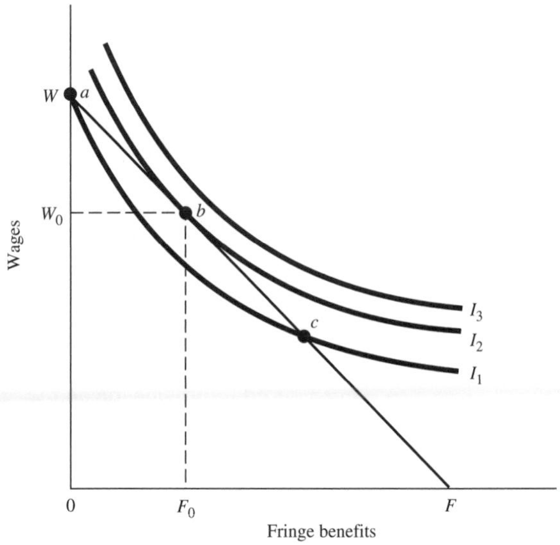

FIGURE 7-5 WAGE–FRINGE OPTIMUM
The optimal combination of wages and fringe benefits is at *b,* where the isoprofit curve is tangent to the highest attainable indifference curve I_2. Here, the firm will provide W_0 wages and F_0 fringe benefits. Points *a* and *c* are also attainable combinations of wages and fringes, but yield less total utility, as is evidenced by their locations on lower indifference curve I_1.

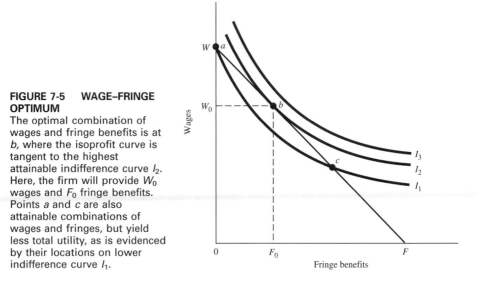

line *WF.* The shift from *WF* to *WF′* tells us that the relative per unit cost or "price" of fringe benefits has fallen. Restated, the firm can now supply more fringe benefits at all but the highest wage without increasing its total compensation. Thus, it can provide more fringe benefits without reducing its profits. The firm can now exchange a dollar's worth of wages for more than a dollar's worth of benefits, even though these benefits only cost a dollar. It will want to offer its workers this better trade-off between wages and fringe benefits to attract and retain the highest-quality employees. In fact, a competitive labor market will dictate that the firm pay compensation to workers as indicated by line *WF′*, because other firms will bid up the level of total compensation to this level.

This new normal-profit isoprofit line results in a new tangency position at point *d* on a higher indifference curve, I_3. Observe that this representative worker now selects a combination of wages and fringes more heavily weighted in favor of fringe benefits. The decline in the price of fringe benefits has both enabled and enticed the worker to "buy" more fringe benefits. He or she now has more real income (wages plus fringes) and views fringe benefits as being a relatively "better buy" than they were before. Consequently, this worker opts for more fringe benefits and achieves a higher level of utility (I_3 at *d* rather than I_2 at *b*).

The obvious question is what might cause the normal-profit isoprofit line to fan outward as indicated in Figure 7-6? What might lower the price of fringe benefits and enable the firm to offer more of them and still retain the same levels of total compensation and normal profits? The answers to these questions provide the basis for a list of reasons fringe benefits have grown historically.

Tax Advantages to the Employer We have observed that fringe benefits confer tax advantages to the worker. These fringe benefits also reduce taxes owed by the em-

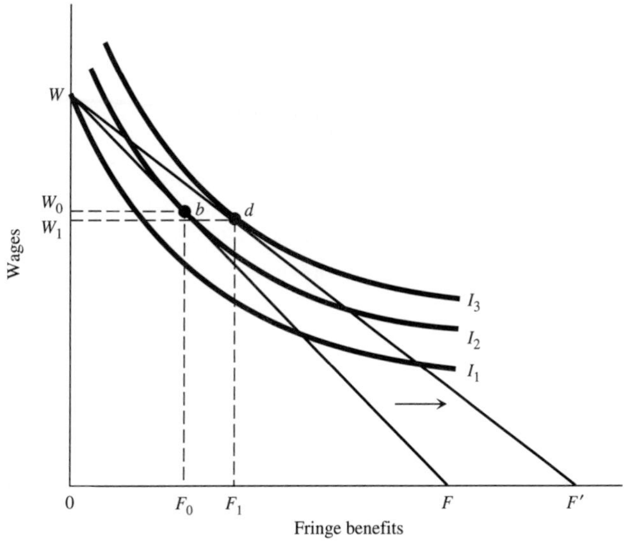

FIGURE 7-6 FRINGE BENEFIT GROWTH
A decrease in the price of fringe benefits due to tax advantages, scale economies, and efficiency considerations fans the normal-profit isoprofit line outward. This allows the worker to attain a higher indifference curve (I_3 rather than I_2). In the process, fringe benefits expand from F_0 to F_1.

ployer. The employer must pay one-half of the 15.3 percent Social Security payroll tax on worker earnings up to \$68,400 (1998) for each employee. For workers earning less than this amount, the firm reduces its payroll tax burden by tilting the pay package away from wage earnings and toward fringe benefits. Example: Suppose a worker earns \$30,000 a year. At the 1998 payroll tax rate of 7.65 percent, the employer would have to pay \$2,295 of tax. But, if the employer instead pays the worker, say \$20,000 in earnings and \$10,000 of fringe benefits, the tax burden for the firm falls to \$1,530 (= \$20,000 × .0765). Multiplied by thousands of workers, the tax saving to a large firm can be considerable. The upshot is that the firm finds that it can offer fringe benefits worth more than a dollar for a dollar reduction in direct pay. In Figure 7-6 the normal-profit isoprofit line fans outward as indicated by the shift from *WF* to *WF′*. Because the Social Security tax base and rate have both increased historically, the optimal level of fringe benefits has risen.

The evidence indicates that taxes play an important role in the provision of fringe benefits. Gentry and Peress report that a 1 percentage point increase in the marginal tax rate would raise the percentage of blue-collar workers (the results were less clear for white-collar workers) who are offered medical insurance by 1.8 percentage points, dental insurance by 1.2 percentage points, and employer-financed pensions 1.3 percentage points.[4]

[4]William Gentry and Eric Peress, "Taxes and Fringe Benefits Offered by Employers," National Bureau of Economic Research Working Paper No. 4764, June 1994.

Economics of Scale Significant economies of scale usually exist in the collective purchase of fringe benefits that lower their prices to buyers. In particular, the administrative costs and agent fees are much less in purchasing medical, life, disability, or dental insurance on a group basis rather than on an individual one.[5] Additionally, group policies eliminate the *adverse selection problem*—the tendency for individuals most likely to draw large benefits to sign up for insurance. As with tax advantages, the "discount prices" on insurance reduce the per unit cost of fringes and rotate the normal-profit isoprofit line outward, as in Figure 7-6. The result is that a worker is enticed to accept more fringe benefits than previously. To the extent that cost savings have increased historically as the size of firms has grown, the optimal amount of fringe benefits has also grown.

Efficiency Considerations Employers are interested in protecting their training investments and reducing their recruiting and training costs. They may see fringe benefits as a way to tie workers to jobs and hence to reduce quits. Pension benefits in particular are effective in reducing employee turnover.[6] Lower turnover means that a higher proportion of the firm's workers are well past the training stage. Consequently, the average productivity of a firm's workforce rises.

7-1

Viewed by the firm, pension benefits thus are less costly than their dollar expense. From a dollar outlay the firm must subtract the added revenue resulting from the enhanced productivity arising from the fringe benefit package. A firm can therefore offer more fringe benefits of this kind without suffering a loss of profits.[7] Because the training investments of firms have risen historically, firms increasingly have had an incentive to use fringe benefits to reduce turnover. More will be said about the economics of deferred payment schemes later in this chapter.

Other Factors There are several other reasons fringe benefits have increased historically. Certain fringe benefits are quite *income elastic*. They involve pension coverage and such services as medical and dental care, purchases of which are quite sensitive to increases in income. Thus, as worker incomes have grown historically, it is not

[5] For studies documenting economies of scale in the administration of pension and health plans, see Emily S. Andrews, *Pension Policy and Small Employers: At What Price Coverage?* (Washington, DC: Employee Benefit Research Institute, 1989); Olivia S. Mitchell and Emily S. Andrews, "Scale Economies in Private Multi-Employer Pension Systems," *Industrial and Labor Relations Review,* July 1981, pp. 522–530; and ICF, Inc., *Health Care Coverage and Costs in Small and Large Businesses,* report prepared for the Office of Advocacy, Small Business Administration, 1987.

[6] For example, see William E. Even and David A. Macpherson, "Employer Size and Labor Turnover: The Role of Pensions," *Industrial and Labor Relations Review,* July 1996, pp. 707–728; Steven Allen, Robert Clark, and Ann McDermed, "Pensions, Bonding, and Lifetime Jobs," *Journal of Human Resources,* Summer 1993, pp. 463–481; and Alan L. Gustman and Thomas L. Steinmeier, "Pension Portability and Labor Mobility: Evidence from the Survey of Income and Program Participation," *Journal of Public Economics,* March 1993, pp. 299–323.

[7] Although the overall productivity-enhancing aspects of fringe benefits are thought to dominate, the reader should be aware that some fringe benefits may reduce productivity. For example, paid sick leave may encourage absenteeism. Also, certain fringe benefits may attract employees who are most likely to draw upon the particular benefits, thus increasing the cost of the fringe benefit program to the employer. For example, a firm that offers parental leave may attract a disproportionate number of employees who have children. For a discussion of the public policy implications of this problem, see Lawrence H. Summers, "Some Simple Economics of Mandated Benefits," *American Economic Review,* May 1989, pp. 177–183.

7-1 World of Work

DOES HEALTH INSURANCE CAUSE "JOB LOCK"?

Health insurance coverage may cause some workers to stay on a job they would prefer to leave. Firms that provide health insurance often require waiting periods before covering new workers or completely exclude a new worker's preexisting medical conditions. As a consequence, some workers may be reluctant to change jobs because of concerns about losing health insurance coverage. This reduced job mobility is known as "job lock."

Buchmueller and Valletta examine the empirical importance of this issue by comparing the job mobility of workers with and without health insurance coverage.* Their results provide fairly strong evidence of job lock for both married and single women. Health insurance coverage reduces job mobility for these workers by 35 to 50 percent. The findings are more mixed among men. Married men whose spouses also work appear to suffer from job lock, but among sole-earner married and single men only weak evidence of job lock exists. The authors speculate that the stronger findings of job lock among women reflect their higher health care use compared to that of men.

One public policy solution to the problem of job lock is "continuation of coverage" mandates. Some states and the federal government require employers to allow ex-employees to purchase health insurance coverage from their former employers for a specified time period after leaving their jobs. To examine the effect of this mandate, Gruber and Madrian compare job mobility for workers across states with different requirements for how long employers must provide coverage (ranging from 2 to 20 months).† Also, they compare job mobility before and after the adoption of these laws. They conclude that the mandates do reduce job lock because a 12-month increase in the required continuation of coverage requirement boosts job mobility by approximately 10 percent.

*Thomas C. Buchmueller and Robert G. Valletta, "The Effects of Employer-Provided Health Insurance on Worker Mobility," *Industrial and Labor Relations Review*, April 1996, pp. 439–455. For a survey of earlier studies, see Alan C. Moheit and Philip F. Cooper, "Health Insurance and Job Mobility: Theory and Evidence," *Industrial and Labor Relations Review*, October 1994, pp. 68–85.

†Jonathan Gruber and Brigette C. Madrian, "Health Insurance and Job Mobility: The Effects of Public Policy on Job-Lock," *Industrial and Labor Relations Review*, October 1994, pp. 86–102.

surprising that the "purchase" of such fringes has also expanded.[8] Also, the federal government has raised mandated fringe benefits such as Social Security and unemployment compensation. Finally, we will find in Chapter 11 that unionization historically has been a factor in the rise in fringe benefits. On average, union workers receive more generous fringe benefits than nonunion workers. Also, nonunion firms often emulate union contracts as a way to deter unionism.

QUICK REVIEW 7-1

- Fringe benefits account for more than one-fourth of the total compensation in private industry.
- In the wage–fringe benefit model, the optimal combination of wages and fringe benefits occurs where the isoprofit curve is tangent to the highest attainable indifference curve.

[8]Stephen Woodbury, "Substitution between Wage and Nonwage Benefits," *American Economic Review*, March 1983, pp. 166–182.

7-1

• Favorable tax treatment, economies of scale, and efficiency considerations have reduced the "price" of fringe benefits, expanding their availability and enhancing worker utility.

7-2

Your Turn: Suppose that government decides to tax fringe benefits as ordinary income. What would happen to the slopes of the typical worker's indifference curves? How would this affect the optimal amount of fringe benefits? (Answers: See page 626.)

THE PRINCIPAL–AGENT PROBLEM

We next turn to a discussion of the relationship between pay and performance. This pay may take the form of either direct cash or fringe benefits. But as a prelude to this topic, we need to explore the nature of the relationship between firms and workers.

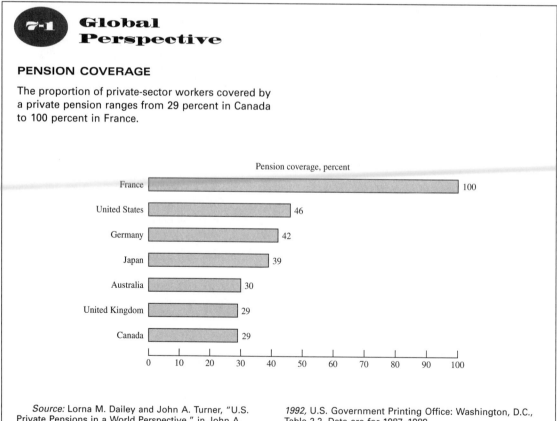

7-1 **Global Perspective**

PENSION COVERAGE

The proportion of private-sector workers covered by a private pension ranges from 29 percent in Canada to 100 percent in France.

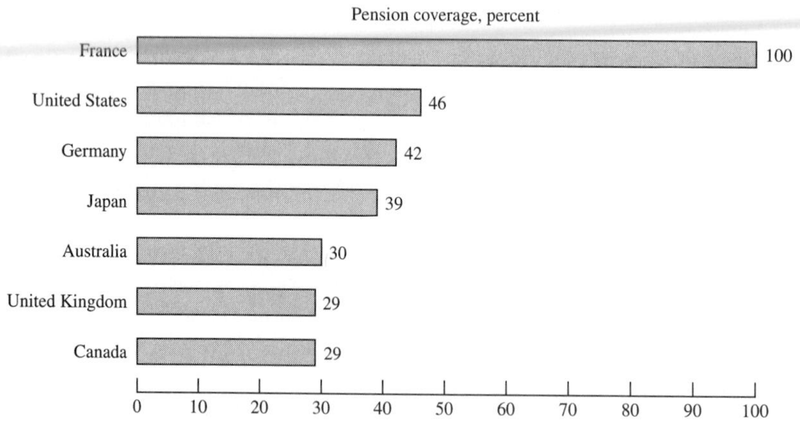

Source: Lorna M. Dailey and John A. Turner, "U.S. Private Pensions in a World Perspective," in John A. Turner and Daniel J. Beller (eds.), *Trends in Pensions, 1992,* U.S. Government Printing Office: Washington, D.C., Table 2.2. Data are for 1987–1989.

7-2 World of Work

THE FALL IN PRIVATE-SECTOR PENSION COVERAGE AMONG MEN*

Since 1979 the percentage of men covered by pension plans in the private sector has significantly declined. This fact is particularly surprising since pension coverage doubled between 1950 and 1979. In 1979 coverage among men was 62 percent; currently it is about 57 percent. The drop in coverage has been particularly pronounced for less-educated, less-skilled young men. Pension coverage for those without a high school degree has decreased from 54 to 32 percent. Coverage for holders of only a high school degree has declined from 63 to 54 percent.

Even and Macpherson attribute the fall in pension coverage to two factors. First, employment has shifted away from jobs offering pension coverage. An important change has been the continuing rapid decline in unionization (Chapter 10). Because union workers have a high incidence of pension coverage, this decline has substantially reduced overall coverage. Another change is the decline in real earnings experienced by less-educated males in the 1980s. Many of these workers can no longer defer part of their present income and still pay day-to-day expenses. The second and more important component is the reduction in participation in pension plans offered to male workers. The main factor in the decline in participation is the growing share of pensions that are 401(k) plans. In contrast to traditional pension plans, participation in 401(k) plans is more voluntary. Of those offered a 401(k) plan, nearly one-quarter of men have declined to participate in the pension plan.

This decline in pension coverage is troublesome. Pension plans are a major source of savings, which fund the private-sector investment necessary for economic growth. Also, the decline in pension coverage bodes ill for many of today's younger workers when they retire. The likelihood is growing that many of these people will have to postpone their retirements, sell off their homes, and rely more heavily on Social Security when they retire.

*Based on William E. Even and David A. Macpherson, "Why Did Male Pension Coverage Decline in the 1980s?" *Industrial and Labor Relations Review,* April 1994, pp. 439–453; and William E. Even and David A. Macpherson, "The Decline in Pension Coverage among Less Educated Workers," Florida State University Working Paper No. 96-03-01, March 1996.

We know from our discussion in previous chapters that firms hire employees because workers help produce goods and services that firms can sell for a profit in the marketplace. In this respect workers might be thought of as the firms' ***agents***—*parties who are hired to advance the interests of others.* Alternatively, firms can be conceived of as ***principals***—*parties who hire others to help them achieve their objectives.* In this case the firms' or principals' objective is profits. Employees are willing to help firms earn profits in return for payments of wage income. This income enables workers to buy goods and services that yield utility. Thus, the relationship between principals (firms) and agents (workers) is based on mutual self-interest; the employment relationship benefits both firms and workers. But to say that principals and agents share common interests is not to say that all their interests are identical. In situations where interests between firms and workers diverge, a so-called "principal–agent problem" might arise.

The ***principal–agent problem*** *occurs when agents (workers) pursue some of their own objectives in conflict with achieving the goals of the principals (firms).* Firms desire to maximize profits (Chapter 6); workers wish to maximize utility (Chapter 2). Profit maximization requires that employees work all agreed-upon hours at agreed-upon effort. Otherwise output will be reduced, and average and marginal costs of production will be higher. But under many employment circumstances, workers can enhance their own utility by engaging in *opportunistic behavior* that directly conflicts with profit maximization. Specifically, workers can increase their "leisure" by ***shirking;*** that is, by either *taking unauthorized work breaks or giving less than agreed-upon effort during work hours.* If undetected by firms, this shirking permits workers to increase their "leisure"—through reduced work time and effort—without forfeiting income. In terms of our earlier income–leisure model (Figure 2-5), workers who neglect or evade work can attain greater total utility than that available along their wage rate lines. In effect, undetected shirking allows workers to attain indifference curves like I_3 in Figure 2-5.

An important proposition derives from the principal–agent perspective. *Quite simply, firms (principals) will have a profit incentive to find ways to reduce or eliminate principal–agent problems.* The remainder of this chapter explores various facets of this proposition.

7-3

PAY FOR PERFORMANCE

One way that firms might attempt to solve the principal–agent problem is to tie pay directly to output or performance. Some so-called ***incentive pay plans*** have become increasingly popular throughout the economy. These pay schemes include piece rates, commissions, and royalties, raises and promotions, bonuses, profit sharing, and tournament pay.[9]

Piece Rates

Piece rates *are compensation paid in proportion to the number of units of personal output.* This compensation often is found in situations where workers control the pace of work and firms find it expensive to monitor worker effort. For example, apple pickers are paid by the bushel; apparel workers are paid by the piece; and typists are paid by the page. Although piece rates are normally associated with low-paying jobs, this type of pay is more ordinary than commonly thought. Surgeons in private practice set fees on a per-operation basis; tax preparers charge fixed amounts for each simple tax return; and lawyers charge set amounts for the various types of wills they draw up.

Evidence indicates that workers who are paid piece rates earn 10 to 15 percent more pay then comparable hourly paid workers in the same industry.[10] Nevertheless, piece rates have several drawbacks that have collectively resulted in their declining importance in American industry. First, in industries where technological change is rapid, it can be very difficult for employers to "find" the profit-maximizing piece rates. Workers

[9]For an analysis of the determinants of method of pay, see Charles Brown, "Firms' Choice of Method of Pay," *Industrial and Labor Relations Review,* February 1990, pp. S165–S182.

[10]Eric Seiler, "Piece Rate vs. Time Rate: The Effect of Incentives on Earnings," *Review of Economics and Statistics,* August 1984, pp. 363–376; and Charles Brown, "Wage Levels and Method of Pay," *Rand Journal of Economics,* Autumn 1992, pp. 366–375. For a study reporting a positive effect on productivity and wages for a firm switching from paying hourly wages to paying piece rates, see Edward P. Lazear, "Performance Pay and Productivity," National Bureau of Economic Research Working Paper No. 5672, July 1996.

7-3 World of Work

PRINCIPALS AND AGENTS: "SOLUTIONS" AS PROBLEMS

As the following two examples suggest, "solutions" to principal–agent problems sometimes produce unintended problems.

Sears admits mistake, reworks auto-repair policy*

In the early 1990s Sears offered its service advisers at its auto-repair shops sales commissions based on the dollar amounts of parts and services recommended and bought. The idea was to align the interest of these service advisers with the profit interest of the corporation. By aggressively identifying and performing needed repairs, the service managers could enhance Sears' profit while adding to their own total pay.

Like a poorly tuned 1972 Vega, the plan backfired. In 1992 government officials detected widespread fraud in Sears' auto-repair shops in California. They found that many Sears service representatives were recommending unneeded repairs, such as new springs and shock absorbers, to increase sales and commissions. This fraud was systematic; it pervaded Sears' auto-repair shops throughout California.

In short, Sears' incentive pay plan produced undesirable outcomes for Sears' customers and ultimately for Sears itself. The revelations resulted in nationwide negative publicity, government legal action, and a large loss of automotive business at Sears.

General Motors riles employees in Flint†

In 1987 workers at the General Motors factory in Flint, Michigan, stamped out body panels for GM cars. As a cooperative gesture and to promote teamwork, GM managers decided to allow 500 workers to leave the factory each day without punching out their timecards. Workers were free to leave when they finished producing the day's quota of parts. To GM's surprise, the new incentive caused productivity to skyrocket. Collectively, workers—some of whom had worked at GM for 20 years—found new ways to meet their joint quota by noon.

GM management thus found itself paying a full-day's salary for what it now considered to be a half-day's work. Management therefore upped the daily production quota. As a result, employees had to work 8-hour days at the faster pace they had established when working under the former incentive to leave early. The workers felt betrayed by management and threatened a local strike. Three years later, at the time of general negotiations between GM and the United Autoworkers, this issue at Flint still had not been fully resolved.

*Based on a combination of news stories.
†Based on Gregory A. Patterson, "UAW and Big Three Face Mutual Distrust as Auto Talks Heat Up," *Wall Street Journal*, August 29, 1990, p. A1.

can artificially boost the piece rate by agreeing among themselves to make the job seem more difficult and time-consuming than is actually the case.[11] Second, piece rates increase the likelihood of weekly, monthly, and even yearly income variability for workers. Thus, to attract workers to piece-rate jobs, firms may have to pay wage premiums (Chapter 8) to compensate workers for this risk of earnings variation. Employers could save the cost of this premium pay by paying a straight hourly wage. Third, where production is complex and team-oriented, it is difficult to ascribe units of output directly to the performance of individuals. Who produces each tube of Colgate toothpaste, can of Campbell's soup, or bottle of Coca-Cola? Fourth, close cooperation among workers is required for successful team performance. Piece rates reward independent work effort and therefore do little to promote this needed cooperation. Finally, piece rates suffer from their own advantage: The rapid production pace they elicit often results in

[11]Stephen Jones, *The Economics of Conformism* (New York: Basil Blackwell, 1984).

poor product quality. For these reasons piece rates have increasingly given way to ***time rates***—*pay based on units of time such as hours, months, or years.*

Commissions and Royalties

Unlike piece rates, which link pay to units of output, commissions and royalties tie pay to the value of sales. ***Commissions*** are commonly received by realtors, insurance agents, stockbrokers, and sales personnel. A glance at the classified sections of big-city newspapers will reveal several columns of help-wanted advertisements for commissioned workers. ***Royalties*** also are set as a percentage of sales revenue. They typically are paid to authors, film producers, recording artists, and similar professionals. For instance, about $8 of the price of this textbook—if it is new—accrues to the authors (and we thank you).

Commissions and royalties are efficient where work effort and work hours are difficult to observe. Time rates in these situations would bring forth attendant shirking problems for the firm because observing the worker would be very expensive. By aligning the interests of the firms and the workers, commissions and royalties help overcome the principal–agent problem.

7-4

Raises and Promotions

A sizable proportion of American workers receive time payments as fixed annual salaries. These workers are typically engaged in team production; thus, it is not easy to monitor their efforts or measure their outputs. Time payments, rather than piece rates, commissions, or royalties, therefore are optimal. But why fixed annual salaries and not fixed hourly pay? The reason is that managers and professionals are ***quasi-fixed resources,*** at least for a 1-year period.[12] A firm's use of salaried workers is largely independent of its level of production. Salaried workers thus are akin to fixed resources such as capital and land (*quasi-* means "as if"). For example, enterprises need accountants, lawyers, managers, and marketing personnel, both when production and sales are brisk and when they are slack. Also, firms incur high search, hiring, and training costs in employing salaried workers. Laying them off would risk quits that would end the firms' opportunities to gain returns on prior expensive investments in specific training [Figure 4-8(b)]. On a more mundane level high-skilled workers may simply be in a position to demand and receive the greater income security associated with fixed annual salaries.

But for all their benefits, annual salaries present a potential shirking problem. Let's describe this problem and then explore its solution.

Salaries and Work Incentives In Figure 7-7 we demonstrate the principal–agent problem associated with salaries. Our methodology will be to compare the optimal hours of work under conditions of hourly pay and an annual salary.

[12]Walter Oi, "Labor as a Quasi-Fixed Factor," *Journal of Political Economy,* December 1962, pp. 538–555.

7-4 World of Work

WHY IS THERE ACADEMIC TENURE?*

Tenure is a unique employment system in which college professors can gain almost complete future job security. Near the end of a tenure candidate's probationary period, a committee of peers assesses the credentials of the candidate and recommends for or against tenure. Recommendations go to the university administration, which decides either to grant tenure or to end the person's employment at the university.

The historical purpose of tenure has been to protect faculty members against arbitrary discharge resulting from controversial research or viewpoints. Supporters of tenure claim that it creates a climate of free inquiry essential to the advancement of human knowledge. But tenure also has some potential drawbacks. The job security it provides may reduce the work effort of some professors. Also, tenure may interfere with the optimal assignment of workers to jobs. It is alleged that older, less productive professors may occupy job "slots" that younger, presumably more productive professors are better qualified to fill. Thus, say critics, tenure reduces the total productive effort of the university.

In view of its supposed deficiencies, why has the tenure system prevailed? While most economists would answer, "Because faculties have sufficient political power within institutions to preserve it," Carmichael provides a more novel answer: Tenure endures precisely because it helps solve an unusual principal–agent problem and thereby enhances the overall quality of the faculty. He emphasizes that incumbent members of academic departments largely decide which new faculty to hire. The university entrusts this task to these individuals because they are uniquely qualified to identify the best possible candidates. But without tenure a unique principal–agent problem would arise: Incumbent professors (agents) would have an incentive to recommend to the university (principal) the weakest applicants for job openings! By doing this, senior faculty would reduce the prospect of being replaced by more productive employees, as happens in, say, professional sports. Senior faculty are willing to participate in identifying the top candidates for new academic openings only because of the tenure system. Because of tenure they do not risk losing their own jobs in the future by helping the university identify and employ promising young professors. In short, says Carmichael, the institution of tenure persists because it aligns the interests of universities (principals) and professors (agents) in the hiring process. The result is an improved overall quality of faculty.

This view of tenure is also consistent with other observed practices by universities. Institutions often provide generous early retirement plans to faculty, occasionally buy out the contracts of poorly performing tenured faculty, and sometimes eliminate entire weak departments when faced with budget cutbacks. Each of these practices addresses problems of tenure while preserving the aspects of the tenure system that allegedly solve the aforementioned principal–agent problem.

*H. Lorne Carmichael, "Incentives in Academics: Why Is There Tenure?" *Journal of Political Economy,* June 1988, pp. 453–472.

1 Hourly Pay First, observe wage rate line *WH,* the slope of which indicates a particular level of hourly pay. Given this hourly wage, the worker characterized by the indifference map shown will choose to work h_1 hours and earn an annual income Y_1. This h_1Y_1 combination of work and income permits the worker to attain indifference curve I_1 at *a,* which represents the highest level of total utility possible along the wage rate line. For illustrative purposes let's suppose that h_1 hours of work symbolize annual hours of work resulting from the normal 40-hour week.

2 Annual Salary Now let's convert the Y_1 income earned by working h_1 hours to an annual salary of the same amount ($= Y_1$). The new budget constraint in Figure 7-7 becomes HSY_1 and indicates this person will receive Y_1 income irrespective of hours of work. Presumably, because of the nature of the job, the number of hours the person

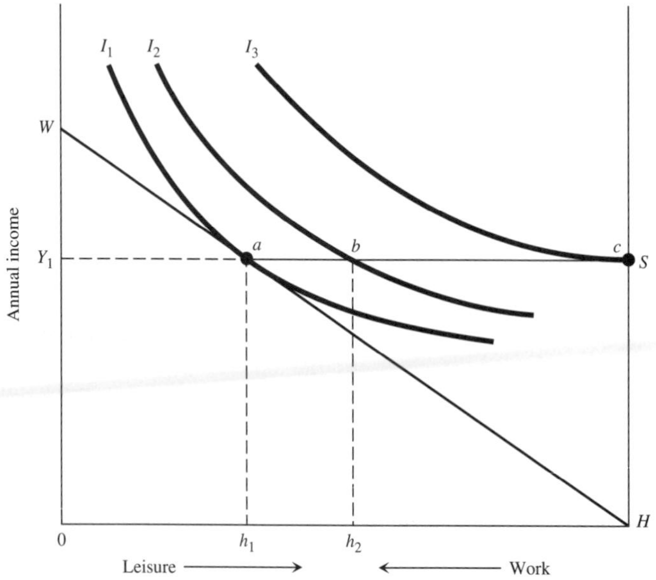

FIGURE 7-7 SALARIES AND WORK INCENTIVES
Wage rate line *WH* indicates a specific level of hourly pay that will provide an annual income equal to Y_1 at h_1 hours of work. An equivalent annual salary of Y_1 will allow the worker to obtain higher indifference curve I_2 or I_3 by reducing the actual number of hours worked to h_2 or *H*. The firm can overcome this incentive problem by offering future raises and promotions to those who work h_1, or more hours.

actually works while on the job is not easily observed. The worker now can achieve a higher level of utility by shirking. That is, the worker has an incentive to reduce work hours from h_1 to, say, h_2, allowing the worker to reach higher indifference curve I_2 at *b*. At the extreme, the worker can achieve a still higher level of utility by working zero hours (*c* on I_3). In both cases the annual salary ensures that the income level remains at Y_1.

Solution: Raises and Promotions One solution to the salary problem posed in Figure 7-7 is for the firm to establish performance-based raises and promotions. The prospect of future raises and promotions means that the worker's decision on hours of work versus leisure in any given year is *not* based on that year's salary alone. Rather, the salaried worker chooses the optimal hours with a view toward maximizing lifetime utility. Desiring to obtain raises and earn promotions, the worker may decide to work more than h_1 hours this year. In fact, salaried employees work more hours weekly than hourly paid workers. One reason may be the importance of raises and promotions to salaried workers. If the worker gains the reputation of being a low producer, advancement within the firm's job hierarchy is unlikely.[13]

[13]A competing explanation for the long hours of salaried workers is that these people may gain direct utility from the work they do, independent of compensation. At the extreme, the total utility of some professional workers would decline if they cut back their hours. For a graphical presentation of this phenomenon, see Bevars D. Mabry, *Economics of Manpower and the Labor Market* (New York: Intext Educational Publishers, 1973), pp. 221–229.

Bonuses

Bonuses are an increasingly popular form of incentive pay. ***Bonuses** are payments beyond the annual salary based on some factor such as personal or firm performance.* Their advantage to the firm is that they may elicit extra work effort. Another advantage is that they do not permanently raise base salaries or hourly wages, as do raises, promotions, or other forms of "merit pay." Therefore, during an economic slump, bonuses can be readily forgone while higher wages or salaries are not readily reduced.

Personal Performance Some bonuses are geared to personal performance that is formally assessed by superiors. If the superior rates the worker highly, the person receives a bonus. In other instances bonuses are based on some quantifiable output. Professional football players, for example, may receive bonuses for passing for more than a certain number of touchdowns or getting more than a specified number of quarterback sacks. Such "piece-rate" bonuses are less common in industries where individual performance is less directly measurable.

Bonuses based on individual performance may solve one form of the principal–agent problem, but they may create other kinds. Although this pay system may increase individual effort, it may channel the effort toward behavior that is counter to the employer's overall goals. Example: A basketball player who receives bonuses for assists may have a tendency to pass the ball rather than take wide-open shots. Second example: A worker whose bonus depends on an evaluation from a superior may spend excessive time pleasing the superior. As a result, the worker may spend less time on, say, developing original product ideas that later might produce higher profits. To repeat: It is relatively easy to structure bonuses to eliminate the shirking problem. But it is difficult to structure bonuses so they do not create other principal–agent problems.

Team Performance One solution to the problem just discussed is to structure individual bonuses on the performance of the team. The team in this case might be an actual team—as in professional sports—or teams such as departments, divisions, or entire enterprises. Once team goals are established, the bonus for each team member depends only on whether the team goals are met. Most formal bonus programs in U.S. enterprises are based on group, rather than personal, contributions to output or profits. Group bonus schemes based on physical output or costs are referred to as *gainsharing schemes.*

Team bonuses have a major drawback in that they create a potential ***free-rider problem.*** As the size of the unit or team increases, the effect of each worker's efforts on achieving the goals of the firm diminishes. Where the number of workers is large, individual workers are tempted to shirk. They realize that their personal shirking will not appreciably reduce the firm's output and profits. Thus, if others work hard, the shirker can still obtain a team bonus. It is unclear how workers who work energetically will respond to free riders. One possibility is that they may "punish" the free riders by reducing their own efforts, in which case the bonus plan will surely fail. Alternatively, it is possible that workers may eventually develop a strategy of cooperation—all agreeing to work hard and all monitoring each other to realize the optimal bonuses for all. The point is that, depending on the severity of the free-rider problem, team bonuses *may* or *may not* increase team productivity.

Team bonuses are more likely to be successful when they are targeted at a relatively small group of top executives whose decisions directly affect profits. In fact, bonuses based on profitability comprise about one-half of the total pay for senior executives. Do these large bonuses improve corporate performance? Recent research tentatively suggests that the answer is yes. But these studies also indicate that the profit increases attributable to bonuses tend to be relatively small.[14]

Profit Sharing

Profit sharing is *a pay system that allocates a specified portion of a firm's profits to employees.* This form of pay increased during the 1980s when workers in basic industries such as autos and primary metals accepted profit sharing in lieu of wage increases. Profit sharing also has become increasingly common for senior executives in large corporations. According to the Bureau of Labor Statistics, 16 percent of all full-time American workers in medium- and large-sized firms participate in profit-sharing plans in 1993.[15] Most participants are in deferred plans, in which profits are credited to employees for distribution at some future date such as retirement.[16]

At first thought the link between profit sharing and productivity seems straightforward. Proponents of profit sharing contend that it transforms workers into minicapitalists who work harder to reap a share of the firm's profits. The extra effort creates extra output and profits, thus making the plan self-financing. Profit sharing therefore aligns the interests of firms and their workforces. That is, profit sharing supposedly overcomes the principal–agent problem.

But in reality the theoretical link between profit sharing and improved efficiency is not so clear-cut.[17] The main reason is that profit sharing is tied to *group* performance. This tie creates the free-rider problem that we identified in our discussion of bonuses. The larger the size of the organization, the greater the possibility that the free-rider problem will short-circuit the profit-sharing–productivity link. The success of a profit-sharing plan depends crucially on how well the free-rider problem is resolved.

The effectiveness of profit-sharing plans therefore is an empirical question. Weitzman and Kruse have provided a detailed summary of the considerable amount of research done on this topic. They conclude: "The available evidence on the connection between profit sharing and productivity is not definitive. Yet it is also not neutral—many sources point towards a positive link; the only quarrel seems to be over magni-

[14]A representative set of these studies is found in the symposium "Do Compensation Policies Matter?" *Industrial and Labor Relations Review,* special issue, February 1990.

[15]U.S. Bureau of Labor Statistics, *Employee Benefits in Medium and Large Establishments, 1993,* Bulletin 2456.

[16]Edward M. Coates III, "Profit Sharing Today: Plans and Provisions," *Monthly Labor Review,* April 1991, pp. 19–25. This source lists and discusses the pros and cons of profit-sharing plans. For an analysis of how peer pressure can operate to overcome potential free-rider problems associated with profit sharing, see Eugene Kandel and Edward P. Lazear, "Peer Pressure and Partnerships," *Journal of Political Economy,* August 1992, pp. 801–817.

[17]Martin L. Weitzman and Douglas L. Kruse provide an excellent discussion of the issues surrounding profit sharing. See their "Profit Sharing and Productivity," in Alan S. Blinder (ed.), *Paying for Productivity* (Washington, DC: Brookings Institution, 1990), pp. 95–141. Our previous discussion of the free-rider problem associated with bonuses drew on this source.

tudes."[18] The Weitzman–Kruse summary suggests that workers under profit-sharing plans are able to overcome the free-rider problem. This conclusion is supported by a major study by Kruse, who reports that the adoption of profit sharing by firms is associated with a 2.5 to 4.2 percent increase in productivity.[19]

7-2

Tournament Pay

Some incentive pay schemes base compensation on relative performance. Such pay plans are known as ***tournament pay.*** For example, tennis or golf tournaments structure pay on the basis of where participants finish in the tournament. Typically, the first prize is extremely high, with pay dropping a bit but still remaining high for the next few places. Rewards then sink rapidly for rankings well below the top spots. One purpose of this pay scheme is to promote greater performance by *all* participants throughout the rankings. Everyone aspires to the top prize; therefore, everyone works hard to

[18]Ibid., p. 139. Studies of employee stock ownership plans (ESOPs) tend to find a positive effect on firm performance, but the results are diverse. ESOPs make workers partial owners of the firms for which they work. For a survey of prior studies, see Douglas Kruse and Joseph Blasi, "Employee Ownership, Employee Attitudes, and Firm Performance," National Bureau of Economic Research Working Paper No. 5277, September 1995. Also see Douglas Kruse and Joseph Blasi, "Employee Ownership and Corporate Performance among Public Companies," *Industrial and Labor Relations Review,* October 1996, pp. 60–79.

[19]Douglas L. Kruse, "Profit Sharing and Productivity: Microeconomic Evidence from the United States," *Economic Journal,* January 1992, pp. 24–36. Other studies finding a positive effect on productivity include Sandeep Bhargava, "Profit Sharing and the Financial Performance of Companies: Evidence from U.K. Panel Data," *Economic Journal,* September 1994, pp. 1044–1056; Subal C. Kumbhakar and Amy E. Dunbar, "The Elusive ESOP-Productivity Link: Evidence from U.S. Firm-Level Data," *Journal of Public Economics,* September 1993, pp. 273–283; Sushil Wadhwani and Martin Wall, "The Effects of Profit-Sharing on Employment, Wages, Stock Returns and Productivity: Evidence from U.K. Micro-Data," *Economic Journal,* March 1990, pp. 1–17; and John Cable and Nicholas Wilson, "Profit-Sharing and Productivity: An Analysis of U.K. Engineering Firms," *Economic Journal,* June 1989, pp. 366–375.

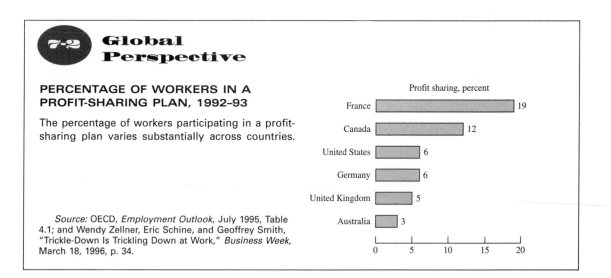

7-2 Global Perspective

PERCENTAGE OF WORKERS IN A PROFIT-SHARING PLAN, 1992–93

The percentage of workers participating in a profit-sharing plan varies substantially across countries.

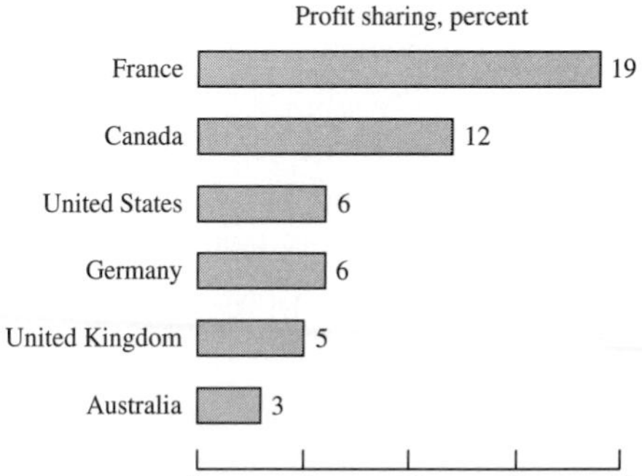

Source: OECD, *Employment Outlook,* July 1995, Table 4.1; and Wendy Zellner, Eric Schine, and Geoffrey Smith, "Trickle-Down Is Trickling Down at Work," *Business Week,* March 18, 1996, p. 34.

achieve it. Lower pay is tolerated by many because of their opportunity to win one of the few big prizes.[20]

Tournament pay may have applications beyond sporting events.[21] Recall from "World of Work" 6-2 that some observers speculate that the multimillion-dollar salaries paid to chief executive officers of large corporations may be equivalent to first-place prizes in a tournament. Indeed, compensation received by CEOs may exceed their personal marginal revenue products, the "excessive" pay (Table 7-1) allegedly may be efficient because it increases the MRPs of younger corporate managers, who have aspirations to one day become the CEO.

This view of CEO pay is controversial, as we will soon detail, but let's first look at some of its possible implications. First, managers who seek the top spot in the corporation but fall somewhat short will also be paid more than their MRPs. The firm may even tolerate "dead wood" at the senior level. Firms that gain reputations for arbitrarily firing older, less-effective executives may not be able to attract a sufficient number of young workers to the tournament pay scheme. These younger workers may be unwilling to incur the risk of falling short of the top spots after expending years of effort to achieve them. The assurances that other high-paying jobs exist in the hierarchy and that employment is relatively secure may be important to the continuing success of this pay scheme.

[20]Edward Lazear and Sherwin Rosen, "Rank Order Tournaments as an Optimum Labor Contract," *Journal of Political Economy,* October 1981, pp. 841–864. The interested reader may also wish to refer to Ronald G. Ehrenberg and Michael L. Bognanno, "The Incentive Effects of Tournaments Revisited: Evidence from the European PGA Tour," *Industrial and Labor Relations Review,* special issue, February 1990, pp. 74S–88S; and Ronald G. Ehrenberg and Michael L. Bognanno, "Do Tournaments Have Incentive Effects?" *Journal of Political Economy,* December 1990, pp. 1307–1324.

[21]For example, the market for broiler chickens lends support to the tournament model. See Charles R. Knoeber and Walter N. Thurman, "Testing the Theory of Tournaments: An Empirical Analysis of Broiler Production" *Journal of Labor Economics,* April 1994, pp. 155–179.

TABLE 7-1 THE 10 HIGHEST-PAID CHIEF EXECUTIVE OFFICERS, 1997

	Company	Total Pay* (in millions)
1. Sanford Weill	Travelers Group	$230.7
2. Roberto Goizueta	Coca-Cola	111.8
3. Richard Scrushy	Healthsouth	106.8
4. Ray Irani	Occidental Petroleum	101.5
5. Eugene Isenberg	Nabors Industries	84.5
6. Joseph Costello	Cadence Design Systems	66.8
7. Andrew Grove	Intel	52.2
8. Charles McCall	HBO and Co.	51.4
9. Philip Purcell	Morgan Stanley Dean Witter	50.8
10. Robert Shapiro	Monsanto	49.3

*Includes salaries, bonuses, and long-term payments such as stock options.
Source: Business Week, April 20, 1998.

Second, tournament pay may help rationalize "golden parachute" provisions in executive compensation contracts. These provisions provide for large lump-sum compensation to executives who lose their jobs as a result of corporate takeovers. Golden parachutes—often worth millions of dollars—allow the executives to float comfortably to the ground.

Several explanations for these provisions have been offered. Perhaps these large sums deter hostile takeovers by making them more expensive. Or perhaps the corporate owners (shareholders) believe that these large awards will discourage CEOs from fending off takeovers that bid up stock prices and increase the shareholders' wealth.

Tournament pay provides a complementary explanation. Perhaps golden parachutes are partly insurance against losing the full amount of the CEO prize, once it is won. People ascending to CEO positions expect to receive high compensation for several years. But an unforeseen corporate takeover that results in discharge of the present CEO will wipe out part of the compensation prize. This possibility may undermine the desired incentive effects of the compensation scheme. The solution: golden parachutes that ensure against at least part of the lost pay resulting from a takeover.

Finally, tournament pay may help explain why many CEOs have relatively short tenures prior to their retirements. Turnover at the top at relatively frequent intervals is important to opening up opportunities for those lower in the corporate hierarchy. Thus, CEOs normally are given generous retirement incentives, usually at age 65. In this way the top-to-bottom work incentives created by the pay scheme are maintained.

Critics of the tournament explanation of high CEO pay dismiss the relevance of the theory to executive pay. They assert that such pay schemes are not optimal in corporations, where participants have opportunities to sabotage one another's performance. In this view, a tournament pay scheme within a corporate setting is more likely to promote detrimental strategic behavior by executives. Teamwork allegedly would erode and overall productivity would decline.

If CEO compensation is not part of a tournament pay scheme, why is this pay so high? Perhaps high CEO pay simply reflects supply-and-demand realities. Because the decisions of CEOs affect entire corporations, their productivity is extremely high. Meanwhile the supply of experienced, top corporate decision makers is low. The labor market result is very high pay, as is true for other superstars, such as those in sports and entertainment.

Critics of high CEO pay dismiss this view, arguing that CEO pay tends to be "excessive" mainly because of the "mutual admiration society" that often develops among CEOs and corporate board members. Many members of corporate boards, themselves CEOs of other corporations, overrate the CEO's importance and worth. In this view some of the profits rightfully belonging to stockholders are instead diverted to extraordinarily high CEO pay. Between 1990 and 1996 chief executive pay increased by 146 percent. During that same period corporate profits rose by only 84 percent and the pay of factory workers increased by 19 percent.[22]

This high and growing CEO compensation has drawn considerable complaint from unions, stockholders, and politicians. In response, the Security and Exchange

[22]Based on *Business Week* surveys.

Commission (SEC) in 1992 established new rules requiring that corporations clearly spell out directly to their stockholders the compensation of their five highest-paid executives. The SEC believes that this informational approach will help stockholders identify and ferret out excessive CEO pay. Also, in 1993 Congress eliminated corporate tax deductions for executive salaries exceeding $1 million annually (with an exception for pay directly tied to the firm's earnings performance).

It is clear that "excessive" CEO pay is highly controversial and will continue to be debated.[23]

EFFICIENCY WAGE PAYMENTS

Pay-for-performance plans are most capable of solving the principal–agent problem in those circumstances where individual output can be readily measured. But in many jobs measuring or assessing individual output is at best difficult and at worst impossible. One solution to the principal–agent problem in these circumstances is direct observation of the agents' actions on the job. Firms can reduce shirking by ***monitoring*** the *efforts* of workers (for example, by hiring supervisors). Fearing the loss of their jobs, most workers will not shirk when they are being observed, since presumably those who do will be identified and replaced. Supervision therefore may be an effective way to reduce the principal–agent problem in some circumstances. For this reason many jobs in the economy are "supervisory."

Monitoring workers, however, is very costly in some employment circumstances. It makes little economic sense, for example, to hire someone to monitor the effort of a security guard, a baby-sitter, a house painter, or a manager. Also, it may be prohibitively costly to hire a sufficient number of supervisors to monitor the quality of each worker's performance in assembly-line work. As a result, some economists suggest that firms search for approaches other than monitoring or pay-for-performance to synchronize the interests of the workers with those of the firm.

How might firms deal with the principal–agent problem when supervision is costly and individual output is difficult to measure? One such approach may be to pay workers a wage that is above the market-clearing level.

Wage-Productivity Dependency

In the models discussed in Chapter 6, we explicitly assumed that labor was homogeneous and implicitly assumed that a change in wage rates did not alter the marginal

[23]Recent research on CEO pay includes Paul L. Joskow, Nancy L. Rose, and Catherine Wolfram, "Political Constraints on Executive Compensation: Evidence from the Electric Utility Industry," *Rand Journal of Economics,* Spring 1996, pp. 165–182; Steven N. Kaplan, "Top Executive Rewards and Firm Performance: A Comparison of Japan and the United States," *Journal of Political Economy,* June 1994, pp. 510–546; Nancy L. Rose and Andrea Shepard, "Firm Diversification and CEO Compensation: Managerial Ability or Executive Entrenchment?" Rand Journal of Economics, Fall 1997, pp. 489–514; Brian G. M. Main, Charles A. O'Reilly III, and James Wade, "Top Executive Pay: Tournament or Teamwork?" *Journal of Labor Economics,* October 1993, pp. 606–628; and Robert Gibbons and Kevin J. Murphy, "Optimal Incentive Contracts in the Presence of Career Concerns: Theory and Evidence," *Journal of Political Economy,* June 1992, pp. 468–505.

product of labor and hence the location of the labor demand curve. Any change in the wage rate therefore resulted in a change in the quantity of labor demanded; it did *not* invoke a change in the location of the demand curve itself. However, under some conditions a wage rise may positively affect labor efficiency, causing a rightward shift of the labor demand curve.

Theories that incorporate the aforementioned possibility—that wage increases may increase productivity—are called efficiency wage theories. An ***efficiency wage*** is *one that minimizes an employer's wage cost per effective unit of labor service employed.* The key phrase is "per *effective* unit of labor service." Under the customary assumptions of competitive labor markets and homogeneous labor inputs, the market-clearing wage (determined where labor supply and demand intersect) *is* the wage that minimizes a firm's wage cost per effective unit of labor service employed. All workers are assumed to be equally and fully effective in the production process. If a firm pays a below-market-clearing wage, the company will not attract the desired number of workers. If it pays an above-market-clearing wage, its wage cost per effective unit of labor will rise, because equally efficient units could have been hired at the lower market wage. We will discover, however, that under assumptions of heterogeneous labor and wage-productivity dependency, a firm may find that it can *lower* its wage cost per effective unit of labor service by paying a *higher* wage rate.

A simple numerical example will help demonstrate this general principle. Suppose that workers who are fully effective at some task can each produce 10 units of a particular output per hour. Next, suppose that the market wage rate is $5 an hour and that for reasons we will discuss shortly, workers each produce only 5 units of output per hour at the $5 wage. In this circumstance, we find that each *effective* unit of labor service costs an employer $10 per hour. The firm needs 2 hours of labor services to obtain 10 units of output ($= 2 \times 5$), and each hour costs $5 in wages.

What if the firm discovers that it can obtain fully effective units of labor—those that produce 10 units of hourly output—by paying $8 an hour? This implies that the hourly wage cost per effective unit of labor declines by $2 (= $10 − $8) as the wage rate rises by $3 (= $8 − $5).

The unusual outcome illustrated by our simple example is possible where a higher wage more than proportionately induces greater employee work effort, improves the worker's capabilities, or increases the proportion of highly skilled workers in a particular workforce.

Shirking Model of Efficiency Wages The shirking model of efficiency wages theorizes that some enterprises pay more than the market-clearing wage to reduce employee shirking. In some situations employers have little information about how diligently workers are performing their duties (for example, night security workers at an office building). Moreover, full supervision and monitoring of such workers may be too costly (hiring other security workers to watch security workers). Under these conditions, the possibility arises that all employees will choose to shirk. To counter this possibility, firms may opt to pay workers more than the market-clearing wage. This higher pay increases the relative value of the job as viewed by each worker. It also raises the cost of being terminated for shirking, should it be detected. In familiar economic wording, the higher opportunity cost (price) of shirking reduces the amount of shirking occurring. Worker productivity improves more than proportionally to the higher wage, the labor demand curve is located further rightward, and wage costs per effective unit of labor decline.[24]

Other Efficiency Wage Theories Although less relevant to the principal–agent problem, there are other variations of the efficiency wage idea, two of which are the *nutritional* and the *labor turnover* models.

1 Nutritional Model In a relatively poor nation, an increase in the real wage might elevate the nutritional and health levels of workers. This will positively affect their physical vigor, mental alertness, and therefore their productivity. Thus, real wage increases could cause labor demand curves to shift rightward, benefiting employers as well as employees.[25]

2 Labor Turnover Model Employers may increase wages to reduce costly ***labor turnover,*** *the rate at which workers quit their jobs, necessitating their replacement by new workers.* We have seen that employers bear the costs of providing firm-specific training to new workers (Chapter 4). Also, because workers normally "learn by doing," new workers are not initially as proficient as the people they replace.

An above-market-clearing wage raises the workers' costs of quitting their jobs and thus lowers the likelihood that they will quit. Lower labor turnover, in turn, increases worker productivity *on the average,* since it increases the proportion of experienced workers relative to those being trained and still "learning by doing." The result is that the higher wage rate shifts the labor demand curve rightward.

7-5

Implication: Nonclearing Labor Markets

Efficiency wage theories produce several interesting implications, one of which is that permanent unemployment may exist under conditions of equilibrium in labor markets.[26] We demonstrate this possibility in Figure 7-8, where the initial equilibrium wage rate and level of employment are W_1 and Q_1. Suppose the firm discovers it can reduce its wage cost per effective unit of labor by increasing the wage to W_2 (from *a* to *b*). This decline in the wage cost per effective unit of labor results from the rightward shift of

[24]The reader interested in a more advanced treatment of efficiency wage theories should consult Joseph E. Stiglitz, "The Causes and Consequences of the Dependency of Quality on Price," *Journal of Economic Literature,* March 1987, pp. 1–48; Lawrence F. Katz, "Efficiency Wage Theories: A Partial Evaluation," in Stanley Fisher (ed.), *NBER Macroeconomics Annual 1986* (Cambridge, MA: MIT Press, 1986), pp. 235–276; George A. Akerlof and Janet L. Yellen (eds.), *Efficiency Wage Models of the Labor Market* (Cambridge: Cambridge University Press, 1986); Andrew Weiss, *Efficiency Wages: Models of Unemployment, Layoffs, and Wage Dispersions* (Princeton, NJ: Princeton University Press, 1991); and Kevin M. Murphy and Robert H. Topel, "Efficiency Wages Reconsidered: Theory and Evidence," in Yoram Weiss and Gideon Fishelson (eds.), *Advances in Theory and Measurement of Unemployment* (London: MacMillan, 1990).

[25]Harvey Leibenstein, "The Theory of Underemployment in Densely Populated Backward Areas," in Harvey Leibenstein (ed.), *Economic Backwardness and Economic Growth* (New York: John Wiley & Sons, 1963), chap. 6.

[26]We explore other implications of the efficiency wage models in later discussions of wage differentials (Chapter 8) and frictional unemployment (Chapter 19).

7-5 **World of Work**

THE FORD MOTOR COMPANY'S $5 PER DAY WAGE*

In 1914 Ford Motor Company made headlines by offering autoworkers the grand sum of $5 per day, up from $2.50 per day. This wage offer was newsworthy because at that time the typical market wage in manufacturing was just $2 to $3 per day.

What was Ford's rationale for offering a higher-than-competitive wage? Statistics indicate that the company was suffering from unusually high quit rates and absenteeism. Ford apparently reasoned that a high wage rate would increase worker productivity by increasing morale and reducing employee turnover. Only workers who had been at Ford for at least 6 months were eligible for the $5 per day wage. Nevertheless, 10,000 workers applied for employment with Ford in the immediate period following the announcement of the wage hike.

According to historians of this era, the Ford strategy succeeded. The $5 wage raised the value of the job to Ford workers, who therefore became loyal to the company and worked hard to retain their high-paying jobs. The quit and absenteeism rates both plummeted, and in 1914 labor productivity at Ford rose by an estimated 51 percent.

How does this increase in productivity relate to economic theory? We know from Chapter 5 that normally a change in the wage rate does not affect labor productivity and therefore does not affect labor demand. Instead, the firm responds to a change in the wage rate by altering the quantity of labor it "purchases." This adjustment is shown graphically as a point-to-point movement along the firm's existing labor demand curve. But in the 1914 Ford situation the $2.50 boost in the daily wage resulted in increased labor productivity. Stated in economic terms, the $5 wage was an *efficiency wage.* The wage increase to $5 per day raised the marginal product of Ford workers. This translated into an increase in Ford's marginal revenue product schedule, which we know is its demand for labor curve.

In brief, Ford's experience with its $5 daily wage is consistent with the theory that efficiency wages may in some situations be optimal for reducing principal–agent problems.

*This application is based in part on Daniel M. G. Raff and Lawrence Summers, "Did Henry Ford Pay Efficiency Wages?" *Journal of Labor Economics,* pt. 2, October 1987, pp. S57–S86.

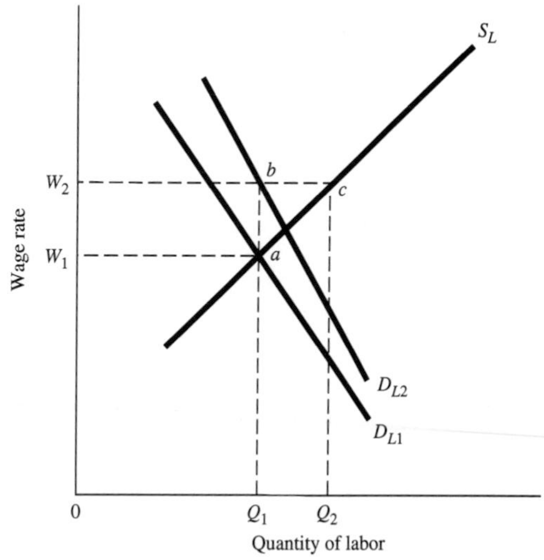

FIGURE 7-8 EFFICIENCY WAGE MODEL
Under some conditions, an increase in the wage may increase worker efficiency and labor demand. In this situation, we suppose that the firm increases the wage from W_1 to W_2, which shifts labor demand from D_{L1} to D_{L2} and minimizes the firm's wage cost per effective unit of labor. Although W_2 is an equilibrium wage, it is not a market-clearing wage, as shown by the surplus of labor *bc*.

the labor demand curve from D_{L1} to D_{L2}, that is, from an increase in the marginal product of labor. The wage cost per effective unit of labor declines because the extra output of workers presumably rises more than the firm's wage expense. Observe that we have drawn the demand increase such that the firm continues to employ Q_1 workers (at *b*) as before, but the efficiency wage just as reasonably could have shifted the curve to a greater or lesser extent than that shown.[27]

Wage rate W_2 is the new equilibrium wage rate in this market; at *b,* the firm has no incentive to reduce the wage rate or to increase it further. But observe that this equilibrium wage is *not* the market-clearing wage. At W_2 the firm employs Q_1 workers, while we see from point *c* on the supply curve that Q_2 workers seek employment. Assuming that workers do not find jobs elsewhere, permanent unemployment of *bc* occurs in this particular labor market. The more elastic the labor demand and supply curves, the greater the unemployment. The closer to *c* that the efficiency demand curve intersects the labor supply curve, the less equilibrium unemployment.

An additional important point: In the shirking efficiency wage model, the *bc* unemployment is partly the reason for the wage-productivity dependency in the first place. The threat of losing a relatively high-paying job and of becoming part of the *bc* unemployed workers serves as a disciplining device to discourage shirking and to encourage full effort. In the absence of the resulting equilibrium unemployment, the labor demand curve might not shift from D_{L1} to D_{L2} in response to the higher wage.

Criticisms

Detractors of efficiency wage theories question whether these models add greatly to our understanding of labor markets in advanced economies. Critics of the shirking model, in particular, point out that several of the pay-for-performance plans discussed earlier in this chapter could serve as options to efficiency wages as ways to guard against poor worker performance. As examples, where monitoring workers is costly, the firm can pay on a piece rate or a commission basis. Where individual performance is difficult to measure, bonus pay based on team performance can be implemented.

Second, critics point out that a firm could require employees to post a bond that they would forfeit if they were found to have been negligent in performing their job duties.

Finally, detractors of the efficiency wage theory note that firms can reduce shirking by establishing pay plans in which part of the workers' pay is deferred until later years or until employees qualify for pensions. Encouraged by the deferred income, workers will work hard to maintain employment within the firm.

[27]A technical note is required here. Each demand curve in Figure 7-8 is a separate "pseudo-demand curve," which holds worker quality and effort constant and assumes that the firm is hiring labor competitively. In fact, this is a "wage-setting firm" and as such does not have a labor demand curve (just as a monopolist does not have a supply curve). Demand in this case is actually the single point *b* on D_{L2}.

Each of these devices, argue the critics, can reduce the principal–agent problem at less expense than paying above-market-clearing wages.[28]

QUICK REVIEW 7-2

- The principal–agent problem is the conflict of interest that occurs when agents pursue their own objectives to the detriment of meeting the principal's objectives.
- Pay-for-performance plans such as piece rates, commissions and royalties, raises and promotions, bonuses, profit sharing, and tournament pay are designed to minimize principal–agent problems.
- Efficiency wages are above-market-clearing wages designed to reduce employee shirking and labor turnover; they are equilibrium wages because, given labor supply and demand, employers have no incentive to change them.
- Because they are set higher than market-clearing wages, efficiency wages may contribute to permanent unemployment.

Your Turn: What is the major difficulty with profit sharing as a means of overcoming the principal–agent problem? (Answer: See page 626.)

DEFERRED PAYMENT SCHEMES

The view that deferred payment contracts are an alternative to the efficiency wage approach merits elaboration. Deferred payment plans seek to reduce principal–agent problems by altering the *timing* of the worker's pay.

Seniority Pay

Researchers have long noted that earnings rise with tenure on the job. The traditional explanation for this relationship derives from the human capital model (Figure 4-1), which hypothesizes that workers gain experience and become more productive as they age. Thus, their pay is higher than when they were younger.

[28]Contrasting views on the efficiency wage notion can be found in H. Lorne Carmichael, "Efficiency Wage Models of Unemployment—One View," *Economic Inquiry,* April 1990, pp. 269–295; and Kevin Lang and Shulamit Kahn, "Efficiency Wage Models of Unemployment: A Second View," *Economic Inquiry,* April 1990, pp. 296–306. Evidence in support of the efficiency wage model can be found in Carl M. Campbell III, "Do Firms Pay Efficiency Wages? Evidence with Data at the Firm Level," *Journal of Labor Economics,* July 1993, pp. 442–470; and Alan B. Krueger, "Ownership, Agency, and Wages: An Examination of Franchising in the Fast Food Industry," *Quarterly Journal of Economics,* February 1991, pp. 75–101.

FIGURE 7-9 DEFERRED PAYMENT CONTRACT
In this figure, MRP is assumed to be the constant over one's work life. Nevertheless, firms and workers may enter into implicit contracts that increase pay as years of service rise. Under this contract, younger workers receive less than their MRPs, and older workers earn more than their MRPs. By offering the prospect of high pay in later years of tenure, these contracts may discourage shirking and reduce turnover. Because of the subsequent increase in productivity, the worker may achieve higher lifetime earnings than if the wage matched MRP in each year.

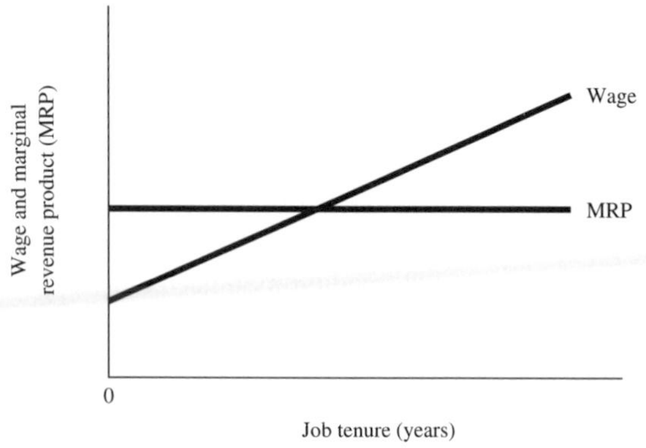

An alternative explanation for the positive relationship between job seniority and pay, at least in specific jobs, has been put forth.[29] This theory contends that, in industries where it is costly to monitor workers, senior workers receive pay above their marginal revenue products. Conversely, junior workers are paid less than their MRPs. This pay pattern is illustrated in Figure 7-9, where we assume for simplicity that MRP is constant for a particular group of workers throughout their work cycles. Observe, however, that the wages of these workers rise as the length of their tenure on the job increases. Although wages are below MRP in early years, they rise substantially above it in later years.[30]

The compensation scheme shown in Figure 7-9 supposedly derives from ***implicit contracts*** between firms and workers. These contracts are "implicit," meaning *they are based on understandings between workers and their firms, not on legal rights.* Unlike *explicit contracts,* which are enforceable by courts, implicit contracts are self-enforcing: Both firms and workers behave in ways to ensure they are heeded. As stated by Carmichael, "Self-enforcing contracts are collections of promises that, while they may not be legally binding, are nonetheless credible. Everyone can be confident that the promises will be kept.[31]

Why would a firm and its workers enter into a ***deferred payment scheme*** like the one suggested in Figure 7-9? The most straightforward answer is that both parties may benefit by the arrangement. This pay scheme may be the least expensive way to re-

[29]Edward P. Lazear, "Agency, Earnings Profiles, and Hours Restrictions," *American Economic Review,* September 1981, pp. 606–620; Lazear, "Why Is There Mandatory Retirement?" *Journal of Political Economy,* December 1979, pp. 1261–1284. Also see Robert M. Hutchens, "Seniority, Wages and Productivity: A Turbulent Decade," *Journal of Economic Perspectives,* Fall 1989, pp. 49–64. Other "internal labor market" explanations of positive age-earnings profiles are discussed in Chapter 16.

[30]This relationship between wage rates and MRPs is just the opposite of that shown in Figure 4-8(b).

[31]H. Lorne Carmichael, "Self-Enforcing Contracts, Shirking, and Life Cycle Incentives," *Journal of Economic Perspectives,* Fall 1989, p. 67.

duce shirking in circumstances where monitoring costs are high. The worker is discouraged from shirking because detection and discharge will mean that he or she must forgo the high seniority pay accruing in the later years of employment. The worker will desire to work hard to maintain employment with the firm and thus to reap the deferred benefits of the contract, that is, wages in excess of MRP. From the firm's standpoint, deferred pay will reduce employee turnover. Workers who quit their jobs will lose the deferred pay they had hoped to obtain.

The reduced shirking and turnover resulting from the deferred pay plan will increase worker productivity. This increase in output is the source of the extra revenue from which the firm and worker, respectively, enhance their profits and lifetime pay. In essence, young workers accept wages that are initially less than the MRPs for the opportunity to participate in a labor market where in time the reverse will be true. The increased work effort and higher average productivity are appealing to the worker because they allow higher lifetime earnings.

Role of Pensions

The seniority pay plan shown in Figure 7-9 also is consistent with the observation that many firms provide generous pension benefits to workers, usually at age 62 or 65, if they agree to retire. In our simplified model, pay grows as workers age, but MRP remains constant. Workers therefore may wish to remain employed with the firm well beyond the usual retirement age because wages exceed MRP for older workers. In fact, seniority pay will continue to rise even though in reality productivity (MRP) can be expected to slacken with old age. Obviously, an open-ended retirement policy is not optimal for firms having the deferred payment plan described in Figure 7-9.

Historically, firms solved this retirement dilemma by requiring retirement at age 65. But federal legislation has outlawed mandatory retirement in most industries. Firms therefore have found another solution to the retirement problem created by deferred pay plans. They offer generous pensions to entice workers to retire at a specific age, say, 62 or 65. Pensions create strong income effects that in most cases induce workers to retire (see Figure 2-9). In addition, most pensions also have strong incentives built into the plan to retire by a particular age. That is, the value of the pension falls if the worker postpones retirement after a certain age.[32]

In summary, the prospect of seniority pay reduces shirking by younger workers while large pensions entice older workers whose wages exceed their MRPs to retire. The combination of seniority pay and large pensions therefore allegedly raises worker productivity.

Pensions, in fact, may increase worker productivity independently of helping solve the retirement problem that deferred payment contracts present. In many pension plans employees must work for the firm for several years before becoming "vested." ***Vesting***

[32]For example, see Richard A. Ippolito, "Toward Explaining Earlier Retirement after 1970," *Industrial and Labor Relations Review,* July 1990, pp. 556–569; and Alan L. Gustman and Thomas L. Steinmeier, "An Analysis of Pension Benefit Formulas, Pension Wealth, and Incentives from Pensions," *Research in Labor Economics,* 1989, pp. 53–106.

means acquiring legal rights to the benefits of the pension plan, regardless of whether employment is continued. Workers are less likely to leave the firm before vesting because doing so will eliminate the pension benefits they have accumulated during their employment. Additionally, many pension plans are "backloaded." This means that even where vesting is in place, pension accrual grows slowly up to a certain age and then grows rapidly after that. Thus, both vesting provisions and "backloading" reduce employee turnover, which, in turn, increases productivity.[33]

Deferred Contracts: Some Final Points

Deferred payment contracts—with their long job tenure, high pay for senior workers, and generous pensions—are most likely to be found in large, well-established firms. Why? First, it may be more difficult for large firms to monitor their workers. We would not expect to find deferred payment contracts where monitoring is relatively inexpensive, as in many smaller firms. Second, workers realize that large firms are less likely than small firms to go bankrupt. Bankruptcy would prevent younger workers from getting the delayed payments available from the implicit contract. Finally, large well-established firms are less likely to cheat on the implicit contract by firing older workers to avoid paying the deferred compensation. Large firms are continuously hiring workers and must keep their reputations intact if they are to attract younger workers to the deferred contract scheme. Cheating on the implicit contract would most likely doom the compensation system itself.

Some indirect empirical support exists for the deferred payment theory. Delayed payment contracts are economical only where the job structure makes monitoring difficult and costly. If this theory is valid, these contracts ought *not* to be found in jobs characterized by relatively inexpensive monitoring of worker effort. Hutchens classified and examined such jobs and found that, holding other factors constant, they tend not to have pensions, mandatory retirement, and comparatively high wages for senior workers. Stated more formally, jobs for which monitoring was inexpensive did not appear to generate self-enforcing deferred payment contracts.[34]

On the other hand, a study by Brown has found that wage growth within firms is mainly determined by productivity growth associated with on-the-job training. Brown concludes that wages rise with tenure primarily because productivity increases with tenure, not because of pay schemes based on implicit contracts.[35] It is therefore fair to say that the theory of deferred payment remains highly controversial.

[33]For a survey of the impacts of pensions, see Alan L. Gustman, Olivia S. Mitchell, and Thomas L. Steinmeier, "The Role of Pensions in the Labor Market: A Survey of the Literature," *Industrial and Labor Relations Review,* April 1994, pp. 417–438. Backloading of pensions is documented in Laurence J. Kotlikoff and David A. Wise, *The Wage Carrot and the Pension Stick* (Kalamazoo, MI: W. E. Upjohn Institute for Employment Research, 1989). Also relevant is Richard A. Ippolito, "Encouraging Long-Term Tenure: Wage Tilt or Pensions?" *Industrial and Labor Relations Review,* April 1991, pp. 520–535.

[34]Robert Hutchens, "A Test of Lazear's Theory of Delayed Payment Contracts," *Journal of Labor Economics,* October 1987, pp. S155–S170.

[35]James N. Brown, "Why Do Wages Increase with Tenure?" *American Economic Review,* December 1989, pp. 971–991.

LABOR MARKET EFFICIENCY REVISITED

The basic supply and demand models in Chapter 6 provide meaningful insights into wages and the efficient allocation of labor. But in this chapter we have seen that the decisions of workers and firms are substantially more complex than our earlier models suggest. A variety of compensation schemes are available, each potentially optimal for a particular type of job and worker. Workers therefore must not only make choices about hours and pay, but about a variety of types of pay. Similarly, firms must not only make hiring and total pay decisions, they must weigh the costs and benefits of a full range of possible compensation schemes. Some schemes may reduce worker productivity; others may greatly enhance it.

In this chapter our previous definition of labor market efficiency has been extended. In Chapter 6 we found the efficiency occurred when no worker could be switched from one *job* to another to produce more economic well-being. Now we must append to that definition by the following phrase: "Neither can any worker be switched from one *compensation scheme* to another to increase economic well-being." Labor market efficiency requires that workers be allocated to optimal work. It also demands that optimal compensation packages be implemented. Privately optimal compensation choices normally are also socially optimal, the exception being where efficiency wages are paid. Recall that these payments may create unemployment.

CHAPTER SUMMARY

1 Total compensation consists of wage and fringe benefits. Fringe benefits include *legally required benefits,* such as Social Security contributions, and *voluntary benefits,* such as paid leaves, insurance benefits, and private pensions. More than one-fourth of total pay takes the form of fringe benefits, broadly defined.
2 An employee's preferences for wages and fringe benefits can be set forth in an indifference map. Each indifference curve shows the various combinations of wages and fringe benefits which yield a given level of utility. An employer's normal-profit isoprofit curve displays the various combinations of wages and fringe benefits that yield a normal profit. The worker achieves an optimal or utility-maximizing combination of wages and fringe benefits by selecting that wage–fringe mix that enables the worker to attain the highest possible indifference curve.
3 Several factors explain the historical growth of fringe benefits. These include: (1) the tax advantages they confer; (2) the scale economies resulting from their collective purchase; (3) their ability to reduce job turnover and motivate workers; (4) the sensitivity of fringe benefits such as medical and dental care to increases in income; (5) legal mandates by the federal government; and (6) the historical growth of union contracts, in which fringe benefits are relatively large.
4 The relationship between firm and workers is one of "principals" (firms) and "agents" (workers). Firms will attempt to take actions to reduce the so-called "principal–agent problem," which occurs when agents pursue their own goals rather than the objectives of the principals.
5 Piece rates, commissions, and royalties are pay schemes designed to tie pay directly to productivity.

6 Workers receiving annual salaries may have an incentive to reduce work hours below levels that they would work if they were paid by the hour. The prospect of raises and promotions reduces this principal–agent problem.

7 Bonuses can elicit greater work effort and thereby increase productivity. But bonuses attached to personal performance may direct behavior away from team goals. Bonuses based upon team or firm performance help solve this problem but create a potential free-rider problem when the team is large. Research indicates that executive bonuses have some positive effect on corporate performance.

8 Assuming minimal free-rider problems, profit-sharing plans synchronize the interests of firms and their workers. Recent research points toward a positive link between profit sharing and productivity.

9 Tournament pay assigns an extraordinarily high reward to the top performer and is designed to maximize performance by all who are striving to achieve the top spot. Some observers view high CEO pay as an efficient aspect of such pay schemes. Critics dismiss this idea as being a rationalization of excessive CEO pay, arguing instead that high CEO pay has resulted from improper corporate board oversight of stockholders' interests.

10 In situations where supervision of workers is minimal, a dependency between the wage paid and productivity may occur. The firm may find that it can increase its profits by paying an efficiency wage—a wage above the market-clearing wage. An interesting implication of efficiency wage theories is that persistent unemployment may be consistent with equilibrium in the labor market.

11 Deferred payment contracts may help explain the observed positive relationship between job tenure and wages. Workers may receive less than their MRPs in earlier years in exchange for wages that exceed their MRPs in later years. These self-enforcing implicit contracts may benefit the firm and worker by increasing work incentives and productivity. Generous employer-provided pensions may be designed to encourage retirement by older workers who are receiving above-MRP wages.

TERMS AND CONCEPTS

fringe benefits
in-kind benefits
isoprofit curve
agents
principals
principal–agent problem
shirking
incentive pay plans
piece rates
time rates
commissions
royalties
quasi-fixed resources
bonuses
free-rider problem
profit sharing
tournament pay
monitoring
efficiency wage
labor turnover
implicit contracts
deferred payment scheme
vesting

QUESTIONS AND STUDY SUGGESTIONS

1 What is an isoprofit curve as it relates to wages and fringe benefits? What is a normal-profit isoprofit curve? In what respect is a normal-profit isoprofit curve a *budget con-*

straint as viewed by a worker? At which point on the employer's isoprofit curve will a rational worker choose to locate? Explain.

2 In Figure 7-6 the reduction in the cost of fringe benefits resulted in an increase in the amount of fringe benefits and a *reduction* in the wage income received. Redraw the worker's indifference map to demonstrate a circumstance in which fringe benefits would not go up by as much, but wage income would *increase*. Explain the difference between the two situations.

3 The U.S. Office of Management and Budget has estimated that the tax-exempt status of fringe benefits such as pensions and group insurance reduces tax revenue to the Treasury by about $50 billion annually. Some economists have suggested that the federal government recover this tax revenue by taxing fringe benefits as ordinary income. Use Figure 7-5 to explain how this proposal would affect *(a)* the slope of the indifference curves and *(b)* the slope of the isoprofit curve. What would be the likely effect on the optimal level of fringe benefits?

4 Explain what is meant by the term *principal–agent problem.* Have you ever worked in a setting where this problem has arisen? If so, do you think that increased monitoring would have eliminated the problem? Why don't firms simply hire more supervisors to eliminate shirking problems?

5 Identify and explain a separate common problem associated with each of the following pairs of compensation plans:

a Piece rates; bonuses tied to individual performance

b Bonuses applied to team performance; profit-sharing plans

6 Demonstrate graphically why someone guaranteed an annual salary might choose to work fewer hours than someone who could earn that same amount through hourly pay. Reconcile your answer with the fact that salaried workers in general work more hours weekly than people receiving hourly pay.

7 Speculate on what actions workers might take to resolve a free-rider problem arising from a profit-sharing plan.

8 People often sell goods (or raffle tickets) as part of a fund-raising project. These projects typically offer valuable prizes to those who sell over a fixed number of units. Often a grand prize, say, a trip to Hawaii, is offered to the person who sells the most units. Why are these prizes offered? Relate this example to the high pay received by chief executive officers of large corporations.

9 Discuss the following statement in relationship to *(a)* the tournament theory of executive pay and *(b)* the "World of Work" 7-4 on faculty tenure: "The new economics of personnel rationalizes whatever exists. If a compensation structure prevails, so goes this view, it *must* be efficient. The policy implication therefore is to 'let it be' *(laissez faire).* Thus, what poses as economic analysis is actually political conservatism."

10 How might payment of an efficiency wage *(a)* reduce shirking by employees and *(b)* reduce employee turnover? What is the implication of the efficiency wage theory for unemployment? In what way are piece rates, commissions, royalties, and profit sharing substitutes for efficiency wages?

11 Distinguish between an implicit contract and a legal contract. What do we mean when we say that an implicit contract is "self-enforcing"? In what sense is a deferred payment contract a self-enforcing implicit contract?

12 Use a work–leisure diagram (Chapter 2) to show how the availability of a pension at age 65 might make a worker want to retire.

13 How does firm-imposed mandatory retirement relate to deferred payment schemes? Analyze: "Implicit deferred payment contracts were dealt a serious blow when the federal government outlawed mandatory retirement."

14 As an employer, suppose you find it costly to monitor employee effort 100 percent of the time. What compensation options are available to ensure that you get appropriate levels of employee effort? What factors would you consider in choosing among these options?

SELECTED REFERENCES

Akerlof, George A., and Janet L. Yellen (eds.): *Efficiency Wage Models of the Labor Market* (Cambridge: Cambridge University Press, 1986).

Blinder, Alan S. (ed.): *Paying for Productivity* (Washington, DC: Brookings Institution, 1990).

"Do Compensation Policies Matter?" *Industrial and Labor Relations Review,* special issue, February 1990.

Dorsey, Stuart, Cornwell, Christopher, and David Macpherson: *Pensions and Producivity,* (Kalamazoo, MI: W. E. Upjohn Institute, 1998).

Ehrenberg, Ronald G., and Robert S. Smith: *Modern Labor Economics,* 6th ed. (Reading, MA: Addison–Wesley, 1997), chap. 11.

Gerhart, Barry, George T. Milkovich, and Brian Murray: "Pay, Performance, and Participation," in David Lewin, Olivia S. Mitchell, and Peter D. Sherer (eds.), *Research Frontiers in Industrial Relations and Human Resources* (Madison, WI: Industrial Relations Research Association, 1992), pp. 193–238.

Gustman, Alan L., and Thomas L. Steinmeier: *Pension Incentives and Job Mobility* (Kalamazoo, MI: W. E. Upjohn Institute, 1995).

Hutchens, Robert M.: "Seniority, Wages and Productivity: A Turbulent Decade," *Journal of Economic Perspectives,* Fall 1989, pp. 49–64.

Kleiner, Morris M., et al.: *Human Resources and the Performance of the Firm* (Madison, WI: Industrial Relations Research Association, 1987).

Kotlikoff, Laurence J., and David A. Wise: *The Wage Carrot and the Pension Stick* (Kalamazoo, MI: W. E. Upjohn Institute, 1989).

Kruse, Douglas L.: *Profit Sharing: Does It Make a Difference?* (Kalamazoo, MI: W. E. Upjohn Institute, 1993).

Lazear, Edward P.: *Personnel Economics* (Cambridge, MA: MIT Press, 1995).

"The New Economics of Personnel," *Journal of Labor Economics,* special issue, October 1987.

"Organizations, Incentives, and Innovation," *Journal of Accounting and Economics,* special issue, March–May 1995.

"A Symposium: The Economics of Human Resource Management," *Industrial Relations,* Spring 1990.

Weiss, Andrew: *Efficiency Wages: Models of Unemployment, Layoffs, and Wage Dispersion* (Princeton, NJ: Princeton University Press, 1991).

Woodbury, Stephen A., and Wei-Jang Huang: *The Tax Treatment of Fringe Benefits* (Kalamazoo, MI: W. E. Upjohn Institute, 1991).

CHAPTER 8

THE WAGE STRUCTURE

As evidence all around us suggests, there are large variations in wages and salaries in the United States. An elite fashion model may earn $2 million annually; her photographer, $60,000; and her makeup artist, $30,000. Meanwhile, a teacher's aide glancing at the model in a magazine ad may earn $8,000. A union tile layer may make $38,000 a year, while the secretary at the tile firm earns $18,000. A lawyer charging $75 per hour may pay her baby-sitter $5.00 per hour. A chemist may earn $50,000 each year; a mixologist (bartender), $15,000. An entertainer from San Diego dressed as a chicken may make $250,000 a year; a deli worker making chicken sandwiches, $15,000.

Many of these wage differences in the economy are ***equilibrium wage differentials***—they do not elicit movement of labor from the lower-paying to the higher-paying jobs. Other wage variations are ***transitional wage differentials***—they promote worker mobility that eventually reduces the wage disparities. In this chapter we examine the wage structure resulting from the working of labor markets and explain why wage differentials occur and persist. In Chapter 9 we look at labor mobility and migration induced by transitory wage differentials and examine the wage narrowing that eventually results.

Our organizational strategy in this chapter is as follows. First, we examine the wage structure that would result if all workers and firms were homogeneous and all labor markets were competitive. Next, some data on the actual wage structure in the United States are presented. The remainder of the chapter discusses the factors producing the observed wage differentials in the economy. More specifically, in the third section of the chapter we examine wage differences due to heterogeneous *jobs;* the fourth section looks at heterogeneous *workers* as a source of earnings differences; the fifth section then combines portions of the previous two sections into a "hedonic" model of wages; and the final section discusses imperfect information and immobilities as each relates to observed wage differences.

PERFECT COMPETITION: HOMOGENEOUS WORKERS AND JOBS

In Chapter 6 we analyzed a perfectly competitive labor market for a *specific type of labor.* Let's now extend the assumption of ***homogeneous workers and jobs*** to *all* employees and firms in the economy. If information is perfect and job searches and migration are costless, labor resources will flow among various employments and regions of the economy until all workers have the same real wage.

The process whereby wages equalize is demonstrated in Figure 8-1. Initially assume that labor demand and supply are D_a and S_a, respectively, in submarket A and D_b and S_b in submarket B. These supply and demand conditions produce a $10 hourly wage in submarket A compared to a $5 wage in B. In each instance the wage rate equals the VMP of labor, but note that the VMP of the Q_b worker in submarket B is less than the wage rate and VMP of the Q_a employee in submarket A. The consequence? Workers will exit submarket B and take jobs in higher-paying A. The decline in labor supply in B from S_b to S'_b and the increase in A from S_a to S'_a will reduce the equilibrium wage in A from $10 to $7.50. The market-clearing wage in submarket B will rise from $5 to $7.50. Following the movement of workers between the two submarkets, (1) the wage rates will be equal ($7.50) and in turn will be equal to the opportunity cost or

FIGURE 8-1 WAGE EQUALIZATION IN PERFECT COMPETITION
If labor supply and demand are S_a and D_a in labor submarket A and S_b and D_b in submarket B, a $5 wage differential (= $10 in A minus $5 in B) will emerge. Assuming that jobs and workers are homogeneous and information and mobility are costless, workers will leave submarket B for the higher-paying submarket A. The decline of labor supply in B from S_b to S'_b and the increase in submarket A from S_a to S'_a will cause the wage rates in each submarket to equalize at $7.50.

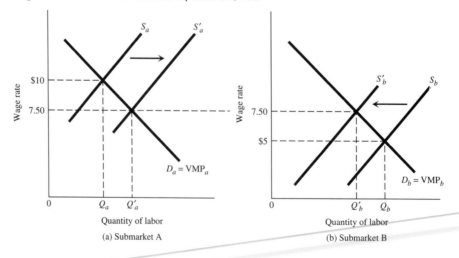

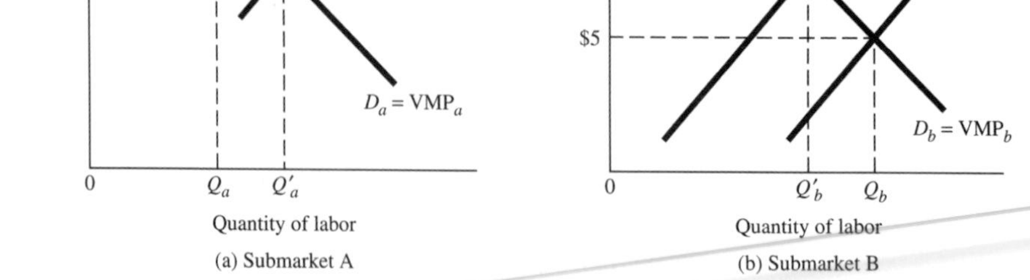

supply price P_L of the last unit of labor ($7.50) in each market; (2) these wages will equal the VMPs in each submarket; and (3) the VMPs will equal each other and the supply price of labor P_L. Symbolically, $W_a = W_b = P_L$; $W_a = \text{VMP}_a$ and $W_b = \text{VMP}_b$; and $\text{VMP}_a = \text{VMP}_b = P_L$. Recall from Chapter 6, specifically equation (6-1), that this equality of VMPs and the price of labor represents an efficient allocation of labor.

We may thus summarize as follows: If all jobs and workers are homogeneous and there is perfect mobility and competition, the ***wage structure***—defined as *the array of wage rates paid to workers*—will evidence no variability. The average wage rate will be the *only* wage rate in the economy.

THE WAGE STRUCTURE: OBSERVED DIFFERENTIAL

Casual observation of the economy reveals that in fact wage differentials *do* exist and that many of them persist over time. Table 8-1 shows an overview of occupational wage differentials. Observe that the average hourly earnings of managerial and professional workers in 1997 were $19.75, while precision production workers received $14.16 and service employees $8.59. Hourly earnings also vary within occupational categories such as those shown in Table 8-1. For example, under the category "service workers," one would discover a difference in hourly earnings between people providing private household services and those providing protective services to, say, corporations. Also, the highest-paid service workers earn more than the lowest-paid workers who are classified as technical, sales, and administrative support workers, even though the average hourly salary is higher for the latter occupational group.

The occupational wage structure is just one of many wage structures that one can isolate for study. Notice from Tables 8-2 and 8-3 that average hourly gross earnings also differ greatly by industry and geographical location. For example, hourly pay

TABLE 8-1 AVERAGE HOURLY EARNINGS BY OCCUPATIONAL GROUP, 1997

Occupational group	Average hourly earnings
Managerial and professional workers	$19.75
Precision production workers	14.16
Technical, sales, and administrative support workers	12.07
Operators, fabricators, and laborers	10.44
Service workers	8.59
Farming, forestry, and fishing workers	7.88

Source: Barry T. Hirsch and David A. Macpherson, *Union Membership and Earnings Data Book: Compilations from the Current Population Survey (1998 Edition)* (Washington, DC: Bureau of National Affairs, 1998).

TABLE 8-2 AVERAGE HOURLY EARNINGS BY INDUSTRY GROUP, 1997

Industry group	Average hourly earnings
Mining	$16.45
Finance, insurance, real estate	15.83
Transportation, public utilities	15.42
Manufacturing	14.51
Wholesale trade	14.17
Services	13.86
Construction	13.69
Retail trade	8.89

Source: Barry T. Hirsch and David A. Macpherson, *Union Membership and Earnings Data Book: Compilations from the Current Population Survey (1998 Edition)* (Washington, DC: Bureau of National Affairs, 1998).

averaged $8.89 in retail trade in 1997 while it was $13.69 in construction. Also observe from Table 8-3 that manufacturing workers in Michigan earned an average of $16.83 per hour; in South Dakota, on the other hand, they received $11.18. Finally, as of 1997 female earnings were about 76 percent of male earnings and the pay for blacks was 79 percent of that paid to whites.

8-1

TABLE 8-3 AVERAGE HOURLY EARNINGS OF PRIVATE WORKERS IN MANUFACTURING INDUSTRIES BY SELECTED STATES, 1997

State	Average hourly earnings
Michigan	$16.83
Colorado	16.81
Massachusetts	16.63
Alaska	16.59
Maryland	16.33
California	16.15
New York	15.73
Pennsylvania	15.37
Texas	14.79
Hawaii	13.89
New Mexico	13.71
Vermont	13.54
North Carolina	12.91
South Dakota	11.18
Mississippi	10.18

Source: Barry T. Hirsch and David A. Macpherson, *Union Membership and Earnings Data Book: Compilations from the Current Population Survey (1998 Edition)* (Washington, DC: Bureau of National Affairs, 1998).

8-1 Global Perspective

HOURLY PAY AROUND THE WORLD

Wage differentials are quite pronounced worldwide. The accompanying chart shows the average hourly pay for production workers in U.S. dollars for various nations for 1996. As defined here, hourly pay comprises all payments made directly to the worker, including pay for time worked; pay for vacations, holidays, and other special payments; and in-kind payments. Also included in the figures are employer expenditures for legally required insurance programs and private benefit plans. All wages are before-tax amounts and are converted to U.S. dollars through appropriate exchange rate adjustments.

Several facts stand out from this chart. First, hourly compensation varies greatly around the world. Second, pay for production workers in the United States is not as high as it is in a number of European nations. Finally, hourly wage rates in nations such as Taiwan, Portugal, Singapore, South Korea, and Hong Kong are exceptionally low relative to pay in the more mature industrial nations. Caution: Prices of goods and services vary widely among these nations. Because exchange rates do not perfectly reflect this fact, these figures are only rough approximations of actual differences in purchasing power and living standards.

Source: Data are from *International Comparisons of Hourly Compensation Costs for Production Workers, 1996,* Bureau of Labor Statistics, Report 98-38, Table 2.

What are the sources of these wage differentials, and how can they persist? Why do some wage differences narrow over time while others remain the same or increase? To answer these and related questions we need to abandon several assumptions made in the previous section of this chapter. More specifically, wage differentials occur because (1) jobs are heterogeneous, (2) workers are heterogeneous, and (3) labor markets are imperfect.

WAGE DIFFERENTIALS: HETEROGENEOUS JOBS

In Figure 8-1 we assumed that jobs were identical to one another in all respects. Utility-maximizing employees thus needed to consider only the wage rate itself in deciding where to work. Higher wages in one submarket would attract workers there. But in reality, jobs are heterogeneous rather than homogeneous. In particular, ***heterogeneous jobs*** have differing nonwage attributes, require different types and degrees of skill, or vary as to the efficacy of paying efficiency wages to increase productivity. Employers also vary with respect to such things as union status, firm size, and discriminatory attitudes.

Compensating Differentials

Nonwage aspects of jobs vary greatly and are the source of ***compensating wage differentials.*** *These differentials consist of the extra pay that an employer must provide to compensate a worker for some undesirable job characteristic that does not exist in an alternative employment.* Compensating wage differentials are thus equilibrium wage differentials since they do *not* cause workers to shift to the higher-paying jobs and thereby cause wage rates to move toward equality.

Figure 8-1 is useful in showing this concept. In our previous discussion of this figure we assumed that the jobs shown in labor submarkets A and B were homogeneous. Now let's suppose instead that the jobs in submarket A are performed outdoors in freezing weather throughout the year while the work in B occurs indoors in pleasant surroundings. Recall from Table 6-1 that one of the categories of determinants of labor supply consists of the nonwage attributes of employment. Because of the indicated differences in nonwage amenities between submarkets A and B, labor supply will be less in A relative to B. If, for example, S_a is the labor supply curve in submarket A while S_b portrays supply in B, the *equilibrium* wage rate in A will be \$10 as contrasted to \$5 in submarket B.

The extra \$5 paid in A is called a wage premium, compensating wage differential, or equalizing difference. No movement of workers from B to A will occur, as happened when jobs were assumed to be homogeneous. This \$5 wage differential will *persist;* it will change only in response to changes in the other determinants of supply and demand in either of the two labor markets.

Several additional points need to be highlighted here. First, the observed wage disparity—\$5—does *not* reflect an actual difference in "net advantage" or net utility between the two jobs. Taking the nonwage characteristics of the two jobs into account, workers Q_a and Q_b are equally paid; they both *net* \$5 of utility from an hour of work:

In A \$10 of wage minus \$5 of extra disutility equals \$5 net; in B \$5 of wage minus \$0 of extra disutility equals \$5 net.

Second, assuming demand is the same in both markets, employment will be lower where the compensating wage differential must be paid. Notice in Figure 8-1 that only Q_a workers are employed in A as contrasted to Q_b in B.

Third, although the marginal revenue product (MRP) and the value of the marginal product (VMP) of worker Q_a in A exceed the MRP (= VMP) in B, the reason for the difference is purely on the supply side. Note that S_a cuts D_a higher on the demand curve than S_b intersects D_b. Workers in A receive \$10 rather than \$5 an hour because supply is limited in that market, rather than because workers there are inherently more productive.

Finally, it is clear that the compensating wage differential performs the socially useful function of allocating labor resources to a productive task that is not as pleasant as others.

Having established the basic principle of compensating wage differentials, we next examine the types of nonwage aspects of jobs that cause differing labor supply curves and therefore compensating payments. Specifically, let's examine each of the following sources of compensating differentials: (1) risk of job injury and death, (2) fringe benefits, (3) job status, (4) job location, (5) the regularity of earnings, (6) the prospect for wage advancement, and (7) the extent of control over the pace of work.

1 Risk of Job Injury or Death The greater the risk of being injured or killed on the job, the less the labor supply to a particular occupation. For this reason, jobs that have high risks of accidents relative to others requiring similar skill will command compensating wage differentials. Viscusi has estimated that the average earnings premium for risk of injury and death in the American economy is about 5 percent. Although other studies have produced mixed findings, collectively they confirm the existence of compensating differentials, particularly those associated with higher probabilities of *fatal* injury on the job.[1]

2 Fringe Benefits Fringe benefits (Chapter 7) vary greatly among employers who hire similar workers and pay similar wage rates. How might this fact relate to wage differentials? Suppose that some firms hiring specific labor pay only \$8 an hour while others pay the \$8 and provide such fringe benefits as sick leave, paid vacations, and medical and dental insurance. Other things being equal, workers will choose to offer

[1]W. Kip Viscusi, *Employment Hazards: An Investigation of Market Performance* (Cambridge, MA: Harvard University Press, 1979). In a review he reaches a similar conclusion; see W. Kip Viscusi, "The Value of Risks to Life and Health," *Journal of Economic Literature,* December 1993, pp. 1912–1946. See also Greg J. Duncan and Bertil Holmlund, "Was Adam Smith Right after All? Another Test of the Theory of Compensating Wage Differentials," *Journal of Labor Economics,* October 1983, pp. 366–379; J. M. Cousineau, R. Lacroix, and A. M. Girard, "Occupational Hazard and Wage Compensating Differentials," *Review of Economics and Statistics,* February 1992, pp. 166–169; Hae-Shin Hwang, W. Robert Reed, and Carlton Hubbard, "Compensating Wage Differentials and Unobserved Productivity," *Journal of Political Economy,* August 1992, pp. 835–838; and W. S. Siebert and X. Wei, "Compensating Wage Differentials for Workplace Accidents: Evidence for Union and Nonunion Workers," *Journal of Risk and Uncertainty,* July 1994, pp. 61–76.

their services to these latter employers. To attract qualified workers, the firms that do not provide fringe benefits will have to pay a compensating wage differential that in effect will equalize the gross hourly compensation between the two groups.[2] This same principle applies in reverse to jobs in which gratuities are customarily received. Other things being equal, wage rates will be *lower* in those occupations than in similar ones in which no tips are received.

3 Job Status Some jobs offer high status and prestige and hence attract a large number of willing suppliers; other employment carries with it the social stigma of being mundane, uninspiring, and dirty. As an extreme example, there is more status in being a semiskilled worker in the burgeoning electronics industry than in being a similarly skilled worker in, say, a sewage disposal plant. To the extent that labor supply behavior is affected by status seeking, compensating wage differentials may emerge between low- and high-prestige work.

Status, of course, is defined culturally, and thus the degree of esteem society places on various jobs is subject to change. For example, in the early 1970s working for the U.S. military commanded limited status, reflecting widespread disapproval of the Vietnam War. On the other hand the successful U.S. military action in Grenada in 1983 boosted public esteem for those in the military. One result was that the supply of labor to the military increased, enabling the armed services to meet recruitment goals more easily. Similarly, the motion picture *Top Gun* and the television show "L. A. Law" are credited with increasing the number of applicants to the Navy flight program and to law schools, respectively.

4 Job Location Similar jobs also differ greatly with respect to their locations, which in turn vary as to their amenities and their living costs. Cities noted for their "livability" may attract a larger supply of workers in a specific occupation than cities mainly noted for their smokestack industries. Consequently, compensating differentials may arise in locations lacking amenities.[3]

[2]Although the evidence is far from conclusive, several studies support the idea of a trade-off between wages and fringe benefits. See Morley Gunderson, Douglas Hyatt, and James E. Pesando, "Wage–Pension Trade-Offs in Collective Agreements," *Industrial and Labor Relations Review,* October 1992, pp. 146–160, particularly Table 1, p. 148. Also see Edward Montgomery, Kathryn Shaw and Mary Ellen Benedict, "Pensions and Wages: An Hedonic Price Theory Approach," *International Economic Review,* February 1992, pp. 111–128. For evidence that a trade-off exists between wages and firm-provided worker's compensation insurance coverage, see Price V. Fishback, and Shawn Everett Kantor, "Did Workers Pay for the Passage of Workers' Compensation Laws?" *Quarterly Journal of Economics,* August 1995, pp. 713–742. A similar conclusion is reached for maternity benefits; see Jonathan Gruber, "The Incidence of Mandated Maternity Benefits," *American Economic Review,* June 1994, pp. 622–641.

[3]For evidence on how locational factors such as crime rates and air pollution affect wage differentials, see Jennifer Roback, "Wages, Rents and the Quality of Life," *Journal of Political Economy,* December 1982, pp. 1257–1278; and Joseph Gyourko and Joseph Tracy, "The Importance of Local Fiscal Conditions in Analyzing Local Labor Markets," *Journal of Political Economy,* October 1989, pp. 1208–1231. Shelby D. Gerking and William N. Weirick find that workers with similar personal characteristics tend to have similar "amenity-adjusted" *real* wages irrespective of where they live. See their "Compensating Differences and Interregional Wage Differentials," *Review of Economics and Statistics,* August 1983, pp. 483–487. Also see J. Michael DuMond, Barry T. Hirsch, and David A. Macpherson, "Wage Differentials across Labor Markets and Workers: Does Cost of Living Matter?" Florida State University Working Paper No. 96-08-1, August 1996.

Differences in price levels between areas of the country may also result in the need to pay compensating money, or *nominal* wage payments. New York City is a good example. Because the cost of living is so high there, a given nominal wage rate is not equal in purchasing power to the same wage rate in, say, Kansas City. Therefore, relative to labor demand, the number of workers who are willing to supply a particular type of labor at *each nominal wage* is less in New York City than in Kansas City. The labor market result is that the equilibrium nominal wage is higher in New York City. Differentials in nominal wage rates are needed to more closely align *real* wage rates among the two geographical labor markets.

5 Job Security: Regularity of Earnings Some jobs provide employment security for long periods and explicit or implicit assurances that one will work full weeks throughout the year. Other positions—for example, construction, consulting, and commissioned sales—are characterized by variability of employment, variability of earnings, or both. Since a specific paycheck is not ensured each week of the year, fewer workers may find these occupations attractive and, all else being equal, people who work in these jobs may receive a compensating wage differential. Restated, the hourly wage may be relatively high as compensation for the low probability that it will be earned 40 hours a week for the entire year.

Empirical evidence supports the theoretical conclusion that compensating wage differentials will arise for jobs in which unemployment is more likely. Abowd and Ashenfelter found that a compensating wage premium of as much as 14 percent may accrue in industries where the workers experience substantial anticipated unemployment and unemployment risk.[4] Li reports a roughly similar wage differential resulting from unemployment risk.[5] A study by Topel concluded that unemployment insurance greatly reduces compensating wage differentials. In the absence of insurance an added percentage point of expected unemployment increases a worker's wage rate by about 2.5 percent.[6] Finally, Hamermesh and Wolfe have decomposed the compensating wage differential for unemployment into two parts: that paid for a higher probability of job loss and that resulting from a longer duration of job loss, should it occur. They conclude that nearly all the compensating differential results from the longer duration of job loss, rather than from the higher probability of losing one's job.[7]

6 Prospect of Wage Advancement Jobs are also heterogeneous with respect to the amount of firm-financed investment in human capital provided over the years. For example, someone entering the banking profession at age 22 might reasonably expect

[4]J. M. Abowd and Orley Ashenfelter, "Anticipated Unemployment, Temporary Layoffs, and Compensating Wage Differentials," in Sherwin Rosen (ed.), *Studies in Labor Markets* (Chicago: University of Chicago Press, 1981).

[5]Elizabeth H. Li, "Compensating Differentials for Cyclical and Noncyclical Unemployment: The Interaction between Investors' and Employees' Risk Aversion," *Journal of Labor Economics,* April 1986, pp. 277–300.

[6]Robert H. Topel, "Equilibrium Earnings, Turnover, and Unemployment: New Evidence," *Journal of Labor Economics,* October 1984, pp. 500–522.

[7]Daniel S. Hamermesh and John R. Wolfe, "Compensating Wage Differentials and the Duration of Job Loss," *Journal of Labor Economics,* January 1990, pp. S175–S197.

to receive rather continuous on-the-job training leading to promotions to successively higher-paying positions over time. A person that same age who decides to be a carpenter is not as likely to experience as large an overall increase in earnings over the years. Assuming that people's time preferences for earnings are the same, at any given wage people will opt for jobs with greater prospects for earnings increases. Thus, labor supply will be greater to these jobs and less to employment with flat lifetime earnings streams. This will necessitate a compensating wage differential for *entry-level* pay in the latter type of occupation. In our example we would expect the beginning pay of the bank employee to be less than that of the carpenter. This type of compensating differential is confirmed by research finding that lower starting salaries across industries are systematically related to higher rates of wage growth as length of time on the job increases.[8]

7 Extent of Control over the Work Pace Some jobs provide less personal control of the work pace and less flexibility in work hours than other positions. More people are likely to prefer the latter jobs to the former, and therefore, an equalizing wage differential may result. In fact, Duncan and Stafford estimate that two-fifths of the union–nonunion wage differential discussed in Chapter 11 is simply an equalizing difference necessitated by the structured work setting, inflexible hours, employer-set overtime, and fast work pace in union jobs.[9]

Differing Skill Requirements

We have established that one reason for wage differentials in a market economy is differing nonwage aspects of jobs. But jobs are clearly heterogeneous in a second major way: They have widely different skill requirements. To illustrate, let's compare two hypothetical occupations. Suppose these two jobs have identical nonwage attributes and all workers have similar preferences for current versus future earnings. But suppose that job X requires 5 years of education beyond high school while job Y demands only a high school diploma. If these two occupations paid an identical wage rate, people would have *no* incentive for making occupational choices to select employment X. Why? The unsurprising answer is that occupation X is more costly to enter than Y. Occupation X necessitates much more investment in human capital to meet the skill requirement, and therefore if the hourly pay is the same in both occupations, the return on the investment for the extra 5 years of education is negative (Chapter 4). That is, the present value of the gained earnings is zero (one receives the same wage after

[8]B. J. Chapman and H. W. Hong, "Specific Training and Inter-Industry Wage Differentials in U.S. Manufacturing," *Review of Economics and Statistics,* August 1980, pp. 371–378. Also of interest is John Garen, "The Trade-Off between Wages and Wage Growth," *Journal of Human Resources,* Fall 1985, pp. 522–539. Garen finds that people "purchase" future wage growth with lower present earnings.

[9]Greg Duncan and Frank Stafford, "Do Union Members Receive Compensating Differentials?" *American Economic Review,* June 1980, pp. 355–371. For a criticism of this research and the authors' rebuttal, see J. M. Barron and D. A. Black, "Do Union Members Receive Compensating Wage Differentials?: Comment" and G. J. Duncan and F. P. Stafford, "Reply," *American Economic Review,* September 1982, pp. 864–872. Also see Timothy J. Gronberg and Robert Reed, "Estimating Workers' Marginal Willingness to Pay for Job Attributes Using Duration Data," *Journal of Human Resources,* Summer 1994, pp. 911–931.

investment as before investment), while the present value of the costs is positive and substantial (tuition, books, sacrificed earnings for 5 years).

The point is that wage equality between occupations X and Y is not sustainable; wage equality would create a disequilibrium. To attract a sufficient flow of people to occupation X, employers must pay these workers more than they pay people in occupation Y. An equilibrium wage differential therefore will persist between the two occupations. The earnings difference created by this wage gap must be just sufficient to produce an internal rate of return r on the investment in 5 years of education equal to the cost of borrowing i, as discussed in Chapter 4. If the wage differential and therefore r were greater than this i, more people would enter college and pursue the advanced degree. This eventually would expand labor supply, reduce the market wage in occupation X, lower the rate of return, and reduce the wage differential between the two occupations to a sustainable level. On the other hand, if the wage differential were insufficient between occupations X and Y, fewer people would enter occupation X, and eventually the wage differential would rise to the equilibrium one.

To reiterate: Other things being equal, jobs that require large amounts of education and training will pay a higher wage rate than those that do not. The wide variety of skill requirements for various jobs constitutes a major source of wage disparity in the economy. The difference in pay between skilled and unskilled workers is called the ***skill differential.***

Wage differentials created by differing skill requirements can either *increase, lessen,* or *reverse* wage variances produced by differences in nonwage aspects of jobs. For example, suppose that job A is characterized by a high risk of injury and hence pays a $3 hourly compensating wage premium relative to safe job B. Now, let's make two alternative assumptions about the skill differentials between the two jobs. First, suppose that the skills necessary to perform dangerous job A are greater than those needed in safe job B. Obviously, the actual wage differential will *exceed* the $3 hourly wage premium paid for the risk of injury. Alternatively, suppose that the risky job A requires little skill while job B demands costly investment in human capital. In this second case, the actual wage differential between A and B will be *less than* $3 hourly and, depending on the size of the skill differential, may even reverse the pay such that safe job B pays more than dangerous job A. Real-world example: Certified public accountants on average earn more than loggers, even though loggers have a much greater risk of being injured on the job.

Conclusion? The oft-made observation that higher-paid workers also seem to have more desirable working conditions does not refute the theory of compensating wage differentials. Rather, this observation simply indicates that in many cases the wage gap created by differences in skills *offsets* the compensating differential working in the opposite direction. Without the compensating differential, the actual wage gap would be even greater. Furthermore, if pleasant working conditions are a normal good ("purchases" of them rise with increases in income), then we would expect to find better working conditions and higher wages positively correlated. Workers who are more highly skilled can afford to "buy" better working conditions as part of their overall compensation package; they can afford to give up some of the relatively high direct wage for more nonwage job amenities. Competition in hiring these highly skilled

8-1

workers will force employers to offer compensation packages that reflect this greater demand for nonwage amenities.

Differences Based on Efficiency Wage Payments

We found in Chapter 7 that under some circumstances employers may find it profitable to pay wages above market-clearing levels. Because these circumstances vary *within* and *among* industries, efficiency wages may help explain wage differentials among workers possessing similar qualifications. Pay differentials resulting from efficiency wage payments will be *equilibrium differentials* since the firms will have no incentive to reduce their wages even though qualified persons offer to work for lower wages.

8-1 **World of Work**

WAGE INEQUALITY AND SKILL-BIASED TECHNOLOGICAL CHANGE*

It is well known that wage inequality among both women and men has increased significantly in the past two decades. Between 1979 and 1989 the hourly earnings of the ninetieth-percentile full-time worker relative to the tenth-percentile full-time worker increased by about 20 percent for men and 25 percent for women. Wage inequality among males is greater today than at any time since 1940.

This growing wage inequality has several dimensions. We know from Chapter 4, specifically Figure 4-3, that the college wage premium has increased sharply in recent years. For those without college degrees the average wages of older workers have increased relative to those of younger workers. Wage inequality has expanded among individuals of the same age, education, and gender. It also has increased among those working in the same industries and occupations.

We will defer a detailed discussion of the various explanations for the changing wage structure until Chapter 17. Nevertheless, one direct cause of the rising skill differential merits comment here. The past two decades have witnessed an explosion of microcomputers and computer-based technology. This new technology is *skill-biased,* meaning that it does not increase the demand for all skill levels of labor equally. Specifically, the computer revolution has increased the productivity of, and thus the demand for, college-educated and other computer-trained workers.

The fraction of all workers using computers increased from 25 to 37 percent between 1984 and 1989. For college graduates, it rose from 42 to 59 percent. Krueger has estimated that workers who use computers earn 10 to 15 percent more than otherwise similar workers who do not. The wage premium is about 20 percent in the nonunion sector and 8 percent for unionized workers. The lower premium for union workers may have to do with the more standardized wages in the union sector. Krueger finds that the increased use of computers has contributed significantly to earnings inequality. Specifically, computer use explains about one-half the increase in the returns to education (Chapter 4) occurring over the 1984–89 period.

In a recent study, Allen confirms the importance of technology improvements in explaining the rise in earnings inequality. Using data from 1979 and 1989, he investigated the impact on wages of measures of technology such as the use of high-tech capital and the intensity of research and development (R&D). Consistent with Krueger's findings, Allen's analysis reveals that the return to schooling is higher in industries that use more R&D and high-tech capital. He concludes that technology variables can explain 30 percent of the rise in the earnings gap between college and high school graduates.

*Based on Lawrence F. Katz, "Understanding Recent Changes in the Wage Structure," *NBER Reporter,* Winter 1992–93, pp. 10–15; Alan B. Krueger, "How Computers Have Changed the Wage Structure: Evidence from Microdata, 1984–1989," *Quarterly Journal of Economics,* February 1993, pp. 33–60; and Steven G. Allen, "Technology and the Wage Structure," National Bureau of Economic Research Working Paper No. 5534, April 1996.

Shirking Model and Wage Differentials The shirking model suggests that firms will pay efficiency wages either where it is costly to monitor the performance of employees or where the employer's cost of poor performance is high. Recall that the above-market wage raises the cost of job loss to workers, which elicits conscientious efforts and reduces the employer's cost per effective unit of labor. On the other hand, where the monitoring of workers is inexpensive or where the cost of malfeasance by individual workers is low, the cost per effective unit of labor will be minimized at the lower market-clearing wage. These differing circumstances will create wage differentials that are unrelated to skill differentials or to differences in nonwage amenities.

Turnover Model and Wage Differentials Recall that the turnover version of the efficiency wage model suggested that firms pay higher than market-clearing wages where hiring and training costs are large. The above-market-clearing wage increases the value of the job to the worker, thus reducing the turnover rate (quit rate). Consequently, the average level of job experience and the productivity of the firm's labor both rise. The point is that wages may vary across and within industries depending on the efficiency gains, if any, arising from pay strategies that purposely increase the value of the job from the standpoint of the worker.

Preliminary Empirical Findings Theories linking efficiency wage payments to wage differentials are relatively recent in origin. It is therefore not surprising that the earliest attempt to test these theories have produced mixed results. Krueger and Summers have found that compensating differences and skill differences do *not* fully explain the interindustry wage structure. They also have presented some direct evidence supporting the efficiency wage explanation.[10]

Using data from the fast-food restaurant industry, Krueger finds that managers whose work is more difficult to supervise receive 9 percent higher wages than managers who can be more easily monitored.[11] In another analysis supportive of the efficiency wage theory, Campbell finds that firms with higher costs from worker turnover pay higher wages.[12]

Leonard, on the other hand, has concluded from a study of 200 firms that there is little empirical support for either the shirking or the turnover versions of efficiency

[10]Alan B. Krueger and Lawrence H. Summers, "Reflections on the Interindustry Wage Structure," in Kevin Lang and Jonathan Leonard (eds.), *Unemployment and the Structure of Labor Markets* (Oxford: Basil Blackwell, 1987), pp. 17–47; and Krueger and Summers, "Efficiency Wages and the Wage Structure," *Econometrica,* March 1988, pp. 259–274. Also see Robert Gibbons and Lawrence F. Katz, "Does Unmeasured Ability Explain Interindustry Wage Differentials?" *Review of Economic Studies,* July 1992, pp. 515–535; and McKinley Blackburn and David Neumark, "Unobserved Ability, Efficiency Wages, and Interindustry Wage Differentials," *Quarterly Journal of Economics,* November 1992, pp. 1421–1436.

[11]Alan B. Krueger, "Ownership, Agency, and Wages: An Examination of Franchising in the Fast Food Industry," *Quarterly Journal of Economics,* February 1991, pp. 75–101. For another study of the impact of supervision on wages, see Erica L. Groshen and Alan B. Krueger, "The Structure of Supervision and Pay in Hospitals," *Industrial and Labor Relations Review,* February 1990, pp. S134–S146. Also see Peter Cappelli and Keith Chauvin, "An Interplant Test of the Efficiency Wage Hypothesis," *Quarterly Journal of Economics,* August 1991, pp. 769–787.

[12]Carl M. Campbell III, "Do Firms Pay Efficiency Wages? Evidence from Data at the Firm Level," *Journal of Labor Economics,* July 1993, pp. 442–470.

wage theory.[13] Likewise, Keane concludes from his research that differences in worker characteristics other than traditional variables such as educational levels explain much of the previously unexplained variance in wages across industries. He thus concludes that the resort to efficiency wage explanations of wage differentials is unnecessary.[14] Finally, Rebitzer and Taylor conclude that efficiency wage theories do *not* explain the wage structure of lawyers employed at large law firms.[15] These earliest findings are preliminary, and further study will be needed to determine whether differences in costs of monitoring and turnover help explain the wage structure.

Other Job or Employer Heterogeneities

Although differences in nonwage amenities and disamenities, variations in skill requirements of alternative employment, and efficiency wage payments appear to be the major heterogeneities of jobs that create wage differentials, several other job or employer differences may contribute to this phenomenon. For instance, employers or jobs differ on such things as (1) union status, (2) tendency to discriminate, and (3) absolute and relative firm size.

1 Union Status We will find in Chapter 11 that empirical evidence suggests that, on the average, unions generate a substantial wage advantage for their members. Part of this differential may be a compensating wage premium for the structured work setting, inflexible hours, and employer-set overtime that are characteristic of unionized firms. Another part may reflect the higher productivity that some economists attribute to unionized labor (Chapter 11). But most economists conclude that the union–nonunion wage differential also includes a separate economic rent component (Chapter 13) deriving from the ability of unions to exert market power. In this latter respect the existence of both union and nonunion jobs creates a distinct job heterogeneity that helps explain wage disparities.

2 Tendency to Discriminate We will discover in Chapter 14 that employers may possess varying tendencies to discriminate; that is, some employers are biased toward or against hiring certain classes of workers, say, blacks, females, or specific ethnic minorities. Thus, direct wage discrimination may occur in some labor markets. The demand for those whom firms prefer will increase; the demand for those whom firms discriminate against will decline; and an observable wage differential will emerge among whites and blacks, males and females, and other groups. Much disagreement exists on whether or not these observed differentials will persist or be eroded by competitive market forces.

[13]Jonathan S. Leonard, "Carrots and Sticks: Pay, Supervision, and Turnover," *Journal of Labor Economics,* October 1987, pp. S136–S152.

[14]Michael P. Keane, "Individual Heterogeneity and Interindustry Wage Differentials," *Journal of Human Resources,* Winter 1993, pp. 134–161. For a similar conclusion, see Jean Helwege, "Sectoral Shifts and Interindustry Wage Differentials," *Journal of Labor Economics,* January 1992, pp. 55–84.

[15]James B. Rebitzer and Lowell J. Taylor, "Efficiency Wages and Employment Rents: The Employer-Size Wage Effect in the Job Market for Lawyers," *Journal of Labor Economics,* October 1995, pp. 678–708.

3 Absolute and Relative Firm Size Several studies indicate that large firms or those with major market shares pay higher wages and salaries in general than smaller firms. There are various possible explanations for this, some involving the previously discussed job heterogeneities. First, large firms are more likely than small firms to be unionized. Second, workers in large firms may be more productive than otherwise comparable workers in small enterprises. This higher productivity may be due to (1) greater amounts and better quality of capital per worker, (2) more on-the-job training necessitated by skill specialization, or (3) the possibility that workers in large firms are "superior" employees who require less supervision than average workers.[16]

A third possibility is that the higher pay observed in large firms is a compensating wage premium. Larger firms may be more bureaucratic and less pleasant places to work than smaller companies.[17] Also, larger firms are more likely to be located in major metropolitan areas, where overall living costs, in addition to commuting and parking expenses, are high.

Finally, firms possessing large market shares often make significant economic profits. This may increase worker bargaining power and consequently enable them to secure higher wage rates.[18]

WAGE DIFFERENTIALS: HETEROGENEOUS WORKERS

Having observed that heterogeneities among jobs and employers constitute a major source of wage disparities, we now turn to an equally important factor influencing the wage structure: ***heterogeneous workers.*** The wage equality initially predicted in Figure 8-1 relied on our assumption not only that all *jobs* were identical but also that all *workers* in the labor force were equally productive. In reality, people have greatly differing stocks of human capital as well as differing preferences for nonwage aspects of jobs.

Differing Human Capital: Noncompeting Groups

In Chapter 17 we will discuss the personal distribution of earnings as it relates to such characteristics as age, years of education, quality of education, native ability, and

[16]For more on this topic, see Charles Brown and James Medoff, "The Employer Size-Wage Effect," *Journal of Political Economy,* October 1989, pp. 1027–1059; David S. Evans and Linda S. Leighton, "Why Do Smaller Firms Pay Less?" *Journal of Human Resources,* Spring 1989, pp. 299–318; C. M. Schmidt and K. F. Zimmerman, "Work Characteristics, Firm Size and Wages," *Review of Economic Statistics,* November 1991, pp. 705–710; Walter Y. Oi, "On Working," *Economic Inquiry,* January 1993, pp. 1–28; William E. Even and David A. Macpherson, "Employer Size and Compensation: The Role of Worker Characteristics," *Applied Economics,* September 1994, pp. 897–907; Timothy Dunne and James A. Schmitz, "Wages, Employment Structure and Employer Size-Wage Premia: Their Relationship to Advanced-Technology Usage at U.S. Manufacturing Establishments," *Economica,* February 1995, pp. 89–107; and Steven J. Davis and John Haltiwanger, "Employer Size and the Wage Structure in U.S. Manufacturing," *Annales d'Economie et de Statistique,* January–June 1996, pp. 323–367.

[17]One study reports that one-third of the effect of employer size on wages can be accounted for by differences in the working conditions in large and small firms. See Douglas Kruse, "Supervision, Working Conditions, and the Employer Size-Wage Effect," *Industrial Relations,* Spring 1992, pp. 229–249.

[18]Jonathan S. Leonard, "Wage Structure and Dynamics in the Electronics Industry," *Industrial Relations,* Spring 1989, pp. 251–275; David Blachflower, Andrew Oswald, and Mario Garrett, "Insider Power in Wage Determination," *Economica,* May 1990, pp. 143–170; and S. Nickell, J. Vainiomaki, and Sushil Wadhwani, "Wages and Product Market Power," *Economica,* November 1994, pp. 457–473.

family background. That approach points out an important reality: People are not homogeneous. Of particular significance to our discussion of the wage structure is the fact that people possess differing stocks of human capital. At any point in time the labor force consists of numerous ***noncompeting groups,*** each one of which represents one or several occupations for which the members of the group qualify.

Differences in stocks of human capital may result from differing innate abilities to learn and perform. Relatively few people possess the required intellectual or physical endowments to be a nuclear physicist, a professional football quarterback, a petroleum engineer, an opera singer, or a professional model. There is no effective competition in the labor market between these groups and larger groups of skilled and unskilled workers. Nor is there substitutability between nuclear physicists and professional athletes. In fact, even within occupational groups, workers are not always perfectly substitutable. For example, some professional football players command salaries far above the average pay for that occupation. The reason: Other players are only imperfect substitutes because of differences in innate abilities.

More significantly, noncompeting groups result from differences in the type, amount, and quality of education and training that people possess (Chapter 4). For instance, the employment options for recent high school graduates include being a farm worker, a gasoline station attendant, a member of the armed forces, an unskilled construction worker, or a fast-food employee. Each of these categories of workers can be classified into one broad group, because each is capable of doing the other jobs. But none of the workers in this group currently offers direct competition to, say, lawyers or accountants, who find themselves in other, more exclusive groups.

Workers can and do move from one noncompeting group to another by investing in human capital.[19] The gasoline attendant may decide to attend college to obtain a degree in accounting. But this presupposes that the person has the financial means and innate intelligence to pursue this degree successfully. To the extent that income, credit worthiness, and native learning skills are unequally distributed, wage differentials between noncompeting groups can persist. Also, bear in mind that the *quality* of education varies. A degree in accounting from a relatively unknown college may not generate the same postinvestment earnings as a degree from a more prestigious university.

To summarize: People have differing stocks of human capital according to native endowments and the type, amount, and quality of education and training they possess. Unsurprisingly, the result is a wide variety of groups, subgroups, or even individuals who are not readily substitutable for one another in the labor market. In the short run, these human capital heterogeneities produce wage differentials due to the varying productivity of workers. People can and do move toward the higher-paying positions in the long run, but the extent of the movements is limited by differing abilities to finance human capital investments and differing inherent abilities to absorb and apply education and training. Therefore, wage differentials remain.

[19]For an analysis of the impact of increasing human capital in the population on a noncompeting group of workers, see Claudia Goldin and Lawrence F. Katz, "The Decline of Non-Competing Groups: Changes in the Premium to Education, 1890 to 1940, National Bureau of Economic Research Working Paper No. 5202, August 1995.

Differing Individual Preferences

In addition to possessing differing stocks of human capital, people also are heterogeneous with respect to their preferences for such things as (1) present versus future income and (2) various nonwage aspects of work.

Differences in Time Preferences Some people are highly present-oriented; they discount the future heavily or ignore it entirely. Other people have a great willingness or ability to sacrifice present satisfaction to obtain greater future rewards. In terms of Chapter 4's investment in human capital framework, we are saying that people have differing discount rates—or "*i*'s" in equation (4-3). Those persons who are highly present-oriented will have high discount rates, or *i*'s. They will not be willing to sacrifice consumption today unless as a result they can obtain substantially more dollars in the future. The higher the *i* in equation (4-3), the lower the net present value of the prospective investment and the less the likelihood that people will undertake a given investment in human capital. On the other hand, people who are more future-oriented will be willing to forgo current consumption for the expectation of obtaining relatively small additions to earnings later. In technical terms, such people will have low discount rate (*i*'s) and will perceive a given investment in human capital to have a higher net present value. Consequently, they will obtain more human capital than the more present-oriented individuals.

These differences in time preferences have a significant implication for the theory of noncompeting groups. Specifically, they help explain why people who possess similar innate abilities and access to financing often choose to obtain differing levels of human capital. We have seen that these disparities in amounts of human capital are a major source of wage differentials. Restated, differences in time preferences, which in themselves represent a worker heterogeneity, help explain an even more significant heterogeneity: differing stocks of human capital.

8-2

Tastes for Nonwage Aspects of Jobs We noted earlier that jobs are heterogeneous with respect to such nonwage features as probability of job accidents, fringe benefits, job status, location, regularity of earnings, prospects for wage advance, and control over the work pace. People also differ as to their preferences for these nonwage amenities and disamenities: workers as well as jobs are heterogeneous in this regard. As examples, some workers value job safety highly while others are far less averse to risks; some people desire positions having paid vacations while others find vacations boring and would gladly forgo paid absences for higher hourly pay; and some individuals seek status while others do not care what people think of their occupations.

QUICK REVIEW 8-1

- A single wage rate would exist if all workers and jobs were homogeneous, markets were perfectly competitive, and mobility and migration were unimpeded.
- Heterogeneous jobs (differing nonwage attributes, skill requirements, and other features) are a major source of wage differentials.

8-2 **World of Work**

SMOKING IS BAD FOR YOUR FINANCIAL HEALTH

Smoking is well known to cause physical health problems such as lung cancer and emphysema. However, it also apparently causes smokers to have worse financial health as well. Levine, Gustafon, and Velenchik have examined the impact of cigarette smoking on labor market outcomes by comparing 4,284 nonsmokers and 2,118 smokers aged 27 to 34 in 1991.* Two conclusions emerged from their study. First, smokers earn 4 to 8 percent less than nonsmokers after accounting for differences between the groups. The lower wages of smokers may come from a variety of causes. They could be the result of discrimination. For example, some smokers may be denied raises and promotions because of their smoking habit. Alternatively, smokers' lower wages may be due to a smoking-related decrease in worker productivity. The productivity decrease could be because of time taken off for smoking breaks or decreased ability to perform manual tasks. Lastly, smokers may cost more due to high absenteeism, higher health and fire insurance premiums, higher maintenance costs, and lower worker morale. These higher employee costs for smokers would lead to a compensating decrease in their wages. The second conclusion from this study is that smoking does not affect the probability of employment.

Smoking also affects other aspects of one's financial health. Evans and Montgomery find that, controlling for other factors, smokers are 6 percent less likely to own a home and have 4 percent less interest and dividend income.† They argue these findings occur because smokers are less concerned about the future and are less willing to engage in future-oriented behaviors such as home ownership and saving money.

*Philip B. Levine, Tara A. Gustafon, and Ann D. Velenchik, "More Bad News for Smokers? The Effects of Cigarette Smoking on Labor Market Outcomes," *Industrial and Labor Relations Review,* April 1997, pp. 493–509.

†William N. Evans and Edward Montgomery, "Education and Health: Where There's Smoke There's an Instrument," National Bureau of Economic Research Working Paper No. 4949, December 1994.

- Sources of compensating wage differentials include differing risks of injury and death, fringe benefits, job status, job location, regularity of earnings, prospects for wage advancement, and control over the pace of work.
- Wage differentials also arise because workers are heterogeneous; their human capital, time preferences, and tastes for nonwage aspects of jobs differ.

8-3 **Your Turn:** Generally, salaries of state governors are far below those of similarly qualified top executives in the private sector. How can these wage differentials persist? (Answer: See page 626.)

THE HEDONIC THEORY OF WAGES

The fact that both jobs *and* workers are heterogeneous is contained in the ***hedonic theory of wages.***[20] The term *hedonic* derives from the philosophical concept of hedonism, which hypothesizes that people pursue utility (pleasure), say, wage income, and avoid disutility (pain), for example, jobs having unpleasant working conditions. According to the hedonic theory, workers are interested in maximizing *net* utility and therefore

[20]Sherwin Rosen, "Hedonic Prices and Implicit Markets," *Journal of Political Economy,* January–February 1974, pp. 34–55.

8-3 World of Work

WAGE DIFFERENTIALS: MARRIED VERSUS SINGLE MALES

One of the more puzzling wage rate differentials in the labor market is that between married and unmarried men. Average wage rates received by married males are anywhere from 8 to 40 percent greater than the hourly pay received by single males.* For example, one study discovered that young married men earn about 10 percent higher wage rates and 33 percent more annual earnings than their unmarried counterparts.† These pay differentials are not just confined to the United States; they are documented in industrial economies throughout the world.

What accounts for this wage differential? At least three explanations have been offered.

1. *Differing personal attributes.* Personality, physical attractiveness, reliability, and other personal attributes may simultaneously contribute to a male's likelihood of being married *and* to his chances of having a high wage, independently of his high level of education and training. Those personal characteristics making one a good (bad) employee may at the same time make one an attractive (unattractive) marriage partner. An unreliable, unmotivated male is neither a desirable employee nor an appealing mate. Marriage and higher wage rates, therefore, may not be related in any causal way, but instead be joint outcomes of hard-to-measure personal characteristics that lead *both* to a higher probability of marriage *and* to a higher wage rate.

2. *Differing incentives to accumulate human capital.* Perhaps males who anticipate being married most of their lives have more of an incentive to accumulate education and training than men who do not contemplate or are uncertain about getting married. If those anticipating being married and having families to support also expect to work more hours over their careers, they will perceive a greater return on human capital. Given the same cost of financing this human capital, they will rationally choose to accumulate relatively more education and training than people expecting to work fewer hours over their lifetimes. For the same reason, married men may have a greater incentive to add to their human capital during marriage. In this explanation, then, the anticipation of marriage and the marriage itself together cause the observed higher wage rates for married males.‡

3. *Differing costs of acquiring human capital.* It is equally plausible that married men tend to acquire relatively more human capital while married because they have lower costs of financing such investments. Males may be able to borrow from household income at lower implicit interest rates (forgone interest on savings) than the bank rates charged to single males. This conforms to the observation that many wives "put their husbands through school" by temporarily working in the labor market. Given equal incentives to invest in human capital (equal internal rates of return), a married male who faces lower financing expenses will choose to accumulate more education and training than a single male. This greater accumulation of human capital will produce higher wage rates.

Recent empirical investigations have reached differing conclusions regarding the relative importance of these explanations. Korenman and Neumark argue that marriage makes men more productive.§ Consistent with their hypothesis, they report wages rise after marriage and the marriage premium grows with the number of years married. Also, they find that the marriage wage differential is largely accounted for by the better performance evaluations that married men receive.

This human capital explanation has been challenged by two other investigations. First, Cornwell and Rupert‖ find that Kornmark and Neumark's findings are sensitive to the age range chosen for the analysis. Also, they report that controlling for the number of years with the current employer eliminates the wage gain associated with becoming married. Thus, Cornwell and Rupert conclude the marriage premium results from better personal attributes among married men. Second, Loh finds married men who are self-employed earn less than their single counterparts.# Also contrary to the productivity hypothesis, he finds that the marriage premium is not affected by the work effort of the spouse or whether the man lived with his future wife before marriage.

*Lawrence W. Kenny, "The Accumulation of Human Capital during Marriage by Males," *Economic Inquiry,* April 1983, pp. 223–231.

†Zvi Griliches, "Wages of Very Young Men," *Journal of Political Economy,* August 1976, part 2, pp. 69–85.

‡Kenny, op. cit., p. 224.

§Sanders Korenman and David Neumark, "Does Marriage Really Make Men More Productive?" *Journal of Human Resources,* Spring 1991, pp. 282–307.

‖Eng Seng Loh, "Productivity Differences and the Marriage Wage Premium for White Males," *Journal of Human Resources,* Summer 1996, pp. 566–589.

#Christopher Cornwell and Peter Rupert, "Marriage and Earnings," *Federal Reserve Bank of Cleveland Economic Review,* 4th Quarter 1995, pp. 10–20.

are willing to "exchange" that which produces utility to get reductions in something that yields disutility.

The Worker's Indifference Map

The hedonic wage theory often is portrayed in terms of a trade-off between a "good" (the wage) and a work-related "bad" (for example, the probability of injury). However, the *absence* of a "bad" (probability that an injury will not occur) is indeed a "good," and therefore, the theory can also be presented in terms of trading off wages and nonwage amenities. This allows the use of standard indifference curve analysis.

It is reasonable to assume that the typical worker places a positive value on (1) the wage rate being paid and (2) the nonwage amenities that a job offers. In a manner similar to the wage–fringe benefit analysis in Chapter 7, a worker faces a subjective trade-off between two things yielding utility.

Figure 8-2 is illustrative, where the wage rate is measured on the vertical axis and a single nonwage amenity is shown on the horizontal axis. This nonwage amenity may be any one of several positive job attributes; for example, the probability of *not* being injured on the job, the advantages associated with the job's location, or the expenses saved and leisure gained as commuting time declines.

Let's suppose that the particular nonwage amenity measured left to right on the horizontal axis is the degree of job safety (the probability of not being injured on the job). Each indifference curve shows the various combinations of wages and degrees of job safety that will yield some given level of utility or satisfaction to this worker. Recall from Chapter 7 that each point on a specific indifference curve is equally satisfactory, but that total utility can be increased by getting to a higher indifference curve, that is, by moving northeasterly from I_1 to I_2 to I_3.

The indifference curves in Figure 8-2 are steep, implying that this individual is highly averse to risks. To understand this conclusion, observe curve I_1 and notice that this person places a high substitution value on extra degrees of job safety. A very large increase in the wage rate is necessary to compensate him or her for a small reduction

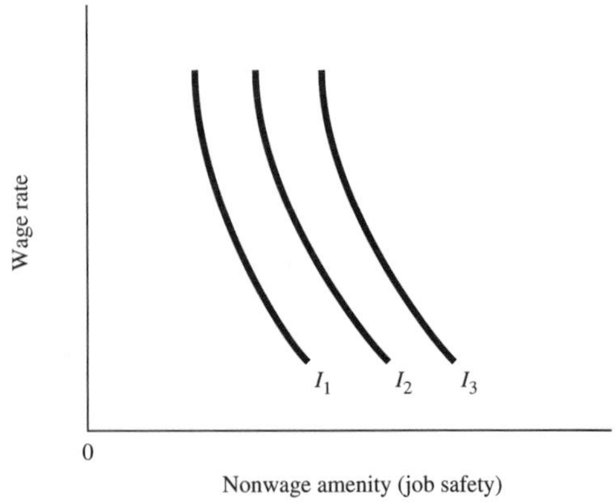

FIGURE 8-2 AN INDIFFERENCE MAP FOR WAGES AND NONWAGE AMENITIES
The "hedonic" indifference map is comprised of a number of indifference curves. Each individual curve shows the various combinations of wage rates and a particular nonwage amenity (for example, job safety) that yield a specific level of total utility. Each successive curve to the northeast reflects a higher level of total utility.

in safety (small increase in the probability of job injury). But indifference maps vary from person to person; another worker may be far less averse to risk and therefore will have relatively flat indifference curves compared to those in Figure 8-2. Succinctly stated, workers are heterogeneous with respect to their preferences for nonwage amenities.

The Employer's Normal-Profit Isoprofit Curve

It is reasonable to assume that an employer can act to reduce the probability of job injury or, alternatively stated, to increase the safety of the workplace. For example, the employer might provide education programs about job safety, purchase safer machinery, provide protective work gear, or slow the pace of work. But because these steps are costly, the employer faces a trade-off between the wages offered and the degree of job safety provided to workers. To maintain any given level of profits, the firm can either (1) pay lower wages and provide a high degree of job safety or (2) pay higher wages and take fewer actions to reduce the risk of job-related accidents.

Figure 8-3 shows a normal-profit isoprofit curve, which in this case indicates the various combinations of wage rates and degrees of job safety yielding a given normal profit. Observe that this curve is concave; it is not a straight line as was the isoprofit curve for wage rates and fringe benefits in Figure 7-4. Why the difference? In Chapter 7 we assumed that the trade-off between wage rates and fringe benefits was constant. But the concave shape of the isoprofit curve in Figure 8-3 derives from the realistic assumption that each unit of added job safety comes at increasing expense and therefore results in a successively larger wage reduction. Successive units of expense (wage reduction) yield diminishing returns to job safety. Marginal costs typically rise as more job safety is produced. Therefore, as one moves rightward on *P*, the curve becomes increasingly steep.

But not all employers have identical isoprofit curves; they too are heterogeneous. The isoprofit curve in Figure 8-3 is relatively flat, indicating that this firm can "purchase" job safety at a low marginal cost. Note from *P* that large increments of job safety are associated with only small reductions in the wage. But other firms may not be so fortunate. Their technological constraints may make it extremely difficult to

FIGURE 8-3 ISOPROFIT CURVE
The employer's isoprofit curve portrays the various combinations of wage rates and job amenities (for example, job safety) that yield a given level of profit. Competition among firms will result in only normal profits (zero-economic profit) in the long run; therefore, firms will be forced to make their "wage rate–job amenity" decisions along a curve such as *P*.

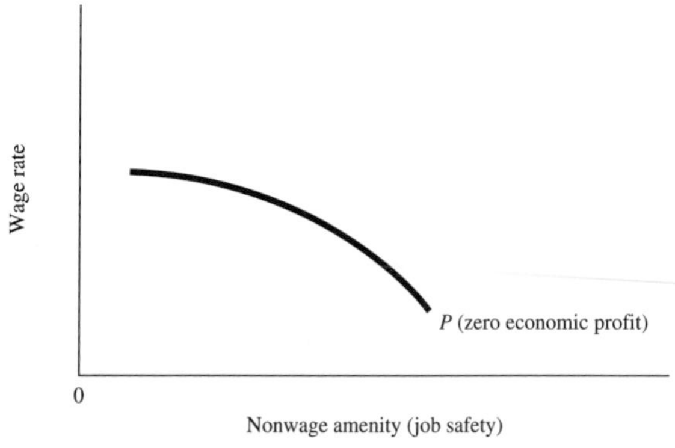

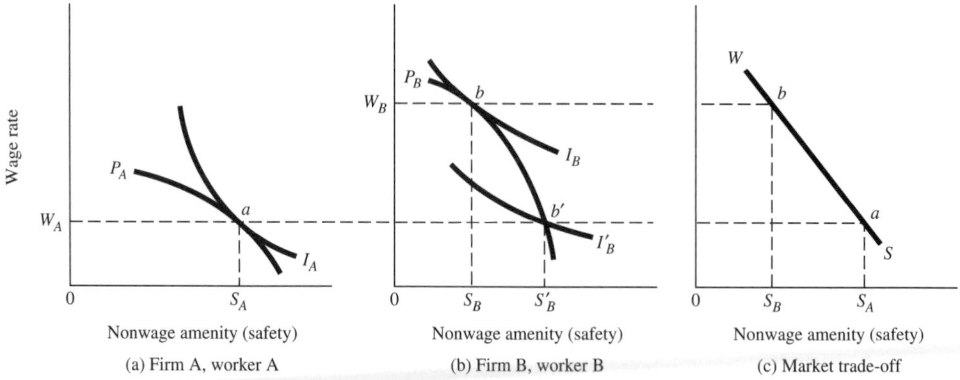

FIGURE 8-4 MATCHING HETEROGENEOUS WORKERS AND JOBS
Graph (a) portrays an optimal job match between worker A who places a high value on job safety at the margin and firm A that can "produce" job safety at relatively low marginal cost. Graph (b) shows the utility-maximizing and profit-maximizing "wage rate–nonwage amenity" combination (point *b*) for a worker who is less averse to risk and a firm that has high marginal costs of making the workplace safer. Graph (c) plots the optimal "wage–job safety" combinations shown in (a) and (b). Line *WS* in graph (c) indicates the general relationship between wage rates and job safety in a labor market characterized by many—not just two—heterogeneous workers and jobs. Higher wage rates are associated with lower levels of nonwage amenities, other things being the same.

reduce the risk of accident and therefore very costly to "produce" a safe work environment. These firms would face steep normal-profit isoprofit curves.

Matching Workers with Jobs

Figure 8-4 portrays the optimal combination of wage rate and job safety for two distinct sets of employers and workers. Workers A and B possess identical stocks of human capital, but have greatly different tastes for the nonwage amenity job safety. The isoprofit curves P_A in graph (a) and P_B in (b) show the highest profit levels attainable for firms A and B, given the competitive nature of their respective industries. The general slope of isoprofit curve P_A is less steep than that of P_B. This indicates that for technological reasons, the marginal cost of producing job safety is more in firm B than in A. Restated, a specific increase in job safety reduces the wage rate more for firm B than for A.

Now observe the indifference curves I_A and I_B in graph (a) and (b). These are the highest attainable indifference curves for each worker. Curve I_A is relatively steep, implying that person A is quite averse to the risk of job injury (he values job safety highly). On the other hand, the curve for person B is relatively flat, indicating that B is less concerned about job injury or death than A. Obviously, workers A and B have differing tastes for this particular job disamenity.

Each worker maximizes total utility where her or his highest indifference curve is tangent to the employer's zero-economic profit isoprofit curve. Worker A will choose to work for employer A and, as indicated by point a in the left-hand graph, will receive wage rate W_A. Along with this low wage, the person will obtain a large quantity of the amenity job safety. Job and worker heterogeneity therefore produce an optimal match between an individual who is highly averse to risk and an employer who has relatively low marginal costs of producing job safety. Similarly, worker B will match up with employer B and receive a higher wage rate W_B, but will be employed in a more dangerous work setting. The matching of laborer B and firm B maximizes the interests of both; employer B has a high marginal cost of producing job safety, and this worker is willing to trade off much of that amenity for a higher wage rate.

8-4

Labor Market Implications

The hedonic wage model has some interesting—and, in some cases, controversial—implications. Let's sample a few.

First, the labor market will generate wage differentials among people who possess identical amounts of human capital. Other things being equal, higher wages will tend

8-4 **World of Work**

COMPENSATING PAY FOR SHIFT WORK*

In the hedonic theory of wages, compensating wage differentials arise for jobs with onerous working conditions. The market wage in these occupations must increase sufficiently to compensate the last worker employed for the disutility that person associates with the poor working conditions. These compensating wage premiums, however, enable some workers to increase their net utility. Specifically, people who are less averse to the poor working conditions or who are comparatively less productive in normal jobs may enhance their net utility by accepting work under the inferior conditions. For these individuals the utility gain from the extra pay may exceed the utility loss from the poor conditions. In this regard, economists say that some workers "self-select" into occupations having poorer working conditions but paying compensating wage premiums.

Kostiuk has found precisely this outcome for work done at night, commonly called "shift work." Shift work is more prevalent than generally supposed, with about 15 percent of full-time wage and salary workers not working a regular daytime schedule. Using data from supplements to the Census Bureau's *Current Population Survey,* Kostiuk found an 8.2 percent wage premium associated with shift work in manufacturing. Union shift workers received an 18.1 percent wage premium; nonunion shift workers, a 4.3 percent differential.

Kostiuk's findings partly reflect the self-selection mentioned earlier. He discovered that workers with less education had a larger wage premium for shift work than did more-educated workers doing similar shift work. This higher relative wage premium for less-educated workers enticed more of them to take shift-work jobs. Thought of differently, if the typical night-work employee had instead worked during the day, his or her pay would be less than the pay of typical day-shift workers. On average, night-shift workers are less educated than day-shift workers doing similar work.

The upshot is that the shift-work sector, with its compensating wage differentials, raises the wage of less-educated workers and reduces overall wage inequality. Shift work narrows the distribution of earnings on two counts: (1) it provides a compensating wage differential for adverse working conditions, and (2) it attracts workers who have a below-average potential for daytime earnings.

*Based on P. F. Kostiuk, "Compensating Differentials for Shift Work," *Journal of Political Economy,* part 1, October 1990, pp. 1054–1075.

to be associated with fewer nonwage amenities. This is shown in graph (c) in Figure 8-4. Line *WS,* which connects points such as *a* and *b* in the two left-hand graphs, indicates the general inverse relationships between wage rates and job safety in a labor market characterized by many—not just two—heterogeneous workers and jobs. The wage differentials possible along this line are persistent, or equilibrium, differentials; they will not create movements of workers among the jobs.

Second, laws that set a minimum standard for nonwage job amenities may actually reduce the utility of some workers. This is shown through reference again to Figure 8-4. If government forces firm B (graph b) to increase its job safety from S_B to, say, S'_B, it will move from point *b* downward on P_B to b', and worker B will be forced to indifference curve I'_B, which clearly is below I_B.

Third, part of the observed male–female earnings differential (Chapter 15) may reflect differing tastes for positive job amenities such as pleasant working conditions, a short commuting distance, and a low probability of job injury. In terms of Figure 8-4, *if* indifference curves for females as a group tend to be more on the order of I_A rather than I_B, women will match up to a greater extent than men with jobs that have lower pay, but also better nonwage amenities. Filer finds evidence to support this possibility. Apparently a portion of the observed male–female earnings differential among similarly trained workers results from compensating differentials.[21]

Finally, the hedonic model extends our earlier discussion of optimal fringe benefits (Figure 7-5) both in terms of worker indifference maps and employer isoprofit curves. Indifference maps of the utility trade-off between wages and fringe benefits vary from worker to worker. Workers who place a high marginal valuation on fringe benefits—that is, have relatively steep indifference curves—will therefore match up with firms offering pay packages containing significant fringe benefits. Conversely, workers whose valuations of cash wages are higher at the margin than valuations of fringe benefits are more likely to opt to work for firms with relatively fewer fringe benefits but higher cash wages.

Additionally, variations in indifference maps among workers help to explain the existence of so-called *cafeteria plans,* which permit workers to choose among a wide range of fringe benefits. These plans allow heterogeneous workers to individually attain higher indifference curves than they could if they had to accept a fixed package of fringe benefits determined by the firm. Examples: A female worker with young children may select child care benefits; an older male worker may opt to have his pension fund enhanced. By increasing the total utility workers receive from any given dollar amount of compensation, cafeteria plans may enable firms to attract and retain higher-quality workers.

The composition of fringe benefits may vary among firms, depending on the marginal cost of providing each fringe benefit. For example, a university may provide free tuition for children of employees, whereas a retail firm may give its workers discounts on merchandise. In each situation, the firm shapes the fringe benefit package in a particular way because of the relatively low marginal cost of providing a specific fringe benefit.

[21]Randall K. Filer, "Male–Female Wage Differences: The Importance of Compensating Differentials," *Industrial and Labor Relations Review,* April 1985, pp. 426–437.

QUICK REVIEW 8-2

- In the hedonic wage model, indifference curves show the various combinations of wage rates and levels of a particular nonwage amenity that yield specific levels of total utility.
- The employer's normal-profit isoprofit curve depicts the various combinations of wage rates and specific nonwage amenities that yield a normal profit.
- The optimal job match occurs where the worker's highest attainable indifference curve is tangent to the employer's normal-profit isoprofit curve.
- Workers who have a strong preference for a particular nonwage amenity will tend to match up with employers who can provide the amenity at a relatively low marginal cost. Other things being equal, these workers will receive lower pay than workers who have weak preferences for the nonwage amenity and match up with employers who provide less of it due to its high marginal cost.

8-5

Your Turn: How might a person who actually enjoys working outdoors in extremely cold temperatures benefit from the more general worker preference for employment in climate-controlled buildings or in mild outdoor temperatures? (Answer: See page 626.)

WAGE DIFFERENTIALS: LABOR MARKET IMPERFECTIONS

Wage differences can be explained largely—but not fully—on the basis of heterogeneous jobs, employers, and workers. They also occur because of labor market imperfections that impede labor mobility. Such factors as imperfect information, costly migration, and various other barriers to mobility interact to create and maintain wage differentials.

Imperfect Labor Market Information

We assumed that labor market information was perfect in Figure 8-1, but in reality it is imperfect and costly to obtain. Recognizing that workers are heterogeneous, firms search the labor market to find those workers who are best suited for employment. Similarly, workers gather information about prospective job opportunities by scanning help-wanted ads, writing letters, inquiring at business establishments, and so forth. These search efforts by firms and prospective employees involve direct costs and opportunity costs of time. Furthermore, the activity of gaining information eventually will yield diminishing returns. Translated into costs, this implies that the marginal cost of obtaining information will increase as more of it is sought. The fact that information is imperfect and increasingly costly to obtain has important implications for labor market activity and the wage structure.[22] Specifically, it implies that (1) a range of wage rates may exist for any given occupation, independently of compensating differentials,

[22]It also has important implications for job search (Chapter 16) and unemployment (Chapter 19).

8-5 World of Work

PLACING A VALUE ON HUMAN LIFE

Agencies such as the Environmental Protection Agency, Federal Aviation Commission, and Occupational Safety and Health Administration are required by law to determine the expected monetary costs and benefits of any new regulations. Because lives saved are an important benefit of many of the regulations, these federal agencies therefore need to estimate the economic value of human life.

The traditional approach to placing an economic value on human life relies on the concept of human capital (Chapter 4). A so-called "wrongful death" from, say, an airline crash eliminates earnings over the remaining years of the person's expected work life. Economists use earnings data on similar individuals in the same occupation to estimate the present value of the amount of wage and fringe benefits lost over these years. Although estimates vary by age and occupation, this method places the value of life on average at between $500,000 and $700,000.

A more recent, controversial approach to attaching a value to human life relies on the hedonic wage theory (Figure 8-4). We know that employers must pay compensating wage differentials to induce people to work at dangerous jobs. The size of these differentials reveals information on the amount of money that firms must pay per job-related death. Suppose, for example, that risk-averse behavior of labor suppliers forces firms to pay compensating wages of $1,000 annually for every 0.1 percent (= .001) increase in the probability of death on the job. On average, every job-related death therefore costs firms $1 million (= $1,000/.001), a sum that could be thought of as the economic value of each life.

The hedonic method typically yields higher estimates of the value of human life than does the human capital approach. For example, hedonic estimates developed by the federal regulatory agencies range upward to $3.5 million per life saved.

and (2) when changes in demand cause wage differentials, long-run supply adjustments are likely to be slow.

1 Wage Rate Distributions Once we introduce costly information, job searches, and heterogeneous workers and employers into our analysis, the likelihood there will be a single equilibrium wage (as in Figure 6-1) for each type of labor greatly diminishes. Rather, we can expect to find a *range* of equilibrium wages for each type of labor. This range may be very narrow or quite broad, depending on the individual circumstances within each occupational labor market.

Figure 8-5 portrays one of many possible wage rate distributions. This particular distribution is symmetrical, but other types of distributions are entirely possible. The horizontal axis shows a range of wages, $6.00 through $7.80, and the vertical axis measures the relative frequency of the occurrence of each subrange of wages in the distribution. The area covered by the wage distribution equals 1; there is a 100 percent probability that the wage will fall within the $6.00 to $7.80 range. Likewise, .05 or 5 percent of all wages will be between $6.00 and $6.19, 8 percent will lie between $6.20 and $6.39, and so forth.

How can a wage rate distribution such as that depicted in Figure 8-5 persist? Won't workers move from lower-paying to higher-paying jobs, with a single equilibrium wage rate eventually resulting? The ideas of costly information and costly job searches provide the answers to these questions. Employers will set wages according to their individual circumstances and their estimates of the "market" wage rate. Some employers may pay slightly more—others, slightly less—than the average wage. But since infor-

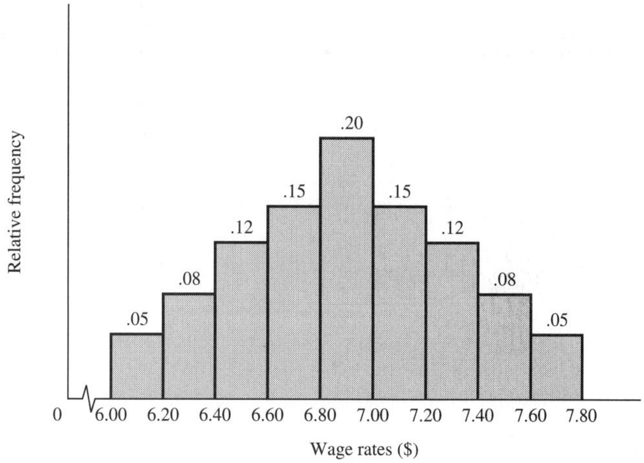

FIGURE 8-5 A WAGE RATE DISTRIBUTION
Under conditions of costly information and job searches, competitive labor markets generate an equilibrium distribution of wage rates within a single occupation, rather than an equilibrium hourly wage. In this example, 20 percent of the workers receive a wage rate between $6.80 and $6.99 an hour, but some workers (5 percent) earn as little as $6.00 to $6.19, while another 5 percent make $7.60 to $7.79 an hour. The area under the frequency distribution sums to 1 (100 percent).

mation is imperfect and costly to obtain, some workers and firms will be unaware that greater or lesser wages are being paid to similar workers. Other employees may recognize that there is a variance in pay but also realize that it is costly to discover which employers of this labor are paying the higher amounts. In technical terms, many workers will judge the marginal cost of obtaining the necessary information to exceed the expected marginal gain from the higher wage. Thus, they will remain in their present places of employment and the wage differentials will persist. *Under conditions of imperfect, costly information, it is entirely possible for wage differences within occupations to be equilibrium differentials, that is, differentials that do not evoke job switching.*[23]

2 Lengthy Adjustment Periods A second implication of imperfect, costly information is that long-run supply adjustments to wage differentials created by changes in demand may take months or even years to occur. Suppose, for example, that the demand for labor in occupation X rises sharply. Given an upward-sloping short-run labor supply curve, a wage increase in occupation X will result. But information concerning this new wage is likely to be incompletely disseminated. Persons making choices on the types and amounts of human capital to obtain will learn *gradually* of the higher wage in occupation X. Of course, as more time transpires, more information will become known. But even then some potential labor suppliers to X will

[23]The classic article on this point is George J. Stigler, "Information in the Labor Market," *Journal of Political Economy,* October 1962, pp. S94–S105.

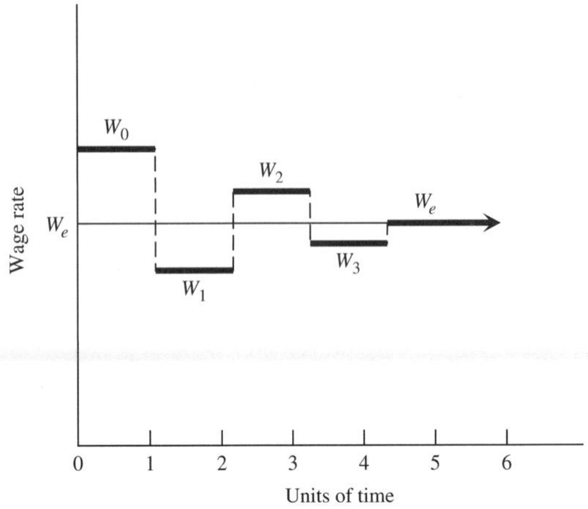

FIGURE 8-6 WAGE RATE ADJUSTMENT PATH
An increase in labor demand initially may cause a substantial wage increase to, say, W_0 in occupations which require long training periods. But the supply response to the higher wage may create a surplus of labor to the occupation in the subsequent period, driving the wage rate lower, say, to W_1. For a time the wage rate may oscillate above and below the long-run equilibrium wage rate W_e before equilibrium in the market is finally restored. During the transition periods, wage differentials between this occupation and others paying W_e will be observed.

wonder if this is indeed a permanent wage differential relative to other occupations or one that will quickly evaporate by the time they become qualified.

Once people *do* begin to recognize that the wage rate in occupation X is permanent, then some will respond and eventually create a flow of labor into X and away from, say, Y and Z. This will cause the wage narrowing predicted by the pure theory. But recall from our discussion of the cobweb model in Chapter 6 (Figure 6-12) that in some occupations requiring long training periods—for example, law and engineering—the supply response may be so great that the wage differential not only is eliminated but turns in the opposite direction. Then, in the next period, still another overadjustment may occur, reducing labor supply so dramatically that a positive wage differential again arises. Thus, as shown by the wage rate adjustment path in Figure 8-6, some wage rates may for a time oscillate above and below the long-run equilibrium wage W_e. Note from the diagram that the wage rate shifts from W_0 to W_1 to W_2, and so forth, as units of time transpire. To summarize: Labor markets in which information is imperfect and costly will be characterized by many transitional wage differentials, which exist because of lengthy and occasionally oscillating adjustment paths to final equilibrium.[24]

Immobilities

Labor immobilities, defined simply as *impediments to the movement of labor,* constitute another major reason that wage differentials occur and sometimes persist. For convenience, we will classify these barriers to labor mobility as geographic, institutional, and sociological.

[24]For a discussion of alternative wage rate adjustment paths, see Belton M. Fleisher and Thomas J. Kniesner, *Labor Economics: Theory, Evidence, and Policy,* 3d ed. (Englewood Cliffs, NJ: Prentice-Hall, Inc., 1984), pp. 186–191. Also of interest is Jean Helwege, "Sectoral Shifts and Interindustry Wage Differentials," *Journal of Labor Economics,* January 1992, pp. 55–84.

1 Geographic Immobilities We will discover in Chapter 9 that wage differences between geographic areas provide an incentive for workers to migrate. By moving to the high-wage location, a worker can enhance lifetime earnings. But moving also involves costs, such as transportation expenses, forgone earnings during the move, the inconvenience of adjusting to a new job and community, the negative aspects of leaving family and friends, and the possible loss of seniority and pension benefits. If these costs deter migration to the extent that an insufficient number of migrants are attracted to the higher-paying locale, geographic wage differentials will persist.

2 Institutional Immobilities Restrictions on mobility imposed by such institutions as government and unions may reinforce geographic immobilities. We previously noted in Chapter 6 that government licensing of occupations can restrict the movement of qualified workers among jobs. Also, differing licensing requirements in various states can limit worker mobility geographically. Craft unions also are a factor here; they impede mobility by limiting the access of nonunion workers to union-controlled apprenticeship programs and union-filled jobs. Other institutional immobilities involve pension plans and seniority rights, which reduce people's incentives to move from one job to another.

3 Sociological Immobilities Finally, there are numerous sociological barriers to labor mobility. In Chapter 14 we examine theories of labor market discrimination by race and gender. For example, females appear to be "crowded" into certain occupations. This drives down the equilibrium wage in these occupations and raises it elsewhere. To the extent that there are barriers that keep qualified women from moving from these lower-paying positions to higher-paying occupations, wage differentials between the sexes can persist. In the same vein, blacks historically were excluded from certain higher-paying occupations either through informal understandings by employers or through formal prohibitions by unions. As an example of the latter, over 20 national unions had constitutional provisions barring blacks from membership in 1930. In fact, some unions such as the Locomotive Engineers and the Railway Conductors still excluded blacks from membership in 1964, when the Civil Rights Act was passed.[25]

Figure 8-7 provides a schematic overview of the major contributing factors to wage differentials. This diagram merits your careful considerations.

CHAPTER SUMMARY

1 Theoretically, if *all* workers and jobs were homogeneous and all labor markets were perfectly competitive, then workers would move among the various jobs until the wages paid in all markets were identical.
2 Casual and empirical examinations of wage rates and weekly earnings reveal that a variety of wage differentials do exist and that many of them persist over time.

[25]F. Ray Marshall, Vernon M. Briggs, Jr., and Allan King, *Labor Economics,* 5th ed. (Homewood, IL: R. D. Irwin, Inc., 1984), p. 567.

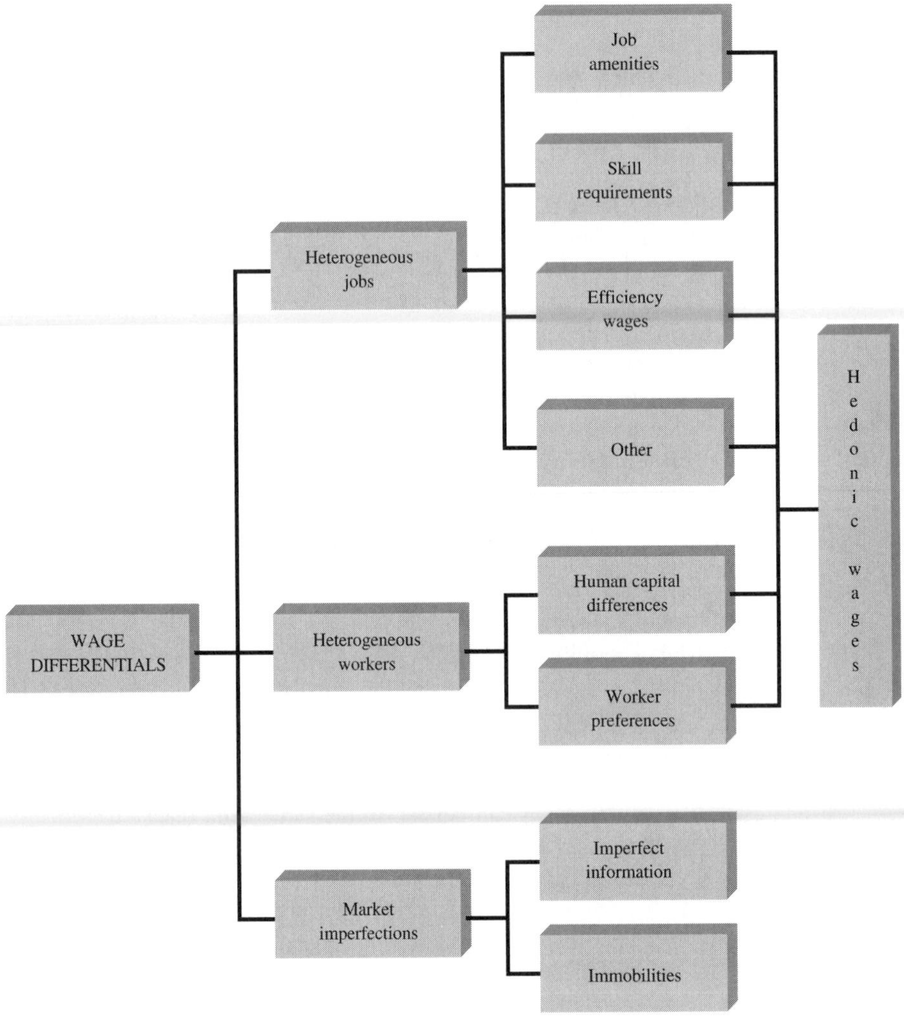

FIGURE 8-7 SOURCES OF WAGE DIFFERENTIALS: A REVIEW
Wage differentials arise because jobs are heterogeneous, workers are heterogeneous, and markets are imperfect. Heterogeneous jobs *and* heterogeneous workers are the underpinning of the hedonic wage, or job-matching, model.

3 Several nonwage aspects of jobs influence supply decisions in ways that generate compensating wage differentials. These nonwage factors include *(a)* risk of job injury and death, *(b)* fringe benefits, *(c)* job status, *(d)* job location, *(e)* the regularity of earnings, *(f)* the prospect for wage advancement, and *(g)* the extent of control over the work pace.

4 Differences in skill requirements also produce wage differences. Other things being equal, to attract a sufficient flow of laborers to an occupation requiring considerable prior investment in human capital, employers must pay these workers more than they pay less-skilled employees.

5 Efficiency wage theories have recently been advanced to explain pay differences within and among industries. These theories predict that wages will be higher where it is difficult to monitor the performance of workers, where the costs to employers of mistakes by individual workers are large, and where high labor turnover significantly reduces productivity.
6 Another major source of wage disparities is heterogeneous workers. Specifically, workers possess greatly varying stocks of human capital and differing preferences for various nonwage aspects of work. Consequently, the overall labor market is composed of numerous submarkets consisting of groups of workers who offer little competition to other groups.
7 The hedonic theory of wages hypothesizes that workers who possess differing subjective preferences for wages compared to nonwage job amenities seek to find optimal matches with employers who differ in their costs of providing those nonwage attributes. Among a wide variety of implications that flow from this model is the basic one that labor markets will generate sustained wage differentials, even among persons who have similar stocks of human capital.
8 Imperfect and costly market information is another reason that wage differentials exist. Imperfect and costly information creates ranges of wage rates, independent of other factors, and explains why transitional wage differentials often are long-lasting.
9 Labor market immobilities—geographic, institutional, and sociological—also help explain persistent earnings differences among workers.

TERMS AND CONCEPTS

equilibrium wage differentials
transitional wage differentials
homogeneous workers and jobs
wage structure
heterogeneous jobs
compensating wage differentials
skill differential
heterogeneous workers
noncompeting groups
hedonic theory of wages
labor immobilities

QUESTIONS AND STUDY SUGGESTIONS

1 Suppose that all workers and jobs in a hypothetical economy are homogeneous. Explain why no wage differentials would exist if this economy were perfectly competitive and information and mobility were costless. Explain why wage differentials would arise if, on the other hand, information and mobility were imperfect and costly.
2 Analyze why college professors generally earn less than their professional Ph.D. counterparts who are employed by corporations.
3 Discuss: "Many of the lowest-paid people in society—for example, short-order cooks—also have relatively poor working conditions. Hence, the theory of compensating wage differentials is disproved."
4 Explain why it may be in a worker's *short-term* best interest to have job titles restated for purposes of adding status: say, becoming a mixologist rather than a bartender or being referred to as a sanitation engineer rather than a garbage worker. Why may such title changes not be in the *long-term* best interest of these workers, however?
5 Explain how the theory of investment in human capital relates to the notion of noncompeting groups and how the latter relates to the presence of equilibrium wage differentials.

6 Referring to Figure 7-8, explain why wage differentials resulting exclusively from efficiency wage payments (shirking model *and* turnover model) will persist rather than erode over time.

7 What is the hedonic theory of wage differentials? Discuss the characteristics of a normal-profit isoprofit curve. Combine isoprofit curves with worker indifference curves to explain how two workers with identical stocks of human capital might be paid different wage rates.

8 Speculate as to why the average hourly wage rate paid by manufacturing firms to production workers is so much lower in South Dakota than in Michigan (Table 8-3).

9 Explain how each of the following relates to wage differentials: *(a)* seniority provisions, *(b)* varying state licensing requirements for occupations, *(c)* racial segregation, and *(d)* regional cost-of-living differences.

10 Explain why "pay comparability" legislation requiring that the public sector remunerate government employees at wages equal to private-sector counterparts might create excess supplies of labor in public-sector labor markets.

11 Suppose that *(a)* employers must pay higher wages to attract workers from wider geographic areas and hence higher wages are associated with longer commuting distances (less of the amenity "closeness of job to home") and *(b)* females have greater tastes for having jobs close to their homes than males. Use the hedonic wage model to show graphically why a male–female wage differential might emerge, independently of skill differences or gender discrimination.

SELECTED REFERENCES

Duncan, Greg, and Bertil Holmlund: "Was Adam Smith Right after All? Another Test of the Theory of Compensating Wage Differentials," *Journal of Labor Economics,* October 1983, pp. 366–379.

Groshen, Erica L.: "Why Do Wages Vary among Employers?" *Economic Review* (Federal Reserve Bank of Cleveland, Quarter 1, 1988), pp. 19–30.

Katz, Lawrence F.: "Efficiency Wage Theories: A Partial Evaluation," in Stanley Fisher (ed.), *NBER Macroeconomics Annual 1986* (Cambridge, MA: MIT Press, 1986), pp. 235–276.

Mabry, Bevars D.: *Economics of Manpower and the Labor Market* (New York: Intex Educational Publishers, 1973), chap. 14.

Rosen, Sherwin: "The Theory of Equalizing Differences," in Orley Ashenfelter and Richard Layard (eds.), *Handbook of Labor Economics,* vol. 1 (Amsterdam: North-Holland, 1986), pp. 641–692.

Smith, Adam: *The Wealth of Nations* (New York: Modern Library, 1957), pp. 99–106.

Toshiaki, Tachibanki (ed.): *Wage Differentials an International Comparison* (London: Macmillian Press, 1998)

Viscusi W. Kip: "The Value of Risks to Life and Health," *Journal of Economic Literature,* December 1993, pp. 1912–1946.

CHAPTER 9

MOBILITY, MIGRATION, AND EFFICIENCY

You most likely know someone who has recently changed employers, occupations, or job locations. Indeed, the movement of workers—***labor mobility***—is one of the striking features of labor markets. Alvarez, an auto mechanic, moves from Arizona to Arkansas. Pearson, a public school teacher, quits to become a private detective. Kioski, an executive of a North Carolina firm, gets transferred to New Mexico.

In the real world, changes are common in such things as product demand, labor productivity, levels of human capital, family circumstances, and personal attitudes toward nonwage amenities. These changes induce some workers to switch employers, occupations, geographical locations, or some combination of all three. Also, employers respond to changing economic circumstances by hiring, transferring, or discharging workers; closing or expanding present facilities; or moving operations to new locations.

Combined, these actions of workers and employers produce much movement of labor from employer to employer, occupation to occupation, and place to place. Careful observation often reveals that this mobility arises in response to transitional wage differentials, which tend to erode as markets move toward equilibrium. Mobility is central to the operation of labor markets; it promotes allocative efficiency by shuffling workers to society's highest-valued employments.

Our discussion of labor mobility proceeds in the following fashion. First, we define various types of labor mobility. Second, we select geographic mobility for special attention and examine migration as an investment in human capital. Next, we take a closer look at factors promoting and impeding mobility. Fourth, the efficiency and distributional consequences of migration and immigration are discussed. Finally, we scrutinize U.S. immigration policies and issues, directing particular attention to illegal immigration.

TYPES OF LABOR MOBILITY

The boxes in Figure 9-1 categorize several important kinds of labor mobility. The columns of the boxes identify locational characteristics of the employment change, while the rows indicate occupational characteristics. Let's describe the kind of labor mobility associated with each box.

Box I: Job Change/No Change in Occupation or Residence

Box I indicates mobility in which neither the worker's occupation nor residence changes. This form of mobility occurs frequently; for example, when electrical engineers switch employers within California's "Silicon Valley" or when automobile salespeople quit one dealership to work for another. This category also includes transfers of employees from one of a firm's units to another in the same local area: for example, when a bank employee is reassigned from one branch of a local bank to another.

Box II: Occupational Change/No Change in Residence

This box identifies changes in occupation not accompanied by changes in residence. Much of this ***occupational mobility*** involves moves to closely related occupations: for example, when a carpenter takes a job in a lumberyard or when a production worker is promoted to a supervisory position within a firm. But in other cases, this mobility is characterized by a significant occupational change: for example, a part-time warehouse employee who completes college might accept a job as a securities broker in the same town. Approximately 1 out of 10 workers in the United States is employed in a different occupation than he or she was in the previous year. A vast majority of these

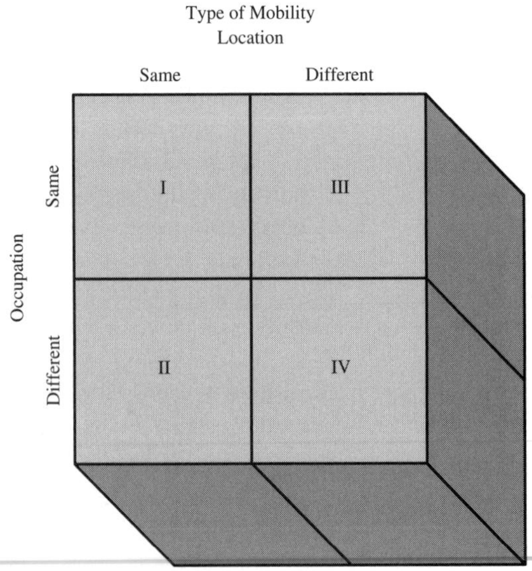

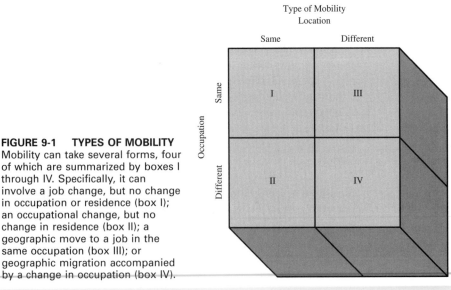

FIGURE 9-1 TYPES OF MOBILITY
Mobility can take several forms, four of which are summarized by boxes I through IV. Specifically, it can involve a job change, but no change in occupation or residence (box I); an occupational change, but no change in residence (box II); a geographic move to a job in the same occupation (box III); or geographic migration accompanied by a change in occupation (box IV).

changes in occupation are accounted for by people who are less than 35 years old. Many of these changes also involve geographic mobility (box IV).

Box III: Geographic Change/No Change in Occupation

Geographic mobility pertains to movements of workers from a job in one city, state, or nation to another. Between 16 and 18 percent of the total U.S. population changes residences each year. Moves from one county or state to another are involved in 37 percent of these residency changes. Transfers of employees by companies range between 400,000 and 500,000 annually. In recent years net immigration to the United States has been about 1 million persons per year.

In many cases geographic moves result in changes in jobs but not changes in occupations. Examples: An executive for an aerospace firm gets transferred from Wichita to Seattle, a farm worker moves from Mexico to the United States, a corporate lawyer leaves a New York City law firm to join one in Boston, a professional football player gets traded from New Orleans to Chicago.

Box IV: Geographic Change/Change in Occupation

Approximately 30 percent of geographic job-related moves are accompanied by changes in occupations. Thus, these changes represent both geographic and occupational mobility. For example, a discharged steelworker might leave Pennsylvania to take a job as a construction worker in Arizona. Or perhaps a high school teacher might move from a small town to take a position as an insurance claims adjuster in a distant
9-1 urban area.

To limit our focus and retain clarity, we will confine our attention to *geographic* mobility (boxes III and IV) in the remainder of the chapter. But much of the analysis that follows can also be directly applied to the other forms of labor mobility.

MIGRATION AS AN INVESTMENT IN HUMAN CAPITAL

Labor migration has been extensively studied by economists, sociologists, demographers, and geographers. One important way economists have contributed to the understanding of geographic mobility is through the development and testing of the human capital model of migration. We know from Chapter 4 that human capital consists of the income-producing skill, knowledge, and experience embodied within individuals. This stock of capital can be increased by specific actions—investments in human capital—that require *present* sacrifices but increase the stream of *future* earnings over one's lifetime. Such actions include obtaining more education, gaining added training, and maintaining one's health. Migration to a higher-paying job is also a human capital investment since it entails present sacrifices to obtain higher future earnings.

Will migration occur in all situations where a potential exists for increased lifetime earnings? The answer is no, because there are costs associated with the migration investment that must be weighed against the expected gains. The main costs are

9-1 **World of Work**

DETERMINANTS OF OCCUPATIONAL TENURE*

On average, Americans change occupations several times during their careers. Median occupational tenure—the cumulative length of time a person has worked in her or his current occupation—is about 6.5 years. But occupational mobility varies considerably around this average. Several important factors affect occupational tenure.

Age. Younger workers tend to change occupations more often than older workers. Median occupational tenure for workers aged 16 to 24 is 2.0 years; for workers aged 55 to 64, it is 17.4 years. Younger workers are still "shopping" for career paths; older workers have settled into their careers.

Employment trends. Occupational tenure is low in industries with rapidly growing employment and high in industries with slowly growing or declining employment. Growing industries are continually adding new workers, which pulls down the average lengths of occupational tenure. Because slowly growing or stagnant industries hire few new workers, the average tenures of their workforces are high. Example: Median occupational tenure in the fast-growing computer and data processing industry is 5.6 years. This compares to 12.5 years in the stagnating blast furnaces and steel products industry.

Education and training. Occupational mobility declines with educational attainment. Workers with large investments in education for specific occupations stay with their occupation longer than workers with little human capital. Median occupational tenure for workers with less than 4 years of high school is 5.2 years, compared to 7.9 years for people with 4 years of college or more.

Compensation and benefits. If all else is equal, high pay and long occupational tenures go hand in hand. High pay encourages workers to remain in an occupation.

Gender, race, and ethnicity. Men have longer median occupational tenure (7.7 years) than do women (5.5 years). Whites of both sexes have longer median tenures than blacks, and blacks have longer tenures than Hispanics.

Self-employed workers. Median occupational tenure is longer for self-employed workers (8.0 years) than for wage and salary workers (5.9 years). Examples of self-employed occupational groups with long tenures include dentists (15.1 years) and barbers (27.2 years).

In short, there are wide variations in occupational mobility among members of the workforce.

*Synopsis of Steven R. Maguire, "Employer and Occupational Tenure: 1991 Update," *Monthly Labor Review,* June 1993, pp. 45–56.

transportation expenses, forgone income during the move, psychic costs of leaving family and friends, and the loss of seniority and pension benefits. According to our analysis of Chapter 4, if the present value of the expected increased earnings exceeds the pres-ent value of these investment costs, the person will choose to move. If the opposite is true, the individual will conclude that it is not worthwhile to migrate, even though the earnings potential in the destination area may be higher than in the present location.[1]

[1]The classic article on this topic is by Larry A. Sjaastad, "The Costs and Returns of Human Migration," *Journal of Political Economy,* suppl., October 1962, pp. 80–93. For reviews of a wide variety of labor mobility models, see Michael J. Greenwood, "Research on Internal Migration in the United States: A Survey," *Journal of Economic Literature,* June 1975, pp. 397–433. Greenwood updated his survey in "Human Migration: Theory, Models, and Empirical Studies," *Journal of Regional Science,* November 1985, pp. 521–543. Also see Charles F. Mueller, *The Economics of Labor Migration: A Behavioral Analysis* (New York: Academic Press, 1982), pp. 1–70.

Equation (9-1)—a modification of equation (4-3) in Chapter 4—gives the net present value of migration.

$$V_p = \sum_{n=1}^{N} \frac{E_2 - E_1}{(1+i)^n} - \sum_{n=1}^{N} \frac{C}{(1+i)^n} - Z \qquad (9\text{-}1)$$

where V_p = present value of net benefits
E_2 = earnings from new job in year n
E_1 = earnings from existing job in year n
N = length of time expected on new job
i = interest rate (discount rate)
n = year in which benefits and costs accrue
C = direct and indirect monetary costs resulting from move in the year n
Z = net psychic costs of move (psychic costs minus psychic gains)

In equation (9-1), if $V_p > 0$, implying that the expected earnings gain exceeds the combined monetary and net psychic investment costs, the person will migrate. If, conversely, $V_p < 0$, the person will remain in his or her present job and location. All else being equal, the greater the annual earnings differential ($E_2 - E_1$) between the two jobs, the higher will be the present value of the net benefits (V_p), and the more likely it will be that an individual will migrate.

THE DETERMINANTS OF MIGRATION: A CLOSER LOOK

Various factors besides the annual earnings differential ($E_2 - E_1$) influence the discounted present value of the total earnings and costs streams in equation (9-1) and thereby affect the present value of the net benefits and the decision to migrate. These factors or ***determinants of migration*** include age, family circumstances, education, distance, and unemployment.

Age

Migration studies consistently find that age is a major factor determining the probability of migration. *All else being equal, the older that a person is, the less likely he or she is to migrate.* There are several reasons for this, each having to do with reducing the gain in net earnings from migrating or increasing the costs of moving.

First, older migrants have fewer years to recoup their investment costs. Given a specific cost of migrating, the shorter the time period one has to gain the annual earnings advantage, the smaller the V_p term in equation (9-1). A young person may view a relatively small wage differential to be significant over his or her lifetime; a person who is 2 or 3 years away from retirement is not likely to incur migration costs to achieve this same short-lived annual differential.

Second, older people tend to have higher levels of human capital that are specific to their present employers. Age, length of time on a job (job tenure), and annual wages are all positively correlated. The longer a person's job tenure, the greater the amount of on-the-job training and employer-financed investment of a specific variety he or she is likely to have. This human capital, by definition, is *not* transferable to other jobs (Chapter 4). Thus, the wage one receives after several years of job tenure partially reflects a return on a specific investment in human capital and is likely to be higher than the wage obtainable elsewhere. Regardless of the length of time available to recoup the investment costs, older people may be less likely to migrate.[2]

The cost of moving is a third age-related consideration affecting migration. Older people often have higher migration costs than younger people. For example, a young person may be able to transport possessions across the country in a 4-by-8-foot U-Haul trailer, whereas an older person may need to hire a professional mover who uses a moving van. Or as another example, a younger person who migrates may lose little seniority or future pension benefits, while an older person may incur very large costs of this type.[3] Also, the psychic costs of migration may rise with age. Older people are more likely than younger workers to have roots in their present communities, children in the local school systems, and an extensive network of workplace friends. The higher these net psychic costs—Z in equation (9-1)—the lower the value of V_p and the less likely one is to migrate.

Finally, the inverse relationship between age and migration exists partially because people are most mobile after completing lengthy investments in human capital. Many people begin "job shopping" at the end of high school—ages 18 to 19—which may result in geographic moves.[4] Migration is even more pronounced for college graduates who enter regional and national labor markets. It therefore is not surprising that the peak age for labor migration in the United States is 23.

Family Factors

The potential costs of migrating multiply as family size increases. Therefore, we would expect married workers to have less tendency to migrate than single people, other factors such as age and education being constant. Furthermore, it seems logical to expect higher migration rates for married workers whose spouses either do not work or work at low pay. If both spouses earn a high wage, the family's cost in forgoing income during the move will be high; and when combined with the possibility that one spouse will not find a job in the destination location, this cost reduces the net present value

[2]Jacob Mincer and Boyan Jovanovic, "Labor Mobility and Wages," in Sherwin Rosen (ed.), *Studies in Labor Markets* (Chicago: University of Chicago Press, 1981), pp. 21–63. There are exceptions to this generalization, however. Charles Mueller found that for people who have *high* incomes, the longer one's job tenure, the *greater* the likelihood of migration. "In the high-paying jobs, it may be that either better opportunities lie with firms other than one's own as experience accumulates or the tendency of job transfer is greater as one's own tenure with a firm increases." See Charles F. Mueller, op. cit., p. 143. Also see Ann P. Bartel, "The Migration Decision: What Role Does Job Mobility Play?" *American Economic Review*, December 1979, pp. 775–786.

[3]For evidence that the prospect of leaving behind an employer-provided pension constitutes a high cost of changing jobs, see Steven Allen, Robert Clark, and Ann McDermed, "Pensions, Bonding, and Lifetime Jobs," *Journal of Human Resources*, Summer 1993, pp. 463–481.

[4]William Johnson, "A Theory of Job Shopping," *Quarterly Journal of Economics*, May 1978, pp. 261–278.

to the family from migration. Finally, the presence of school-age children can be expected to reduce the likelihood of migration. The parents and children may conclude that the psychic costs associated with the move are too great relative to the expected monetary gain.

These particular predictions from the human capital model are borne out by empirical evidence. Mincer has found that (1) unmarried persons are more likely to move; (2) the wife's employment inhibits family migration; (3) the longer the wife's tenure, the less likely a family will migrate; and (4) the presence of school-age children in the family reduces migration.[5]

Education

Within age groupings, the level of educational attainment beyond high school is a major predictor of how likely one is to migrate within the United States. *The higher one's educational attainment, all else being equal, the more likely it is that one will migrate.*[6] Several reasons have been offered for this relationship. College graduates and those with postgraduate training—MBAs, Ph.D.s, lawyers, CPAs—search for employment in regional and national labor markets in which employers seek qualified employees. These markets often have substantial job information and participants who possess excellent ability to analyze and assess the available information. The potential for economic gain from migration also may be increased by the heterogeneity of many of the workers and positions (Chapter 8).[7] Union wage scales and minimum-wage rates reduce wage differentials within occupations not requiring college training. On the other hand, the wide disparities of pay for professional and managerial employees provide more opportunity to move to jobs entailing greater responsibility and pay. Less-specialized workers may have a greater opportunity to increase their earnings through *occupational* mobility within their present locale (box II in Figure 9-1). That route may not be open to highly specialized workers, who therefore may use *geographic* migration to achieve gains in earnings.

Other factors are also at work here. College-educated workers are more apt to get transferred to new geographic locations and, if not transferred, are more likely than those with fewer years of schooling to have new jobs already in place upon migrating. Thus, the probability of their failing to find a job once they move to the new area is zero, and the expected earnings gain over their lifetimes is increased. Finally, people who have college degrees may attach fewer psychic costs Z to leaving their hometowns. Many college students initially migrate to new areas to attend school in the first

[5]Jacob Mincer, "Family Migration Decisions," *Journal of Political Economy,* October 1978, pp. 749–774. Julie DaVanzo also found that the labor force participation by wives has a negative effect on mobility. The higher the *percentage* of total family income earned by the wife, however, the greater the likelihood of family migration. See *Why Families Move: A Model of the Geographic Mobility of Married Couples.* Monograph 48, Employment and Training Administration, U.S. Department of Labor, 1977.

[6]Larry H. Long, "Migration Differentials by Education and Occupation: Trends and Variations," *Demography,* May 1973, p. 245.

[7]For evidence that regional variations in the returns to schooling are important determinants of migration flows among skilled workers, see George J. Borjas, Stephen G. Bronars, and Stephen J. Trejo, "Self-Selection and Internal Migration in the United States," *Journal of Urban Economics,* September 1992, pp. 159–185.

place, and this experience may make it easier for them to move again when new economic opportunities are present. Or perhaps the fact that these people moved geographically to attend college indicates that they have lower innate psychic costs of or stronger preferences for migration than those who did not make that same choice initially. For whatever reasons, studies show that people who move once are more inclined to migrate again.

Distance

The probability of migrating varies inversely with the distance a person must move. The greater the distance, the less information a potential migrant is likely to possess about the job opportunities available. Also, transportation costs usually increase with distance. Finally, the longer the physical distance of the move, the more probable it is that psychic costs will be substantial. With respect to such costs, it is one matter to move across town, another to move to a nearby state, and still another to migrate across the country or to another nation. Psychic costs may be partially reduced, but not necessarily eliminated, by following "beaten paths" and congregating in specific neighborhoods within the destination area. Migrants often follow the routes previously taken by family, friends, and relatives. These earlier migrants ease the transition for those who follow by providing job information, employment contacts, temporary living quarters, and cultural continuity. But the longer the distance of the move, the less available the information about wage disparities and the greater the psychic cost. Thus, the likelihood is less that one will migrate.[8]

Unemployment Rates

On the basis of the human capital model, high unemployment rates in an "origin" location should increase the net benefits from migrating and *push* workers away. That is, an unemployed person must assess the probability of gaining employment in the *origin* location relative to the probability of gaining employment at the potential *destination.* Although evidence on this matter is surprisingly mixed, studies support the following generalizations: (1) *Families headed by unemployed persons are more likely to migrate than others, and* (2) *the rate of unemployment at the origin positively affects out-migration.*[9] Such out-migration may not always be as great as we might expect, however, when the decision makers are mainly older and less-educated workers or when unemployment compensation and other income transfers are relatively high.

Does the unemployment rate at the possible destination influence the migration decision by affecting the probability of getting employment and therefore increasing the *expected value* of discounted net benefits? No definitive conclusion can be reached on this question. For one thing, the general unemployment rate does not always reflect

[8]Henry W. Herzog, Jr., and Alan M. Schlottmann, "Labor Force Migration and Allocative Efficiency in the United States: The Roles of Information and Psychic Costs," *Economic Inquiry,* July 1981, pp. 459–475. Also see Bernt Bratsberg, "Legal versus Illegal U.S. Immigration and Source Country Characteristics," *Southern Economic Journal,* January 1995, pp. 715–727.

[9]See DaVanzo, op. cit.; and DaVanzo, "Does Unemployment Affect Migration?—Evidence from Micro Data," *Review of Economics and Statistics,* November 1978, pp. 32–37.

the probability that a specific *individual* will find employment. Also, in-migration itself can increase unemployment rates at the destination. Nevertheless, one generalization is possible: Currently unemployed workers tend to migrate to destinations with lower-than-average unemployment rates.

Other Factors

Many other factors may influence migration, and we list only a few of them here. First, studies show that home ownership deters migration.[10] Second, occupational licensure reduces migration by impeding the flow of licensed practitioners among states having differing licensing requirements.[11] Third, state and local government policies may influence labor migration. Examples: (1) High personal tax rates that reduce disposable income may impede migration to the high-tax area, (2) high levels of per capita government spending on services may increase in-migration, and (3) government policies that attract new industries are likely to result in greater migration to a particular locale. Fourth, federal defense contracts appear to shift labor regionally in the United States.[12] Fifth, in the case of international migration, the language spoken at the destination is a prime factor affecting mobility. Immigration quotas and emigration prohibitions also greatly influence international migration. Additionally, many international migrants are pushed from their present places of residence by political repression and war. Sixth, union membership may be a determining factor. By providing workers with a voice with which to change undesirable working conditions, unions may reduce voluntary "exits" and reduce mobility and migration (Chapter 11). Or from a different perspective, perhaps the wage gains that unions secure for workers reduce the incentive for members to migrate to new jobs. Seventh, some scholars suggest that people increasingly have placed a high priority on environmental quality and climate in their migration decisions.[13] Although extremely diverse, these factors share a common feature: They all influence V_p in equation (9-1) by affecting the expected gains from migrating, the expected costs, or some combination of each.[14]

THE CONSEQUENCES OF MIGRATION

The consequences of domestic and international migration have several dimensions. Initially, we will examine the individual gains from migration by asking: What is the return on this form of investment in human capital? We then will analyze the increased

[10] DaVanzo, op. cit.

[11] For the effect of occupational licensure on the mobility of lawyers, see B. Peter Pashigian, "Occupational Licensing and the Interstate Mobility of Professionals," *Journal of Law and Economics,* April 1979, pp. 1–26.

[12] Philip L. Rones, "Moving to the Sun: Regional Job Growth, 1968–1978," *Monthly Labor Review,* March 1980, p. 15.

[13] Larry H. Long and Kristen A. Hansen, "Reasons for Interstate Migration," *Current Population Reports, Special Studies,* no. 81, Bureau of the Census, March 1979, p. 78. Also see Philip E. Graves, "Migration and Climate," *Journal of Regional Science,* 1980, pp. 227–237.

[14] William J. Kahley provides a very readable summary of the various factors affecting migration in his "Population Migration in the United States: A Survey of Research," *Economic Review* (Federal Reserve Bank of Atlanta), January–February 1991, pp. 12–21.

output accruing to society from migration. There we will also attempt to sort out the distribution of net gains. Who benefits? Who loses?

Personal Gains

People expect to increase their lifetime utility when they *voluntarily* decide to migrate from one area to another. One interesting way to conceptualize this expected gain is to ask: What amount of money would we have to pay to entice the migrant to reject the job opportunity? This dollar amount is an estimate of the migrant's expected gain from moving to the new location.

Empirical Evidence Empirical studies confirm that migration increases the lifetime earnings of the average mover.[15] The estimated rate of return is similar to that on other forms of investment in human capital, meaning it generally lies in the 10 to 15 percent range.

Caveats At least five cautions or complications must be mentioned when generalizing about rates of return to migration.

1 Uncertainty and Imperfect Information Migration decisions are based on *expected* net benefits, and most are made under circumstances of uncertainty and imperfect information. High *average* rates of return do not imply positive returns for *all* migrants. In many instances the expected gain from migration simply does not materialize—the anticipated job is not found at the destination, the living costs are higher in the new area than anticipated, the psychic costs of being away from family and friends are greater than expected, the anticipated raises and promotions are not forthcoming. Thus, there are major *backflows* in migration patterns.[16] Although this return migration is costly to those involved, it does perform a useful economic function: It increases the availability of information about the destination to other potential migrants, enabling them to assess better the benefits and costs of moving. This makes subsequent migration more efficient.

Also, not all return migration indicates an unprofitable investment in human capital. Some people temporarily migrate to accumulate wealth or enhance their stock of human capital via on-the-job training or after-work education. Most return to their original locations on reaching their financial or human capital goals. For example, most of those who built the Alaskan pipeline returned to the lower 48 states after completion of their task. Also, many illegal aliens who cross the U.S.–Mexican border return to Mexico.[17]

[15]For example, see John B. Lansing and J. N. Morgan, "The Effect of Geographical Mobility on Income," *Journal of Human Resources,* Fall 1967, pp. 475–494. For a more recent article on this subject see Stephen C. Farber, "Post-Migration Earnings Profiles: An Application of Human Capital and Job Search Models," *Southern Economic Journal,* January 1983, pp. 693–705.

[16]Among foreign-born immigrants, return migration is more likely among those who do not perform well in the U.S. labor market. See George J. Borjas, "Immigrant and Emigrant Earnings: A Longitudinal Study," *Economic Inquiry,* January 1989, pp. 21–37. Also see George J. Borjas and Bernt Bratsberg, "Who Leaves? The Outmigration of the Foreign-Born," *Review of Economics and Statistics,* February 1996, pp. 165–176.

[17]Michael J. Piore, *Birds of Passage: Migrant Labor and Industrial Societies* (Cambridge: Cambridge University Press, 1979), pp. 149–154.

2 Timing of Earnings Gains Lifetime income gains from migration do not necessarily mean that migrants receive gains from earnings during the first few postmigration years. Studies show that some migrants experience lower than previous earnings in the first few years after moving. These reductions, however, tend to be followed by more than commensurate increases in earnings in later years. Stated differently, some migrants accept a short-term postmigration reduction in earnings as an investment cost for faster rate of growth of future earnings.

3 Earnings Disparities Increases in lifetime earnings do not imply that migrants necessarily will receive annual earnings equal to those received by people already at the destination. The skills that migrants possess are not always perfectly transferable between regions (because of occupational licensure), between employers (because of specific training), or between nations (because of language and other factors). This lack of ***skill transferability*** may mean that migrants—although perhaps improving their own wage—may be paid less than similarly trained, educated, and employed workers at the destination. For example, McManus has found that differences in English language skills explain a large portion of differences in earnings among U.S. ethnic groups. His research indicates that the cost of English deficiency for most immigrant groups is quite large. The cost of English deficiency, however, appears to be ethnically and occupationally specific. Kossoudji, for example, finds that Hispanics have a higher cost of English language deficiency than Asians at every skill level.[18] A recent study finds that immigrants who have a lesser incentive to learn English—for example, those who anticipate returning to their home country or who live in an area where their native language is used extensively—are less likely to learn the new language.[19]

On the other hand, migration tends to be characterized by ***self-selection.*** Because some migrants choose to move while others with similar skills do not, it is possible that the former have greater motivation for personal economic achievement and greater willingness to sacrifice current consumption for higher levels of later consumption. As Chiswick has pointed out:

> Such self-selected immigrants would tend to have higher earnings than the native born in the destination, if it were not for the disadvantage of being foreign born. Combining the [negative] effects of skill transferability and favorable self-selection suggests that the earnings of the foreign born may eventually equal and then surpass those of the native born.[20]

Do the earnings of immigrants, in fact, eventually exceed those of native-born Americans? For earlier immigrants, Chiswick found that, given equal amounts of education and premigration labor experience, male immigrants on average achieved

[18]Walter S. McManus, "Labor Market Assimilation of Immigrants: The Importance of Language Skills," *Contemporary Policy Issues,* Spring 1985, pp. 77–89; and Sherrie A. Kossoudji, "English Language Ability and the Labor Market Opportunities of Hispanic and East Asian Immigrant Men," *Journal of Labor Economics,* April 1988, pp. 205–228. Also see, Geoffrey Carliner, "The Language Ability of U.S. Immigrants: Assimilation and Cohort Effects," National Bureau of Economic Research Working Paper No. 5222, August 1995.

[19]Barry R. Chiswick and Paul W. Miller, "The Endogeneity between Language and Earnings: International Analyses," *Journal of Labor Economics,* April 1995, pp. 246–288.

[20]Barry R. Chiswick, "Immigrant Earning Patterns by Sex, Race, and Ethnic Groupings," *Monthly Labor Review,* October 1980, p. 22.

earnings parity with their native-born cohorts after 11 to 15 years and after that had higher earnings by as much as 5 percent.[21] However, recent studies have discovered that immigrants arriving in the United States during the second half of the 1970s and the 1980s were on average less skilled than previous immigrants. In addition, the skill disadvantage of new immigrants was larger in the 1980s than in the 1970s. The earnings of these more recent immigrants remain 12 to 20 percent below those of comparable native-born workers. Borjas concludes that these newer immigrants are not likely to achieve wage parity with native workers, even after several decades.[22]

Internal migrants within the United States—as distinct from immigrants from abroad—rather quickly assimilate in their new locales. A recent study indicates that young internal migrants initially earn less than similar natives in the area to which they migrate, but this wage differential disappears within a few years. The initial wage disadvantage is greater the longer the distance moved and the poorer the economic conditions in the destination locale.[23]

4 Earnings of Spouses A gain in family earnings from migration does not necessarily mean a gain in earnings for both working spouses. On the average, migration increases the earnings of husbands but tends to reduce the earnings for wives, at least over the following 5-year period.[24] Apparently the higher average earnings and stronger labor force attachment of husbands relative to that of wives entices families to migrate in response to improved earnings for the husband. These moves, on the average, increase the family's income; but they also reduce either the wife's incentive to work (income effect), her market opportunities, or some combination of the two.

5 Wage Reductions from Job Losses A positive rate of return to migration does not necessarily imply higher earnings than would have accrued had past wage rates continued to be earned. Some migrants are pushed into moving by job loss or political repression. For these people job mobility is not totally voluntary. For example, suppose that Smith, a 50-year-old Ohio steelworker, earns $18 an hour in wages and fringe benefits, has children in college, and has lived all of his life in the same locale. If Smith is displaced from his job because of a factory shutdown, exhausts his unemployment benefits, and eventually finds a job at $12 an hour in a new occupation in the Southwest, can we conclude that migration enhanced his well-being? Considerable misunderstanding exists on this very point. The job loss and its consequences for Smith and his

[21]Ibid., p. 23. Also see Chiswick's "The Effect of Americanization of Foreign-Born Men," *Journal of Political Economy,* October 1978, pp. 897–921; and James Long, "The Effect of Americanization on Earnings: Some Evidence for Women," *Journal of Political Economy,* June 1980, pp. 620–629.

[22]George J. Borjas, *Friends or Strangers: The Impact of Immigrants on the U.S. Economy* (New York: Basic Books, 1990), chap. 6; and George J. Borjas, "Assimilation and Changes in Cohort Quality Revisited: What Happened to Immigrant Earnings in the 1980s?" *Journal of Labor Economics,* April 1995, pp. 201–245. However, some evidence exists that the skill of new immigrants increased during the late 1980s. See Edward Funkhouser and Stephen J. Trejo, "The Labor Market Skills of Recent Male Immigrants: Evidence from the Current Population Survey," *Industrial and Labor Relations Review,* July 1995, pp. 792–811.

[23]George J. Borjas, Stephen G. Bonars, and Stephen J. Trejo, "Assimilation and the Earnings of Young Internal Migrants," *Review of Economics and Statistics,* February 1992, pp. 170–175.

[24]For example, see Solomon Polachek and Francis Horvath, "A Life Cycle Approach to Migration," in Ronald G. Ehrenberg (ed.), *Research in Labor Economics* (Greenwich, CN: JAI Press, 1971), pp. 103–149; and Stephen Sandell, "Women and the Economics of Migration," *Review of Economics and Statistics,* November 1977, p. 410.

family are indeed severe in that income from work falls to zero. But once this event occurs, Smith faces a new set of prospective earnings streams over the remainder of his work life. For illustrative purposes, let's assume that the highest-paying job he can find in his present locale is at $8 an hour. By migrating to the Southwest where he can earn $12 an hour, Smith does increase his lifetime earnings, other things being equal, even though these earnings are considerably lower than those that would have accrued in the absence of the job loss. Migration increases lifetime earnings for most movers; it does not always increase earnings above levels that existed prior to a job loss.

Wage Narrowing and Efficiency Gains

Economic efficiency exists when a nation achieves the greatest possible real domestic output or income from its available land, labor, capital, and entrepreneurial resources. Labor mobility is crucial in approaching this goal. To illustrate, let's suppose, first, that there are only two labor markets, each perfectly competitive and each situated in a different geographic location. Second, suppose that each labor market contains a fixed number of workers and there is no unemployment in either market. Third, we assume that nonwage job amenities and locational attributes are the same in both areas. A fourth assumption is that capital is immobile. Finally, we assume that workers possess perfect information about wages and working conditions in both markets and that migration between the two markets is costless.

Numerical Illustration Columns 1_A and 2_A in Table 9-1 display the demand for labor in market A, while columns 1_B and 2_B show it for B. Notice that the wages are given in *annual* terms and that, because of our assumption of perfect competition in the product and labor markets, these wages equal the value of the marginal product

TABLE 9-1 ALLOCATIVE EFFICIENCY: THE ROLE OF LABOR MOBILITY

Labor market A			Labor market B		
(1_A) Workers	(2_A) VMP_A Annual wage	(3_A) VTP_A	(1_B) Workers	(2_B) VMP_B Annual wage	(3_B) VTP_B
1	$25,000	$ 25,000	1	$21,000	$ 21,000
2	23,000	48,000	2	19,000	40,000
3	21,000	69,000	3	17,000	57,000
4	19,000	88,000	4	15,000	72,000
5	17,000	105,000	5	13,000	85,000
6	15,000	120,000	6	11,000	96,000
7	13,000	133,000	7	9,000	105,000
8	11,000	144,000	8	7,000	112,000
9	9,000	153,000	9	5,000	117,000
10	7,000	160,000	10	3,000	120,000

(VMP) of labor.[25] Columns 3_A and 3_B cumulate the VMP data to show the value of the total product (VTP) associated with each level of employment. Also, notice that the VMP is greater for each labor input in labor market A than in B. This difference in the strength of labor demand is not crucial to our analysis but presumably arises from a greater capital and technological endowment in A than in B, so that the marginal product of labor is higher in market A.

Now suppose that initially, two workers are employed in market A and each earns \$23,000 annually (boxed figure), while eight workers, earning \$7,000 apiece, are working in B (boxed figure). Next, we relax the assumption that these are separate markets and observe that given our other assumptions, workers in B will migrate to labor market A in pursuit of higher earnings.

What will happen to annual earnings in the respective markets as this migration occurs? The number of workers in A will increase, causing the market wage there to fall. In region B, the corresponding decline in the quantity of labor will increase the equilibrium wage. Migration will continue until the wage advantage in A is totally eliminated. This occurs in Table 9-1 at \$15,000 (circled data). At this annual wage, employers in the highly capital-endowed region A will hire six workers, while those in the less-endowed area B will hire four workers. To generalize: *Assuming perfect competition, costless information, and costless migration, market wages will equal the value of the marginal product of labor* (W = VMP), *and labor will relocate until* VMP*s are equal in all labor markets* ($VMP_A = VMP_B$).

Does this migration of labor enhance the total value of output in our hypothetical nation? To determine the answer, again note Table 9-1, columns 3_A and 3_B. Before migration, the value of the total product (VTP) was \$48,000 in labor market A and \$112,000 in B. Thus, the combined premigration VTP was \$160,000 (= \$48,000 + \$112,000). And after migration? A glance at the table shows it to be \$192,000. The six workers in A produce a combined output valued at \$120,000, while the four workers in B produce \$72,000. In this simple model, then, we observe that wage differentials create an incentive for labor to move from one market to another. This mobility, or migration, equalizes wages and results in allocative efficiency [equation (6-1)]; it generates the highest possible value of total output from the available resources.

Graphic Portrayal We can easily show graphically both the wage narrowing and the ***efficiency gains from migration*** that arise. For variety and to extend our focus, let's now employ an international, rather than an interregional, example. Figure 9-2(a) shows the demand for labor in the United States, and graph (b) portrays the labor demand curve for Mexico.

Suppose that the employment and wage levels in the United States and Mexico are $0e$, W_u, and $0l$, W_m, respectively. Because information is assumed to be perfect and migration is assumed to be costless, labor will flow from Mexico to the United States until the equilibrium wage of W_e is achieved in each nation. Notice the positive efficiency gains accruing to the "world" from this migration. The United States *gains* domestic output equal to the area *ebcf* in graph (a), and Mexico *loses* domestic output equiva-

[25]If this is not clear, you may want to review the discussion pertinent to Table 5-2.

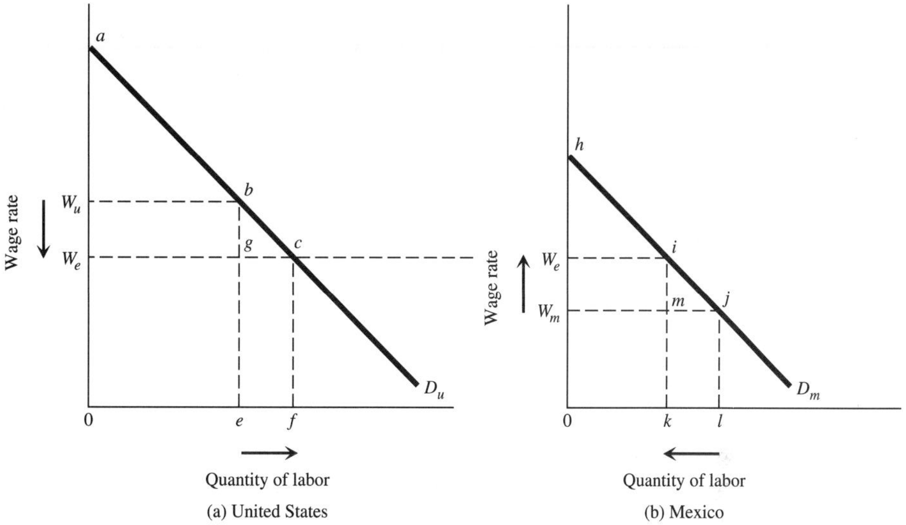

FIGURE 9-2 **THE EFFICIENCY GAINS FROM MIGRATION**
The migration of labor from low-wage Mexico (b) to high-wage United States (a) will increase the domestic output and reduce the average wage rate in the United States and produce the opposite effects in Mexico. The output gain of *ebcf* in the United States exceeds the loss of *kijl* in Mexico; therefore, the net value of the combined outputs from the two nations rises.

lent to the area *kijl* in graph (b). Because the U.S. gain exceeds the Mexican loss, the total value of the combined output produced by the two nations rises. Stated differently, the sum of the areas 0*acf* in graph (a) and 0*hik* in (b) exceeds the premigration areas 0*abe* plus 0*hjl*. Conclusion? Given our assumptions, wage-induced labor migration—whether internal or international—increases the total income and output in the *combined* origin and destination. Quite simply, migration enables a larger total real output to be achieved from a given available amount of resources.

External Effects

The generalization drawn from Table 9-1 and Figure 9-2 raises an important question: If the efficiency gains from migration are so direct and evident, why do so many people in origin and destination locales view migration negatively? Although numerous noneconomic factors are also at work, much of the explanation is economic in character and can be understood by analyzing ***migration externalities,*** or third-party effects. These externalities can be ***"real"*** or ***"pecuniary"*** and either positive or negative.

1 Real Negative Externalities Real negative externalities are effects of private actions spilling over to third parties and creating misallocations of resources (economic inefficiency). An example is water pollution. If a firm produces a product and in the process pollutes a river used by downstream municipalities, recreational enthusiasts, and industries, then the firm fails to cover all the costs of its actions. The price of the firm's product is too low, more resources are devoted to producing this output than is socially optimal, and downstream users incur costs that absorb further resources. In some circumstances mass migration generates similar negative spillovers. As Thurow points out:

> Private incomes may increase enough to more than make up for the costs of moving, but the social costs of accommodating people in a crowded urban area may exceed the net private gain. More public services must be provided, and congestion may increase. Excess capacity, and hence waste, may develop in the production of social services (schools, etc.) in areas from which people are moving, and new investment in social services may be needed in areas to which they are moving.[26]

Put simply, where negative externalities from migration are substantial and diffuse, the private gains to migrants and employers will overstate the net gain to society. Under these circumstances, more migration will occur than is consistent with an optimal allocation of society's resources. For example, this outcome occasionally occurs when substantial migration to a "boom town" creates increases in congestion, crime, and other external costs.

2 Pecuniary Externalities: Income Redistribution Most of the expressed opposition to emigration and immigration, however, arises not from these potential real externalities but rather from numerous pecuniary—or financial—ones. *Pecuniary externalities may be defined as acts that redistribute income among individuals and groups.* Such redistributive effects typically give rise to active resistance on the part of adversely affected groups and engender heated political debate. Careful analysis of Figure 9-2 reveals several redistributive impacts of migration.

Losses in the Origin Nation Although immigration from Mexico to the United States *increases* the total product in the United States, it *reduces* it in Mexico. Stated more generally, migration increases the value of the total product produced in the combined economies of the origin and destination; but under most conditions these gains accrue to the destination. There are exceptions, of course. As an extreme example, if the *kl* workers who migrate to the United States are unemployable (value of marginal product = 0), then no increased output is forthcoming, and the destination nation will be the loser by virtue of having to support the migrants. Conversely, the origin nation will gain because its fixed domestic output will be shared among fewer people. Also, many migrants save a large portion of their wages and send these funds home or bring them back as a lump sum at the end of their temporary stay. In these cases the origin nation captures a share of the efficiency gains. But when migration is permanent, is in response to higher wages in the destination nation, and involves migrants who leave jobs in the origin nation, the destination nation experiences an increase in national income while the origin nation loses. These distributional impacts partially explain why

[26] Lester C. Thurow, *Investment in Human Capital* (Belmont, CA: Wadsworth Publishing Company, 1970), p. 33.

"brain drains"—the emigration of highly skilled workers—are a source of economic concern for some nations of the world.[27]

Reduced Wage Income to Native Workers A second income distribution consequence of migration is also evident from Figure 9-2. Immigration increases the supply of labor in the United States from $0e$ to $0f$, driving down the average wage rate from W_u to W_e and reducing the wage income to native U.S. workers from $0W_ube$ to $0W_ege$. Notice that immigration may or may not increase the total wage income in the United States: That depends on the elasticity of labor demand (Figure 5-8). It is clear, however, that the influx of the *ef* workers reduces the wage income accruing to the $0e$ native U.S. workers. In Mexico the reduction in labor supply *increases* the wage rate (W_e rather than W_m) for those who remain. Another generalization thus emerges: Immigration is likely to be opposed by laborers in the destination region or nation, while workers in the place of origin are likely to support emigration.

The above generalization, however, must be accompanied by an important caution relating to our distinction made in Chapter 5 between gross substitutes and gross complements. Immigrants to the United States are *gross substitutes* (substitution effect > output effect) for some labor market groups, reducing the labor demand and wages for these groups. On the other hand, the immigrants are *gross complements* (output effect > substitution effect) for other domestic workers, causing labor demand and wages for these groups to rise. Therefore, not all groups of workers are equally affected by immigration. Overall, a survey of empirical studies concludes that a 10 percent increase in the fraction of immigrants creates at most a 1 percent decrease in the wages of native workers.[28] Immigrants appear to have the largest impact on the wages of high school dropouts and other immigrants.[29]

In this regard, Borjas has shown through an analysis of 1980 census data that immigrants do *not* substantially affect the earnings of *native-born* workers, but instead reduce the earnings of *natives who themselves were immigrants.*[30]

Gains to Owners of Capital A third potential for opposition to migration by some groups in origin and destination locales arises from the impact of migration on labor income relative to capital income. We again return to Figure 9-2, graph (a). Immigration

[27]Brain drains also are viewed negatively because the origin nation loses the return on investments in human capital that it may have either paid for in full or partially subsidized. For a theoretical discussion of brain drains, see Viem Kevok and Hayne Leland, "An Economic Model of the Brain Drain," *American Economic Review,* March 1982, pp. 91–100.

[28]Rachel M. Friedberg and Jennifer Hunt, "The Impact of Immigrants on Host Country Wages, Employment and Growth," *Journal of Economic Perspectives,* Spring 1995, pp. 23–44. For a study concluding that the overall impact of immigration on national income is minimal, see George J. Borjas, "The Economic Benefits from Immigration," *Journal of Economic Perspectives,* Spring 1995, pp. 3–22. Also, see Timothy J. Hatton and Jeffrey G. Williamson, "The Impact of Immigration on American Labor Markets Prior to Quotas," National Bureau of Economic Research Working Paper No. 5185, July 1995.

[29]See George J. Borjas, Richard B. Freeman, and Lawrence Katz, "Searching for the Effect of Immigration on the Labor Market," *American Economic Review,* May 1996, pp. 246–251.

[30]George J. Borjas, "Immigrants, Minorities, and Labor Market Competition," *Industrial and Labor Relations Review,* April 1987, pp. 382–392.

increases the total nonimmigrant national income in the United States by the triangle *gbc*. To see why, note that the value of the total product rises from 0*abe* to 0*acf* in the United States. Of the total gain (*ebcf*), migrants receive *egcf*. This leaves triangle *gbc* as the increase in total nonimmigrant income. Now recall that in the previous paragraph we concluded that the wage bill to native U.S. workers falls. So who receives the gain that native workers lose? The answer, of course, is U.S. businesses. They gain area W_eW_ubg at the expense of native U.S. workers and also obtain the added product shown by the triangle *gbc*. Thus, this simple model suggests that "business interests" gain added income from immigration—at least in the short run—and conversely actually lose income when substantial out-migration occurs. This helps explain why some U.S. businesses historically have recruited foreign workers to come to the United States. For example, Chinese workers were recruited to help build the railroads, and migrant agricultural workers presently are recruited to help harvest U.S. crops and produce.

The conclusion that businesses gain from migration at the expense of domestic workers must be tempered by the fact that this is a short-run, partial-equilibrium model. The theoretical possibilities become more complicated when a long-run, general-equilibrium approach is used and when various assumptions are relaxed. For example, the new migrants are likely to spend portions of their earnings in the United States. This will increase the demand for many types of labor and may increase wages for workers who are not close substitutes in production for the specific immigrant labor. Additionally, the gain in business income relative to the stock of U.S. capital increases the rate of return on capital. This increase tends to raise domestic investment spending and consequently enlarges the stock of U.S. capital. Under normal production conditions, the marginal product of labor therefore will rise and labor demand will increase. Thus, in the long run, part of the negative impact of immigration on the wage rate may be lessened or eliminated. But the basic point is clear: Differing views on the desirability of open migration policies, illegal-alien problems, and brain drains can partially be understood in the context of the actual and perceived redistributional effects of migration.

Fiscal Impacts One final distributional outcome merits discussion. An inflow of immigrants can affect the distribution of disposable income in a destination nation or area through its effect on transfer payments and tax collections. If the immigrants to the United States in Figure 9-2 are highly educated and skilled professionals, for example, we would expect little opposition from the general U.S. public. These workers most probably will be net taxpayers and not major recipients of cash and in-kind transfer payments. However, if the immigrants are illiterate, low-skilled individuals who are not likely to find permanent employment in the United States, then this influx may necessitate increased government spending on transfer payments and social service programs. As a consequence, this specific immigration may produce higher taxes for U.S. citizens, lower average transfer payments to native low-income residents, or some combination of each. Thus, taxpayers and low-income residents in the United States may oppose the migration. A real externality might even result from the increased taxes and transfers through a disincentive impact on labor supply (Chapters 2 and 12). This rests on the assumption, of course, that the immigrants are eligible for the transfer programs and extensively use them.

Historically, the immigrant population in the United States was less likely than the native population to receive welfare benefits.[31] But welfare participation by immigrants has greatly increased since the late 1970s and is now greater for immigrants than for natives. Borjas and Trejo attribute this turnabout to the changing mix of immigrants, with fewer skilled immigrants coming from European countries and many unskilled immigrants arriving from Asia and Latin America.[32]

QUICK REVIEW 9-1

- Occupational mobility involves workers changing occupations; geographic mobility involves workers moving to jobs in another city, state, or nation.
- The decision to move geographically can be viewed through the investment in human capital framework; a worker will move when the net present value of migration, V_p, is positive.
- Along with the annual earnings differential, important determinants of migration include age, family factors, education, distance, and unemployment rates.
- Migration produces earnings gains for movers, wage narrowing among regions, and real output gains for society. Generally, migration reduces wage income to native workers with skills similar to those of the immigrants and increases the income of owners of capital.

Your Turn: Suppose the E_2 and N values in the net present value equation (equation 9-1) fall while the Z value rises. What will happen to V_p and the likelihood of migration? (Answer: See page 626.)

CAPITAL AND PRODUCT FLOWS

Table 9-1 and Figure 9-2 overstate the probable extent of labor migration between two regions or nations for reasons other than those associated with the costs of obtaining information and migrating. Through differing rates of investment capital itself is mobile in the long run. Also, products made in one locale are sold in many others. These facts have considerable significance for labor migration.

[31]Francine Blau, "The Use of Transfer Payments for Immigrants," *Industrial and Labor Relations Review,* January 1984, pp. 222–239; and Julian L. Simon, "Immigrants, Taxes, and Welfare in the United States," *Population Development Review,* March 1984, pp. 55–69.

[32]Borjas, *Friends or Strangers,* chap. 9. Also relevant is George J. Borjas and Stephen J. Trejo, "Immigrant Participation in the Welfare System," *Industrial and Labor Relations Review,* January 1991, pp. 195–211; George J. Borjas and Lynette Hilton, "Immigration and the Welfare State: Immigrant Participation in Means-Tested Entitlement Programs," *Quarterly Journal of Economics,* May 1996, pp. 575–604; and Janet Currie, "Do Children of Immigrants Make Differential Use of Public Health Insurance?" National Bureau of Economic Research Working Paper No. 5388, December 1995.

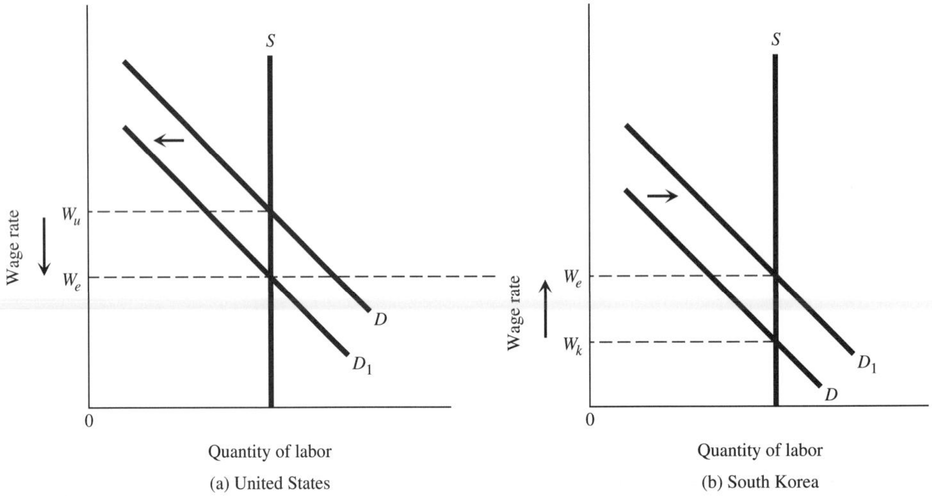

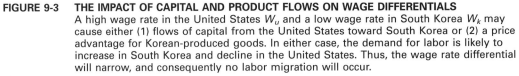

FIGURE 9-3 **THE IMPACT OF CAPITAL AND PRODUCT FLOWS ON WAGE DIFFERENTIALS**
A high wage rate in the United States W_u and a low wage rate in South Korea W_k may cause either (1) flows of capital from the United States toward South Korea or (2) a price advantage for Korean-produced goods. In either case, the demand for labor is likely to increase in South Korea and decline in the United States. Thus, the wage rate differential will narrow, and consequently no labor migration will occur.

Capital Flows

The impacts of ***capital mobility*** and interregional or international trade on wage differentials and therefore on labor migration are illustrated in Figure 9-3. Here, we use the United States and South Korea in a simplified example. Notice initially that given the labor demand curves D in each nation, wages in the United States W_u exceed those in South Korea W_k. Our previous analysis implied that this wage differential would induce Korean workers to migrate to the United States. But other forces are also at work. The lower Korean wage rate might cause some U.S. producers to abandon production facilities in the United States and construct new facilities in Korea. We would expect this increase in capital in Korea to increase the marginal product and value of marginal product of labor there. The labor demand curve therefore would shift outward, say to D_1 as shown in graph (b) of Figure 9-3. Conversely, the lower stock of capital in the United States would reduce labor demand from D to D_1 here (graph a).

The increase in labor demand from D to D_1 in South Korea raises the market wage from W_k to W_e. In the United States the decline in demand from D to D_1 lowers the wage from W_u to W_e. Capital mobility thus has removed the wage disparity in our model and eliminated the incentive for labor to migrate. But as is true with labor mobility, migration of capital is very costly and is impeded by many real-world economic, political, and legal obstacles. For example, U.S. meat producers would not likely find it profitable to move to South Korea to realize savings in labor costs. Other costs such as transporting livestock in Korean facilities and shipping meat products back to U.S. markets would be too high. Thus, while significant flows of capital *have* occurred (for example, from the northeast United States to the South and Southwest and from the United States to South Korea, Mexico, and elsewhere), their role in narrowing wage differentials has been somewhat limited. But to the extent that capital is mobile, wage differentials between areas are smaller, and thus, less labor migration will occur than if investment is confined to the domestic economy.[33]

Product Flows

Interregional and international trade has a similar potential effect on wage differences and labor mobility. Again return to Figure 9-3. Now suppose that capital and labor are immobile, U.S. and South Korean workers are homogeneous, and the costs of transporting goods between the two nations are zero. What effect will the low Korean wage W_k compared to the high U.S. wage W_u have on the relative competitiveness of Korean versus U.S. goods? Assuming that competition forces product prices down to marginal costs in both nations, U.S. consumers would reallocate their expenditures toward the lower-priced Korean goods. This would increase the total demand for these imports and eventually raise the derived demand for Korean labor. As shown by the outward shift of the labor demand curve from D to D_1 in Figure 9-3(b), this would increase the Korean wage rate. The opposite chain of events would occur in the United States. Here, reduced product demand would shift the derived demand for U.S. labor leftward from D to D_1 and reduce the wage to W_e. This wage narrowing via product flows diminishes the extent of labor migration, once we relax the assumption that labor is immobile. But in reality, transportation costs are so high for many goods and services that shipping them long distances is not economical. Thus, trade can be expected to narrow, but not equalize, wages in the long run.

Conclusion: *Labor migration, capital mobility, and trade between regions and nations all complement one another in promoting an efficient allocation of resources.* Labor mobility simply is one aspect of the broader mobility of resources and commodities in the economy. In fact, the U.S. government has at times promoted investment in less-developed nations and has reduced trade barriers to slow immigration from those nations into the United States. The ***Mexican Border Industrialization Program***—

9-2 the subject of "World at Work" 9-2—is a case in point.

U.S. IMMIGRATION POLICY AND ISSUES

Our analysis of the motivations for migration, the efficiency gains produced by this mobility, and the problem of gainers versus losers provides the tools necessary for understanding some of the controversies surrounding U.S. immigration patterns and policies.

History and Scope

Before World War I, immigration to the United States was virtually unimpeded. The great influx of foreign labor occurring in the nineteenth century contributed to

[33]For critical discussion of American capital exports, see Seymour Melman, *Profits without Production* (New York: Alfred A. Knopf, 1983), chap. 1.

9-2 World of Work

THE MEXICAN *MAQUILADORAS*

Under provisions of the Mexican Border Industrialization Program and U.S. trade law, U.S. firms are permitted to ship raw materials and components duty-free across the Mexican border, where Mexican workers assemble products in factories called *maquiladoras*. In turn, most of the products are brought back to the United States for sale, taxed at only the relatively low value added by Mexican workers. The approximately 1,800 *maquiladoras* are growing in number at a 15 percent annual rate and employ roughly 400,000 workers who receive on average $1.50 to $2.00 an hour. About 90 percent of these manufacturing plants are within 10 miles of the U.S. border.

The main purpose of the *maquiladora* program is to stimulate economic development in Mexico. This objective has clearly been met. *Maquiladoras* contribute nearly $3 billion annually to the Mexican economy and collectively have replaced tourism as Mexico's second largest source of foreign exchange (oil is its first).

A secondary purpose of the *maquiladora* program is to reduce illegal immigration to the United States. In theory, greater job opportunities in Mexico should reduce illegal immigration. However, *maquiladora* jobs have also lured more Mexicans from the interior to a closer proximity to the U.S. border. It is possible that some of these internal migrants become aware for the first time of the still-greater economic opportunities farther to the north. If so, the Mexican Border Industrialization Program could actually increase illegal immigration, at least until Mexican wages rise to levels more comparable to those of low-wage workers in the United States.

The *maquiladoras* are controversial. Organized labor in the United States has strongly criticized the *maquiladora* program, claiming that it has resulted in a sizable loss of jobs for U.S. workers. Advocates counter that any loss of U.S. jobs would have occurred in any event to other low-wage countries such as South Korea, Taiwan, and Hong Kong.*

Two recent studies by Gordon Hanson indicate that the concern about job loss due to the Mexican Border Industrialization Program may be overblown.† He finds that while manufacturing employment in the 1980s was nearly constant, it grew substantially in U.S. border areas. Hanson notes that the North American Free Trade Agreement eliminates the need for *maquiladoras* since all Mexican exports will enter duty-free under the agreement. He argues that the United States will benefit from NAFTA since it has a comparative advantage in components production, while Mexico has an advantage in assembly. The expansion of assembly plants in Mexico under NAFTA is likely to increase the demand for U.S.-made components.

*William C. Gruben, "Mexican Maquiladora Growth: Does It Cost U.S. Jobs?" *Economic Review* (Dallas: Federal Reserve Bank of Dallas, January 1990), pp. 15–29. For a critical appraisal of the *maquiladora* program, see Philip Mirowski and Susan Helper, "Maquiladoras: Mexico's Tiger by the Tail?" *Challenge,* May/June 1989, pp. 24–30.

†Gordon Hanson, "The Effects of Offshore Assembly on U.S. Industry Location," National Bureau of Economic Research Working Paper No. 5400, December 1995; and Gordon Hanson, "U.S.–Mexico Integration and Regional Economies," National Bureau of Economic Research Working Paper No. 5425, January 1996.

economic growth and to rising levels of per capita income. The flow of immigrants was slowed by World War I and the restrictive Immigration Acts of 1921 and 1924. These acts established immigration quotas for various nationalities based on the number of foreign-born persons of that nationality in the United States in specific census years. Additionally, the laws allowed several categories of nonquota immigrants to enter the United States. Between 1921 and 1965 only 10 million people entered the United States, and over one-half were nonquota immigrants, including 900,000 Canadians, 500,000 Mexicans, and thousands of spouses and children of U.S. citizens.

In 1965 amendments to the 1952 Immigration and Nationality Act shifted the preferences of the quota system away from northern and western European immigrants and toward a more evenly balanced set of nationalities. Further amendments established a

TABLE 9-2 LEGAL IMMIGRATION TO THE UNITED STATES, SELECTED YEARS

Year	Total (thousands)	Year	Total (thousands)
1970	373	1988	643
1980	531	1989	1091
1981	597	1990	1536
1982	594	1991	1827
1983	560	1992	974
1984	544	1993	904
1985	570	1994	804
1986	602	1995	720
1987	602	1996	916

Sources: U.S. Bureau of the Census, *Statistical Abstract of the United States, 1996,* p. 10; and U.S. Immigration and Naturalization Service, *Statistical Yearbook,* 1996.

worldwide annual ceiling of 270,000 immigrants, set an annual limit of 20,000 individuals per nation, and developed a six-point preference system giving priority to people who have specific job skills. Immediate relatives of U.S. citizens, refugees, and people seeking political asylum, however, were exempt from these provisions and ceilings.

Table 9-2 lists the number of legal immigrants to the United States in selected years. Note that during the 1980s legal immigration ranged from a low of 531,000 in 1980 to a high of 1,091,000 in 1989, but generally was 550,000 to 600,000 each year. The number of legal immigrants jumped considerably in 1989, 1990, and 1991—three years when many former illegal immigrants were granted permanent residence under the amnesty provisions of the Immigration Reform and Control Act of 1986.

To the numbers in Table 9-2 we must add the illegal aliens who arrived mainly from Mexico, the Caribbean, and Central and South America. The U.S. Census Bureau estimates that the net inflow of illegal aliens averaged about 200,000 annually between 1980 and 1990. Therefore, it was not uncommon for total immigration (legal and illegal) to exceed 750,000 annually during that period.

Immigration has further increased during the 1990s. In late 1990 Congress passed an immigration law raising the legal immigration cap from about 500,000 to 700,000 people annually, not counting refugees. This new law reserves 140,000 permanent residency visas each year for high-skilled professional workers. It also grants 10,000 residency slots to immigrants who either invest at least $1 million in the U.S. economy and create 10 or more full-time jobs or who invest $500,000 in targeted depressed areas in the United States.

Meanwhile, despite the passage of the Immigration Reform and Control Act, the flow of illegal immigrants has continued. This law granted amnesty and legal status to undocumented individuals who had lived in the United States since 1982. It also made it illegal for employers to hire undocumented workers.[34] The idea behind the employer sanctions was to diminish or eliminate the demand for the services of undocumented workers, thereby reducing their incentive to enter the country. But illegal immigrants have skirted this law by obtaining counterfeited documents. Thus, studies indicate that the law has reduced illegal immigration by, at best, 20 percent.

9-1 Coupled with the liberalized provisions of the 1990 immigration law, the continued flow of illegal immigrants means that on average about 865,000 immigrants have entered the United States each year since 1992.

Effects of Illegal Immigration

The inflow of ***illegal aliens*** into the United States over the past two decades has made immigration and immigration policy a major public issue in the United States. The main reason for the general concern is that most undocumented immigrants are unskilled workers. People fear that these individuals and their families reduce employment opportunities for the existing workforce, depress wage rates in already low-wage labor markets, and financially strain U.S. taxpayers via their receipt of transfer payments and use of social service programs. Are these concerns justified? Unfortunately, a simple yes or no answer cannot be provided.

1 Employment Effects Some observers contend that the employment of illegal aliens decrease the employment of domestic workers on a one-for-one basis. They argue that a given number of jobs exist in the economy and that if one of these positions is taken by an illegal worker, then that job is no longer available for a legal resident. At the other extreme is the claim that illegal aliens only accept work that resident workers are unwilling to perform and thus take no jobs from native workers. As we will demonstrate, both views are somewhat simplistic.

Figure 9-4 illustrates a market for unskilled agricultural workers. The curve D is the typical labor demand curve with which we are familiar. Supply curve S_d portrays the labor supply of domestic workers, while curve S_t reflects the total supply of domestic *and* illegal workers. Thus, the horizontal distance between S_t and S_d is the number of undocumented workers who will offer their labor services at each wage rate.

Given the presence of the illegal workers, the market wage and level of employment are W_t and Q_t. At this low wage, *no* domestic workers are willing to work. In this case, the reservation wage of domestic workers is simply too high. Perhaps this results from the availability of nonwage income, a high marginal value or opportunity cost associated with leisure, or a perceived lack of possibilities for advancement in the job. Can we therefore conclude that illegal aliens take work that U.S. workers do not want?

[34]For a study examining the wage effects of the Immigration Reform and Control Act, see Deborah A. Cobb-Clark, Clinton R. Shiells, and B. Lindsay Lowell, "Immigration Reform: The Effects of Employer Sanctions and Legalization on Wages," *Journal of Labor Economics,* July 1995, pp. 472–498. For evidence of the act's impact on illegal immigration, see Katherine Donato, Jorge Durand, and Douglas S. Massey, "Stemming the Tide? Assessing the Deterrent Effects of the Immigration Reform and Control Act," *Demography,* May 1992, pp. 139–157; and Sherrie A. Kossoudji, "Playing Cat and Mouse at the U.S.–Mexican Border," *Demography,* May 1992, pp. 159–180.

9-1 Global Perspective

IMMIGRANTS AS A PERCENT OF THE POPULATION, 1991–93

The percentage of the population who are immigrants ranges from a low of 1.1 in Japan to 22.7 in Australia.

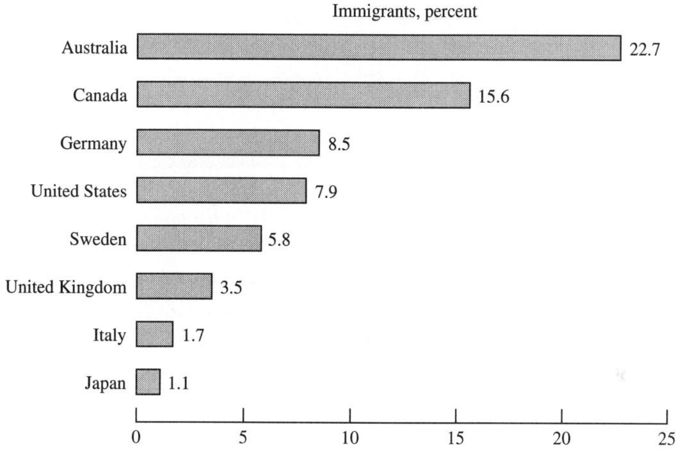

Source: Organization for Economic Cooperation on Development, *Trends in International Migration,* 1995, Table 1.2

In Figure 9-4 the answer is yes, *but* only if we add "at the low wage W_t." If all the illegal aliens were deported, the wage would rise to W_d in this market, and *some* U.S. workers, specifically $0Q_d$, would indeed be willing to do this work. The point is this: So-called "undesirable" work will attract U.S. workers if the compensating wage premium is sufficiently high (Chapter 8). If the illegal aliens were deported and if employers continue to offer wage rate W_t, there will be a shortage $0Q_t$. But this shortage occurs because the wage rate has not been allowed to rise to its equilibrium, not because U.S. workers are unwilling to do work that illegal aliens are willing to perform. The willingness to work at any given job depends partly on the wage rate being paid.

The opposite argument, that illegal aliens reduce domestic employment by an amount equal to the employment of illegal aliens, is also misleading. As shown in Figure 9-4,

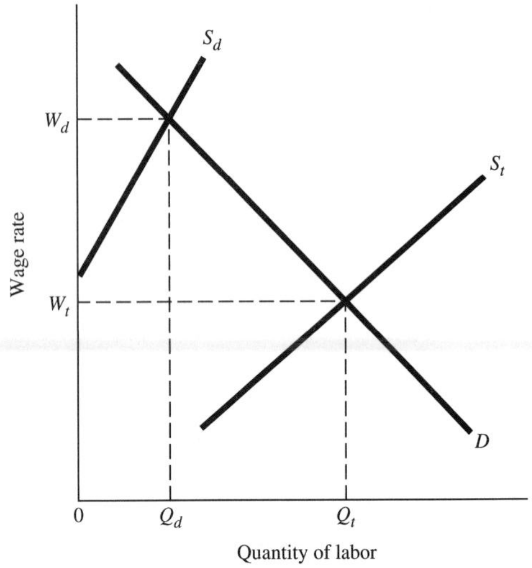

FIGURE 9-4 THE IMPACT OF ILLEGAL ALIENS ON DOMESTIC JOBS AND WAGES
The presence of illegal aliens in this low-wage labor market shifts the labor supply curve to S_t and reduces the market wage from W_d to W_t. At W_t, all workers hired are illegal aliens. If the illegal aliens were deported, however, Q_d domestic workers would be employed. Thus, it is misleading to conclude that illegal aliens accept jobs that domestic workers will not take. It is also misleading to conclude that the deportation of illegal aliens would create employment for native workers on a one-for-one basis.

the presence of the undocumented laborers *increases* the total number of jobs in this low-skilled labor market. With the illegal migration, the number of jobs is Q_t; without the inflow, it is only Q_d. It is erroneous to contend that deportation of the Q_t illegal migrants would result in an increase in domestic employment of Q_t. But it is correct to say that native employment would increase by the amount Q_d in this labor market. We conclude that illegal immigration does cause some substitution of illegal aliens for domestic workers but that the amount of displacement most likely is less than the total employment of the illegal aliens.[35]

2 Wage Effects There is little doubt that large inflows of migrants—be they legal or illegal—can depress some wage rates. Note in Figure 9-4 that the increase in labor supply reduces the U.S. market wage from W_d to W_t. In this regard, Smith and Newman found that real wage rates in towns in Texas that border Mexico were about 8 percent lower than those in Texas towns farther inland from the border.[36]

The overall effect of illegal immigration on the average wage rate in the economy is less clear. Some native workers and illegal immigrants are gross complements. This means that the reduced wage rate associated with the illegal immigration lowers production costs, creating an output effect that results in an increased labor demand for certain native workers. As one example, it is possible that illegal immigration raises

[35]For an empirical investigation indicating a low amount of job displacement, see George E. Johnson, "The Labor Market Effects of Immigration," *Industrial and Labor Relations Review,* April 1980, pp. 331–341. A more recent article of interest is Julian L. Simon, Stephen Moore, and Richard Sullivan, "The Effect of Immigration on Aggregate Native Unemployment: An Across-City Estimation," *Journal of Labor Research,* Summer 1993, pp. 299–316.

[36]Barton S. Smith and Robert Newman, "Depressed Wages along the U.S.–Mexican Border: An Empirical Analysis," *Economic Inquiry,* January 1977, pp. 51–66. Also relevant is Frank D. Bean, B. Lindsay Lowell, and Lowell J. Taylor, "Undocumented Mexican Immigrants and the Earnings of Other Workers in the United States," *Demography,* February 1988, pp. 35–52.

the demand for native workers who help transport and merchandise fruit. Also, spending by illegal aliens in the United States adds to the demand for products and therefore increases the derived demand for labor. For example, the demand for many workers in the barrios of Los Angeles may be greater because of the presence of illegal workers. On the other hand, this impact is reduced because many illegal aliens remit large portions of their pay to their families living abroad.[37]

So what can we conclude concerning the impact of illegal immigration on wage rates? The safest conclusion—given real-world complexities—is that *large-scale* illegal immigration does reduce the wage rate for substitutable low-skilled domestic workers. But illegal immigration probably has little *net* impact on the average level of wages in the United States.

3 Fiscal Effects Finally, what are the effects of illegal immigrants on tax revenues, transfer expenditures, and public services? Illegal immigrants legally do not qualify for public assistance from such programs as Medicaid and food stamps. Nevertheless, the easy availability of forged documents has recently increased participation in these programs. Evidence exists that current illegal immigrants and the families of illegal immigrants granted amnesty in the early 1990s are burdening the social welfare systems of some localities such as Los Angeles. Also, if immigrants display low-paid native workers, then immigrants may impose an indirect cost on the U.S. welfare and income maintenance programs.[38]

On the other hand, we must remember that most illegal immigrants are young workers without families, while eligibility for the major transfer programs depends on such characteristics as old age, illness, disability, or position as female head of a household. Also, while illegal immigrants do use many local public services such as schools, roads, and parks, most also pay Social Security taxes, user fees, and sales taxes. Most scholars of illegal immigration conclude that these immigrants remain net taxpayers.

CHAPTER SUMMARY

1. Mobility takes numerous forms, including occupational mobility and geographic mobility.
2. The decision to migrate can be viewed from a human capital perspective, by which the present value of expected gains in lifetime earnings is compared to investment costs (transportation expenses, forgone income during the move, and psychic costs).
3. Various factors can influence the decision to migrate: Age is inversely related to the probability of migrating; family status influences the migration decision in several ways; educational attainment and mobility are positively related; the likelihood of migration and the distance of the move are negatively related; unemployed people are more likely to

[37]For evidence on these large remittances, see David North and Marion Houstown, *The Characteristics and Role of Illegal Aliens in the U.S. Labor Market: An Exploratory Study* (Washington, DC: Linton and Co., Inc., 1976).

[38]Evidence suggests, however, that illegal immigration has had very little impact on the unemployment of youth and minority groups. See C. R. Winegarden and Lay B. Khors, "Undocumented Immigration and Unemployment of U.S. Youth and Minority Workers: Econometric Evidence," *Review of Economics and Statistics,* February 1991, pp. 105–112.

move than those who have jobs; and a high unemployment rate in the destination area reduces the probability that an unemployed worker will migrate there.

4 The average lifetime rate of return on migration is positive and is estimated to be in the 10 to 15 percent range.

5 Labor mobility contributes to allocative efficiency by relocating labor resources away from lower-valued and toward higher-valued employment. Under conditions of perfect competition and costless migration, workers of a given type will relocate until the value of the marginal product of labor (VMP) is the same in all similar employments ($VMP_a = VMP_b = \ldots = VMP_n$), at which point labor is being allocated efficiently.

6 Along with the positive outcomes, migration may generate negative externalities, which if real may reduce the efficiency gains of migration and if pecuniary may alter the distribution of income among various individuals and groups in origin and destination areas.

7 Wage differentials may generate capital and product flows that tend to equalize wages in the long run and reduce the extent of labor migration.

8 Total annual immigration (legal plus illegal) to the United States has averaged about 750,000 during the 1980s and has averaged about 865,000 since 1992.

9 Illegal aliens in the United States do not reduce native employment by the full extent of the employment of the illegals, but they do depress wage rates in some labor markets. The overall wage effect of illegal immigration is thought to be slight.

TERMS AND CONCEPTS

labor mobility
occupational mobility
geographic mobility
determinants of migration
skill transferability
self-selection
efficiency gains from migration
migration externalities (real versus pecuniary)
capital mobility
Mexican Border Industrialization Program
illegal aliens (employment, wage rate, and fiscal impacts)

QUESTIONS AND STUDY SUGGESTIONS

1 Use equation (9-1) to explain the likely effect of each of the following on the present value of net benefits from migration: *(a)* age, *(b)* distance, *(c)* education, *(d)* marital status, and *(e)* the discount rate (interest rate).

2 What is meant by the term "beaten paths"? How do such paths increase V_p in equation (9-1) and thereby increase the likelihood of migration?

3 Why are people who possess *specific* human capital less likely to change jobs, other things being equal, than those who possess *general* human capital? Does this imply that people who possess large amounts of specific human capital will never migrate? Explain.

4 Use Table 9-1 to determine the impact of wage-induced labor migration on:

a The combined output of the two regions
b Capital versus wage income in the destination region
c The average wage rate in the origin region
d The total wage bill for the native workers in the destination region

5 Use the variables in equation (9-1) to cite at least two reasons it may be rational for a family to migrate from one part of the country to another, even though the hypothetical move produces a decline in family earnings in the first year of work following the move.

6 How might a wage differential between two regions be reduced via movements of capital to the low-wage area? How does the U.S. government's support for the Mexican *maquiladora* program relate to your answer? In what circumstances might the *maquiladora* program *increase* illegal immigration to the United States?

7 Comment on this statement: "If we deported all illegal aliens who are now in the United States, our total national unemployment would decline by the same number of people."

8 How might labor mobility and migration affect the degree of monopsony power (Chapter 6) in labor markets?

9 Is it consistent to favor the free movement of labor *within* the United States and be opposed to immigration *into* the United States?

10 If one believes in free international trade, then to be consistent, must one also advocate unrestricted international migration of labor?

11 Analyze this statement: "U.S. tariffs on imported products from low-wage foreign nations create an incentive for migration of low-skilled immigrants into the United States." Relate this idea to the North American Free Trade Agreement, discussed in "World of Work" 6-6.

SELECTED REFERENCES

Borjas, George J.: "The Economics of Immigration," *Journal of Economic Literature,* December 1994, pp. 1667–1717.

Borjas, George J.: *Friends or Strangers: The Impact of Immigrants on the U.S. Economy* (New York: Basic Books, 1990).

Borjas, George J., and Richard B. Freeman (eds.): *Immigration and the Work Force* (Chicago: University of Chicago Press, 1992).

Briggs, Vernon M. Jr.: *Immigration and the American Labor Force* (Baltimore: Johns Hopkins University Press, 1984).

Chiswick, Barry R. (ed.): *The Gateway: U.S. Immigration Issues and Policies* (Washington, DC: American Enterprise Institute for Public Policy Research, 1982).

Chiswick, Barry R.: *Illegal Aliens: Their Employment and Employers* (Kalamazoo, MI: W. E. Upjohn Institute for Employment Research, 1988).

Freeman, Richard B., and John M. Abowd (eds.): *Immigration, Trade, and the Labor Market* (Chicago: University of Chicago Press, 1990).

Greenwood, Michael J.: "Research on Internal Migration in the United States: A Survey," *Journal of Economic Literature,* June 1975, pp. 397–433.

Greenwood, Michael J., and John M. McDowell: "Factor Market Consequences of U.S. Immigration," *Journal of Economic Literature,* December 1986, pp. 1738–1772.

Kritz, Mary M. (ed.): *U.S. Immigration and Refugee Policy* (Lexington, MA: D. C. Heath and Company, 1983).

Mueller, Charles F.: *The Economics of Labor Migration: A Behavioral Analysis* (New York: Academic Press, 1982).

Pozo, Susan (ed.): *Essays on Legal and Illegal Immigration* (Kalamazoo, MI: W. E. Upjohn Institute, 1986).

Simon, Julian L.: *The Economic Consequences of Immigration* (New York: Basil Blackwell, 1989).

Sjaastad, Larry A.: "The Cost and Returns of Human Migration," *Journal of Political Economy,* October 1962, pp. 80–93.

CHAPTER 10

LABOR UNIONS AND COLLECTIVE BARGAINING

Experts on etiquette agree that it is unwise to bring up certain topics—politics and religion, for example—in social conversations with new acquaintances. These topics often evoke strong emotions, differing opinions, and the potential for unwanted debate. Unionism is another such topic. A strongly expressed opinion on this subject stated in a social setting may well generate unwanted verbal fireworks!

Opinion, of course, is not fact; nor is opinion always based on sound analysis. In Chapter 6 we examined ways that workers can collectively influence wage rates through unionization. The main objective in this chapter and Chapter 11 is to deepen our understanding of unions, their goals, and their activities. Our approach will be factual and analytical. Thus, these two chapters will provide useful information that will help you develop an informed opinion on unionism in America.

In the present chapter we initially address such questions as: Why do unions exist? How large is the labor movement in the United States? What kinds of workers are most likely to be union members? In what industries are unions concentrated? Has union membership grown or declined in recent decades? Second, we ask what, if anything, unions attempt to maximize. What are the goals of unions? Third, we discuss how collective bargaining differs from ordinary market transactions, that is, how the "buying" and "selling" of labor services differ from the buying and selling of, say, a carton of milk at a supermarket. Finally, we inquire how wage rate indeterminacy (Figure 6-11) gets resolved through collective bargaining in situations where there is economic power on both sides of the labor market. More specifically, in the final section of this chapter a simple bargaining model is presented and discussed.

In Chapter 11 our concern turns to the economic impacts of collective bargaining. There, we attempt to determine whether unions and bargaining are effective means for raising wages, whether unions have a positive or negative impact on efficiency and productivity and on firm profitability, and whether unions increase or diminish inequality in the distribution of earnings.

WHY UNIONS?

A myriad of theories have been designed to explain the origins and evolution of labor unions.[1] We will settle for the straightforward historical view that unions are essentially the offspring of industrialization. Most preindustrial workers were self-sufficient, self-employed artisans, craftspeople, or farmers who worked in their own homes and on their own land. These workers were simultaneously employers and employees. Industrialization, however, undermined this system of self-employment and made many workers dependent on factory owners for employment and income. Industrialization also separated the functions of management and labor.

Although employers may not have purposely mistreated labor, competitive pressures in the product market often forced them to pay meager wages, to work their employees "long and hard," to provide minimal on-the-job amenities, and to terminate workers when lagging product demand made them redundant. In short, industrialization forced workers into a position of dependency where their earnings, working conditions, and security were largely beyond their control as individuals. To represent, protect, and enhance their interests, workers formed unions to bargain collectively with employers.

LABOR UNIONISM: FACTS AND FIGURES

Before analyzing the collective bargaining process and its economic implications, it is important that we gain a basic understanding of the scope and character of unionization in the United States. Specifically, let's discuss (1) the distribution of unionized labor by industry, occupation, gender, race, age, and location; (2) the structure of organized labor; and (3) the decline in the relative size of the unionized sector that has occurred over the past several decades.

Who Belongs to Unions?

10-1

In 1997 approximately 16.1 million of the 122 million civilian nonagricultural workers belonged to unions. In other words, about 13 percent of American workers were union members. But the likelihood that any given worker will be a union member depends on the occupation and industry with which the worker is associated, personal characteristics (gender, race, and age), and geographic location.

1 Industry and Occupation Table 10-1 shows the percentage of wage and salary workers who are unionized by industry and occupational classification. Union

[1]See, for example, Simeon Larson and Bruce Nissen (eds.), *Theories of the Labor Movement* (Detroit: Wayne State University Press, 1987). Ray Marshall and Brian Rungeling, *The Role of Unions in the American Economy,* 2d ed. (New York: Joint Council on Economic Education, 1985), presents an excellent elaboration of the theory presented here and a succinct history of the American labor movement.

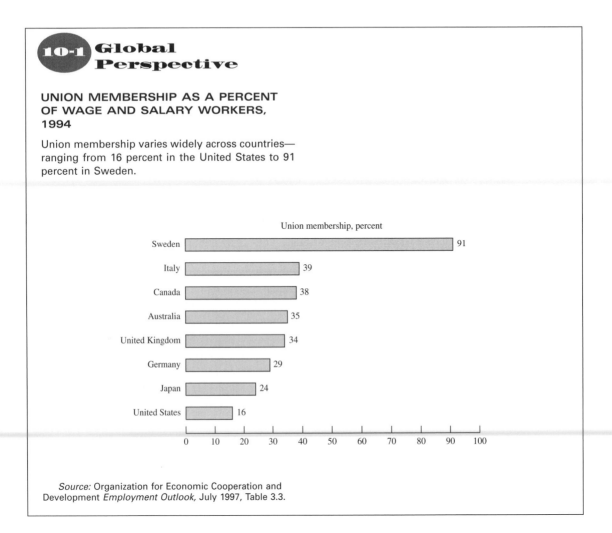

10-1 Global Perspective

UNION MEMBERSHIP AS A PERCENT OF WAGE AND SALARY WORKERS, 1994

Union membership varies widely across countries—ranging from 16 percent in the United States to 91 percent in Sweden.

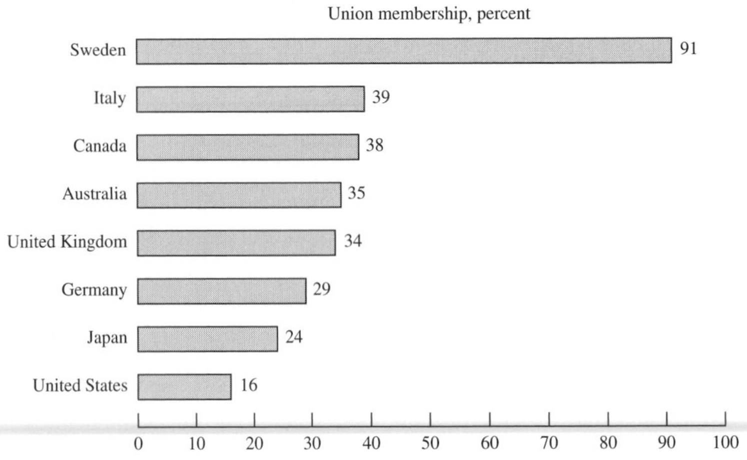

Source: Organization for Economic Cooperation and Development *Employment Outlook,* July 1997, Table 3.3.

membership is heavily concentrated in goods-producing industries (mining, construction, and manufacturing) and is relatively low in most service-oriented industries (wholesale and retail trade; finance, insurance, and real estate; and services). The exceptions are the low level of unionization in goods-producing agriculture and the high level in the service-providing transportation, communication, and public utilities industries. The high union density in transportation, communications, and public utilities partially results because these industries "are typically publicly regulated, highly concentrated within individual labor markets, and capital intensive—all of which lead to low labor demand elasticities, large expected benefits from union representation, and low organizing costs."[2] Also no-

[2] Barry T. Hirsch and John T. Addison, *The Economic Analysis of Unions* (Boston: Allen and Unwin, 1986), p. 63.

TABLE 10-1 UNION MEMBERSHIP BY INDUSTRY AND OCCUPATION, 1997

Industry	Percent union*	Occupation	Percent union*
Goods-producing:		White-collar:	
Agriculture	2	Professional and technical	20
Mining	14	Managers and administrators	5
Construction	20	Technicians	10
Manufacturing	16	Clerical workers	13
Services-producing:		Sales workers	4
Transportation, communication,		Blue-collar:	
and public utilities	32	Craft workers	23
Wholesale and retail trade	6	Operatives	22
Finance, insurance, and		Transportation	24
real estate	3	Nonfarm laborers	18
Services	13	Service	13
Public administration	32		

*Percent of employed wage and salary workers who belong to unions.

Source: Barry T. Hirsch and David A. Macpherson, *Union Membership and Earnings Data Book: Compilations from the Current Population Survey (1998 Edition)* (Washington, DC: Bureau of National Affairs, 1998).

table is the high level of unionization in public administration, which reflects the facts that almost three-fourths of all postal workers are organized and there has been vigorous growth of public-sector unionism at the state and local levels during the past few decades.

Table 10-1 also makes clear that blue-collar workers are much more heavily unionized than white-collar workers. The reasons for this difference include the following: First, some white-collar workers are managers, and under existing labor law, employers are not obligated to bargain with supervisory employees. Second, many white-collar workers identify with management and aspire to move upward from worker to management status. They feel that union membership is "unprofessional" and a potential obstacle to their ambitions. Finally, on the average, white-collar workers enjoy higher wages and better working conditions than blue-collar workers; hence, the former may feel they have less need for unions.

With some important exceptions, the industrial–occupational pattern of unionization was established by the late 1940s. Industries that were heavily unionized by that time remain so now. Today most workers do *not* become union members by organizing their employers, but rather join a union because they take a job with an already unionized employer. "A blue-collar worker who finds himself in the automobile industry will almost certainly work under a union contract. A worker who takes a job in banking almost certainly will not."[3]

The previously noted high level of unionization in the public sector merits additional attention. Prior to the 1960s government workers were weakly organized and seemed

[3]Daniel J. B. Mitchell, *Unions, Wages, and Inflation* (Washington, DC: Brookings Institution, 1980), p. 214.

destined to remain so because most public-sector employment entailed white-collar service jobs *and* a high proportion of government workers were women. Nevertheless, between the mid-1960s and the early 1970s, public-sector union membership more than quadrupled, and today we find union density in the public sector to be more than twice as great as for the economy as a whole. This expansion is quite remarkable in view of the fact that private-sector unionism has been declining significantly.

What caused this striking spurt of union growth among government workers? Most important, in the 1960s and 1970s a variety of state and local laws were passed that established mechanisms for government employees to vote for or against unionism and required government employers to bargain with unionized workers. Executive orders at the federal level accomplished much the same for federal employees. In short, a new legislative climate provided public-sector workers in the 1960s and 1970s with the opportunity to join unions—an opportunity private-sector workers had enjoyed since the 1930s.

Despite this new legal environment, why did public-sector unionism experience such rapid growth while private-sector unionism was on the wane? On the one hand a "pent-up" demand for unionization may have existed that the favorable legal environment simply unleashed. On the other hand private employers have typically demonstrated considerable resistance to unionization to the extent that they have frequently broken both the spirit and the letter of labor law. In contrast public-sector employers have not fought the unionization of their workers.[4]

The rapid growth of public-sector unionism occurred largely in the 1960–76 period. Since 1976 there has been little or no growth as membership has leveled off at about 37 percent of all public-sector employees. It is probably correct to say that the era of dramatic public-sector union growth is now behind us.[5]

2 Personal Characteristics: Gender, Race, and Age Table 10-2 indicates that personal characteristics are associated with the likelihood of union membership. We observe that men are much more likely to be union members than women. This difference is *not* attributable to any fundamental attitudinal differences based on gender, but largely because women are disproportionately represented in less-unionized industries and occupations. For example, many women are employed in retail sales, food service, and office work, where the levels of unionization are very low. Furthermore, women on average have a less permanent attachment to the labor force than men. Thus, the present value of the *lifetime* wage gains from unionization will be lower for women than for men, making union membership relatively less attractive to women.[6]

[4]This paragraph is based upon Richard B. Freeman, "Unionism Comes to the Public Sector," *Journal of Economic Literature,* March 1986, pp. 41–86.

[5]Linda N. Edwards, "The Future of Public Sector Unions: Stagnation or Growth?" *American Economic Review,* May 1989, pp. 161–165.

[6]Three articles addressing the topic of this paragraph are Richard B. Freeman and Jonathan S. Leonard, "Union Maids: Unions and the Female Work Force," in Clair Brown and Joseph A. Pechman (eds.), *Gender in the Workplace* (Washington, DC: Brookings Institution, 1987); William E. Even and David A. Macpherson, "The Decline of Private-Sector Unionism and the Gender Wage Gap," *Journal of Human Resources,* Spring 1993, pp. 279–296; and Diane S. Sinclair, "The Importance of Sex for the Propensity to Unionize," *British Journal of Industrial Relations,* June 1995, pp. 173–190.

TABLE 10-2 UNION MEMBERSHIP BY GENDER, RACE, AND AGE, 1996

Personal Characteristic	Percent union*
Gender:	
Male	16
Female	12
Race:	
White	14
Black	18
Age:	
Under 25	5
25 and over	16

*Percent of employed wage and salary workers who belong to unions.

Source: Barry T. Hirsch and David A. Macpherson, *Union Membership and Earnings Data Book: Compilations from the Current Population Survey (1998 Edition)* (Washington, DC: Bureau of National Affairs 1998).

We also see from Table 10-2 that a larger proportion of blacks than whites belong to unions. This difference is also partly a reflection of the industrial distribution of workers. Specifically, a disproportionately larger number of blacks have blue-collar jobs. Another explanatory factor is that unionization results in larger relative wage gains for black workers than for white workers.[7] Blacks stand to benefit relatively more than whites by belonging to unions.

Table 10-2 also reveals that young workers (under 25 years of age) are less likely than older workers to have union cards. Once again, this is largely explainable in terms of the kinds of jobs young workers acquire. Specifically, as we will see momentarily, the traditional blue-collar, goods-producing, unionized sectors of the economy have *not* been expanding rapidly in recent years and therefore have *not* been a major source of jobs to youths entering the labor force. Rather, the largely nonunion service sectors have been growing and providing more jobs. Today high school graduates are more likely to take jobs with nonunion fast-food chains; 25 years ago many high school graduates found work in unionized automobile or steel manufacturing plants.

3 Location To a considerable degree the labor movement in the United States is an urban phenomenon. Six heavily urbanized, heavily industrialized states—New York, California, Pennsylvania, Illinois, Ohio, and Michigan—account for approximately one-half of all union members.[8] Furthermore, the percentage of workers who are unionized in the South is only about two-thirds of what it is in the rest of the country. This may

[7]For evidence that blacks have a stronger demand for unionization than other groups, see Gregory Defreitas, "Unionization among Racial and Ethnic Minorities," *Industrial and Labor Relations Review,* January 1993, pp. 284–301.

[8]Marten Estey, *The Unions,* 3d ed. (New York: Harcourt Brace Jovanovich, 1981), p. 10.

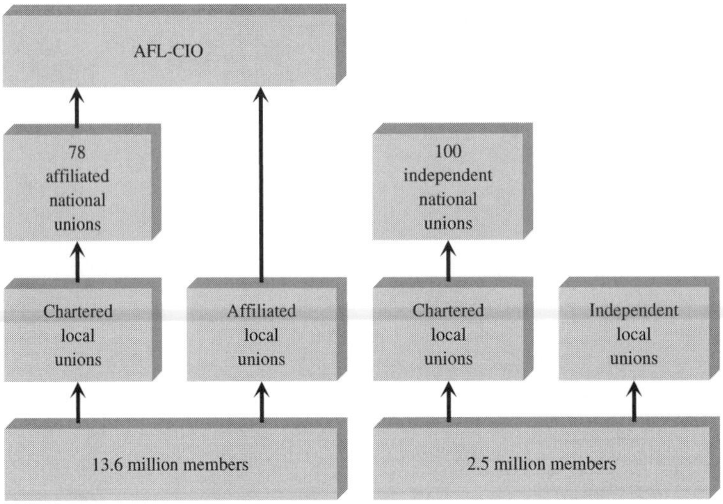

FIGURE 10-1 **THE INSTITUTIONAL ORGANIZATION OF AMERICAN UNIONISM**
Organized labor in the United States consists of the AFL-CIO and numerous independent unions. The AFL-CIO's basic function is to formulate and promote labor's views on a wide range of economic, social, and political issues. The national unions generally have responsibility for negotiating collective bargaining agreements, while the locals are concerned with administering those agreements.

stem in part from the occupational and industrial makeup of jobs in the South, but it is also claimed that employers and the general populace there simply are more inclined to be antiunion.

Structure of Organized Labor[9]

Figure 10-1 provides a thumbnail sketch of the structure of American labor organizations. You will observe there are three major levels of union organizations: the federation, national unions,[10] and local unions.

AFL-CIO The ***American Federation of Labor and Congress of Industrial Organizations,*** better known as the ***AFL-CIO,*** is a loose and voluntary federation of independent and autonomous national unions. We note in Figure 10-1 that 78 national unions with a combined membership of about 13.6 million workers belong to the AFL-CIO in 1997, while approximately 100 national unions possessing an aggregate mem-

[9]The ensuing discussion draws upon ibid., chap. 3. For a discussion of the evolution of the labor movement and a more detailed consideration of its structure, see Gordon F. Bloom and Herbert R. Northrup, *Economics of Labor Relations,* 9th ed. (Homewood, IL: Richard D. Irwin, Inc., 1981), chaps. 2 and 3.

[10]Some national unions call themselves "international" unions—for example, the International Brotherhood of Electrical Workers (IBEW)—which usually means that there are some affiliated locals in Canada or Puerto Rico.

bership of about 2.5 million were independent of the AFL-CIO. The AFL-CIO does *not* engage in collective bargaining but is the primary political organ of organized labor. The AFL-CIO formulates labor's view on a spectrum of political issues ranging from the minimum wage to foreign policy, publicizes labor's positions, and engages in political lobbying.[11] The AFL-CIO is also responsible for settling jurisdictional disputes among affiliated national unions; that is, it determines which union has the "right" to organize a particular group of nonunion workers.

National Unions The ***national unions*** are federations of local unions that are typically in either the same industry ("industrial unions" such as those made up of autoworkers or steelworkers) or the same skilled occupation ("craft unions" such as those representing carpenters and electricians). Table 10-3 lists the largest national unions and indicates which are, and which are not, affiliated with the AFL-CIO. Those not identified as independent are affiliated with the AFL-CIO.

A national union has two primary functions: (1) organizing the unorganized workers in its craft or industry and (2) negotiating collective bargaining agreements. Responsibility for the latter function, however, may be shared in some cases with

[11]For an analysis of organized labor's effectiveness in the political sphere, see Richard B. Freeman and James L. Medoff, *What Do Unions Do?* (New York: Basic Books, Inc., 1984), chap. 13.

TABLE 10-3 LABOR ORGANIZATIONS REPORTING 100,000 MEMBERS OR MORE (IN THOUSANDS)

Labor organization*	Members	Labor organization	Members
National Education Association (independent)	2,200	Paperworkers	252
Teamsters	1,440	Police (independent)	250
Food and commercial workers	1,400	Hotel Employees and Restaurant Employees	241
State, county and municipal employees	1,300	Firefighters	225
Service Employees (SEIU)	1,112	Nurses (independent)	205
Teachers	907	Government Workers	200
Aerospace and Auto Workers	790	Transport Workers	159
Laborers	750	Federal Government Workers (independent)	150
Electrical Workers	679	Electronic Workers	135
Machinists	675	Painters	125
Communication Workers	600	Bakery	122
Carpenters	500	Transportation, Communication Workers	120
Steelworkers	403	Musicians	120
Operating Engineers	365	Health Workers	117
Letter Carriers	311	Sheet Metal Workers	106
Plumbers	300	Ironworkers	105
Postal Workers	300		
Textile Workers	285		

*All organizations not identified as independent are affiliated with the AFL-CIO.
Source: Courtney D. Gifford, *Directory of U.S. Labor Organizations (1997 Edition)* (Washington, DC: Bureau of National Affairs, 1997), pp. 47–80.

local unions, depending on the size of the local and the industry involved. For example, if the relevant product market is local (such as housing construction), the local carpenters, bricklayers, and other craft unions are likely to negotiate their own bargaining contracts. But where the product market is regional or national in scope (for example, textiles or automobiles), contract negotiation is usually performed by the national union rather than its locals. The reasons for this are twofold. Most important, the national union wants to standardize wages—to "take wages out of competition"—so that employers who would pay high union wages would not be penalized by losing sales to other firms paying low union wages. Furthermore, collective bargaining has become very complex and legalistic, requiring skilled negotiators, lawyers, and so forth. Consequently, it is likely that "economies of scale" are to be gained by relying on national negotiators.

Local Unions Generally, the approximately 45,000 ***local unions*** are essentially branches or components of the respective national unions. We do observe in Figure 10-1, however, that some locals are directly affiliated with the AFL-CIO, and a few are not affiliated with either a national union or the AFL-CIO. The relationship between the locals and the national unions is significantly different from that between the AFL-CIO and the nationals. When they join the federation, the national unions retain their sovereignty and autonomy over their internal affairs. But a local union is usually subservient to its national union. For example, locals are often required to clear a decision to strike with the national before undertaking such action. Furthermore, the national union has the power to suspend or to disband one of its locals.

This is not to downgrade the role of the local union. Locals perform the important functions of administering or policing the bargaining contract and seeking the resolution of worker grievances that may arise in interpreting the contract. As Estey points out:

> The local union is judged primarily on its handling of the grievance procedure, the process by which the collective bargaining agreement is administered and interpreted. It is the local-union officer, not the international representative or someone from the Federation, who gets the individual member's complaints about how he or she is treated in the plant. And it is the local-union officer who, in effect, is responsible for winning or losing the grievance for the worker. If the grievance is settled in favor of the worker, the local—and through it the national union and unions generally—looks good; and if the grievance is lost, unionism may suffer. . . .
>
> Active, interested, and effective local leadership tends to produce a favorable reaction from the members, and vice versa. In short, the local union *is* the union to the members. Its performance is the basis for the opinions of unions.[12]

Diversity of Bargaining Structures The term ***bargaining structure*** refers to *the scope of the employees and employers covered by a collective bargaining agreement;*

[12]Estey, op. cit., pp. 50–51.

the bargaining structure tells us who bargains with whom. In the United States a great diversity of bargaining structures exists. The diversity is implicit in Figure 10-1 and in the fact that nearly 2,000 major collective bargaining contracts (those involving 1,000 or more workers) are currently in force. Thousands of other collective bargaining agreements cover smaller employers.

Many unions negotiate with a single-plant employer. Others bargain on a more centralized basis with multiplant employers. In this case firms with many plants negotiate a "master agreement" with one or more unions, which then applies to workers in all of the firm's plants.[13] Still greater centralization is involved in ***pattern bargaining,*** where the union negotiates a contract with a particular firm in an industry, and this contract—or a slightly modified version—comprises the demands the union seeks to impose on all other employers in that industry. In still other instances, multiemployer bargaining occurs; employers in a given industry will form an employers' association (for example, the Bituminous Coal Owners Association) and bargain as a group with the union.

Although the determinants of a bargaining structure are manifold and complex,[14] pragmatic considerations and perceived effects on each party's bargaining power are important. For example, where employers are numerous and small and their markets are highly localized, unions are likely to bargain a citywide agreement with an employers' association. Both employers and the union may see advantages in such a bargaining structure. First, there may be some economies of scale in negotiations; it would be very costly for the union to have to negotiate separate agreements with a larger number of employers. Second, employers may feel that they can enhance their bargaining power by negotiating as a group rather than individually. Finally—and perhaps most important—by standardizing wage rates through a citywide agreement, each employer avoids the risk of incurring a competitive disadvantage vis-à-vis other firms because of higher wage costs. Similarly, the union "takes wages out of competition" and avoids the problem of job loss in higher-wage union firms.[15] Thus, in building construction, hotels and motels, retail trade, and local trucking, citywide agreements are quite common. Regional multiemployer bargaining has also been practiced in over-the-road trucking, bituminous coal, and the basic steel industry, among others.

Single-company bargaining is common in many of the basic manufacturing industries where large oligopolistic corporations feel sufficiently strong to "go it alone" in negotiating with the union. But frequently the negotiation of a contract with one firm will establish a pattern for other firms in the same industry. The automobile industry is the most publicized example of pattern bargaining. When contracts terminate every 3 years, the United Auto Workers selects one of the "Big Three" manufacturers for

[13]The master agreement is often supplemented by a local agreement that deals with issues and conditions unique to particular plants.

[14]For a systematic discussion of the determination of bargaining structure, see Thomas A. Kochan and Harry C. Katz, *Collective Bargaining and Industrial Relations,* 2d ed. (Homewood, IL: Richard D. Irwin, Inc., 1988), chap. 4.

[15]By lessening the ability of consumers to substitute nonunion products for union products, increased union coverage in an industry will lower the elasticity of demand for the products sold by the unionized firms. We know from Chapter 5 that reduced elasticity of product demand lessens the elasticity of labor demand, enabling the union to increase wage rates without experiencing large losses of employment.

contract renegotiation. The negotiated contract serves as the standard for dealing with the other automakers. This bargaining structure is advantageous to the union because lost wages during a possible strike will be less if only one firm is struck rather than the entire industry. Furthermore, the firm experiencing the work stoppage will lose sales to its nonstruck competitors, creating pressure on the former to accept the union's demands. The basic point is that there is no such thing as a "typical" bargaining structure in the United States.

QUICK REVIEW 10-1

- Unions are a by-product of industrialization through which workers' earnings, working conditions, and security became dependent on decisions of business owners. Unions arose to represent, protect, and enhance the interests of workers.
- In 1997 approximately 16.1 million of the 122 million members of the American nonagricultural workforce belonged to unions.
- Unionization varies greatly by industry, occupation, gender, race, age, and location.
- Organized labor in the United States consists of the AFL-CIO (a federation of 78 affiliated national unions) and about 100 independent national unions.

Your Turn: Based on national statistics, who would most likely be a union member: Susan, a white female, age 23, who is a sales worker in Iowa, or Isaiah, a black male, age 53, who is a transportation worker in Ohio? (Answer: See page 626.)

UNIONISM'S DECLINE

We have just noted that some 16.1 million workers—about 13 percent of civilian nonagricultural workers—belonged to unions in 1997. Table 10-4 provides a historical overview of trends in union membership. Two points stand out. First, the unionized sector is clearly the minority component of the labor force. Union membership has never exceeded 30 percent of the total labor force. The United States, incidentally, is relatively "nonunion" compared to most other industrially advanced Western economies. For example, estimates indicate that 91 percent of all nonagricultural wage and salary workers are organized in Sweden. Comparable figures for Australia, Canada, and Japan are 35, 38, and 24 percent, respectively.

The second point is that unionism in the United States is on the decline. The *relative* size of the labor movement peaked in the early 1970s and since then has been declining.[16] In the 1970s this decline resulted from union membership's failing to grow as fast as the labor force. But between 1980 and 1990 the *absolute* number of active union members also declined sharply and has declined slowly since 1990.

[16] If members of professional organizations that bargain collectively with employers are excluded from the figures, the labor movement reached its relative peak in the mid-1950s.

TABLE 10-4 UNION MEMBERSHIP IN THE UNITED STATES, SELECTED YEARS, 1880–1997

Year	Union membership (in thousands)	Percentage of nonagricultural workers
1880	149	2
1890	722	6
1900	1,028	7
1910	1,993	9
1920	4,551	17
1930	3,284	11
1940	8,416	26
1950	13,775	30
1960	16,461	30
1970	18,713	26
1980	20,095	22
1990	16,740	15
1997	16,110	13

Source: Richard B. Freeman, "Spurts in Union Growth: Defining Moments and Social Processes," National Bureau of Economic Research Working Paper No. 6012, April 1997, and Barry T. Hirsch and David A. Macpherson, *Union Membership and Earnings Data Book: Compilations from the Current Population Survey (1998 Edition)* (Washington, DC: Bureau of National Affairs, 1998).

Why has this happened? A variety of explanations have been put forth. We will examine the three most widely discussed hypotheses and briefly note several other potential contributors to the wane of unionism.[17]

Structural Changes

The most publicized view, the ***structural-change hypothesis,*** is that a variety of structural changes have occurred both in our economy and in the labor force that have been unfavorable to the expansion of union membership. This view embraces a number of interrelated observations.

First, consumer demand and therefore employment patterns have shifted away from traditional union strongholds. Generally speaking, domestic output has been shifting away from blue-collar manufactured goods (where unions have been strong) to

[17]The reader who seeks more detail on this topic should consult Jack Fiorito and Cheryl L. Maranto, "The Contemporary Decline of Union Strength," *Contemporary Policy Issues,* October 1987, pp. 12–27; Edward P. Lazear et al., "Symposium on Public and Private Unionization," *Journal of Economic Perspectives,* Spring 1988, pp. 59–110; Henry S. Farber, "The Decline of Unionization in the United States: What Can Be Learned from Recent Experience?" *Journal of Labor Economics,* January 1990, pp. S75–S105; and Henry S. Farber and Alan B. Krueger, "Union Membership in the United States: The Decline Continues," in Bruce E. Kaufman and Morris M. Kleiner (eds.), *Employee Representation: Alternatives and Future Directions* (Madison, WI: Industrial Relations Research Association, 1993), pp. 105–134.

white-collar services (where unions have been weak). This change in the mix of industrial output may be reinforced by increased competition from imports in highly unionized sectors such as automobiles and steel. Growing import competition in these industries has curtailed domestic employment and therefore union membership. As our economy has become increasingly open to low-labor-cost foreign competition, American unionized firms have found themselves at a serious competitive disadvantage.

Second, a disproportionate share of employment growth in recent years has been provided by small firms, which are less likely to be unionized than large firms. Even and Macpherson have estimated that declining plant size accounted for 28 percent of the decline in unionism over the 1979–83 period.[18]

Third, an unusually large proportion of the increase in employment in recent years has been concentrated among women, youths, and part-time workers—groups that have allegedly been difficult to organize because of their less firm attachment to the labor force.

Fourth, spurred by rising energy costs, the long-run trend for industry to shift from the Northeast and the Midwest where unionism is a "way of life" to "hard-to-organize" areas of the South and Southwest may have impeded the expansion of union membership.

A final and ironic possibility is that the relative decline of unionism may be in part a reflection of the greater success unions apparently have had in gaining a wage advantage over nonunion workers. As we will find in the next chapter, there is evidence suggesting that on the average union workers in the 1970s realized an enlarged wage advantage over their nonunion counterparts. Confronted with a growing wage-cost disadvantage vis-à-vis nonunion employers, we would expect union employers to accelerate the substitution of capital for labor, subcontract more work to nonunion suppliers, open nonunion plants in less-industrialized areas, or have components produced in low-wage nations. These actions reduce the growth of employment opportunities in the union sector as compared to the nonunion sector. Perhaps more important, we would also expect output and employment in lower-cost nonunion firms and industries to increase at the expense of output and employment in higher-cost union firms and industries. In short, union success in raising wages may have changed the composition of industry to the disadvantage of union employment and membership.[19]

Several potential flaws in the structural-change hypothesis have been noted.[20] First, other advanced capitalistic countries have experienced structural changes similar to those that have occurred in the United States, and their labor movements continue to

[18]William E. Even and David A. Macpherson, "Plant Size and the Decline of Unionism," *Economic Letters,* August 1990, pp. 393–398.

[19]For a discussion and empirical evidence on this point, see Peter Linneman and Michael L. Wachter, "Rising Union Premiums and the Declining Boundaries among Noncompeting Groups," *American Economic Review,* May 1986, pp. 103–108; Richard Edwards and Paul Swaim, "Union–Nonunion Earnings Differentials and the Decline of Private-Sector Unionism," *American Economic Review,* May 1986, pp. 97–102; Peter D. Linneman, Michael L. Wachter, and William H. Carter, "Evaluating the Evidence on Union Employment and Wages," *Industrial and Labor Relations Review,* October 1990, pp. 34–53; and David G. Blachflower and Richard B. Freeman, "Unionism in the United States and Other Advanced OECD Countries," *Industrial Relations,* Winter 1992, pp. 56–79.

[20]Freeman and Medoff, op. cit., chap. 15.

grow both absolutely and relatively. Canada is perhaps the most relevant example. Second, historically union growth has been realized in good measure by the unionization of groups of workers who were once regarded as traditionally "nonunion." The unionization of blue-collar workers in the mass-production industries such as automobiles and steel in the 1930s and the organizing of public-sector workers more recently are cases in point. Given this history, why can't women workers, young workers, immigrants, and southern workers be brought into the labor movement to spur its continued growth? Finally, surveys indicate that young and female workers—who, we found in Table 10-2, are now less unionized—are in fact as much, or more, prounion as more heavily unionized older and male workers. Yet unions are losing an increasing proportion of National Labor Relations Board (NLRB) elections where workers vote to determine whether they want to be unionized.

Managerial-Opposition Hypothesis

Such criticisms have led Freeman and Medoff to question the adequacy of the structural-change explanation, arguing that intensified ***managerial opposition*** to unions has also been a major deterrent to union growth. Freeman and Medoff contend that beginning in the 1970s unions have increased the union wage advantage they enjoy vis-à-vis nonunion workers (Chapter 11) and, as a result, union firms have become less profitable than nonunion firms.[21] As a reaction, managerial opposition to unions has crystallized and become more aggressive. This opposition takes a variety of forms, both legal and illegal. Legal antiunion tactics include written and verbal communications with workers indicating that unionism will create an adversarial relationship between labor and management that will be generally detrimental to workers. Similarly, management may suggest that with unionization, strikes will be frequent and costly to workers. Also, as explained in "World of Work" 10-1, firms may hire permanent strikebreakers to replace striking workers. Or management may use various tactics to delay the NLRB union certification election, reasoning correctly that an extension of the election period tends to reduce worker enthusiasm for unionization. It is increasingly common for employers to hire labor–management consultants who specialize in mounting aggressive antiunion drives to dissuade workers from unionizing or, alternatively, to persuade union workers to decertify their union.[22]

Freeman and Medoff contend that the use of illegal antiunion tactics has risen dramatically. In particular, they argue that it has become increasingly common for management to identify and dismiss leading prounion workers, even though this is

[21]Although substantial union wage differentials (Chapter 11) induce workers to join unions, the same union wage differentials reduce profits and increase managerial opposition to unionization. Freeman contends that the latter effect outweighs the former and that "as much as one-quarter of the decline in the proportion [of workers] organized through NLRB elections may be attributed to the increased union wage premium of the 1970s and its adverse effects on firm profitability which raised management opposition." See Richard B. Freeman, "The Effect of the Union Wage Differential on Management Opposition and Union Organizing Success," *American Economic Review,* May 1986, pp. 92–96.

[22]A 1984 brochure from an organization called Executive Enterprises, Inc., boasts that it had over 20,000 management representatives attend its seminars on "How to Maintain Nonunion Status" and "The Process of Decertification."

prohibited by the Wagner Act. The increasing popularity of this tactic stems from the fact that when proved guilty, the employers receive only light penalties. Given these antiunion strategies, the labor movement has gone into relative eclipse.

Freeman cites 13 studies on the impact of management antiunion activities on the outcomes of union organizational drives and representation elections. He observes that in 12 of the 13 studies such management activity was found to be effective. He concludes that managerial opposition is critical in determining the success or failure of union organizational campaigns and is a major factor in explaining the deunionization 10-1 of the American economy.[23]

The Substitution Hypothesis

The ***substitution hypothesis*** is the notion that other institutions—specifically, government and employers—have come to provide the services, benefits, and employment conditions that were historically available to workers only through unionization. This substitution of employer- and government-provided services to workers has allegedly reduced the need for and attractiveness of union membership. Thus, Neumann and Rissman note that many of today's public programs that relate to the labor market—such as unemployment insurance, workers' compensation, Social Security, and health and safety laws—were once important goals of labor unions. Their empirical analysis leads them to conclude that historically government has been responsible for providing more and more "unionlike" services, and this has simply lessened the need for workers to join unions.[24]

Similarly, some employers have attempted to install "progressive" labor policies to usurp worker demand for union representation. Such employers establish two-way communication channels with workers, provide for the orderly handling of worker grievances, create worker-participation schemes, offer seniority protection, pay attractive wages and fringe benefits, and so forth. By averting the major source of prounion sentiments—job dissatisfaction—employers remain union-free. Here, employers are substituting their own benefits for those ordinarily sought through unions and thereby beat unions at their own game.

Examining data on worker attitudes toward unions, Farber observes that workers who are satisfied with their jobs are much less likely to vote for union representation than are dissatisfied workers. His data indicate that the reported levels of satisfaction of nonunion workers with their pay and job security rose dramatically over the 1977–84 period he examined. Furthermore, nonunion workers' perception of the effectiveness of unions in improving wages and working conditions has diminished. Farber's con-

[23]Richard B. Freeman, "Contraction and Expansion: The Divergence of Private Sector and Public Unionism in the United States," *Journal of Economic Perspectives,* Spring 1988, pp. 82–83; and Richard B. Freeman and Morris M. Kleiner, "Employer Behavior in the Face of Union Organizing Drives," *Industrial and Labor Relations Review,* April 1990, pp. 351–365.

[24]George R. Neumann and Ellen R. Rissman, "Where Have All the Union Members Gone?" *Journal of Labor Economics,* April 1984, pp. 175–192. From their empirical work, Neumann and Rissman find that about half of the decrease in union membership that has occurred since 1956 is explainable in terms of changes in the structure of industry.

10-1 World of Work

SHOULD THE RIGHT TO HIRE PERMANENT STRIKEBREAKERS BE RESCINDED?

Managerial opposition to unions has increasingly taken the form of threats to hire permanent strikebreakers or the actual employment of such workers. For example, in 1992 Caterpillar broke a 5-month strike by the United Auto Workers by threatening to hire permanent replacements for strikers who did not return to work on the company's terms. Fearing the unalterable loss of their jobs, thousands of UAW workers returned to work. The union then directed all its workers back to work, without a signed labor contract.

Earlier, Phelps Dodge, the Chicago *Tribune,* Hormel, Continental Airlines, International Paper, Eastern Airlines, Greyhound, and several other major firms had hired permanent replacements for their striking workers. A few of these firms allegedly "baited" their unions into striking by demanding large, unacceptable wage concessions. The firms then replaced the striking workers with new, permanent employees.

Unions have vigorously sought to change labor relations law to counter these business tactics. In 1992 the House of Representatives passed legislation banning firms from hiring permanent strikebreakers, but the legislation failed in the Senate. Under the proposed law, firms could not promise their strikebreakers permanent jobs and would have to hire back striking workers when they individually or collectively opted to return to work. The Clinton administration has endorsed this legislation, but passage by Congress remains elusive.

Proponents of the ban on hiring permanent strikebreakers argue that hiring such replacements is akin to firing striking workers. Firing these workers is expressly prohibited under current labor laws; permanently replacing them is not. Unions and firms must legally bargain with each other in "good faith." But, as noted by one commentator, "you can't bargain with a striker whose job is no more." Proponents also note that Japan, Germany, and other key trade competitors bar firms from hiring permanent replacements.

Opponents of the legislation counter that a ban on hiring permanent strikebreakers will mean that unions with exorbitant demands could force firms either into bankruptcy or out of the country. They say that the possibility of being permanently replaced is simply one of the risks that workers should consider in voting to strike. Also, say opponents, the fact that some corporations can find thousands of qualified permanent replacements reveals the unreasonableness of many union wage demands.

A study by Peter Cramton and Joseph Tracy of over 300 strikes during the 1980s indicates that a ban on the hiring of replacement workers would have a substantial impact on strike activity.* They estimate that such a ban would have resulted in a 30 percent increase in the number of strikes for the period of 1982–89. They also report that the use of replacement workers is lower when the labor market is tight and the workers are more experienced.

*Peter C. Cramton and Joseph S. Tracy, "The Use of Replacement Workers in Union Contract Negotiations: The U.S. Experience, 1980–89," National Bureau of Economic Research Working Paper No. 5106, May 1995.

clusion is that there has been a significant decline in the demand for union representation among nonunion workers that is independent of structural changes in the labor force and in industry.[25] Farber further supports his view with additional evidence in a controversial paper coauthored with Krueger.[26] The two find that virtually all of the decline in union membership between 1977 and 1991 was caused by a decline in worker

[25]Henry S. Farber, "Trends in Worker Demand for Union Representation," *American Economic Review,* May 1989, pp. 166–171.

[26]Henry S. Farber and Alan B. Krueger, "Union Membership in the United States: The Decline Continues," in Bruce E. Kaufman and Morris M. Kleiner (eds.), *Employee Representation: Alternatives and Future Directions* (Madison, WI: Industrial Relations Research Association, 1993), pp. 105–134.

10-2

demand for union representation, as compared to a decline in the availability of traditionally unionized jobs.

Other Factors

Our three hypotheses do not exhaust the factors that might be contributing to the decline of unionism. For example, evidence exists to suggest that union efforts to organize the unorganized have been insufficient.[27] It has also been argued that the basic values of American society, which stress the free market and competitive individualism, do not provide a fertile environment for a strong labor movement.[28] Finally, the public policy environment became increasingly promanagement during the Reagan–Bush era. In particular, NLRB rulings became increasingly antilabor, creating an administrative–legal environment hostile to union growth.

Relative Importance

Interesting attempts have been made to quantify the significance of the various factors that may have contributed to unionism's decline. How important are structural changes—as compared to, say, enhanced managerial opposition or a diminished effort by unions to organize workers—in explaining the labor movement's eclipse? While

[27]Paula B. Voos, "Union Organizing: Costs and Benefits," *Industrial and Labor Relations Review,* July 1983, pp. 576–591; and Gary N. Chaison and Dileep G. Dahvale, "A Note on the Severity of the Decline in Union Organizing Activity," *Industrial and Labor Relations Review,* April 1990, pp. 366–373.

[28]See Seymour Martin Lipset, "North American Labor Movements: A Comparative Perspective," in Seymour Martin Lipset (ed.), *Unions in Transition* (San Francisco: ICS Press, 1986), pp. 421–452.

10-2 World of Work

REVITALIZATION OF UNIONS?*

The proportion of the labor force that is unionized has fallen by more than one-half over the past four decades. An important contributing factor to this decline has been a decrease in attempts by unions to gain new members. For example, the number of union representation elections has decreased by one-half since 1980. If unions do not gain more new members, union workers will continue to decline as a percentage of the labor force.

This bleak situation has led unions to devote more resources to getting new members. The AFL-CIO has increased its spending on organizing from nearly zero to $20 million—one-third of its $60 million total annual spending.

In addition, unions are undertaking a new strategy toward organizing. The historical union base of well-paid industrial workers has been shrinking over time. As a result, unions are now focusing on organizing low-wage workers such as janitors and manual laborers. It is more difficult to organize such workers since labor laws do not cover temporary and contract workers. Furthermore, low-wage workers typically have low job attachment and may not be willing to fight to improve their jobs.

Some evidence exists that this tack has a chance for success. The Service Employees International Union, which targeted low-wage workers for organizations, is one of the few unions to have gained membership over time. In fact, it has increased its membership by 50 percent over the past 10 years. How successful this new approach will be, however, remains to be seen.

*Based on G. Pascal Zachary, "Signs of Revival" *Wall Street Journal,* September 1, 1995, p. 1.

quantification is difficult and estimates must be treated with some caution, some reasonable measures are available. For example, Farber has confirmed that structural changes in the economy have been of some significance. He estimates that about 40 percent of the decline in organized labor's relative share of the labor force over the 1956–78 period resulted from shifts toward more workers in nonmanufacturing jobs, more white-collar workers, more female workers, and the South.[29]

Similarly, Kochan, McKersie, and Chalykoff studied several hundred partially unionized firms to assess the effects of management policies and practices toward unionization on union membership and the probability that new plants will be unionized. For the average firm in this sample, the number of union workers declined by 977 over the 1977–83 period. In a firm of equivalent size that placed a high priority on union avoidance, the reduction in union workers was 2,647, or almost two and one-half times the decline experienced by average firms. In addition, the probability that a new plant would be organized was 15 percent for an average firm but less than 1 percent for firms that evidenced strong managerial opposition to unions.[30]

Freeman[31] has studied the declining success of unions in winning NLRB (Chapter 13) certification elections and estimates that over one-fourth to almost one-half of the decline in union success in organizing workers through NLRB elections is attributable to managerial opposition. Freeman's overall rough assessment is that about 40 percent of the total decline in unionism is attributable to increased managerial opposition; another 20 percent is the result of reduced efforts by unions to organize nonunion workers; and the remaining 40 percent is due to structural changes in the economy and unknown forces.

10-3

Union Responses

How have unions reacted to their declines?

Mergers One of the basic responses of unions to the relative decline of organized labor has been for unions with similar jurisdictions to merge with one another. Of the more than 85 labor organization mergers that have occurred since the AFL and CIO combined in 1955, about 35 percent took place between 1979 and 1984. While it is true that trade union ideology stresses unity, practical considerations have clearly been paramount in recent mergers. Shrinking membership, declining income from dues, and the desire to achieve a strong and united voice in collective bargaining negotiations have all contributed to the recent impetus for merger.[32]

[29]Henry S. Farber, "The Extent of Unionization in the United States," in Thomas A. Kochan (ed.), *Challenges and Choices Facing American Labor* (Cambridge, MA: MIT Press, 1985), pp. 15–43.

[30]Thomas A. Kochan, Robert B. McKersie, and John Chalykoff, "The Effects of Corporate Strategy and Workplace Innovations on Union Representation," *Industrial and Labor Relations Review,* July 1986, pp. 487–501.

[31]Richard B. Freeman, "Why Are Unions Faring Poorly in NLRB Representation Elections?" in Thomas A. Kochan (ed.), *Challenges and Choices Facing American Labor* (Cambridge, MA: MIT Press, 1985), pp. 45–64.

[32]Larry T. Adams, "Labor Organization Mergers 1979–84: Adapting to Change," *Monthly Labor Review,* September 1984, pp. 21–27.

10-3 World of Work

UNIONISM'S DECLINE: UNIQUE TO THE UNITED STATES?

Supporters of the managerial-opposition hypothesis contend that the decline of unionism is unique to the United States. They discount the role of structural changes by arguing that Canada and the nations of Western Europe have experienced industrial and labor market changes very similar to the United States and that unionism in these countries has continued to flourish and grow.

But evidence presented by Troy* leads him to challenge the managerial-opposition hypothesis. He makes two essential points. First, the structural and labor market changes that have occurred in Canada and Western Europe in fact have differed from those experienced by the United States. Second, a careful analysis of the data shows that private-sector unionism actually has declined in Canada and Western Europe.

Troy points out that Canadian and most Western European labor markets have lagged the United States by a decade or more in shifting from the production of goods to the production of services. Furthermore, within manufacturing the United States has led Canada and Europe in the substitution of high-tech manufacturing (such as computer equipment, semiconductors, and radio and television communications equipment) for "traditional" manufacturing (such as steel and automobiles). The result in the United States has been an enormous substitution of nonunion white-collar jobs for union blue-collar jobs, as the structural-change hypothesis would suggest. According to Troy: "Structural changes in labor markets began sooner, proceeded more rapidly, and their scope was more extensive in the U.S. than in Canada and Western Europe. . . . In union terms, the nonunion labor market grew sooner and much more rapidly in the U.S. than in Canada and Western Europe."†

Troy also alleges that any comparison of American and Canadian unionism is greatly complicated by the fact that in 1985 *public*-sector unions accounted for almost 60 percent of total union membership in Canada, while *private*-sector unions accounted for over 70 percent of total union membership in the United States. He notes that *private*-sector union membership in Canada actually declined from about 26 to only 21 percent of all such workers over the 1975–85 period. Indeed, he presents data that indicate that private-sector unionism has fallen in virtually all of Western Europe.

In summary, Troy argues that the structural changes in Canada and Western Europe have differed from those in the United States in both timing and extensiveness. Additionally, the structural changes that have occurred in Canada and Western Europe have brought about declines in private-sector unionism in those nations. These observations are at odds with the managerial-opposition hypothesis and supportive of the structural-change hypothesis.

*Leo Troy, "Is the U.S. Unique in the Decline of Private Sector Unionism?" *Journal of Labor Research,* Spring 1990, pp. 111–143.

†Ibid., p. 124.

Changes in Strategies Another response by unions to the decline in membership has been changes in union organizing and negotiation strategies.

Unions have increased their efforts to train union organizers and have attempted to define bargaining demands that have appeal to white-collar professionals and to an increasingly female labor force (Chapter 3). For example, some unions are giving a lower priority to wages and working conditions and putting more emphasis on such objectives as parenting leave, child care, and flexible work schedules. Many unions have formulated positions on issues such as worker drug testing and AIDS protection that are of concern to potential members. Moreover, unions have begun to offer several nontraditional services, such as low-interest credit cards and job counseling, to both union and nonunion members. The idea is to create union allegiance and associate membership even though a worker may not presently hold a job in a union bargaining unit.

On the negotiation front, unions increasingly have chosen to avoid strikes, which employers frequently countered by hiring permanent strikebreakers who later voted to decertify the union. One alternative to the strike that has gained prominence and some success is the union-sponsored *work slowdown* or "working sitdown." Rather than proceed with their work as usual, union members "go by the book," which implies working to the very minimum of their job requirements. The decline in production reduces the firm's profitability, much as a strike would, but the employees do not lose their pay or risk replacement by strikebreakers. The goal is to convince management that it is in the firm's interest to negotiate seriously with the union.

ARE UNIONS MAXIMIZERS?

Given some understanding of (1) the size of the labor movement, (2) the kinds of workers who are most likely to belong to unions, (3) the structure of organized labor, and (4) the possible causes of the relative decline in union membership, let's now turn to the thorny question of union objectives.

In Chapter 6 we considered how unions might increase wage rates by manipulating labor supply and demand. One of the "loose ends" in that discussion is the issue of union goals. For what end does a union formulate its wage policy? What are unions trying to achieve in terms of wage and employment outcomes? In terms of Figures 6-8 and 6-9, the question is: To what extent and for what purposes will unions attempt to enhance labor demand or restrict labor supply? Or in terms of Figure 6-10: Why might the union seek the wage rate W_u rather than some higher or lower wage rate?

Economic Models

Most economists view individuals and institutions as attempting to maximize some magnitude or another. Thus, for example, in models of consumer behavior the goal is to maximize utility or satisfaction. Similarly, business firms presumably seek to maximize profits. Thus, it is not surprising that economists have attempted to apply the maximizing concept to unions in explaining their wage policies. As we will now find, attempts to isolate single maximizing goals have *not* been particularly successful.

1 Wage Rate Samuel Gompers, founder of the AFL, is reported to have said that unions want "more, more, more!" But attempts by a union to maximize the wage rate per worker makes no sense. Assuming a union is able to impose its wage demand unilaterally on a totally submissive employer, the logical outcome would be the employment of one worker at an extremely high wage rate! To *maximize* the wage rate would be to *minimize* employment. Unions are concerned with their institutional survival and growth. And their members are concerned with having jobs. Given the reality of a downward-sloping labor demand curve as shown in Figure 10-2, a policy of aggressively pushing up wage rates will cause unemployment among union members. As it

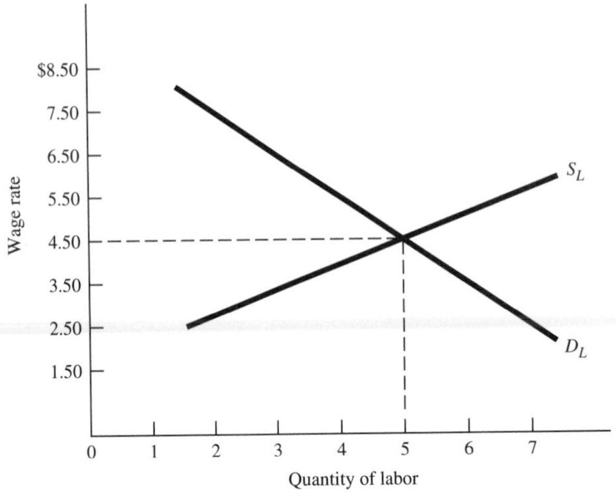

FIGURE 10-2 ARE UNIONS MAXIMIZERS?
Simple maximizing objectives do not adequately describe union behavior. Concern about employment and institutional survival constrains unions from the goal of maximizing—or even dramatically increasing—wage rates. And if the current combination of wage rate and employment were on the elastic segment of the labor demand curve, a union seeking to maximize the wage bill would need to reduce wages. Similarly, the maximization of employment and union membership would occur at the equilibrium wage rate, implying that a union is redundant.

is reasonable to suppose that in time these unemployed workers will seek and obtain alternative jobs and cease to be affiliated with the union, we can conclude that union wage demands eventually will be constrained by unemployment effects. Indeed, the widespread "concession bargaining" of the 1980s, whereby unions accepted wage freezes or agreed to wage cuts, provides rather compelling evidence that unions and their members are concerned with being employed.

2 Wage Bill Given concern with employment, another possible goal might be to maximize the wage bill—the wage rate multiplied by the number of employed workers. But this objective runs into difficulties where the demand for labor is elastic. In Figure 10-2 the labor demand curve is constructed so that demand is elastic at all wage rates above $4.50 and inelastic at all wage rates below $4.50. Now if the union currently enjoys a wage rate above $4.50—say $6.50—it will be obligated to request a wage *reduction* to maximize the wage bill. Why so? Recall from Figure 5-7 that where the demand curve is elastic—as it is at $6.50—a reduction in the wage rate will *increase* the wage bill because the resulting percentage increase in employment will be larger than the percentage reduction in the wage rate per worker.[33] With the labor supply curve in Figure 10-2, the union would maximize the wage bill at the equilibrium

[33]Remember from the discussion of the elasticity coefficient in Chapter 5 that, by definition, demand is elastic when the percentage change in the quantity of labor demanded is greater than the associated percentage change in the wage rate.

wage rate of \$4.50. More precisely, by lowering the wage rate from \$6.50 to \$4.50 the union's wage bill will increase from \$19.50 (= \$6.50 × 3) to \$22.50 (= \$4.50 × 5). In this instance, the union would be irrelevant insofar as wage determination is concerned because the market would yield the combination of wage rate and employment that would maximize the wage bill. Why should workers pay union dues when the market yields the desired result? "The goal of maximizing wages per member is deficient because it implies that unions have no concern for members who become unemployed and no interest in remaining in existence as organizations. The goal of maximizing the wage bill has the opposite difficulty: It implies that unions can be interested in increasing membership to the point of leaving the original members no better off than they would have been without a union."[34]

3 Employment and Membership Because unions are concerned with institutional survival and growth and because union leaders derive prestige and power from presiding over large organizations, perhaps unions seek to maximize the employment of their (dues-paying) members. If in Figure 10-2 we assume that all available workers are union members and the curves reflect the demand for and the supply of *union* workers, the realization of this goal would require the union to seek the competitive equilibrium wage of \$4.50. At any higher wage rate, the constraint of the demand curve would be pertinent and employment would fall below five workers. At any wage rate below the \$4.50, the restraint of the supply curve becomes relevant and employment again falls below five. In other words, at any wage rate above equilibrium, employers will choose to employ fewer than the equilibrium number of workers. At any below-equilibrium wage rate, fewer than the equilibrium number of workers will want to be employed in this market. Again, why have a union if the market will achieve your goal in the union's absence?

Political Models

In view of the problems associated with simple maximizing models of union goals, it is not surprising that some economists have argued that it is more appropriate to treat unions as essentially political rather than economic institutions (Chapter 16).[35] Thus, union wage–employment policies are envisioned as entailing a series of political compromises as union leaders respond to pressures from their constituents, employers, government, and rival unions. Furthermore, a union's wage–employment policy must consider not only the economic well-being of its members but also the survival and growth of the union as an institution and the ability of the union's leadership to remain in office. This political model eschews simple maximizing goals to argue that in reality union wage demands are usually formulated in terms of "equitable comparisons," that is, in terms of what comparable groups of workers are being paid. Thus, for example,

[34]Albert Rees, *The Economics of Trade Unions* (Chicago: University of Chicago Press, 1962), pp. 53–54.
[35]The classic work is Arthur M. Ross, *Trade Union Wage Policy* (Berkeley: University of California Press, 1948).

unions in the fabricated metals industry may base their wage demands on what the steelworkers are being paid.[36]

Synopsis

Our conclusion is that while unions do engage in purposeful behavior, their goals are multidimensional and impossible to analyze through one-dimensional maximization assumptions. Indeed, by glancing at Table 10-5's synopsis of the contents of a typical collective bargaining agreement, the multiplicity of areas of concern to unions becomes apparent. There is some agreement that while unions are ordinarily concerned with both wages and employment, the former is probably of paramount interest. Although economists take the notion of a trade-off between wages and employment for granted, that relationship is not always evident to union workers and their leaders. To them, the links between wage rates, production costs, product prices, and product sales are far from precise or dependable. For example, workers observe that fluctuations in a firm's sales and therefore in employment seem to be linked to the general state of the economy and have little to do with the level of wage rates in their particular firm. Similarly,

[36]For in-depth discussions of union objectives, see Allan M. Cartter, *Theory of Wages and Employment* (Homewood, IL: Richard D. Irwin, Inc., 1959), chap. 7; and Hirsch and Addison, op. cit., chap. 2. For empirical studies of union goals, see Felice Martinello, "Wage and Employment Determination in a Unionized Industry: The IWA and the British Columbia Wood Products Industry," *Journal of Labor Economics,* July 1989, pp. 303–330; Janet Currie, "Employment Determination in a Unionized Public Sector Labor Market: The Case of Ontario's School Teachers," *Journal of Labor Economics,* January 1991, pp. 45–66; and Walter J. Wessels, "Do Unions Contract for Added Employment?" *Industrial and Labor Relations Review,* October 1991, pp. 181–193.

TABLE 10-5 ABBREVIATED CONTENTS OF A COLLECTIVE BARGAINING AGREEMENT

The agreement and its administration	**Job security, promotions, and layoffs**
Managerial rights and obligations	Seniority provisions
Union security and status	Hiring and layoff procedures
Contract enforcement	Training and retraining
Grievance procedure	Severance pay
Mediation and arbitration	Promotion procedures
Wage determination	Allocation of overtime work
Basic wage rates and wage structure	**Fringe benefits**
Incentive systems	Pension plans
Pay for overtime work	Health and insurance plans
Shift differentials	Sick leave
Cost-of-living adjustments	Vacations and holidays
Company operations	Profit-sharing stock-purchase plans
Work rules	Parenting leave
Disciplinary procedures	Child care facilities
Production rates and standards	
Safety and health	

the decline in employment resulting from the substitution of capital for labor may be interpreted by workers as the consequence of an "unfortunate" management decision rather than a response to higher wages. Furthermore, workers may feel that wage rates are a factor over which they can collectively exert some degree of control. Employment, on the other hand, depends on the decisions of others and the general state of the economy.[37]

With these points in mind, let's turn to the unique characteristics of the collective bargaining transaction.

QUICK REVIEW 10-2

- Union membership as a percent of the labor force has fallen steadily over recent decades; also, the absolute number of union members is lower today than in 1980.
- Three hypotheses—perhaps complementary—have been offered to explain the decline in unionism: *(a)* structural changes in industry composition and location, *(b)* renewed managerial opposition to unions, and *(c)* substitution by government and employers of services formerly provided by unions.
- Unions have responded to their decline by merging and developing creative strategies to serve members' needs.
- Union goals are multidimensional and impossible to analyze adequately through one-dimensional economic assumptions such as maximizing the wage bill or maximizing employment and membership.

Your Turn: Which of the following would most likely *increase* union membership as a percent of the labor force? *(a)* the movement of manufacturing firms from the Northeast to the Southwest, *(b)* a decline in imports, *(c)* expansion of high-technology industries such as computer chips and software, or *(d)* a relative decline in employment in the public sector. (Answer: See page 626.)

COLLECTIVE BARGAINING: A COMPLEX TRANSACTION[38]

Economic transactions range from the exceedingly simple to the highly complex. Buying a loaf of bread at a supermarket or obtaining a Coke from a vending machine is a clearly uncomplicated transaction. In contrast, the negotiation of a collective bargaining agreement is undoubtedly one of the most complex transactions occurring in our economy. This complexity derives from a number of unique characteristics of the collective bargaining transaction.

[37]For more on the union view of the relationship between the wage rate and employment, see Mitchell, op. cit., pp. 64–68.

[38]Instructors wishing to move immediately to a discussion of union impacts (Chapter 11) can skip the remainder of this chapter.

Delivering Labor Services

Labor services are inseparably tied up with the worker who is "selling" or "renting" those services to an employer. While the buyer and seller of a used car may never see each other again after their transaction, the seller of labor services must spend 40 or so hours per week in an office or factory delivering those services to the buyer. Collective bargaining thus involves much more than wage determination. Working conditions, work rules, promotion and training, job safety, seniority, level of job risk, fringe benefits, and a spectrum of other issues must be mutually approved by the union and management. Table 10-5 illustrates the range and complexity of bargainable issues. While our discussion will focus on the wage aspects of bargaining, it is important to keep in mind that the bargaining agenda is extensive and that many of the bargaining subjects affect the cost of employing workers.

Long-Term Relationship

The relationship between labor and management is long-term. The parties will negotiate a contract this year, a new contract 2 or 3 years hence, and so forth. This long-term relationship is important because what transpires in negotiating this year's contract can have an impact on succeeding agreements. For example, suppose that in the present negotiations the union flatly threatens to strike if the employer does not double its contribution to the pension plan. If the employer rejects this demand and the union does *not* strike, the credibility of the union's threats will be diminished in future negotiations.

Negotiations

Many buyers and sellers confront each other on a simple "take-it-or-leave-it" basis. A supermarket manager will not negotiate the price of a loaf of bread, and a vending machine stands mute as you consider dropping in $.60 for a Coke. If you decide not to buy the bread or the Coke, no great damage is inflicted on either potential buyer or seller.

But labor and management are highly dependent on each other, and this changes their transaction from a take-it-or-leave-it situation to one of *negotiation.* If labor and management do not reach agreement and a strike therefore results, significant costs will be imposed on both parties. More positively, collective bargaining involves a ***symbiotic relationship*** between the two parties, that is, a relationship that simultaneously involves elements of both *cooperation* and *competition.* On the one hand, both parties gain by cooperating and reaching agreement. By agreeing, the two parties combine their resources in the production of some good or service and share the revenues derived therefrom. Hence, there is a strong mutual interest in reaching agreement. On the other hand, the two parties are in a competitive position because the "terms of trade" under which agreement is reached determine how the revenues stemming from their cooperative efforts in the production process will be shared between the two parties.

Given these several characteristics of the bargaining transaction, let's next examine the bargaining process. This process is a means for resolving the opposing interests of the union and the employer. We will see that the key to this resolution is the symbiotic relationship just described.

A MODEL OF THE BARGAINING PROCESS

Although models of collective bargaining are numerous,[39] we will confine our attention to a conceptually simple, but very insightful, bargaining model developed by Chamberlain.[40] This model focuses on the determinants of bargaining power and the ways changes in these determinants lead to settlement in the majority of collective bargaining situations.

The Model

Chamberlain defines ***bargaining power*** as the ability to secure your opponent's agreement to your terms. Thus, a ***union's bargaining power*** can be defined as management's willingness to agree to the union's terms or demands. But what determines the willingness (or unwillingness) of management to agree to the union's terms? The answer, according to Chamberlain, depends on how costly disagreeing will be relative to how costly agreeing will be. That is:

$$\text{Union's bargaining power (UBP)} = \frac{\text{management's perceived cost of disagreeing with the union's terms (MCD)}}{\text{management's perceived cost of agreeing with the union's terms (MCA)}} \tag{10-1}$$

If management estimates that it is more costly to agree than to disagree (that is, if the union's bargaining power is less than 1), management will choose to disagree and reject the union's terms. If, however, management judges that it is more costly to disagree than to agree (that is, if the union's bargaining power is greater than 1), management will choose to agree.

But what constitutes the "cost of agreeing" and the "cost of disagreeing"? If we simplify by assuming the wage rate is the only bargainable issue, then ***management's cost of disagreeing*** is the probable or estimated loss of profits during the strike that *may* follow its rejection of the union's stated wage demand. This perceived cost is probabilistic in that management's estimate of the cost of disagreeing depends on its estimate of both (1) the probability that a strike will occur if the wage demand is rejected

[39]The ambitious reader may want to consult Charles Mulvey, *The Economic Analysis of Trade Unions* (New York: St. Martin's Press, 1978), chap. 7; Bevars D. Mabry, *Economics of Manpower and the Labor Market* (New York: Intext Educational Publishers, 1973), chap. 13; John G. Cross, *The Economics of Bargaining* (New York: Basic Books, Inc., 1969); Richard B. Peterson and Lane Tracy, *Models of the Bargaining Process: With Special Reference to Collective Bargaining* (Seattle: University of Washington, Graduate School of Business Administration, 1977); and Terry L. Leap and David W. Grisby, "A Conceptualization of Collective Bargaining Power," *Industrial and Labor Relations Review,* January 1986, pp. 202–213.

[40]Neil W. Chamberlain, *A General Theory of Economic Process* (New York: Harper & Row, 1955), particularly chaps. 6–8.

and (2) the probable length of the strike should it occur. ***Management's cost of agreeing***—that is, the perceived cost of accepting the union's wage demand—is the estimated reduction in the flow of profits resulting from the payment of a higher than intended wage rate.

Management's bargaining power can be similarly defined:

$$\text{Management's bargaining power (MBP)} = \frac{\text{union's perceived cost of disagreeing with management's terms (UCD)}}{\text{union's perceived cost of agreeing with management's terms (UCA)}} \qquad (10\text{-}2)$$

Once again, if the union believes it is more costly to agree than to disagree, the union will disagree with management's offer. Whenever the denominator is greater than the numerator in equation (10-2)—that is, whenever management's bargaining power is less than 1—the union will choose to reject management's offer. Conversely, if the union judges it to be more costly to disagree than to agree, the union will choose to agree. In other words, when management's bargaining power is greater than 1, the union will be willing to accept management's offer.

The union's costs of disagreeing and agreeing can be defined similarly to those of management. The ***union's cost of disagreeing*** is the probable loss of wage income during a strike. This estimate depends on the probability that a strike will occur *and* on the estimated length of the strike. The ***union's cost of agreeing*** is a reduced flow of wage income. Given that the union seeks a higher wage rate than management is now willing to offer, the decision to accept the lower wage offered by management entails forgoing the larger flow of wage income to which the union and its constituents aspire.

Implications

Several significant observations can be derived directly from these concepts of bargaining power.[41]

1 Requirement for Agreement The necessary condition for a settlement is that one party must be willing to agree to the terms put forward by the other party. More specifically, management (the union) will be willing to agree to the union's (management's) terms when management (the union) feels that the cost of disagreeing with those terms is greater than the cost of agreeing. As previously noted, in the bargaining power ratios of equations (10-1) and (10-2), the ratio would have to exceed unity, or 1, for agreement to be possible.

To illustrate, suppose negotiations begin with the union asking for a $1.00 per hour wage increase. Consulting equation (10-1), if management perceives that the cost of disagreeing to this wage demand will exceed the cost of agreeing, then management

[41]For a survey of empirical research on strikes and bargaining, see David Card, "Strikes and Bargaining: A Survey of the Recent Empirical Literature," *American Economic Review,* May 1990, pp. 410–415.

will be willing to accept the union's wage demand. Needless to say, the $1.00 wage increase is presumably also acceptable to the union because it is the union's proposal. On the other hand, if management perceives that the costs of agreeing will exceed the costs of disagreeing, the union's wage demand will be unacceptable to management. At this point several things may happen: The union may alter (lower) its wage demand, management may put an alternative (higher) wage offer on the table for consideration by the union, or a stalemate (strike) may result. The implications of these developments are discussed below.

2 Relative Bargaining Power Individuals normally think of the bargaining power of a union or an employer as being in some sense absolute. But Chamberlain's model correctly suggests that a party's bargaining power is *relative* in the sense that it will depend on what is being demanded or offered. For example, equation (10-1) implies that the union's bargaining power will be much less when it is asking for, say, a $1.00 per hour wage increase than when it is asking for only $.20 more per hour. Why so? Because it is very costly for management to agree to a $1.00 wage increase, while it costs relatively little to agree to a $.20 per hour wage boost. In equation (10-1) the denominator will be small for the $.20 wage demand, tending to cause the union's bargaining power to exceed unity and inducing management's acceptance of the union's terms. Conversely, the denominator of equation (10-1) will be large for the $1.00 wage demand, tending to cause the union's bargaining power to be less than unity so that the necessary condition for agreement is not realized. The important generalization is that *the greater the union's wage demand, the greater the management's resistance to it and therefore the less the union's bargaining power.*

3 "Unnecessary" Strikes We have stressed that the necessary condition for agreement is that one party must find it more costly to disagree than to agree with the other party's wage demand or offer. But this is not a sufficient condition for agreement. Work stoppages may arise because one party misjudges the other's position *or* because the parties become committed to irreconcilable positions during the negotiation process.

Misjudgment Let's suppose that, in fact, management would be willing to grant a maximum hourly wage increase of, say, $.50 per hour. That is, $.50 is the maximum wage increase at which management perceives the cost of disagreeing to exceed the cost of agreeing. Similarly, suppose the union is willing to accept as little as a $.25 hourly increase. This is the minimum wage increase at which the union perceives the cost of disagreeing to exceed the cost of agreeing. We thus have a range or zone of potential agreement where the necessary condition for agreement is present. Either party would rather agree than disagree with the opponent's terms within the $.25 to $.50 range.

But the negotiation process occurs in an environment of incomplete knowledge. Specifically, the union does *not* know the maximum wage increase ($.50) to which management will agree because this depends on management's estimates of the costs of agreeing and disagreeing to the union's wage demands. Similarly, management does *not* know the minimum wage increase ($.25) the union will accept. Now assume the union misjudges the maximum wage increase that management will concede. For example, suppose the exchange of information that occurs in the bargaining process leads the union to believe that management will eventually concede $.60 per hour rather than the actual $.50. If the union adamantly demands $.60 during negotiations, time may run out, and the cost of this misjudgment will be an unwanted and unnecessary strike. A similar outcome would occur if management misjudged the lowest acceptable wage increase to the union to be, say, $.15.[42]

Commitments The other possibility is that the union and management might become "committed" to irreconcilable positions within the $.50 to $.25 range of potential agreements. That is, the parties may establish a wage demand and a wage offer from which neither can retreat without "loss of face" and the undermining of its credibility in future negotiations. For example, management might become committed to a $.30 wage increase on the grounds that it is noninflationary, and management accepts social responsibility to behave in a noninflationary manner. Conversely, the union may become committed to a $.40 hourly increase on the grounds that it is justified on the basis of "what other peer groups of workers are getting." These commitments, clearly tied to publicized "principles," may put both parties in a position where they cannot retreat from their stated terms without bringing into question the credibility of the positions they may take in future negotiations. We have here a range of mutually acceptable wage increases but no actual agreement. By becoming committed, the parties blunder into a strike that neither wants. To the layperson it appears highly irrational to engage in a perhaps long and mutually costly strike over a few cents an hour. However, such an outcome is more understandable when one recognizes that if, for example, the union adamantly says it will strike should it not receive $.40 per hour and then fails to do so, its bargaining power in future negotiations will be decreased because the credibility of its demands has been diminished.[43]

4 Reaching Agreement Let's assume that initially the bargaining power of neither party exceeds unity. That is, at the outset of the negotiation period both parties feel it is more costly to agree than to disagree with its opponent's terms. As the bargaining process proceeds, two developments may occur that cause the parties to move toward agreement. In the first place, collective bargaining negotiations are characterized by a *deadline*. For example, the parties begin to bargain, say, 60 days prior to the termination of their current collective bargaining agreement. It is generally understood that if no agreement is reached during the negotiating period, a work stoppage in the form of either a strike or a lockout will occur. The general rule is "no contract, no work." Now recall that an important ingredient of each party's perceived cost of disagreeing is the

[42]The empirical evidence indicates that strikes occur because of mistakes. For example, one study indicates that the length and probability of a strike decline as the experience level of the bargainers rises. See Edward Montgomery and Mary Ellen Benedict, "The Impact of Bargainer Experience on Teacher Strikes," *Industrial and Labor Relations Review,* April 1989, pp. 380–392. Also see Martin J. Mauro, "Strikes as a Result of Imperfect Information," *Industrial and Labor Relations Review,* July 1982, pp. 522–538; and John F. Schnell and Cynthia L. Gramm, "Learning by Striking: Estimates of the Teetotaler Effect," *Journal of Labor Economics,* April 1987, pp. 221–241.

[43]For a perceptive discussion of the "commitment" issue in particular and the bargaining process in general, see Carl M. Stevens, *Strategy and Collective Bargaining Negotiations* (New York: McGraw-Hill Book Company, Inc., 1963).

probability that a strike will occur. One can expect that as the strike deadline approaches, both parties will revise upward their estimate that a strike will in fact occur. In equations (10-1) and (10-2), this means that as the prestrike negotiating period diminishes, the estimated costs of disagreeing for labor and management will rise, increasing the likelihood that the bargaining power of one or both parties will exceed unity and therefore create the necessary condition for agreement. The purpose of a deadline in collective bargaining is to create pressures on both parties to reach agreement. In Chamberlain's model this function is reflected in upward revisions of the perceived costs of disagreeing for both parties.

The second and perhaps most evident factor that may move the bargainers toward agreement is revision of the terms of both parties. Compromise demands and offers promote agreement. Specifically, the union may lower its wage demand and management may increase its wage offer. If the union lowers its wage demand, management's cost of agreeing is reduced in equation (10-1), pushing the union's bargaining power toward unity and making for agreement. Similarly, an increase in management's wage offer will reduce the union's cost of agreeing in equation (10-2), driving management's bargaining power toward unity and thereby agreement.

There is, however, a potential problem with compromise offers and demands. While they reduce the opponent's costs of agreeing and increase one's own bargaining power, the risk exists that a compromise offer or demand will be interpreted by the opponent as a sign of weakness. Should this happen, the opponent's cost of disagreeing will also decrease, reducing one's own bargaining power and impeding agreement. For example, if the union reduces its wage demand, management might interpret this to mean that the union is very anxious to reach agreement and therefore a strike is less likely to occur than management had thought. Thus, management revises its estimate of the cost of disagreeing downward. The point is that by reducing its wage demand, the union may reduce *both* management's cost of agreeing and its cost of disagreeing. Declines in both the numerator and denominator of equation (10-1) do not necessarily move the negotiators toward agreement.

5 Negotiating Tactics: Coercion and Persuasion Chamberlain's model encompasses the use of negotiating tactics as a means of improving one's bargaining power. Given equations (10-1) and (10-2), either party can increase its bargaining power by increasing its opponent's perception of the cost of disagreeing *and* by decreasing the opponent's estimate of the cost of agreeing.

Coercive Tactics Tactics designed to increase the opponent's cost of disagreeing might be termed ***coercive bargaining tactics*** since they suggest that some negative or undesirable outcomes, which have been either ignored or underestimated, will occur if the opponent does not agree to the other party's terms. Thus, the union might take a strike vote or emphasize the availability of strike funds to induce management to increase its estimate of the probability that a strike will occur if it rejects the union's wage demand. If successful, management's estimate of the cost of disagreeing will increase in equation (10-1), and hence, so will the union's bargaining power. Conversely, in terms of equation (10-2) the company may threaten to automate or close the plant to prompt the union to increase its estimate of the cost of disagreeing to management's wage offer.

Strikes and lockouts, of course, are coercive tactics in and of themselves. As the length of a work stoppage increases, the actual loss of wage income rises and this increases the union's cost of disagreeing. Similarly, the lengthening impasse increases the amount of revenues and profits lost by the firm and therefore increases its cost of disagreeing. Furthermore, during a strike coercive tactics may be employed in an attempt to increase a party's bargaining power. For example, unions may picket the firm to reduce patronage and to keep other employees from working. In both instances the picketing imposes higher costs of disagreeing on the firm. It is important to note that in collective bargaining, a strike or lockout can play a positive role in that it impels the two parties toward agreement by increasing their costs of disagreeing.

Persuasive Tactics Tactics designed to decrease the opponent's estimate of the costs of agreeing can be labeled *conciliatory* or ***persuasive bargaining tactics*** because they imply that certain desirable outcomes, which have been ignored or underestimated, will occur if the opponent agrees to the other party's terms. Thus, the union may stress that higher wages will improve worker morale and productivity, enhance the prosperity of the community and hence of the firm itself, improve worker discipline, reduce turnover, and so forth. Similarly, management may argue that the acceptance of its wage offer will make the firm more competitive in its industry, increasing employment security for workers and providing them with greater opportunities for overtime work. And, of course, we have already noted that either party usually can reduce the other's cost of agreeing by altering the wage demand or offer. The union can reduce management's cost of agreeing and increase the probability of settlement by asking for a smaller wage increase; management can reduce the union's cost of agreeing by offering a larger wage increase. In fact, this process of compromise in wage demands and offers is typically involved in the resolution of strikes.

QUICK REVIEW 10-3

- Collective bargaining is a complex transaction because labor services are tied to human beings, the union and the firm have a long-term relationship, and contract decisions are made through negotiations.
- In the Chamberlain bargaining model, bargaining power is the ability of one party to get the other party to agree with its terms.
- The union's (management's) bargaining power depends on the strength of management's (the union's) cost of disagreeing relative to its cost of agreeing, the higher management's (the union's) cost of disagreeing relative to its cost of agreeing, the greater is the union's (management's) bargaining power.
- The union (management) can increase its bargaining power through coercive tactics that *(a)* increase management's (the union's) cost of agreeing; the higher management's (the union's) costs of disagreeing relative to its cost of disagreeing or via persuasive tactics that *(b)* decrease management's (the union's) cost of agreeing.

Your Turn: Suppose that in a particular negotiation the union's bargaining power is 1.3 while management's bargaining power is .8 (Chamberlain model). Will settlement occur? Why or why not? If so, on whose terms? Explain. (Answers: See page 626.)

10-4

10-4 World of Work

AND FINALLY THE CONTRACT WAS SIGNED!

The collective bargaining process often is long and tedious, involving much strategy and the use of coercive and persuasive tactics. Some of these tactics work; others do not. People who are unfamiliar with the art of bargaining often view the actions of negotiators as being frivolous and even immature. In reality, most of these actions are purposeful, being part of the collective bargaining "game."

The following anonymously written poem, although supplied in jest, provides a central insight about the collective bargaining process.

We wheedled and threatened and blustered,
We ranted and wrangled and roared;
We chided and fretted, we scoffed and we petted,
We snickered and wept and implored;
We groveled and swore and demanded,
We spurned and we fawned and we brayed,
We trampled on data, and tossed ultimata,
We grumped and we stamped and inveighed;
We whimpered and simpered and shouted,
Pretended, defended, and doubted;
We smiled and we jested, reviled and protested,
Debated, orated, and shouted;
We fumed and we sneered and we whined,
We flattered, cajoled, and maligned,
Consented, revoked, and declined . . .
And finally the contract was signed!*

*Anonymous, quoted by Henry Mayer, "Should Politics Make Mediators Expendable? *Labor Law Journal,* May 1953, p. 317.

6 The Economic Environment Economic forces are not circumvented by collective bargaining. On the contrary, the character of the economic environment within which workers and employers negotiate affects the bargaining power of the two parties. In our discussion we will consider (1) the overall condition of the national economy and (2) the structure of the employer's industry.

Prosperity and Recession Generally speaking, the bargaining power of a union is procyclical and that of an employer is countercyclical. A strong economy enhances a union's bargaining strength while weakening the bargaining power of the employer.

If the economy has been prosperous and operating at, or close to, full employment for a period of time, we can expect the bargaining power of the union to be strong. In the first place, if workers actually strike the employer, they will have a good chance of obtaining alternative employment. This means that workers will be in a good position to prolong a strike. Conversely, the employer will have few alternative sources of labor in the event of a work stoppage. A second and related point is that a period of prosperity will have provided workers with an opportunity to build their personal savings and their union with an opportunity to enlarge its strike fund. Finally, if the firm has been operating at capacity for some time, its inventories will be low. This means that if a strike occurs, the firm will not be able to service its customers for any length of time. The employer will lose profitable business and, perhaps more important, may lose established customers to other producers who are not experiencing labor disputes. The impact of all of these considerations is to increase management's perceived cost of disagreeing to the union's terms (equation 10-1), which clearly has the effect of increasing the union's bargaining power.

When the economy is experiencing a recession, the tables will be turned. In a recession the employer is likely to have overly large inventories of unsold goods so that at least for a time, customers could be served during a strike. In fact, a firm that is losing money by operating at a loss during a recession may find the cost of a strike to be virtually nil. Similarly, unemployed nonstriking workers may be readily available to operate the employer's plant in the event of a strike. And the high unemployment rate means that it will be difficult for striking workers to find alternative jobs. All of these factors suggest that the union's perceived cost of disagreeing with the employer's terms will be high in equation (10-2) and that management's bargaining power will be enhanced.[44]

Industry Structure No clear agreement exists among economists as to how industry structure affects bargaining power. Is bargaining power greater for firms functioning in a heavily concentrated, oligopolistic industry such as the automobile industry or in unconcentrated, more competitive environments such as the clothing and shoe industries? On the one hand, we would expect a corporate giant in a concentrated industry to have great financial resources to draw on in meeting the costs associated with a strike. One could argue that a union, realizing this, will estimate the cost of disagreeing with the employer's terms to be high and, therefore, that management's bargaining power in equation (10-2) will be large. On the other hand, large firms in concentrated industries may possess a degree of monopoly power enabling them to practice administered pricing and to pass increases in labor costs on to consumers via higher product prices. This exercise of market power allows management to "escape" union attempts to encroach upon profits. Such firms may find it convenient to acquiesce to the union's wage demand. If the union feels that the "will to resist" of such firms is weak, its perceived cost of disagreeing with management's terms will be small in equation (10-2) and so will management's bargaining power.

The scope or coverage of a collective bargaining agreement *and* the extent to which an industry is unionized can also have important effects on bargaining power. For example, if a union is bargaining simultaneously with all three or four firms in an oligopolistic industry, the resistance shown to the union's wage demand may be less than if the union were bargaining with one of the firms separately. For the firms as a group, a 5 percent increase in labor costs and in product price will put none of the firms at a competitive disadvantage vis-à-vis its rivals. But a single firm might exhibit greater resistance when faced with the prospect of raising its price by 5 percent while its rivals do not. Similarly, when the degree of unionization in an industry is small, the union's bargaining power will tend to be weak. If only a few firms are organized in the industry, those firms will find themselves at an obvious competitive disadvantage vis-à-vis nonunion firms if they accept union wage demands significantly above those paid by nonunion firms. In equation (10-1) this competitive disadvantage may be re-

[44]For evidence that strikes are procyclical, see Susan B. Vroman, "A Longitudinal Analysis of Strike Activity in U.S. Manufacturing: 1957–1984," *American Economic Review,* September 1989, pp. 816–826; and Peter C. Cramton and Joseph S. Tracy, "The Determinants of U.S. Labor Disputes," *Journal of Labor Economics,* April 1994, pp. 180–209.

garded as increasing management's cost of agreeing to the union's terms and therefore reducing the union's bargaining power.

CHAPTER SUMMARY

1 Unions are in part the consequence of industrialization, which changed the economy from one dominated by self-employment to one where labor depends on management for employment and earnings.

2 Approximately 16.1 million workers—about one worker in eight—belong to a labor union. Membership is relatively strong in goods-producing industries and weak in service-providing industries. Unionization is also relatively strong in the public sector.

3 Male, older, and black workers are more likely to belong to unions than female, young, and white workers. These differences are largely explained by the industrial and occupational affiliations of these demographic groups.

4 Labor unions are strongest in the heavily urbanized, heavily industrialized states and are relatively weak in the South.

5 The structure of the labor movements reveals three basic levels of union organization. The American Federation of Labor and Congress of Industrial Organizations (AFL-CIO) is concerned with formulating and expressing labor's political views and resolving jurisdictional disputes among national unions. The primary functions of the national unions are to organize unorganized workers and negotiate collective bargaining agreements. The task of administering bargaining agreements falls primarily to the local unions. Bargaining structures are many and diverse.

6 Unionism has been declining relatively in the United States. Some labor economists attribute this to changes in the composition of domestic output and in the demographic structure of the labor force that have been uncongenial to union growth. Others contend that employers, recognizing that unionization results in lower profitability, have more aggressively sought by both legal and illegal means to dissuade workers from being union members. Still others feel that government programs and "progressive" labor relations by employers have usurped many of organized labor's traditional functions, lessening workers' perceived need for union membership.

7 Union bargaining behavior cannot be readily interpreted in terms of the maximization of such magnitudes as wage rates, the wage bill, or employment.

8 Collective bargaining embodies several unique characteristics: *(a)* Workers must deliver their labor services over time, which makes working conditions, work rules, and a variety of other issues bargainable; *(b)* because a long-term relationship exists between management and a union, the negotiations involved in the present contract have an impact upon future negotiations; *(c)* a symbiotic relationship exists between the union and management in that both parties benefit from cooperating (agreeing) but simultaneously are competing for shares of the revenue they jointly produce.

9 Chamberlain has defined bargaining power as the ability to secure your opponent's agreement to your terms. The willingness of your opponent to accept your terms depends on the comparative costs of disagreeing and agreeing. That is:

$$\text{Your bargaining power} = \frac{\text{opponent's cost of disagreeing to your terms}}{\text{opponent's cost of agreeing to your terms}}$$

10 The Chamberlain bargaining power model has a number of salient implications: *(a)* At least one party must perceive disagreement to be more costly than agreement in order for agreement to occur; *(b)* one's bargaining power is relative in that it depends on the size of the wage increase one is asking for or offering; *(c)* misjudgment of the maximum offer the employer will make (or the minimum offer the union will accept) or the commitment of the parties to irreconcilable positions may result in a strike, even though a range of mutually acceptable settlements exists; *(d)* compromise offers (and demands) and the approach of the bargaining deadline both tend to move the parties toward agreement; *(e)* the model allows for coercive tactics (which increase your opponent's costs of disagreeing) and for persuasive tactics (which reduce your opponent's cost of agreeing); and *(f)* the economic environment, including both the state of the macroeconomy and industry structure, can affect the bargaining power of the two parties.

TERMS AND CONCEPTS

American Federation of Labor and Congress of Industrial Organizations (AFL-CIO)
national unions
local unions
bargaining structure
pattern bargaining
structural-change hypothesis
managerial-opposition hypothesis
substitution hypothesis
symbiotic relationship
Chamberlain's bargaining power model
union's (management's) bargaining power
management's (union's) cost of agreeing and disagreeing
coercive bargaining tactics
persuasive bargaining tactics

QUESTIONS AND STUDY SUGGESTIONS

1 Why have unions evolved? To what extent is the civilian labor force unionized? Indicate the *(a)* industrial and *(b)* occupational distribution of union members. Why are relatively fewer white-collar workers organized than blue-collar workers? Briefly explain union membership differences as related to gender, race, and age. Evaluate this statement: "Whether an individual worker is a union member depends not so much on the worker's feelings toward membership, as on her or his occupational choice."

2 Summarize the organizational structure of the American labor movement, indicating the functions of the AFL-CIO, the national unions, and the local unions.

3 Describe the variety of bargaining structures that exist in the United States. What might be the advantages of multiemployer bargaining to a union? To employers? What is "pattern bargaining"?

4 Critically evaluate each of these statements:

a "The relative decline of the American labor movement can be explained by the shift from goods-producing to service-providing industries and by the closely related shifts from blue- to white-collar occupations and from male to female employers."

b "The success of unions in raising their wages relative to nonunion workers has contributed to the decline of unionism."

c "Unionized firms have tended to become less profitable, and therefore, employers are more resistant to unionization."

5 Explain the rapid growth of public-sector unionism in the 1960s and early 1970s, despite the general deunionization of the economy during this period.

6 What are some of the difficulties encountered in using maximizing models to explain trade union behavior? Specifically, using the elasticity of demand concept, explain how the goal of maximizing the wage bill might prompt a union to prefer lower wages.

7 In what ways does collective bargaining differ from most transactions between buyers and sellers? What is the nature of the "symbiotic relationship" existing between a union and management?

8 How does Chamberlain define bargaining power from the union's point of view? From management's standpoint? Explain this statement: "No agreement will be possible unless for at least one of the parties the cost of agreeing to the opponent's terms is less than the cost of disagreeing to those terms." Explain how coercive and persuasive tactics might be employed within Chamberlain's model. Is it rational for a party to engage in coercive and persuasive tactics simultaneously?

9 Explain in terms of Chamberlain's model: "Bargaining power depends on how much is demanded of the opponent." If there is no basis for agreement initially under the Chamberlain model, what developments might occur over time to create conditions favorable to settlement? Explain how a strike might occur even though a range of potential agreement exists. "Negotiation deadlines and strikes play *positive* roles in collective bargaining." Do you agree? Explain.

10 Use Chamberlain's conception of a union's bargaining power to explain the rationale for each of the following union tactics:

a The union announces a strike vote wherein workers overwhelmingly endorse striking.

b The union places a full-page newspaper ad explaining the reasonableness of its wage demand.

c The union threatens to encourage a buyer's boycott of the firm's product.

d The union pickets the firm.

e The union promises to accept the removal of certain provisions of the old bargaining agreement that management claims diminish labor productivity.

f The union eliminates its demand for a 5-day increase in sick leaves.

g The union reduces its hourly wage demand by $.20.

Indicate which of the above actions or tactics are coercive and which are persuasive.

11 How does the bargaining power of labor and management vary over the business cycle? What is the effect of industry structure on the bargaining power of a union?

12 Explain the impact on a union's bargaining power of *(a)* welfare programs and *(b)* the federal commitment to maintain full employment.

SELECTED REFERENCES

Chamberlain, Neil W.: *A General Theory of Economic Process* (New York: Harper & Row, 1955).

Freeman, Richard B., and Casey Ichniowski (eds.): *When Public Sector Workers Unionize* (Chicago: University of Chicago Press, 1988).

Goldfield, Michael: *The Decline of Organized Labor in the United States* (Chicago: University of Chicago Press, 1987).

Huang, Wei-Chiao (ed.): *Organized Labor at the Crossroads* (Kalamazoo, MI: W. E. Upjohn Institute, 1989).

Kennan, John: "Strikes and Bargaining," in Orley Ashenfelter and Richard Layard (eds.), *Handbook of Labor Economics* (Amsterdam: North-Holland, 1986).

Kerr, Clark, and Paul D. Staudohar (eds.): *Industrial Relations in a New Age* (San Francisco: Jossey-Bass Publishers, 1986).

Kochan, Thomas A. (ed.): *Challenges and Choices Facing American Labor* (Cambridge, MA: MIT Press, 1985).

Lazear, Edward P., Richard B. Freeman, and Melvin W. Reder: "Symposium on Public and Private Unionization," *Journal of Economic Perspectives,* Spring 1988, pp. 59–110.

Lipset, Seymour Martin (ed.): *Unions in Transition* (San Francisco: ICS Press, 1986).

Mulvey, Charles: *The Economic Analysis of Trade Unions* (New York: St. Martin's Press, 1978).

Strauss, George, Daniel G. Gallagher, and Jack Fiorito (eds.): *The State of the Unions* (Madison, WI: Industrial Relations Research Association, 1991).

CHAPTER 11

THE ECONOMIC IMPACT OF UNIONS

In the previous chapter we focused on (1) the industrial, occupational, and demographic characteristics of organized labor; (2) the institutional structure of the American labor movement; (3) the unique characteristics of collective bargaining negotiations; and (4) a model of the negotiation process.

In this chapter we direct our attention to the economic effects of unions and collective bargaining. The specific issues we want to examine are as follows. First, are unions able to gain a wage advantage through collective bargaining? Other things being equal, do union workers in a given occupation receive higher wages than nonunion workers in the same occupation? And what of fringe benefits? Are they more or less generous when unions are present? Second, what are the implications of unions and collective bargaining for productivity and allocative efficiency? Is our economy more or less efficient because of the presence of unions? Third, how do unions affect profitability? Do organized firms and industries earn larger or smaller profits than those that are nonunion? Fourth, what is the impact of union wage determination on the distribution of earnings? Do unions cause wage income to be more or less equally distributed? Finally, the chapter concludes with brief summaries of the effects of unions on the price level, aggregate employment, and labor's share of the national income.

THE UNION WAGE ADVANTAGE

Most people undoubtedly assume that union workers are paid more than nonunion workers. That is, they assume that unions gain a wage differential or *wage advantage* for their constituents. A union, after all, is able to deprive a firm of its workforce b striking and can thus impose associated costs on the firm. Presumably an employer, within limits, will pay the "price" of higher wage rates to avoid the costs of a strike. And, indeed, Bureau of Labor Statistics data reveal that average hourly earnings of union members were \$16.30 in 1997 compared to \$13.10 for nonunion workers.

Preliminary Complications

Closer examination suggests that this issue is not so clear-cut. In the first place, envision a unionized employer in a perfectly (or at least a "highly") competitive industry. If rival firms in the industry are nonunion, other things being equal, this firm will *not* be able to survive if it pays a higher wage to its employees than competitors are paying to their nonunion workers. Despite its potential to impose strike costs on the employer, the union would be faced with the dilemma of "no wage advantage" or "no firm" in these circumstances! A wage advantage would imply a higher average cost of production than the market-determined product price, that is, an economic loss.

The competitive model implies two additional points. On the one hand, the model tells us why unions are anxious to organize not just single firms but entire industries. If *all* firms are unionized and have higher wage costs, then no single firm will be at a competitive disadvantage and therefore faced with the prospect of losing market share to rivals. The United Automobile Workers' intense desire to organize workers of new automobile plants established by foreign manufacturers in the United States is prompted by much more than the goal of adding thousands of workers to the UAW's ranks. On the other hand, the model implies that unions may fare better in industries where product markets are imperfect; for example, government-regulated industries and the oligopolistic industries dominating much of the manufacturing sector of our economy. Such firms realize economic or surplus profits that in part can be expropriated by unions through higher wages without necessarily reducing output and employment.

This leads us to a second complication. Suppose that we do find a positive association between the degree of unionization and the average level of wage rates in various industries. That is, we discover that strongly unionized industries do in fact pay higher wage rates than weakly unionized industries. How do we know that unions are responsible for the higher wages? Do unions cause higher wages, *or* are unions prone to organize industries that already pay high wages? The automobile industry, for example, was renowned for paying relatively high wages long before it was unionized in the late 1930s. In fact, one can cite considerations other than the presence of unions that might explain at least a part of the wage advantage that is enjoyed by highly unionized industries.[1] First, female workers generally constitute a larger proportion of the work force in weakly unionized industries than they do in strongly unionized industries. We will find in Chapter 15 that women—because of discrimination and other considerations—are paid less than men. One can therefore argue that at least some portion of the wage differential found between strongly and weakly unionized industries is due not to the existence of unions but to the differing demographic makeup of the

[1]The following discussion is based on Daniel J. B. Mitchell, *Unions, Wages, and Inflation* (Washington, DC: Brookings Institution, 1980), pp. 83–85.

workforces in these industries. Second, strongly unionized industries usually have larger plants *and* are more capital-intensive than weakly unionized industries. The fact that unionized plants tend to be larger raises the possibility that supervision and monitoring may be more costly in such firms, causing employers to seek out and hire "superior" workers who can work effectively with less supervision. Such workers would be paid relatively high wages even if the union were not present. Similarly, capital-intensive production often requires more highly skilled workers who naturally command higher wages.[2] Our basic point is that higher wages in unionized industries might be attributable—at least in part—to factors other than the existence of the union.

Measuring the Wage Advantage

Aside from the complications just discussed, there is also a basic conceptual problem in measuring the *pure* union–nonunion differential. This arises because unionization may affect wage rates in nonunion labor markets, pushing them upward or downward and creating a bias in the measurement of the union wage advantage.

To begin, the ***pure union wage advantage*** is the amount by which the union wage exceeds the nonunion wage that would exist without the union. This difference is expressed as a percentage. In equation (11-1) the pure union wage advantage is *A*:

$$A = \frac{W_u - W_n}{W_n} \times 100 \qquad (11\text{-}1)$$

where W_u is the union wage and W_n is the nonunion wage. The $(W_u - W_n)/W_n$ term is multiplied by 100 to express the union wage advantage as a percentage. For example, if the union wage were \$12 per hour and the nonunion wage were \$10, the union wage advantage would be 20 percent $[(12 - 10)/10 \times 100]$.

Ideally, the union wage advantage should be determined under "laboratory conditions" in which we compare union and nonunion wages with all other possible influences on wages being constant. Thus, in Figure 11-1 we first would want to observe the level of wages "before" the presence of the union (W_n) and then compare this with the wage rate "after" the union was added (W_u). We would then use the relevant numbers in our union wage advantage formula as just described. The problem, of course, is that there is no way of conducting such a controlled experiment. In particular, it is impossible to observe what the earnings of unionized workers would be in a given labor market if the union did not exist. We must therefore make "real-world" comparisons of a more complex and tentative nature.

The best that can be done in this regard is to compare the wages of workers of a specific kind in unionized (or strongly unionized) markets with the wages of workers in nonunion (or weakly unionized) markets. But in making this comparison, our aforementioned conceptual difficulty intrudes. *Unions may influence the wage rates of*

[2]Of course, one can push the causal relationship back one step further by arguing that highly unionized industries are capital-intensive *because* of union wage pressure that prompts employers to substitute capital for labor.

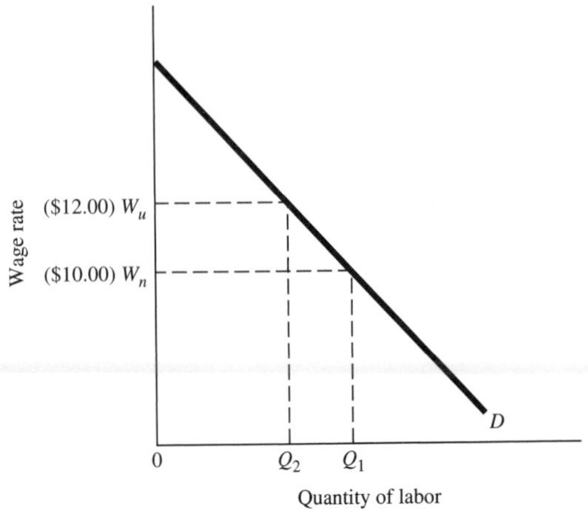

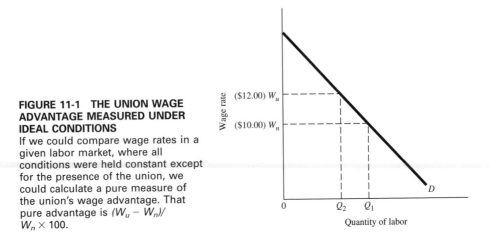

FIGURE 11-1 THE UNION WAGE ADVANTAGE MEASURED UNDER IDEAL CONDITIONS
If we could compare wage rates in a given labor market, where all conditions were held constant except for the presence of the union, we could calculate a pure measure of the union's wage advantage. That pure advantage is $(W_u - W_n)/W_n \times 100$.

nonunion workers as well as the wage rates of their own workers. Furthermore, the potential influence of unions on nonunion wages can take several different forms, so that the overall impact is ambiguous. We are theoretically uncertain whether an increase in union wages will cause nonunion wages to rise or fall. Additionally, the union wage may result in more productive workers in union firms. Let's briefly explore several different "effects" that describe various ways union wage setting may affect nonunion wages and may influence the quality of the unionized workforce.

1 Spillover Effects The ***spillover effect*** refers to the decline in nonunion wages that results from displaced union workers supplying their services in nonunion labor markets. The higher wages achieved in the unionized sector of the labor market will be accompanied by a loss of jobs, and displaced workers will "spill over" into the nonunion sector and depress nonunion wages.

The basics of the spillover effect are portrayed in Figure 11-2. Assume that both sectors are initially nonunion and that movement between the two sectors entails a common equilibrium wage rate of W_n for this labor. Now assume that sector 1 becomes unionized and that the union is successful in increasing the wage rate to W_u. We observe that the higher wage rate in this sector causes unemployment of Q_1Q_2. The spillover effect assumes that some or all of these unemployed workers will seek and find employment in the nonunion sector. This movement of workers from the union to the nonunion sector will reduce the supply of labor in the union sector and increase the supply in the nonunion sector. If we assume downward flexibility of wages, then, in time, wages will fall in the nonunion sector to W_s.

To the extent that the spillover effect occurs, our ***measured union wage advantage,*** which is the amount by which the union wage exceeds the *observed* nonunion wage, will *overstate* the pure union wage advantage. This can be grasped by comparing our hypothetical "laboratory experiment" of Figure 11-1 with the real-world comparison of Figure 11-2 embodying the spillover effect. Specifically, instead of comparing the union wage W_u with the nonunion wage W_n in Figure 11-1 to get the pure union wage

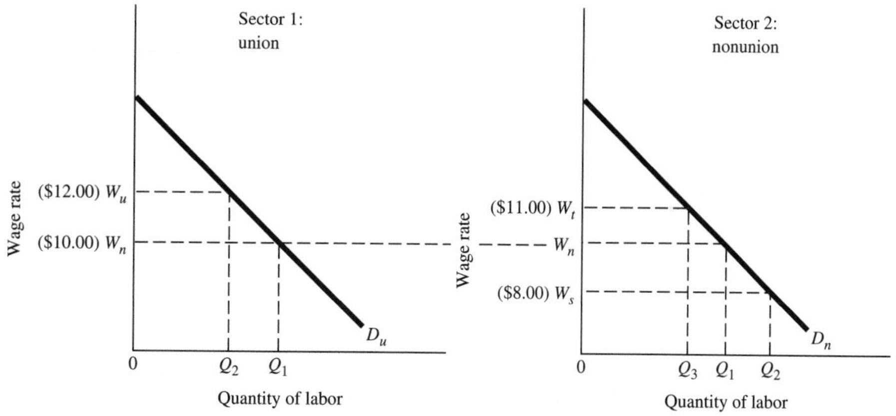

FIGURE 11-2 THE SPILLOVER EFFECT, THE THREAT EFFECT, AND THE MEASURED WAGE ADVANTAGE
The spillover effect suggests that as a union is able to raise wage rates from W_n to W_u in sector 1, it will reduce employment by Q_1Q_2. Assuming downward wage flexibility, the reemployment of these workers in sector 2 will reduce wages there from W_n to W_s. The measured union wage advantage will be $(W_u - W_s)/W_s \times 100$, which overstates the pure advantage of $(W_u - W_n)/W_n \times 100$. The threat effect indicates that as the union raises wages from W_n to W_u in sector 1, nonunion employers will grant a wage increase from, say, W_n to W_t in sector 2 to counter the threat of unionization. The measured wage advantage will be $(W_u - W_t)/W_t \times 100$, which understates the pure advantage of $(W_u - W_n)/W_n \times 100$.

advantage of 20 percent, we must compare the union wage W_u ($12) with the nonunion wage W_s ($8). Because W_s is less than W_n due to the spillover effect, the measured wage advantage in this case is 50 percent $[(12 - 8)/8 \times 100]$. Because the spillover effect depresses observed nonunion wages, the measured union wage advantage is larger than the pure union wage advantage of 20 percent. To repeat, a spillover effect will cause the union wage advantage to be *overstated.*[3]

2 Threat Effect In contrast, some labor economists, labeled "institutionalists," argue that market forces, as described by the spillover effect, are largely subverted or set aside by collective bargaining and that wage rates are determined mainly on the basis of "equitable comparisons." This implies that wages for any group of workers will be determined on the basis of wages being paid to comparable workers and that union and nonunion wages may be positively linked.

More specifically, the ***threat effect*** refers to an increase in nonunion wages that a nonunion employer offers as a response to the threat of unionization. The reasoning is that nonunion employers will feel increasingly threatened with unionization when workers in union firms obtain wage increases. An enlarged union–nonunion differential will increase the incentive for the workers in the nonunion firms to organize. To meet this

[3]For an empirical examination of the spillover effect, see Lawrence M. Kahn, "Union Spillover Effects on Unorganized Labor Markets," *Journal of Human Resources,* Winter 1980, pp. 87–98.

threat, the nonunion employer will grant wage increases. Thus, if we once again start from the W_n equilibrium wage in both sectors (Figure 11-2), the wage increase from \$10 to \$12 resulting from the unionization of sector 1 might *increase* nonunion wages in sector 2 from W_n (\$10) to, say, W_t (\$11). Now the measured union wage advantage will be about 9 percent [(12 − 11)/11 × 100] rather than the pure advantage of 20 percent (Figure 11-1). To recapitulate: If the threat effect causes union wage increases to pull up nonunion wages, then the measured union wage advantage will *understate* the pure union advantage.

3 Other Effects Our brief discussions of the spillover and threat effects do not exhaust all the possible ways union wages may influence nonunion wages. For example, there may be a ***product market effect*** that indicates an increase in nonunion wages caused by consumer demand shifting away from relatively high-priced union-produced goods and toward relatively low-priced goods produced by nonunion workers. The product market effect works as follows: A "union pay increase, through its effect on costs and prices, shifts demand to firms in the nonunion sector. The added demand for nonunion output is translated into added demand for nonunion labor, which could have a pay-raising influence."[4]

Other economists question the relevance of the spillover effect by citing the phenomenon of ***wait unemployment.*** The argument here is that when the union achieves a wage increase in sector 1 of Figure 11-2, the resulting unemployed workers may well remain in sector 1 hoping to be recalled to their high-paying jobs. Encouraged perhaps by the availability of unemployment insurance, they might prefer the probability of being recalled at higher union wages to the alternative of accepting lower-wage jobs in the nonunion sector. If wait unemployment occurs, the downward spillover pressure on nonunion wages does not occur to any great degree in sector 2. This implies that the measured union wage advantage more accurately portrays the pure wage advantage.

There is also the notion of the ***superior-worker effect.*** This idea is that the higher wages paid by union firms will cause workers to queue up for these "good" union jobs. (Note back in Figure 6-10 that the quantity of labor supplied exceeds the quantity demanded by *be* workers at the union wage rate W_u). Given the availability of many job seekers, unionized employers will carefully screen these prospective workers for those having the greatest ability, the most motivation, the least need for costly supervision, and other worker traits contributing to high productivity. This means that, in time, high-wage union firms may acquire superior workforces in comparison to nonunion firms.[5] Thus, in seeking to measure the union wage advantage accurately, the researcher is confronted with determining how much of an observed union wage advantage is due to the presence of the union as an institution and how much it reflects the presence of more highly productive workers in the unionized firms. To the extent that "superior workers" acquire the high-wage union jobs, the measured union wage advantage would

[4]Mitchell, op. cit., p. 87.

[5]On the other hand, unions may seek higher wages in the future if worker quality improves. See Walter J. Wessels, "Do Unionized Firms Hire Better Workers?" *Economic Inquiry,* October 1994, pp. 616–629.

TABLE 11-1 DIFFICULTIES IN MEASURING THE PURE UNION WAGE ADVANTAGE

Effect	Consequence
Spillover	Lowers nonunion wages, causing measured wage advantage to overstate pure advantage
Threat	Increases nonunion wages, causing measured wage advantage to understate pure advantage
Product market	Increases nonunion wages, causing measured wage advantage to understate pure advantage
Superior-worker	Results in more productive workers in union firms, causing measured wage advantage to overstate pure wage advantage

be *overstated*. Part of the higher wages paid such workers is attributable to their higher productivity rather than to the union.

Finally, a part of the union wage advantage may be a "compensating wage differential" that accounts for the fewer amenities in the workplace encountered by union workers. Alternatively stated, some portion of the wage advantage enjoyed by union members may be compensation for the fact that their working conditions are more structured, working hours are less flexible, and the work pace is faster.[6]

Table 11-1 lists the various "effects" and summarizes how each biases the measured wage advantage from the pure wage advantage. Although unanimity does not exist on the issue, most studies indicate that the threat and product market effects dominate the spillover effect, meaning that the overall impact of unions on nonunion wages is positive. Furthermore, this positive impact on nonunion wages is more than sufficient to counter any superior-worker effect that might be present. As a result, the measured union wage advantage probably understates the pure union wage advantage.[7]

Empirical Evidence

Now that we have some appreciation of the practical and conceptual difficulties in estimating the union wage advantage, let's turn to the available empirical evidence. Hirsch and Macpherson have examined the union wage premium for the 1973–97 period using a consistent methodology and data source.[8] Their findings are summarized in Table 11-2. The average overall union wage advantage was 18 percent. This estimate is somewhat higher than the 10-to-15 percent range that Lewis estimated for the 1923–58

[6]Greg J. Duncan and Frank P. Stafford, "Do Union Members Receive Compensating Wage Differentials?" *American Economic Review,* June 1980, pp. 355–371.

[7]Barry T. Hirsch and John T. Addison, *The Economic Analysis of Unions* (Boston: Allen & Unwin, 1986), pp. 120, 176. For some recent evidence that questions the strength of the threat effect, however, see David Neumark and Michael L. Watcher, "Union Effects on Nonunion Wages: Evidence from Panel Data on Industries and Cities," *Industrial and Labor Relations Review,* October 1995, pp. 20–38.

[8]Barry T. Hirsch and David A. Macpherson, *Union Membership and Earnings Data Book: Compilations from Current Population Survey (1998 Edition)* (Washington, DC: Bureau of National Affairs, 1998).

TABLE 11-2 HIRSCH AND MACPHERSON'S ESTIMATES OF THE UNION WAGE ADVANTAGE

Year	Wage advantage (percent)
1973	18
1974	18
1975	19
1976	21
1977	23
1978	22
1979	15
1980	15
1981	15
1983	19
1984	20
1985	19
1986	19
1987	18
1988	17
1989	19
1990	18
1991	17
1992	17
1993	18
1994	19
1995	18
1996	17
1997	18
1973–97 average	18

Source: Barry T. Hirsch and David A. Macpherson, *Union Membership and Earnings Data Book: Compilations from Current Population Survey (1998 Edition)* (Washington, DC: Bureau of National Affairs, 1998).

period.[9] Hirsch and Macpherson also examined the union wage advantage in the public sector, as opposed to the overall wage advantage. They estimate that, all else being equal, the pay of unionized government workers is 14 percent higher than that of nonunionized government workers. This union wage advantage is 6 percentage points lower than the advantage commanded by union workers in the private sector.

Observe in Table 11-2 that Hirsch and Macpherson estimate that the union wage advantages for 1976, 1977, and 1978 were well above average, peaking at 23 percent in 1977. Other studies have confirmed this finding. Lewis found that the union wage ad-

[9]H. Gregg Lewis, *Unionism and Relative Wages in the United States* (Chicago: University of Chicago Press, 1963).

vantage peaked at 20 percent in 1976.[10] Other researchers have found an even higher union wage premium in the mid-1970s. Mitchell,[11] using three different data sets, surmised that the union wage premium in the mid-1970s was in the range of 20 to 30 percent. Also, Freeman and Medoff, using six data sets for individual workers, found union wage advantages ranging from 21 to 32 percent and concluded that "in the 1970s the archetypical union wage advantage was on the order of 20–30 percent."[12]

The period in question was one of stagflation—simultaneous inflation and high unemployment—resulting largely from dramatic oil price increases. Through collective bargaining and cost-of-living adjustments (COLAs) in contracts, union workers were better able than nonunion workers to keep their nominal wages rising with inflation. The loose labor markets (high unemployment) apparently slowed the relative pace of nominal wage increases for nonunion workers. Recall from Chapter 10 that the high union wage advantage of the 1970s is cited as a possible cause of the decline in union employment during the 1980s.

The union wage advantage has fallen from its lofty heights in the mid-1970s but remains high today compared to historical standards. The union wage advantage has averaged about 17 to 18 percent in the 1990s. The handful of highly publicized wage concessions won by management in the 1980s do not appear to have been sufficiently
11-1 widespread to reduce the overall average size of the union wage advantage.[13]

Union wage advantages vary greatly by industry, occupation, race, gender, and state of the economy. Although no unassailable generalizations can be drawn from the studies that try to sort out these differences, the following comments seem to be defensible.[14]

1 The union wage advantage moves countercyclically, increasing during recessions and narrowing during expansions. Specifically, the advantage increased during the Great Depression (1931–33) as union contracts provided a bulwark against wage cuts that affected many nonunion workers. Conversely, during periods of unanticipated demand-pull inflation, such as the immediate post-World War II period (1945–49), the union wage advantage diminished. Union wages were locked in by long-term bargaining agreements that were not readily adjusted upward. At the same time, nonunion wages were free to respond to the buoyant labor market, and therefore, nonunion wages rose relative to union wages. On the other hand, we have seen that the union wage premium increased during the mid-1970s, a period of severe cost-push inflation and high unemployment.

2 Craft unions in the construction industry have achieved union wage advantages that are much larger than average. Some of these advantages range upwards to 70

[10]H. Gregg Lewis, *Union Relative Wage Effects* (Chicago: University of Chicago Press, 1986).

[11]Mitchell, op. cit., p. 95.

[12]Richard B. Freeman and James L. Medoff, *What Do Unions Do?* (New York: Basic Books, Inc., 1984), p. 46.

[13]For supporting evidence, see Mark E. Haggerty and Duane E. Leigh, "The Impact of Union Wage Concessions on Union Premiums," *Industrial Relations,* Winter 1993, pp. 111–123.

[14]For example, see C. J. Parsley, "Labor Union Effects on Wage Gains: A Survey of Recent Literature," *Journal of Economic Literature,* March 1980, pp. 1–31; Javed Ashraf, "Recent Trends in the Union Wage Premium," *Journal of Labor Research,* Fall 1990, pp. 435–451; and Javed Ashraf, "The Effects of Unions on Wages: Findings from Pooled Data," *Eastern Economic Journal,* April–June 1991, pp. 549–569.

11-1 World of Work

TWO-TIER WAGE SYSTEMS*

In the 1980s a new phenomenon—two-tier wage systems—came into being in a number of important unionized industries such as air and truck transportation, automobile production, and retail stores.

Let's focus on three questions. First, what is a two-tier wage system (TTWS)? Second, why did such wage systems evolve in the 1980s? Finally, what potential problems are embodied in the TTWS?

Two-tier wage systems. Simply put, a TTWS is one wherein an employer provides two different compensation systems to workers who are doing the same work. Typically, "new" workers—those who are employed after a specified date—are paid less than "old" workers who were employed prior to that date. Thus, for example, "new" American Airlines flight attendants hired after November 9, 1983, were paid a base wage of $14.50 per hour, while "old" attendants received a $17.82 base wage.

Causes. Although causal factors are complex,† the immediate reason for adopting a TTWS usually is to contain labor costs and bolster firm profits. In the late 1970s and early 1980s a number of factors converged to increase competition and reduce profits in many unionized industries. Some industries, including the air and motor transport industries, experienced government deregulation and thereby found themselves in a much more competitive environment. For example, many of the new airlines that came into being after deregulation employed lost-cost nonunion labor. In other industries enhanced competition from foreign producers reduced the profitability of American firms. And in some instances—for example, construction, meatpacking, and retail stores—competitive pressures came from new domestic firms that are nonunion and pay lower wages. Furthermore, the union–nonunion wage differential apparently rose in the 1970s to the detriment of the relative profitability of union firms. Finally, back-to-back recessions in the early 1980s also contributed to diminished profits.

Given traditional union adherence to the principle of "equal pay for equal work," why would unions accept a TTWS? The answer is that such wage systems were established under duress and appeared preferable to the alternatives of substantial wage concessions or significant job loss for current workers. Observe that a TTWS is a means of protecting the jobs and wage rates of *current* union members; the cost of such systems is borne by *new* workers. A TTWS shifts the burden of lower wages to new workers.

Potential problems. While the TTWS has provided short-run wage cost relief to many firms and industries, such schemes have potential problems. In particular, workers tend to regard the TTWS as being inherently unfair, and it is reasonable to expect that the impact on worker morale may be negative, especially among new workers. Our earlier discussion of efficiency wages (Chapter 7) reminds us that unit labor costs depend not only on wage rates but also on worker productivity. If lower worker morale adversely affects productivity, unit labor costs might rise despite the TTWS. In short, while the TTWS might reduce labor costs in the short run, those cost reductions might be lost to employers through lower productivity in the long run. And, indeed, there is evidence to suggest that a TTWS generates dissatisfaction among low-tier workers. They are less satisfied with their pay, think the wage structure is unfair, are less committed to the firm, and trust management less than do high-tier workers.‡

Another "fairness" issue involves the goal of equal employment opportunity. If "new" workers are heavily comprised of female and minority workers, the question arises as to whether the TTWS will perpetuate wage and earnings inequality for women and minorities.

*This synopsis is based on Richard S. Belous, "Two-Tier Wage Systems in the U.S. Economy," Report N. 85-165 E, Congressional Research Service, mimeographed, August 12, 1985. The interested reader should also see James E. Martin, *Two-Tier Compensation Structures: Their Impact on Unions, Employers, and Employees* (Kalamazoo, MI: W. E. Upjohn Institute for Employment Research, 1990).

†David J. Walsh, "Accounting for the Proliferation of Two-Tier Wage Settlements in the U.S. Airline Industry, 1983–1986," *Industrial and Labor Relations Review,* October 1988, pp. 50–62.

‡Dean B. McFarlin and Michael R. Frone, "A Two-Tier Wage Structure in a Nonunion Firm," *Industrial Relations,* Winter 1990, pp. 145–153. Also see Peter Cappelli and Peter D. Sherer, "Assessing Worker Attitudes under a Two-Tier Wage Plan," *Industrial and Labor Relations Review,* January 1990, pp. 225–244.

percent. The bargaining power of such unions is great because each craft union represents a small proportion of total building costs (Chapter 5) and construction workers can often find employment in other firms during a strike.

3 Black males, on average, gain more from being union members than do whites and females.

4 Unions achieve higher wage advantages for blue-collar workers (craftspersons, operatives, laborers) than for white-collar workers (clerical workers, salespersons).

11-2 **5** Less-educated workers have higher union wage premiums than better-educated workers.

Total Compensation: Wages plus Fringe Benefits

We would be remiss not to examine the impact of unions on fringe benefits. Recall from Chapter 7 that ***fringe benefits*** include public (legally mandated) programs such as Social Security, unemployment compensation, and workers' compensation as well as a wide variety of private nonmandatory programs, including private pensions,

---

11-2 World of Work

THE EFFECT OF INTERNATIONAL COMPETITION ON THE UNION WAGE ADVANTAGE*

Many American firms and industries have experienced a dramatic increase in international competition during the past two decades. This competition—in steel, autos, electronics, sporting goods, textiles, and elsewhere—has placed downward pressure on both union and nonunion wages in the affected industries. Has this downward wage pressure had equal impacts on union and nonunion wages? If so, the total impact on the union wage advantage would be nil, since this advantage is defined in relative terms.

MacPherson and Stewart have addressed this issue by comparing the wages of 13,194 union and 12,786 nonunion workers in 75 blue-collar manufacturing industries between 1975 and 1981, a period during which import competition grew rapidly. Two findings emerged from their study. First, international competition had a greater effect on the wages of unionized workers than of nonunion workers. Apparently, international competition pushed union wages closer to their competitive levels. Nonunion wages suffered less of an impact since they presumably were already at or near their competitive levels. Thus, the growth of international competition over this period reduced the union wage advantage. According to MacPherson and Stewart, a 10 percent rise in the import share in an industry on average lowered the union wage advantage by about 2 percent.

A bit more surprising, the researchers found that the impact of international competition on wages decreased sharply as the percentage of an industry that was unionized increased. Heavily unionized industries did not experience as high a decline in the union wage differential as did less-unionized industries. Apparently, workers in heavily unionized industries were better able to resist—at least for a time—the downward wage pressure accompanying the international competition. But this lack of wage adjustment in heavily unionized industries may also have had a negative long-run effect. To the extent that it reduced the competitiveness of American firms, it may have contributed to the decline in union employment and membership during the 1980s (Chapter 10).

*Based on David A. MacPherson and James B. Stewart, "The Effect of International Competition on Union and Nonunion Wages," *Industrial and Labor Relations Review,* April 1990, pp. 434–446.

medical and dental insurance, and paid vacations and sick leave. *Total compensation* is simply the sum of wage earnings and the value of fringe benefits. If union workers enjoy more generous fringe benefits than nonunion workers, then the overall economic advantage that union workers have over nonunion workers is greater than the wage advantage suggests. On the other hand, if union wage gains are realized at the expense of fringe benefits and nonunion workers receive larger fringe benefits, then the union wage advantage overstates the economic advantage of union workers.

Evidence

How do union fringe benefits compare to those of nonunion workers? The answer is that union workers enjoy a greater variety and higher overall level of fringe benefits than nonunion workers. Even and Macpherson report that in 1988 union workers in the private sector were 103 percent and 42 percent more likely than their nonunion counterparts to have pension and health insurance coverage, respectively.[15] Wiatrowski finds that the union advantage exists for a wide variety of fringe benefits.[16] Freeman and Medoff have shown that unions gain a larger fringe benefit advantage than wage advantage. Finally, Lewis contends that the inclusion of fringe benefits would raise estimates of the union compensation advantage by 2 or 3 percentage points. In short, substantial agreement exists that union workers generally achieve not only a wage advantage but also a considerable fringe benefit advantage compared to nonunion workers.

Role of Unions Why do union members receive more generous fringe benefits than nonunion workers? A number of interrelated reasons may be involved. First, union fringes may be higher for the same reason that union wage rates are higher. The union is able to deprive management of its workforce, and the employer is willing to pay both higher wages *and* larger fringe benefits to avoid the costs of a strike. Second, union workers, by virtue of their higher earnings, may simply choose to "buy" more fringes than lower-income nonunion workers. Third, as a collective-voice institution, a union may formulate fringe benefit proposals, inform its constituents of the details of such proposals, and crystallize worker preferences; the union then communicates these preferences to management. Fourth, older workers are usually more active in the internal politics of a union and are therefore more influential in determining union goals. These older workers are typically more interested in pensions and insurance programs than are younger workers. Fifth, as we will discover momentarily, unionism reduces worker quit rates and thus increases job tenure. Greater tenure in turn increases the probability that workers will actually receive benefits from such fringes as nonvested pensions and life insurance. Finally, there is the simple fact that under collective bargaining law, fringe benefits are a mandatory item on the bargaining agenda, which accords them more serious and systematic attention than in nonunion labor markets.

[15]William E. Even and David A. Macpherson, "The Impact of Unionism of Fringe Benefit Coverage," *Economics Letters,* May 1991, pp. 87–91.

[16]William J. Wiatrowski, "Employee Benefits for Union and Nonunion Workers," *Monthly Labor Review,* February 1994, pp. 34–38.

QUICK REVIEW 11-1

- The pure union wage advantage is the percentage by which the union wage exceeds the wage that would exist if there were no union.
- If the spillover and superior-worker effects are dominant, the measured union wage advantage will overstate the pure advantage; if the threat and product market effects are dominant, the measured union wage advantage will understate the pure wage advantage.
- Overall, the union wage advantage is an estimated 18 percent. This advantage rises by 2 to 3 percentage points when fringe benefits are considered.
- The union wage advantage *(a)* moves countercyclically, *(b)* is particularly high for craft unions in the construction industry, *(c)* is higher for black males than for other racial or gender groups, and *(d)* is higher for less-educated workers than for better-educated workers.

Your Turn: Suppose the union wage is $10 an hour; the current nonunion wage, $9 an hour; and the nonunion wage that would exist without the union, $8 an hour. What is the measured union wage advantage? The pure wage advantage? (Answers: See page 626.)

EFFICIENCY AND PRODUCTIVITY

Are unions a positive or a negative force insofar as economic efficiency and productivity are concerned? How do unions affect the allocation of resources? While much disagreement exists as to the efficiency aspects of unionism, it is useful to consider some of the ways unions might affect efficiency both negatively and positively. We will consider the negative view first.

Negative View

Unions might exert a negative impact on efficiency in three basic ways. First, unions may impose work rules that diminish productivity *within* union firms. Second, strikes may entail a loss of output. Finally, the union wage advantage is a distortion of the wage structure, causing a misallocation of labor *between* union and nonunion firms and industries.

1 Restrictive Work Rules Perhaps the most apparent way unions might impair productivity and efficiency is by imposing various work rules on management. These "make-work" rules can take a variety of interrelated forms. First, the union may obtain a direct limit on hourly, daily, or weekly output per worker. Example: Allegedly to control output quality, the bricklayers have sought to restrict the number of bricks laid per hour or per day. Second, the union may insist on the use of time-consuming production methods. Illustrations: Painters' unions may prohibit the use of spray guns or limit the width of paint brushes. In past years, the typographers' unions resisted the introduction of computers in setting type. Third, a union may require that unnecessary work be done. Example: Craft unions have sometimes promoted the enactment of building codes that require that prefabricated housing units be broken down and reassembled on the construction site. Fourth, work crews of excessive size may be required. Examples: Historically, the musicians' union insisted on oversized orchestras for musical shows and required that a union standby orchestra be paid by employers using nonunion orchestras. For many years the Brotherhood of Locomotive Firemen and Engineers was able to retain a fireman on train crews, even though the worker's function was eliminated by the shift from steam to diesel engines. Such practices are labeled *featherbedding.* Fifth, unions may impose jurisdictional restrictions on the kinds of jobs workers may perform. Illustration: Sheet metal workers or bricklayers may be prohibited from performing the simple carpentry work often associated with their jobs. Observance of such rules means, in this instance, that unneeded and underutilized carpenters must be available. Finally, unions may restrain management in the assignment of workers to jobs. The most prevalent example is that unions typically insist that workers be promoted in accordance with seniority rather than ability and efficiency.

This recitation of reasons that union work rules might impede intrafirm efficiency merits modification in several respects. To begin with, one must not make the mistake of assuming that productivity will necessarily be enhanced by "speeding up the assembly line." A speedup may in fact cause workers to tire and become demoralized and therefore be *less* efficient. Similarly, it is also incorrect to associate featherbedding, unnecessarily large work crews, make-work rules, and the like solely with unionized workers. While unions may be responsible for codifying and enforcing such practices, the practices themselves are quite common in both union and nonunion sectors of the economy. Peer pressure and the threat of social ostracism can be as effective as a clause in a collective bargaining agreement in controlling the pace of production.[17] Finally, the productivity-reducing practices just outlined often come into being against a backdrop of technological change. Labor and management may agree to a crew size that is reasonable and appropriate at the time the agreement is concluded. But labor-saving technology may then emerge that renders the crew "too large." The union is likely to resist the potential loss of jobs.[18]

2 Strikes A second way unions may adversely affect efficiency is through strikes. If union and management reach an impasse in their negotiations, a strike will result and the firm's production will generally cease for the strike's duration. The firm will forgo sales and profits, and workers will sacrifice income.

Simple statistics on strike activity suggest that strikes are relatively rare and the associated aggregate economic losses are relatively minimal. Table 11-3 provides data on major work stoppages, defined as those involving 1,000 or more workers and lasting at least one full day or one work shift. Given that about 700 major collective bar-

[17]See Paul A. Weinstein (ed.), *Featherbedding and Technological Change* (Boston: D. C. Heath and Company, 1965).

[18]For an analysis of when unions are likely to resist labor-saving technology, see Steve Dowrick and Barbara J. Spencer, "Union Attitudes to Labor-Saving Innovation: When Are Unions Luddites?" *Journal of Labor Economics,* April 1994, pp. 316–344.

TABLE 11-3 MAJOR WORK STOPPAGES IN THE UNITED STATES, SELECTED YEARS, 1960–96

			Days idle	
(1) Year	(2) Work stoppages (number)	(3) Workers involved (number in thousands)	(4) Number (in thousands)	(5) Percent of estimated total working time
1960	222	896	13,260	.09
1962	211	793	11,760	.08
1964	246	1,183	16,220	.11
1966	321	1,300	16,000	.10
1968	392	1,855	35,567	.20
1970	381	2,468	52,761	.29
1972	250	975	16,764	.09
1974	424	1,796	31,809	.16
1976	231	1,519	23,962	.12
1978	219	1,006	23,774	.11
1980	187	795	20,844	.09
1982	96	656	9,061	.04
1984	62	376	8,499	.04
1986	69	533	8,995	.04
1988	40	118	4,364	.02
1990	44	185	5,926	.02
1992	35	364	3,989	.01
1994	45	322	5.020	.02
1996	37	273	4,887	.02

Source: U.S. Department of Labor, "Major Work Stoppages, 1996," News Release 97–44, February 12, 1997.

gaining agreements are negotiated each year, the number of major work stoppages is surprisingly small. Furthermore, most strikes last only a few days. Thus, we find in column 5 that for the 1960–96 period, the lost work time from major strikes has been quite consistently far less than one-half of 1 percent of total work time. In fact, over this period the amount of work time lost is typically less than two-tenths of 1 percent of total work time. This loss is the equivalent of 4 hours per worker per year, which is
11-1 less than 5 minutes per worker per week.[19]

But these data on time lost from work stoppages can be misleading as a measure of the costliness of a strike. On the one hand, employers in the struck industry may have anticipated the strike and worked their labor force overtime to accumulate inventories to supply customers during the strike period. This means that the overall loss of work time, production, profits, and wages is less than the work-time loss figures suggest. Similarly, other nonstruck producers in an industry may have increased their output to offset the loss of production by those firms engaged in a strike. In other words, while

[19]Marten Estey, *The Unions,* 3d ed. (New York: Harcourt Brace Jovanovich, 1981), p. 140.

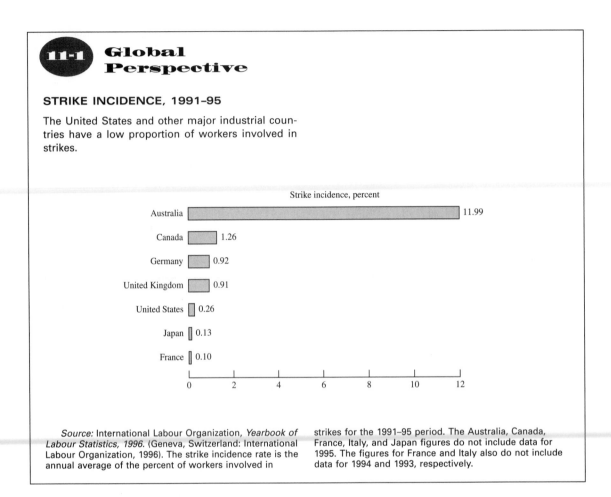

11-1 **Global Perspective**

STRIKE INCIDENCE, 1991–95

The United States and other major industrial countries have a low proportion of workers involved in strikes.

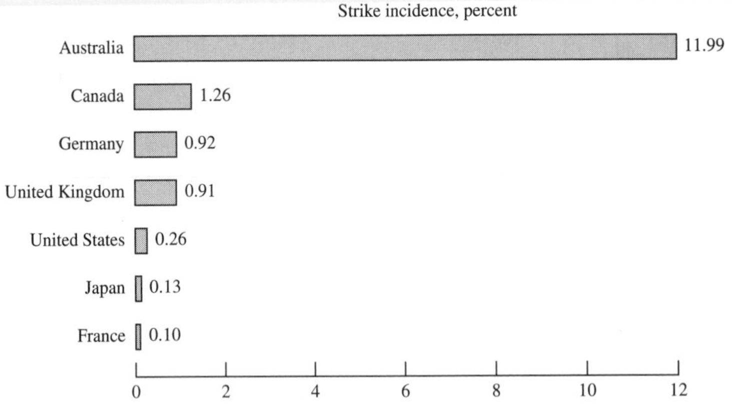

Source: International Labour Organization, *Yearbook of Labour Statistics, 1996.* (Geneva, Switzerland: International Labour Organization, 1996). The strike incidence rate is the annual average of the percent of workers involved in strikes for the 1991–95 period. The Australia, Canada, France, Italy, and Japan figures do not include data for 1995. The figures for France and Italy also do not include data for 1994 and 1993, respectively.

a strike may impose significant losses on participants, the total output loss to the industry or to society at large may be minuscule or nonexistent. Note, however, that the production adjustments made in anticipation of, or as a consequence of, a strike may entail some efficiency losses. If firms that suffered a strike were able to anticipate perfectly the loss of output and sales and therefore accumulate inventories prior to the strike, this additional production would likely entail the overutilization of productive facilities and, thus, higher costs (less-productivity efficiency) per unit of output. Similar efficiency losses may be incurred by firms replacing the output of the firm that is struck. While the data on worker days lost because of strikes may overstate the output loss, a consequent efficiency loss may be concealed.

Furthermore, the amount of production and income lost because of strikes will be greater than suggested by work-time loss data when a work stoppage in a specific industry disrupts production in associated industries. These affected industries may either buy inputs from the struck industry or sell output to it. Nonstriking workers in the affected industries may lose work time and the economy may lose their output if a strike depletes these industries of essential inputs or essential buyers. In some instances, a strike could force affected firms to cease or curtail operations.

Alternatively, output in industries linked as purchasers or suppliers to struck industries may decline while paid work-time remains steady. If so, labor productivity (output per worker) in the affected industries will fall and the average cost of the output will rise. McHugh[20] finds empirical support for this possible outcome. He suggests that many employers in nonstruck firms affected by strikes retain their workforces during the strike. This "hoarded" labor is redundant; since output falls, these firms experience declines in labor productivity.

As a broad generalization, the adverse effects of a strike on nonstriking firms and customers are likely to be greater when services are involved and less when products are involved. As Estey has pointed out, the impact on the public of strikes in durable goods industries tends to be negligible. For example, although the General Motors strike of 1970 resulted in the loss of 17.8 million worker days and contributed to an unusually high loss of 0.29 percent for national loss of work time in that year (Table 11-3), the consuming public was not severely affected. The public was able to buy other makes of cars or used GM cars.[21] And, of course, within limits the purchase of consumer durables such as autos is postponable. In contrast, a strike of a major airline or a public transit system might impose significant economic costs on consumers, workers, and businesses who are not party to the strike.

Overall it is appropriate to say that, on the average, the costs imposed on the immediate parties to a strike and affected firms and consumers are not as great as one might surmise. A study of some 63 manufacturing industries over the 1955–77 period
11-3 concluded that strike costs were significant in only 19 of these industries.[22] Furthermore, in these 19 industries the amount of output lost was typically a small fraction of 1 percent of total annual output. The ability of struck firms to draw on inventories and the capacity of nonstruck firms to increase their output apparently make industry output losses minimal.

Postscript: Strikes are precipitated by the failure of *two* parties—union and management—to reach agreement. In fact, a growing number of work stoppages in recent years have taken the form of lockouts initiated by employers. Popular opinion to the contrary, it is unfair to attribute all of the costs associated with a strike to labor alone.

3 Wage Advantage and Labor Misallocation A third major way unions may adversely affect efficiency is through the wage advantage itself.

[20]Richard McHugh, "Productivity Effects of Strikes in Struck and Nonstruck Industries," *Industrial and Labor Relations Review,* July 1991, pp. 722–732.

[21]Estey, op. cit., pp. 140–141.

[22]George R. Neumann and Melvin W. Reder, "Output and Strike Activity in U.S. Manufacturing: How Large Are the Losses?" *Industrial and Labor Relations Review,* January 1984, pp. 197–211. Another study also concludes that the intertemporal adjustments in sales and production in the North American automobile industry caused the output loss of strikes to be minimal. See Morley Gunderson and Angelo Melino, "Estimating Strike Effects in a General Model of Prices and Quantities," *Journal of Labor Economics,* January 1987, pp. 1–19.

11-3 World of Work

THE IMPACT OF A STRIKE ON OTHER WORKERS

In March 1996 2,700 workers at two General Motors brake plants in Dayton, Ohio, went on strike over the future of fewer than 100 workers and affected tens of thousands of other workers. Over the course of a few days the brake plant shutdown caused a parts shortage for other GM plants. As a result, 21 of 29 GM car and truck assembly plants were closed, and nearly 90,000 workers were laid off. Workers at other GM parts plants also were laid off since they mostly manufacture parts for GM vehicles of which production had been stopped.

If the strike had lasted longer, workers at GM dealerships would have been laid off as well. These layoffs would have occurred since customers would not have been able to custom-order a car or truck, and the inventory of popular vehicles would have decreased.

The strike also affected workers at other firms. It slowed production at the more than 1,600 firms that provided parts for GM vehicles. These firms laid off workers and reduced their purchases of raw materials and parts from other firms.

This strike clearly illustrates how work stoppages can affect workers at other firms. Thus, the loss in output can be greater than the amount directly lost due to the striking employees not working.

A Simple Model This effect can be seen through reconsideration and extension of the spillover model in Figure 11-2. In Figure 11-3 we have drawn (for simplicity's sake) identical labor demand curves for the unionized and nonunion sectors of the labor market for some particular labor. We assume that the relevant product market is purely competitive so that the labor demand curves reflect not only marginal revenue product (MRP) but also value of marginal product (VMP).[23] If there is no union present, then the wage rate that would result from competition in the hire of labor is W_n. Now assume that a union establishes itself in sector 1 and increases the wage rate from W_n to W_u. In accordance with our analysis of the spillover effect, the result is that the $Q'_1Q'_2$ workers who lose their jobs in the union sector move to nonunion sector 2, where we assume they secure employment. These additional workers depress the wage rate from W_n to W_s in the nonunion sector 2.

Because we have kept the level of employment unchanged, this simple model allows us to isolate the efficiency or allocative effect of the union wage differential. The area $Q'_2abQ'_1$ represents the loss of domestic output caused by the $Q'_1Q'_2$ employment decline in the union sector. This area is the sum of the VMPs—the total contribution to the domestic output—of the workers displaced by the W_n to W_u wage increase achieved by the union. As these workers spill over into nonunion sector 2 and are reemployed, they add to the domestic output the amount indicated by the Q_1cdQ_2 area. Because $Q'_2abQ'_1$ exceeds Q_1cdQ_2, there is a net loss of domestic output. More precisely, because the shaded areas are equal in each diagram, the net loss of output attributable to the union wage advantage is equal to area $c'abd'$ as shown in the union sector diagram. Since the same amount of employed labor is now producing a smaller output, labor is obviously misallocated and inefficiently used. Viewed from a slightly

[23]Recall from Chapter 5 that MRP measures the amount that an additional worker adds to a firm's total revenue, while VMP indicates the value of a worker's extra output to society. VMP tells us the dollar amount an extra worker contributes to the domestic output.

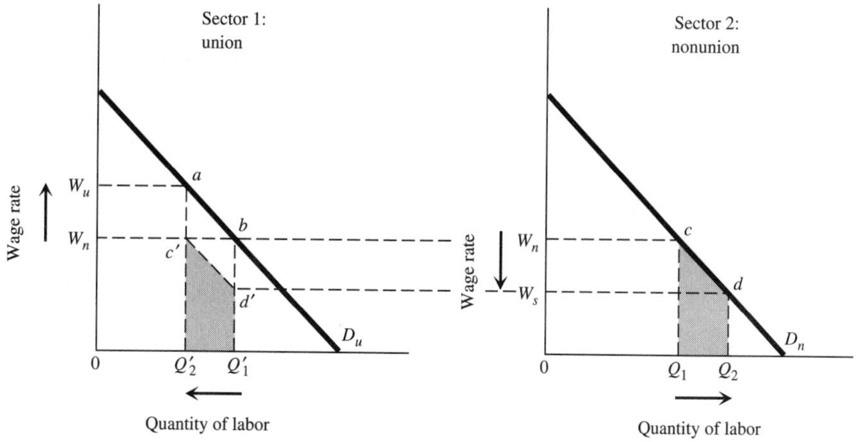

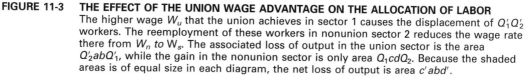

FIGURE 11-3 **THE EFFECT OF THE UNION WAGE ADVANTAGE ON THE ALLOCATION OF LABOR**
The higher wage W_u that the union achieves in sector 1 causes the displacement of $Q'_1Q'_2$ workers. The reemployment of these workers in nonunion sector 2 reduces the wage rate there from W_n *to* W_s. The associated loss of output in the union sector is the area $Q'_2abQ'_1$, while the gain in the nonunion sector is only area Q_1cdQ_2. Because the shaded areas is of equal size in each diagram, the net loss of output is area $c'abd'$.

different perspective, *after* the spillover of Q_1Q_2 workers from the union to the nonunion sector has occurred, workers will be paid a wage rate equal to their VMPs in both sectors. But the VMPs of the union workers will be higher than the VMPs of the nonunion workers. The economy will always benefit from a larger domestic output when any given type of labor is reallocated from a relatively low-VMP use to a relatively high-VMP use. But, given the union's presence and its ability to maintain the W_u wage rate in its sector, this reallocation from sector 2 to 1 will not occur.

Qualifications Our model of the allocative inefficiency stemming from a union wage advantage is very simplified. Let's briefly call attention to several additional real-world considerations that might cause the efficiency loss to be greater or less than our model suggests.

1 Unemployment. Recalling our earlier comments on "wait unemployment," what if some of those workers who lost their jobs because of higher wages in the union sector decided to remain in that sector in the hope of reemployment? The consequence is a net loss of output in excess of $c'abd'$ in Figure 11-3. The reason? While output would decline by area $Q'_2abQ'_1$ in the union sector, it would increase by *less than* Q_1cdQ_2 in the nonunion sector. In the extreme, if the entire $Q'_1Q'_2$ displaced workers remained unemployed in the union sector, the loss of output to society would be $Q'_2abQ'_1$. The same result might stem from downward wage rigidity in sector 2. If for some reason wages would not decline to W_s, then it would not be profitable for sector 2 firms to hire additional workers beyond Q_1. Finally, to the extent that the threat and product market effects increase nonunion wages, workers will be displaced in that sector as well as in the union sector.

2 Job search costs. A second and related point is that our model understates the loss of output because it implicitly assumes that workers instantly and costlessly shift from the union to the nonunion sector. Job search by unemployed workers takes time and entails both out-of-pocket costs (paying for advertisements and for the service of employment agencies) and opportunity costs (earnings forgone during the search period). And as we discovered in Chapter 9, the geographic movement that may be involved in shifting from the union to the nonunion sector is also costly.

3 Bilateral monopoly. On the other hand, our discussion tends to overstate the detrimental effect that unions may have on allocative efficiency to the extent that unions engage in bargaining with monopsonistic employers. Recall from the discussion of bilateral monopoly in Figure 6-11 that union wage determination may in effect "correct" the underallocation of labor resources that a monopsonistic employer would find profitable.

4 Investment behavior and productivity growth. The model discussed in the preceding section (Figure 11-3) portrays only the *static* or short-run efficiency effects of the union wage advantage. The union wage differential may also have an adverse *dynamic* or long-run effect on efficiency. Specifically, unions may very well reduce firm and industry profitability, thereby exerting a retarding effect on investment and economic growth. If a powerful union is capable of expropriating a sizable portion of the returns from a firm's investment in either physical capital (machinery and equipment) or in research and development, such investments may diminish. Because the path of labor productivity over time depends heavily on the stock of capital goods per worker and technological progress (Chapters 5 and 18), any significant union encroachment on profits from such investments could be expected to reduce the growth of labor productivity.

Empirical Estimates Several estimates have been made of the static efficiency loss associated with union wage gains. They are in agreement that the loss is small. In a pioneering study Rees assumed a 15 percent union wage advantage and estimated that approximately 0.14 percent—only about one-seventh of 1 percent—of the domestic output was lost.[24] A more recent estimate by Freeman and Medoff indicates that "union monopoly wage gains cost the economy 0.02 to 0.04 percent of gross national product, which in 1980 amounted to about $5 to $10 billion or $20.00 to $40.00 per person."[25] And in a 1983 study, DeFina estimated that a 15 percent union wage advantage would result in only a 0.08 to 0.09 percentage loss of output.[26]

Positive View

Other economists believe that on balance, unions make a positive contribution to productivity and efficiency.

[24] Albert Rees, "The Effects of Unions on Resource Allocation," *Journal of Law and Economics,* October 1963, pp. 69–78.

[25] Freeman and Medoff, op. cit., p. 57.

[26] Robert H. DeFina, "Unions, Relative Wages, and Economic Efficiency," *Journal of Labor Economics,* October 1983, pp. 408–429.

1 Investment and Technological Progress One may carry Figure 11-3's discussion of the labor misallocation that stems from the union wage advantage a step further and argue that union wage increases may *accelerate* the substitution of capital for labor and *hasten* the search for cost-reducing (productivity-increasing) technologies. When faced with higher production costs due to the union wage advantage, employers will be prompted to reduce costs by using more machinery and by seeking improved production techniques that use less of both labor and capital per unit of output. In fact, if the product market is reasonably competitive, a unionized firm with labor costs that are, say, 15 to 20 percent higher than those of nonunion competitors will not survive unless productivity can be raised. In short, union wage pressure may inadvertently generate managerial actions that increase domestic productivity. This is essentially the opposite of the argument made a moment ago that higher union wages will reduce profits, inhibit investment in capital goods and innovation, and reduce labor productivity.

2 Unions as a Collective Voice Freeman and Medoff have stressed the view that on balance, unions contribute to rising productivity in firms by voicing worker grievances and through their effects on labor turnover, worker security, and managerial efficiency.[27]

The Voice Mechanism In their view, the positive impact of unions on productivity occurs in part because unions function as a ***collective voice*** for their members in resolving disputes, improving working conditions, and so forth. If a group of workers are dissatisfied with their conditions of employment, they have two potential means of response. These are the "exit mechanism" and the "voice mechanism." The ***exit mechanism*** refers to the use of the labor market—by leaving or exiting the present job in search of a better one—as a means of reacting to "bad" employers and "bad" working conditions. In contrast, the ***voice mechanism*** entails communication between workers and the employer to improve working conditions and resolve worker grievances. It may well be risky for *individual* workers to express their dissatisfaction to employers because employers may retaliate by firing such workers as "troublemakers." But unions can provide workers with a *collective* voice to communicate problems and grievances to management and to press for their satisfactory resolution. This enhances worker job satisfaction and morale and therefore increases productivity. According to Freeman and Medoff, unions can positively affect productivity not only through the voice mechanism but also in a variety of other ways.

Reduced Turnover Substantial evidence exists that unionization reduces quits and turnovers. On the one hand, the collective voice of the union may be effective in correcting job dissatisfactions that otherwise would be "resolved" by workers through the exit mechanism of changing jobs. On the other hand, other things being the same, the union wage advantage will tend to reduce the quit rates of union workers.

A variety of studies suggest that the decline in quit rates attributable to unionism is very substantial, ranging from 31 to 65 percent.[28] A lower quit rate increases efficiency by producing a more experienced labor force within unionized firms and by reducing

[27]Freeman and Medoff, op. cit., chap. 11.
[28]Ibid., pp. 95–96.

the firm's recruitment, screening, and hiring costs. Furthermore, the reduced turnover makes investments in specific training by employers more attractive. Reduced turnover increases the likelihood that the employer will capture a positive return on worker training (Chapter 4).

Seniority and Informal Training Because of union insistence on the primacy of seniority in such matters as promotion and layoff, worker security is enhanced. Given this security, workers are more willing to pass on their job knowledge and skills to new or subordinate workers through informal on-the-job training (Chapter 16). Obviously, this enhances labor quality and productivity.[29]

Managerial Performance Union wage pressure may precipitate a ***shock effect*** that is favorable to productivity. Confronted with a strong union and higher wage demands, firms may be forced to adopt better personnel and production methods to meet the union's wage demands and maintain profitability. For example, in his study of the impact of unionization on productivity in the cement industry, Clark observes that after unionization, plant management was improved.[30] He documents a managerial shift to "a more professional, businesslike approach to labor relations." Furthermore, after unionization, greater stress was placed on production goals and the monitoring of worker performance. "Perhaps the most cogent description of the differences in the management process before and after unionization was given by a plant manager who remarked: '. . . before the union this place was run like a family; now we run it like a business.' "[31] Finally, it is worth noting that collective bargaining provides a potential avenue of communication through which the union can point out to management ways of enhancing productivity.

Recapitulation: Unions may improve efficiency by (1) functioning as a collective-voice mechanism for resolving worker grievances; (2) reducing worker turnover; (3) enhancing worker security and thereby creating an environment favorable to on-the-job training; and (4) stimulating managerial efficiency through the shock effect.

Mixed Empirical Evidence

Many studies have been undertaken to measure the impact of unionization on productivity. These studies attempt to control for labor quality, capital–labor ratios, the newness of capital equipment, and other variables aside from unionization that might contribute to productivity differences. The empirical score on the union-productivity issue is about even. For every study that finds a positive union effect on productivity, another study using different data or techniques concludes that there is a negative effect. Let's selectively examine some of the evidence, looking first at economywide studies and then at case studies of specific industries.

[29]The "lifetime" job security that some Japanese firms provide for a portion of their labor force is often cited as an important determinant of their rapid productivity growth. It should be noted, however, that the contention that unionization increases on-the-job training lacks empirical support. See John M. Barron, Scott M. Fuess, Jr., and Mark A. Loewenstein, "Further Analysis of the Effects of Unions on Training," *Journal of Political Economy,* July 1987, pp. 632–640.

[30]Kim B. Clark, "The Impact of Unionization on Productivity: A Case Study," *Industrial and Labor Relations Review,* July 1980, pp. 451–469.

[31]Ibid., p. 467.

An economywide study of manufacturing industries by Brown and Medoff[32] concluded that productivity was 20 to 25 percent higher in a given industry if workers were heavily unionized. However, Warren's[33] study of the private business sector over the 1948–73 period found that increases in unionization significantly reduced labor productivity.

Case studies of specific industries also reflect mixed results. For example, Allen's[34] 1984 study of the construction industry yielded an estimate that union workers are 20 percent more productive than nonunion workers. In a more recent study Allen found that union labor was at least 30 percent more productive in the construction of office buildings, and he attributed much of this higher productivity to a lower ratio of supervisory to production workers and to the use of labor-saving techniques and materials. On the other hand, Allen[35] found "no clear picture" of the effects of unions on labor productivity in the construction of elementary and secondary schools. Clark's previously mentioned study of the cement industry concluded that unionism increased productivity by 6 to 8 percent.[36] In contrast, Pencavel[37] has presented evidence showing that in the 1900–13 period the growth of trade unionism in the British coal industry contributed to declining productivity. Likewise, Mitchell and Stone[38] find that in 1986 unionized sawmills in the western United States were between 12 and 21 percent less productive than nonunionized mills. Finally, we note that Freeman has reviewed 11 studies of public-sector unionism, including firefighters, librarians, teachers, and mass-transit and hospital workers. Two report that unions have positive effects on productivity, two report negative effects, and the remaining seven show essentially no effect.[39]

11-4

Although evidence on the long-run effects of unions on productivity is scanty, Addison and Hirsch[40] summarize two studies that suggest that innovative (research and development) activity is weaker in unionized firms and a third study that indicates "that unionized firms invest significantly less in research and development and physical capital than do similar nonunion firms." Similarly, in examining some 19 manufacturing

[32]Charles Brown and James Medoff, "Trade Unions in the Production Process," *Journal of Political Economy,* June 1978, pp. 355–378.

[33]Ronald S. Warren, Jr., "The Effect of Unionization on Labor Productivity: Some Time Series Evidence," *Journal of Labor Research,* Spring 1985, pp. 199–207.

[34]Steven G. Allen, "Unionized Construction Workers Are More Productive," *Quarterly Journal of Economics,* May 1984, pp. 251–273.

[35]Steven G. Allen, "Unionization and Productivity in Office Building and School Construction," *Industrial and Labor Relations Review,* January 1986, pp. 187–201.

[36]Clark, op. cit., p. 467.

[37]John H. Pencavel, "The Distributional and Efficiency Effects of Trade Unions in Britain," *British Journal of Industrial Relations,* July 1977, pp. 137–156.

[38]Merwin W. Mitchell and Joe E. Stone, "Union Effects on Productivity: Evidence from Western U.S. Sawmills," *Industrial and Labor Relations Review,* October 1992, pp. 135–145.

[39]Richard B. Freeman, "Unionism Comes to the Public Sector," *Journal of Economic Literature,* March 1986, pp. 62–65.

[40] John T. Addison and Barry T. Hirsch, "Union Effects on Productivity, Profits, and Growth: Has the Long Run Arrived?" *Journal of Labor Economics,* January 1989, pp. 96–97. Also relevant is Barry T. Hirsch, *Labor Unions and the Economic Performance of Firms* (Kalamazoo, MI: W. E. Upjohn Institute, 1991), chaps. 5 and 6, pp. 69–112.

11-4 World of Work

THE EFFECTS OF TEACHER UNIONS ON PRODUCTIVITY*

Eberts and Stone have analyzed the effect of teacher unions on the productivity of public schools as measured by increases in student achievement. More specifically, they compared the increase in student achievement in mathematics of some 14,000 fourth graders attending 328 elementary schools nationwide. For the entire sample of students, the overall relative productivity or achievement gain for students taught by unionized teachers was 3 percent greater than for students taught by nonunion teachers. However, the gain varied by student quality. For students of average ability the advantage for students in unionized schools was about 7 percent. On the other hand, for students who were extremely above or below average the productivity advantage was reversed. That is, students taught by *nonunion* teachers had approximately a 7 percent greater achievement gain than those taught by union teachers.

How might these findings be explained? Eberts and Stone speculate and present data to suggest that unionized school districts "rely to a greater degree than nonunion districts on standard classroom instruction as a uniform teaching mode, reducing the use of specialized techniques and resources. Standard classroom instruction is tailored to the abilities and problems of the majority of students and, not surprisingly, works best for average students."†

Eberts and Stone also found that "instructional leadership"—that is, the time spent by school principals on curriculum development, program planning and evaluation, and the like—is significantly different between union and nonunion schools. In particular, these leadership activities on the part of school principals are associated with *higher* student achievement in union schools but with *lower* achievement in nonunion schools. This curious finding is explained in terms of the collective-voice function of unions. That is, in unionized schools "instructional leadership by school principals may be much more effective than otherwise, both because specific principal actions are conditioned by teacher opinion and because the effectiveness of particular actions is enhanced by improved communication and coordination."‡

*Randall W. Eberts and Joe E. Stone, "Teacher Unions and the Productivity of Public Schools," *Industrial and Labor Relations Review,* April 1987, pp. 354–363.

†Ibid., p. 361.

‡Ibid., p. 362.

industries, Hirsch and Link[41] have concluded that productivity growth is slower in industries characterized by (1) a greater proportion of union coverage and (2) faster union growth.

There is obviously no neat summing up of this discussion of the efficiency effects of unions. Systematic analysis of the impact of unions on productivity is a relatively new endeavor, and there are no unassailable conclusions. The relationship between unionism and productivity is multifaceted, complex, and imperfectly understood at this point in time. Yet some agreement exists that the "state of industrial relations" may be critical in determining whether unionization is accompanied by higher or lower labor productivity. "If industrial relations are good, with management and unions working together to produce a bigger 'pie' as well as fighting over the size of their slices, productivity is likely to be higher under unionism. If industrial relations are poor, with management and labor ignoring common goals to battle one another, productivity is likely to be lower under unionism."[42]

[41]Barry T. Hirsch and Albert N. Link, "Unions, Productivity, and Productivity Growth," *Journal of Labor Research,* Winter 1984, pp. 29–37.

[42]Freeman and Medoff, op. cit., p. 165. On this point, see also Brian Bemmels, "How Unions Affect Productivity in Manufacturing Plants," *Industrial and Labor Relations Review,* January 1987, pp. 241–253. For more on the union-productivity relationship, see Hirsch and Addison, op. cit., chap. 7; John T. Addison, "Are Unions Good for Productivity?" *Journal of Labor Research,* Spring 1982, pp. 125–138; and W. H. Hutt, "The Face and Mask of Unionism," *Journal of Labor Research,* Summer 1983, pp. 197–211.

FIRM PROFITABILITY

Does unionization raise or lower firm and industry profitability? Do the wage gains of union workers come at the expense of business profits? Or do productivity increases that *may* accompany unionization offset higher wages so that profits are unaffected? Or are unionized firms and industries able to shift their higher wage costs on to consumers through higher product prices and thereby preserve profitability?

Virtually all empirical studies associate unionization with diminished profitability. (Indeed, it would be difficult to reconcile employer resistance to unions if the opposite were true.) Freeman and Medoff, for example, report significant (17 to 37 percent) reductions in profits due to unionization.[43] Using data for some 139 manufacturing industries, Voos and Mishell have concluded that unionization reduces profitability by 20 to 23 percent.[44] Two recent studies using firm-level data report that unionization reduces profitability.[45] Similarly, after examining 16 studies of the union impact on profitability, Addison and Hirsch conclude, "The most striking result of the studies is the common theme of lower profitability in union regimes. . . . Moreover, the magnitude of the reduction in profits is large."[46]

Is this redistribution from profits to wages desirable? There are two polar scenarios. Scenario 1: If the unionized industry is highly concentrated or "monopolistic," then the effect of a union may simply be to transfer unwarranted "excess" or "monopoly" profits from the pockets of capitalists to those of workers, with no negative effects on economic efficiency. Scenario 2: If the unionized industry is quite highly competitive and profits are therefore about "normal," then higher union wage costs may have adverse effects. Specifically, higher wage costs will mean below-normal profits and the impairment of investment in capital equipment and technological progress, and in the long run, firms will leave the industry. The resulting smaller output will mean higher product prices for consumers and less employment for workers. Declining investment in the industry will mean a lower overall rate of economic growth.

Which scenario is more relevant? Researchers disagree. For example, Freeman and Medoff have compared the impact of unions on profitability in highly concentrated or monopolistic industries and in less-concentrated or "competitive" industries. They find little difference between profitability in union and nonunion industries that are competitive. But for monopolistic industries, unions significantly reduce profits. In other words, according to Freeman and Medoff, the more socially desirable scenario 1 seems to be more descriptive of our economy than the less desirable scenario 2.[47] In direct comparison, Clark has reached the opposite conclusion. He finds that unions reduce

[43]Freeman and Medoff, op. cit., Table 12-1, p. 183.

[44]Paul B. Voos and Lawrence R. Mishel, "The Union Impact on Profits: Evidence from Industry Price-Cost Margin Data," *Journal of Labor Economics,* January 1986, pp. 105–133.

[45]Barry T. Hirsch, "Union Coverage and Profitability among U.S. Firms," *Review of Economics and Statistics,* February 1991, pp. 69–77; and Stephen G. Bronars, Donald R. Deere, and Joseph S. Tracy, "The Effects of Unions on Firm Behavior: An Empirical Analysis Using Firm-Level Data," *Industrial Relations,* October 1994, pp. 426–451.

[46]Addison and Hirsch, op. cit., p. 87. Hirsch, op. cit., chap. 4, pp. 35–68, provides a concise, readable discussion of this topic.

[47]Freeman and Medoff, op. cit., pp. 184–187.

significantly the profits of less-concentrated employers but not of concentrated employers.[48] This, of course, lends credence to scenario 2.

To summarize: There is agreement that, overall, unions reduce firm profitability. But there is no consensus as to whether this redistribution reduces economic efficiency.

QUICK REVIEW 11-2

- Unions may negatively affect efficiency and productivity through *(a)* restrictive work rules, *(b)* strikes, and *(c)* labor misallocation resulting from the union wage advantage.
- The static efficiency loss from unionism is thought to be relatively small.
- Unions may positively contribute to efficiency and productivity through *(a)* inadvertently accelerating the substitution of capital for labor and hastening the search for cost-reducing technologies and *(b)* serving as a collective-voice mechanism that reduces labor turnover, enhances worker security, and induces managerial efficiency.
- Empirical evidence on the union impact on productivity is mixed and inconclusive.
- Studies indicate that unions significantly reduce the profitability of firms.

Your Turn: Explain why the following two statements could be consistent: "Unions enhance productivity"; "Unions reduce firm profitability." (Answer: See page 626.)

DISTRIBUTION OF EARNINGS

Some disagreement also arises as to the impact of unions on the distribution of earnings. A few economists reason that unions contribute to earnings inequality; most take precisely the opposite view.

Increasing Inequality

Those who argue that unions increase inequality in the distribution of wages contend that unions (1) simultaneously increase the wages of union workers and depress the wages of nonunion workers through the spillover effect; (2) raise the wages of skilled blue-collar workers relative to unskilled blue-collar workers; and (3) increase the demand for skilled labor within unionized firms.

Union–Nonunion Wages Perhaps the simplest argument in support of the position that unions enhance inequality is based on the spillover effect. Recall once again

[48]Kim B. Clark, "Unionization and Firm Performance: The Impact on Profits, Growth, and Productivity," *American Economic Review,* December 1984, pp. 893–919. See also Barry T. Hirsch and Robert A. Connolly, "Do Unions Capture Monopoly Profits?" *Industrial and Labor Relations Review,* October 1987, pp. 118–136; and Brian E. Becker and Craig A. Olson, "Unions and Firm Profits," *Industrial Relations,* Fall 1992, pp. 395–415.

that the higher wage rates realized in the union sector of Figure 11-2 displace workers who then seek reemployment in the nonunion sector. The result of this displacement is that nonunion wage rates are depressed. Thus, while we began with equal rates of W_n in both submarkets, the effect of unionism is to generate higher wage rates of W_u for union workers but lower wages of W_s for nonunion workers.

Blue-Collar Wages The fact that unionization is more extensive among the more highly skilled, higher-paid blue-collar workers than among less-skilled, lower-paid blue-collar workers also suggests that the obtaining of a wage advantage by unions increases the dispersion of earnings.

Skilled Labor Demand Pettengill[49] has argued that when unions force employers to pay above-equilibrium wage rates, the long-run response is to hire higher-quality workers. This constitutes a shift in the structure of labor demand away from low-quality and toward high-quality workers. The net result is a widening of the dispersion of wages or, in short, greater wage inequality.

Pettengill elaborates his reasoning with the following example shown in Table 11-4. Here, we assume that *A, B,* and *C* designate various levels of labor quality—say, high school graduates, high school dropouts, and workers with no high school education, respectively—that are available to a nonunion employer. The productivity or output per hour of each quality level is given in column 2, and wage rates are specified in column 3. By dividing productivity into the wage rate, we obtain wage cost per unit of output as shown in column 4. Given these options, the firm will hire *B*-quality labor at $4 per hour because the associated wage costs per unit of output are minimized.

Now suppose that the firm is unionized and the wages of *B*-quality labor are increased to $6. What are the consequences? In the short run, the per unit cost of production rises to $1.50 and the lifetime earnings prospects of *B*-quality workers are enhanced. In the long run, the normal attrition of *B*-quality workers through retirement, voluntary quits, deaths, and so forth will prompt the firm to replace such workers with *A*-quality workers. That is, if the union forces the employer to pay $6 per hour for labor, then the firm will seek the best-qualified workers obtainable at that wage rate.

[49]John S. Pettengill, *Labor Unions and the Inequality of Earned Income* (Amsterdam: North-Holland Publishing Company, 1980).

TABLE 11-4 LABOR QUALITY, PRODUCTIVITY, AND WAGE RATES

(1) Type of labor	(2) Output per hour	(3) Wage rate	(4) = (3) ÷ (2) Wage cost per unit of output
A	5	$6.00	$1.20
B	4	4.00	1.00
C	2	2.50	1.25

Specifically, the firm will now require all of its new employees to have a high school diploma. Note that when all *B* workers are eventually replaced with *A* workers at the \$6 wage rate, labor costs per unit of output will have fallen from \$1.50 to \$1.20 because *A* workers are more productive.

If this scenario is repeated on a wide scale, we find that an increase in the demand for high-quality *A* workers and a decline in the demand for lower-quality *B* workers occur. This causes the ratio of the "going wage" of high school graduates to increase relative to the "going wage" of high school dropouts, widening the dispersion of wages and increasing earnings inequality. Less obviously, the higher wages for high school graduates will reduce the incremental income received by college graduates in comparison with high school graduates (see Figure 4-2). This decline in the "college premium" will reduce the rate of return on an investment in a college education and in time reduce the supply of college graduates. As a result, the wages and salaries received by college graduates will tend to rise, further increasing the dispersion of wages and increasing earnings inequality.

Promoting Equality

Other aspects of union wage policies, however, suggest that unionism promotes greater, not less, equality in the distribution of earnings. What are these other ways unions tend to equalize wages?

1 Uniform Wages within Firms Without unions, employers are apt to pay different wages to individual workers on the same job. These wage differences are based on perceived differences in job performance, length of job tenure, and, perhaps, favoritism. Unions, on the other hand, have a tradition of seeking uniform wage rates for all workers performing a particular job. In short, while nonunion firms usually assign wage rates to *individual workers,* unions—in the interest of worker allegiance and solidarity—seek to assign wage rates to *jobs.* To the extent that unions are successful, wage and earnings differentials based on supervisory judgments of individual worker performance are eliminated. An important side effect of this standard-wage policy is that wage discrimination against blacks, other minorities, and women is likely to be less when a union is present. Recall from Chapter 10 that black male workers tend to benefit more from unionization than any other demographic group.

Wage and earnings inequality within a firm may be reduced by unionism for another reason. Industrial unions—those comprised of a variety of workers, ranging from unskilled to highly skilled—frequently follow a wage policy of seeking equal *absolute* wage increases for all of their constituents. This means that larger *percentage* increases are realized by less-skilled workers, and the earnings gap between unskilled and skilled workers is reduced. Consider this simple illustration. Assume that skilled workers are initially paid \$10 and unskilled workers \$5 per hour. Suppose the union negotiates equal \$2 increases for both groups so that skilled workers now receive \$12 and unskilled \$7 per hour. Originally, unskilled workers earned 50 percent (= \$5/\$10) of what skilled workers received. But after the wage increase, unskilled workers get about 58 percent (= \$7/\$12) of skilled wages. Relative wage inequality has diminished.

Why would an industrial union adopt a policy of equal absolute wage increases for workers of different skills? The answer is twofold. On the one hand, it reflects the union's egalitarian ideology. On the other hand, it allows union leaders to largely sidestep politically awkward and potentially divisive decisions concerning the relative worth of various groups of constituents.

2 Uniform Wages among Firms In addition to seeking standard wage rates for given occupational classes *within* firms, unions also seek standard wage rates *among* firms. The rationale for this policy is almost self-evident. The existence of substantial wage differences among competing firms in an industry may undermine the ability of unions to sustain and enhance wage advantages. For example, if one firm in a four-firm oligopoly is allowed to pay significantly lower wages to its union workers, the union is likely to find it difficult to maintain the union wage advantage in the other three firms. In particular, during a recession the high-wage firms are likely to put great pressure on the union to lower wages to the level of the low-wage firm. To avoid this problem, unions seek to "take labor (wages) out of competition" by standardizing wage rates among firms, thereby reducing the degree of wage dispersion. You may recall from Chapter 10 that multiemployer bargaining that culminates in an industrywide contract is an important means of standardizing wage rates.

3 Reducing the White-Collar to Blue-Collar Differential In examining the empirical evidence on the union wage advantage, we observed that unions achieve larger wage gains for blue-collar workers than for white-collar workers. Because on the average white-collar workers enjoy higher earnings than blue-collar workers, the larger wage gains that unions achieve for the latter reduce earnings inequalities between blue- and white-collar workers.

Increased Equality?

What is the *net* effect of unionism on the distribution of earnings? There is a rather strong consensus that unions decrease the degree of wage dispersion. Freeman and Medoff have used empirical analysis to conclude that the spillover effect *increases* earnings inequality by about 1 percent, but the standardization of wage rates within and among firms *decreases* inequality by about 4 percent. The net result is a 3 percent decline in earnings inequality due to unionism. Noting that only a relatively small percentage of the labor force is unionized, the authors contend that this 3 percent reduction in inequality should be regarded as "substantial."[50] This conclusion is reinforced

[50]Freeman and Medoff, op. cit., pp. 90–93, and additional studies cited therein. For a succinct summary of nine studies of the impact of unions on wage inequality, see Richard B. Freeman, "Effects of Unions on the Economy," in Seymour Martin Lipset (ed.), *Unions in Transition* (San Francisco: ICS Press, 1986), pp. 183–188. See also Nguyen T. Quan, "Unionism and the Size Distribution of Earnings," *Industrial Relations,* Spring 1984, pp. 270–277; and Hirsch and Addison, op. cit., chap. 6.

by more recent research by Card,[51] who estimates that unions reduced wage inequality by 7 percent in 1987. He also points to the decline in unionism as a contributor to the recent increase in wage inequality in the United States ("World of Work" 8-1 and Chapter 17). Card finds that about 20 percent of the increase in wage inequality occurring between 1973 and 1987 is attributable to the decline in unionism.

OTHER ISSUES: INFLATION, UNEMPLOYMENT, AND INCOME SHARES

Our discussion of the possible economic impact of unions is not complete. Unions could conceivably affect inflation, employment and unemployment, and the share of national income paid as wages. Let's briefly assess each, deferring detailed discussion in some cases to later chapters.

Inflation

Economists generally agree that union wage determination is *not* a basic cause of inflation. Most of our serious inflationary episodes have been associated with excess aggregate demand or supply shocks rather than wage-push considerations. Specifically, recent inflations can be attributed largely to expansionary fiscal or monetary policies or supply shocks, such as the dramatic Organization of Petroleum Exporting Countries oil price increases of the 1970s. On the other hand, wage determination under collective bargaining may well perpetuate an ongoing inflation since unions may seek and receive wage gains in anticipation of future inflation. These actions hinder the effectiveness of anti-inflationary policies.

Unions and Unemployment

The relationship between unionism and unemployment is complex and highly controversial. One view is that unions are a major cause of downward wage inflexibility in our economy.[52] As a result, declines in labor demand affect employment almost exclusively and not wages. Because of the downward inflexibility of wages, wage reduction cannot cushion or ameliorate the impact of recession on unemployment. The counterview is that downward wage rigidity is largely attributable to factors other than unionism. For example, nonunion workers have informal understandings or "implicit contracts" with employers that obligate employers to maintain wage rates unless economic conditions are so severe as to threaten the firm with bankruptcy. Furthermore, firms may prefer selective layoffs to across-the-board wage reductions during an economic slump. The reason is that the latter might cause higher-skilled, more-experienced workers in whom the firm has made large training investments to quit and take other

[51] David Card, "The Effect of Unions on the Structure of Wages: A Longitudinal Analysis," *Econometrica,* July 1996, pp. 957–979. Also see John Dinardo and Thomas Lemieux, "Diverging Male Wage Inequality in the United States and Canada, 1981–1988: Do Institutions Explain the Difference?" *Industrial and Labor Relations Review,* July 1997, pp. 629–651.

[52] See Chapter 19 for a fuller discussion.

jobs. A fixed-wage-with-layoffs strategy allows employers to "hoard" these more valuable workers during an economic downturn and to lay off less-trained workers who can be more easily and less expensively replaced.

Apart from cyclical changes in labor demand, unions may affect employment in at least two other ways. First, unionism is associated with lower worker turnover, which tends to reduce unemployment rates. Second, by raising wages unions may increase unemployment by attracting additional workers into the labor force (see Figure 6-10 and the accompanying discussion).

Overall, the unionism–unemployment picture is mixed, and no consensus exists as to the net effect. It is relevant to note, however, that in one study Montgomery examines data for some 42 metropolitan areas in an attempt to assess the impact of union strength (as measured by both the percentage of workers organized and the size of the union–nonunion wage differential) on employment. He does find that greater union strength is associated with a lesser likelihood of employment, but the quantitative effects are very small. For example, a 10 percent increase in the percentage of workers unionized reduces the likelihood of being employed by only 0.2 percent. Similarly, a 10 percent increase in the union wage premium reduces the likelihood of being employed by just 0.06 percent.[53]

Labor's Share

There is no significant evidence to suggest that unions have been able to increase labor's share and decrease the capitalist share of national income. The reasons for this are several. In the first place, as our analysis of the spillover effect implies, higher wages for union workers may come largely at the expense of the wages of nonunion workers (Figure 11-2) and not out of the capitalist share. Second, union wage increases may induce the substitution of capital for labor. Therefore, the potential positive effect that higher union wages have on labor's share in the unionized sector may be offset by the negative effect associated with fewer union jobs. Finally, management may largely escape a redistribution of national income from capital to labor through productivity and price increases. The potential encroachment on profits stemming from wage increases may partially be absorbed or offset by productivity increases or by price increases. The lack of any significant impact on labor's share is undoubtedly related to the fact that only a relatively small percentage of the labor force is unionized.

CHAPTER SUMMARY

1 Considerations other than the presence of unions may explain at least in part why strongly unionized industries pay higher wages than weakly organized industries. These factors include relatively fewer female workers, larger-scale plants, and more capital-intensive production methods in the strongly unionized industries.

[53]Edward Montgomery, "Employment and Unemployment Effects of Unions," *Journal of Labor Economics,* April 1989, pp. 170–190.

2 The pure union wage advantage A is equal to $(W_u - W_n)/W_n \times 100$, where W_u is the union wage and W_n the nonunion wage that would exist without unions.
3 The spillover and superior-worker effects cause the measured union wage advantage to overstate the pure wage advantage; the threat and product market effects cause the measured union wage advantage to understate the pure wage advantage.
4 Research evidence consistently indicates that unions do achieve a wage advantage for their constituents, although the size of the advantage varies substantially by occupation, industry, race, and gender. Estimates by Lewis for the 1923–58 period suggest that the average union wage advantage was on the order of 10 to 15 percent, but that the advantage widens during depression and diminishes when unexpected inflation occurs. The union wage advantage widened in the mid-1970s. Although the advantage has fallen since then, it remains at the high range of its 15 to 20 percent contemporary level.
5 Union workers also generally receive a higher level and greater variety of fringe benefits, causing the union total compensation advantage to exceed the wage advantage.
6 Disagreement exists as to whether the net effect of unions on allocative efficiency and productivity is positive or negative. The negative view cites *(a)* the inefficiencies associated with union-imposed work rules, *(b)* the loss of output through strikes, and *(c)* the misallocation of labor to which the union wage advantage gives rise.
7 The positive view contends that *(a)* union wage pressure spurs technological advance and the mechanization of the production process and *(b)* as collective-voice institutions, unions contribute to rising productivity by resolving worker grievances, reducing labor turnover, enhancing worker security, and inducing greater managerial efficiency.
8 Consensus exists that unions reduce firm profitability, but disagreement arises as to whether this reduction has undesirable effects on economic efficiency.
9 Those who contend that unions increase earnings inequality argue that *(a)* unionization increases the wages of union workers but lowers the wages of nonunion workers; *(b)* unions are strongest among highly paid, skilled blue-collar workers but are relatively weak among low-paid, unskilled blue-collar workers; and *(c)* union wage increases generate an increase in the demand for high-quality workers and a decline in the demand for low-quality workers. The opposing view is that unions contribute to greater earnings equality because *(a)* unions seek uniform wages for given jobs within firms, *(b)* unions favor uniform wages among firms, and *(c)* unions have achieved higher wage gains for relatively low-paid blue-collar workers than for relatively high-paid white-collar workers. Recent empirical evidence finds that unionism does reduce wage inequality and that the decline of unionism has contributed to growing wage inequality.

TERMS AND CONCEPTS

pure versus measured union wage advantages
spillover effect
threat effect
A product market effect
wait unemployment
A superior-worker effect
fringe benefits
collective voice
exit and voice mechanisms
A shock effect

QUESTIONS AND STUDY SUGGESTIONS

1 What is the "commonsense" basis for expecting a union wage advantage? Explain how each of the following differences between union and nonunion firms might complicate one's determination of whether unions actually are responsible for an observed wage advantage: *(a)* the demographic makeup of the labor forces, *(b)* plant sizes, and *(c)* the amount of capital equipment used per worker.

2 Evidence suggests that the union wage advantage varies directly with the proportion of a given industry that is organized. Why is this?

3 How is the "pure" union wage advantage defined? If in a given labor market the wage rate would be $8 without a union and $10 with a union, then what is the pure union wage advantage? Explain how, and in what direction, each of the following might cause the "measured" union wage advantage to vary from the pure advantage: *(a)* the spillover effect, *(b)* the threat effect, *(c)* the product market effect, and *(d)* the superior-worker effect.

4 Indicate the overall size of the measured union wage advantage. Does recent evidence suggest that the advantage has increased or decreased? Comment on and explain cyclical changes in the union wage advantage.

5 Compare the size of the fringe benefits received by union and nonunion workers and indicate why unions might be responsible for any differences.

6 Comment on each of the following statements:

a "Unions tie the hands of management and inhibit efficient decision making."

b "Unions contribute to economic efficiency in that union wage pressure hastens the weeding out of the high-cost, least-efficient producers in each industry."

c "Although unions may reduce wage inequality, to the extent they reduce wage differentials based upon individual merit and effort, the outcome may be rightly perceived as both inequitable and inefficient."

d "Unions impair the efficiency of our economy indirectly by diminishing profits and thereby reducing investment and economic expansion."

7 Indicate the amount of work time lost each year because of strikes. Cite circumstances under which the amount of work time lost during a specific strike might be a poor indicator of the amount of lost output.

8 "There is an inherent cost to society that accompanies any union wage gain. That cost is the diminished efficiency with which labor resources are allocated." Explain this contention. Do you agree? In your response, distinguish between static and dynamic efficiency.

9 Evidence suggests that firms that sell their products in less-competitive product markets are more likely to be unionized than firms selling in highly competitive markets. Recalling from Chapter 5 that the elasticity of product demand is an important determinant of the elasticity of labor demand, how might this affect *(a)* the elasticities of the union and nonunion demand curve in Figure 11-3 and *(b)* the net loss of output due to the union wage advantage?

10 In what specific ways might the presence of a union raise productivity within a firm? Use the "exit mechanism" and "voice mechanism" concepts in your response.

11 Describe the various avenues through which unions might alter the distribution of earnings. On balance, do unions enhance or mitigate wage dispersion?

12 Would our economy function better if it were union-free? Explain your answer. Next, provide a counterargument to your position.

SELECTED REFERENCES

Booth, Allison L.: *The Economics of the Trade Union* (Cambridge, England: Cambridge University Press, 1995).

Burton, John F., Jr., et al.: "Review Symposium on *What Do Unions Do?*" *Industrial and Labor Relations Review,* January 1985, pp. 244–263.

Freeman, Richard B., and James L. Medoff: *What Do Unions Do?* (New York: Basic Books, Inc., 1984).

Hirsch, Barry T.: *Labor Unions and the Economic Performance of Firms* (Kalamazoo, MI: W. E. Upjohn Institute, 1991).

Hirsch, Barry T., and John T. Addison: *The Economic Analysis of Unions* (London: Allen & Unwin, 1986), chaps. 5–7.

Lewis, H. Gregg: *Union Relative Wage Effects* (Chicago: University of Chicago Press, 1986).

Lipset, Seymour Martin (ed.): *Unions in Transition* (San Francisco: ICS Press, 1986), chaps. 7–9.

Mitchell, Daniel J. B.: *Unions, Wages, and Inflation* (Washington, DC: Brookings Institution, 1980), chap. 3.

Parsley, C. J.: "Labor Union Effects on Wage Gains: A Survey of Recent Literature," *Journal of Economic Literature,* March 1980, pp. 1–31.

Pencavel, John: *Labor Markets under Trade Unionism: Employment, Wages, and Hours* (Cambridge, MA: Basil Blackwell, 1991).

Pettengill, John S.: *Labor Unions and the Inequality of Earned Income* (Amsterdam: North-Holland Publishing Company, 1980).

Rees, Albert: *The Economics of Trade Unions,* rev. ed. (Chicago: University of Chicago Press, 1977), chaps. 4 and 7.

Reynolds, Morgan: *Making America Poorer* (Washington, DC: Cato Institute, 1987).

CHAPTER 12

GOVERNMENT AND THE LABOR MARKET: EMPLOYMENT, EXPENDITURES, AND TAXATION

In Chapters 6, 10, and 11, we discussed the role of unions in influencing wage rates and employment levels in labor markets. We now turn our attention to another major institution—government—and the various ways it affects wages and employment throughout the economy. Government's participation in the labor market is very substantial. For example, in 1997 the number of Americans working for federal, state, and local governments exceeded the number of workers in manufacturing jobs!

This chapter examines public-sector employment and the impacts of government spending and selected taxes on wages and employment in the private sector. In the following chapter we discuss examples of direct government intervention in labor markets via laws and regulations.

Our present discussion proceeds as follows. First, we examine the extent and growth of government employment and compare public-sector and private-sector pay. Next, the labor market aspects of the draft versus those of the voluntary army are analyzed. Third, we take a look at the labor market effects of government's nonpayroll spending, that is, its purchases of private-sector output and its transfers and subsidies. This is followed by a discussion of how the *presence* of publicly provided goods and services can influence labor supply and demand, independently of the hiring of workers needed to produce these items. The final section of the chapter analyzes the labor market consequences of the personal income tax. There, we answer the question: Does the personal income tax affect wage rates and employment levels?

PUBLIC-SECTOR EMPLOYMENT AND WAGES

Government is a major—or even the sole—employer of specific types of workers in many labor markets. For example, it hires military personnel, antitrust prosecutors, postal workers, air traffic controllers, park rangers, schoolteachers, agency managers, firefighters, and highway maintenance personnel. The demand for these employees is derived from society's demand for the public-sector goods and services that these workers help provide. When government employs workers, it "exhausts" or "absorbs" economic resources. More precisely, government employment makes a direct claim on the nation's productive capabilities. For example, when government employs postal workers, those laborers are no longer available to produce other goods and services. Likewise, when the military either drafts personnel or persuades them to enlist voluntarily, society forgoes the private-sector output that those resources could have produced. Presumably, society values the public-sector output or services more highly than the alternative uses for these resources.

Government Employment: Extent and Growth

Table 12-1 demonstrates the extent and growth of government employment in the United States since 1950. Close examination of the columns in the table reveals several generalizations. First, the absolute number of federal civilian (column 2) and state and local government employees (column 4) increased over the 47-year period. This is not surprising because total employment in the economy (column 5) also rose considerably. Second, the growth of federal government employment was much less dramatic than the increase in state and local government employment. Clearly, most of

TABLE 12-1 EXTENT AND GROWTH OF GOVERNMENT EMPLOYMENT IN THE UNITED STATES, 1950–97

	Government employment (in millions)				(6)	(7)
(1) Year	(2) Federal civilian	(3) Armed services*	(4) State and local	(5) Total U.S. employment (in millions)	Federal civilian employment as a percent of total U.S. employment	State and local employment as a percent of total U.S. employment
1950	1.9	1.5	4.1	58.9	3.2%	7.0%
1955	2.2	2.9	4.7	62.2	3.5	7.6
1960	2.3	2.5	6.1	65.8	3.5	9.3
1965	2.4	2.7	7.7	71.1	3.4	10.8
1970	2.7	3.0	10.0	78.7	3.4	12.7
1975	2.7	2.1	12.0	85.8	3.1	14.0
1980	2.9	2.1	13.3	99.3	2.9	13.4
1985	2.9	2.2	13.5	107.2	2.7	12.6
1990	3.1	2.0	15.2	118.5	2.6	12.8
1997	2.7	1.8	17.0	129.6	2.1	13.1

*Active duty personnel.

Source: Compiled from U.S. Bureau of the Census, *Statistical Abstract of the United States, 1993, 1997;* and *Economic Report of the President, 1998,* Tables B-36 and B-46.

the growth of employment in the public sector since 1950 has occurred at the state and local levels of government. Federal civilian employment as a percentage of total employment (column 6) fell from 3.2 percent in 1950 to 2.1 percent in 1997. During those same years state and local employment rose from 7.0 to 13.1 percent of total employment (column 7). Third, in 1950, one out of 7 U.S. workers was employed by government; by 1997 that figure had risen to about one out of six workers. Finally, the number of active-duty personnel in the armed services (column 3) varied between 1.5 and 3 million during these selected years.

12-1

12-1

The relative growth of public-sector employment over the past several decades can be envisioned in terms of our familiar labor demand and supply model (Figure 6-2). Although labor supply has increased at roughly the same pace in both the public and

12-1 World of Work

WHAT DO GOVERNMENT WORKERS DO?

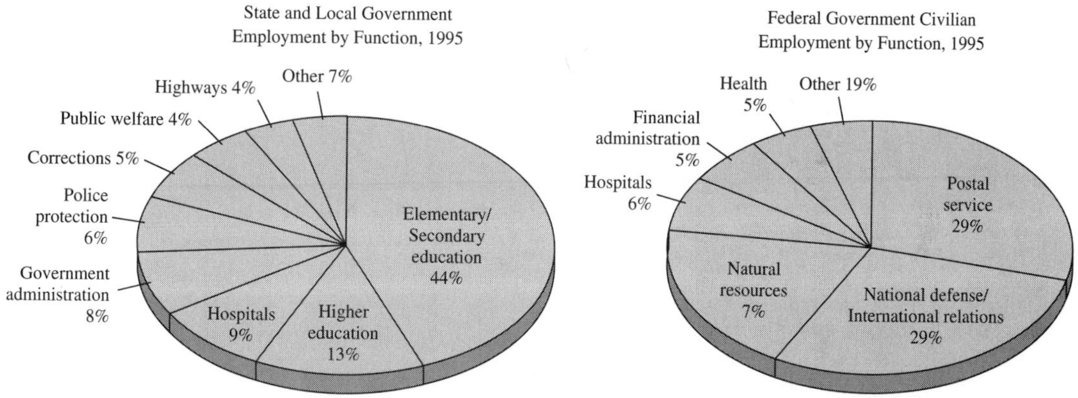

The types of jobs government workers hold depend on the level of government. State and local government employment is focused in education, with over one-half of the workers in that sector. Other large areas of employment include hospitals and law enforcement, each of which account for about one-tenth of state and local government employment. Smaller sectors include public welfare and highways, which together total less than one-tenth of total employment.

Federal government civilian workers are concentrated in different areas than state and local government workers. Nearly three-fifths of federal government workers are in defense and postal service jobs. The natural resources, hospitals, health, and financial administration sectors each account for 5 to 7 percent of total employment. The "other" category is composed of workers in areas such as judicial and legal, corrections, air transportation, and social insurance administration.

Source: U.S. Census Bureau, "Federal Government Civilian Employment by Function," October 1995 and "Total State and Local Government Employment and Payroll Data," October, 1995.

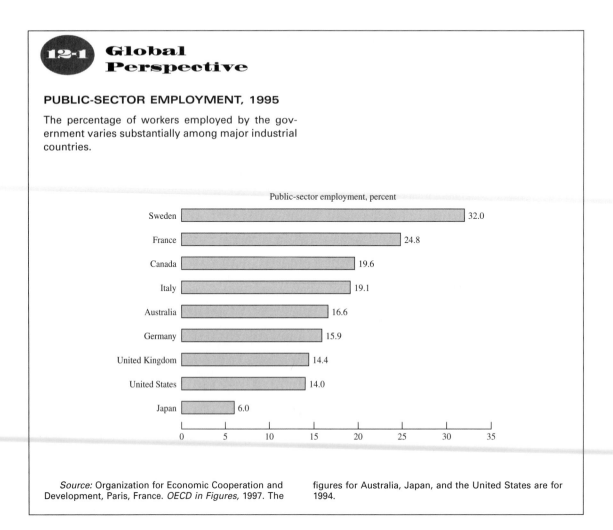

12-1 **Global Perspective**

PUBLIC-SECTOR EMPLOYMENT, 1995

The percentage of workers employed by the government varies substantially among major industrial countries.

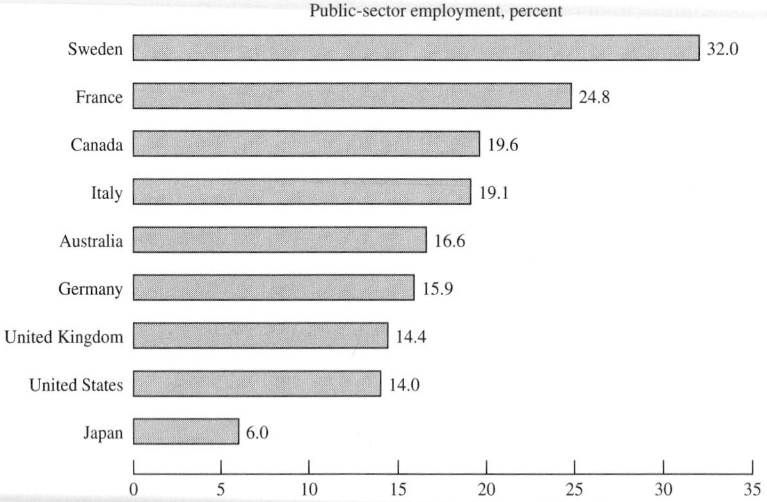

Source: Organization for Economic Cooperation and Development, Paris, France. *OECD in Figures,* 1997. The figures for Australia, Japan, and the United States are for 1994.

private sectors, the labor demand curve has shifted to the right more rapidly in the public sector than in the private sector. The result has been a faster rate of equilibrium employment growth in the public sector.

Economists cite several reasons for this relative growth of labor demand in the public sector. In the first place, the attendant needs and problems associated with population growth, urbanization, and urban sprawl increased the demand for many state and local government services. Furthermore, the age composition of the population dramatically changed over the 47-year period. The post–World War II baby boom caused a considerable increase in school-age children, which in turn caused a marked increase in the demand for public school teachers. A third factor at work was the growth of real income in the society, which increased the demand for such income-elastic government services as higher education, health services, parks, and a clean environment. Additionally, public-sector unions emerged as a more powerful and militant force in the public-sector labor market. Some observers contend that public employee unions and professional groups increasingly used their political power—via campaign contributions, organizational support, endorsements, and votes—to elect government officials who favored greater spending for governmentally provided goods and services. This may have increased the derived demand for public employees.[1] Finally, government's regulatory role in the economy has expanded over the past four decades, and this has also increased the demand for government workers.

12-2

[1]See Paul Courant, Edward Gramlich, and Daniel Rubinfeld, "Public Employee Market Power and the Level of Government Spending." *American Economic Review,* December 1979, pp. 806–817. Marick F. Masters and John Thomas Delaney provide a good review of the scholarly literature on labor's role in U.S. national politics since 1945 in "Union Political Activities: A Review of the Empirical Literature," *Industrial and Labor Relations Review,* April 1987, pp. 336–353. In particular, see table 1, pp. 339–342.

12-2 World of Work

THE 10 MOST UNUSUAL FEDERAL JOBS*

In Table 12-1 we saw that the federal government employs 2.7 million civilian workers. Many of these jobs are familiar: Postal workers deliver the mail, judges sentence offenders, and IRS agents audit tax returns. There are other federal jobs—some important, some not—that are much more obscure. *Wall Street Journal* reporter David Wessel set out to find the 10 most unusual jobs in the federal government. Here is his list.

1. *Smokey the Bear's manager.* The U.S. Forest Service employs a full-time official to protect the government's trademark on Smokey the Bear. Private uses of this symbol might dilute its effectiveness in creating awareness of fire dangers to our national forests.
2. *The Army's civilian marksmanship chief.* An army officer oversees an annual budget of $5 million to support the training of civilians in rifle marksmanship. These civilian sharpshooters presumably would be helpful if war broke out.
3. *The fish watcher.* Federal marine biologists spend 2 or 3 months at a time living aboard foreign fish-processing vessels off the coast of Alaska. Their task is to detect any illegal taking of prohibited species such as salmon.
4. *The Supreme Court seamstress.* A seamstress is employed by the federal government to keep the robes of Supreme Court justices in good repair.
5. *The gold stacker.* Much of the gold owned by foreign governments is stored in vaults in the basement of the Federal Reserve Bank of New York. When an international gold transaction occurs, the gold stacker wheels gold bars from one nation's chicken-wire cage to another's.
6. *The (legal) cocaine importer.* A worker for the Drug Enforcement Administration grants licenses to import coca leaves for extracting cocaine. This legal cocaine is used in medicines.
7. *The condom tester.* Employees of the Food and Drug Administration place condoms on equipment to test them for defects.
8. *The currency reconstructor.* The Bureau of Engraving and Printing has an employee who reconstructs torn currency from fragments. Once the job is completed, the damaged bills are replaced with new currency.
9. *The air force curator.* This person oversees the air force's collection of 7,000 paintings, drawings, and sculptures.
10. *The White House gift appraiser.* The White House assigns a person to appraise the value of all gifts given to the president and his family. These gifts include everything from $12,000 crystal bowls to $10 bottles of wine.

*Based on David Wessel, "How Your Tax Dollars Go to Protecting Smokey and Keeping Supreme Court Justices in Stitches," *Wall Street Journal,* October 9, 1989, p. 16.

Public- versus Private-Sector Pay

The increase in public-sector employment over the 1950–97 period was accompanied by an increase in public-sector pay. In theory, most governmental units adhere to a ***prevailing-wage rule*** (or "comparable-wage" rule). That is, they attempt to set public employees' wages equal to those earned by comparably trained and employed private-sector workers.[2] In 1997, the average hourly pay of public-sector workers was $15.46, while the average for private-sector workers was $13.19.[3] But these averages fail to adjust for such factors as differences in union status, education and training, and demographic characteristics (gender, race). Smith undertook a comprehensive study in the mid-1970s to test empirically whether public-sector employees did in fact achieve wages comparable to private counterparts, once these other factors were accounted for. She found that in 1975 federal employees received wages that were 13 to 20 percent *higher* than those earned by comparably educated and experienced private-sector workers. At the state level, female workers received 6 to 7 percent more and males 3 to 11 percent less than similar private-sector employees. Local government workers appeared to earn wages nearly equal to their private-sector counterparts.[4]

Subsequent studies using data from the mid-1970s to 1982 suggest that the federal pay differential found by Smith persisted into that period. For example, Gyourko and Tracy estimated there was about an 18 percent federal pay premium in 1977.[5] Venti found that the federal pay premium for *male* workers relative to comparable private-sector workers was about 4 percent in 1982, while the pay differential for *female* workers was approximately 22 percent.[6] Krueger discovered that the average increase in the real wage of individual workers who moved from the private to the public sector in the late 1970s was 12 percent. He also found that the application rate for federal jobs in 1982 was 25 to 33 percent higher than for private-sector jobs. This difference in application rates is consistent with a federal pay premium.[7]

Does the wage differential indicated by these earlier studies still exist? The available evidence indicates that the wage premium for public-sector workers has appreciably declined since the mid-1970s. Moulton replicated the procedures of Smith, Gyourko and Tracy, and Krueger, using late-1988 data. He discovered that the federal pay differential had dropped by between 8 and 14 percentage points between 1977–79 and 1988.[8]

[2]The prevailing-wage principle was codified for federal workers in the Federal Pay Comparability Act of 1970. Many state and local governments have similar formal policies.

[3]Barry T. Hirsch and David A. Macpherson, *Union Membership and Earnings Data Book: Compilations from Current Population Survey (1998 Edition)* (Washington, DC: Bureau of National Affairs, 1998).

[4]Sharon P. Smith, *Equal Pay in the Public Sector: Fact or Fantasy* (Princeton, NJ: Princeton University Press, 1977).

[5]Joseph Gyourko and Joseph Tracy, "An Analysis of Public- and Private-Sector Wages Allowing for Endogenous Choices of Both Government and Union Status," *Journal of Labor Economics,* April 1988, pp. 229–249.

[6]Steven F. Venti, "Wages in the Federal and Private Sectors," in David A. Wise (ed.), *Public Sector Payrolls* (Chicago: University of Chicago Press, 1987), pp. 147–177.

[7]Alan B. Krueger, "Are Public Sector Workers Paid More Than Their Alternative Wages? Evidence from Longitudinal Data and Job Queues," in Richard B. Freeman and Casey Ichniowski (eds.), *When Public Sector Workers Unionize* (Chicago: University of Chicago Press, 1988), pp. 217–240.

[8]Brent R. Moulton, "A Re-Examination of the Federal-Private Wage Differential in the United States," *Journal of Labor Economics,* April 1990, pp. 270–293. For a similar conclusion about state and local government workers, see Richard B. Freeman, "How Do Public Sector Wages and Employment Respond to Economic Conditions?" in Wise, op. cit., pp. 183–207.

Moulton concludes that the federal pay premium is about 3 percent nationally and has disappeared entirely in high-wage urban areas and for administrative and professional occupations.[9] Other studies also indicate that wage differential has changed by skill levels since the 1970s. Katz and Krueger report that the public sector has not altered relative pay in response to the rising return to education that has occurred in the private sector. As a result, the public-sector wage differential has risen for low-skilled workers but fallen for high-skilled workers.[10]

Several additional points are worth noting about public- versus private-sector pay. First, the percent of total compensation paid in the form of fringe benefits is higher for public employees than for private workers. Thus, wage and salary comparisons alone may be misleading. Second, the rate at which federal government employees quit their jobs is lower than for comparable workers in the private sector. Some economists conclude that this is an indication that federal workers are overpaid.[11] But others point out that the portion of federal pay taking the form of pensions is very high, which may encourage federal workers to remain in their jobs. If this is the case, quit rates may be poor indexes for judging the adequacy of pay.[12] Third, the occupational wage structure is more egalitarian within government than in the private sector (Chapter 17). Political considerations apparently cause government to pay lower-skilled workers relatively more, and elected and appointed officials relatively less, than comparably trained and experienced private-sector workers. Finally, studies indicate that female and black workers in government receive higher pay than their counterparts in the private sector. Rather than indicating overpayment to workers, however, this higher pay may be the result of a greater relative commitment by government to equal treatment of minorities and women.[13]

12-3

THE MILITARY SECTOR: THE DRAFT VERSUS THE VOLUNTARY ARMY

As indicated earlier in column 3 of Table 12-1, the number of active-duty military personnel employed by the United States during the selected years shown varied between a high of 3 million in 1970 to a low of 1.5 million in 1950. Before 1973, the United States used the selective service system—commonly called the "draft"—to compel people to serve in the military. These draftees worked alongside "volunteers," some of whom offered their labor services to the military rather than waiting to be drafted. Under this system of military conscription, wages were below those that many draftees and enlisted

[9]For a study indicating that state and local government professional and administrative workers earn less than comparable private-sector workers, see Michael Miller, "The Public-Private Pay Debate: What Do the Data Show?" *Monthly Labor Review,* May 1996, pp. 18–29.

[10]Lawrence F. Katz and Alan B. Krueger, "Changes in the Structure of Wages in Public and Private Sectors," *Research in Labor Economics,* 1991, pp. 137–172.

[11]James Long, "Are Government Workers Overpaid? Alternative Evidence," *Journal of Human Resources,* Winter 1982, pp. 123–131.

[12]Richard A. Ippolito, "Why Federal Workers Don't Quit," *Journal of Human Resources,* Spring 1987, pp. 281–299.

[13]This point is made by Martin Asher and Joel Popkin in "The Effect of Gender and Race Differentials on Public–Private Wage Comparisons: A Study of Postal Workers," *Industrial and Labor Relations Review,* October 1984, pp. 16–25.

12-3 World of Work

PUBLIC-SECTOR UNIONS: ARE THEY UNIQUE?*

The public sector differs from the private sector in an important way: Governments provide monopoly services in their particular jurisdictions. As a result, the demand for public goods and services in a particular locale is quite inelastic. That is, consumers cannot substitute one provider for another as is true for most private goods and services. The upshot, according to some observers, is that the derived demand for public employees is also highly inelastic. This inelastic demand allegedly gives public-sector unions extraordinary bargaining power.

Freeman rejects this claim of extraordinary bargaining power on four grounds.

1 Governments face tax and budget constraints that serve as "disciplinary" devices similar to market demand in the private sector. Given a fixed budget, any increase in wages will require a reduction in employment.

2 Cities and states are not really monopolies because people who are unhappy with the level of public services in one area can move elsewhere. An exodus of citizens from a particular jurisdiction will reduce the taxable population there and limit the ability of a particular government to pay public-sector wages.

3 Workers are almost always forbidden to strike when essential services such as police and fire protection will be disrupted.

4 Strikes by public workers do not block revenue flows to government, while strikes by private workers stop these flows to firms. Government may therefore be more willing than private-sector firms to resist union demands.

The uniqueness of public-sector unions, states Freeman, does not lie in differences in elasticity of labor demand between the private and public sectors. Rather, it derives from the political nature of public-sector collective bargaining. Unions use their political power to increase the demand for public services, as well as employ their bargaining power to achieve higher wages. Also, public-sector unions place a heavy emphasis on employment because additional employees increase the political power of the unions. Finally, public-sector unions operate in a multilateral bargaining environment. Union appeals are made not only to people who sit across the negotiating table but also to elected officials and citizen groups.

In sum, says Freeman, differences between public- and private-sector unions do indeed exist. Nevertheless, the relative strength of unions in the two sectors cannot be determined by prior logic alone.

*Based on Richard B. Freeman, "Unionism Comes to the Public Sector," *Journal of Economic Literature,* March 1986, pp. 41–86.

personnel could have earned in civilian-sector jobs. In 1973, the federal government abandoned the draft in favor of armed services staffed by people recruited voluntarily through wages and benefits that were sufficiently high to attract the required number of employees. In a sense, the military has become a professional, market-based entity, much like the U.S. Postal Service, the Federal Bureau of Investigation, and the National Park Service. In fact, Phillips and Wise estimated in 1987 that the total potential lifetime compensation of the average career military enlistee exceeded the average lifetime earnings of high school graduates by 40 to 70 percent, while the total potential compensation of career officers exceeded the average lifetime compensation of college graduates by 60 to 90 percent.[14] We

[14]Douglas W. Phillips and David A. Wise, "Military versus Civilian Pay," in Wise, op. cit., pp. 19–46. Total potential compensation includes the basic pay, the basic allowance for quarters, the basic allowance for subsistence, the federal income tax advantage resulting from tax-exempt status of the basic allowances, the military retirement pension, and the potential earnings of military personnel after retirement from military service.

might add that these differences in potential lifetime earnings may be compensating wage payments (Chapter 8) for the added risk and poorer working conditions generally associated with jobs in the military.

The voluntary, wage-based army remains somewhat controversial. Calls for a return to the peacetime draft or for establishment of a new system of universal national service are commonplace. Critics of the modern voluntary army argue that it produces an army drawn mainly from the ranks of low-income citizens, creates a racially imbalanced military force, reduces the overall sense of duty to one's country, and increases the cost of the military to taxpayers.

Defenders of the voluntary approach counter that the professional army is better prepared to achieve its goals, minimizes society's overall cost of allocating labor to the services, promotes the use of a more efficient combination of labor and capital in the military, creates employment opportunities for low-skilled workers, provides on-the-job training that is transferable to the private sector, and maximizes individual freedom. These defenders also argue that it is more equitable to have taxpayers, rather than draftees, bear the costs of the armed services; that the voluntary army reduces the military's training costs by lessening the turnover of personnel; and that shortages of skilled personnel or reservists can be eliminated by raising wages in the areas where more personnel are needed.

A comprehensive examination of these pros and cons is well beyond our present discussion. Because our interest is government's role in the labor market, we limit our analysis here to the *labor market* aspects of the two alternatives.

The Economics of Military Conscription

Figure 12-1 shows labor supply and demand as viewed by the military. For the sake of simplicity, we assume that the market from which the military drafts personnel is perfectly competitive and that the nation is not at war. Initially, disregard the labor demand curve labeled D_v and instead concentrate on curves S and D_d. The curve S is a conventional competitive supply curve as *viewed by an employer.* The perfectly inelastic demand curve D_d is drawn on the assumption that Congress authorizes the armed services to conscript or *draft* 0*G* people and pay each of them wage rate 0*A*. Initially, suppose that those drafted are the specific individuals who would have voluntarily enlisted had the wage rate been at the equilibrium level 0*B* rather than 0*A*.

Let's now address two questions. First, what is the total wage bill that the military (taxpayers) will have to pay under this draft authorization? Second, given our assumptions, what is the overall cost to society of drafting these specific 0*G* workers? The answer to the first question is very simple and straightforward. The military's wage bill is the area 0*AfG*, which is found by multiplying the authorized wage 0*A* times the authorized employment level 0*G*.

Is this wage bill also the total cost to society? The answer is no, and this can be understood by examining the labor supply curve. The vertical height of curve *S* measures the opportunity cost of using each unit of labor in this employment or, in other words, the forgone civilian earnings for each of the 0*G* workers drafted. For example, suppose that these workers would earn $12,500 a year at wage rate 0*B* and only $5,000

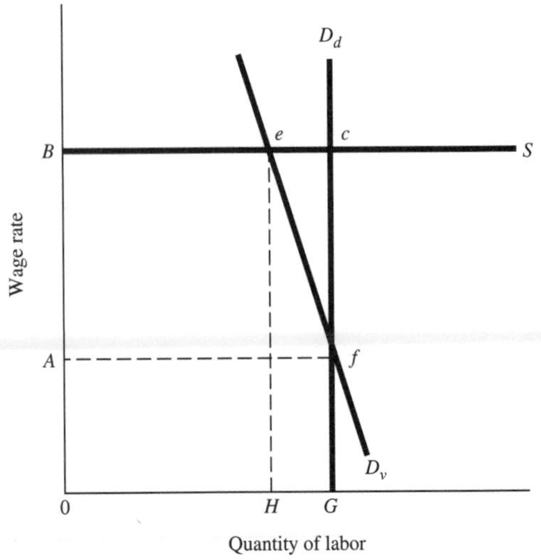

FIGURE 12-1 THE DRAFT VERSUS THE VOLUNTARY ARMY
If the military drafts the specific group of workers 0*G* and pays each of them 0*A*, the wage bill to taxpayers (0*AfG*) will be less than the total opportunity costs to those drafted (0*BcG*). Under a voluntary or market-based system, the relevant demand curve becomes D_v, the cost to taxpayers increases (0*BeH* as compared to 0*AfG*), those who volunteer are fully compensated for their opportunity costs (0*BeH*), and the military is likely to reduce its total workforce (0*G* to 0*H*). The true cost of employing any specific group of workers is *independent* of the wage bill.

at the military wage rate 0*A*. The annual income these individuals sacrifice and the output forgone by society from drafting them is $12,500 times 0*G* draftees. The fact that the military pays these workers $5,000 does *not* reflect the actual costs to either these individuals or to society. By drafting 0*G* workers, the military imposes an opportunity cost on draftees and society equal to the area under the labor supply curve, 0*BcG*. It pays the draftees 0*AfG* and imposes the remainder of the cost—*ABcf*—on those drafted. This cost is the difference between what draftees could earn as civilians and the amount earned in the military. To generalize: The true social cost of drafting any specific group of workers into the military is *independent* of the total wage rate that the military pays them. The actual cost consists of the income (output) sacrificed by draftees. ***Military conscription*** at low pay reduces the military's (taxpayer's) personnel costs, but it does *not* lower the costs of the military to society. Rather, it shifts a portion of the true costs—$7,500 per draftee in this case—from taxpayers to those drafted.[15]

Thus far, we have assumed that draftees are people who have opportunity costs that are reflected by the perfectly elastic supply curve in Figure 12-1. This assumes that government drafts only those from the low-skilled labor market—people who have low civilian earnings. But what if the military imposes a *lottery* to select the 0*G* draftees? Many of those selected will have higher civilian wage opportunities than 0*B*. Stated differently, the collective civilian wage opportunities of the 0*G* draftees selected through

[15]An additional cost to draftees is that military service may lower future civilian earnings. See Joshua D. Angrist, "Lifetime Earnings and the Vietnam Era Draft Lottery: Evidence from Social Security Administrative Records," *American Economic Review,* June 1990, pp. 313–335; and Joshua D. Angrist and Alan B. Krueger, "Why Do World War Two Veterans Earn More Than Nonveterans?" *Journal of Labor Economics,* January 1994, pp. 74–97. On the other hand, voluntary military service (i.e., after the end of the draft) appears to raise the postmilitary earnings of nonwhites and lower the earnings of white veterans. See Joshua D. Angrist, "Estimating the Labor Market Impact of Voluntary Military Service Using Social Security Data on Military Applicants," *Econometrica,* March 1998, pp. 249–288.

a lottery will exceed area 0*BcG*. The relevant generalization here is that the true cost to individuals and society of a lottery draft will exceed that of a draft of low-paid civilian workers.

The Voluntary, Market-Based Approach

We can analyze the economic implications of a ***voluntary or market-based army*** by turning to the demand curve D_v in Figure 12-1. Notice that we have drawn a typical downward-sloping demand curve, as opposed to the perfectly inelastic one used to analyze the draft. This downward-sloping curve reflects a realistic expectation that higher market wages for military personnel will cause the armed services to reduce the number of its employees. As seen by the intersection of D_v and *S,* the equilibrium military wage and quantity of labor will be 0*B* and 0*H,* respectively. The total wage bill to the military will be 0*BeH,* which is considerably greater than 0*AfG,* the total wage bill under the draft. Assuming that the military's demand for personnel is relatively inelastic, we conclude that a voluntary army will increase the money cost of military personnel to taxpayers. Notice that a voluntary army transfers income from taxpayers to military personnel such that the latter are totally compensated for their opportunity costs 0*BeH.*

Figure 12-1 shows that *if* the wage rate were at the draft level of 0*A,* the voluntary army would hire the same number of employees that it previously drafted (0*G*). But the existence of the voluntary army with a market-determined wage rate reduces military employment from 0*G* to 0*H.* We assume that this occurs for two reasons. First, as the wage rises from 0*A* to 0*B,* the military will likely *substitute* capital for labor. The military can lower its costs by engaging in such activities as purchasing dishwashing machines, procuring more weapons, and computerizing routine paperwork. This will enable the armed services to economize on the use of the now-higher-priced labor. Second, although the higher wage bill adds nothing to the true cost of the military, it does raise the price of the armed services *as perceived by Congress and taxpayers.* We would expect this increase in price to cause Congress to reduce its "output" of military services or reduce the *scale* of the total military establishment, which then would reduce military employment. The alert reader will recognize that we are here referring to both substitution and output effects of a wage rate increase.

A final point is germane to our discussion. The payment to enlistees of an amount equal to the supply price of labor rather than an artificially low wage can be expected to improve military morale and reduce labor turnover. These factors may join those previously discussed in lowering the costs of the military to society.

To summarize: Government's conscription or hiring of personnel for the military is another example of how government influences specific labor markets in the economy. Labor market analysis suggests that (1) the true cost of allocating personnel to the military is independent of the wage paid to those workers, (2) the methods (a lottery versus a draft of low-wage workers) used to obtain labor may affect the total cost of acquiring a given amount of military personnel, (3) the cost of a voluntary army may be less than that of a drafted army because of higher productivity related to reduced turnover and higher morale, (4) a voluntary army is likely to increase the "price" of the military as viewed by taxpayers, and (5) society can be expected to allocate fewer labor resources to the military under a higher-pay voluntary system than a lower-pay compulsory one. Finally, while labor market analysis *can* help us understand the costs and benefits of various public policy options, it *cannot* determine which option society should select.

12-4

NONPAYROLL SPENDING BY GOVERNMENT: IMPACT ON LABOR

We have established that government employment of civilian and military workers is a major factor in the overall labor market. Government's nonpayroll spending also influences wages and employment. This spending is substantial and takes two forms: (1) purchases of private-sector goods and services and (2) transfer payments and subsidies. In 1996 government purchased $1,182 billion of labor, goods, and services. About one-half of this amount was for goods produced by private industry. Also, government transfers and subsidies exceeded $1,000 billion in 1996. Let's briefly examine selected labor market impacts of each category of expenditure.

Government Purchases of Private-Sector Output

Government purchases include procurement of such items as word processors, tanks, medical supplies, textbooks, buses, submarines, paper clips, furniture, and weather

12-4 **World of Work**

THE EFFECT OF RETENTION BONUSES ON REENLISTMENT IN THE U.S. ARMY*

The military offers bonuses to personnel in selected occupations who are eligible to reenlist in the army, navy, and air force. The amount of the bonus depends on (1) the monthly basic pay at the date of reenlistment, (2) the number of years of reenlistment, and (3) a multiplier that ranges from 1 to 6. Example: A soldier who reenlists for 3 years in an occupation that has a monthly basic pay of $1,000 and a multiplier of 4 will get a lump-sum bonus of $12,000 (= $1,000 × 3 × 4). The military *decreases* the multiplier when the number of people seeking reenlistment exceeds the number of soldiers needed; it *increases* the multiplier when shortages of personnel occur.

How well do these retention bonuses work? Lakhani has found that a boost in reenlistment bonuses increases reenlistment, as economic theory would predict. However, the reenlistment bonuses are more effective for soldiers in combat occupations than for those in noncombat roles. A 5 percent increase in the average reenlistment bonus increases the reenlistment rate in combat jobs by 1.0 percent, while it increases the reenlistment rate in noncombat jobs by only 0.4 percent.

Why the difference? Lakhani speculates that soldiers in combat occupations acquire what is equivalent to *firm-specific training* (Chapter 4) that is not easily transferable to the private sector. Alternatively, soldiers in noncombat roles receive *general training* that is more marketable in the civilian labor market. Thus, soldiers in noncombat occupations have higher opportunity costs of staying in the military and therefore are less responsive to a given monetary incentive for reenlisting. Lakhani's research suggests that apart from the base pay, relatively higher reenlistment bonuses for noncombat personnel are needed to equalize the reenlistment rates between the two groups.

*Based on Hyder Lakhani, "The Effect of Pay and Retention Bonuses on Quit Rates in the U.S. Army," *Industrial and Labor Relations Review,* April 1988, pp. 430–438.

satellites. This type of spending by government creates a derived demand for specific kinds of private-sector workers. In some cases, it creates demands for labor that would not otherwise exist—or at least not be nearly as great—without government. We could expect such changes in demand to affect equilibrium wage rates and employment levels. For example, *cuts* in government spending on strategic missiles could be expected eventually to reduce the wages and employment levels of aerospace engineers. Similarly, *increases* in federal construction spending would likely increase the demand for—and the collective bargaining position of—a wide range of construction workers.

Transfer Payments and Subsidies

Government payroll expenditures and nonpayroll spending for private-sector goods and services have one common feature. Both are *exhaustive* or resource-absorbing expenditures in that they account for the employment of labor and other economic resources. In contrast, transfer payments and subsidies are *nonexhaustive* because, as such, they do not directly absorb resources or account for production. More precisely, as their name implies, ***transfer payments***—such as Social Security benefits to the retired, unemployment compensation, welfare payments, and veterans' benefits—merely transfer income from government to individuals and families. The recipients perform no current productive activities in return: hence, transfers are nonexhaustive. Similarly, a ***subsidy*** is a transfer payment to a firm, institution, or household that consumes or produces some specific product or service. Medicare for the elderly, price supports for farmers, and public education for youth are all examples of governmental subsidies.

Demand Effects Although transfers and subsidies do not directly exhaust or absorb labor or other resources, they do alter the structure of total demand in the economy and therefore affect the derived demands for specific types of labor. For example, cash and in-kind medical transfers provided to older Americans under provisions of the Social Security program increase the demand for products and services that older Americans tend to purchase. More specifically, the transfers increase the demand for such items as prescription and over-the-counter drugs, nursing home services, hospital care, and retirement property. This demand, in turn, increases the derived demand for workers who help produce, deliver, or sell these goods and services. In a similar sense, the cash transfers provided through welfare programs for low-income families increase the demand for a variety of products, including children's clothing, toys, and foodstuffs. Other things being equal, these increases in product demand boost product prices, which then increase the demand for labor in the affected industries (demand determinant 1, Table 6-1).

Subsidies provided to private firms and nonprofit organizations also increase the demand for specific types of workers. For instance, the U.S. government, through the Export–Import Bank, provides loans at below-market interest rates to some foreign buyers of U.S. exports. This reduces the effective price of U.S. exports while leaving the price charged by the exporters intact, thus increasing foreign purchases and ultimately the derived demand for labor in the U.S. export sector. Similarly, the federal government provides subsidies to such nonprofit organizations as private universities, which then demand more workers to deliver their services.

Supply Effects In addition to their impact on labor demand, transfer payments and subsidies affect short- and long-run labor supply. Recall from our discussion of individual labor supply in Chapter 2 that transfers (for example, a guaranteed income program) generate an *income effect* that tends to reduce the optimal number of work hours offered by the recipient. Put simply, transfer income induces the recipient to buy more normal goods and services, including leisure (Figure 2-12). Also, if the amount of the cash transfer is inversely related to work income—that is, if a benefit-reduction rate applies to earned income—then the program creates an accompanying *substitution effect* that further reduces work effort. By reducing the opportunity cost—or price—of leisure, the transfer payment encourages the substitution of the lower-priced leisure for the now relatively higher-priced work.

Transfers and subsidies also influence long-run labor supply decisions (Chapter 4). For example, the existence of cash and in-kind transfers may reduce incentives to invest in human capital. In essence, the present value of the net returns to the investor is reduced because future gains in earned income that result from the training or education are accompanied by the loss of future transfers. Other things being equal, the higher the benefit-reduction rate of a transfer plan, the less the actual net rate of return on any given investment in human capital.

Not all transfers and subsidy programs, however, reduce long-run labor supply. Those transfers and subsidies that reduce the private cost of investing in human capital produce just the opposite effect. For example, government provides subsidized, below-market interest rates on loans to many college students. Recall that the economic rationale for these loans was outlined in Chapter 4. This subsidy reduces the private cost of investing in a college education, which increases the personal rate of return on this form of human capital. As a direct consequence, the long-run labor supply in various skilled and professional labor markets increases. Additionally, we know that better-educated people stay in the labor force longer than people who have less education. We therefore conclude that government transfers and subsidies may either positively or negatively affect supply in specific labor markets.

LABOR MARKET EFFECTS OF PUBLICLY PROVIDED GOODS AND SERVICES

Thus far, we have established that government employment and public-sector purchases of private-sector output influence wage rates and employment levels in specific labor markets. We next raise an interesting related question: Do publicly provided goods and services affect labor demand and supply *independently* of the public and private employment necessary to provide these items? Publicly provided goods and services range from ***pure public goods,*** whose benefits are indivisible and therefore impossible to deny to those who have not paid for them, to goods and services provided by government but also sold in the private sector. An example of the former is national defense, while an example of the latter is college education. It is clear that some publicly provided goods *do* affect private-sector demand for labor. It is also conceivable that these goods and services reduce overall labor supply in the economy. Let's examine each possibility.

Effects on Labor Demand

The provision of public-sector goods and services influences labor demand in a variety of ways. For example, suppose that government builds a major dam on a river. Assume that this project creates multiple benefits such as electricity generation, flood control, irrigation, and recreational opportunities. Government affects the labor market by employing labor and private-sector products to construct the dam, power station, irrigation network, and adjacent recreational areas. But the *existence* of the dam also independently affects labor demand. For example, the irrigation system will likely increase the demand for farm workers; the new recreational opportunities will increase the demand for fishing boats, motors, and water skis, which will increase the derived demand for workers who help produce these products; the availability of cheap electric power may entice manufacturing firms to the area, thereby increasing the demand for specific skilled and unskilled workers; and control of downriver flooding may actually *reduce* the demand for flood insurance agents and claims adjusters. In fact, we may generalize as follows: Other things being equal, the provision of a public good that is a *complement* in either production or consumption to a specific private good will *increase* the derived demand for workers who help produce the private good. Conversely, the provision of a public good that is a *substitute* in production or consumption to a specific private good will *reduce* the derived demand for workers who help produce the private good.

Effects on Labor Supply

A modified version of the basic income–leisure model of short-run individual labor supply suggests that publicly provided goods and services may reduce the quantity of labor supplied. Recall from Chapter 2 that the basic model income–leisure choice contains a preference map composed of indifference curves, each one showing the various combinations of real income and leisure that yield some specific level of utility. Also recall that the model contains a wage rate, or budget, line indicating the *actual* combination of income and leisure that the individual can obtain given his or her wage.

Figure 12-2 presents a modified version of the basic model. Notice from the vertical axis that we are defining real income as the total amount of private- *and* public-sector goods and services obtainable from any specific level of work. Suppose that Y_{pu} ($= WW_1$) of public-sector goods is available to Green regardless of how much he works. The real income available to him will be Y_{pu} plus the level of private goods that his work income will allow him to obtain. Prior to the provision of Y_{pu} public goods, Green's budget constraint was WW', but the existence of the publicly provided output means that his effective budget constraint is $W_1W'_1$. This latter line shows the combinations of leisure and goods (private- and public-sector) available to Green at each level of work, given his wage rate. The vertical distance between the two budget lines measures the value of the public goods available to Green.

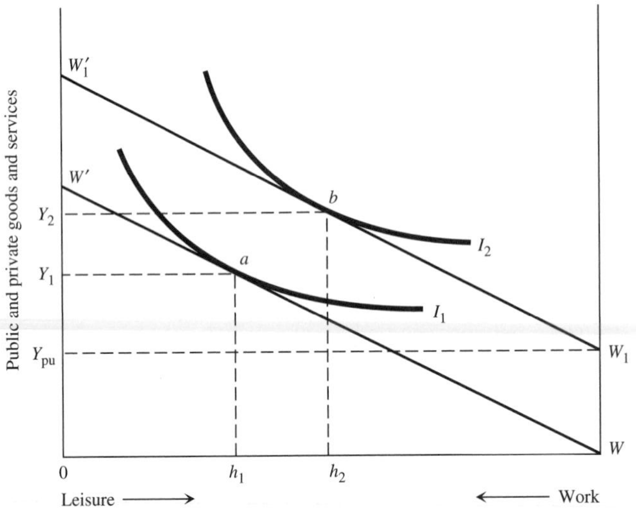

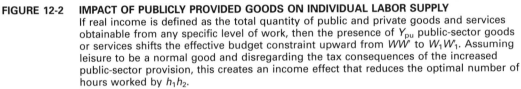

FIGURE 12-2 IMPACT OF PUBLICLY PROVIDED GOODS ON INDIVIDUAL LABOR SUPPLY
If real income is defined as the total quantity of public and private goods and services obtainable from any specific level of work, then the presence of Y_{pu} public-sector goods or services shifts the effective budget constraint upward from WW' to W_1W_1'. Assuming leisure to be a normal good and disregarding the tax consequences of the increased public-sector provision, this creates an income effect that reduces the optimal number of hours worked by h_1h_2.

If no public goods were available to this individual, he would maximize his utility at a by working h_1 hours, from which he would earn Y_1 goods (real income). The existence of the public goods, however, creates an income effect that allows Green to "buy" more leisure. The provision of the public-sector goods Y_{pu} increases his total utility by moving him from a on indifference curve I_1 to b on curve I_2. But in achieving this gain in utility, Green *reduces* his labor hours from h_1 to h_2.

We thus conclude that the existence of publicly provided goods and services may reduce individual and overall labor supply in the economy. The more closely the public goods are substitutable for private goods, the greater the reduction in labor supply. Example: Free food provided by the public sector may reduce the incentive to earn income to buy food. In fact, a 1988 study estimated that the federal Food Stamp program reduced the labor supply of female heads of households by 9 percent.[16] On the other hand, the more complementary the public goods are to leisure, the greater the decline in labor supply. Example: A public golf course conceivably could reduce labor supply by encouraging more leisure. Finally, the more complementary the public goods are to work, the less the reduction in labor supply. Example: By reducing the cost of getting to work, a mass-transit system may augment labor supply.

[16]Thomas Fraker and Robert Moffitt, "The Effect of Food Stamps on Labor Supply: A Bivariate Selection Model," *Journal of Public Economics*, February 1988, pp. 25–56.

Our discussion of the labor supply effects of public goods overlooks an important fact. Government must collect taxes from people in order to provide the public goods in question, and these taxes also have potential labor supply impacts. It is to this topic that we turn next.

QUICK REVIEW 12-1

- Most of the sizable growth of public-sector employment occurring since 1950 has been at the state and local levels of government.
- Although a large federal pay advantage existed a decade or so ago, it is thought to have largely evaporated in recent years.
- A conscripted army at below-market pay does not reduce the cost of the military to society; it simply shifts part of the cost to those drafted. A voluntary, market-based army is likely to be less costly to society because it *(a)* reduces turnover, *(b)* creates higher morale, and *(c)* induces the military to use socially optimal combinations of labor and capital.
- Government transfers (and subsidies) and the existence of publicly provided goods have widespread impacts on labor supply and labor demand.

Your Turn: How might Figure 12-2 relate to the lack of work effort observed under the old Communist regimes of Eastern Europe and Russia? (Answer: See page 626.)

INCOME TAXATION AND THE LABOR MARKET

12-2

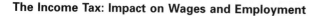

To this point, our emphasis has been on government's influence on labor markets through its spending and hiring decisions. We now examine the effects of selected taxes on the labor market, focusing on the personal ***income tax.*** Income from wages and salaries constitutes approximately 75 percent of national income in the United States. Because a large portion of this income is subjected to the personal income tax, it is particularly important to ascertain the impact of this tax on labor markets. Specifically, do workers bear the full burden of the tax in the form of lower net, or after-tax, wage rates? Or is it possible that part or all of the tax is borne by employers, who must pay higher market wage rates to attract profit-maximizing quantities of labor? What impact does the income tax have on employment?

The Income Tax: Impact on Wages and Employment

We will discover from the following discussion that given the elasticity of labor demand, the effects of the personal income tax on wages and employment depend principally on the elasticity of labor supply. Figure 12-3(a) and (b) demonstrate this proposition. The labor supply curve in graph (a) is perfectly inelastic, indicating that workers do not collectively change the extent of their labor force participation in response to wage rate changes. In graph (b) the labor supply curve displays some elasticity;

12-2 Global Perspective

INCOME TAX RATES

The average income tax rate for the average production worker who is married and has two children ranges from 10 percent in Japan to 23.2 percent in Germany.

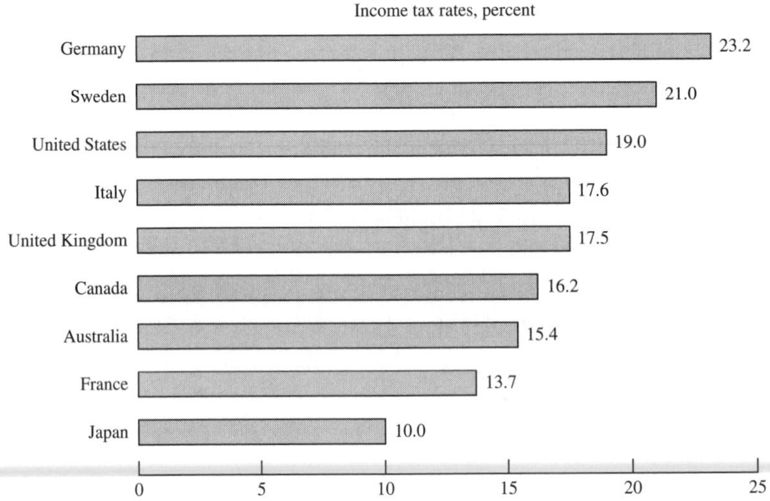

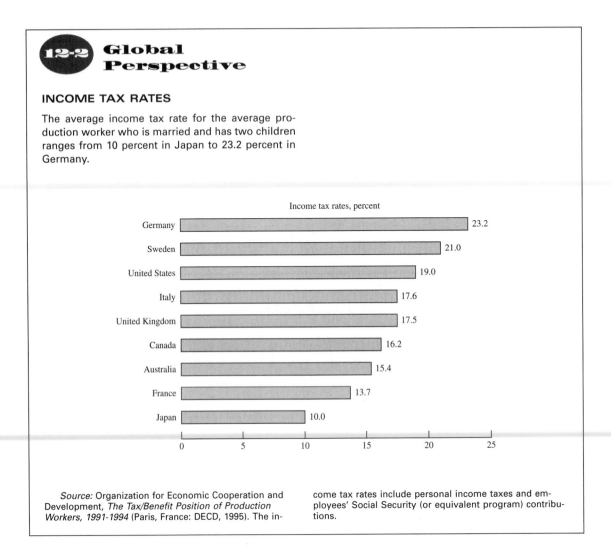

Source: Organization for Economic Cooperation and Development, *The Tax/Benefit Position of Production Workers, 1991-1994* (Paris, France: DECD, 1995). The income tax rates include personal income taxes and employees' Social Security (or equivalent program) contributions.

people collectively increase their labor hour offerings when the wage rises and reduce them when it falls.

The demand curves in the two graphs are identical and reflect the *before-tax* wage rates and corresponding quantities of labor that firms will desire to employ. The curves labeled D_t lie below the conventional demand curves in each graph and show the *after-tax* wages as viewed by workers. The progressive income tax on labor earnings pivots the after-tax wage rate lines downward from D to D_t by the amount of the tax per hour of work.

Table 12-2 helps us better understand the crucial distinction between the conventional labor demand curve D and the after-tax wage-rate line D_t in Figure 12-3(a) and

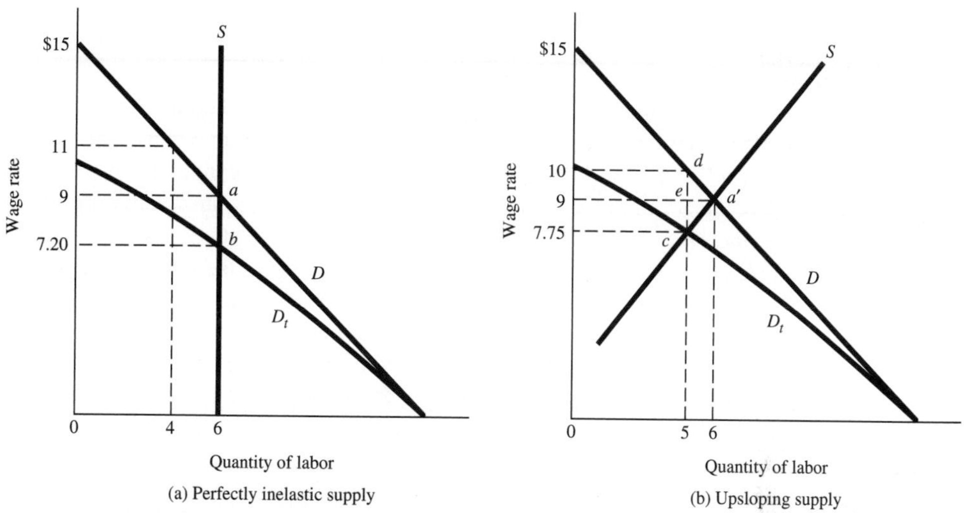

FIGURE 12-3 IMPACT OF THE PERSONAL INCOME TAX ON WAGES AND EMPLOYMENT
If the aggregate labor supply curve in the economy is perfectly inelastic as in (a), then the personal income tax—measured by the vertical distance between *D* and D_t—will not affect the market wage ($9), but will reduce the after-tax wage by the amount of the tax per hour. If the labor supply curve displays some elasticity as in (b), the tax reduces the quantity of labor hours supplied and raises the before-tax market wage—in this case from $9 to $10. Given labor demand, the greater the elasticity of labor supply, the greater the increase in the wage rate and the greater the reduction in employment resulting from the tax.

TABLE 12-2 BEFORE-TAX VERSUS AFTER-TAX EARNINGS PER UNIT OF LABOR (HYPOTHETICAL DATA)

(1) *W*	(2) *Q*	(3) *T*	(4) *W* – *T*	(5) *T/W* (%)
$14	1	$4.25	$9.75	30.4
13	2	3.75	9.25	28.8
12	3	3.25	8.75	27.1
11	4	2.75	8.25	25.0
10	5	2.25	7.75	22.5
9	6	1.80	7.20	20.0
8	7	1.40	6.60	17.5
7	8	1.05	5.95	15.0
6	9	.75	5.25	12.5
5	10	.50	4.50	10.0
4	11	.30	3.70	7.5
3	12	.15	2.85	5.0
2	13	.05	1.95	2.5

(b). Notice that columns (1) and (2) constitute the before-tax labor demand schedule, which graphically is shown as curve *D* in each of the figures. Columns (2) and (4) establish the after-tax wage rate lines D_t in the two graphs. Example: If the wage rate is \$12 (column 1), firms will employ 3 workers (column 2). Observe from column (3) that the tax per hour is \$3.25 at the \$12 wage rate. Hence, the *net* or *after-tax wage rate* is \$8.75 (= \$12 − \$3.25), as shown in column (4). When plotted graphically against the quantity of labor, the after-tax wage rates shown in column (4) establish the D_t curves in Figure 12-3(a) and (b). The vertical distances between the demand curves and the after-tax wage-rate lines measure the tax per hour of work at each particular market wage rate (and at each particular quantity of labor demanded).

Column 5 of Table 12-2 shows the average hourly tax rate (= *T/W*) for each wage rate. Notice that the average tax rate rises as earnings per hour increase, indicating that this tax is progressive. In terms of Figure 12-3(a) and (b), this progressivity is reflected in the fact that the distances between *D* and D_t increase as a percentage of the wage as the wage rises.

Perfectly Inelastic Labor Supply Let's now focus on graph (a) in Figure 12-3. The before-tax equilibrium market wage and quantity of labor are \$9 and 6 units, respectively (point *a*). Once the tax is introduced, however, workers perceive their net wage to be only \$7.20 (= \$9 − \$1.80), as shown by point *b*. But because the supply is perfectly inelastic, the income tax will not affect the collective quantity of labor supplied. Therefore, workers bear the entire burden of the tax; the before-tax wage rate remains at \$9, and the after-tax hourly pay falls by the full amount of the tax, \$1.80 (= \$9 − \$7.20).

To confirm this proposition, suppose that workers are angered by their *net* wage decline and try to shift the tax to their employers. If they demand, say, \$11 (= \$9 + \$2), employers will seek only 4 units of labor, while workers will continue to offer 6 units. Assuming competition, the excess supply of workers will drive the before-tax wage down to \$9, where the labor market will once again clear. It is evident that if the labor supply curve is perfectly inelastic, employees will be unable to pass the tax forward to their employers and the tax will have no impact on either the market wage rate or equilibrium employment.[17]

Positively Sloped Labor Supply We next turn our attention to graph (b) in Figure 12-3, where we discover a labor supply curve that displays a positive slope. This implies that workers collectively will respond to wage or income tax changes by adjusting the amount of labor supplied. In the absence of the income tax, the equilibrium wage rate and quantity of labor are \$9 and 6 units (point *a*′). How will these workers react to a newly imposed income tax? As we see from the intersection of D_t and *S*, workers will reduce the amount of labor supplied from 6 to 5 units (point *c*). Employers will encounter a shortage of labor of 1 unit (= 6 − 5) *at the \$9 market wage.* This ex-

[17]This is true even in the presence of a strong union, assuming that the union has already bargained for its optimal contract package. If it has squeezed all it can extract from the employers, the sudden enactment of an income tax can do nothing to enhance its ability to gain still more.

cess demand will drive the wage to \$10, and the market will again clear at point *d*—this time at 5 units of labor. Those still working following the tax will receive a before-tax wage rate of \$10 rather than \$9. The workers' after-tax wage will fall by \$1.25 (= \$9 − \$7.75) to \$7.75. Notice that this decline is less than the tax per hour of \$2.25 (= \$10 − \$7.75). The reason is that \$1 of the tax is borne indirectly by employers as higher wage rates. That is, of the total tax *dc* in Figure 12-3, *ec* is borne by workers as lower after-tax pay while *ed* is borne by employers as higher wage costs.

To summarize: Other things being equal, if the overall labor supply curve slopes upward, a personal income tax will reduce the quantity of labor supplied, cause the wage rate to rise, and decrease employment. Given the elasticity of demand, the greater the elasticity of supply, the greater the portion of the income tax borne by employers in the form of a higher market wage. You might want to rework the analysis for a *perfectly elastic* labor supply curve to demonstrate that under these conditions the *entire* tax will be borne by employers and that the employment effect will be greater.

The Income Tax and Individual Labor Supply

Which of the two graphs in Figure 12-3 best portrays reality? How elastic is the overall supply of labor? Economists have approached this question both theoretically and empirically.

Theoretical Analysis The income tax is similar in impact to a wage rate decrease—both reduce the actual return from an hour of work and lower total net income from any specific number of hours of work. The tax generates income and substitution effects that act in opposing directions. By reducing income at any specific level of work, the tax lowers consumption of all normal goods, including leisure; and therefore, the incentive to work increases (the income effect). But the tax also reduces the net return from work or, stated alternatively, decreases the opportunity cost (price) of leisure. This creates an incentive to substitute the relatively lower-priced leisure for the now relatively higher-priced work, and therefore, work declines (the substitution effect).

Graphical Depiction Figure 12-4 illustrates this graphically. The figure shows the indifference maps and budget constraints for Smith (graph a) and Jones (graph b). Notice that each graph portrays two budget lines: *HW,* which is linear, and HW_t which lies below *HW* and increases at a diminishing rate as work hours increase from 0 to 24. The *HW* curves shows the *before-tax* income for Smith and Jones at each level of work hours, and the HW_t curves depict the *after-tax* income from that specific work effort. The vertical distances between *HW* and HW_t measure the income tax paid at each work–income combination. These distances increase as a percentage of income as income rises, again indicating that the tax is progressive.

Without the tax, Smith (graph a) will choose to work h_1 hours, earn income Y_b, and maximize her utility at point *a* on indifference curve I_2. Once the income tax is imposed, Smith's after-tax wage rate falls as shown by the downward shift of *HW* to HW_t, and she reacts by *reducing* her work effort to h_2 (point *b*). At this level of work she earns a gross income of Y_g, pays a total tax of Y_gY_a, and receives an after-tax income of Y_a. For Smith, the income tax *reduces* the number of labor hours supplied by h_1h_2.

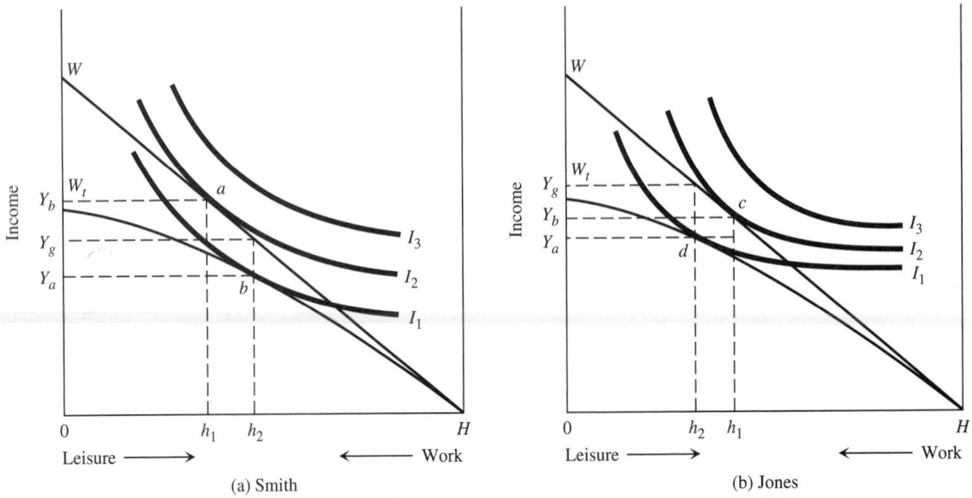

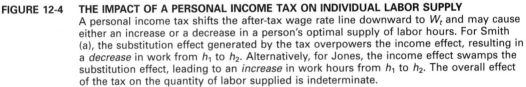

FIGURE 12-4 THE IMPACT OF A PERSONAL INCOME TAX ON INDIVIDUAL LABOR SUPPLY
A personal income tax shifts the after-tax wage rate line downward to W_t and may cause either an increase or a decrease in a person's optimal supply of labor hours. For Smith (a), the substitution effect generated by the tax overpowers the income effect, resulting in a *decrease* in work from h_1 to h_2. Alternatively, for Jones, the income effect swamps the substitution effect, leading to an *increase* in work hours from h_1 to h_2. The overall effect of the tax on the quantity of labor supplied is indeterminate.

What is the outcome for Jones (graph b)? By employing the same logic, we find that he reacts to the tax by *increasing* his labor hours. Given his subjective preferences for income versus leisure, he discovers it to be in his interest to increase work from h_1 to h_2 (point *d* rather than *c*), earn a gross income of Y_g, pay a tax equal to the vertical distance of Y_gY_a, and retain an after-tax income of Y_a. Thus, Figure 12-4 illustrates a basic point: The progressive income tax (and changes in tax rates) causes some workers to work less, others to work more, and still others to maintain their pretax level of work. For Smith (graph a), the substitution effect outweighs the income effect and she works less; but for Jones (graph b), the income effect swamps the substitution effect, leading him to work more. (Remember from Chapter 2 that the income effect increases hours of work and the substitution effect decreases hours of work when we are considering a reduction in wages.) The basic work–leisure theory of individual labor supply does not permit us to predict whether the aggregate labor supply curve is negatively sloped, perfectly inelastic, or positively sloped. Thus, we are uncertain as to whether the aggregate amount of labor supplied will increase or decrease in response to, say, an income tax reduction.

Caveat We must note, however, that this matter is not entirely settled. Recall from our previous analysis that government's provision of public goods theoretically can produce income effects that reduce labor hour offerings. These goods are financed partially through the personal income tax and are available to people independently of their work effort. Consequently, workers need not work as much to achieve a given level of real goods or total utility. This income effect may reduce labor hours offered and offset any added work effort generated by the income effect from the imposition of the tax. If so, only a substitution effect remains, and the overall outcome may be a reduced quantity of labor supplied.[18]

Empirical Analysis Many economists have tried to measure the relative strengths of the income and substitution effects and thereby estimate the elasticity of aggregate labor supply in the economy. The task of designing these studies so that they incorporate and control properly for the many intercorrelated influences on labor supply behavior is extremely complex and difficult. The success of existing studies in accomplishing this task is subject to some debate, so the findings must be regarded with caution. Recall from Chapter 2 that most of the studies reveal that the income effect slightly exceeds the substitution effect for adult males as a group. This implies that the supply curve for this group is negatively sloped; that is, tax increases (net wage decreases) cause males to increase their work hours slightly. For females, the substitution effect appears to dominate the income effect so that the tax increases (wage decreases) create reductions in hours worked.[19] The studies generally find that aggregating various individual labor supply curves yields an overall supply curve that is extremely inelastic. The major portion of U.S. income tax falls squarely on workers. Therefore, the tax has a minimal net impact on work effort, the market wage rate, and equilibrium employment, as seen in Figure 12-3(a).

QUICK REVIEW 12-2

- If labor supply is perfectly inelastic, workers will bear the full burden of the personal income tax; if labor supply is positively sloped, some of the tax will be borne by the employer through higher wages.
- The impact of the income tax on individual labor supply is indeterminate in terms of theory because the tax creates income and substitution effects having opposite impacts on desired hours of work.
- Empirical studies suggest that labor supply is highly inelastic, meaning that *(a)* workers bear nearly all of the personal income tax and *(b)* the tax has little impact on market wages and employment levels.

[18]The view that a tax change produces only a substitution effect on economywide labor supply is found in James Gwartney and Richard Stroup, "Labor Supply and Tax Rates: A Correction of the Record," *American Economic Review,* June 1983, pp. 446–451. The Gwartney–Stroup criticism of the traditional model (Figure 12-4), in turn, has been challenged by several economists. For example, see Firouz Gahvari, "Labor Supply and Tax Rates: Comment," *American Economic Review,* March 1986, pp. 280–283; and David M. Betson and David Greenberg, "Labor Supply and Tax Rates: Comment," *American Economic Review,* June 1986, pp. 551–556.

[19]For example, Eissa finds that the reduction of the top marginal tax rate from 50 to 28 percent in 1986 increased the labor supply of high-income married women. See Nada Eissa, "Taxation and Labor Supply of Married Women: The Tax Reform Act of 1986 as a Natural Experiment," National Bureau of Economic Research Working Paper No. 5023, February 1995.

12-5

Your Turn: In 1992 Congress increased the maximum marginal tax rate on income from 31 to 39.6 percent. Explain why Stone may work more as a result, whereas Smythe may work less. (Answer: See page 626.)

Specific Individuals and Markets Although the overall impact of the income tax on labor supply may be negligible, impacts on specific individuals and on specific labor markets may be considerable. Examples: Variations in income taxes among states may cause some workers to migrate from high- to low-tax geographic areas;[20] high

[20]James E. Long, "Income Taxation and the Allocation of Labor," *Journal of Labor Research,* Summer 1982, pp. 259–276.

12-5 **World of Work**

WHO PAYS THE SOCIAL SECURITY PAYROLL TAX?

The federal government levies a flat-rate payroll tax on all earnings below a set minimum to finance the Social Security program (old age, survivors, disability, and health insurance). In 1998 employers and employees each paid a Social Security tax of 7.65 percent of the first $68,400 of wage and salary earnings. Because these taxes are significant and are levied directly on earnings, labor economists are interested in their impact on wages.

The consensus expert opinion is that workers bear more than one-half of the Social Security tax. How can this be? We have just said that employers and employees are assessed equal Social Security taxes. The answer is that firms "collect" some or all of these tax proceeds from their workers. They "collect" this money by reducing the employees' wages below levels they would have received without the tax.

That part of the Social Security tax levied on employers reduces the after-tax marginal revenue product of labor, as viewed by firms. Suppose, for example, that the pretax wage rate is $10 an hour and that the employer is assessed a 7.65 percent Social Security tax (one-half of 15.3 percent). From the firm's perspective, the workers' MRP thus becomes $9.23 [= $10 − $.77 (= .0765 × $10)]. If labor supply is perfectly inelastic [Figure 12-3(a)] and the wage rate equals MRP, the after-tax hourly pay becomes $9.23, not $10. In this case workers have indirectly paid the employer's $.77 per hour Social Security tax through a $.77 per hour pay cut.

Also, employees must pay the 7.65 percent tax directly levied on their earnings. With the $9.23 market wage, this tax is $.71 per hour (.0765 × $9.23). The after-tax hourly wage therefore falls to $8.52. The Social Security tax reduces the workers' market wage from $10 to $9.23 per hour and lowers their after-tax wage from $10 to $8.52. Thus, under these circumstances the workers in effect pay the full Social Security tax.

Empirical studies confirm that employers do not pay their full one-half of the Social Security tax, although they apparently do pay a small part of it.* These findings imply that the overall labor supply curve may be somewhat elastic rather than perfectly inelastic. As the Social Security tax rises, spouses, teenagers, semi-retired workers, and others who do not have strong attachments to the labor force may reduce their labor offerings. If the overall labor supply curve is somewhat elastic [Figure 12-3(b)], employers cannot reduce workers' wages by the full amount of the employers' portion of the Social Security tax. They will have to bear some of the tax themselves to continue to attract a profit-maximizing number of workers.

*The classic research is John A. Brittain, *The Payroll Tax for Social Security* (Washington, DC: Brookings Institution, 1972). Other research includes Wayne Vroman, "Employer Payroll Tax Incidence: Empirical Tests with Cross Country Data," *Public Finance,* vol. 29, 1974, pp. 184–200; and Daniel Hamermesh, "New Estimates of the Incidence of the Payroll Tax," *Southern Economic Journal,* February 1979, pp. 1208–1219.

marginal tax rates may entice some salaried workers to switch to "underground" activity to avoid paying income taxes; and exclusions, deductions, and credits—which are part of the tax code—may influence the composition of labor demand by affecting spending patterns of consumers. With regard to this third example, we point out that the tax deductibility of interest paid on mortgages increases the demand for residential construction workers; the tax deduction for charitable contributions enhances the ability of colleges to provide financial aid, which in turn increases the supply of graduates to such occupations as teaching, medicine, and law; and the complexity of the tax code increases the demand for tax accountants, tax lawyers, and IRS agents.

CHAPTER SUMMARY

1 Government employment has increased both absolutely and as a percentage of total employment since 1950. The rate of growth of public-sector employment has been greatest at the state and local levels of government.
2 Federal workers had higher wage rates in the 1970s than comparably educated and experienced private-sector employees, but that pay differential largely eroded during the 1980s.
3 The total economic cost of allocating labor to the military consists of the total value of the alternative output (income) that is forgone. A "voluntary" army requires that economic costs be paid by taxpayers; a "drafted" army at below-market wage rates imposes some of the costs on those who are conscripted.
4 Taken alone, government's provision of goods and services may create an income effect that reduces one's optimal supply of hours of work.
5 Government transfer payments and subsidies affect the composition of labor demand in the economy and also influence labor supply decisions.
6 Other things being equal, the more elastic the overall labor supply in the economy, the greater the extent to which a personal income tax will cause *(a)* a decline in the hours of labor supplied, *(b)* an increase in the market wage, and *(c)* lower overall employment. Most economists, however, judge the aggregate labor supply curve to be highly inelastic.
7 The impact of an income tax on an individual's optimal supply of labor is theoretically indeterminate in that the tax generates income and substitution effects that work in opposite directions with respect to the quantity of labor supplied.

TERMS AND CONCEPTS

prevailing-wage rule
military conscription
✓ voluntary or market-based army
government purchases
transfer payments
subsidy
pure public goods
income tax

QUESTIONS AND STUDY SUGGESTIONS

1 List and discuss factors that help explain why public-sector employment rose faster than private-sector employment between 1950 and 1997. At what levels of government has public-sector employment increased most dramatically?

2 Comment on this statement: "In general, federal government employees are underpaid compared to similar private-sector workers. This is due to the monopsony power of government."

3 Speculate as to the reason(s) for each of the following facts about public-sector pay:
  a The pay premium received by federal employees declined in the mid- and late-1980s.
  b Local governments tend to pay less-skilled workers more and more-skilled workers less than comparably trained and experienced private-sector workers.
  c Female and black workers in government receive higher pay on the average than their equally qualified counterparts in the private sector.

4 Explain why a voluntary army may be less expensive to society than an army composed of draftees. Which will likely be less expensive to taxpayers?

5 Explain why a draft system might cause the U.S. military to overemploy labor and underemploy capital (from society's perspective). Speculate as to why the army increasingly "contracts out" construction and maintenance work to private firms now that it is voluntary.

6 Assuming that "income" includes both private and public goods, and that leisure is a normal good, explain how a major reduction in governmentally provided goods might increase a person's optimal number of hours of work.

7 Explain how the existence of national, state, and city parks might affect:
  a Labor demand in the recreational vehicle industry
  b The demand for workers who build and maintain equipment for private recreational "theme" parks
  c The overall supply of labor

8 Use the following labor market data to determine the answers to *(a)* through *(d)*.

(1) Wage rate	(2) Quantity demanded	(3) Quantity supplied	(4) Tax per hour
$10	14	22	$3.33
8	18	22	2.67
6	22	22	2.00
4	26	22	1.33
2	30	22	.67

  a Is this tax progressive? Explain.
  b What is the before-tax equilibrium wage rate?
  c What effect does the tax have on the number of hours of work supplied and the market wage rate?
  d If the labor supply curve were highly elastic, rather than perfectly inelastic, how would your answers to *(c)* change?

SELECTED REFERENCES

Brown, Charles V.: *Taxation and the Incentive to Work,* 2d ed. (New York: Oxford University Press, 1983).

Freeman, Richard B., and Casey Ichniowski (eds.): *When Public Sector Workers Unionize* (Chicago: University of Chicago Press, 1988).

Journal of Human Resources, Special Issue on Taxation and Labor Supply in Industrial Countries, Summer 1990.

Musgrave, Richard A., and Peggy B. Musgrave: *Public Finance in Theory and Practice,* 5th ed. (New York: McGraw-Hill Book Company, 1989), chap. 15.

Rosen, Harvey S.: *Public Finance,* 5th ed. (Burr Ridge, IL: Irwin/McGraw-Hill, 1999), chaps. 16 and 17.

Smith, Sharon, P.: *Equal Pay in the Public Sector: Fact or Fantasy* (Princeton, NJ: Princeton University Press, 1977).

Wise, David A. (ed.): *Public Sector Payrolls* (Chicago: University of Chicago Press, 1987).

CHAPTER 13

GOVERNMENT AND THE LABOR MARKET: LEGISLATION AND REGULATION

Besides directly employing labor, providing public goods, transferring income, and levying taxes (Chapter 12), government engages in the important task of establishing the legal rules for the economy. Many of these laws and regulations directly or indirectly affect wage and employment outcomes. We examine such laws throughout this book; for example, in Chapter 9 we discussed immigration laws. In later chapters we discuss laws outlawing discrimination (Chapter 15) and promoting full employment (Chapter 19).

Laws affecting labor markets are so numerous that we must be highly selective. We limit our analysis here to four main topics. First, we discuss the influence of labor relations laws on union membership, bargaining power, and labor markets. Second, we examine the wage, employment, and income distribution effects of the federal minimum wage law. Next, our focus turns to the Occupational Safety and Health Act of 1970 and the question of the proper role of the government in promoting workplace safety. This law is an interesting example of the wide variety of ways in which government directly intervenes in the labor market. Finally, we discuss government laws that provide workers with increases in economic "rent." In that section we extend the discussion of occupational licensure presented in Chapter 6 and also look at the rent aspects of tariffs, quotas, and "domestic content" laws.

LABOR LAW[1]

Laws governing labor relations in general and collective bargaining in particular constitute a significant institutional factor influencing wages, employment, and resource

[1] Instructors in colleges that offer a separate course in labor relations may wish to skip this section.

TABLE 13-1 A SUMMARY OF BASIC LABOR RELATIONS LAWS

The Norris–LaGuardia Act of 1932

1. Increased the difficulty for employers to obtain injunctions against union activity.
2. Declared that yellow-dog contracts were unenforceable. These contracts required employees to agree as a condition of continued employment that they would not join a union.

The Wagner Act of 1935 (National Labor Relations Act—NLRA)

1. Guaranteed the "twin rights" of labor: the right of self-organization and the right to bargain with employers engaged in interstate commerce.
2. Listed a number of "unfair labor practices" on the part of management. Specifically, it *(a)* forbids employers to interfere with the right of workers to form unions; *(b)* outlaws company unions, that is, pseudo-unions, established by firms to discourage the establishment of worker-controlled unions; *(c)* prohibits antiunion discrimination by employers in hiring, firing, and promoting; *(d)* outlaws discrimination against any worker who files charges or gives testimony under the act; and *(e)* obligates employers to bargain in good faith.
3. Established the National Labor Relations Board (NLRB), which was given the authority to investigate unfair labor practices occurring under the act, to issue cease-and-desist orders, and to conduct elections by workers on whether or not they desire union representation.
4. Made strikes by federal employees illegal and grounds for dismissal.

The Taft–Hartley Act of 1947 (Amendment to the NLRA of 1935)

1. Established "unfair labor practices" on the part of unions. Specifically, it prohibits *(a)* coercion of employees to become union members; *(b)* jurisdictional strikes (disputes between unions over who is authorized to perform a specific job); *(c)* secondary boycotts (refusing to buy or handle products produced by another union or group of workers); *(d)* sympathy strikes (work stoppages by one union designed to assist some other union in gaining employer recognition or some other objective); *(e)* excessive union dues; and *(f)* featherbedding (forcing payment for work not actually performed).
2. Regulated the internal administration of unions; e.g., required detailed financial reports to the NLRB.
3. Outlawed the closed shop but made union shops legal in those states that do not expressly prohibit them (state "right-to-work" laws).
4. Set up emergency strike procedures allowing the government to stop for up to 80 days a strike that imperils the nation's health and safety.
5. Created the Federal Mediation and Conciliation Service to provide mediators for labor disputes.

The Landrum–Griffin Act of 1959 (Amendment to the NLRA of 1935)

1. Required regularly scheduled elections of union officers and excluded Communists and people convicted of felonies from holding union office.
2. Held union officers strictly accountable for union funds and property.
3. Prevented union leaders from infringing on the individual worker's rights to participate in union meetings, to vote in union proceedings, and to nominate officers.

allocation. The major laws in this category are summarized in Table 13-1. A careful reading of this table will complement the discussion that follows. The labor relations laws summarized in the table affect the labor market in diverse ways, two of which are (1) by influencing the extent and growth of union membership, which in turn influences the ability of unions to secure wage gains; and (2) by establishing the rules under which collective bargaining transpires.

Labor Law and Union Membership

The effect of labor relations laws and regulations, or the absence thereof, on union membership is not always easy to determine. Such factors as changes in industry structure and altered worker attitudes may create conditions that simultaneously foster both new labor laws *and* changes in union membership. That is, observed changes in union membership may not necessarily result from the changes in the labor laws. Untangling cause and effect therefore is not an easy task. Nevertheless, there can be no doubt that labor law per se can be an important determinant of union membership. This relationship between labor law and union membership is observable in both the private and public sectors.

1 Labor Law and Private-Sector Union Membership A glance back at Table 10-4 reveals that union membership was 1 million in 1900 (7 percent of the labor force) and only 3.3 million in 1930 (11 percent of the labor force). Two decades later, union membership stood at nearly 14 million workers (30 percent of the labor force). After cresting in absolute numbers in the 1970s, union membership declined absolutely during the 1980s and 1990s. Relative to total employment, union membership peaked in the mid-1950s (or in 1970 if members of professional associations are included) and has since declined. Although the reasons for this pattern of union growth and decline are many and varied, the imprint of labor law on these trends is readily discernible.

Pre-1930 Period Prior to the 1930s, union organizers and members were legally unprotected against reprisals by employers or even government itself. Stated bluntly, joining a union might involve job loss, fines, or even bodily harm. Attempts to unionize were met with ***discriminatory discharge*** in many instances. Those dismissed often were placed on ***blacklists*** and therefore denied opportunities to gain alternative employment. Workers sometimes were required to sign ***yellow-dog contracts*** that as a condition of continued employment, legally prohibited them from joining unions. Violation could result not only in discharge but also in a lawsuit initiated by the employer and a court-imposed fine. Firms also used ***lockouts*** (plant closedowns) as a way to stop organizing attempts in their infancies. By closing down the plant for a few weeks, employers could impose high costs on those contemplating joining labor unions. Where workers did successfully organize and attempt to force their employers to bargain, firms often countered strikes by employing ***strikebreakers,*** who sometimes clashed violently with union workers. The Homestead Strike of 1892 and the Pullman Strike of 1894 are cases in point. Often government intervened with police action on the side of employers during these confrontations.

Court hostility toward unionization was a related factor explaining the low union membership during this period. Without labor laws, courts relied on common law interpretations. This placed unions in the weak position of seeking new legal rights for labor at the expense of long-standing property rights of firms. This court hostility manifested itself in several ways, including (1) the courts' interpretation of antitrust laws and (2) the use of ***injunctions.*** For example, the Supreme Court held that the Sherman Antitrust Act of 1890 applied to unions, even though the intent of the legislation was clearly directed toward prohibiting price fixing and monopolization by firms. Injunctions were readily dispensed as a way of stopping actions such as picketing, striking, and boycotting, which employers claimed would reduce their profits. Lower profits would reduce the capitalized value of the firm's assets and, according to the courts, violate the firm's property rights.

To summarize: Prior to the 1930s, the absence of protective labor legislation allowed firms and the courts to repress union activity and growth. The low union membership translated into an inability of unions, in general, to make a significant impact on the overall labor market.

Post-1930 Period As evidenced in the summary of labor legislation in Table 13-1, Congress enacted significant labor relations laws during the 1930s. The Norris–LaGuardia Act of 1932 and the Wagner Act of 1935 placed a protective umbrella over the union movement and greatly encouraged growth of union membership. By outlawing yellow-dog contracts, the ***Norris–LaGuardia Act*** significantly reduced the personal costs of becoming a union member and thus made it easier to organize a firm's workforce. Previously, the cost of joining a union might be the loss of one's job. Also, the act's provision limiting the use of the court-issued injunction to halt normal union activities such as striking increased the ability of unions to impose costs on firms as a way to obtain higher wage offers. Larger union wage gains, in turn, increased the incentive for workers to become union members.

The ***Wagner Act*** had even greater impact on union membership. In fact, one of the expressed purposes of this law was to promote the growth of unionism. Table 13-1 informs us that this legislation guaranteed unions (1) the right to self-organization, free of interference from employers, and (2) the right to bargain as a unit with employers. Furthermore, the act delineated several "unfair labor practices" that management had used successfully to thwart unionism. The Wagner Act enabled the American Federation of Labor (AFL) to solidify its power within various crafts and also permitted the rapid growth of industrial unions affiliated with the Congress of Industrial Organizations (CIO). These CIO unions organized millions of less-skilled workers employed in mass-production industries such as steel, rubber, and automobiles. By the time of the merger between the AFL and CIO in 1955, union membership had risen to about 17 million.

The dramatic surge in union membership in the two decades following the pro-union legislation of the mid-1930s strengthened the ability of unions to achieve dominance (Chapter 6) of many labor markets and thus secure improvements in wage rates and working conditions. That is, increases in union membership translated into increased union bargaining power and a greater overall impact of unionism on labor market outcomes.

The growing strength of labor unions produced a political backlash against unions, resulting in passage of the ***Taft–Hartley Act*** of 1947 and the ***Landrum–Griffin Act*** of 1959, both of which are annotated in Table 13-1. Union membership continued to grow, however, until the more recent decline in unionism discussed in detail in Chapter 10. Recall that some observers contend that part of the recent decline in unionism can be traced to an increased use of illegal antiunion tactics by management. If this assertion is true, then it might be argued that the *degree of enforcement* of labor laws is also a factor in explaining trends in union membership within the private sector.

2 Labor Law and Public-Sector Union Membership Recall from Chapter 10 that membership in public employee unions spurted during the 1960s and 1970s. The driving force for this growth at the federal level was a set of presidential executive orders that provided for the recognition of unions composed of federal workers. At the state level, the main factors explaining the rapid rise in public employee unionism were (1) laws recognizing the rights of state workers to organize and (2) laws establishing public employee relations boards to conduct elections to determine whether workers desire union representation.[2]

Labor Law and Bargaining Power

The overall body of labor law and specific provisions of the law influence bargaining power independently of effects on the level of union membership. Many provisions of labor law enhance the bargaining power of unions, enabling them to secure higher wage gains; other provisions strengthen the negotiating positions of employers. Let's briefly examine an example of each outcome.

1 Limitation on the Use of the Injunction The Norris–LaGuardia Act of 1932 placed into effect a limitation on the use of court-issued injunctions to enjoin picketing, striking, and related union activities. This prohibition clearly strengthened union bargaining power. Because firms could no longer gain legal relief from, say, a work stoppage, threats by unions to strike now became more credible. Previously, firms knew they could get the courts to enjoin the strike once it began. In terms of the bargaining power model discussed in Chapter 10, the limitation on the issuance of these back-to-work orders increased management's costs of disagreeing. This higher cost of disagreeing raised union bargaining power, which, you will recall, is the union's ability to get management to accept its wage demand.

2 Prohibition of Secondary Boycotts ***Secondary boycotts*** are actions by one union to refuse to handle, or to get one's employer to refuse to buy, products made by a firm that is party to a labor dispute. Although the Taft–Hartley Act of 1947 presumably made these secondary pressures illegal, trucking unions continued to demand and obtain "hot-cargo" clauses in their contracts. The courts ruled that such clauses technically did not constitute an illegal secondary boycott. What were these clauses and how did they affect union bargaining power?

Hot-cargo clauses declared that trucking firms would not require unionized truckers to handle or transport products made by an "unfair" employer involved in a labor dispute. For example, suppose that a manufacturer of fabricated steel products was being struck by its employees. Unionized transportation firms governed by hot-cargo provisions would refuse to transport these fabricated steel items while the labor dispute was in progress. The union representing the steel fabricators therefore had more bar-

[2]Richard Freeman, "Unionism Comes to the Public Sector," *Journal of Economic Literature,* March 1986, pp. 41–86. Table 4 in this article summarizes empirical work that supports the thesis that changes in the legal environment independently encourage membership in public-sector unions. Also relevant is Casey Ichniowski, "Public Sector Union Growth and Bargaining Laws: A Proportional Hazards Approach with Time-Varying Treatments," in Richard Freeman and Casey Ichniowski (eds.), *When Public Sector Workers Unionize* (Chicago: University of Chicago Press, 1988, pp. 19–38).

gaining power than it might otherwise have possessed. The reason is that, as a result of the hot-cargo provisions, the strike would effectively curtail all revenue to the firm, thus causing it to suffer losses; it could not maintain its sales and profits through such actions as hiring strikebreakers, using supervisory personnel, or selling from its inventory. Once struck by a union, the firm could not get its products transported to its customers. Management's costs of disagreeing therefore would increase, causing a corresponding rise in the union's bargaining power [equation (10-1)].

The Landrum–Griffin Act of 1959 declared hot-cargo contracts illegal. Specifically, the act stated that it was an unfair labor practice for a union and employer "to enter into any contract or agreement, express or implied, whereby the employer ceases or refrains or agrees to cease or refrain from handling; using; selling; transporting; or otherwise dealing in any products of any other employer, or to cease doing business with any other persons." Once passed and enforced, this prohibition increased management bargaining power by increasing the union's cost of disagreeing in many labor disputes. Many firms now could continue to maintain their profits during strikes by hiring strikebreakers, using supervisory personnel, or selling previously produced goods.

MINIMUM-WAGE LAW

The ***Fair Labor Standards Act*** of 1938, which established a ***minimum wage*** of $.25 per hour, is another way government legislation affects the labor market. Before undertaking a detailed analysis of these effects, it will be useful to establish some facts about the minimum-wage law and provide a brief synopsis of the alternative positions taken on the wisdom of this government intervention into the labor market.

Facts and Controversy

Congress has amended the Fair Labor Standards Act many times to increase the legal minimum wage in monetary terms. Between 1991 and 1996 the legal minimum wage was $4.25 per hour. Because inflation occurred during this period, the ratio of the minimum wage to the average wage fell from 37.3 percent to 32.4 percent.[3] As a result, Congress passed legislation in 1996 that initially increased the minimum wage to $4.75 an hour and then to $5.15 an hour after September 1, 1997.

Congress has extended the coverage of the minimum-wage law over the years. The original legislation placed about 44 percent of all nonsupervisory workers under its coverage; today about 88 percent of all such workers are included. Recent statistics reveal that 36 percent of workers earning the minimum wage are teenagers, 63 percent are women, and 16 percent are black. About 81 percent of minimum-wage employees work in private-sector service-producing industries. Approximately 67 percent of those receiving the minimum wage work part-time.[4]

[3]Barry T. Hirsch and David A. Macpherson, *Union Membership and Earnings Data Book: Compilations from Current Population Survey (1997 Edition)* (Washington, DC: Bureau of National Affairs, 1997).

[4]*Statistical Abstract of the United States, 1997* (Washington, DC: U.S. Government Printing Office, 1997), p. 433.

The minimum wage has been controversial since its inception. Proponents argue that it is needed to ensure that workers receive a "living wage"—one that will provide full-time workers an annual income sufficient to purchase the bare necessities of life. They also contend that this wage floor prevents monopsonistic employers from exploiting low-skilled labor, a disproportionate number of whom are minorities and women. Finally, proponents point to the possibility that the minimum wage "shocks" employers into greater technical efficiency, raising labor productivity and mitigating much of the unemployment consequence predicted by conventional economic theory.

Opponents of the minimum wage, on the other hand, argue that it increases unemployment, particularly among teenagers, females, and minorities. Second, opponents cite the possibility that the legal wage floor causes a spillover effect (Figure 11-2) that reduces wage rates in those sectors of the economy that are not covered by the law. Third, detractors argue that it encourages teenagers to drop out of school. Finally, critics contend that the minimum wage is poorly targeted to reduce poverty; that is, a majority of minimum-wage workers do *not* live in poverty households.

The Competitive Model

The competitive labor supply and demand model is the best starting place for analyzing the possible labor market effects of the minimum wage. We will first assume that all workers are covered by the law and then relax that assumption to allow for incomplete coverage.

1 Complete Coverage Considering Figure 13-1, suppose that all employees in the economy are covered by the minimum-wage law and that labor and product markets are perfectly competitive (MRP = VMP = MWC = P_L). The figure depicts the impact of a specific minimum wage W_m on a labor market in which the equilibrium wage and employment levels are W_0 and Q_0. One point needs to be stressed at the outset. *If* the minimum wage W_m is at or below the equilibrium wage W_0, which is true for higher-wage labor markets, then the law is irrelevant and has *no* direct wage and employment consequence. The actual wage and employment outcome will remain at W_0 and Q_0. This is *not* the situation in Figure 13-1, where W_m exceeds the equilibrium wage W_0.

What employment, unemployment, and allocation effects will this government-imposed minimum wage produce? First, observe that at W_m, employers will hire only Q_d workers rather than the original Q_0. Stated differently, the marginal revenue product of the Q_d through Q_0 workers will be less than the minimum wage, and therefore, profit-maximizing employers will reduce employment.

Second, the supply curve suggests that the minimum wage will attract Q_s as opposed to Q_0 workers to the market. The minimum wage changes the behavior of employers and labor suppliers such that employment declines by the amount *ba* and unemployment increases by the larger amount *ac*.

Third, the minimum wage W_m creates allocative inefficiency. Notice from segment *ae* of the labor demand curve that the value of the marginal product (VMP) for each of the Q_d to Q_0 workers exceeds the supply price of these individuals (as shown by segment *fe* of S_L). This implies that society is giving up output of greater value ($Q_d aeQ_0$)

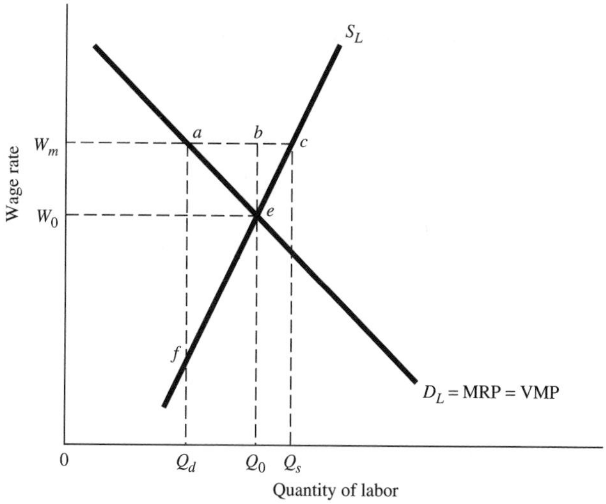

FIGURE 13-1 **MINIMUM-WAGE EFFECTS: BASIC MODEL**
The above-equilibrium minimum wage W_m reduces employment in this low-wage labor market by *ab* and creates unemployment of *ac*. The more elastic the labor supply and demand curves, the greater the unemployment consequences of the law.

than the Q_dQ_0 displaced workers can contribute in their next most productive employment (Q_dfeQ_0). The *net* loss of domestic output is shown then by area *fae* (= Q_daeQ_0 − Q_dfeQ_0). You should use Figure 13-1 to verify the following generalizations: (1) Other things being equal, the higher the minimum wage relative to the equilibrium wage, the greater the negative employment and allocation effects; and (2) the more elastic the labor supply and demand curves, the greater the unemployment consequences of the law.

Two factors, of course, might dampen the minimum-wage effects just mentioned. One such factor is failure on the part of some firms to comply with the minimum-wage law.[5] The other factor is the possibility that some firms offset the minimum wage by reducing fringe benefits (say, sick leave or health insurance).[6] In either case, hourly labor cost would not rise in Figure 13-1 by the full amount W_0W_m, and therefore, the indicated employment and efficiency effects would be lessened.

2 Incomplete Coverage Although the overall coverage of the minimum wage for employees is about 88 percent, it is much less in such industries as agriculture and services. Moreover, self-employed workers are not covered. What impact might incomplete coverage have on the employment and efficiency effects that we have just discussed?

[5]For evidence of this possibility see Orley Ashenfelter and Robert S. Smith, "Compliance with the Minimum Wage Law," *Journal of Political Economy,* April 1979, pp. 335–350.

[6]Walter J. Wessels, "The Effect of Minimum Wages in the Presence of Fringe Benefits: An Expanded Model," *Economic Inquiry,* April 1980, pp. 293–313.

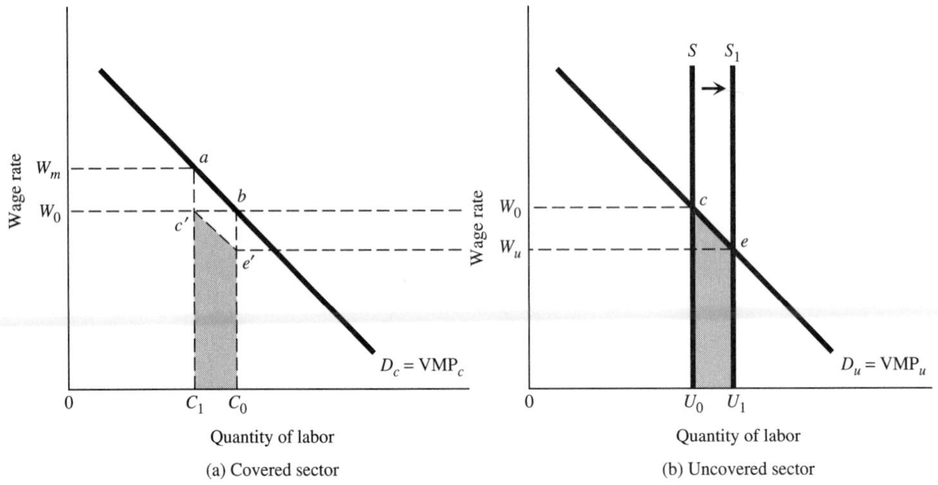

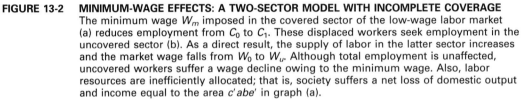

FIGURE 13-2 MINIMUM-WAGE EFFECTS: A TWO-SECTOR MODEL WITH INCOMPLETE COVERAGE
The minimum wage W_m imposed in the covered sector of the low-wage labor market (a) reduces employment from C_0 to C_1. These displaced workers seek employment in the uncovered sector (b). As a direct result, the supply of labor in the latter sector increases and the market wage falls from W_0 to W_u. Although total employment is unaffected, uncovered workers suffer a wage decline owing to the minimum wage. Also, labor resources are inefficiently allocated; that is, society suffers a net loss of domestic output and income equal to the area *c′abe′* in graph (a).

Figure 13-2(a) and (b) portrays two purely competitive labor markets for unskilled workers. One of these (a) is covered by the minimum-wage law and the other (b) is not. To simplify the analysis, assume that jobs are equally attractive in both markets and that the total quantity of labor hours supplied remains constant. In the absence of the minimum wage and in the presence of costless migration and perfect information, workers will migrate between the two sectors until a single equilibrium wage, say W_0, emerges. Employment at that wage will be C_0 in the soon-to-be "covered" sector (a) and U_0 in the sector shown in graph (b). Now suppose that government establishes a minimum wage of W_m for the covered sector (a) of the unskilled labor market. Assuming there is not a shock effect, firms in the newly covered sector will respond to the law by reducing employment from C_0 to C_1. Because of our assumption that the total level of worker hours remains constant, all of the displaced employees will then migrate to the uncovered sector, where labor supply will shift rightward from S to S_1. This will increase the equilibrium employment from U_0 to U_1, where $U_1 = U_0 + (C_0 - C_1)$, and drive down the equilibrium wage to W_u in the uncovered sector.

This spillover model is analytically the same as the union–nonunion spillover model discussed earlier (Figure 11-3). The overall outcomes can be summarized as follows. First, the minimum wage will benefit those workers in the covered sector who are fortunate enough to retain their jobs (C_1). Second, the law will reduce employment in the covered sector (C_0 to C_1), which will increase employment in the uncovered sector (U_0 to U_1). The net employment effect will be zero. Third, the legal minimum will *reduce* the wage of unskilled workers in the uncovered sector (W_0 to W_u). Finally, the law will cause a misallocation of labor resources. Society will gain total output and income of area U_0ceU_1 in the uncovered sector (shaded area under the VMP_u curve) but will lose output and income equal to area C_1abC_0 in the covered sector. Since the shaded areas are equal in each graph, the *net* loss to society is area $c'abe'$, as shown in graph (a). A reallocation of the U_0U_1 workers from the uncovered sector to the covered one, where the VMP is higher, would increase the total value of output in the economy.[7]

The Shock Effect

In Chapter 7, the possibility was raised that in some situations an increase in the wage rate could increase the marginal product of labor and therefore increase labor demand. This possibility *may* be applicable to the imposition of a legal minimum wage. Presumably, the increased wage rate could shock firms employing low-wage labor into improving their management, employing better technology, or making better use of their existing capital. This so-called ***shock effect*** is shown in Figure 13-3, where we assume that the minimum wage rate W_m has resulted in the rightward shift of the labor demand curve from D to D'. Notice that this increase in labor demand mitigates some of the unemployment that otherwise would have resulted. Without the shock effect, unemployment would be *ac;* with this effect, it is only *xc*.

A shock effect produced by a minimum wage theoretically could completely offset any negative unemployment and resource allocation consequences, but the likelihood of this outcome is small. First, for inefficiency initially to exist, competition in the

[7]In reference to the foregoing outcomes, keep in mind that the assumptions of this model are quite rigid. In reality, as the wage sinks from W_0 to W_u, some workers may decide to withdraw from the labor force. Also, some workers may choose to "wait" for jobs to open at the minimum wage. Finally, as we saw in Chapter 9, worker mobility involves costs that may reduce the spillover effect shown in Figure 13-2(a) and (b).

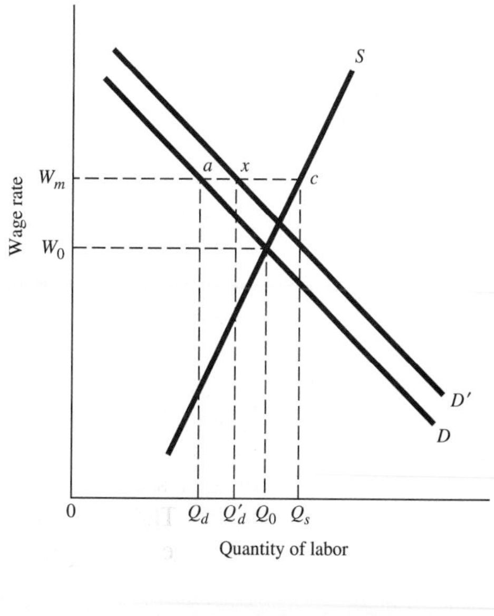

FIGURE 13-3 MINIMUM-WAGE EFFECTS: THE SHOCK EFFECT
A minimum wage such as W_m may "shock" firms out of their organizational inefficiency. As a result, the marginal product of labor may rise, shifting the labor demand curve rightward (D to D'). Consequently, a portion of the unemployment predicted by the basic model may be mitigated (*xc* rather than *ac*).

product market must be quite weak. In competitive product markets, inefficient firms—those which do not achieve minimum average cost—are driven out of business or acquired by firms that are efficient. In fact, the minimum wage rate generally applies in firms operating in highly competitive product markets.

Second, where inefficiency does exist, firms are just as likely to be *overemploying* labor as they are to be underutilizing capital and technology. Some economists point out that the minimum wage might shock firms into discharging redundant labor.[8]

Monopsony

Thus far we have assumed that the low-wage labor market is perfectly competitive. We now dispose of this assumption and analyze the potential employment effects of the minimum wage under conditions of nondiscriminating monopsony. Figure 13-4 portrays a labor market comprising only a single employer of labor services or several employers colluding to set a below-competitive wage. Recall from Figure 6-7 that a monopsonist's marginal wage cost (MWC) exceeds its average wage cost (AWC) at each level of employment. Because it is the only buyer of labor services, the monopsonist faces the typical upward-sloping market supply of labor curve. To hire more workers it must attract them away from other occupations, and it accomplishes this by raising the wage it pays. But because the nondiscriminating monopsonist must pay *all* its workers the same wage, it discovers that its extra cost of hiring one more worker (MWC) exceeds the higher wage payment to that worker alone (AWC).

[8]Charles Brown, Curtis Gilroy, and Andrew Kohen, "The Effect of the Minimum Wage on Employment and Unemployment," *Journal of Economic Literature*, June 1982, p. 489. Also see E. G. West and Michael McKee, "Monopsony and the 'Shock' Arguments for Minimum Wages," *Southern Economic Journal*, January 1980, pp. 888–891.

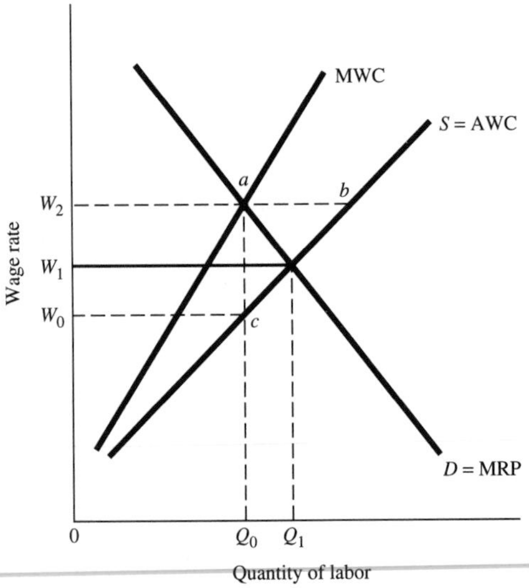

FIGURE 13-4 MINIMUM-WAGE EFFECTS: MONOPSONY
Without the minimum wage, this monopsonist will choose to hire Q_0 workers and pay a wage equal to W_0. Any legal minimum wage above W_0 and below W_2 will transform the firm into a "wage-taker," and the firm will choose to increase its level of employment. For example, if the minimum wage is W_1, this firm will hire the same number of workers as if competition existed in this labor market. Thus, it is possible that a minimum wage might cause employment to increase in some industries.

The monopsonist depicted in Figure 13-4 will use the profit-maximizing hiring rule—MRP = MWC—and employ Q_0 workers. As we see from point *c* on the labor supply curve, to attract that number of workers it has to pay a wage of W_0. But now suppose that government sets a minimum wage somewhere between W_0 and W_2—say W_1. In effect, the labor supply curve becomes perfectly horizontal at W_1 over the $0Q_1$ range of employment. Because the firm can hire up to Q_1 extra workers at the minimum wage, its marginal wage cost equals its average wage cost over this entire range. Contrast this to the previous situation where it has to raise the wage to attract more workers (MWC > AWC).

With the legal minimum wage of W_1, the monopsonist becomes a "wage-taker" rather than a "wage-setter" and maximizes its profits by hiring Q_1 workers. The additional Q_0 through Q_1 workers are now hired because their MRPs exceed the minimum wage (MWC). In this case, the minimum wage *increases* employment from Q_0 to Q_1 by perfectly countervailing the monopsony power of the employer. Close scrutiny of Figure 13-4 shows that any legal wage above W_0 and below W_2 will increase employment above Q_0. It therefore is possible that a well-chosen and selectively implemented minimum wage might increase employment and improve allocative efficiency. This outcome is the same analytically as Chapter 6's discussion of bilateral monopoly in which a union-imposed wage rate might increase employment and enhance efficiency (Figure 6-11).

But much caution is needed here. First, if government sets the minimum wage above W_2, employment will decline. Second, even though *employment* may be equal to or greater than Q_0 at minimum-wage levels above the monopsony wage W_0, *unemployment* could easily be higher. For example, *b* laborers seek employment in this market at wage rate W_2, while firms hire only *a* workers. At W_2, although *employment* is the same as at the monopsony wage W_0, the excess supply of workers—*unemployment*—rises from zero to *ab.* Third, being the only employer of a specific type of low-wage labor, a monopsonist might be able to discriminate, that is, to pay each worker a wage just sufficient to attract her or his employment. If so, the MWC curve will coincide with the labor supply curve, and the firm's profit-maximizing level of employment (MRP = MWC) will be the competitive one, Q_1, rather than Q_0. This is true because the firm must pay the higher wage that is necessary to attract each extra worker only to that particular worker. Where discriminating monopsony exists, a minimum wage will either be ineffective or reduce employment; it cannot increase employment. Fourth, empirical studies on this subject find little evidence of monopsony in most labor markets.

Other Considerations

Two additional considerations concerning the minimum wage merit mention.

1 Union Support Minimum-wage legislation may promote the economic self-interest of high-wage union labor. The minimum wage increases production costs and prices in the nonunion sector, while leaving costs and prices in the unionized sector unchanged. Consumers therefore may buy more goods produced by unionized firms, increasing the derived demand for union labor and, by extension, union wages.[9] In view of this union benefit from increases in the minimum wage, it is not surprising that senators from states with high proportions of unionized employees are more likely to vote for minimum-wage increases. This is equally true for Republican and Democratic senators.[10]

2 Efficiency Wage Considerations The shirking theory of efficiency wages examined earlier (Figure 7-8) implies that firms having high costs of monitoring or high costs of employee malfeasance will pay above-market-clearing wages in order to elicit conscientious effort. Both the high wage and resulting pool of unemployed workers encourage those employed to work more diligently.

In the theoretical world of efficiency wages, the introduction of a minimum wage could have a salutary effect. The unemployment created by the wage floor has the beneficial effect of discouraging shirking by low-paid workers throughout the economy. A worker fired for shirking will have a more difficult time finding a job because of the high volume of unemployment created by the minimum wage. Reduced shirking means that firms can lower their efficiency wage payments and still elicit optimal work efforts from their employees. Lower efficiency wage payments in turn reduce the equilibrium unemployment associated with high efficiency wage payments (Figure 7-8). Conceivably, this *reduction* in unemployment could more than offset the *increase* in unemployment created by the minimum wage. The minimum wage therefore could *reduce* total unemployment.[11]

Empirical Evidence

It should be evident from our discussion that the overall employment and unemployment consequences of the minimum wage are theoretically ambiguous. For this reason, economists have devoted much effort to estimating these consequences through empirical research. Additionally, they have used statistical studies to try to determine whether the minimum wage influences human capital investment decisions and achieves its goal of creating more equality in the distribution of earnings and household income. The results of several of these studies are summarized as follows.

1 Employment and Unemployment The employment and unemployment consequences of the minimum wage vary by age group.

Teenagers On the basis of the prediction of the basic labor market model, we would expect that the minimum wage would increase teenage unemployment by more

[9]James C. Cox and Ronald L. Oaxaca, "The Political Economy of Minimum Wage Legislation," *Economic Inquiry,* October 1982, pp. 533–555. Also see their "Minimum Wage Effects with Output Stabilization," *Economic Inquiry,* July 1986, pp. 443–453.

[10]Farrell E. Block, "Political Support for Minimum Wage Legislation," *Journal of Labor Research,* Fall 1980, pp. 245–253; and idem, "Political Support for Minimum Wage Legislation: 1989," *Journal of Labor Research,* Spring 1993, pp. 187–190.

[11]Jeremy I. Bulow and Lawrence H. Summers, "A Theory of Dual Labor Markets with Application to Industrial Policy, Discrimination, and Keynesian Unemployment," *Journal of Labor Economics,* July 1986, pp. 376–414. Also relevant is James B. Rebitzer and Lowell J. Taylor, "The Consequences of Minimum Wage Laws: Some New Theoretical Ideas," *Journal of Public Economics,* February 1995, pp. 245–255.

than the reduction in employment (*ac* in Figure 13-1 as compared to *ab*). Empirical research, however, yields the opposite finding: Teenage unemployment resulting from the minimum wage is less than the reduction of teenage employment. Two simultaneous effects help explain this outcome. We know from our discussion of labor supply elasticity that taken alone, a wage increase associated with a minimum wage would draw more teenagers into the labor force (*bc* in Figure 13-1). But this positive *elasticity response* is swamped by a negative *probability effect.* Because of the minimum wage, teenage jobs are fewer (*ab* in Figure 13-1) and teenage unemployment is higher. The combined result is a reduced probability for teenagers of successfully finding work. Some teenagers may concede that it no longer is worth their time and effort to seek a job. Other teenagers who are unsuccessful in their early efforts to find a job may withdraw from the labor force (for example, return to school) rather than continue to search for work. In both cases, these teenagers are not actively searching for work and therefore not officially unemployed.[12] In Figure 13-1, the net outcome is that teenage unemployment rises by less than *ab,* the amount that teenage employment falls. In effect, the labor supply curve shifts leftward by a distance greater than *cb* because of the perceived reduction in the likelihood of finding a job.

13-1

Young Adults Young adults aged 20 to 24 also suffer adverse employment and unemployment effects from the minimum wage, but these impacts are smaller than for teenagers.[13]

Older Adults The effect of the minimum wage on the employment and unemployment of older adults "is uncertain in empirical work, as it is in theory."[14] Some older adults probably are displaced by the minimum wage, but others may owe their employment to reduced job competition from teenagers. An employer who would have hired a teenager at, say, $3 an hour rather than an adult at $5.15 an hour may decide to hire the adult once the minimum wage requires that both be paid the legal minimum of $5.15 (1997).

Researchers generally agree that the current minimum wage has had at most a mild negative effect on adult employment. The legal minimum wage is not sufficiently high to cause large-scale reductions in employment. This conclusion is in contrast to Puerto Rico, where the United States has imposed a relatively high minimum wage on a low-productivity, low-wage economy. The result has been an extraordinarily high minimum wage relative to the average wage and a very substantial reduction in employment.[15]

[12]Jacob Mincer, "Unemployment Effects of Minimum Wages," *Journal of Political Economy,* August 1976, p. S104; and C. Brown, C. Gilroy, and A. Kohen, "Time-Series Evidence of the Effect of the Minimum Wage on Youth Employment and Unemployment," *Journal of Human Resources,* Winter 1983, pp. 3–31.

[13]Brown, Gilroy, and Kohen, "The Effects of the Minimum Wage on Employment and Unemployment," *Journal of Economic Literature,* June 1982, p. 524.

[14]Ibid.

[15]Alida J. Castillo-Freeman and Richard B. Freeman, "When the Minimum Wage Really Bites: The Effect of the U.S.-Level Minimum Wage on Puerto Rico," in George J. Borjas and Richard B. Freeman (eds.), *Immigration and the Work Force* (Chicago: University of Chicago Press, 1992), pp. 177–211. The authors find that the high unemployment resulting from the U.S. minimum wage in Puerto Rico has contributed to the massive migration from there to the United States. For critical review of this study see Alan B. Krueger, "The Effect of the Minimum Wage When It Really Bites: A Reexamination of the Evidence from Puerto Rico," in Solomon Polachek (ed.), *Research in Labor Economics,* (Greenwich, CT: JAI Press), 1995, pp. 1–22.

13-1 World of Work

SURPRISING NEW FINDINGS ON THE MINIMUM WAGE

A large increase in the minimum wage, either at the federal or state level, gives researchers a unique opportunity to ascertain subsequent employment effects. Past studies have found negative (albeit small) employment declines, particularly for teenagers. Labor economists therefore were surprised by recent studies suggesting that large increases in the minimum wage in the 1980s and early 1990s may have *increased* employment.

Card and Krueger have examined the impact of the 1992 rise in the New Jersey minimum wage on employment in fast-food restaurants in the state.[*] To conduct their research, the authors surveyed managers of 410 fast-food restaurants in New Jersey and eastern Pennsylvania before and after the rise in the minimum wage. They report employment rose faster in New Jersey than Pennsylvania restaurants (where the minimum wage did not change). The results also revealed that restaurants in New Jersey that paid high wages before the minimum-wage hike did not have faster employment growth than those that paid low wages. Thus, the authors concluded that the minimum wage did not decrease employment.

A study by Card of another state minimum wage increase found similar results.[†] He reports that the boost in the minimum wage raised the earnings of California teenagers, but it did not lower their employment rate relative to workers in other states.

Although these and other studies by Card and Krueger have generated strong interest from policy makers, they have also produced warnings that these results should be considered tentative.[‡] One criticism of the New Jersey study is that the quality of the data collected by Card and Krueger may be poor. A study by Neumark and Wascher, using actual payroll data collected from fast-food restaurants in New Jersey and Pennsylvania, finds that the minimum-wage increase had a negative effect on employment.[§] However, a follow-up study by Card and Krueger, also using a payroll data set, confirms their original conclusion.[||] Another researcher argues that the California study did not appropriately account for the boom that was occurring in that state at the time of the minimum-wage increase.[#] Critics also point out that the employment declines from new minimum-wage legislation could occur before the law takes effect since the laws are announced well in advance. Alternatively, declines could lag many years behind hikes in the minimum wage. Nevertheless, these findings have renewed empirical interest in the employment effects of minimum-wage increases.

[*] David Card and Alan B. Krueger, "Minimum Wages and Employment: A Case Study of the Fast-Food Industry in New Jersey and Pennsylvania," *American Economic Review,* September 1994, pp. 772–793.

[†] David Card, "Do Minimum Wages Reduce Employment? A Case Study of California, 1987–89," *Industrial and Labor Relations Review,* October 1992, pp. 38–54.

[‡] Much of their research on this topic is summarized in David Card and Alan B. Krueger, *Myth and Measurement: The New Economics of the Minimum Wage,* (Princeton, NJ: Princeton University Press, 1995). For a critical review, see John Kennan, "The Elusive Effects of Minimum Wages," *Journal of Economic Literature,* December 1995, pp. 1949–1965; and idem, "Review Symposium on *Myth and Mismeasurement: The New Economics of the Minimum Wage* by David Card and Alan B. Krueger," *Industrial and Labor Relations Review,* July 1995, pp. 842–848.

[§] David Neumark and William Wascher, "The Effect of New Jersey's Minimum Wage Increase on Fast-Food Employment: A Re-Evaluation Using Payroll Records," unpublished manuscript, March 1997.

[||] David Card and Alan B. Krueger," A Reanalysis of the Effect of the New Jersey Minimum Wage Increase on the Fast Food Industry with Representative Payroll Data," Princeton University, Industrial Relations Section Working Paper No. 393, December 1997.

[#] See Taeil Kim and Lowell J. Taylor, "The Employment Effect in Retail Trade of California's 1988 Minimum Wage Increase," *Journal of Business and Economics Statistics,* April 1995, pp. 175–182.

2 Investment in Human Capital The effect of the minimum wage on investment in human capital is likely negative. The minimum wage probably *reduces* on-the-job training. Recall from Chapter 4 that firms sometimes hire workers and provide them with general on-the-job training. To cover the expense, they pay a lower wage during the training period. But the minimum wage places a floor on the wage that firms are able to offer. Therefore, some firms may decide against providing general job training under these circumstances, and thus, the minimum wage may reduce the formation of this type of human capital. Also, empirical evidence indicates that a higher minimum wage encourages teenagers to seek employment and drop out of school.[16]

3 Income Inequality and Poverty The minimum wage does *not* generally alter the overall distribution of family income or appreciably reduce poverty. This somewhat surprising conclusion rests on the empirical evidence that people paid a minimum wage are more likely to be members of middle- or high-income families than low-income families. About 70 percent of minimum-wage workers reside in families that have family income above 300 percent of the poverty line. Thus, the minimum wage appears to be poorly targeted as an antipoverty weapon.[17]

Final Remarks

The minimum wage *does* offset monopsony power in some circumstances, say, where undetected collusion by employers would otherwise result in a wage rate below the minimum wage and below the marginal revenue productivity of workers. Also, the minimum wage *does* increase the annual earnings of some low-income workers. Perhaps these are the reasons for the strong public support for the minimum wage and the fact that the debate over it has largely moved away from the question of whether it should exist and toward the issue of how high it should be set. Economists commonly agree that there is some real minimum wage that would be so high that it would severely reduce employment and economic efficiency. But based on the evidence summarized above, it does not appear that this level has yet been reached. In this regard, one knowledgeable reviewer of the minimum-wage literature has recently concluded that "the minimum wage is overrated: by its critics as well as its supporters."[18]

QUICK REVIEW 13-1

- The Norris–LaGuardia Act of 1932 and the Wagner Act of 1935 encouraged the growth of U.S. unionism; the Taft–Hartley Act of 1947 and the Landrum–Griffin Act of 1959 sought to restrain union power.
- In a competitive labor market, an above-equilibrium minimum wage will reduce employment, increase unemployment, and create an efficiency loss.
- Where monopsony is present in a labor market, a government-set minimum wage can increase employment and promote allocative efficiency.

[16]See David Neumark and William Wascher, "Minimum-Wage Effects on School and Work Transitions of Teenagers," *American Economic Review,* May 1995, pp. 244–249.

[17]See Richard V. Burkhauser, Kenneth A. Couch, and David C. Wittenburg, "Who Gets What from Minimum Wage Hikes: A Re-estimation of Card and Krueger's Distributional Analysis in *Myth and Measurement: The New Economics of the Minimum Wage,*" *Industrial and Labor Relations Review,* April 1996, pp. 547–552. Also see William E. Even and David A. Macpherson, "Consequences of Minimum Wage Indexing," *Contemporary Economic Policy,* October 1996, pp. 67–77.

[18]Charles Brown, "Minimum Wage Laws: Are They Overrated?" *Journal of Economic Perspectives,* Summer 1988, pp. 133–145.

• Researchers have estimated that a 10 percent increase in the minimum wage causes a 1 to 3 percent decline in teenage employment. Some question exists, however, of whether the most recent increases in the minimum wage followed this pattern ("World of Work" 13-1).

Your Turn: Suppose the federal government increases the minimum wage by 25 percent. Based on theory and traditional evidence, predict the impact of this increase on *(a)* the average wage of teenagers, *(b)* teenage employment, *(c)* teenage unemployment, and *(d)* adult employment. (Answers: See page 627.)

OCCUPATIONAL HEALTH AND SAFETY REGULATION

Another important and controversial area of direct government intervention into the labor market is the regulation of occupational health and safety. This intervention has taken several forms, including state workers' compensation programs and the federal ***Occupational Safety and Health Act*** of 1970. The former mandated that firms purchase insurance that pays specified benefits to workers injured on the job. The latter, which will be our main focus, requires employers to comply with workplace health and safety standards established under the legislation.

Government regulation of workplace health and safety is worthy of discussion for several reasons. First, statistics show that work is more dangerous than generally perceived. In 1995 5,300 workers died in job-related accidents in the United States, and roughly 3.6 million people incurred injuries that precluded work for a full day or more. As observed in Table 13-2, these accidents varied greatly by industry. Note, for ex-

TABLE 13-2 OCCUPATIONAL FATALITIES AND DISABILITIES BY INDUSTRY, 1995

	Deaths		
Industry group	Number (in thousands)	Rate per 100,000 workers	Number of disabling injuries* (in thousands)
Total	5.3	4	3,600
Agriculture	0.8	24	140
Mining and quarrying	0.2	30	20
Construction	1.0	16	350
Manufacturing	0.7	4	600
Transportation and utilities	0.9	13	300
Trade	0.5	2	840
Service	0.7	2	800
Government	0.5	3	550

*Defined as injuries resulting in death, physical impairment, or inability to perform regular duties for a full day beyond the day of injury.

Source: Statistical Abstract of the United States, 1997, (Washington, DC: U.S. Government Printing Office, 1997), p. 437.

ample, that there were 24 deaths per 100,000 workers in "agriculture" as compared to 2 deaths per 100,000 employees in "trade." Second, job safety—or lack thereof—is an important nonwage aspect of work, which is an important determinant of labor supply (Chapter 6). Therefore, degrees of workplace safety help explain wage differentials among certain occupations (Chapter 8). Finally, just as with such labor market interventions as the minimum wage and affirmative-action legislation (Chapter 15), controversy exists over the appropriateness and effectiveness of regulation of workplace health and safety.

This topic will be approached as follows. First, we will discuss how a profit-maximizing firm determines how much job safety to provide its workers. Then, we will analyze why this level of protection against workplace hazards might be less than society's optimal amount. Finally, we will discuss the controversies surrounding the Occupational Safety and Health Act of 1970.

Profit-Maximizing Level of Job Safety[19]

13-1 Competition in the product market will force a profit-maximizing firm to minimize its internal costs of producing any specific amount of output. One cost of production is the expenditure necessary to make the workplace safe. The "production" of job safety normally involves diminishing returns, which, translated into cost terms, means that each dollar of additional expenditure yields successively smaller increases in job safety. More concretely, firms will first use such relatively inexpensive techniques as disseminating safety information and issuing protective gear (say, hard hats) to make the job safer; but to make further gains, they may have to resort to such increasingly costly actions as purchasing safer equipment and slowing the work pace. Therefore, most firms experience a rising ***marginal cost of job safety;*** successively higher amounts of direct expense, reduced output, or both will be required to gain additional "units" of job safety. We depict a marginal cost of safety curve MC_s in Figure 13-5. Each additional unit of job safety, measured on the horizontal axis, costs more than previous units.

Knowing that it is costly to provide job safety, why would a firm choose to offer workers *any* protection from workplace hazards? The answer is provided by the marginal benefit of safety curve MB_s (disregard the curve labeled MB'_s for now). An employer benefits from creating a relatively safe workplace; job safety reduces certain costs that the firm might otherwise incur. Notice, however, that as more units of job safety are produced by this firm, the ***marginal benefit from job safety*** (MB_s) to the firm falls. Just as individuals experience diminishing marginal utility as successive units of a good are consumed, firms find that the extra benefit (cost saving) of job safety diminishes with every increase in the amount of job safety.

Just what are these benefits to the firm? First, lower risks of injury or death enable employers to attract workers at lower wage rates. Because workers value job safety,

[19]The basic analytical framework for this section and the section that follows was developed by Walter Oi in "An Essay on Workmen's Compensation and Industrial Safety," in *Supplemental Studies for the National Commission on State Workmen's Compensation Laws,* vol. 1, 1974, pp. 41–106.

13-1 Global Perspective

OCCUPATIONAL INJURIES, 1991–93

Denmark and Sweden have relatively low proportions of workers affected by occupational injuries, while Germany has a substantially higher rate of job injury.

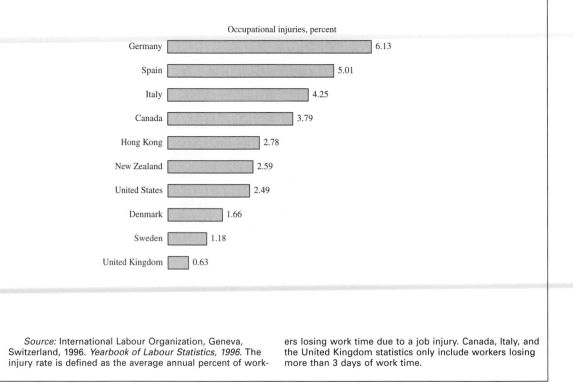

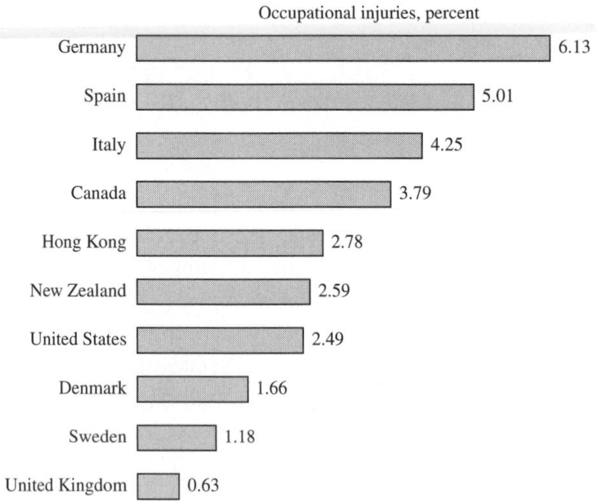

Source: International Labour Organization, Geneva, Switzerland, 1996. *Yearbook of Labour Statistics, 1996.* The injury rate is defined as the average annual percent of workers losing work time due to a job injury. Canada, Italy, and the United Kingdom statistics only include workers losing more than 3 days of work time.

they are willing to accept a lower wage for work performed in a healthy, relatively safe environment (Chapter 8). Second, a safer workplace reduces the amount of disruption of the production process that job accidents create. Workplace mishaps and the absence of key employees during rehabilitation often halt or slow the production process. Third, a safer workplace reduces the cost of recruiting, screening, and training workers. The fewer the number of workers injured on the job, the fewer the resources required to hire and train new employees. Fourth, workplace safety helps maintain the firm's return on its specific investment in human capital. Job fatalities and injuries terminate or reduce the firm's returns on its previously financed specific formal and on-the-job training. Finally, fewer job-related accidents translate into lower workers' compensa-

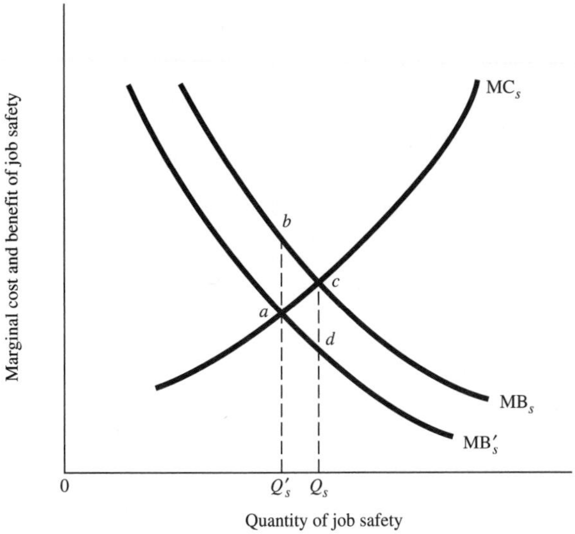

FIGURE 13-5 THE OPTIMAL LEVEL OF JOB SAFETY
A profit-maximizing firm will provide a level of job safety at which its marginal benefit and marginal cost of safety are equal, say at Q_s, which is determined by the intersection of MB_s and MC_s. If workers have full information about possible work hazards and accurately assess job risks, this level of output will optimize society's well-being. If workers are unaware of workplace danger or underestimate it, they will not be paid a proper wage premium, and the firm will not gain the benefit of lower wages as it provides more safety. Thus, the marginal benefit of each unit of job safety will be less (MB'_s rather than MB_s), and the firm will underprovide job safety from society's viewpoint (Q'_s rather than Q_s).

tion insurance rates. Such rates are determined by the probability and types of accidents experienced in a given firm.

To determine the profit-maximizing level of workplace safety, the cost-minimizing firm will compare the marginal benefit of safety (MB_s) against the marginal cost (MC_s). In so doing, it will use the following decision rule: Provide additional job safety so long as the marginal benefit exceeds the marginal cost. In Figure 13-5 we see that the profit-maximizing level of job safety is Q_s units, at which $MB_s = MC_s$. Conclusion? Even in the absence of government intervention, this firm will find it cost-effective and profitable to provide some degree of job safety. In this case, our firm will provide Q_s units.

Another observation merits comment here. The perception that some jobs, say coal mining and construction, are *inherently* dangerous while others, say accounting and teaching, are innately safe is slightly misleading. A more accurate statement is that given present technology, it is inherently more costly to provide job safety in some occupations than others. Therefore, firms with similar marginal benefit schedules but different marginal costs of safety will offer differing levels of job safety. A firm with the same marginal benefits curve as that in Figure 13-5 but with significantly higher marginal costs of providing job safety than those shown by MC_s would provide much less job safety than Q_s units.

13-2

13-2 World of Work

DO COMPUTERS EXPAND JOB OPPORTUNITIES FOR PEOPLE WITH SPINAL CORD INJURIES?*

The computer revolution has dramatically changed the labor market: 46 percent of workers now use computers on their jobs.† Workers using computers on the job earn 10 to 15 percent more than similar workers who do not use a computer.‡ Krueger, Kruse, and Drastal investigate whether the emergence of computers in the workplace has lessened the negative labor market effects of spinal cord injuries, which lead to severe disability because mobility requires the use of a wheelchair or crutches.

The researchers conducted their analysis on a sample of 391 New Jersey residents who had a spinal cord injury in the prior 10 years. Not surprisingly, they find that a spinal cord injury lowers the probability that a person is employed by 40 to 50 percentage points and reduces hours worked and weekly earnings by about one-quarter. On the other hand, it has little effect on the wage rate for those who do work.

Computers do improve the situation of those with spinal cord injuries. Computer skills are associated with increased wages, a quicker return to work, and faster earnings growth. Among workers using computers on the job, those with spinal cord injuries report similar earnings to those without such injuries. However, workers with spinal cord injuries who do not use computers have lower earnings than their injury-free counterparts. Despite the advantages gained from computers, people with spinal cord injuries are no more likely to use computers than the average person.

*Based on Alan B. Krueger, Douglas Kruse, and Susan Drastal, "Labor Market Effects of Spinal Cord Injuries in the Dawn of the Computer Age?" National Bureau of Economic Research Working Paper No. 5302, October 1995.

†See *Statistical Abstract of the United States, 1996* (Washington, DC: U.S. Government Printing Office, 1996), p. 423.

‡See Alan B. Krueger, "Why Computers Have Changed the Wage Structure: Evidence from Microdata, 1984–89," *Quarterly Journal of Economics,* February 1993, pp. 33–61.

Society's Optimal Level of Job Safety

A firm's profit-maximizing level of job safety *may* or *may not* be society's optimal level of job safety. In addressing this topic, let's first assume that there is perfect information and assessment of job risk, and then examine a situation where this is not the case.

1 Perfect Information and Assessment *If workers have full information about possible work hazards and accurately assess the likelihood of occupational fatality, injury, or disease, then the amount of job safety offered by employers will match that level required to maximize society's well-being.* Where workers have full knowledge of job risk, employers providing hazardous work environments will have to pay a wage premium to attract a sufficient number of employees (Chapter 8). The existence of the compensating wage differential will ensure that the employer's extra benefit from providing a safer workplace (including a *reduced* wage premium) will match the extra benefit of job safety from society's perspective.

In Figure 13-5 we are saying that given our assumption of perfect information and assessment, curve MB_s depicts both the private *and* social marginal benefits of job safety. The number of units of job safety shown as Q_s will maximize the firm's profits *and* optimize society's well-being.

2 Imperfect Information and Assessment *Where information about job hazards is limited and/or workers underestimate the personal risk of occupational fatality, injury, or disease, employers will provide less job safety than is socially optimal.*

To demonstrate this generalization, suppose that workers mistakenly judge the job in question to be risk-free, when in reality one of the substances handled by workers is highly hazardous. Because employees are unaware of the long-term danger, the job hazard will *not* reduce labor supply to this occupation and employer. The market wage therefore will *not* contain a wage premium required to compensate workers for the added job risk. Consequently, the firm's marginal benefit from reducing the health hazard—that is, from providing a safer workplace—will be smaller than it would be if workers had full information about the job danger. Extra units of job safety will fail to reduce the wages paid by our firm, because the labor market has not dictated payment of a wage premium to compensate workers for their true risk. From the firm's perspective, the marginal benefits from providing job safety is less than it would be if full information about the long-term health consequences of the job were known.

The marginal benefit schedule of job safety as viewed by the firm in this situation is shown in Figure 13-5 as curve MB_s'. The firm compares MB_s' with its marginal cost of providing safety (MC_s) and settles for Q_s' units of job safety. Result: *Job safety is underprovided from society's viewpoint.* Suppose that the true marginal benefits of each added unit of safety are those shown as MB_s rather than MB_s'. Given full information and accurate assessment by workers of the job danger, the firm's relevant marginal benefit curve would be MB_s, and both the profit-maximizing and socially optimal levels of job safety would be Q_s units. As can be observed by extending a vertical line upward from Q_s' to MB_s, and observing the triangle *abc,* the $Q_s'Q_s$ units of job safety generate marginal benefit to society that exceed the marginal costs MC_s. But under conditions of incomplete information or underestimation of risk by workers, and therefore no market wage premium, the firm has no incentive to provide these extra units. From its perspective the marginal benefit is less than the marginal cost. We conclude that a firm's maximizing level of job safety may not always conform to society's optimal level of job safety. In our example, society's welfare loss from this inefficiency is area *abc.*

The Occupational Safety and Health Act

The Occupational Safety and Health Act of 1970 interjected the federal government directly into regulation of workplace hazards. The act's purpose was to reduce the incidence of job injury and illness by identifying and eliminating hazards found in the workplace. The Occupational Safety and Health Administration (OSHA) was given the responsibility of developing safety and health standards and enforcing them through workplace inspections and fines for violations.

The Case for OSHA OSHA was controversial when passed and remains subject to debate today. Those who support the legislation contend that the costs of providing a healthy and safe workplace are legitimate business costs that should not be transferred to workers. According to this view, imperfect information, underestimation of risk, and barriers to occupational mobility prevent the labor market from making the adjustments that would provide adequate wage premiums for hazardous jobs. Thus, for reasons described earlier, government standards are needed to force firms to provide more job safety than is dictated by their own self-interests. Finally, supporters of OSHA regulation point out that much of the criticism has originated in the corporate community, where resistance is predictable and understandable. To see why, note in Figure 13-5 that under conditions of incomplete information and improper assessment of risk, a minimum safety standard, say of Q_s units, would force this firm to provide $Q_s'Q_s$ units of safety, which, from its perspective, cost more to produce than they generate in private benefits. This is seen by comparing the *ac* segment of MC_s to the *ad* segment of MB_s'.

Criticisms of OSHA Critics of OSHA counter that safety standards and inspections represent an unwarranted, costly government intrusion into the private sector. They point out that even though information about job hazards may be imperfect and workers may inaccurately assess personal risk, no a priori reason exists to expect that workers systematically will underestimate the risk of job hazards. Rather, workers could just as well overestimate the likelihood that they will be the unlucky party affected by occupational death, injury, or illness, just as many purchasers of state lottery tickets or sweepstake entrants overestimate the probability that they will win. According to this line of reasoning, it is possible that wage premiums for hazardous jobs are greater than they would be if there were perfect information and risk assessment. Restated, the perspective that "it will probably happen to me" may dissuade people from hazardous occupations, driving up the wage rate for those who perform such work. Recall that when such wage premiums exist, the firm's marginal benefit from reducing the job hazard is greater than otherwise, and an underallocation of resources to job safety is not likely.

Critics of OSHA also assert that workplace standards often bear no relationship to reductions in injury and illness. They point to the numerous trivial standards—wall-height rules for fire extinguishers, specified shapes of toilet seats, and so forth—to support this assertion. Additionally, opponents of OSHA cite the complexity of determining just what the standards are. Wiedenbaum has noted OSHA's original definition of an "exit": "That portion of a means of egress which is separated from all other spaces of the building or structure by construction or equipment as required in this subpart to provide a protected way of travel to the exit discharge." Wiedenbaum contrasts this definition with one from a dictionary: An exit is "a passage or way out."[20] In the face of criticism over trivial rules and bureaucratic language, OSHA revoked over 1,100 standards in 1978 and attempted to rewrite remaining standards in simple terms.

Findings and Implications The controversy over OSHA has been heightened by the mixed findings on whether OSHA standards and inspections have reduced occupational accidents and injuries. Since the passage of OSHA, the rate of fatal injury on the job has declined, but the rate of workdays lost per year from nonfatal injuries has risen.

Studies attempting to sort out OSHA's role in the overall workplace fatality and accident trends are fraught with data and interpretation problems. Nevertheless, several noteworthy attempts have been made. Research looking at early years following passage of OSHA found little indication that OSHA reduced industrial injury rates. Specifically, Viscusi[21] found that OSHA had no significant effect on workplace safety

[20]Murray L. Wiedenbaum, *Business, Government, and the Public* (Englewood Cliffs, NJ: Prentice-Hall, Inc., 1977), pp. 64–65.

[21]W. Kip Viscusi, "The Impact of Occupational Safety and Health Regulation," *Bell Journal of Economics*, Spring 1978, pp. 117–140.

for the years 1972–75, and Smith and McCaffrey[22] found no effects of OSHA inspections during 1974–76. These scholars warned, however, that caution needed to be exercised in interpreting their findings. The results may be due to lack of enforcement of the law or inadequate penalties for firms failing to meet the safety standards.

Studies of more recent periods are mixed. In a follow-up study to the earlier Smith and McCaffrey research, Ruser and Smith[23] found that OSHA had little impact on workplace injuries in the early 1980s. On the other hand, a 1986 study by Viscusi[24] covering the 1973–83 period discovered that OSHA inspections modestly reduced the rate of both occupational injury and lost workdays. Gray and Jones[25] have found that OSHA inspections within the manufacturing sector have reduced the number of OSHA citations of safety violations by one-half. Also, Gray and Scholz[26] have recently tested for the effects of OSHA safety enforcement using a unique data set on injuries and OSHA inspection for 6,842 manufacturing plants between 1979 and 1985. They found that plants that were inspected and penalized for violations experienced a 22 percent decline in their injuries in the following few years.

If OSHA becomes increasingly effective in reducing workplace fatalities, injuries, and diseases in hazardous jobs, existing wage differentials between "hazardous" and "safe" jobs should decline over time. Recall from Chapter 6 that one of the determinants of labor supply to an occupation is the nonwage aspects of employment. By making dangerous jobs safer, effective OSHA standards may result in an increased supply of labor to the formerly hazardous jobs, eventually reducing the wage premiums paid in those lines of work. Wage premiums for risk of workplace death or injury are one of several sources of wage differentials among workers. Thus, over the long run, highly effective OSHA regulations conceivably could reduce some of the wage disparity among jobs in the economy.

Other subtle labor market effects may possibly result from government regulation of occupational health and safety. For example, the high cost of complying with OSHA standards in some industries may result in the demise of smaller nonunion firms, increased product market share for larger unionized producers, and enhanced bargaining power and wages for union workers.[27] As a second example, the amount of money

[22]Robert Smith and David McCaffrey, "An Assessment of OSHA's Recent Effect on Injury Rates," *Journal of Human Resources,* Winter 1983, pp. 131–145.

[23]John W. Ruser and Robert S. Smith, "Reestimating OSHA's Effects: Have the Data Changed?" *Journal of Human Resources,* Spring 1991, pp. 212–235.

[24]W. Kip Viscusi, "Reforming OSHA Regulation of Workplace Risks," in Leonard W. Weiss and Michael W. Klass (eds.), *Regulary Reform: What Actually Happened?* (Boston: Little, Brown, 1986), p. 262.

[25]Wayne B. Gray and Carol Adaire Jones, "Longitudinal Patterns of Compliance with OSHA in the Manufacturing Sector," *Journal of Human Resources,* Fall 1991, pp. 623–653. Of related interest is Wayne B. Gray and Carol Adaire Jones, "Are OSHA Health Inspections Effective? A Longitudinal Study in the Manufacturing Sector," *Review of Economics and Statistics,* August 1991, pp. 504–508.

[26]Wayne B. Gray and John T. Scholz, "Does Regulatory Enforcement Work?" *Law and Society Review,* 1993, vol. 27, no. 1, pp. 177–213.

[27]For empirical support for this scenario as it relates to the Federal Coal Mine Health and Safety Act of 1969, see Scott Fuess and Mark Lowenstein, "Further Analysis of the Effects of Government Safety Regulation: The Case of the 1969 Coal Mine Health and Safety Act," *Economic Inquiry,* April 1990, pp. 354–389.

13-3 firms spend to comply with OSHA standards may directly compete with more productive expenditures to improve job safety.[28]

Questions about the effectiveness of OSHA in relationship to its costs have led some economists to call for alternative or complementary approaches to promoting job safety. As one option, government could accumulate and directly provide information to workers about the injury experience of various employers, much as it publishes the on-time performance of airlines. Alternatively, it could mandate that firms develop and disclose information about known workplace hazards. In either case, the availability of information would help workers assess risk. This in turn would enable labor markets to establish more appropriate compensating wage differentials.

[28]Ann P. Bartel and Lacy Glenn Thomas, "Direct and Indirect Effects of Regulation: A New Look at OSHA's Impact," *Journal of Law and Economics*, April 1985, pp. 1–25.

13-3 World of Work

THE EFFECT OF WORKERS' COMPENSATION ON JOB SAFETY

Each of the 50 states has workers' compensation laws requiring employers to pay legally established benefits to workers injured on the job (or to families of workers who die from work-related accidents). Firms are mandated by law to purchase insurance to finance these benefits.* The insurance premiums the firms must pay vary directly with the risk of accident at their establishments. For example, logging firms, which typically have higher-than-average accident rates, have larger workers' compensation premiums than, say, fast-food establishments, which have better safety records.

What are the effects of workers' compensation laws on workplace safety? These laws produce two opposing effects. First, the insurance premiums required under the laws create an incentive for firms to make their workplaces safer. By reducing accident rates, firms can lower the workers' compensation premium they must pay. Thus, the marginal benefit of providing any given level of safety is greater for the firm in the presence of workers' compensation. Firms therefore discover that it is in their profit interest to increase their levels of job safety. (You should use Figure 13-5 to demonstrate this effect.)

But workers' compensation laws also create an opposing effect—a *moral-hazard problem.* Generally defined, this problem is the tendency of one party to a contract to alter his or her behavior in ways which are costly to the other party. As it relates to workers' compensation insurance, the moral-hazard problem is that workers may be less careful as they go about their work, knowing they are insured against on-the-job accidents. Taken alone, this change in behavior would lead to higher incidences of job accidents.

In a major study, Moore and Viscusi have found that the workers' compensation laws have had a dramatic effect in reducing job fatalities.† This finding implies that the positive incentive effect of the laws swamps the negative moral-hazard effect. Specifically, Moore and Viscusi show that fatality risks in American industries would rise by over 40 percent if the workers' compensation program were not in place. They also conclude that the program saves almost 2,000 lives per year. Finally, Moore and Viscusi note that these sizable positive effects stand in contrast to the smaller effects identified in other studies as resulting from direct workplace regulation by the Occupational Safety and Health Administration. This fact suggests that an "injury tax" imposed on employers might be a more efficient way to reduce on-the-job accidents than the present regulatory approach.

*Depending on the state, this insurance may be purchased from a state agency or from private insurance firms. Also, some states allow firms to "self-insure," which means that they may establish an insurance plan within their own enterprises.

†Michael J. Moore and W. Kip Viscusi, *Compensating Mechanisms for Job Risks: Wages, Workers' Compensation, and Product Liability* (Princeton, NJ: Princeton University Press, 1990).

As a second option, government could impose an "injury tax" on employers based on their incidences of work-related injuries and deaths. By boosting the employers' marginal benefit of job safety, such a tax would provide an incentive for firms to make their workplaces safer.

QUICK REVIEW 13-2

- Each year about 5.3 thousand occupational fatalities and about 3.6 million occupational injuries occur in the United States.
- A firm's profit-maximizing level of workplace safety occurs where its marginal cost and marginal benefit of providing safety are equal.
- Profit-maximizing levels of job safety may be lower than socially optimal levels where workers lack information about job risk or underestimate the probability of being hurt or killed.
- The Occupational Safety and Health Act of 1970 remains somewhat controversial; only recently has preliminary evidence emerged finding that OSHA standards and inspections are effective in reducing job injuries.

Your Turn: Suppose that a firm's marginal cost of an extra unit of job safety is $250,000; the marginal private benefit, $200,000; and the marginal social benefit, $300,000. Will the firm provide this extra unit of job safety? Should government intervene? If so, what are its policy options? (Answers: See page 627.)

GOVERNMENT AS A RENT PROVIDER

Government influences wages and employment in labor markets in more subtle ways than establishing labor laws, imposing a legal minimum wage, or setting occupational safety standards. One such method is through providing economic rent to labor market participants. ***Economic rent*** *in the labor market is the difference between the wage paid to a particular worker and the wage just sufficient to keep that person in his or her present employment.* Recall from Chapter 6 that a market labor supply curve such as the one shown in Figure 13-6 is essentially a marginal opportunity cost curve. The curve reflects the value of each worker's next best alternative, whether that be another job, household production, or leisure. Given the market wage of $8 in Figure 13-6, all employed workers with the exception of the marginal one, Q_0, receive economic rent, the total of which is area *abc*. To clarify further, suppose that Jones is the worker shown by Q_j and that her marginal opportunity cost is $6 an hour. We can see then that Jones is receiving a $2 per hour "rent" (= $8 − $6).

What would happen to Jones' economic rent if government passed a law that had the effect of increasing the market wage to $10 an hour? She and all other workers who remain employed would receive an *increase* in economic rent of $2 (= $10 − $8). But why might government be interested in providing increases in economic rent to

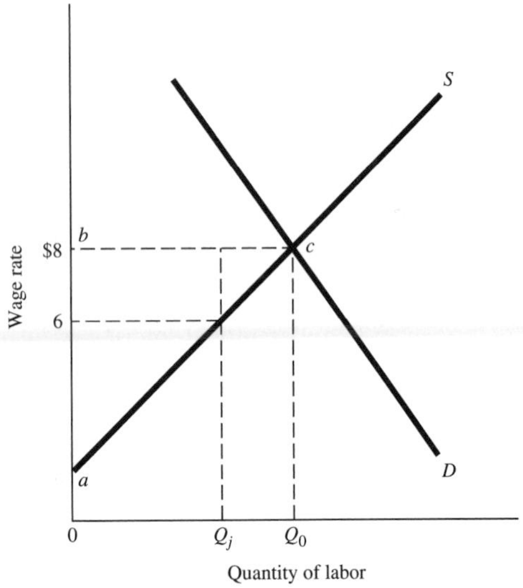

FIGURE 13-6 ECONOMIC RENT IN LABOR MARKETS
At the market wage of $8, employers will hire Q_0 workers. The labor supply curve indicates that these Q_0 workers collectively receive economic rent equal to the area *abc*. The Q_j worker receives a $2 per hour rent ($8 minus the person's opportunity cost of $6).

workers? According to some economic and political theorists, the main goal of politicians is to get and stay elected. Consequently, they offer and provide a wide range of publicly provided goods and services that enhance the utility of their constituents. One such service may be the provision or the enhancement of economic rents. According to this controversial theory, groups of workers—for example, professional groups or unions—have a demand for economic rent; that is, they are ***rent seekers.*** Elected officials respond to this demand by supplying the publicly provided service, economic rent; they are ***rent providers.***[29]

Admittedly, care must be taken not to oversimplify here. Higher wages provided by law or regulation may produce lower market-determined wages for other workers, higher product prices for consumers, lower corporate dividends for common stockholders, or some combination of all three. These groups are interested in their own rents and may intervene politically to block the provision of rents to a group of workers. But because acquisition of information and political lobbying are costly, people have little incentive to try to block rent provision when they perceive their personal losses to be small. Hence, elected officials may find it beneficial to dispense economic rent to highly organized groups of workers.

This concept of rent provision is apparent in some instances of occupational licensure and in legislation that establishes tariffs, quotas, and "domestic content" laws.

[29]A political scientist once defined politics as "who gets what, when, and how." This view of politics has been formalized into a theory of regulation by several economists. See, for example, George J. Stigler, "The Theory of Economic Regulation," *Bell Journal of Economics and Management Science,* Spring 1971, pp. 3–21. Also see Sam Peltzman, "Toward a More General Theory of Regulation," *Journal of Law and Economics,* August 1976, pp. 181–210.

Occupational Licensure

In the United States there are 1,500 separate state licensing boards, 600 licensed occupations, and another 400 occupations subject to some other form of state regulations.[30] Table 13-3 provides a partial list of occupations requiring licenses in one state.

In many instances, licensing of occupational groups (pharmacists, surgeons) is held to be necessary to protect consumers against incompetents who might do irreparable damage. In these circumstances governmental licensing may be the most efficient way to minimize the costs of obtaining information needed by consumers to make optimal buying decisions. But, as we first indicated in Chapter 6, in other situations the occupational groups themselves, not consumers, generate the demand for licensing. These groups may wish to restrict access to licenses as a way to obtain economic rent for licensees.

Figure 13-7 demonstrates how occupational licensure can confer economic rent. Suppose that the prelicensing equilibrium wage and employment level are \$8 and 10,000 workers, respectively. Next assume that licensing has the effect of restricting the total number of licensed workers to 7,000. In effect, the postlicensing labor supply curve is SgS_1, compared to the old curve of SS_0. Notice that licensing increases the market wage to \$11 an hour and that total employment falls from 10,000 to 7,000. The \$11 wage attracts another 4,000 workers (= 14,000 − 10,000) who would like to work

[30] *Employment and Training Report of the President, 1982* (Washington, DC: U.S. Government Printing Office, 1983), p. 94.

TABLE 13-3 SELECTED LICENSED OCCUPATIONS: STATE OF WASHINGTON

Accountants	Dentists	Osteopaths
Agricultural brokers	Dispensing opticians	Oyster farmers
Aircraft pilots	Egg dealers	Pesticide applicators
Ambulance drivers	Embalmers	Pharmacists
Architects	Engineers	Physical therapists
Auditors	Fish dealers	Physician assistants
Barbers	Funeral directors	Physicians and surgeons
Beauticians	Harbor pilots	Proprietary school agents
Blasters	Insurance adjusters	Psychologists
Boathouse operators	Insurance agents	Real estate brokers
Boiler workers	Landscape architects	Real estate sales agents
Boxers	Law clerks	Sanitarians
Boxing managers	Lawyers	Security advisors
Chiropodists	Librarians	Security brokers
Chiropractors	Livestock dealers	Surveyors
Commercial fishers	Marine pilots (inland)	Teachers
Commercial guides	Milk vendors	Veterinarians
Dairy technicians	Naturopaths	Wrestlers
Debt adjustors	Nurses	Weighers and graders
Dental hygienists	Optometrists	Well diggers

Source: Employment Security Department, state of Washington.

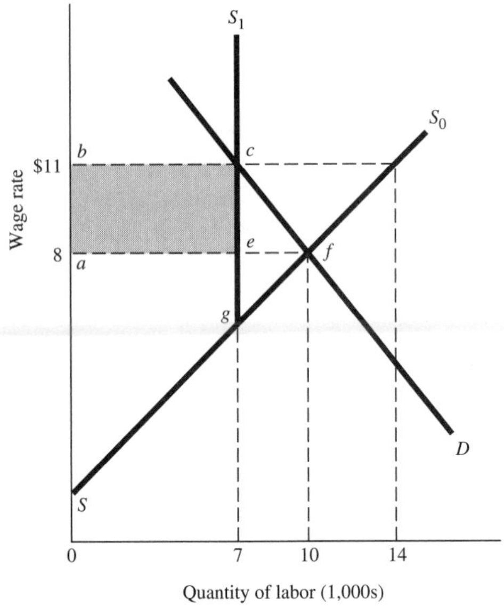

FIGURE 13-7 RENT PROVISION THROUGH OCCUPATIONAL LICENSURE
By setting a limit of 7,000 licenses in this labor market, government indirectly increases the wage from $8 to $11, thereby providing licensees collectively with an increase in economic rent of *abce* and creating an efficiency loss of *gcf.*

in this occupation. These 14,000 workers see 7,000 licenses, and those who get the license receive increases in economic rent of $3 for every hour worked. As a consequence, the government's action *raises* the total rent *to those employed* by $21,000. This can be determined by noting that the total rent was area *Saf* prior to the licensing. Following licensing, the total economic rent increases to *Sbcg.* Thus, the *gain* in rent is *abce*—the shaded area in the figure—and the loss of rent to the workers displaced by the licensing is area *gef.*

Close inspection of Figure 13-7 reveals that occupational licensure of a type that restricts labor supply creates an efficiency loss for society, in this case, triangle *gcf.* The 3,000 additional employees who would have been employed in this occupation would contribute more to the value of society's output in this employment (as shown by segment *cf* of the demand curve) than in their most productive alternative uses of time (as shown by segment *gf* of the supply curve). Additionally, the true efficiency loss to society may be greater than area *gcf.* To secure the licensing law and thus the added economic rent, this particular occupational group most likely had to spend large amounts for political lobbying, public relations advertising, and other activities. From society's perspective, these expenditures diverted resources away from potentially higher-valued uses, adding to the overall efficiency cost of the occupational licensing.

To summarize: Occupational licensure of the type restricting labor supply increases the market wage, confers economic rent to licensees, and causes economic inefficiency. We might add that it is possible that the competition for the limited number of licenses will cause the new licensees to expend dollars in an amount equal to the expected rents.
13-4 Thus, those who are automatically granted licenses at the time the law is passed and those who train potential licensees will be the major beneficiaries of the law.[31]

Tariffs, Quotas, and Domestic Content Rules

Collectively, tariffs, quotas, and domestic content rules provide a second example of governmental provision of economic rent to groups of workers. *Tariffs* are excise duties on imported products; *import quotas* are limits on the quantity or total value of imports; and *domestic content rules* are requirements that a specified portion of imported products contain domestically produced or domestically assembled components. These laws and regulations tend to increase the prices of foreign goods, raise the sales of the competing "protected" domestic products, and increase the derived demand for the U.S. workers who help produce the domestic goods. Assuming a competitive labor market in which there is a normal upward-sloping labor supply curve, the increased domestic demand for labor increases the equilibrium wage and employment. If the labor market is imperfectly competitive, the increase in labor demand enhances the bargaining position of the union and increases the probability that the union-negotiated wage will rise. It is therefore perfectly understandable why some U.S. unions—for example, the United Steelworkers and the United Auto Workers—strongly support tariffs, quotas, and domestic content rules. Quite simply, these laws increase economic rent for domestic workers at the expense of foreign producers and domestic consumers.

It is a fairly simple matter to portray this gain in economic rent graphically. Figure 13-8 depicts an initial equilibrium wage of \$10 per hour at which firms hire Q_1 workers. The tariff, import quota, or domestic content law increases the derived demand for labor from D to D_1. The increase in labor demand raises the equilibrium wage from \$10 to \$12 an hour and causes the level of employment to rise to Q_2. Prior to the trade restriction, the total economic rent to workers was *abf.* After the law, it is *ace.* The workers in this market thus collectively gain an increase in economic rent equal to the shaded area *bcef.*

CHAPTER SUMMARY

1 Labor relations laws and regulations have influenced the growth of both private- and public-sector unionism in the United States. To the extent that union membership and union bargaining power are positively correlated, labor law influences the determination of wages and employment in labor markets.

[31]Existing empirical evidence is consistent with these hypotheses. Kleiner and Krudle, using data on incoming air force personnel, report that states with tougher licensing requirements for dentists do not have better dental health. However, prices for dental services are higher in states with stricter licensing requirements due to competition being reduced. See Morris M. Kleiner and Robert T. Krudle, "Does Regulation Improve Outputs and Increase Prices? The Case of Dentistry," National Bureau of Economic Research Working Paper No. 5869, January 1997. For a study finding that stricter licensing requirements deter entry into the dental profession, see Morris M. Kleiner and Robert T. Krudle, "Do Tougher Licensing Requirements Limit Occupational Entry? The Case of Dentistry," National Bureau of Economic Research Working Paper No. 3984, January 1992. For empirical evidence that more restrictive state licensing laws reduce immigration and, as a consequence, raise economic rent to incumbents within various occupations, see Morris M. Kleiner, Robert S. Gay, and Karen Greene, "Barriers to Labor Migration: The Case of Occupational Licensing," *Industrial Relations,* Fall 1982, pp. 383–391.

13-4 World of Work

TURF WARS*

Occupational licensing determines who can and who cannot legally provide certain labor services. It is only natural, therefore, that groups of people who are currently licensed oppose allowing closely related unlicensed groups to perform similar work. Conversely, it is understandable why occupational groups whose work is closely related to higher-paying groups would like to perform the licensed tasks. Such is the stuff of occupational turf wars.

Two recent turf battles, both involving licensing, match architects against interior designers and psychiatrists against psychologists. The work of architects and interior designers is converging and, in some cases, overlapping in designing offices, stores, and other interior spaces. Interior designers now specify fabrics and finishes, plan lighting and acoustical systems, arrange fire-code compliance, and manage interior projects. This growing role of interior designers has encouraged the American Association of Interior Designers to campaign for state licensing. Such licensing would specify qualifications and standards and require prospective interior designers to pass a written examination. The association claims that this licensing is needed to protect the public from the many charlatans who now claim to be interior designers. Skeptics say that the hidden goal is to limit supply in this occupation.

Licensing of interior designers has met with legislative resistance, partly because it is vigorously opposed by architects. Architects argue that interior designers are seeking to further invade the domain of architecture, without having the extensive training of these professionals. They also contend that state licensing laws would prevent them from practicing interior design, a growing part of their business.

A second recent turf battle involves psychiatrists and psychologists. Psychiatrists are licensed medical doctors who treat mental illness. Psychologists also treat mental problems but do not have medical training and cannot prescribe medication. Because of the success of new prescription drugs in treating mental illness, many psychologists advocate establishing training programs that would give them the necessary pharmaceutical expertise to prescribe medication.

The American Psychiatric Association and the American Medical Association are strongly opposed to this idea. Psychiatrists contend that diagnosing mental illness and prescribing brain-altering drugs are sophisticated services requiring a medical degree. Such degrees ensure intensive training in anatomy, physiology, and biochemistry, as well as in pharmacology. Also, the medical degree requires extensive clinical training.

Psychologists counter that many general medical practitioners currently treat such mental illnesses as anxiety and depression and are allowed to prescribe medication. Psychologists assert they are often better trained to diagnose and treat these mental disorders than are general medical practitioners. Also, some elected officials argue that giving psychologists the right to prescribe psychoactive medication would help relieve the shortage of psychiatrists in rural areas.

The final decisions in these occupational turf battles rest with state legislatures, which establish the licensing requirements.

*Based in part on Stephen MacDonald, "Building Battle: Interior Designers Pitted against Architects in Licensing Dispute," *Wall Street Journal,* May 6, 1987; and Sally Squires, "Psychiatry, Psychology in Turf War," *Minneapolis Star-Tribune,* August 6, 1990.

2 Labor law in general and specific provisions of labor law in particular influence union bargaining power—and therefore labor market results—independently of impacts on union membership.

3 The basic model of a competitive labor market predicts that an above-equilibrium minimum wage applied to all sections of the economy will reduce employment. The more elastic the supply and demand for labor, the greater the resulting unemployment.

4 The possibility that workers who lose jobs because of the minimum wage will find employment in sectors not covered by minimum-wage requirements, the presence of a shock effect, and the existence of nondiscriminating monopsony each explain why the negative employment and efficiency consequences predicted by the basic competitive model might not fully materialize.

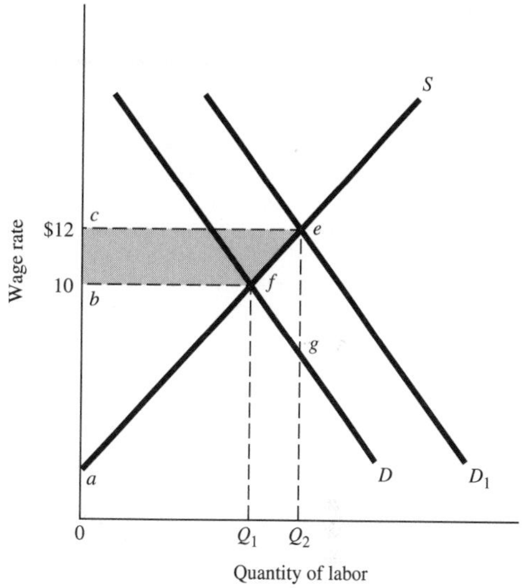

FIGURE 13-8 RENT PROVISION: TARIFFS, QUOTAS, AND DOMESTIC CONTENT LAWS
Import restrictions reduce labor demand in foreign nations and increase the demand for specific types of labor in the protected country. These restrictions, therefore, cause increases in wages in these specific labor markets. In this case the wage rises from $10 to $12, and economic rent increases by the amount of *bcef.*

5 Theoretically, a minimum wage can promote the economic self-interest of high-wage union labor by increasing the costs incurred by nonunion producers. By causing unemployment, it can also reduce the need to pay above-market-clearing efficiency wages where they otherwise would be needed to elicit full work effort.

6 Empirical evidence indicates that the minimum wage *(a)* reduces employment, particularly for teenagers; *(b)* increases unemployment of teenagers by less than the reduction in employment; *(c)* reduces the amount of on-the-job training offered to low-wage workers but encourages school attendance for those unable to find work; and *(d)* does not greatly alter the degree of family income inequality and extent of poverty.

7 A firm incurs both costs and benefits when it improves the safety of its workplace. A profit-maximizing firm will provide a level of job safety at which its marginal benefit and marginal cost of safety are equal.

8 If workers have full information about possible work hazards and accurately assess job risks, the profit-maximizing level of job safety will tend to be optimal from society's viewpoint. If information is incomplete and job risks are inaccurately assessed, then society's optimal level of job safety may be greater than the level willingly provided by profit-maximizing firms.

9 The Occupational Safety and Health Act imposed a set of workplace safety standards on individual firms. The act is controversial, and the debate over its provisions and methods of enforcement has been heightened by studies that present mixed findings on its effect on the number of work-related accidents.

10 Government affects wages and employment in specific occupations through its "rent provision" activities. Two examples are *(a)* occupational licensure of the kind that restricts labor supply; and *(b)* tariffs, import quotas, and domestic content laws, which increase labor demand for protected domestic workers.

TERMS AND CONCEPTS

discriminatory discharge
blacklists
yellow-dog contracts
lockouts
strikebreakers
injunctions
Norris–LaGuardia Act of 1932
Wagner Act of 1935
Taft–Hartley Act of 1947
Landrum–Griffin Act of 1959
secondary boycotts
hot-cargo clauses
Fair Labor Standards Act of 1938
minimum wage
shock effect
Occupational Safety and Health Act of 1970
marginal cost of job safety
marginal benefit from job safety
economic rent
rent seekers and rent providers

QUESTIONS AND STUDY SUGGESTIONS

1 Explain each of the following statements:
   a "The Wagner Act of 1935 reduced the costs of providing union services and thereby increased the number of union members."
   b "The Wagner Act of 1935 increased the demand for union services by increasing the relative bargaining power of unions. This increased union membership."

2 Use the Chamberlain bargaining power model [equations (10-1) and (10-2)] to predict the impact of each of the following hypothetical changes in labor law on union bargaining power:
   a Legalization of all forms of secondary boycotts
   b Legislation making it an "unfair labor practice" to employ strikebreakers
   c Repeal of the prohibition against strikes by federal employees

3 Show graphically how an increase in the minimum wage might affect employment in *(a)* a competitive labor market and *(b)* a labor market characterized by monopsony.

4 Explain how an increase in the minimum wage could:
   a Reduce teenage employment but leave the teenage unemployment rate unaffected
   b Reduce one type of investment in human capital but increase another
   c Reduce above-market-clearing efficiency wages paid to some workers in the economy

5 Why are most labor unions—whose constituents receive wages substantially above the minimum wage—strong supporters of the minimum wage? Why might unions composed of skilled workers who are *pure complements in production* (Chapter 5) with raw materials produced by low-skilled workers *oppose* a large increase in the minimum wage?

6 Evaluate this statement: "Profit-maximizing firms lack an incentive to provide job safety, and consequently, the federal government must intervene legislatively to protect workers against the unsafe working conditions that will surely result."

7 Answer these questions on the basis of the following information for a competitive firm.
   a What is the profit-maximizing level of job safety as viewed by the firm? Explain.
   b Assume that information is perfect and that workers accurately assess personal risk. What is the optimal level of job safety from society's perspective? Explain.
   c Suppose that government imposed a minimum safety standard of 5 units. Why would the firm object? Speculate as to why some workers might object.
   d Suppose that new technology reduced this firm's marginal cost data to \$1, \$2, \$3, \$4, and \$5 for the first through fifth units of safety. How would this firm respond?

Marginal benefit from safety	Amount of safety provided	Marginal cost of safety
$60	1	$1
40	2	3
20	3	6
10	4	9
6	5	15

8 How might each of the following be interpreted to be an example of "rent provision" by government?

a State laws that require out-of-state big-game hunters to be accompanied by one of a limited number of licensed in-state hunting guides

b An increase in the minimum wage that increases the likelihood that firms will hire skilled unionized labor rather than unskilled labor.

c A state law that requires that graduates of dental schools pass a stringent examination, established by a panel of dentists, in order to practice dentistry.

SELECTED REFERENCES

Brown, Charles: "Minimum Wage Laws: Are They Overrated?" *Journal of Economic Perspectives,* Summer 1988, pp. 133–145.

Brown, Charles, Curtis Gilroy, and Andrew Kohen: "The Effect of the Minimum Wage on Employment and Unemployment," *Journal of Economic Literature,* June 1982, pp. 487–528.

Card, David, and Alan B. Krueger: *Myth and Measurement: The New Economics of the Minimum Wage* (Princeton, NJ: Princeton University Press, 1995).

Levitan, Sar, Peter E. Carlson, and Isaac Shapiro: *Protecting American Workers: An Assessment of Government Programs* (Washington, DC: Bureau of National Affairs, 1986).

Petersen, H. Craig: *Business and Government,* 4th ed. (New York: Harper & Row, 1993), chap. 18.

Rottenberg, Simon (ed.): *Occupational Licensure and Regulation* (Washington, DC: American Enterprise Institute for Public Policy Research, 1980).

Smith, Robert S.: "Have OSHA and Workers' Compensation Made the Workplace Safer?" in David Lewin, Olivia S. Mitchell, and Peter Sherer (eds.), *Research Frontiers in Industrial Relations and Human Resources* (Madison, WI: Industrial Relations Research Association, 1992), pp. 557–586.

Taylor, B. J., and F. Witney: *Labor Relations Law,* 6th ed. (Englewood Cliffs, NJ: Prentice-Hall, Inc., 1992).

Viscusi, W. Kip: *Risk by Choice: Regulating Health and Safety in the Workplace* (Cambridge, MA: Harvard University Press, 1983).

CHAPTER 14

THEORIES OF LABOR MARKET DISCRIMINATION

Few would seriously question the assertion that discrimination based on race, gender, religion, and ethnic background is a fact of American life. Abundant statistical evidence exists to suggest discrimination: Comparison of blacks and whites and women and men reveal substantial differences in earnings, unemployment rates, allocations among various occupations, and accumulations of human capital. Also, anecdotal evidence of discrimination can be found in newspaper headlines on an almost daily basis: "Court upholds racial discrimination suit against grocery chain"; "Few jobs for black teenagers"; "Minorities excluded from top executive positions"; "Wage gap for women persists"; "Sexual harassment in the workplace."

Because of the importance and complexity of labor market discrimination as an institutional feature of labor markets, we will devote two chapters to this subject. In the present chapter we will define discrimination, delineate the various types of discrimination, and then explain four important labor market models of discrimination. In Chapter 15 we turn to the outcomes of labor market discrimination; there, we present and assess evidence of discrimination against women and racial minorities. We also examine antidiscrimination policies, note some of the controversies they have generated, and consider their effectiveness.

Several caveats must be made explicit at the outset. Discrimination is complex, multifaceted, and deeply ingrained in behavior. It is also difficult to measure or quantify. Furthermore, any reasonably complete explanation of discrimination must be interdisciplinary; economic analysis can contribute only insights rather than a full-blown explanation of the phenomenon. In fact, we will find a number of contrasting explanations of discrimination within economics, and these frequently imply different policy prescriptions. Bluntly stated, discrimination constitutes an untidy area of study that is characterized by controversy and a lack of consensus. Finally, to achieve a degree of focus in our discussion, discrimination based on gender (sex) and race is emphasized in this chapter. But keep in mind that age, ethnic origin, religious background, physical disability, and sexual orientation are equally important bases for discrimination and are neglected here only for the sake of brevity.

14-1

DISCRIMINATION AND ITS DIMENSIONS

Discrimination is easier to define than to discern. *Economic discrimination exists when female or minority workers—who have the same abilities, education, training, and experience as white male workers—are accorded inferior treatment with respect to hiring, occupational access, promotion, wage rate, or working conditions.* Note that

14-1 **World of Work**

SEXUAL HARASSMENT GLOBAL PROBLEM*

WASHINGTON (AP)—Sexual harassment plagues working women throughout the industrialized world and many countries lack the legal means to combat the problem, the International Labor Organization said Monday.

The ILO, in a 300-page report, said only seven of 23 nations surveyed—Australia, Canada, France, New Zealand, Spain, Sweden and the United States—have statutes that specifically refer to or define sexual harassment.

Studies cited by the report said that sexual harassment caused 6 percent to 8 percent of working women to change their jobs and that 15 percent to 30 percent have experienced serious problems such as unwanted touching, offensive sexual commentary and unwelcome requests for sexual intercourse.

"Sexual harassment is one of the most offensive and demeaning experiences an employee can suffer. For those who are its victims, it often produces feelings of revulsion, violation, disgust, anger and powerlessness," Michael Rubenstein, a consultant on sexual harassment to the European Community, writes in the report.

Among the findings:

- The term "sexual harassment" originated in the United States and U.S. federal courts were the first to recognize it, in 1975, as a prohibited form of sexual discrimination.

  ILO civil rights lawyer Constance Thomas said it's her belief that, "in general, American women are fairly intolerant and perhaps more strenuous in their perseverance" in pursuing harassment charges.
- In Austria, a 1986 survey said that 30.5 percent of women reported serious incidents of sexual harassment.
- In Czechoslovakia, a survey said that 17.5 percent of women said they had been harassed physically, 35.8 percent verbally. No court cases have dealt with the issue.
- In Denmark, 11 percent of women questioned in 1991 said they had experienced sexual harassment at work and 8 percent said they had lost their jobs as a consequence.
- In Germany, 6 percent of women in a 1990 survey said they had resigned from at least one job as a result of being sexually harassed.
- Surveys said that 21 percent of French women, 58 percent of Dutch women and 74 percent of British women said they had experienced sexual harassment at work, and that 27 percent of Spanish women said they had encountered strong verbal advances and unwanted touching.

*"Sex Harassment Global Problem," *Lincoln Star* (Lincoln, Nebraska), December 1, 1992. Reprinted by permission.

discrimination may also take the form of unequal access to formal education, apprenticeships, or on-the-job training programs, each of which enhances one's stock of human capital (Chapter 4).

Types of Discrimination

This definition is sufficiently important to merit elaboration. Implicit in our definition, labor market discrimination can be classified into four general types.[1]

1 ***Wage discrimination*** means that female (black) workers are paid less than male (white) workers for doing the same work. More technically, wage discrimination exists when wage differentials are based on considerations other than productivity differentials.

2 ***Employment discrimination*** occurs when, other things being equal, blacks and women bear a disproportionate share of the burden of unemployment. Blacks in particular have long faced the problem of being the last hired and the first fired.

3 ***Occupational*** or ***job discrimination*** means that females (blacks) have been arbitrarily restricted or prohibited from entering certain occupations, even though they are as capable as male (white) workers of performing those jobs, and are conversely "crowded" into other occupations for which they are frequently overqualified.

4 ***Human capital discrimination*** is in evidence when females (blacks) have less access to productivity-increasing opportunities such as formal schooling or on-the-job training. Blacks in particular often obtain less education and education of inferior quality compared to whites.

The first three categories of discrimination are frequently designated as *postmarket* (also "current" or "direct") *discrimination* because they are encountered *after* the individual has entered the labor market. Similarly, the fourth category is called *premarket* (also "past" or "indirect") *discrimination* because it occurs *before* the individual seeks employment.[2]

These distinctions among the various kinds of discrimination are useful for at least two reasons. First, the significance of the various kinds of discrimination varies among blacks and women. Generally speaking, blacks are subject to a much greater degree of employment discrimination than women. And although blacks and women are both subject to occupational segregation, this form of discrimination is especially relevant with respect to women. Second, awareness of the various forms of discrimination helps one understand how discrimination may be self-reinforcing and therefore perpetuate itself. For example, if blacks and women anticipate that occupational discrimination

[1]We are concerned here only with those kinds of discrimination that are relevant to the labor market. While discrimination in access to housing or consumer credit is important, it is less germane to the subject matter of labor economics.

[2]On-the-job training poses a bit of a problem for our pre- and postmarket classification. While such training is a human capital investment, people do not have access to it until they have entered the labor market. A very useful and more detailed taxonomy of discrimination is presented by Brian Chiplin and Peter J. Sloane, "Sexual Discrimination in the Labor Market," in Alice H. Amsden (ed.), *The Economics of Women and Work* (New York: St. Martin's Press, 1980), p. 285.

will confine them to low-wage, dead-end jobs or that they will be exposed to frequent and prolonged periods of unemployment, they will rationally choose to invest less than otherwise in schooling (Chapter 4). That is, the expectation of postmarket discrimination will reduce the rate of return expected on investments in education and training, which will aggravate the premarket condition of inadequate preparation for many jobs.

14-2

Theories of Labor Market Discrimination

As indicated earlier, there is no generally accepted economic theory of discrimination. There are undoubtedly a variety of reasons for this. First, the interest of economists in explaining the phenomenon of discrimination is relatively recent. The pioneering book in the field, Gary Becker's *The Economics of Discrimination,*[3] was published in 1957. Second, discrimination may assume a variety of guises and take different forms for different groups. For example, blacks traditionally have been at a substantial disadvantage in obtaining employment, while women have had access to jobs but only in a restricted number of occupations. Finally, we noted at the outset that the roots of

[3]Chicago: University of Chicago Press, 1957.

14-2 World of Work

IT PAYS TO BE GOOD-LOOKING

Better-looking men and women earn more than their less beautiful counterparts. Using data from three labor market surveys in which the interviewer rated the respondent on physical looks, Hamermesh and Biddle report that plain people earn 5 to 10 percent less than average-looking people.* Workers with above-average looks earn a 5 percent premium relative to average-looking people. About one-half of the men and women were rated average looking, while one-third were rated as above average in looks. The effects of appearance are somewhat stronger for men than women.

Why does beauty affect worker's earnings? Hamermesh and Biddle find that attractive people enter occupations in which appearance may be productive (such as a model or flight attendant). However, good looks increase the earnings of individuals even in jobs in which they should not affect productivity (such as a janitor). This result suggests employers discriminate in favor of better-looking individuals.

Beauty has other effects as well, particularly for women. Hamermesh and Biddle find that less-attractive women are more likely not to be in the labor force and their spouses are more likely to be less educated. They did not find such an effect for men. Consistent with these results, Averett and Korenman report that obese women have lower family incomes than women who have a normal weight-to-height ratio.† They find that obese women, like the women in the Hamermesh and Biddle study, have lower earnings, all else being equal. However, the lower marriage rate and husband's earnings of obese women account for 50 to 95 percent of their lower economic status. Averett and Korenman's results were more mixed and weaker for men.

*Daniel S. Hamermesh and Jeff E. Biddle. "Beauty and the Labor Market," *American Economic Review,* December 1994, pp. 1174–1194. For a study on the effects of beauty for lawyers, see Jeff E. Biddle and Daniel S. Hamermesh, "Beauty, Productivity and Discrimination: Lawyers' Looks and Lucre," *Journal of Labor Economics,* January 1998, pp. 172–201. For an analysis reporting similar findings for MBAs, see Irene H. Frieze, Josephine E. Olson, and June R. Russell, "Attractiveness and Income for Men and Women," *Journal of Applied Social Psychology,* July 1991, pp. 1039–1057.

†Susan Averett and Sanders Korenman, "The Economic Reality of the Beauty Myth," *Journal of Human Resources,* Spring 1996, pp. 304–330.

discrimination are diverse and complex, ranging beyond the boundaries of economics. A discipline such as economics, which predicates its analysis on rational behavior, may be at a severe disadvantage in explaining a phenomenon that many regard as irrational. Nevertheless, economists have contributed important analytical and empirical work on the problem of discrimination, and our immediate goal is to summarize several of the more prominent theories: (1) the taste-for-discrimination model, (2) the monopsony or market power model, (3) statistical discrimination, and (4) the crowding model. You should be aware that, for the most part, the models to be discussed apply to all types of discrimination. For example, although we will present the market power model in terms of sexual discrimination, the model is also useful in explaining racial discrimination.

TASTE-FOR-DISCRIMINATION MODEL

Becker's ***taste-for-discrimination model*** envisions discrimination as a preference or "taste" for which the discriminator is willing to pay. Becker uses an analogy based on the theory of international trade. It is well known that a nation can maximize its total output by engaging in free trade based on the principle of comparative advantage. But in fact nations obstruct trade through the use of tariffs, quotas, and a variety of other techniques. Nations are apparently willing to sacrifice economic efficiency to have certain goods produced domestically rather than imported. Society seems to have a preference or taste for domestically produced goods, even though it must pay the "price" of a diminished national income in exercising that taste. Similarly, Becker argues that, unfortunately, society also has a taste for discrimination and is willing to forgo productive efficiency—and, therefore, maximum output and profits—to exercise its prejudices. The price—or opportunity cost—of racial discrimination alone may be on the order of 4 percent of the domestic output.[4]

Becker's theory is general since it can be applied to, say, white (male) workers who discriminate against black (female) workers, *or* white consumers who discriminate against firms that employ black workers or salespersons, *or* white employers who discriminate against black workers. The latter aspect of this theory—white employers who exercise their taste for discrimination against black workers—is the most relevant to our discussion, and therefore, we will concentrate on it. Why do employers discriminate? Employers' tastes for discrimination are based on the idea that they and their employees want to maintain a physical or "social" distance from certain groups; for example, that white employers and their workers do not want to associate with black workers. These employers may then choose not to hire black workers because they and their employees do not want to work alongside them.

The Discrimination Coefficient

Assuming that black and white (male and female) workers are equally productive, a nondiscriminating employer will regard them as perfect substitutes and will hire them

[4]Joint Economic Committee, *The Cost of Racial Discrimination* (Washington, DC: U.S. Government Printing Office, 1980), pp. 2–5.

at random if their wages are the same. But if a white employer is prejudiced against blacks, then the situation is significantly altered. According to Becker, prejudiced white employers have "tastes for discrimination" and behave as if employing black workers imposed subjective or psychic costs on the employer. The strength of this psychic cost is reflected in a ***discrimination coefficient*** *d,* which can be measured in monetary terms. Given that the employer is *not* prejudiced against other whites, the cost of employing a white worker will simply be the wage rate W_w. However, the cost of employing a black worker to a prejudiced employer will be regarded as the black worker's wage W_b plus the monetary value of the discrimination coefficient—in other words, $W_b + d$. The prejudiced white employer will be indifferent as to hiring black and white workers when the total cost per worker is the same, that is, when $W_w = W_b + d$. It follows that our prejudiced white employer will hire blacks only if their wage rate is *below* that of whites. More precisely, for the prejudiced employer to employ blacks, their wage must be less than the wages of whites by the amount of the discrimination coefficient—in other words, $W_b = W_w - d$. For example, if we suppose that the going wage rate for whites is \$10 and that the monetary value of the psychic costs the employer attaches to hiring blacks is \$2 (that is, d = \$2), then that employer will be indifferent as to hiring blacks or whites only when the black wage is \$8 ($W_b = W_w - d$ or \$8 = \$10 − \$2).

It is apparent that the larger a white employer's taste for discrimination as reflected in the value of *d,* the larger the disparity between white wages and the wages at which blacks will be hired. As noted earlier, for a nondiscriminating or "color-blind" employer ($d = 0$), equally productive blacks and whites will be hired randomly if their wage rates are the same. At the other extreme, the white employer whose *d* was infinity would refuse to hire blacks at any wage rate, no matter how low that wage was in comparison to white wages. But note carefully that we are *not* saying prejudiced employers will refuse to hire blacks under all conditions. Thus, in our initial example where the monetary value of *d* was \$2, the white employer would prefer to hire blacks if the actual white–black wage gap exceeded \$2. For example, if in fact whites could be hired at \$10 and equally productive blacks at only \$7.50 per hour, the employer would choose to hire blacks. The prejudiced employer would be willing to pay a wage premium of up to \$2 per hour for whites in order to satisfy his or her taste for discrimination, but no more than that. At the \$2.50 differential, the employer would choose to hire blacks. Conversely, if whites could be hired at \$10 and blacks at \$8.50, whites would be hired. The employer would be willing to pay a wage premium of up to \$2 for whites; having to pay only a \$1.50 premium means that hiring whites is a "bargain."

Demand and Supply Interpretation

Modified demand and supply analysis is useful in deepening our understanding of Becker's model and, more specifically, in explaining the prevailing wage differential between black and white workers. In Figure 14-1 we assume a competitive labor market for some particular occupation. The vertical axis differs from the usual labor market representation in that it measures the ratio of black to white wages W_b/W_w, and the horizontal axis shows the quantity of *black* workers. The quantity of white workers and

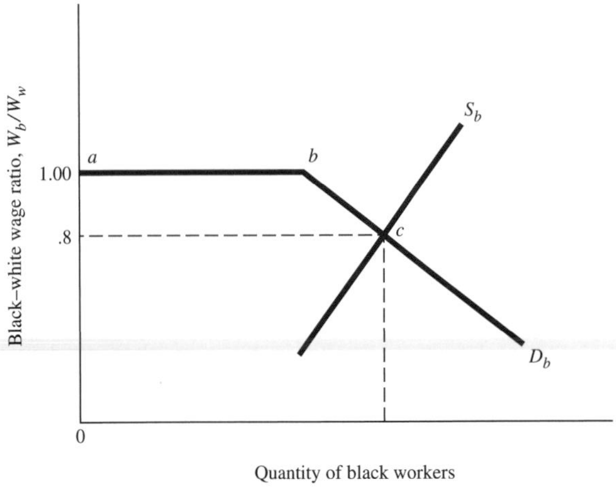

FIGURE 14-1 WAGE DISCRIMINATION IN THE LABOR MARKET
The D_b and S_b curves show the demand for and the supply of black labor. Their intersection determines the black–white wage ratio and the number of black workers employed.

their wage rate are assumed to be given. The kinked demand curve for black workers D_b is constructed by arraying white employers left to right from lowest to highest discrimination coefficients. Thus, we find that the horizontal portion *(ab)* of the demand curve where W_b/W_w equals 1.00 reflects nondiscriminating white employers—those whose *d*'s are zero. These employers do not discriminate between equally productive black and white workers so long as the wage rates of the two groups are equal. The downward-sloping portion of the demand curve (bD_b) reflects discriminating employers, whose *d*'s increase as we move down that segment. On this segment of the curve, W_b/W_w is less than 1.00 and diminishes as we move to the southeast.

To this demand curve we now add the supply of black labor. Not surprisingly, this curve is upward-sloping; the quantity of black labor supplied increases as W_b/W_w increases. The intersection of the two curves establishes the actual W_b/W_w ratio—that is, the extent of wage discrimination—and the number of black workers who will be employed in this occupation. Using the numbers from our initial illustration, let's assume that the actual wage rates being paid to blacks and whites are \$8 and \$10, respectively, so that W_b/W_w is 8/10 or .8. This model suggests that nondiscriminating white employers (segment *ab* of the demand curve) and those whose *d*'s are less than \$2 (segment *bc*) will hire all black workers in this occupation; those shown by the cD_b range of the demand curve have *d*'s greater than \$2 and will hire only whites.

Two Generalizations

Two generalizations concerning the size of the black–white wage differential emerge from the taste-for-discrimination model.

1 A change in the shape or location of the demand curve will alter the W_b/W_w ratio. For example, suppose that a change in societal attitudes or antidiscrimination legislation has the effect of reducing the discrimination coefficient of employers. This will extend the horizontal portion of the demand curve further to the right *and* reduce the slope of the remaining downward-sloping segment. Given the supply of black labor, the effect will be to raise the equilibrium W_b/W_w ratio, that is, to reduce the discriminatory wage differential and increase the employment of black workers. For example, the equilibrium W_b/W_w ratio in Figure 14-1 may rise from .8 to, say, .85.

2 The size of the discriminatory wage differential varies directly with the supply of minority (black) workers. If the supply of black labor in Figure 14-1 were so small as to intersect the horizontal segment of the demand curve, there would be no discriminatory wage differential. If the supply of black labor increased to the position shown on the diagram, the differential would be .8 or 8/10. A further increase in supply will lower the W_b/W_w ratio, indicating a widening of the wage differential.

These two generalizations raise an interesting question: Is the greater observed wage differential between black and white workers in the South as compared to the North the consequence of a stronger taste for discrimination in the South, that is, a further leftward demand curve? Or, alternatively, is it the result of a greater relative supply of black workers in the South? In either case, of course, the *source* of the discrimination is white prejudice, not the size of the black labor force.

Gainers, Losers, and the Persistence of Discrimination

Becker's taste-for-discrimination model indicates that white workers will gain from discrimination because their wage rates will be higher than otherwise. The reason for this is that just as import restrictions reduce foreign competition to the benefit of domestic producers, discrimination by employers protects white workers from the competition of black workers. Blacks, of course, are losers in that they receive lower wages because of discrimination. Finally, employers who discriminate may injure themselves since they will experience higher costs than necessary. Let's explain why this is so.

Returning to Figure 14-1 once again, let's further assume that all of the employers arrayed on the demand curve are producing the same product. All of the non- or less-discriminating employers on the demand curve to the left of the intersection point will find themselves with a competitive cost advantage relative to the more-discriminating employers on the segment of the demand curve to the right of the intersection. To illustrate: In equilibrium, the W_b/W_w ratio is .8, that is, whites are paid \$10 and blacks only \$8. Remembering the assumption that blacks and whites are equally productive workers, a nondiscriminating employer on the horizontal segment would hire a black labor force at \$8 per hour, while a discriminator far down the demand curve would hire all white workers at \$10 per hour. The discriminating employer will incur higher wage costs than the nondiscriminating employer. Therefore, nondiscriminating firms will have lower average total costs and product prices than discriminating producers.

One of the important implications of Becker's model is that competitive market forces will cause discrimination to diminish and disappear over time because the lower-cost nondiscriminating firms can gain a larger share of the market at the expense of less-efficient discriminating firms. In fact, in a highly competitive product market, only nondiscriminating firms (least-cost producers) will survive; discriminators will have average total costs that will exceed product price. Thus, Becker's theory is consistent with a "conservative" or laissez-faire position toward discrimination; that is, in the long run, the operation of the competitive market will resolve the problem of discrimination, and therefore, the only governmental action required is that which promotes free occupational choice.[5] Discriminating employers will either have to become nondiscriminators or be driven out of business.

A fundamental criticism of this perspective is that, in fact, progress in eliminating discrimination has been modest. The functioning of the market has *not* eliminated employers' prejudices. Discrimination based on both race and gender has persisted decade after decade. Thus, alternative models have been proposed to explain why discrimination has continued.

QUICK REVIEW 14-1

- Labor market discrimination occurs when workers who have the same abilities, education, training, and experience as other workers receive inferior treatment with respect to hiring, occupational access, promotion, or wages.
- Labor market discrimination can be classified as either *(a)* wage discrimination, *(b)* employment discrimination, *(c)* occupational or job discrimination, or *(d)* human capital discrimination.
- Becker's taste-for-discrimination model views discrimination as a preference or "taste" for which the discriminator is willing to pay; the greater this preference, the larger is Becker's discrimination coefficient.
- Employers with high discrimination coefficients will incur higher labor costs than nondiscriminating employers; thus, the nondiscriminators will have a cost advantage in competing with discriminators in the marketplace.

Your Turn: Suppose that the hourly market wage for specific white workers is $16, while the wage for equally productive black workers is $12. What can be inferred about the dollar value of the discrimination coefficient for an employer that hires all white workers under these circumstances? All black workers? (Answers: See page 627.)

MARKET POWER: THE MONOPSONY MODEL

A second discrimination theory rests on the monopsonistic or market power of employers. You may recall from your introductory economics course that a monopolistic

[5]That government will be unsuccessful in eliminating discrimination is the major theme of Thomas Sowell, *Markets and Minorities* (New York: Basic Books, Inc., 1981). See also William A. Darity, Jr., and Rhonda M. Williams, "Peddlers Forever? Culture, Competition, and Discrimination," *American Economic Review,* May 1985, pp. 256–261.

seller of a product may be able to enhance profits by practicing price discrimination. Specifically, the seller will find it profitable to charge buyers whose demand for a given product is less elastic a higher price than those whose demand is more elastic. The monopsony or ***market power model*** of discrimination is similar in that it suggests that an employer may find it profitable to practice wage discrimination, that is, to pay different wage rates to equally productive males and females (whites and blacks). As we will see momentarily, with wage discrimination, the lower wage will be paid to those workers whose labor supply curve is less elastic. In this model, the employer need not be prejudiced; a white male employer need not dislike blacks or females as employees or on any other grounds. Wage discrimination simply "pays" in terms of maximizing profits.

The Model

A disaggregation of the simple monopsony model presented in Chapter 6 to allow for payment of differing wages to different groups reveals the essence of this theory. Figure 14-2, then, is simply one version of a "discriminating monopsony" model.[6] In graph (a) we have reproduced the monopsony model of Figure 6-7. The firm's total labor

[6]The discussion here is based on Janice Fanning Madden, "Discrimination—A Manifestation of Male Market Power?" in Cynthia B. Lloyd, editor, "Sex, Discrimination and the Division of Labor," (New York: Columbia University Press, 1975).

FIGURE 14-2 THE MARKET POWER (MONOPSONY) MODEL OF DISCRIMINATION
Under monopsony, the disaggregation of total labor supply (a) on the basis of gender (b and c) will result in lower wage rates for women, provided the labor supply curve for women is less elastic than for men. In this case, the monopsonist will increase profits by hiring 9 workers *(Q_t)*, of whom 3 *(Q_f)* are females and 6 *(Q_m)* are males. Projecting these quantities off the female and male labor supply curves S_t and S_m, we determine that the wage rates of women and men are \$6 and \$10, respectively.

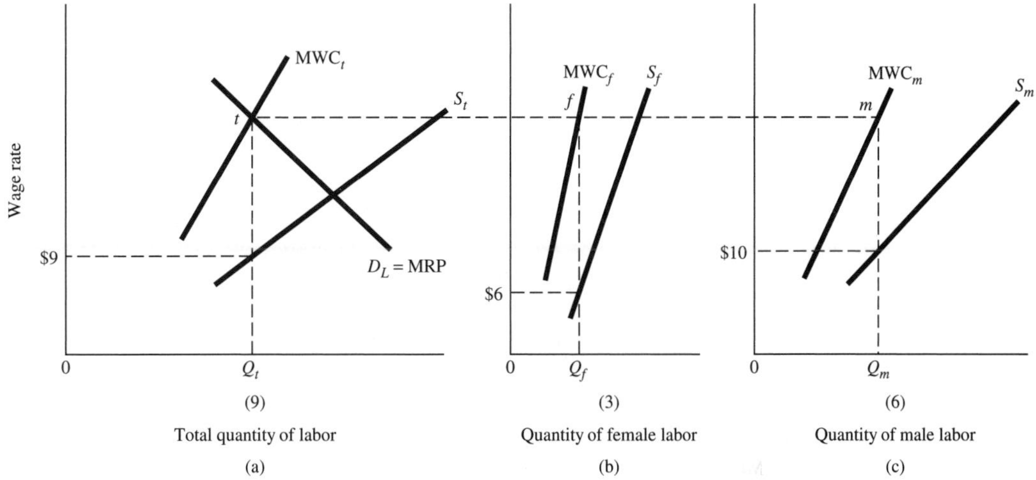

supply is represented by S_t, the associated marginal wage cost curve is MWC_t, and D_L is the demand for labor. Note that equilibrium is at point *t,* where nine workers are employed and the wage rate is \$9. Now observe in graphs (b) and (c) that we have disaggregated the monopsonist's labor supply on the basis of gender. In graph (b) the supply and marginal wage cost curves of female workers are S_f and MWC_f. Similarly, S_m and MWC_m in graph (c) show these same curves for male workers. The labor supply curve for women is purposely drawn to be less elastic than that for men.

By extending the horizontal (dashed) line rightward from equilibrium point *t* in graph (a), we can show how total employment will be divided among men and women. That is, the dashed line reflects the MRP associated with the profit-maximizing total quantity of labor. Its intersection with MWC_f and MWC_m tells us how many female and male workers, respectively, it is profitable to employ. Specifically, by dropping vertical (dashed) lines from equilibrium points *f* and *m,* we find that the firm will employ three women and six men. The wage rates paid to women and men are determined where the vertical lines intersect the female and male labor supply curves S_f and S_m. The discriminating monopsonist will pay rates equal to the supply prices of Q_f (three) females and Q_m (six) males. Here, we find that women are paid a \$6 wage and men a \$10 wage.

Implications

The implications of this model are both straightforward and interesting. First, the male wage rate is higher than it would be without sex discrimination (\$10 as compared to \$9). Second, the female wage of \$6 is lower than both the male wage (\$10) and the wage that would prevail without sex discrimination (\$9). Third, the profits of the firm have increased. In discriminating, the firm hires the same number of workers and, because female and male workers are assumed to be equally productive, realizes the same total output and total revenue. However, discrimination reduces total wage costs from \$81 (= 9 × \$9) to \$78 [= (3 × \$6) + (6 × \$10)]. Unlike the Becker model, this model shows that it is profitable to discriminate. A fourth and closely related point is that in contrast to Becker's model, the monopsonist need not be malicious, that is, unfavorably disposed toward women. Becker's employer pays to exercise his or her prejudices; the monopsonistic employer discriminates because it enhances profits. Fifth, assuming competition in the product market, if this firm does *not* engage in sex discrimination while its rivals do, it will have higher production costs and will ultimately be driven out of business by its discriminating rivals. Note that circumstances are precisely the reverse of those implicit in Becker's taste-for-discrimination model. In Becker's model, nondiscriminators would drive discriminators out of business. In the monopsonist model, discriminators would drive nondiscriminators from the market. Finally, a corollary of our fifth point is that while the taste-for-discrimination model implies that the pursuit of profits by employers will reduce discrimination over time, the market power model suggests that there is no necessary reason market forces would cause discrimination to diminish. The monopsony model implies that public policy action is required to deal with discrimination.

Elasticity Assumptions

As noted, these outcomes depend on a situation in which the female labor supply curve S_f is less elastic than the male supply curve S_m. This might be the case for two reasons. First, some women are less mobile than men, both geographically and occupationally. If a woman's husband has a job in a particular locality, she may be unwilling to accept a job in another locality. Similarly, because of the prevalence of occupational segregation, women do not have access to as wide a range of occupations and job opportunities as men do. (Note that occupational mobility often involves geographic mobility as well.) Because some women have less geographic and occupational mobility, if wage rates in this particular market were, say, reduced, we would expect more males than females to leave this work for alternative jobs. Given these conditions, the conclusion might be that women are less responsive to wage changes than men; or, in technical terms, the supply curve of women is less elastic. Stated differently, more employment alternatives may exist for male workers than for female workers, making the supply curve of male workers more elastic. The end result would be that male workers would be paid more than equally productive female workers because the supply elasticity of female workers would be such that they would be willing to work for less.

A second reason for the less elastic supply curve for female workers has to do with unionization. Specifically, male workers are more likely to be unionized than female workers. While 16 percent of male wage and salary workers are unionized, only about 12 percent of such female workers belong to unions (Table 10-2). You may recall from Figure 6-10 that industrial unions establish a uniform wage that makes the labor supply curve perfectly elastic at that wage. The significance of this is that the union reduces the monopsonistic employer's ability to exploit workers. Thus, in firms where men are unionized and women are not, the labor supply of women will be less elastic than that of men, resulting in wage differentials that are unfavorable to women.[7]

Assessment

Some economists find the monopsony model of discrimination to be unpersuasive, particularly as it relates to married women. Specifically, the critical assumption that the female labor supply is less elastic than that for males can be questioned. Although the job and occupational mobility of women may be less than that of men, women may perceive work within the home to be a more relevant alternative than men. In our earlier illustration, while discrimination may limit the reallocation of women to other jobs when wage rates fall, it does not prevent relatively large numbers of women from becoming nonparticipants. Therefore, when the option of work within the home is included, the quantitative response of women to a wage change could well be as large as or larger than that of males. And, in fact, considerable empirical evidence exists to suggest that the supply responses of women to wage rate changes may be greater than those of men (Chapter 2).[8]

[7]It is a worthwhile exercise to reanalyze Figure 14-2(a) on the assumption that a union of male workers is able to establish a wage that is above $9.

[8]Mark R. Killingsworth, *Labor Supply* (Cambridge, England: Cambridge University Press, 1983), p. 102.

THEORY OF STATISTICAL DISCRIMINATION

Still another theory centers on the concept of ***statistical discrimination.***[9] By way of definition, we can say that statistical discrimination

> . . . occurs whenever an individual is judged on the basis of the average characteristics of the group, or groups, to which he or she belongs rather than upon his or her own personal characteristics. The judgments are correct, factual, and objective in the sense that the group actually has the characteristics that are ascribed to it, but the judgments are incorrect with respect to many individuals within the group.[10]

A commonplace non-labor market example of statistical discrimination involves automobile insurance. Insurance rates for teenage males are higher than those for teenage females. This rate differential is based on accumulated factual evidence indicating that, on the average, young males are more likely than females to be involved in accidents. However, many young male drivers are equally or less accident prone than the average of young females, and these males are discriminated against by having to pay higher insurance rates.

It is easy to understand how statistical discrimination would function in labor markets. Employers with job vacancies want to hire the most productive workers available to fill open positions. Thus, their personnel departments collect a variety of information concerning each job applicant: for example, an individual's age, education, and prior work experience. Employers supplement this information with scores on preemployment tests that they feel are helpful indicators of potential job performance. But two interrelated considerations pertain to this employee screening process. First, because it is very expensive to collect detailed information about each job applicant, only limited data are collected. Second, the limited information available to the employer from job application forms and test scores will *not* permit the employer to predict perfectly which of the job applicants will prove to be the most productive employees. As a consequence of these two considerations, it is common for employers to use "subjective" considerations such as race or gender or age in determining who is hired. In practicing statistical discrimination, the employer is not satisfying a taste for discrimination, but rather is using gender or race or age as a proxy for production-related attributes of workers that are not easily discernible. Gender, for example, may be used as a proxy for physical strength or job commitment.

To illustrate: An employer may assume that *on the average,* young married women are more likely to quit their jobs within, say 2 years after hire than males because they may become pregnant or their husband may take a job in a different locality. All other things being equal, when confronted with a married female and a male job applicant, the employer may hire the male. Similarly, when considering whether to employ a black or a white high school graduate whose age, work experience, and test scores are identical, the employer may hire the white youth because the employer knows that *on*

[9]See Edmund S. Phelps, "The Statistical Theory of Racism and Sexism," *American Economic Review,* September 1972, pp. 659–661; and Dennis J. Aigner and Glen G. Cain, "Statistical Theories of Discrimination in Labor Markets," *Industrial and Labor Relations Review,* January 1977, pp. 175–187.

[10]Lester Thurow, *Generating Inequality* (New York: Basic Books, Inc., 1975), p. 172. This entire section draws on chapter 7 of Thurow's work.

the average blacks receive schooling that is qualitatively inferior to that obtained by whites. Note what is happening here: Characteristics that apply to a group are being applied to individuals. *Each* married woman is assumed to behave with respect to employment tenure as the "average" married woman. Similarly, *every* black youth is assumed to have the same quality of education as the "average" black youth. It is assumed that group or average differences apply in each individual case. As a result, married women who do not plan to have children (or do not plan to quit work if they do) and black youths who receive a quality education will be discriminated against.

Three further aspects of statistical discrimination merit comment. In the first place, unlike in the taste-for-discrimination model, the employer is *not* harmed by practicing discrimination. On the contrary, the employer is a beneficiary. An employer will enhance profits by minimizing hiring costs. Given that the gathering of detailed information on each job applicant is costly, the application of perceived group characteristics to job seekers is an inexpensive means of screening employees. Some economists feel that the statistical discrimination theory, which envisions employers as "gainers," is more plausible than the taste-for-discrimination model, which conceives of them as "losers."

Second, as suggested earlier, the statistical discrimination model does not necessarily indicate that an employer is being malicious in his or her hiring behavior. The decisions made may very well be correct, rational, and, as noted, profitable *on the average.* The only problem is that many workers who differ from the group average will be discriminated against.

Finally, as noted at the outset, there is no compelling reason statistical discrimination need diminish over time. In contrast to the taste-for-discrimination model, statistical discrimination may persist because those who practice it are beneficiaries.

Our first and third points merit qualification in one important sense. If the average characteristics of any two groups converge over time—perhaps because of a decline in other aspects of discrimination—the application of statistical discrimination may become increasingly costly to employers. For example, suppose human capital discrimination diminishes and black youths now obtain high school educations equal in quality to those acquired by white youths. By applying statistical discrimination to employ only whites, the employer will now be making more hiring mistakes. These mistakes will be of two types: hiring more whites who are not qualified and failing to hire blacks who are qualified.

Similarly, the increasing availability of child care facilities, higher female pay, and changing female preferences have meant that having children no longer seriously interrupts the work careers of many women. Also, studies reveal that the difference in turnover rates of men and women in similar jobs with similar advancement opportunities is small.[11] Thus, employers who base their hiring decisions on the average turnover rate of females may make costly hiring mistakes. The cost to the employer of such mistakes is that the most productive workers available are not being selected.

[11]Francine D. Blau and Lawrence M. Kahn, "Race and Sex Differences in Quits by Young Workers," *Industrial and Labor Relations Review,* October 1981, pp. 563–577. Also see Audrey Light and Manuelita Ureta, "Panel Estimates of Male and Female Job Turnover Behavior: Can Female Nonquitters Be Identified?" *Journal of Labor Economics,* April 1992, pp. 156–181.

Employers who make fewer mistakes will have lower production costs and will increase their market share at the expense of rivals.

THE CROWDING MODEL: OCCUPATIONAL SEGREGATION

A glance ahead to Table 15-3 will reveal that occupational distributions of whites and blacks *and* of males and females are substantially different. We have also noted that job segregation is a factor underlying the less elastic female labor supply curve, which is critical in explaining gender-based wage differences in the market power model. Thus, it is no surprise to find that an entire theory of discrimination has been based on the concept of occupational segregation. This ***crowding model*** uses simply supply and demand concepts to explore the consequences of confining women and blacks to a limited number of occupations.[12]

Why does crowding occur? Why do employers practice job segregation based on gender or race? One important reason is that worker productivity is the result of a group or "team" effort. If social interactions on the job are unfavorable, productivity will suffer. Some male (white) workers may become disgruntled when obligated to work along with or to take orders from women (blacks). Thus, in the interest of productivity and profits, employers decide to segregate men and women (blacks and whites) on the job. Furthermore, many employers have preconceived notions concerning the job capabilities of women and minorities. As a result, very few women, for example, have jobs driving trucks or selling electronics equipment or automobiles.

Assumptions and Predictions

The following simplifying assumptions will facilitate our discussion of the crowding model.

1 The labor force is equally divided between male and female (or white and black) workers. Let's say there are 6 million male and 6 million female workers.

2 The total labor market is composed of three occupations—X, Y, and Z—each having identical labor demand curves as shown in Figure 14-3.

3 Men and women have homogeneous labor force characteristics; males and females are equally productive in each of the three occupations.

4 Product markets are competitive so that the demand curves reflect not only marginal revenue product (MRP) but also value of marginal product (VMP) (Chapter 5).

5 We assume that as a result of occupational segregation, occupations X and Y are "men's jobs" and occupation Z is a "woman's job." Women are confined to occupation Z and systematically excluded from occupations X and Y.

[12]For a detailed discussion of the "crowding hypothesis" by one of its leading exponents, see Barbara Bergmann, *The Economic Emergence of Women* (New York: Basic Books, Inc., 1986), chaps 4–6 and, more specifically, pp. 128–132 and appendix B. Bergmann's book contains a number of case studies of occupational crowding. Also see her "Does the Market for Women's Labor Need Fixing?" *Journal of Economic Perspectives,* Winter 1989, pp. 43–60.

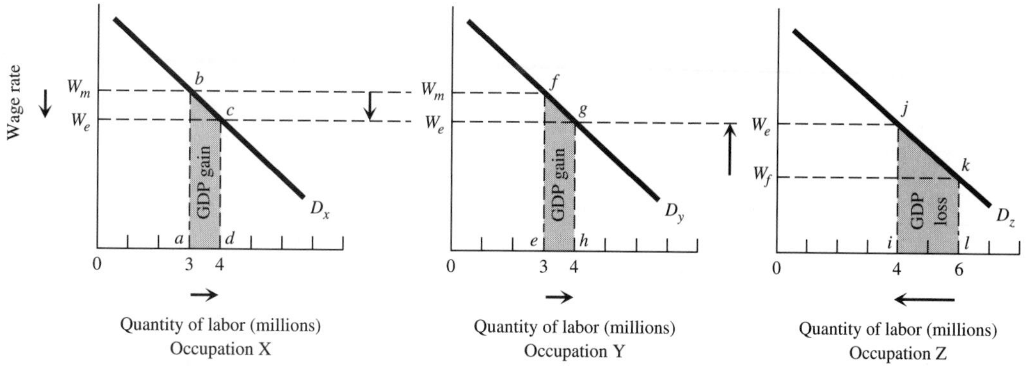

FIGURE 14-3 OCCUPATIONAL SEGREGATION: THE CROWDING MODEL
By crowding women into occupation Z, men will receive high wage rates of W_m in occupations X and Y, while women receive low wage rates of W_f in occupation Z. The abandonment of discrimination will equalize wage rates at W_e and result in a net increase in the domestic output [*(abcd + efgh) − ijkl*].

Men will distribute themselves equally among occupations X and Y so that there are 3 million male workers in each and the resulting common wage rate for men is W_m. Assuming no barriers to mobility, any initially different distribution of males between X and Y would result in a wage differential that would prompt labor shifts from low- to high-wage occupations until wage equality was realized. Note that all 6 million women, on the other hand, are crowded into occupation Z and, as a consequence of this occupational segregation, receive a much lower wage rate W_f. Given the reality of discrimination, this is an "equilibrium" situation. Women *cannot,* because of discrimination, reallocate themselves to occupations X and Y in the pursuit of higher wage rates. Although men could presumably enter occupation Z if they so chose, they would not want to do so in the face of Z's lower wage rates.

The net result of occupational segregation is obvious: Men realize higher wage rates and incomes at the expense of women. Note, however, that women are not being disadvantaged as the result of exploitation; they are *not* being paid a wage rate less than their marginal revenue product. In occupation Z women *are* being paid a wage rate equal to their MRP *and* to their contribution to society's output (VMP). Their problem is that by being restricted to only occupation Z, their supply is great relative to demand and their wage rate is therefore low compared to that of males.

Ending Discrimination

Suppose that through legislation or sweeping changes in social attitudes, discrimination disappears. What are the results? Women, attracted by higher wage rates, will shift from Z to X and Y. Specifically, if we assume occupational shifts are costless, 1 million women will shift into X and another 1 million into Y, leaving 4 million workers in Z. At this point, 4 million workers will be in each occupation and wage rates will be equal to W_e in all three occupations, and therefore, there is no incentive for further reallocation. This new, nondiscriminatory equilibrium is to the advantage of women, who now receive higher wages, and to the disadvantage of men, who now receive lower wages.

If the elimination of occupational segregation results in both winners (women) and losers (men), it is pertinent to ask whether the gains exceed the losses. That is, does society reap an economic gain by ending occupational segregation? Figure 14-3 reveals that there *is* a net gain to society. Our labor demand curves reflect value of marginal product, the contribution of each successive worker to the domestic output. Hence, the movement of 2 million women out of occupation Z yields a *decrease* in domestic output shown by area *ijkl*. But the areas *abcd* and *efgh* for occupations X and Y show the *increases* in domestic output—the market values of the marginal products—realized by adding 1 million women to each of these occupations. We observe that the sum of the additions to domestic output in occupations X and Y exceeds the decline in domestic output that occurs when women leave occupation Z. The conclusion that society gains from the termination of occupational segregation is not unexpected. Women reallocate themselves from occupation Z, where their VMP is relatively low, to occupations X and Y, where their VMPs are relatively high. This reallocation continues until the VMPs of labor in each alternative use are equal, a condition that defines the efficient allocation of labor (Chapter 6). Thus, our analysis underscores that discrimination has both equity and efficiency connotations. Discrimination influences not only the distribution but also the size of the domestic income.

QUICK REVIEW 14-2

- The market power (monopsony) model of discrimination allows for the payment of lower wages to groups with a less-elastic labor supply.
- The theory of statistical discrimination holds that employers often wrongly judge individuals on the basis of the average characteristics of the group to which they belong rather than on their own personal characteristics.
- The crowding model of discrimination suggests that women and minorities are systematically excluded from high-paying occupations and crowded into low-paying ones.

14-3

Your Turn: How might statistical discrimination reinforce occupational segregation? (Answer: See page 627.)

Index of Segregation

How extensive is crowding or occupational segregation? An ***index of segregation*** has been devised to quantify occupational segregation. As applied to sex discrimination, *this index is designed to show the percentage of women (or men) who would have to change occupations for women to be distributed among occupations in the same proportions as men.* The hypothetical figures of Table 14-1 are instructive. Suppose that the occupational

14-3 World of Work

JOHN S. MILL AND HARRIET TAYLOR MILL ON OCCUPATIONAL SEGREGATION*

John Stuart Mill, the last of the great classical economists, was one of the major contributors to the development of economic thought. He made several original contributions and systematized the entire body of his predecessors' economic thought. Mill attributed to Harriet Taylor, his long-term friend and eventually his wife, his love of liberty and his passionate defense of the rights of women. The two were among the first to recognize the costs to society of occupational segregation. In the essay "Enfranchisement of Women," published in 1851, they stated:

> Let every occupation be open to all, without favour or discouragement to any, and employments will fall into the hands of those men and women who are found by experience to be most capable of worthy exercising them. There need be no fear that women will take out of the hands of men any occupation which men perform better than they. Each individual will prove his or her capacities, in the only way in which capacities can be proved—by trial; and the world will have the benefit of all the best faculties of all its inhabitants. But to interfere beforehand by arbitrary limit, and declare that whatever be the genius, talent, energy, or force of mind of an individual of a certain sex or class, those faculties shall not be exerted, or shall be exerted only in some of the few of the many modes in which others are permitted to use theirs, is not only an injustice to the individual, and a detriment to society, which loses what it can ill spare, but is also the most effectual mode of providing that, in the sex or class so fettered, the qualities which are not permitted to be exercised shall not exist.†

In the *Subjection of Women,* published in 1869, the Mills argued that equal rights for women would actually benefit men. Men growing up with the idea of superiority to women face a problem similar to that of a hereditary king, said the Mills. The relation between husband and wife becomes like that between a lord and vassal. "However the vassal's character may have been affected, for better or worse, by his subordination, who can help see that the lord's [character] was affected greatly for the worse."‡

*Based on Stanley L. Brue, *The Evolution of Economic Thought,* 5th ed. (Fort Worth, TX: Dryden Press, 1994), p. 150.

†John Stuart Mill, "Enfranchisement of Women," *Dissertations and Discussions* (London: 1859), vol. 2, p. 423.

‡John Stuart Mill and Harriet Taylor Mill, *Essays on Sex Equality,* Alice S. Rossi (ed.), (Chicago: University of Chicago Press, 1970), p. 219.

TABLE 14-1 DETERMINING THE INDEX OF SEGREGATION (HYPOTHETICAL DATA)

(1) Occupation	(2) Male	(3) Female	(4) = (2) − (3) Absolute differences
A	50%	30%	20%
B	30	20	10
C	20	50	30
	100%	100%	60%

$$\text{Index of segregation} = \frac{60\%}{2} = 30\% \text{ or } .30.$$

distributions of male and female workers are as shown in columns 2 and 3. To make the distributions identical, *either* 30 percent of the total of *female* workers would have to move *from* occupation C (20 percent going to A and 10 percent to B) *or* 30 percent of the total of *male* workers would have to move *to* occupation C (20 percent coming from A and 10 percent coming from B). Because 30 percent of either female or male workers would have to change occupations for males and females to be distributed in the same proportions among occupations, the index of segregation is 30 percent, or simply, .30. For more numerous occupational categories, the index can be calculated by determining the absolute value of the percentage differences for each occupation (without regard to sign) and summing these differences as shown in column 4. To obtain the index of segregation, the resulting 60 percent is then divided by 2 because any movement of workers is counted twice, as a movement *out of* one occupation and as a movement *into* another occupation.

The conclusion from our simple hypothetical illustration is that 30 percent of the female (or male) labor force must change occupations for the proportions of men and women in each occupation to be the same. Note that this new distribution would result in an index of segregation of zero. The other extreme where, say, occupations A and B are each populated 50 percent by men and occupation C 100 percent by women yields an index of 100 percent or 1.00. Hence, the index of segregation may take on any value ranging from 0 to 1.00, and the higher the value, the greater the extent of occupational segregation.

Evidence

What are the magnitudes of the indexes of occupational segregation based on gender and race for the United States? And what, if anything, has happened to these indexes over time? Albelda[13] has demonstrated that occupational segregation between all (white and nonwhite) men and all (white and nonwhite) women was quite high and fell by only 7 percentage points over the 1958–81 period. Subsequent research has found that the index of occupational segregation has moderately declined between 1973–74 and 1993.[14] The index of occupational segregation by *gender* was 68.5 percent in 1973–74 and declined to 54.6 percent by 1993. More than half the women (or men) in the United States would have to change occupations for women to be distributed among occupations in the same proportions as men. This moderate decline in the index is consistent with growing evidence that women have made substantial occupational gains in such professions as dentistry, medicine, pharmacy, and law ("World of Work" 14-4).[15]

14-1

14-4

[13]Randy P. Albelda, "Occupational Segregation by Race and Gender, 1958–1981," *Industrial and Labor Relations Review,* April 1986, pp. 404–411. Similarly, in considering some 503 occupations, Victor Fuchs has calculated the overall male–female indexes of occupational segregation for full-time workers to be 55 percent in 1980 for both blacks and whites; 28 percent in comparing white women and black women; and 33 percent in comparing white men and black men. See his "Women's Quest for Economic Equality," *Journal of Economic Perspectives,* Winter 1989, pp. 26–27.

[14]David A. Macpherson and Barry T. Hirsch, "Wages and Gender Composition: Why Do Women's Jobs Pay Less?" *Journal of Labor Economics,* July 1995, pp. 426–471. Also see Francine D. Blau, "Trends in the Well-Being of American Women: 1970–95," *Journal of Economic Literature,* March 1998, pp. 112–165.

[15]John B. Parrish, "Are Women Taking over the Professions?" *Challenge,* January–February 1986, pp. 54–58; and Francine D. Blau, Marianne A. Ferber, and Anne E. Winkler, *The Economics of Women, Men, and Work,* 3d ed. (Englewood Cliffs, NJ: Prentice–Hall, 1998).

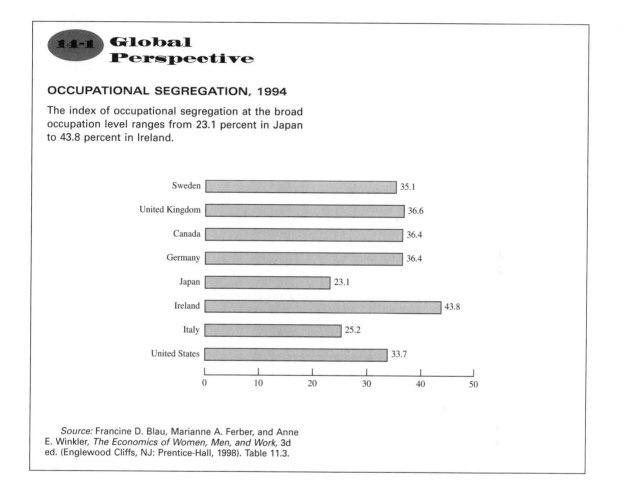

14-1 **Global Perspective**

OCCUPATIONAL SEGREGATION, 1994

The index of occupational segregation at the broad occupation level ranges from 23.1 percent in Japan to 43.8 percent in Ireland.

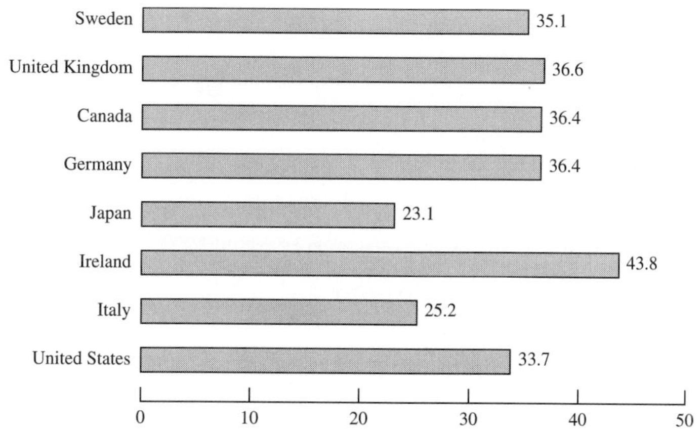

Source: Francine D. Blau, Marianne A. Ferber, and Anne E. Winkler, *The Economics of Women, Men, and Work,* 3d ed. (Englewood Cliffs, NJ: Prentice-Hall, 1998). Table 11.3.

Occupational segregation based on race is less pronounced than that based on gender. In addition, has it declined modestly over time. Comparing white women and black women, the index of segregation was found to be 36.7 percent in 1973–74 and fell to 27.4 percent in 1992.[16] This is consistent with a general integration of black women into occupations traditionally held by white women. When white men and black men are analyzed, the change was more modest as the index fell from 36.7 percent in 1973–74 to 29.6 percent in 1992.

[16]Barry T. Hirsch and David A. Macpherson, "Wages, Racial Composition, and Quality Sorting in Labor Markets," Florida State University Working Paper No. 94-1-01. Also see Barry T. Hirsch and Edward J. Schumacher, "Labor Earnings, Discrimination, and the Racial Composition of Jobs," *Journal of Human Resources,* Fall 1992, pp. 602–628; Andrew M. Gill, "Incorporating the Cause of Occupational Differences in Studies of Racial Wage Differentials," *Journal of Human Resources,* Winter 1994, pp. 20–41.

14-4 World of Work

WOMEN'S ENTRY INTO SELECTED PROFESSIONS*

Consistent with the decline in the overall index of occupational segregation during the 1980s and 1990s, women made considerable gains in entering selected professions. This fact is evident from several studies and is implied in the accompanying figure. The gray bars in the figure indicate the overall percent of women in each particular profession in 1996; the black bars show women as a percentage of *new graduates* in each field in 1995.

Note, for example, that while women constituted only 13.7 percent of dentists in 1996, they made up 36.4 percent of the graduates from dental school in the preceding year. In 1995 women were nearly two-thirds of the graduates from pharmacy school, compared to 42.6 percent of pharmacists in general in 1996. More than 40 percent of all law school graduates in 1995 were women, which is substantially more than the overall percentage of women lawyers in 1996.

The increase in the number of women entering the professions, of course, is very encouraging. Nevertheless, the true test of equality will come as these women progress in their careers. Will some of them drop out of their professions for reasons related to family responsibilities and child-raising? Will they experience discriminatory barriers—so called "glass ceilings"—impeding their advancement to the top positions in their professions? Studies of the hierarchies of professions continue to show that males often dominate the higher-paying professional positions.

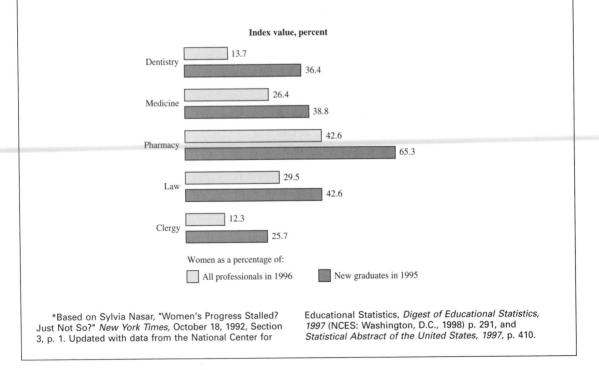

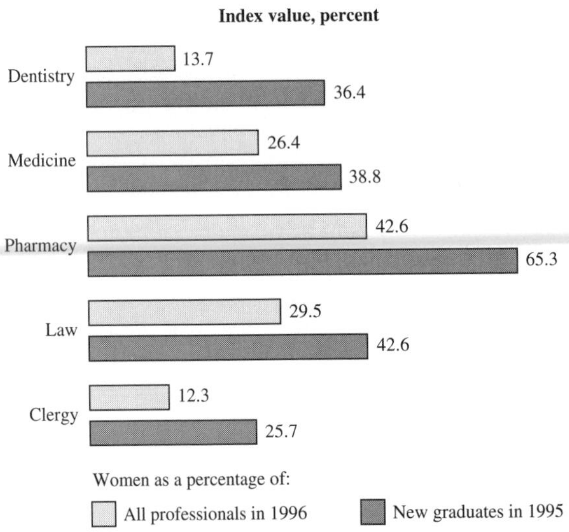

*Based on Sylvia Nasar, "Women's Progress Stalled? Just Not So?" *New York Times*, October 18, 1992, Section 3, p. 1. Updated with data from the National Center for Educational Statistics, *Digest of Educational Statistics, 1997* (NCES: Washington, D.C., 1998) p. 291, and *Statistical Abstract of the United States, 1997,* p. 410.

CHAPTER SUMMARY

1 Discrimination occurs when female or black workers—who have the same abilities, education, training, and experience as male or white workers—are accorded inferior treatment with respect to hiring, occupational access, promotion, or wage rate.

2 Forms of labor market discrimination include *(a)* wage, *(b)* employment, *(c)* occupational, and *(d)* human capital discrimination.
3 According to Becker, some white employers have a "taste for discrimination" that can be measured by the discrimination coefficient *d*. Prejudiced white employers will be indifferent to hiring blacks only when the wage rate of blacks is less than that of whites by the monetary value of *d*. In supply and demand form, the model indicates *(a)* that a decline in the discrimination coefficient will increase the ratio of black to white wages and increase black employment, and *(b)* that the size of the black–white wage differential will vary directly with the supply of black workers.
4 Market power models indicate that employers with monopsony power will find it profitable to pay female workers less than male workers. The reason is that the labor supply curve of female workers is allegedly less elastic than that of male workers because females have fewer alternative job opportunities due to occupational segregation.
5 The theory of statistical discrimination indicates that because detailed information concerning the potential productivity of job applicants is costly to obtain, profit-seeking employers base employment decisions on the perceived characteristics of groups of workers. The imputation of group characteristics to individuals discriminates against many individuals within those groups.
6 The crowding model focuses on occupational segregation. Using supply and demand analysis, it demonstrates that occupational crowding results in lower wages for women (blacks), higher wages for men (whites), and a net loss of domestic output. The index of occupational segregation measures the percentage of women or men who would have to change occupations for the occupational distribution of women to be the same as for men. The index for the United States has declined somewhat in recent decades.

TERMS AND CONCEPTS

discrimination
wage, employment, occupational, and human capital discrimination
taste-for-discrimination mode
discrimination coefficient
market power model
statistical discrimination
crowding model
index of segregation

QUESTIONS AND STUDY SUGGESTIONS

1 Women have increased the amount of education they have achieved relative to men, and average years of schooling completed are now approximately the same for males and females. Human capital theory predicts that this would close the male–female earnings gap. In fact, this has not happened. How can you explain it?
2 In Becker's taste-for-discrimination model, what is the meaning of the discrimination coefficient *d*? If the monetary value of *d* is, say, $3 for a given white employer, will that employer hire black or white workers if their actual wage rates are $8 and $10, respectively? Explain. In Becker's model, what effect would a decrease in the supply of black labor have on the black–white wage ratio and the employment of black workers? Use the model to explain the economic effects of an increase in employer prejudice. What are the basic public policy implications of this model?
3 Use the market power model to explain why women might be paid lower wages than men. What assumption concerning the elasticity of the female labor supply curve is requisite to this conclusion? Do you feel this assumption is justified?

4 What is statistical discrimination and why does it occur? The theory of statistical discrimination implies that discrimination can persist indefinitely, while the taste-for-discrimination model suggests that discrimination will tend to disappear. Explain the difference.

5 Use simple supply and demand analysis to explain the impact of occupational segregation or "crowding" on the relative wage rates of men and women. Who gains and who loses as a consequence of eliminating occupational segregation? Explain the following statement: "A gender-blind labor market would allocate labor more efficiently throughout the economy, and productivity would be higher on average."

6 Explain the following statement: "In the taste-for-discrimination model, discrimination is practiced even though it is costly to do so. But in the monopsony and statistical discrimination models, it is clear that discrimination pays."

7 Assume that the occupational distribution of males and females is as follows:

Occupation	Male	Female
E	60%	5%
F	20	5
G	10	40
H	10	50

Calculate the index of segregation and explain its meaning. Compare the meaning of an index of .40 with indexes of 1.00 and 0. As applied to gender, has the index changed significantly over time?

SELECTED REFERENCES

Amsden, Alice H. (ed.): *The Economics of Women and Work* (New York: St. Martin's Press, 1980).

Becker, Gary: *The Economics of Discrimination* (Chicago: University of Chicago Press, 1957).

Bergmann, Barbara R.: *The Economic Emergence of Women* (New York: Basic Books, Inc., 1986).

Blau, Francine D.: "Trends in the Well-Being of American Women, 1970–1995," *Journal of Economic Literature,* March 1998, pp. 112–165.

Blau, Francine D., Marianne A. Ferber and Anne E. Winkler: *The Economics of Women, Men, and Work,* 3d ed. (Englewood Cliffs, NJ: Prentice-Hall, 1998).

Lloyd, Cynthia B., and Beth T. Niemi: *The Economics of Sex Differentials* (New York: Columbia University Press, 1979).

CHAPTER 15

WOMEN, BLACKS, AND THE LABOR MARKET

In Chapter 14 our main goal was to define discrimination and present a number of theories of labor market discrimination. Building on that base, we now want to examine the evidence of discrimination and discuss antidiscrimination policies. How do earnings and occupational distributions of women and blacks differ from those of men and whites? How many of these differences are attributable to nondiscriminatory factors such as occupational choice, educational attainment, and job tenure? How many to discrimination? How can society prevent discrimination or, where it has occurred, rectify it? What are the major governmental antidiscrimination policies, and why do they remain highly controversial?

Our organizational strategy for answering these and related questions is as follows: First, we will compare gender and racial differences in key economic variables, including earnings, unemployment rates, occupational distribution, educational attainment, and earnings at each educational level. Second, we will discuss and assess nondiscriminatory factors that may explain some of these differences. Next, findings from empirical studies that try to control for the nondiscriminatory factors will be summarized. Finally, the chapter will end with a discussion of governmental antidiscrimination policies and issues.

While our focus in this chapter remains on women and blacks, bear in mind that the general nature of the statistical discrepancies identified and the issues discussed apply equally to other disadvantaged groups, particularly Hispanics.

GENDER AND RACIAL DIFFERENCES

It is not difficult to find statistical discrepancies that lead one to suspect the presence of discrimination based on gender and race.

TABLE 15-1 MEDIAN WEEKLY EARNINGS OF FULL-TIME WORKERS BY GENDER AND RACE FOR SELECTED YEARS, 1967–96 (IN CURRENT DOLLARS)

	Gender			Race		
Year	Males	Females	Ratio of female to male	Whites	Blacks	Ratio of blacks to whites
1967	$125	$ 78	.62	$113	$ 79	.70
1969	142	86	.61	125	90	.72
1971	162	100	.62	142	107	.75
1973	188	116	.62	162	129	.80
1975	221	137	.62	190	156	.82
1977	253	156	.62	217	171	.79
1978	272	166	.61	232	186	.80
1981	345	217	.63	292	236	.81
1986	419	290	.69	370	291	.79
1989	468	328	.70	409	319	.78
1992	505	381	.75	462	357	.77
1996	579	431	.74	519	400	.77

Source: U.S. Department of Labor, *Handbook of Labor Statistics, 1980,* p. 118; and *Employment and Earnings,* January 1998, Table 37.

Earnings

Table 15-1 shows the median weekly earnings of full-time workers by gender and race. We observe that from 1967 through 1981 the weekly earnings of women workers were about 62 percent of those of men. Since 1981 the percentage has increased significantly, rising to 74 percent in 1997. Several explanations have been given for this narrowing of the gender gap in earnings. First, evidence exists that the skill levels of female workers have increased. Second, labor market discrimination perhaps has declined. Also, the industrial restructuring of the economy away from manufacturing jobs and toward services may have negatively affected the earnings of men more than women. Fourth, the decline in unionism (Chapter 10) may have reduced male pay more than female pay. Finally, the occupational distribution of men and women workers may have changed positively in favor of women.[1]

15-1

[1]This list is drawn from Elaine Sorensen, *Exploring the Reasons behind the Narrowing Gender Gap in Earnings* (Washington, DC: Urban Institute Press, 1991, pp. 129–130. For more on recent earnings trends see William E. Even and David A. Macpherson, "The Decline in Private-Sector Unionism and the Gender Wage Gap," *Journal of Human Resources,* Spring 1993, pp. 279–296; David A. Macpherson and Barry T. Hirsch, "Wages and Gender Composition: Why Do Women's Jobs Pay Less?" *Journal of Labor Economics,* July 1995, pp. 426–471; Francine D. Blau and Lawrence M. Kahn, "Rising Wage Inequality and the U.S. Gender Wage Gap," *American Economic Review,* May 1994, pp. 23–28. Francine D. Blau and Lawrence M. Kahn, "Swimming Upstream: Trends in the Gender Wage Differentials in the 1980s," *Journal of Labor Economics,* January 1997, pp. 1–42; and Francine D. Blau, "Trends in the Well-being of American Women: 1970–95," *Journal of Economic Literature,* March 1998, pp. 112–165.

15-1 World of Work

THE GENDER PAY GAP: AN INTERNATIONAL COMPARISON*

The gender pay gap is larger in the United States than in most industrial nations. Specifically, Blau and Kahn find that the female–male hourly wage ratio is 80 to 90 percent in Australia, Denmark, France, New Zealand, Norway, and Sweden, compared to 65 percent in the United States. Only Japan, with a 50 percent ratio, has consistently had a larger gender pay gap than the United States. The relatively high U.S. pay gap is particularly surprising since American women compare favorably with women in other countries in terms of education and occupational status. Also, the United States has historically been more committed to equal pay and equal opportunity policy for women than have most other countries.

Blau and Kahn help resolve this seeming paradox. They note that pay for lower-skilled workers relative to higher-skilled workers is lower in the United States than in most other nations. Because women are disproportionately represented in the lower-skill ranks, the gender wage gap is higher in the United States. In fact, this greater overall wage inequality accounts for nearly all the differences in the female–male pay ratios between the United States and countries with higher ratios. That is, the gender earnings gap in the United States would be approximately the same as the gaps in Australia, Sweden, and Norway if the overall distribution of wages were the same as in those countries.

One of the main reasons Australia, Norway, Sweden, and other nations have less overall wage inequality and thus smaller gender pay gaps is because they have more centralized wage setting than exists in the United States. For example, in Norway and Sweden nearly all workers are unionized and a single union federation signs wage agreements directly with a single employers' federation. Wage setting is also quite centralized in Australia, where minimum wages are set for various industries by government tribunals. Centralized wage setting by union federations and governmental tribunals tends to compress the market-based wage distribution.

Blau and Kahn point out: "Given growing wage inequality in the United States in the 1970s and 1980s [Chapter 17], American women have been swimming upstream in a labor market increasingly unfavorable to low-wage workers."†

*Based on "U.S. Gender Pay Gap Reflects Overall Wage Inequality," *NBER Digest,* April 1993, pp. 1–2; Francine D. Blau and Lawrence M. Kahn, "The Gender Earnings Gap: Some International Evidence," in Richard B. Freeman and Lawrence F. Katz (eds.), *Differences and Changes in Wage Structure* (Chicago: University of Chicago Press, 1995); and Francine D. Blau and Lawrence M. Kahn, "The Gender Earnings Gap: Learning from International Comparisons," *American Economic Review,* May 1992, pp. 533–538.

†Blau and Kahn, p. 538.

We also see in Table 15-1 that, while the ratio of black to white weekly earnings has increased somewhat since the 1960s, the increase has been unsteady over time and a substantial earnings gap remains. In fact, in the last decade, the black–white pay gap of young black males has considerably widened.[2]

Unemployment

Table 15-2 shows selected data on the distribution of unemployment over the past several decades. A comparison of columns 2 and 3 reveals that while white females seem to have been at some disadvantage compared to white males, the differential is not

[2]John Bound and Richard B. Freeman, "What Went Wrong? The Erosion of Relative Earnings and Employment among Black Men in the 1980s," *Quarterly Journal of Economics,* February 1992, pp. 201–232. Also relevant to the discussion of racial differences in pay is Francine D. Blau and Andrea H. Beller, "Black–White Earnings over the 1970s and 1980s: Gender Differences in Trends," *Review of Economics and Statistics,* May 1992, pp. 533–538.

TABLE 15-2 UNEMPLOYMENT RATES BY RACE AND GENDER, SELECTED YEARS, 1950–96

(1) Year	(2) White male	(3) White female	(4) Black male	(5) Black female
1950	4.7%	5.3%	9.4%	8.4%
1955	3.7	4.3	8.8	8.4
1960	4.8	5.3	10.7	9.4
1965	3.6	5.0	7.4	9.2
1970	4.0	5.4	7.3	9.3
1975	7.2	8.6	14.8	14.8
1978	4.5	6.2	11.8	13.8
1981	6.5	6.9	15.7	15.6
1983	8.8	7.9	20.3	18.6
1987	5.4	5.2	13.0	13.2
1989	4.5	4.5	11.5	11.4
1992	6.9	6.0	15.2	13.0
1997	4.2	4.2	10.2	9.9

Source: Employment and Training Report of the President, 1982, p. 190; and *Economic Report of the President, 1998,* Table B-43.

dramatic. In fact, in 1983, 1987, and 1992 the unemployment rate for women dipped below that for men.

Blacks, however, have consistently had unemployment rates that have been roughly twice as great as those of whites. Furthermore, the data understate the disadvantage of blacks because a larger percentage of blacks than whites have been discouraged workers (Chapter 3 and 19); they have dropped out of the labor force because of poor job prospects and are therefore not counted among the unemployed.

Occupational Distribution

Substantial differences in the occupational distribution of workers by gender and race are revealed in Table 15-3. Women, who constitute about 46 percent of the employed labor force, have been disproportionately concentrated in the following occupations: nursing, public school teaching, clerical work, retail sales, services, secretarial work, and private household employment. All these occupations rank low in relative earnings. It must be added, however, that women have recently made significant gains in the professions ("World of Work" 14-4).

Blacks constitute about 11 percent of the total labor force and have also been concentrated in a limited number of low-paying jobs as laundry workers, cleaners, hospital orderlies, and other manual workers. Conversely, note that women and blacks have both been underrepresented among such highly paid professionals as dentists and physicians.

Education

Table 15-4 provides some basic insights into differentials in human capital accumulation, although the data provide no information on apprenticeship programs and on-the-

TABLE 15-3 OCCUPATIONAL DISTRIBUTION OF EMPLOYED WORKERS BY GENDER AND RACE, 1997

Occupation	Percent female	Percent black
Total employment	46	11
Administrative and managerial workers	44	7
Construction inspectors	10	9
Underwriters	70	9
Professional workers	53	8
Physicians	26	4
Dentists	17	3
Registered nurses	94	8
Elementary school teachers	84	11
Sales occupations	50	8
Retail sales workers	66	12
Clerical workers	79	13
Secretaries	99	9
Typists	94	17
Receptionists	97	9
Service workers	59	18
Waiters and waitresses	78	5
Nursing aides and orderlies	89	35
Janitors and cleaners	34	20
Child care workers (in homes)	98	11
Machine operators, assemblers, and inspectors	38	15
Pressing machine operators	71	22
Laundering and dry cleaning machine operators	59	19
Transportation and material moving workers	9	15
Crane and tower operators	2	22
Taxicab drivers and chauffeurs	8	26
Handlers, equipment cleaners, helpers, and laborers	20	16
Construction laborers	5	13

Source: U.S. Department of Labor, *Employment and Earnings,* January 1998, Table 11.

job training. We found in Chapter 4 that those individuals who acquire the most formal education also tend to receive the most on-the-job training. The advantages that white males have enjoyed compared to females and blacks in obtaining a college education have been magnified through the greater access these white males have had to postmarket job training that has increased their productivity and earnings. Furthermore, studies indicate that the quality of education received by blacks has been generally inferior to that acquired by whites.

Average Earnings by Educational Attainment

Although Table 15-4 clearly indicates differences in educational levels by gender and race, it is important to note that these differences do not fully explain the earnings

TABLE 15-4 SELECTED MEASURES OF THE EDUCATIONAL ATTAINMENT OF THE POPULATION BY GENDER AND RACE, 1996

Percent completing 4 years of high school or more	
White males	82.7
White females	82.8
Black males	74.3
Black females	74.2
Percent completing 4 years of college or more	
White males	26.9
White females	21.8
Black males	12.4
Black females	14.6

Source: Statistical Abstract of the United States 1997, p. 159.

differences observed earlier in Table 15-1. As shown in Table 15-5, full-time women workers and black workers have significantly lower average earnings levels than white men workers at each level of educational attainment. The pattern is clear: On average, white males who work full-time earn more than black males at each educational level. Black males, in turn, earn more than white females and black females. These data mean that the age-earnings profiles for women and blacks lie significantly below those displayed earlier in Figure 4-1 (all males).

TABLE 15-5 AVERAGE EARNINGS OF FULL-TIME WORKERS (25 YEARS OF AGE OR OLDER) BY EDUCATIONAL ATTAINMENT, 1995

	Whites		Blacks	
	Males	Females	Males	Females
Average earnings, total	$ 43,311	$27,964	$31,514	$23,693
Not a high school graduate	23,715	15,919	21,730	18,529
High school degree	33,796	22,368	25,388	19,726
College:				
Associate degree	38,868	29,836	40,504	26,570
Bachelor's degree	54,252	35,017	40,166	29,282
Master's degree	65,076	42,281	44,284	36,662
Doctorate degree	79,830	52,249	u	u
Professional degree	109,883	61,192	u	u

u = Data unavailable.
Source: U.S. Bureau of the Census, *Educational Attainment in the United States, March 1996,* pp. 52–62.

Related Points

Three additional points must be made concerning this survey of empirical data, each point clarifying potential misinterpretations of the raw numbers.

Nondiscriminatory Factors While it is tempting to conclude that Tables 15-1 through 15-5 prove the existence of wage, employment, occupational, and human capital discrimination, the situation is in fact far more complex than this. As will soon become clear from our discussion, a variety of factors other than discrimination may bear on the differences shown in the tables. For example, perhaps women earn less than men not as a result of discrimination, but rather because they freely choose academic programs and jobs that are less valued in the labor market than those chosen by men. Similarly, if black professors on average earn less than white professors, is this the result of discrimination or some other factor such as choice of academic discipline or blacks having gotten their training and degrees from less prestigious institutions? The point is that simple, raw data comparing incomes, unemployment, and occupational distribution by gender or race must be regarded with caution as evidence of discrimination. ***Nondiscriminatory factors*** may explain part or all of the indicated differentials. Conversely, as demonstrated in "World of Work" 15-2, in some instances raw data indicating workforce integration and comparable *average* salaries can disguise underlying discrimination, once productivity differences are introduced.

15-2

Interrelated Data The second point is that the various gender and racial differences evidenced in Tables 15-1 through 15-5 are interrelated. For example, differences in human capital accumulation shown in Table 15-4 are undoubtedly an important causal factor in explaining the earnings, unemployment, and occupational differences revealed in Tables 15-1, 15-2, and 15-3. Also, the occupational differences shown in Table 15-3 help explain the differences in earnings by education shown in Table 15-5.

Efficiency Loss Finally, you might be inclined to infer from our tabular comparisons that the economic impact of discrimination is essentially distributional, that discrimination simply transfers benefits from women and blacks to men and whites. But as Chapter 14's discussion of the crowding theory of discrimination revealed, the size of the domestic output is also adversely affected. Where it exists, discrimination influences the distribution of a diminished national income. An understanding of basic economics suggests on intuitive grounds that this would be the case. Discrimination is like a tariff or any other artificial barrier to free competition that diminishes economic efficiency and reduces economic output and income. It arbitrarily keeps women and minorities out of high-productivity, high-wage jobs and prohibits them from making the maximum contribution to society's well-being.

One rather simple estimate suggests that gross domestic product would be about 4.4 percent higher if *racial* discrimination were eliminated.[3] In absolute terms, this would have amounted to about $333 billion of goods and services in 1996. This estimate was

[3]Joint Economic Committee, *The Cost of Racial Discrimination* (Washington, DC: U.S. Government Printing Office, 1980), pp. 2–5.

15-2 World of Work

DISCRIMINATION IN PROFESSIONAL SPORTS

Casual observation of the number of nonwhite players and their high salaries would suggest an absence of racial discrimination in professional sports. For example, nonwhite athletes constitute about 75 percent of NBA basketball players, 60 percent of NFL football players, and 30 percent of major league baseball players. Nevertheless, researchers have identified several areas of discrimination.

Studies of professional sports lend themselves to isolating discrimination because there are extensive public data on salaries and performance can be measured more precisely than in many other occupations. Here are some conclusions gleaned from several recent studies on this topic:

1 Productivity being equal (number of seasons played, games played per season, career points, field goal percentage, rebounds, assists, and so forth), black professional basketball players on average earn about the same as white players. This is in contrast to the 20 percent penalty observed for black players in the mid 1980s. However, the star white players do appear to earn a premium.*

2 Team customers (fans) may be the source of discrimination in professional and college basketball. Home attendance and team revenues increase with the number of white players on the team.†

3 The wage advantage for whites in professional football is negligible, once salaries are adjusted for productivity. But a significant white wage advantage exists in metropolitan areas with larger than average percentages of whites in the population. Similarly, nonwhite players earned proportionately more in metropolitan areas with relatively high numbers of nonwhites in the population.‡

4 The implication that consumers might be the source of discrimination in professional sports is bolstered by evidence that discrimination exists in the market for sports memorabilia. For example, baseball cards for nonwhite hitters sell for about 10 percent less than the cards of white players of comparable ability. Among pitchers, the discount for cards for nonwhite is about 13 percent. On the bright side, there is no race differential for recently issued "rookie" cards.**

5 In professional baseball there are "unexplained racial differences in career lengths and persistent, though slowly falling, segregation by [playing] position."§

6 Segregation by position continues in professional football, particularly among quarterbacks.

7 Although nonwhites comprise large percentages of players in baseball, basketball, and football, they constitute very small percentages of managers, coaches, and team executives. Both customers and employers may be sources of this possible discrimination.

*See Barton Hughes Hamilton, "Racial Discrimination and Professional Basketball Salaries in the 1990s," *Applied Economics,* March 1997, pp. 287–296; Orn B. Bodvarsson and Raymond T. Brastow, "Do Employers Pay for Consistent Performance: Evidence from the NBA," *Economic Inquiry,* January 1998, pp. 145–160; and Peter D. Sherer and Lawrence M. Kahn, "Racial Differences in Professional Basketball Players' Compensation," *Journal of Labor Economics,* January 1988, pp. 40–61.

†Sherer and Kahn, op. cit. and Robert W. Brown and R. Todd Jewell, "Race, Revenues, and College Basketball," *Review of Black Political Economy,* Winter 1995, pp. 75–90.

‡Lawrence M. Kahn, "The Effects of Race on Professional Football Players' Compensation," *Industrial and Labor Relations Review,* January 1992, pp. 295–310.

**See Clark Nardinelli and Curtis Simon, "Customer Racial Discrimination in the Market for Memorabilia," *Quarterly Journal of Economics,* August 1990, pp. 575–595 and Paul E. Gabriel, Curtis Johnson, and Timothy J. Stanton, "An Examination of Customer Racial Discrimination in the Market for Baseball Memorabilia," *Journal of Business,* April 1995, pp. 215–230.

§Lawrence M. Kahn, "Discrimination in Professional Sports: A Survey of the Literature," *Industrial and Labor Relations Review,* April 1991, pp. 414–415.

made essentially by assuming that (1) the unemployment rate of blacks was reduced to the same level as whites and (2) the annual earnings of black workers were increased to the level received by whites. A more statistically complex study has concluded that the elimination of *gender* discrimination would increase gross domestic product by 2.57 percent.[4]

QUICK REVIEW 15-1

- The ratios of median weekly earnings of women to men and of blacks to whites are higher today than they were in 1967.
- Unemployment rates of blacks are roughly twice those of whites; unemployment rates of women and men are quite similar.
- About 27 percent of white males have completed 4 or more years of college compared to 22 percent of white females, 12 percent of black males, and 15 percent of black males.
- Compared to white men, women and blacks who work full-time have lower average earnings at each level of educational attainment.
- Discrimination not only redistributes national income but also reduces it through an efficiency loss.

Your Turn: Compare the average earnings of black males to white males in Table 15-5. Explain how this difference might be responsible for the difference in the percentage of black males and white males attending college (Table 15-4). (Answer: See page 627.)

CAUSE AND EFFECT: NONDISCRIMINATORY FACTORS

As we have indicated, economists are well aware that many factors other than discrimination may bear on female–male and black–white earnings differentials. To find that Ms. Anderson earns $20,000 a year while Mr. Alvarez earns $30,000 annually is not necessarily evidence of gender discrimination. This is true even where Ms. Anderson and Mr. Alvarez have equal levels of education or where they work for the same employer. A variety of considerations have nothing to do with prejudice may simply cause Alvarez to be more productive than Anderson. More generally, cause-and-effect considerations are difficult to unravel in attempting to isolate the role of discrimination in explaining differences in socioeconomic status. Let's consider this issue in terms of gender discrimination.

[4]Estelle James, "Income and Employment Effects of Women's Liberation," in Cynthia B. Lloyd (ed.), *Sex, Discrimination, and the Division of Labor* (New York: Columbia University Press, 1975), pp. 379–400.

Rational Choice

Some economists argue that the inferior economic position of women is basically the result of rational and freely rendered decisions by women. The thrust of this view is that most women anticipate marriage and childbearing, and this generates for women a conflict between labor market careers and marriage that explains much of women's economic disadvantage. For example, Sorensen[5] has found that "over 85 percent of the female workforce between the ages of 35 and 41 have worked intermittently. These women earn 30 percent less than women in this age group who have worked continuously."

In this regard, Fuchs recognizes that some of the economic disadvantage borne by women undoubtedly is due to discrimination, but he also argues that:

> In addition, there are powerful forces rooted in biology and culture. Women's greater role in reproduction and gender differences in upper body strength probably play a large role in pre-industrial societies, but in modern society they have been amplified by socialization. From infancy onward, the experiences of girls and boys in families, schools, churches, and their exposure to the media significantly affect their behavior as adult women and men. Historically, one of the primary objectives of socialization has been to direct women to the roles of wife, mother, and homemaker, and to direct men to the roles of husband, father, and provider. Not surprisingly, the jobs women have taken are more likely to be located in residential areas, more likely to afford opportunities for part-time work, and in general to be more compatible with the traditional primary roles.[6]

In short, in attempting to make their traditional homemaking role more compatible with labor market work, women make decisions concerning human capital investments, hours of work, and job location that result in incomes lower than those earned by men.

Participation and Human Capital Decisions The traditional childbearing–childrearing role of women means that their participation in the labor market will be discontinuous and truncated. This fact has a variety of implications.

First, since women will work fewer lifetime hours, their expected rate of return on human capital investments (education and job training) will be lower than that for men. It might therefore be rational for women to choose to invest less in education and training. Because of smaller investments in human capital, the productivity and thus the earnings of women will be less than for men. Similarly, anticipating greater turnover among female workers as they move from the labor market to work in the home, employers may act rationally in investing in less on-the-job training for women.

Second, the stock of human capital that women possess may deteriorate when they are out of the labor force. For example, a professional nurse who temporarily withdraws from the labor force to have and rear children may find that technological advances in medicine have rendered her skills largely obsolete during her 10- or 15-year absence from the labor market. Again, this means lower productivity and lower earnings.

[5]Sorensen, op. cit., p. 2.
[6]Victor F. Fuchs, *How We Live* (Cambridge, MA: Harvard University Press, 1983), pp. 28–29.

Third, it can be argued that occupational segregation is also the result of rational choice. Knowing they will not be in the labor force continuously, women may have a preference for occupations such as nursing or elementary school teaching, which will have the greatest relevance or carryover value for productive activity within the home. The overall implication here is that some substantial portion, if not all, of the female–male earnings differential results from considerations other than discrimination.

Heterogeneous Jobs and Preferences We noted in Chapter 8 that wage and earnings differentials may arise because jobs and workers are heterogeneous. On one hand, jobs differ in terms of such factors as social status, hours of work, location, and risk of accident or death. On the other hand, workers have different job preferences or "tastes." Compensating wage differentials arise in part as a consequence of these heterogeneities. If women put a high value on, say, shorter hours, job safety, and the location of jobs close to their homes, then the exercise of these preferences may result in lower wages and earnings for women. Stated differently, some portion of the higher earnings of males *may* be a wage differential that compensates them for longer hours and for performing more hazardous and inconveniently located jobs and thus is unrelated to sex discrimination. In fact, women—particularly married women—are much more likely to hold part-time jobs than are men. Additionally, in comparing "full-time" male and female workers, we find that on the average men work more hours per week than do women. Fuchs contends that the desire of women to work part-time or shorter hours contributes to occupational segregation—and consequently to lower female earnings—because occupations differ in the opportunities they afford for part-time work and relatively shorter workweeks.

Becker[7] has extended this line of reasoning by pointing out that women remain largely responsible for child care and household production, activities that are highly effort-intensive. Married women react to this by seeking jobs and occupations that require less effort. The consequences are twofold. First, by choice, women segregate themselves into less-demanding (less effort-intensive) jobs and occupations. As we know from the crowding model, this leads to lower earnings for women. Second, wage rates paid by employers depend not only on time worked but also on effort expended. Because women allegedly choose less effort-intensive jobs, their wages and earnings
15-3 are lower than those of men.

Discrimination as a Cause

The "rational choice" view suggests that voluntary decisions by women concerning the amounts and types of education and training they receive and the kinds of jobs they choose *cause* them to realize lower earnings than men. Skeptics argue that it is more plausible to reverse the implied cause-effect sequence and thereby assign a primary role to discrimination in explaining female–male earnings differentials. To facilitate our discussion, we will concentrate on the rational choice contention that women freely

[7] Gary S. Becker, "Human Capital, Effort, and the Sexual Division of Labor," *Journal of Labor Economics,* January 1985, pp. S33–S58.

15-3 World of Work

WOMEN IN MANAGEMENT: A "MOMMY TRACK"?*

Felice N. Schwartz, a leading authority on career women, has boldly proposed that firms should recognize that women in management positions fit into two general categories. "Career-primary" women are those female managers who put their careers first. They are willing to make sacrifices in their family lives; to work extra hours and on weekends; and to pursue all available opportunities for professional development. Some of these women will remain single; others will be married but childless; and still others will marry and have children but be willing to have others raise their children. "Career-and-family" women are those who want to pursue careers but also want to have children and actively participate in the rearing of those children. These women, who are on what has been dubbed the "mommy track," are willing to accept more limited career and compensation growth in exchange for more free time to engage in the bearing and nurturing of children.

Schwartz contends that in general it is more costly to hire female managers than male managers because career-and-family women frequently leave a firm after it has invested in their recruitment, training, and development. To reduce or eliminate this cost, Schwartz argues, firms should recognize the two categories of women managers and provide the job flexibility which will allow the retention of career-and-family women as middle managers. Specifically, firms should make available part-time employment; greater flexibility in scheduling work hours; "job sharing," where two workers split a single job; and high-quality child care. Schwartz asserts that career-and-family women are valuable assets to firms and can be retained by such measures. In short, companies should adopt policies which accommodate motherhood and child rearing as a means of retaining skilled managers and workers. Schwartz predicted correctly that labor force growth would be substantially less in the 1990s than it was in the 1970s and 1980s and that the available supplies of quality managerial talent would diminish.

The "mommy track" proposal has generated considerable controversy. Perhaps the main point of contention is that the recognition of a "mommy track" tends to reinforce and solidify business prejudices about women. A "mommy track" makes it explicit that women are potentially more expensive to hire and train and implicitly says to employers that, if you have the option, hire men.

*Felice N. Schwartz, "Management and Women and the New Facts of Life," *Harvard Business Review*, January–February 1989, pp. 65–79.

choose to truncate their labor market careers with the result that it is rational for employers and women themselves to invest less in human capital.

One can argue that women invest in less education and training or invest in types of training that have the greatest carryover value for household production *because* of labor market discrimination and manifest income disparities. For example, the decision of many women to withdraw from the labor force for extended periods of time may be the consequence of the low opportunity cost of nonparticipation, the latter being the result of low market pay due to discrimination. Poor labor market opportunities for women lower their earnings and increase the relative attractiveness of work in the home. In more positive terms, if job opportunities and the earnings potential for women in the labor market were improved because of a decline in discrimination, more women might decide to remain single or childless if they did marry. Or if they were to marry and have children, the higher earnings due to less discrimination might make it rational for them to employ domestic help or use child care facilities and remain continuously in the labor force. In this interpretation, labor market discrimination *causes* women to choose the amounts and kinds of human capital investment that they do and to withdraw from the labor market for extended periods.

It is also possible that many women who experience sexual harassment ("World of Work" 14-1) and discrimination in the workplace respond by changing careers or having children and working in the home. Thus, the truncated careers of women and their resulting lower earnings may be an outcome of discrimination, not the consequence of truly free choice.[8]

Bergmann stresses the role of discrimination in explaining female–male income differences by examining a list of 25 narrowly defined occupations (for example, hotel clerks, apparel sales workers, secretaries, bus drivers, stock clerks, painters, printing machine operators) that require similar duties and human capital for both male and female workers. These are occupations in which we would expect prolonged experience to have little or no impact on productivity and earnings. In all of these occupations, she notes, men are paid more than women and in some cases men receive as much as 60 to 70 percent more than women. She contends that such consistent and substantial male wage advantages can be explained on no other grounds than discrimination. Bergmann also counters the argument that child care is responsible for the inferior economic position of women by noting that female workers with no children earn much less than male workers of equivalent education and work experience.[9]

A Complex Intermingling

Which position is correct? Perhaps the most balanced response is provided by Lloyd and Niemi:

> Do the lower earnings, higher unemployment, and occupational segregation of women result from their higher turnover and lack of continuous job experience? Or are discontinuous work histories and high turnover the inevitable result of being restricted to secondary occupations, characterized by low earnings, unstable employment and little or no opportunity for advancement? The answer to both questions is *yes*. The same observed variables, such as occupation and work experience, simultaneously represent both different opportunities *and* different qualifications. Different opportunities arise in part because of employers' perceptions of the different qualifications of women and men, and different qualifications, in turn, are the result of different opportunities for skill acquisition.[10]

The point, of course, is that discrimination entails a complex intermingling of cause and effect. Differences in supply decisions with respect to human capital investment and occupational choice of males and females may *result* from labor market

[8]For evidence of this effect, see David Neumark and Michele McLennon, "Sex Discrimination and Women's Labor Market Interruptions," *Journal of Human Resources,* Fall 1995, pp. 713–740.

[9]Barbara R. Bergmann, "Does the Market for Women's Labor Need Fixing?" *Journal of Economic Perspectives,* Winter 1989, pp. 46–48. Also see Andrew M. Gill, "The Role of Discrimination in Determining Occupational Structure," *Industrial and Labor Relations Review,* July 1989, pp. 610–623. Examining racial differences in occupational structure, Gill finds that "much of the underrepresentation of blacks in managerial, sales and clerical, and craft occupations can be attributed to discrimination."

[10]Cynthia B. Lloyd and Beth T. Niemi, *The Economics of Sex Differentials* (New York: Columbia University Press, 1979), p. 13.

discrimination and existing earnings disparities and simultaneously be a *cause* of these earnings differentials.

Evidence

Despite the difficult cause-effect interrelationships involved, a large number of empirical studies have attempted to disaggregate female–male and black–white earnings differentials in the hope of determining what portion of them is due to productivity differences as opposed to discrimination per se. These studies attempt to control for such factors as education, age, training, industry and occupation, union membership, location and continuity of workforce experience, health, and so forth. The reasoning is that these are allegedly "nondiscriminatory" considerations that cause productivity differences and therefore earnings differences. A comprehensive study by Blau and Kahn found that approximately two-thirds of the female–male earnings differential is attributable to such factors as differences in years of work experience (26 percent), industry (23 percent), occupation (8 percent), and union status (4 percent).[11] That is, males have more work experience, are more likely to be union members, and are in higher-paying industries and occupations. Consequently, their productivity was higher, and this justified two-thirds of the earnings advantage they enjoyed. The remaining one-third of the earnings gap was "unexplained" and presumably due, wholly or in part, to discrimination. Consistent with other studies, Blau and Kahn report that the gender earnings gap is falling over time.[12] They find that the female–male earning ratio rose from 62 percent in 1979 to 72 percent in 1988. The earnings differential fell equally due to an increase in the relative productivity characteristics of women and a decline in the unexplained gap.

Regarding the black–white gap, a study by Blau and Kahn found that productivity differences account for 89 percent of the pay differential between black and white men.[13] A study by Neal and Johnson found that racial differences in cognitive achievement as measured by the Armed Forces Qualifying Test (AFQT) score alone appears to "explain" about two-thirds of the pay gap between young black and white men.[14] They find that black men have lower AFQT scores due to lower-quality schooling and

[11]Francine D. Blau and Lawrence M. Kahn, "Swimming Upstream: Trends in the Gender Wage Differential in the 1980s," *Journal of Labor Economics,* January 1997, pp. 1–42. They also report that the productivity differences only account for one-third of the gap when only human capital variables are included in the statistical model (i.e., gender differences in industry, occupation, and union status are not accounted for).

[12]For example, see William E. Even and David A. Macpherson, "The Decline of Private Sector Unionism and the Gender Wage Gap," *Journal of Human Resources,* Spring 1993, pp. 279–296; June O'Neill and Solomon Polachek, "Why the Gender Gap Narrowed in the 1980s," *Journal of Labor Economics,* January 1993, pp. S205–S228; and Alison J. Wellington, "Changes in the Male/Female Wage Gap, 1976–1985," *Journal of Human Resources,* Spring 1993, pp. 383–411.

[13]Francine D. Blau and Lawrence M. Kahn, "Race and Gender Pay Differentials," in David Lewin, Olivia S. Mitchell, and Peter D. Scherer (eds.), *Research Frontiers in Industrial Relations and Human Resources* (Madison, WI: Industrial Relations Research Association, 1992), pp. 381–416.

[14]Derek Neal and William Johnson, "The Role of Premarket Factors in Black–White Wage Differences," *Journal of Political Economy,* October 1996, pp. 869–895. Also see June O'Neill, "The Role of Human Capital in Earnings Differences between Black and White Men," *Journal of Economic Perspectives,* Fall 1990, pp. 25–46.

other environmental factors. In contrast to the gender pay gap, the black–white pay differential has not narrowed in recent years.[15] The stall in progress for black men appears to be partly the result of offsetting factors. On one hand, black men have, on average, less education than white men, and so the increased payoff to education in the 1980s has caused the black–white pay gap to expand. On the other hand, the black–white gap in education has shrunk, which has tended to diminish the black–white earnings differential. The net result has been little change in the black–white earnings differential.

Controversy

But the interpretation of such studies has been controversial. Some economists feel that the "unexplained" earnings differential overstates the role of discrimination; others contend that it is an underestimation. Those who feel that the discrimination estimate is too high argue that there may be other productivity-influencing considerations (such as worker motivation, quantitative skills, or course of study in school) that have not been taken into account. These factors allegedly increase the productivity of males relative to females and, if included, would reduce the unexplained (discriminatory) portion of the wage differential.[16]

Others, however, take the opposite view and contend that certain omitted variables (for example, men are more likely to smoke and abuse alcohol and drugs, have criminal records, and have bad driving records) suggest that the job performance and productivity of men should be lower than that of females. Taking such variables into account would increase the size of the "unexplained" female–male earnings gap. A second argument is that in fact many of the control variables—such as formal education, on-the-job training, and occupational placement—reflect discriminatory decisions. Although male productivity may exceed that of females, that higher productivity reflects discriminatory decisions with respect to (1) the quantity and type of education and job training provided men and women and (2) occupational segregation.

Conclusion? "When all is said and done, we cannot make a precise estimate of the proportion of the wage gap that is due to discrimination, but we can say with

[15]See, for example, Francine D. Blau and Andrea H. Beller, "Black–White Earnings over the 1970s and 1980s, Gender Differences in Trends," *Review of Economics and Statistics,* May 1992, pp. 276–286; and John Bound and Richard B. Freeman, "What Went Wrong? The Erosion of Relative Earnings among Young Black Men in the 1980s," *Quarterly Journal of Economics,* February 1992, pp. 201–232.

[16]See, for example, Thomas N. Daymont and Paul J. Andrisiani, "Job Preferences, College Major, and the Gender Gap in Earnings," *Journal of Human Resources,* Summer 1984, pp. 408–428; and Randall K. Filer, "Male–Female Wage Differences: The Importance of Compensating Differentials," *Industrial and Labor Relations Review,* April 1985, pp. 426–437. Also see Morton Paglin and Anthony M. Rufolo, "Heterogeneous Human Capital, Occupational Choice, and Male–Female Earnings Differences," *Journal of Labor Economics,* January 1990, pp. 123–144. Paglin and Rufolo find that "mathematical ability is an important determinant of field choices for college students and that differences in earnings across fields are largely explained as a return to the use of scarce quantitative abilities in the production of each type of human capital." Differences between females and males in quantitative skills purportedly explain a significant portion of the previously unexplained earnings differences between females and males.

considerable confidence that the statistical evidence points strongly to discrimination as an important factor in the labor market.[17]

QUICK REVIEW 15-2

- Some economists contend that the inferior economic position of women has resulted mainly from educational decisions, occupational choices, interrupted careers, and other voluntary choices made by women.
- Other economists stress discrimination as being the root cause of the inferior economic position of women; discriminatory outcomes help explain the economic choices made by women.
- After sorting out nondiscriminatory sources, empirical studies typically find a large, unexplained residual in pay by gender and race; many researchers attribute most of this residual to discrimination.
- Controversy remains on the question of how successfully empirical studies have isolated true discriminatory outcomes.

Your Turn: On average, women have less mathematical and quantitative training than men. Jobs demanding high levels of such training often pay exceptionally high salaries. Relates these factors to each of the arguments made in the first two review points above. (Answers: See page 627.)

ANTIDISCRIMINATION POLICIES AND ISSUES

There are several avenues through which government might attack the problem of discrimination.[18] One very general policy is to achieve a tight labor market through the use of appropriate monetary and fiscal policies. On the one hand, an expanding economy makes it increasingly expensive for employers to indulge their "tastes for discrimination." On the other hand, tight labor markets help to overcome stereotyping. For example, the over-full employment of World War II simultaneously created new labor market opportunities for minorities and women and made it clear that fe-

[17]Barbara Bergmann, *The Economic Emergence of Women* (New York: Basic Books, Inc., 1986), p. 81. Also relevant to this overall discussion is Robert G. Wood, Mary E. Corcoran, and Paul Courant, "Pay Differences among the Highly Paid: The Male–Female Gap in Lawyers' Salaries," *Journal of Labor Economics,* July 1993, pp. 417–441; David Neumark, with the assistance of Roy J. Blank and Kyle D. Van Nort, "Sex Discrimination in Restaurant Hiring: An Audit Study," *Quarterly Journal of Economics,* August 1996, pp. 915–942; William R. Carrington and Kenneth R. Troske, "Gender Segregation in Small Firms," *Journal of Human Resources,* Summer 1995, pp. 503–533; Andrew M. Gill, "Incorporating the Cause of Occupational Differences in Studies of Racial Wage Differentials," *Journal of Human Resources,* Winter 1994, pp. 20–41; and Edwin A. Sexton and Reed Neil Olsen, "The Return to On-the-Job Training: Are They the Same for Blacks and Whites?" *Southern Economic Journal,* October 1994, pp. 328–342.

[18]For a more detailed discussion of antidiscrimination policies, see Bergmann, *The Economic Emergence of Women,* chaps. 7 and 8.

TABLE 15-6 A SUMMARY OF ANTIDISCRIMINATION LAWS AND POLICIES RELATING TO GENDER AND RACE

Equal Pay Act of 1963
Mandates equal pay for women and men who perform the same, or highly similar, jobs.
Civil Rights Act of 1964, Title VII
Seeks to eliminate discrimination based on race, gender, color, religion, or national origin in hiring, promoting, firing, and compensating workers.
Executive orders (1965–68)
Prohibit federal contractors from discriminating among workers on the basis of race, gender, color, religion, or national origin; require affirmative-action programs for firms that underuse women and minorities.

males and blacks could effectively perform in jobs that heretofore had been closed to them.

A second general policy is to improve the education and training opportunities of those who have been discriminated against. For example, by upgrading the quantity and quality of schooling received by blacks, they can become more competitive with white workers.

The third and most obvious means of dealing with discrimination is through direct governmental intervention. We will focus on this aspect of policy.

Direct governmental intervention has stressed equal employment opportunities for minorities and for women. The purpose has been to deal directly with labor market inequalities by prohibiting certain practices in hiring, promotion, and compensation. Table 15-6 provides a summary of the salient legislation and policies that are the focal point for our discussion.

Equal Pay Act of 1963

This was the first major federal act to deal with sex discrimination. The act makes it illegal for employers to pay men and women different wage rates if they "do equal work on jobs, the performance of which requires equal skill, effort and responsibility, and which are performed under similar working conditions." While the ***Equal Pay Act of 1963*** was clearly a landmark piece of legislation, it did not comprehensively deal with all forms of gender discrimination. In particular, we have seen that women workers are plagued with the problem of occupational segregation as indicated by the crowding model. A discriminating employer could simply dodge the provisions of the act by practicing strict occupational segregation, that is, by *not* employing women and men on the same jobs. In fact, an employer with an all-male labor force would be in compliance with the law.

Civil Rights Act of 1964

Title VII of the ***Civil Rights Act of 1964*** is the centerpiece of U.S. antidiscrimination policy. This law applies to not only discriminatory wages but also discrimination in hiring and promotions. Specifically, the act made it illegal for any employer "to refuse to hire or to discharge any individual, or otherwise to discriminate against any individual with respect to his compensation, terms, conditions, or privileges or employment, because of such individual's race, color, religion, sex, or national origin." By requiring equal treatment in hiring, firing, promotion, and compensation (including fringe benefits), the law virtually eliminated the ability of employers to practice overt discrimination legally. As amended, the act applies to all employers in interstate commerce with 15 or more workers, to all labor unions with 15 or more members, and to workers employed by educational institutions, state and local governments, and federal agencies. Enforcement rests primarily with the Equal Employment Opportunity Commission (EEOC).

Executive Orders and Federal Contracts

Executive orders issued in 1965 and 1968 attempted to eliminate all discriminatory policies that might be practiced by businesses or other institutions holding government contracts. Thus, the executive order of 1968 specifies:

> The contractor will not discriminate against any employee or applicant for employment because of race, color, religion or national origin. The contractor will take *affirmative action* to ensure that applicants are employed, and that employees are treated during employment, without regard to their race, color, religion, sex or national origin. Such action shall include, but not be limited to the following: employment, upgrading, demotion, or transfer; recruitment or recruitment advertising; layoff or termination; rates of pay or other forms of compensation; and selection for training, including apprenticeship.

As revised, the executive orders require firms with contracts totaling $50,000 or more to develop ***affirmative-action programs.*** If on examination it is found that a firm underuses women and minorities compared to their proportions in the available labor force, the firm must establish a program embodying numerical goals and timetables for increasing its employment of women and minorities. In a series of important decisions in 1986 and 1987 involving, among others, sheet metal workers in New York City, firefighters in Cleveland, and the Alabama state police, the Supreme Court upheld the constitutionality of affirmative-action programs. More recently, however, the Court's decisions have threatened to undermine affirmative-action plans. For example, in early 1989 the Court declared illegal a program by the city of Richmond, Virginia, to provide a specified proportion of its construction work to minority-owned firms, arguing that the program constitutes reverse discrimination. Similarly, another 1989 ruling permitted white Birmingham, Alabama, firefighters to challenge an existing affirmative-action program on the grounds that the program denied them promotions in favor of less-qualified blacks. The Birmingham ruling has triggered a number of reverse-discrimination lawsuits throughout the country. On the political scene, in 1996 California voters passed a constitutional amendment ending all state programs that give gender or racial preferences in government hiring and contracting, as well as public education. It is fair to say that affirmative action is under legal and political attack.

Comparable Worth Controversy[19]

The last decade has spawned a heated debate over the concept of comparable worth or "pay equity." This is partly the consequence of the persistence of the female–male earnings gap (Table 15-1) *and* partly the result of the continued occupational segregation of women. Equal pay for equal work as specified by the Equal Pay Act of 1963 will be of little or no help to women and minorities if they are unable to gain access to the jobs now dominated by white males.

The Concept The comparable worth doctrine attempts to broaden the concept of equal pay for equal work to the notion of equal pay for work of comparable value to a firm or government agency. The essence of the ***comparable worth doctrine*** is that female secretaries, nurses, and clerks should receive the same salaries as male truck drivers or construction workers *if* the knowledge, skills, effort, and working conditions in these disparate jobs are comparable. This concept is made operational by applying job evaluations to determine the worth and the wage rates to be assigned to various jobs. Job evaluation entails the assigning of points to the aforementioned job characteristics. Hence, if a job evaluation program determines that the jobs of transportation engineer and registered nurse entail the same number of points—that is, if they are of comparable worth—then the rates of pay should be equal.[20]

The Debate The arguments for and against comparable worth have solidified along the following lines. Proponents argue, first, that job evaluation, although admittedly imperfect, will provide a better indication of female and minority worth than existing wages. The latter are distorted by such institutional factors as unions, seniority provisions, statistical discrimination, barriers to occupational choice, imperfect information, and tradition. According to this view, it is incorrect to argue that existing earnings disparities between males and females largely reflect differences in productivity, varying degrees of job attachment, and differing job preferences. Second, supporters of comparable worth note that numerous public agencies and private firms presently base their internal wage structures on job evaluation. Comparable worth, therefore, merely extends an existing practice. Finally, those advocating comparable worth contend that its

[19]The reader who is especially interested in this topic should consult Michael E. Gold, *A Dialogue on Comparable Worth* (Ithaca, NY: ILR Press, 1983); Henry J. Aaron and Cameran M. Lougy, *The Comparable Worth Controversy* (Washington, DC: Brookings Institution, 1986); Frances C. Hutner, *Equal Pay for Comparable Worth* (New York: Praeger, 1986); Mark Aldrich and Robert Buchele, *The Economics of Comparable Worth* (Cambridge, MA: Ballinger Publishing Company, 1986); Ellen Frankel Paul, *Equity and Gender: The Comparable Worth Debate* (Washington, DC: Cato Institute, 1988); M. Anne Hill and Mark R. Killingsworth (eds.), *Comparable Worth: Analysis and Evidence* (Ithaca, NY: ILR Press, 1989); Mark R. Killingsworth, *The Economics of Comparable Worth* (Kalamazoo, MI: W. E. Upjohn Institute, 1990); and Steven E. Rhoads, *Incomparable Worth* (Cambridge, England: Cambridge University Press, 1993).

[20]Job evaluation is discussed in more detail in Chapter 16 of this text.

implementation is essential if current wage discrimination is to be corrected within any reasonable time frame.

But comparable worth is not without its critics. First, it is held that job evaluation is necessarily subjective and arbitrary; no two evaluations seem to produce the same results. Thus, the resulting pay scales have no claim to equity or fairness. Detractors predict that once wage scales are set through job evaluation, occupational groups will bicker over the accuracy of the methods used to calculate point totals and innumerable lawsuits are certain to follow. Second, critics argue that if comparable worth results in substantial pay hikes for female-dominated jobs, employers will respond by hiring fewer (female) workers. That is, comparable worth may hurt female workers by reducing their employment opportunities. Finally, opponents of comparable worth assert that it will entail an efficiency loss for the economy as a whole. The contention is that reasonably competitive labor markets will tend to allocate labor efficiently (Chapter 6). But under comparable worth the use of job evaluations will almost invariably determine wages at levels that deviate from their true market worth. The result will be shortages of workers where wages are set below, and surpluses where wages are established above, their true market value. In short, critics contend that the application of comparable worth will undermine the ability of labor markets to allocate labor to its highest valued employments and thereby will generate economic *in*efficiency.

You have probably sensed that the debate over comparable worth rests rather heavily on one's conception of labor markets prior to the imposition of comparable worth. Opponents of comparable worth assume that labor markets are competitive; therefore, workers are paid what they are worth *and* labor is initially allocated efficiently. Proponents of comparable worth envision labor markets as riddled with the imperfections caused by various forms of discrimination, not to mention custom and tradition. In the former view, a comparable worth plan necessarily entails harmful economic effects; in the latter model, the economic implications of comparable worth need not be adverse and, in fact, may be beneficial.[21]

Opponents of comparable worth suggest that public policy might be better directed toward enforcement of existing laws—or enactment of stricter laws, if necessary—that grant and guarantee equal access of females, free from harassment, to job-training programs, employment opportunities, and job advancement in *all* occupations. Therefore, females desiring to enter the higher-paying "mostly male" occupations could do so. This would improve female pay directly and, by reducing labor supply to traditional female jobs, eventually would increase pay there as well. Any remaining differentials would reflect preferences for particular types of work, not discrimination. Proponents of comparable worth, however, quickly counter that this "equal access" approach has not resolved the female–male pay gap to date and that even if it were more successful in the future, it would take decades to accomplish what comparable worth can quickly achieve.

Evidence

Although empirical evidence on the effects of comparable worth is rather limited, a study of its impact on government workers in the state of Washington reaches the fol-

[21]See Aaron and Lougy, op. cit., pp. 16–24.

lowing conclusions. First, as expected, the implementation of comparable worth reduced the gender pay gap. Specifically, the female-to-male hourly pay rose from 80.2 to 85.6 percent, although it is recognized that a part of this gain might be due to more general considerations that are reducing the female–male earnings gap (Table 15-1). Second, comparable worth imposes unemployment effects. The share of state government employment going to those occupations that received significant comparable worth pay increases declined. Third, it was found that under comparable worth the returns to human capital investments declined. In particular, the contributions of the level of schooling (such as having a high school diploma or college degree) and length of work experience to one's pay were reduced under comparable worth.[22]

A study of comparable worth in Iowa found that the substantial gains to women under its original plan were significantly diluted during the political process of finalizing and implementing the plan: ". . . initial gains to women were ultimately reduced and redirected toward constituencies that stood to lose or gain little as a result of the initial plan: union members, professionals, supervisors, and those with the highest market wage." While women were to gain 8.8 percentage points in female pay relative to male pay under the original plan, that gain was reduced to only 1.4 percentage points by the time it was finalized.[23]

QUICK REVIEW 15-3

- The three main facets of antidiscrimination laws and policies relating to gender and race are *(a)* the Equal Pay Act of 1963, *(b)* the Civil Rights Act of 1964 (Title VII), and *(c)* executive orders rendered between 1965 and 1968.
- The comparable worth doctrine is the notion that women in one occupation should receive the same salaries as men in another if the level of skill, effort, responsibilities, and working conditions are comparable.
- Proponents of comparable worth policy see it as the quickest and most efficient way to close the earnings gap between women and men.
- Critics contend that the implementation of a nationwide comparable worth policy would severely reduce female employment, distort market pay, and thereby cause allocative inefficiency.

Your Turn: Affirmative-action policy emerged from which one of the laws and policies listed in the first review point above—*a, b,* or *c*? (Answer: See page 627.)

Controversy and Conflict

To say that government antidiscrimination legislation and policies have been controversial is an understatement. Making no pretense at being comprehensive, let's note

[22]June O'Neill, Michael Brien, and James Cunningham, "Effects of Comparable Worth Policy: Evidence from Washington State," *American Economic Review,* May 1989, pp. 305–309.

[23]Peter F. Orazem and J. Peter Mattila, "The Implementation Process of Comparable Worth: Winners and Losers," *Journal of Political Economy,* February 1990, pp. 134–152.

some of the controversies and criticisms surrounding antidiscrimination measures and their application.

Free-Market View Some economists take the position that direct governmental intervention is at best unnecessary and at worst counterproductive in eliminating discrimination. Friedman has argued that the competitive market system is quite capable of eliminating discrimination:

> There is an economic incentive in a free market to separate economic efficiency from other characteristics of the individual. A businessman or an entrepreneur who expresses preferences in his business activities that are not related to productive efficiency is at a disadvantage compared to other individuals who do not. Such an individual is in effect imposing higher costs on himself than are other individuals who do not have such preferences. Hence, in a free market they will tend to drive him out.[24]

Sowell, a black economist, has gone further to argue that legislation and policies designed to aid disadvantaged groups have often worked to their detriment. He notes that American Indians, who have had the longest and most intimate involvement with the federal government, have persistently been on the lowest rung of the economic ladder. Furthermore, Sowell observes that some groups—for example, Jewish and Japanese Americans—have realized highly favorable socioeconomic positions in our society "despite a well documented record of anti-Semitism and anti-Oriental feelings, policies, and laws."[25] Sowell's view is that the socioeconomic positions of various racial and ethnic groups in our society are not due primarily to discrimination but rather to culturally produced attitudes and work patterns.

Interventionist View Others take the opposite view that the market has clearly failed to make reasonable progress in eliminating discrimination and that while present laws and policies are helpful, they do not go far enough. For example, some critics contend that legislation and public policies have been too narrowly focused. As our enumeration of the various types of discrimination at the outset of this chapter suggests, discrimination is a multifaceted and deeply rooted problem that will not quickly be resolved by laws that apply primarily to compensation, hiring, and promotion. More specifically, these policies function only on the demand side of the labor market, while much of the problem lies on the supply side. Minorities and women have been discriminated against in acquiring the human capital—that is, the formal education and job training—required to compete on equal terms with white males. What good is a firm's affirmative-action program to hire more blacks and women for middle-management positions or a university's efforts to employ more black and female faculty if qualified candidates are simply not available? More generally, the argument is that discrimination assumes many forms and is highly institutionalized and that the var-

[24]Milton Friedman, *Capitalism and Freedom* (Chicago: University of Chicago Press, 1962), pp. 109–110. For a detailed presentation of "conservative," "liberal," and "radical" views of discrimination, see Robert Cherry, *Discrimination: Its Economic Impact on Blacks, Women, and Jews* (Lexington, MA: Lexington Books, 1989).

[25]Thomas Sowell, *Markets and Minorities* (New York: Basic Books, Inc., 1981), p. 126.

ious types of discrimination tend to reinforce one another. Therefore, a more comprehensive and more aggressive government program against discrimination is required.

Another related criticism is that *current* legislation and policies designed to create equal opportunities for all workers do little to correct the effects of *past* discrimination. While recent legislation may keep existing income differentials based on gender and race from widening, it will allegedly do little to lessen those disparities in the foreseeable future. Minorities and women have been forced to carry the extra burden of discrimination in the "race" for socioeconomic status; thus, they find themselves far behind. Merely to remove the discrimination burden does nothing to close the present gap in the socioeconomic race. It is argued that something more than equal opportunity—positive preferential treatment—is required if women and minorities are to catch up. For example, job segregation is currently so pervasive that it will persist for decades if we are content to accept only the marginal changes in the occupational allocation of labor that equal opportunity legislation allows. Furthermore, white male workers typically have achieved seniority, which protects them from layoffs and thereby puts the burden of unemployment on women and minorities. Those who accept this line of reasoning endorse affirmative action, quotas, and other forms of preferential treatment as appropriate means for hastening the elimination of discrimination. The counterargument is that such practices will frequently force employers to hire less-qualified female or minority workers to achieve affirmative-action targets or quotas, and therefore, economic efficiency will be impaired. Another counterargument is that quotas and preferential treatment are a form of "reverse discrimination." It is held that preferential treatment and discrimination are simply two ways of viewing the same phenomenon. Showing preference for A is to discriminate against B.

Have Antidiscrimination Policies Worked?

In Table 15-1 we observed that the black–white and female–male earnings ratios have increased during the past 25 years. How much of these increases are explained by antidiscrimination policy? The simple answer is that empirical evidence is mixed, and therefore, opinions are divided.

This lack of consensus is not surprising because it is extremely difficult to isolate the effect of antidiscrimination policies from other factors and polices that might have impacted the relative economic status of women, men, blacks, and whites. For example, the increase in the ratio of black to white earnings might be interpreted as the result of, say, the Civil Rights Act of 1964, which has presumably reduced discrimination and therefore raised the demand for, and wages and earnings of, black workers. An alternative explanation might be that increases in the quantity and improvements in the quality of the education of black workers relative to whites have been the cause of the slight rise in the black–white earnings ratio. Or perhaps the improved relative earnings of blacks have derived from labor supply adjustments having little or nothing to do with antidiscrimination policies. Aware of such difficulties, let's touch on some of the relevant empirical evidence.

An influential study by Freeman concluded that federal antidiscrimination efforts have been instrumental in reducing black–white income differentials. His analysis indicates that specific groups of black workers—women, young men, and young male college graduates—have realized very large economic gains since World War II, while the progress of older black workers has been more modest. Freeman estimates that overall, the incomes of black males and black females were 15 and 22 percent higher, respectively, in 1971 than they would have been in the absence of the antidiscrimination laws and policies of the mid-1960s. Although the attainment of more education and the general economic boom of the late 1960s were undoubtedly helpful in improving the relative economic status of blacks, Freeman concludes that most of the relative gain realized by blacks during the 1960s was "the result of governmental and related antidiscriminatory activity associated with the 1964 Civil Rights Act."[26]

Butler and Heckman, however, have critically examined Freeman's study, along with several others, and concluded that there is no real evidence that the tightening of the black–white earnings ratio is attributable to government's antidiscrimination activities.[27] Their basic argument is that although black–white wage and earnings differentials did begin to decline in the mid-1960s when antidiscrimination legislation was put into place, the relationship is quite coincidental rather than causal. Butler and Heckman contend that the relative improvement in the economic status of blacks was attributable to a decline in the participation rates of low-income blacks (Chapter 3), caused by various income maintenance programs that were inaugurated and expanded as a part of the War on Poverty in the 1960s. As our analysis in Chapter 2 suggests, the increased availability of more generous income transfer payments encourages low-income receivers of both races to withdraw from the labor force. But, because relatively more blacks have low incomes than whites, a greater relative decline occurred in the supply of black workers, which caused the average wages and earnings of blacks to increase in comparison to those of whites.

In turn, the Butler–Heckman conclusion is challenged by new evidence from Card and Krueger[28] which supports the view that antidiscrimination legislation per se has increased the earnings of black men. Using data derived from current population surveys and Social Security earnings records, they find a distinct upward break in the rising trend of the relative wages of black men after 1964. They conclude that the Civil Rights Act of 1964 contributed significantly to the narrowing of the black–white earnings gap in the years immediately following enactment of the law.

The picture painted by the empirical literature on the impact of affirmative action is a bit clearer. Leonard [29] has concluded from a series of studies that affirmative action led to improvements in the employment opportunities of both minorities and females between 1974 and 1980 but that this progress largely ended in the 1980s. Specifically, he statistically compared the changes in the demographic composition of

[26]Richard B. Freeman, "Changes in the Labor Market for Black Americans, 1948–1972," *Brookings Papers on Economic Activity,* no. 1, 1973, pp. 67–120.

[27]Richard Butler and James J. Heckman, "The Government's Impact on the Labor Market Status of Black Americans: A Critical Review," in Hausman et al. (eds.), op. cit., pp. 235–281.

[28]Card and Krueger, op. cit.

[29]Jonathan S. Leonard, "The Impact of Affirmative Action on Employment," *Journal of Labor Economics,* October 1984, pp. 439–463; Leonard, "What Promises Are Worth: The Impact of Affirmative Action Goals," *Journal of Human Resources,* Winter 1985, pp. 3–20; and Leonard, "Women and Affirmative Action," *Journal of Economic Perspectives,* Winter 1989, pp. 61–75.

the workforce in more than 68,000 firms, isolating the role of affirmative action by controlling for other factors that might have brought about these changes in demographic composition. Between 1974 and 1980, female and minority shares of employment grew faster in firms obligated to undertake affirmative action than in establishments not subject to this requirement. In this period affirmative action increased the demand for black males by 6.5 percent, for nonblack minority males by 11.9 percent, and for white females by 3.5 percent.

But the positive effects of affirmative action apparently ended during the 1980s, when the government's enforcement slackened under the Reagan administration. Leonard reports that, after accounting for other factors, the employment shares of blacks actually grew less rapidly over the 1980–84 period in companies required to practice affirmative action than in firms not covered by the law.

A final comment: We can be quite certain that controversy will continue to surround not only the scope and techniques of antidiscrimination policies but also the question of their actual effectiveness. But these debates should not obfuscate the clear reality that discrimination in America continues to influence labor supply and demand, and therefore wage rates and the allocation of labor. An understanding of discrimination and antidiscrimination policies is essential to a realistic conception of how labor markets work.

CHAPTER SUMMARY

1 Empirical data suggest that *(a)* the earnings of full-time female and black workers are substantially less than those of white male workers; *(b)* blacks have higher unemployment rates than whites; *(c)* occupational distributions differ significantly by gender and race; *(d)* there are gender and racial differences in human capital acquisition; and *(e)* women and blacks have lower total earnings than white men at each level of educational attainment.
2 The effect of gender and racial discrimination is to redistribute national income and, by creating allocative inefficiency, diminish its size.
3 Much disagreement exists about the extent to which earnings differentials based on gender or race are rooted in discrimination per se as opposed to rational decision making by women and blacks.
4 Economists have found several nondiscriminatory factors that help explain gender and racial pay differentials. Nevertheless, even after these factors are accounted for, large unexplained pay disadvantages for blacks and women remain. Many economists attribute these unexplained pay differences to discrimination.
5 Governmental antidiscrimination legislation, policies, and proposals involving direct labor market intervention include the Equal Pay Act of 1963, the Civil Rights Act of 1964, and executive orders applicable to federal contractors.
6 The comparable worth doctrine is the idea that women in "women's occupations" should receive the same pay as men in "men's occupations" if the skills, effort, responsibilities, and working conditions are comparable.
7 Proponents of comparable worth policy contend that *(a)* job evaluation will provide a better indication of female and minority worth than existing wages; *(b)* job evaluation is common in many large firms and public agencies, and thus, comparable worth merely extends an accepted practice; *(c)* implementation of comparable worth policy would be the quickest and most efficient way to correct current wage discrimination.

8 Critics of comparable worth policy argue that *(a)* job evaluation is necessarily subjective and arbitrary; *(b)* it would reduce employment for women and blacks; *(c)* it would distort wage differentials, create numerous shortages and surpluses of workers, and cause allocative inefficiency.

9 Statistical evidence reveals no clear picture as to the impact of antidiscrimination policy on the gender and racial pay gaps. But there is evidence suggesting that affirmative-action programs have increased black employment and earnings in affected industries.

TERMS AND CONCEPTS

nondiscriminatory factors
Equal Pay Act of 1963
Civil Rights Act of 1964
affirmative-action programs
comparable worth doctrine

QUESTIONS AND STUDY SUGGESTIONS

1 What has been the general secular trend of the weekly earnings of full-time female workers compared to male workers? What factors help explain this trend?

2 Is the following statement true or false? If false, explain why. "The unemployment rates for white females and black men are considerably higher than the rate for white men."

3 Table 15-5 reveals significant earnings differences by gender and race at each level of education. What nondiscriminatory factors might explain part of the earnings differences between females and males? Between blacks and whites? Do you think that nondiscriminatory factors explain all the earnings differences in the table?

4 In what way does discrimination redistribute national income? How does it reduce national income?

5 There has been considerable controversy over the fact that certain pension plans into which males and females make equal contributions pay smaller monthly benefits to women than to men on the grounds that women live longer on the average than men. Is this practice discriminatory? Explain. The use of female military personnel in most forms of combat is currently prohibited. Do you favor this ban?

6 It has been argued that to correct the inequalities of past discrimination, blacks and females should be given preference in employment and promotion. Do you agree? In the celebrated *Bakke* case, the plaintiff argued that he had been unjustly denied admission to medical school because less-qualified black applicants were given preference under a quota system. Evaluate the plaintiff's argument: "To discriminate in favor of one individual or group is necessarily to discriminate against some other individual or group." Do you agree?

7 "Wage differences between men and women do not reflect discrimination but rather differences in job continuity and rational decisions with respect to education and on-the-job training." Explain why you agree or disagree.

8 Some economists have argued that the unemployment effects associated with the minimum wage have been greater for blacks than for whites. Explain why this might be the case.

9 Critically evaluate each of the following statements:

a "Affirmative-action plans have not worked; there is no evidence that they have increased black or female employment and wages."

b "The greatest barriers to economic equality between men and women are marriage and children."

10 Although the labor market opportunities for women have improved greatly over the past 30 years, poverty has become increasingly concentrated among women. How can you reconcile these two developments?

11 Professors in universities normally are paid according to their professional specialties, based on market pay, and not simply according to their degrees, number of courses they teach, and their research. Thus, professors of accounting and engineering usually receive significantly higher salaries than professors of nursing, art, and languages. Is this fair? What would be the impact of implementing a comparable worth pay policy in this situation: that is, paying all professors with comparable academic degrees, teaching loads, and research achievements the same salary? Assuming that the university does not increase its total payroll, which departments would eventually be strongest? Which weakest? Explain.

12 Explain why those who believe that labor markets generate wages based on marginal productivity typically oppose comparable worth policy, whereas those who believe that current wage patterns reflect overt and institutional discrimination are more likely to favor this policy.

SELECTED REFERENCES

Bergmann, Barbara R.: *In Defense of Affirmative Action* (New York: Basic Books, Inc., 1996).

Blau, Francine D., Marianne A. Ferber and Anne E. Winkler: *The Economics of Women, Men, and Work,* 3d ed. (Englewood Cliffs, NJ: Prentice-Hall, 1998).

Cherry, Robert: *Discrimination: Its Economic Impact on Blacks, Women, and Jews* (Lexington, MA: Lexington Books, 1989).

Fuchs, Victor R: *Women's Quest for Economic Equality* (Cambridge, MA: Harvard University Press, 1988).

Hoffman, Emily P. (ed.): *Essays on the Economics of Discrimination* (Kalamazoo, MI: W. E. Upjohn Institute, 1991).

Killingsworth, Mark R.: *The Economics of Comparable Worth* (Kalamazoo, MI: W. E. Upjohn Institute, 1990).

Lazear, Edward P., et al.: "Symposium on Women in the Labor Market," *Journal of Economic Perspectives,* Winter 1989, pp. 3–75.

Sorensen, Elaine: *Exploring the Reasons behind the Narrowing Gender Gap in Earnings* (Washington, DC: Urban Institute Press, 1991).

Sowell, Thomas: *Markets and Minorities* (New York: Basic Books, Inc., 1981).

"Symposium on the Economic Status of African-Americans," *Journal of Economic Perspectives,* Fall 1990, pp. 3–84.

CHAPTER 16

JOB SEARCH: EXTERNAL AND INTERNAL

A large amount of job switching occurs in the labor market. Nearly two-thirds of young people will work for three or more different employers in their first five years of work experience.[1] Between the ages of 16 and 64, the average male will change employers over 10 times.[2] Individuals also switch jobs without changing employers.

Individuals search for jobs for a variety of reasons. Firms may suffer a decrease in demand and lay off workers who then search for new employment. New high school and college graduates will search for their first permanent employment. Individuals who dropped out of the labor force to raise children may reenter the job market. Workers may search for jobs that are a better match with their abilities.[3] For a given occupation, earnings and other working conditions differ widely within a city or even a firm.[4] As a result, workers search for jobs that offer them better combinations of wages and job characteristics.

Our discussion of the job search process will proceed as follows: We first analyze how workers attempt to find jobs at a new employer (external job search). In our dis-

[1]Henry S. Farber, "The Analysis of Interfirm Worker Mobility," *Journal of Labor Economics,* October 1994, pp. 554–593.

[2]Robert E. Hall, "The Importance of Lifetime Jobs in the U.S. Economy," *American Economic Review,* September 1982, pp. 716–724.

[3]For an analysis of the job matching process, see Boyan Jovanovic, "Job Matching and the Theory of Turnover," *Journal of Political Economy,* October 1979, pp. 972–990; and Kenneth J. McLaughlin, "Rent Sharing in an Equilibrium Model of Matching and Turnover," *Journal of Labor Economics,* October 1994, pp. 499–523.

[4]For evidence on the variation of earnings, see John E. Buckley, "Wage Differences among Workers in the Same Job and Establishment," *Monthly Labor Review,* March 1985, pp. 11–16.

jects an offer, that wage opportunity is lost; most wage offers cannot be "stored." Therefore, *a major cost of continued job search is the forgone earnings of the best known opportunity.* As higher wage offers are received, the *marginal* cost of continued search rises.

What decision rule might this person employ in accepting or rejecting a particular wage offer? One approach is to establish a reservation wage (Chapter 2) or, in this context, an ***acceptance wage*** and reject any wage offer that falls below it. But how would one rationally select such a wage? Theoretically, if a person knows the frequency distribution in Figure 16-1 and can estimate the cost of generating new job offers, she or he can find the wage that equates the *expected* marginal benefit (MB) and *expected* marginal cost (MC) from search. If the job seeker is offered an hourly wage above this acceptance wage, that person will conclude that it is not worthwhile to continue searching (MB $<$ MC); if offered a wage below this amount, the person will reject the offer and continue to look for new offers, because the expected marginal benefit of the activity exceeds the expected extra cost (MB $>$ MC).

This optimal acceptance wage is shown as the vertical line W_a in Figure 16-1. The shaded area of the frequency distribution indicates the probability that any single offer will be above the acceptance wage. In this case, the probability is 80 percent (= .30 + .30 + .15 + .05). The probability that this person will accept any wage offer in the *c* to *g* range is 100 percent, and the probability that she or he will accept offers in the 0 to *c* range is zero. During the period of searching for a wage offer that exceeds the acceptance wage, this person is actively seeking work and therefore is officially unemployed. Because of the continuous nature of the labor force flows in the economy, this type of unemployment is always present.

Several important implications arise from our search model. We will examine two
16-1 in detail and then briefly list several others.

Inflation and Job Search

Will inflation have an impact on the length of time people search for jobs? To answer this question, we assume initially that the rate of inflation is zero and that the economy is operating at its natural levels of output and employment. Now, suppose that expansionary fiscal and monetary policies increase aggregate demand such that the general price level rises by 5 percent. Also assume that increases in nominal wage offers match this increase in the price level so that real wage offers remain unchanged.

Figure 16-2(a) repeats the frequency distribution of wage offers discussed previously, indicating again that, given the acceptance wage W_a, the probability that the job searcher will accept any specific offer is 80 percent. But now observe from graph (b) that the entire frequency distribution has shifted rightward because nominal wage offers are now 5 percent higher than previously. What impact will this shift have on a person's length of job search? Let's examine two distinct circumstances.

1 Expected Inflation If the job searcher represented by Figure 16-2(a) and (b) fully anticipates the 5 percent rate of inflation, she or he will simply raise the acceptance wage by 5 percent to keep it constant in real terms. This is shown in graph (b)

16-1 World of Work

HOW DO THE UNEMPLOYED SEARCH FOR WORK?

Unemployed workers use a wide variety of methods to search for employment. As the table shows, the most common method is to directly contact potential employers through a phone call, visit, or letter. Almost one-half send out résumés or fill out an application. Less widely used methods include placing or answering a newspaper ad, checking with friends or relatives, or using an employment agency. The average job seeker uses 1.8 methods per month to search for work.

The number and type of methods used differ across demographic groups. Prime-age job seekers (age 25 to 54) use nearly two methods on average, while teenagers and those 65 and older use only 1.5 methods. The number of methods used is often employed as an imperfect measure of job search intensity. Ports points out that the less-intense search by teenagers is likely caused by the demands on their time such as school work.* Older workers may search less intensively than prime-age job seekers because they place a higher value on leisure and flexible work schedules. Prime-age job seekers are much more likely to use employment agencies than those who are younger or older. Individuals searching for white-collar jobs are more likely to use newspaper advertisements than those looking for blue-collar jobs.

Methods used by job seekers have changed over time. Ports finds that the percentage of individuals placing or answering job advertisements has doubled since 1970. On the other hand, the fraction of job seekers using a public employment agency has fallen.

Not all search methods are equally successful. Bortnick and Ports report that job seekers using private employment agencies are the most likely to find employment in the following month.† On the other hand, those placing or answering ads or using a public employment agency are least likely to find a job. Those using more methods are slightly more likely to find a job.

*Michelle Harrison Ports, "Trends in Job Search Methods, 1970–92," *Monthly Labor Review,* October 1993, pp. 63–67.

†Steven M. Bortnick and Michelle Harrison Ports, "Job Search Methods and Results: Tracking the Unemployed, 1991," *Monthly Labor Review,* December 1992, pp. 29–35.

JOB SEARCH METHODS OF THE UNEMPLOYED, 1997

Method	Percent
Contacted employer directly	65.0
Sent out résumés or filled out applications	48.4
Placed or answered ads	16.9
Contacted friends or relatives	16.1
Used a public employment agency	18.7
Used a private employment agency	6.9

Source: U.S. Department of Labor, *Employment and Earnings,* January 1998, Table 33. The sum of the percents using each method will total more than 100 since job seekers often use more than one method in a given month.

as the rightward shift of line W_a to W'_a. In this case the worker's expectation that inflation will rise by 5 percent offsets the 5 percent increase in the nominal wage distribution and leaves the probability that any specific wage offer will be accepted at 80 percent (= .30 + .30 + .15 + .05).

To generalize: When the actual rate of inflation matches the expected rate, job searchers will *not* be influenced by the inflation. Their average length of job search

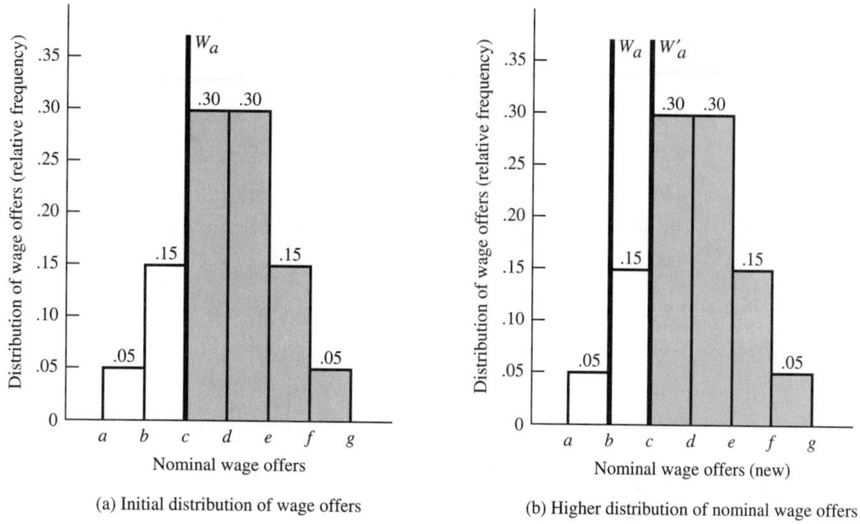

FIGURE 16-2 THE IMPACT OF UNEXPECTED INFLATION ON JOB SEARCH
Unexpected inflation results in higher nominal wage offers, and the frequency distribution shifts from that shown in (a) to that seen in (b). Because this person's acceptance wage initially remains at W_a, he or she is more likely to accept the next wage offer—a probability of 95 percent versus 80 percent—and hence, the length of job search falls. But once people recognize that the nominal wage offers are no higher in real terms than previously, they adjust their acceptance wages (for example, W_a to W'_a), and the job search length returns to normal.

will remain constant and, therefore, the unemployment level will stay at the natural rate.

2 Unexpected Inflation Suppose that the present rate of inflation is zero and that our job searcher expects this price stability to continue. Also, suppose that, in the short run, this person does not adjust her expectation to the reality of higher inflation. Under these circumstances, the 5 percent inflation will lead our unemployed job seeker to reduce her search time. As a result, unemployment will decline temporarily below its natural rate.

This is easily demonstrated in Figure 16-2. Expecting inflation to be zero, this individual holds the acceptance wage rate at W_a. But the 5 percent inflation shifts the wage distribution rightward as shown in Figure 16-2(b). We observe that the probability that a new wage offer will be accepted increases from 80 percent to 95 percent $(= .15 + .30 + .30 + .15 + .05)$. This person's duration of job search therefore falls, and if this pattern is widespread, unemployment declines. But according to this ***adaptive expectations theory,*** the unemployment decline will be short-lived. In the long run, unemployed job searchers will adjust their expectations of future inflation to the actual 5 percent rate. Consequently, they will increase their acceptance wages and lengthen their job searches, causing the unemployment rate to return to its natural level.

Generalization: Actual rates of inflation that exceed expected rates may temporarily reduce unemployment below its natural rate.

Unemployment Compensation and Job Search

A second major implication of our search model is that unemployment benefits provided by government, past employers, or both will increase the extent of unemployment by enabling unemployed people to search for higher wage offers at less *net* cost.[9] Recall that a person's acceptance wage is established at the level where the expected gain from more search just equals the expected cost. Quite understandably, the presence of unemployment compensation increases one's acceptance wage, because it *reduces* the expected *net* cost of searching for a higher wage offer. The opportunity cost of continued search is reduced to the existing highest offer *minus* the unemployment benefits. As portrayed in Figure 16-3, an individual who qualifies for unemployment benefits may have an acceptance wage W'_a rather than W_a, and given the distribution of wage offers, the probability that this person will accept the next job offer falls to 20 percent (= .15 + .05) compared to the previous probability of 80 percent (= .30 + .30 + .15 + .05). This person's optimal length of job search therefore increases, and the overall rate of unemployment in the economy rises.

[9]This is *not* to suggest that such programs are undesirable; in fact, one expressed purpose of these payments is to allow workers to search for positions commensurate with their skills and experience, rather than being forced through economic necessity to take jobs in which they are underemployed. Also, much unemployment occurs in the form of layoffs, and unemployment compensation cushions the decline in earnings while workers wait to be called back.

FIGURE 16-3 THE IMPACT OF UNEMPLOYMENT BENEFITS ON UNEMPLOYMENT
Unemployment benefits reduce the *net* opportunity cost of rejecting wage offers and continuing to search for higher-paying employment and thus allow people to increase their acceptance wages. For the person shown, the increase in the acceptance wage from W_a to W'_a means that the probability of receiving an acceptable wage offer in the next attempt falls from 80 to 20 percent (.15 + .05). The length of job search and the amount of unemployment therefore rise.

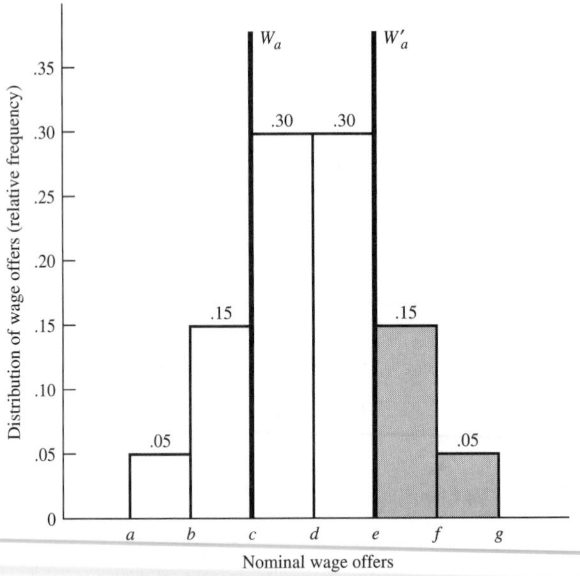

Other Implications of the Search Model

Let's briefly consider several other important implications of the job search theory. First, a prospective worker may not accept the initial job offer or even seek available jobs that pay below the acceptance wage. This fact helps explain the presence of numerous unfilled job vacancies in the presence of considerable overall unemployment. Second, the longer the expected length of tenure on the job, the higher a person's acceptance wage, all else being equal. For instance, suppose that a person expects to be employed on a new job for 20 years. The anticipated gain from searching for a high wage offer is greater in this case, and the acceptance wage higher, than if the job searcher expects to work only a month or two for the new employer. Third, random luck will play a part in the wage and earnings distribution in the economy (Chapter 17). One person may receive the highest wage offer in the frequency distribution on the first try; another may get a lower offer, continue to search, and finally accept an offer above the acceptance wage but below the highest wage in the distribution. Fourth, the level of unemployment is partly a function of the overall demand for labor. During recessions, the length of time required to discover each wage offer rises because so few firms are hiring workers. Also, if job searchers perceive a recession to be temporary, they may retain their acceptance wages, thereby prolonging their job search and contributing to a rise in unemployment.

Empirical Evidence

There have been two major strands in studies of the job search process. One line has focused on determinants of the acceptance wage and the other on the length of the job search. Several patterns have emerged regarding the acceptance wage. The acceptance wage falls with time unemployed as individuals become more realistic about the available wage offers.[10] The acceptance wage rates also fall—one estimate is by 15 percent—when people exhaust their unemployment benefits.[11] More highly educated and union workers have a higher acceptance wage.[12] Black male youth tend to have higher acceptance wages than white male youth.[13]

In a summary of the available evidence, Devine and Kiefer conclude that most studies find that the average acceptance rate of offers is between 80 and 100 percent.[14] Thus, most of the variation in the rate of exiting from unemployment appears to be due to variations in the rate at which workers receive offers.

Numerous empirical studies indicate that unemployment insurance lengthens the job search process. The consensus estimate is that a 10 percent increase in real monthly

[10]Nicholas M. Kiefer and George R. Neumann, "An Empirical Job Search Model with a Test of the Empirical Reservation Wage Hypothesis," *Journal of Political Economy,* February 1979, pp. 89–107.

[11]Raymond Fishe, "Unemployment Insurance and the Reservation Wage of the Unemployed," *Review of Economics and Statistics,* February 1982, pp. 12–17.

[12]Keifer and Neumann, op. cit.; and John T. Warner, J. Carl Poindexter, Jr., and Robert M. Fearn, "Employer-Employee Interaction and Duration of Unemployment," *Quarterly Journal of Economics,* May 1980, pp. 211–233.

[13]Harry J. Holzer, "Reservation Wages and Their Labor Markets Effects for Black and White Male Youth," *Journal of Human Resources,* Spring 1986, pp. 157–177.

[14]Devine and Kiefer, 1993, op. cit. However, one study finds a substantially lower acceptance rate. See David M. Blau, "An Empirical Analysis of Employed and Unemployed Job Search Behavior," *Industrial and Labor Relations Review,* July 1992, pp. 738–752.

unemployment benefits on average lengthens a person's unemployment duration by one-half to 1 week.[15] This is consistent with evidence that the probability of finding work rises sharply after unemployment benefits end.[16]

Other factors also influence the duration of job search. Blacks tend to have a longer job search than whites. Though union workers have a higher acceptance wage, there is only weak evidence that they have a longer job search than nonunion workers.[17] Older workers tend to have longer job searches than younger workers. This likely occurs because they face a wider range in wage offers than younger workers and thus the return to job search is greater.[18]

QUICK REVIEW 16-1

- The unemployed worker looking for work determines an acceptance wage based on the expected marginal costs and marginal benefits of longer searches. If a given wage offer exceeds the acceptance wage, the person takes the job; if the wage offer is less than the acceptance wage, the individual rejects the offer.

Your Turn: How do unexpected inflation, anticipated inflation, and unemployment insurance each affect the optimal length of a person's job search? (Answer: See page 627.)

INTERNAL LABOR MARKETS

A strict interpretation of neoclassical theory evokes the notion of an auction market in which workers are openly and continuously competing for jobs *and,* conversely, firms

[15]For a review of some of these studies, see Anthony B. Atkinson and John Micklewright, "Unemployment Compensation and Labor Market Transitions: A Critical Review," *Journal of Economic Literature,* December 1991, pp. 1679–1727; Bruce D. Meyer, "Lessons from U.S. Unemployment Insurance Experiments," *Journal of Economic Literature,* March 1995, pp. 99–131; and Gary S. Burtless, "Unemployment Insurance and Labor Supply: A Survey," in W. Lee Hansen and James F. Byers (eds.), *Unemployment Insurance* (Madison: University of Wisconsin Press, 1990). A related article of interest is Patricia M. Anderson and Bruce D. Meyer, "Unemployment Insurance in the United States: Layoff Incentives and Cross Subsidies," *Journal of Labor Economics,* January 1993, Part 2, pp. S70–S95. A positive relationship between unemployment compensation and unemployment duration has been found in Canada. See John C. Ham and Samuel A. Rea, Jr., "Unemployment Insurance and Male Unemployment Duration in Canada," *Journal of Labor Economics,* July 1987, pp. 325–353. In fact, David Card and W. Craig Riddell contend that most of the rise in the unemployment gap between Canada and the United States is due to the more generous Canadian unemployment compensation provisions. See David Card and W. Craig Riddell, "Unemployment in Canada and the United States: A Further Analysis," Working Paper No. 352, Industrial Relations Section, Princeton University, November 1995. For evidence of the impact of unemployment insurance in Germany, see Jennifer Hunt, "The Effects of Unemployment Compensation of Unemployment Duration in Germany," *Journal of Labor Economics,* January 1995, pp. 88–120.

[16]Lawrence Katz and Bruce Meyer, "Unemployment Insurance, Recall Expectations and Unemployment Outcomes," *Quarterly Journal of Economics,* November 1990, pp. 993–1002.

[17]Devine and Kiefer, 1993, op. cit.

[18]Solomon W. Polachek and W. Stanley Siebert, *The Economics of Earnings* (Cambridge, England: Cambridge University Press, 1993), pp. 235–236.

persistently bid to attract and retain labor services. Orthodox theory assumes that the firm, as an institution, poses no obstacle or barrier to the competitive pressures of the labor market. It is assumed that the wage rates of every type of labor employed by the firm are determined by market forces. Therefore, the wage structures of all firms employing the same types of workers would be identical. Workers would have access to jobs at all skill levels for which they are qualified, and mobility between firms would be unimpeded and extensive.

But critics of orthodox theory contend, and many mainstream economists increasingly agree, that this portrayal is sorely at odds with the real world. The public school teacher, the skilled machinist, and the government bureaucrat, to cite but a few, are *not* faced with the daily prospect of being displaced from their jobs by someone who is equally capable and who is willing to work for a slightly lower salary. Workers, on the one hand, enjoy "job rights," and employers, on the other hand, seek to maintain stable workforces. Although there is considerable occupational and geographic mobility in our economy, the average worker's employment is in fact quite stable. As indicated
16-2 in "World of Work" 16-2, Hall has concluded that today the typical worker is holding a job that will last for 8 years. A quarter of all workers hold jobs that will last 25 years or more. Even for women—who we know have problems in achieving access to more desirable jobs (Chapter 15)—some 15 percent hold jobs that will last 20 years or more. Indeed, perhaps as much as 80 percent of the labor force participates in "internal labor markets" in which they are substantially shielded from the competitive pressures
16-1 of the "external labor market."[19]

Characteristics of Internal Labor Markets

What is an internal labor market? How and why do such markets evolve? What are their implications? An ***internal labor market*** is "an administrative unit, such as a manufacturing plant, within which the pricing and allocation of labor is governed by a set of administrative rules and procedures" rather than by economic variables.[20] Within many firms we find more or less elaborate hierarchies of jobs, each of which centers on a certain skill (machinist), a common function (building maintenance), or a single focus of work (the computer). Furthermore, each job hierarchy entails a sequence or progression of jobs that forms what is called a mobility chain or ***job ladder.*** As suggested by Figure 16-4, a new worker will typically enter this job ladder as a trainee in the least-skilled job at the bottom of the ladder. The position at which workers gain

[19]Peter B. Doeringer and Michael J. Piore, *Internal Labor Markets and Manpower Analysis* (Lexington, MA: D. C. Heath and Company, 1971), pp. 41–42. A more recent estimate by David M. Gordon, Richard Edwards, and Michael Reich, *Segmented Work, Divided Workers* (Cambridge, England: Cambridge University Press, 1982), pp. 211–212, suggests that about two-thirds of all workers are employed in internal labor markets. John T. Dunlop's "The Task of Contemporary Wage Theory," in George W. Taylor and Frank C. Pierson (eds.), *New Concepts in Wage Determination* (New York: McGraw-Hill Book Company, 1957), pp. 128–139, is a pioneering statement on the structure of jobs and wages within firms. The Doeringer and Piore book is a comprehensive discussion of the evolution and character of internal labor markets. For a critical assessment of internal labor market theory, see George Baker and Bengt Holmstrom, "Internal Labor Markets: Too Many Theories, Too Few Facts," *American Economic Review,* May 1995, pp. 255–259.

[20]Doeringer and Piore, op. cit., pp. 1–2.

16-2 World of Work

LONG-TERM JOBS IN THE U.S. ECONOMY*

Although the U.S. labor market is characterized by a high degree of occupational and geographic mobility, there is also a surprising amount of stable, long-term employment. Many changes in occupations do not entail changes in employers. For example, a football coach at a high school may become an administrator within the same school district, or a production worker may obtain a college degree and be promoted to a supervisory position in the same firm. Also, as indicated in Chapter 9, some of the geographic mobility in the economy consists of intracorporate transfers of employees. Finally, the often-cited statistic that the median number of years of job tenure is only 3.5 is misleading. Young workers, who make up a large proportion of the labor force, cannot possibly have long job tenures.

To gain a better picture of the degree of long-term jobs in the United States, Hall projected what he calls the "eventual tenure" of jobs currently being held. He defines a job as a continuous employment with the same employer or, for those self-employed, continuous activity in the same line of work. Job tenure simply is the number of years since the worker's present job began. Eventual tenure is determined by summing actual present tenure and the projected additional time on the job. Hall estimates the latter by analyzing the number of workers in one age-tenure category who advance to higher age-tenure categories.

The accompanying table shows the distribution of eventual tenure across all age and tenure categories. It reveals that a significant proportion of workers *do* change jobs quite frequently. Notice that 23.5 percent of the workers have eventual job tenures of less than 2 years. But the table also discloses other interesting facts. Nearly 60 percent of U.S. workers are currently employed on jobs that eventually will last 5 years or more. More strikingly, almost 28 percent of the workforce is in jobs that will last 20 years or more. About 17 percent of present workers have jobs that, when ended, will be 30 or more years in length. Further analysis by Hall shows that among workers who are 30 years or older, about 40 percent are in employment that eventually will last 20 or more years. Hall also finds that job tenure for blacks is nearly identical to that for whites.

Conclusion: While ours is definitely a mobile society, it also is a society characterized by stable, near-lifetime employment for a significant proportion of the labor force.

THE DISTRIBUTION OF EVENTUAL JOB TENURE

Years	Percent			
0 – 0.5	9.8			
0.5 – 1	6.7	23.5		
1 – 2	7.0			
2 – 3	5.0			
3 – 5	13.5			
5 – 10	14.8			
10 – 15	10.4			
15 – 20	4.7			
20 – 25	4.7	58.0		
25 – 30	6.2			
30 – 35	10.0		27.9	
35+	7.0			17.0

*Robert E. Hall, "The Importance of Lifetime Jobs in the U.S. Economy," *American Economic Review,* September 1982, pp. 716–724. Although Hall's study is now more than a decade old, subsequent research has tended to confirm similar patterns for more recent periods. For example, see Francis X. Diebold, David Neumark, and Daniel Polsky, "Job Stability in the United States," *Journal of Labor Economics,* April 1997, pp. 206–233; and Kenneth A. Swinnerton and Howard Wial, "Is Job Stability Declining in the U.S. Economy?" *Industrial and Labor Relations Review,* January 1995, pp. 293–304.

access to the job ladder is called, for obvious reasons, a ***port of entry.*** It is through the port of entry that the sequence of jobs that constitute the job ladder makes contact with the ***external labor market.*** This external labor market is the "auction market" of orthodox theory. That is, in recruiting workers to fill vacancies for the least-skilled position in a job ladder, the firm must compete with other firms that are hiring the same kind of labor. While the market forces of supply and demand may be paramount in de-

16-1 **Global Perspective**

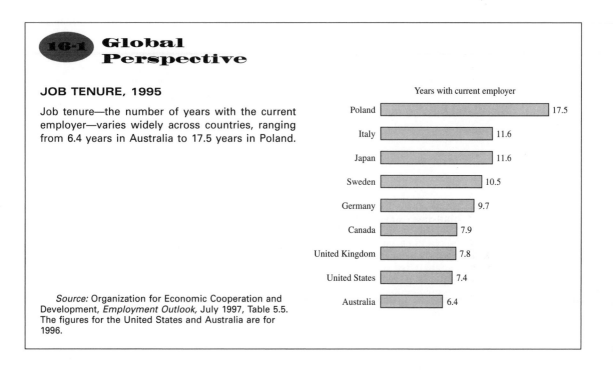

JOB TENURE, 1995

Job tenure—the number of years with the current employer—varies widely across countries, ranging from 6.4 years in Australia to 17.5 years in Poland.

Source: Organization for Economic Cooperation and Development, *Employment Outlook,* July 1997, Table 5.5. The figures for the United States and Australia are for 1996.

termining the wage rate paid for the port-of-entry position, market forces are held to be superseded by administrative rules and procedures in explaining the wages paid for other jobs constituting the job ladder of the internal labor market. The point to be stressed is that within the internal labor market, it is institutionalized rules and procedures, along with custom and tradition, that are foremost in determining how workers are allocated in the job hierarchy and what wage rates they are paid.

Reasons for Internal Labor Markets

Why do internal labor markets exist? The basic answer to this question is that firms typically encounter significant costs in the recruiting and training of workers and that these costs can be minimized by reducing labor turnover. Let's first consider the matter of training. Internal labor market theorists contend that many job skills are unique and specific to individual enterprises.

> Almost every job involves some specific skills. Even the simplest custodial tasks are facilitated by familiarity with the physical environment specific to the workplace in which they are performed. The apparent routine operation of standard machines can be importantly aided by familiarity with a particular piece of operating equipment. . . . Moreover, performance in some production and most managerial jobs involves a team element, and a critical skill is the ability to operate effectively with the given members of the team. This ability is dependent upon the interaction of the personalities of the

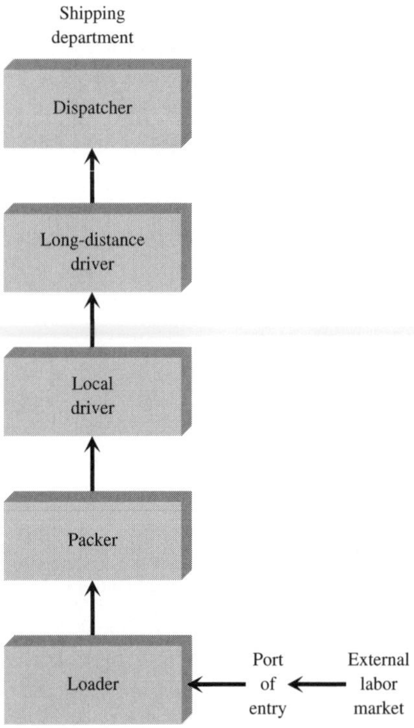

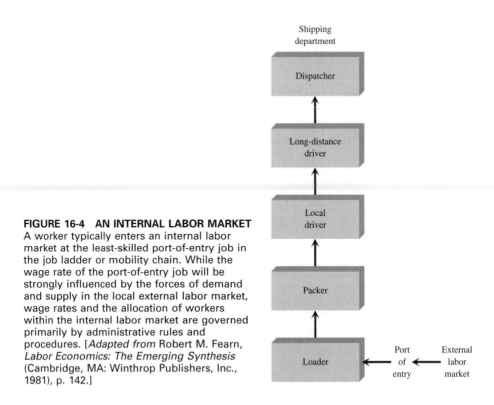

FIGURE 16-4 AN INTERNAL LABOR MARKET
A worker typically enters an internal labor market at the least-skilled port-of-entry job in the job ladder or mobility chain. While the wage rate of the port-of-entry job will be strongly influenced by the forces of demand and supply in the local external labor market, wage rates and the allocation of workers within the internal labor market are governed primarily by administrative rules and procedures. [*Adapted from* Robert M. Fearn, *Labor Economics: The Emerging Synthesis* (Cambridge, MA: Winthrop Publishers, Inc., 1981), p. 142.]

members, and the individual's work "skills" are specific in the sense that skills necessary to work on one team are never quite the same as those required on another.[21]

The specificity of job skills and technology to individual firms means that workers require *specific training* that is most efficiently acquired on the job. The cost of such training, you will recall from Chapter 4, is borne by the employer. But to obtain a return on this investment in human capital, the employer must *retain* specifically trained workers *over a period of time.* The job ladder—the core characteristic of internal labor markets—is the mechanism by which the desired workforce stability is achieved.

Advantages to Employers The mutual advantageousness of the internal labor market to both the firm and the workers merits further comment. As just noted, the reduction of worker turnover increases the return the firm receives on its investments in specific training. Furthermore, the amount of training that a firm needs to provide will be reduced by the presence of the internal labor market. If the firm fills a vacancy from the external labor market, it will have to finance *all* of the specific training that the worker requires. It can avoid much of this cost by simply promoting an internal applicant who, by virtue of having worked for the firm for some time, has already ac-

[21]Ibid., pp. 15–16.

quired a portion of the specific training that is prerequisite to the job opening. Similarly, recruitment costs will be larger if a position is filled from the external labor market. The firm—even after interviewing and screening—will have only limited knowledge about the quality of workers in the external labor market. But it will have accumulated a great deal of information about members of its present workforce. Thus, promoting from within will greatly reduce recruitment and screening costs and lessen the chances of making an error in filling the job. Another advantage of the internal labor market to the firm is that the existence of a clearly defined job ladder will provide an incentive for its existing workforce to be disciplined, productive, and continuously motivated to seek new skills. That is, the internal labor market will help solve the principal–agent problem discussed in Chapter 7. Finally, and related, internal labor market configurations may induce greater employee identification with the goals of the organization. Osterman asserts that "this heightened commitment may in turn lead to more effort, more attention to quality, lower turnover rates, and other behaviors which enhance productivity.[22]

Advantages to Workers Internal labor markets also confer advantages on workers who are accepted into them. Workers who are admitted receive benefits in the form of enhanced job security and built-in opportunities for job training and promotion. Workers need not leave the firm to secure better jobs but rather may ascend a well-defined sequence of jobs that constitute the job ladder. Furthermore, those in the internal labor market are shielded from the competition of workers in the external labor market. In addition, the formalization and codification of the rules and procedures governing both worker allocation and wage rates within the internal labor market protect workers from favoritism and capricious managerial decisions. Workers in internal labor markets are more likely to enjoy due process and equitable treatment with respect to layoffs, promotion, and access to training opportunities.[23]

The Role of Unions

Although the presence of a labor union can accelerate the development of internal labor markets, the cause-effect relationship is rather complicated. Internal labor markets tend to invite unionization; conversely, unions promote or accelerate the evolution of internal labor markets.

On the one hand, several reasons make an internal labor market conducive to unionization. First, the enhanced stability of the labor force resulting from an internal labor market promotes unionization. A fluid, unstable workforce is an obstacle to organization, but a stable group of workers develops a community spirit and perhaps a

[22]Paul Osterman, "Internal Labor Markets in a Changing Environment: Models and Evidence," in David Lewin, Olivia S. Mitchell, and Peter D. Sherer (eds.), *Research Frontiers in Industrial Relations and Human Resources* (Madison, WI: Industrial Relations Research Association, 1992), pp. 273–337.

[23]For more on the potential benefits of internal labor markets to both employers and employees, see Peter B. Doeringer, "Internal Labor Markets and Noncompeting Groups," *American Economic Review,* May 1986, pp. 48–56. Michael J. Carter and Susan B. Carter detail two interesting case studies of the evolution of internal labor markets in their "Internal Labor Markets in Retailing: The Early Years," *Industrial and Labor Relations Review,* July 1985, pp. 586–598.

common set of grievances that lead to formalization through a union. Second, workers in internal labor markets possess specific training that endows them with considerable bargaining power. Remember: Employers must retain specifically trained workers to realize a return on their human capital investments. It is only natural that workers might want to express this bargaining power collectively through a union. Finally, the administrative rules and procedures that prevail in the internal labor market define quite clearly the scope and character of managerial decisions. Unionization is a logical response to those instances where managerial actions are at odds with customary rules and procedures.

On the other hand, the presence of a union can be important in reinforcing the development of an internal labor market. A written collective bargaining agreement codifies, formalizes, and makes more rigid the rules and procedures that prevail in the functioning of an existing internal labor market.

Labor Allocation and the Wage Structure

Let's consider in more detail the promotion process—the allocation of labor—*and* the determination of wages within the internal labor market. The critical point to recall is that in the internal labor market, the pricing and allocation of labor are determined not by the forces of supply and demand but rather by administrative rules and procedures. Thus, in the case of promotions, the typical administrative rule is that, other things being roughly equal, the worker who has been on a particular rung of a job ladder for the longest period of time will be promoted to the next rung when an opening occurs. That is, promotions are generally determined on the basis of ***seniority.*** Seniority is typically tempered, however, by the presumed ability of the individual to perform the job satisfactorily after a trial period. In short, the rules indicate that the "right" to the promotion resides with the most experienced worker, not necessarily the most able worker available from either the internal or the external labor market. Similarly, layoffs are allocated on the basis of reverse seniority; the newest workers are laid off first (Chapter 19).

The wage structure within an internal labor market is also determined by administrative procedures, through custom and tradition, and by the pattern of mobility that is sought. In terms of Figure 16-4, how should the wage rate of a packer in the shipping department, for example, compare with that of a local driver? Very frequently a system of job evaluation is used to establish the wage rate attached to each job in a job ladder. ***Job evaluation*** is a procedure by which jobs are ranked and wage rates assigned in terms of a set of job characteristics and worker traits. Table 16-1 shows an illustrative job evaluation scheme where points have been assigned, undoubtedly with some degree of arbitrariness, to various job characteristics and traits. Thus, using this system, the actual points assigned to a packer's job and a driver's job might be 50 and 75, respectively. This ranking implies that the wage rate of a driver should be 50 percent higher than that of a packer. For example, if packers receive \$8 per hour, then drivers should be paid \$12. Note in particular that in the internal labor market, wage rates frequently are attached to jobs rather than individuals. Internal labor market theorists are suggesting in effect that productivity often resides in jobs rather than in workers. Also observe that administrative procedure has supplanted the forces of demand and supply.

TABLE 16-1 MODEL JOB EVALUATION SYSTEM

Factor		Maximum points
Working conditions		15
Noise	5	
Dirt	5	
Smell	5	
Responsibility for equipment		25
Responsibility for other workers		20
Skill		20
Manual dexterity	10	
Experience	10	
Education		35
Physical effort		10
Total points		125

Source: Peter B. Doeringer and Michael J. Piore, *Internal Labor Markets and Manpower Analysis* (Lexington, MA: D. C. Heath and Company), p. 67.

Once established, custom and tradition intervene to make the internal wage structure rigid: "Any wage rate, set of wage relationships, or wage setting procedure which prevails over a period of time tends to become customary; changes are then viewed as unjust or inequitable, and the work group will exert economic pressure in opposition to them.[24] Recalling the notion of equitable comparisons, we should note that custom and rigidity evolve around wage *relationships* as opposed to specific wage *rates*.

The wage structure is not determined in isolation from the allocative function of the internal labor market. One of the important constraints that applies is that the wage structure must foster and facilitate the internal allocation of labor that the employer seeks. "The wage on every job must be high enough relative to the job or jobs from which it is supposed to draw its labor and low enough relative to the jobs to which it is supposed to supply labor to induce the desired pattern of internal mobility."[25] In Figure 16-4 the wage of the packer must be sufficiently higher than that of a loader so that the latter will aspire to become the former.

The Efficiency Issue

The question of whether internal labor markets are efficient is intriguing and important. The basic premise of orthodox economics is that competitive pressures result in the efficient use of labor and other inputs. When competition prevails, any given firm must combine labor and other productive resources in the most efficient way, or it will be driven out of business by other firms that are efficient. But the critical feature of

[24]Doeringer and Piore, op. cit., p. 85.
[25]Ibid., p. 78.

the internal labor market is that aside from port-of-entry jobs, workers are shielded from competition. Wages in internal labor markets are determined not by market forces but by rather arbitrary administrative procedures embodied in job evaluation, through custom and tradition, and so forth. Thus, say orthodox economists, it would be only by chance that the various kinds of workers would be paid in accordance with their productivities. Furthermore, workers are promoted (allocated) largely on the basis of seniority, rather than in terms of worker ability (productivity). More senior workers may or may not be more productive than some junior workers. These characteristics imply that the existence of internal labor markets conflicts with society's interest in allocative efficiency.

But for several reasons most internal labor market theorists and some mainstream economists rebut this line of reasoning. Internal labor markets and the wage structures embodied in them may exist precisely because they efficiently allocate labor.

In the first place, recall that the internal labor market reduces labor turnover, reducing the costs of training, recruitment, screening, and hiring. Of particular significance, the job ladders of internal labor markets provide the employer with abundant information on the quality of its workers. Therefore, the firm is less likely to promote a nonproductive worker if it selects that worker from within the internal labor market. In comparison, hiring from the external labor market is based on more limited information, which may increase the risk of obtaining an unproductive worker. It is also noteworthy that the use of seniority in the allocation of labor is *not* necessarily at odds with efficiency. The worker who has been on the job the longest is probably a suitable candidate for promotion. Also, only in a very few instances is internal labor market promotion based *solely* on seniority. The senior worker with the requisite ability and an acceptable performance record typically gets promoted, rather than simply the most senior employee.[26]

A second reason that internal labor markets may be efficient centers on the distinction between static and dynamic efficiency. ***Static efficiency*** refers to the combining of labor and other resources *of given quality* in the most efficient (least costly) way. ***Dynamic efficiency,*** on the other hand, has to do with increases in productive efficiency that arise from *improvements in the quality* of labor and other resources. For present purposes, the relevant contention is that internal labor markets promote dynamic efficiency, which is held to be of greater consequence than realizing static efficiency. The gain from using *existing* skills of workers more efficiently is a "one-shot" gain, while the gains from *improving* worker knowledge and skills can go on indefinitely.[27] Furthermore, internal labor markets are conducive to dynamic efficiency because providing a greater amount of security to more-skilled senior workers makes those workers willing to pass along their knowledge and skills to less-skilled colleagues. Highly skilled senior workers will want to conceal their knowledge from less-skilled junior workers *if* the latter can become competitors for the formers' jobs. But senior-

[26]It should be noted, however, that length of service frequently takes priority over ability and performance in promotion. See D. Quinn Mills, "Seniority versus Ability in Promotion Decisions," *Industrial and Labor Relations Review,* April 1985, pp. 421–425.

[27]Thurow, op. cit., pp. 194–195.

ity rules and other security provisions embodied in internal labor markets guarantee that this will not happen. If senior workers are assured that they have priority in promotions, that their wages will not be reduced as more workers acquire knowledge of their job, and that they will be the last to be laid off, then senior workers will be amenable to sharing their skills with fellow workers. Internal labor markets may provide these assurances.

Finally, some economists point out that the pay structures within typical internal labor markets may be effective incentive-generating devices, particularly in large firms where it is difficult to monitor the work effort of employees. As indicated in our discussion of deferred payment schemes (Figure 7-9), the wage structure of the internal labor market may be such that not only are senior workers paid more than junior workers but senior workers are paid more than their marginal revenue products (MRPs), while junior workers are paid less than their MRPs.[28] The "premium" paid to senior workers is an inducement for younger employees to work hard. By being productive, young workers demonstrate to employers that they deserve to be retained and to progress up the job ladder to higher-paying jobs in which they, too, will enjoy the "premium" of a wage rate in excess of their MRPs. Young workers presumably accept wages that are initially less than their MRPs for the privilege of participating in a labor market where in time the reverse will be true. This wage structure is also appealing to young workers in that it offers the prospect of higher lifetime earnings. The greater work effort and higher average worker productivity that result from this wage structure increase the firm's profits, in which workers may share through wage bargaining.[29]

QUICK REVIEW 16-2

• Evidence indicates that many people work for the same employer for numerous years and, in effect, "search" for improved pay and job characteristics through promotions and reassignments within their existing firms.

• Internal labor markets are characterized by hierarchies of jobs called job ladders, which workers enter via ports of entry. Only the wages at the ports of entry are truly market-based.

• Some economists think that internal labor markets contribute to inefficiency because wages are determined by rigid administrative procedures and rules.

• Other economists argue that internal labor markets enhance productivity by *(a)* reducing recruitment, screening, and training costs; *(b)* inducing senior workers to

[28]This implies a relationship between wage rate and MRPs that is just the opposite of that shown in Figure 4-8(b).

[29]Edward P. Lazear, "Agency, Earnings Profiles, Productivity, and Hours Restriction," *American Economic Review,* September 1981, pp. 606–620; Lazear, "Why Is There Mandatory Retirement?" *Journal of Political Economy,* December 1979, pp. 1261–1284; and Lazear and Sherwin Rosen, "Rank-Order Tournaments as Optimum Labor Contracts," *Journal of Political Economy,* October 1981, pp. 841–864. Also see Michael L. Wachter and Randall D. Wright, "The Economics of Internal Labor Markets," *Industrial Relations,* Spring 1990, pp. 240–262.

share their skills and knowledge with junior workers; and *(c)* providing younger workers with greater incentives to work productively.

Your Turn: Have you worked in a firm that has a clearly defined job ladder? If so, how much upward mobility did you observe along the ladder? (Answer: See page 627.)

CHAPTER SUMMARY

1 Job search is a natural and often constructive occurrence in a dynamic economy characterized by heterogeneous workers and jobs and by imperfect information.

2 The rational job seeker forms an acceptance wage at a level where the expected marginal costs and benefits of continued search are equal and then compares this wage to actual wage offers.

3 Fully anticipated inflation has no impact on the optimal length of job search because job seekers will adjust their acceptance wages upward at the same rate as nominal wage offers rise. But if job searchers mistakenly view inflation-caused rises in nominal wage offers as real wage increases, they will shorten their job search, and unemployment will temporarily fall.

4 Unemployment benefits extend the optimal length of job search by reducing the *net* opportunity cost of continuing to seek still higher wage offers.

5 Most firms and plants embody internal labor markets in which wages and the allocation of labor are determined by administrative rules and procedures rather than strictly by supply and demand.

6 Internal labor markets entail hierarchies of jobs called job ladders, which focus on a certain job skill, function or technology. Having entered the job ladder through a port of entry, internal labor market workers are largely shielded from the competitive pressure of external labor markets.

7 Internal labor markets exist because they generate advantages for both employers and workers. For employers, internal labor markets reduce worker turnover and thereby increase the return on specific training and reduce recruitment and training costs. For workers, internal labor markets provide job security, opportunities for training and promotion, and protection from arbitrary managerial decisions.

8 By providing labor force stability, internal labor markets attract unions; conversely, unions promote and accelerate the development of internal labor markets.

9 It is unclear whether internal labor markets diminish or enhance productive efficiency.

TERMS AND CONCEPTS

job search model
acceptance wage
internal labor market
job ladder
port of entry
external labor market
seniority
job evaluation
static and dynamic efficiency

QUESTIONS AND STUDY SUGGESTIONS

1 What are the benefits and costs of job search? Why don't job seekers endlessly search for a higher wage offer?

2 What is meant by the term "acceptance wage"? How does a job seeker determine his or her acceptance wage? Why might the acceptance wage for one new college graduate differ from another new college graduate?

3 Explain how each of the following would affect the probability that a job searcher will accept the next wage offer and thus affect the expected length of his or her unemployment: *(a)* a decline in the rate of inflation below the expected one and *(b)* a decrease in unemployment benefits.

4 How do you explain the existence of internal labor markets? What are their advantages to employers? To workers?

5 How does a worker go about "searching" for a better job in an internal labor market? What is the employer's search process within internal labor markets?

6 Explain the following statement: "Unions are both a consequence and a cause of internal labor markets." Why might the presence of internal labor markets in a firm encourage unionization?

7 Do you think internal labor markets enhance or detract from efficiency? How might one argue that the realization of dynamic efficiency is more important than achieving static efficiency? Do you agree?

SELECTED REFERENCES

Baker, George, and Bengt Holmstrom: "Internal Labor Markets: Too Many Theories, Too Few Facts," *American Economic Review,* May 1995, pp. 255–259.

Devine, Theresa J., and Nicholas M. Kiefer: *Empirical Labor Economics: The Search Approach* (Oxford, England: Oxford University Press, 1990).

Devine, Theresa J., and Nicholas M. Kiefer: "The Empirical Status of Job Search Theory," *Labour Economics,* June 1993, pp. 3–24.

Doeringer, Peter B., and Michael J. Poire: *Internal Labor Markets and Manpower Analysis* (Lexington, MA: D. C. Heath and Company, 1971).

Osterman, Paul (ed.): *Internal Labor Markets* (Cambridge, MA: MIT Press, 1984).

Osterman, Paul (ed.): "Internal Labor Markets: Theory and Change," in Clark Kerr and Paul D. Staudohar (eds.), *Labor Economics and Industrial Relations: Markets and Institutions* (Cambridge, MA: Harvard University Press, 1994).

Siebert, W. S., and J. T. Addison: "Internal Labour Markets: Causes and Consequences," *Oxford Review of Economic Policy,* Spring 1991, pp. 76–92.

Watcher, Michael L., and Randall Wright: "The Economics of Internal Labor Markets," *University of Pennsylvania Law Review,* Spring 1990, pp. 240–262.

CHAPTER 17

THE PERSONAL DISTRIBUTION OF EARNINGS

Thus far our focus has been mainly on microeconomic aspects of labor markets. Specifically, we have discussed in some detail the labor market decisions of individuals, families, and firms. As illustrated in Figure 1-1, the next three chapters examine the *macroeconomics* of labor markets. Recall that macroeconomics deals with broad aggregates or collections of specific economic units treated as if they were one. The topics in these three chapters include the personal distribution of earnings, aggregate labor productivity, and employment and unemployment.

The micro–macro distinction is clearly evident in the present chapter, where our attention turns away from an analysis of specific wages and toward an examination of the ***personal distribution of earnings.*** This distribution is the national pattern of the shares of individual wage earnings. How unequal is the distribution of wages and salaries? What general factors explain the observed pattern? How much mobility is there within the overall distribution? Why has this distribution become more unequal over the past two decades?

In pursuing these questions we first will discuss alternative ways of describing the earnings distribution and measuring the degree of observed inequality. Second, we will examine theories that help explain the pattern of the distribution of U.S. earnings. Our focus then shifts to personal earnings mobility, or movements within the aggregate earnings distribution. The chapter concludes with a discussion of the trend toward greater inequality in the earnings distribution over the past 25 years.

DESCRIBING THE DISTRIBUTION OF EARNINGS

The degree of inequality in the distribution of earnings can be described in several ways. Let's examine two graphic portrayals: the frequency distribution and the Lorenz curve.

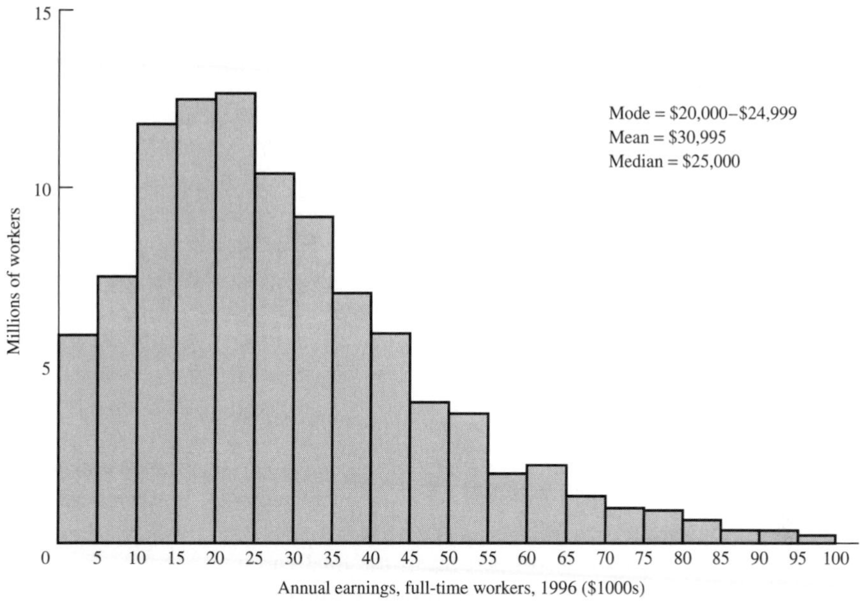

FIGURE 17-1 THE DISTRIBUTION OF ANNUAL EARNINGS FOR FULL-TIME WORKERS, 1996
The personal distribution of annual earnings is highly unequal and is skewed to the right. The histogram (absolute frequency distribution) of earnings is characterized by (1) much bunching around the leftward mode, (2) an extended rightward tail, and (3) a mean (arithmetic average) that exceeds the median (one-half above, one-half below). Author calculations from March 1997 Current Population Survey.)

Frequency Distribution

The distribution of annual earnings received by full-time U.S. workers in 1996 is shown in Figure 17-1. This absolute ***frequency distribution***—or ***histogram***—shows the number of full-time wage and salary workers (measured on the vertical axis) whose annual earnings fell within each $5,000 earnings range shown on the horizontal axis. For example, the third bar from the left represents earnings within the $10,000-to-$14,999 range. We would then know from the height of this bar that about 11.8 million people had annual earnings in this category in 1996. Or, as a second example, the bar representing the wider $55,000-to-$59,999 earnings range tells us that 1.9 million people received work income between $55,000 and $59,999 in 1996.

It is equally common to represent the distribution of income in terms of *relative* frequencies, in which case the vertical axis is converted to percent of total earners, rather than being the *absolute* number of such workers, as shown here.

Three measures of location, or central tendency, are commonly used to summarize histograms or absolute frequency distributions such as that in Figure 17-1. The *mode* is the income category occurring with the greatest frequency. The *mean* is the arithmetic average, obtained by dividing the total earnings by the number of workers. Finally, the *median* is the amount of annual work income received by the individual who stands at the midpoint of the array of earnings. One-half of those earning wages and salaries receive more than the median, while the other one-half receive less. With these definitions in mind, note from Figure 17-1 that the distribution of annual earnings for full-time U.S. workers is concentrated around a single leftward mode ($20,000 to $24,999 in 1996); has a median level of earnings ($25,000 in 1996) that is to the right of the mode; and possesses a mean, or average ($30,995 in 1996), which is greater than both the mode and median. The mean exceeds the median because the average is pulled upward by the extremely high earnings of the relatively few workers who have earnings in the long rightward tail of the histogram. This tail is so long that our truncated diagram prevents it from reaching the horizontal axis. These characteristics correctly suggest that most U.S. workers receive earnings in the leftward two-thirds of the overall distribution, while some people receive extraordinarily large annual earnings relative to the median and mean.

Lorenz Curve

The degree of earnings inequality can also be shown by a ***Lorenz curve,*** such as the one portrayed in Figure 17-2. This curve indicates the *cumulative* percent of all full-time wage and salary earners from left to right on the horizontal axis and the corresponding *cumulative* percent of the total earnings accruing to that percent of earners on the vertical axis. If each full-time worker received the average earnings, the Lorenz curve would be the diagonal (45°) line that bisects the graph. Twenty percent of all full-time earners would receive 20 percent of all earnings, 40 percent of the workers would get 40 percent, and so forth. All these points would fall on the diagonal line that we appropriately label "perfect equality."

The actual Lorenz curve in Figure 17-2 is derived by plotting the data for 1996 from Table 17-1. This table shows the percent of total earnings accruing to five numerically equal groups, or *quintiles.* For 1996 we see that the bottom 20 percent of all full-time

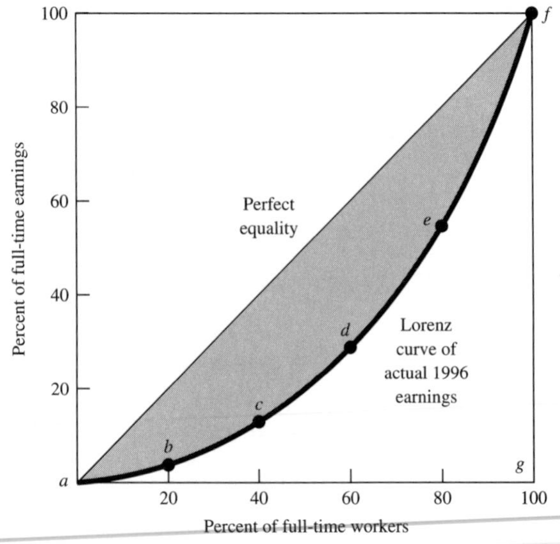

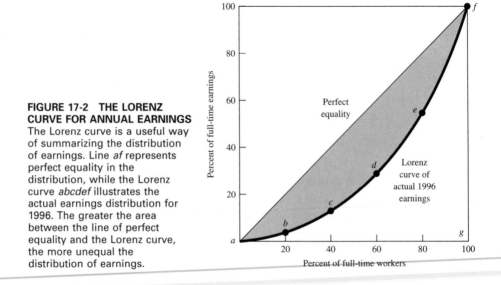

FIGURE 17-2 THE LORENZ CURVE FOR ANNUAL EARNINGS
The Lorenz curve is a useful way of summarizing the distribution of earnings. Line *af* represents perfect equality in the distribution, while the Lorenz curve *abcdef* illustrates the actual earnings distribution for 1996. The greater the area between the line of perfect equality and the Lorenz curve, the more unequal the distribution of earnings.

TABLE 17-1 THE DISTRIBUTION OF ANNUAL WAGE AND SALARY EARNINGS FOR FULL-TIME WORKERS, 1996

Quintile	Percent
Lowest 20 percent	4.7
Second 20 percent	10.7
Third 20 percent	18.9
Fourth 20 percent	19.8
Highest 20 percent	45.9
Total	100.0

Source: Author calculations from the March 1997 Current Population Survey.

workers received 4.7 percent of the total earnings, which plots as point *b* on the Lorenz curve. The bottom 40 percent of the earners received 15.4 percent (= 4.7 + 10.7) of the total earnings, which yields point *c* on the curve, and so forth. The shaded area between the diagonal line of perfect equality of earnings and the Lorenz curve provides a visual measure of the extent of earnings inequality. The larger this area, the greater the degree of disparity in annual earnings. If there were complete inequality—if one person had 100 percent of total earnings—the Lorenz curve would coincide with the horizontal and right vertical axis, forming a 90° angle at point *g*.

Gini Coefficient

The visual measure of earnings inequality just described can be easily transformed into a mathematical measure. The ***Gini coefficient*** (equation 17-1) is the ratio of the shaded area of Figure 17-2 to the entire triangle below the diagonal.

$$\text{Gini coefficient} = \frac{\text{area between Lorenz curve and diagonal}}{\text{total area below diagonal}} \tag{17-1}$$

If there were complete equality of earnings, the distance between the diagonal and the Lorenz curve would be zero, and therefore, the Gini coefficient also would be zero (= 0/*afg*). On the other hand, if one person had all the income, the area between the Lorenz curve and the diagonal would be equal to *afg,* and the Gini coefficient would be 1 (= *afg/afg*). The larger the Gini coefficient, the greater the degree of earnings inequality. The Gini coefficient for the 1996 data shown in Table 17-1 and the Lorenz curve in Figure 17-2 is .40.

Cautions

Great care must be exercised in interpreting frequency distributions, Lorenz curves, and Gini coefficients.

1 Full- versus Part-Time Workers Annual earnings are a product of both wages per hour *and* the number of hours worked in a year. A distribution that includes part-time workers and people who work full-time only portions of the year will display greater variability than distributions that include only full-time workers. The histogram in Figure 17-1 and the Lorenz curve in Figure 17-2 include only *full-time* wage and salary earners.

2 Fringe Benefits Most earnings data do not include fringe benefits (Chapter 7). The addition of these benefits increases the skewness of the frequency distribution of earnings or, stated differently, increases the sag of the Lorenz curve away from the diagonal and raises the Gini coefficient. Workers who have above-average annual earnings also tend to have higher-than-average fringe benefits as a percentage of their total compensation.[1]

3 Individual versus Family Distributions Earnings distributions can be shown by either *individual* or *family* wages and salaries. Although the general shape of the family distribution is similar to that for individual workers, the median and average incomes are higher in the family formulation. Also, the family distribution is tighter; that is, the Gini coefficient is lower. The reason is that the income effect (Chapters 2 and 3) produced by the high incomes of some men reduces the likelihood that their wives are labor force participants. This income effect is offset somewhat by the tendency for men with higher earnings to marry women who earn more than the average female salary when they do choose to work.[2]

4 Static Portrayals Frequency distributions, Lorenz curves, and Gini coefficients are all *static* portrayals or measures of earnings inequality. They do not provide information about the extent of personal movement within the distribution from year to year or over people's lifetimes. We discuss this important topic later in the chapter.

5 Other Income Sources A final important caution is that annual earnings are only one of several possible sources of individual or family income. People who have high earnings from salaries tend to have disproportionately higher rental, interest, and dividend income than lower-wage workers. Taken alone, the inclusion of these nonwage incomes would make the distribution of individual or family income even more unequal than the distribution of wages and salaries. But government transfer payments such as Social Security benefits, welfare payments, and veterans' benefits offset this added inequality. Individuals and families who have zero or very low wage earnings receive proportionately more transfer income than higher-earnings individuals. The out-

[1]Timothy M. Smeeding, "The Size Distribution of Wage and Nonwage Compensation: Employer Cost versus Employer Value," in Jack E. Triplett (ed.), *The Measurement of Labor Cost* (Chicago: University of Chicago Press, 1983), pp. 237–277.

[2]James Smith, "The Distribution of Family Earnings," *Journal of Political Economy,* October 1979, pp. S163–S192; Evelyn Lehrer and Marc Nerlove, "A Life-Cycle Analysis of Family Income Distribution," *Economic Inquiry,* July 1984, pp. 360–374; and David Betson and J. VanDerGagg, "Working Married Women and the Distribution of Income," *Journal of Human Resources,* Fall 1984, pp. 532–543.

come is a slightly less unequal distribution of individual and family income than that based solely on individual or family wage and salary earnings (full-time and part-time workers).

QUICK REVIEW 17-1

- The absolute frequency distribution (histogram) of earnings is a graphical depiction showing the number of employees whose earnings fall within various earnings ranges.
- The Lorenz curve graphically displays the cumulative percent of all wage and salary earners on the horizontal axis and the corresponding cumulative percentage of total earnings accruing to that group; the farther the curve from the diagonal line of perfect equality, the greater the earnings inequality.
- The Gini coefficient is an arithmetic measure of earning inequality; it is the area between the Lorenz curve and the diagonal line, divided by the total area beneath the diagonal line. The higher the Gini coefficient, the greater the earnings inequality.
- As measured by the histogram, Lorenz curve, and Gini coefficient, the degree of earnings inequality in the United States is high.

Your Turn: Suppose the Lorenz curve of earnings moves closer to the diagonal line. What has likely happened to the histogram of earnings and the Gini coefficient? (Answer: See page 627.)

EXPLAINING THE DISTRIBUTION OF EARNINGS

Human characteristics that we might associate with earnings—intelligence, physical strength, motivation, determination—are thought to be distributed according to the familiar bell-shaped normal curve. So why aren't earnings also distributed in this manner? Numerous theories attempt to explain this paradox.[3] Rather than describing each of these theories, we will approach this topic by first discussing the basic human capital explanation for earnings inequality and then exploring the diversity of alternative explanations by synthesizing several of them into a modified, multifactor model.

Human Capital Theory

The ***human capital model*** (Chapter 4) provides valuable insights into why the personal distribution of earnings is unequal and has a long rightward tail. Recall that human capital investments take various forms, the two most critical for present purposes being formal education and on-the-job training. Each relates to the earnings distribution.

[3]For a review of these theories, see Gian S. Sahota, "Theories of Personal Income Distribution: A Survey," *Journal of Economic Literature,* March 1978, pp. 1–55.

1 Formal Education: Amount and Quality Formal education has an investment component in that it requires present sacrifice to enhance future productivity and therefore lifetime earnings. A review of Figure 4-2 reminds us that a given investment will be undertaken only if the present value of the expected stream of enhanced earnings (area 3) equals or exceeds the present value of the sum of the direct and indirect costs (areas 1 + 2). Other things being equal, the greater the amount of formal schooling and the better its quality, the higher the investment costs (areas 1 + 2), and thus the greater the enhancement of productivity and the future earnings stream needed to justify the investment. Thus, we have a rudimentary theory of earnings inequality. If other things such as ability, nonwage aspects of jobs, uncertainty of earnings, and life expectancies are held constant, earnings will be systematically and positively related to the amount and quality of a person's formal education. An unequal distribution of educational attainment will produce an unequal distribution of personal earnings.

A glance back at Table 15-5 offers casual evidence of the link between the amount of education undertaken and average annual earnings. It reveals that men and women—both blacks and whites—who have high school diplomas earn more than people who have obtained 9 or fewer years of education. Observe that workers with doctorates and professional degrees earn more than those with master's degrees, those with master's degrees earn more than those with bachelor's degrees, and those with bachelor's degrees earn more than those with associate degrees.

Econometric studies that account for other factors confirm the positive relationship between education and earnings shown in Table 15-5. Also, a few studies have found a direct relationship between the quality of formal education and subsequent earnings. For example, Card and Krueger[4] have recently discovered that, all else being equal, men who were educated in states with higher-quality public schools and who had better-educated teachers experienced a higher average rate of return on their investments in education. Care must be taken, however, not to overstate the importance of the link between education and earnings. Formal schooling explains only about 7 to 12 percent of the observed differences in individual earnings.

2 On-the-Job Training The explanatory power of the basic human capital model rises appreciably once on-the-job training is added to the analysis. On-the-job training varies from simple "learning by doing" to formal apprenticeships and training programs and, as indicated in Chapter 4, may either be general or specific to the firm. In the case of *general training,* the worker usually bears the investment cost through a reduced wage. The worker's expected gain in the future wages, therefore, must be sufficient to produce a rate of return on the investment cost (reduced present wage) equal to what the worker could obtain through alternative investments. With nontransferable *specific training,* the firm will be forced to pay the investment expense. The employer will un-

[4]David Card and Alan B. Krueger, "Does School Quality Matter? Returns to Education and the Characteristics of Public Schools in the United States," *Journal of Political Economy,* February 1992, pp. 31–39. For earlier studies finding that educational quality matters, see Paul Taubman and Terence Wales, *Higher Education and Earnings* (New York: McGraw-Hill Book Company, 1974); and George E. Johnson and Frank Stafford, "Social Returns to Quantity and Quality of Schooling," *Journal of Human Resources,* Spring 1973, pp. 139–155.

dertake this investment only if the expected increase in the worker's productivity justifies it. Training is undertaken in both cases on the expectation of an increase in productivity and enhanced future earnings. Therefore, we would expect to observe a direct relationship between the amount and quality of on-the-job training and a person's annual earnings.

Mincer has shown that about one-half to two-thirds of the variation of personal earnings is explained once postschooling on-the-job training investment is included in the definition of human capital.[5] This inclusion adds so much explanatory power for two reasons. First, taken alone, formal schooling does little to explain why people's earnings typically *rise* with age. That is, education explains why postschooling earnings exceed preschooling pay, but it alone does not explain why earnings rise more rapidly for educated people over their work lives. After all, most people conclude their formal education relatively early in their lives. On-the-job training, on the other hand, provides a basic explanation for the age variations in earnings that are so apparent in the distribution. As a person accumulates more training on the job, productivity and earnings rise. Furthermore, evidence shows that people who possess greater amounts of formal education also receive more on-the-job training from employers. Those people with the most formal education have demonstrated their ability to absorb training and are the workers firms choose for on-the-job training. Those who have more education therefore have disproportionately greater earnings than less-educated workers.

A second reason postschooling investment helps explain the observed inequality in the distribution of earnings is its impact on hours of work. Assuming that in the aggregate the substitution effect dominates the income effect (Chapter 2), people who have more schooling and on-the-job training not only will have higher hourly wage rates but also will choose to work more hours annually than less-educated and less-trained workers. This will mean that the annual earnings—wage rate × hours worked—will be *disproportionately* greater than the differences in schooling and on-the-job training, implying that the earnings distribution will be skewed to the right.

A Modified Human Capital Model: A Multifactor Approach

The basic human capital explanation of earnings disparities is not without its critics. Of particular interest to our topic is the criticism that schooling and on-the-job training do not sufficiently explain the long, extended rightward tail of the earnings distribution. Many economists believe that we can better understand why the earnings distribution is skewed rightward by modifying the human capital model to include elements beyond the traditional ones of education and on-the-job training. In this ***multifactor approach to the earnings distribution,*** we specifically consider (1) ability, (2) family background, (3) discrimination, and (4) chance and risk taking, as well as education and training.

1 Ability Ability is broadly defined as "the power to do" and, as used here, consists of something separate and distinct from the skills gained through formal education

[5]Jacob Mincer, *Schooling, Experience, and Earnings* (New York: Columbia University Press, 1974).

or on-the-job training. Ability is difficult to isolate and measure but is thought to be normally distributed. In addition, ability is multidimensional; that is, it takes several forms, including intelligence (IQ), physical dexterity, and motivation. It may be either genetic or environmental in origin. Our interest in this discussion is not the source of observed differences in ability but rather the consequences of these differences for the distribution of earnings. Ability can influence earnings directly—in other words, independently of human capital investments—and indirectly, through its impact on the optimal amount and quality of human capital acquired.

Direct Impact Those who envision a direct effect of ability on earnings argue that in a market economy, people are rewarded in a general way according to their ability to contribute to a firm's output. Other things being equal, the greater one's ability, the greater one's productivity and therefore earnings. Recall from the discussion of the "ability problem" in Chapter 4 that some critics of the human capital theory contend that the observed positive relationship between formal education and earnings largely reflects ***self-selection,*** which is based on differences in ability. People who possess more intelligence are more likely to choose to attend college than those with less intelligence. Even if these highly intelligent people did not go to college, they could be expected to have higher earnings than less-intelligent people who did not attend college. In other words, if we could somehow control the skills and knowledge gained during college, this high-quality group still would have substantially higher earnings than their less-able counterparts. Consequently, much of the inequality of earnings normally attributed to differences in education and training could be the result of differences in ability.

Complementary Elements A related possibility is that *elements* of differences in ability are complements to one another in the "production" of earnings. This implies that the addition of one factor will increase the productivity of other elements of ability. In other words, ability differences may act *multiplicatively* to generate the exceptionally high earnings that some people receive. To illustrate, let's suppose that ability consists of several normally distributed complementary elements, two of which are intelligence and the ***D-factor,*** where *D* represents drive, dynamism, doggedness, or determination.[6]

With these assumptions, a person who is fortunate enough to be located in the rightward tail of both the normal distribution of intelligence *and* the normal distribution of the *D*-factor will have earnings that are disproportionately greater than her or his relative position in either of the two distributions. This idea can be illustrated by a simple example. Suppose that we could place a cardinal value on intelligence and the *D*-factor. Next, suppose that Assad's intelligence is 4 on a scale of 1 to 5 (where 5 is high and 1 is low) while Bates' is 1. Also, assume that Assad's *D*-factor is 4 compared to a rating of 1 for Bates. If intelligence and the *D*-factor interacted in an *additive* way to determine earnings, we would add 4 + 4 for Assad (= 8) and 1 + 1 for Bates (= 2) and note that Assad could be expected to earn 4 times as much as Bates (= 8/2). But we have speculated that the two factors might interact *multiplicatively* to deter-

[6]Howard F. Lydall, "Theories of the Distribution of Earnings," in A. B. Atkinson (ed.), *The Personal Distribution of Income* (Boulder, CO: Westview Press, 1976), p. 35.

mine earnings; that is, Assad's score will be 16 (= 4 × 4) while Bates' will be 1 (= 1 × 1). In this case, Assad's earnings will be 16 times those of Bates (= 16/1). The point is that if elements of ability are positively correlated and interact in a complementary fashion, a skewed distribution of earnings is entirely consistent with normal distributions of the elements.

Effect on Human Capital Decisions Perhaps of greater significance is the notion that ability can influence earnings through its effect on the human capital investment decision. You may recall from Figure 4-6 that greater ability enables some people to translate any given investment in human capital, say a year of college or a year of on-the-job training, into a larger increase in labor market productivity and earnings than others. Therefore, the rate of return on each year of schooling or training will be higher for those who possess greater ability.[7] Consequently, these people will have a greater demand for formal education *and* their employers will possess a stronger desire to train them on the job than will be the case for less-able people. The result? People possessing greater ability will tend to have disproportionately greater stocks of human capital and earnings than simple differences in abilities would suggest. Stated simply, people who do well in school because of ability tend to get more schooling, and people who get more education, in turn, tend to receive more on-the-job training than others. These tendencies skew the overall distribution of earnings to the right.

2 Family Background Differences in family background—indicated by such variables as family income, father's and mother's years of education, father's and mother's occupations, number of children, and so forth—also influence earnings both directly and indirectly.

Direct Effect The direct effect of family background on earnings often comes through employment of family members in family-owned businesses. A youth born into a family owning a prosperous Mercedes dealership stands a good chance of earning a sizable income later in life. Also, family "connections" may enable sons and daughters of the wealthy to gain high-paying positions in firms that are owned or managed by their parents' close friends or business associates. Sometimes these networks simply increase a job seeker's access to information about job openings, but in other instances they generate jobs for adult children through intricate reciprocity arrangements among those who interact both socially and commercially with one another.

Effect on Human Capital Decisions Of perhaps greater significance, however, is the role of family background in influencing the decision of how much formal education to obtain. This influence affects both the demand for human capital and the supply price of investment funds. High-income families tend to provide more preschool education for children, are more likely to live in areas which have better schools, and often stress the importance of higher education as a route toward a professional career.

[7]This conclusion must be viewed cautiously. Greater ability also may imply larger forgone earnings during the investment period, in which case the observed greater postinvestment earnings may *not* yield higher rates of return. See John Hause, "Ability and Schooling as Determinants of Lifetime Earnings, or If You're So Smart, Why Ain't You Rich?" in F. Thomas Juster (ed.), *Education, Income and Human Behavior* (New York: McGraw-Hill Book Company, 1975), pp. 123–149.

Their children also may be socialized to think in terms of attending higher-quality educational institutions. Consequently, high-income parents on average have a greater *demand* for human capital for their children, and therefore, these offspring obtain more formal education.[8]

Family background may also provide easier financial access to higher education. Wealthier families may be able to finance their children's education from annual earnings or personal savings, incurring only the opportunity cost of forgone goods or interest. Lower-income families most probably will need to borrow funds from imperfect financial markets at high interest rates. Because of these differing supply costs of human capital, the children of wealthier parents will find it optimal to obtain more formal education than children of poorer families (Figure 4-7).[9] These differences in education will combine with *direct* family influences to produce an unequal, rightwardly skewed distribution of earnings.

3 Discrimination In Chapter 15 we saw that discrimination explains part of the wage inequality between males and females and between whites and minorities in the United States. Discrimination adds to earnings inequality in a number of ways. First, overt pay discrimination and discrimination in promotion directly reduce the pay of those discriminated against. Second, occupational crowding or segregation not only reduces the pay of females and minorities but also increases the pay of males and whites. Both outcomes contribute to greater earnings inequality. Finally, poorer black and other minority families are often segregated into city neighborhoods where there is low-cost or public housing. These areas often have lower-quality schools and contain few adult role models with college degrees. Thus, children from these areas are much less likely to obtain higher education than are children growing up in higher-income neighborhoods. Adding to this problem is the sheer expense of attending college. This expense deters many blacks and Hispanics from obtaining college degrees.

In short, wage and occupational discrimination contribute directly to earnings inequality while human capital discrimination, by reducing the quantity and quality of education and training, further contributes to this inequality.

4 Chance and Risk Taking Some economists have incorporated the role of random elements such as chance or luck into theories of the distribution of earnings and

[8]The mathematically minded reader who desires a more detailed presentation of this general perspective should see Gary Becker and Nigel Tomes, "Child Endowments and the Quality and Quantity of Children," *Journal of Political Economy,* August 1976, pp. 143–162; and Nigel Tomes, "The Family, Inheritance and the Intergenerational Transmission of Inequality," *Journal of Political Economy,* October 1981, pp. 928–958. Also of interest is a set of conference papers presented under the title "The Family and the Distribution of Economic Rewards" in the supplementary July 1986 issue of the *Journal of Labor Economics.* Finally, an article by Charles M. Beach and Ross E. Finnie is relevant. The authors report a significant positive relationship between family background characteristics and the educational and earnings attainment of children. See their "Family Background in an Extended Earnings Generation Model: Further Evidence," *Eastern Economic Journal,* January–March, 1988, pp. 39–49.

[9]Care must be taken not to overstate this effect, however. Financial aid—low-interest loans, scholarships, and so forth—received by students from lower-income families reduces the cost of investment funds for this group. Also, the *implicit* borrowing costs to the rich may not be that much lower than the *actual* borrowing costs to the poor. For evidence of this latter possibility, see Edward Lazear, "Family Background and Optimal Schooling Decisions," *Review of Economics and Statistics,* February 1980, pp. 42–51.

income. These ***stochastic theories*** demonstrate how the cumulative impacts of random fortune tend to produce a long rightward tail in the distribution of such nonwage income as profits, rents, and capital gains. Because this is a text in labor economics, our interest, of course, is strictly in the distribution of earnings, and thus many of the stochastic theories have little relevance.

Nevertheless, according to some economists, stochastic elements offer important insights as to why earnings are unequal and why the earnings distribution is skewed to the right. Three examples of ways in which risk and luck might enter into the earnings determination process are as follows. First, suppose that at a specific instant, all people possess a given level of normally distributed earnings plus an opportunity to participate in a lottery. Further suppose that the lottery winnings consist of opportunities to be a premier professional athlete, a rock star, a motion picture celebrity, a major corporate executive, or a best-selling author. These positions are few in number but pay considerably more than the average salaries in society. But there is a catch: You must incur *risk* if you wish to play the lottery; that is, you must buy a lottery ticket. The ticket price may be say, the cost associated with advocating bold business ventures to your employer only to have one of them fail; the direct and indirect costs of refining your acting, musical, or athletic skills only to discover that the investment does not result in stardom; or the cost of forgoing present job security to become a writer whose uncertain earnings derive from book royalties.

Will all workers of equal ability participate in this lottery? Obviously not. Some people simply are much too averse to risk. Only those who are less averse to risk will decide that the chance of winning the few big prizes is worth the price of the ticket. How then might the distribution of earnings be affected by the lottery? Three distributions, each individually symmetrical, would be observable. First, there would be a distribution of earnings for the many nonparticipants in the lottery. Second, we would observe a distribution, possibly lying to the left of the one for nonparticipants, indicating the earnings of lottery losers. Finally, there would be a distribution lying to the right of that for nonparticipants displaying the very large average earnings of the relatively few lottery winners. Even though each of these three distributions might be normally distributed, the composite distribution of earnings would be skewed to the right.[10]

In Chapter 8, we implied a way chance may account for differences in personal earnings. In Figure 8-5 it was observed that differences in pay for the same type of work can exist under circumstances of imperfect wage information and costly job search. Who receives which wage in the frequency distribution shown in the figure is in part determined randomly. For example, suppose that Gomez and Green are equally qualified job seekers who both have the same reservation wage (minimum acceptable wage). Also, assume that each is searching in a random fashion for job openings in the frequency distribution shown in Figure 8-5. Through good luck, Gomez may receive the highest wage offer in the distribution on her first try, while the less fortunate Green may get an offer above her reservation wage but well below the pay received by Gomez.

[10]This example is based on a more complex model presented by Milton Friedman, "Choice, Chance, and the Personal Distribution of Income," *Journal of Political Economy,* August 1953, pp. 273–290. For a highly technical criticism of Friedman's article, see S. M. Kanbur, "Of Risk Taking and the Personal Distribution of Income," *Journal of Political Economy,* August 1979, pp. 769–797.

A final example of the role of chance in theories of personal earnings is provided by Thurow. He contends that "marginal products are inherent in jobs and not individuals. The individual will be trained into the marginal productivity of the job he is slated to hold, but he does not have this marginal productivity independent of the job in question."[11] The implication of this thesis is that workers possessing a particular set of general background characteristics—that is, being equally trainable—will make up a labor pool from which employers will draw randomly. Those who are fortunate will get selected for jobs with high marginal productivity and annual earnings, but because such jobs are few, other equally qualified people will end up in lower-paying occupations. Thus, according to Thurow, "similar individuals will be distributed across a range of job opportunities and earnings. In effect, they will participate in a lottery."[12]

Schematic Summary

Figure 17-3 summarizes the major determinants of earnings just discussed.[13] The basic human capital explanation of earnings is represented by the thick solid line connecting *education and training* with earnings. The more comprehensive multifactor explanation is portrayed by the entire figure. *Ability* (independent of education) affects earnings directly, as shown by the thick line connecting the two, and indirectly via its impact on the optimal amount and quality of education and training (thin line). Likewise, *family background* and *discrimination* have direct and indirect effects on

[11]Lester C. Thurow, *Generating Inequality: Mechanisms of Distribution in the U.S. Economy* (New York: Basic Books, Inc., 1975), p. 85.

[12]Ibid., p. 92.

[13]For a fuller discussion of this representation, see A. B. Atkinson, *The Economics of Inequality,* 2d ed. (Oxford: Clarendon Press, 1983), p. 122.

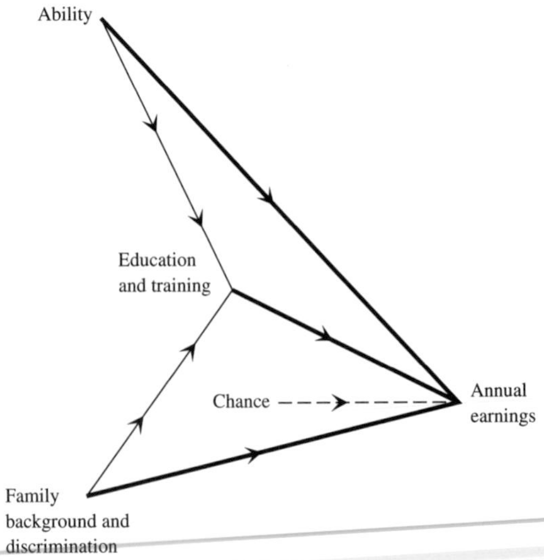

FIGURE 17-3 FACTORS AFFECTING PERSONAL ANNUAL EARNINGS
The basic human capital explanation of the personal distribution of annual earnings is shown by the heavy solid arrow that connects education and training to annual earnings. The multifactor approach adds ability, family background, and discrimination as variables that can directly influence earnings (heavy lines) or indirectly affect earnings by having an impact on the amount and quality of education and training that a person receives (thin lines). Luck, or chance, also plays a role in affecting annual earnings (broken line). [Adapted from A. B. Atkinson, *The Economics of Inequality,* 2d ed. (Oxford: Oxford University Press, 1983), p. 122.]

personal earnings. The solid arrow between these factors and earnings represents the roles of family firms, family connections, and wage and occupational discrimination. The thin line from family background and discrimination to education and training illustrates the impact of family education and wealth on the demand for, and the supply price of, human capital. It also captures the effect of racial and gender discrimination on human capital and therefore indirectly on earnings. Finally, the role of *chance* is portrayed by the broken line leading directly to earnings.

We could easily add more complexity to Figure 17-3. For example, we could connect chance with family background and ability, for in a sense both are partly products of luck. Also, we could add a *feedback loop* from earnings to education and training, inasmuch as present earnings may help determine how much subsequent education one might find optimal. Then, too, we could recognize the role of compensating wage premiums in causing earnings differences (Chapter 8). Finally, as pointed out by Lydall, Rosen, and others, hierarchical structures of organizations may create large earnings disparities.[14] But these important considerations aside, Figure 17-3 adequately summarizes the major determinants of the personal distribution of earnings.

MOBILITY WITHIN THE EARNINGS DISTRIBUTION

The aggregate personal distribution of earnings is quite rigid from one year to the next and changes only slightly from one decade to the next. But this fact masks the degree of individual movement within that fixed distribution. As Schiller colorfully points out, on the one hand, individuals may be highly mobile from year to year and over their lifetimes within the static aggregate distribution, suggesting a game of musical chairs in which the positions of the chairs remain the same but the occupants regularly change. On the other hand, "the rigid shape of the aggregate distribution is equally compatible with a total lack of personal mobility—a game, as it were, that individuals play by remaining in their chairs until the music . . . is over."[15]

Which of these two possibilities best describes reality? The answer appears to be the musical chairs scenario. The evidence suggests that considerable movement or mobility occurs within the rather rigid static distribution. This ***earnings mobility*** is of two
17-1 main types: life-cycle mobility and a "churning" that is independent of age.

Life-Cycle Mobility

We know from our previous discussions of age-earnings profiles (Figure 4-1) that people's earnings typically vary systematically with age over the course of the life cycle. Most people have relatively low earnings when they are young; later, during their prime earning years, their earnings rise substantially; and finally, their earnings fall near the time of retirement. Thus, even if everyone had an identical stream of earnings over her

[14]Howard Lydall, *The Structure of Earnings* (London: Oxford University Press, 1968); and Sherwin Rosen, "Authority, Control, and the Distribution of Earnings," *Bell Journal of Economics,* Autumn 1982, pp. 311–323.

[15]Bradley R. Schiller, "Relative Earnings Mobility in the United States," *American Economic Review,* December 1977, p. 926.

17-1 World of Work

ARE EARNINGS BECOMING LESS STABLE?*

An issue related to earnings mobility that has received little attention is earnings instability. That is, temporary year-to-year changes in earnings. For example, a person may have high sales commissions or bonuses in one year but not in the next. To examine changes in earnings stability over time, Gottschalk and Moffitt have compared the temporary instability of earnings of white males in the 1970-to-1979 period to their counterparts in the 1979-to-1987 period. They report that the size of temporary changes in earnings increased 42 percent during the 1980s.

This rise in earnings instability varied across different types of workers but was concentrated among those with lower incomes. For example, those in the bottom quartile of earnings had a 47 percent increase in earnings instability, while those in the top quartile had only a 20 percent increase. The increase in instability was also greater among those with less education—96 percent for high school dropouts and 43 percent for college graduates. Interestingly, earnings instability rose by more than one-third for those who changed jobs as well as those who did not.

No definitive explanation appears to exist for the increased instability. Employment shifts away from the manufacturing and unionized sectors can account for only 12 percent of the rise in instability. In addition, shifts toward greater job mobility and the rise in self-employment and part-time work can explain only a part of the increase. Thus, most of the rise cannot be explained.

An important outcome of the rise in earnings instability is that it accounts for one-third to one-half of the rise in earnings inequality discussed in the next section. Thus, inequality appears to be rising partly because individuals' earnings are rocketing up one year and back down the next.

*Based on Peter Gottschalk and Robert Moffitt, "The Growth of Earnings Instability in the U.S. Labor Market," *Brookings Papers on Economic Activity,* 1994–2, pp. 217–272.

or his lifetime, we still would observe age-related inequality in the distribution of earnings. In any specific year, the static annual distribution of earnings would include, say, young (low-earnings) workers just beginning their labor force participation, middle-aged (high-earnings) employees in the prime of their careers, and older workers who were phasing into retirement. This inequality of *annual* earnings for a specific year would be present despite complete equality of *lifetime* earnings.

The evidence suggests that there is much ***life-cycle mobility*** of earnings *and* that this mobility contributes to more equality in lifetime earnings than is observed using static cross-sectional annual data. The degree of inequality of lifetime earnings may be as much as 45 percent less than the annual inequality shown earlier in Table 17-1.[16]

"Churning" within the Distribution

Is there movement within the earnings distribution that is independent of age itself? Do people's relative age-adjusted earnings positions change during their lifetimes? Is there sufficient ***"churning" within the earnings distribution*** to allow the "cream" to rise? To answer this question, Schiller drew a sample from the Social Security records

[16]Lee A. Lillard, "Inequality: Earnings vs. Human Wealth," *American Economic Review,* March 1977, pp. 42–53. Also see Peter Friesen and Danny Miller, "Annual Inequality and Lifetime Inequality," *Quarterly Journal of Economics,* February 1983, pp. 139–155. For a discussion of how age affects the Gini coefficient of family income, see Morton Paglin, "The Measurement and Trend of Inequality: A Basic Revision," *American Economic Review,* September 1975, pp. 598–609.

of nearly 75,000 males who were 16 to 49 years of age and earned at least $1,000 in 1957. He divided the sample into 20 earnings categories (ventiles), each containing 5 percent of the workers, and then observed the movements of individuals among the categories between 1957 and 1971. Controlling for the effects of age, Schiller found that about 70 percent of the workers were mobile across at least two earnings categories and that on the average, workers moved about four categories, or one-fifth of the way from one end of the earnings distribution to the other. Schiller concluded that "the longitudinal earnings data . . . unambiguously demonstrate that individuals are highly mobile across relative positions in the earnings distribution."[17]

The finding that people are mobile within the earnings distribution is significant in that it implies that this churning joins with the age factor to reduce the degree of lifetime inequality. In terms of Schiller's "chair" analogy, the same workers *do not* always remain in the same earnings chairs. For example, a salesperson may have relatively small commissions and earnings in the first year of a new job but receive considerably larger annual commissions in subsequent years. Or a manager may get promoted to a job that pays considerably more than the job previously held. Or, as an example of churning in a downward direction, a performer who is highly paid one year may earn much less annually during following years. And, as stated by Blinder, "Americans seem quite willing to tolerate gross disparities in [earnings] so long as there is a reasonable chance that low-income families in one year can become high-income families in another. . . . While ghetto dwellers rarely trade places with Rockefellers, ours is not a stratified society."[18]

Nevertheless, one must not overstate the extent of churning in the earnings distribution. Schiller, for example, found that (1) mobility in and out of the *lowest* and *highest* 5 percent (ventile) categories was lower than to and from other categories and that (2) although blacks were also mobile, their *rate* of mobility was less than that for whites. Conclusion? Although Schiller's evidence and more recent data confirm that much churning occurs within the earnings distribution, the extent of this type of mobility is
17-1 neither uniform throughout the distribution nor equal for all groups of workers.[19]

QUICK REVIEW 17-2

- The human capital theory looks to differences in the amount and quality of education and the extent of on-the-job training as the major reasons for earnings inequality.

[17]Schiller, op. cit., p. 938.

[18]Alan S. Blinder, "The Level and Distribution of Economic Well-Being," in Martin Feldstein (ed.), *The American Economy in Transition* (Chicago: University of Chicago Press, 1980), p. 454.

[19]Recent studies have reached mixed conclusions on whether the rate of earnings mobility has changed over time. For example, see Moshe Buchinsky and Jennifer Hunt, "Wage Mobility in the United States," National Bureau of Economic Research Working Paper No. 5455, February 1996; and Peter Gottschalk and Robert Moffitt, "The Growth of Earnings Instability in the U.S. Labor Market," *Brookings Papers on Economic Activity,* 1994–2, pp. 217–272. For a survey of earnings mobility studies, see Anthony Barnes; François Bourguignon; and Christian Morrisson, *Empirical Studies of Earnings Mobility* (Philadelphia: Harwood Academic Publishers, 1992).

- The multifactor approach to earnings distribution takes into account ability, family background, discrimination, chance, and risk taking, in addition to education and training.
- Workers exhibit considerable earnings mobility over their work lives; earnings typically are low in earlier years, rise in prime working years, and then decline.
- There is much year-to-year movement of workers across earnings categories, independent of life-cycle aspects of earnings. This mobility is lower for blacks than whites and less in the lowest and highest earnings categories.

17-2

Your Turn: Of all the factors explaining earnings inequality, which one do you think is the most significant? (Answer: See page 627.)

RISING EARNINGS INEQUALITY

During the past two decades labor economists have devoted much research to tracking and explaining changes in the distribution of earnings in the United States. The initial

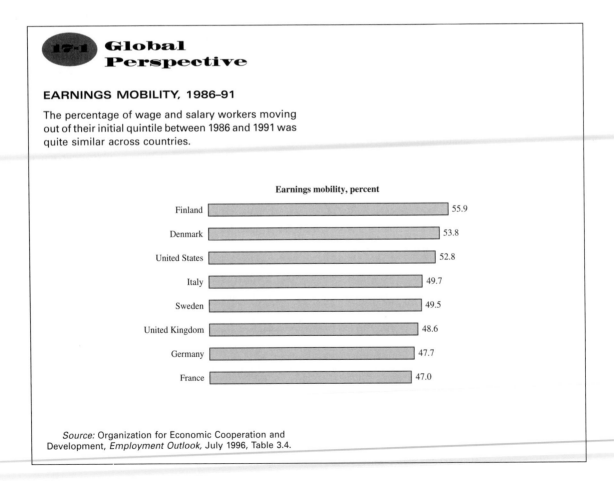

17-1 **Global Perspective**

EARNINGS MOBILITY, 1986–91

The percentage of wage and salary workers moving out of their initial quintile between 1986 and 1991 was quite similar across countries.

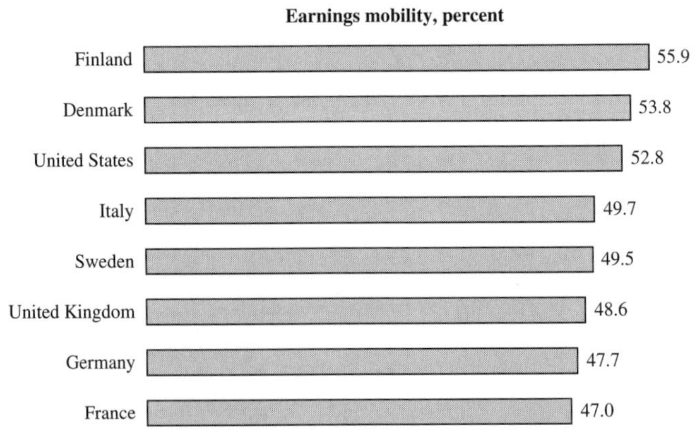

Source: Organization for Economic Cooperation and Development, *Employment Outlook,* July 1996, Table 3.4.

17-2 **World of Work**

GOVERNMENT EMPLOYMENT AND THE EARNINGS DISTRIBUTION

One out of six U.S. workers is employed by the government. How do the wages paid to these employees affect the distribution of earnings? The answer is that government employment and remuneration reduce overall earnings inequality.

Government agencies and government contractors usually adhere to a prevailing wage rule under which the wages paid to public employees are comparable to the earnings of similar workers in the private sector. But this rule tends to be modified at both the bottom and the top ends of the government pay structure. Blue-collar public employees are paid more than their private-sector counterparts, while white-collar workers in government—particularly executives—are paid much less. As a consequence, the personal distribution of earnings in the public sector is more egalitarian than in the private sector, causing the overall distribution in society to also be less unequal.

The reasons for the compression of earnings in the public sector are many. For example, elected officials may pay low-wage workers more than their private-sector counterparts to avoid the potentially politically embarrassing circumstance of having full-time government workers qualify for government cash and in-kind welfare benefits. Also, it seems probable that low- to middle-wage-earning employees, who are large in number and strong politically, are more likely to secure wage increases than higher-paid managers and professionals, who are few in number. Furthermore, it may be that the large salaries paid to executives in corporations (Table 7-2) simply are not politically feasible when paid to top governmental administrators and elected officials. In this regard, we might note that in a typical year, the total of the combined salaries and bonuses of the 10 highest-paid corporate executives in the United States exceeds the combined salaries of the following government officials: the president of the United States, the vice president, the 100 U.S. senators, the 50 state governors, the 9 Supreme Court justices, and the 50 heads of major regulatory agencies.

motivation for this research was the controversial hypothesis expressed in the early 1980s that the middle class in America is shrinking. In its extreme form, this view holds that American employment is being polarized between high-paying positions requiring considerable education and low-paying jobs in the service sector.[20]

Although most labor economists reject the extreme polarization view, a consensus has arisen that the distribution of work and salary earnings has indeed become more unequal. Evidence indicates that earnings inequality has increased over the past 25 years and that this trend has accelerated since 1980.[21]

Trends in Wage Inequality

A useful measure of wage inequality is the ratio of the wages at different parts of the wage distribution. For example, a commonly used differential is the 90–10 ratio; that is, the wage at the 90th percentile divided by the wage at the 10th percentile. Figure 17-4

[20]Barry Bluestone and Bennett Harrison, *The Deindustrialization of America* (New York: Basic Books, Inc., 1982). Also see Bennett Harrison and Barry Bluestone, *The Great U-Turn: Corporate Restructuring and Polarization of America* (New York: Basic Books, Inc., 1988).

[21]Frank Levy and Richard J. Murnane, "U.S. Earnings Levels and Earnings Inequality: A Review of Recent Trends and Proposed Explanations," *Journal of Economic Literature*, September 1992, pp. 1333–1381; Symposium on "Wage Inequality," *Journal of Economic Perspectives*, Spring 1997; Jared Berstein and Lawrence Mishel, "Has Wage Inequality Stopped Growing?" *Monthly Labor Review*, December 1997, pp. 3–16; and Council of Economic Advisors, *Economic Report of the President* (Washington, DC: U.S. Government Printing Office, February 1997), chap. 5.

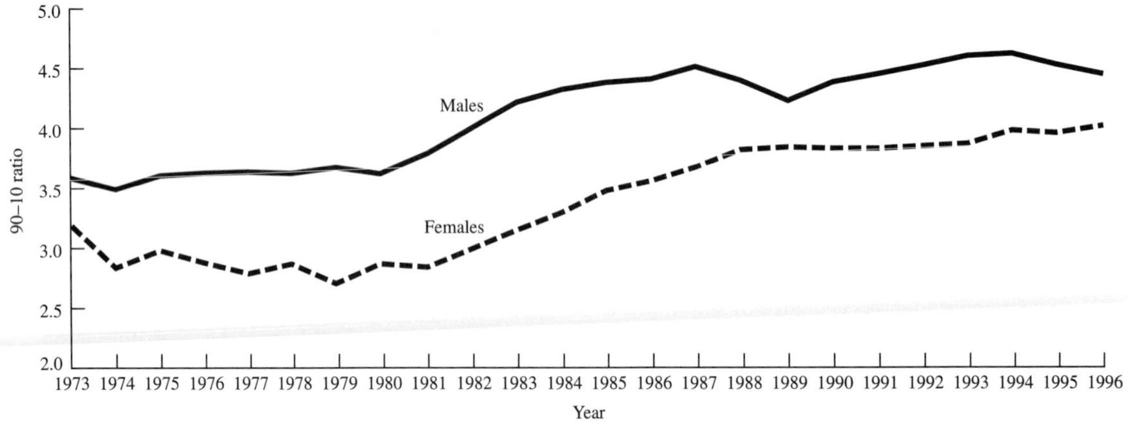

FIGURE 17-4 WAGE INEQUALITY, 90–10 RATIO, 1973–96
Wage inequality for both men and women has increased in recent decades.
Source: Jared Berstein and Lawrence Mishel, "Has Wage Inequality Stopped Growing?" *Monthly Labor Review,* December 1997, pp. 3–16.

shows the ratio of the hourly wage for wage and salary workers by gender. For men in 1973 the 90–10 ratio was 3.59.[22] This indicates that the men at the 90th percentile earned 3.59 times as much as men at the 10th percentile. The ratio rose to 4.45 in 1996, indicating inequality increased.[23]

The rate of increase, however, was not steady over this period. It rose at a modest pace of .013 points per year between 1973 and 1979, then accelerated. It increased by .056 points per year between 1979 and 1989 and .031 points per year between 1989 and 1996. A further breakdown of the 90–10 ratio into the 90–50 and 50–10 ratios reveals that the recent slowdown in the rise in inequality is caused by a slight decline in the 50–10 ratio. That is, wages for men at the 10 percentile have risen slightly relative to those at the 50th percentile. Wages of men at the 90th percentile have steadily risen relative to those at the 50th percentile.

Wage inequality has also risen among women. The 90–10 ratio rose from 3.18 in 1973 to 4.02 in 1996. The change in inequality across time was different for women: the 90–10 ratio fell between 1973 to 1979, in contrast to the slight rise for men. On the other hand, the ratio rose twice as fast as for men between 1979 and 1989.

Why the Increase in Earnings Inequality?

Economists have advanced several explanations as to why earnings inequality has grown over the past two and a half decades. Let's briefly assess four potential explanations.

[22]The source of the statistics in this section is Berstein and Mishel, op. cit.

[23]Evidence shows that inequality measures are sensitive to the sample of workers examined and the earnings measure. See Robert I. Lerman, "Reassessing Trends in U.S. Earnings Inequality," *Monthly Labor Review,* December 1997, pp. 17–25.

1 Deindustrialization Since the mid-1970s employment in the service sector has increased dramatically relative to employment in manufacturing. Because the service sector has a lower average wage and a higher variance of earnings than the manufacturing sector, this tilt toward services has undoubtedly increased earnings inequality.[24]

But economists warn that this is an incomplete explanation. The change in the mix of employment toward services accounts for only a small portion of the overall rise in wage inequality. As much as 80 percent of the total rise in earnings inequality is explained by increased wage and salary dispersion *within* industries.[25] This intraindustry increase in earnings inequality is not easily explained by the shift from manufacturing to service employment. Moreover, it is important to remember that several high-growth service industries—for example, law, consulting, accounting, medicine, and education—are high-pay sectors, not low-pay ones.

2 Import Competition and the Decline of Unionism Strong import competition has severely reduced the demand for workers in several high-wage, unionized industries, including autos and steel. Because union wages have been relatively inflexible downward, these declines in labor demand have produced massive reductions in unionized employment. One result has been a direct decline in the average wage of workers with lower levels of education. Also, the many workers displaced from unionized jobs have increased the labor supply in lower-paying industries. Thus, there has been a downward pressure on wages in these industries as well. Another factor is that import competition has induced some high-pay industries to move their operations to nonunion, lower-paying regions of the country. These relocations have further widened earnings inequality and contributed to the decline of unionism.

Research evidence supports this perspective on growing wage inequality. Increases in the trade deficit (more imports than exports) and the related decline of unionism (Chapter 10) have contributed to the rise in earnings inequality.[26]

3 Increased Demand for Skilled Workers Recall that the college wage premium rose substantially in the 1980s (Chapter 4), implying a growing wage gap between more-skilled workers and less-skilled workers. One potential explanation for the rising rate of return to higher education and therefore for increased earnings inequality

[24]Bluestone and Harrison, op. cit.; and Harrison and Bluestone, op. cit. Also relevant is Barry Bluestone, "The Impact of Schooling and Industrial Restructuring on Recent Trends in Wage Inequality in the United States," *American Economic Review,* May 1990, pp. 303–307.

[25]McKinley L. Blackburn, David E. Bloom, and Richard B. Freeman, "The Declining Economic Position of Less Skilled American Men," in Gary Burtless (ed.), *A Future of Lousy Jobs? The Changing Structure of U.S. Wages* (Washington, DC: Brookings Institution, 1990), pp. 77–122.

[26]For a survey on the link between the trade imbalance and rising inequality, see Gary Burtless, "International Trade and the Rise in Earnings Inequality," *Journal of Economic Literature,* June 1995, pp. 800–816. Also see Symposium on "Income Inequality and Trade," *Journal of Economic Perspectives,* Summer 1995. For evidence that the decline in unionism has contributed to rising earnings inequality, see John Dinardo, Nicole Fortin, and Thomas Lemieux, "Labor Market Institutions and the Distribution of Wages, 1973–1993: A Semiparametric Approach," *Econometrica,* September 1996, pp. 1001–1044; David Card, "The Effect of Unions on the Structure of Wages: A Longitudinal Analysis," *Econometrica,* July 1996, pp. 957–979; and Nicole M. Fortin and Thomas Lemieux, "Institutional Changes and Rising Wage Inequality," *Journal of Economic Perspectives,* Spring 1997, pp. 75–96.

is that the demand for more-skilled workers may have sharply increased relative to the demand for less-skilled workers. Other things being equal, a relative increase in the demand for more-skilled, higher-paid workers will widen the earnings distribution.

Increased demand for more-skilled workers may have evidenced itself in two ways. First, the demand for more-skilled workers may have occurred *within* industries. Responding to new technologies, industries in general may have changed their production techniques in ways that require comparatively more college-educated workers. For example, manufacturing and service industries alike have expanded their use of computer-aided technologies.[27] Second, a shift in product demand may have occurred *among* industries. Specifically, the derived demand for labor may have shifted in favor of industries that employ a higher proportion of more-skilled workers. For instance, the emergence of high-tech industries such as the computer software and biomedicine industries may have increased the overall demand for highly trained workers.

It is also possible that the rise in the college pay premium has resulted from a relative slowdown in the historical increase in the proportion of young people who are attending college. Together with a rising demand for college-educated workers, this would further explain the increase in earnings inequality.

4 Demographic Changes Some economists have looked to the supply side of the aggregate labor market to explain rising earnings inequality. Specifically, they cite changes in the composition of labor supply between more-skilled and less-skilled workers as an important factor. In particular, the entrance of large numbers of less-skilled baby boomers and female workers into the labor market during the 1970s and 1980s may have contributed to increased earnings inequality.

The link between the surge in the number of inexperienced, less-skilled workers and earnings inequality has two dimensions. First, this surge may have raised the proportion of low-wage workers to high-wage workers in *all industries,* creating greater wage disparity. Second, the increased supply of young workers and inexperienced female workers in various *lower-wage labor markets* may have depressed the relative earnings of workers in those markets. In either case, the predicted impact would be a rise in the pay differential between less-skilled (less-experienced) and more-skilled workers.

The demographic explanation for rising earnings inequality is logically appealing and often cited. But it is difficult to reconcile this explanation with evidence that increases in aggregate inequality largely result from growing earnings inequality *within* each age group. The research consensus is that the baby boom, the surge of female labor force entrants, and immigration have only modestly contributed to the growing
17-1 earnings inequality.[28]

[27]See, for instance, "World of Work" 8-1. Also see George E. Johnson, "Changes in Earnings Inequality: The Role of Demand Shifts," *Journal of Economic Perspectives,* Spring 1997, pp. 41–54.

[28]Burtless, op. cit., p. 109. Also see Robert H. Topel, "Factor Proportions and Relative Wages: The Supply-Side Determinants of Wage Inequality," *Journal of Economic Perspectives,* Spring 1997, pp. 55–74.

17-1 Global Perspective

MALE EARNINGS INEQUALITY

Earnings inequality among males has increased in some but not all major industrial countries.

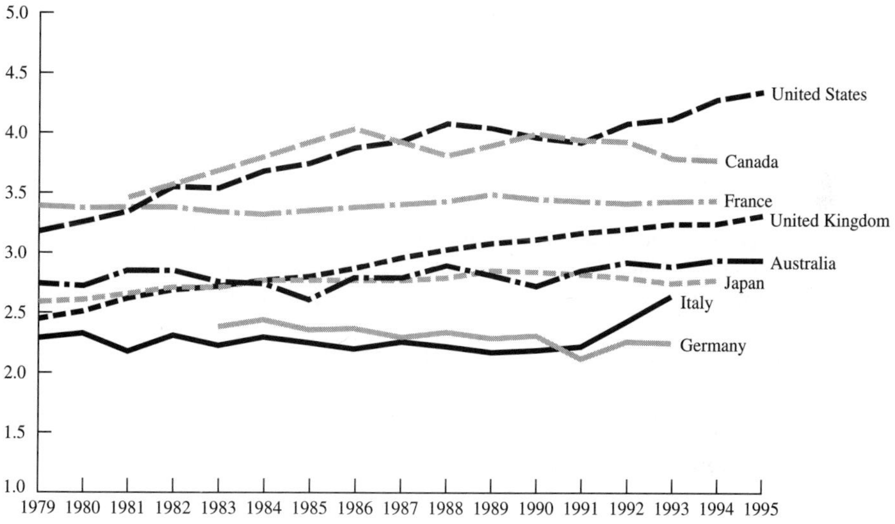

Source: Organization for Economic Cooperation and Development, *Employment Outlook,* July 1996, Table 3.4.

Conclusions and Future Prospects

What can we conclude from our discussion of possible sources of growing wage inequality? The main conclusion is that there appears to be no single cause of this phenomenon. The evidence on this matter points to demand-side, supply-side, and institutional factors being at work. The demand for college-trained workers appears to have risen relative to the supply of these workers. The supply of less-skilled workers appears to have increased relative to the demand for less-skilled workers. Meanwhile, trade deficits and the decline of unionism have reduced traditional mid-paying jobs and channeled workers into lower-paying employment. The result has been a widening distribution of earnings for both women and men.[29]

Will the distribution of earnings continue to widen during the next decade? The tentative answer provided by experts in this area is "probably not." Declining labor force growth (Chapter 3) should tighten the aggregate labor market in the future and increase wages for less-skilled workers. Also, the rising rate of return to investment in education and training should entice more people to enroll in colleges and encourage firms to invest more in training their employees. Eventually, we would expect the increased supply of more-skilled workers to reduce the earnings premium paid to this group.[30] But keep in mind that the factors affecting earnings inequality are manifold and complex. Therefore, predicting the future course of earnings inequality is highly speculative.

CHAPTER SUMMARY

1 The degree of inequality in personal earnings can be shown by either a histogram (absolute frequency distribution), a relative frequency distribution, or a Lorenz curve. A frequency distribution shows either the absolute or the relative number of employed whose annual earnings fall within various ranges of annual earnings. The Lorenz curve portrays the cumulative percentage of all wage and salary earners and their corresponding cumulative percentage of total earnings.
2 The frequency distribution for U.S. earnings evidences considerable bunching around a single mode that is to the left of the median and mean and displays a long rightwardly skewed tail, indicating rather wide disparities in personal earnings.
3 The Gini coefficient measures the degree of earnings inequality on a scale of zero (complete equality) to one (complete inequality). It can be found graphically by comparing the area between the diagonal line and the Lorenz curve to the entire area below the diagonal.
4 Frequency distributions, Lorenz curves, and Gini coefficients of *personal* earnings must be interpreted cautiously because they *(a)* differ depending on whether part-time workers are included or excluded, *(b)* fail to include fringe benefits, *(c)* do not provide information on *family* earnings, and *(d)* display more inequality than when based on income after taxes and transfers.
5 According to human capital theorists, approximately one-half to two-thirds of earnings inequality is explained by the interactive differences in people's formal education and on-the-job training.
6 Ability *(a)* is thought by some economists to influence earnings *directly* through enhancement of productivity, *(b)* may take several forms that interact multiplicatively to produce the observed skewed distribution of earnings, and *(c)* may *indirectly* have an im-

[29]A few attempts have been made to evaluate the relative importance of the factors cited. For example, John Bound and George Johnson have concluded from such a study that the major cause of the relative wages changes was a shift in the skill structure of labor demand brought about by technological change that has called for the use of more highly skilled labor. See John Bound and George Johnson, "Changes in the Structure of Wages in the 1980s: An Evaluation of Alternative Explanations," *American Economic Review,* June 1992, pp. 371–392. This conclusion is consistent with other studies on this issue. See Council of Economics Advisors, op. cit.

[30]For a discussion of this point, see Topel, op. cit.

pact on earnings by determining the return from—and hence the optimal amount of—investment in human capital.

7 Family background, discrimination, extent of risk taking, and degree of luck also are variables that help explain earnings inequality and the rightwardly skewed tail of the earnings distribution.

8 There is considerable movement by individuals within the overall distribution of earnings. This mobility is related to the life cycle, reflecting the generally positive relationship between age and earnings. It can also be of a "churning" nature, in which people with more education, training, ability, or luck rise from lower to higher levels of age-adjusted earnings.

9 The distribution of earnings in the United States has become more unequal over the past two decades. Potential causes that have been cited include *(a)* deindustrialization, *(b)* import competition and the decline of unionism, *(c)* increased demand for skilled workers, and *(d)* demographic changes. None of these factors alone can explain the increase in wage and salary inequality. It would appear that demand-side, supply-side, and institutional factors all are involved.

TERMS AND CONCEPTS

personal distribution of earnings
frequency distribution
histogram
Lorenz curve
Gini coefficient
human capital model
multifactor approach to the earnings distribution
self-selection
D-factor
stochastic theories
earnings mobility
life-cycle mobility
"churning" within the earnings distribution

QUESTIONS AND STUDY SUGGESTIONS

1 Suppose that a hypothetical economy consists of 20 nonunionized private-sector workers who have the following annual earnings: $18,000, $9,000, $82,000, $12,000, $13,000, $76,000, $61,000, $14,000, $22,000, $23,000, $21,000, $46,000, $59,000, $26,000, $27,000, $37,000, $6,000, $41,000, $3,000, and $24,000.

a Using annual earnings ranges of $10,000—that is, 0–$10,000, $10,000–$20,000, and so forth—construct a histogram (absolute frequency distribution) of this nation's distribution of personal earnings. What is the mode of the histogram? What is the average (mean) level of earnings? What is the median level of earnings? Characterize the distribution as being (1) normal, (2) skewed leftward, or (3) skewed rightward. Explain.

b Construct a Lorenz curve showing the quintile distribution of earnings for this economy.

c What would be the likely impact of unionization of this entire work force on the Lorenz curve? Explain.

2 Speculate about why a given Gini coefficient is compatible with more than one particular Lorenz curve. Illustrate graphically.

3 Why is it that people who have more formal education than others also in general tend to receive more on-the-job training during their careers? What is the implication of this fact for the distribution of earnings?

4 Critically evaluate this statement: "Lifetime earnings are less equally distributed than annual earnings."

5 Speculate as to how successful attempts by government to tighten the distribution of family *income* through transfers might inadvertently make the distribution of annual *earnings* more unequal.

6 Explain how both *ability* and *family background* can *directly* influence earnings, independently of education and training. How do ability and family background *indirectly* determine earnings through the human capital investment decision? How does *discrimination* contribute to earnings inequality?

7 What has happened to the location of the Lorenz curve of annual earnings over the past 25 years? Make a case that the Lorenz curve will shift leftward over the next 25 years. Make a case that it will shift further to the right than its present location. Which of your two scenarios do you think is most realistic?

8 Which two of the text's possible explanations for increasing wage and salary inequality seem least consistent with the following fact: The distribution of earnings has become more unequal *within* industries (both goods and service industries) and *within* age groups? Explain.

9 In the light of new information presented in this chapter, answer question 10 at the end of Chapter 4.

SELECTED REFERENCES

Atkinson, A. B.: *The Economics of Inequality,* 2d ed. (London: Oxford University Press, 1983).

Atkinson, A. B. (ed.): *The Personal Distribution of Income* (Boulder, CO: Westview Press, Inc., 1976).

Blinder, Alan S.: *Toward an Economic Theory of Income Distribution* (Chicago: University of Chicago Press, 1974).

Bluestone, Barry, and Bennett Harrison: *The Great U-Turn: Corporate Restructuring and Polarization of America* (New York: Basic Books, Inc., 1988).

Burtless, Gary (ed.): *A Future of Lousy Jobs? The Changing Structure of U.S. Wages* (Washington, DC: Brookings Institution, 1990).

Danzinger, Sheldon, and Peter Gottschalk (eds.): *Uneven Tides: Rising Inequality in America* (New York: Russell Sage Foundation, 1993).

Freeman, Richard, and Lawrence F. Katz (eds.): *Differences and Changes in Wage Structure* (Chicago: University of Chicago Press, 1995).

Gottschalk, Peter, and Timothy M. Smeeding: "Cross-National Comparisons of Earnings and Income Inequality," *Journal of Economic Literature,* June 1997, pp. 633–687.

Levy, Frank, and Richard J. Murnane: "U.S. Earnings Levels and Earnings Inequality: A Review of Recent Trends and Proposed Explanations," *Journal of Economic Literature,* September 1992, pp. 1333–1381.

Mincer, Jacob: *Schooling, Experience and Earnings* (New York: Columbia University Press, 1974).

Osberg, Lars: *Economic Inequality in the United States* (Armonk, NY: M. E. Sharp, Inc., 1984).

Sahota, Gian S.: "Theories of Personal Income Distribution: A Survey," *Journal of Economic Literature,* March 1978, pp. 1–55.

Symposium on "Wage Inequality," *Journal of Economic Perspectives,* Spring 1997.

Thurow, Lester C.: *Generating Inequality: Mechanisms of Distribution in the U.S. Economy* (New York: Basic Books, Inc., Publishers, 1975).

CHAPTER 18

LABOR PRODUCTIVITY: WAGES, PRICES, AND EMPLOYMENT

Previous chapters emphasized the determination of wage rates for specific types of workers, explained the complex cluster of individual wages that constitute the wage structure, and examined the distribution of personal earnings. The spotlight now shifts to the long-term trend of the average level of real wages. What has propelled the increase in average real wages occurring during this century? Why has real wage growth in America slowed so dramatically since 1979 ("World of Work" 6-1)?

In answering these questions we will find that the secular expansion of the level of real wages is intimately linked to the growth of labor productivity. Much of the present chapter is thus devoted to productivity growth and its various ramifications.

In more specific terms, this chapter is organized as follows. First, the concept of labor productivity is introduced and its measurement is briefly discussed. Second, the various economic implications of productivity growth are examined, with emphasis on the relationship between productivity and real wages. A third and major segment of the chapter examines the primary factors that contribute to the growth of labor productivity. Next, cyclical changes in labor productivity are briefly considered. Fifth, the relationship between productivity growth and employment growth is analyzed. Do industries characterized by rapid productivity growth provide more or fewer jobs than do industries with slow productivity growth? Finally, we survey explanations of the slowdown in the rate of productivity growth that began in the mid-1960s.

THE PRODUCTIVITY CONCEPT

In essence, productivity is a simple concept. It is merely a relationship between real output—the quantity of goods and services produced—and the quantity of input used to produce that output. Productivity, in other words, is a measure of resource or input efficiency expressed in terms of a ratio:

$$\text{Productivity} = \frac{\text{output}}{\text{input}} \tag{18-1}$$

Productivity tells us how many units of output we can obtain from a unit of input. If output per unit of input increases, productivity has risen.

As you might sense from this definition, there is a whole family of productivity measures that vary depending on the specific data chosen for insertion in the numerator and denominator of the productivity equation. The output in the numerator might be the real gross domestic product (GDP), the real output of the private sector, or the real output of a particular industry or plant. Whatever output measure is used in the numerator, it must be stated in *real* rather than nominal terms. The production of more goods and services per unit of input constitutes an increase in productivity; higher prices on a fixed or even declining quantity of output clearly do not. As for the denominator, some productivity analysts combine inputs of both labor and capital to derive a measure of *total factor productivity.* Because labor is the focal point of our discussion, we will be concerned with ***labor productivity,*** in which worker hours are related to total product, or real GDP.[1]

Measurement

Figure 18-1 provides information enabling us to calculate labor productivity for each of two specific years for a hypothetical economy. The figure shows two aggregate production functions, TP_1 and TP_2, each of which represents a specific year and relates quantities of worker hours to total annual real GDP for that period. We will initially focus on the aggregate production function labeled TP_1. This curve reflects two assumptions: first, that the quality of labor, amount of capital, and methods of production are fixed; and second, that production is subject to diminishing marginal returns (Chapter 5). To simplify, we assume diminishing returns over the entire range of output. Thus, TP_1 indicates the relationship between worker hours and total product, *other things being equal,* and shows that total product rises at a diminishing rate as added units of labor are used in conjunction with the fixed capital stock.

The input–output information provided by curve TP_1 allows us to measure labor productivity for this hypothetical economy for this particular year. Specifically,

$$\text{Labor productivity} = \frac{\text{total product (real GDP)}}{\text{number of worker hours}} \tag{18-2}$$

[1]For a brief survey of available productivity measures, see Jerome A. Mark, "Productivity Measurement," in Jerome M. Rosow (ed.), *Productivity: Prospect for Growth* (New York: Van Nostrand Reinhold Company, 1981), pp. 54–75. Also of interest is Solomon Fabricant, "Productivity Measurement and Analysis: An Overview," in *Measuring Productivity: Trends and Comparisons from the First International Productivity Symposium* (New York: UNIPUB, 1984), pp. 1–19; and Roy H. Webb, "National Productivity Statistics," Federal Reserve Bank of Richmond Economic Quarterly, Winter 1998, pp. 45–64.

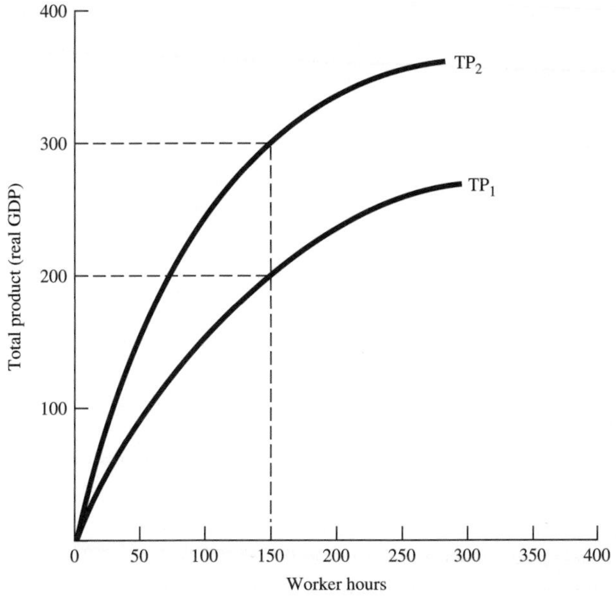

FIGURE 18-1 **THE AGGREGATE PRODUCTION FUNCTION AND LABOR PRODUCTIVITY**
The aggregate production functions TP_1 and TP_2 portray the relationship between worker-hour inputs and total product, or real GDP, for two time periods and differing capital stocks. Assuming no change in labor hours, the upward shift of the production function portrays a 50 percent increase in labor productivity.

Equation (18-2) confirms that labor productivity is simply the average productivity of labor inputs for the economy as a whole. For illustrative purposes, we assume that the number of worker hours—the denominator in equation (18-2)—is 150. The aggregate production function of Figure 18-1 reveals that the corresponding total product is 200. Dividing 200 by 150, we conclude that labor productivity is 1.33. Equation (18-3) allows us to convert this labor productivity figure to an index number, using this specific year as the base year.

$$\text{Productivity index}_{\text{base year}} = \frac{\text{productivity}_{\text{year 1}}}{\text{productivity}_{\text{base year}}} \times 100 \qquad (18\text{-}3)$$

Equation (18-3) simply sets labor productivity equal to 100 for the base year. That is, $100 = (1.33/1.33) \times 100$.

We now can turn our attention to the upward shift of the aggregate production function from TP_1 to TP_2 in Figure 18-1. In the long run, other things are *not* equal; that is, labor quality can improve, the capital stock can increase, and more efficient methods for combining resources may be discovered. For example, suppose that this economy enlarged its stock of capital goods, which in turn enabled workers to use more machinery and tools in the production process. As illustrated by the upward shift of the aggregate production function from TP_1 to TP_2, this would increase output per unit of labor input. Assuming that the number of worker hours remains constant at 150, total product would rise to 300, and labor productivity would increase to 2 (= 300/150). By comparing this new productivity level, 2, to productivity for the base year, 1.33, we can determine the productivity index in year 2.

$$\text{Productivity index}_{\text{year 2}} = \frac{\text{productivity}_{\text{year 2}}}{\text{productivity}_{\text{base year}}} \times 100 \qquad (18\text{-}4)$$

The new index is 150 [= (2/1.33) × 100], which represents a 50 percent increase relative to the base year index of 100.

The BLS Index

The Bureau of Labor Statistics (BLS) publishes an official index of labor productivity for the United States economy. Table 18-1 shows the course of the BLS index of output per worker hour since 1960 and indicates the percentage change in productivity from the previous year. Note that 1992 is the base year for the index. Because this ***BLS productivity index*** is widely used and cited, it is important to be familiar with its characteristics.

TABLE 18-1 INDEX OF LABOR PRODUCTIVITY* AND PERCENTAGE CHANGE OVER PREVIOUS YEAR, 1960–97

Year	Output per worker hour	Annual percentage change	Year	Output per worker hour	Annual percentage change
1960	51.4	1.7	1979	84.5	−0.4
1961	53.2	3.5	1980	84.2	−0.3
1962	55.7	4.7	1981	85.7	1.8
1963	57.9	3.9	1982	85.3	−0.5
1964	60.5	4.6	1983	88.0	3.2
1965	62.7	3.5	1984	90.2	2.5
1966	65.2	4.0	1985	91.7	1.6
1967	66.6	2.2	1986	94.0	2.6
1968	68.9	3.4	1987	94.0	−0.1
1969	69.2	0.4	1988	94.6	0.6
1970	70.5	2.0	1989	95.4	0.8
1971	73.6	4.3	1990	96.1	0.7
1972	76.0	3.3	1991	96.7	0.7
1973	78.4	3.2	1992	100.0	3.4
1974	77.1	−1.7	1993	100.2	0.2
1975	79.8	3.5	1994	100.6	0.4
1976	82.5	3.4	1995	100.5	0.0
1977	83.9	1.7	1996	102.6	2.1
1978	84.9	1.1	1997	104.5	1.9

*Business sector.
Source: Economic Report of the President 1998, Tables B-49 and B-50, and Bureau of Labor Statistics.

First, the index is calculated by dividing constant dollar (real) GDP originating in the private sector by the number of worker hours employed in the private sector. The public sector is excluded from the BLS index for a very practical reason: The public goods and services provided by government—such things as national defense, flood control, police and fire protection—are not sold in a market to individual buyers. Therefore, it is extremely difficult to estimate the economic value of the public-sector output. Most productivity experts believe that productivity has grown less rapidly in the public sector than in the private sector. For this reason, the BLS data tend to overstate the entire economy's productivity growth.

Second, the index understates productivity growth in that improvements in the *quality* of output are not taken into account. This, of course, is merely a reflection of a shortcoming involved in calculating real output or GDP for the private sector; GDP measures changes in the quantity, but not the quality, of output.

Third, the use of output per worker hour subtly implies that labor alone is responsible for rising productivity. This is not true. As we already indicated in our discussion of Figure 18-1, the factors affecting labor productivity are manifold and diverse. They include improvements in the quality of labor, the use of more capital equipment, improvements in production technologies and managerial organizational techniques, increased specialization as the result of expanding markets, shifts in the structure of the economy, public policies, and societal attitudes. While the BLS index of labor productivity provides information about changes in labor productivity, it does not explain the *causes* of these changes.

Despite its limitations and biases, the BLS index of labor productivity provides a reasonable approximation of how private-sector efficiency has changed through time. Indeed, the official BLS measure has certain notable virtues. First, the index is conceptually simple and can quite easily be calculated from available data. Second, because it is calculated on a per worker-*hour* basis, the index automatically takes into account changes in the length of the workweek. In contrast, an index of output per worker per year would understate the growth of labor productivity if the length of the average workweek decreased through time. Finally, as a measure of hourly output, the index can be directly compared with hourly wage rates.[2]

IMPORTANCE OF PRODUCTIVITY INCREASES

The growth of labor productivity is important for at least two reasons.

1 Productivity growth is the basic source of improvements in real wages and living standards.

2 Productivity growth is an anti-inflationary force in that it offsets or absorbs increases in nominal wages.

Let's consider these two points in the order stated.

[2]For a succinct discussion of the problems involved in measuring productivity, see Sar A. Levitan and Diane Werneke, *Productivity: Problems, Prospects, and Policies* (Baltimore: Johns Hopkins University Press, 1984), pp. 12–23. The more ambitious reader may also want to consult Solomon Fabricant, "Problems of Productivity Measurement," in *Measuring Productivity,* pp. 21–39.

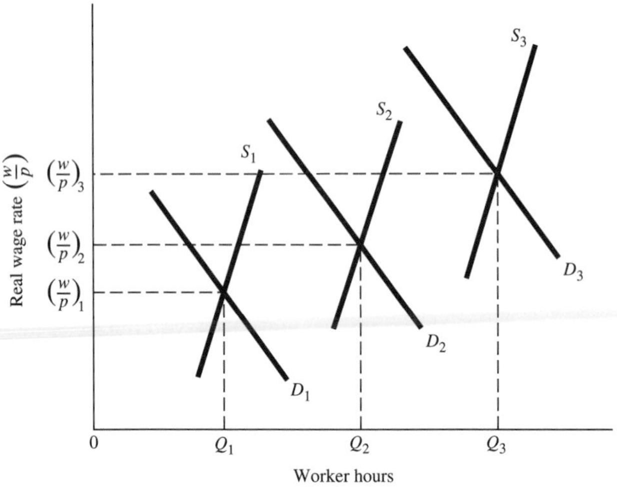

FIGURE 18-2 REAL WAGE INCREASES: LABOR SUPPLY AND DEMAND EXPLANATION
Increases in real wages occur when the demand for labor rises more rapidly than the labor supply.

Productivity and Real Wages

Real wage rates have increased in the United States over the past century at an average annual rate of 2 to 3 percent. Figure 18-2 provides an accurate but somewhat superficial explanation for that secular trend. The figure shows that increases in real wages—for example, from $(w/p)_1$ to $(w/p)_2$ to $(w/p)_3$—occur when the demand for labor rises more rapidly than labor supply. As seen in the figure, these rising real wages are fully compatible with increases in the number of worker hours (Q_1 to Q_3).

This simple supply and demand explanation for rising real wages naturally raises a more penetrating question: Why has labor demand increased over the decades? Figure 18-3 identifies the primary source of this increase: rising labor productivity. Notice the extremely close relationship between the increase in output per worker hour and the growth of average real hourly compensation. Increases in labor productivity have increased the demand for labor relative to labor supply and therefore have boosted the average real wage rate. When one recognizes that society's real output *is* its real income, the close relationship between productivity and real compensation is no surprise. Generally, for the economy as a whole, real income per worker per hour can only increase at the same rate as real output per worker per hour; more output per hour means more real income to distribute for each hour worked. The simplest case is the classic one of Robinson Crusoe on his deserted island. The number of coconuts he can pick or fish he can catch per hour *is* his real income or wage per hour. Crudely stated, what you produce is what you get.

The importance of the contribution that the growth of labor productivity has made to the overall growth of our economy can hardly be overstated. We can rearrange the labor productivity equation (18-2) as follows:

$$\text{Real GDP} = \text{worker hours} \times \text{labor productivity} \qquad (18\text{-}5)$$

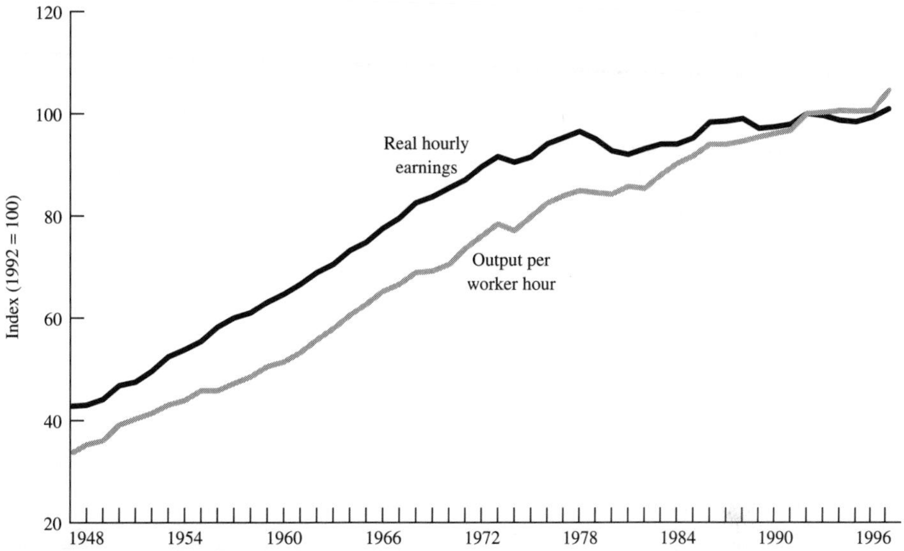

FIGURE 18-3 LABOR PRODUCTIVITY AND THE AVERAGE LEVEL OF REAL COMPENSATION
Because real output *is* real income, the growth of real output per worker hour and the growth of real compensation per hour are very closely related.

Equation (18-5) implies that real output can increase because of an increase in inputs of worker hours *or* because each of those hours of work generates more output. In other words, total product as shown in Figure 18-1 can rise because of a rightward movement along an existing aggregate production function (more inputs of labor hours) or as a result of an upward shift of the function (rising labor productivity). Data indicate that rising productivity has been the more important of the two contributors to the growth of real GDP in the United States. Over the 1960–97 period, for example, real output increased by 245 percent. During this same period, labor productivity rose by 104 percent, while worker hours of labor increased by 70 percent.

Inflation and Productivity

Although the causes of inflation are complex and controversial, economists acknowledge a link between the rate of productivity growth and the rate of inflation. Other things being equal, rapid productivity growth helps limit the rate of inflation, and slow productivity growth causes the inflation rate to be higher than would otherwise be the case. More specifically, productivity gains offset increases in nominal wages and thereby help restrain increases in unit labor costs and ultimately product prices.

Let's employ several simple numerical examples to grasp the relationship between changes in nominal wages, productivity, and unit labor costs. If, for example, hourly nominal wages are $5.00 and a worker produces 10 units per hour, then unit labor costs—that is, labor cost per unit of output—will be $.50. Now, if nominal wages increase by 10 percent to $5.50 per hour and productivity also increases by 10 percent to 11 units per hour, then unit labor costs will be unchanged. That is,

\$5.00/10 = \$5.50/11 = \$.50. Generalization: *Equal percentage increases in nominal wages and productivity leave unit labor costs unchanged.*

Similarly, if nominal wages rise by 10 percent and labor productivity does not rise at all, unit labor costs will rise by 10 percent. That is, if the wage is \$5.00 initially and output per hour is 10 units, unit labor costs will be \$.50. But with wages now at \$5.50 and output still at 10 units per hour, unit labor costs will be \$.55, which is a 10 percent increase. Generalization: *If nominal wage increases exceed the increase in labor productivity, unit labor costs will rise.*

Finally, suppose the nominal wage rate does not rise, but productivity increases by 10 percent. Specifically, if wages remain at \$5.00 and productivity increases from 10 to 11 units per hour, then unit labor costs will decline from \$.50 to about \$.45. Generalization: *If productivity increases exceed the increase in nominal wages, unit labor costs will fall.*

Columns 1 through 4 of Table 18-2 show the indicated relationships between changes in the hourly compensation of workers, productivity, and unit labor costs for the 1960–97 period.

TABLE 18-2 THE RELATIONSHIP BETWEEN CHANGES IN WAGES, PRODUCTIVITY, UNIT LABOR COSTS, AND THE PRICE LEVEL, 1960–97 (ANNUAL PERCENTAGE CHANGES)

(1) Year	(2) Change in compensation per hour worked	minus	(3) Change in output per hour worked (productivity)	roughly equals	(4) Change in unit labor costs	(5) Change in price level*
1960	4.3		1.7		2.5	1.1
1962	4.5		4.7		−0.2	0.9
1964	5.2		4.6		0.5	1.0
1966	6.7		4.0		2.6	2.5
1968	8.1		3.4		4.6	3.9
1970	7.8		2.0		5.7	4.4
1972	6.3		3.3		2.9	3.3
1974	9.7		−1.7		11.6	9.4
1976	8.8		3.4		5.2	5.4
1978	8.9		1.1		7.7	7.3
1980	10.8		−0.3		11.1	9.1
1982	7.5		−0.5		8.0	5.9
1984	4.4		2.5		1.8	3.0
1986	5.2		2.6		2.5	2.1
1988	4.6		0.6		4.0	3.5
1990	5.7		0.7		5.0	4.0
1992	5.2		3.4		1.7	2.4
1994	1.6		0.4		1.2	2.2
1996	3.9		2.0		1.8	1.9
1997	3.9		1.9		2.0	1.7

*GDP implicit price deflator.
Source: Bureau of Labor Statistics. Data are for the private business sector.

Because labor costs on the average constitute 70 to 75 percent of total production costs and higher production costs eventually cause higher product prices, the link between productivity increases and the rate of inflation is clear. Other things being equal, the 10 percent increase in unit labor costs in our example would translate into a 7 to 7.5 percent increase in total costs. As the data in Table 18-2 suggest, with important exceptions, changes in unit labor costs (column 4) and the rate of inflation (column 5) do track closely. As a rough rule of thumb, in most years changes in unit labor costs are associated with roughly similar changes in the rate of inflation.

One must be careful not to infer from Table 18-2 that the relationship between the growth of nominal wages and the increase in labor productivity is necessarily a primary cause of inflation. Many other factors—the money supply, inappropriate fiscal policy, expectations, supply "shocks"—are all held by various economists to be of greater significance. Indeed, some economists would argue that the relationship between the growth of real output and increases in the money supply is the primary determinant of changes in the price level. They contend that excessive growth of the money supply causes all prices to rise, including the price of labor: the nominal wage. The great majority of economists believe that both demand and supply (cost) factors can cause inflation, at least in the short term. They believe that the relationship between nominal wages and productivity is an important determinant of the price level. In fact, the U.S. government has at times implemented wage–price policies designed to restrict nominal wage increases to the average labor productivity increase as a means of controlling inflation.

The question of whether increases in unit labor costs cause inflation or are simply a symptom of inflation is subject to debate. Suffice it to say that given the rate of increase in nominal wage rates, the higher the rate of labor productivity, the smaller the rate of inflation.

LONG-RUN TREND OF LABOR PRODUCTIVITY[3]

Data suggest that in the long run—say, over the past century—average annual increases in output per worker hour have been on the order of 2 to 3 percent. Although these figures may not seem particularly impressive, the "miracle" of compounding translates this annual increase into very large increases in hourly output and income over a period of time. Specifically, a 2.5 percent annual increase in hourly output will double output per worker hour in about 28 years. We will find later in this chapter, however,

[3]Among the numerous economists who have contributed to the economic literature on productivity trends, Edward F. Denison and John W. Kendrick stand out. See, for example, Denison's *Trends in American Economic Growth, 1929–1982* (Washington, DC: Brookings Institution, 1985); and *Accounting for Slower Economic Growth: The United States in the 1970s* (Washington, DC: Brookings Institution, 1979). Also see Kendrick's *Productivity Trends in the United States* (Princeton, NJ: Princeton University Press, 1961); *Postwar Productivity Trends in the United States, 1948–1969* (New York: Columbia University Press, 1973); and (with Elliot S. Grossman) *Productivity in the United States: Trends and Cycles* (Baltimore: Johns Hopkins University Press, 1980). Also see Angus Maddison, "Explaining the Economic Performance of Nations, 1820–1989," in William J. Baumol, Richard R. Nelson, and Edward N. Wolff, (eds.), *Convergence of Productivity: Cross National Studies and Historical Evidence* (New York: Oxford University Press, 1994).

TABLE 18-3 RELATIVE IMPORTANCE OF THE CAUSES OF PRODUCTIVITY GROWTH, 1929–82

(1) Improved labor quality		20%
(2) Quantity of physical capital		28
(3) Increased efficiency		53
(3a) Technological advance	41	
(3b) Economies of scale	13	
(3c) Improved resource allocation	12	
(3d) Legal–human environment and other	−13	
Increase in labor productivity		100%

Source: Adapted from Edward F. Denison, *Trends in American Economic Growth, 1929–1982* (Washington, DC: Brookings Institution, 1985), p. 30. Details may not add to totals because of rounding.

that productivity growth during the past two decades has fallen significantly below its long-run or secular rate.

What causes productivity growth? Generally speaking, the critical determinants of productivity growth can be classified under three headings: (1) the average quality of the labor force, (2) the amount of capital goods employed with each worker hour of labor, and (3) the efficiency with which labor, capital, and other inputs are combined. Edward F. Denison spent most of his professional career attempting to quantify the various factors that contribute to the growth of productivity and real gross domestic product. Table 18-3 presents his latest (1929–82) estimates of the contributors to the growth of labor productivity. These factors, listed in ascending order of importance, are the focal point for the following discussion.

Improved Labor Quality

The quality of labor depends on its education and training, its health and vitality, and its age–gender composition. Other things being the same, a better-educated, better-trained workforce can produce more output per hour than a less-educated, inadequately trained one. Indeed, Chapter 4's discussion of education and training as investments in human capital that increase labor productivity and earnings is highly relevant. Table 18-4 provides a general overview of the increases in formal educational attainment of the population (25 years of age and older) since 1950. For the 1929–82 period, Denison estimates that approximately 20 percent of the growth of labor productivity was due to enhanced worker education and training (item 1 in Table 18-3).

Investments in human capital that enhance the health and vitality of workers also improve the average quality of labor. Improved nutrition, more and better medical care, and better general living conditions improve the physical vigor and morale of the labor force. These same factors enhance worker longevity and contribute to a workforce that is more productive because it is more experienced.

Finally, changes in the age–gender composition of the labor force may also affect average labor force quality and therefore productivity. For example, historically, in-

TABLE 18-4 YEARS OF SCHOOL COMPLETED BY THE POPULATION, 1950–92 (25 YEARS OF AGE OR OLDER)

Year	Percent high school graduates or more	Percent college graduates or more	Median years of school completed
1950	34.3	6.2	9.3
1960	41.1	7.7	10.6
1970	52.3	10.7	12.1
1980	66.5	16.2	12.5
1990	77.6	21.3	12.7
1997	81.7	23.6	NA

Source: U.S. Bureau of the Census, *Statistical Abstract of the United States, 1993,* p. 152 and *Statistical Abstract of the United States, 1997,* p. 159.

creasingly stringent child labor and school attendance legislation has kept potential young workers—workers who would be unskilled and relatively unproductive by virtue of their lack of education and work experience—out of the labor force. This exclusion has increased the *average* quality of the labor force. We will find later in this chapter that recent changes in the age–gender composition of the labor force may have lowered productivity growth.

A benevolent circle of feedback and self-reinforcement may evolve historically with respect to labor quality. If the productivity of labor rises, real wages also rise. These enhanced earnings permit workers to improve their health and education, which leads to further improvements in labor quality and productivity. And so the cycle repeats itself. This circular interaction may be strengthened because the demands for education and health care are both elastic with respect to income. This means that rising national income generates more than proportionate percentage increases in expenditures on these items.

Quantity of Physical Capital

The productivity of any given worker will depend on the amount of capital equipment with which he or she is equipped. A construction worker can dig a basement in a much shorter period of time with a bulldozer than with a hand shovel! A critical relationship with respect to labor productivity is the amount of capital available per unit of labor or, more technically, the capital–labor ratio. This ratio has increased historically. For example, in the 1889–1969 period, the stock of capital goods is estimated to have increased sixfold, and over the same period, labor hours are estimated to have doubled. Thus, the quantity of capital goods per labor hour was three times as large in 1969 as in 1889. Stated differently, the capital–labor ratio increased threefold over this 81-year period.[4] Denison's estimates for 1929–82 indicate that approximately 28 percent of the

[4]Solomon Fabricant, *A Primer on Productivity* (New York: Random House, Inc., 1969), chap. 5.

growth of labor productivity was the result of increases in the stock of physical capital (item 2 in Table 18-3).

Increased Efficiency

The third and quantitatively most important source of rising productivity is greater efficiency in the use of labor and capital. In the present context, "increased efficiency" is a comprehensive term that includes a variety of both obvious and subtle factors that enhance labor productivity. At a minimum, increased efficiency encompasses (1) technological progress, including that embodied within both improved capital and improved business organization and managerial techniques; (2) greater specialization as the result of scale economies; (3) the reallocation of labor from less to more productive uses; and (4) changes in a society's institutional, cultural, and environmental setting and in its public policies. Note in Table 18-3 (item 3) that increased efficiency accounts for over half of the productivity gains that occurred over the 1929–82 period.

Let's comment briefly on each of these factors. First, technological advance (item 3a) involves the development of more efficient techniques of production. The evolution of mass-production assembly-line techniques immediately comes to mind, as do computers, biotechnical developments, xerography, robotics, and containerized shipping. The switch from the old open-hearth process of steel making to the oxygen method enhanced productivity in that industry, as did the supplanting of the distillation process by the newer cracking process in petroleum refining. Improved managerial techniques—time-and-motion studies and the creation of new systems of managerial control of production—have similarly enhanced productive efficiency. A variety of "worker participation," "job enrichment," and "profit-sharing" plans are being experimented with in the hope that they will enhance worker productivity.

Second, production efficiencies called "economies of scale" (item 3b) are typically derived from growing market and firm size. Market growth allows firms to become mass producers, which in turn permits greater specialization in the use of labor and therefore greater output per worker. Market expansion also enables firms to avail themselves of the most efficient production techniques. For example, a large manufacturer of automobiles can use elaborate assembly lines, featuring computerization and robotics, while small producers have to settle for less-advanced technologies. The contribution of economies of scale shown in Table 18-3 means that markets have increased in scope and firms have increased in size so that greater labor specialization is realized and more efficient production methods are being used. Accordingly, labor productivity increases.

Third, productivity has also been stimulated by the reallocation of labor from less-productive to more-productive employments. Thus, for example, productivity gains have been realized historically by the reallocation of labor from agriculture, where the average productivity of labor is relatively low, to manufacturing, where the average productivity of labor is relatively high. Item 3c in Table 18-3 reveals that 12 percent of the 1929–82 productivity increase stemmed from improved resource allocation.

Finally, the cultural values of a society, the nature of its institutions, and the character of its public policies affect labor productivity in myriad ways. The fact that

American values condone material advance and that the successful inventor, innovator, and business executive are accorded high levels of respect and prestige has been important historically for productivity growth. Similarly, the "work ethic" is generally held in high esteem. Equally critical is the existence of a complex array of financial institutions that marshal the funds of savers and make them available to investors. On the other hand, recall from Chapter 11 that the impact of unions on productivity is unclear.

Public policies and social attitudes provides a mixed picture with respect to their implications for productivity. For example, while the long-run trend toward freer international trade and the general policy of promoting domestic competition bode well for productivity growth, the many exceptions to both free trade and procompetition policies do not. Tariffs and import quotas shelter American producers from competition and can have the effect of retaining labor and other inputs in relatively inefficient industries. Similarly, we know from Chapter 15 that discrimination based on race, gender, or age is an artificial impediment to allocative efficiency and therefore a barrier to productivity growth.

Turning to item 3d in Table 18-3, we note that changes in the "legal–human environment" were in fact a detriment to productivity growth in the 1929–82 period. Over this period considerable changes were made in the regulation of industry, environmental pollution, worker health and safety, and so forth, which have negatively affected productivity growth. The expansion of government regulation of business in such areas as pollution control and worker health and safety diverted investment spending away from the productivity-increasing capital goods and toward equipment that provides cleaner air and water and greater worker protection from accident and illness. A firm required to spend $1 million on a new scrubber to meet government standards for air pollution does not have that $1 million available to spend on machinery and equipment that would enhance worker productivity.[5] The diversion of resources to deal with dishonesty and crime and the effects of such considerations as work stoppages because of labor disputes and the impact of bad weather on agricultural output are also included in item 3d.

Two final comments are in order. First, while Denison concludes that about half of the increase in labor productivity is due to greater efficiency and the other half is the result of improved labor quality and the use of more capital goods, other experts offer somewhat different estimates. For example, Fabricant attributes approximately two-thirds of the productivity increase to enhanced efficiency, with labor quality and capital goods accounting for the remaining third.[6] The second point is that in fact the factors in productivity growth are interrelated. For example, investment in capital equipment is stimulated by technological advance. Similarly, highly educated and well-trained workers cannot be used productively in the absence of sophisticated capital goods.

[5]This raises an important point. Workplace safety, clean air and water, and the general "quality of life" may come at the expense of productivity. But the converse is also true. That is, we cannot assume that productivity advances automatically enhance society's welfare; they may come with opportunity costs of other things that we value more highly. Productivity measures output per hour of work, not utility per hour of work.

[6]Fabricant, *A Primer on Productivity,* pp. 52, 66, and 73.

QUICK REVIEW 18-1

- Labor productivity is a measure of output per unit of labor input (worker hours).
- Productivity growth is important for two reasons: *(a)* It is the basic source of improvements in real wages and living standards, and *(b)* it helps offset inflationary forces by holding down unit labor costs when nominal wages are rising.
- Productivity growth has averaged between 2 and 3 percent annually since the turn of the century.
- The critical determinants of productivity growth include *(a)* the average quality of the labor force; *(b)* the amount of capital goods per worker hour; and *(c)* the efficiency with which labor, capital, and other inputs are combined. This last category includes technology, economies of scale, improved resource organization, and the legal–human environment.
- Table 18-3 summarizes the relative weights of the various factors that have contributed to American productivity growth.

Your Turn: Suppose that real output in a hypothetical economy is 10 units, 5 units of labor are needed to produce this output, and the price of labor is $2 per unit. What is the economy's labor productivity? What is its unit or average labor cost? (Answers: See page 627.)

18-1

CYCLICAL CHANGES IN PRODUCTIVITY

Emphasis thus far has been on the long-term trend of labor productivity. Because of the close relationship between productivity growth and real wages, this attention is entirely appropriate. However, productivity also exhibits a rather systematic short-run or cyclical pattern around the long-term trend.

Labor productivity generally displays a procyclical pattern. That is, productivity growth falls below the long-term trend during a cyclical downturn or recession and rises above the trend during an economic upturn or recovery. For example, over the 1889–1969 period, total real output declined in 17 years and increased in the remaining 63 years. In the 17 years of declining real output, the rate of productivity growth was *negative,* averaging –0.6 percent per year; in the 63 years of expanding aggregate output, labor productivity rose by 3.4 percent per year.[7] Examining data for eight industrially advanced economies, Kendrick has estimated that a 1 percent increase in the unemployment rate will decrease productivity by 1.5 percent.[8]

The reasons for these cyclical changes in productivity are quite detailed. We will simplify the discussion by considering just three factors: (1) changes in the utilization of labor, (2) changes in the utilization of plant and capital equipment, and (3) changes in the composition of aggregate output.

[7]Ibid., p. 90.

[8]John W. Kendrick, "International Comparisons of Recent Productivity Trends," in *Measuring Productivity,* p. 124.

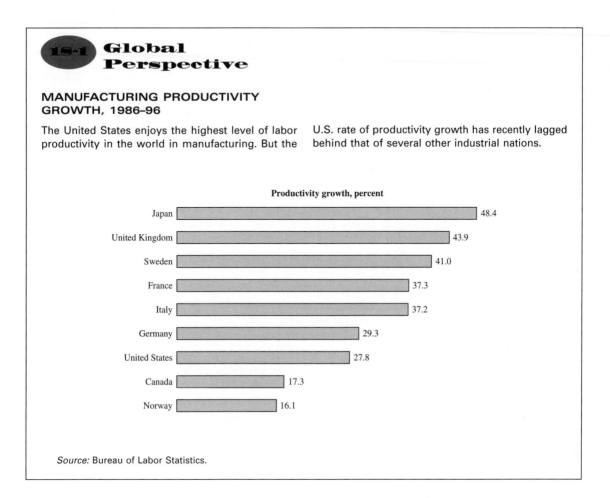

18-1 **Global Perspective**

MANUFACTURING PRODUCTIVITY GROWTH, 1986–96

The United States enjoys the highest level of labor productivity in the world in manufacturing. But the U.S. rate of productivity growth has recently lagged behind that of several other industrial nations.

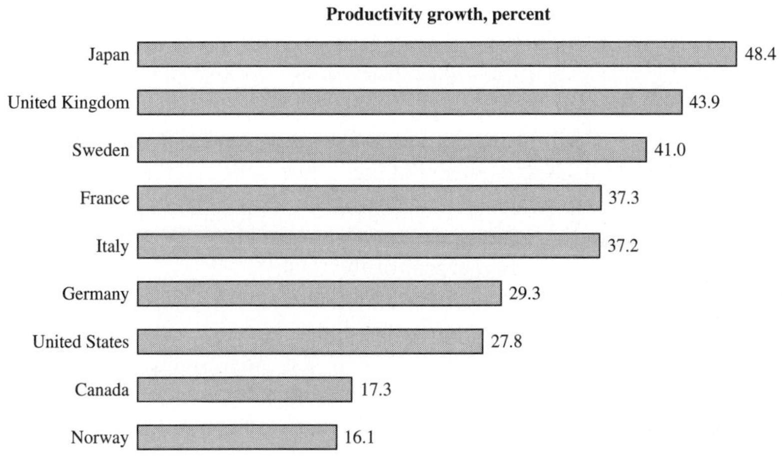

Source: Bureau of Labor Statistics.

Utilization of Labor

As the economy moves into a downturn or recession, a firm's sales and output will decline more rapidly than its inputs of labor.

Specifically, during cyclical contractions, employers normally are loath to fire workers—preferring instead to shunt labor into maintenance and other less essential tasks rather than the production of goods—until they are convinced that the downturn is not a temporary aberration. As a consequence, *measured* productivity (the ratio of output to *employed* labor) declines. Analogously, once a recovery starts, employers put these underutilized labor resources back on the production line. So output can expand briskly with little need for new hiring, and measured productivity registers dramatic gains.[9]

Why the reluctance to fire workers during a downswing? Why is labor a quasi-fixed, rather than a completely variable, input? Some employees, of course, are

[9]Alan S. Blinder, *Economic Policy and the Great Stagflation* (New York: Academic Press, 1981), pp. 65–66.

salaried workers or "overhead" labor. Few firms will dispense with top- or middle-level executives during a downturn. An internal auditor, a marketing manager, and a personnel director will all be needed, even though output is currently down. Also, the typical firm will have invested in the specific training of its skilled and semiskilled workers. Remember from Chapter 4 that such workers must be retained for the firm to realize a return on its human capital investment. If these workers are furloughed, the firm runs the risk of losing them to other employers. Finally, there are layoff and rehiring costs to contend with, and within limits, it may be less expensive to retain and underutilize workers if layoff and rehiring costs can be avoided by so doing. Thus, firms find it to be in their long-run profit-maximizing interest to hoard labor during recession and, from a social perspective, use labor less productively than previously.

Fay and Medoff have provided direct evidence of ***labor hoarding*** during cyclical downturns. Using survey data from some 168 manufacturing firms, they found that "the typical plant paid for 8 percent more blue-collar labor hours than were technically necessary to perform regular production work during the trough quarter of its most recent downturn." Some portion of these blue-collar workers were used to perform other valuable nonproduction tasks such as plant and equipment maintenance, cleaning, training, and so forth. When such work was taken into account, the amount of "hoarded" blue-collar labor was 4 percent of the total.[10]

But during the upswing or recovery phase of the cycle, output can be increased substantially by simply correcting this underutilization. Within limits, firms can increase output by taking up the slack in their currently employed labor forces. More output can be obtained from the number of worker hours now being employed so that productivity will rise sharply. It has also been observed that workers are generally more productive when there is more work to be done. For example, checkout personnel at supermarkets work faster when the queues of shoppers are long.[11]

Utilization of Plant and Equipment

A similar point can be made with respect to capital equipment. Competition forces firms to design their plants so that they operate with maximum efficiency during "normal times." This means that during a recession, falling output causes the plant and equipment to be used at less than the optimal level, and productivity consequently falls. Conversely, during recovery, plant utilization moves back in the direction of the most efficient level of output, and productivity tends to rise.

[10]Jon A. Fay and James L. Medoff, "Labor and Output over the Business Cycle: Some Direct Evidence," *American Economic Review,* September 1985, pp. 638–655. For additional studies finding evidence of labor hoarding, see Craig Burnside, Martin Eichenbaum, and Sergio Rebelo, "Labor Hoarding and the Business Cycle," *Journal of Political Economy,* April 1993, pp. 245–273; and Argia M. Sbordone, "Interpreting the Procyclical Productivity of Manufacturing Sectors: External Effects or Labor Hoarding?" *Journal of Money, Credit, and Banking,* February 1997, pp. 26–45.

[11]George A. Akerlof and Janet L. Yellen, "Introduction," in Akerlof and Yellen (eds.), *Efficiency Wage Models of the Labor Market* (Cambridge, England: Cambridge University Press, 1986), p. 5.

Composition of Output

Cyclical fluctuations affect the various sectors of the economy with differing degrees of severity. Specifically, the demand for durable manufactured goods—machinery and equipment and such consumer goods as automobiles, refrigerators, and microwave ovens—is very sensitive to cyclical changes. By way of contrast, the demand for most services is much less responsive to cyclical changes. Thus, the *relative* share of manufactured goods in domestic output declines during cyclical downswings and increases during upswings. Because the level of productivity in manufacturing is among the highest of all sectors of the economy, it follows that the relative decline in manufacturing during a recession will reduce overall labor productivity.

Conversely, the relative expansion of manufacturing as a proportion of total output during recovery causes average labor productivity to rise. Note that this effect is independent of other cyclical influences on productivity. Even if no individual firm or industry experienced a productivity change due to a change in the use of labor and capital, the indicated relative shift in the composition of output would cause average labor productivity to vary procyclically.

Implications

Of what consequences are these cyclical changes in productivity? In the first place, they are not merely the result of cyclical fluctuations but rather an integral part of the business cycle. When the economy lapses into a recession, productivity falls sharply, and this tends to increase unit labor costs. If nominal wage rates continue to rise during the recession, unit labor costs will rise by an even larger amount. Rising costs typically squeeze business profits. This profit decline deters investment spending in two ways: It diminishes the financial resources (undistributed profits) that firms have for investing, *and* it generates pessimistic business expectations. Falling investments, of course, intensifies the cyclical downswing. Conversely, rising productivity during recovery stimulates the upturn. Rapidly increasing productivity keeps unit labor costs down and contributes to rising profits. Profit growth is conducive to expanded investment spending, which accelerates the economic expansion.

A second related point is that cyclical changes in productivity have important implications for economic policy. For example, some economists are more or less resigned to the view that to arrest rapid inflation, it is necessary to create a recession through the application of restrictive monetary and fiscal policies. But an understanding of cyclical changes in productivity suggests that any such recession may have to be deep and long to produce its intended effects. Specifically, the decline in productivity that accompanies recession may contribute to rising unit costs, which in turn may contribute to supply, or cost-push, inflation. On the other hand, if the economy is already in a recession and unemployment is high, then the rapid labor productivity increase that occurs in the early stages of recovery may permit policy makers to increase output and employment through expansionary monetary and fiscal measures with less fear of generating added inflation. The reason is that high productivity growth tends to limit cost and price increases.[12]

PRODUCTIVITY AND EMPLOYMENT

Let's now consider the impact of productivity growth on the level of employment. Do employees "work themselves out of their jobs" as they become more productive?

Superficial consideration of the relationship between productivity and employment often leads people to conclude erroneously that productivity growth causes unemployment. The reasoning normally is that an increase in labor productivity means that fewer workers are needed to produce any given level of real output. For example, if a firm employs 50 workers whose average productivity is \$10 worth of real output per hour, then \$500 worth of output can be produced. If the productivity of the 50 employees were to increase by 25 percent to \$12.50 worth of output per hour, the same output could now be produced with only 40 workers (= 40 × \$12.50). Thus, 10 of the 50 workers would seem to be redundant.

But this illustration is too simple because it ignores society's desire for additional output and the fact that rising productivity increases aggregate demand. Society's wants tend to exceed its available resources. Productivity increases allow society to achieve higher levels of output, that is, to fulfill more wants, given these limited resources. In terms of the previous example, the 25 percent productivity increase enables society to gain \$125 worth of output. The 50 workers now can produce \$625 worth of output (= 50 × \$12.50) compared to \$500 (= 50 × \$10 = \$500). But will there be sufficient aggregate spending to take this additional output off the market? We know that productivity and real wages are closely correlated. Thus, the 25 percent increase in productivity can be expected to increase real incomes, which would increase aggregate spending and generate additional jobs. Although our economy has been characterized by cyclical fluctuations in output and employment (Chapter 19), the long-term historical trend of productivity growth in the United States has *not* given rise to a growing stockpile of unemployed workers. Rather, increases in labor productivity have been associated in the aggregate with both higher real wages *and* higher levels of employment.

Does this positive relationship between productivity and employment also apply on an industry-by-industry basis? In answering this question it will be useful to (1) ascertain the relationship between productivity growth and changes in employment in an industry, given the locations and elasticity of the product demand curves; (2) indicate the complexities that arise once these demand assumptions are relaxed; and (3) present actual data on the relationship between industrial productivity and employment growth in the United States.

[12]A more detailed discussion of cyclical changes in productivity can be found in John W. Kendrick, *Understanding Productivity: An Introduction to the Dynamics of Productivity Change* (Baltimore: Johns Hopkins University Press, 1977), pp. 87–89.

Demand Factors Constant

Let's analyze how productivity growth and employment changes in an industry would be related without shifts in, and varying elasticities of, product demand. We must first establish that wage rates in various U.S. industries move more in accord with *national* productivity than with *industry* productivity. As indicated in the right-hand column of Figure 18.4, compensation per hour rises more or less evenly in all industries, even though output per worker hour varies greatly by industry (left-hand column). Why is this the case? If wages began to diverge—rising rapidly in high-productivity-growth

FIGURE 18-4 OUTPUT PER WORKER HOUR AND COMPENSATION PER WORKER HOUR, SELECTED INDUSTRIES, 1972–85

Changes in labor productivity vary considerably by industry on an annual basis, but compensation increases per hour of work tend to be closely matched across industries. Hourly increases in pay per year are more closely related to the average increase in labor productivity for the entire economy than to the change in productivity within specific industries. (Bureau of Labor Statistics, *Productivity and the Economy: A Chartbook,* 1988, p. 41.)

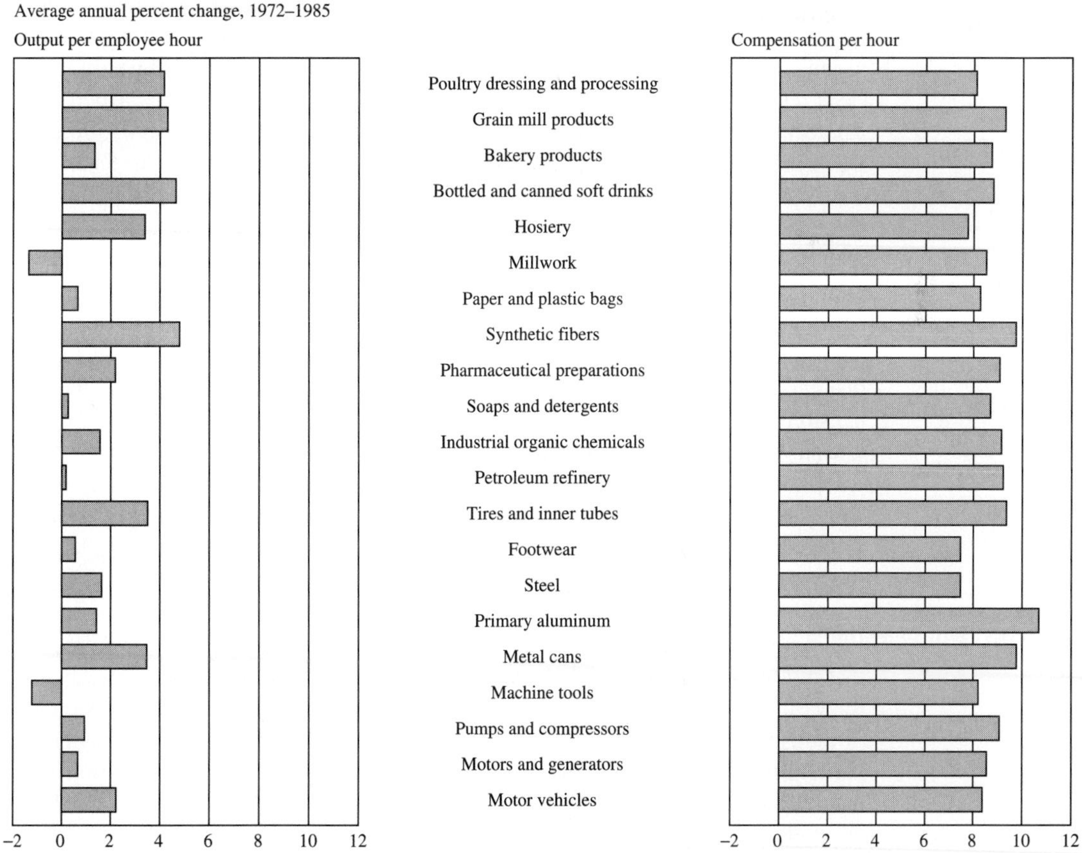

industries and increasing slowly in low-productivity-growth industries—the wage structure would be pulled apart. But this doesn't occur because workers respond to the growing wage differentials by leaving the low-growth, low-wage industries to seek the higher wages in the high-growth industries. Similarly, new labor force entrants would choose employment in the high-growth industries and shun the low-growth industries. The increased labor supply would tend to reduce wages in the high-productivity industries, and the diminished labor supply would increase wages in the low-productivity industries. In short, labor supply responses would prevent wages from diverging in the various industries. To repeat: The trend of wages paid by specific industries is dominated by the nationwide trend of productivity primarily because workers are responsive to wage differentials (Chapter 8).

With this fact in mind, let's now reconsider the productivity–unit labor cost relationship in the context of a simple numerical example designed to illustrate the relationship between productivity growth and employment changes in an industry, *all else being constant.* Assume that (1) the annual rate of productivity growth for the economy as a whole is 3 percent; (2) industry X realizes a 6 percent annual productivity increase, while productivity growth in industry Y is 0 percent; and (3) nominal wage rates and earnings in both industries increase by 3 percent in accordance with the economy's overall rate of productivity growth. We find that unit labor costs would *decrease* in industry X and *increase* in industry Y. Further assuming that changes in unit labor costs result in roughly equivalent price changes, we can expect prices to *fall* by about 3 percent in industry X and to *rise* by approximately 3 percent in industry Y. Specifically, a 3 percent increase in nominal wages in industry X coupled with its 6 percent productivity increase would cause its unit labor costs and product price to fall by about 3 percent. Similarly, the 3 percent increase in nominal wages in industry Y combined with its zero rate of productivity growth would cause unit labor costs and product price to increase by approximately 3 percent. Given the locations and elasticities of the product demand curves for the two industries, output and sales would rise in industry X and decline in Y. Provided that the increase in sales more than compensates for the fact that each unit of output can now be produced with a smaller quantity of labor, an expansion of employment in industry X would result. Conversely, the price increase for industry Y's product would reduce output and sales, implying the need for fewer workers. Therefore, other things being the same, industries with rapid productivity growth would employ more workers, while industries with slow productivity growth would provide less employment.

Demand Factors Variable

It is *not* realistic to expect that product demand conditions are similar and unchanging for various industries in the economy. In our example, the demands for the products of industries X and Y may have different elasticity characteristics *and* may be changing (shifting) through time in such a way as to undermine the generalization that productivity growth and employment growth are positively related. The price and income elasticities of, and shifts in, product demand curves can and do have profound effects on the cause-effect chain that links productivity and employment.

Industry Growth and Decline Once again, consider industry X, where productivity is rising by 6 percent and product price is falling by about 3 percent. The consequent increase in output and employment would be especially large *if* the demand for its product is elastic with respect to both price and income. If demand is elastic with respect to price, then the price decline will generate a relatively larger increase in sales. For example, the 3 percent decrease in price may increase sales by 8 or 9 percent. This suggests a relatively large increase in employment. Similarly, if demand is elastic with respect to income,[13] then the growth of income in this economy will cause relatively larger increases in the demand for product X. For example, a 3 percent increase in income—which is the amount by which real income is increasing in our hypothetical two-industry economy—might shift the demand curve to the right so that perhaps 9 or 10 percent more of the product would be purchased at any given price. Of course, industry X's demand curve may shift rightward for reasons other than rising incomes. For example, consumer preferences for the product may become stronger, or the imposition of tariffs or quotas on competing foreign products may have deflected consumer purchases from imports and in favor of domestic production. The point is that increases (rightward shifts) in product demand will enhance output and therefore employment in the industry so as to offset any declines in employment due to the fact that less labor is needed per unit of output.

In contrast, if the demand for industry X's product is inelastic with respect to both price and income, the increases in output would tend to be small. If sufficiently small, the increase occasioned by the enhancement in sales may fail to offset the fact that rising productivity has reduced labor requirements per unit of output. In this case, employment in industry X will decline, despite the high rate of productivity growth.

The worst scenario in terms of adverse employment effects would occur if product X were an *inferior good*—a product of which people buy *less* as their incomes rise—because the resulting decrease (leftward shift) of the product demand curve would reduce employment even though product price is falling. Enhanced foreign competition or declines in the prices of substitute goods are other developments that could also cause decreases in demand and diminished output and employment. To recapitulate: The conditions most conducive to employment growth in an industry experiencing rapid productivity growth are (1) a price- and income-elastic product demand curve and (2) fortuitous circumstances that increase product demand.

Conversely, recall that industry Y, achieving no productivity growth, would find that the price of its product is *rising* by about 3 percent. The adverse effect of this price increase on output and employment will be minimized, or perhaps completely offset, if product demand is inelastic with respect to price and elastic with respect to income. The employment-diminishing effect would be aggravated, however, if demand is price-elastic and income-inelastic. Once again, changes in product demand stemming from

[13]Income elasticity is measured as the percentage change in quantity demanded relative to a given percentage change in income. If the percentage increase in the quantity demanded is greater than the percentage increase in the income that triggered the increase in the amount demanded, then we say that demand is "income-elastic" or "income-sensitive." If the percentage increase in quantity demanded is less than the percentage increase in income, then demand is "income-inelastic" or "income-insensitive." In the special case of an *inferior good,* an *increase* in income *decreases* the demand for the product.

a variety of causes other than rising real income may intensify or alleviate the impact on output and employment.

Illustrations Our analysis can be used to gain insight into the waxing and waning—particularly the waning—of various industries in our economy. For example, productivity in higher education—particularly in teaching—has been relatively constant. The result has been rising educational costs and rising tuition. But the demand for higher education is inelastic with respect to price and elastic with respect to income. As a consequence, higher education has absorbed an expanding proportion of per capita income. Furthermore, the production of certain highly crafted goods—fine pottery, glassware, and furniture—has also experienced little or no productivity growth. This has resulted in sharply rising prices for such products. But the demand for these products is price-elastic, and the result has been a decline in the total production of high-quality products. A similar analysis applies to the performing arts. (Given the size of the audience, how does one increase the productivity of a string quartet?) The symphonies and community theaters of most cities and towns are dependent on public and private subsidization. Furthermore, the financial problems of many large cities may be intimately tied to the fact that they provide services—of police, hospital workers, social workers—for which it is difficult to raise productivity. As the wages of public employees rise in accordance with the (higher) productivity growth of the national economy, the cost of government services will necessarily increase. The source of soaring government budgets may lie much more in the low productivity growth associated with public services than with bureaucratic mismanagement or malfeasance.[14]

Observed Productivity–Employment Relationship

Figure 18-5 compares for a 14-year period the average annual percentage changes in employment with the average annual percentage changes in productivity for some 89 industries. You will observe that the scattering of industry data points is random; one simply cannot generalize on the relationship between productivity growth and employment growth by industry.

While productivity increased for 71 of the 89 industries over the 1973–86 period, employment increased in 31 industries, declined in 54, and remained unchanged in 1. In some industries rapid productivity growth is associated with declines in employment (radio and television sets, and railroad transportation), while other industries experienced both rapid productivity growth and employment growth (semiconductors). Similarly, some industries that have been comparatively stagnant with respect to productivity growth have experienced large employment increases (eating and drinking places) while employment has declined in others (footwear, laundry and cleaning services).

It is challenging to speculate about the productivity and employment changes shown for specific industries in Figure 18-5. For example, the large rise in employ-

[14]These examples are from William J. Baumol, "Macro-Economics of Unbalanced Growth: The Anatomy of Urban Crisis," *American Economic Review*, June 1967, pp. 415–426.

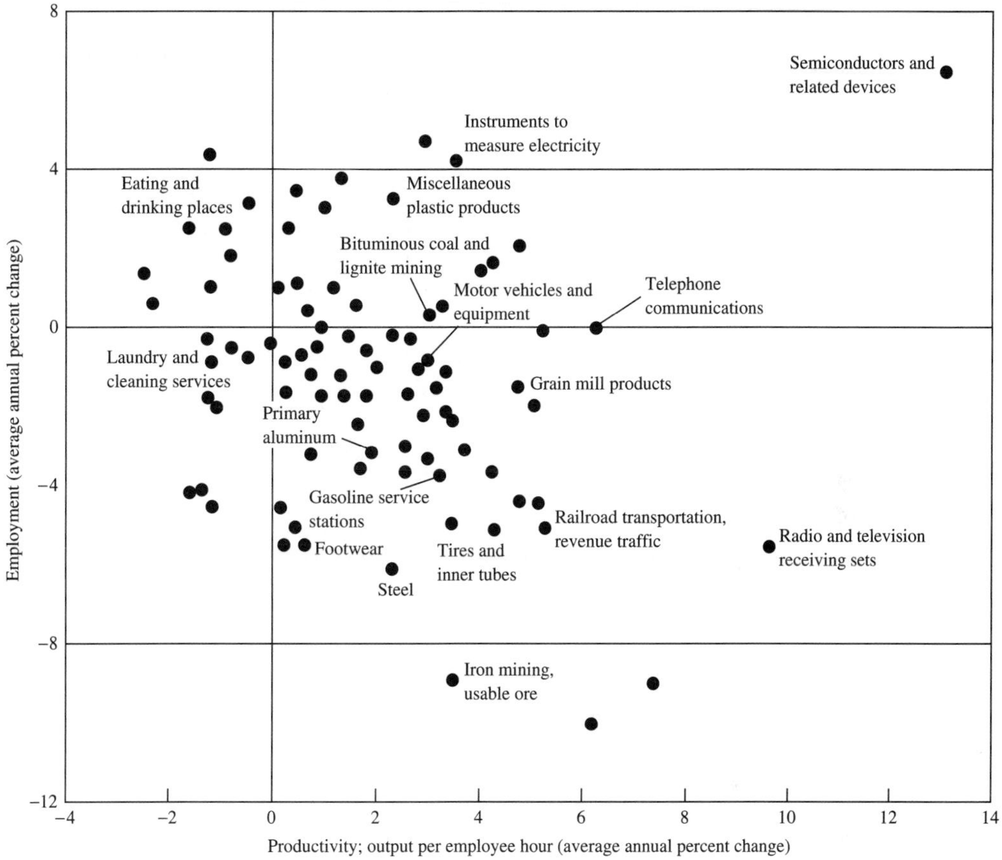

FIGURE 18-5 OUTPUT PER WORKER HOUR AND EMPLOYMENT, SELECTED INDUSTRIES, 1973–86
Average annual percentage changes in employment within industries are not systematically related to industry average annual productivity changes. (Bureau of Labor Statistics, *Productivity and the Economy: A Chartbook,* 1988, p. 45.)

ment in the "eating and drinking" industry, where productivity growth has been negligible, might well reflect large increases in consumer demand related to changing labor market participation rates for married women. If we recall the time allocation model of Chapter 3, we can see how the increasing value of women's time in the labor market may have induced families to substitute time-saving meals in restaurants for time-intensive meals prepared in the home. Similarly, we note that in the manufacture of radio and television sets, productivity growth has been quite dramatic. The accompanying decline in employment undoubtedly reflects strong foreign competition. You are urged to use your general knowledge of the economy to ponder the production and employment changes of various other industries shown in Figure 18-5.

QUICK REVIEW 18-2

- The rate of productivity growth fluctuates with the business cycle, falling as the economy recedes and rising as the economy expands.
- While productivity growth means that society can produce its existing output with fewer workers, it also permits society to obtain more total output. Overall, productivity growth has been associated with growing employment, not rising unemployment.
- Compensation per hour rises more or less evenly in all industries, even though output per worker hour varies greatly by industry. Other things being equal, this fact implies rising per unit costs and reduced output and employment in industries with slow productivity growth, and falling per unit costs and increased output and employment in industries with high productivity growth.
- Variable demand factors confound the actual relationship between productivity and employment growth within industries; data reveal no systematic relationship between industry productivity growth and industry employment growth.

Your Turn: Productivity growth in both 1990 and 1991 was 0.7 percent; in 1992 it rose to 3.4 percent. Can you think of a possible explanation for this abrupt change? (*Hint:* A recession occurred in 1990–91.) (Answer: See page 628.)

THE PRODUCTIVITY SLOWDOWN

In the past three decades the United States has experienced a much-publicized productivity slowdown. The rate of productivity growth began to fall in the mid-1960s and then declined quite precipitously in the 1970s. In Table 18-5 we observe vigorous productivity growth in the 1948–66 era, followed by slower productivity growth in the 1966–73 period and even slower growth during the 1973–97 period.

TABLE 18-5 LABOR PRODUCTIVITY GROWTH RATES, 1948–97

Period	Productivity growth rate
1948–66	3.5%
1967–73	2.7
1974–81	1.1
1982–90	1.3
1991–97	1.2
Postwar trend:	
1948–97	2.3

Source: Bureau of Labor Statistics. Endpoints of calculations are cyclical peaks (except 1997, the last year of data available for this edition of the book).

The effects of this slowdown are those discussed earlier. The standard of living in the United States rose less rapidly than it had in the past and less rapidly than in several other nations. For example, real compensation per hour rose by 39 percent over the 1958–70 period, but over the equally long 1970–82 time span it increased by only 7 percent. Over the 1973–97 period the annual rate of productivity growth in the United States was significantly less than that experienced by virtually all other major market economies. Also, according to many economists, the slowdown in productivity growth contributed to the unusually high inflation rate of the 1970s.

Possible Causes

No consensus exists among experts as to why U.S. productivity growth has slowed and fallen behind the rates of Japan and Western Europe.[15] Nevertheless, it is enlightening to survey some of the possible causes of the slowdown. In doing so it is helpful to distinguish between economic and institutional factors.

Economic Factors Because so many factors affect a country's productivity performance, a simple economic explanation of the slowdown is unlikely.[16] The following are some of the primary explanations that economists have considered.

1 Labor Quality One possibility is that slower improvements in the quality of labor may have dampened productivity growth. In the first place, the experience level of the labor force may have declined. A large number of baby boom workers entered the labor force in the late 1960s and the 1970s. Such workers were less experienced than veteran workers and therefore less productive. A similar observation applies to many of the large number of females who entered the labor force in the 1960s and 1970s. Second, concern has been expressed that the declining scores of students on standardized examinations over the 1967–80 period signaled a decline in worker quality and contributed to the productivity slowdown. Bishop has concluded that the test score decline was not a cause of the slowdown but has clearly contributed to its

[15]There is also disagreement as to whether a slowdown has actually occurred. Michael R. Darby has contended that "the productivity panic is based on statistical myopia" and that in fact the long-term trend of productivity in the United States has been quite constant. See his "The U.S. Productivity Slowdown: A Case of Statistical Myopia," *American Economic Review,* June 1984, pp. 301–322. Also see William J. Baumol, "Productivity Growth, Convergence, and Welfare: What the Long-Run Data Show," *American Economic Review,* December 1986, pp. 1072–1085; and William E. Cullison, "The U.S. Productivity Slowdown: What the Experts Say," *Economic Review* (Federal Reserve Bank of Richmond), July–August 1989, pp. 10–21.

[16]For empirical analysis of possible causes of the slowdown, see Denison, *Accounting for Slower Economic Growth*; J. R. Norsworthy, Michael J. Harper, and Kent Dunze, "The Slowdown in Productivity Growth: Analysis of Some Contributing Factors," *Brookings Papers on Economic Activity,* no. 2, 1979, pp. 387–421; John W. Kendrick, "Productivity Trends and the Recent Slowdown: Historical Perspectives, Causal Factors, and Policy Options," in William Fellner (ed.), *Contemporary Economic Problems* (Washington, DC: American Enterprise Institute for Public Policy Research, 1979), pp. 17–69; John W. Kendrick, "International Comparisons of Recent Productivity Trends," pp. 95–140; "Symposium on the Slowdown in Productivity Growth," *Journal of Economic Perspectives,* Fall 1988, pp. 3–97; and Daniel E. Sichel, "The Productivity Slowdown: Is a Growing Unmeasurable Sector the Culprit?" *Review of Economics and Statistics,* August 1997, pp. 367–370; and Edward N. Wolff, "The Productivity Slowdown: The Culprit at Last? Follow-Up on Hulten and Wolff," *American Economic Review,* December 1996, pp. 1239–1252.

perpetuation.[17] And recall from Table 18-4 that the median number of years of school completed by the civilian labor force has increased only very modestly in the last 20 years. Finally, as noted earlier, the growth of labor productivity may also have slowed because the historical shift of labor from low-productivity employments such as agriculture to high-productivity employments such as manufacturing has greatly diminished in recent years.

2 Technological Progress Still other economists have argued that technological advance—usually reflected in improvements in the quality of capital goods and improvements in the efficiency with which inputs are combined—may have faltered in the 1960s and 1970s to cause the productivity decline. Technological progress is fueled by expenditures for formal research and development (R & D) programs, and R & D spending in the United States declined as a percentage of GDP between the mid-1960s and the late 1970s. Specifically, R & D outlays rose steadily in the postwar period to a peak of 3 percent of the GDP by the mid-1960s, only to decline to about 1 percent by the late 1970s. But this explanation has been discounted for at least two reasons. First, the R & D slowdown was less pronounced in other industrially advanced countries than it was in the United States, and those countries experienced larger productivity declines than did the United States. Second, calculations of the contribution of R & D to productivity growth suggest that the slowdown in R & D can explain only a very small portion of the productivity decline.[18]

3 Net Investment Diminished growth of the nation's stock of capital goods may also have contributed to the productivity slowdown. Figure 18-6 chronicles the decline of real net investment in machinery and equipment as a percent of gross domestic product. Note the decline in the 1970s and the even more pronounced fall in the 1980s and 1990s. Combined with rapid labor force growth, sluggish net investment spending tends to restrain growth of the capital–labor ratio.

A number of factors may have contributed to the weak growth of real net investment. First, the United States has had a relatively low savings rate, which, coupled with strong private and public demands for credit, has resulted in interest rates that have been high by historical standards. High interest rates in turn mean that the financial cost of investing is high, and therefore, investment spending is discouraged.

[17]See John H. Bishop, "Is the Test Score Decline Responsible for the Productivity Growth Decline?" *American Economic Review,* March 1989, pp. 178–197.

[18]Zvi Griliches, "Productivity Puzzles and R & D: Another Nonexplanation," *Journal of Economic Perspectives,* Fall 1988, pp. 13–19. Also see Zvi Griliches, "R & D and the Productivity Slowdown," *American Economic Review,* May 1980, pp. 343–348; and Frederick M. Scherer, "R & D and Declining Productivity Growth," *American Economic Review,* May 1983, pp. 215–218. For a study finding a larger role of R & D spending in the productivity slowdown, see Gordon R. Richards, "An Econometric Model With Endogenous Technological Advance: Implications for Productivity and Potential Growth," National Association of Manufacturers, Working Paper, 1997. On a related note, some studies indicate that technological progress raises productivity in the long run, but possibly lowers it in the short run since it may take a substantial amount of time for individuals to learn how to use the new technology effectively. For a study examining the impact of computer innovations, see Andreas Hornstein and Per Krussel, "Can Technology Improvements Cause Productivity Slowdowns?" in Ben S. Bernanke and Julio J. Rotemberg (eds.) *NBER Macroeconomics Annual 1996* (Cambridge, MA: MIT Press, 1996), pp. 202–259. For a historical study investigating the adoption of electricity, see Paul A. David, "The Dynamo and the Computer: An Historical Perspective on the Modern Productivity Paradox," *American Economic Review,* May 1990, pp. 355–361.

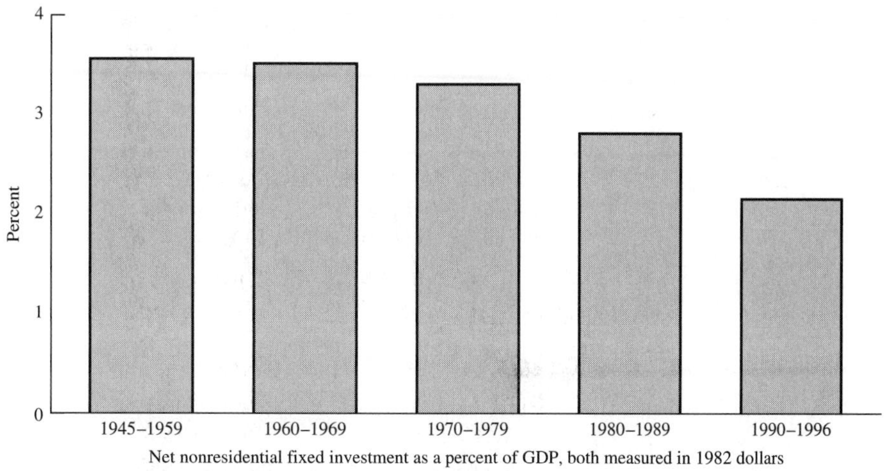

FIGURE 18-6 NET INVESTMENT AS A PERCENT OF GDP, SELECTED PERIOD AVERAGES
Real net investment in the United States declined for a variety of reasons in the 1970s and diminished even more significantly in the 1980s and 1990s. These declines may have contributed to the slow growth of labor productivity.

Second, strong import competition may have made American producers less anxious to invest in new capital equipment.

Third, as noted earlier, the expansion of government regulations of businesses in the areas of pollution control and worker health and safety diverted some investment spending away from output-increasing capital goods and toward capital that may have increased total utility to society but did not directly increase output itself. Stated differently, the composition of investment may have shifted toward uses that do not increase *measured* productivity.

Fourth, reduced spending on the economy's ***infrastructure,*** that is, on highways, airports, harbors, power installations, and similar facilities, may have slowed productivity growth. Such public capital goods are complementary to private capital goods. For example, public investments in new highways and bridges increase the productivity of business travelers and the efficiency with which inputs and finished products are transported. Similarly, public spending on power plants lowers energy costs and therefore the costs of running private manufacturing plants. Data show that in the 1947–69 period the public capital stock or infrastructure grew at a 3.5 percent annual rate and labor productivity growth was 2.5 percent per year. In the 1970–92 era, however, the yearly increase in the infrastructure fell to only 3.3 percent and the annual productivity increase plummeted to 1.6 percent. In short, a slowing of spending on public investment goods may have contributed to diminishing private investment and thereby to declines in labor productivity growth.

Finally, the dramatic runup of energy prices that occurred in the 1970s may have had negative effects on investment. This factor is of sufficient importance to merit separate treatment.

18-1

18-1 World of Work

IS PUBLIC CAPITAL PRODUCTIVE?*

The role of the decline in spending on public-sector capital such as highways and airports in the productivity slowdown is controversial. The debate is centered around the impact of public-sector capital on productivity. The results from empirical investigations range from public capital having no effect on productivity to it having triple the productivity effect of private capital.

The wide range of productivity estimates arise from several factors. The largest estimates arise from studies based on national data. One should be skeptical of these findings since the studies treat all public-capital goods the same, and the results are sensitive to the estimation methodology. Investigations using state or regional data and narrower definitions of public capital yield substantially smaller productivity estimates, but they ignore the impact of infrastructure on other states. However, a study by Holtz-Eaken and Schwartz indicates that this bias is small. It is worth noting that all of the empirical estimates are biased downward since they do not account for the complementary effects between public capital and private capital and labor. In summary, public capital likely does increase productivity, but the exact magnitude of this effect is unclear.

Should government spending on public capital goods be increased? Not surprisingly, estimates vary widely of the ideal amount of spending on public-sector goods. One study suggests the best amount is 4 percent of GDP, while another indicates that it is nearly 20 percent of GDP. Given the uncertainty regarding the optimal amount of public capital goods spending, Lansing argues that one should be wary about increasing investment in public-sector capital.

*Based on Kevin J. Lansing, "Is Public Capital Productive? A Review of the Evidence," Federal Reserve Bank of Cleveland *Economic Commentary,* March 1, 1995, and Douglas Holtz-Eakin and Amy Ellen Schwartz, "Spatial Productivity Spillovers from Public Infrastructure: Evidence from State Highways," National Bureau of Economic Research Working Paper No. 5004, February 1995.

4 Energy Prices Perhaps the prime suspect in the productivity slowdown was the sizable increases in energy (oil) prices that occurred in 1973–75 and 1978–80. At the outset we might note two points that give credence to rising energy prices as an important cause of the productivity slowdown. First, the timing is right. That is, productivity growth did fall off sharply after the quadrupling of oil prices in 1973–75 (see Table 18-5). Second, the impact of skyrocketing energy prices was worldwide, as has been the productivity slowdown.

Less clear are the mechanisms through which higher energy prices impaired productivity growth. On the one hand, the direct impact of higher oil prices was to cause some highly productive capital-insensitive technologies to become relatively less attractive or even obsolete. In particular, high energy prices increased the costs of operating capital equipment. This in effect raised the price of capital relative to the price of labor. Producers were therefore more inclined to use less-productive labor-intensive techniques. On the other hand, the indirect macroeconomic effects of dramatically higher energy prices may have been even more important in causing the decline in productivity growth. Bluntly put, the two episodes of soaring energy prices precipitated periods of stagflation, that is, inflationary recessions. Government's use of restrictive macroeconomic policies to control inflation undoubtedly worsened and prolonged the periods of recession and slow economic growth. You will recall from our earlier discussion that recession causes productivity to fall for a variety of reasons. Thus, prolonged periods of the underutilization of productive capacity in many industries may have been the immediate cause of the productivity slowdown.[19]

Institutional and Behavioral Factors A very different view of the productivity slowdown stresses that forces of an institutional nature—the way work is organized, the attitudes and behavior of workers and managers, communication between labor and management, and the division of authority among managers and workers—account for much of our poor productivity performance vis-à-vis Japan and Western Europe. The argument here is that American industrial relations are characterized by an adversarial relationship between managers and their employees. Feeling alienated from their employers, workers do not participate in the decisions that govern their daily work lives; they do not identify with the objectives of their firms, and they therefore are not motivated to work hard and productively. Managers are judged, rewarded, and motivated by short-term profit performance and thus, it is argued, give little attention to long-term plans and strategies that are critical to the realization of high rates of productivity growth. Japanese industries, by way of contrast, provide lifetime employment security for a sizable portion of their workforce, allow for worker participation in decision making, and use profit sharing or bonuses to provide a direct link between the economic success of a firm and worker incomes. Furthermore, the direct interest that workers have in the competitiveness and profitability of their enterprise reduces the need for supervisory personnel. The result of all this is a commonality of interest and cooperation between management and labor, greater flexibility in job assignment, and enhanced willingness of workers to accept technological change. Lifetime employment is also conducive to heavy investment by employers in the training and retraining of their workers.[20] The implication is that an overhaul of our industrial relations systems may be a key to revitalizing our productivity growth.

There is, in fact, a growing body of evidence that does suggest that profit sharing (Chapter 7) and organized programs of worker participation have positive effects on productivity. For example, in reviewing some 15 studies of the effects of profit sharing on productivity, Weitzman and Kruse find positive effects in all cases. Similarly, a study by Mitchell, Lewin, and Lawler concludes that, first, productivity is 5 to 10 percent higher in firms with profit sharing schemes and, second, productivity is higher in
18-2 companies with formalized worker participation programs.[21]

CHAPTER SUMMARY

1 Productivity is the relationship between real output and inputs. The "official" Bureau of Labor Statistics (BLS) index of labor productivity is the ratio of real GDP originating in the private sector to the number of worker hours employed in the private sector.

[19]Griliches, "Productivity Puzzles and R & D, op. cit., p. 19.

[20]For an interesting elaboration of these points, see Levitan and Werneke, op. cit., chap. 3.

[21]See Martin L. Weitzman and Douglas L. Kruse, "Profit Sharing and Productivity," pp. 95–142; and Daniel J. B. Mitchell, David Lewin, and Edward E. Lawler III, "Alternative Pay Systems, Firm Performance, and Productivity," pp. 15–94, both in Alan S. Blinder (ed.), *Paying for Productivity* (Washington, DC: Brookings Institution, 1990).

18-2 World of Work

SERVICES AND PRODUCTIVITY*

One striking feature of the productivity slowdown is that productivity growth in the service sector has lagged seriously behind productivity growth in the manufacturing (goods-producing) sector. Since 1973 productivity in manufacturing has increased by about 2.75 percent annually, while productivity growth in the service-producing sector has been about 0.7 percent.

Why the differences? There are several possible reasons. First, it simply may be more difficult for service companies to increase their productivity by substituting capital for workers. How do you substitute machinery for a barber, dentist, tax preparer, day care worker, or retail clerk?

Second, the competitive pressure to enhance productivity may be weaker in services than in manufacturing. It is possible that customers are more loyal to service providers than to brands of manufactured products. Also, it may be more costly for consumers to switch banks, accountants, or law firms than to switch from Levi's to Wranglers or from Colgate to Crest toothpaste. Finally, the U.S. service sector has been relatively immune from stiff foreign competition.

Third, as consumers become wealthier they often demand higher-quality services, which often means more—not less—labor intensity. Service firms may need to employ more retail clerks, pizza deliverers, maintenance workers, or financial planners to stay competitive.

Fourth, the influx of women into the labor force—specifically into the service sector—has kept wages in services relatively low. Also, the minimum wage remained constant at $3.35 per hour over the 1981–90 period and, because of inflation, declined in real terms. With relatively cheap labor available, U.S. service firms in such areas as retail trade, health care, finance, insurance, and real estate may have hired low-wage workers rather than investing in productivity increasing capital equipment or in new methods of using labor more efficiently.

Finally, perhaps the slow productivity growth in services is at least partly illusory. Unlike manufacturing, in services there are no physical "products" to count in determining output. Improvements in real output depend largely on improvements in quality. Existing techniques for collecting data on output do not easily capture these improvements. In fact, in such services as banking and recreation, changes in the level of production are estimated using measures of inputs such as the number of employees. When labor inputs are used as a proxy for real output, then by definition an industry will show no productivity growth (output per input). These and other measurement problems have led some productivity experts to question whether productivity growth in services is as dismal as officially stated.

*Compiled from various sources, including *Business Week, The Economist,* the *Wall Street Journal,* and the *Weekly Letter* (Federal Reserve Bank of San Francisco).

2 The BLS index overstates productivity growth because it excludes the public sector. On the other hand, it understates productivity growth in that quality improvements in output are ignored. The BLS index measures, but does not reveal the causes of, productivity growth.

3 The advantages of the BLS index are that *(a)* it is conceptually simple, *(b)* it automatically takes changes in the length of the workweek into account, and *(c)* it is directly comparable to hourly wage rates.

4 Economists are interested in labor productivity primarily because changes in productivity correlate very closely with changes in real wage rates.

5 Other things being equal, productivity growth offsets increases in nominal wages and thereby restrains increases in unit labor costs and product prices.

6 The basic factors that determine productivity growth are *(a)* improvements in the quality of labor, *(b)* increases in the capital–labor ratio, and *(c)* increased efficiency in the use of labor and capital inputs. Increased efficiency is quantitatively the most important factor.

7 Labor productivity falls below the long-term rate of growth during recession and rises above that rate during recovery. Causal factors include cyclical changes in the use of labor and capital and changes in the relative importance of the manufacturing sector.
8 There is no easily discernible relationship between productivity growth and employment changes in various industries. Price and income elasticities of product demand, coupled with demand shifts from changes in such factors as consumer tastes or public policy, make it virtually impossible to predict whether a productivity increase will be associated with increasing or declining employment in any given industry.
9 The rate of productivity growth has slowed dramatically, particularly since 1973. Possible economic factors in the slowdown include *(a)* diminishing improvements in the quality of labor, *(b)* a declining rate of technological progress, *(c)* diminished growth of the nation's stock of capital goods, and *(d)* the direct and indirect effects of higher energy prices. Others argue that productivity growth will be stimulated if the present adversarial relationship between labor and management is replaced by profit-sharing programs and greater worker participation.

TERMS AND CONCEPTS

labor productivity	labor hoarding
BLS productivity index	infrastructure

QUESTIONS AND STUDY SUGGESTIONS

1 How is labor productivity defined? Comment on the shortcomings and advantages of the Bureau of Labor Statistics index of labor productivity.
2 Suppose that in an economy 100 labor hours produce 160 units of output in year 1. In years 2 and 3 labor hours are 120 and 130 and units of output are 216 and 260, respectively. Using year 2 as the base year, calculate *(a)* the productivity index for all 3 years and *(b)* the rates of productivity growth.
3 How do you account for the close correlation between changes in the rate of productivity growth and changes in real wage rates for the economy as a whole? Does this relationship also hold true on an industry-by-industry basis? Explain.
4 Explain this statement: "High wage rates are both an effect and a cause of high labor productivity."
5 Discuss the relationship between aggregate productivity growth and price inflation. Draw a diagram (similar to Figure 18-5), putting average annual productivity growth on the horizontal axis and average annual price changes on the vertical axis. If you were to plot relevant data for, say, 60 or 70 major industries, what general relationship would you expect? Explain.
6 Suppose in a given year a firm's productivity increases by 2 percent and its nominal wages rise by 5 percent. What would you expect to happen to the firm's unit labor costs and product price?
7 Briefly comment in quantitative terms on the long-term trend of labor productivity in the United States; cite the three primary factors that contributed to that growth and indicate the relative quantitative importance of each. Discuss the specific factors that have contributed to increased efficiency in the use of labor and capital.
8 Describe and explain the cyclical changes that occur in labor productivity. Of what significance are these changes?

9 Explain the relationship between changes in *(a)* nominal wage rates, *(b)* productivity, *(c)* unit labor costs, and *(d)* product price. What does this relationship suggest about the expected impact of productivity growth on employment in a particular industry? Can you reconcile your generalization with Figure 18-5?

10 Assume that labor productivity is rising by 6 percent in the economy as a whole, but by only 1 percent in industry X. Also assume that nominal wages for all industries rise in accordance with the economy's overall rate of productivity increase. Labor costs are 90 percent of total costs in industry X. The demand for industry X's product is highly elastic with respect to price and inelastic with respect to income. Assuming no shifts in demand curves for products in the economy other than those associated with changes in income, forecast the future growth or decline of industry X, specifying all of the steps in your reasoning.

11 Comment on each of the following statements:

a "While most highly productive companies are profitable, not all profitable companies are highly productive."

b "Increased public demand for such amenities as clean air and safer workplaces has complicated the difficulties of comparing productivity rates over time."

c "Rising productivity means that it takes fewer workers to produce a given level of output. Productivity increases are therefore a source of unemployment."

12 The rate of increase in the productivity of U.S. labor has been declining, particularly since 1973. How do you account for this slowdown? Explain how rising energy prices might have directly *and* indirectly contributed to this slowdown. What specific policy changes do you think might help to reverse this trend?

13 The accompanying diagram contains average annual data for the 1960–82 period. Interpret this diagram and relate it to the slowdown of U.S. productivity growth. What *specific* policies to increase productivity growth do these data imply?

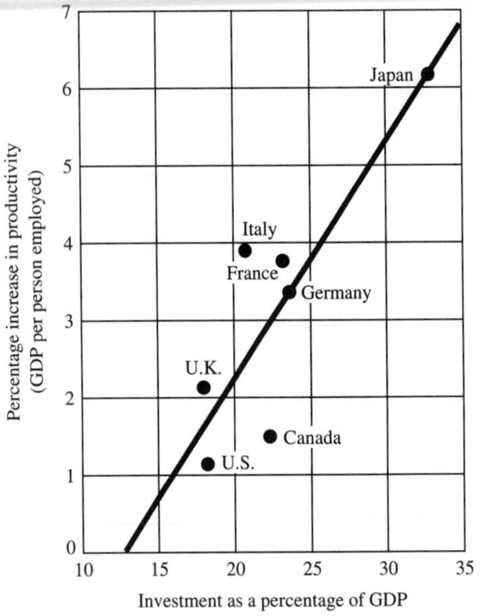

SELECTED REFERENCES

Baumol, William J., Sue Anne Batey Blackman, and Edward N. Wolff: *Productivity and American Leadership* (Cambridge, MA: MIT Press, 1989).

Blinder, Alan S. (ed.): *Paying for Productivity* (Washington, DC: Brookings Institution, 1990).

Denison, Edward F.: *Trends in American Economic Growth, 1929–1982* (Washington, DC: Brookings Institution, 1985).

Dertouzos, Michael L., Richard K. Lester, and Robert M. Solow: *Made in America: Regaining the Productive Edge* (Cambridge, MA: MIT Press, 1990).

Griliches, Zvi (ed.): *R & D, Patents, and Productivity* (Chicago: University of Chicago Press, 1984).

Kendrick, John W.: *Understanding Productivity* (Baltimore: Johns Hopkins University Press, 1977).

Kendrick, John W., and Elliot S. Grossman: *Productivity in the United States: Trends and Cycles* (Baltimore: Johns Hopkins University Press, 1980).

Kerr, Clark, and Paul D. Staudohar (eds.): *Economics of Labor in Industrial Society* (San Francisco: Jossey-Bass Publishers, 1986), parts 4 and 5.

Levitan, Sar A., and Diane Werneke: *Productivity: Problems, Prospects, and Policies* (Baltimore: Johns Hopkins University Press, 1984).

Measuring Productivity: Trends and Comparisons from the First International Productivity Symposium (New York: UNIPUB, 1984).

Nelson, Richard R.: "Research on Productivity Growth and Productivity Differences: Dead Ends and New Departures," *Journal of Economic Literature,* September 1981, pp. 1029–1064.

"Symposium on the Slowdown in Productivity Growth," *Journal of Economic Perspectives,* Fall 1988, pp. 3–97.

CHAPTER 19

EMPLOYMENT AND UNEMPLOYMENT

Facts: In the 1980s the U.S. economy created 18 million new jobs; an additional 11 million jobs came into existence between 1990 and 1997. In 1997, 4.9 percent of the U.S. labor force was unemployed, down 2 full percentage points from just 4 years earlier. Unemployment rates in 1997 fell to 9.2 percent in Canada, 8.6 percent in Australia, and 10 percent in the United Kingdom. Meanwhile, only 3.4 percent of the Japanese labor force was unemployed in 1997.

Questions: What explains the growth of employment over time? How much unemployment is natural for an economy? What causes higher-than-usual unemployment rates? Who are the unemployed? How long do they remain unemployed? What policies does government use to try to reduce unemployment?

In earlier chapters we analyzed how individuals make short- and long-term labor supply decisions and how firms determine their profit-maximizing levels of employment under varying conditions in labor and product markets. We also examined how unemployment might arise in specific labor markets where a union wage, a legal minimum wage, or an efficiency wage exceeded the market-clearing wage. We now turn our attention to the *aggregate* labor market and to the determinants of the *total* levels of employment and unemployment in the economy.

We first examine the procedures for measuring employment and unemployment, problems associated with gathering and interpreting the data, and difficulties in defining full employment. Next, a macroeconomic model is developed that allows us to analyze how the level of total employment is determined. We then delineate and discuss frictional, structural, and cyclical unemployment. In our discussion of frictional unemployment, we examine unemployment associated with searching for work or waiting for a job expected to be available in the future. The section on structural unemployment includes a discussion of job losses from plant closedowns. Sources of wage rigidity command much of our attention in the section on cyclical unemployment. In the concluding sections of the chapter, we examine the distribution of unemployment and the public policies used to minimize unemployment.

EMPLOYMENT AND UNEMPLOYMENT STATISTICS

Employment and unemployment statistics are widely used to assess the macroeconomic health of the economy. It is important to have knowledge of how total employment and unemployment are measured, to be aware of the recent employment and unemployment record, and to understand the limitations of the data as guides to public policy.

Measurement

Each month the Bureau of the Census conducts a current population survey (CPS) commonly referred to as the ***Household Survey.*** About 50,000 households are selected to represent the U.S. population 16 years of age or older and are interviewed to determine the proportions of the population employed, unemployed, or not in the labor force. The Bureau of Labor Statistics of the U.S. Labor Department then uses the sample data to estimate the number of people in each category in the survey week.

Employed Persons Those officially *employed* include people who, during the survey week, were 16 years or older and either (1) were employed by a private firm or government unit, (2) were self-employed, or (3) had jobs but were not working because of illness, bad weather, labor disputes, or vacations.

Once the total employment for the survey week is known, the ***employment–population ratio*** is easily computed. As shown by equation (19-1), this ratio is total employment as a percent of the total noninstitutional population.

$$\text{Employment–population ratio} = \frac{\text{employment}}{\text{noninstitutional population}} \times 100 \qquad (19\text{-}1)$$

Recall from the discussion of the labor force participation rate in Chapter 3 that the noninstitutional population comprises all persons 16 years of age and older who are not in institutions such as prisons, mental hospitals, or homes for the aged.

Unemployed Persons People are considered officially *unemployed* if during the survey week they were 16 years of age or older, were not institutionalized, and did not work, *but* were available for work *and* (1) had engaged in some specific job-seeking activity during the past 4 weeks, (2) were waiting to be called back to a job from which they were temporarily laid off, (3) would have been looking for a job but were temporarily ill, or (4) were waiting to report to a new job within 30 days.

Those, who are 16 years or older and not institutionalized but officially neither employed nor unemployed are classified as "not in the labor force." The labor force itself therefore consists of those employed and unemployed.

$$\text{Labor force} = \text{employment} + \text{unemployment} \tag{19-2}$$

The ***unemployment rate,*** then, is the percentage of the labor force that is unemployed.

$$\text{Unemployment rate (\%)} = \frac{\text{unemployment}}{\text{labor force}} \times 100 \tag{19-3}$$

Recap Figure 19-1 helps clarify how the BLS breaks down the total population into various components; it also provides a basis for computing values for equations (19-1) through (19-3). The *employment–population ratio* [equation (19-1)] for 1997 was 67.1 percent. This number is found by dividing the number of people employed (= 129.6 million) by the noninstitutional population of 203.1 million (= 267.6 million − 64.5 million) and multiplying by 100. Consistent with equation 19-2, we observe that the size of the *labor force* in 1997 was 136.3 million. It is found by adding the number of those employed (= 129.6 million) and the number unemployed (= 6.7 million). The *unemployment rate* [equation (19-3)] in 1997 was 4.9 percent, calculated by

FIGURE 19-1 TOTAL POPULATION, LABOR FORCE, EMPLOYMENT, AND UNEMPLOYMENT, IN MILLIONS, 1997
Of the total population of 267.6 million people in the United States in 1997, 136.3 million were in the labor force. Of this latter group, 129.6 million workers were employed and 6.7 million people were unemployed. The unemployment rate for 1997 was 4.9 percent, and the employment-population ratio was 63.8 percent.

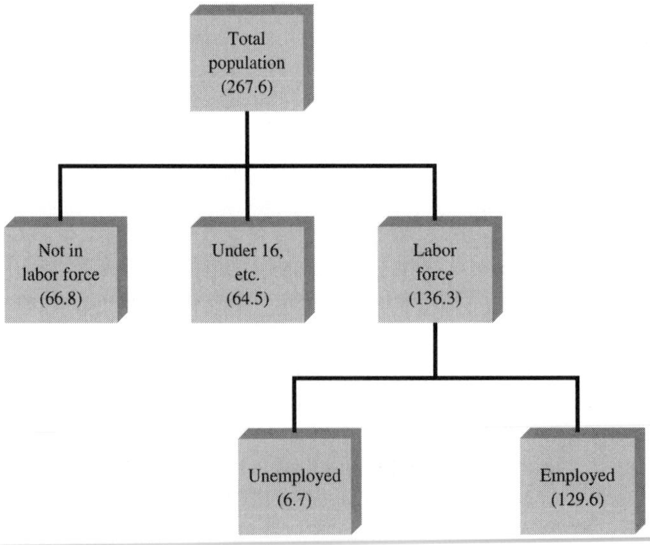

TABLE 19-1 EMPLOYMENT AND UNEMPLOYMENT, SELECTED YEARS

Year	Employment (millions)	Employment–population ratio (%)	Unemployment (millions)	Unemployment rate (%)
1960	65.8	56.1	3.9	5.5
1962	66.7	55.5	3.9	5.5
1964	69.3	55.7	3.8	5.2
1966	72.9	56.9	2.9	3.8
1968	75.9	57.5	2.8	3.6
1970	78.7	57.4	4.1	4.9
1972	82.2	57.0	4.9	5.6
1974	86.8	57.8	5.2	5.6
1976	88.8	56.8	7.4	7.7
1978	96.0	59.3	6.2	6.1
1980	99.3	59.2	7.6	7.1
1982	99.5	57.8	10.7	9.7
1984	105.0	59.5	8.5	7.5
1986	109.6	60.7	8.2	7.0
1988	115.0	62.3	6.7	5.5
1990	118.8	62.8	7.0	5.6
1992	118.5	61.5	9.6	7.5
1994	123.1	62.5	8.0	6.1
1996	126.7	63.2	7.2	5.4
1997	129.6	63.8	6.7	4.9

Source: Bureau of Labor Statistics, *Employment and Earnings,* January 1998, Table 1.

dividing the number of people unemployed (= 6.7 million) by the size of the labor force (= 136.3 million) and multiplying by 100.

Historical Record

Table 19-1 provides information on employment and unemployment for selected years since 1960. Particularly striking is the extent to which total employment increased over these years. Between 1990 and 1997 alone, 10.8 million new jobs were created. We see that the employment–population ratio also was higher in recent years than in 1960. The 1997 rate of 63.8 percent was 7.7 percentage points above that in 1960. On the other hand, the unemployment rate has been highly variable during these years; its low was 3.5 percent in 1968 and its high was 9.7 percent in 1982. Observe that the unemployment rate fell steadily between 1992 and 1997. The 1997 rate of 4.9 percent was the lowest unemployment rate since the early 1970s.

A Critique of the Household Data

The official employment-related statistics based on the CPS household interviews and reported by the BLS possess several notable virtues that make them useful to economists. First, the sampling technique is uniform throughout the nation and, with the exception of minor changes, has remained consistent over the years. Therefore, economists can compare employment and unemployment rates between periods and track cyclical and secular trends. Second, the time lag between the survey and the reporting of the data is short, and the information is highly accessible through government publications. Third, the data are reported in disaggregated as well as overall forms; for example, unemployment rates are provided by race, age, gender, marital status, occupation, reasons for unemployment, and duration of unemployment. This aids in analyzing the distribution of the burden of unemployment. Finally, the data provide useful clues as to the direction of the overall economy during the course of a business cycle.

Unfortunately, however, these official statistics also have limitations. In the first place, the official data include all *part-time workers as fully employed,* when in reality some of these people desire to work full-time. In 1997 about 18.1 million people worked part-time because of personal choice. Another 4.1 million part-time workers either wanted to work full-time but could not find suitable full-time work or were on short hours because of a temporary slack in consumer demand.[1]

A second limitation is that to be counted as unemployed, a person must be actively seeking work. But studies show that after many people unsuccessfully look for work for a time, they become discouraged and then abandon their job search. Specifically, an estimated .34 million people fell into this category in 1997. These ***discouraged workers*** (Chapter 3) constitute "hidden unemployment."

A third problem is that the data do not measure the ***subemployed;*** the statistics fail to include people who are forced by economic circumstances to accept employment in occupations that pay lower wages than those they would qualify for in periods of full employment. Each of these three limitations causes the official unemployment statistics to *understate* the extent of underutilization of labor resources and the degree of economic hardship associated with a particular "official" overall rate of unemployment.

But other problems with the data cause some observers to conclude that the true extent of economic hardship in the nation may be *overstated* by the "official" unemployment rate. First, it is likely that some respondents to the monthly Household Survey provide false information that increases the official unemployment rate. To present a good image of themselves and family members, interviewees may indicate that household members are actively seeking work when in fact they are not in the labor force.

A second problem is that each unemployed person is counted equally whether he or she is, say, normally a full-time worker who has a strong attachment to the labor force, a semiretired person who wishes to work part-time, or a teenager seeking an after-school job. To the extent that the unemployment statistics include people in the latter two categories, the official unemployment rate may be misleading.[2]

Moreover, the household data do not contain information on the *minimum acceptable* wages (reservation wages) for those unemployed, some of whom may have recently been discharged from high-paying jobs in declining sectors of the economy.

[1]For research indicating that the Bureau of Labor Statistics classification of these workers as "involuntarily" part-time is correct, see Leslie S. Stratton, "Are 'Involuntary' Part-Time Workers Indeed Involuntary?" *Industrial and Labor Relations Review,* April 1996, pp. 522–536.

[2]Well over one-half of all teenagers who are unemployed are enrolled in school and seeking only part-time work.

These people may remain unemployed until they accept the reality that they no longer can command their initial reservation wages. Unemployment insurance benefits, supplemental unemployment benefits (SUBs) provided by firms, and severance pay may increase the length of this adjustment period. A closely related criticism of using the official data as an indicator of the social impact of unemployment is that the increase in the number of multiearner families over the past few decades has reduced the amount of poverty corresponding to any specific level of unemployment. The loss of a job by one family member greatly lessens the standard of living of most families, but it does not push as many families into poverty as it once did.[3]

The Stock-Flow Model

One final limitation of the overall unemployment rate requires comment. This rate does not distinguish between people who are experiencing short—perhaps less serious—unemployment spells and those who are going through long periods of unemployment. Suppose, as a simple illustration, that an economy has only 12 members in the labor force. In situation A, each person is unemployed for 1 separate month during a year; while in situation B, one person is unemployed and the rest employed for the entire year. The Household Survey would discover that in each case, one out of 12 workers is unemployed *in each month* and therefore the annual employment rate is 8.3 percent (1/12). Yet most observers would judge situation B to be of greater social concern; it leaves one person without any wage income for a full year.

This example demonstrates an important fact: The household data measure *stocks* of people in each of the three important labor force categories—employed, unemployed, and not in the labor force—but do not reveal the continuous movement—or *flows*—of people between the various categories. This movement is captured in the ***stock-flow model*** of unemployment shown in Figure 19-2. Two things to note from this diagram are that (1) the unemployment rate [$= U/(E + U)$] can remain constant even though the specific people in the unemployment "pool" change, and (2) several distinct flow factors can act independently or interact with one another to cause the unemployment rate to change. As one example of the latter, suppose that the rate of inflow to the unemployment category U by way of layoffs, flow 2, increased, while all other flow rates remained constant. Obviously, this would increase the absolute number of people who are unemployed while leaving the size of the labor force $(E + U)$ unchanged, thereby causing the unemployment rate to rise.

As a second and more complex example, suppose that the rate of exit from the employed category E via retirements and withdrawals, flow 4, increased while all other flow rates remained unchanged. Once again the unemployment *rate* would rise, but in this case the *absolute* number of unemployed persons would remain at its previous level. The size of the labor force $(E + U)$ would shrink, and since unemployment (U) would remain constant, the unemployment rate [$= U/(E + U)$] would rise.

[3]S. L. Terry, "Unemployment and Its Effects on Family Income," *Monthly Labor Review,* April 1982, pp. 35–43.

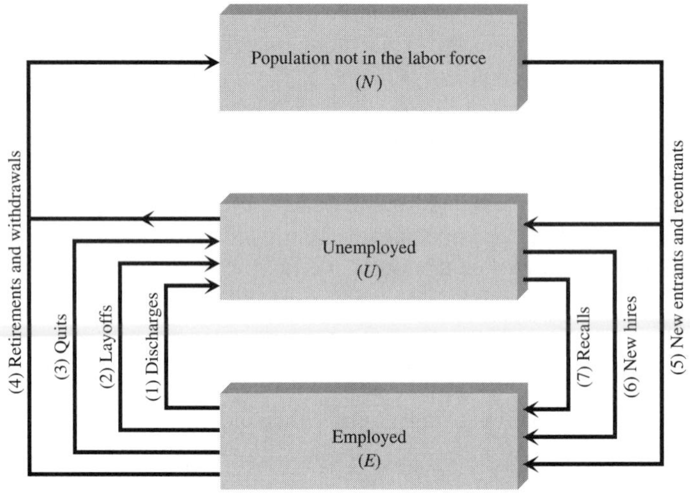

FIGURE 19-2 THE STOCK-FLOW MODEL OF UNEMPLOYMENT
At any point in time, there is a measurable *stock* of people in each of the three boxes that represent categories of labor force status. But these stocks are simultaneously being depleted and replenished by numerous *flows* into and out of each category. Changes in the rates of these flows can significantly affect the unemployment rate.

An analysis of the flows between the categories of labor force status helps us understand the length of unemployment spells of individuals and the reasons why unemployment rates rise and fall. The following are examples of insights gleaned from the stock-flow analysis of unemployment rates: (1) Empirical evidence suggests that a considerable amount of unemployment is due to prolonged spells of unemployment for relatively few people.[4] (2) During recessions, the rates of layoffs and discharges rise and the rates of "new hires" and "recalls" fall, more than compensating for the decline in voluntary job quits. Consequently, the overall unemployment rate rises. (3) First-time labor force entrants and people reentering the labor force from the "not in the labor force" category typically constitute over one-third of the unemployed. (4) Unemployment rates stay higher than expected during earlier phases of an economic recovery because improved job prospects entice people who are out of the labor force to seek work, that is, to become officially unemployed (Chapter 3).

Defining Full Employment

Not only is a zero rate of unemployment unachievable in a dynamic economy where information is imperfect and workers and firms heterogeneous, but it may in fact be undesirable. Later in this chapter we will find that some *voluntary* unemployment is a way individuals increase their personal earnings and is part of the process through

[4]Kim B. Clark and Lawrence H. Summers, "Labor-Market Dynamics and Unemployment: A Reconsideration," *Brookings Papers on Economic Activity,* no. 1, 1979, pp. 13–60.

which society enhances its real output and income. We also will observe that some *involuntary* unemployment is an unavoidable by-product of changes in tastes, population shifts, and technological advance. These changes create structural mismatches between labor demand and supply and require adjustments in the allocation of labor resources from some occupations and regions to others.

How much voluntary and unavoidable involuntary unemployment is there in the U.S. economy? What rate of unemployment constitutes ***full employment?*** In the 1960s, economists concluded that a 4 percent unemployment rate was an achievable full-employment policy goal. But in the 1970s and 1980s, numerous factors led economists to boost this figure to 5.5 or even 6 percent. Two of the more important factors were (1) a changed composition of the labor force such that groups having high unemployment rates—teenagers, for example—constituted a larger fraction of the overall labor force and (2) evidence that rates of unemployment in the 4 percent range were associated with accelerating rates of inflation.

Today the consensus appears to be that an unemployment rate of 5.5 percent constitutes "practical" full employment and that attempts to reduce the rate below this level through policies that increase aggregate demand will cause the existing rate of inflation to accelerate. This 5.5 percent rate is sometimes called the equilibrium or ***natural rate of unemployment*** and is defined as (1) *the unemployment rate at which there is neither excess demand nor excess supply in the overall labor market* or (2) *the unemployment rate that will occur in the long run if expected and actual rates of inflation are equal.* We will defer explanations of the economic rationales for these two definitions to later in this chapter.
19-1

MACROECONOMIC OUTPUT AND EMPLOYMENT DETERMINATION

The macroeconomic models shown as graphs (a) and (b) in Figure 19-3 are central to much of the discussion in this chapter. Therefore, a close look at their components is imperative.

Aggregate Demand and Supply

Graph (a) depicts the familiar aggregate demand and supply curves introduced in principles of macroeconomics textbooks to discuss price level and real output determination. The vertical axis shows the *price level* for a hypothetical economy, and the horizontal axis measures *real output.* Conceptually, real output always equals real income; $1 of output generates $1 of income as wages, rent, interest, and profits. The horizontal axis therefore also measures real income.

Aggregate Demand ***Aggregate demand*** *for goods and services is shown as curve D in Figure 19-3(a) and indicates the total quantity of real output that domestic consumers, businesses, government, and foreign buyers will collectively desire to purchase at each price level.* As the price level falls (rises), the quantity of goods and services demanded rises (falls).

19-1 Global Perspective

COMPARATIVE UNEMPLOYMENT RATES, 1985–97

Unemployment rates vary greatly among nations of the world over specific periods. The major reasons for these differences are that nations have different natural rates of unemployment and they may be in different phases of their business cycles.

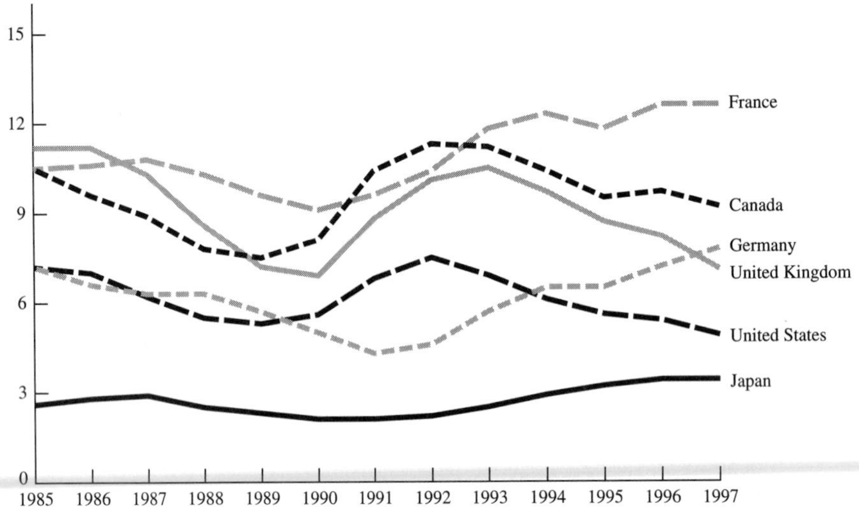

Source: Bureau of Labor Statistics, "Comparative Labor Force Statistics, 10 Countries, 1959–1997," March 1998.

The negative slope of the aggregate demand curve results from three interacting effects, the first being the *interest rate effect.* As the price level declines, the demand for money drops because fewer dollars are needed to purchase any given quantity of goods and services. If the money supply is fixed, this decrease in money demand will reduce interest rates, which then will increase spending on such interest-sensitive commodities as new autos, homes, and plants and equipment. Thus, other things being equal, the lower the price level, the greater the quantity of output demanded.

The second effect that helps explain the downward slope of the aggregate demand curve is the *wealth* or *real balances effect.* Lower price levels increase the *real value* of such assets as currency, checking deposits, and savings deposits, whose values are fixed in money terms. As the price level falls, the purchasing power of dollar-

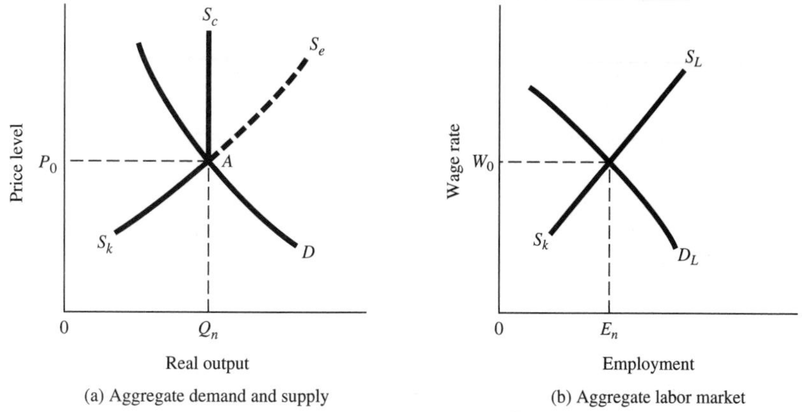

FIGURE 19-3 **REAL OUTPUT AND TOTAL EMPLOYMENT DETERMINATION**
The intersection of the aggregate demand and supply curves D and S_kAS_c in graph (a) produces equilibrium price and real output levels P_0 and Q_n. In the aggregate labor market (b), the equilibrium wage rate and level of total employment are determined at the intersection of the aggregate labor demand and supply curves. Employment level E_n is the natural level of employment; it is the amount of labor needed to produce the natural level of real output Q_n.

denominated wealth held by consumers rises, and people increase their spending on normal goods and services.

The final effect at work is the *foreign purchases effect.* As the domestic price level falls relative to prices of products produced abroad, foreign consumers will shift their spending toward U.S. goods. Hence, the lower price level will be associated with a greater amount of U.S. real output and income.

Aggregate Supply ***Aggregate supply*** *of goods and services is the relationship between the price level and the total quantity of real output that firms are willing to produce and offer for sale.* The curve in Figure 19-3(a) is a synthesis of varying interpretations of aggregate supply. The solid curve labeled S_kAS_c incorporates traditional Keynesian (S_kA) and classical (AS_c) assumptions about the working of the economy. The curve's segment S_kA is explained as follows: As aggregate demand falls (D shifts leftward), firms experience declines in sales and increases in inventories of unsold goods. Because wages are relatively inflexible downward, firms respond by laying off or discharging workers and reducing production. Consequently, output falls.

On the other hand, the AS_c segment of the aggregate supply curve shows that when labor and capital resources are being fully used, as is assumed to be true at the full-employment output level Q_n, increases in aggregate demand boost only the price level. The greater demand and higher prices cannot generate greater output. The *monetary* value of the Q_n output rises because of the higher price level, but *real* output remains constant at Q_n.

Other economists envision a short-run aggregate supply curve as shown by S_kAS_e. They assume that, in the long run, the economy generates a natural level of output Q_n, but that, in the short run, output can be less or greater than that amount depending on the relationship between the actual and expected price levels. We must defer a full discussion of this interpretation to later, but the following constitutes its essence. Suppose that the price level is P_0 and workers expect it to remain there. Now suppose that unanticipated inflation occurs so that the price level rises above P_0. As a result, the prices that firms receive for their products will rise, while nominal wage rates, at least temporarily, will remain fixed at their previously contracted levels. This will mean that real wages will fall and profits will rise, causing firms collectively to increase their employment and output.

Meanwhile, unemployed workers who are searching for jobs will begin to receive inflation-induced higher nominal wage offers and mistakenly think that they are being offered higher real wages. Consequently, they will begin to accept job offers more quickly; the level of employment will rise, unemployment will fall, and real output temporarily will rise above Q_n. Thus, the aggregate supply curve will extend upward as shown by the broken line AS_e.

Equilibrium Price Level and Real Output The equilibrium levels of price and real output occur where the quantities of total output demanded and supplied are equal, that is, where D and $S_k S_c$ in Figure 19-3(a) intersect. Real output and income level Q_n is the full-employment level of real output or, rephrased, the natural level of real output and income.

The Aggregate Labor Market

Graph (b) in Figure 19-3 shows the aggregate labor market. This graph is our familiar labor market diagram "writ large." The labor demand curve D_L in the figure can be thought of as the aggregate marginal revenue product curve for the economy. This curve is found by multiplying the aggregate marginal product of labor by the price level, in this case P_0. This curve tells us the profit-maximizing level of employment associated with each wage rate. Alternatively, the aggregate labor supply curve S_L indicates the amount of labor services people collectively are willing to offer at each nominal wage rate, given the price level. We assume that in the short run, workers expect the existing price level to remain. We observe that the equilibrium wage rate is W_0 and the equilibrium level of employment is E_n. This level of employment is the natural level of employment—or "full employment"—and is just sufficient to produce the Q_n level of real output shown in graph (a). As noted earlier, most economists feel that the natural rate of unemployment associated with E_n and Q_n is about 5.5 percent.

Why is this natural rate of unemployment so high? Why has the actual rate of unemployment in the United States greatly exceeded the natural rate in some years? To answer these questions we must next consider the three major types of unemployment and their causes. Throughout the discussion, bear in mind that the boundaries between unemployment categories are not absolute and that the extent of one type of unemployment may be a function of the amount of one or both of the other types.

FRICTIONAL UNEMPLOYMENT

Even when aggregate demand is sufficient to employ all the labor force and when those who are unemployed possess skills matching those required by firms with job openings, the nation's unemployment rate will remain positive. As implied in our stock-flow model (Figure 19-2), people continuously (1) quit present jobs to shop for new ones, (2) look for new jobs after losing previous ones, (3) enter the labor force to seek work for the first time, (4) reenter the labor force after periods of absence, and (5) move from one job to take another within the next 30 days. Likewise, employers continuously (1) search for replacements for workers who quit or retire, (2) discharge some employees in hopes of finding better ones, and (3) seek new workers to fill jobs created by expansion of their firms. Thus, unlike "auction" markets such as stock and wheat exchanges, the overall labor market never fully "clears." At any moment there is considerable ***frictional unemployment;*** that is, not all active job searchers will have yet found or accepted employment and not all employers will have yet filled their job vacancies.

Search unemployment is an important source of frictional unemployment. This type of unemployment is created by individuals searching for the best job offer and firms searching for workers to fill job openings. The job search process and its relationship to unemployment compensation and inflation is discussed in Chapter 16.

Not all frictional unemployment is of the search variety. In some instances, unemployed workers willingly wait to be recalled from temporary layoffs or willingly wait in job queues to obtain union jobs (Chapter 11). Additionally, efficiency wages (Chapter 7) may attract workers into the labor force who are forced to wait for such jobs to open. These types of frictional unemployment collectively might best be described as ***wait unemployment,*** rather than search unemployment. Let's briefly examine each of these potential sources of frictional unemployment.

1 Temporary Layoffs Although large layoffs are normally associated with recessions, temporary layoffs by firms occur throughout the economy even during periods of robust overall aggregate demand. Such layoffs may account for as much as 1 to 1.5 percentage points of the natural rate of unemployment.[5] Workers on temporary layoff normally do not search for new employment; rather, they wait to be recalled to their former jobs. We know from our discussion of the Household Survey that these workers are counted as unemployed.

Seasonal unemployment might also be thought of as temporary layoff and therefore a type of wait unemployment. Examples: Construction workers often are unemployed during the winter, farm workers occasionally are unemployed between planting and harvesting seasons, and professional athletes may be unemployed during parts of the year. In each case, these workers are waiting to resume their jobs.

2 Union Job Queues Unions also contribute to frictional unemployment. Analysis in Chapter 6 demonstrated that union wage scales may contribute to wait unemployment

[5]D. M. Lilien, "The Cyclical Pattern of Temporary Layoffs in United States Manufacturing," *Review of Economics and Statistics,* February 1980, pp. 24–31.

by reducing the number of workers demanded by firms and increasing the number of willing suppliers of labor (Figure 6-10). In brief, some workers may be willing to wait in the employment queue for union jobs, rather than take nonunion jobs available at lower pay.

3 Efficiency Wages Finally, efficiency wages may contribute to the relatively high rate of frictional unemployment. Recall that efficiency wages are those that firms set above the market-clearing levels as a way to either elicit hard work, reduce costly labor turnover, or achieve some other desirable end that adds to worker productivity. We observed earlier in Figure 7-8 that efficiency wage payments and permanent frictional unemployment go hand in hand. As concisely stated by DeFina:

> Unemployed individuals, whether they have quit, have been fired, or have entered the labor force for the first time, might try to get jobs by bidding down the wages of current workers. But in contrast to the simple competitive market situation, firms will not accept those offers. Firms have already weighed the benefits and costs of lower wages and decided that keeping wages high yields them their greatest profit. And because the unemployed cannot bid their way into jobs, they must instead wait until new openings arise from quits, firings, or increases in firms' demands for workers. They must then hope to be chosen over other jobless persons. On the whole, unemployed persons might remain jobless for quite some time.[6]

QUICK REVIEW 19-1

- The employment–population ratio measures total employment as a percent of the total noninstitutional population; the unemployment rate is the percentage of the labor force which is unemployed.
- The total level of employment is largely determined by aggregate demand and aggregate supply. Full employment exists when the rate of unemployment is 5.5 percent.
- Frictional unemployment is the unemployment mainly resulting from voluntary job quits, job switches, and new entrants and reentrants into the labor force.

Your Turn: What factors cause the "official" unemployment rate to overstate the true extent of economic hardship in the United States? What factors cause it to understate economic hardship? (Answer: See page 628.)

STRUCTURAL UNEMPLOYMENT

Another type of unemployment that is part of a nation's natural rate of unemployment is ***structural unemployment.*** This unemployment shares many of the same features as frictional unemployment but is differentiated by being long-lived. It therefore can in-

[6]Robert H. DeFina, "Explaining Long-Term Unemployment," *Business Review* (Federal Reserve Bank of Philadelphia), May–June 1987, p. 19.

volve considerable costs to those unemployed and substantial loss of forgone output to society.

Structural unemployment is caused by changes in the *composition* of labor supply and demand; it is a "square pegs, round holes" phenomenon. This unemployment generally has one or both of the following dimensions. First, it may result from a mismatch between the skills needed for available jobs and the skills possessed by those seeking work. Second, structural unemployment may occur because of a geographic mismatch between the locations of job openings and job seekers. Examples of structural unemployment abound: Robotics technology and the increase in the market share of imports greatly reduced employment in the U.S. auto industry in the 1970s. Many of the workers who were displaced did not have the skills required for positions that were open, for example, in accounting and computer programming. Similarly, improvements in agricultural technology over the past 100 years caused job losses for many farm operators and laborers who did not possess readily transferable job skills in expanding areas of employment and who were not geographically mobile. Unemployment resulting from job losses associated with the spate of mergers in the United States over the last decade is another example of structural unemployment, as is unemployment resulting from the deregulation of the trucking and airline industries.

Displaced Workers

During the 1980s and 1990s many of the people who were structurally unemployed were ***displaced workers***—individuals who had lost their jobs specifically because of permanent plant closings or job cutbacks. A total of about 2.4 million workers 20 years of age and over who had been at their jobs at least 3 years were displaced between January 1993 and January 1994. By February 1996, 78.5 percent of these workers were reemployed in new jobs. Another 14.2 percent of them had left the labor force. Seven percent of the displaced workers thus were still unemployed and looking for work. This 7 percent figure was higher than the overall unemployment rate in 1996. Of those full-time workers who were back at work, 53.5 percent were earning less than before they were displaced. About one-fifth were earning 0 to 19 percent more than before, and one-quarter were earning at least 20 percent more.[7]

Not all plant closures and job cutbacks occur where we would most expect them: in declining industries or industries hurt by import competition. The level of employment within firms is surprisingly volatile from one year to the next, *independently* of the business cycle or major industry trends. Jobs themselves are more unstable than generally thought, implying that much of structural unemployment results from workers

[7]Steven Hipple, "Worker Displacement in an Expanding Economy," *Monthly Labor Review,* December 1997, pp. 26–39. These statistics are summarized for the 1980s and 1990s in Henry S. Farber, "The Changing Face of Job Loss in the United States, 1981–1995," *Brookings Papers on Economic Activity, Microeconomics Issue,* 1997, pp. 55–142. For a survey of studies examining laid-off workers, see Bruce Fallick, "A Review of Recent Empirical Literature on Displaced Workers," *Industrial and Labor Relations Review,* October 1996, pp. 5–16; and Lori G. Kletzer, "Job Displacement," *Journal of Economic Perspectives,* Winter 1998, pp. 115–136.

being in the wrong place at the wrong time. Changes in labor demand within firms alone may account for as much as one-fourth of the natural rate of unemployment.[8]

The extent of structural unemployment depends on the *degree* of the compositional changes in labor demand and supply and the *speed* of the adjustments of the imbalances and mismatches. Training and retraining play a key role in this adjustment process, and efforts to shorten the duration of structural unemployment normally involve retooling of skills to match job vacancies.

Additional Observations

Several additional observations about structural unemployment deserve mention. In the first place, higher levels of general education are associated with lower levels of structural unemployment. For instance, college graduates who are displaced from their employment because of changes in demand or technology have a wider range of job options and usually find retraining to be easier than persons who have little formal education.[9]

A second observation is that structural and cyclical unemployment overlap. When the economy is at full employment and rapidly expanding, firms experiencing shortages of skilled workers often find it profitable to hire people who do not possess the required job skills but who can be trained while on the job. This training reduces the amount of structural unemployment. But when a recession occurs and the overall rate of unemployment rises, firms hiring new or replacement workers can draw skilled workers from the large unemployment pool. Workers who do not possess the required job skills will stay unemployed longer, and structural unemployment will rise.

A final observation is that futurists in nearly every historical period have warned of impending massive increases in technological unemployment. To date, however, the historical record indicates that, on the average, technological change creates more jobs than it destroys and does not greatly alter the overall rate of structural unemployment. More generally, recall the discussion surrounding Figure 18-5, which suggested that no systematic relationship exists between productivity changes and employment changes on an industry-by-industry basis.

But might not the high-technology revolution change this pattern? Most economists doubt that it will. They point out that although specific workers will lose their jobs—and many firms, communities, and perhaps even regions will suffer negative consequences—the new technologies will spur capital investment, spawn secondary industries, and generate output effects that will increase overall labor demand. To fill available positions in the expanding sectors, firms there may need to engage in more concerted on-the-job training. Most economists view the current explosion of new technology as presenting a major challenge to society but not one that is fundamentally different from previous challenges posed by other new technologies.

19-1

[8]Jonathan S. Leonard, "In the Wrong Place at the Wrong Time: The Extent of Frictional and Structural Unemployment," in Kevin Lang and Jonathan S. Leonard (eds.), *Unemployment and the Structure of Labor Markets* (New York: Basil Blackwell, 1987), pp. 141–163.

[9]W. R. Johnson, "The Demand for General and Specific Education with Occupational Mobility," *Review of Economic Studies,* October 1979, pp. 695–705; and Paul Swaim and Michael Podgursky, "Do More-Educated Workers Fare Better Following Job Displacement?" *Monthly Labor Review,* August 1989, pp. 43–46.

19-1 World of Work

ADVANCED NOTIFICATION OF PLANT CLOSURE OR SIZABLE DISMISSAL

Two important sources of frictional and structural unemployment are plant closings and large permanent dismissals (often referred to as permanent layoffs). When firms without warning close one of their plants or announce sizable dismissals, the displaced workers are immediately unemployed. On the other hand, with advance warning they would be able to begin job searches or undertake retraining prior to losing their jobs. Such job searches or retraining might lead to new jobs, therefore reducing or eliminating intervening periods of frictional or structural unemployment.

In response to the problem of abrupt mass dismissals, Congress passed the Worker Adjustment and Retraining Notification Act of 1988 (WARN). This act requires that firms with 100 or more full-time employees provide 60-day advanced notice to workers in the event of an expected (1) plant closing that will result in an employment loss for 50 or more workers at any site, (2) layoff involving at least 33 percent of the workforce, or (3) layoff involving 500 or more employees. Exempt from the provisions are companies facing lockouts or strikes, acute financial distress, unforeseeable economic circumstances, or natural disasters.

Preliminary studies confirm that the prenotification requirements have reduced the lengths of unemployment spells of displaced workers. In particular, prenotification has reduced unemployment duration for household heads, women, nonwhites, and workers in local labor markets with high unemployment rates. On average, however, the reduction in unemployment is rather slight. One study suggests that WARN has reduced the average unemployment spell of displaced workers by only 3 to 5 working days.*

WARN has also been weakly enforced. A study by the federal government's General Accounting Office (GAO) found that 54 percent of the employers that closed plants in 1990 did not properly comply with the WARN provisions. The GAO has recommended to Congress that the Labor Department be given authority to enforce the law.

*Christopher J. Ruhm, "Advanced Notice and Postdisplacement Joblessness," *Journal of Labor Economics,* January 1992, pp. 1–32. Other recent studies relating to this topic include Jane Friesen, "Mandatory Notice and the Jobless Durations of Displaced Workers," *Industrial and Labor Relations Review,* July 1997, pp. 652–666; John T. Addison and McKinley L. Blackburn, "A Puzzling Aspect of the Effect of Advance Notice on Unemployment," *Industrial and Labor Relations Review,* January 1997, pp. 268–288; John T. Addison and McKinley L. Blackburn, "Advance Notice and Job Search: More on the Value of an Early Start," *Industrial Relations,* April 1995, pp. 242–262; and Stephen R. G. Jones and Peter Kuhn, "Mandatory Notice and Unemployment," *Journal of Labor Economics,* October 1995, pp. 599–622.

DEMAND-DEFICIENT UNEMPLOYMENT

In many years the unemployment rate greatly exceeds the 5.5 percent natural rate. For example, unemployment was 8.3 percent in 1975, 9.5 percent in 1982, and 7.3 percent in 1992. In the depth of the Great Depression—1933—24.9 percent of the labor force was unemployed. These high unemployment rates are by-products of recessions and depressions and result from deficiencies in aggregate demand that force firms to lay off and discharge workers. The evidence strongly suggests that decline in aggregate demand—rather than, say, differences between expected and actual inflation rates—are the *primary* cause of cyclical unemployment.[10]

Graphic Analysis

The analytical framework that we developed earlier helps clarify ***demand-deficient*** or ***cyclical unemployment.*** In Figure 19-4(a) we depict a sharp, unexpected decline in

[10]Ronald S. Warren, Jr., "Labor Market Contracts, Unanticipated Wages, and Employment Growth," *American Economic Review,* June 1983, pp. 389–397.

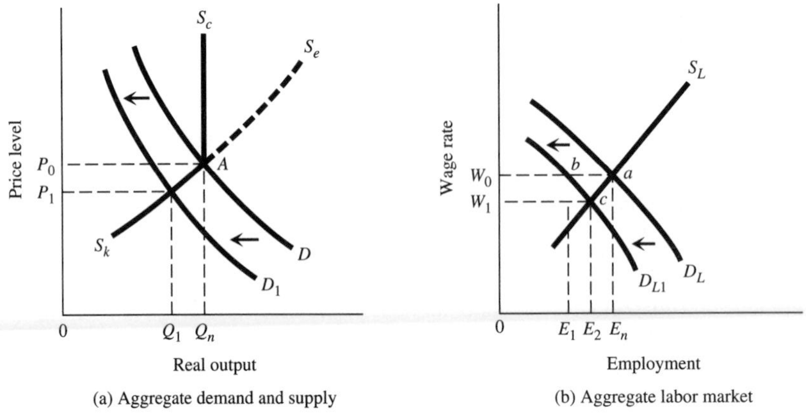

FIGURE 19-4 **DEMAND-DEFICIENT UNEMPLOYMENT**
A decline in the aggregate demand for output [D to D_1 in (a)] reduces the demand for labor [D_L to D_{L1} in (b)]. Assuming a rigid nominal wage W_0, the decline in labor demand results in involuntary demand-deficient unemployment by the amount *ab* in graph (b).

aggregate demand, as shown as the movement from D to D_1. Keynesians view a decline in investment or consumption spending as the usual cause of such a shift, while monetarists look to a reduction in the money supply as the underlying culprit. Irrespective of the cause, the fall in the aggregate demand decreases real output from the full-employment level Q_n by the amount Q_nQ_1.

As shown in graph (b) of Figure 19-4, the decline in aggregate demand in graph (a) reduces the derived aggregate demand for labor from D_L to D_{L1}. In technical terms, this decline in labor demand occurs because the lower price level P_1 in graph (a) reduces revenue to producers; that is, marginal revenue product in the aggregate falls. More generally, firms experience rapid rises in their inventories because they are unable to sell their existing output. They therefore curtail their production and reduce their demand for labor. Put simply, they no longer wish to hire as many workers at each wage rate as previously.

Let's assume, for reasons we will explore shortly, that the wage rate in graph (b) remains at W_0. We note that employment declines from the natural level E_n to the smaller amount E_1. At wage W_0, *a* individuals desire work—and previously were working—but firms employ only *b* workers. Thus, *ab* workers are cyclically unemployed.

The full decline in employment and emergence of unemployment rest on the crucial assumption that the wage rate in our model does not fall. For if it were to decline to W_1, firms would adjust their employment to E_2 (point *c*). We note that employment is only E_2 at W_1, compared to E_n at the original W_0 equilibrium. The E_2E_n decline in employment, however, would be voluntary on the part of these workers. As shown by segment *ca* of the labor supply curve, these workers have reservation wages that exceed the new lower wage W_1. Because the E_2E_n workers voluntarily withdraw from the labor force, they are not officially unemployed.

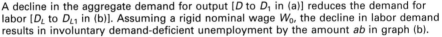

Just how flexible downward are nominal wages in the U.S. economy? Although nominal wages eventually do fall under pressure of slack aggregate demand, they are relatively rigid downward in the short run. Declines in aggregate demand therefore produce demand-deficient or cyclical unemployment.[11]

Wage Rigidity

Why are nominal wages relatively inflexible downward? Several diverse explanations have been cited.

1 Unions Unions are one reason why nominal wages are rigid downward. Unions view wage cuts as "givebacks" of previous hard-earned collective bargaining gains and thus vigorously resist wage reductions. Reductions in nominal wages do occur in unionized industries, but normally only *after* severe cutbacks in employment have occurred. Unions appear to prefer layoffs to temporary wage reductions. The latter affect all workers, while layoffs usually affect only a small percentage of the firm's workforce and normally involve people with little seniority. Thus, a *majority* of workers benefit by a layoff policy as contrasted to wage cuts, and elected union leaders are likely to be responsive to this majority when negotiating wage and layoff provisions.

2 Bias toward Layoffs by Firms Another reason that nominal wages are inflexible downward is that firms themselves may favor temporary selective layoffs to across-the-board temporary wage reductions. The latter might cause higher-skilled, more-experienced workers in whom a firm has invested large amounts of training to quit and take jobs elsewhere. The layoff strategy allows the firm to "inventory" or "hoard" this skilled labor and instead lay off workers who are more easily replaced if they happen to take alternative employment rather than wait for a callback. Furthermore, the existence of unemployment compensation and the way it is financed bias the decision toward layoffs. Those laid off experience a *net* loss of income that is much less than the full decline in wages, and therefore, they will be less likely to accept other permanent jobs during this period. Also, because the tax payments paid by firms to the unemployment compensation program are not perfectly related to layoff experience, firms that dismiss substantial numbers of workers are subsidized by the tax payments of other firms. Stated technically, the unemployment benefits received by workers who are temporarily unemployed exceed the *incremental* tax cost to the firms that lay them off.[12]

3 Implicit Contracts A closely related reason that wages appear to be inflexible downward during recessions is that implicit contracts govern many employment relationships. ***Implicit contracts*** are informal, often unstated, understandings that are

[11]According to Keynes, even if nominal wages did fall, so too would product costs and prices. Therefore, the *real* wage—the nominal wage divided by the price level—would remain constant, and employment would not increase.

[12]See Martin Feldstein, "The Importance of Temporary Layoffs: An Empirical Analysis," *Brookings Papers on Economic Activity,* no. 3, 1975, pp. 725–744; and Robert H. Topel, "On Layoffs and Unemployment Insurance," *American Economic Review,* September 1983, pp. 541–559. Also see Anderson and Meyer, op. cit.; and Donald R. Deere, "Unemployment Insurance and Employment," *Journal of Labor Economics,* October 1991, pp. 307–324.

"invisible handshakes."[13] One common feature of many implicit contracts is an understanding that the firm will maintain existing nominal wages and pay cost-of-living wage increases except under severe economic conditions, such as impending bankruptcy. In return for this guarantee, employers obtain the right to lay off workers in response to cyclical declines in the demand for their products. By providing "insurance" against wage declines during recessions, employers can attract workers at a lower average wage. Additionally, the "fixed wage–variable employment" contract provides firms with certainty in the reduction of the wage bill (wage $\times$ number of worker hours) compared to the uncertainty associated with a wage reduction, which might cause some highly valued workers to quit. Finally, these contracts may produce positive "reputation effects" that may allow firms to attract better-quality workers who require less supervision.

4 Insider–Outsider Theories Recently a set of so-called ***insider–outsider theories*** has emerged that purports to explain downward wage rigidity on the basis of "insiders" and "outsiders."[14] *Insiders* are employed workers who have some degree of market power; *outsiders* are unemployed persons who are unable or unwilling to underbid the existing wage rate to gain employment. In terms of Figure 19-4(b), outsiders are represented by distance *ab* at wage W_0.

Why are outsiders unable or unwilling to secure jobs for themselves by bidding down the wage rate to, say, W_1 in Figure 19-4(b)? They may be *unable* to do this because firms may view the cost of hiring them as being prohibitive. Firms may expect that, upon hiring outsiders at less than the existing wage rate, the remaining incumbent workers will withhold cooperation from those who "stole" jobs. Where workplace cooperation is important in the production process, the firms' output and profits will most surely suffer. Moreover, even if firms were willing to hire outsiders, this group may be *unwilling* to offer their services for less than the present wage rate for fear of being harassed by remaining incumbent workers. Outsiders may thus opt to wait for an increase in aggregate demand to obtain or regain employment. Meanwhile, the cyclical unemployment described in Figure 19-4(b) will persist.

19-2

THE DISTRIBUTION OF UNEMPLOYMENT

The distribution of unemployment is uneven over the labor force and changes as demand-deficient unemployment rises and falls. In Table 19-2 we present disaggregated civilian unemployment rates by race, age, gender, and duration of unemployment for 2 different years. These years were selected for contrast: In 1992, a major recession in the previous year had driven the overall unemployment rate to 7.4 percent (civil-

[13]A voluminous, but difficult, literature on implicit contracts has developed. The major contributions are surveyed in Costas Azariadis and Joseph E. Stiglitz, "Implicit Contracts and Fixed-Price Equilibria," *Quarterly Journal of Economics,* vol. 98, suppl. 1983, pp. 1–22.

[14]Assar Lindbeck and Dennis Snower, "Wage Setting, Unemployment, and Insider–Outsider Relations," *American Economic Review,* May 1986, pp. 235–239; and Lindbeck and Snower, "Cooperation, Harassment, and Involuntary Unemployment: An Insider–Outsider Approach," *American Economic Review,* March 1988, pp. 167–188. For empirical evidence against the insider–outsider model, see Denise J. Doiron, "A Test of the Insider–Outsider Hypothesis in Union Preferences," *Economica,* August 1995, pp. 281–290.

19-2 World of Work

THE SHARE ECONOMY*

Martin Weitzman of the Massachusetts Institute of Technology has offered an interesting proposal that would make wages flexible downward and therefore reduce the impact of a decline in aggregate product demand on employment. In essence, Weitzman's proposal—which he calls "gainsharing"—is that a part of each worker's compensation should come as a share of the firm's profit. For example, instead of paying workers a guaranteed wage rate of $10 per hour, workers might be guaranteed $5 per hour (the base wage) and paid additional compensation equal to some predetermined percentage of the firm's profits (the share wage). Total compensation (base wage + share wage) then might exceed or fall short of $10 per hour, depending on the firm's economic fortunes. Presumably, if the firm earned its usual profits, the total wage would be $10 per hour; if profits slide below their usual level, the wage rate would be less than $10; and if profits exceeded the normal level, the worker would get more than $10 per hour.

How would employment be affected by this plan? Assume initially that workers are receiving $10 per hour—$5 as a guaranteed wage and another $5 as compensation from profit sharing. Now suppose that aggregate product demand declines and the employer's sales and profits both drop. As a result, the $5 of profit-sharing income will fall and might decline to zero so that the actual hourly wage paid by the firm drops from $10 to $5. In view of the newly depressed demand for labor, the firm would clearly choose to retain more workers at $5 per hour than if the wage were fixed at $10. In effect, a decline in product demand that reduces profits *automatically* reduces a firm's wage rate. Weitzman therefore claims that his wage proposal will create an incentive for employers to retain larger workforces.

Weitzman suggests that Congress implement the plan through tax incentives to encourage firms and workers to agree to gainsharing arrangements. Specifically, he proposes that wage income from the share wage be taxed at a lower tax rate than income from fixed wage rates. This lower tax rate would encourage workers to agree to having a larger percentage of their wage income granted as share wages and less as base wages.

There are a number of criticisms of the profit-sharing wage plan. For example, the plan could jeopardize the wage uniformity and wage gains achieved by organized labor. A further criticism is that in response to lower base wages, employers will adopt production techniques that use relatively more labor and less capital. Because the amount of capital equipment per worker is critical to labor productivity and economic growth (Chapter 18), the long-run expansion of real gross domestic product might be impaired. At the pragmatic level, critics point out that Weitzman's plan to link pay to profits eliminates the present certainty that workers have as to whether the labor contract has been properly fulfilled. Wage avoidance and evasion by employers through accounting and other techniques might become commonplace.

Finally, there is the fundamental question as to whether workers will accept more jobs and greater employment stability in exchange for a reduced hourly wage guarantee and higher annual variability of earnings. But it should be noted in this regard that over the past decade a growing number of union and nonunion contracts *have* contained profit-sharing arrangements. Thus, although the emergence of a full-blown share economy seems improbable, profit sharing appears to be an idea that is spreading.

*Martin L. Weitzman, *The Share Economy* (Cambridge, MA: Harvard University Press, 1984). The December 1986 issue of the *Journal of Comparative Economics* contains the proceedings of an interesting symposium on the proposal for a share economy. For empirical evidence on Weitzman's theory, see Douglas L. Kruse, *Profit-Sharing: Does It Make a Difference? The Productivity and Stability Effects of Employee Profit-Sharing Plans* (Kalamazoo, MI: W. E. Upjohn Institute for Employment Research, 1993); and Linda A. Bell and David Neumark, "Lump-Sum Payments and Profit-Sharing Plans in the Union Sector of the United States Economy," *Economic Journal,* May 1993, pp. 602–619.

ian workforce); while in 1997 the economy reached full employment, experiencing a 4.9 percent unemployment rate.

Observation of the large variance in the disaggregated rates of unemployment *within each year* and comparison of the rates *between* the 2 years support several generalizations drawn from more extensive studies of unemployment data. First, the unemployment

TABLE 19-2 UNEMPLOYMENT RATES FOR LABOR FORCE SUBCLASSIFICATIONS, 1997 (FULL EMPLOYMENT) VERSUS 1992 (RECESSION)*

Category	Unemployment rate, 1997 (%)	Unemployment rate, 1992 (%)
Overall	4.9	7.4
Occupation		
Managerial and professional	2.0	3.1
Operators, fabricators, and laborers	7.5	11.0
Age		
16–19	16.0	20.0
Black, 16–19	32.4	39.8
White, 16–19	13.6	17.1
Males, 20+	4.2	7.0
Females, 20+	4.4	6.3
Race		
Black	10.2	14.1
White	4.2	6.5
Gender		
Female	5.0	6.9
Male	4.9	7.8
Duration		
15 weeks +	1.5	2.6

*Civilian labor force data. In 1992 the economy was suffering the lingering unemployment effects of the 1990–91 recession.

Source: Employment and Earnings, January 1993, 1998.

rates for people in occupations requiring less human capital tend to be higher than those for people in positions requiring more skills. For example, in 1997 the unemployment rate for managers and professionals was 2.0 percent compared to 7.5 percent for operators, fabricators, and laborers.

As a corollary, the unemployment rate usually is disproportionately higher for lower-skilled workers, during a recession. We say "usually" because this generalization is not without exception. In the 1990–91 recession, firms moved toward leaner management structures and laid off many white-collar workers. Observe in Table 19-2 that the unemployment rate in 1992 for operators, fabricators, and laborers was 11.0 percent compared to the 3.1 percent for managerial and professional workers. This 11.0-to-3.1 ratio is lower than the 7.5-to-2 ratio occurring in full-employment year 1997.

The reasons for the differential rates between workers of various skills and the normally rising relative rates for lower-skilled workers during recessions include: (1) lower-skilled workers are often subject to more technologically caused unemployment and longer spells of structural unemployment; (2) higher-skilled workers are more likely to be self-employed; and (3) during periods of falling product demand, firms lay off or discharge workers in whom they have invested the least amount of human capital over the years and retain more-skilled workers, managers, and professionals.

A second generalization concerning the disaggregated unemployment data shown in Table 19-2 is that the rate of unemployment for 16- to 19-year-olds is considerably higher than that for adults. Additionally, the black teenage unemployment rate greatly exceeds that for white teenagers. The overall teenage unemployment rate was 7.4 percent in 1992 and 16.0 percent in 1997, but the black teenage rates for the 2 years were 39.8 and 32.4 percent. Teenagers have low skill levels, high rates of job quits and discharges, little geographic mobility, and frequent transitions to and from the labor force. They therefore have numerous spells of frictional and structural unemployment. Also, some teenage unemployment is attributable to the minimum wage (Chapter 13).[15]

A third broad generalization based on Table 19-2 is that over the years, the unemployment rate for all blacks—teenage and adult—has been about two times that for whites. For example, in 1997 the black unemployment rate was 10.2 percent compared to the white rate of 4.2 percent. The reasons for the higher rates of black unemployment are difficult to sort out, but one factor is that blacks are more heavily represented in lower-skilled occupations. Recall from our prior discussion that such occupations have high rates of frictional and structural unemployment. Also, blacks live disproportionately in declining inner cities, where the demand for labor is often insufficient to employ all those seeking work. Finally, discrimination undoubtedly plays an important role in explaining the black–white unemployment rate gap. Only 20 to 40 percent of the unemployment rate differential between black and white men can be explained by observable characteristics such as education and job experience.[16]

A fourth generalization from the disaggregated unemployment data is that female unemployment rates are quickly approaching those of males. This has occurred over the past decade as females have moved into positions that are career-oriented and characterized by lower unemployment rates. We see in Table 19-2 that in 1997 the overall unemployment rate for females was 5.0 percent and for males, 4.9 percent. In 1992, the female unemployment rate actually was lower than that for males. This is explained by the impact of the 1990–91 recession on unemployment rates in such specific industries as wood products, autos, construction, and steel, which have high male-to-female employment ratios.

A final generalization concerning the disaggregated data illustrated in Table 19-2 is that the number of persons unemployed for long periods—say 15 weeks or more—as a percentage of the labor force is much less than the overall unemployment rate but rises during recessions. The unemployment rate for people without work for 15 weeks or longer was only 1.5 percent in 1997, compared to the overall rate of 4.9 percent. But this rate was 2.6 percent in 1992, indicating that recessions tend to create longer

[15]The causes and consequences of unemployment among black youths are analyzed in Richard B. Freeman and Harry J. Holzer, *The Black Youth Employment Crisis* (Chicago: University of Chicago Press, 1986). Also of interest are Harry J. Holzer, "Can We Solve Black Youth Unemployment?" *Challenge*, November/December 1988, pp. 43–49; and John Bound and Richard B. Freeman, "What Went Wrong? The Erosion of Relative Earnings and Employment among Young Black Men in the 1980s," *Quarterly Journal of Economics*, February 1992, pp. 201–232.

[16]See Leslie S. Stratton, "Racial Differences in Men's Unemployment," *Industrial and Labor Relations Review*, April 1993, pp. 451–463.

periods of idleness of labor resources and much more social hardship than does the unemployment we associated with the natural rate of unemployment.

QUICK REVIEW 19-2

- Structural unemployment results from the mismatch between the skills required for available job openings and the skills possessed by those seeking work; it also results from a geographical mismatch between jobs and job seekers.
- Many displaced workers—those who lose their jobs because of permanent plant closings or job cutbacks—become structurally unemployed.
- Demand-deficient unemployment (also called "cyclical unemployment") results from declines in aggregate demand and thus is associated with recessions and depressions.
- Unemployment rates vary by race, age, and occupation; specifically, blacks, youth, and lower-skilled workers have disproportionately high unemployment rates.

Your Turn: True or false? The unemployment rate of women typically has been twice that of men in recent years. (Answer: See page 628.)

REDUCING UNEMPLOYMENT: PUBLIC POLICIES

The U.S. government is officially committed to the goal of full employment. The Employment Act of 1946 proclaimed among other things that "it is the continuing policy of the Federal Government to use all practical means consistent with its needs and obligations and other essential considerations of national policy . . . to promote maximum employment, production, and purchasing power." The Full Employment and Balanced Growth Act of 1978 reaffirmed this goal and required that government (1) establish 5-year employment and inflation goals and (2) formulate programs to achieve them.

Table 19-3 deserves careful examination because it summarizes the wide variety of government programs that in full or in part are designed to reduce frictional, structural, and cyclical unemployment. Analysis of each of these approaches is impossible in a single chapter. Therefore, we will confine our attention in the remainder of this chapter to a single topic: stabilization (fiscal and monetary) policy.

Fiscal and Monetary Policy

As defined in Table 19-3, ***fiscal policy*** is the deliberate manipulation of expenditures and taxes by the federal government for purposes of promoting full employment, price stability, and economic growth. Alternatively, ***monetary policy*** consists of the deliberate actions taken by the Federal Reserve Bank to adjust the nation's money supply and interest rates to promote these same goals.

TABLE 19-3 GOVERNMENT POLICIES AND PROGRAMS TO REDUCE UNEMPLOYMENT*

Frictional unemployment

Job information and matching: government programs that increase the availability of information concerning job vacancies and skills of those seeking work and help match job applicants and employers. Examples: U.S. Job Service (state employment agencies).

Structural unemployment

1. *Educational subsidies:* government programs and expenditures that reduce the investment costs of obtaining human capital and thereby enhance people's ability to obtain jobs that are less likely to become obsolete as new technology emerges. Examples: Pell Grants and Guaranteed Student Loans for college students; subsidies under the Vocational Educational Act; funding of primary and secondary schools, community colleges, and state universities.
2. *Equal employment opportunity laws:* laws making it illegal to discriminate in hiring and promotion on the basis of race or gender, thus removing an institutional barrier that creates structural unemployment. Examples: Title VII of Civil Rights Act of 1964; Executive Order 11246.
3. *Job training and retraining:* programs designed to provide skills and work experience for those structurally unemployed. Examples: Manpower Development and Training Act (MDTA), occupational training at skill centers; MDTA on-the-job training programs; Job Corps; Comprehensive Employment and Training Act (CETA) programs aimed at youth, Native Americans, and displaced homemakers; Job Training Partnership Act; Trade Adjustment Assistance.
4. *Public service employment:* direct government hiring and on-the-job training of the long-term structurally unemployed. Examples: CETA, Title II as amended in 1978.
5. *Directed wage subsidies or employment tax credits:* direct payments or tax credits to firms that hire members of specific disadvantaged groups that experience high rates of structural unemployment. Example: Targeted Employment Tax Credit program of 1979; AFDC–WIN program.
6. *Layoff warning:* requirement that firms anticipating plant closures or major layoffs provide advance notice, thus enabling workers to immediately search for new jobs or enroll in retraining programs. Example: Worker Adjustment and Retraining Notification Act of 1988.

Demand-deficient unemployment

1. *Fiscal policy:* deliberate manipulations of expenditures and taxes by government for the purposes of increasing aggregate demand and thereby increasing domestic output and employment. Examples: tax cuts in 1964, 1970, and 1974.
2. *Monetary policy:* deliberate actions taken by the Federal Reserve to increase the nation's supply of money to reduce interest rates and increase aggregate demand for products and services. Examples: monetary expansions in 1974–75, 1982, and 1991–93.
3. *Supply-side policies:* deliberate actions taken by the government to increase labor supply, savings, and investment and to reduce the costs of goods and services so that the aggregate supply curve shifts rightward. Examples: Reagan administration 1981 tax cuts, Individual Retirement Accounts, deregulation.
4. *Public service unemployment:* direct government hiring of people unable to find jobs. Examples: Works Progress Administration in the 1930s; Comprehensive Employment and Training Act; Title VII, Public Service Employment in the 1970s.
5. *Wage subsidies or employment tax credits:* direct payments or tax credits to firms that expand their employment. Example: New Jobs Tax Credit program of 1977.

*Not all of the programs cited as specific examples are currently operating; some of the examples are historical.

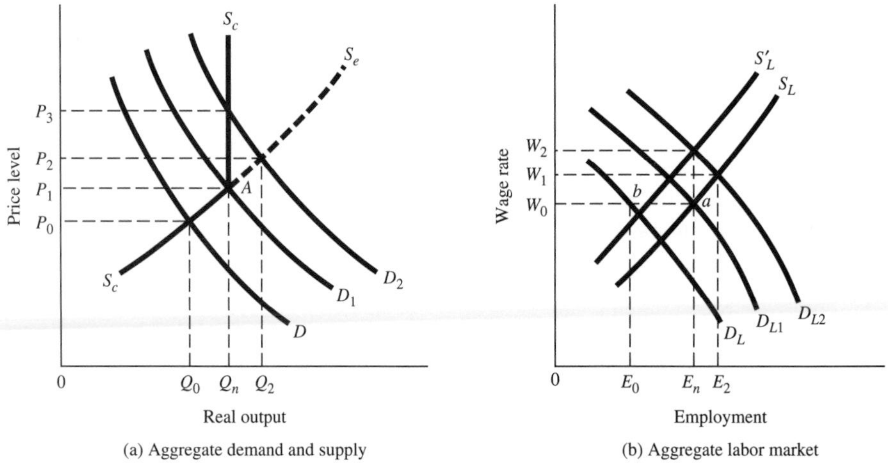

FIGURE 19-5 **FISCAL AND MONETARY POLICY TO REDUCE UNEMPLOYMENT**
Expansionary fiscal and monetary policy that increases aggregate demand from D to D_1 in graph (a) increases real output from Q_0 to Q_n. In the labor market, the corresponding rise in labor demand from D_L to D_{L1} eliminates cyclical unemployment and raises employment to E_n. But if policymakers mistakenly increase aggregate demand to D_2, labor demand will rise to D_{L2}. Eventually, labor suppliers will adjust their behavior to the higher expected price level, their labor supply will decline from S_L to S'_L, and unemployment will then move to its natural level E_n.

The impact of expansionary fiscal and monetary policy on domestic output and unemployment is shown in Figure 19-5. Suppose initially that aggregate demand has fallen from D_1 to D, reducing real output to Q_0 (graph a). This decline in aggregate demand is accompanied by a decline in the demand for labor from D_{L1} to D_L (graph b). For the moment, suppose that labor supply is shown by curve S_L. Because the nominal wage is assumed to be inflexible downward at W_0, the decline in the demand for labor to D_L produces demand-deficient unemployment of *ab*. If the full-employment level of output in graph (a) is Q_n and the natural rate of employment in graph (b) is E_n, then E_0E_n represents cyclical unemployment.

Successful fiscal and monetary policy would increase aggregate demand to D_1, which would raise domestic output to its natural level Q_n and, as seen by the intersection of D_{L1} and S_L in graph (b), restore total employment to its natural level E_n.

The increase in aggregate demand to D_1 and the corresponding rise in labor demand to D_L can be accomplished through some combination of (1) tax cuts for individuals to increase personal consumption spending, (2) expansion of the money supply to reduce interest rates and promote investment spending, (3) tax reductions or direct subsidies to firms to increase investment spending, and (4) increases in government expenditures.

Complications

What appears simple in theory—shifting the aggregate demand curve rightward precisely to D_1—is difficult in reality. Timing is crucial, and several time lags make the precise management of aggregate demand difficult. Once the administration has recognized that aggregate demand has declined, it must formulate a fiscal policy and submit it to Congress. Next, Congress must hold hearings on the proposed policy and pass it as law. Then, once in place, the policy itself takes time to have full impact on the economy. During these lags, factors independent of the fiscal policy can shift the aggregate demand curve further inward or rightward. Thus, a specific dose of fiscal policy may turn out to be either inappropriately large or small.

Careful coordination of fiscal and monetary policy is needed to avoid another potential complication of stabilization policy: the ***crowding-out effect.*** This is a problem arising from the federal government's need to borrow funds from the money market to finance the deficits accompanying expansionary fiscal policy. Government borrowing may compete with private borrowing, increasing interest rates and reducing private investment spending. Thus, the stimulus of the fiscal policy may be weakened or canceled. To keep this crowding out from occurring, the monetary authorities need to increase the money supply by just enough to offset the deficient-caused rise in the equilibrium interest rate.

Another complication of stabilization policy is that government may overshoot its mark. Because this overshooting has happened in the past, it will be worthwhile to examine the implications in aggregate product and labor markets. Let's suppose that expansionary fiscal and monetary policies shift the aggregate demand curve further to the right than expected, say to D_2 rather than D_1, thus causing a higher than expected price level (P_2 rather than P_1). In the short run, this unexpectedly high inflation temporarily may increase real output above its natural level; the economy may move upward along the broken-line segment of AS_e. In the long run, however, real output will return to its natural level Q_n. In the meantime, with aggregate demand at D_2, the price level will continue to rise to its equilibrium level at P_3.

We need to examine closely what is happening in the labor market to understand why real output temporarily rises to Q_2, only eventually to fall back to Q_n. The expansion of aggregate demand to D_2 (graph a) increases the demand for labor to D_{L2} (graph b). Employment temporarily rises above its natural level as firms, which have contracted for existing labor at W_0, expand their hiring. Also, job searchers, who now are being offered nominal wages at W_1, reduce their search time. To repeat: The reason for the rise in employment is that the actual rate of inflation has exceeded the expected rate, reducing frictional unemployment (recall our previous discussion of this topic). But once suppliers of labor recognize that the new price level is higher than previously expected, they readjust their behavior such that labor supply shifts from S_L to S'_L. Why is this so? The answer is that workers will no longer supply as much labor *at each nominal wage* now that the price level is P_2 rather than the expected level of P_1. The *real wage* (nominal wage/price level) associated with *each* nominal wage is now *lower,* and this fact translates into a leftward shift of the labor supply curve.

Observe from the intersection of D_{L2} and S'_L that the nominal wage, which *is* flexible upward, has increased to W_2. At this higher nominal wage, employment returns to its natural level E_n. This employment decline corresponds to the return of real output from Q_2 to Q_n in graph (a). Observe also that both the price level *and* the nominal wage are now higher than previously. The inappropriately expansionary fiscal and monetary policy eliminated cyclical unemployment but also produced price and wage inflation.

CHAPTER SUMMARY

1 A person is officially unemployed if she or he is 16 years or older, is not institutionalized, and is either actively seeking work, waiting to be called back to a job after being laid off, or waiting to report to a new job within 30 days.

2 The official unemployment data have several limitations as measures of economic hardship and as guides to public policy. The stock-flow model sorts out causes of changes in the unemployment rate and provides information on the duration of employment spells for individuals.

3 An unemployment rate of 5.5 percent represents a "full" or natural rate of unemployment. At this rate neither an excess demand nor an excess supply of labor occurs, and the actual and expected rates of inflation are equal.

4 Frictional unemployment is a natural and often constructive occurrence in a dynamic economy characterized by heterogeneous workers and jobs, imperfect information, and continuous movements of people among the various categories of labor force status. It can take two basic forms: search unemployment, which is associated with the time required to find a job; and wait unemployment, where workers either wait to be recalled to former jobs or remain in job queues resulting from above-market-clearing wages.

5 Structural unemployment results from a mismatch between the skills needed for available jobs and the skills possessed by those seeking employment. Many of those structurally unemployed are displaced workers who specifically lose their jobs because of permanent plant closings or job cutbacks.

6 Declines in the aggregate demand for goods and services cause a deficiency in the aggregate demand for labor. Wage rates tend to be inflexible downward for a variety of reasons, including the presence of unions, a bias toward layoffs by firms, implicit contracts, and "insider–outsider" relationships. As a result, involuntary demand-deficient unemployment arises when aggregate demand declines.

7 Unemployment is distributed unevenly over the labor force. For example, the unemployment rate for blacks is about twice that for whites.

8 Fiscal policy is a major tool used to combat demand-deficient unemployment, but it is fraught with several complications, including *(a)* time lags, *(b)* the need to coordinate fiscal and monetary policies to avoid the crowding-out effect, and *(c)* tendencies to create inflation.

TERMS AND CONCEPTS

Household Survey (CPS)
employment–population ratio
unemployment rate
discouraged workers
subemployed
stock-flow model
full employment
natural rate of unemployment
aggregate demand and aggregate supply
frictional unemployment
search unemployment
wait unemployment
structural unemployment
displaced workers
demand-deficient (cyclical) unemployment
implicit contracts
insider–outsider theories
fiscal policy
monetary policy
crowding-out effect

QUESTIONS AND STUDY SUGGESTIONS

1 Use the following data to calculate *(a)* the size of the labor force, *(b)* the official unemployment rate, and *(c)* the labor force participation rate (Chapter 3) for a hypothetical economy: population = 500; population 16 years or older and noninstitutionalized = 400; persons employed full- or part-time = 200; persons unemployed and actively seeking work = 20; persons who have quit seeking work due to lack of success = 10; part-time workers seeking full-time jobs = 30.

2 What factors tend to *understate* the extent to which the official unemployment rate accurately measures the degree of economic hardship in the nation? What factors lead some observers to conclude that the official unemployment rate *overstates* economic hardship?

3 Use the basic model shown in Figure 19-3 to illustrate graphically each of the following: *(a)* demand-deficient unemployment and *(b)* temporary increases in output and employment beyond their natural, or full-employment, levels.

4 Define the term *structural unemployment* and distinguish it from frictional and demand-deficient unemployment. Why might structural unemployment fall when demand-deficient unemployment declines?

5 Suppose you are economic adviser to the president, who has asked you to design a program to reduce the amount of unemployment associated with displaced workers. What major elements would your plan include?

6 Why are nominal wages inflexible downward? What is the implication of this characteristic for the ability of involuntary demand-deficient unemployment to persist for a considerable length of time?

7 Assume that the official national unemployment rate rises from 6 percent to 11 percent because of a major recession. What impact do you predict this would have on *(a)* the black–white unemployment rate ratio, *(b)* the labor force participation rate, and *(c)* the teenage–adult unemployment rate ratio? Explain.

8 Do you expect the natural rate of unemployment to *(a)* increase, *(b)* decrease, or *(c)* remain at the present level over the next decade? Explain your reasoning.

9 Examine critically this statement: "Unemployment in the United States can be resolved quickly and efficiently. The government should simply provide jobs for everyone who wants to work and cannot find suitable employment in the private sector."

SELECTED REFERENCES

Belous, Richard S.: *The Contingent Economy: The Growth of the Temporary, Part-Time and Subcontracted Workforce* (Washington, DC: National Planning Association, 1989).

Dornbusch, Rudiger, and Stanley Fischer: *Macroeconomics,* 6th ed. (New York: McGraw-Hill, 1993).

Economic Report of the President: various years.

Ehrenberg, Ronald G., and George H. Jakubson: *Advanced Notice Provisions in Plant Closing Legislation* (Kalamazoo, MI: W. E. Upjohn Institute for Employment Research, 1988).

Gordon, Robert J.: *Macroeconomics,* 7th ed. (Reading, MA: Addison-Wesley, 1998), Chap. 7.

Hall, Robert E., and John B. Taylor: *Macroeconomics,* 5th ed. (New York: W.W. Norton, 1997), Chap. 5.

Jacobson, Louis S., Robert J. LaLonde, and Daniel J. Sullivan: *The Costs of Worker Dislocation* (Kalamazoo, MI: W. E. Upjohn Institute for Employment Research, 1993).

Kniesner, Thomas J., and Arthur H. Goldsmith: "A Survey of Alternative Models of the Aggregate U.S. Labor Market," *Journal of Economic Literature,* September 1987, pp. 1241–1280.

Lang, Kevin, and Jonathan S. Leonard (eds.): *Unemployment and the Structure of Labor Markets* (New York: Basil Blackwell, 1987).

Leigh, Duane E.: *Assisting Displaced Workers* (Kalamazoo, MI: W. E. Upjohn Institute for Employment Research, 1989).

Leigh, Duane E.: *Assisting Workers Displaced by Structural Change: An International Perspective* (Kalamazoo, MI: W. E. Upjohn Institute for Employment Research, 1995).

Lindbeck, Assar, and Dennis J. Snower: *The Insider–Outsider Theory of Employment and Unemployment* (Cambridge, MA: MIT Press, 1989).

APPENDIX

INFORMATION SOURCES IN LABOR ECONOMICS

The purpose of this appendix is to survey significant sources of information about labor economics. This information should prove useful to individuals preparing term papers in this or subsequent courses. In this regard, note the list of potential term paper topics in Appendix Table 1. Also, this appendix provides valuable information on how you might keep your personal and professional knowledge of labor economics current in the years ahead. If you are a business or economics major, we urge you to keep this book (or at least a copy of this appendix) in your personal library.

An overview of the appendix will point our way. First, we identify and briefly describe key Internet sites relating to labor economics and labor statistics. Then we annotate print sources of labor statistics. Third, we call your attention to various publications containing articles on labor economics and policy. There, we annotate bibliographic indexes, professional journals, compendiums of invited essays, and nontechnical publications. Next, several advanced textbooks in labor economics are briefly described. Finally, mention is made of textbooks that cover closely related fields such as labor law, collective bargaining, labor relations, and labor history.

SOURCES OF LABOR STATISTICS

Statistical sources can be classified as being either primary or secondary and as providing either time-series or cross-sectional data. A ***primary statistical source*** is an original source of data such as that generated from the U.S. Bureau of Census' *Current Population Survey* (CPS) and reported by the U.S. Bureau of Labor Statistics (BLS). You may recall from Chapter 19 that this particular survey samples about 50,000 households nationwide each month to obtain information on labor force participation,

APPENDIX TABLE 1 A SELECTED LIST OF TERM PAPER TOPICS

- Worker Absenteeism
- Multiple Job Holding (Moonlighting)
- The Retirement Decision
- The Social Security Earnings Test
- Female Labor Force Participation Rates
- Discouraged- versus Added-Worker Effects
- Cyclical and Secular Changes in the Average Workweek
- Racial Differences in Labor Force Participation
- Educational Attainment and Earnings, Hours of Work, and Unemployment
- Trends in Labor Force Participation of Older Males
- The Economics of Student Loans
- Criticisms of Human Capital Theory
- Economic Value of Life
- The Firm's Investment in Human Capital: On-the-Job Training
- Corporate Sponsorship of Education
- The Economics of Pensions
- CEO Pay
- Effectiveness of Public-Sector Training Programs
- Monopsony in Labor Markets
- The Market for Nurses
- Occupational Licensing
- Efficiency Wage Theories
- Should Fringe Benefits Be Taxed?
- The Decline of Unionism
- Determinants of Union Membership
- Deregulation and the Labor Market
- Theories of Collective Bargaining
- Collective Bargaining in Professional Sports
- The Economics of Seniority
- Labor-Owned Enterprises
- Incentive Pay Systems
- Employee Stock Option Plans (ESOPs)
- Compulsory Arbitration
- Effects of Right-to-Work Laws
- The Economics of Fringe Benefits
- Pay, Performance, and Productivity
- Unions and Job Turnover
- Economic Impacts of Strikes
- Trends in Government Employment
- Public versus Private Pay
- The Impact of Taxes on Labor Supply
- National Service Plans
- Effects of the Minimum Wage
- Labor Market Impacts of OSHA
- Sexual Harrassment in the Workplace
- Earnings Disparities by Race
- Trends in the Female–Male Earnings Ratio
- Occupational Discrimination
- The Comparable Worth Issue
- Effectiveness of Antidiscrimination Laws
- Compensating Wage Differentials
- Firm Size and Pay Levels
- Two-Tiered Wage Systems
- The Earnings of "Superstars"
- Family Background and Human Capital Investment in Children
- Trends in the Distribution of Earnings
- Unions and the Distribution of Earnings
- Occupational Mobility
- Earnings of Recent Immigrants
- Immigration Reform: Labor Market Issues
- Plant Closures and Displaced Workers
- Are Internal Labor Markets Efficient?
- Trends in Real Wage Rates
- International Comparisons of Real Wages
- The Productivity Slowdown
- International Trends in Productivity Growth
- Trends in Self-Employment
- What Is "Full" Employment
- Theories of Job Search
- Technological Unemployment
- Implicit Contracts: Theory and Implications
- Teenage Unemployment
- Black Unemployment
- The Public Service Employment Issue
- Wage Subsidy Programs
- Rational Expectations and Labor Markets
- The Macroeconomics of Profit Sharing
- Labor Market Effects of Unemployment Insurance Benefits
- International Differences in Unemployment Rates
- Alternative Work Arrangements: Compressed Work, Flextime, and Work Sharing
- The North American Free Trade Agreement and American Labor
- Lifetime Employment in Japan
- Cost-of-Living Adjustment Clauses (COLAs)
- Unemployment and Underemployment in the Developing Countries

employment, and unemployment. The CPS data are replicated or summarized in numerous ***secondary statistical sources*** such as handbooks of statistics, business periodicals, and textbooks. Secondary sources are normally reliable, but you should be aware that they usually present truncated versions of the data. Therefore, you can often obtain more information by going to the primary source.

Labor statistics are reported as time-series data, cross-sectional data, or some combination of the two. ***Time-series data*** are ordered chronologically, that is, by some period of time such as month or year. Examples are Figure 3-2, which graphs population and the labor force since 1950; Table 11-3, which shows the number of work stoppages in the United States for selected years since 1960; and Table 18-1, which chronicles the BLS's annual labor productivity index since 1960.

Cross-sectional data, on the other hand, are measurements of a particular variable at a specific time, but for different economic units or groups. For example, Table 13-2 reports occupational fatalities and injuries in 1995 *by industry.* Similarly, Table 8-3 presents data on the average hourly wage of production workers in 1997 by *selected state,* and Table 19-2 summarizes unemployment rates for specific years *by occupation, race, gender, age, and duration.*

What are the major (primary and secondary) sources of time-series and cross-sectional labor statistics? We will approach this topic by annotating each of the following: Internet sites, bibliographies of statistical sources, print sources of general U.S. statistics, print sources of statistics specific to labor economics, and data sets available from research institutes. Where possible, we paraphrase the descriptions supplied by the sources themselves.[1]

Internet Sites

The Internet contains several excellent sources that provide information and statistics relating to labor economics. We list and annotate these sites in Appendix Table 2. We urge you to "try out" several of the sites listed in the table. (Some of these Internet sites contain full copies of the print sources described below).

Bibliographies of Statistical Sources

Bibliographies of statistical publications index sources of statistical series by topical heading such as the familiar *Reader's Guide to Periodical Literature* lists magazine articles. Just as the *Reader's Guide* contains no articles itself, bibliographies of statistical sources contain no statistical series themselves. These bibliographies or indexes complement the Internet as a good place to begin a search for statistical series. For labor economics, you might fruitfully seek out listings under such topics as unions, employment, labor, and productivity. Of the several bibliographic guides, the following are particularly useful.

[1]Our organization in this section roughly follows that used by Charles Helppie, James Gibbons, and Donald Pearson, *Research Guide in Economics* (Morristown, NJ: General Learning Press, 1974), pp. 69–91.

APPENDIX TABLE 2 INTERNET SITES RELATING TO LABOR ECONOMICS

Asset and Health Dynamics among The Oldest-Old (AHEAD)
[http://www.umich.edu/~hrswww]
Provides survey data that focuses on the relationship between economic and family resources and later life behavior.

Bureau of Economic Analysis
[http://www.bea.doc.gov]
Provides data on GDP and selected tables in the *Survey of Current Business.*

Bureau of Labor Statistics
[http://www.bls.gov]
Includes detailed data on employment, unemployment, prices, productivity, and foreign labor statistics.

Data on the Net
[http://odwin.ucsd.edu/idata]
Permits search by keyword of over 800 Internet sites with downloadable social science statistical data.

Dismal Scientist
[http://www.dismal.com]
Contains data at the national and regional level as well as forecasts of some economic series.

Economic Chart Dispenser
[http://www.economic-charts.com/cgi-bin/charter.exe/CGI?fedstl\currdd]
Provides custom charts of monthly and quarterly data from the Federal Reserve Bank of St. Louis database.

Economic Journals on the Web
[http://www.oswego.edu/~economic/journals/html]
Provides an index to web locations of numerous economics journals.

Economic Report of the President 1998
[http://www.gpo.ucop.edu/catalog/erp98.html]
The entire report for years 1998 and beyond are online. This site also includes statistical tables summarizing important economic data series.

Economic Statistics Briefing Room
[http://www.whitehouse.gov/fsbr/esbr.html]
Contains up-to-date data and historical charts for the major economic data series.

Fedstats
[http://www.fedstats.gov]
Searchable site with links to over 70 Federal agencies with statistical data.

Health and Retirement Survey (HRS)
[http://www.umich.edu/~hrswww]
Provides survey data on the economic, demographic, and health characteristics of individuals.

Immigration and Naturalization Service
[http://www.ins.usdoj.gov/index.html]
Provides comprehensive annual immigration statistics for recent years.

Integrated Public Use Micro Data Center
[http://www.ipums.umn.edu]
Contains census data from 1850 to 1990.

National Labor Relations Board
[http://www.nlrb/gov/]
Contains information about the NLRB and its decisions relating to alleged unfair labor practices of firms and unions.

Mining Co. Guide to Economics
[http://economics.miningco.com]
Provides Internet links to current economics information. For example, it includes links to economic articles in online versions of magazines such as *Business Week.*

Organization for Economic Cooperation and Development
[http://www.oecd.org]
Includes data on selected economic measures for OECD countries.

Panel Study of Income Dynamics
[http://www.isr.umich.edu/src/psid]
Consists of longitudinal data on the characteristics and labor market behavior of the survey respondents.

Resources for Economists on the Internet
[http://rfe.wustl.edu]
Provides links to more than 700 economics related Internet sites.

Social Security Administration
[http://www.ssa.gov]
Provides statistical information on Social Security programs (e.g., benefit formulas, number of beneficiaries, trust funds, average benefits, etc.)

APPENDIX TABLE 2 INTERNET SITES RELATING TO LABOR ECONOMICS *(Continued)*

Statistical Abstract of the United States
[http://www.census/gov/statab/www]
Tables from the statistical abstract are downloadable.

Uncover
[http://www.uncweb.carl.org]
Searchable database of journal articles in economics as well as other fields.

W. E. Upjohn Institute
[http://upjohninst.org]
Provides an online catalogue of their publications as well as working papers.

U.S. Census Bureau
[http://www.census.gov]
Comprehensive site with extensive data on topics such as population, earnings, and demographic characteristics. It also provides all data Census Bureau Publications since January 1996. Finally, it includes links to data extraction from data sources such as the Current Population Survey (CPS), American Housing Survey (AHS), and Public Use of Microdata Samples (PUMS) of the census.

American Statistics Index (Washington, DC: Congressional Information Service). Annual with monthly supplements.

This index provides the most comprehensive print access to U.S. government statistical publications available. It indexes and abstracts all of the statistical publications issued by federal agencies and therefore provides a starting point in searching for specific statistical series.

U.S. Bureau of the Census: *Directory of Federal Statistics for Local Areas: A Guide to Sources* (Washington, DC: U.S. Government Printing Office).

This directory lists sources of federal statistics for metropolitan statistical areas (MSAs). An MSA is a geographic area containing either (1) one city having 50,000 or more inhabitants or (2) an urbanized area of at least 50,000 people *and* a total MSA population of at least 100,000.

U.S. Bureau of the Census: *Statistical Abstract of the United States* (Washington, DC: U.S. Government Printing Office). Appendix, "Guide to Sources of Statistics."

Alphabetically arranged by subject, this appendix contains references to the primary and secondary sources of data summarized in the body of this national data book. Publications listed under each subject are divided into two main groups: "U.S. Government" and "Other."

General Summary Statistics

Several excellent volumes contain summaries of statistical series on a full range of political, economic, social, and demographic variables. These "data books," "statistical abstracts," or "statistical handbooks" contain numerous tables of interest to students of labor economics. A few of the more significant works are the following.

U.S. Bureau of the Census: *Statistical Abstract of the United States* (Washington, DC: U.S. Government Printing Office). Annual

This previously cited annual edition provides comprehensive summaries of statistics on the social, political, and economic organizations of the United States. It draws on both government and private sources, and many of the more than 1,400 tables present statistics relevant to labor and labor markets. A section of particular significance is titled "Labor Force, Employment, and Earnings." Other useful sections are "Population," "Education," and "Federal Government Finances and Employment."

U.S. Bureau of the Census: *Historical Statistics of the United States, Colonial Times to 1970* (Washington, DC: U.S. Government Printing Office). Issued 1976.

This book contains more than 12,500 statistical time series, largely annual, on American social, economic, political, and geographic developments covering periods from 1610 to 1970. This is an excellent source for back-dating series found in the *Statistical Abstract.*

U.S. Office of the President: *Economic Report of the President* (Washington, DC: U.S. Government Printing Office). Annual.

This annual report has an extensive appendix containing statistical data relating to income, the labor force, employment, and production. A section of the appendix that is particularly useful to labor economists is "Population, Employment, Wages and Productivity." Furthermore, the text of the *Report* usually contains sections or chapters pertaining to recent labor market developments. For example, the 1997 *Report* contains an entire chapter on income inequality.

Labor-Specific Statistical Sources

Considerable overlap of tables occurs in the various statistical sources. For example, the *Statistical Abstract of the United States* contains many labor-related series also found in the more specialized sources that we are about to annotate. But in general, labor-specific sources contain a wider range of data and statistical series that relate directly to labor economics. Awareness of these specialized sources is therefore critical for finding data that may not be presented elsewhere. Let's examine several excellent publications.

Eva E. Jacobs (ed.): *Handbook of U.S. Labor Statistics* (Bernan Press, MD: Bernan Press). Periodically.

This publication presents the major series of statistics generated annually by the Bureau of Labor Statistics. The most recent edition (1998) contained tables grouped into the following categories: (1) population, labor force, and employment status; (2) employment and unemployment by industry; (3) hourly and weekly earnings; (4) consumer and producer prices; (5) export and import prices; (6) consumer expenditures by household type; (7) employment costs; (8) productivity; (9) employee benefits; and (10) international comparisons.

Barry T. Hirsch and David A. Macpherson: *Union Membership and Earnings Data Book: Compilations from the Current Population Survey (1998 Edition)* (Washington, DC: Bureau of National Affairs). Annual.

This annual report presents current and historical data on union membership as well as earnings for union and nonunion workers. Breakdowns of these and related measures are provided by state, industry, occupation, and demographic group.

Directory of U.S. Labor Organizations (Washington, DC: Bureau of National Affairs, Inc.). Periodically.

In addition to providing aggregate union membership data for American labor, this publication presents detailed statistics concerning the membership of individual unions and the demographic, occupational, industrial, and geographic characteristics of union members.

U.S. Department of Labor, Bureau of Labor Statistics: *Monthly Labor Review* (Washington, DC: U.S. Government Printing Office). Monthly.

This periodical is a source of current statistics on labor force participation, productivity, employment, unemployment, and consumer prices. An appendix reports the results of the (1) Current Population Survey, (2) Establishment Payroll Survey, and (3) Consumer Price Survey, all of which are conducted monthly.

U.S. Department of Labor, Bureau of Labor Statistics: *Employment and Earnings* (Washington, DC: U.S. Government Printing Office). Monthly.

Employment and Earnings is a monthly publication that provides current information on employment status, characteristics of the employed and unemployed, hours and earnings, productivity, and state and area labor force data. It is worth noting that in 1985 this publication introduced a valuable new series—reported in January issues—showing union membership by age, race, gender, occupation, and industry.

U.S. Department of Labor, Bureau of Labor Statistics: *Compensation and Working Conditions* (Washington, DC: U.S. Government Printing Office). Monthly.

This publication, previously titled *Current Wage Developments,* includes data and brief articles on the total compensation package and other aspects of the work environment, such as major collective bargaining settlements, employer costs for employee compensation, union membership, employee benefits, and area wages.

U.S. Department of Commerce, Bureau of the Census: *Money Income of Households, Families, and Persons in the United States.* Current Population Report P–60. Annual.

This publication, found in libraries that are depositories for federal government publications, reports detailed statistics on the functional and personal distribution of income in the United States. The tables summarize data from the Census Bureau's annual *Current Population Survey.*

International Labour Office: *Yearbook of Labour Statistics* (Geneva, Switzerland: ILO Publications). Annual.

This international yearbook contains time series of labor-related data classified by 180 countries or territories.

Research Institute Survey Data

Several sets of primary data from surveys conducted by research institutes are available to scholars wishing to do original research. Three such sources are the following.

Survey Research Center, Institute for Social Research, University of Michigan: *Health and Retirement Survey.*

This survey, conducted biannually, provides information on aspects of work such as working conditions and earnings for people who were age 51 to 62 in 1992.

Survey Research Center, Institute for Social Research, University of Michigan: *Panel Study on Income Dynamics (PSID).*

This survey provides information on employment, earnings, unemployment, fringe benefits, and so forth. Nearly 5,000 families were first surveyed in 1968 and were interviewed annually each year thereafter. When family members leave home and set up new families, the latter also become part of the annual surveys.

U.S. Department of Labor, Employment and Training Administration: *National Longitudinal Survey (NLS).* Conducted by the Center for Human Resource Research, Ohio State University.

The *NLS* collects information from the same group of people periodically over an extended period of time. It provides information on union status, wages, fringe benefits, job separations, and job satisfaction. The availability of extensive personal information allows researchers to control for such factors as education, age, and parents' income.

Updating and Augmenting Tables

Most of the statistical tables found in *Contemporary Labor Economics* are drawn from the general abstracts or labor-specific statistical sources just discussed. These tables can be updated by noting the source cited for each and then finding the most recent edition of that particular publication. Normally, series found in earlier editions are included somewhere within the new ones. Alternatively, you can update many of these tables via the Internet.

For such purposes as writing term papers, tables in the text may not be sufficiently detailed to meet your needs. But keep in mind that the source cited in the table likely contains many more data than those summarized in the table. For example, Table 9-2 provides statistics of legal immigration into the United States for selected years. By referring to the source, *Statistical Abstract of the United States,* you would discover a wealth of additional information on immigration, for example, (1) immigrants by country of birth and (2) immigrants admitted as permanent residents under refugee acts. Furthermore, you would discover there that a *primary* source of immigration data is the *Statistical Yearbook of the Immigration and Naturalization Service* (Washington, DC: Government Printing Office), or the INS Internet site, both of which contains still more information on this subject.

APPLICATIONS, NEW THEORIES, EMERGING EVIDENCE

Our attention now turns to those sources in which new developments in labor economics are reported. We will annotate numerous professional journals, compendiums of invited essays, and nontechnical publications in the discussion that follows. But first, let's highlight works that provide indexes or bibliographies of labor-related publications.

Indexes and Bibliographies

Several publications help direct interested people toward specific books and journal articles that treat labor economics. Three of the more useful sources are the following:

American Economic Association: *Index of Economic Articles* (Homewood, IL: Richard D. Irwin). Updated via new volumes.

This series contains bibliographic citations to articles from over 250 economics journals, with each volume covering a particular period. For example, Volume I covers the 1886–1924 period while Volume XIX indexes articles published in 1977. This index is not current, however, and thus those interested in recently published articles should consult the source that follows.

American Economic Association: *Journal of Economic Literature (JEL).* Quarterly.

This publication contains (1) review articles of research on particular topics, (2) reviews of selected books, (3) an annotated listing of new books in economics, and (4) a listing of the most recent journal articles, indexed by topic. Brief abstracts are provided for selected journal articles in the list. The "J" listing in the ***Journal of Economic Literature classification system,*** shown in Appendix Table 3, defines subtopics in labor and demographic economics.

Professional Journals

Scholarly journals contain articles in which economists report new theories, new evidence, new techniques for testing established theories, and the like. The main audiences for these articles are other specialists in economics. Therefore, most undergraduates will find the mathematical models and econometric techniques employed to be formidable. However, the basic conclusions of the articles can be gleaned through careful reading.

Articles on labor economics are found in *general* economics journals and labor-specific journals. Examples of the former include *The American Economic Review, Journal of Political Economy, Review of Economics and Statistics, Quarterly Journal of Economics, Brookings Papers on Economic Activity, Economic Inquiry, Journal of Economic Issues, Southern Economic Journal, Canadian Journal of Economics,* and *Oxford Economic Papers.*[2]

[2]For a listing of 107 economics journals, see S. J. Liebowitz and J. P. Palmer, "Assessing the Relative Impacts of Economic Journals," *Journal of Economic Literature,* March 1984, p. 80.

APPENDIX TABLE 3 *JOURNAL OF ECONOMIC LITERATURE* CLASSIFICATION SYSTEM: "J" LISTINGS

J Labor and Demographic Economics

J00 General

J1 Demographic Economics
- J10 General
- J11 Demographic Trends and Forecasts
- J12 Marriage; Marital Dissolution
- J13 Fertility; Child Care; Children
- J14 Economics of the Elderly
- J15 Economics of Minorities
- J16 Economics of Gender
- J17 Value of Life; Forgone Income
- J18 Public Policy
- J19 Other

J2 Time Allocation, Work Behavior, and Employment Determination
- J20 General
- J21 Labor Force and Employment, Size, and Structure
- J22 Time Allocation and Labor Supply
- J23 Employment Determination; Demand for Labor
- J24 Human Capital Formation; Occupational Choice; Labor Productivity
- J26 Retirement; Retirement Policies
- J28 Safety; Accidents; Industrial Health; Job Satisfaction; Related Public Policy
- J29 Other

J3 Wages, Compensation, and Labor Costs
- J30 General
- J31 Wage Level and Structure: Wage Differentials by Skill, Training, Occupation, etc.
- J32 Nonwage Labor Costs and Benefits
- J33 Compensation Packages; Payment Methods
- J38 Public Policy
- J39 Other

J4 Particular Labor Markets
- J40 General
- J41 Contracts: Specific Human Capital, Matching Models, Efficiency Wage Models, and Internal Labor Markets
- J42 Monopsony; Segmented Labor Markets
- J43 Agricultural Labor Markets
- J44 Professional Labor Markets and Occupations
- J45 Public Sector Labor Markets
- J49 Others

J5 Labor–Management Relations, Trade Unions, and Collective Bargaining
- J50 General
- J51 Trade Unions: Objectives, Structure, and Effects
- J52 Dispute Resolution: Strikes, Arbitration, and Mediation
- J53 Labor–Management Relations; Industrial Jurisprudence
- J54 Producer Cooperatives; Labor Managed Firms
- J58 Public Policy
- J59 Other

J6 Mobility, Unemployment, and Vacancies
- J60 General
- J61 Geographic Labor Mobility; Immigrant Workers
- J62 Occupational and Intergenerational Mobility
- J63 Turnover; Vacancies
- J64 Unemployment: Models, Duration, Incidence, and Job Search
- J65 Unemployment Insurance; Severance Pay; Plant Closings
- J68 Public Policy
- J69 Other

J7 Discrimination
- J70 General
- J71 Discrimination
- J78 Public Policy
- J79 Other

The following are important *labor-specific* journals.

New York State School of Industrial and Labor Relations, Cornell University: *Industrial and Labor Relations Review.* Quarterly.

For example, the April 1998 issue presented research on displaced workers, occupational sex segregation, the return to human capital, labor market assimilation of female and male immigrants, and Spanish labor unions. As a second example, a special October 1994 issue focused on the labor market impacts of health insurance.

University of Chicago: *Journal of Labor Economics.* Quarterly.

This journal publishes theoretical and applied research on the supply and demand for labor services, compensation, labor markets, the distribution of earnings, labor demographics, unions and collective bargaining, and policy issues in labor economics.

Basil Blackwell: *Industrial Relations.* Triannually.

This cross-disciplinary international journal is a publication of the Institute of Industrial Relations, University of California at Berkeley. It contains papers and original articles, as well as research notes and "current topic" articles, on the employment relationship.

University of Wisconsin: *Journal of Human Resources.* Quarterly.

This excellent journal publishes articles on the role of education and training in enhancing production skills, employment opportunities, and income, as well as human resource development, health, and welfare policies as they relate to the labor market.

International Labour Office, Geneva, Switzerland: *International Labour Review.* Monthly.

This journal contains articles, comparative studies, and research reports on such topics as employment and unemployment, wages and conditions of work, industrial relations, and workers' participation. Authors are international scholars.

George Mason University: *Journal of Labor Research.* Quarterly.

Articles on labor unions, labor economics, labor relations, and related topics appear in this quarterly. Interdisciplinary studies are common, and many papers have a public policy orientation. Occasionally it includes papers from symposia, conferences, and seminars sponsored by the journal.

North-Holland: *Labour Economics: An International Journal.* Quarterly.

This new international journal publishes research in micro and macro labor economics in a balanced mix of theory, empirical testing, and policy applications. Of particular interest are articles that explain the origin of institutional arrangements of national labor markets and the impacts of these institutions on labor market outcomes.

Basil Blackwell: *British Journal of Industrial Relations.* Triannually.

Articles on labor economics, labor relations, and collective bargaining are published in this British journal. For example, a typical issue contained articles titled

"Management Strategy and the Reform of Collective Bargaining: Cases from the British Steel Corporation"; "Product and Labour Markets in Wage Determination: Some Australian Evidence"; and "The U.S. Automobile Collective Bargaining System in Transition."

New York University: *Labor History.* Quarterly.

This journal is concerned with research in labor history, the impact of labor problems on ethnic and minority groups, theories of the labor movement, comparative analysis of foreign labor movements, studies of specific unions, and biographical portraits of important labor leaders.

Industrial Relations Research Association: *Proceedings of the Industrial Relations Research Association.* Biannually.

These proceedings consist of addresses by distinguished labor experts, contributed papers, and invited papers on topics of interest to industrial and labor relations specialists and practitioners.

Commerce Clearing House: *Labor Law Journal.* Monthly.

This journal contains a survey of important legislative, administrative, and judicial developments in labor law. Articles on subjects pertaining to legal problems in the labor relations field are featured.

Our annotated listing of labor-specific journals is far from exhaustive. Other English-language journals that relate to labor include *Labor Studies Journal, Human Resource Planning, Economic and Industrial Democracy, Women at Work, Journal of Collective Negotiations in the Public Sector, International Journal of Manpower, Journal of Productivity Analysis, Government Union Review, Labour and Society, Japan Labor Bulletin, Journal of Industrial Relations, Work and Occupations,* and *Journal of Population Economics.*

Compendiums of Invited Essays

Several organizations and publishers regularly release edited books that contain invited papers or chapters on current aspects of labor economics. Three examples are as follows.

Research in Labor Economics: A Research Annual (Greenwich, CN: JAI Press). Annual. Solomon Polochek, series editor.

Contributions to this series consist of original papers that are longer than the normal journal articles but shorter than traditional monographs. The series began in 1977. Contributors include many of the more prominent researchers in labor economics.

Industrial Relations Research Association Series. Annual.

The Industrial Relations Research Association (IRRA) annually publishes a book made up of papers on a specific topic. Examples include *Contemporary Collective*

Bargaining in the Private Sector, edited by Paula B. Voos; *The Comparative Political Economy of Industrial Relations,* edited by Kirsten S. Wever and Lowell Turner; and *Employee Representation: Alternatives and Future Directions,* edited by Bruce E. Kaufman and Morris M. Kleiner.

Matthew Bender Publisher: *Proceedings of New York University Conference on Labor.* Annual. Richard Adelman, editor.

This annual publication, which began in 1948, stresses collective bargaining and the labor relations field. Thus, recent volumes contain chapters on developments in labor law, arbitration, worker absenteeism and incompetence, age and gender discrimination, public-sector bargaining, comparable worth, two-tier wage systems, and so forth.

Nontechnical Publications

Although articles in professional journals are useful, their specialized language and esoteric statistical techniques often diminish their accessibility to undergraduate students. Sometimes of greater usefulness are nontechnical books, journals, magazines, and even newspapers that report and summarize recent theory and research.

1 Nontechnical Books Many important books in labor economics are directed to wide audiences, not just labor specialists. Most of the works listed in the "Selected References" at the end of each chapter in this book can be comprehended by readers who are taking, or have completed, the undergraduate labor economics course.

Some publishing houses specialize in publishing analytical books that are accessible to nonspecialists. The W. E. Upjohn Institute of Employment Research (Kalamazoo, Mich.), in particular, is noted for books on timely employment topics. Recent examples are Dave M. O'Neill and June Ellenoff O'Neill, *Lessons for Welfare Reform: An Analysis of the AFDC Caseload and Past Welfare-to-Work Programs;* Stuart Dorsey, Christopher Cornwell, and David Macpherson, *Pensions and Productivity;* and Duane E. Leigh, *Assisting Workers Displaced by Structural Change: An International Perspective.* Also, the Brookings Institution occasionally publishes books of interest to students of labor economics. An example is Gary Burtless (ed.), *A Future of Lousy Jobs?*

2 Hearings Testimony Testimony before congressional committees is a valuable source of information on important research in labor economics. These volumes, published by the U.S. Government Printing Office, are located in libraries that are depositories of federal government publications. While numerous committees hold hearings on legislation relating to labor, two of the more relevant ones are the Senate Human Resources Committee and the House Education and Labor Committee (and subcommittees of each).

3 Nontechnical Journals A few nontechnical journals are also of interest to students of labor economics. The *Monthly Labor Review* mentioned earlier is of particular importance in this regard. It contains informative and readable articles on such topics as labor markets, wages and earnings, fringe benefits, mobility, unionism, and collective bargaining. Also, the AFL-CIO *Federationist* is a good source of information on organized labor's position on policy issues. Third, the May issue of the *American Economic Review* (previously cited) contains papers delivered at the annual meeting of the American Economics Association. Usually one or two sessions of the conference pertain to labor economics, and because presentors are instructed to keep their papers noneconometric, these discussions usually are accessible to undergraduates. Finally, two journals that contain articles on current economic policy issues are worth checking for discussions of labor topics: *Contemporary Policy Issues* and *Journal of Economic Perspectives.*

4 Magazines and Newspapers The "economics" or "labor" sections of popular magazines such as *Business Week, Newsweek, Time,* and *U.S. News and World Report* occasionally contain stories on current labor economics issues. By mentioning economists who have done research on a particular topic, these articles serve as helpful starting points for identifying academic sources. This is also true of newspaper articles, particularly those found in financial papers such as the *Wall Street Journal.* Listed below are a nontechnical magazine devoted exclusively to economics and two important indexes through which one can identify specific nontechnical magazine and newspaper articles.

Challenge: A Magazine of Economic Affairs. Six issues yearly.
Among other things, *Challenge* contains invited articles on economic policy issues, interviews with leading economists, and a comment section called "The Growlery." It is not uncommon for an issue to contain one or two articles pertinent to labor economics. The articles are written by economics experts but are directed toward all people interested in the topics, not just specialists in the field.

Reader's Guide to Periodical Literature, 1900–present.
This familiar reference source provides a cumulative topic index for articles in over 160 U.S. nontechnical, general, and popular magazines.

The Wall Street Journal Index.
Wall Street Journal articles are listed by topic and corporation in this index.

TEXTBOOKS AND RESEARCH SURVEYS

There are several advanced textbooks in the "new" labor economics and numerous undergraduate texts in closely related fields. The former strengthen one's *depth* of understanding of labor economics, while the latter add *breadth* beyond the topics included in this textbook.

Advanced Texts and Surveys

Advanced textbooks presume more knowledge of mathematics, econometrics, and economic theory than this text. Nevertheless, the diligent reader whose preparation in those areas is modest can gain much from them. The following books are particularly useful in this regard.

Addison, John T., and W. Stanley Siebert: *The Market for Labor: An Analytical Treatment* (Santa Monica, CA: Goodyear Publishing Co., 1979).

This book covers many of the topics found in *Contemporary Labor Economics* but treats them with considerably greater analytical rigor. Mathematical appendixes follow several chapters.

Robert F. Elliott: *Labor Economics: A Comparative Text* (London: McGraw-Hill, 1991).

Using extensive graphical analysis and some calculus, this British publication treats the economics of labor markets at a slightly higher level than traditional American undergraduate texts. It also contains many tables comparing labor market data among the industrialized nations.

Joll, Caroline, Chris McKenna, Robert McNabb, and John Shorey: *Developments in Labour Market Analysis* (London: Allen & Unwin, 1983).

This British publication employs a rigorous graphic approach to analyze developments in labor economics. It presupposes that the reader has had several courses in economics, including intermediate microeconomic theory.

Fleisher, Belton M., and Thomas J. Kniesner: *Labor Economics: Theory, Evidence, and Policy,* 3d ed. (Englewood Cliffs, NJ: Prentice-Hall, Inc., 1984).

Exceptionally well written, this advanced textbook assumes that readers have completed intermediate microeconomics and are familiar with quantitative research techniques. Of special interest are the sections entitled "Frontiers of Labor Economics" and the extensive citations in the end-of-chapter "References and Selected Readings" sections.

Ashenfelter, Orley, and Richard Layard (eds.): *Handbook of Labor Economics,* 2 vols. (Amsterdam: North-Holland, 1986).

The 22 chapters of this two-volume advanced survey of labor economics are written by prominent labor economists. In volume I, the supply of labor, the demand for labor, and the wage structure are examined. Volume II looks at labor market equilibrium and frictions and discusses institutional structures of labor markets.

Alison L. Booth: *The Economics of the Trade Union* (Cambridge, England: Cambridge University Press, 1995).

This book surveys, synthesizes, and critically analyzes theoretical and econometric work on the economic effects of unions in the United States and Great Britain.

Texts in Related Fields

High-quality textbooks abound for courses of study related to labor economics. One good way to discover them is to browse in your college bookstore for textbooks required for courses in such fields as collective bargaining, labor law, labor history,

APPENDIX TABLE 4 REPRESENTATIVE TEXTBOOKS, SUBJECTS RELATED TO CONTEMPORARY LABOR ECONOMICS

Collective Bargaining

Mills, D. Q.: *Labor Management Relations,* 5th ed., Irwin/McGraw-Hill, 1993.

Kochan, T. A., and H. C. Katz: *Introduction to Collective Bargaining and Industrial Relations,* Richard D. Irwin, Inc., 1992.

Labor Economics and Labor Relations

Reynolds, L. G., S. H. Masters, and C. H. Moser: *Labor Economics and Labor Relations,* 11th ed., Prentice-Hall, Inc., 1998.

Human Resource Economics

Levitan, S. A., G. Mangum, and R. Marshall: *Human Resources and Labor Markets: Employment and Training in the American Economy,* 3d ed., Harper & Row, Publishers, 1981.

Labor Law

Twomey, D. P.: *Labor Law and Employment Law,* 8th ed., South-Western, 1994.

Taylor, B. J., and F. Witney: *Labor Relations Law,* 6th ed., Prentice-Hall, Inc., 1992.

Social Insurance

Rejda, G. E.: *Social Insurance and Economic Security,* 5th ed., Prentice-Hall, Inc., 1994.

Labor History

Cohen, S.: *Labor in the United States,* 5th ed., Charles E. Merrill Books, Inc., 1979.

Dulles, R. F. and M. Dubofsky: *Labor in America,* 5th ed., Harlan Davidson, 1993.

labor relations, human resource economics, and social insurance. Appendix Table 4 lists several such books by topic. Numerous other texts are available in each of these subject areas and could be identified by visiting with a professor who specializes in the particular field. These textbooks typically are revised on 3- to 5-year cycles.

GLOSSARY

Ability problem The tendency to overestimate rates of return to education if those with more ability tend to obtain more schooling. Earnings differences may reflect differences in ability rather than in education.

Absence rate The ratio of full-time workers with absences from work in a typical work to total full-employment. It is usually expressed as a percentage.

Absolute frequency distribution A graphic portrayal (histogram) of the earnings distribution. The horizontal axis shows the various earnings classes, while the heights of the bars indicate the actual number of earnings recipients which have earnings in the particular class. ***Compare to*** Relative frequency distribution.

Acceptance wage The lowest wage required to induce an individual to accept an employment offer.

Actual labor force Those who are either employed or are unemployed but actively seeking work.

Actual subsidy payment The subsidy received by a participant in an income maintenance plan. It is calculated by multiplying the benefit-reduction rate times the person's earned income and subtracting the product from the plan's basic benefit.

Added-worker effect The change in the labor force that results from other family members entering the labor force when the primary worker loses his or her job.

Administered price A price or wage rate that established institutionally rather than through the market forces of supply and demand.

Affirmative-action programs Policies that establish targets of employment for women and minorities and a timetable for meeting them.

AFL-CIO The American Federation of Labor and Congress of Industrial Organizations. It is the largest U.S. federation of autonomous national unions.

Age-earnings profile A graph showing the earnings level of a specific worker or group of workers at various ages over the life span.

Agents Parties who are hired to help advance the objectives of others. ***Compare to*** Principals.

Aggregate demand curve The curve indicating the total quantity of goods and services consumers, businesses, government, and foreigners are willing and able to purchase at each price level.

Aggregate supply curve The curve indicating the total real output producers are willing and able to provide at each price level.

Average product (AP) Output per unit of labor. It

is found by dividing total product by the number of labor units or may be measured as the slope of a straight line drawn from the origin to a particular point on the total product curve.

Average wage cost The firm's total wage cost divided by the number of units of labor employed. If all workers are paid the same, it is simply the wage rate.

Backloading Structuring a pension plan such that accruals to the plan grow slowly up to a certain age and then rapidly thereafter.

Backward-bending labor supply curve The hours of work supplied as a function of the wage, where the substitution effect dominates at relatively low wages, and the income effect dominates at high wages. In the latter region, the supply curve will be negatively sloped.

Bargaining power A measure of the ability of one side to secure, on its own terms, its opponent's agreement to a labor contact. ***See*** Union bargaining power and Management bargaining power.

Bargaining structure The scope of the employees and employers covered by a collective bargaining agreement; the structure determines who bargains with whom.

Basic benefit The amount of subsidy a household receives from an income maintenance plan if it has no earned income.

Beaten paths Migration routes of previous job changers. The information provided by these movers typically reduces the costs of migration and explains why various racial and ethnic groups may cluster in a given area.

Benefit-reduction rate The rate at which the household's basic income maintenance benefit is reduced as earned income increases.

Bilateral monopoly A market structure consisting of a monopsonist and a strong industrial union. The wage outcome in such a situation is indeterminate.

Blacklist A directory of individuals who were known to be union members or sympathizers. Individuals on the list were often denied employment.

Bonus Payment in addition to the annual salary based upon some factor such as personal, team, or firm performance.

Break-even income The level of income at which the household's subsidy from an income maintenance plan is reduced to zero. It is calculated by dividing the basic benefit by the benefit-reduction rate.

Budget constraint A line plotted on a graph that shows all the combinations of market goods (real income) and leisure that the consumer can obtain at any given wage rate.

Bureau of Labor Statistics productivity index The measure of productivity reported by the Bureau of Labor Statistics. It is found by dividing real gross domestic product for the private sector by private-sector worker hours; it is scaled so as to have a value of 100 in the base year.

Cafeteria plan A fringe benefit package that permits workers to choose among a wide range of particular benefits.

Capital market imperfections The bias against lending money for investments in human capital that occurs largely because human beings cannot be used as collateral for loans.

Capital mobility The movement of capital (plant and equipment) from one region or nation to another in response to higher rates of return on investment.

Chamberlain's bargaining power model A model of the bargaining process developed by Neil Chamberlain that relates union's (management's) bargaining power to its opponent's relative costs of disagreeing and agreeing with the union's (management's) demands.

Churning Mobility of individuals within a static earnings distribution independent of life-cycle effects. ***Compare to*** Life-cycle mobility.

Civil Rights Act of 1964 An act of Congress that, among other things, made it illegal to hire, fire, or discriminate on the basis of race, color, religion, gender, or national origin.

Coalescing power The ability of a bilateral monopoly, through tacit collusion between the monopsonist and the union, to suppress competition in the firm's product market.

Cobweb model A labor market characterized by labor supply adjustments that lag behind changes in demand because of the lengthy training periods required. The path of wages and employment in such models traces out a cobweb pattern when plotted on a supply and demand diagram.

Coercive bargaining tactics Bargaining strategies that increase the opponent's cost of disagreeing.

Collective voice The role of unions as representatives or agents that speak on behalf of their members in negotiating contracts and resolving disputes.

College wage premium The average earnings differential enjoyed by college graduates compared to high school graduates.

Commissions Compensation paid to an agent in proportion to the value of sales.

Commodity As defined by Becker, a combination of goods and time that yields utility to the consumer.

Comparable worth doctrine The notion that females in one occupation should receive the same salaries as males in another if the levels of skill, effort, and responsibility and the working conditions in the two occupations are comparable.

Compensating wage differential The extra amount an employer must pay to "reimburse" a worker for an undesirable job characteristic that does not exist in alternative employment. Also called "wage premium" or "equalizing difference."

Consumer Price Index (CPI) An index number that measures a weighted average of the prices of goods and services consumed by representative consumer families. The percentage change in its level is the most commonly used measure of the rate of inflation.

Cost of agreeing The perceived cost of accepting a bargaining opponent's terms. For the union it is the reduced flow of wage income; for management it is the diminished profits that result from paying higher wages.

Cost of disagreeing The perceived cost of not accepting a bargaining opponent's terms. For the union it is the anticipated loss of wages during a strike; for management it is the potential loss of profits from a strike.

Cost-of-living adjustment (COLA) A labor contract clause that provides for automatic increases in nominal wages when the price level rises.

Countervailing power The ability of a union to offset the power of a monopsonist in bilateral monopoly in such a way that the resulting wage and employment outcome enhances allocative efficiency.

Cross-sectional data A collection of observations of a group of variables at a specific time but for different economic units or groups.

Crowding The segregation of women and minorities into low-paying jobs.

Crowding model A supply and demand model that suggests that if women (minorities) are crowded into "female" ("minority") occupations, their wages will be driven down by the relatively greater supply of labor to such occupations.

D-factor A combination of several personal traits thought to influence an individual's earnings potential. It represents drive, dynamism, doggedness, or determination.

Davis-Bacon Act A law passed in 1931 that requires contractors engaged in federally financed projects to pay prevailing wages, which have primarily been union scale.

Deadline The data of termination of a union contract; the probable starting time of a work stoppage if no agreement is reached.

Deferred payment scheme A method of payment by which workers are paid an amount less than their marginal revenue product early in their careers but are rewarded with wages in excess of their marginal revenue product in later years. Such a scheme may reduce shirking and labor turnover.

Demand-deficient unemployment Unemployment caused by a decline in aggregate demand. Also called "cyclical unemployment."

Demand for human capital curve A curve displaying a negative relationship between the marginal rate of return on investment in human capital and the optimal amount of such investment undertaken.

Derived demand The notion that demand curves for labor and other productive inputs are derived from the demand for the product that they are used to produce. For example, the demand for autoworkers is derived from the demand for automobiles.

Determinants of labor demand Factors that cause shifts in the labor demand curve, as opposed to a movement along the curve. These include product demand, productivity, number of employers, and the prices of other resources.

Determinants of labor supply Factors that cause shifts in the labor supply curve, as opposed to a movement along the curve. These include other wage rates, nonwage income, preferences for work versus leisure, nonwage aspects of jobs, and the number of qualified labor suppliers.

Determinants of migration Those personal and geographic characteristics, such as age, education, wages, and distance, that have an impact on the decision to migrate.

Discount formula The mathematical relationship that defines net present value (V_p) in terms of future values (E_t) and the rate of interest (i):

$$V_p = E_0 + E_1/(1 + i) + E_2/(1 + i)^2 + \dots + E_n/(1 + i)^n$$

Discouraged worker effect The change in the labor force due to job seekers who drop out of the labor force after becoming pessimistic about their chances of finding suitable employment.

Discouraged workers Individuals who have searched unsuccessfully for work, become discouraged, and then abandoned their job search. They are not officially counted as "unemployed" because they are not in the labor force.

Discrimination According inferior treatment with respect to hiring, occupational access, training, promotion, or wages to the members of one group having the same abilities, education, training, and experience as others.

Discrimination coefficient The amount by which a black's (or female's) wage rate is perceived to exceed that of an equally productive white's (or male's). If an employer acts as though the black's (female's) wage is equal to $W + d$, d is the discrimination coefficient.

Discriminatory discharge Dismissal of an employee for participation in union activity.

Displaced workers People who lost their jobs specifically because of permanent plant closings or job cutbacks.

Domestic content rules Requirements that imported products contain a specified portion of domestically produced or domestically assembled components.

Dynamic efficiency The combination of resources that produces goods and services at their lowest possible costs over a long period of time. ***Compare to*** Static efficiency.

Earnings mobility Year-to-year movement by individuals from one portion of the earnings distribution to another.

Economic perspective An analytical approach that assumes that resources are scarce relative to wants, individuals make choices by comparing benefits and costs, and people respond to incentives and disincentives.

Economic rent The return to a factor of production in excess of its opportunity cost. Specifically, the difference between a worker's wage and the wage that would be just sufficient to keep that person in his or her present employment. ***Compare to*** Rent.

Efficiency gains from migration The net increase in total output that accrues to society when labor relocates from regions or nations in which its value of marginal product is relatively low to regions or nations in which it is higher.

Efficiency wage A wage rate that minimizes the employer's cost per effective unit of labor employed.

Efficient allocation of labor The state of the economy achieved when the value of goods and services produced is the highest possible given the amount of labor available. This state occurs when the value of marginal product of a given type of labor is the same in all its potential uses and is equal to its opportunity cost (the price of this type of labor).

Elasticity of labor demand The responsiveness of the quantity of labor demanded to a change in the wage rate.

Employed An individual who is 16 years of age or older, not institutionalized, and at any time during the survey week is *(a)* employed by a firm or government, *(b)* self-employed, or *(c)* has a job but is not working due to illness, inclement weather, vacation, or a labor dispute.

Employee compensation The national income account comprised of wages and salaries, plus payments into social insurance, and worker pension, health, and welfare funds.

Employment Act of 1946 An act of Congress proclaiming the federal government's goal of promoting "maximum employment, production, and purchasing power."

Employment discrimination Higher-than-average unemployment rates for a particular group after adjusting for differences in education and experience.

Employment–population ratio Total employment as a percent of the total noninstitutional population.

Equal Pay Act of 1963 A law that made illegal the payment of unequal wages to women and men for equal work.

Equilibrium wage differential A wage differential that does not cause workers to shift their labor supplies to alternative employments.

Excess demand The excess of quantity demanded over quantity supplied at a given wage rate or price.

Excess supply The excess of quantity supplied over quantity demanded at a given wage rate or price.

Exclusive unionism A union structure wherein the members seek to restrict labor supply by excluding potential workers from participating in the trade or profession.

Exit mechanism The process of leaving one's job as a response to dissatisfaction with present working conditions. ***Compare to*** Voice mechanism.

External benefit A benefit that accrues to a party other than the buyer or seller; also called "social benefit."

External labor market The labor market of orthodox economic theory in which wages and employment are determined by the forces of supply and demand.

Fair Labor Standards Act of 1938 A law that established the legal minimum wage, maximum hours, and mandated time-and-a-half pay for overtime work.

Family and Medical Leave Act of 1993 Legislation that permits workers in firms employing more than 75 workers to take up to 12 weeks a year of unpaid leave to care for a spouse, a child, or their own health. Upon return, those having taken these leaves are guaranteed their original or equivalent positions.

Featherbedding Employment of workers in unnecessary or redundant jobs.

Fiscal policy Deliberate manipulation of federal expenditures and taxes to promote full employment, price stability, and economic growth.

Foreign purchases effect As the domestic price level falls relative to prices abroad, both domestic and foreign consumers will shift their spending toward U.S. goods, thereby increasing the aggregate quantity demanded.

Free-rider problem The incentive for each worker to shirk when individual compensation is based on team performance. As team size grows, each worker's contribution to the team has an increasingly negligible effect on team performance.

Frictional unemployment Unemployment that is due to voluntary quits, job switches, and new entrants or reentrants into the labor force. It is composed of search unemployment and wait unemployment.

Fringe benefits That part of employee compensation other than wages or salary. This includes pensions, insurance benefits, paid vacations, and sick leave.

Full employment The amount of employment consistent with the natural rate of unemployment.

Full Employment and Balanced Growth Act of 1978 A reaffirmation of the Employment Act of 1946, this act also required the federal government to set 5-year employment and price-level goals and design programs to achieve them.

General training The creation of worker skills that are equally valuable in a number of firms or industries.

Geographic mobility Movement of workers from a job in one city, state, or nation to another. This may or may not also involve a change in occupation.

Gini coefficient An arithmetic measure of earnings inequality. It is the area between the Lorenz curve and the diagonal line of perfect equality, divided by the total area beneath the diagonal.

Golden parachute A contract provision that provides for a large lump-sum payoff to executives who lose their jobs as a result of a corporate takeover.

Goods-intensive commodities Those commodities that are comprised of a relatively large amount of goods and a small amount of time. ***Compare to*** Time-intensive commodities.

Government purchases Expenditures by federal, state, and local governments on goods, services, and resources.

Gross complements Inputs such that when the price of one changes, the demand for the other changes in the opposite direction because the output effect exceeds the substitution effect.

Gross substitutes Inputs such that when the price of one changes, the demand for the other changes in the same direction because the substitution effect exceeds the output effect.

Hedonic theory of wages A model of equilibrium wage differentials that hypothesizes that workers maximize the net utility of their employment by trading changes in wages for changes in nonwage job attributes.

Heterogeneous workers and jobs An assumption that not all workers and not all jobs are identical. As a result, wages will differ to compensate for job and worker differences.

Histogram *See* Absolute frequency distribution.

Homogeneous workers and jobs An assumption that all workers and all jobs have identical characteristics. If information were perfect and mobility costless, all workers would receive the same real wage.

Hot-cargo clause A labor contract provision that states that trucking firms will not require unionized truckers to handle or transport products made by an employer involved in a labor dispute. Such clauses were made illegal by the Landrum-Griffin Act of 1959.

Household Survey A monthly survey conducted by the Bureau of Labor Statistics to determine the number of people who are employed, unemployed, or not in the labor force; also called the "Current Population Survey."

Human capital The accumulation of prior investments in education, on-the-job training, health, and other factors that increase productivity.

Human capital discrimination Unequal access to productivity-increasing opportunities such as formal schooling or on-the-job training.

Human capital investment demand curve The relationship between human capital investment and the marginal rate of return on that investment. It reflects the (individual) optimal amount invested at any given opportunity cost of funds.

Human capital investment supply curve The relationship between human capital investment and the marginal opportunity cost of funds required to finance that investment.

Illegal aliens Individuals who unlawfully immigrate into the United States, usually to work; also called "undocumented workers."

Immediate-market-period labor supply curve A vertical line at the number of workers attracted into a given market by the current wage rate. This number is derived from the "Long-run supply curve" ***(see).***

Immigration Reform and Control Act of 1986 A sweeping immigration reform bill that granted amnesty to certain illegal aliens, provided for sanctions on employers who knowingly hire illegal aliens, and allowed temporary farm workers into the country to harvest perishable crops.

Implicit contract An informal, often unstated, understanding between workers and their firms concerning compensation and working conditions. Both workers and firms behave in ways to ensure that terms of the contract are heeded, making the contract self-enforcing.

In-kind benefits Benefits that take the form of a specific good or service rather than money; insurance benefits, for example, or a company car.

Incentive pay plan A compensation scheme that ties workers' pay directly to performance. Such plans may include piece rates, commissions and royalties, raises and promotions, bonuses, profit sharing, and tournament pay.

Inclusive unionism A union structure wherein the members seek to include all workers employed in a specific industry.

Income effect The change in the desired hours of work resulting from a change in income, holding the wage rate constant.

Income elasticity The percentage change in quantity demanded divided by the percentage change in income.

Income tax A broad-based tax on income received from many sources, not just wages and salaries.

Indeterminacy problem The notion that, if a change in the wage rate changes labor productivity, the position of the labor demand curve becomes indeterminate.

Index of Compensation per Hour (ICH) An index number that measures average hourly compensation of workers, including employer contributions to Social Security and private fringe benefits. The percentage change in its level is a measure of wage inflation.

Index of segregation The percentage of women (minorities) who would have to change occupations in order for them to be distributed across occupations in the same proportion as men (whites).

Indifference curve A curve that shows the various combinations of two goods (real income and leisure or cash wages and fringe benefits) that will yield some given level of utility or satisfaction to the individual.

Indifference map A set of indifference curves that collectively specify an individual's preferences for two goods such as income and leisure or cash wages and fringe benefits.

Inferior good A product for which the quantity demanded falls when income rises.

Inflation A rising general level of prices in the economy.

Infrastructure A nation's stock of public capital such as highways, airports, harbors, and power plants.

Injunction A court order to stop a particular activity, especially a strike, boycott, or picketing.

Insider–outsider theories Theories that purport to explain downward wage rigidity and thus cyclical unemployment on the basis of the relationships between incumbent workers ("insiders") and unemployed workers ("outsiders") who might be expected to bid down the wage rate to obtain employment.

Interest rate effect As the price level falls, the demand for money falls, which in turn reduces interest rates. The subsequent rise in spending on interest-sensitive goods and services increases the aggregate amount of output demanded.

Internal labor market A firm or other administrative unit characterized by job ladders. Except for those at the port of entry, jobs are shielded from competitive market pressures in that wages and employment are determined by administrative rules and procedures rather than by the forces of supply and demand.

Internal rate of return *(r)* That rate of discount that equates the present value of future costs and benefits. An investment is profitable if its internal rate of return exceeds the marginal opportunity cost of the funds as measured by the interest rate *(i)*.

Investment in human capital Any action taken to increase the productivity (by improving the skills and abilities) of workers; expenditures made to improve the education, health, or mobility of workers.

Isocost curve A curve showing the various combinations of capital and labor that can be purchased with a given outlay, given the prices of capital and labor.

Isoprofit curve A curve portraying the various combinations of wages and fringe benefits (or some other nonwage amenity) that yield a specific level of profits.

Isoquant A curve showing the various combinations of capital and labor that are capable of producing a specific quantity of total output.

Job evaluation The procedure by which jobs are ranked and wage rates assigned in terms of a set of job characteristics and worker traits.

Job ladder A sequence of jobs within an internal labor market, beginning at a port of entry and progressing through higher levels of skill, responsibility, and wages.

Job search model A theory of how workers and firms acquire information concerning employment prospects.

Joint monopsony *See* Monopsony.

***Journal of Economic Literature* classification system** The system used to classify subfields within economics. The "J" classification identifies labor economics.

Labor economics The field of economics that examines the organization, functioning, and outcomes of labor markets; the decisions of prospective and present labor market participants; and the public policies relating to the employment and payment of labor resources.

Labor force participation rate The percentage of the potential force that is either employed or unemployed.

Labor hoarding The practice by which firms retain more workers during recessions than would be technically necessary, specifically "overhead" workers such as executives, managers, and skilled laborers on whom the firms have spent large sums to recruit and train.

Labor immobilities Geographic, institutional, or sociological barriers to labor mobility. These barriers are a major reason why wage differentials occur and persist.

Labor turnover The rate at which workers quit their jobs, necessitating their replacement by new workers.

Landrum-Griffin Act of 1959 An amendment to the Wagner Act that declared "hot-cargo clauses" illegal, required regularly scheduled elections of union officers, excluded communists and convicted felons from holding union office, held union officers accountable for union funds and property, and prevented union leaders from infringing on individual workers' rights to participate in the governance of the union.

Law of diminishing marginal returns The principle that if technology is unchanged, as more units of a variable resource are combined with one or more fixed resources, the marginal product of the variable resource must eventually decline.

Least-cost combination of capital and labor The point of tangency of an isocost line to a given isoquant. At this point the marginal rate of technical substitution equals the ratio of the price of labor to the price of capital.

Life-cycle mobility The movement of specific individuals within the income distribution over their lifetimes. ***Compare to*** Churning.

Line of perfect equality The Lorenz curve that would result if all individuals in the economy had the same earnings. It is a diagonal line through the origin.

Local union The basic unit of organized labor. Its main functions are administering the labor contract and resolving worker grievances.

Lockout A plant closedown used as a means of imposing costs on workers who are engaged in union-organizing activity or any other union activity such as a strike.

Long run A period of time sufficient for the firm to vary the levels of all of its factors of production.

Long-run demand for labor The schedule or curve indicating the amount of labor that firms will employ at each possible wage rate when all factors of production are variable.

Long-run supply curve In the cobweb model, this curve indicates the eventual response of labor suppliers to changes in the wage rate.

Lorenz curve A graphical depiction of the earnings distribution. It indicates the cumulative percentage of all wage and salary earners (ranked from lowest to highest earnings) on the horizontal axis; the vertical axis measures the corresponding cumulative percentage of earnings accruing to that group.

Macroeconomics The subfield of economics concerned with the economy as a whole or with basic aggregates that comprise the economy.

Management bargaining power (MBP) The ratio of the union's "cost of disagreeing" ***(see)*** to its "cost of agreeing" ***(see).***

Managerial-opposition hypothesis The notion that increased managerial opposition to unions has lead to the decline in union membership and growth.

Marginal cost (benefit) of safety The cost (benefit) to the firm of increasing job safety by 1 unit.

Marginal internal rate of return The internal rate of return ***(see)*** on additional human capital. Optimal investment occurs where the marginal internal rate of return equals the marginal opportunity cost of the funds.

Marginal product (MP) The change in total product that results from changing labor input by 1 unit.

Marginal rate of substitution of leisure for income (MRS *L,Y*) The amount of income one must give up to compensate for the gain of 1 more unit (hour) of leisure.

Marginal rate of technical substitution of labor for capital (MRTS, *L,K*) The amount by which capital must decline when labor is increased by 1 unit along an isoquant (equal output curve); the absolute value of the slope of an isoquant.

Marginal resource cost (MRC) The change in the firm's total cost that results from changing its employment of a particular resource by 1 unit. It is equal to the per unit cost of the resource in competitive input markets.

Marginal revenue product (MRP) The change in total revenue that results from changing labor input by 1 unit.

Marginal wage cost (MWC) The change in the firm's total wage cost that results from changing labor input by 1 unit. It is equal to the wage rate in competitive labor markets.

Market demand for labor The relationship between the quantity of labor demanded by all firms employing a given type of labor and the wage rate for this labor. It is assumed that the amount of labor employed at various wages may have an impact on product price, which is held constant in the derivation of the individual firm's demand for labor.

Market power (monopsony) model A model of employer profit-maximizing behavior whereby groups with lower elasticities of labor supply are paid lower wages.

Market sector That part of the private sector consisting of the millions of small businesses. Firms in this sector are subject to strong competitive forces and have few economies of scale. This sector is associated primarily with the secondary labor market. ***Compare to*** Planning sector.

Master agreement A contract struck between management and one or more local unions that then applies to workers in all of the firm's plants.

Mean The arithmetic average of a distribution. With respect to earnings, it is found by dividing total earnings by the number of earnings recipients.

Measured union wage advantage ***See*** Union wage advantage.

Median The midpoint of a distribution. With respect to earnings, half earn less and half earn more.

Mexican Border Industrialization Plan A program intended to reduce inflows of Mexican workers into the United States by allowing U.S. companies to ship materials duty-free across the border for assembly; the goods are returned for sale, taxed at relatively low rates.

Microeconomics The subfield of economics concerned with the decisions of individual economic units and the functioning of specific markets.

Midpoints formula A method employed to calculate the elasticity coefficient:

$$E_d = \frac{(Q_2 - Q_1)/(\text{average } Q)}{(W_2 - W_1)/(\text{average } W)}$$

Military conscription A method of obtaining labor resources for military service that relies on the ability of government to compel persons to serve. The alternative is a volunteer or market-based military.

Minimum wage A legally specified minimum rate of pay for labor employed in covered occupations.

Mode That class of a distribution with the greatest frequency.

Monetary policy Deliberate manipulation of the money supply by the Federal Reserve Bank, intended to promote full employment, price stability, and economic growth.

Monitoring Employing supervisors and using other methods to determine which workers, if any, are shirking.

Monopoly power The ability of a firm to set its price, rather than being forced to accept a market-determined price.

Monopsony A labor market in which a single firm is the sole employer of a particular type of labor (pure monopsony), or when two or more firms, through collusion, act as the sole employer of a particular type of labor (joint monopsony).

Moral-hazard problem As it relates to workers' compensation insurance, the tendency of workers to be less careful in their jobs, knowing they are insured against workplace accidents.

MRP = MWC rule A rule specifying the profit-maximizing level of labor employment. With capital fixed, profits are maximized when labor is employed to the point where MRP = MWC.

Multiemployer bargaining A bargaining structure in which employers in a particular industry organize as a group to bargain with the union.

Multifactor approach A method of explaining the earnings distribution that accounts for innate ability, family background, risk taking, chance, and many other factors in addition to schooling and on-the-job training.

National Labor Relations Board A group of individuals empowered by the Wagner Act to ensure that its provisions are carried out.

National union A federation of local unions that typically are either in the same industry or the same skilled occupation.

Natural rate of unemployment *(a)* The unemployment rate at which there is neither excess demand nor excess supply in the aggregate labor market; *(b)* the unemployment rate that will occur in the long run if expected and actual rates of inflation are equal. Currently estimated to be about 5.5 percent.

Net present value The dollar difference between streams of future costs and benefits of an investment that have been discounted to the present at some appropriate rate of interest. ***See*** Discount formula.

Noncompeting groups Categories of labor market participants whose members, because of differences in education, training, and skill, are imperfect labor market substitutes for members of other groups.

Normal-profit isoprofit curve The isoprofit curve consistent with zero economic profits.

Norris-LaGuardia Act of 1932 A law that severely limited the use of injunctions to enjoin labor union activity and outlawed yellow-dog contracts ***(see).***

Occupational discrimination Arbitrarily restricting or prohibiting the members of a group from entering certain occupations even though the group members have the requisite skills; also called "job discrimination."

Occupational licensure Laws or regulations by a governmental unit that workers meet certain requirements to practice a specific trade or profession. Tests, standards, and other requirements are established that often have the effect of restricting labor supply to the licensed occupation.

Occupational Safety and Health Act of 1970 Legislation that created the Occupational Safety and Health Administration (OSHA), an agency that establishes and enforces workplace health and safety standards.

Old Age, Survivors, Disability, and Health Insurance (OASDHI) A government transfer program. Commonly referred to as the Social Security system, it is financed through a payroll tax on employers and employees.

On-the-job training The accumulation of skills acquired while working at a job.

Optimal wage rate–job safety combination The point of tangency between the worker's highest attainable indifference curve and an employer's normal-profit isoprofit curve.

Optimal work–leisure position That point on the worker's budget constraint at which the marginal rate of substitution of leisure for income is equal to the wage rate. At this point the budget constraint is tangent to the individual's highest attainable indifference curve.

Output effect The change in labor input resulting from the effect of a change in the wage rate on the firm's cost of production and the subsequent change in the desired level of output.

Overemployment A situation in which the worker could increase utility by taking more leisure and less income; a level of work where the marginal rate of substitution of leisure for income exceeds the wage rate.

Pattern bargaining A bargaining structure in which a union negotiates a contract with a particular firm in an industry and then seeks to impose similar terms on all other employers in that industry.

Payroll tax A tax on the amount of wages and salaries received.

Pecuniary externality Effects of private actions that impose monetary costs or benefits on third parties. Such externalities do not affect economic efficiency but rather redistribute a constant real income.

Perfectly competitive labor market A labor market characterized by a large pool of similarly qualified workers independently offering their labor services to a large number of firms, none of which has the power to influence the wage rate. Workers and firms have perfect information, and mobility is costless.

Personal distribution of income The division of income among households and individuals.

Persuasive bargaining tactics Bargaining strategies that decrease the opponent's cost of agreeing.

Piece rates Compensation paid in proportion to the number of units of personal output.

Planning sector That part of the private sector consisting of the largest major corporations that carry on the bulk of economic activity. This sector is associated with the primary labor market. ***Compare to*** Market sector.

Port of entry The link between the external market and a job ladder within the internal labor market. The market forces of supply and demand determine wages at this lowest level of a job ladder, and those who obtain jobs here are allowed future access to the higher job levels in the internal labor market.

Potential labor force All noninstitutionalized persons age 16 and over; also called the "age-eligible population."

Prevailing-wage rule The practice by governments of setting public employee wage rates equal to those received by comparably trained and employed private-sector workers; also called "the comparable-wage rule."

Price of labor (*P_L*) The marginal value of alternative work, non-labor market production, or leisure for a given type of labor. P_L measures the opportunity cost of labor.

Primary statistical source An original source of data, such as the *Current Population Survey.*

Principal–agent problem A conflict of interest that occurs when agents pursue their own objectives to the detriment of meeting the principal's objectives.

Principals Parties who hire others to help them advance their objectives. ***Compare to*** Agents.

Product market effect The increase in nonunion wages that is caused by consumer demand shifting away from relatively higher-priced union-produced goods and toward relatively lower-priced goods produced by nonunion workers.

Production function The relationship between the various quantities of inputs and the corresponding output, assuming the resources are combined in a technically efficient manner.

Productivity Output per unit of input; it is a measure of efficiency of resource use.

Profit sharing A compensation scheme that allocates a specified portion of a firm's profits to employees.

Progressive tax A tax for which the rate increases with the size of the tax base (particularly if income is the base).

Proprietor's income The national income account comprised of income received by owners of unincorporated businesses (sole proprietorships and partnerships).

Pure complements in production A pair of resources, such as capital and labor, that must be used in direct proportion to one another in producing output. Pure complements in production are always gross complements.

Pure monopsony ***See*** Monopsony.

Pure public goods Collectively consumed goods or services. For these products use by one person does not diminish the amount available for another's consumption. An example is national defense.

Pure union wage advantage ***See*** Union wage advantage.

Quality circles Joint labor–management committees on productivity.

Quasi-fixed resource A productive resource that has some of the characteristics of both fixed and variable factors. Once made, specific training investments are fixed costs to the firm; thus, workers with such training constitute quasi-fixed resources.

Quota Limits on the quantity or total value of specific imported goods.

Real balance effect As the price level falls, the real value of dollar-denominated assets increases. This increase in wealth increases consumption spending and the aggregate amount of output demanded.

Real externality Effects of private actions that spill over to third parties, either adding to (external benefits) or detracting from (external costs) economic efficiency.

Real wage Worker earnings expressed in terms of purchasing power. It is found by dividing the money or nominal wage by the average price level.

Relative frequency distribution A graphic portrayal (histogram) of the earnings distribution. The horizontal axis shows the various earnings classes, while the heights of the bars indicate the percentage of the total number of earnings recipients that have earnings in the particular class. ***Compare to*** Absolute frequency distribution.

Relative share The proportion of national income accruing to a particular productive factor.

Rent The return to nonreproducible resources (land) that are provided in fixed quantities in nature. ***Compare to*** Economic rent.

Rent provision Practices, particularly by government, that yield economic rent to a specific group or individual. Examples include the minimum wage and occupational licensure.

Rent-seeking activity Actions by individuals or specific groups that have the effect of increasing their economic rent.

Reservation wage The highest wage rate at which an individual chooses not to work; the lowest wage rate at which an individual chooses to enter the labor market.

Right-to-work laws State laws (protected by Section 14b of the National Labor Relations Act) that make union shop and agency shop agreements illegal.

Royalties An amount, proportional to sales, paid in compensation for allowing an agent to market the principal's product.

Screening hypothesis The view that education only identifies individuals who are trainable or of high ability rather than increasing productivity per se.

Secondary boycott Actions by a union to refuse to handle or to get an employer to refuse to buy products made by a firm that is party to a labor dispute. ***See*** Hot-cargo clause.

Secondary statistical source A source that contains data from original sources in abridged or truncated form, such as the *Statistical Abstract of the United States.*

Self-selection A type of statistical bias encountered when the effects of individual choices are improperly measured or unaccounted for. For example, if people with more ability are more likely to obtain high earnings, independently of education, and also are more likely to obtain education, failing to account for differences in ability will tend to overstate the effects of education on earnings. With respect to immigration, the notion that those who choose to move tend to have greater motivation for economic gain or greater willingness to sacrifice current for future consumption than those of similar skills who choose not to migrate.

Seniority A system of granting economic amenities (higher wage rates, better jobs, protection from layoff) based on length of service (job tenure).

Shift work Work done at night, as opposed to during usual daytime work hours.

Shirking Attempts by workers to increase utility by taking unauthorized breaks or by giving less than agreed-upon effort during work hours; the act of neglecting or evading work.

Shock effect The upward shift in the marginal product schedule that results from managerial responses to an increase in the wage rate.

Short run A period of time sufficiently short that the quantity of capital employed by the firm cannot be varied.

Short-run labor demand curve The schedule or curve indicating the amount of labor that firms will employ at each possible wage rate assuming a fixed capital stock. It is that part of the marginal revenue product curve that is positive and lies below the average revenue product curve.

Skill differential The difference in wages between skilled and unskilled workers.

Skill transferability The ability of skills that are appropriate for one job or location to apply in another job or location.

Specific training The creation of worker skills that are of value only to the particular firm providing the training.

Spillover effect The decline in nonunion wages that results from displaced union workers supplying their services in nonunion labor markets.

Static efficiency The combination of resources of a fixed quality that produces output at the lowest possible cost at a given point in time. ***Compare to*** Dynamic efficiency.

Statistical discrimination Judging an individual on the basis of the average characteristics of the group to which he or she belongs rather than on his or her personal characteristics.

Stochastic theories Theories of income distribution that are based on change rather than individual choice or institutional structure.

Stock-flow model A model of labor flows into and out of various categories of labor force status. It is used to analyze changes in the unemployment rate.

Straight-time equivalent wage The wage that would yield the same income at the same number of hours as the income and hour combination actually chosen by an individual paid an overtime premium.

Strikebreaker A nonunion worker hired by the firm to continue operations during a strike.

Structural-change hypothesis The notion that changes in the composition of the labor force and the industrial mix have led to the decline in union growth and membership.

Structural unemployment Unemployment due to a mismatch between the skills required for available job openings and the skills possessed by those seeking work; a geographical mismatch between jobs and job seekers; displaced workers.

Subemployed Those who are forced by economic circumstances to work in occupations that pay lower wages than those for which they would qualify in periods of full employment.

Subminimum training wage A legally specified minimum rate of pay for teenagers established below the minimum rate for older workers.

Subsidy A transfer payment provided to consumers or producers of a specific good or service.

Substitutes in production A pair of inputs, such as capital and labor, such that a given amount of output can be produced with many different combinations of the two. Substitutes in production will be gross substitutes if the substitution effect outweighs the output effect; the inputs will be gross complements if the output effect outweighs the substitution effect.

Substitution effect As it relates to labor supply, the change in the desired hours of work resulting from a change in the wage rate, keeping income constant. As it relates to production, the change in employment resulting solely from a change in the relative price of labor, output being held constant.

Substitution hypothesis The notion that benefits provided by the government and some employers have substituted for their provision by unions, leading to the decline in union growth and membership.

Superior-worker effect The increase in average union wages that arises when union employers carefully screen prospective employees and hire only the most productive workers. This practice is made possible by the queuing of employees for the higher-paying union jobs.

Supply of investment funds A schedule or curve showing the relationship between the marginal opportunity cost of investment funds (the interest rate) and the amount of such funds made available for financing various levels of human capital.

Symbiotic relationship In collective bargaining the notion that both parties to the bargain must cooperate with one another to reach an agreement but compete directly to determine the distribution of the gains from their cooperation.

Taft-Hartley Act of 1947 An amendment to the Wagner Act, it established unfair labor practices on the part of unions, regulated the internal administration of unions, outlawed the closed shop while upholding state "right-to-work" laws, and established emergency strike provisions.

Tariff An excise duty on an imported good.

Taste-for-discrimination model A theory of discrimination developed by Gary Becker that views discrimination as a preference for which employers are willing to pay.

Tax incidence The economic location of the burden of a tax, or the determination of who ultimately pays a tax. The redistributive effects of a tax.

Threat effect The increase in nonunion wage rates that a nonunion employer offers as a response to the threat of unionization.

Time-intensive commodities Those commodities that are comprised of a relatively large amount of time and a small amount of goods. ***Compare to*** Goods-intensive commodities.

Time preference The notion that most people prefer present consumption to future consumption.

Time rates Compensation paid in proportion to time worked such as hours, months, or years.

Time-series data A collection of observations of a group of variables ordered sequentially with respect to time.

Total compensation The sum of wage earnings and the value of fringe benefits.

Total factor productivity Output per standardized unit of combined labor and capital input.

Total product (TP) The total output of the firm, expressed as a function of labor input.

Total wage bill The total wage cost to the firm; the wage rate multiplied by the quantity of labor hours employed.

Total wage bill rules Rules for determining the elasticity of labor demand. Labor demand is elastic (inelastic) if a change in the wage rate causes the total wage bill to move in the opposite (same) direction. If labor demand is unit elastic, then the total wage bill remains constant when the wage rate changes.

Tournament pay A compensation scheme that bases payments on relative performance. Typically, first prize is very high, with subsequent prizes sinking rapidly for ranks below the top. If everyone aspires to the top, productivity in the lower ranks is enhanced.

Transfer payment A government expenditure that merely reflects a transfer of income from government to households. Recipients perform no productive activities in exchange.

Transitional wage differential Short-run wage differences that arise from imperfect and costly information as labor markets move toward final equilibrium.

Underemployment A situation in which the worker could increase utility by taking less leisure and more income; a level of work wherein the wage rate exceeds the marginal rate of substitution of leisure for income. This term may also refer to a situation in which the worker is employed in a position for which he or she is overqualified.

Unemployed An individual who is 16 years of age or older, is not institutionalized, did not work during the previous week but was available for work, and *(a)* has engaged in some specific job-seeking activity within the previous 4 weeks, *(b)* is waiting to be called back to a job from which she or he has been laid off, *(c)* would have been looking for a job but was temporarily ill, or *(d)* is waiting to report to a new job within 30 days.

Unemployment rate The percentage of the labor force that is unemployed. It is the ratio of total unemployment to the total labor force, where the latter is the sum of employment and unemployment.

Union bargaining power (UBP) The ratio of management's "cost of disagreeing" ***(see)*** to its "cost of agreeing" ***(see)***.

Union shop clause A bargaining agreement that specifies that nonunion workers may be hired but requires that all employees must join the union or pay union dues following a probationary period, usually 60 days.

Union wage advantage The percentage amount by which the union wage exceeds the nonunion wage. The *measured union wage advantage* is $(W_u - W_n)/W_n \times 100$, where W_u is the observed union wage and W_n is the observed nonunion wage. The *pure union wage advantage* is computed in the same manner, but W_n is the nonunion wage that would be observed in the absence of the union.

Unit labor cost Total labor cost divided by the quantity of output. It is alternatively computed as the wage rate divided by labor productivity.

Utility The ability of goods or leisure to satisfy wants: want-satisfying power.

Value of marginal product (VMP) The change in the total value of output that results to society from changing labor input by 1 unit. VMP equals the price of the product times the marginal product ($P \times$ MP).

Vesting Acquiring legal rights to the benefits of the worker's pension plan, irrespective of whether employment is continued.

Voice mechanism The process of using communication channels between the employer and employees to express dissatisfaction with present working conditions. Typically, these channels are institutionalized through collective bargaining and union grievance procedures. ***Compare to*** Exit mechanism.

Voluntary or market-based army An army in which the requisite number of military personnel are attracted through payment of wage rates that are sufficiently high to cover the opportunity costs of those taking the jobs.

Wage bill The total amount of wages paid by the firm; the wage rate times the number of worker hours.

Wage discrimination Basing wage rate differentials upon considerations other than productivity differentials.

Wage elasticity coefficient (E_d) A measure of the responsiveness of the quantity of labor demanded to a change in the wage rate. E_d equals the percentage change in the quantity of labor demanded divided by the percentage change in the wage rate.

Wage elasticity of labor supply *(E_s)* A measure of the responsiveness of the quantity of labor supplied to a change in the wage rate. E_s equals the percentage change in the quantity of labor supplied divided by the percentage change in the wage rate.

Wage–fringe optimum The composition of total compensation that provides maximum attainable utility to the worker.

Wage narrowing The overall impact on wages in both the area of origin and area of destination as a result of migration. Wages tend to rise in the (initially low wage) origin and fall in the (initially high wage) destination area.

Wage-push inflation An increase in the general level of prices due primarily to decreases in aggregate supply, specifically when total worker compensation rises faster than productivity.

Wage structure The observed wage differentials of the economy, broken down by industry, occupation, geographical location, or other job or worker differences.

Wage subsidy A direct payment or a reduction in taxes from the government to a firm that expands its employment of low-wage or structurally unemployed workers.

Wagner Act of 1935 (National Labor Relations Act) A law that guaranteed the rights of self-organization and collective bargaining, outlined unfair labor practices on the part of management, established the National Labor Relations Board, and made strikes by federal employees illegal.

Wait unemployment The excess supply of workers that results from nonmarket-clearing wage rates. Workers displaced by union wage gains may prefer unemployment with the likelihood of regaining union employment to employment at the lower nonunion wage rate. Also, the unemployed workers who are forced by efficiency wage payments to wait for jobs to open.

Work–leisure optimum The combination of leisure and income that provides the maximum attainable total utility. The point at which the worker is on the highest possible indifference curve given the budget constraint.

Yellow-dog contract A labor contract clause that as a condition of continued employment, prohibited workers from joining a union. These clauses were declared unenforceable by the Norris-LaGuardia Act of 1932.

Zone of production Stage II of the production function. Those quantities of labor input beyond the point of maximum average product but prior to a negative marginal product. In this stage, changes in labor input contribute to increase efficiency by either labor or capital.

ANSWERS TO "YOUR TURN" QUESTIONS

Your Turn 1-1: The second statement reflects the economic perspective. Those retiring at age 65 are comparing costs and benefits—that is, responding to incentives and disincentives. Although retirees sacrifice their work earnings, they gain private pension benefits, Social Security benefits, and added leisure, which more than compensate for these foregone earnings.

Your Turn 2-1: If the slope of the budget line is steeper than the slope of the indifference curve that it intersects, the worker should work more hours than those identified by the intersection. Working more hours will allow the person to achieve greater total utility (attain a higher indifference curve). The worker will maximize total utility where the slopes of the budget line and the highest attainable indifference curve are equal.

Your Turn 2-2: When a worker's wage rate declines and the income effect dominates the substitution effect, the person will work more hours. The backward-bending portion of the labor supply curve is the relevant segment here.

Your Turn 2-3: Other things being equal, we would prefer jobs where we can select our work hours. That way we can choose to work the precise number of hours that will maximize our total utility. This optimal number of work hours may differ from that prescribed by an employer. Employer-required hours can lead to either underemployment or overemployment; worker-determined hours cannot.

Your Turn 3-1: The fact that women's real wages and rates of labor force participation have simultaneously increased implies that the Becker substitution effect has exceeded the Becker income effect.

Your Turn 3-2: The labor force size in this hypothetical nation is 60 million (= 53 million employed *plus* 7 million unemployed who are actively seeking work). The potential labor force is 85 million (= 60 million in the labor force *plus* 25 million eligible persons who are not in the labor force). The LFPR is 70.6 percent [= (60 million/85 million) × 100].

Your Turn 4-1: If the net present value of an investment is highly positive, then the internal rate of return on the investment typically exceeds the interest cost of borrowing funds to finance the investment.

Your Turn 4-2: The marginal rate of return, r, is indeed the same for each person at the optimal level of education. Both r's equal the cost of borrowing, i. But the person with more ability has a greater r at any particular level of education, leading that person to obtain more education than the individual with less ability.

Your Turn 4-3: MBA education is mainly general training that is applicable to numerous employers. The firm's employees probably indirectly pay for this training through lower dollar salaries than would be paid without this fringe benefit.

Your Turn 5-1: In the competitive situation, MRP is \$32 (= 8 units × the price of \$4). Where there is monopoly, MRP will be less than \$32. The firm's marginal revenue from each of the extra 8 units sold will be less than \$4.

Your Turn 5-2: The high wages paid autoworkers may have accelerated the substitution of industrial robots for workers (substitution effect). Also, these high wages may have contributed to the cost advantage experienced by Japanese auto producers. Partly because of this cost advantage, imports of autos from Japan surged and employment in the American auto industry declined (output effect).

Your Turn 5-3: Capital and labor are gross complements in this scenario. The decline in the price of capital increased the amount of capital purchased, which increased the demand for labor. The output effect of the decline in the price of capital exceeded the substitution effect.

Your Turn 6-1: The increase in labor supply will reduce the market wage rate [the perfectly competitive firms' marginal wage cost (MWC)]. This decline in MWC will entice firms to employ more units of labor. They will stop adding new workers when MRP declines sufficiently to equal the new lower wage rate (= MWC). Equilibrium will be restored where MRP = MWC.

Your Turn 6-2: The monopsonist's MWC curve lies above the market labor supply curve because the monopsonist must pay a higher wage to attract an extra worker and must pay this higher wage to all workers, including those whom otherwise could have been paid less. Monopsony is *not* a disadvantage to an employer; it is an advantage since it allows the monopsonist to reduce its wage rate by restricting the number of workers employed.

Your Turn 7-1: The slopes of the typical worker's indifference curves would become flatter. Workers would be less willing to trade off wage earnings for fringe benefits. Thus, the optimal amount of fringe benefits would decline.

Your Turn 7-2: The major difficulty of profit sharing as a means of overcoming the principal–agent problem is that it can give rise to free riders who know that they will share in any profits even though they shirk. Seeing free riders, other workers may abandon their efforts to increase productivity, thus undermining the objective of the profit-sharing plan.

Your Turn 8-1: State governors receive compensating wage differentials such as fame, prestige, and power not available to most executives in the private sector. There is a ready supply of qualified, willing candidates for governor, even though the pay is far below that of otherwise similar private-sector positions.

Your Turn 8-2: Because most people do not like to work outdoors in freezing temperatures, a compensating wage premium will arise for this type of work. A person who enjoys working in cold temperatures will receive this higher wage without suffering the utility loss experienced by the marginal worker enticed to this occupation by the compensating wage.

Your Turn 9-1: The V_p in the net present value equation will fall, reducing the likelihood that V_p will be positive and that migration will occur.

Your Turn 10-1: Based on personal characteristics, occupation, and location of employment, Isaiah is clearly more likely than Susan to be a union member.

Your Turn 10-2: The correct answer is *(b)*. A decline in imports would probably boost output and sales by domestic, unionized manufacturers. Consequently, domestic employment and union membership would rise.

Your Turn 10-3: Settlement should occur on the union's terms. Management views its own costs of disagreeing to exceed its costs of agreeing.

Your Turn 11-1: The measured union wage advantage is \$1 an hour, or 11.1 percent [= (\$10 – \$9/\$9) × 100]; the pure union wage advantage is \$2 an hour, or 25 percent [= (\$10 – \$8/\$8) × 100].

Your Turn 11-2: Unions could simultaneously increase the firm's productivity (output per worker) while extracting wage rate increases beyond the productivity gains. If so, the firm's profitability would decline.

Your Turn 12-1: People's incentives to work hard were reduced because the state provided many goods at no charge or at low, highly subsidized prices.

Your Turn 12-2: Smith may work more hours to maintain the same after-tax standard of living as before; for Smith the income effect of the tax increase (after-tax wage decrease) may exceed the substitution effect. Smythe may work fewer hours, responding to the fact that leisure is now less expensive. Because of the tax hike, less after-tax pay is sacrificed in "buying" leisure. For Smythe the substitution effect of the tax may exceed the income effect.

Your Turn 13-1: The average wage of teenagers would increase, teenage employment would fall, and teenage unemployment would rise. It is unlikely that adult employment would change.

Your Turn 13-2: The firm will not provide this extra unit of job safety; the marginal benefit of $250,000 is less than the marginal cost of $300,000. But the marginal cost of $250,000 is less than the marginal social benefit of $300,000. Thus, a strong case can be made for government intervention. Government could simply require the firm to provide this extra job safety, or alternatively, government could provide workers with information about the safety hazards in their workplaces. Greater awareness by workers of job risks create compensating wage differences that increase the firm's private benefits of providing job safety.

Your Turn 14-1: The dollar value of the discrimination coefficient for an employer hiring all white workers must be greater than $4. The coefficient for an employer hiring all black workers must be less than $4.

Your Turn 14-2: Statistical differences in group averages might lead employers to reject qualified women and minorities for some jobs, confining those discriminated against to lower-paying, stereotypical jobs. For example, women might be excluded from career tracks in management based on the assumption that family responsibilities will interfere with transfers to new locations and other aspects of job performance. Instead, women may be segregated into administrative assistant positions.

Your Turn 15-1: Because black males earn less than white males at higher levels of education, blacks may have a reduced incentive to obtain more education.

Your Turn 15-2: The inferior economic position of women may spring partly from their relative lack of mathematical and quantitative interest and training. Perhaps women have freely chosen to avoid preparing for higher-paying professions requiring these skills. On the other hand, women may possibly have less mathematical training than men because of discrimination. That is, socialization, advising in education, and stereotypical hiring may have pushed them away from this type of training and toward training for "women's jobs."

Your Turn 15-3: Affirmative-action policy has emerged from presidential executive orders applying to private firms working under federal contracts or receiving federal funds.

Your Turn 16-1: Unexpected inflation reduces the length of job search; anticipated inflation has no effect on the length of job search; and unemployment insurance increases the length of job search.

Your Turn 16-2: The job ladder in academia involves only three rungs: assistant professor, associate professor, and full professor. There is considerable upward mobility along the ladder.

Your Turn 17-1: A shift of the Lorenz curve toward the diagonal line represents a decline in earnings inequality. Most likely the histogram of earnings will be compressed, and the Gini coefficient of earnings will decline.

Your Turn 17-2: While all the factors shown in Figure 17-3 are important, if forced to select one set of factors, we would pick differences in education and training.

Your Turn 18-1: Productivity is 2 (= 10 units of output/5 units of labor). Average labor cost is $1 (= $10 of labor cost/10 units of output).

Your Turn 18-2: As the economy emerged from the recession of 1990–91, firms collectively increased their output more rapidly than their employment. Therefore, output per worker increased.

Your Turn 19-1: The unemployment rate overstates economic hardship because some survey respondents may falsely claim they are searching for work, it counts people with weak labor market attachment the same as their strongly attached counterparts, and a large number of families have more than one earner. The unemployment rate understates economic hardship because it counts involuntarily part-time workers as fully employed and does not measure either discouraged or subemployed workers.

Your Turn 19-2: False. Recently, men and women in the United States have had very similar unemployment rates.

AUTHOR INDEX

Note: References followed by *n* appear in footnotes.

SUBJECT INDEX

Note: References followed by *f* refer to figures; references followed by *n* refer to footnotes.

LABOR STATISTICS FOR SELECTED YEARS, 1980–1997

	1980	1981	1982	1983	1984	1985
1. Noninstitutional population, 16 yrs. or older (millions)[a]	167.7	170.1	172.3	174.2	176.4	178.2
2. Labor force (millions)[a]	106.9	108.7	110.2	111.6	113.5	115.7
3. Labor force participation rate (%)[a]	63.8	63.9	64.0	64.0	64.4	64.8
3a male (%)[a]	77.4	77.0	76.6	76.4	76.4	76.3
3b female (%)[a]	51.5	52.1	52.6	52.9	53.6	54.5
3c white (%)[a]	64.1	64.3	64.3	64.3	64.6	65.0
3d black and other (%)[a]	61.7	61.3	61.6	62.1	62.6	63.3
4. Employment (millions)[a]	99.3	100.4	99.5	100.8	105.0	107.2
5. Unemployment (millions)[a]	7.6	8.3	10.7	10.7	8.5	8.3
6. Unemployment rate (%)[a]	7.1	7.6	9.7	9.6	7.5	7.2
6a male (%)[a]	6.9	7.4	9.9	9.9	7.4	7.0
6b female (%)[a]	7.4	7.9	9.4	9.2	7.6	7.4
6c white (%)[a]	6.3	6.7	8.6	8.4	6.5	6.2
6d black and other (%)[a]	13.1	14.2	17.3	17.8	14.4	13.7
6e 16–19 yr. olds[a]	17.8	19.6	23.2	122.4	18.9	18.6
7. Average hourly earnings (current $)[b]	6.66	7.25	7.68	8.02	8.32	8.57
8. Average hours worked per week[b]	35.3	35.2	34.8	35.0	35.2	34.9
9. Average earnings per week (1982 $)[b]	275	271	267	273	275	271
10. Change in earnings per week from year earlier (% in 1982 $)[b]	−5.8	−1.5	−1.2	2.0	.8	−1.3
11. Federal minimum wage rate (current $)	3.10	3.35	3.35	3.35	3.35	3.35
12. Change in productivity from year earlier (%)[c]	−.3	1.8	.5	3.2	2.5	1.6
13. Change in hourly compensation from year earlier (%)[c]	10.8	9.5	7.5	4.2	4.4	4.9
14. Change in unit labor cost from year earlier (%)[c]	11.1	7.6	8.0	0.9	1.8	3.2
15. Labor union membership (millions)[d]	22.4	na	19.8	17.7	17.3	17.0
16. Union membership as percent of civilian labor force	20.9	na	17.9	15.9	15.3	14.7
17. Work stoppages involving 1,000 or more workers	187	145	96	81	62	54
18. Strike time as percent of total work time[e]	.09	.07	.04	.08	.04	.03
19. Employee compensation as percent of national income	73.7	73.1	74.1	73.2	71.3	71.7

[a]civilian [b]total private, nonagricultural industries [c]business sector [d]includes members of professional associations, 1970–1997